PENGUIN BOOKS

DICTIONARY OF HORTICULTURE

The National Gardening Association, one of the most influential horticulture organizations in the United States, is the publisher of *National Gardening* magazine, which reaches a growing subscriber base of over 200,000 readers each month. A national clearinghouse for gardening information, the NGA is also a leading compiler of statistical surveys on gardening topics and trends. The NGA is based in Burlington, Vermont.

Executive Editor: *David Els*

Editor-in-Chief: *Jack Ruttle*

Managing Editor: *Barbara Radcliffe Rogers*

Principal Lexicographer: *Sara Godwin*

Compilers: *John R. Dunmire, Kathleen Hatt, Joanne H. Lemieux, Lance Walheim, Rex Wolf*

Senior Editorial Staff: *Lee Ann Chearneyi, Norma Ledbetter*
Editorial Staff: *Julia Banks, Basil Daley, Kelli Daley, Jennifer Hirshlag, Jim Luckett, Anne Pierce, Laura-Ann Robb, Midge Smith, Gary Sunshine, Emile Wamsteker, Phillip Ward, Kelley Williams*
Senior Research Associate: *Cathy Hasher*
Research Staff: *Lauren Hartz-Lewis, Stephen Leiper, Lauren Bonar Swezey, Karen Woodward*
Design: *Jeannette Jacobs*

THE NATIONAL GARDENING ASSOCIATION

DICTIONARY OF HORTICULTURE

PRODUCED BY

THE PHILIP LIEF GROUP, INC.

PENGUIN BOOKS

PENGUIN BOOKS

Published by the Penguin Group

Penguin Books USA Inc., 375 Hudson Street, New York, New York 10014, U.S.A.

Penguin Books Ltd, 27 Wrights Lane, London W8 5TZ, England

Penguin Books Australia Ltd, Ringwood, Victoria, Australia

Penguin Books Canada Ltd, 10 Alcorn Avenue, Toronto, Ontario, Canada M4V 3B2

Penguin Books (N.Z.) Ltd, 182–190 Wairau Road, Auckland 10, New Zealand

Penguin Books Ltd, Registered Offices: Harmondsworth, Middlesex, England

First published in the United States of America by Viking Penguin,
a division of Penguin Books USA Inc. 1994
Published in Penguin Books 1996

3 5 7 9 10 8 6 4 2

Published by arrangement with
The Philip Lief Group, Inc.
6 West 20th Street
New York, NY 10011

ISBN 0-670-84982-8 (hc.)
ISBN 0 14 01.7882 1 (pbk.)
(CIP data available)

Printed in the United States of America
Set in Bembo

About the National Gardening Association

The National Gardening Association, founded in 1972, is one of the largest and most influential gardening authorities in the United States. The association publishes a monthly magazine, *National Gardening*, to a growing subscriber base of over 200,000 gardeners, and is a leading compiler of statistical surveys on gardening topics and trends. NGA surveys are frequently cited in national newspapers and magazines like *USA Today*. NGA also publishes the *National Gardening Association Directory of Seed and Nursery Catalogs: Retail, Mail-Order Sources of Vegetable Seed, Fruit Trees, Herbs, Wild Flowers and Garden Products in North America*.

A clearinghouse for home, school, community, and institutional gardening information, NGA also conducts programs providing technical assistance, materials, and grants to community gardens nationwide and operates a national Seed Search Service.

The National Gardening Association holds that gardening adds joy and health to living while improving the environment, encouraging an appreciation for the proper stewardship of the earth, and enabling people to grow a portion of their own food.

Contributors

DAVID ELS is executive director of the National Gardening Association and publisher of *National Gardening* magazine. He lives in Vermont.

JACK RUTTLE is senior editor of *National Gardening* magazine. Also a science writer, Ruttle has concentrated on cutting-edge research about aquaculture, solar greenhouses, coldframes, and amaranth. He has studied garden design and fruit tree training in England and initiated an organic apple research project at the Rodale Research Center. He is formerly managing editor of *Organic Gardening*. Ruttle lives in southeastern Pennsylvania.

BARBARA RADCLIFFE ROGERS has written numerous books on horticultural topics, most recently, *The Encyclopaedia of Everlastings*, *Fresh Herbs*, and *Drying Flowers*. She is a co-author of *The Gardener's Home Companion*, which received a 1992 Honorable Mention in the Garden Writer's Association of America's Quill & Trowel competition. Rogers is a regular contributor to periodicals such as *Yankee*, *Organic Gardening*, *New England Living*, and *The Herb Companion*. She lives in New Hampshire.

SARA GOODWIN is the writer and editor of several best-selling gardening books including *The World of Trees*, *Gardening with Color*, *All About Groundcover*, *The World of Cactus and Succulents*, *All About Perennials*, and *The Gardener's Companion*, a *New York Times Review* garden book club selection. Godwin has written cover stories for such nationally recognized magazines as *Metropolitan Home* and contributed feature articles to numerous periodicals. She is the former editor of a popular newspaper column on California gardening and host of a local radio show, "Ask the Gardener." Godwin has taught organic gardening and designed private gardens in the United States, England, and Mexico. She is a consultant on the restoration of a 14-acre nineteenth-century garden at Oolompali State Park in Novato, California, recently given the Governor's Award, and the xeriscape garden at the Frank Lloyd Wright-designed Civic Center in San Rafael, California. Godwin is a member of the Garden Writers Association of America. She lives in California.

JOHN R. DUNMIRE, a gardening editor and writer, is a former president of the Western and California Horticultural Societies. A retired senior editor at *Sunset* magazine, he is most recently editor of *The Sunset Western Garden Book*. Dunmire lives in California.

KATHLEEN HATT has written for many agricultural trade magazines and contributed articles to *Turf* and *Flower and Garden*. She lives in New Hampshire.

JOANNE H. LEMIEUX holds degrees in Agricultural Engineering and Environmental Conservation Education and is the author of numerous newspaper columns on gardening subjects. Lemieux lives in New Hampshire.

LANCE WALHEIM is an expert in pest control, including pesticide registration, pest identification, and alternative control methods. He is a contributing editor/author to over forty gardening books. Walheim is part owner of California Citrus Specialties, marketers of specialty citrus. He currently operates a seventeen-acre citrus ranch in Exeter, California.

REX WOLF is the author of *Landscaping for Privacy*, published by Sunset Books and co-author of *All About Roses* for Ortho. A specialist in horticultural marketing, consulting, and writing, he lives in the San Francisco Bay Area.

INTRODUCTION

All who have worked the soil and waited for begonias, peonies and rhododendrons to bloom or anticipated the hearty succulence of freshly-picked tomatoes and snap beans know the glorious truth of the ancient Chinese proverb, "Life begins in the garden." The garden welcomes young and old, urban and rural dweller, those with busy schedules and those with time on their hands . . . all it takes is the desire and determination to make things grow, a space to grow in, the proper tools and equipment, and a working knowledge of basic gardening processes.

The National Gardening Association has created in its *Dictionary of Horticulture* a unique, all-inclusive gardening reference for all who delight in making things grow. This one-of-a-kind dictionary is a truly user-friendly sourcebook of horticulture written in accessible and vivid language. Invaluable to the entire spectrum of gardeners, from the beginner to the experienced amateur, and up to professionals in the horticultural trade—garden center sales clerks, wholesale growers, landscape contractors, garden designers, gardening writers, and more, the thousands of concise definitions in the *Dictionary of Horticulture* will aid any gardening enthusiast in deciphering the language and terminology used in gardening magazines, greenhouses, seed catalogs, horticulture books, and backyards everywhere.

No matter what the degree of proficiency or area of interest, this dictionary helps users break the taxonomical and linguistic codes of horticulture.

The *Dictionary of Horticulture* is more complete than regional horticultural references and easier to understand than standard national references like *Hortus Third*. It includes over 15,000 main entries featuring an extensive selection of plants and their varieties, fruits, herbs, and vegetables, botanical terms, pests, diseases, pesticides, fertilizers, soils, tools and materials, and techniques. Main entries reflect the vocabulary regularly used by the widest range of contemporary gardeners—in short, every word the gardener needs to know.

Users just beginning to garden can benefit from entries on plants that are simple to grow, like petunias, marigolds, geraniums, and pansies. The more serious horticulturist can research terms specific to a field of expertise and will appreciate, for example, the rich selection of collectors' plants including alpine plants, cacti, orchids, ornamental grasses, and succulents.

PLANTS AND BOTANICAL TERMS

The selection of plants defined in the *Dictionary of Horticulture* covers every region of North America spanning the North, Northeast, South, Southeast, Midwest, Far West, Southwest, West Coast and the Pacific Northwest including Canada, the United States, and Mexico. Plants listed as main entries in the *Dictionary of Horticulture* will thrive and bloom in any one of a diverse set of climates and terrains: mountains, plains, deserts, and forests. The dictionary showcases a larger proportion of plants that are native to America than other gardening references. Native plants are naturally inclined to grow well and bring a garden that is less demanding or time-consuming for some, and yet greatly rewarding.

Every plant defined in the *Dictionary of Horticulture* lists the scientific name, the most common name(s), family, genus, and species. Difficult main entry words are also pronounced. The plant's growth habit is established, whether it is found as a flower, vine, shrub or tree. Colorful, animated prose descriptions bring distinguishing characteristics of leaves, flowers, or fruit to life, as in the dame violet's "long, thin, toothed leaves and small fragrant single or double white, lilac, or lavender flowers." Hardiness is given, as well as the plant's most suitable habitat.

In addition to taxonomy and appearance, users are familiarized with the plant's specific qualities, whether it is long-blooming, fast-growing, long-lived, pest-free, drought-tolerant, or fragrant, for example. They will discover whether a plant self-sows or grows from cuttings, or whether it is inclined to be invasive. Poisonous or rash-causing properties are also noted.

The combined elements of the definition explain the particular traits of a plant and inform gardeners about how it is grown and used in the garden, placing a wealth of information into each main entry. For example, if a plant is native to marshes or streamsides or recommended for a bog garden, the gardener understands that it needs moist soil to thrive. If it is recommended for the woodland garden, it prefers dappled shade and soil rich in organic matter. If it is native to the desert, the gardener recognizes that it will tolerate high heat and needs little water. A tender perennial is one that may be grown in warm winter climates as a perennial, in cold winter climates as an annual, or as an indoor/outdoor potted plant that summers out-of-doors and comes in for the winter. If the definition notes that the plant can become invasive or has naturalized, the gardener stands warned that it may become a weed. A plant that is traditional in herb gardens or cottage gardens probably has more to recommend it than simple beauty, perhaps a culinary use or exceptional fragrance.

Fruits, vegetables, and herbs common to this part of the world are defined, also reflecting a wide variety of climates and terrains. These entries appear under a plant's common name; they describe and identify plants used as food by humans and also include the habitat and conditions under which a plant will thrive. Many native edible plants are featured. Definitions provide nutritional information whenever particularly relevant.

While botanical terms may not be used in the garden on an everyday basis, they are certain to appear in diverse horticultural texts. The *Dictionary of Horticulture* defines the important terms botanists use to describe the structure and functions of a plant's anatomy in clear, easy-to-understand language that benefits both the layperson and professional alike.

PESTS AND PESTICIDES
The selection of pests like mealybugs and aphids, and diseases ranging from brown rot to root rot and downy mildew, speaks to the problems affecting gardeners throughout the continent. In compiling entries describing solutions to these problems, the editors have emphasized non-synthetic pest controls, but have also included chemical controls.

Botanical and biological pest controls like bacillus and the nemm all do their jobs without having a debilitating effect on the environment. Also, because the government has stepped up efforts to regulate the sale of chemical pesticides, many of the products on the market today may not be available in ten years—aphids and parasitic nematodes will always be at work.

A dictionary format cannot provide in-depth descriptions for the products of particular manufacturers. Rather, in the selection of chemical pesticides, users are provided with generic names of products and cautionary instructions on how to read a product's label, rather than a delineation of the toxicity of specific product brands. Consult your state or local agency for more extensive information and guidelines.

SOIL
Soil science entries determine the composition of soil, be it acidic or alkaline. Terms that deal with

the quality of soil are distributed throughout, as are terms describing how substances and materials are absorbed or used by plants in certain types of soil. Entries are also included for soil components, like phosphate and nitrogen, as well as types of soils you will use for various plantings, as in adobe and woodland soil.

TOOLS, MATERIALS, AND TECHNIQUES

An expansive array of definitions for tools, hardware, containers, and accessories common to contemporary American and Canadian gardeners reflect the ever-widening, technologically advanced spectrum of materials and equipment currently at the gardener's disposal. Scores of terms identifying gardening procedures—like "heeling in" or "hardening off"—are also defined with concise explanations that quickly demystify common techniques.

How to use
the *Dictionary of Horticulture* and
the Common Name Index

Most gardeners are far more familiar with the common name for a plant than the scientific botanical Latin name. To make the *Dictionary of Horticulture* as gardener-friendly as possible, all main entries are listed under the name by which a plant is best known—be it the common or scientific name.

The Common Name Index

Located at the back of the dictionary, this index works as a further aid to gardeners in searching for a particular plant, species, or genus. It forms a complete listing of all common names appearing in the book, cross-referenced to the correct scientific name. For example, a gardener who does not find a main entry in the dictionary for "bitterwood" need only consult the *Common Name Index* to discover that the scientific name for the genus is "Quassia." Turning to "Quassia," she or he finds the correct description.

Genera and species names appear in italic unless they are a main entry word. Main entries always appear in boldface roman type. Family names appear in roman type within parentheses in the text of particular entries.

A Note on Taxonomy and Accuracy

Botanical taxonomy, or the classification of plants, is a complicated and ever-evolving process. Each year, at botanical congresses around the world, taxonomists review and alter their system of naming plants to reflect new discoveries, theories, and horticultural innovations. Add to this that it is common practice for the nursery trade to continue to sell plants under their established former names, which are often more recognizable to consumers. While this state of unpredictable flux inherent to taxonomy makes a compiler's goal of total accuracy impossible, the *Dictionary of Horticulture* is as current and all-inclusive as possible, and speaks today's gardening parlance. Common or scientific names that have become superannuated, but are still used popularly, are noted in the text. As names continue to change, users should be able to find enough information in the *Dictionary of Horticulture* to lead them to the proper definitions.

The editors hope that gardeners will use the *Dictionary of Horticulture* to cultivate their knowledge of and fervor for gardening, and to coax a deeper understanding of our fragile and wondrous natural environment.

Pronunciation Guide

Pronunciations based upon the phonetic system below appear to aid users in the correct pronunciations of Latin names, botanical terms, or difficult-to-pronounce entries in the dictionary.

KEY SYMBOL	SAMPLE WORD	PRONUNCIATION	KEY SYMBOL	SAMPLE WORD	PRONUNCIATION
a	flat	flat		spore	spor
	catkin	kat'kihn		floor	flor
ay	date	dayt	ow	flower	flow'er
	ray	ray		out	owt
	daisy	day'zee	u	bush	bush
ah	star	stahr		wood	wud
	heart	hahrt	uh	plum	pluhm
	log	lahg		flood	fluhd
	palm	pahm	yoo	yew	yoo
ai	hair	hair		use	yooz
	pear	pair	ch	cherry	cher'ee
	rare	rair		peach	peech
aw	straw	straw	g	grow	groh
	haul	hawl		dig	digh
eh	edge	ehj	j	jonquil	jahn'kwihl
	stem	stehm		gentian	jehn'shuhn
ee	leaf	leef		sedge	sehj
	tree	tree	k	kiwi	kee'wee
er	fern	fern		cup	kuhp
	bur	ber	ks	fix	fihks
	dirt	dert		sticks	stihks
	earth	erth	kw	queen	kween
	worm	werm		kumquat	kuhm'kwaht
ih	pit	piht	ng	spring	sprihng
igh	spike	spighk	s	seed	seed
	bright	bright		cedar	seed'er
	cyme	sighm		raceme	ray seem'
oh	rose	rohz	sh	show	shoh
	oak	ohk		fresh	frehsh
	hoe	hoh	th	thorn	thorn
	mow	moh		mouth	mowth
oi	soil	soil	y	yellow	yehl'oh
	royal	roi'uhl		onion	uhn'yuhn
oo	root	root	z	zinnia	zihn'ee uh
	fruit	froot		leaves	leevz
oe	corn	korn	zh	measure	meh'zher

abaca (ab′a ka) *n.* The native Philippine name of the banana plant, *Musa textilis,* which yields manila hemp, much used in making rope and cord. Also spelled abaka.

ABC soil *n.* A soil that has a complete profile or series of layers, of surface, subsoil, and lower loose rock material, known as its A, B, and C horizons.

abele (uh beel′) *n.* The white poplar, *Populus alba,* which takes its name from the color of its twigs and leaves. Its wood is used to make wooden matches and excelsior. Also called silver-leaved poplar.

Abelia (uh bee′lee uh) *n.* A genus of about 30 summer-blooming shrubs (Caprifoliaceae), with pairs of opposite leaves and many small pink or white flowers.

Abeliophyllum (uh bee′oh fihl′uhm) *n.* A genus of shrubs of the olive family (Oleaceae) with bluish-green leaves and fragrant white flowers. Commonly known as white forsythia.

Abelmoschus (ay′behl mahs′kuhs) *n.* A small genus of plants, including okra *(A. esculentus)* and musk mallow *(A. moschatus).* Name formerly applied to some species of plants now referred to as *Hibiscus.* (See **Hibiscus** and **okra**.)

aberrant (a ber′ehnt) *a.* In botany, an individual plant or species, genus, etc. that differs in some of its characters from the group in which it is placed.

Abies (ayb′ee eez) *n.* A genus of about 40 evergreen, coniferous (cone bearing) trees *(Pinaceae),* the true firs, some of which are valuable for their timber. They are distinguished by their erect female cones and are found throughout the temperate zone of the northern hemisphere. Included in this genus are *A. alba* (silver fir) and *A. procera* (noble fir). (See **fir**.)

ablastous (uh blas′tuhs) *a.* Without germ or bud.

abruptly pinnate (pihn′ayt) *a.* Terminating without an odd leaflet or a tendril; said of a leaf made up of a number of small leaflets ending in a matched pair.

abruptly pinnate leaf

Abrus (ay′bruhs) *n.* A small genus of leguminous plants (Leguminosae). Indian licorice is a woody twining vine, found in tropical regions, including Florida. Its root is often used as a substitute for licorice, but the seeds are extremely poisonous. The polished, particolored, pea-sized seeds, commonly called crabs′-eyes, jumble-beads, jequirity, or John Crow beans, are strung into rosaries, necklaces, etc.

absinthium (ab sihn′thee uhm) *n.* The common wormwood, containing a volatile oil that is the principal ingredient in the French liqueur absinthe.

absorption *n.* The process by which plants take up water through their roots.

Abutilon (uh byoot′ihl ahn) *n.* A genus of 150 soft, woody perennial shrubs (Malvaceae). They have palmate, or fan-shaped, leaves and white, yellow, orange, or reddish-purple flowers. Many are very ornamental and can be grown in mild-winter climates or greenhouses. Commonly known as flowering maple. *A. hybridum* is known as Chinese lantern.

AC soil (ay see soil) *n.* 1. A young soil with an incomplete profile. 2. A soil that includes an A and a C horizon.

Acacia (uh kay′shuh) *n.* A genus of perhaps 800 shrubs and trees (Leguminosae), natives of warm regions. They have small, fluffy, fragrant yellow flowers. The leaves are alternate, bipinnate (doubly divided), or reduced to leaflike stems. *A. nilotica* is used to make gum arabic. *A. catechu* once provided the brown dye used for khaki. Those species cultivated for ornament tend to be fast-growing and short-lived, and all are attractive to birds. *A. cornigera* is naturalized in Southern Florida and is sometimes grown as a curiosity for its large paired thorns, resembling cattle horns. Commonly known as wattle; *A. dealbata* is called mimosa.

1

Acacia nilotica
(gum arabic tree)

Acaena (uh see′nuh) *n.* A genus of trailing, mostly evergreen, perennial plants *(Rosaceae),* grown as a ground cover for their mats of attractive gray-green or pale green divided leaves. Commonly known as sheep-bur.

acajou (ak′uh zhoo) *n.* 1. The fruit of the cashew tree *(Anacardium occidentale).* (See **cashew nut.**) 2. A gum or resin extracted from the bark of the cashew tree. 3. A common name that may refer to any of several mahoganies *(Meliaceae)* or laurel-oak *(Quercus)* as well as the cashew tree *(Anacardium).*

Acalypha (ak uh ligh′fuh) *n.* A genus of mostly shrubs, native to warm regions, grown primarily for their mottled foliage. The chenille plant *(A. hispida)* is grown for its curious 18-inch flowers that resemble long tassels of crimson chenille. Jacob's-Coat, or copperleaf *(A. wilkesiana),* has leaves more colorful than many flowers.

acantha (uh kna′thuh) *n.* In botany, a prickle, thorn, or spine.

Acanthaceae (a kan thay′see ee) *n. pl.* A large family of herbaceous, shrubby tropical plants with opposite leaves and irregular flowers. Several genera are very ornamental and are widely grown, particularly *Acanthus, Aphelandra,* and *Thunbergia.*

Acantholimon (uh kan′thuh ligh′mahn) *n.* A genus of 150 species of tufted, evergreen perennial plants (Plumbaginaceae) native to rocky, gravelly places in the mountains of Eurasia. The leaves grow in basal tufts or rosettes, and the flowers may be single or in clusters. Most often grown in rock gardens. Commonly known as prickly thrift.

Acanthopanax (uh kan thah′puh naks) *n.* A genus of hardy prickly shrubs or trees of which only *A. Sieboldianus* is grown ornamentally. It has small leaves, slender, arching branches, greenish-white flowers, and rarely, black fruit.

Acanthus (uh kan′thuhs) *n.* A genus of tall, herbaceous, drought-resistant perennial plants (Acanthaceae). They have large, glossy, broadly lobed leaves and tall spikes of snapdragon-shaped flowers, though they are cultivated primarily for their beautiful foliage. The bold leaves of *Acanthus* have inspired important decorative features in Western art and architecture, especially ancient Greek capitals on columns. Commonly known as bear's-breech. *A. mollis* is called artist's acanthus.

acarpous (ay kar′puhs) *a.* In botany, not producing fruit; sterile.

acaulescent (ay koh lehs′ehnt) *a.* In botany, stemless; applied to a plant in which the stem is apparently absent. The term acauline is also used.

accretive (uh kreet′ihv) *a.* Of or pertaining to accretion; increasing or adding by growth; continued development from within.

accumbent (uh kuhm′behnt) *a.* In botany, lying against; applied to the first sprouts of an embryo when they lie against the body of a seed, as in sprouting beans.

accumbent ovule

-aceae (ay′see ee) *n. pl. suffix* New Latin suffix, meaning "plants of the nature of," which is used to form names of families of plants, such as *Liliaceae,* Rosaceae, etc.

acephate (as′uh fayt) *n.* A synthetic, systemic insecticide used to control a variety of pests, including aphids, scale, and thrips, of most ornamental plants.

Acer (ay′ser) *n.* A genus of about 200 species of mostly deciduous (lose leaves seasonally) trees and shrubs, commonly known as maples (Aceraceae), that are native to northern temperate regions. Maples have opposite, usually fan-shaped, leaves, inconspicuous flowers, and double-winged seed capsules. Many maples are widely cultivated for shade and ornament: Among the most useful in the garden are the Japanese maple, *A.palmatum;* the vine maple, *A. circinatum;* and the scarlet maple, *A.rubrum.* Maple syrup and maple sugar are made in North America from the sap of the native sugar maple, *A.saccharum.* (See **maple.**)

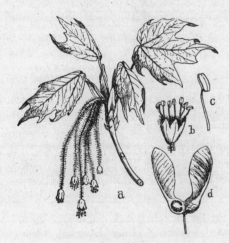

Acer saccharum
(sugar maple)
a flowering branch, *b* sterile flower, *c* stamen, *d* fruit, cut open to show the seed

acervate (uh ser′vayt) *a.* In botany, heaped; growing in heaps or in close, compact clusters.

achene (uh keen′) *n.* In botany, a small, dry, hard, 1-celled, 1-seeded fruit that remains closed at maturity. Also written achenium, achaenium, akene, and akenium.

Achillea (uh kuh lee′uh) *n.* A genus of 60 to 100 species of hardy, often aromatic perennials (Compositae). They grow from 6 inches to 5 feet, depending on species, with finely divided, fernlike gray-green leaves and flat, round clusters of tiny yellow, rose, or white flowers. Traditional in cottage gardens, herb gardens, the matlike species in rock gardens, the taller species in beds and borders. They are drought tolerant once established and fire retardant as well. Commonly known as yarrow and achillea.

Achimenes (uh kihm′uh neez) *n.* A genus of 26 perennial flowers (Gesneraceae). They have small, conelike rhizomes (root swellings); crisp, bright green, hairy leaves; and showy, flaring tubular pink, blue, orchid, lavender, or purple flowers to 3 inches across. Related to African violets and gloxinia, they are grown primarily as summer-flowering houseplants or in greenhouses. *Achimenes* has a wealth of lovely common names: orchid pansy, Japanese pansy, kimono plant, Cupid′s-bower, mother′s-tears, widow′s-tears, nut orchid, and magic flower.

Achras (ak′ruhs) *n.* Formerly, a genus of plants consisting of a single species (Sapotaceae); now classified as *Manilkara Zapota.* It is an evergreen tree with papery leaves, solitary flowers, and a milky sap, chicle, which was the original base for chewing gum. It is cultivated for its edible fruit, the sapodilla.

Acidanthera (as uh dan′thuh ruh) *n.* A genus of summer-blooming, tender corms (bulblike growths) with creamy-white and chocolate-brown flowers. Now classified as *Gladiolus callianthus.* Commonly known as Abyssinian sword lily.

acidify *v.* To lower the soil′s pH to meet the characteristics of acid soil.

acidity *n.* The level of acid in the soil.

acidity test *n.* A comprehensive test taken on a soil sample to determine if the soil′s pH meets the requirement of an acid soil and to what degree.

acid soil *n.* A soil with a low level of pH (between 1 and 6.9).

acinaceous (as ih nay′shuhs) *a.* Consisting of or full of kernels.

acinacifolious (uh sih′nuh sih foh′lee uhs) *a.* Having scimitar-shaped leaves.

acinaciform (uh sih′nuh sih form) *a.* In botany, shaped like a scimitar, usually said of a leaf. An acinaciform leaf is a leaf with one edge convex and

3

thin and the other edge straighter and thick. The term is also used to describe the pods of some beans.

acinaciform leaf

acinarious (a sih nair′ee uhs) *a.* In botany, covered with little round, stalked, grapelike sacs, as in some algae.

Acineta (as uh neet′uh) *n.* A genus of about 15 tropical epiphytic (living on, but not taking nourishment from, a host plant) orchids (Orchidaceae). *Acineta superba* has large pseudobulbs, 3 leaves to 16 inches long, and multicolored flowers in pendulous loose spikes to 3 inches across.

aciniform (as′ih nih form) *a.* Having the form of grapes, or growing in grapelike clusters; acinose.

Acmena (ak meen′uh) *n.* A genus of about 11 species of Asian trees. *A. smithii,* the only species grown ornamentally, has opposite leaves, clusters of many small white flowers at the ends of stems, and showy white, lavender, or lavender-pink edible berries. *A. smithii* is commonly known as lillipilli tree.

Acoelorrhaphe (uh seel lohr ahf′ee) *n.* A genus of palm with a single species, *A. wrightii* (Palmae), native to warm moist areas, including Southern Florida. Slow-growing to 15 to 25 feet, it has fan-shaped leaves, green above and silvery below, and a slender trunk. Excellent in clusters in the landscape in warm climates or as a tub plant anywhere. Commonly known as Everglades palm, silver saw palm, and saw cabbage palm.

aconite, winter (ak′uh night) *n.* Any of several species of low perennial herbs with white or yellow single flowers.

Aconitum (ak′uh night um) *n.* A genus of 100 or more species of hardy perennials (Ranunculaceae), some species native to North America. They grow from 18 inches to 6 feet, depending on species, with lobed leaves in basal clusters and tall spikes of helmet-shaped deep purple, violet, blue, white, or yellow flowers. Useful in moist soils and dappled shade; traditional in cottage gardens. All parts of the plant are extremely poisonous. Commonly known as monkshood and aconite. (See **monkshood**.)

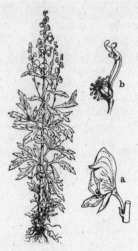

Aconitum
a flower, *b* same, calyx removed

acorn *n.* The fruit of the oak *(Quercus)*; a 1-celled, 1-seeded, rounded or elongated nut, the base of which is surrounded by a scaly cup.

acorn squash *n.* A variety of dark green, deeply ribbed winter squash, 4 to 6 inches long, with deep orange flesh. They are usually baked, and keep well in winter storage.

Acorus (ak′uh ruhs) *n.* A genus of 2 species of perennial grasslike plants *(Araceae)* native to marshy areas. Used as foliage plants, usually in wet areas. Irislike or grasslike leaves grow from a rhizome (swollen root); the flowers are inconspicuous. *A. Calamus* is aromatic, grows to 6 feet, and the root has been used medicinally; commonly known as sweet flag or calamus. *A. gramineus* grows to 18 inches and is used as a pot plant as well as in bog gardens; commonly known as grassy-leaved sweet flag.

Acroclimium (ak ruh klihn′ee uhm) *n.* A name retained by florists for *Helipterum,* a daisylike everlasting flower.

Acrocomia (ak ruh koh′mee uh) *n.* A genus of tropical American feather palms with a tall, prickly trunk with long, black spines, bearing a tuft of very large divided leaves. The fruit is sweet and edible. Commonly known as grugru palm or coyoli palm.

acrogen (ak′ruh gehn) *n.* A plant that increases by growth at the summit or by terminal buds only. The acrogens form a division of the Cryptogams, including ferns, fern allies, liverworts, and mosses.

Actinidia (ak tuh nihd′ee uh) *n.* A genus of deciduous (lose leaves seasonally) woody vines to 30 feet. They bear edible fruit known as kiwifruit or Chinese gooseberry. The round leaves of *A. deliciosa* are dark green above, white below; the flowers are cream-colored; and the fruit is egg-sized and covered with brown fuzz. Fruit requires both male and female plants, though single plants are used ornamentally. See kiwi.

activator *n.* Any of various substances such as microorganisms and nutrients, which, when added to a compost pile, speed the breakdown of organic matter. Also called compost activator and compost inoculant.

acuminate (uh kyoo′mih nayt) *a.* Pointed; acute. In botany, having a long, tapering point; applied to leaves and other organs.

acuminate leaf

acute *a.* In botany, specifically applied to a leaf or other organ ending in a sharp point.

Adam's-needle *n.* A common name of both *Yucca filamentosa* and *Y. Smalliana.*

adder's-tongue *n.* The fern *Ophioglossum vulgatum,* so called from the form of its fruiting spike. Also called adder's spear. The name yellow adder's-tongue is given to the plant *Erythronium americanum.*

adder's-violet *n.* The rattlesnake plantain, a low-growing orchid of North America, with conspicuous white-veined leaves. *Goodyera* spp.

adder's-wort *n.* Snakeweed, so named from its writhing, twisted roots. Also called bistort. *Polygonum bistorta* and *P. bistortoides.*

additive *n.* Something added to a fertilizer to improve its chemical or physical condition.

-adelphous (ih dehl′fihs) *a. comb. form.* Related. In botany, having stamens united into sets; used mostly in combination, as in monadelphous.

Adenanthera (ad uh nan′ther uh) *n.* A genus of 4 species of trees and shrubs (Leguminosae). *A. pavonina,* one of the largest and handsomest of them, yields hard, solid timber, called red sandalwood, which is used in cabinetwork. The bright scarlet seeds are used by goldsmiths in India as weights because of their equality in weight (each equals 4 grains). Used as a street tree in wet, warm regions. Common names include coralwood, coral pea, peacock flower-fence, and Barbados-pride.

Adiantum (ad ee an′tuhm) *n.* A large genus of 200 or more species of ferns, widely distributed. It includes the common maidenhair ferns, *A. Capillus-Veneris* and *A. pedatum,* the latter native to North America. Grown for their delicate and lovely fronds.

Adlumia (ad loo′mee uh) *n.* A genus with a single species, the climbing fumitory, a delicate climbing herbaceous biennial, with clusters of drooping flowers. It is a native of the Alleghenies and is often cultivated.

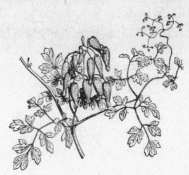

Adlumia
(climbing fumitory)

adnate (ad′nayt) *a.* In botany, grown together or attached.

5

adnexed (ad nehkst´) *a.* In botany, annexed or touching, but not attached.

adobe soil *n.* A dense, claylike soil, also called gumbo, that is also a high-alkaline soil.

Adonis *n.* In botany, a small genus of about 40 species of Eurasian plants (Ranunculaceae) with narrow, divided, alternate leaves and red or yellow flowers. In the corn-adonis, or pheasant's-eye, the bright scarlet petals are considered symbolic of the blood of Adonis, from which, according to Greek mythology, the plant is fabled to have sprung. Used in borders and rock gardens.

adosculation (a dahs kyoo lay´shuhn) *n.* In botany, the fertilization of plants by the falling of the pollen on the pistils.

Adoxa (uh dahk´suh) *n.* A genus of plants (Adoxaceae). The only species, *A. Moschatellina,* (muskroot), is a small, inconspicuous plant, 4 or 5 inches high, found in woods and moist, shady places in the cooler regions of America. The summer-blooming, pale green flowers have a musky smell, which gives the plant its common name of moschatel. Used in rock gardens.

adsorb *v.* To accumulate on a soil surface.

adsortion *n.* Condensation on the soil's surface.

adventitious (ad vehn tih´shihs) *a.* In botany, appearing in an abnormal or unusual position or place; occurring as a straggler or away from its natural position, such as roots on aerial stems.

adventitious buds (ad vehn tih´shihs) *n.* Buds appearing in an unusual place; for example, buds on leaves.

adventive *a.* Said of a plant that has been introduced but is not yet completely naturalized.

Adzuki bean (ad zoo´kee) *n.* A tiny red bean grown for drying. Because it has a long growing season, 120 days at its earliest, it is suitable for warmer climates. It is used in Japanese dishes.

Aechmea (eek mee´uh) *n.* A genus of about 168 species of tropical American epiphytic (growing on a host plant, but not taking nutrients from it) bromeliads (Bromilaceae) with strikingly patterned foliage and handsome flowers. The long, stiff, spiny leaves grow in basal rosettes with yellow, red, or blue flowers that emerge from brightly colored bracts. Most often used as houseplants, they are very easy to grow. Commonly known as vase plants.

Aegopodium (ee guh pohd´ee uhm) *n.* A genus of fast-spreading perennials that spread by creeping rootstocks. *A. Podagraria* and its variegated form, *A.P.* Cv. 'Varigatum', are both used as ground covers and edgings. It is vigorous and invasive, with light green divided leaves and small white or yellow flowers. Commonly known as goutweed, bishop's weed, and herb Gerard.

aerate (air´ayt) *v.* 1. To expose to the air. 2. To charge with air.

aeration (air ay´shihn) *n.* An exchange of air in the soil with air from the atmosphere. Earthworms accomplish this, as does digging and turning the soil to loosen it.

aerator (air´ay ter) *n.* Any of various implements used to break up compacted soil and facilitate air and gas exchange.

aerator sandals (air´ay ter) *n.* Sandal-type shoes or spikes strapped onto regular shoes used to break up compacted soil in lawns.

aerobic (air oh´bihk) *a.* Living or acting only in the presence of air.

Aesculus Hippocastanum
(horse chestnut)
a flower, *b* seed, *c* seed, cut lengthwise

Aesculus (ehs′kyoo luhs) *n*. A genus of 13 species of trees and shrubs (Hippocastanaceae), chiefly North American, with broad hand-shaped leaves and showy flowers in large clusters. The seeds are large, of the shape and color of chestnuts, but too bitter to be eaten. The horse chestnut (*A. Hippocastanum*) is extensively cultivated as an ornamental shade tree. The American species, native to the western and southern United States, share the common name buckeye.

Aethionema (ee thee oh nee′muh) *n*. A genus of 30 to 40 species of low-growing plants with smooth, simple leaves and showy pink, yellow, lilac, or white flowers (Cruciferae). Used in rock gardens. Commonly known as stone cress.

African daisy *n*. A daisy-shaped flower, *Arctotis stoechadifolia,* grown as an everlasting.

African hemp *n*. The common name for *Sparmannia africana* (Tiliaceae), a multistemmed shrub 20 feet high at maturity, with 9-inch heart-shaped leaves and white flowers with purple stamens growing in umbels (clusters with flower stems radiating from a central point).

African tulip tree *n*. The common name for *Spathodea campanulata* (Bignonaceae), a tree to 70 feet high, with leaves 18 inches long and showy scarlet flowers 8 inches long. Also known as flame-of-the-forest.

African violet *n*. The common name for *Saintpaulia ionantha* (Gesneriaceae). A very popular, long-flowering houseplant with fuzzy, thick, heart-shaped leaves growing in rosettes and small pink, white, lavender, or purple flowers in clusters of 3 or more. Hybrids may have doubled flowers and ruffled or scalloped leaves.

Agalinis (ag uh ligh′nihs) *n*. About 60 species of mostly parasitic (taking nourishment from a host) plants (Scrophulariaceae) native to eastern North America with short, linear leaves and rose-pink, purple-spotted flowers. Commonly known as Gerardia.

Agaricus (uh gar′ih kuhs) *n*. A large and important genus of mushrooms characterized by a fleshy cap and radiating gills. Many of the species are edible, such as *A. campestris,* the meadow mushroom or *champignon,* whereas others vary in toxicity from mild to poisonous. (See **mushroom**.)

Agricus campestris
(meadow mushroom)

Agathosma (ag uh thohz′muh) *n*. A large genus of heathlike shrubs (Rutaceae). Several species are cultivated for their flowers.

Agave (uh gah′vee) *n*. A large American genus of plants (Amaryllidaceae). They are slow-growing, often large, consisting of a dense cluster of rigid, thick, juicy leaves, which are tipped and edged with spines. Agave often sucker (grow new plants from the roots of a parent), flower once at maturity, and then die. Commonly known as the century plant or American aloe, agave is frequently cultivated for ornament. It lives many years, 10 to 50 or more, before flowering. At maturity it throws up rapidly from its center a tall stem many feet high bearing a large inflorescence (flower), and dies after ripening its fruit. It is extensively cultivated in Mexico under the name of *maguey,* and the fermented sap produces a drink, called *pulque,* that resembles cider.

Agave
(century plant)

Ageratum (aj ih rayt′ihm) *n*. A genus of plants (Compositae) native to tropical America. *A. Houstonianum* is a well-known annual with dense lavender-blue flowers. Often used in borders, ageratums hold their color well. Many hybrids are dwarf and compact. Commonly known as floss-flower or pussy-foot.

aggregate *n.* Fine soil particles that are held together in a single mass.

Aglaomorpha (ag lay oh mor'fuh) *n.* A genus of about 10 species of large epiphytic (living on a host but not drawing nutrients from it) ferns (Polypodaceae). The fronds resemble those of conventional ferns but broaden toward the base into brown shieldlike organs similar to staghorn ferns. The fronds are 3 to 6 feet long. Usually grown on bark slabs or wooden plaques in a greenhouse, as it is tender to frost.

Aglaonema (ag lay oh nee'muh) *n.* A genus of about 50 tropical plants (Araceae) valued mostly for their ornamental foliage, featuring narrow, pointed dark green leaves, often mottled; the flowers resemble small greenish-white callas. Excellent low-light houseplants. An exudation that drips from the leaf tip will spot furniture finishes. *A. modestum* is commonly known as Chinese evergreen.

Agonis (a gon'is) *n.* About 12 species of evergreen shrubs (Myrtaceae) with willowlike leaves and weeping branches. *A. flexuosa* bears many small white flowers in June, and its leaves smell like peppermint when crushed. One of the best small trees for warm climates; tender below 27° F. Commonly known as Australian willow myrtle or peppermint tree.

agricultural experiment station *n.* One of 50 government-financed U.S. facilities where personnel promote and answer questions about agricultural practices and problems.

Agrimonia (ag rih moh'neeuh) *n.* A genus of 15 perennial herbs (Rosaceae) with divided leaves, yellow flowers, and bristly burs; native to the northern temperate zone. They are commonly known as agrimony or cocklebur.

agrimony *n.* The general name of plants of the genus *Agrimonia*, (Rosaceae), which includes several species. They are perennial herbs with yellow flowers. The common agrimony of Europe and the United States has been used medicinally. Its roots yield a yellow dye.

Agropyron (ag'roh pigh'rahn) *n.* A genus of nearly 40 species of perennial grasses (Gramineae). Tough plants, a few (particularly crested wheatgrass, *A. cristatum*) used as low-maintenance lawns. Commonly known as wheatgrass. *A. repens*, often called quack grass, is an invasive weed.

Agrostemma (ag roh stehm'uh) *n.* A genus of 3 species (Caryophyllaceae) native to the eastern Mediterranean, with opposite, entire leaves and flowers with large purple petals. Widely naturalized in most temperate regions, it is considered a weed in cultivated fields, and the seeds are poisonous. Commonly known as corn cockle.

Agrotis (uh groh'tihs) *n.* A genus of more than 200 annual and perennial grasses (Gramineae) native to many areas. Two perennials, *A. stolonifera* and *A. tenuis*, called creeping and colonial bent grass, respectively, are commonly used as fine-textured, cool-season lawns. *A. nebulosa*, an annual called cloud grass, is grown as an ornamental, valued for its wispy blooms.

A horizon *n.* A surface layer of a mineral soil having maximum biological activity; topsoil.

Ailanthus (ay lan'thuhs) *n.* A genus of trees (Simarubaceae), the only commonly grown species of which, *A. altissima*, the tree of heaven, is frequently planted as a shade tree. It grows rapidly to 50 feet, has very long divided leaves, and throws up abundant root suckers. The flowers are ill-scented. Often condemned as a weed tree because it suckers profusely and self-seeds, it is redeemed by its ability to create beauty and shade under adverse conditions: drought, hot winds, extreme air pollution, and every type of difficult soil.

air layering *n.* A method of plant propagation in which new roots are encouraged to form around a sliver cut from the plant's stem and wrapped with moss.

air plant *n.* An epiphyte; a plant that grows in the branches of trees rather than on the ground, but does not take nourishment from its host. Many epiphytic orchids and bromeliads in cultivation are popularly called air plants.

air-potato yam *n.* A common name for *Dioscorea bulbifera*.

Aizoaceae (ay igh zuh way'see ee) *n.* A family of low-growing succulent herbs and shrubs (Caryophyllales) with single or clustered flowers and capsular fruit. Commonly known as carpetweed or fig marigold.

Ajuga (a joo'guh) *n.* A genus of about 40 species of temperate climates (Labiatae) with square stems, opposite leaves, and blue, white, or rose flowers at the ends of spikes. Ajugas spread by runners, which makes them good ground covers, particularly *A. reptans. A. genevensis* is used in rock gardens. Commonly known as carpet bugle and bugleweed.

Akebia (a kee'bee uh) *n.* A genus of fast-growing woody climbing plants. Commonly known as 5-leaf akebia.

akee (a kee') *n.* A common name for *Blighia sapidia* (Sapindaceae). It was carried by Captain Bligh to Jamaica in 1793, and from there disseminated over the West Indies and South America. It is a small tree, with ashlike leaves and a fleshy fruit containing several large jet-black seeds partly embedded in a white spongy coating. When cooked, the fleshy coating tastes very much like custard or scrambled eggs; however, the pink fiber that attaches the flesh to the seed, and the flesh of unripe or fallen fruit are poisonous.

akee fruit

Albizia (al bihts'ee uh) *n.* A large genus of fast-growing trees and shrubs (Leguminosae), allied to *Acacia. A. Julibrissin,* commonly known as mimosa or silk tree, has fernlike foliage that folds at night and masses of fluffy pink flowers. Also spelled albizzia.

Albuca (al byoo'kuh) *n.* A genus of about 130 bulbs (Liliaceae) with cylindrical to flat leaves growing from the base of the plant and spikes of white or yellow flowers.

albumen (al byoo'mihn) *n.* In botany, any form of nutritive matter stored within the seed. Also called endosperm.

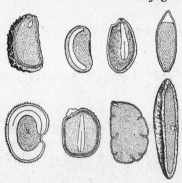

albumen
seeds cut vertically to show embryos and albumen

Alcea (al see'uh) *n.* A genus of about 60 species of tall herbaceous plants (Malvaceae), popularly known as hollyhock. *A. rosea* can grow to 10 feet with big, rough, roundish, heart-shaped leaves and white, pink, rose, red, purple, yellow, or apricot flowers. Hybrids tend to be shorter and may have single, semidouble, or double flowers.

Alchemilla (al keh'mil uh) *n.* A genus of 200 species of low-growing annuals and perennials (Rosaceae). They grow from 4 inches to 2 feet with attractive lobed or divided leaves, often hand-shaped, and clusters of small green or yellow flowers. Used for edging borders or as a small-scale groundcover. The common name for *A. vulgaris,* (lady's mantle), whose mounds of wide leaves are attractive in perennial beds.

alder *n.* The popular name of shrubs and trees. The black alder is *Alnus glutinosa.* In the eastern United States, the native *A. rugosa* is known as hazel alder. These are usually tall shrubs, rarely small trees. The alder of the Pacific coast, *A. oregona,* is called red alder and grows to be a medium-sized tree.

black alder

9

Aletris (al'eh trihs) *n.* A genus of plants that are natives of the eastern United States. They are low, smooth, stemless, bitter herbs with fibrous roots, a cluster of spreading, flat, lance-shaped leaves, and a spiked cluster of small white or yellow flowers. Commonly known as colicroot or star-grass.

Alexandrian laurel *n.* A common name for *Danae racemosa,* an evergreen shrub native to Southwest Asia with branches modified to look like leaves, white flowers on short terminal racemes (clusters), and attractive red berries.

algae *n. pl.* Algae are among the simplest organisms of the plant kingdom, lacking roots, stems, leaves, and flowers. Most grow in water, such as seaweeds or pondweeds. Seaweeds are valuable as fertilizers.

Alisma (a lihz'muh) *n.* A small genus of aquatic plants. The common water plantain.

alkali soil (al'kih ligh) *n.* 1. A highly alkaline soil with a pH of 8.5 or higher. 2. A soluble salt or a mixture of soluble salts present in a soil.

alkaline soil (al'kih lihn) *n.* Soil with a high-level pH (between 7.1 and 9).

alkanet (al'kuh neht) *n.* 1. A common name for *Anchusa,* the root of which yields a red dye, for which the plant was once commercially cultivated. Now grown in herb gardens, chiefly for its historical interest.

Allamanda (al uh man'duh) *n.* A genus of woody climbers. The flowers are large and handsome, and several species are cultivated in greenhouses. In warm-climate areas, they are used to cover walls.

All American selections *n. pl.* New hybrids selected annually from seeds grown in test gardens throughout the United States for form, vigor, disease resistance, and novelty. Often featured in seed catalogs as AAS choices.

Alliaria (al ee ar'ee uh) *n.* A genus of Old World herbs (Cruciferae) with broad leaves and white flowers. Commonly known as garlic mustard.

Allium (al'ee uhm) *n.* A genus of more than 400 species of perennial bulbs or rhizomes (Liliaceae, Amaryllidaceae), some species native to North America. They grow from 12 inches to 5 feet, depending on species, with narrow, basal leaves that smell strongly of onion or garlic when bruised and stalkes with clusters of small white, yellow, purple, blue, violet, pink, or red flowers. Many species are grown ornamentally like bulbs for their attractive spring and summer flowers such as giant allium *(A. giganteum)* and golden garlic *(A. moly).* Others are grown for their edible bulbs, such as onions, garlic, leeks, and shallots. Chives are grown for their edible, onion-flavored leaves. Commonly known as onion.

allogamy (uh lahg'uh mee) *n.* The process of cross-fertilization in which the pollen of 1 plant fertilizes the flower of another plant.

allspice *n.* The fruit of a tree of the West Indies and Central America, *Pimenta dioica,* which is dried, unripe, as a spice. Carolina allspice is the sweet shrub *Calycanthus floridus.*

alluvial soil (uh loo'vee uhl) *n.* Soil transported and recently deposited with little or no modification, such as the soil left by floodwaters.

alluvium (uh loo'vee uhm) *n.* Clay, silt, sand and/or gravel deposited on land by running water.

almond *n.* The stone or kernel of the fruit of the almond tree. There are two kinds, the sweet and the bitter. Sweet almonds are a favorite nut.

almond

almond tree *n.* A species of *Prunus* the produces the almond (Rosaceae). The leaves and flowers resemble those of the peach, with a thin, tough, and fibrous deciduous husk when ripe, and with a thinner and more fragile shell. Most garden almonds are grown on grafted stock, *P. domestica* on *P. dulcis* rootstock. The common flowering almond is a dwarf double-flowered species, *P. glandulosa,* grown for ornament on account of its large, early flowers.

Alnus (al'nuhs) *n.* A genus of 30 species of deciduous shrubs and small trees (Betulaceae) that grow in moist places in northern temperate regions. The leaves are alternate and toothed; it produces pale yellow flowers in catkins, and small cones in winter. Several species are cultivated for ornament. Commonly known as alder.

Alocasia (al uh kayzh'ee uh) *n.* A genus of 70 species of plants (Araceae). They grow from rhizomes (swollen roots) with large, dramatic, heart-shaped leaves and small, calla-shaped flowers. Grown primarily as a houseplant, it is commonly known as elephant's ear.

Aloe (al'oh) *n.* 1. A genus of between 200 and 250 species of tender succulent perennials, shrubs, and trees (Liliaceae). They grow from 6-inch miniatures to 60-foot trees, depending on species, with thick, fleshy, pointed leaves and spikes with clusters of small yellow, orange, cream, or red flowers. Grown in dry, warm-winter regions, in containers, as indoor/outdoor plants, and smaller species as houseplants. 2. The common name for plants of the genus *Aloe*. The American aloe is the century plant. Many species are cultivated for ornament, growing readily on very dry soil. *Aloe vera* is used medicinally.

Alonsoa (uh lahn'zuh wuh) *n.* A genus of 7 to 10 flowers and shrubs (Scrophulodariaceae) native to tropical America with 4-sided stems, opposite leaves (sometimes in 3), and orange or red flowers in terminal clusters. Used as a houseplant or an annual for showy winter bloom. Commonly known as maskflower.

Alopecurus (uh lahp'uh kyoo'ruhs) *n.* A genus of nearly 35 annual and perennial grasses (Gramineae) native to temperate regions. A few varieties of *A. pratensis*, notably 'Aureus', are grown as ornamentals for their colorful variegated foliage. Commonly known as foxtail or meadow foxtail.

Aloysia (al uh wihsh'ee uh) *n.* A genus of 30 species of aromatic herbs (Verbenaceae) native to the warm climates of the Americas with opposite or whorled simple leaves and inconspicuous, spiky flowers. *A. triphylla,* lemon verbena, is a gangly herb with lemon-scented foliage. Grown in sunny herb gardens. (See **lemon verbena.**)

alpencross *n.* A common name for *Hutchinsia alpina,* a perennial herb used as a rock-garden or alpine-garden plant.

alpine *a.* Of, pertaining to, or connected with the Alps or any lofty mountain. Specifically applied to plants growing on mountains above tree line, that is, above the line where the climate becomes too cold for trees to grow.

alpine azalea *n.* A common name for *Loiseleuria procumbens* (Ericaceae), an evergreen prostrate shrub of the polar regions.

Alpinia (al pihn'ee uh) *n.* A genus of 250 species of perennial herbs (Zingerberaceae), related to ginger. *A. zerumbet* grows 8 to 9 feet tall, with shiny 2-foot-long leaves with maroon stems and with showy, waxy, shell-like fragrant flowers in drooping clusters. Commonly known as shell ginger or shell flower.

Alsophila (al sahf'uh luh) *n.* A genus of 200 species of evergreen tropical tree ferns. *A. australis* has a straight, slender trunk and divided leaves 12 feet long. Their slender trunk and large leaves makes them effective as specimen plants in frost-free climates or elsewhere in containers or in greenhouses. Commonly known as tree ferns.

Alstroemeria (al ztruh mee'ree uh) *n.* A genus of 60 species of bulbs (Alstroemeriaceae) with long, thin, lancelike leaves topped with loose clusters of azalea-shaped flowers streaked in a myriad of colors. Used for massing or in borders. Commonly known as Peruvian lily.

Alternanthera (al ter nan'thuh ruh) *n.* A genus of perennial plants (Amaranthaceae) with opposite, richly colored leaves. Several cultivars of *A. ficoidea* are grown as annuals for their foliage, similar to that of *Coleus.* Commonly known as Joseph's-coat or copperleaf.

alternate leaves

alternate *a.* In botany: 1. Placed at uneven sequences upon the stem, as alternate leaves, which are solitary at the junction with the stem, in distinction from opposite or whorled. 2. Opposite to the intervals between organs, as petals that are alternate with sepals, or stamens with petals.

alternate generation *n.* In botany, the passage of a plant through a succession of unlike generations before the original form is reproduced. Usually the succession is one in which one sexually produced form alternates with another produced asexually, as in some ferns.

Althaea (al thee'uh) *n.* 1. A genus of plants, including the marsh mallow, with deeply lobed leaves and pink, bluish, or purple flowers in clusters. The marsh mallow *(A. officinalis)* has naturalized in the eastern United States. Some *Althaea* are now classified as *Alcea,* including the hollyhock, *Alcea rosea.* 2. [l.c.] A common name of the shrubby althaea and rose-of-Sharon *(Hibiscus syriacus).*

aluminum *n.* A silverlike metallic chemical element that can be found in soil.

aluminum plant *n.* A common name for *Pilea Cadierei* (Urticaceae), a small, plant with thick, fleshy, dark green ribbed leaves variegated with silver stripes; grown for its foliage. It is grown primarily as a houseplant.

aluminum silicates (sihl'ih kaytes) *n. pl.* Compounds that contain aluminum, silicon, and oxygen.

aluminum sulfate *n.* A colorless salt used as a soil amendment to increase soil acidity.

alumroot *n.* A common name given to the astringent root of several plants, such as *Heuchera* spp. and *Geranium maculatum.*

Alyssum (uh lihs'uhm) *n.* A genus of plants (Cruciferae) containing several white- or yellow-flowered species, often grown on stone walls and in rock gardens. This genus has been reorganized, and sweet alyssum is now classified as *Lobularia maritima. Alyssum saxatile,* commonly known as basket-of-gold, is now *Aurinia saxatilis.* Hoary alyssum is now classified as *Berteoa incana.*

amaranth *n.* A common name for the globe amaranth, *Gomphrena globosa.*

Amaranthus (am uh ran'thuhs) *n.* A genus of about 50 species of plants (Amarantaceae), including several old-fashioned cottage-garden flowers, such as love-lies-bleeding, *A. caudatus,* and prince's-feather, *A. hybridus erythrostachys.* Most species are coarse, sometimes weedy, plants grown as annuals for their brightly colored foliage or flowers.

Amaryllidaceae (am uh rihl ih day'see ee) *n. pl.* A family of 90 genera and 1,200 species, resembling the lilies. It includes many well-known ornamental plants: the amaryllis, narcissus (with the daffodil and jonquil), etc. The bulbs of some are poisonous.

Amaryllis (am uh rihl'ihs) *n.* 1. A genus of bulbous plants (Amaryllidaceae) with large, bright-colored lily-shaped flowers on a stout stem. The belladonna lily *(A. hallii)* from southern Africa, now regarded as the only species, is widely grown and has naturalized in some areas of the United States. The African amaryllis is classified as *Hippeastrum.*

Amberboa (am ber boh'uh) *n.* A genus of about 20 species of annual herbs (Compositae) with bristly bracts, tubular flowers, and alternate divided leaves. Also known as star of the desert.

Ambrosia (am broh'zhuh) *n.* A genus of coarse annual weeds (Compositae), commonly known as ragweed. Widely distributed throughout the Americas, its pollen is notorious as a cause of hay fever.

Amelanchier (am uh lang'kee er) *n.* A genus of small trees and shrubs (Rosaceae) with clusters of showy white flowers, alternate, toothed leaves, and small dark purple or black fruits; native to northern temperate zones. Commonly known as serviceberry or shadblow.

amendment *n.* A term for any conditioner or material (like lime, gypsum, etc.) that is added or worked into the soil to make it more productive.

ament *n.* A catkin; a slim, spikelike, and often drooping flower cluster, such as those found on birch, willow, and poplar, as well as oak, walnut, and hazel. Aments may be male or female. In some plants (cottonwoods, willows), male catkins are borne on one individual plant, female on another; in others (alders, birches), a single plant may produce both male and female aments. Also written amentum.

aments of the willow

American aloe (al'oh) *n.* Also called century plant. (See **Agave**.)

Amherstia (am hers'tee uh) *n.* A leguminous genus of tree with a single species, *A. nobilis,* which has large, showy tubular flowers of bright vermilion spotted with yellow, in long, pendulous hanging clusters. It grows to 40 feet. The flowers are considered sacred and are sometimes laid as an offering on Buddhist shrines.

amianthium (am ih an'thee uhm) *n.* A perennial bulb (Liliaceae) native to eastern North America. The narrow leaves which grow from the base of the plant, are 2 feet long, and the flower stalk is 4 feet high, topped with white flowers. The bulb is extremely poisonous if eaten. Commonly known as fly-poison.

amino acid (uh mee'noh) *n.* A nitrogen-containing organic compound that is linked together to form a protein molecule.

Ammobium (uh moh'bee uhm) *n.* A genus of 2 or 3 species of perennials (Compositae). The common name for *Ammobium alatum,* frequently cultivated for its daisylike flower heads, which dry well for everlasting arrangements. The blossoms, with several rows of silvery-white petals around a large yellow center, grow profusely to 3 feet on thickened, fleshy stems, which are often too heavy to support their own weight in the garden. The *Grandiflorum* cultivar has larger flowers and is sometimes erroniously labeled *Alatum grandiflorum.*

ammonia *n.* 1. A colorless gas made up of 1 part nitrogen and 3 parts hydrogen. 2. A gas that can be liquified under pressure to be used as a fertilizer.

ammonification (uh mahn'ih fih kay'shuhn) *n.* The act of forming ammonium compounds from organic material by various organisms.

ammonium ion *n.* 1. The positively charged $NH_4 +$ ion. 2. A form that nitrogen takes in many commercial fertilizers.

ammonium nitrate *n.* 1. An inorganic fertilizer that will add nitrogen to the soil. 2. The form that nitrogen takes in numerous commerical fertilizers.

ammonium sulfate *n.* An inorganic fertilizer applied to soil (20.6% N).

Amomum (uh moh'muhm) *n.* A genus of plants (Zingiberaceae) allied to the ginger plant. They are herbaceous, with creeping aromatic rhizomes (swollen roots) and large leaves. They are remarkable for the pungency and aromatic properties of their seeds, and several species are used as substitutes for true cardamoms (*Elettaria* spp.).

Amorpha (uh mor'fuh) *n.* A genus of 20 species of deciduous (loose leaves seasonally) shrubs (Leguminosae) native to the United States. They have leaves divided into leaflets and long, dense clusters of blue-violet flowers. *A. fruticosa* is commonly known as false indigo and wild indigo.

Amorphophallus (uh mor fuh fal'uhs) *n.* A genus of about 90 species (Araceae) of perennial herbs with huge umbrellalike leaves, native to Old World tropics. The corms (bulblike swellings) of some species are edible. Also known as leopard palm, snake palm.

Ampelopsis (am peh lahp'sihs) *n.* A genus of vigorous, woody vines (Vitaceae), closely related to grapes, that climb by tendrils. Porcelain ampelopsis, *A. brevipunduculata,* has striking porcelain-blue berries and excellent fall color. Pepper vine, *A. arborea,* is native to North America. Both are used for fast cover on slopes, fences, walls, and arbors. (Virginia creeper and Boston ivy, formerly classified as *Ampelopsis,* are now classified as *Parthenocissus.*)

Amphicarpaea (am fih kar pee'uh) *n.* A genus of twining, beanlike vines (Leguminosae) with 3-part leaves, small white or violet flowers, and fruit pods that can grow both on the plant or underground on the roots. Native to North America. Commonly known as hog peanut.

amphicarpous (am fih kahr′puhs) *a.* In botany, producing two classes of fruit, differing either in form or in time of ripening.

amphitropous (am fiht′roh puhs) *a.* In botany, having the seed embryo curved or coiled back along the supporting stalk so that its base and the opening of the pollen tube bend close to each other.

amplexicaul (em plehk′sih kuhl) *a.* In botany, nearly surrounding or embracing the stem, as the base of some leaves.

amplexicaul leaves

amplexifoliate (am plehk sih foh′lee iht) *a.* In botany, having leaves that clasp the stem.

ampulla (am pul′uh) *n.* In botany, a small bladder or flask-shaped organ attached to the roots or immersed leaves of some aquatic plants, as in *Nepenthes* or *Utricularia*.

ampulla

Amsonia (am sohn′ee uh) *n.* About 20 species of perennial herbs (Apocynaceae) characterized by milky sap, alternate leaves, and clusters of small steel-blue flowers at the end of each stem. Native to North America. Commonly known as bluestar.

anacard (an′uh kard) *n.* The cashew nut; the fruit of the *Anacardium occidentale*.

Anacardiaceae (an uh kar dee ay′see ee) *n. pl.* A family of shrubs and trees with compound, alternate leaves and clusters of small flowers. Most are native of tropical and warm regions and are characterized by an acrid, resinous, milky sap. Plants in

this family include the sumac *(Rhus)*, some species of which cause itchy skin rashes (poison oak and poison ivy); the pistachio *(Pistacia vera)*; the mango *(Manifera indica)*; the cashew *(Anacardium occidentale)*; and the Japan lacquer *(Rhus vernicifera)*.

anacardiaceous (an uh kar dee ay′shuhs) *a.* In botany, relating or belonging to the Anacardiaceae.

anacardic (an uh kar′dikh) *a.* Pertaining to the shell of the cashew nut.

Anacardium (an uh kar′dee uhm) *n.* A genus of shrubs and trees (Anacardiaceae). Each fruit contains a single nut. In the cashew tree *(A. occidentale,* the principal species), the fruitlike receptacle resembles a pear in shape and size and is edible, having an acid, though somewhat astringent, flavor. The nuts are roasted to destroy their natural intense bitterness. The tree also yields a gum similar to gum arabic, called acajou.

Anacharis (uh nak′uh rihs) *n.* A small genus of underwater plants with long, branching leafy stems; little, opposite leaves; and small flowers growing out of a 2-cleft covering. Synonym for *Elodea*. Commonly called waterweed.

Anacyclus (an uh sihk′luhs) *n.* A small genus of herbs (Compositae) with finely cut leaves and daisylike white or yellow flowers.

anaerobic (an uh roh′bihk) *a.* Functioning in the absence or air or oxygen.

Anagallis (an uh gal′ihs) *n.* A genus of herbs, with simple leaves and small flowers that may be red, blue, pink, or white. Commonly known as pimpernel and scarlet pimpernel *(A. arvensis)*.

anagua (an a′gwah) *n.* A common name for *Ehretia elliptica* (Boraginaceae), a deciduous (looses leaves seasonally) tree with rough-surfaced, 2-inch-long, pointed leaves and clusters of fragrant white flowers. Commonly called the knackaway. Also spelled anaqua or anacua.

Anaheim pepper (an′uh highm) *n.* A meaty variety of green hot pepper. Its mildly hot flavor is best when eaten fresh.

Ananas (an′uh nuhs) *n.* A genus of 9 species of stiff-leaved, terrestrial tropical bromeliads (Bromeliaceae), native to tropical America. They grow to 4 feet with rigid, spiny leaves in basal rosettes, tall leafless stalks topped by violet or red flowers, and large, thick-skinned, edible, sweet, juicy fruit. Grown as a novelty houseplant in temperate climates, grown commercially for its fruit in tropical climates. Commonly known as pineapple.

Anaphalis (uh naf'uh lihs) *n*. 1. A genus of 35 species of hardy perennials (Compositae). They grow from 8 inches to 3 feet, depending on species, with gray or white woolly leaves and clusters of tubular yellow flowers. The flowers are used in dried arrangements. 2. A common name for *A. margaritacea,* the pearly everlasting common to North American roadsides.

Anastatica (an uh stat'ih kuh) *n*. A genus of a single species, *A. hierochuntina* (Cruciferae). Commonly known as rose-of-Jericho or resurrection plant, it is remarkable for the power of the dormant, dried-up plant to absorb water and appear to revive when placed in it. It is sometimes grown as a novelty.

Anastatica
(rose-of-Jericho)
1 the living plant, *2* the plant withered, *3* the same expanded by moisture

ancho (ahn'choh) *n*. A mildly pungent, 4-inch-long pepper, which ripens from dark green to brownish-red. Also known as poblano.

androdioecious (an'dro dih ee'shuhs) *a*. In botany, having hermaphrodite (bisexual) flowers only upon one plant and male only upon another of the same species, but no corresponding form with only female flowers.

androecium (an dreesh'ee uhm) *n., pl.* **androecia** In botany, the male organs of a flower; the assemblage of stamens.

Andromeda (an drahm'ih duh) *n*. A genus of hardy, evergreen, low-growing, cold-climate shrubs (Ericaceae) with leathery, alternate leaves and nodding clusters of pale pink or white flowers. Some species are native to North America. Some are cultivated for ornament in rock gardens and borders, particularly in cold climates; several are poisonous to sheep and goats, such as *A. polifolia*. Commonly known as bog rosemary.

androphore (an'droh for) *n*. In botany, the stalk or column supporting the stamens of certain flowers, usually formed by a union of the filaments, as in the Malvaceae and in many genera of Leguminosae.

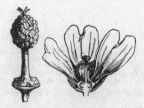

tubular androphore
section of flower, *Malva*

Andropogon (an drah poh'gahn) *n*. A genus of about 100 species of annual and perennial grasses (Gramineae) grown in warm climates. *A. scoparius,* known as little bluestem, is grown as an ornamental for its red blossom and blue-green foliage, which turns reddish in winter.

Androsace (an drahs'uh kee or an drahs'uh see) *n*. A genus of tufted herbs, usually with leaves growing from the base and red or white flowers (Primulaceae). Some species are native to North America. They are grown in rock gardens or low borders. Commonly known as rock jasmine.

Anemone (The Latin generic name is pronounced a nay moh'nay, the English common name, uh nehm'oh nee.) *n*. A widely distributed genus of 120 species of herbaceous perennials; the windflowers (Ranunculaceae). The leaves are lobed or divided. The flowers are showy, varying in color from whites and yellows to reds, blues, and purples, and may be single or double. Several species are widely grown in gardens, such as the poppy anemone, *A. coronaria;* the star anemone, *A. hortensis;* the pasqueflower, *A. pulsatilla;* and the fall-blooming Japanese anemone, *A. × hybrida*. The European wood-anemone (*A. nemorosa),* is an attractive spring woodland wildflower.

15

wood-anemone

Anemonella (a nehm oh nehl'uh) *n*. A single species of spring-flowering perennial (Ranunculaceae) with tuberous roots, leaves growing from the base of the plant, and clusters of white to pale pink or lavender flowers. Commonly known as rue anemone.

anemophilous (an uh mahf'ih luhs) *a*. Wind pollinated, said of flowers that are dependent on the wind for fertilization. Anemophilous flowers, as a rule, are small, uncolored, and inconspicuous; they do not secrete honey, but produce a great abundance of pollen. The flowers of the grasses, sedges, pines, etc. are examples.

Angelica (an jehl'ih kuh) *n*. A genus of 50 species of hardy perennials (Umbelliferae). They grow from 12 inches to 10 feet, depending on species, with large, divided, yellow-green leaves and large umbrellalike clusters of small white flowers. *A. Archangelica* is grown as a culinary herb in herb and cottage gardens. Stems may be candied and leaves cooked as a vegetable.

angelica tree *n*. The American name of *Aralia spinosa* (Araliaceae). It is a small, clump-forming tree to 30 feet high with dense, stout prickles and umbrellalike clusters of small white or greenish flowers. The foliage gives a subtropical effect. Both the berries and the bark have been used medicinally. Also called Hercules'-club and devil's-walking-stick.

angelin (an'jeh lin) *n*. The common name of 25 to 35 species of timber trees belonging to the genus *Andira* (Leguminosae). They are grown as shade trees and for their fragrant, attractive flowers.

angelique *n*. Any plant of the genus *Angelica*, particularly *A. archangelica*, a biennial herb cultivated for its roots and seeds, which yield a flavoring oil. The roots can be candied to form an excellent confection.

angel's-tears *n*. A common name applied to plants of 3 genera: *Datura sanguinea*, a tropical shrub or small tree; *Narcissus triandrus*, a miniature daffodil; and *Soleirolia Soleirolii*, a shade-loving ground cover.

angel's trumpet *n*. A common name for several different plants: *Brugmansia suaveolens*, *B. arborea*, and red angel's trumpet, *B. sanguinea*, as well as *Datura inoxia*. *Brugmansia* spp. are tropical or subtropical shrubs or small trees with trumpet-shaped flowers 6 to 20 inches long, all richly fragrant at night except *B. sanguinea*. *D. inoxia* is a spiny perennial herb, 3-feet high, with 8-inch-long pink or lavender trumpet-shaped flowers.

angiocarpian (an'jee oh kar'pee uhn) *n*. A plant that has its fruit enclosed in a husk.

angiocarpous (an jee oh kar'puhs) *a*. In botany, having a fruit enclosed within a distinct covering, as the filbert within its husk.

angiosperm *n*. Any flowering plant that reproduces by seeds enclosed in a protecting seed vessel. The term angiosperms is applied to the larger of the two divisions of seed-bearing plants, in contrast to the gymnosperms, which lack flowers and in which the seeds are naked (Coniferae, Cycadaceae, etc.).

Angiospermia (an jee uh sper'mee uh) *n. pl.* In botany, the second family of the Linnean class Didynamia, having numerous seeds enclosed in an obvious seed vessel, as in foxglove (*Digitalis*).

angiospermous (an'jee uh sper'muhs) *a*. Having seeds enclosed in a seed vessel, for example, the poppy, the rose, and most flowering plants; opposed to gynmospermous, or naked-seeded. Equivalent forms are angiospermal and angiospermatous.

anglepod *n*. The name of a twining vine, *Gonolobus gonocarpos* (Asclepiadaceae), of the southern United States.

Angraecum (an greek'uhm) *n.* A genus of about 250 species of tropical epiphytic (living on a host plant, but not drawing nourishment from it) orchids (Orchidaceae), some species of which have bizarre and showy flowers. Also spelled *Angrecum.*

anhydrous (an high'druhs) *a.* Dry or lacking water.

animated oat *n.* An oat grass *(Avens sterilis)* characterized by spikelets that twist and move in response to dampness. This twisting reaction to moisture has led to its use in making flies for fishing. It is sometimes grown as a curiosity. (See **Avena**.)

anion (an'igh uhn) *n.* An ion that is carrying a negative charge of electricity.

anise *n.* An annual plant, *Pimpinella Anisum.* The seeds, which have an aromatic smell and a pleasant warm taste, are used largely in the manufacture of cordials. Star anise, *Illicium verum,* produces a star shaped spice from its dried, unripe seeds.

anise hyssop (an'ihs hih'suhp) *n.* An herb, *Agastache foeniculum,* related to the mints, with a mild licorice flavor and scent. It is grown in herb gardens for its fragrance and in perennial borders, where it forms compact mounds up to 3 feet tall, surmounted by spikes of purple flowers. A quick-growing plant, it will often bloom the same year when planted from seed. The dried leaves and flowers are used in potpourri and dried arrangements.

anise tree *n.* The common name for a genus of evergreen shrubs and small trees *(Illicium)* with fragrant flowers; grown in warm climates as ornamentals. Previously classified with magnolias because of their close resemblance.

anisophyllous (a nigh suh fihl'uhs) *a.* In botany, having the leaves of a pair of two different shapes and sizes, as in conifers and many aquatic plants.

annatto (uh nah'to) *n.* The seed of *Blixa orellana.* (See **arnotto.**)

Annona (uh noh'nuh) *n.* A genus of about 50 species of trees and shrubs (Annonaceae) with simple leaves and odd, dull-colored flowers. Most species are grown for the dessert fruits. *A. squamosa* (sweetsop or sugar apple) yields an edible fruit with a thick, sweet, luscious pulp. *A. muricata* (soursop or guanabana), produces a large, pear-shaped, greenish fruit with slightly acid pulp. The genus produces other edible fruits, such as the common custard apple or bullock's-heart, *A. reticulata,* and the cherimoya (sometimes also called custard apple) of Peru, *A. Cherimola.*

Annonaceae (an uh nay'see ee) *n. pl.* A family of tropical or subtropical trees and bushes with alternate leaves and simple flowers; allied to the magnolias. They are grown for ornamental use, for their edible fruit, and for a powerful aromatic secretion used in making perfumes. The soursop, sweetsop, custard apple, and Ethiopian pepper are yielded by these trees. The pawpaw *(Asimina)* represents the family in the United States.

annual *n.* A plant whose natural term of life is 1 year or 1 season; especially, any plant that grows from seed, blooms, fruits, and dies in the course of the same year. Annuals may be carried over 2 or more years by preventing them from setting seed, as is frequently done with the mignonette. Many species that are perennials in warm climates are used as annuals in climates where winters are severe. Winter annuals, frequent in warm regions with dry summers, germinate from seed with the rains of autumn, grow through the winter, and die after setting seed in the spring. Annuals are used for bedding, massing, and for filling gaps in perennial borders.

annual ring *n.* In trees and other woody plants, the layer of wood produced each year that appears when the wood is cut into a cross section. The number of rings equals the age of the tree.

annulus *n.* 1. A ringlike part, structure, or membrane. 2. In botany: the elastic ring that surrounds the sporecase of most ferns.

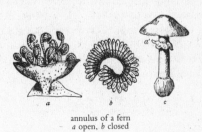

annulus of a fern
a open, *b* closed

Anoda (an oh'duh) *n.* A genus of plants (Malvaceae) native to the Americas with simple, often furry, leaves that vary widely in shape and flowers that range in color from white and yellow to blue and lavender.

Anredera (an ree'dair uh) *n.* A genus of fast-growing, twining, perennial vines with fleshy leaves and fragrant white flowers; (Basellaceae). Small tubers (root swellings) grow in the leaf stems from which the vine can be propagated. Commonly known as madeira vine or mignonette vine.

Ansellia (an suh'lee uh) *n.* A genus of epiphytic (growing on, but not taking nourishment from a host plant) orchids (Orchidaceae) with canelike stems and numerous flowers in terminal clusters.

ant (ant) *n.* A crawling insect known mostly as household pest. It can effect garden plants by fostering other pests, such as aphids and scale, to harvest their secretions, known as honeydew.

antelope brush *n.* A silvery-leaved shrub *(Purshia tridentata)* with 3-part leaves and yellow flowers; native to arid regions of western North America.

Antennaria (an teh na'ree uh) *n.* A genus of white or gray woolly perennial plants (Compositae) grown in rock gardens or for dried flowers. Commonly known as everlasting, pussy-toes, and ladies'-tobacco.

anterior (an tee'ree or) *a.* In botany, the under side of a leaf; otherwise called inferior or lower; the opposite of the posterior. Also used in flowers, as on a snapdragon, where the lower lip is anterior, the upper lip posterior.

Anthemis (an'thuh mis) *n.* A genus of 100 species of mostly aromatic, low-growing annuals or perennials (Compositae). Some form mats, others form cushions to 3 feet with finely divided leaves and daisylike or buttonlike yellow, pink, deep orange, or white flowers. Traditional in cottage and herb gardens, in rock gardens, or the mat-forming species as a small scale groundcover. Commonly known as camomile.

anther (an'ther) *n.* In botany, the part of a stamen that contains the pollen, usually located at the end of a slender stalk often in the center of a blossom.

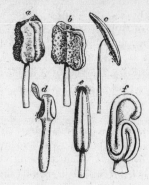

anthers of various flowers
a Aquilegia, b same, expanded, *c Lilium, d Berberis, e Solanum, f Ecbalium*

Anthericum (an ther'ih kuhm) *n.* A genus of perennial herbs (Liliaceae) with fleshy or tuberous roots, narrow leaves, and clusters of small white flowers. *A. Liliastrum* is commonly known as St. Bernard's lily. Spider plant, *A. comosum,* is now classified as *Chlorophytum comosum.*

antheridium (an ther ih'dee uhm) *n., pl.* **antheridia** In botany, the male reproductive organ in spore-bearing plants such as ferns, mosses, algae, and fungi. Corresponds to the anther in seed-bearing plants.

antherozoid (an ther oh zoh'ihd) *n.* In botany, the threadlike substance produced by the male with which the female organs are fertilized.

anthesis (an thee'sihs) *n.* The period during which a flower opens or the act of a flower opening; coming to full bloom.

anthocyanin (an thoh sigh'uh nihn) *n.* The dissolved coloring matter (glycoside pigments) in blue flowers. Also anthocyan.

anthography (an thah'gruh fee) *n.* The description of flowers.

antholeucin (an thoh loo'sihn) *n.* The dissolved coloring matter in white flowers.

Antholyza paniculata (an thuh ligh'zuh pan ihk yoo lah'tuh) *n.* A perennial corm now classified as *Curtonus paniculatus.*

anthophore (an'thoh for) *n.* In botany, an elongated segment at the base of a flower, betweeen the stem and the base of the petals, stamens, and pistil, as in pinks *(Dianthus)* or catch-fly *(Silene)*. Also called anthophorum.

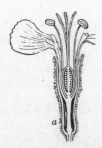

anthophore of a *Silene* blossom

anthoropic soil (an thoh roh'pihk) *n.* Soil worked by humans in a way to produce new characteristics that make it different from the original natural soil.

anthoxanthin (an thoh zan'thihn) *n.* The yellow or orange coloring matter of yellow flowers and fruit.

Anthoxanthum (an thoh zan'thuhm) *n.* A genus of aromatic grasses (Poaceae) grown for dry bouquets. Commonly known as sweet vernal grass.

anthracnose (an thrak'nohs) *n.* A difficult-to-control bacterial disease that causes leaf-spotting and twig dieback in many species, especially trees such as Chinese elm, ash, and sycamore. Planting resistant varieties is the best control.

Anthurium (an thoo'ree uhm) *n.* A large genus of tropical American epiphytes (growing on, but not taking nourishment from a host plant) (Araceae) that grow on forest trees. The flowers are arranged on a fleshy spike, rising out of a green or often richly colored spathe (a wide leaflike covering that surrounds the spike). It is widely cultivated as an ornamental plant in greenhouses.

Anthyllis (an thihl'uhs) *n.* A genus of plants (Leguminosae) with pea-shaped yellow to red flowers in dense, cloverlike heads. Commonly known as kidney vetch, woundwort, and lady's-fingers.

Antiaris (an tee ahr'ihs) *n.* A genus of trees with clustered flowers and fleshy purple fruits (Mora-

ceae). It includes the famous upas tree, *A. toxicaria,* which towers to 250 feet. The sap is used locally as a dart and arrow poison, and the inner bark is made into bark cloth.

antibiosis (an tih bigh oh'sihs) *n.* 1. Not alive. 2. The absence of life.

Antigonon (an tihg'uh nahn) *n.* A genus of tropical and subtropical tendril-clinging vines with alternate leaves and showy flowers. *A. leptopus* is remarkable for the number of delightful common names by which it is known: corallita, coral vine, pink vine, love vine, chain-of-love, queen's-jewels, queen's wreath, mountain rose, rosa montana, confederate vine, and Mexican creeper.

antipetalous (an tih peht'uh luhs) *a.* In botany, having stamens opposite the petals.

antipetalous flower
cross section showing *a* stamens, *b* petals

Antirrhinum (an tih'ri nuhm) *n.* A genus of 40 species of annuals and perennials (Scrophulariaceae). They grow from 14 inches to 5 feet, depending on species, with oval leaves and spikes densely clustered with flowers that resemble a dragon's head. Pinching the sides opens the dragon's jaws and is guaranteed to charm children. Used in beds and borders, and traditional in cottage gardens. Commonly known as snapdragon.

antisepalous (an tih sehp'uh luhs) *a.* In botany, standing opposite to sepals; applied to stamens.

antisepalous flower
a stamens, *b* alternating with petals

Apache plume *n.* A common name for *Fallugia paradoxa* (Rosaceae), a low deciduous shrub with showy, feathery purple plumes; native to the southwestern United States and Mexico.

apatite (ap′a tight) *n.* 1. The chief mineral found in phosphate rock. 2. An inorganic compound found in bones; a component of the fertilizer, bone meal.

Apetalae (ay peht′uh lee) *n. pl.* 1. Plants without petals. 2. A group of the Archichlamydeae comprising plants whose flowers have no petals, such as willow and oak.

apetalous (ay peht′uh luhs) *a.* In botany, without petals or corolla; pertaining to the Apetalae.

Aphanostephus (a fa noh′steh phus) *n.* A genus of American flowers (Compositae) with soft, gray foliage and daisylike white flowers that are red or rosy on the underside. Commonly known as lazy daisy.

Aphelandra (a fuh lan′druh) *n.* A genus of American shrubs and herbs (Acanthaceae) with large, handsome leaves and spikes of showy bracts. Grown primarily as houseplants. The most common species, *A. squarrosa,* is commonly known as zebra plant.

apheliotropic (uh fee′lee oh troh′pihk) *a.* In botany, turning away from the light; applied to shoots or other parts of plants, as in roots that turn away from the sun; opposed to heliotropic.

aphid (ay′fihd) *n.* Any of several kinds of small, many-colored sucking insects, usually congregate on new growth (which often becomes distorted) of a great variety of plants, including ornamentals, like roses, and vegetables, like cabbage and broccoli. Easily controlled by insect predators, insecticidal soap, botanical insecticides, or traditional pesticides.

aphid trap (ay′fihd) *n.* A pheromone-baited (scent-baited) device to lure and capture aphids.

Aphyllanthes (ay fihl an′theez) *n.* A genus consisting of a single species, *A. monospeliensis,* a fibrous-rooted perennial bulb (Liliaceae) with single, light blue or white flowers and almost no leaves.

aphyllous (ay fihl′uhs) *a.* In botany, without leaves; applied to flowering plants that are naturally leafless, such as many species of cactus.

Aphytis wasp (ah figh′tihs) *n.* (See **scale parasite**.)

Apiaceae (ay pee ay′see ee) *n.* A synonym of Umbelliferae, a family of plants including anise, caraway, carrot, celery, dill, and parsley.

Apios (ay′pee ahs) *n.* A North American genus of leguminous climbing plants, producing numerous, small, edible tubers on underground shoots. The only species, *A. tuberosa,* is a native of the Atlantic States; it is called groundnut, or wild bean.

Apium (ay′pee uhm) *n.* A genus of Eurasian herbs related to carrots, having leaves composed of many leaflets and white or yellow flowers in compound umbels (umbrella shaped clusters). Celery *(A. dulce)* and celeriac are in this genus.

Aplectrum (ay plehk truhm) *n.* A genus consisting of a single species, *A. hyemale,* a North American terrestrial orchid that grows from a corm (a bulblike growth). It has 7-inch leaves and a 20-inch flower group with yellowish-brown flowers. It blooms in late spring from Southern Quebec to North Carolina and west Saskatchewan and Arizona. Commonly known as puttyroot and Adam-and-Eve.

apocarpous (ap oh kar′puhs) *a.* In botany, an ovary of a fruit composed of 1 or more simple and distinct pistils, as in buttercups.

apocarpous fruit

Apocynum (uh pahs′us nuhm) *n.* A genus of 7 species of hardy perennials (Apocynaceae). They grow to 4 feet with entire leaves and cluters of small pink or white flowers. Used in hardy perennial border. Commonly known as dogbane.

Apocynaceae (uh pahs uh nay′see ee) *n. pl.* A family of plants, which derives its name from the dogbane *(Apocynum).* The species are largely tropical and have a milky juice that is often acrid and sometimes very poisonous. Among ornamentals, the family includes the periwinkle, *Vinca;* oleander, *Nerium oleander;* star jasmine, *Trachelospermum;* and the frangipani tree, *Plumeria.*

apogamous (uh pahg'uh muhs) *a.* In botany, of the nature of or characterized by apogamy.

apogamy (uh pagh'uh mee) *n.* In botany; Generally, the absence of sexual reproductive power, the plant perpetuating itself only by vegetative means, as buds, bulbs, etc.

apomixis (ap oh mihks'ihs) *n.* Reproduction involving generative tissues but not dependent on fertilization.

Aponogeton (ap uh noh jee'tahn) *n.* A genus of water plants (Aponogetonaceae) more likely to be used in an aquarium than in a greenhouse pond. Two of the most common are *A. distachyus,* cape pondweed, or water hawthorn, and *A. madagascariensis,* latticeleaf, or Madagascar lace plant.

apophyllous (uh pah'fihl uhs) *a.* In botany, having distinct leaves, applied to a whorled flower with distinct sepals and petals; opposed to gamophyllous.

Aporocactus (a por oh kak'tuhs) *n.* A genus of slender, creeping Mexican cacti (Cactaceae) with aerial roots, ribbed stems, numerous small spines, and pink or red funnel-shaped flowers. *A. flagelliformis* is commonly known as rattail cactus.

apostle plant *n.* The common name for two different species of *Neomarica; N. gracilis* and *N. Northiana* (Iridaceae). Both are native to Brazil and have sword-shaped leaves and blue to violet flowers; they are used primarily as houseplants.

appendage *n.* That which is attached to something as a proper part of it; a subordinate, attached part of anything. Specifically, in botany, any subsidiary part added to another part, as hairs and glands to a stem or leaf.

applanate (ap'la nayt) *a.* In botany, flattened out or horizontally expanded.

apple *n.* 1. The fruit of the tree *Pyrus Malus,* now cultivated in nearly all temperate regions, in numerous varieties; its fruit is in universal use. It was introduced into America from England in 1629, by the governor of Massachusetts Bay. It is scarcely known in its wild state, but is often found as an escape from cultivation. The cultivated crab apple is the fruit of other species of *Pyrus.* 2. A name popularly given to various fruits or trees having little or nothing in common with the apple. Among them are Adam's apple, the lime, a variety of *Citrus medica,* and the custard apple.

apple maggot *n.* A wormlike fly larva that infests apples, turning them to mush. Usually controlled with carefully timed sprays of traditional pesticides; botanical insecticides are sometimes effective.

apple mint *n.* A common name used for *Mentha suaveolens,* that is sweet scented and slightly hairy; its leaves are used to make a favorite tea.

apple-of-peru *n.* The common name used for *Nicandra Physalodes* (Solanaceae), a Peruvian plant with coarse alternate leaves, large, solitary blue or white flowers, and a bladderlike fruit. Also called shoo-fly plant.

application *n.* 1. The act of applying fertilizer to the soil. 2. The amount of fertilizer added to the soil.

appressed *a.* Pressed closely against; fitting closely to; lying flat against.

apricot

apricot *n.* The common name for *Prunus armeniaca* (Rosaceae), a roundish, orange-colored fruit, of a rich aromatic flavor, closely related to the plum. The tree grows to the height of 15 to 30 feet, and its flowers appear before its leaves. In cultivation, it is often propagated by budding upon plum stocks.

Aptenia (ap ten'ee uh) *n.* A fast-spreading succulent (fleshy leaved) ground cover (Aizoaceae) with cylindrical, 1-inch-long leaves and numerous red-purple flowers; easily propagated by cuttings. *A. cordifolia* is commonly known as baby sun rose or hot apple.

aqua ammonia *n.* A water solution of ammonia.

aquatic plants *n.* Plants that grow in water, usually fresh water. The term may also be used for plants that grow in bogs, swamps, and at the edges of ponds and lakes. Some may be completely submerged, whereas others may float on the surface, for example, waterlilies (Nympheaceae).

aquifer *n.* A water-bearing formation, usually underground, through which water can move easily.

Aquifoliaceae (ak wih foh lee ay'see ee) *n.* The name of the holly family, consisting of 2 genera - *Ilex* and *Nemopanthus* - and approximately 400 species. Hollies may be trees or shrubs with simple, often spiny leaves, small flowers, and bright berries.

Aquilegia (ak wih lee'jee uh) *n.* A genus of hardy, branching perennial plants (Ranunculaceae), widely distributed over the temperate parts of the Northern Hemisphere. The flowers have 5 flat, elliptical, colored sepals, alternating with 5 spurred petals; the fruit consists of 5 segments with numerous seeds. Commonly known as columbine (from the Latin *columba,* a dove) because the spurred petals with incurved heads resemble doves, the sepals representing the wing. Many species are common in cultivation, and, as they

Aquilegia
(columbine)

are prone to hybridize, the varieties of form and color are numerous.

Arabis (ar'uh bihs) *n.* A large genus of low-growing, spreading plants (Cruciferae) cultivated for edgings, ground covers, alpine rock gardens, and flower borders; commonly known as wall cress or rock cress. They require sun, and many grow well in poor soil. *A. caucasia,* wall rock cress, has gray leaves and small white flowers.

Araceae (uh ray'see ee) *n. pl.* The arum family contains plants varying from tuberous or rhizomatous perennials to tropical climbers grown for their foliage. The leaves are usually arrow-shaped, often huge, and highly ornamental. The inconspicuous flowers are crowded upon a long spike surrounded by a broad, petallike spathe. The family includes 15 genera and about 2,000 species, most of which are found in the tropics. Examples of genera include *Anthurium, Philodendron,* and *Pothos.* The tuberous roots of many species are edible, and some, such as taro or dasheen *(Colocasia esculenta),* are extensively cultivated in tropical countries for food. Some are poisonous, such as the popular houseplant dumb cane *(Dieffenbachia),* which receives its popular name from the fact that when it is chewed, the tongue swells, making it difficult or impossible to talk. Also called aroids.

Arachis (uh'ruh kihs) *n.* A genus of 12 to 15 species of mostly annuals (Luguminosae), native to South America. *A. hypogaea,* the peanut, has trailing stems about two feet long with leaves divided into four oval leaflets, yellow pealike flowers, and fruit with a brittle shell that ripens underground. Grown for its seed, the peanut. Commonly known as peanut, groundnut, goober, grass nut, earth nut, monkey nut, and pindar.

Aralia (uh ray'lee uh) *n.* A large genus of widely distributed herbs, shrubs, and trees with compound leaves, small flowers in rounded clusters, and succulent berries; the type of the family Araliaceae.

Araliaceae (uh ray lee ay'see ee) *n. pl.* The Aralia or ginseng family of plants, comprising 84 genera of herbs, shrubs, trees, and vines. Among the better-known members of the family are ivy, *Hedera Helix;* ginseng, *Panax quinquefolius,* which is used as a stimulant; and *Tetrapanax papyriferus,* from which rice paper is made.

Araucaria (a raw ka′ree uh) *n*. A genus of about 15 species of conifer, large evergreen trees with spreading branches covered with stiff, narrow, pointed leaves and bearing large cones, each scale having a single large seed. The species best known in cultivation is the Chilean pine or monkey-puzzle tree, *A. araucana,* which is quite hardy. A native of the mountains of southern Chile, it forms vast forests. The Norfolk Island pine, *A. heterophylla,* attains a height of 200 feet, but is most often grown in its juvenile form as a houseplant.

arbor *n*. A bower formed by trees, shrubs, or vines intertwined or trained over a latticework trellis, so as to make a leafy roof, and usually provided with seats; any shaded walk. Arbors are used to provide support for plants, to create shade, or to frame a view.

arboraceous (ar buh ray′shuhs) *a*. Pertaining to or of the nature of trees.

Arbor Day *n*. In parts of the United States, a day of each year set apart by law or tradition for the planting of trees.

arborescent (ar buh res′ehnt) *a*. Resembling a tree; treelike in growth, size, or appearance; having the nature and habits of a tree; branching like a tree.

arboretum (ar buh ree′tuhm) *n*. A place in which trees and shrubs, especially rare ones, are cultivated for scientific or other purposes; a botanical tree garden.

arboriculture *n*. The cultivation of trees; the art of planting, training, pruning, and cultivating trees and shrubs for ornamental purposes.

arborist *n*. A specialist in the planting, transplanting, and pruning of trees as well as in diagnosing tree diseases, performing tree surgery, and maintaining trees.

arborvitae (ar′ber vee′tee) *n*. A common name for certain species of *Thuja, Thujopsis,* and *Libocedrus,* all conifers of the Cupressaceae. *Thuja occidentalis,* the American arborvitae, or white cedar, is widely planted for ornament and for hedges.

arbuscle (ar′buhs uhl) *n*. A dwarf tree or treelike shrub, in size between a shrub and a tree.

arbutus (ar byoo′tuhs) *n*. 1. A plant of the genus *Arbutus.* 2. [cap.] A genus of evergreen shrubs or small trees of western North America (Ericaceae) characterized by a many-seeded berry. The strawberry tree, *A. Unedo,* cultivated for ornament, takes its name from its bright scarlet berries. The picturesque and striking madrone of Oregon and California, *A. Menziesii,* sometimes reaches a height of 80 feet or more. 3. The trailing arbutus, *Epigaea repens* is a creeper native to North America with fragrant pink or white flowers that bloom in the spring; also known as mayflower.

Arbutus unedo
(strawberry tree)

Archontophoenix (ar kawn′toh fee′niks) *n*. A genus of 2 species of palms. Commonly known as king palm, they are among the fastest growing palms in cutivation, eventually attaining a height of 80 feet. Widely grown as tub plants in warm winter climates, they sprout easily from seed but are difficult to transplant. Also known as Alexander palm, Barbel palm, piccabean bangalow palm, piccabean palm, step palm.

Arctium (ark′tee uhm) *n*. A genus of 5 species of biennials or short-lived perennials (Compositae) with stout taproots. They grow from 5 feet to 10 feet with large, oval, heart-shaped leaves, spikes or clusters of tubular purple flowers and bristly fruit. Generally considered a weed, they have naturalized in North America. Commonly known as burdock.

Arctostaphylos (ark toh staf′uh luhs) *n*. A genus of evergreen ground covers, shrubs, and small trees, mostly natives of California and Mexico, where the larger species are known as manzanita and sometimes grow from 10 to 20 feet high. Branches tend to be reddish-brown, crooked, and smooth-barked; the flowers are white to pink in clusters at the ends of the stems. Berries are smooth and vary from red to brown. The bearberry or kinnikinnick *(A. Uva-ursi)* is a trailing plant, found in the arctic and in mountainous regions.

Arctotheca (ark′toh thee kuh) *n*. A fast-growing evergreen perennial ground cover (Compositae) with gray-green divided leaves and yellow daisy-like flowers. Commonly known as cape weed.

Arctotis (ark tuh′tihs) *n.* A genus of about 30 species of flowers (Compositae) with a rosette of woolly, lobed leaves growing from the base of the plant and solitary daisylike flowers, which often have a contrasting ring of color around a dark eye in the center. Commonly known as African daisy, a name also applied to *Dimorphotheca* and *Osteospermum.*

Ardisia (ar deezh′eeuh) *n.* A genus of evergreen tropical shrubs and trees (Myrsinaceae) with clusters of small flowers followed by bright red berries. Most often grown as a houseplant.

Areca (ar′eh kuh) *n.* 1. A genus of palms, natives of tropical Asia and the Malay archipelago, with a slender, ringed trunk, leaves composed of a series of leaflets, and solid, orange-colored, pungent, fibrous-coated nuts. There are about 50 species, the most important of which is the pinang or betel palm, *A. Catechu,* which furnishes the betel nut. 2. The houseplant commonly called the Areca palm, formerly *Arecalutescens,* is *Chrysalidocarpus lutescens.*

Arecastrum (ar ee kas′truhm) *n.* A genus of a single species, *A. Romanzoffanum* (Palmae), a fast-growing palm with arching, feathery, glossy green leaves and an exceptionally straight trunk to 50 feet tall. Also known as queen palm.

Arenga, with fruit

Arenga (uh reng′uh) *n.* A genus of 17 species of dwarf to large palms. They grow from 6 to 30 feet, depending on the species, and have divided leaves, often pale beneath. Several species are grown ornamentally.

Arethusa (ar uh thyoo′zuh) *n.* A genus of orchids consisting of a single species, *A. bulbosa* (Orchidaceae), a small North American swamp plant with a single leaf and a handsome, rosy-purple, sweet-scented flower, with yellow and purple markings, that blooms in spring and summer. Commonly known as swamp pink, dragon's mouth, or bog rose.

Argemone (ar jeh moh′nee) *n.* A small genus of about 30 species of poppy (Papaveraceae), all native to North America and Hawaii. They are very ornamental, with spiny leaves and large white, yellow, or lavender flowers 6 inches across. Argemone oil, a semidrying oil useful to painters, is obtained from the seeds of *A. mexicana.* Commonly known as horned poppy or prickly poppy.

aril (ar′ihl) *n.* In botany, a term applied to the coverings or appendages of seeds.

Ariocarpus (ar ee oh kar′puhs) *n.* A genus of 6 species of cactus that look more like rocks than plants (Cactaceae). Commonly known as living-rock or star cactus.

Arisaema (ar ih see′muh) *n.* More than 190 species of tuberous-rooted herbs with 1 to 3-lobed leaves and, often, a purple spathe (broad, leaflike covering) (Araceae). Grown ornamentally for their curious flowers, handsome summer foliage, and colorful fruits. The best-known members of the genus are jack-in-the pulpit *(A. triphyllum)* and green-dragon *(A. Draconitum).*

Aristolochia (ar ihs′toh loh′kee uh) *n.* A large genus of mostly tropical woody climbers and perennial herbs (Aristolochiaceae). There are about 200 species, of which only a few are found in the United States. They are remarkable for their curiously shaped, dull-colored flowers, which vary greatly in form and size. The pipe-vine, or Dutchman's-pipe *A. durior,* is a native of the Alleghenies; it has large heart-shaped leaves and is cultivated as fast-growing ornamental climber on sun porches and verandas. Commonly known as birthwort.

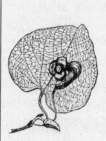

Aristolochia durior
(Dutchman's pipe)

Aristolochiaceae (ar ihs'toh loh kee ay'see ee) *n. pl.* Five genera of herbs or woody climbing vines, widely distributed through temperate and tropical regions. The principal genera are *Aristolochia* and *Asarum,* with about 275 species between them. (See **Aristolochia** and **Asarum**.)

Aristotelia (ar ihs'toh teel'ee uh) *n.* About 11 species of evergreen, berried trees or shrubs native to the Southern Hemisphere. The berries of *A. chilensis* are edible.

Armeria (ar mair'ee uh) *n.* About 35 species of low-growing, tufted, widely adapted, evergreen perennials. *A. maritima,* best known as common thrift, has stiff, narrow leaves and white-to-rose-pink flowers; it is particularly long-blooming in seaside plantings.

Armillaria root rot (ar mih lar'ee uh) *n.* (See **oak root fungus**.)

Armoracia (ar mor ay'shuh) *n.* The botanical name for horseradish, *A. rusticana,* a large, coarse, weedy-looking perennial grown for its thick, heavy, sharply flavored roots. A member of the mustard family (Cruciferae), it is related to cabbage and broccoli.

armyworm *n.* A night-feeding larva of the gray-brown moth. It attacks a variety of vegetable plants. Control with parasitic nematodes or *Bacillus thuringiensis* var. *kurstaki.*

Arnica (ar'nihk uh) *n.* A genus of 30 species of very hardy, hairy perennials (Compositae), many species native to North America. They grow from rhizomes from 3 inches to 2 feet, depending on species, with opposite leaves and yellow daisylike flowers. Grown in borders, rock gardens, or colonized in woodsy places.

Arnotto (ar naht'oh) *n.* 1. A common name for *Bixa Orellana,* a small tree, (Bixaceae), a native of tropical America, also known as the lipstick tree. It has been introduced into south Florida from the West Indies. 2. The dye or coloring matter obtained from the seeds of this tree. It is used in Latin American recipes to add an orange color. Also spelled arnotta and annatto.

aroeira (ar oh air'uh) *n.* A common name for *Schinus terebinthifolius,* a small tree with dark green

Arnica montana
(mountain tobacco)

glossy leaves and bright red winter berries. The branches and berries are used for holiday wreaths, and the resin, bark, and leaves have been used medicinally. Commonly known as Brazilian pepper, it is widely naturalized in Florida and Hawaii.

aroid (ar'oid) *n.* Any plant of the family Araceae, such as *Calla* or *Caladium.*

Aronia (uh roh'nee uh) *n.* A genus of small deciduous shrubs native to North America with alternate, simple leaves with toothed edges, and clusters of small white or pink flowers. Related to roses (Rosaceae), its small, berrylike fruit gives it its common name of chokeberry.

Arrhenatherum (ar uh nath'uh ruhm) *n.* A genus of 6 species of tall, erect, slender, ornamental perennial grasses (Gramineae), used as a meadow grass. It has naturalized in the northern and eastern regions of the United States. Most can be invasive. *A. elatius bulbosum* 'Variegatum', called oat grass, is a more restrained ornamental grown for its white-marked foliage.

arrow arum *n.* The common name for *Peltandra virginica,* a 3-foot-tall, hardy, North American perennial marsh plant. Also known as Virginian wake-robin.

arrowhead *n.* An aquatic plant of the genus *Sagittaria*, so called from the shape of the leaves. (See **Sagittaria**.)

arrowleaf *n.* A common name for *Sagittaria montevidensis*, an aquatic plant with large, arrow-shaped leaves. Also known as swamp potato.

arrowroot *n.* A starch obtained from the horizontal rhizomes (root swellings) of several species of *Maranta*. The most common is *M. arundinacea*, known as the arrowroot plant. This starch is commonly used as a thickening agent in cooking.

arrowroot
a rhizomes

arrowwood *n.* A name given in the United States to several species of shrubs or small trees used by the Indians for making their arrows, as *Viburnum dentatum* and *V. acerifolium, Euonymus atropurpurea,* and *Cornus florida.*

Artemisia (ar tuh′misz ee uh) *n.* 1. A genus of 200 species of annuals, biennials, or perennials (Compositae), many species native to North America. They grow from 6 inches to 10 feet, depending on species, with mostly aromatic, alternate leaves and spikes or clusters of daisylike or buttonlike wihte, yellow, purple or brown flowers. Grown for their aromatic foliage, they thrive on poor, dry soil. 2. A common name for several members of the genus, especially *A. Absinthium,* (wormwood), *A. Abrotanum,* (the herb southernwood), and for the ornamentals commonly known as silver king, silver queen, and silver mound.

artichoke *n.* 1. The common name for *Cynara scolymus* (Compositae), somewhat resembling a thistle. The fleshy bases of the scales are used as food. Artichokes are grown in warmer regions of the United States, requiring about 5 frost-free months to develop. The plants, which may grow to 5 feet tall, have attractive foliage and can be used as a background planting in an ornamental border. 2. Jerusalem artichoke, the *Helianthus tuberosus,* a species of sunflower cultivated for its sweet, tuberous roots.

artichoke
a top of plant, *b* flowering head

articulate *a.* Provided with joints or nodes, at which points separation takes place naturally; jointed, consisting of segments united by joints. An example is Christmas cactus *(Schlumbergera bridgesii).*

artificial light *n.* Light other than sunlight, often fluorescent tubes, used to grow plants.

artillery plant *n.* A name given to some cultivated species of *Pilea,* such as *P. microphylla.* The name refers to the forcible shooting of the pollen from the anther by the sudden straightening of the elastic filaments.

Artocarpus (ar toh kar′puhs) *n.* A genus of about 50 tropical trees (Moraceae). The most important species is *A. altilis,* the breadfruit tree.

arugula (uh roo′guhl uh) *n.* A leafy salad green, *Eruca vesicaria,* with a robust peppery flavor. It is a cool-weather crop, becoming tough and strong flavored with warm weather. Also known as roquette, rocket, and rucola.

Aruncus (uh ruhn'kuhs) *n.* A genus of 2 to 3 species of 4-to-7-foot tall North American perennials with airy, plumelike flowers that grow well in moist, shaded locations. An excellent back-of-the-border plant. Commonly known as goatsbeard.

Arundinaria (uh ruhn deh'nah ree uh) *n.* A genus of woody grasses (Gramineae), many native to North America, growing to 30 feet. The leaves are long and narrow, growing along a usually thick stem. Known as bamboo, these plants flower infrequently; all of the plants in a particular area flower at the same time and all of the plants die. *A. gigantea* is the common cane of the southern United States, growing to 15 feet in cane brakes and known as southern cane.

Arundo (uh ruhn'doh) *n.* A genus of about 5 vigorous, tall-growing, reedlike grasses (Gramineae) native to wet areas. *A. donax* and several of its variegated varieties are sometimes grown as ornamentals, but they are extremely invasive and have become pests. Commonly known as giant reed.

Asarina (a sa ree'nuh) *n.* A small genus of tender, climbing perennial vines native to North America and Europe with triangular leaves and showy white, rose, purple, or blue snapdragonlike flowers. Distinguished from snapdragons *(Antirrhinum)* by their climbing habit.

Asarum (as'air uhm) *n.* A genus of 75 species of mostly hardy low-growing perennials (Aristolochiaceae). They rarely grow as much as 12 inches high with attractive, heart-shaped leaves and purple or brown bell-shaped flowers. Used as a woodland or wild garden groundcover; useful in shady moist situations. Commonly known as wild ginger.

ascidium (uh sihd'ee um) *n.* In botany, any tubular, horn-shaped, or pitcherlike formation of a plant, usually arising from the union of the margins of a leaf or other organ. The ascidium, ordinarily known as a pitcher, is often covered by a lid and contains a fluid in which insects are drowned and macerated; for example, as in the pitcher plants (*Nepenthes* and *Sarracenia*).

ascidium of pitcher plant

Asclepiadaceae (as kleh'pee uh day'see eeu) *n. pl.* The milkweed family, a family of about 130 genera and 2,000 species of perennial plants, shrubs, and vines, mostly succulent with milky sap. It includes *Asclepias* (milkweed), *Stapelia* (carrione flower), and *Hoya* (wax plant).

Asclepias (as kleh'pee uhs) *n.* 1. A genus of 200 species of perennials and shrubs (Asclepiadaceae), some species native to North America. They grow from 1 foot to 6 feet, depending on species, with simple, opposite, sometimes whorled leaves and large clusters of white, red, yellow, orange, or purple flowers. Some have showy puffy seed capsules that split open to reveal silky, white-haired seeds. *A. tuberosa,* (butterfly weed), the most commonly cultivated species, has large clusters of orange flowers that attract butterflies, particularly the migratory monarch butterfly. Used in prairie gardens, wild gardens or in borders. Commonly known as milkweed.

asexual *a.* 1. Not sexual; not sexed; having no sex. 2. Effected or produced by other than sexual processes, as asexual reproduction. Asexual reproduction: any process of propagation that is not effected by means of sexual organs, as, in botany, when propagation is carried on by buds, offshoots, bulbs, etc.

ash (ash) *n.* 1. The popular name of trees belonging to the genus *Fraxinus*. The common ash of Europe, *F. excelsior,* is a handsome ornamental tree,

which grows to 140 feet. 2. Yellow ash, a leguminous tree of the United States, *Cladrastis lutea.* (See
yellowwood; also **hoop ash, mountain ash, wafer ash**.)

Asian hand cultivator *n.* A long- or short-
handled implement with a sharp, pointed, concave,
triangular blade used for digging and cultivating.

Asiatic sweetleaf *n.* The common name for *Symplochos paniculata;* also known as sapphire berry. A
deciduous tree to 40 feet at maturity with variably
shaped leaves, clusters of fragrant white flowers,
and small blue fruits.

Asimina (uh sihm'ih nuh) *n.* A genus of 8 species
of shrubs and small trees native to North America
(Annonaceae). The most widely distributed is the
common papaw, *A. triloba,* which becomes a small
tree and bears a large edible fruit.

asparagus (us spar uh guhs) *n.* The common asparagus, *A. officinalis,* has a much-branched stem
rising from thick and matted perennial root stocks.
The narrow, thread like so-called leaves are in re-
ality branchlets growing in clusters. The part eaten
is the young shoot covered with scales at the top in
place of leaves. The foliage is commonly used in
floral arrangements, particularly in combination
with roses.

asparagus bean (uh spar'uh guhs) *n.* A subspecies
of the black-eyed pea, *Vigna unguiculata sesquipeda-
lis,* an annual of the bean family with green pods up
to 18 inches long. The young pods are cooked as
green beans. Seeds are available from companies
specializing in Asian vegetables. Also known as
yard-long bean.

asparagus beetle *n.* A small beetle that feeds (in
both larval and adult stages) on emerging asparagus
spears, causing scarring and deformities. Control
with sanitation, row covers, handpicking, rotenone, predators, or traditional pesticides.

asparagus fern *n.* Several species of ornamental
asparagus (Liliaceae) with airy, fernlike foliage,
tiny white flowers, red berries, and matted or tuberous roots. Often used as houseplants or
hanging-basket plants.

asparagus knife *n.* An implement for prying and
pulling out long-rooted plants. Also called dandelion weeder or fishtail weeder.

Aspasia (as pas'ee uh) *n.* A genus of 5 species of
epiphytic (growing on, but not taking nourishment
from a host plant) orchids (Orchidaceae). Most
have long leaves and spikes of greenish-yellow
flowers. Best grown in greenhouses or conservatories in a shady location; culture similar to that of
Oncidium.

aspen *n.* The common name for certain trees of
the genus *Populus,* such as *P. tremuloides,* the quaking aspen.

asperifoliate (as'per ih foh'lee iht) *a.* Having
leaves rough to the touch.

Asperula (a spair'uh luh) *n.* A genus of about 90
species of square-stemmed herbs of the woodruff
family (Rubiaceae). Some of the common woo-
druffs have been reclassified as *Galium;* for example, sweet woodruff *(A. odorata)* is now *Galium
odoratum.*

asphodel (as'fuh dehl) *n.* The common name for
some species of *Asphodeline* and *Asphodelus* (Liliaceae). The yellow asphodel or king's-spear,
Asphodeline lutea, is the handsomest and best-
known species. The asphodel referred to by some
early English and French poets is the daffodil, *Narcissus pseudo-narcissus.* In Greek mythology, the asphodel was considered the plant of the dead, and its
pale blossoms were said to cover the meadows of
Hades. The bog asphodel refers to the genus *Narthecium,* the yellow asphodel to *N. Americanum.* False
asphodel is the American name of plants of the genus *Tofieldia.*

Asphodeline (as fuh dehl'uh nee) *n.* A genus of
perennial flowers (Liliaceae). They grow from rhizomes (root swellings), having linear leaves and
clusters of white or yellow flowers. Formerly classified as *Asphodelus.* Commonly known as Jacob's-
rod.

Asphodelus (as fahd'uh luhs) *n.* A genus of flowers (Liliaceae) with basal leaves and cylindrical clusters of white-to-pink flowers. Commonly known
as asphodel.

Aspidistra (as pih dihs'truh) *n.* A genus of evergreen perennials with thick roots and rhizomes;
leathery, glossy leaves; and dull brown-to-green
flowers borne singly next to the ground. Frequently

grown as a houseplant. Because of its tolerance of neglect, low light, and poor soil, it is commonly known as cast-iron plant.

Aspidium (as pihd′ee um) *n.* Formerly a genus of about 20 ferns *(Arachniodes),* now variously reclassified as *Cyrtomium, Dryopteris, Polystichum,* and *Thelypteris.* The common species are usually known as wood ferns or shield ferns. (See **shield fern.**)

Asplenium (as plee′nee uhm) *n.* A genus of about 700 species of ferns (Polypodiaceae). Its species are found in all parts of the world, wherever ferns grow. It includes widely varied forms; many of the species are evergreen, and several are grown as houseplants or greenhouse specimens. Commonly known as spleenwort, the species include *A. nidus,* bird's-nest fern; *A. bulbiferum,* mother fern; *A. rutamuraria,* wall rue; and *A. platyneuron,* ebony spleenwort.

assai (uh sigh′) *n.* The common name of several species of palms of the genus *Euterpe.* Best known as the source of hearts of palm.

assai palm (uh sigh′) *n.* A common name for two species of *Euterpe, E. edulis* and *E. oleracea.*

assimilation *n.* The conversion of a substance taken into the living tissues of plants.

Aster *n.* 1. A genus of between 250 and 500 species of summer- and fall-blooming perennials (Compositae). They have white to lilac-blue or purple daisylike flowers with yellow or purple centers. Commonly known as Michaelmas daisy. 2. [l.c.] A plant of the genus *Aster.* 3. A name of plants of some allied genera, as the China aster *(Callistephus chinensis),* the false aster *(Boltonia asteroides),* and the golden aster *(Chrysopsis).*

Asteraceae (as tuh ray′see ee) *n. pl.* A synonym for Compositae.

Astilbe (as tihl′buh) *n.* A genus of 14 species of hardy perennials (Saxifragaceae). They grow from 2 feet to 6 feet with leaves divided into toothed or finely cut leaflets and airy, plumelike white, pink, rose, or red flowers. Used in beds, borders, under high-branching trees, beside streams and pools, or in pots. Excellent on moist, shady places. Com-

monly known as meadowsweet, spirea, perennial spirea, and false spirea.

Astragalus (uh strag′uh luhs) *n.* A genus of 1,000 species of perennials, some very hardy (Leguminosae), many species native to North America. They grow from 4 inches to 5 feet, depending on species, with leaves divided into leaflets, pealike purple, white, or yellow flowers, and fleshy or papery pods. Used in borders or rock gardens. Commonly known as milk vetch.

Astrantia (uh stran′shee uh) *n.* About 9 species of perennial plants (Umbelliferae), with hand-shaped leaves and showy clusters of small starlike flowers. A few species are suitable for borders. Commonly known as masterworts.

Astrocaryum (as troh ka′ree uhm) *n.* A genus of more than 40 species of palms from 10 to 40 feet in height, with beautiful feathery leaves. Prickly on all or most parts, the stems are covered with stiff and sharp spines, sometimes a foot in length. The seed is enclosed in a hard, stony nut, and the nut is enveloped by a fleshy, fibrous husk. The fruits of several species have been used as a source for palm oil. Commonly known as Mexican feather palms.

astrological gardening *n.* A theory of gardening that orders the timing of garden activities, such as planting and harvesting, according to the position of certain heavenly bodies, especially the waxing and waning of the moon.

Astrophytum (as troh figh′tuhm) *n.* A genus of small, green, globular cacti (Cactaceae) with 4 to 10 ribs, growing from 1½ inches to 3 feet in height. All except *A. ornatum* and *A. capricorne* are spineless, and several have tufts of hair. The yellow flowers are pungent, funnel- or wheel-shaped, and are borne on the top of the cactus. Common varieties are bishop's cap, *A. myriostigma;* star cactus, *A. ornatum;* and sea-urchin cactus, *A. asterias.*

Athyrium (uh thee′ree uhm) *n.* A genus of deciduous ferns (Polypodaceae) growing on short rhizomes (thickened roots) *A. Filix-femina* (lady fern) has bright green leaves to 3 feet long, and there are many varieties and cultivars. It is widely distributed, and many species are hardy.

Atropa (a′truh puh) *n.* A small genus of plants of 4 species (Solanaceae), of which the best known is the deadly nightshade, *A. Belladonna,* a native of Europe and western Asia. (See **lily, belladonna** .)

attar *n.* A general term for a perfume from flowers. In Europe, it generally denotes only the attar (or otto) of roses, an essential oil. The yield is very small, 150 pounds of rose flowers yielding less than an ounce of attar. The odor is agreeable only when diffused, being too powerful when it is concentrated.

attenuate (uh tehn′yoo ayt) *a.* In botany, tapering gradually to a narrow point.

atypical *a.* Having no distinct typical character; not typical; not conformable to the type.

Aubrietia (aw′breesh ee uh) *n.* A genus of 12 species of matlike plants with many colorful spring flowers. Common aubrietia *(A. deltoidea),* with rose-pink to purple flowers is grown as a rock-garden plant. Most species of *Aubretia* are now classified as *Deltoidea.*

Aucuba (aw′kyoo buh) *n.* 1. A small genus of plants (Cornaceae). They are evergreen branching shrubs, with smooth opposite leaves and small unisexual flowers. *A. Japonica* commonly called gold dust plant, has long been in cultivation; it is prized for its mass of glossy, leathery green leaves, splotched with yellow, and its coral-red berries. 2. A shrub of the genus *Aucuba.*

auger (aw′ger) *n.* A tool for boring a hole in the soil. Different-sized augers, powered by hand or electric drills, are used in planting or transplanting seeds, seedlings, or bulbs or in fertilizing shrubs, trees, and ground covers.

auriculate (aw rik′yoo liht) *a.* In botany, said of a leaf or petal with a pair of small, blunt, ear-shaped projections at the base. Also auriculated.

Aurinia (aw rihn′ee uh) *n.* A genus of about 7 species of biennial or perennial plants. *Aurinia* was once combined with *Alyssum.* Commonly known as basket-of-gold, *Aurinia saxatilis* has gray leaves and masses of tiny golden yellow flowers. It is used in the border, rock garden, and on stone walls.

Australian tea tree *n.* The common name for *Leptospermum laevagatum,* a small shrub or tree to 20 feet with a muscular, twisted trunk and shredding bark, long, narrow leaves, and white flowers. Used as a solitary specimen or closely planted as a hedge or windbreak.

autocarpous (awt oh kar′puhs) *a.* In botany, consisting of ripened pericarp alone, having no adnate parts; applied to fruits that are free from the perianth. Same as superior.

autogamous (aw tahg′uh muhs) *a.* Self-fertilized; applied to flowers that are fertilized by their own pollen.

autogamy (aw tahg′uh mee) *n.* In botany, self-fertilization; the fertilization of a flower by its own pollen. (See **allogamy.**)

autotrophic (awt oh trahf′ihk) *a.* The ability to use simple chemical elements or compounds to obtain energy for growth.

autumn crocus *n.* A common name for *Colchicum autumnale,* or meadow saffron. A crocuslike perennial corm with lavender, rose-pink, or white flowers to 4 inches across. The poisonous corm is the source of the drug colchicine.

auxin (awk′sin) *n.* An organic substance characterized by its ability to promote growth, particularly of roots. It is an active ingredient in rooting compounds.

auxotonic (awk suh tahn′ihk) *a.* Determined by growth. In botany, applied to those movements of plants that are the result of growth, rather than of external stimulation.

availability *n.* A term used to refer to the amount of a given nutrient in the soil or in a fertilizer that plants can absorb immediately; it may differ from the amount of the nutrient present.

available nutrient *n.* Nutrients found in the soil that can be taken in by plants at rates and amounts that are significant to the plants' growth.

Avena (uh vee′nuh) *n.* A genus of nearly 25 species of annual grasses (Gramineae). Several are grown as grain crops. *A. sterilis,* known as wild oat or animated oat, has drooping, hairy spikes that are prized for use in dried bouquets; sometimes used as a garden plant.

avens (av'ehnz) *n.* The popular English name of species of plants of the genus *Geum.* The common, or yellow, avens, also called herb Bennet, is G. *urbanum;* the water avens, or chocolate root, G. *rivale.* The mountain avens is *Dryas octopetala.*

Averrhoa (av er oh'uh) *n.* A genus of small trees (Oxalidaceae), containing two species, cultivated for their very acid fruit. The leaves are alternate, divided, and somewhat sensitive. The flowers grow in small, fragrant clusters. *A. Bilimbi,* the bilimbi, is made into pickles, jams, jellies, and drinks and can be candied as well. *A. Carambola,* the carambola has a yellow, deeply ridged, sweet fruit.

avocado *n.* The fruit of *Persea americana,* a tree common in tropical America and the West Indies. The pear-shaped, brownish-green or purple fruit weighs from 1 to 2 pounds; the pulp is firm. The tree is an evergreen, growing to the height of 30 feet.

awn (awn) *n.* In botany, a bristle-shaped terminal appendage, such as the beard of wheat, barley, and many grasses.

ax (aks) *n.* An implement having a wedge-shaped, bladed head mounted on a handle; used for cutting or chopping roots and trees.

axil (ak'sihl) *n.* In botany, the angle formed between the upper side of a leaf and the stem of branch to which it is atttached; in ferns, the angle formed by the branching of a frond.

a axils

axillary (ak'sih ler ee) *a.* In botany, pertaining to or growing from the axil of plants.

axis (ak'sihs) *n.* In botany, the stem; the central part or upright support of a plant to which organs or parts are attached.

Axonopus (ak'sahn uh puhs) *n.* A genus of American grasses. Commonly known as carpet grass.

azadirachtin (uh zad'uh rak'tihn) *n.* (See **neem**.)

Azalea (uh zail'yuh) *n.* 1. Formerly, a genus of showy ericaceous plants, now referred to as *Rhododendron.* 2. [l.c.] A plant or flower belonging to this genus. The plants commonly referred to as azaleas tend to be shorter and more complete in habit, with smaller leaves and smaller flowers than the plants commonly known as rhododendrons; both, however, belong to the genus **Rhododendron.** (See **Rhododendron.**) 3. [l.c.] A name of a species of plants of the genus *Loiseleuria,* the alpine azalea, *L. procumbens.*

azaleamum (uh zail'yuh muhm) *n.* Any of several profusely flowering dwarf chrysanthemums.

Azara (a za'ruh) *n.* A genus of 4 small evergreen trees and shrubs, with simple, shiny, alternate leaves and clusters of fluffy, sweetly fragrant flowers that smell like chocolate to some, vanilla to others. Blooms in early spring, February to April.

Azolla (a'zohl uh) *n.* A genus of 6 species of tiny free-floating water ferns native to the Americas. They are symbiotic with blue-green alga, *Anabaena,* and grow in outdoor pools and aquariums. Commonly known as mosquito plant.

azonal soil (ay'zohn'uhl) *n.* 1. A young soil. 2. A soil having very little or no soil profile development (layers not formed). 3. A soil lacking a well-developed horizon.

 B

Babiana (ba bee an'uh) *n.* A genus of about 61 fibrous corms (Iridaceae) with several pleated, ribbed, slim leaves and white, cream, red, blue, and purple fragrant flowers. Grown as far north as middle Atlantic States. Commonly known as baboon flower and baboonroot.

baboonroot *n.* A common name for *Babiana.*

baby blue-eyes *n.* A common name for *Nemophila menziesii.* A small, low-growing flower with rounded leaves and cup-shaped sky-blue flowers with a white center. Used as a border edging, for massing, or as a cover for bulbs.

baby orchid *n.* A common name for *Odontoglossum grande.* Has large orange-yellow flowers and is popular in hothouses.

baby's breath *n.* 1. *Gypsophila elegans,* a delicate, multibranched annual highly prized by florists as a filler material. Its tiny white or pink blossoms dry well for everlasting arrangements. The plant is large and bushy, easily grown from seed. 2. *G. paniculata,* a perennial plant, larger, but with the same characteristics and uses as *G. elegans.*

baby's tears *n.* A common name for both *Hypoestes phyllostachya* and *Soleirolia soleirolii. H. phyllostachya* has long, thin, dark green leaves marked with lavender-pink spots. Grown primarily as a houseplant, *S. soleirolii* is a dense, low-growing perennial ground cover with tiny, shiny, round leaves. Good in moist shady places, in frost-free gardens.

Baccharis (bak'uh ruhs) *n.* A very large genus of plants (Compositae) native to the Americas. They are mostly evergreen shrubs, sometimes small trees, with small, toothed, dark green leaves often coated with a resinous secretion, and whitish or yellowish flowers. *B. pilularis* is exceptionally useful as a drought-tolerant ground cover.

Baccharis halimifolia
(groundsel tree)

bacciferous (bak sihf'uh rus) *a.* In botany, bearing or producing berries.

bachelor's button *n.* The popular name of *Centaurea canus;* a tall annual, 1 to 2½ feet, with narrow, gray-green leaves and tufted blue, pink, rose, wine-red, or white flowers. Used as a cottage garden plant or massed in borders. Also known as cornflower, these are an easily grown old fashioned favorite.

Bacillus (buh sihl'uhs) *n.* A genus of nontoxic biological (bacterial) insecticides. *B. thuringiensis* var. *kurstaki* controls caterpillars, such as cabbageworm. *B. t.* var. San Diego controls Colorado potato beetle. *B.t.* var.*isralensis* controls mosquito larvae. *B. popilliae,* also called milky spore, controls Japanese beetle larvae.

backcross *n.* 1. In hybridizing, the process of crossing a first generation hybrid with one of its own parents to produce a better variety. 2. A plant produced by backcrossing.

backpack sprayer *n.* A device consisting of a tank worn on the back, a pump, and a wand with nozzle used to apply any of various substances, such as herbicides or pesticides, to plants.

Bacopa (buh koh'puh) *n.* A genus of tropical aquatic plants (Scrophulariaceae) with pairs of opposite leaves and small, single flowers. Commonly known as water hyssop.

bacterial canker *n.* A bacterial disease, common to many fruit trees, that causes a gummy excretion on the trunk and lower branches and, eventually, dead limbs. Best controlled by removing the infected parts with sterile pruning shears.

bacterial wilt *n.* A bacterial disease that infects cucumbers, melons, pumpkins, and sometimes corn. It causes all or part of the plant to wilt and eventually die. Usually transmitted by insects, most often cucumber beetles (except in corn). The best control is to plant resistant varieties and to control cucumber beetles.

bactericide (bak ter'uh sighd) *n.* An agent that kills bacteria; specifically, that which kills bacterial plant disesases.

bagworm *n.* A small brown caterpillar that defoliates many deciduous and evergreen tree species, mostly in the eastern United States. The name comes from small silken bags spun and dragged by the pest. Control with nontoxic *Bacillus thuringiensis* or traditional insecticides.

Bahia grass (buh hee′uh) *n.* (See **Paspalum.**)

Baileya (bai′lee uh) *n.* A genus of 3 or 4 species of herbs (Compositae) with furry, alternate leaves and daisylike yellow flowers; native to dry regions of western North America. Commonly known as desert marigold.

bait (bayt) *n.* Any material used to lure insects, usually to a poisonous substance such as a pesticide. Commonly used to control snails and earwigs.

baking potato *n.* Any variety of potato with dry flesh, suitable for baking.

baking soda *n.* Sodium or potassium bicarbonate. Sometimes mixed with horticultural oils and applied to plants (usually roses) to prevent fungal diseases, such as black spot and powdery mildew.

bald cypress *n.* A common name for *Taxodium distichum*, a tall, cone-bearing, deciduous tree native to the southeastern United States. It grows to 100 feet at maturity, with delicate, feathery yellow-green foliage that turns bright orange-brown in autumn before dropping.

Baldwin *n.* A large, round, bright red variety of apple, which keeps well and is popular for cooking as well as for eating.

ball fern *n.* A common name for *Davallia bullata*, a feathery fern with creeping rhizomes (enlarged underground stems); native to tropical Asia. When planted in a hanging basket, the rhizomes tend to grow on all sides, creating a ball.

balloon flower *n.* A common name for *Platycodon grandiflorus*, a long-lived perennial flower, with oval- to lance-shaped leaves and blue, white, or pink flowers. The buds resemble little inflated balloons.

balloon vine *n.* A common name for the tropical vine *Cardiospermum Halicacabum* (Sapindaceae), native to the tropical regions of the Americas and now naturalized in the southeastern United States. It bears a large, 3-celled, bladderlike pod. Also called heartseed.

balloon vine

balm (bahm) *n.* 1. An oily, aromatic resin or other substance, exuding from trees; hence, by extension, any aromatic substance given off from plants. 2. One of several aromatic plants, particularly those of the genus *Melissa*. The sweet balm, or lemon balm, is *M. officinalis*. Plants of other genera so named are the bee balm, *Monarda didyma;* the horse balm, *Collinsonia canadensis;* the Molucca balm, *Moluccella laevis;* and balm of Gilead, *Cedronella canariense*. Balm of heaven is the *Umbellularia californica*, an evergreen with strongly aromatic foliage.

balsam *n.* 1. An oily, aromatic, resinous substance, exuding from trees. (See **balm.**) Balsam is the name often applied to the balsam fir, *Abies balsamea*, an evenly shaped aromatic tree favored as a Christmas tree. 3. The *Impatiens balsamina*, a common flowering annual cultivated as a bedding plant, is often called garden balsam. Its white, red, and yellow flowers, which may be single or double, look like miniature camelias.

balsam apple *n.* A common name for an annual tropical vine, *Momordica Balsamina* (Cucurbitaceae). It climbs by tendrils and bears a small, warty fruit of a red or orange color. The mature fruits make interesting decorative arrangements.

Balsaminaceae (bahl suh muh nay′see ee) *n. pl.* A family of 2 genera and 500 species of herbaceous herbs or subshrubs native to tropical and subtropical Asia and Africa.

balsam pear *n.* A common name for *Momordica Charantia* (Cucurbitaceae), a climbing vine with deeply lobed leaves and oblong orange-yellow fruit. Also known as bitter gourd and bitter cucumber. Has been used medicinally.

balsam tree *n*. A name given in North America to *Populus balsamifera* and on the West Coast to *P. trichocarpa*. It is also given to the firs *Abies balsamea, A. Fraseri* (the latter tree being distinguished as the she-balsam), and *A. concolor*.

bamboo
1 showing growth, *2* flowers, leaves, and stem

bamboo *n*. 1. The common name of the treelike grasses belonging to the genus *Bambusa* and its allies. 2. A stick or cane from the stem of the bamboo. Often refers to sacred bamboo, the *Nandina domestica* is a handsome evergreen shrub (Berberidaceae) that bears red berries in winter; its leaves turn red in autumn, but do not fall; used, like bamboo, to create an Oriental effect in arrangements.

bamboo-brier *n*. A common name for *Smilax rotundifolia*, a tall, thorny climber native to the United States. Also known as greenbrier or bullbrier.

bamboo grass *n*. (See **Chasmanthium**.)

banana *n*. A plant of the genus *Musa, M. acuminata*, cultivated for its fruit in the tropics. The trunklike stem, formed of the compact, sheathing leaf stalks, grows to a height of 8 or 10 feet, bearing its oblong fruit in a dense cluster 2 or 3 feet long and sometimes weighing 70 or 80 pounds. Several varieties are cultivated, differing in size, color, and flavor. After fruiting, the stem decays, or is cut

down, and new shoots spring from the root and produce a new crop in a few months. The banana is an excellent source of dietary potassium. *a*. Used in naming hybrid varieties or others that have long, thin shapes and creamy or yellow color, such as Hungarian banana peppers.

banana

banana shrub *n*. A common name for *Michelia figo*, an evergreen shrub with small creamy-yellow flowers that smell strongly of ripe bananas.

banding *n*. 1. Placing fertilizer in continuous narrow bands and then covering it with soil. 2. Encircling part of a plant (usually the trunk) or a portion of a garden with some type of material that traps, kills, or excludes pests. Common types include sticky materials, copper stripping, and poisonous baits.

banding trees *n*. The act of fastening a barrier around the trunk of a tree to mark the tree for some attention, such as pruning, or to discourage infestation by crawling insects.

baneberry (bayn'ber ee) *n*. A common name of plants of the genus *Actaea*, so called because of their poisonous berries.

Banksia (bangk'see uh) *n*. A genus of small evergreen shrubs or trees (Proteaceae). The foliage is hard and dry and extremely variable in form, and the flowers form close, cylindrical heads resembling bottlebrushes. Many species are grown, especially in Southwestern gardens, and used in floral arrangements, also in dried arrangements.

banner *n*. 1. The upper petal, usually broad and growing straight up, of some flowers. 2. One of the usually erect petals of the inner upright section of an iris. Also called the standard.

banner of pea-blossom

banner plant *n.* A name given to some cultivated species of *Anthurium* (Araceae), in which the bright scarlet spathe (petal-like upper leaf) is broadly expanded at right angles to the spadix, or central spike of the blossom.

banyan *n.* An East Indian fig tree, *Ficus benghalensis* (Moraceae), remarkable for the area that individual trees cover through the development of aerial roots from the branches, which descend to the ground and become trunks for the support and nourishment of the extending crown. It grows rapidly, frequently covering a space 100 yards in diameter and reaching a height of 80 or 100 feet. It is extensively planted as a shade tree. Also spelled bania or banian.

Baptisia (bahp teez'ee uh) *n.* A genus of 30 to 35 species of hardy drought-tolerant perennials (Leguminosae), native to North America. *B. australis* (plains false indigo or wild blue indigo) forms large clumps to 6 feet with bluish-green leaves divided into oval leaflets and tall spikes of deep purple sweet-pea-shaped flowers. Used in sunny borders and wild gardens. Commonly known as false indigo and wild indigo.

barb *n.* In botany, a stiff bristle or hair terminating an awn or prickle, usually slanted downward or backward.

barbados cherry *n.* A common name for any of several West Indian shrubs of the genera *Malpighia* and *Bunchosia*.

Barbarea (bahr buh ree'uh) *n.* A genus of weedy herbs (Cruciferae) commonly known as winter cress, native to the Northern Hemisphere. The leaves are divided into leaflets, and the small yellow flowers grow in terminal clusters.

barbate (bahr'bayt) *n.* In botany, bearded; furnished with long and weak hairs.

barberry *n.* 1. A spiny shrub of the genus *Berberis, B. vulgaris,* bearing racemes (long clusters) of yellow, ill-smelling flowers, which produce elongated red berries of a pleasantly acid flavor; a native of Europe that has naturalized in New England. (See **Berberis.**) 2. The fruit of this shrub.

bark (bahrk) *n.* Generally, the dry and dead outer covering of woody stems, branches, and roots of plants, as distinct and separable from the wood itself; considered to include all tissue outside the true cambium (the growth layer between bark and wood).

bark beetle *n.* An insect whose larvae (often called borers) bore beneath the bark of a variety of species, girdling trunk and limbs, thus causing dieback and often killing the plant. Difficult to control, but healthy, vigorous plants are less likely to be attacked than stressed ones. Lindane is a sometimes effective, although toxic, chemical control.

bark-ringing *n.* A procedure used to try to force fruit trees and some other woody plants to bloom. It is done by cutting a complete ring around the trunk below the lowest branch and another ring directly beneath the first. The bark between the two rings is removed and the scar covered with grafting wax.

Barleria (bahr-lair'ee uh) *n.* About 230 species of tropical shrubs and herbs (Acanthaceae), many drought-tolerant. They have showy blue or white flowers, and some species have spines.

barley *n.* The grain of the barley plant, eaten and used to prepare ales, beers, and whiskey. (See **Horteum.**)

barrel cactus *n.* A common name for 3 different cacti: *Echinocactus Garusonii, Ferocactus ancanthoides, and F. wislizenii.*

barren strawberry *n. Waldsteinia fragarioides,* a creeping, strawberrylike herb sometimes grown in rock gardens.

barrenwort (bahr'ehn wert) *n.* The common name of *Epimedium,* a genus of about 21 species of low, herbaceous perennial plants (Berberidaceae) having creeping roots, small leaves divided into leaflets, and small white or yellow flowers. Used primarily in rock gardens.

barrier *n.* Some type of physical obstruction to keep pests from reaching plants. Barriers include copper stripping to exclude snails, row covers to exclude many pests from vegetables, and sticky materials used to keep pests from climbing tree trunks.

Bartlett *n.* A type of pear with a round base, soft, juicy flesh, and a sweet flavor. This is the most popular pear of home orchards.

basal leaves *n.* Leaves growing at the base or bottom of a plant.

base *n.* 1. An alkaline solution. 2. A solution with a pH of 7.1 or higher.

basifixed (bay'sih fihkst) *a.* In botany, attached at the base or lower end.

basifixed anthers
a anthers, *b* filaments

basifugal (bay sihf'yoo guhl) *a.* In botany, said of the growth of leaves that develop from the base upward.

basil (bay'sihl) *n.* 1. A common name for *Ocimum basilicum,* a fragrant, tender annual herb grown for culinary uses, known as sweet or common basil. Bush or lesser basil is *O. basilicum,* 'minimum'. 2. The tender and highly flavored leaves are often used with tomatoes. Basil is highly sensitive to cold and will not survive even a light frost. Varieties include anise basil, cinnamon basil, and lemon-scented basil, which have overtones of those flowers, as well as purple basil, which has deep purple leaves and stems. Mexican basil has a smaller leaf and a milder flavor.

basin irrigation (level borders) *n.* The irrigation of level areas that are surrounded by ridges or levees to retain the water.

basket fern *n.* The common name for *Nephrolepis pectinata,* a popular indoor fern for hanging baskets. Its fronds are about 18 inches long and grow in a compact, neat shape.

basket flower *n.* A common name for 2 different flowers, *Centaurea americana* and *Hymenocallis narcissiflora.*

basket-of-gold *n.* The common name for yellow alyssum, *Aurinia saxatile,* often planted in stone walls. It is a low growing plant.

basswood *n.* The common name of the American linden, or lime tree, *Tilia Americana.* The white basswood is *T. heterophylla.* Also called bass.

bast *n.* 1. In botany, a woody fiber obtained from the phloem, or inner bark, used to make hemp, jute, ramie, etc.

batata (buh tah'tuh) *n.* Another name for the sweet potato. (See **sweet potato**.)

bat house *n.* A rectangular box, similar to a birdhouse, to attract and shelter an ecologically safe form of insect control, the bat.

Bauhinia leaf and flower

Bauhinia (boh ihn'ee uh) *n.* A genus of 300 species of trees, shrubs, and vines, woody lianas (Leguminosae). *B. blakeana,* the Hong Kong orchid tree, is a small, umbrella-shaped tree with twin-

beam tree, flowers and leaves

lobed leaves and huge, orchidlike multicolored flowers of maroon, purple, rose, and pink, often all in one blossom. Several species are used in frost-free climates as spectacular flowering garden or street trees.

bay (bay) *n.* 1. The berry of the *Myrica pensylvanica.* 2. The sweet bay, *Laurus nobilis,* an aromatic evergreen shrub or tree native to the Mediterranean; it may grow to 40 feet in height. Its elliptical, dark green leaves are tough, glossy, and as long as 4 inches. Its leaves are used in cooking and their oil in perfumery. The flavor of bay is mild and easily lost in long cooking, so a whole leaf is added to soups or stews toward the end of cooking time and then removed before serving. Bay leaf should not be broken into foods, because the fragments, which remain hard and sharp, can cause injury.

bayberry *n.* 1. The fruit of the wax myrtle, *Myrica pensylvanica,* which yields wax for candle making. Also called candleberry. 2. *M. Californica,* California bayberry or California wax myrtle. 3. *Pimenta racemosa,* from which an oil is obtained, which is used in the manufacture of bay rum.

baygon (bay'gahn) *n.* (See **propoxur.**)

bay leaf *n.* The leaf of the herb bay, *Laurus nobilis.* (See **bay.**)

Bayleton (bay'lee tuhn) *n.* (See **triadimefon.**)

beach heather *n.* A common name for *Hudsonia tomentosa,* native to northeastern North America as far south as the Carolinas. Short-lived, it grows in dry, sandy soil. The mound-shaped evergreen shrubs are grown in seaside gardens, but are very difficult to transplant sucessfully. It has yellow flowers in May and June.

bead plant (beed plant) *n.* A common name for *Nertera granadensis,* a low-growing matted plant with tiny egg-shaped leaves, minute greenish flowers, and a small orange berry. Grown as a ground cover in warm-winter climates.

beaked (beekt) *a.* Having a beak, or something resembling a beak; beak-shaped. In botany, rostrate; or ending in a beaklike point.

beam tree (beem tree) *n.* A common name for the tree *Sorbus Aria,* also called whitebeam. It is of moderate size, bearing an abundance of white flowers and showy red fruit.

bean (been) *n.* 1. A smooth, kidney-shaped seed, flattened at the sides, borne in long pods by a leguminous plant; usually of the genus *Phaseolus Vicia,* and, with a descriptive names, of other genera. 2. The plant producing beans. The bean known to the ancients from prehistoric times was the *Vicia Faba,* a broad bean native to western Asia. Numerous other kinds of cultivated beans belong chiefly to the genus *Phaseolus.* Among the *P. vulgaris* are the common kidney bean, the haricot and French beans, the stringbean, and the pole bean; to *P. lunatus,* the lima and Carolina beans and the butter bean. To the genus *Vigna* belong the asparagus, adzuki, and mung beans. Beans are very nutritious, containing much starch and a large percentage of a nitrogen compound called legumin, similar to the casein in cheese. The name bean is also given to many leguminous seeds that are not cultivated or used as food, and to certain other plants and their seeds that are not in the legume family: the coffee bean; castor bean, the seed of *Ricinus communis,* yielding castor oil: soy beans, *Glycine Max:* and the vanilla bean, the fragrant pod of *Vanilla planifolia,* used for flavoring.

bean leaf beetle *n.* A small, 4-spotted ladybug relative that attacks beans and peas. The adults skeletonize leaves, the larvae infest roots. Control with pyrethrins or traditional insecticides.

bean sprout *n.* The edible sprout of the bean seed, primarily of mung beans, grown in a moist, dark environment. Commonly used in Asian cooking, especially Chinese.

beanstalk *n.* The stem of a bean, or the whole plant, as Jack and the beanstalk.

bean tree (been tree) *n.* A name given to *Castanospermum australe,* also called the Moreton Bay chestnut. It is grown in southern California for its dark evergreen foliage and showy red and yellow blossoms in July; also to *Laburnum* spp.

bean-trefoil *n*. A common name for *Anagyris foetida*.

bearberry *n*. 1. A trailing evergreen shrub, *Arctostaphylos uva-ursi*, found throughout the arctic and mountainous portions of the Northern Hemisphere, and bearing small, bright red berrylike fruit. The leaves are very astringent and slightly bitter. It is also called kinnikinick.

beard (beerd) *n*. In botany: 1. A crest, tuft, or covering of spreading hairs. 2. The awn or bristlelike appendage upon the chaff of grain and other grasses.

beard grass *n*. (See **Polypogon**.)

beard moss *n*. A common name for the lichen *Usnea barbata*, which hangs like a greenish-gray shaggy beard from the branches of trees.

beardtongue *n*. A common name given to plants of the genus *Pentstemon*, with reference to the bearded stamen, which sticks out of the center of the blossom.

bear's-breech *n*. A common name of *Acanthus spinosus*. (See *Acanthus*.)

bear's-ear *n*. A common name for *Primula Auricula*, in referring to the shape of its leaf. Their spring-blooming flowers are available in a variety of colors, some with contrasting centers, and the round leaves form as rosette close to the ground.

bear's-foot *n*. A plant of the genus *Helleborus*, *H. foetidus*. (See *Helleborus*.)

bear's-grape *n*. (See **bearberry**.)

Beaucarnea (boh kar'nee uh) *n*. A genus of drought-tolerant, tall, treelike plants, swollen at the base; native to deserts of North America. Commonly known as pony tail plant or bottle palm. Often grown as a houseplant or in desert gardens.

Beaumontia (boh mahn'shee uh) *n*. A small genus of tropical and subtropical woody vines with opposite, entire leaves and large trumpet-shaped flowers. Grown ornamentally in Florida and a popular greenhouse plant.

beaumont root (boh'mahnt) *n*. Same as culber's-root or bowman's-root, common names for *Gillenia trifoliata* and *Veronicastrum virginicum*.

beautyberry *n*. A common name for *Callicarpa americana*, a shrub with toothed, hairy 6-inch-long leaves, blue flowers, and violet fruit in late spring and early summer.

beautybush *n*. A common name for *Kolkwitzia amabilis*, a shrub with egg-shaped leaves, small pink and yellow flowers, and tiny bristly fruits.

bed (behd) *n*. An area within a garden or lawn in which plants are grown.

bedding plant *n*. An ornamental flowering plant or foliage plant suited by habit for growing in beds or masses. Often used as a synonym for annual.

bedstraw *n*. A popular name for the different species of the genus *Galium*, from the old practice of using it as a mattress filling in beds. Our Lady's or yellow bedstraw is *G. verum;* white bedstraw is *G. Mollugo*. (See **Galium**.) Yellow bedstraw was also used as a coloring for butter and cheese but is now grown in herb gardens for its ornamental and historical interest.

bee *n*. An insect welcome in the garden for its ability to polinate plants as it moves from flower to flower.

bee balm *n*. A flowering herb, *Monarda didyma*, of the mint family. Its red, pink, or white blossoms grow on tall stems and attract bees. The leaves are used as a tea, which gives rise to another common name, Oswego tea, and are the source of the oil that gives Earl Grey tea its distinctive flavor. Also known as monarda and bergamot.

beech *n*. A tree of the genus *Fagus* (Fagaceae), large deciduous trees native to the northern temperate zone. The common or European beech, *F. sylvatica*, grows to 80 feet, with branches forming a beautiful head with thick foliage; the bark is smooth. Ornamental hybrid varieties are grown, such as the copper beech (*F.s.*'Atropurpurea') with wine-colored leaves, the weeping beech (*F.s.* 'Pendula'), and the fern-leafed beech (*F.s.*'Laciniata') with divided leaves. The American beech, *F. grandiflora*, is a very similar tree, sometimes 100 feet in height and 3 or 4 feet in diameter.

beechdrops *n.* A low, wiry annual plant, *Epifagus Virginiana,* without green foliage, parasitic upon the roots of the beech in the United States.

beech fern *n.* A common name for the fern *Thelypteris phegopteris.*

beeflower *n.* A common name for the North American wildflowers *Cleome serrulata* and *C. lutea.* Also called bee orchis or bee orchid.

beefsteak *n.* A large tomato, very fleshy and particularly popular for slicing.

bee skep (bee skehp) *n.* A traditional beehive made of twisted grass, now used ornamentally.

beet (beet) *n.* A plant of the genus *Beta.* The various forms are a single species, *B. vulgaris.* The common beet is extensively cultivated in many varieties for the use of its sweetish, succulent root as a vegetable and as feed for cattle. The mangel is a large coarse form raised exclusively for cattle. The sugar beet is a large, white, and very sweet variety, from the root of which sugar is manufactured. Called beetroot in British books, to distinguish it from the beetgreen, which is prized as a pot herb and is occasionally used in salads when it is very small. Beetroots are high in sugar but low in calories and are a good source of potassium and iron. The greens are rich in calcium.

bee tree *n.* A hollow tree occupied by wild bees.

beetroot *n.* The root of the beet plant. (See **beet**.) This usage is common in Britain and in older American books.

beggar's-lice *n.* The name given to species of *Bidens,* the seeds of which cling persistently to clothing. Also called beggar's-ticks.

beggar-weed *n.* A name sometimes given to such weeds as knotweed, spurry, and dodder.

Begonia (beh gohn'yuh) *n.* A very large genus of many-petaled flowers (Begoniaceae). Most are natives of the warmer regions of the globe, and are frequently cultivated as foliage plants and for their showy flowers. Some, such as the Rex begonias, are grown for their beautifully patterned leaves. Others, such as the tuberous begonias, are grown as hanging-basket plants or summer pot plants for their spectacular red, yellow, or orange flowers.

The fibrous begonias are used as annuals, primarily for massing or bedding out in the garden.

Begonia

Begoniaceae (beh goh nee ay'see ee) *n. pl.* A family of plants of 3 genera and more than 1,000 species. The genera are *Begonia, Hillbrandia,* and *Synbegonia.*

begonias, tuberous (beh gohn yuhz, too' ber uhs) *n.* Summer-blooming tender perennials that grow from thick, round, brown tubers, die back in fall, and go dormant during winter. The leaves are toothed, and the thick stems are succulent. The brilliant red, yellow, and orange flowers are massive, many-petaled, and heavy. They are excellent hanging-basket, window-box, or conservatory plants.

Belamcanda (behl am kan'uh) *n.* A genus of 2 species of hardy perennial flowers (Iridaceae) with stout rhizomes (enlarged underground stems), broad, irislike leaves, clusters of orange flowers dotted with red, and shiny black seeds exposed when the seed capsules split. Commonly known as blackberry lily.

Belgian endive (behl'juhn en'dighv) *n.* A leafy green vegetable, *Cichorium intybus,* used in salads and cooking. Its small, elongated heads are compact and slightly bitter in flavor. The roots are grown outdoors in summer, then brought into a dark place, where they are grown in boxes or pots to produce almost white leaves. Although the vegetable is known as Belgian endive, the plant is witloof chicory.

belladonna *n.* A plant, *Atropa Belladonna* (Solanaceae), or deadly nightshade, a native of central and southern Europe. All parts of the plant are poisonous.

belladonna
a flowering branch, b fruit

bellflower *n.* A common name for the species of *Campanula,* a name derived from the shape of the flower, which resembles a bell. (See cut under *Campanula.*)

Bellis (behl′ihs) *n.* The daisy, a small genus of annual or perennial flowers (Compositae), native to the temperate and cold regions of the Northern Hemisphere. The English daisy, *B. perennis,* often grows in lawns. The plump, fully double ones are horticultural varieties with rosettes of dark green leaves and with pink, rose, red, or white double flowers on short stems. Used as a low edging plant or in pots. (See **daisy.**)

Bellium (behl′ee uhm) *n.* A small genus of low-growing flowers (Compositae) with leaves at the base of the plant and asterlike white or pinkish flowers.

bell pepper *n.* Any of several blocky, squarish, meaty varieties of sweet pepper.

bells of Ireland *n. Molucella laevis,* an ornamental annual herb, native to Asia Minor, with round, bright green bell-shaped bracts (flower bases) crowded along an upright stem. When dried, they turn a pale straw color, and they are popular for use in dried arrangements.

bellwort (behl′wert) *n.* A common name for spring lilies (Liliaceae) of the genus *Uvularia.*

Beloperone guttata (behl uh per oh′ nuh guh tah-′tuh) *n.* The former classification for the shrimp plants, now classified as *Justicia Brandegeana.* Shrimp plants are small evergreen shrubs with soft

green leaves and bronze, rose, or yellow-green shrimp-shaped flowers in terminal, drooping, 6-inch spikes. Grown ornamentally in warm weather regions, it has naturalized in southern Florida.

belvedere (behl′vuh deer) *n.* 1. A common name for the summer annual *Kochia scoparia.* Grown for its foliage, it is widely naturalized in the United States. Also called summer cypress. 2. A garden summerhouse with a view, or a terrace overlooking a view.

ben (behn) *n.* The seed of any of the trees of the genus *Moringa. Moringa pteryogosperma,* the horseradish tree, yields oil of ben, or ben oil. (See **horseradish tree.**)

bendiocarb (behn′dee oh karb) *n.* A synthetic insecticide used to control a variety of house and garden pests including earwigs and ants.

beneficial insect *n.* Any insect whose presence has a positive effect on plants growing nearby. They include bees, which act as pollinator; earthworms, which improve soil structure; and lacewing larvae, which prey on plant pests. Encouraging or releasing beneficial insects is an important part of organic gardening.

beneficial organisms *n.* An animal or plant used to control garden pests.

Benlate (behn layt′) *n.* (See **benomyl.**)

benne (behn′ee) *n.* An annual plant, *Sesamum Indicum* (Pedaliaceoe), a native of India, but largely cultivated in most tropical and subtropical countries for the sake of the seeds and their oil. From ancient times, the seeds have been classed with the most nutritious grains, and they are still used for food. Also benni or bene. They are sold as sesame seeds, except in the southern United States, where benne is a more common name.

benomyl (behn′oh mihl) *n.* A systemic fungicide used to control a variety of diseases of ornamentals, usually foliar. It is absorbed into the system of the plant to fight off infection. Common trade name: Benlate.

bent grass (behnt gras) *n.* (See **Agrotis.**)

benzoin (behn′zuh wihn) *n.* Gum benjamin; the concrete resinous juice of *Styrax officinalis,* a tree of

Southeast Asia. It is chiefly used in cosmetics, perfumes, and incense. Although the tree is not grown in the United States, benzoin can be purchased from herb suppliers as an ingredient for potpourri.

Berberidaceae (ber'ber ih day'see ee) *n. pl.* A family of plants with 13 cultivated genera, including *Mahonia* (Oregon grape) and *Nandina* (sacred bamboo). Commonly known as the barberry family.

Berberis (ber'ber ihs) *n.* A genus of the family Berberidaceae that contains about 500 species of shrubby plants, including the common barberry. The common barberry, *B. vulgaris,* is used for hedges and as specimen shrubs for its foliage, attractive spring-blooming flowers, and bright red winter berries.

Berberus vulgaris
(barberry)
fruit, flower, and anther

Berchemia (ber kee'mee uh) *n.* A genus of tropical, twining, deciduous, woody vines (Rhamnaceae) with alternate, leaves and with small flowers in clusters at the end of the stems. Commonly known as supplejack.

bergamot (ber'guh maht) *n.* 1. A variety of orange, *Citrus aurantium,* subsp. *bergamia,* with a very aromatic rind, from which oil of bergamot is obtained. The essence is a product chiefly of southern Italy and is much employed in perfumery. 2. A popular name for *Monarda didyma.* (See **bee balm.**)

Bergenia (ber gee'nee uh) *n.* A genus of 12 or more species of perennial plants (Saxifragaceae) with thick rhizomes (enlarged underground stems) that develop into large clumps. They have attractive, broad, wavy leaves and small pink or white clusters of flowers. Grown as a ground cover in

shady situations. They are attractive to snails and slugs.

Bergerocactus (ber ger oh kak'tus) *n.* A genus of a single species, *B. Emmoryi* (Cactaceae), a slender cactus with sprawling, ribbed stems branching from the base and with yellow flowers that close at night; native to southern California and northern Baja, California.

Bermuda grass *n.* (See **Cynodon.**)

Bermuda onion *n.* A type of onion characterized by its white skin, round shape, and mild flavor.

berry *n.* In botany: 1. In ordinary use, any small pulpy and usually edible fruit, as the huckleberry, strawberry, blackberry, mulberry, and checkerberry, of which only the first is a berry in the technical sense. 2. Technically, a simple fruit in which the entire pericarp (inside) is fleshy, except the outer skin or epicarp; for example, banana, tomato, grape, and currant. 3. The dry kernel of certain kinds of grain, such as the berry of wheat and barley, or the coffeeberry.

Berteroa (ber tee roh'uh) *n.* A genus of several species of drought-tolerant plants that grow in stony or rocky places. *B. incana,* the only species in cultivation, has naturalized in parts of the United States. Commonly known as hoary alyssum, it has pale, 2-foot-long leaves and white or yellow flowers.

Bertholletia (ber thuh leesh'ee uh) *n.* A small genus of which only 1 species, *B. excelsa* (Lecythidaceae), is grown. It is a large tropical tree; the fruit is known as the Brazil nut.

Bertolonia (ber toh loh'nee uh) *n.* A genus of 14 species of dwarf, creeping herbs (Melastomataceae) grown as houseplants for their foliage, which is often metallic above and purplish beneath.

Bessera (behs'eh ruh) *n.* A genus of Mexican bulbs (Amaryllidaceae) consisting of 2 species, of which only *B. elegans* is cultivated. It grows from corms (sprouting bulblike bases), has leaves nearly 3 feet long, and bears clusters of showy, bell-shaped, crimson flowers on a 3-foot-tall stalk. Commonly called coral-drops.

bethlehem sage *n. Pulmonaria saccharata.*

betony (beht'uh nee) *n.* The common name for *Stachys officinalis,* an ornamental herb with furry gray leaves. (See **lamb's ears**.) Wood betony is the common name of *Pedicularis Canadensis*.

Betula (beht'yoo luh) *n.* A genus of 50 or 60 species of hardy deciduous trees or shrubs native to the Northern Hemisphere; the birches (Betulaceae). Closely related to alders *(Alnus).*

Betulaceae (beht yo lay'see ee) *n.* A family of 6 genera and more than 100 species of hardy deciduous trees and shrubs. Commonly known as the birch family.

B horizon *n.* 1. A soil layer underneath the surface soil. 2. A subsoil.

bi- (bigh) *prefix.* Two, twice, double, or twofold, as in *biennial,* a plant requiring two seasons to produce flowers.

bibb *n.* A popular variety of butterhead lettuce.

bicolor *n.* A sweet hybrid corn with both white and yellow kernels on the same ear.

Bidens (bigh'dehnz) *n.* A genus of 200 species of herbaceous composite plants (Compositae) closely related to *Cosmos* and *Coreopsis.* The wild species are weeds, infamous for their burs. The persistency with which the seeds adhere to clothing and the coats of animals has given rise to the common names of beggar's-ticks, beggar's-lice, stick-tight, tickseed, and bur-marigold.

biennial *n.* A plant that requires 2 seasons of growth to produce its flowers and fruit, growing leaves the first year, flowering, fruiting, and going to seed, and dying the next.

bifarious (bigh fa'ree uhs) *n.* Divided into 2 parts. Specifically, in botany, pointing in 2 ways, or arranged in 2 opposite rows, as leaves that grow only on opposite sides of a branch.

bifid (bigh'fihd) *a.* Divided into 2 equal lobes or parts by a space in the center; forked, like a snake's tongue.

bifoliate (bigh-foh'lee iht) *a.* Having 2 leaves.

bifoliolate (bigh foh'lee oh liht) *a.* Having 2 leaflets; as in a compound (many parted) leaf.

bifollicular (bigh foh lihk'yoo ler) *a.* Having 2 seed cases, or twin pods, especially in milkweed *(Asclepias).*

biforate (bigh fohr'iht) *a.* Having 2 pores or perforations. Also biforous.

Big Boy *n.* A hybrid tomato producing large, flavorful tomatoes with thick walls, among the best-known varieties for home gardens.

Bignonia (bihg noh'nee uh) *n.* A genus of 1 species of woody, evergreen vine, *B. capreolata* (Bignoniaceae), native to eastern North America. It grows to 50 feet, has entire 6-inch leaves, branching tendrils, and trumpet-shaped yellow-red flowers. Commonly called trumpet flower.

Bignoniaceae (bihg-noh'nee ay'see ee) *n. pl.* A family of 110 genera and 750 species of trees, shrubs or woody vines, mostly tropical and subtropical. Of the many genera, the best known are *Bignonia, Tecoma, Campsis, Catalpa,* and *Jacaranda.*

Bignoniaceae
flowering branch of trumpet creeper
a open follicle showing seeds, *b* seed of *Catalpa bignoniodes*

big tree (bihg tree) *n.* A common name for the redwood tree, *Sequoiadendron giganteum,* which grows to 300 feet and more, reputed to be the largest living thing on the planet.

bilabiate (bigh lay'bee iht) *a.* Possessing, or having the appearance of possessing, 2 lips. In botany, the two-lipped center of a flower. This characteristic is typical of the family Labiatae and can be seen in the blossoms of *Salvia*.

bilabiate calyx of *Salvia*

bilberry (bihl′ber ee) *n.* A shrub and its fruit, *Vaccinium Myrtillus. V. uliginosum* is known as the bog bilberry; *V. caespitosum,* the dwarf bilberry. (See **Vaccinium** and **whortleberry**.)

Billardiera (bihl ahrd ee er′uh) *n.* A genus of 8 species of small tender shrubs (Pittosporaceae) with twining branches and alternate leaves; greenish-yellow flowers, either solitary or clustered; and a blue or violet berry.

Billbergia (bihl ber′jee uh) *n.* A genus of about 52 species of tropical epiphytic plants (Bromeliaceae). (Epiphytes are plants which live on a host plant, but do not rob it of nourishment.) They grow in stiff, tall, slender rosettes with crowded, spiny, toothed leaves and spikes of often drooping, colorful flowers. Used outdoors in the south, and as houseplants elsewhere.

bilobate (bigh loh′bayt) *a.* Having or divided into 2 lobes, as a bilobate leaf.

bilocular (bigh lahk′yuh ler) *a.* Divided into 2 cells, or compartments, such as a walnut.

binate (bigh′nayt) *a.* Being double or in couples; having only 2 leaflets to a group; growing in pairs.

Bing cherry *n.* A big heart-shaped cherry, dark red to black in color. It is very sweet and juicy, and is popular with home gardeners.

binomial (bigh noh′mee uhl) *a.* In botany: 1. Using or having 2 names: applied to the system of naming plants introduced by Linnaeus, in which every plant receives 2 names, 1 indicating the genus, the other the species; for example, as *Bellis*

perennis, the English daisy. The genus is always written first, and with a capital initial letter; it is, or is used, as a noun. The specific word follows, which is usually an adjective, or used as an adjective, though it may be a noun. 2. Consisting of 2 names, as binomial terms.

biodynamic (bigh′oh digh nam′ihk) *a.* Of, or concerned with, the dynamic relation between organisms and their environment.

biological control *n.* A method of taking advantage of natural living predators and parasites as nontoxic controls of garden pests. They include insects like lacewings, bacterium such as *Bacillus thuringiensis,* and viruses.

biota (bigh oh′tuh) *n.* The plant and animal life of a region or period.

biotype *n.* All the plants in a specific genotype, or group, all of which resemble one another in some specific way.

bipinnate (bigh pihn′ayt) *a.* Doubly pinnate, or double divided. In botany, applied to a pinnate (divided) leaf when its divisions are themselves again divided. Also bipinnated.

bipinnate leaf

biplicate (bigh′pligh kayt) *a.* Doubly folded; twice folded together, transversely, as the new first leaves that sprout from a germinating bean.

biramous (bigh ray′muhs) *a.* Possessing or consisting of 2 branches; dividing into 2 branches. Also biramose.

birch *n.* A tree or shrub belonging to the genus *Betula.* Several varieties of this species, such as the weeping, cut-leafed, and purple birches, are much cultivated ornamentally. (See **Betula**.)

bird *n.* Mostly a beneficial animal that eats many destructive garden pests and adds beauty to the garden. Sometimes birds become garden pests of fruit-bearing plants and young seedlings. The best control is to use protective coverings like netting or row covers over plants.

birdbath *n.* A basin-shaped garden ornament for birds to bathe in or drink from.

bird feeder *n.* Any of several variously decorated platforms or tubes attached to a tree or pole or suspended from a branch used to hold food for birds.

bird-foot *a.* Leaves or flowers divided like a bird's foot; pedate, as the leaves of the bird's-foot violet, *Viola pedata.*

birdhouse *n.* A box or other home-made or manufactered container used as a nesting site for birds. Birdhouses designed to attract insect-eating birds are particularly useful in the garden.

bird netting *n.* Nylon or plastic mesh used as a drape to keep birds out of fruit trees, berry patches, or vegetable gardens. Smaller mesh netting is placed directly on strawberries, raspberries, and corn; larger mesh netting may be draped over trees, bushes, grapes, or over a supporting structure.

bird-of-paradise flower *n.* A common name for *Caesalpinia mexicana, Strelitzia reginae,* and *S. nicolai,* the last called giant bird-of-paradise.

bird-plant *n.* A common name for *Heterotoma lobelioides* (Lobeliaceae), with yellow and purple irregular flowers somewhat resembling a bird; native to Mexico. Also called canary-bird flower.

bird's-eye *n.* A common name for several different flowers: the pheasant's-eye, *Adonis annua;* the speedwell, *Veronica Chamaedrys,* so named from its bright-blue flower; and species of primrose, *Primula farinosa.*

bird's-foot *n.* A common name for several plants including bird's-foot trefoil, *Lotus corniculatus* (see **Lotus**); also bird's-foot fern, *Pellaea mucronata* (see **Pellaea**); also bird's-foot violet, *Viola pedata* (see **Viola**).

bird's-nest *n.* 1. A name popularly given to several plants, from some suggestion of a bird's nest in their form or manner of growth; bird's-nest orchid, *Neottia Nidusavis,* so called because of the mass of stout, interlaced fibers that form its roots; *Asple-*

nium nidus, from the manner in which the fronds (foliage) grow, leaving a nestlike hollow in the center; and the wild carrot, *Daucus Carota,* from the form of the umbel (cluster of flower stems, as in dill) in fruit. 2. Same as crow's-nest.

bird's-nest fern *n.* A common name for two ferns, *Asplenium nidus* and *Pycnodoria vittata.*

birimose (bigh righ′mohs) *a.* Opening by two slits, as the anthers (pollen sacs) of most plants.

birthroot (berth′root) *n.* A common name given to various species of the genus *Trillium.* Has been used medicinally.

birthwort (berth′wert) *n.* In botany, the common name for the European species of *Aristolochia.*

bisetose (bigh see′tohs) *a.* Having 2 bristles.

bisexual (bigh seks shoo uhl) *a.* Said of flowers that have both male and female parts within a single flower.

bishop's-cap *n.* A common name for the genus *Mitella,* native to the United States. It takes its common name from the form of the pod. Also called miterwort.

bishop's-elder *n.* Same as bishop's-weed, *Aegopodum podagraria.*

bishop's-weed *n.* 1. *Aegopodum podagraria.* (See **goutweed**.) Also called bishop's-elder and bishop-weed. 2. A name given to the plants of the genus *Ammi,* especially *Ammi majus.*

bispinous (bigh spigh′nuhs) *a.* Having 2 spines.

bitterbloom *n.* A common name for the American centaury, *Sabbatia angularis.*

bitter-herb *n.* 1. The European centaury, *Erythroea centaurium.* 2. The balmony of the United States, *Chelone glabra.*

bitter melon *n.* A fast-growing vine, *Momordica charantia,* bearing a cucumber-shaped melon, 6 to 10 inches long. Although somewhat sour in flavor, the young melon is cooked as a vegetable, especially in Chinese dishes. Also called bitter gourd and balsam pear. The vine, which may grow to 12 feet, has become naturalized in some parts of southeastern United States.

bitternut *n*. The swamp hickory of the United States, *Carya cordiformis*. Its nuts are very thin-shelled, with an intensely bitter kernel.

bitter root *n*. A common name for *Lewisia rediviva*, a plant native to the Bitter Root Mountains lying between Idaho and Montana.

bittersweet *n*. 1. The climbing bittersweet of the United States, *Celastrus scandens*, whose orange berries retain their color when dry. The vines are prized by florists and wreath makers. 2. The deadly nightshade, *Solanum Dulcamara*, a trailing plant native to Europe and Asia and naturalized as a weed in the United States. It bears a purple flower with yellow stamens. Its small scarlet berries, resembling red currants, as well as other parts of the plant, are poisonous.

Bixa (bihk′suh) *n*. A genus of 1 species, *Bixa Orellana*, which yields the spice annotto.

Bixaceae (bihk say′see ee) *n. pl.* A family with a single genus of a single species, *Bixa Orellana*.

blackberry *n*. 1. The fruit of those species of *Rubus* in which the receptacle (the white center of the berry) becomes juicy and falls off with the rest of the berry (called the drupelet), in distinction from the raspberry, which comes off the vine with a hollow center. Blackberries are extensively cultivated, and they grow wild in northern regions. In Britain, often called bramble. The berries are eaten raw, baked in pies, and made into jams and jellies. They are rich in vitamin C.

black-eyed Susan *n*. A common name for *Rudbeckia hirta* (Compositae), a tough, easy-to-grow plant with rough, hairy leaves and showy, daisylike yellow-orange flowers with a black-purple center. Excellent in summer and fall borders and for cutting.

black gum *n*. A North American tree, *Nyssa sylvatica*, which grows to 100 feet, bearing a dark blue berry. Also called pepperidge and sour-gum.

black haw *n*. A common name for *Viburnum prunifolium*. Has been used medicinally, but is primarily grown as a small ornamental tree for its brilliant red fall foliage and white spring blossoms. The small blue-black fruits are used to make preserves.

blackheart *n*. 1. Any of several species of cherry having heart-shaped fruit and nearly black skin. 2. A name for 2 different plant diseases, one that afflicts maple and ash, the other that attacks the inside of potatoes.

black plastic *n*. Sheet plastic placed around plants as a mulch to discourage weeds, retain moisture, and absorb heat. Also called black poly sheeting or black polyethylene.

black radish *n*. A winter-keeping radish with a black skin and pure white flesh. One of the oldest known radishes, it has a slightly pungent flavor and can be eaten raw, although it is most commonly boiled like a turnip.

black raspberry *n*. A sweet, black or purple fruited raspberry.

black-seeded Simpson *n*. A classic leaf lettuce with frilled outer leaves and crinkly, juicy, light green inner leaves.

black spot (blak spaht) *n*. A fungal disease causing black spotting on foliage and stems, usually of roses. Most common in areas with summer rain and/or high humidity. Good winter cleanup (destroying infected leaves and prunings) and spring fungicide sprays are effective controls.

blackthorn *n*. The sloe, *Prunus spinosa*. The fruit is used for flavoring liquors. (See **sloe**.)

black tartarian (tahr ta′ree uhn) *n*. A type of cherry grown on an ornamental tree, with high yield. Colors range from purplish-black to bright red, and the fruit is very flavorful.

black turtle bean *n*. A small black kidney bean usually grown for drying and used in soups.

black vine weevil *n*. A night-feeding insect that eats the foliage and roots (the adult insects eat the foliage; the larvae eat the roots) of many plants, including rhododendrons, yew, and azalea. Crescent-shaped holes along the edges of leaves indicate the presence of adults. Difficult to control. Rotenone or parasitic nematodes can be effective, but usually combinations of traditional insecticides are required.

bladder campion *n.* The popular name of the plant *Silene vulgaris,* so called from its inflated calyx, a balloon-like growth at the base of the flower.

bladder fern *n.* The common name of *Cystopteris,* a genus of ferns.

bladdernut *n.* The popular name of plants of the genus *Staphylea* (Staphyleaceae), given on account of their inflated fruit capsule.

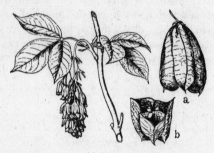

bladdernut
a fruit, *b* section of fruit

bladderpod *n.* A common name for the genus *Alyssoides,* which has 3 species of perennial flowers that grow in rocky places, on cliffs, and on walls. They have entire leaves, long-clawed yellow flowers, and inflated, saclike fruit, which suggests the common name.

bladder snout *n.* The common bladderwort, *Utricularia vulgaris,* a pondweed that grows to 6 feet in length.

bladderwort *n.* The common name of members of the genus *Utricularia,* slender aquatic plants (plants that live in water), the leaves of which are furnished with floating bladders. Often grown in aquariums. (See **Utricularia**.)

blade (blayd) *n.* 1. The leaf of a plant, such as a grass. 2. In botany, the lamina, or broad part, of a leaf, petal, sepal, etc., as distinguished from the petiole, or leafstalk.

blanch (blanch) *v.* In horticulture, to whiten or prevent from becoming green by excluding light, a process applied to the stems or leaves of plants, such as celery, lettuce, and endive. Blanching is done by banking up earth about the stems of the plants, tying the leaves together to keep the inner

ones from light, or covering with pots, boxes, or the like.

blanching *n.* The act of making a plant blanched, or white.

Blandfordia (blan for′dee uh) *n.* A genus of 4 species of fibrous-rooted perennial herbs (Liliaceae) native to Australia and Tasmania. They have long, thin leaves that grow from the base of the plant and drooping long clusters of funnel- or bell-shaped red, yellow, or orange flowers. Suitable for mild climates.

blanketflower *n.* A common name for *Gaillardia grandiflora* (Compositae), a 2- to 4-foot-tall perennial with rough, gray-green leaves and daisylike yellow, bronze, and scarlet flowers; native to central and western North America. Somewhat drought-tolerant once established.

blastema (blas tee′muh) *n. pl.* blastemata. In botany, the point of growth from which any organ or part of an organ is developed.

blazing star *n.* A common name for several very different plants: (a) the genus *Liatris* (Compositae), (b) *Chamaelirium luteum* (Liliaceae), and (c) *Mentzelia laevicaulis* (Loasaceae).

Blechnum (blehk′nuhm) *n.* A genus of 200 species of evenly shaped evergreen ferns (Polypodiaceae) with divided leaves; native mostly to the Southern Hemisphere. Some, such as *B. brasiliense* and *B. gibbum,* are dwarf tree ferns, growing to no more than 4 feet in height. Others are useful in shaded, formal borders or in mild-climate woodland gardens.

bleeding *n.* The drawing of sap from a tree or plant.

bleeding heart *n.* 1. In England, a name of the wallflower, *Cheiranthus Cheiri.* 2. A common name of some species of *Dicentra,* especially *D. spectabilis* from China, so called from the shape of the flowers. 3. A name sometimes applied to cultivated forms of *Colocasia* with colored leaves.

Blephilia (bleh fihl′ee uh) *n.* A genus of 2 species of North American perennial wildflowers (Labiatae) with square stems, simple, hairy leaves, and dense clusters of bluish or purplish flowers. *B. hirsuta* is commonly known as wood mint. Both species are suitable to the wild garden.

blessed thistle *n.* A common name for the genus *Cnicus*, of which there is 1 species, *C. benedictus*, a thistlelike annual herb of Mediterranean origin. It bears prickly yellow flowers.

Bletia (blee'shuh) *n.* A genus of terrestrial tropical American land orchids (Orchidaceae) that grow from corms (fleshy stem bases); they have long, pleated leaves and a slender stalk of large purple or pink flowers.

Bletilla (bleh tihl uh) *n.* A genus of 9 species of Asiatic land-growing orchids (Orchidaceae) of which only 1, *B. striata*, is widely cultivated. It grows to 2 feet, has 3 to 5 upright leaves, and long stalks of purple or white flowers. Commonly known as Chinese ground orchid.

Blighia (bligh'hee uh) *n.* A genus of 4 species of tropical evergreen trees and shrubs (Sapindaceae). *B. sapida*, with divided clusters of greenish-white flowers, and edible fruits, is the only cultivated species. The unripe fruit and some parts of the plant are poisonous. Grown in zones 9 and 10, it is commonly known as akee-akee.

Bliss *n.* An old-fashioned variety of potato grown in northern areas and into Canada. It has a superior flavor and light red skin.

blister beetle *n.* A voracious feeding, swarming insect that devours many garden vegetables, including tomatoes, beans, and peas, and attacks ornamentals. When crushed, irritants exuding from the beetle can cause blisters on the skin, hence the name. Wear gloves when handling. Pyrethrum-rotenone combinations, parasitic nematodes, and traditional insecticides are effective controls.

blister cress *n.* A common name for pungent cresses, especially *Erysimum* and *Cheiranthus*.

blite *n.* A common name for strawberry blite, *Chenopodium capitatum*, so called from its red fleshy clusters of fruit.

Blitum (bli'tum) *n.* A former genus of the family Chenopodiaceae, now included in *Chenopodium*. (See **blite**.)

bloodflower *n.* A common name for *Asclepias curassavica*, a member of the milkweed family with crimson flowers.

bloodleaf *n.* A common name for the genus *Iresine*, planted in beds for its red leaves. Although it produces flowers, these rarely form in seasonal bedding plants.

bloodroot *n.* The common name in North America for a perennial native herb, *Sanguinaria Canadensis*, 1 of the earliest spring woodland flowers. It has simple white blossoms and fleshy roots, which yield a dark red bitter and acrid juice. It is commonly used in shaded wildflower gardens.

bloodroot

bloom (bloom) *n.* 1. A blossom; the flower of a plant, especially of an ornamental plant; an expanded bud. 2. The state of blossoming; the opening of flowers in general; flowers collectively: such as, the plant is in bloom, or covered with bloom. 3. A powdery deposit or coating of various kinds. The delicate, powdery, waxy coating on certain fruits, such as apples, grapes and plums, and leaves, such as cabbage. 4. *v.* To blossom.

Bloomeria (bloo mer'ee uh) *n.* A genus of 2 species of flowers (Amaryllidaceae) native to California. The only species in cultivation, *B. crocea*, grows from corms (fleshy stem bases); it has grasslike leaves and wheel-shaped yellow flowers. It is commonly known as yellow stars.

blooming-sally *n.* A common name for the willow-herb, *Epilobium angustifolium*.

bloomless *a.* Having no bloom or blossom, or being incapable of blooming.

bloomy *a.* 1. Full of bloom or blossoms; flowery. 2. Having a bloom, or delicate powdery appearance, as fresh fruit.

blossom *n*. 1. The flower of a plant, usually more or less conspicuous because of the colored leaflets that form it and that are generally of more delicate texture than the leaves of the plant. It is a general term, applicable to the essential organs of reproduction, with their appendages, of every species of tree or plant. It is often preferred to *flower* or *bloom* when referring to plants that produce edible fruits. 2. The state of flowering or bearing flowers; bloom; as the apple tree is in blossom. 3. *v*. To put forth blossoms or flowers; to come into bloom.

blossomed *a*. Covered with blossoms; flowering; in bloom.

blowball *n*. The downy head of the dandelion, salsify, etc., formed by the tufted seeds after the flower has died.

bluebeard *n*. A common name for the genus *Caryopteris*, a deciduous shrub with fluffy blue flowers. (Deciduous plants lose their leaves seasonally.)

bluebell *n*. The popular name of several different plants: 1. *Campanula rotundifolia*, a plant bearing a loose cluster of bell-shaped blue flowers. Also called bluebell of Scotland and harebell. (See **harebell**.) 2. *Endymion non-scriptus*, the wild hyacinth, so called from the bell shape of its drooping flowers. Also called wood hyacinth and English bluebell. (See **bluebell, English**.) 3. Occasionally, the name of other plants with bell-shaped blue flowers.

bluebell, California *n*. A common name for *Phacelia campanularia*, an annual flower native to California deserts. It grows to 18 inches, with egg-shaped, coarsely toothed leaves and loose clusters of deep blue bell-shaped flowers. Used in flower beds with well-drained soil. Also known as desert bluebells.

bluebell, Clanwilliam *n*. A common name for *Ixia incarnata*, a tender perennial bulb. It grows to 1 foot, with narrow, sword-shaped leaves and loose spikes of lilac to red-purple trumpet-shaped flowers.

bluebell, English *n*. A common name for *Endymion non-scriptus*, a prolific, vigorous, hardy perennial bulb. It grows to 1 foot, with narrow, basal leaves and loose spikes of nodding blue, white, pink, or rose bell-shaped flowers. Used to naturalize in drifts under deciduous trees or under shrubs. They thrive in pots and make good cut flowers. Also known as wood hyaching and harebell (often sold under the name *Scilla*).

bluebell, Spanish *n*. A common name for *Endymion hispanicus*, a hardy perennial bulb. It grows to 20 inches, with narrow pointed basal leaves and loose spikes of blue, pink, white or rose nodding, bell-like flowers. Used to naturalize in drifts under deciduous trees or under shrubs. They thrive in pots and make good cut flowers. Also known as Spanish jacinth and bell-flowered squill (often sold under the name *Scilla*).

bluebell, Australian *n*. A common name for *Sollya heterophyla*, a tender climbing shrub with small, narrow leaves and many blue or white bell-shaped flowers. Drought tolerant once established; dies if drainage is poor. Also called Australian bluebell creeper and bluebell creeper.

blueberry *n*. The fruit of several species of *Vaccinium*, ordinarily distinguished from the various kinds of huckleberry by its light blue color and smaller seeds, but a common name for the huckleberry in some regions. The swamp or high bush blueberry is the *Baccinium corymbosum;* the low-bush blueberry is *V. vacillans;* and the dwarf blueberry, *V. Pennsylvanicum*. Also known as bilberry. Blueberries, rich in vitamin C, are widely cultivated. The choicest are the smaller wild berries gathered in northern New England, especially in Maine, and sold commercially for making pies and other baked goods and jams and jellies.

blueblossom *n*. A common name for *Ceanothus thyrsiflorus*, an evergreen shrub, native to California, with masses of blue flowers.

bluebonnet *n*. A common name for *Lupinus subcarnosus*. Also called Texas bluebonnet.

bluebottle *n*. A common name for *Centaurea Cyanus*, an annual with gray leaves and bright blue flowers. Also called cornflower or bachelor's button.

bluebush *n*. A common name for *Eucalyptus macrocarpa*.

blue corn *n.* A popular Southwest variety of corn that has blue kernels. It is most commonly dried and ground into meal.

blue creeper *n.* A common name for *Bredemeyera volubilis,* a graceful, twining vine, bearing an abundance of showy, bright blue flowers, grown in western gardens.

blue-curls *n.* A common name for the genus *Trichostema,* which has blue flowers with very long coiled filaments. Also a common name for *Phacelia congesta.*

blue daisy *n.* A common name for *Felicia amelloides,* a long-blooming, shrubby perennial covered with blue summer flowers. Excellent as a container plant or as a short, flowering hedge bordering a path.

blue-dicks *n.* A common name for *Dichelostemma pulchellum,* a drought-tolerant Western native that grows from a corm (fleshy stem base) and has stalks with deep blue flowers in tight clusters at the ends. Often classified as *Brodiaea.*

blue-eyed grass *n.* The common name for *Sisyrinchium bellum,* a bulb native to much of North America with narrow, grasslike bluish-green leaves and stems with clusters of purple to bluish-purple flowers at the ends. They are easily grown in border gardens.

blue-eyed Mary *n.* The common name for two different plants, *Omphalodes verna* and *Tradescantia virginiana.* *O. verna* has small blue flowers, resembling the forget-me-not, and is also called creeping forget-me-not. *T. virginiana* has clusters of 3-petaled flowers, each flower blooming for only 1 day.

blue fescue (fehs′kyoo) *n.* (See **Festuca.**)

blue gramma grass *n.* (See **Bouteloua.**)

bluegrass *n.* (See **Poa.**)

blue-gum tree *n.* The *Eucalyptus globulus,* of extremely rapid growth, and known to have attained a height of 350 feet. It has naturalized in California. Its leaves and seed capsules are fragrant when rubbed or rained upon.

blueheart *n.* The common name of the genus *Buchnera,* a perennial herb with deep-purple flowers, often parasitic on roots.

blue Hubbard *n.* A large, blue-skinned winter squash suitable for baking. Its bright yellow-orange flesh is fine grained, dry, and sweet. It keeps well in a cool place.

bluejack *n.* A species of oak, *Quercus cinerea,* a small tree with hard, strong, and heavy wood, native to the coasts of the southern United States.

blue palm *n.* A common name for 2 palms, *Sabal minor* and *Brahea armata.*

blue palmetto *n.* A common name for *Rhapodophyllum hystrix,* native to the southern United States. It is a slow-growing, suckering (producing new stems from underground roots) ornamental palm useful in temperate areas where most palms cannot be grown.

blue poppy *n.* A common name for *Meconopsis betonicifolia,* a perennial with toothed leaves and clusters of blue-violet to purple poppy-shaped flowers 2 inches across.

blue potato *n.* Any of several varieties of potatoes characterized by blue or purple skin. Some have white interior flesh and others are blue inside. Blue Victor is a popular variety for home gardeners.

blue oat grass *n.* (See **Helictotrichon.**)

bluet (bloo′eht) *n.* A common name given to several plants with blue flowers: (a) to bachelor's button, *Centaurea Cyanus;* (b) to farkleberry, *Houstonia coerulea* and *H. patens;* and (c) to bilberry, *Vaccinum* spp.

blueweed *n.* A common name for *Echium vulgare,* the viper's bugloss, a European weed with showy blue flowers, which has naturalized in the United States. It is invasive, it has even been called pernicious.

blue wild ryegrass *n.* (See **Elymus.**)

blushwort *n.* A name given to the genus *Aeschynanthus,* epiphytic (growing on, but not taking nourishment from, a host plant) subshrubs or vines native from China to New Guinea.

Bocconia (buh koh′nee uh) *n.* A genus of 9 species of tropical and subtropical small trees or large shrubs (Papaveraceae), with large lobed leaves and large clusters of flowers. Some species, such as *B. arborea* and *B. frutescens,* are grown for their showy, 18-inch leaves. Other *Bocconia* species are now classified as *Macleaya.*

bog asphodel (bahg as'foh dehl) *n.* A common name for the genus *Narthecium,* with grasslike leaves growing from the base of the plant and greenish-yellow flowers in clusters at the end of the stem.

bogbean *n.* The common name of the *Menyanthes trifoliata* (Gentianaceae, *Menyanthaceae*), a bog plant, a native of the more temperate parts of the Northern Hemisphere. Used in bog gardens. Also called buckbean.

bogberry *n.* The cranberry, *Vaccinium Oxycoccus;* name now rarely used.

bog gardening *n.* The cultivation of an ornamental garden devoted to moisture-loving plants; good for low-lying, marshy sites.

bog oak *n.* Trunks and large branches of oak found embedded in bogs and preserved by the antiseptic properties of peat. It is of a shining black or ebony color, or of a deep greenish-gray, mottled, and shading into black, derived from its impregnation with iron. It is frequently converted into ornamental pieces of furniture or jewelry. Also called bogwood.

bog rush *n.* The name of various cyperaceous plants, including those of the genus *Juncus.* (See **rush**.)

Bok choy (bahk) *n.* A green leafy vegetable that is a member of the Chinensis Group of *Brassica Rapa.* It has white or light green stalks, and smooth or wavy slightly glossy leaves, of various shades of green. It is rich in vitamins C and A. Also spelled Pak choy and pakchoi, it is a common ingredient of Chinese dishes and is often sold under the general name of Chinese cabbage. Also called Chinese mustard cabbage.

Bolandra (boh lan'druh) *n.* A genus of 2 species of perennial herbs (Saxifragaceae) native to the northwest United States. They grow from bulblike rhizomes (enlarged underground stems) and have leafy stems and small clusters of purple flowers. Suitable for the rock garden or wild garden.

bole (bohl) *n.* The body, or trunk, of a tree.

Boletus (boh lee'tuhs) *n.* An extensive genus of mushrooms, generally found growing on the ground in woods, especially in pine woods. A few species are edible, including *Boletus edulis,* often considered among the choicest of wild mushrooms. Called *cepe* in French, *porcini* in Italian, *steinpilz* in German, and king bolete in English.

Boletus mushroom entire, and cut lengthwise

Boltonia (bohl toh'nee uh) *n.* A genus of about 10 species of tall asterlike perennials (Compositae) native to North America. It has long, alternate leaves and large clusters of asterlike flowers—purple, violet, or white, with yellow centers. A good back-of-the-border plant or tall meadow-garden specimen.

Bomarea (boh ma'ree uh) *n.* A genus of 100 species of perennial twining climbers (Alstroemeriaceae), natives to high elevations of southern America. The tubular flowers, which are often showy, grow in simple or compound umbels (clusters of flower stems spreading from a central point).

Bombacaceae (bahm buh kay'see ee) *n. pl.* A family of 27 genera of tropical trees with leaves like palms and large dry or fleshy fruit with woolly seeds. Commonly known as bombax.

Bombax (bahm'baks) *n.* A genus of 8 species of silk-cotton trees (Bombacaceae). It has alternate palmlike leaves and large red, yellow, purple, or white flowers.

bone meal (bohn meel) *n.* Ground bone, raw or steamed, that is used as a fertilizer to add phosphoric acid to the soil. It is the preferred fertilizer in herb gardens.

boneset (bohn'seht) *n.* The thoroughwort, *Eupatorium perfoliatum,* a perennial herb native to wet grounds in eastern North America. Cultivated only as a specimen in historic and medical herb gardens.

bonsai (bohn'sigh) *n.* A tree or shrub grown in a container and dwarfed by pruning, pinching, and wiring to produce a desired shape.

bonsai dish (bohn'sigh) *n.* A planter for holding a miniaturized tree or shrub.

borage (bor'ihj) *n.* A European and North African annual, *Borago officinalis,* the principle representative of the genus; cultivated in herb gardens for its blue flowers, which are used in salads and cold drinks. The leaves, which have a slight cucumber flavor, may be cooked as a green. Its loose sprawling shape is a little untidy for formal beds, so it is often grown in the vegetable garden.

Boraginaceae (buh raj uh nay'see ee) *n. pl.* A large family of 100 genera and 2,000 species of plants, shrubs, trees, or, even occasionally, lianas, found all over the world. The leaves are often rough and hairy, the flowers are regular, and the fruit usually consists of 4 distinct nutlets. The ornamental genera include *Heliotropium* (heliotrope), *Myosotis* (forget-me-not), *Anchusa* (alkanet), *Symphytum* (comfrey), and *Lithospermum* (gromwell). Commonly called borage.

Bordeaux mixture (bor doh) *n.* A mixture of copper sulfate and lime used as a fungicide, particularly against powdery mildew on grapes.

border *n.* A narrow bed or strip of garden that encloses or separates a portion of lawn or other land form by a path, walk, driveway, street, or building. Typically planted with perennials or flowering shrubs for spring and summer bloom.

border fence *n.* A short fence, usually only 12 to 18 inches high, of wood or metal, used to mark and separate flower beds from foot traffic and lawn mowers.

border fork *n.* A 4-tined implement used for close work in existing plantings and raised beds. A border fork is lighter, shorter, and has smaller tines than a digging fork.

border shears *n. pl.* Long-bladed scissors used to trim the horizontal growth of border plants. Those with long handles may be used from a standing position.

border spade *n.* A D-handled shovel used for close work in existing plantings and raised beds. A border spade is shorter, lighter, and has a smaller blade than a digging spade.

borer *n.* A beetle or moth larva that bores beneath the bark of a variety of species, often trees, girdling trunks and branches, causing dieback or death of the plant. Difficult to control, but healthy, vigorous plants are less likely to be attacked than stressed ones. Injecting parasitic nematodes into holes may help. Lindane is sometimes an effective control but is also a very toxic chemical. (See also **bark beetle**.)

boric acid *n.* A salt that can be effectively used as a barrier against some crawling household pests such as ants. If kept dry, it can also be used outdoors.

boron *n.* A trace element usually present in most soils but sometimes added by applying fertilizer.

Boronia (buh roh'nee uh) *n.* A genus of between 60 and 70 species of shrubs and subshrubs (Rutaceae). They have opposite leaves with glandular dots and clusters of white, pink, red, blue, or purple flowers that are often fragrant. Grown as a summer annual or as a houseplant.

Bosc (bahsk) *n.* A versatile pear variety prized for its resistance to both heat and cold. It has attractive cinnamon-colored skin and an aromatic flavor.

boscage (bahs'kihj) *n.* Sylvan scenery, specifically woods, groves, or thickets of trees or shrubs. Also spelled boskage.

bosket (bahs'keht) *n.* A grove; a thicket or small plantation in a garden, park, etc., formed of trees, shrubs, or tall plants. Also spelled bosquet.

Boston fern *n.* A common name for *Nephrolepis exaltata* cv. 'Bostoniensis'. A popular houseplant, also used outdoors in summer as a hanging plant.

Boston ivy *n.* A common name for *Parthenocissus tricuspidata,* a deciduous clinging vine, with simple leaves, that attaches itself with disks. Often used on walls and buildings, it colors brilliant crimson in fall. This is the ivy of college campuses.

botanic *a.* Pertaining to botany, or the scientific study of plants. For example, a botanic garden is a garden devoted to the culture of plants collected for scientific and display purposes. Also botanical.

botanical insecticide *n.* Any of various natural insecticides derived from plants. They include pyrethrum, neem, rotenone, rynia, sabadilla, and nicotine sulfate. They break down quickly when

51

exposed to sun and must be applied frequently. They usually are nontoxic but not always (see **nicotine sulfate**).

botany *n.* The science of plants, their classification and study.

bo tree (boh) *n.* The *Ficus religiosa*, or pipal tree, under which the Buddha Siddartha Gautama, the founder of Buddhism, is said to have become "enlightened."

Botrychium
(moonwort)
a entire plant, *b* branch of the fertile frond

Botrychium (boh trihk'ee uhm) *n.* A genus of about 40 species of somewhat fleshy ferns (Ophioglossaceae). Some species are commonly known as moonwort, others as grape fern; *B. virginianum* is called rattlesnake fern.

botryoid (bah'tree oid) *a.* Having the form of a bunch of grapes. Also botryoidal.

bottle-brush *n.* A common name for the *Callistemon* and some varieties of *Melaleuca*. The latter flower is quite similar in appearance, looking much like a bottle brush, with tiny florets around the end of a stiff stem. Both are dried for flower arranging.

bottlebrush grass *n.* (See **Hystrix**.)

bottle gentian (jehn'shuhn) *n.* A common name for *Gentiana Andrewsii;* also called closed gentian, after the unusual shape of its flower, which consists of a cluster of small tube shapes.

bottle gourd *n.* The fruit of *Lagenaria siceraria* (Cucurbitaceoe), 1 of several names based on their shapes.

Bougainvillea (boo gehn vihl'yuh) *n.* A genus of 14 species of vines or small trees (Nyctaginaceae). The branches are woody and thorny, with simple leaves. The flowers grow in clusters of 3, growing out of spectacularly showy red, purple, orange, or white bracts. It is a highly ornamental perennial vine in mild winter climates, commonly grown in Florida.

bough *n.* An arm or branch of a tree.

bouncing bet *n.* A popular name for the common soapwort, *Saponaria officinalis,* a Eurasian native naturalized in North America.

Bourbon rose *n.* A common name for *Rosa xbarboniana* (a hybridization of *R. chinensis* and *R. damascena*), a fragrant rose growing on compact plants. It is an older variety, but still available from rose nurseries.

Bouteloua (boo tuh loo'uh) *n.* A genus of at least 25 species of annual and perennial grasses (Gramineae) native to the Americas. The most common is *B. gracilis,* native to the central plains of North America, where it is sometimes used as a low-maintenance lawn. Commonly known as blue gramma grass.

Bouvardia (boo vahr'dee uh) *n.* A genus of 30 or more species of shrubs and herbs (Rubiaceae). They have opposite or whorled leaves with clusters of large, showy red, yellow, or white flowers. *B. longiflora* has a jasminelike fragrance. Grown in mild winter climates or as greenhouse plants.

bowman's root *n.* 1. A common name for perennial herbs of the genus *Gillenia*. 2. A common name for *Veronicastrum virginicum,* a tall, slender herb with long clusters of pale blue or white flowers; native to North America.

bow saw *n.* An implement having a straight blade attached at both ends to a curved handle, in all making the shape of the letter D; used for cutting branches.

bowerplant *n.* A common name for *Pandorea jasminoïdes,* a tender vine with clusters of white, fragrant flowers to 2 inches long.

Bowiea (bow'ee uh) *n.* A genus with 2 species of tropical bulbous perennials. It has an exposed bulb to 7 inches across, fleshy, twining, leafless stems to

15 feet long, and small greenish-white flowers. Grown as a novelty in greenhouses. Commonly called Zulu potato or climbing onion.

Bowle's golden grass (bohlz) *n.* (See **Milium**.)

box (bahks) *n.* A common name for *Buxus,* a genus of evergreen shrubs and small trees widely grown for hedges. May be clipped for a formal effect or left unclipped for a soft, billowing effect. Also known as boxwood.

box elder *n.* A common name for *Acer Negundo,* a tree, with divided, finely notched leaves and with flowers that appear before the leaves in spring.

box huckleberry *n.* A common name for *Gaylussacia brachycera,* native to eastern North America. It is a prostrate, creeping evergreen shrub with small, shiny, boxwoodlike leaves, white or pink flowers, and blue fruit. Now considered rare.

box thorn *n.* A name given to plants of the genus *Lycium,* particularly *L. europaeum. Lycium* species are tropical woody shrubs with narrow, alternate grayish-green leaves and numerous small flowers.

boxwood *n.* 1. The fine, hard-grained timber of the genus *Buxus,* much used by wood engravers and in the manufacture of musical and mathematical instruments, tool handles, etc. 2. The name given to several trees with hard, compact wood, that takes a fine polish. Some species of *Eucalyptus* are also called boxwood.

Boykinia (boi kihn'ee uh) *n.* A genus of about 8 species of perennial herbs (Saxifragaceae), some native to the mountains and woods of the western United States. They have toothed or lobed leaves and white tubular flowers.

boysenberry *n.* A common name for a cultivar of the *loganobaccus* variety of *Rubus ursinus,* a berry sometimes reaching 2 inches in length, grown along the Pacific coast. It resembles a large blackberry in both appearance and flavor.

Brachychiton (brak'uh kigh'tuhn) *n.* A genus of 12 species of tall shrubs or trees (Sterculiaceae). The leaves are handsome, glossy, 10-inch-wide bright green fans. In bloom, the tree is covered with masses of red or orange-red bells. Commonly called bottletree from the shape of its trunk, which resembles a soda-water bottle. Makes a spectacular red-flowering tree specimen in mild-winter climates.

Brachycome (bra kihk'uh mee) *n.* A genus of flowers (Compositae) native to Australia and New Zealand. It grows in neat mounds with finely divided leaves that are covered in spring and summer with masses of small, daisylike purple blossoms. Good as an edging, in massed beds, in rock gardens, and in containers.

Brachysema (bra kihs'uh muh) *n.* A genus of 15 species of shrubs (Leguminosae) native to Australia. They have simple leaves and clusters of sweet pea-shaped red flowers. They tend to be long-blooming and do well in mild-winter climates.

bracken *n.* A common name for a wild fern, especially the *Pteridium aquilinum,* and other large ferns. (See **brake**.)

bract (brakt) *n.* A leaf in a flower cluster or a leaf base of a flower, usually differing somewhat from an ordinary leaf in size, form, or texture; often much reduced but occasionally large and showy. Sometimes petallike, highly colored, and very conspicuous, as in dogwood *(Cornus)* and *Bouganvillea.*

bracts
1 Campanula, 2 Calendula

bracteate (brak'tee ayt) *a.* Having bracts.

bracteolate (brak tee'oh liht) *a.* Having bracteoles.

bracteole (brak'tee ohl) *n.* A little bract, especially one on a flower stem. Also called bractlet. (See cut under **bract**.)

Brahea (bra′hee uh) *n*. A genus of about 12 species of drought-tolerant fan palms (Palmae). *B. armata*, the Mexican blue palm, grows slowly to 40 feet; it has silvery-blue leaves and conspicuous creamy flowers, which drape dramatically nearly half the height of the tree. Hardy to 18° F and tolerant of drought, heat, and wind. Also known as Franceschi palm, Guadalupe palm, hesper palm, rock palm.

brake (brayk) *n*. The name given to *Pteridium aquilinum* and other large ferns. Buckhorn brake is a name sometimes applied to the royal fern, *Osmunda regalis;* cliff brake, a common name for the genus *Pellea;* rock brake, a common name for the genus *Cryptogama* and some species of *Polypodium,* especially *P. vulgare.*

bramble *n*. A name used to describe plants of the genus *Rubus,* especially and usually in England for the common blackberry, occasionally (because they are armed with prickles), any rough, prickly shrub, even roses.

brambleberry *n*. 1. An old name for the berry of a bramble, especially the blackberry. 2. The plant itself. (See **bramble** and **blackberry**.)

branch (branch) *n*. A stem growing from the trunk of a tree, shrub, or other plant (the smaller offshoots being called branchlets, twigs, or shoots); a bough.

Brassaia (bra sigh′uh) *n*. A genus of about 40 species of trees and shrubs (Araliaceae), most native to the Southern Hemisphere, with crowded, palm-shaped, glossy leaves. Grown for its foliage, usually as a large houseplant or greenhouse specimen. Formerly classified as *Schefflera* and often still sold as *Schefflera.*

Brassavola (bra sa′vuh luh) *n*. A genus of 15 species of epiphytic orchids (Orchidaceae), native to tropical America. They have stemlike pseudobulbs with long, fleshy leaves and small clusters of green, white, or yellow flowers.

Brassia (bras′ee uh) *n*. A genus of about 50 species of epiphytic orchids (Orchidaceae) native to tropical America. They have psuedobulbs, 1 to 3 leaves, and olive-green, yellow, or ochre spidery flowers, often spotted. Commonly known as spider orchids.

Brassicaceae (bras ih kay see ee) *n. pl*. A synonym for Cruciferae, a family of plants including many vegetables, such as cabbage, and many ornamental plants. Commonly known as the mustard family.

Brazil nut *n*. An edible nut, the seed of the fruit of *Bertholletia excelsa* (Myrtaceae), a native of Guiana, Venezuela, and Brazil. (See **Bertholletia**.)

breadfruit *n*. The fruit of the tree *Artocarpus altilis,* the breadfruit tree, a native of Java and the neighboring islands, but long in cultivation in all the tropical islands in the Pacific and introduced in the West Indies and other parts of tropical America. The fruit is composed of the numerous small female flowers united into 1 large fleshy mass. It is roasted before being eaten, and though virtually tasteless, it forms the principle article of food in the South Sea islands.

breed *n*. A group of plants under cultivation by man, incapable of keeping its characteristics in the wild.

Breynia (brayn′yuh) *n*. A genus of between 20 and 30 species of tropical shrubs and trees (Euphorbiaceae). They have alternate, simple leaves, flowers without petals, and a berrylike fruit. Used in subtropical climates for hedges.

Brickellia (brih kehl′ee uh) *n*. A genus of about 100 species of herbaceous plants (Compositae) many native to the western United States. *B. grandiflora* grows to 3 feet, with 4-inch-long triangular leaves and clusters of 20 to 30 white flowers. It grows well in moist, shady places.

bridal wreath *n*. 1. The common name of the genus *Spiraea,* with long, curved branches and numerous small white double flowers. 2. The *Francoa ramosa,* a clumping saxifragaceous plant, with long, crowded stalks of white flowers.

brier *n*. In general, a prickly plant or shrub; specifically, the sweetbrier or the greenbrier (See **greenbrier**). Also spelled briar.

brier, Austrian *n*. A common name for the single, bright yellow rose, *Rosa foetida.*

brierroot *n*. The root of the white heath, *Erica arborea.* The roots are gathered and used to make tobacco pipes, commonly called brierwood pipes.

brisbane box *n*. A common name for *Tristania*

conferta, an evergreen tree with handsome, 6-inch-long leaves and clusters of small white summer flowers. The outer bark peels, revealing an attractive reddish-brown trunk. Grown in mild-winter climates as an ornamental.

bristle *n.* A stiff, sharp hair on a plant.

bristle fern *n.* The common name of the genus *Trichomanes,* especially *T. radicans.*

brittlebush, white (briht uhl bush, wight) *n.* A common name for *Encelia farinosa,* a rounded desert shrub with silvery, hairy leaves and small yellow flowers. A fragrant resin exuded by the stems was used by Spanish padres as incense.

brittle fern *n.* A common name for *Cystopteris fragilis,* also known as fragile fern.

Briza (brigh'zuh) *n.* A genus of about 20 species of annual and perennial grasses (Gramineae) native to temperate regions. Several annual species are grown as ornamentals for their interesting seed heads, which resemble rattlesnake rattles and tremble in the wind. Also used in dried arrangements. Commonly known as quaking grass and rattlesnake grass.

broad-base terrace *n.* A low embankment that is constructed across a slope to reduce runoff and/or erosion.

broad bean *n.* A variety of garden bean, *Vicia Faba,* grown for its edible seeds. This is the oldest known bean, referred to by the earliest writers of antiquity.

broadcast *a.* Cast or dispersed upon the ground with the hand, as seed in sowing; opposed to sowed in drills or rows. *v.* To scatter or sow.

broadleaf evergreen *n.* A broadleaf tree that is not deciduous (does not lose foliage seasonally), such as magnolia *(Magnolia grandiflora)* or coast live-oak *(Quercus agrifolia).*

broadleaf tree *n.* Any deciduous tree having broad flat leaves, as distinguished from the conifers.

broad-spectrum pesticide *n.* A pesticide that is effective against many pests.

broccoli *n.* A garden vegetable of the *Italica* variety of *Brassica oleracea,* similar to the cauliflower, but green and not compacted closely into a fleshy head. Sometimes called sprouting broccoli, it was introduced from Italy at the beginning of the twentieth century. A cool-weather crop, it is grown in spring and fall in warm climates. Broccoli is rich in calcium.

broccoflower (brahk'uh flow'er) *n.* A new vegetable that looks like a cauliflower with green heads.

broccoli raab (rahb) *n.* A sharp-flavored variety of *Brassica Rapa,* Group Ruvo that combines the qualities of broccoli and mustard greens. It has small florets and edible pungent leaves, which can be steamed or used raw in salads.

Brodiaea (broh dee uh) *n.* A genus of 10 species of North American bulbs (Amaryllidaceae) that grow from fibrous corms (bulblike swellings). They have long, slim, almost cylindrical leaves and stalks with terminal clusters of dark blue flowers.

brome (brohm) *n.* (See **Bromus.**)

Bromelia (broh meel'yuh) *n.* A genus of American tropical plants (Bromeliaceae), including 4 or 5 species with rigid, spiny-margined leaves closely packed upon a short stem. Grown as houseplants or greenhouse specimens.

Bromeliaceae (broh meel ee ay'see ee) *n. pl.* A family of 45 genera and 2,000 species, all but 1 native to tropical America. Usually epiphytic plants (growing on, but not taking nourishment from a host plant), with rigid leaves, often spiny, growing in rosettes. The family includes *Ananas,* the pineapple, *Tillandsia* (to which the Spanish moss of the southern United States belongs), *Pitcairnia, Aechmea,* and *Billbergia,* many species of which are cultivated as houseplants for their curious habit and showy flowers.

bromeliads (broh'meel ee adz) *n. pl.* A common name for the genus *Bromelia.*

Bromus (broh'muhs) *n.* A genus of nearly 150 species of annual, biennial, and perennial grasses (Gramineae) native to temperate regions. Some are troublesome weeds; others are grown as ornamentals for their triangular stems and drooping seed heads. Known as bromes.

bronze fennel (fehn'uhl) *n.* A variety of the herb fennel, with striking, deep burgundy-brown colored foliage. It is used as an ornamental background plant for its color and plumes of feathery foliage.

brooklime *n.* A common name for the genus *Veronica.* The American brooklime is *V. americana. Veronica* is also called speedwell.

brookweed *n.* A plant, the water pimpernel, *Samolus Valerandi.* Used as an aquarium plant. (See **Samolus.**)

broom (broom) *n.* The popular name for several plants, mostly shrubs, characterized by long, slender branches and numerous yellow flowers. The most common, Scotch broom is the *Cytisus scoparius,* abundant throughout Europe and grown as a showy garden plant in North America. Spanish broom, *Spartium junceum* is a closely allied species, as is also the dyer's broom, *Genista tinctoria,* which was formerly used as a yellow dye.

broomcorn *n.* Common name for *Sorghum bicolor* var. *techinum,* a tall, reed-like grass, rising to a height of 8 or 10 feet. The branched clusters of its upper stems are made into brooms and brushes, for which purpose the plant is still cultivated.

broom, Spanish *n.* A common name for *Spartium junceum,* which grows to 10 feet with rushlike, leafless branches and clusters of fragrant yellow flowers.

Broughtonia (brow tohn'yuh) *n.* A genus of a single species of epiphytic (growing on, but not taking nourishment from a host plant) orchid (Orchidaceae). It grows from a pseudobulb and has stiff, hard, fleshy leaves and long stalks with crimson flowers at the ends.

Broussonetia
(paper mulberry)

Broussonetia (broo suh nee'shuh) *n.* A genus of plants of about 7 species of deciduous trees and shrubs (Moraceae). The leaves are alternate, toothed, and often lobed; the flowers grow in drooping catkins; and the fruit is small and orange. The paper mulberry, *B. papyrifera,* is used as a street tree. It tolerates poor soil, wind, desert heat, and drought.

Browallia (bruh wahl'ee uh) *n.* A genus of 8 species of tropical American herbaceous plants (Solanaceae), some species of which are cultivated for ornament. The leaves are mostly simple, and the blue and white flowers can be solitary or in clusters. Commonly known as amethyst flower or bush violet.

brown-eyed Susan *n.* A common name for 2 different species, *Rudbeckia hirta* and *Gaillardia aristata.*

brown forest soil *n.* A soil rich in humus with a dark brown surface soil.

brown patch *n.* A fungal disease causing large, circular, brownish-gray spots in lawns. Common in high heat and humidity and in southern lawn grasses. Thrives in overwatered, overfertilized, thatchy turf. Control with corrected cultural practices, fungicides, or by planting resistant varieties.

brown podzolic soil (pahd zahl'ihk) *n.* A mixed humus and mineral soil with a thin mat of decayed leaves; usually found under a deciduous (leafy) or mixed deciduous and coniferous forest.

brown rot *n.* A fungal disease causing light brown spoiled areas on ripening fruit. The effected fruit gradually dries into a hard, dark "mummy." Common in wet weather. Control with copper, sulfur, and other fungicide sprays just prior to blossom. Destroying mummies and pruning for better ventilation are also good preventative practices.

brown soil *n.* A brown surface soil found under grasses and shrubs that gets lighter in color the deeper you dig.

Bruckenthalia (bruhk ehn thal'ee uh) *n.* A genus with 1 species, a very hardy evergreen heathlike shrub (Ericaceae). It has small, simple, crowded leaves and spikes of tiny, bell-shaped, pink flowers. It is often used as a rock-garden specimen. Commonly known as spike heath.

Brugmansia (bruhg man'see uh) *n*. A genus of 5 species of perennial shrubs and small trees (Solanaceae). They have large, dull-green leaves and huge, fragrant, tubular flowers, which can be white, yellow, peach, or orange-red. Both flowers and seeds are poisonous. Some were previously classified as *Datura*. Commonly known as angel's trumpet.

Brunfelsia (broon fehl'zee uh) *n*. A genus of about 40 species of tropical shrubs and small trees (Solanaceae) native to the Americas. The leaves are alternate, simple, and entire. The flowers are showy and often fragrant, growing in terminal clusters and fading from purple to lavender to white; the common name for *B.australis* and *B. floribunda* is yesterday-today-and-tomorrow, since the bush often has flowers of all 3 colors at any one time.

Brunnera (broo nair'uh) *n*. A genus of 3 species of herbs (Boraginaceae) with hairy stems; simple, alternate, and veined dark green leaves; and clusters of tiny, clear blue, forget-me-not-like flowers. It is used as an informal ground cover. Commonly known as Siberian bugloss.

Brunsvigia rosea (bruhnz vihg' ee uh roh zay'uh) *n*. An archaic classification for *Amaryllis belladonna*.

brush *n*. 1. The small trees and shrubs of a wood; a thicket of small trees; scrub. 2. Branches of trees lopped off. 3. Brushland; brushwood.

Brussels sprout *n*. The common garden vegetable, *Brassica oleracea*, var. *gemmifera*. The plant consists of a thick green stem covered with small round heads, like miniature cabbages. It requires a long, cool growing season and has the best flavor after it has been exposed to a frost.

Bucida (byoo sigh'duh) *n*. A genus of 6 species of tropical trees (Combretaceae), of which only *B. buceras* is grown ornamentally. It is native to the tropical Americas. The branches are thorny, and the leaves are 3 inches long, with spikes of greenish-yellow flowers. Commonly known as black olive tree.

buckeye *n*. An American name for the different species of horse chestnut, *Aesculus*, native to the United States.

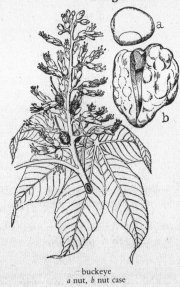

buckeye
a nut, b nut case

buckler fern *n*. A common name for *Nephrolepis exaltata*.

buckthorn *n*. The popular name of species for *Rhamnus*. The common buckthorn is *R. catharticus*.

buckwheat tree *n*. The *Cliftonia monophylla* (Cyrillaceae), a small evergreen with showy, fragrant white flowers and wing-angled fruit; a native of Georgia and the Gulf States. It grows in very moist soils. Also called titi and ironwood.

bud *n*. 1. In plants, a growing point enclosed by closely overlaid rudimentary leaves. Besides foliage, the bud may also contain the rudimentary flower. Bulbs and bulblets are forms of leaf buds. Flower buds are unexpanded blossoms. 2. The state of budding or putting forth buds; for example, the trees are in bud. *v.* 1. To graft a bud of 1 plant on the stem of another; for example, to bud a garden rose on a brier, or a brier with a garden rose. 2. To put forth by or as if by the natural process of budding. 3. To produce buds; be in bud. 4. To sprout or to begin to grow.

budding *n*. In botany: 1. The putting forth or producing of buds. 2. A form of asexual propagation in which a single bud is grafted to the stock. Also known as bud grafting.

budding, or bud grafting

budding *a.* 1. Producing buds; such as a budding tree. 2. Being in the condition of a bud; figuratively, being in an early stage of growth.

budding strip *n.* A rubber strip, typically ⅛ to ⅜ inches wide and up to 8 inches long, used to hold grafts.

Buddleia (buhd'lee uh) *n.* A genus of 100 or more species of shrubs or trees (Loganiaceae) native to the American tropics. Its grayish-green leaves are long, narrow, and usually opposite, and its pink, lilac, blue, purple, or white flowers grow in spikes or clusters and attract butterflies. Commonly known as butterfly bush or summer lilac.

bud mutation *n.* A bud variation resulting from local genetic alteration and producing a permanent modification that usually can be retained by grafting. Example: navel orange.

bud sport (buhd sport) *n.* The product of bud mutation or bud variation.

bud variation *n.* In the outgrowth of a bud, the deviation in any respect from the ordinary growth of the plant, producing what is commonly known as a sport. Many remarkable varieties in cultivated plants arise in this way—for example, Red Delicious apples—and these are perpetuated by bud propagation.

budworm *n.* A moth larva that bores into unopened flower buds to feed on young petals, distorting flowers or greatly reducing bloom. It infests geraniums, petunias, nicotiana, roses, and many other plants. Control with *Bacillus thuringiensis,* handpicking, pyrethrum, or traditional insecticides.

buffalo berry *n.* 1. A common name for *Shepherdia argentea* and *S. canadensis,* a shrub or small tree native to western North America. 2. The fruit of the tree, which is edible.

buffer *n.* A substance in the soil that will chemically act to resist changes in the soil's reaction or pH, usually clay or fine organic matter.

buffer strips *n. pl.* Strips of perennial grass or other erosion-resisting vegetation.

bugbane *n.* A name given to *Cimicifuga,* from its reputed virtues as a destroyer of insects. 2. False bugbane, the North American genus *Trautvetteria,* is very similar to *Cimicifuga.*

bugleweed *n.* The common name for the North American plant *Lycopus virginicus* and the ground cover *Ajuga reptans,* more commonly know as ajuga.

bugloss (byoo'glahs) *n.* The popular name for the biennial or perennial *Anchusa officinalis.* The viper's bugloss is *Echium vulgare.* They are plants of the borage family, with rough leaves, popular in flower borders for their blue and purple blossoms. Also called alkanet.

bug zapper *n.* An electronic device used to lure, trap, and kill insects.

Buglossoides (byoo glahs oi'deez) *n.* A genus of about 7 species of herbaceous plants or subshrubs (Boraginaceae). *B. purpureocaeruleum* is the only species grown ornamentally. It grows from a rhizome (root swelling) and has 2-foot-long trailing stems, long, narrow leaves, and clusters of flowers that emerge purple, then turn blue. Previously classified as *Lithospermum.* Grown in rock gardens.

bulb of a *Hyacinth,* and cross section

bulb (buhlb) *n.* 1. The resting phase of plants such as the onion and tulip, which have membranous or fleshy leaves forming a rounded underground mass, and which can develop into new plants. Some types of underground stems, such as the crocus and gladiolus, are commonly called bulbs but are more properly called corms. Others are more accurately called rhizomes, tubers, or tuberous roots. 2. A plant that has or develops from bulbs. (See **bulbs**.)

bulb drill *n*. A tool for digging holes for bulbs.

bulbil (buhl'bihl) *n*. Same as bulblet.

Bulbinella (buhl bihn ehl'uh) *n*. A genus of about 13 species of perennial bulbs (Liliaceae). They grow from a rhizome (root swelling) and have basal leaves and stalks of white or yellow flowers.

bulblet *n*. A little or secondary bulb; specifically, in botany, a small aerial bulb or bud with fleshy scales, growing in the axils of leaves, as in the tiger lily, or taking the place of flower buds, as in the common onion. Also known as bulbil.

bulblet fern (buhlb leht fern) *n*. A common name for *Cystopteris bulbifera,* which has long, tapering leaves with green bulblets on the lower surface that drop off to form new plants. Also called bladder fern.

bulb lifter *n*. A 2-pronged, fork-shaped digging implement used to remove bulbs for winter storage or for dividing.

Bulbocodium (buhl buh koh'dee uhm) *n*. A genus of 2 species of spring-flowering crocuslike corms (Liliaceae). They have leaves growing at the base of the plant and violet flowers that grow on a short stem directly from the corm. *B. vernum* is commonly known as spring meadow saffron.

Bulbophyllum (buhl buh fighl'uhm) *n*. A genus of 1,200 pantropical epiphytic (growing on, but not taking nourishment from a host plant) orchids (Orchidaceae) with pseudobulbs, 1 or 2 leaves, and a spike of flowers arising directly from the pseudobulb.

bulb planter *n*. A sharp-edged, tapered, and calibrated cylinder used to remove a plug of sod or soil. A bulb is placed in the resulting hole, and the plug is returned to the hole to cover the bulb. It may be either short- or long-handled.

bulb planting tray *n*. A galvanized wire container in which tender bulbs can be planted and then lifted at the end of the season.

bulbs *n. pl*. A term commonly used in gardening for a whole category of spring- or summer-blooming perennial plants that may grow from bulbs, corms, rhizomes, tubers, and tuberous roots. Examples: daffodil, crocus, summer lily, tulip.

bulk density *n*. 1. Volume weight. 2. Apparent density. 3. The weight of dry soil per unit of bulk volume, which also includes air found in the soil.

bullate (bul'ayt) *a*. In botany, appearing to be blistered.

bull-bay *n*. A common name for *Magnolia grandiflora,* a tall, handsome tree with glossy leaves and large, fragrant white flowers.

bullnut *n*. A species of hickory, *Carya tomentosa,* of the southern United States.

bullweed *n*. A common name for *Centaurea nigra;* also called knapweed.

bullwort *n*. The bishop's-weed, *Ammi majus,* a perennial that has naturalized widely in North America. It grows to 2½ feet and has sharply notched leaves and umbrella-shaped clusters of white flowers. Excellent as a cut flower.

bulrush *n*. The popular name for large, rushlike plants growing in marshes. The bulrush of Egypt is the *Cyperus Papyrus.*

Bumelia (byoo mee'lee uh) *n*. A genus of 25 species of trees or shrubs (Sapotaceae). They are often thorny with a milky sap, small, alternate leaves, and small white or greenish flowers. They are native to the United States. They have many common names including mock orange, blackhaw, and gum elastic.

bunchberry *n*. A common name of *Cornus canadensis,* on account of its dense clusters of bright red berries.

bunchflower *n*. A common name for the *Melanthium virginicum* (Liliaceae), native to the eastern United States. It has grasslike leaves and a tall stem, with a broad cluster of small greenish flowers.

bunching onions *n*. Scallions; white, bulbless onions that take up little garden space.

Buphthalum (byoof thal'uhm) *n*. A genus of 2 species of hardy perennial plants, with yellow daisylike flowers. Commonly known as oxeye. Used in borders.

bur (ber) *n*. The rough, prickly case or covering of the seeds of certain plants, such as the chestnut and burdock. Also spelled burr.

burdock (ber'dahk) *n.* A field weed, a common name for *Arctium lappa,* sometimes cultivated for its long edible root. The roots, which store well under refrigeration, are cooked in soups and stews. The root may become invasive in a vegetable garden, where the plant's large leaves may shade other plants, so it is often planted elsewhere.

burl (berl) *n.* A hard, woody growth occurring on the trunks or branches of trees; sometimes used for making bowls, veneer, and coffee tables, such as from the redwood.

burlap *n.* A loosely woven fabric made of jute or hemp used to protect newly seeded lawns from wind, water, and birds.

burnet *n.* 1. The common or garden burnet is *Poterium Sanguisorba,* also called salad burnet. It is grown in herb gardens for the cucumberlike flavor of its leaves. This flavor, which is quite strong when the leaves are fresh, is lost in drying. 2. The great burnet, *Sanguisorba officinalis,* which is less commonly grown.

burning bush *n.* 1. The American species of *Euonymus atropurpurea,* hardy deciduous shrubs or small trees with bright crimson, pendulous, 4-lobed capsules, often cultivated for ornament. Also known as wahoo. (See **Euonymus.**) 2. The plant *Dictamnus albus,* gas plant or faxinella, so called because its volatile oils are inflammable. Also, *Kochia scoparia,* summer cypress, and *Pilea microphylla,* artillery plant.

burnt lime (CaO) *n.* A caustic solid used to neutralize acid soil or to raise the pH of soil.

burpless cucumber *n.* Sometimes called Oriental cucumber, it is a Chinese variety recommended for those who have trouble digesting regular cucumbers. It has a sweet flavor and is used in salads and for making all types of pickles.

bur reed *n.* The common name for species of *Sparganium,* so called from their narrow, reedlike leaves and burlike heads of fruit. *S. erectum* may be grown in a water garden. The floating bur reed is *S. angustifolium.*

bursiculate (ber sihk'yuh liht) *a.* In botany, resembling a small pouch, or having a small, pouch-like cavity.

burstwort *n.* The *Herniaria glabra,* a low weed of European origin, formerly used in the treatment of hernia. Also called rupturewort.

bush *n.* 1. A thicket; a clump of shrubs or trees. 2. A shrub with branches; a thick shrub; technically, a low and much-branched shrub. 3. A stretch of forest or of shrubby vegetation; a district covered with brushwood, or shrubs, trees, etc.; a wide uncultivated tract of country covered with scrub.

bush bean *n.* Any of several bean varieties that grow on compact plants about 20 inches tall. These varieties do not require support in the garden as the pole varieties do.

bush cherry *n.* A cherry variety grown on an ornamental shrub. The fruit is large and black, with a flavor like that of a tree cherry.

bush clover *n.* A common name for the genus *Lespedeza,* hardy perennial plants or low shrubs with leaves divided into 3 leaflets and dense clusters of flowers. Some are grown for forage, others for ornament.

bush honeysuckle *n.* A common name for the genus *Diervilla,* especially *D. Lonicera.*

bush poppy *n.* A common name for the genus *Dendromecon,* especially *D. rigida,* a drought-tolerant open shrub, to 8 feet, with pale shredding bark, gray-green leaves, and bright yellow poppy-like flowers.

bustic (buhs'tihk) *n.* The common name for *Dipholis salicifolia* (Sapotaceae), a tree native to Florida, with shiny, long, narrow leaves and white flowers.

Butea (byoo'tee uh) *n.* A genus of about 7 tropical small trees or shrubs (Leguminosae). Only 1 species, *B. monosperma,* is grown ornamentally. It is a tree that grows to 50 feet, with a crooked trunk, leaves divided into leaflets, showy orange-red flowers, and silvery-gray fruit. Commonly known as flame-of-the-forest, jelly palm.

Butomus (byoo'tuh muhs) *n.* A genus of 1 species of erect water plant, *B. umbellatus* (Butomaceae), which grows from rhizomes (root swellings); it has long tufts of leaves and umbrella-shaped clusters of showy rose-colored flowers. It has naturalized in northeastern North America. Grown in pools and ponds, it is commonly known as water gladiolus.

Butte (byoot) *n.* A white russet potato, used for baking. As well as having a high yield, it contains up to 20% more protein than any other potato.

butter-and-eggs *n.* The common name for toad flax, *Linaria vulgaris;* from the color of the flowers, which are of two shades of yellow.

butterbur *n.* A common name for the genus *Petasites,* creeping perennials with large basal leaves and white or purplish flowers. Also known as sweet coltsfoot.

buttercup *n.* A name given to many of the common species of *Ranunculus* with bright yellow cup-shaped flowers and divided leaves, such as *R. acris* and *R. bulbosus.* Also called butter flower and crowfoot.

buttercup squash *n.* A turban-shaped winter squash with an exceptionally thick flesh, which cooks, freezes, and stores well.

butterfly bush *n.* A common name for the genus *Buddleia.* It has long, narrow, grayish-green leaves and spikes or clusters of pink, lilac, blue, purple, or white flowers that attract butterflies.

butterfly flower *n.* 1. A common name for the genus *Schizanthus,* which has attractive ferny foliage and great quantities of orchidlike blooms that look like butterflies. Also called poor man's orchid. 2. A common name for the genus *Asclepias,* which has hairy, lance-shaped, dark green leaves and clusters of brilliant orange-red flowers that attract butterflies.

butterfly garden *n.* A garden planted for the specific purpose of attracting butterflies by using plants whose flowers provide nectar for butterflies, such as butterfly bush *(Buddleia)* and butterfly flower *(Asclepias).*

butterfly orchid *n.* A common name for *Epidendrum tampense,* which grows to 1 to 2 feet from a pseudobulb. It has narrow, linear leaves and stalks of yellowish-green flowers with a magenta lip. It is native to Florida. 2. A common name for both *Oncidium Krameranum* and *O. papilio,* which grow from a flattened pseudobulb, have a single mottled leaf, and showy reddish-brown flowers on stalks from 2½ to 4 feet long.

butterfly weed *n.* A name for the North American plant *Asclepias tuberosa,* which has hairy, lance-shaped, dark green leaves and clusters of brilliant orange-red flowers that attract butterflies. Its seed cases resemble those of common milkweed, but are smaller and more prized for dried arrangements. Also called pleurisy root.

butterhead *n.* A variety of tender head lettuce. It has soft, pliable leaves and a buttery texture.

butternut *n.* 1. A gourd-shaped winter squash with orange flesh. It is more resistant to squash borers than other types of squash. 2. The fruit of *Juglans cinerea,* an American tree, so called from the oil it contains; also, the tree itself. The tree grows to 100 feet, has 5-inch-long oblong leaves, and bears furrowed and sharply jagged nuts.

butterwort *n.* A name common to the species of *Pinguicula.* The butterworts grow on wet ground, are apparently stemless, and have showy spurred flowers. The name is due to the greasy-looking surface of the leaves, which are covered with soft hairs, secreting a sticky substance that catches small insects. The edges of the leaf roll over on the insect and retain it.

buttonball *n.* A common name for the genus *Platanus,* the plane tree, or sycamore, especially the North American tree, *P. occidentalis;* so called from its small, round, hanging fruit. Also called buttonwood.

buttonbush *n.* 1. A common name for *Cephalanthus occidentalis,* a North American shrub, on account of its globular flower heads. (See **Cephalanthus.**) 2. Also *Platanus,* the plane tree, or sycamore.

buttonwood *n.* 1. A common name for *Conocarpus erecta,* a tropical tree, which grows to 60 feet, with heads of greenish flowers and greenish-purple cones. Also called button tree. 2. A common name for the genus *Platanus,* the plane tree or sycamore, especially the North American tree *P. occidentalis.*

Buxaceae (buhk say'see ee) *n. pl.* A family of about 7 genera and 40 species, known as the box family. The leaves are alternate, the flowers small, and the fruit berrylike. Several species are grown ornamentally, including *Buxus, Pachysandra,* and *Sarcococca.*

Buxus (buhk'suhs) *n.* A genus of evergreen shrubs or small trees (Buxaceae), commonly called box-wood or box. It is widely used for hedging and edging.

Buxus
(boxwood)

Byttneriaceae (biht'ner ee ay' see ee) *n. pl.* A family of 50 genera of tropical trees and shrubs, of which 9 are grown ornamentally. It includes *Dombeya* and *Hermannia,* which are grown in mild climates, and also the plant that produces cocoa and chocolate.

 C

cabbage *n.* 1. A variety of *Brassica oleracea* in which the thick, rounded, and strongly veined leaves are crowded in a large compact head on a short, stout stem. Many kinds are extensively cultivated as a vegetable. From the prominence of this species, the whole order of Cruciferae is sometimes called the cabbage family. The major types of cabbage are smooth, Savoy (with thin, crinkly leaves), red, and Chinese—the latter is a term loosely applied to a number of varities of Asian *brassicas*. 2. The large terminal bud of some kinds of palms, as the cabbage palm.

cabbage, Chinese *n.* (See **Chinese cabbage.**)

cabbage looper *n.* A small green caterpillar that eats the foliage (usually creating small round holes or ragged leaf edges) of brassicaceous plants and some ornamentals. Control with *Bacillus thuringien-*

sis, trichogramma wasps, protective row covers, or traditional insecticides. Also known as cabbage-worm.

cabbage maggot *n.* A small white fly larva that attacks the roots of members of the cabbage family and some other vegetables. It causes plants to wilt even when they are well watered. Crop rotation and protective row covers may help, but soil applications of traditional insecticides are most effective.

cabbage rose *n.* A species of rose, *Rosa centifolia,* of many varieties, with a large, round, compact flower, supposed to have been cultivated from ancient times, and especially suited from its fragrance for the manufacture of rose water and rose oil.

cabbage tree *n.* A name given to many species of palms, of which the tender growing leaf buds are used as a vegetable. The cabbage is the terminal leaf bud, the removal of which, though often done, destroys the tree. It is sold as hearts of palm. Includes the species *Andira inermis, Cordyline australis, Cussonia paniculata, C. spicata, Livistona australis,* and *Sabal palmetto.*

cabbage worm *n.* (See **cabbage looper**.)

Cabomba (kuh bahm'buh) *n.* A genus of 7 species of water plants (Nymphaeaceae) known as water shields, with both small, shield-shaped floating leaves and finely dissected submerged ones, and small flowers; native to the Americas.

cacao
(chocolate)

cacao (kuh kay'oh) *n.* The chocolate tree, *Theobroma Cacao,* (Byttneriaceae). The cacao is a small evergreen tree. Its fruit is a somewhat pear-shaped pointed pod, 10-furrowed, from 5 to 10 inches long, which contains numerous large seeds embedded in a sweet pulp. The seeds yield cacao and chocolate. Cacao husks are used as a mulch.

cacao nut (kuh kay'oh nuht) *n.* The fruit of the *Theobroma Cacáo.* (See **cacao**.)

Cactaceae (kak tay'see ee) *n. pl.* A large family of 50 to 220 genera and 800 to 2,000 species of succulent plants; the cactus family. They are green and fleshy, mostly without true leaves, globular or columnar or jointed, and usually spiny. The flowers are often large and showy. The fruit is usually a pulpy berry, with numerous seeds, sometimes edible. They are natives mostly to dry and hot regions of the Americas. The principal genera are *Mammillaria, Melocactus,* and *Echinocactus,* which are round or oval plants, sometimes gigantic; *Cereus,* often climbing or erect and columnar, sometimes treelike and 30 to 50 feet high; *Opuntia,* jointed and with the joints often flattened; and *Epiphyllum,* frequently grown for its large flowers, commonly known as orchid cactus.

cactus *n., pl.* **cacti** or **cactuses**. The common name for plants in the family *Cactaceae;* for example, the night-blooming cactus (or night-blooming cereus), *Selenicereus grandiflorus* and the old-man cactus, *Cephalocereus senilis.*

Caesalpinia (sez al pihn'ee uh) *n.* A genus of tropical or subtropical trees or shrubs (Leguminosae) with showy yellow or red flowers, bipinnate (doubly divided) leaves, and usually prickly stems.

caespitose (sehs' puh tohs) *a.* Tufted; growing in clumps or clusters; sod-forming. Also spelled cespitose.

Cajanus (kuh jay'nuhs) *n.* A genus of 2 species of shrubs (Leguminosae), 1 species of which, *C. Indicus,* is grown for its edible seeds, as a cover crop, and as green manure in tropical regions. The plant has many common names including cajan, pigeon pea, Angola pea, and Congo pea.

cajeput (kaj'uh puht) *n.* A common name for *Melaleuca Leucadendron* and *M. quinquenervia* (Myrtaceae), which have small trees or shrubs. They have long, narrow, leathery leaves and flowers that resemble those of the bottlebrush. Also a common name for *Umbellaria californica.*

calabash (kal'uh bash) *n.* 1. A fruit of the tree *Crescentia cujete* hollowed out, dried, and used as a vessel to contain liquids. These shells are so close-grained and hard that when containing liquid, they may be used several times as kettles upon a fire without injury. 2. A gourd of any kind used in the same way. 3. A popular name for the gourd plant, *Lagenaria vulgaris.*

Caladium (kuh lay'dee uhm) *n.* A genus of 15 species of tuberous-rooted herbaceous plants (Araceae) with large arrow-shaped leaves, which are spectacularly variegated; native to tropical America. They are widely grown for their foliage and are used as container plants, bedding plants, or houseplants.

Calamagrotis (kal'uh muh grahs'tihs) *n.* A genus of more than 250 species of perennial grasses (Gramineae) native to moist areas in temperate zones. A few are used as ornamentals, grown for their nodding, feathery plumes, which are good in dried arrangements. Known as reeds or reed grasses.

calamondin (kal uh mahn'dihn) *n.* A common name for the citrus hybrid *Citrofortunella mitis,* a small evergreen tree and its acid, loose-skinned fruit. It has dense, glossy leaves and bright orange fruit, which is very ornamental and used like lemon or lime. One of the hardiest citrus.

Calandrinia (kal uhn drihn'ee uh) *n.* A large genus of more than 150 species of succulent (fleshy) herbs native mostly to the Americas, with basal or alternate narrow leaves and stalks of red, rose, or purplish flowers; native mostly to the Americas. Grown as annuals in borders or rock gardens. Commonly known as rock purslane.

Calanthe (kuh lan'thee) *n.* A genus of about 120 species of tropical terrestrial orchids (Orchidaceae) with broad, folded leaves and showy white, yellow, or rose-colored flowers.

Calathea (kal uh thee'uh) *n.* A genus of 100 species of tropical plants (Maranthacea) with exotically patterned leaves in shades of green, white, and pink. Grown for their foliage as a houseplant or greenhouse specimen.

calcareous soil (kal ka'ree uhs) *n.* A soil that is alkaliine in its reaction because of the presence of calcium carbonate.

Calceolaria (kal see uh lar'ee uh) *n.* A large genus of 500 species of tender, ornamental herbaceous or shrubby plants (Scrophulariaceae). They are distinguished by an unusual pouch-shaped flower. They are grown as summer annuals for bedding or as houseplants. Commonly known as slipperwort, slipper flower, pocketbook flower, and pouch flower.

calcium (kal'see uhm) *n.* An element needed by plants. An element that can also be added to soil.

calcium carbonate (kal'see uhm kahr'buh nayt) *n.* A salt CaCo3 found in plant ashes, bones, shells, calcite and aragonite.

calcium chloride (kal'see uhm klor'ighd) *n.* A deliquescent salt CaCl2 used as a drying and dehumidifying agent.

calcium cyanamide (kal'see uhm sigh an'uh mighd) *n.* A compound CaCN2 used as a fertilizer and weed killer.

calcium phosphate (kal'see uhm fah'sfayt) *n.* 1. A phosphate used as a fertilizer; 2. A naturally occurring phosphate of calcium occurring as the main constituent of phosphate rock.

calcium polysulfide (kal'see um pol ee suhl'fighd) *n.* (See **lime sulfur**.)

caliche (kuh leesh'ee) *n.* A term used to identify cemented deposits of calcium carbonate.

calico bush *n.* A common name of the *Kalmia latifolia,* the mountain laurel; native to North America.

calico flower (kal'ih koh flow'er) *n.* A common name for *Kalmia latifolia,* the mountain laurel, as well as for *Aristolochia elegans,* a vine.

California bluebell *n.* A common name for *Phacelia minor,* a desert flower with broad, oval, notched leaves and clusters of blue or purple tubular flowers. Grown for massing in beds.

California fuschia (fyoo'shuh) *n.* A common name for the genus *Zauschneria,* drought-tolerant perennials or subshrubs with small, gray-green, narrow leaves and tiny, trumpet-shaped, bright scarlet flowers. The flowers attract hummingbirds.

California laurel *n.* A common name for the tree *Umbellaria californica,* with long, narrow, fragrant leaves, small yellow flowers, and olivelike fruits called bay nuts. Sometimes grown as a drought-tolerant ornamental tree, providing dense shade.

California nutmeg *n.* A common name for *Toryea californica,* a slow-growing, moderately sized evergreen conifer (cone-bearing) with horizontal, drooping branches, dark green leaves in white-banded sprays, and pale green plumlike fruit; native to California.

California pitcher plant *n.* A common name for *Darlingtonia californica,* an insect-devouring flower found in bogs and marshes. Also known as cobra lily, cobra orchid, and cobra plant.

California poppy *n.* A common name for *Escholizia californica,* a low-growing plant with finely divided gray-green leaves and cream, pale yellow, orange, or gold poppylike flowers.

Calla (kal'uh) *n.* 1. A genus of a single species, *C. palustris* (Araceae), the water arum, which occurs in cold marshes in North America. It has heart-shaped leaves from a creeping rootstock, an open white spathe, and red berries. Also known as water dragon and wild calla. 2. [l.c.] A plant of the genus *Calla.* 3. A plant of the genus *Zantedeschia;* the common calla lily of garden cultivation, so called from the lilylike appearance of its pure-white flowers. (See **lily, Calla**.)

Calliandra (kal ee an'druh) *n.* A genus of about 250 species of tropical and subtropical evergreen trees and shrubs (Leguminosae) with alternate, divided leaves and showy, fluffy, round pink or red flowers. Commonly known as powderpuff, fairy duster, false mesquite, Trinidad flame bush, and Brazilian flame bush.

Callicarpa (kal uh kar'puh) *n.* A genus of 135 species of shrubs (Verbenaceae). The best-known species is *C. americana,* of the United States, called French mulberry, which is cultivated for ornament on account of its abundant violet-colored berries. Also called beautyberry.

Calliopsis (kal ee ahp'sihs) *n.* A former genus now reclassified as *Coreopsis.*

Callirhoe (kuh ler′uh wee) *n.* A small genus of 8 species of flowers (Malvaceae) native to the United States. They have lobed leaves and showy white, crimson, or purple flowers. Commonly known as poppy mallow.

Callistemon (kal uh stee′muhn) *n.* A genus of about 20 species of shrubs or small trees (Myrtaceae). They have long, narrow, simple leaves and striking red or yellow flowers in showy heads or spikes. Tolerant of drought, heat, poor soil, and air pollution, they are widely used in the West in public plantings; also grown in gardens. Commonly known as bottlebrush.

Callistephus (ku lihs′tuh fuhs) *n.* A genus of 1 species, *C. chinensis* (Compositae), a late-summer and autumn-blooming flower. It grows 1 to 3 feet tall, has alternate leaves, and dense, round clusters of brightly colored flowers in shades of violet to rose or white. Tolerates drought, but does better with moist, rich soil. Commonly known as the China aster or garden aster.

Callitris (kal′uh trihs) *n.* A genus of 16 species of coniferous (cone-bearing) trees (Cupressaceae). They have scalelike leaves and both catkinlike and woody cones. Useful in arid regions. Commonly known as cypress pine.

Calluna (kuh lyoo′nuh) *n.* A genus of 1 species, *C. vulgaris* (Ericaceae), the common heather, with many cultivars. It has opposite, 4-ranked leaves and spikes of tiny flowers in white, pink, deep pink, lavender, or purple.

Calluna vulgaris
(heather)

callus (kal′uhs) *n., pl.* **calli.** In botany, any unusually hard thickened area or swelling on a plant; also, the thickening that is formed over wounds, by which the inner tissues are protected and healing is effected.

Calocedrus (kal uh seed′ruhs) *n.* A genus of 3 species of evergreen conifers (Cupressaceae), some native to North America. A symmetrical tree that grows as high as 90 feet, it has rich green foliage in flat sprays that give off a pungent fragrance in warm weather. It has reddish-brown bark and unusual cones, which look like ducks' bills and open on the tree. Commonly known as incense cedar.

Calochortus (kal uh kor′tuhs) *n.* A genus of about 60 species of perennial bulbs (Liliaceae), native to the western United States. The leaves grow from the base of the plant, and the flowers are large, showy, and variously colored. Commonly known as butterfly lily, sego lily, mariposa, star tulip, globe tulip, and mariposa lily.

Calopogon (kal uh poh′gahn) *n.* A small genus of American wild orchids found in bogs and marshes. The leaves are grasslike, and the flowers are pink and bearded. Commonly known as grass pink.

Caltha (kal′thuh) *n.* A genus of 15 to 20 species of early-blooming marsh plants (Ranunculaceae) with stout, creeping rootstocks, flowers with showy yellow sepals but no petals, and clusters of many-seeded pods. *C. palustris* is known as the common marsh marigold and cowslip.

Calycanthaceae (kal uh kan thay′see ee) *n. pl.* A family of 2 genera and 6 species of hardy shrubs. The 2 genera are *Calycanthus,* of the United States, and *Chimonanthus,* of Asia. They are well known for the delicious fragrance of their blossoms.

calycanthemy (kal uh kan′thuh mee) *n.* An abnormality of form in a flower, in which the calyx lobes have become petallike, as in some varieties of primrose.

Calycanthus (kal uh kan′thuhs) *n.* A genus of 4 species of aromatic shrubs with large, fragrant reddish-brown or purple flowers that have the odor of strawberries. The bruised leaves and bark are also fragrant. The most common species in cultivation are *C. floridus* and *C. occidentalis.* Also called strawberry plant or strawberry shrub.

Calycanthus floridus
(strawberry plant)

Calypso (kuh lihp'soh) *n.* A genus of beautiful orchids, consisting of a single species, *C. bulbosa,* a small circumboreal tuberous plant found in bogs and wet woods in North America. It has a single thin leaf and a slender stalk with a single, variegated purple-and-yellow flower with a large lip similar to that of the lady's slipper, *Cypripedium.* Also known as fairy slipper, calypso, cytherea, and pink slipper orchid.

calyptra (kuh lihp'truh) *n.* A hood or covering on a flower or fruit. Also called calypter.

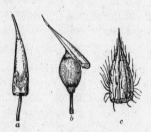

calyptra
a conical, *b* dimidiate, *c* mitriform

calyptrate (kuh lihp'trayt) *a.* In botany, furnished with a calyptra, as a capsule or a flower; resembling a calyptra, as a calyx that comes off like a lid.

Calyptridium (kal ihp trihd'ee uhm) *n.* A genus of about 6 species of perennial plants. *C. umbellatum* has spreading stems, leaves growing from the base of the plant, and white or pink flowers. It is used in rock gardens. Commonly known as pussy paws.

calyptrogen (kuh lihp'truh juhn) *n.* In botany, the cell layer from which the root cap originates.

calyx (kay'lihks) *n., pl.* **calyxes**, or **calyces**. In botany, in general, the outer set of the envelopes that form or enclose the base of a flower. It is usually more green and leaflike than the corolla, but it is often highly colored and corollalike and is sometimes the first to fall.

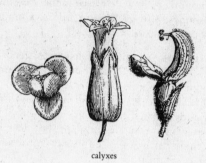

calyxes

camas (kam'uhs) *n.* 1. The common name for *Camassia, especially C. Quamash* and *C. Leichtlinii,* which are native to moist meadows from northern California to British Columbia and east to western Montana. It has large, clustered bulbs, 20-inch leaves, and pale blue-to-blue flowers on 3-foot stalks. 2. A common name for *Zigadenus venenosus.* Also called death camas; the root is poisonous. Also spelled camass.

Camassia (kuh mas'ee uh) *n.* A genus of hardy bulbs (Liliaceae) native to North America. They have long linear leaves and a stalk that bears numerous blue or white flowers. *C. scilloides,* commonly known as meadow hyacinth or indigo squill, is found in the Atlantic states, and there are 3 others west of the Rocky Mountains. (See **camas.**)

cambium (kam'bee uhm) *n.* In botany, a layer of tissue, 1-cell thick, formed between the wood and the bark of vascular plants, that is capable of giving rise to new cells. Cambium develops on the 1 side into a layer of new wood and on the other into new bark while, at the same time, fresh cambium is formed. The renewal of this process year after year brings about the increase of growth in the diameter of the trunk of trees, as indicated by its concentric rings.

Camellia (kuh meel'yuh) *n.* 1. A genus of about 80 species of long-lived, handsome, tender evergreen shrubs or small trees (Theaceae). They grow from 8 to 45 feet, depending on the species, with glossy, leathery, simple leaves and white, pink, rose, red, or variegated flowers. There are more than 3,000 named camelias. *C. Japonica,* is the most widely grown. It has elegant, laurellike leaves and 8 distinct flower forms, of which the formal double is best known. Camelias are members of the tea family; tea is *C. sinensis.* Used in filtered shade in mild-climate gardens for fall and winter bloom. 2. [l.c.] A flower of the genus *Camellia,* especially of *C. Japonica.*

camomile (kam'oh meel) *n.* (See **chamomile**.)

Campanula (kam pan'yuh luh) *n.* A large genus of nearly 300 species of mmostly perennial plants (Campanulaceae), the bell-flower family. They have large blue, white, or pink bell-shaped flowers. Many species are cultivated for their showy flowers; the most common are *C. Medium,* known as canterbury bells, and *C. M.* 'Calycanthema', often called cup-and-saucer. The best-known wild species is *C. rotundifolia,* the bluebells of Scotland. Some species are useful in borders, others as ground covers, and still others as hanging-basket plants.

Campanula
(bell flowers)

Campanulaceae (kam pan yuh lay'see ee) *n. pl.* A family of about 40 genera and more than 700 species of herbaceous plants (occasionally shrubs or trees), the bellflowers. Most have milky sap, alternate, simple leaves, and regular bell-shaped flowers. The principal genus is *Campanula.*

campanulate (kam pan'yuh layt) *a.* Bell-shaped.

campernelle (kam'per nehl) *n.* A common name for *Narcissus* × *odorus,* also called campernelle jonquil.

campion (kam'pee uhn) *n.* The popular name of certain plants belonging to the genera *Lychnis* and *Silene.* Bladder campion, or maiden's tears, is *Silene vulgaris;* moss campion, *S. acaulis;* starry campion, *S. stellata;* white, or evening, campion, *S. alba;* red alpine campion, *Lychnis alpina;* rose campion, *L. Coronaria;* flower-of-Jove, *L. Flos-Jovis;* red, or morning, campion, *L. dioica.*

Campsis (kamp'sihs) *n.* A genus of 2 species of vines (Bignoniaceae), which climb by aerial rootlets. They have opposite, divided leaves with toothed leaflets and clusters of bright orange, orange-yellow, or scarlet flowers that attract hummingbirds. Commonly known as trumpet creeper, trumpet vine, or crown plant.

Camptosorus (kamp tuh sor'uhs) *n.* A genus of 2 species of small, hardy evergreen ferns (Polypodiaceae). *C. rhizophyllus* is native to eastern North America from Quebec to Georgia, west to Oklahoma and Alabama. Commonly known as walking fern because the tip of the frond bends over and takes root, giving origin to a new plant. Used in rock gardens and wild gardens.

Cananga (kuh nang'uh) *n.* A genus of 2 species of large tropical evergreen trees. The only species grown ornamentally is *C. odorata,* the ilang-ilang. It grows to 80 Feet, with large, oval, pointed leaves and very fragrant drooping flowers which yield an oil often used in perfume.

candlenut tree *n.* A common name for *Aleurites moluccana,* a large tropical tree. It grows to 60 feet, with large, lobed, white-haired leaves and 9-inch long white flowers. Grown ornamentally as a shade tree, it appears white from a distance. Also called candleberry tree.

candle plant *n.* A common name for *Plectranthus Oertendahlii* and *Senecio articulatus. P. Oertendahlii* is a semisucculent plant with draping stems; it is usually used as a hanging-basket houseplant. *S. articulatus* is a drought-tolerant succulent perennial with sausagelike joints to 2 feet tall.

candle tree *n.* 1. A common name for a tropical tree, *Parmentiera cereifera* (Bignoniaceae). Its fruit, of which is nearly 4 feet long, has the appearance of a yellow wax candle and a peculiar applelike smell. It is grown ornamentally as an oddity. 2. Also the tree *Catalpa bignonioides,* so called from its long round pods.

candlewood *n.* A common name given to several resinous trees or shrubs from their usefulness as torches for illumination, such as the genus *Fouquiera,* especially the ocotillo; the torchwood, *Amyris balsamifera;* and a West Indian tree, *Dacryodes excelsa.*

candytuft *n.* The common name for the genus *Iberis,* widely grown garden flowers, some of which are annuals, others perennials. They grow to 18 inches, with clusters of white, lavender, lilac, pink, rose, purple, or crimson flowers. The annuals are grown for borders and for use as cut flowers. The perennials are low-growing and useful for rock gardens, edging, small scale ground covers, and containers. (See **Iberis**.)

cane *n.* 1. A long and slender jointed woody stem, more or less rigid, hollow or pithy, as that of some palms, grasses, and other plants, such as the rattan, bamboo, and sugarcane; also, the stem of raspberries or blackberries. 2. Sugarcane. 3. Plants of the genus *Arundinaria.*

Canellaceae (kan uh lay′see ee) *n. pl.* A small family of 5 genera of fragrant and aromatic tropical trees and shrubs. *Canella Winterana,* wild cinnamon, has glossy leaves and purple, red, or violet flowers. It is the source of canella bark, a spice. Used in frost-free gardens.

canescent (kuh nehs′ehnt) *a.* Growing white or gray; tending or approaching to white; whitish. Applied to plants with grayish-white, short, soft leaf hairs.

canker (kang′ker) *n.* A lesion or an oozing point of decay in the tissue of a plant, usually on the trunk or branches. Caused by disease, wounds, or insects.

cankerworm *n.* A small caterpillar that feeds on the foliage of fruit and shade trees in spring or fall, swinging from tree to tree by silken threads. Control with *Bacillus thuringiensis* or traditional insecticides. Also known as inchworm.

cankerworm
a adult moth

Canna (kan′uh) *n.* A genus of 60 species of tall, erect, tropical perennials (Cannaceae). They grow from rhizomes, with large, simple, entire leaves and showy rose, scarlet, or yellow flowers, sometimes striped or spotted. Most garden varieties are hybrids.

Canna
(canna lily)
a foliage, *b* flower, *c* fruit

Cannabaceae (kan uh bay′see ee) *n. pl.* A family of 2 genera and 3 species; the hemp family. The 2 genera are *Cannabis,* true hemp, or marijuana, and *Humulus,* commonly known as hops. It is illegal to grow *Cannabis sativa* in the United States without a government permit. *Humulus lupulus* is grown as a summer vine and is an important ingredient in beer.

Cannabis (kan′uh bihs) *n.* A genus of a single species, *C. sativa,* with long, toothed leaves and spikes or clusters of flowers. Best known for its hallucinatory properties, it is illegal to cultivate it in the United States. Commonly known as pot, or marijuana. (See **hemp**.)

cannonball tree *n.* A common name for *Couroupita Guianensis,* a tree native to tropical America. It grows to 50 feet, with long, somewhat downy leaves, 3-foot-long stalks of large, showy, fragrant, red and yellow flowers, and large, round, woody fruit. Grown as a novelty in tropical gardens.

can sprayer *n.* (See **hand sprayer**.)

cantaloupe *n.* A variety of of muskmelon, almost spherical in shape, ribbed, of orange or yellow color, and of a delicate flavor. Also spelled cantaloup, cantalope, or cantelope.

canterbury bell *n.* The common name for *Campanula Medium,* of which there are several varieties.

Cantua (kan'tyoo uh) *n.* A genus of 6 species of shrubs and trees (Polemoniaceae). They have simple, alternate leaves and white, violet, or red flowers, often in many-flowered clusters. *C. buxifolia* is commonly known as sacred-flower-of-the-Incas.

Cape Cod weeder *n.* An angled, pointed-tipped, knifelike implement used for weeding and cultivation.

Cape cowslip *n.* A common name for *Lachenalia,* a genus of small bulbs that have two spotted basal leaves and spikes of yellow, white, or red flowers.

Cape fuschia (fyoo'shuh) *n.* A common name for *Phygelius capensis,* a subshrub. It has oval, toothed leaves, and large clusters of scarlet flowers.

Cape Gooseberry *n. Physalis peruviana,* a small dense shrub with oval or triangular leaves, yellow flowers with purple markings, and small yellow berries. It is grown for its edible fruit, encased in a ribbed husk similar in appearance to that of the tomatillo (husk tomato).

Cape honeysuckle *n.* A common name for *Tecomaria capensis,* a tender evergreen vine or shrub. It grows to 25 feet with leaves divided into many glistening dark green leaflets and clusters of brilliant orange-red tubular flowers, which attract hummingbirds.

cape marigold *n.* A common name for the genus *Dimorphotheca,* a tender, drought-tolerant ground cover, with brilliantly colored free-blooming, daisylike flowers, often multicolored. Grows best in dry, warm-winter areas.

cape primrose *n.* A common name for the genus *Streptocarpus,* flowering plants with fleshy, hairy leaves and trumpet-shaped, wide-mouthed white, blue, pink, purple, rose, or red flowers. Most garden varieties are hybrids. Related to African violets and gloxinias, they can be used as a houseplant anywhere, a garden plant in warm-winter climates.

caper (kay'per) *n.* A plant, *Capparis spinosa,* the buds of which (called capers) are pickled as a condiment. The bush is a low shrub, growing on old walls in Mediterranean countries. Nasturtium buds are sometimes used as a substitute for real capers.

capillary (kap'uh lair ee) *n.* 1. Water movement within the soil; 2. Water held by or found in the soil resulting from surface tension.

capillary attraction (kap'uh lair ee) *n.* Is responsible for water moving against gravity and moving up to the soil's surface.

capillary matting (kap'uh ler ee mat'ihng) *n.* An interwoven fabric that wicks water from a reservoir. Used in propagators, seed flats, pots, or English baskets to provide plants with a continuous supply of moisture.

capillary porosity (kap'uh lair ee puh rahs'uh dee) *n.* The volume of small pores in the soil that holds water.

capillary water (kap'uh lair ee) *n.* The movable water retained by surface tension in the small pores found in the soil.

capitate (kap'uh tayt) *a.* In botany, head-shaped, or collected in a head.

Capparaceae (kap uh ray'see ee) *n. pl.* A family of about 37 genera of temperate, tropical, and subtropical plants, sometimes shrubs or trees. The principal genera are *Capparis* and *Cleome.* Some species of *Crateva* and *Polanisia,* other genera of this family, are cultivated for ornament. (See cut under **caper** and *Cleome.*)

Capparis (kap'uh rihs) *n.* A genus of perhaps 300 species of tropical and subtropical shrubs or trees, of which the most familiar species is the caper, *C. spinosa.*

caprifig (kap'ruh fihg) *n.* The common name for the male form of the wild fig, *Ficus carica sylvestris.* The fruit of the caprifig is hard and inedible, but it is the home of a small gnatlike gall insect, *Blastophaga* (commonly called the fig wasp). In escaping from the orifice of the caprifig, the insect covers itself with pollen, thus becoming the essential means for effecting the fertilization of the edible fig, *F. Smyrna.*

caprifoil (kap'rih foil) *n.* A common name for woodbine; honeysuckle. Also called caprifole.

Caprifoliaceae (kap rih foh lee ay'see ee) *n. pl.* A family of 12 to 15 genera and 400 to 450 species of erect or twining shrubs; the honeysuckle family. The ornamental genera, in addition to *Lonicera* (honeysuckle), includes *Abelia, Viburnum,* and *Weigela.*

Capsella (kap sehl'uh) *n.* A small genus of low-growing plants (Cruciferae). Commonly known as shepherd's purse.

capsule *n.* In botany, a pod or seed vessel, either membranous or woody, composed of 2 or more carpels, which at maturity becomes dry and opens. The term is sometimes applied to any dry, wide-opening fruit, and even to the spore cases of plants.

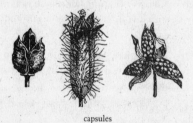

capsules

captan (kap'tan) *n.* A synthetic fungicide used to control many diseases, including damping-off and leaf spots.

Caragana (kar uh gah'nuh) *n.* A genus of more than 60 species of hardy deciduous shrubs or trees (Leguminosae), with feathery, pale green foliage and sweet-pea-shaped yellow flowers appearing in early spring. Grown for their showy bright yellow flowers, they endure all privation, tolerating cold,

heat, wind, and desert sun. Used as a windbreak, clipped hedge, or cover for wildlife.

Caralluma (kair uh loo'muh) *n.* A genus of about 100 species of dwarf, succulent (fleshy), leafless plants (Asclepiadaceae) They have 4-to-6-angled jointed spiny stems and tight clusters of large, showy, star-shaped cream, yellow, deep red, or purple flowers, some to 4 inches across. The flowers have a carrion scent. Grown as a succulent in rock gardens.

carambola (kar uhm boh'luh) *n.* The acid fruit of the *Averrhoa Carambola* of tropical Asia, which is used for making tarts, etc.

caraway (kar'uh way) *n.* A biennial plant, *Carum Carvi* (Umbelliferae). It is cultivated for its fruit, or so-called seeds, which have a warm, pungent taste and are frequently used to flavor rye bread.

carbaryl (kar'buh rihl) *n.* A broad-spectrum, synthetic insecticide that kills insects (including beneficial ones) on contact. Very toxic to bees. Common trade name: Sevin.

carbohydrate (kar boh high'drayt) *n.* A compound containing carbon, hydrogen and oxygen.

carbon *n.* One of the most common chemical elements found in soil and air that is needed by living plants.

carbon dioxide (CO_2) *n.* A colorless gas found in the air.

carbon-nitrogen ratio *n.* The ratio of weight of organic carbon to the weight of nitrogen found in the soil.

Cardamine (kahr dam'uh nee) *n.* A genus of annual or perennial flowers (Cruciferae). The plants have divided leaves and stalks of white or rose-colored, often double, flowers. The genus includes the cuckooflower, or lady's-smock, *C. pratensis,* a perennial traditional in cottage gardens and useful in rock gardens, bog gardens, and cool, moist borders.

cardamom (kar'duh muhm) *n.* Capsules of *Elettaria cardomomum,* which are thin and filled with brown aromatic seeds, are used in curries and breads.

cardinal climber *n.* A common name for *Ipomoea Quamoclit* and *I.* ×*multifida.* Both are annual twining vines with scarlet flowers. *I. Quamoclit* is also known as star-glory. *I.* × *multifida* is also known as hearts-and-honey vine.

cardinal flower *n.* The name commonly given to *Lobelia Cardinalis* because of its large, showy, intensely red flowers. It is a native of North America and is often cultivated. A similar species, *L. syphilitica,* but with bright blue flowers, is sometimes called blue cardinal flower. Useful in bog gardens and moist borders.

Cardiocrinum (kahr′dee oh krigh′nuhm) *n.* A genus of 3 species of perennial bulbs (Liliaceae). They have heart-shaped leaves and stalks of funnel-shaped, creamy white, fragrant flowers, some to 6 inches long.

Cardiospermum (kahr′dee oh sper′muhm) *n.* A genus of 12 species of shrubby tropical vines (Sapindaceae) native mostly to tropical America. They have alternate, coarsely toothed leaflets in sets of 3 and clusters of tiny white fragrant flowers. Grown as an annual on trellises or other support.

cardoon (kar doon′) *n.* The *Cynara cardunculus,* the same genus as the artichoke, and somewhat resembling it. Its thick, fleshy stalks and the ribs of its leaves are cooked quickly and eaten as a vegetable. Also called chardoon.

Carex (kah′reks) *n.* A genus of about 2,000 species of grasslike, clumping, perennial herbs (Cyperaceae) native mostly to temperate and cold regions of the world. Many are grown as ornamentals for their straplike foliage, which is often brightly colored or variegated. Commonly known as sedges.

carices (ka′ri-seez) *n. pl.* Any plant of this genus.

Carica (kar′uh kuh) *n.* A genus of about 25 species of semisucculent trees (Caricaceae) native to tropical America. They have straight trunks and a crown of palmate (palmlike) leaves. Their fruit, the papaya, is technically a large berry that resembles a melon. The best-known is *C. Papaya,* grown in tropical gardens for its fruit.

caricature plant *n.* A common name for the tropical shrub *Graptophyllum pictum* (Acanthaceae); so called from the curious variegation of the leaves, which are often so lined as to present grotesque likenesses of the human profile. The leaves are entire, elliptical and variegated green, purple, and yellow.

Carissa (kuh rihs′uh) *n.* A genus of about 35 species of tender evergreen, often spiny, shrubs or small trees (Apocynaceae). *C. macrocarpa* has glossy, dark green leaves, very fragrant pinwheel-shaped white flowers, and showy purplish berries. Commonly known as Natal plum.

Carlina (kahr ligh′nuh) *n.* A genus of thistlelike plants (Compositae). The spiny leaves grow in rosettes at the base of the plant and look as though covered in cobwebs; the flowers are white, yellow, or red.

Carludovica (kahr′lyoo duh vee′kuh) *n.* A small genus of 3 species of tropical American palmlike plants (Cyclanthaceae). The large fanlike leaves of *C. palmata* are the material of which the well-known Panama hats are made, each hat being woven from a single leaf.

carnation *n.* The common name for the pink *Dianthus Caryophyllus,* cultivated from very ancient times for its fragrance and beauty.

Carnegiea (kahr neh′gee uh) *n.* A genus of 1 species, *C. gigantea,* a slow-growing giant cactus that is native to the American West. It is columnar and branching, with fluted, spiny, columns, which grow to 50 feet, and large, white, night-blooming flowers. The state flower of Arizona, it is commonly known as saguaro.

carob (kar′ohb) *n.* The common English name of the plant *Ceratonia Siliqua,* cultivated as a substitute for chocolate.

Carolina-allspice *n.* (See **Calycanthus**.)

carosella (kar uh sehl′uh) *n.* A popular name of the common fennel, *Foeniculum vulgare.* It has delicate, dark green, fernlike leaves and flat clusters of yellow flowers. Also called finocchio and anise.

carpels

carpel (kahr'puhl) *n.* In botany, a simple pistil, or one of the several members composing a compound pistil or fruit. In a general sense, it is the organ of a plant that bears ovules.

Carpenteria (kahr pehn tee'ree uh) *n.* A genus of 1 species of evergreen shrub, *C. californica* (Saxifragaceae), native to the central Sierra Nevada mountains of California. It has opposed, leathery leaves and large white flowers. Commonly known as bush or tree, anemone.

carpet bugle *n.* A common name for the genus *Ajuga*, a blue-flowered ground cover.

Carpinus
(hornbeam)

Carpinus (kahr pigh'nuhs) *n.* A genus of 35 species of very hardy deciduous trees or tall shrubs (Betulaceae). They have gray bark, alternate, toothed leaves, and catkins. Commonly known as hornbeam.

Carpobrotus (kahr poh broht'uhs) *n.* A genus 29 species of low-growing, succulent plants (Aizoaceae), some native to North America. They have stubby, fleshy, 3-sided leaves and lightly fragrant, daisylike brilliant magenta or pale yellow flowers. They tolerate everything but frost and foot traffic, including drought, heat, poor soil, and air pollution. Widely used in mild climates along freeways. Commonly known as ice plant.

carpogenic (kahr poh jehn'ihk) *a.* In botany, fruit-producing. Also carpogenous.

carpophore (kahr'poh for) *n.* In botany, the wiry stalk that bears the carpels of some compound fruits, as in *Geranium* and many Umbelliferae.

carpophore with carpels

carrion flower *n.* A name given to various plants, especially to species of the genus *Stapelia* and to *Smilax herbacea,* whose flowers have an offensive, carrionlike odor. The odor draws flies, which are pollinators for these plants.

carrot *n.* 1. The common name of plants of the genus *Daucus*. The best-known species, *D. Carota* has been used as a vegetable since ancient times. Carrots are a garden favorite, especially in gardens with sandy soil. They vary in shape from almost round to the long, tapered varieties known as Nantes.

cart *n.* A 2-wheeled vehicle for pushing or pulling heavy loads. The bed of the cart is typically of wood or polyethylene; the wheels, standing brace, and U-shaped handle are of metal. Smaller carts hold up to 200 lbs; larger ones up to 400 lbs.

caruncle (kar'uhng kuhl) *n.* In botany, an outgrowth surrounding the scar on a seed.

Caruncle
whole and cross section

Carya (ka'ree uh) *n.* A genus of about 25 species of deciduous American trees (Juglandaceae) mostly native to eastern North America; hickory trees. The leaves are alternate, divided into odd-numbered leaflets; the flowers occur in drooping catkins; and the nuts are edible. Several species are grown ornamentally. Commonly known as hickory and shagbark.

Caryophyllaceae (kar′ee oh fih lay′see ee) *n. pl.* A family of 70 genera of flowers, best known as pinks, found all over the world. They have stems that are generally swollen at the nodes (leaf joints), simple, opposite leaves, and tightly ruffled flowers that grow at the end of slender stalks. Many are old-fashioned favorites in gardens, such as the pink, florists' carnation, and sweet william. The ornamental genera include *Dianthus, Silene, Lychnis,* and *Arenaria.*

caryopsis (kar ee ahp′sihs) *n.* In botany, a small, 1-seeded, dry fruit, in which the fruit and seed are incorporated into a single grain, as in wheat and all other cereal grains.

Caryopteris (kar ee ahp′tuh rihs) *n.* A genus of about 6 species of tender, deciduous shrubs or perennial plants (Verbenaceae). They have opposite, simple leaves and white, lavender, or blue flowers in terminal clusters. Commonly known as bluebeard.

Caryota (kar ee oht′uh) *n.* A small genus of tropical palms (Palmae), with leaves divided into wedge-shaped leaflets, strongly toothed at the ends; the fishtail palms. Grown outdoors in warm-winter climates and a choice houseplant or greenhouse specimen anywhere. Also known as jaggery palm, sago palm, toddy palm, winw palm.

cash crop *n.* Plants grown for sale in a market, as distinguished from plants grown for home consumption or ornament.

cashew nut

cashew *n.* The tree *Anacardium occidentale* and its fruit, an edible nut. The kidney-shaped nut causes skin rashes in its raw state, but the toxicity is removed by roasting. (See **Anacardium.**)

Casimiroa (kaz uh mih roh′uh) *n.* A genus of about 6 species of large shrubs or trees (Rutaceae) native to highland Mexico and Central America. *C. edulis* has luxuriant, glossy green leaves divided fanlike into leaflets, and bears a round pale-green-to-yellow edible fruit. The fruit has a custardlike texture, and the taste is variously described as similar to that of peaches, bananas, or pears, but the consensus is banana-peach. Each tree can bear several hundred pounds of fruit. Commonly known as white sapote.

cassabanana (kas′uh buh nan′uh) *n.* A common name for *Sicana odorifera,* a tall-growing annual vine with huge leaves, yellow bell-shaped flowers, and 2-foot-long, fragrant, orange-red edible fruits. Grown as an annual for its ornamental, edible fruit.

cassava (kuh sah′vuh) *n.* 1. The name of several species of *Manihot,* extensively cultivated for food in tropical America. Its roots are made into bread, starch, and tapioca. Also known as manioc or maniocca. 2. The starch prepared from the roots of the cassava plant.

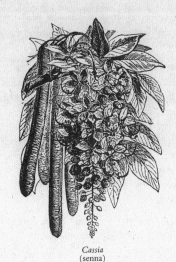

Cassia
(senna)

Cassia (kas′ee uh) *n.* A very large genus of more than 500 species of plants, shrubs, and trees (Leguminosae), native mostly to tropical or warm regions; the senna family. They have handsome alternate leaves, divided into leaflets, and large clusters of conspicuous yellow flowers. Numerous species are grown as ornamental flowering shrubs and trees. Commonly known as senna.

Cassine (kas ee′nuh) *n.* A genus of about 80 species of trees and shrubs (Celastraceae). They have simple, leathery leaves and clusters of small greenish or white flowers.

Cassiope (kuh sigh′oh pee) *n.* A small genus of 12 species of low evergreen shrubs (Ericaceae) resembling heather. They have small, scalelike, overlapping leaves and white or pinkish nodding flowers. *C. Mertensiana,* native to the western United States, is commonly called white heather.

Castanea (ka stay′nee uh) *n.* A genus of 12 species of hardy, deciduous trees and shrubs (Fagaceae) native to north temperate regions. They have alternate, oblong, toothed leaves, flowers in catkins, and large brown nuts encased in a prickly bur. The American chestnut, *C. dentata,* was nearly exterminated by chestnut blight, but efforts are being made to save it. The Japanese species, *C. crenata,* is blight-resistant.

Castanopsis (kas tuh nahp′sihs) *n.* A genus of 110 species of evergreen shrubs and trees (Fagaceae) with 2 species, *C. chrysotophylla* and *C. sempervirens,* native to the Pacific slope of North America. Commonly known as giant chestnut or chinquapin.

Castanospermum (kas′tuh noh sper′muhm) *n.* A genus of 1 species of handsome broadleaf evergreen tree (Leguminosae). *C. australe* has beautiful large, shiny dark green leaves divided into numerous leaflets and spectacular red and yellow flowers on stiff spikes that grow from twigs, branches, and the main trunk. The cylindrical fruit grows to 9 inches long. A superb shade and flowering tree for warm-winter climates. Commonly known as Moreton Bay chestnut.

Castilleja (kas tuh lee′yuh) *n.* A large genus of 200 species of mostly perennial plants (Scrophulariaceae), most are native to North America. Their yellow, purple, or scarlet flowers are in terminal spikes, with large, colored bracts often more showy than the flowers, which attract hummingbirds. Commonly known as paintbrush.

cast-iron plant *n.* A common name for *Aspidistra eliator,* widely grown as a houseplant. It tolerates low light, minimal water, and general neglect, hence its name; however, it looks much better when given good care.

castor bean *n.* A common name for *Ricinus communis.* It grows as an annual to a height of 15 feet, with broad, hand-shaped leaves and inconspicuous flowers. The leaves and beans can cause skin rashes, and the shiny, mottled, attractive beans are highly poisonous. Also known as palma christi.

castor bean

castor oil *n.* The oil yielded by the seeds of *Ricinus communis* (the castor-oil plant).

Casuarina (ka zhuh wuh ree′nuh) *n.* 1. A genus of about 30 peculiar, tender trees and shrubs (Casuarinaceae). They have long, thin, jointed barnches, similar to pine needles, and woody, conelike fruit. They tolerate difficult conditions, including dry soil, wet soil, salinity, heat, and wind and are hardy to 15° F. Many are useful in the desert, and some are good at the seashore. Commonly known as she-oak, beefwood, and Australian pine. 2. [l.c.] A plant of this genus.

catalase (kat′uh layz) *n.* An enzyme capable of decomposing hydrogen peroxide into water and oxygen.

Catalpa (kuh tal′puh) *n.* 1. A genus of 13 species of trees (Bignoniaceae) with large simple leaves, clusters of showy flowers, and long woody pods. *C. bignonioides* and *C. speciosa,* are native to the

United States. Commonly called Indian bean or Western catalpa. 2. [l.c.] A tree of the genus *Catalpa.*

catalyst *n.* Something that will increase the rate of a chemical reaction.

Catananche (kat uh nang'kee) *n.* A small genus of flowers (Compositae). *C. coerulea* has long gray-green leaves and lavender-blue flowers resembling cornflowers. The flowers dry well for use in everlasting bouquets. Commonly known as cupid's-dart.

cataphyll
corm of a crocus with cataphylls

cataphyll (kat'uh fihl) *n., pl.* **cataphylls**. In botany, 1 of the rudimentary leaves that precede a stage of growth; for example, the cotyledons of an embryo, the scales of a bud, or the scales of a rhizome.

Catasetum (kat uh seet'uhm) *n.* A genus of 70 species of tropical orchids (Orchidaceae) native to the Americas. They grow from a pseudobulb with folded leaves and stalks of white, yellow, yellow, orange, or maroon flowers, which may be spotted or dotted with purple or maroon. Grown in a warm greenhouse or conservatory.

catawba (kuh taw'buh) *n.* A variety of native grape, with red fruit, much cultivated in the middle United States, taking its name from the Catawba River in the Carolinas, where it was first raised.

catbrier (kat'brigh'er) *n.* A common name for several species of *Smilax,* woody vines that have numerous small clawlike prickles.

catch crop *n.* A method of increasing garden production in which the blank spaces created when slower-growing vegetables are harvested are filled in with fast-growing crops. Radishes or green onions, for example, may be grown in the space created when a broccoli plant is cut.

catchfly *n.* The common name for several species of flowers belonging to the genus *Silene* and for *Lychnis Viscaria*. Both have sticky stems, which sometimes trap small insects. The sleepy catchfly is *Silene antirrhina.*

catclaw *n.* The common name for several species of *Acacia* with hooked thorns, such as *A. Greggi.*

catena (kuh tee'nuh) *n.* A term used to describe soil formed from similar parent materials but do not have like soil characteristics because of the differences in relief or drainage.

caterpillar *n.* Any of various larvae of true moths or butterflies. They are destructive to the foliage of many plants. Control with *Bacillus thuringiensis,* trichogramma wasps, handpicking, or traditional insecticides.

caterpillar tape *n.* Band of adhesive material, typically 5 inches to 2 feet wide, which is wrapped around a tree trunk to prevent gypsy moth caterpillars from crawling upward to eat the leaves. (See also **tree guard**.)

Catha (kath'uh) *n.* A genus of 1 species of evergreen shrub (Celastraceae). *C. edulis* grows to about 20 feet in height, with long, elliptical, toothed leaves about 4 inches in length. The leaves and tender shoots are used in the preparation of a beverage similar to tea and coffee; they are also chewed fresh. Commonly known as khat.

Catharanthus (kath uh ran'thuhs) *n.* A genus of about 5 species of bushy flowers with glossy leaves and white, blush-pink, or rose phloxlike flowers with a red eye. Used primarily as bedding plants, container plants, or as small-scale ground covers. Grown as annuals except in frost-free gardens. Commonly known as Madagascar periwinkle.

cation (kad'igh uhn) *n.* An ion that carries a positive charge of electricity like calcium, magnesium, sodium, potassium and hydrogen.

cation exchange (kad'igh uhn) *n.* The exchange of cations, held by a soil absorbing complex, with other cations.

cation exchange capacity (kad'igh uhn) *n.* The measurement of the total amounts of exchangable cations that can be held by the soil. Expressed as milliequivalents per 100 grams of soil.

catkin *n.* In botany, a scaly spike of unisexual flowers that fall after flowering or fruiting, as in the willow and birch; an ament.

catkins of birch tree

catmint *n.* Same as catnip.

cattail *n.* (See **Typha.**)

Cattleya (kat'lee uh) *n.* A genus of highly ornamental epiphytic (growing on, but not taking nourishment from a host plant) orchids (Orchidaceae) native to tropical America. They have broad, fleshy leaves and clusters of large, ruffled, showy, sometimes fragrant white, yellow, maroon, or purple flowers. The species is highly prized, and their flowers are among the largest and handsomest of the orchid family. This is the classic prom corsage orchid.

caudate (kah'dayt) *a.* Having a taillike appendage.

caulescent (kah lehs'ehnt) *a.* In botany, having an obvious stem that rises above the ground.

cauliflower *n.* A garden variety of *Brassica oleracea,* of the cabbage family, the blossom of which is condensed while young into a tight, fleshy head, cultivated as a vegetable. Most varieties have heads 6 to 8 inches in diameter, although miniature varieties have heads the size of a single serving.

caulocarpous (kahl oh kar'puhs) *a.* In botany, bearing a fruit repeatedly upon the same stem; ap-

plied to such plants as have perennial stems. Also caulocarpic.

Caulophyllum (kah loh fighl'uhm) *n.* A genus of 2 species of perennial rhizomatous-rooted plants (Berberidaceae), one native to North America. They usually have a single basal leaf and a stalk or cluster of yellowish flowers, succeeded by blue berries. The American species, *C. thalictroides,* is commonly known as blue cohosh or papooseroot.

Cayenne (kigh ehn') *n.* A very hot pepper variety, 5 inches long, narrow, and often curled and twisted. It is often dried and ground into powder for use as seasoning.

Ceanothus (see uh noh'thuhs) *n.* A genus of about 55 species of flowering ground covers, shrubs, or small trees (Rhamnaceae) native to North America, particularly California. They have small, toothed, alternate leaves and masses of small flowers in all shades of blue to deep violet, as well as white. *C. Americanus,* the common eastern species, is known as New Jersey tea or redroot. *C. thyrsiflorus* is commonly known as California lilac, or wild lilac.

Cecropia (sih kroh'pee uh) *n.* A genus of 20 species of fast-growing, beautiful tropical American trees (Moraceae). They have lobed dark green leaves, white below, and dense spikes of yellow flowers.

cedar *n.* 1. A commmon name for *Cedrus,* a genus of evergreen conifers (cone bearers). Cedar-of-Lebanon, C. libani, grows slowly to 80 feet, with dense, short, bright green needles; it is majestic in old age. Deodar cedar, *C. Deodara,* is a fast-growing tree to 80 feet, with branches that sweep gracefully to the ground. 2. The common name given to various coniferous trees, for example, the white cedar, *Chamaecyparis thyoides,* and the American arborvitae, *Thuja occidentalis;* the incense cedar, *Libocedrus decurrens,* and the Port Orford cedar, *Chamaecyparis Lawsoniana.* The red cedar is *Juniperus virginiana;* the Japanese cedar, *Cryptomeria Japonica.*

cedar apple rust *n.* A fungus that attacks cedar trees, causing globular distortions, with appendages turning to yellow gelatinous masses in spring rains. Control with traditional fungicides.

cedar apple rust

cedar-of-Lebanon *n.* A common name for the evergreen coniferous tree *Cedrus libani.* (See **cedar**.)

cedar planter *n.* A container of durable, rot-resistant wood for growing and displaying plants, primarily flowers. Also called cedar tub or tub.

Cedrela (sih dree′luh) *n.* A genus of about 20 species of large tropical trees. They grow to 50 feet or more, with leaves divided into oval, pointed leaflets and with dense, drooping clusters of white or yellow flowers. The fragrant wood of *C. odorata;* commonly known as cedar, was once used to make cigar boxes.

Cedrus (see′druhs) *n.* A genus of evergreen coniferous trees with erect cones and needlelike leaves that grow in tufts or bunches. The genus includes only 3 species; the cedar-of-Lebanon, *C. libani;* the deodar cedar, *C. Deodara;* and the atlas cedar, *C. atlantica.* (See **cedar**.)

Ceiba (say′buh) *n.* A genus of about 10 species of deciduous, tropical trees (Bombacacea), mostly native to the Americas. They are large, usually spiny trees and have hand-shaped compound leaves and showy red or white flowers. From the abundant cottony covering of the seeds, *C. pentandra* is known as the silk-cotton tree. 2. [l.c.] A common name for *Bombax Ceiba,* also known as the red silk-cotton tree.

celandine (sehl′uhn dign) *n.* 1. An herb of the genus *Chelidonium,* European biennials and perennials naturalized in the United States. The greater celandine, so named to distinguish it from the pilewort, has bright yellow flowers. 2. The pilewort, *Ranunculus Ficaria,* called the lesser or small celandine, also naturalized in North America.

Celastraceae (sehl uhs tray′see ee) *n. pl.* A family of 55 genera and 800 species of shrubs or trees. The most widely grown genera are *Celastrus* (bittersweet) and *Euonymus* (spindle tree).

Celastrus (seh las′truhs) *n.* A genus of hardy deciduous twining shrubby vines or trees (Celastraceae); some species native to America. *C. scandens,* native to the eastern United States, is a climbing vine to 25 feet, with light green oval leaves and showy fruit, its orange-colored capsules splitting to reveal 2 bright red seeds; Commonly known as American bittersweet. The genus is commonly known as bittersweet.

celeriac (suh lair′ee ak) *n. Apium graveolens* var. *rapaceum,* grown for its bulbous root. The root has a potatolike texture and a mild celery flavor.

celery *n. Apium graveolens* var. *dulce,* a native of Europe, and long cultivated in gardens for table use. The green leaves and stalks are used as an ingredient in soups, and the tender, blanched inside stalks are used in salads. Ordinarily the stems are covered with soil as they grow to keep them light colored and tender, a process known as blanching. Celery requires abundant water during growing.

celery cabbage *n.* (See **Chinese cabbage**.)

cell *n.* A small, usually microscopic mass of protoplasm, usually with 1 or more nuclei and some nonliving material, with an external membrane; the basic structural and functional unit of life.

cell tray *n.* (See **growing tray**.)

celosia (see lohzh′ee uh) *n.* Any of several annual plants of the genus *Celosia,* grown for their bright-colored flowers, which retain their colors in dried arrangements. Two varieties are common, known as plume and cockscomb, for their quite different shapes. Plume celosia, available in shades of red, orange, and yellow, is also grown as an ornamental bedding plant. Cockscomb has a deep red color and is grown only in cutting gardens for use in dried arrangements.

Celsia (sehl′see uh) *n.* A genus of between 30 and 40 species of flowers (Scrophulariaceae), mostly Mediterranean, with yellow snapdragon-shaped flowers. Commonly known as Cretan bear's-tail or Cretan mullein.

Celtis (sehl'tihs) *n.* A genus of 70 species of hardy deciduous (loses leaves seasonally) trees (Ulmaceae). They have alternate, elmlike leaves that turn yellow in fall, small flowers, and small, round dark purple or red fruit. Used as shade trees, once established, will tolerate drought, wind, heat, and alkaline soil. Often used near paved areas as their roots do not disturb the surface. Commonly known as nettle tree and hackberry. (See **nettle tree** and **hackberry**.)

celtuce (sehl'tuhs) n. A variety of lettuce with a thicker, fleshier stem than ordinary head and leaf varieties. The leaves are eaten raw when young; when the plant matures, the stalks can be used like celery. The leaves are crisper and firmer than the usual salad lettuces and need to be harvested when very young, or they turn bitter. The stem remains flavorful until the flower head begins to develop. It is a cool-weather crop and should not be transplanted.

Centaurea (sehn tah'ree uh) *n.* A genus of 500 species of annuals or perrenials (Compositae) found throughout the world. They have alternate leaves and flowers of many colors. The annuals, such as *C. cyanus* (cornflowers, or bachelor's buttons) and *C. moschata* (sweet sultan), are grown for their flowers in borders and cottage gardens. The perennials, often known as dusty miller, are grown for their silvery, gray, or nearly white foliage, for example, *C. cineraria.* Commonly known as centaurea.

Centaurium (sehn tah'ree uhm) *n.* A genus of 30 species of slender, low-growing flowers (Gentianaceae). They have opposite, simple, and entire leaves and clusters of pink or rose flowers. Used in rock gardens and borders. Commonly known as centaury.

centipede grass (sehn'tih peed gras) (See **Eremochloa.**)

Centradenia (sehn truh deen'yuh) *n.* A genus of 5 species of plants or small shrubs (Melastomataceae). They have attractive long, narrow, lance-shaped leaves and clusters of small pink or white flowers. Grown for their showy colored leaves and flowers as houseplants or greenhouse specimens.

Centranthus (sehn tran'thus) *n.* A genus of 12 species of perennials and annuals (Valerianaceae) widely naturalized on the West Coast. They have simple, opposite leaves and dense clusters of rose, white or red flowers. Red valerian, or jupiter's-Beard *(C. ruber),* is a sweet-scented, long-blooming plant with long, narrow, opposite leaves and spikes of fluffy red, pink, or white flowers that attract humingbirds and butterflies. It tolerates drought and poor soil, and it self-sows. Used on slopes, banks, and walls.

Centropogon (sehn trahp'uh gahn) *n.* A genus of more than 200 species that range from robust flowers to small shrubs (Lobeliaceae) native to tropical America. They have alternate, toothed leaves; white, red, pink, orange, or yellow-green solitary flowers; and a berrylike fruit. Grown as a hanging-basket plant.

Ceaphaelis (sehf uh ee'lihs) *n.* A genus of 100 species of shrubs or small trees (Rubiaceae) mostly native to tropical America. *C. tomentosa* is a shrub to 15 feet, with narrow, opposite leaves, yellow flowers surrounded by red bracts, and blue fruit. *C. Ipecacuanha,* is the source for the medicine ipecac.

century plant *n.* A name given to the American aloe, *Agave Americana,* which was formerly thought to flower only after it had grown a century. (See **Agave**.)

Cephalanthus (sehf uh lan'thuhs) *n.* A genus of 6 or more shrubs (Rubiaceae) with opposite or whorled leaves and showy, dense, round heads with small white flowers. *C. occidentalis,* native to North America, is commonly known as buttonbush.

Cephalaria (sehf uh lar'ee uh) *n.* A genus of 65 species of annuals and perennials (Dipsacaceae). They have opposite leaves and white, yellow, or blue cup-shaped flowers on long, prominent stalks.

Cephalocereus (sehf uh loh see'ree uhs) *n.* A genus of about 50 species of tall, ribbed, spiny, cylindrical, columnar cacti (Cactaceae) native to tropical and subtropical America. Some of the spines are long and sharp; others are soft and hairy. The night-blooming flowers are small, tubular, or bell-shaped. The soft, woolly spines and flowers are typically not produced until the plant is 15 to 20 years old, though *C. senilis* (old-man cactus) develops soft hairs much sooner.

Cephalophyllum (sehf uh loh figh'luhm) *n.* A genus of more than 70 species of dwarf succulents (Aizoaceae). They have nearly cylindrical to 3-angled fleshy leaves in crowded tufts; and cerise-red, pale rose, coppery, or golden-yellow 2-inch wide flowers that open in bright sunlight and close at night or on an overcast day. Used as a drought-tolerant, fire-retardant ground cover in mild-winter climates. Commonly called ice plant.

Cephalotaxus (sehf uh loh tak'suhs) *n.* A genus of 7 species of tender, evergreen, coniferous shrubs or trees (Cephalotaxaceae) that resemble yew, but with clustered flowers and large plumlike fruit. They are slow-growing, to 30 feet or less, with bright green needles and small green or brown plumlike fruit. They are undemanding and shade-tolerant. Commonly known as plum yew.

ceraceous (sih ray'shuhs) *a.* In botany, waxy; applied to bodies that have the texture and color of new wax, as the pollen masses of many orchids.

Cerastium (sih ras'chee uhm) *n.* A genus of about 60 plants (Caryophyllaceae) with small leaves and white flowers. *C. tomentosum,* commonly known as snow-in-summer, is grown in rock gardens, as a small-scale ground cover, as an edging, and on walls. It is drought-tolerant once established. Commonly known as chickweed.

Cerastium
(chickweed)

Ceratonia (ser uh toh'nee uh) *n.* A genus of 1 species of drought-tolerant and fire-retardant ever-green tree, *C. siliqua* (Leguminosae). It has dense, dark green alternate leaves divided into round leaflets, and spring-blooming small red flowers. The pods, often called locust beans, contain a sweet pulp used as a substitute for chocolate. Also known as carob tree.

Ceratonia
(carob tree)

Ceratophyllaceae (ser'uh toh fih lay'see ee) *n. pl.* A family of plants of 1 genus with 3 or 4 species; the hornwort family. It is a slender aquatic herb, with whorled, finely dissected, rigid leaves and small, solitary flowers. It is used in pools or aquariums and grows in slow streams.

Ceratophyllum (ser'uh toh fihl'uhm) *n.* The only genus of plants of the family Ceratophyllaceae, with 3 or 4 species. All are submersed pondweeds with floating, leafy branches, whorled leaves, and minute flowers. Commonly known as hornwort.

Ceratopteris (ser uh tahp'tuh rihs) *n.* A genus of 4 species of annual tropical ferns (Parkeraceae) that float in water, sending roots into the mud. They have thick, fleshy, floating leaves. Commonly known as water fern or floating fern.

Ceratostigma (ser a'toh stihg'muh) *n.* A genus of about 8 species of evergreen perennials and small shrubs (Plumbaginaceae). They have alternate, often bristly, leaves and dense clusters of rich deep blue phloxlike flowers. They tolerate a wide variety of soils, degrees of moisture, and amounts of sun or shade. Prized for their blue flowers, they are used in borders and beds. Commonly known as Burmese plumbago, Chinese plumbago, or dwarf plumbago. Cape plumbago is *Plumbago auriculata*.

Ceratozamia (ser'uh toh zaym'yuh) *n.* A genus of 2 species of cycad (Zamiaceae), a slow-growing, palmlike tree with a short trunk and divided, gracefully recurved leaves at the crown. Grown as a container plant in mild climates or as a greenhouse specimen.

Cercidiphyllum (ser'sih dih fighl'uhm) *n.* A genus of 1 or 2 species of deciduous (loses leaves seasonally) trees (Cercidiphyllaceae). *C. Japonicum* has dainty, heart-shaped, blue-green leaves that color beautifully in red or yellow in autumn. Grown in parks or gardens as a specimen tree. Commonly known as katsura tree.

Cercis (ser'sihs) *n.* A small genus of 7 species of deciduous (loses leaves seasonally) trees or shrubs (Leguminosae). They have simple, broad, generally two-lobed leaves, and clusters of sweet, pea-shaped pink, mauve, or white flowers, which appear before the leaves. *C. Siliquastrum* is commonly called the judas tree. *C. canadensis* is popularly known as the redbud. They are grown for their great profusion of showy, early flowers.

Cercocarpus (ser koh kahr'puhs) *n.* A genus of shrubs or small trees (Rosaceae) native to North America. They have a handsome, open branching pattern, thick, leathery leaves, little flowers, and long-lasting small fruit. They make an excellent hedge or small tree of fine character. Commonly known as mountain mahogany.

Cereus (see'ree uhs) *n.* 1. A genus of 36 species of night-blooming cactus (Cactaceae) native to tropical America. They are oval or columnar plants, with spiny ribs or angles and large, tubular, funnel-shaped flowers. They vary greatly in size and shape and can be either erect or climbing. The flowers are often very large, such as the 6-inch-long flowers of *C. peruvianus*. They grow from 10 to 80 feet, depending on the species. 2. [l.c.] Any plant of the genus *Cereus*.

ceriman (ser'uh man) *n.* A common name for *Monstera deliciosa*, a tropical American vine with huge, deeply cut leaves, often grown as a houseplant. Also known as swiss cheese plant.

Cerinthe (ser ihn'thee) *n.* A genus of 14 species of flowers (Boraginaceae). They have rough, simple, alternate leaves and flat clusters of yellow or yellow-and-purple flowers. Commonly known as honeywort.

cernuous (ser'nyoo uhs) *a.* Drooping; hanging; pendulous; having the top curved or bent down.

Ceropegia (ser oh pihg'yuh) *n.* A genus of 150 species of twining vines or small shrubs (Asclepiadaceae). They have opposite, gray-green, white-spotted leaves and flat clusters of curiously structured, tiny pink or purplish flowers. Grown as a hanging-basket houseplant or a greenhouse specimen. Commonly known as rosary vine or string-of-hearts.

Ceroxylon (sih rahk'sih lahn) *n.* A genus of 15 or more species of tall palms with divided leaves and small berries with 1 hard seed. *C. alpinum*, is 1 of the tallest of American palms (190 feet), has leaves 20 feet long. Commonly known as wax palm.

Cestrum (sehs'truhm) *n.* A genus of about 150 species of fast-growing evergreen vines, shrubs, and trees (Solanaceae), native to tropical America. They have clusters of funnel-shaped, richly fragrant red, yellow, white, or greenish flowers. Both flowers and fruit attract birds. *C. nocturnum*, commonly known as night jessamine has clusters of powerfully fragrant, creamy-white night-blooming flowers and white berries. Used on trellises or as an espalier in frost-free climates.

Chaenomeles (kee'nuh mee'leez) *n.* A genus of 3 species of deciduous or semievergreen shrubs (Rosaceae). They have alternate, toothed, shiny green leaves tinged with red and many early-blooming, large, deep rose-pink flowers. They are picturesque and practically indestructible, tolerating extremes of cold and heat and light-to-heavy soil. The flowers attract birds. There are many hybrids available. This is the traditional flower of the Chinese New Year. Used for hedges and barriers. Commonly known as flowering quince.

Chaenorrhinum (chuh nor'ee nuhm) *n.* A genus of 20 species of flowers (Scrophulariaceae) with branching stems, small oval leaves, and white, blue, or purple snapdragon-shaped flowers. Commonly known as dwarf snapdragon.

chaff *n.* The glumes, husks, or other pieces of leaves and stems of wheat, oats, or other grains and grasses, especially when separated from the seed by threshing and winnowing.

chain fern *n.* The common name of ferns of the genus *Woodwardia,* from the chainlike rows formed by the fruit dots on each side of the midrib and midveins.

chalaza (kuh lay'zuh) *n., pl.* **chalazae** or **chalazas**. In botany, that part of the ovule where the seed stalk and the outer coverings attach to each other.

chalice vine *n.* A common name for *Solandra maxima* and *S. guttata,* heavy, twining subtropical vines with thick, evergreen leaves and large, cup-shaped gold flowers. They tolerate salt spray, wind, and fog and are used on large walls, along eaves, to cover pergolas, and as a ground cover on steep slopes. Also known as cup-of-gold.

Chamaecereus (kam uh see'ree uhs) *n.* A genus of 1 species of dwarf cactus (Cactaceae). It is jointed, with peanut-shaped segments that are ribbed, cylindrical, and spiny. The red, tubular flowers are 3 inches long. Commonly known as peanut cactus.

Chamaecyparis (kam uh sihp'uh rihs) *n.* A genus of large evergreen coniferous trees (Cupressaceae); the false-cypress family. *C. thyoides,* (white cedar) is native to the eastern United States, *C. Nootkatensis* (yellow or Sitka cypress) and the *(C. Lawsoniana)* (Port Orford cedar) to the Pacific Coast. They have scalelike leaves in flattened sprays and round cones. Excellent as large specimen trees, as hedge or screening material, or as container plants; sometimes used for bonsai.

Chamaedaphne (kam uh daf'nee) *n.* A genus of a single species, *C. calyculata,* a low, evergreen bog shrub (Ericaceae). It has small leathery leaves— green above, rusty beneath—and small, 5-petaled white flowers. Grown in rock gardens or moist situations. Commonly known as leatherleaf or cassandra.

Chamaedorea (kam uh dor ay'uh) *n.* A genus of more than 100 species of palms (Palmae) native to Mexico and Central America. They are small, feathery-leaved palms. They grow well in containers and are often grown as pot plants in a protected situation or as houseplants. Known as bamboo

palm. *C. elegans* is commonly known as parlor palm.

Chamaelirium (kam uh ler'ee uhm) *n.* A genus with 1 species, *C. luteum* (Melanthaceae), (formerly Liliaceae), native to eastern North America. It has tuberous roots, wide, basal leaves 1 to 4 feet tall, and spikes of white flowers. It is grown as a shade plant. Commonly known as blazing star, fairy wand, and rattlesnake root.

Chamaemelum (kam uh mee'luhm) *n.* A genus of 3 species of perennial herbs (Compositae). It is a low-growing plant, with aromatic feathery leaves and flowerheads that resemble small yellow buttons. Grown as an herb and a lawn substitute; used in rock gardens and to fill in between stepping stones. The flower heads are used to make a calming tea. Commonly known as chamomile.

Chamaerops (kuh mee'rahps) *n.* A genus of palms of a single species, *C. humilis* (Palmae). It is a dwarf tree with fan-shaped leaves and prickly stems and has a small berrylike fruit. It is inclined to form clumps. Commonly known as fan palm, hair palm, windmill palm.

chamomile (kam'oh meel) *n.* 1. The common name for *Chamaemelum nobilis,* (formerly *Anthemis nobilis*), a low, creeping composite plant of Europe, with strongly scented foliage, which has long been in cultivation and is often distinguished as Roman chamomile. A low-growing plant, it was formerly imagined to flourish best where it was trodden upon, a favorite subject of ancient writers. It is used as a lawn cover in moist climates, such as Great Britain. 2. Dyer's chamomile, *Anthemis tinctoria,* with yellow-rayed flowers, is sometimes cultivated for ornament and yields a yellow dye. 3. German chamomile, *Matricaria recutita,* is a taller plant of similar flower and scent. Also spelled camomile.

channeled *a.* In botany, hollowed out; troughlike; canaliculate. Applied to petioles, leaves, etc.

chanterelle (shan tuh rehl') *n.* A common name for the edible mushroom *Cantharellus cibarius.* It is golden orange, vase-shaped, with thick, shallow, blunt gills that extend down onto the stipe; it has a fragrant fruity smell, reminiscent of ripe apricots. Also spelled chantarelle.

chanterelle

chaparral (chap uh ral′) *n.* 1. A close growth, more or less extensive, of low evergreen oaks. 2. Any very dense thicket of low stiff or thorny shrubs. 3. A community of shrubby plants in the American West and Southwest that are adapted to dry summers and wet winters. Also spelled chaparal.

chard *n.* The leaf stalks and midribs of a variety of white beet, *Beta Vulgaris Cicla,* in which these parts are greatly developed. Grown as an early crop, they provide some of the first vegetables of spring. Also called Swiss chard.

charentais (shar ehn tay′) *n.* A very sweet variety of cantaloupe with no netted pattern on its skin. Some hybrid varieties are available with some of the charentais deep color and flavor, but the true variety can be distinguished by its smooth skin.

Chasmanthium (chas man′thee uhm) *n.* A genus of about 6 species of grasses (Gramineae) native to the eastern United States. *C. latifolium,* called sea oats or bamboo grass, is grown as an ornamental for its tall flower spikelets, which look like oats; its overall appearance is similar to bamboo.

chaste tree *n.* A common name for *Vitex Agnus-castus,* an aromatic shrub or small tree with divided, fanlike leaves that are green above and gray beneath and with showy spikes of lavender-blue flowers. Also known as the agnus castus, hemp tree, monk's pepper tree, sage tree, Indian-spice, and wild pepper.

chaulmoogra (chahl moog′ruh) *n.* A common name for the handsome tropical tree *Hydnocarpus Kurzii,* (Flacourtiaseae), which has fragrant flowers and a large round, wrinkled, hard fruit. Also spelled chaulmugra or chaulmaugra.

chayote (chigh oh′tee) *n. Sechium edule,* a pear-shaped vegetable with a furrowed surface and pale green skin. Its flavor is very mild, and its texture is similar to that of a summer squash. It grows on a vine native to tropical America, where the tuberous root is perennial. Grown in the Southwest as an annual from seed, it reqires a 6-month growing season to produce ripe fruit. The tubers are also edible.

checkerberry *n.* The American wintergreen, *Gaultheria procumbens,* a low-growing evergreen creeper with shiny leaves and white, nodding flowers. Once a source of oil of wintergreen, now popular in winter berry bowls and terrariums.

checkerbloom *n.* A common name for *Sidalcea malvaflora,* a 3-foot tall perennial with fleshy, lobed leaves and stalks of pink flowers.

Cheilanthes (kigh lan′theez) *n.* A genus of 180 species of ferns (Polypodiaceae) widely distributed in tropical and temperate regions. They have hairy, woolly, or scaly fronds with pinnate (divided) leaves. Commonly known as lip fern.

Cheiranthus (kigh ran′thuhs) *n.* A genus of 10 species of pubescent herbs or small shrubs (Cruciferae) with large, sweet-scented, richly colored yellow, rose, pink, or burgundy flowers. *C. Cheiri,* (wallflower) is an old-fashioned favorite, often grown in cottage gardens and borders; also known as English wallflower.

Cheiridopsis (kigh rih dahp′sihs) *n.* A genus of about 100 species of clumping succulents (Aizoaceae). They have pairs of opposite leaves which may be green, white, or dotted, and yellow or pink many-petaled flowers.

chelates (kee′laytz) *n.* A chemical compound that combines a metallic atom with a molecule using multiple chemical bonds.

Chelidonium (kehl uh doh′ee uhm) *n.* A genus of 2 or more species (Papaveraceae). *C. majus* (common celandine) stands 4 feet tall and has deeply divided leaves and clusters of yellow flowers. It has naturalized in the eastern United States.

Chelone (keh loh′nee) *n.* A genus of 5 or 6 species of perennials (Scrophulariaceae) native to North America. The flowers are inflated, arched, and nearly closed, so as to resemble the head of a turtle. *C. glabra,* which grows to 6 feet, with narrow, 6-inch leaves and pink or white flowers, is popularly known as snakehead, turtlehead, or balmony.

The genus is commonly known as turtlehead or snakehead.

chemical drenches *n.* Can be used to control soil-borne diseases.

chemical gardening *n.* A method of growing plants in which chemicals are used to control undesirable pests or weeds.

chenille plant (shuh neel′) *n.* A common name for several plants, including *Acalypha hispida, Echeveria leucotrichia,* and *E. pulvinata. A. hispida* is a shrub with simple, alternate, toothed leaves and showy long, drooping, fluffy white, red, or purple flowers. *E. leucotrichia* is a succulent with a rosette of densely hairy leaves growing from the base and spikes of numerous red flowers. *E. pulvinata* is a perennial succulent with densely hairy leaves and spikes of red and yellow flowers.

Chenopodiaceae (kee nuh poh dee ay′see ee) *n. pl.* A family of about 75 genera of plants or shrubs, for the most part native to coasts, salt marshes, and to alkaline deserts; the goosefoot family. It includes the beet, *Beta,* and spinach *Spinacia,* as well as the Mexican herb epazote, *Chenopodium ambroisiodes.*

Chenopodium (kee nuh poh′dee uhm) *n.* A genus of 250 species of plants (Chenopodiaceae). It includes various common weeds, known as goosefoot, pigweed, good-king-henry, etc., which have naturalized throughout North America.

cherimoyar (cher ih moi′er) *n.* The fruit of *Annona Cherimola,* a native of Peru. It is a heart-shaped fruit, with a scaly exterior and numerous seeds buried in a smooth pulp. It is sometimes called custard apple, to which it bears a strong resemblance, although that is properly *A. reticulata.* Although it is rarely grown in the United States, it is now available in grocery stores.

chernozem soils (cher nuh zhawm′) *n.* A deep dark black rich organic surface soil.

cherry *n.* 1. The fruit *Prunus cerasus, P. avium,* or *P. besseyi,* consisting of a round, pulpy friut enclosing a smooth seed. The cultivated varieties of the garden cherry probably all belong to 2 natives of Europe. Cherries are eaten raw, preserved in brandy, cooked in pies and pastries, and preserved in jam. 2. A name given to many different kinds of fruit that bear some resemblance to the common cherry, such as the ground cherry.

chert (chat) *n.* A structureless form of silica.

chervil (cher′vihl) *n.* 1. A garden herb, *Anthriscus cerefolium* (Umbelliferae). Chervil is a hardy annual, grown as a spring and fall herb in hot climates and as a summer herb in the north. It is used in French cooking. Sweet cicily, *Myrrhis odorata,* an aromatic perennial herb is also occasionally called sweet chervil.

chestnut *n.* 1. A common name for *Castanea sativa* (Fagaceae), the European chestnut a large, handsome, hardy deciduous tree. It grows to a height of 80 to 100 feet, with long slender catkins and nuts that are enclosed, 2 or 3 together, in a round, prickly husk called the bur. 2. The fruit of trees of the genus *Castanea.* 3. The common name for the American chestnut, *Castanea dentata,* which was rendered nearly extinct by chestnut blight, but is slowly making a comeback. 4. A name given to certain trees or plants of other genera and to their fruit: the cape chestnut, the *Calodendron capense,* a large ornamental tree; the horse chestnut, *Aesculus Hippocastanum,* native to California (see **Aesculus**); the Moreton Bay chestnut; and the seed of the *Castanospermum australe,* which somewhat resembles the chestnut in flavor.

chestnut branch and nut

chestnut blight *n.* A devastating fungal disease that has destroyed most of the native American chestnuts. Resistant varieties are being developed.

chestnut soils *n*. A dark brown surface soil.

chicken manure *n*. A strong organic fertilizer derived from chickens droppings. Also called hen manure.

chick-pea *n*. The popular name for the plant *Cicer arietinum*. It grows wild around the shores of the Mediterranean, producing a short, puffy pod, containing 1 or 2 small seeds. It can be grown like field beans in temperate climates, where the beans are allowed to mature and dry on the plant. Also called ceci, cici, and garbanzo.

chick-pea

chicory (chihk′uh ree) *n*. The popular name for *Cichorium Intybus,* a composite plant common in waste places, found throughout Europe and naturalized in the United States. It grows 1- to 3-feet high, with spreading branches and bright blue flowers. The roots are used as a substitute for coffee, or to mix with coffee, first roasted and ground. The Witloof chicory is the root from which Belgian endive is forced as a winter crop. (See **Belgian endive**.) Also spelled chiccory or chickory.

Chilean jasmine *n*. A common name for *Mandevilla laxa,* a subtropical deciduous vine with narrow, pointed leaves and clusters of white, powerfully fragrant, gardenia-scented flowers.

Chile-bells *n*. A common name for *Lapageria rosea,* a tropical evergreen woody vine with showy rose to rose-crimson bell-shaped flowers. The national flower of Chile. Grown out of doors in frost-free climates or as a greenhouse specimen. Also called Chilean bellflower.

chili *n*. A pepper variety well known for its bright red color and very hot flavor.

chimera (kigh mer′uh) *n*. A plant composed of 2 or more genetically distinct tissues or an artificially produced plant having tissues of several species.

chimney bellflower *n*. A common name for *Campanula pyramidalis,* a tall 4- to 6-foot tall flower with nearly heart-shaped leaves and dense spikes of flat, saucer-shaped blue or white flowers. Used in the back of perennial borders; a good substitute where delphiniums do not do well.

Chimonanthus (kigh muh nan′thuhs) *n*. A genus of 4 species of deciduous shrubs (Calycanthaceae). *C. praecox,* popularly called wintersweet has aromatic, tapering, medium-green leaves and early, sweet-scented yellow and chocolate-colored flowers, which appear before the leaves. It is generally trained against walls, where its winter fragrance can be enjoyed.

china aster *n*. A common name for the annual flower *Callistephus chinensis*. It grows to 2 1/2 feet, has toothed or lobed leaves, and flowers profusely. Hybridization has resulted in a wide variety of flower forms—among them, quilled, curled, and incurved—in a broad range of colors, including white, pink, wine, scarlet, lavender, and blue. Used for bedding or massing for seasonal color.

chinaberry *n*. A common name for 2 different species, *Sipindus saponaria* and *Melia Azedarach*. *S. saponaria* is a small evergreen tropical tree with 7-foot-long leaves divided into leaflets, white flowers, and round, orange-brown, glossy fruits, which can be used as soap. *M. Azedarach* is a small deciduous spreading tree with finely cut 7-to-3-foot-long leaves, loose clusters of lilac-colored flowers, which give off a fragrant perfume in the evening, and hard, yellow fruit. The fruit is poisonous if eaten, but birds enjoy it.

china fir *n*. A common name for *Cunninghamia lanceolate*. It is a small, picturesque, evergreen conifer with stiff needles that are green above and white below and with a few brown cones. The palest of the evergreen conifers, it turns red-bronze where winters are cold.

china rose *n*. 1. A common name for *Rosa chinensis,* noted for blooming frequently, and one of the parents of the recurrent-blooming cultivars, particularly the Hybrid Perpetuals and Polyanthas. *R. chinensis minima* is the parent of modern miniature roses. Old-rose specialists still offer the original China rose 'Old Blush', also called 'Parson's Pink China'. 2. A common name for the tropical shrub *Hibiscus Rosa-sinensis.*

chinar tree (chih naahr′) *n.* A common name for the Oriental plane tree, *Platanus orientalis.* Also spelled chenar tree.

chinch bug *n.* A heat-loving insect that sucks the juices of lawn grasses, particularly St. Augustine, causing yellow patches with brown centers in sunny areas. To check for chinch bugs, cut both ends from a tin can, push it 2 to 3 inches into the lawn at the edge of the damaged area, and fill it with water. The insects will float to the surface. Control by applying soap sprays, sabadilla, pyrethrins, or traditional insecticides to the entire lawn.

chincherinchee (chihn chuh rihn′chee) *n.* A common name for *Ornithogalum thyrsoides;* the giant chincherinchee is *O. Saundersiae.* Both are tender bulbs with basal leaves and have stalks clustered with white or cream-colored flowers that bloom in winter and spring. Grown as pot plants, they make long-lasting cut flowers.

Chinese artichoke (ahrt′ih chohk) *n.* A spreading, hardy, nettlelike plant, *Stachys affinis,* grown for its potatolike roots. The plant grows to 12 inches and produces the tubers just beneath the surface of the soil, so they are easily dug. The roots can be eaten raw in salads or pickled, but are more frequently boiled briefly, then fried.

Chinese cabbage *n.* A loose term used to describe many annual leafy vegetables, *Brassica Rapa,* including wongbok and Michihli, as well as the related vegetables pakchoi and bokchoi. Chinese cabbage usually refers to those vegetables with tight, elongated heads. In grocery stores, the term is generally used to describe any Asain green, so it is of no real use to the gardener as a descriptive term.

Chinese date *n.* 1. A common name for the *Ziziphus Jujuba,* also known as the jujube: a tree or large bush with long, narrow leaves and a fleshy, plumlike fruit called jujube. 2. Also the name for the jujube fruit, which may be preserved, dried, sweetpickled, stewed, or used in sweets.

Chinese evergreen *n.* A common name for *Aglaonema modestum,* a foliage plant that tolerates both low light conditions and drought. Widely grown as a houseplant.

Chinese hat plant *n.* A common name for *Holmskioldia sanguinea,* a large, rangy evergreen tropical shrub with oval leaves and red or orange flowers. Also known as Mandarin's-hat and cup-and-saucer plant.

Chinese-houses *n.* A common name for *Collinsia heterophylla,* an attractive North American annual with opposite, long, narrow leaves and clusters of violet and white flowers.

Chinese lantern *n.* 1. *Physalis alkekenji,* a persistent perennial, about 2 feet tall, which is cultivated for its ripened bright orange calyxes-thin, papery globes that completely enclose the seed in a bright lantern-shaped covering. They are highly prized as a dried flower because they retain both shape and color when dried. 2. A common name for *Abutilon hybridum,* a tender evergreen flowering shrub with upright, arching branches, maplelike leaves, and drooping, curiously shaped white, yellow, pink, and red flowers shaped like Chinese paper lanterns. Grown as a specimen shrub. Also known as flowering maple and Chinese bellflower.

Chinese mustard *n. Brassica Rapa,* an annual or biennial vegetable grown for its stalk and leaves.

Chinese parasol tree *n.* A common name for *Firmiana simplex,* a deciduous tree with large, handshaped leaves and showy lemon-yellow flowers. Used as a street, shade, or lawn tree in warm-winter regions.

Chinese scholar tree *n.* A common name for *Sophora japonica,* a round-headed deciduous tree with pairs of sharply pointed leaves and long, loose clusters of yellowish-white flowers in late summer. Also called Japanese pagoda tree.

Chinese spinach *n.* An edible form of amaranth, *Amaranthus tricolor,* grown for its paddle-shaped leaves. An easy-to-grow annual, its young leaves and stems are cooked as a green vegetable. Also sold as *Amaranthus gangeticus.*

Chinese tallow tree *n.* A common name for *Sapium sebiferum,* a dense, round-headed deciduous tree, which has poplarlike leaves that color brilliant, translucent red or yellow in autumn. Used as a lawn tree, a street tree, a patio or terrace tree and to screen out objectional views.

chinquapin (chihng'kuh pihn) *n*. 1. A common name for *Castanea pumila,* the dwarf chestnut of the United States, a shrub or tree native from Pennsylvania to Texas that bears a smaller, usually solitary nut. 2. A common name for *Castanopsis chrysophylla,* a tree or shrub of the Sierra Nevada and Cascade mountains in the Western United States. Also called the giant chestnut, it has a small nut, which is enclosed in a chestnut-like spiny bur. 3. The nut of *Castanea pumila.* Also spelled chinkapin.

Chiococca (kigh uh kahk'uh) *n*. A genus of small tropical American shrubs and vines (Rubiaceae) with opposite, leathery leaves and funnel-shaped yellow or white flowers. The fruit is a white berry, which gives the genus its common name of snowberry.

Chionanthus (kigh uh nan'thuhs) *n*. A genus of low trees or shrubs (Oleaceae), some species native to eastern North America. The principal species is *C. virginicus,* the fringe tree of the eastern United States. Also known as old-man's-beard.

Chionodoxa (kigh uh noh dahk'suh) *n*. A genus of 5 or 6 species of hardy early-spring-blooming perennial bulbs (Liliaceae) native to alpine meadows. They have narrow, leaves growing from the base of the plant and stalks that bear clusters of blue, white, or pink flowers. Commonly known as glory-of-the-snow.

chipper *n*. A device composed of a chute, blades, and an electric or gas motor; used for turning branches into wood chips. (See **shredder**.)

chitin (kigh'tihn) *n*. A natural pesticide made from ground-up crustacean shells. It is added to soil to increase the feeding of soil organisms on nematode eggs, thus providing an effective control of a troublesome pest.

chive *n*. The perennial herb *Allium Schoenoprasum,* used as seasoning for its delicate onion flavor. The clumps of round, hollow leaves do not form distinct bulbs. The flower is pink, also used as seasoning, especially in egg dishes. The buds of chives are used in chinese cooking. The garlic chive has a mild garlic flavor, flat leaves, and a white blossom.

Chlidanthus (klih dan'thus) *n*. A genus of 2 species of tropical American bulbs (Amaryllidaceae) with strap-shaped, leaves rising from the base and a 10-inch stalk that bears clusters of fragrant, 3-inch long yellow flowers. *C. fragrans* is commonly known as perfumed fairy lily.

chlorophyll (kloh'ruh fihl) *n*. The green coloring matter of plants, which is essential to photosynthesis. Also spelled chlorophyl.

Chlorophytum (kloh ruh figh'tuhm) *n*. A genus of anout 215 species of perennial plants (Liliaceae). They grow from rhizomes (root swelling) and have long, slim, leaves growing from the plant's base and long arching stalks with tiny greenish or white flowers. *C. comosum* is widely grown as a houseplant and is commonly known as spider plant, airplane plant, or ribbon plant. It is notable for its tendency to produce plantlets at the end of the flower stalks that root wherever they touch soil. They are also grown outdoors in warm regions.

chlorothalonil (klor'oh thal'oh nihl) *n*. A multipurpose fungicide used to treat a variety of plant diseases. Common trade name: Daconil.

chlorpyrifos (klor pigh'rih fahs) *n*. (See **Dursban**.)

chocolate-root *n*. A common name for *Geum rivali,* a flower with leaves divided into toothed leaflets and small, nodding purple and pink flowers.

chocolate tree *n*. The common name for *Theobroma Cacao,* an evergreen tropical tree, the fruit of which is used to make chocolate. (See **cacao**.)

Choisya (choi'syuh) *n*. A genus of evergreen shrubs with glossy yellow-green leaves divided into 3 leaflets and extremely fragrant, showy clusters of white flowers. A handsome, useful specimen shrub in warm-winter regions. *C. ternata* is commonly called Mexican orange.

choke cherry *n*. The popular name for an American species of wild cherry, *Prunus virginiana,* remarkable for the astringency of its fruit, which is used for making jelly.

choripetalous (koh rih peht'uh luhs) *a.* In botany, having the petals unconnected. Also polypetalous.

Chorisia (kor ihs'yuh) *n.* A genus of about 3 species of deciduous tropical and subtropical trees (Bombacaceae) native to South America. The trees grow to 50 feet with thorn-studded trunks. The leaves are divided into leaflets like the fingers of a hand and the large, showy flowers resemble narrow-petaled hibiscus. Tender to frost. Commonly known as floss-silk tree.

chorisis (koh'rih sihs) *n.* In botany, the multiplication, by congenital division during development, of a leaf or floral organ that is ordinarily entire. It may be either collateral when the parts are side by side, as in the stamens of *Dicentra*, or parallel or median when the parts are one in front of another.

Chorizema (kor ighz'uh muh) *n.* A genus of 15 species of evergreen shrubs (Leguminosae). They have alternate, simple leaves and flamboyantly showy clusters of orange- and purplish-red flowers. Used in warm climates as small shrubs to drape over walls, or in borders. A showy indoor plant in cold climates. Commonly known as flame pea.

C horizon *n.* The unconsolidated rock material found in the lower part of the soil profile.

Christmasberry *n.* A common name for *Heteromeles arbutifolia*, which has toothed, leathery green leaves and large clusters of bright red winter berries. Also known as toyon or California holly.

Christmas cactus *n.* A comon name for *Schlumbergera Bridgesii*, a sprawling, jointed, spineless cactus with bright pink or red 3-inch-long flowers that can be forced for midwinter bloom.

Christmas fern *n.* A common name for *Polystichum acrostichoides*, a fern with firm-textured, divided fronds, 2 feet long and 5 inches wide, which remain green through the winter.

Christmas rose *n.* A common name for *Helleborus niger*. It has winter-blooming flowers, which resemble single roses. Also called Christmas flower. (See **Helleborus**.)

Christ's-thorn *n.* A common name for *Paliurus Spina-Christi*, a hardy, thorny deciduous shrub, with small oval leaves, yellow-green flowers, and yellow-brown fruit. (See **Paliurus**.)

chromosomes (kroh'muh sohmz) *n. pl.* The bodies that contain the essential material of genetic coding.

Chrysalidocarpus (krih sal ih doh kahr'puhs) *n.* A genus of about 20 species of tropical palms (Palmae). They grow slowly to about 30 feet, with graceful, slender, yellow-green divided leaves. Most commonly used as a houseplant; often sold as *Areca lutescens*. Commonly known as areca palm, golden feather palm.

Chrysanthemum (krih san'thuh muhm) *n.* 1. A large genus of flowers (Compositae). The perennial garden chrysanthemum, *C. indicum*, has been hybridized into a great many attractive varieties. It is the national flower of Japan, where an open, 16-petaled chrysanthemum is the imperial emblem. Botanists have recently split *Chrysanthemum* into 4 genera, but the new classifications have neither been welcomed nor have they received wide acceptance in the nursery trade or among gardeners. *C. frutescens*, the marguerite, or Paris daisy, is now classified as *Argyranthemum frutescens*; *C. morifolium*, the florist's chrysanthemum, is now classified as *Dendrathema morifolium*; *C. maximum*, the Shasta daisy, is now *Leucanthemum maximum*; *C. coccineum*, the painted daisy, or pyrethrum, is now *Thanacetum coccineum*. Still classified as *Chrysanthemum* are *C. balsamita* (costmary), *C. parthenium* (feverfew), and *C. ptarmiciflorum* (dusty miller or silver lace), among others less commonly grown. 2. A plant of the genus *Chrysanthemum*.

Chrysobalanus (krihs oh bal'uh nuhs) *n.* A genus of 4 species of tropical trees and shrubs (Rosaceae) with simple entire leaves, small white flowers, and a fleshy 1-seeded fruit. The cocoa plum, *C. Icaco*, is found throughout tropical America and in southern Florida. Its fruit is edible, resembling a plum, and is used as a preserve.

Chrysogonum (krihs ahg'uh nuhm) *n.* A genus of 1 species, *C. virginianum*, a low-growing North American perennial with opposite leaves and yellow sunflower-shaped flowers. Commonly known as golden star.

Chrysophyllum (krihs oh fihl'uhm) *n.* A genus of 80 species of tropical evergreen trees (Sapotaceae), some species native to North America. They have beautiful, alternate, entire leaves that are covered below with golden hairs, small clusters of purplish-white flowers, and fruit, which is edible *in some species*. *C. Cainito* produces a delicious tropical fruit called the star apple. Some are cultivated as foliage plants, such as *C. oliviform,* commonly known as satinleaf.

Chrysopsis (krihs ahp'sihs) *n*. A genus of about 30 species of perennial North American flowers with simple, entire, alternate leaves and flat clusters of golden asterlike flowers. Grown in borders, rock gardens, and wild gardens. Commonly known as golden aster.

Chrysosplenium (krihs oh spleen'ee uhm) *n*. A genus of about 55 species of small, creeping, semi-aquatic plants (Saxifragaceae). They have alternate, coarsely toothed tufts of leaves and small greenish-yellow flowers. Used as a small-scale ground cover in moist situations such as stream banks and bog gardens. Commonly known as garden saxifrage.

Chrysothamnus (krihs oh tham'nuhs) *n*. A genus of about 13 species of low-branching, drought-tolerant shrubs and subshrubs (Compositae) native to North America. They have alternate, entire, long leaves and yellow or white tubular flowers. Useful in arid regions. Commonly known as rabbit brush.

Chysis (kigh'sihs) *n*. A genus of 3 species of epiphytic (growing on, but not taking nourishment from a host plant) orchids (Orchidaceae). They have draping, jointed stems and folded leaves. *C. aurea* has bell-shaped, golden-yellow flowers 2 inches across, the lip striped with red.

Cibotium (sih boh'tee uhm) *n*. A genus of large tree ferns (Dicksoniaceae), some species native to tropical America. They have soft, furry trunks that grow to as much as 30 feet tall and long, drooping, feathery green fronds. Used outdoors in frost-free climates to create a tropical effect and also as pot plants or greenhouse specimens. Commonly known as tree fern.

cicadas (sih kay'duhz) *n.pl.* A popular name for a group of large, clear-winged, grasshopperlike insects that make a loud, rhythmical creaking or chirping sound. The juveniles live underground, usually for long periods, often emerging in swarming masses. They can damage many types of plants, particularly trees and shrubs, but usually are just

annoying. Difficult to control without using large amounts of traditional pesticides. Prized shrubs can be protected with covers. Also called locust.

Cicer (sigh'ser) *n*. A genus of about 14 species of annual or perennials (Leguminosae). Commonly known as chick-pea or garbanzo.

Cichorium (sih koh'ree uhm) *n*. A genus of 9 species of annuals, biennials, and perennials (Compositae). They have mostly basal leaves and blue, purple, pink, or white flowers. The genus includes common garden chicory, *C. Intybus* and the endive *C. Endivia.* (See **chicory** and **endive.**)

Cicuta (sih kyoo'tuh) *n*. A small genus of about 8 perennial plants (Umbelliferae), some species native to North America; water hemlock. They are tall, graceful, heavy-scented plants with finely divided, feathery leaves and rounded clusters of small white flowers. The common American species, *C. maculata,* is known as water hemlock or poison hemlock. The roots of all are a deadly poison. The genus is commonly known as water hemlock. (See **hemlock.**)

cigar plant *n*. A common name for *Cuphea ignea,* a small evergreen shrub. It has narrow dark-green leaves, with bright scarlet tubular flowers tipped with black and white. Used outdoors in warm climates for edging, bedding, and borders; in cold climates as an indoor/outdoor pot plant. Also known as cigar flower.

cigar tree *n*. A common name of the western catalpa, from the shape of its pods.

cilantro (chih lan'troh) *n*. The leaf of the coriander plant, used as an herb for flavorings. (See **coriander.**)

ciliate (sihl'ee ayt) *a*. Furnished with cilia; bearing cilia. In botany, marginally fringed with hairs, as leaves, petals, etc.

ciliolate (sihl'ee uh layt) *a*. Marginally fringed with tiny hairs.

Cimicifuga (sihm uh sihf'yuh guh) *n*. A genus of tall, upright perennials (Ranunculaceae) the bugbanes, or rattletop. *C. racemosa,* native to the eastern United States, the black snakeroot, or black cohosh, has attractive, much-divided shiny, dark green leaves and tall spikes of small white flowers.

It is useful in the back of the border as a background plant and for its flowers.

Cinchona (sihn koh'nuh) *n.* A genus of evergreen trees (Rubiaceae), growing chiefly altitude of 5,000 to 8,000 feet. They are the source of the medicine quinine.

cincinnus (sihn sihn'uhs) *n.* In botany, a form of definite flowering in which the successive axes arise alternately to the right and left of the preceding one, in distinction from the bostryx, in which the growth is all on one side; a scorpioid cyme. Also cicinnus.

cineraria (sihn uh ra'ree uh) *n.* A common name given by horticulturalists and florists to plants of the genus *Senecio,* particularly *S. hybridus.* They have lush, broad, green leaves and clusters of white, deep blue, or purple flowers. Excellent in shady beds or as potted plants.

cinnamon *n.* 1. A tree of the genus *Cinnamomum,* especially *C. zeylanicum.* This tree is cultivated for its bark in Ceylon, Sumatra, and Borneo, and on the Malabar coast. 2. The inner bark of *C. Zeylanicum.* It is stripped from the branches and, in drying, takes the form of rolls, called quills. The bark of *C. Cassia,* being cheaper, is often substituted for true cinnamon, but it is thicker, coarser, and less delicate in flavor.

cinnamon

cinnamon vine *n.* A common name for *Dioscorea batatas,* a twining vine with glossy, heart-shaped leaves, clusters of small flowers, and edible tubers; the true yam. Grown as perennial ornamental vines in warm climates and for the edible yam.

cinquefoil (sihngk'foil) n. The common name of several species of plants of the genus *Potentilla,* from their 5-part leaves. Also called five-finger.

Circaea (ser see'uh) *n.* A genus of about 12 species of low-growing perennials (Onagraceae), mostly native to northern woodlands. They have opposite, delicate leaves and stalks of white or rosy pairs of flowers. Useful as a shade plant or in moist rock gardens. Commonly known as enchanter's nightshade.

circinate (ser sih nayt) *a.* Circular or ring-shaped: specifically, in botany, applied to leaves in which the leaf is rolled up on itself from the top toward the bottom, like a shepherd's crook, as in the fronds of ferns and the leaves of the sundew.

circinate
a flowers of forget-me-not, *b* young fronds of a fern

circumnutation (ser'kuhm nyoo tay'shuhn) *n.* In botany, the continuous motion of some part of a plant, as the top of the stem or a tendril, in which it describes irregular ellipses or circles.

circumscissile pod of pimpernel

circumscissile (ser'kuhm sihs'ihl) *a.* In botany, opening or divided by a transverse circular line; applied to pods or seed capsules that open with a lid, like a box, as in monkeypot. The fruit in such cases is called a pyxidium.

cirrose (sihr'uhs) *a*. In botany: 1. Having a cirrus or tendril; specifically applied to a leaf tipped with a tendril, or, in mosses, with a very narrow or hairlike sinuous point. 2. Resembling tendrils, or coiling like them. Also cirrate, cirrous, cirrhous, cirrhose.

cirrus (sir'us) *n., pl.* **cirri**. In botany, a tendril; a long threadlike part by which some plants climb. Also cirrhus.

cirri of passion flower

Cirsium (ser'see uhm) n. A genus of between 100 and 200 tall, spiny perennials thistles (Compositae). Most are noxious weeds; a few are grown ornamentally for their bold effect and large purple flowers.

Cissus (sihs'uhs) *n*. A genus of perhaps 350 species of tropical and subtropical tendril-climbing vines and shrubs (Vitaceae). The toothed leaves are alternate, and the flowers are inconspicuous. Grown mainly as very easy-to-grow houseplants, particularly grape ivy, *C. rhombifolia,* and Kangaroo treebine, *C. antarctica.*

Cistaceae (sihs-tay'see ee) *n. pl.* A family of 8 genera and 175 species of low evergreen shrubs or plants, with opposite, simple, entire leaves and showy, flowers that resemble single roses in shape and last only a day. The principal genera are *Cistus* and *Helianthemum,* commonly called rockrose.

Cistus (sihs'tuhs) *n*. 1. A genus of 17 species of beautiful, tender, evergreen flowering shrubs (Cis-

taceae) the rockroses. They are both ornamental and useful, being extremely tolerant of difficult conditions: They are drought-resistant and fire-retardant; they contribute effectively to erosion control on steep banks; and they tolerate salt spray, cold ocean winds, and desert heat. 2. [l.c.] A rockrose; a plant of the genus *Cistus.*

Cistus
(rock rose)

citrange (siht'rihnj) *n*. A hybrid fruit, a cross between the sweet orange and the trifoliate orange, with a more acid flavor than the orange.

Citrofortunella (siht ruh for tyoo'nehl uh) *n*. A genus of hybrid crosses between *Citrus* and *Fortunella,* resulting in such fruits as the limequat and calamondin.

citron (siht'ruhn) *n*. 1. The fruit of the citron tree, a variety of *Citrus medica,* distinguished from the lemon by the absence of an umbo (a pointed knob) at the end and by its very thick rind. The rind is candied and used in confections and pastries. The fingered citron is a variety in which the fruit is curiously divided into large fingerlike lobes. 2. The citron tree, *C. medica.* 3. A round and nearly solid variety of the watermelon *Citrullus lanatus* var. *citroides,* with white and almost flavorless flesh, candied as a confection.

citronella (siht ruh nehl'uh) *n*. A fragrant plant, *Collinsonia canadensis,* a strongly scented perennial herb of North America, usually planted in herb or wildflower gardens.

citronella candle (siht'ruh nehl'uh) *n*. A candle made of pungent oil, used to repel insects.

citron tree (siht ruhn) *n.* The tree *Citrus medica,* which produces the citron. It has an upright, smooth stem, with a branchy head, rising from 5 to 15 feet, adorned with large, oval, spear-shaped leaves.

Citrullus (siht′ruh luhs) *n.* A genus of 3 species of tendril-climbing vines (Cucurbitaceae). *C. lannatus* is the watermelon.

Citrus (siht′ruhs) *n.* A genus of small, tender evergreen trees (Rutaceae) with glossy, alternate leaves and winter-blooming, fragrant, white flowers. The fruit is pulpy with a spongy rind. Included in this genus are the sweet orange, *C. sinensis,* the lemon, *C. Limon,* and the lime, *C. aurantiifolia.* Used in warm-winter climates as a fruit tree, lawn tree, or container plant. Most varieties of citrus fruit are available on dwarf rootstock, especially suitable to the residential garden.

citrus fruits (siht′ruhs) *n. pl.* The fruits of about 15 species of broadleafed evergreens of the genus *Citrus,* including lime, orange, lemon, grapefruit, tangerine, kumquat, among others.

city garden *n.* A garden, often long and narrow and often shaded by nearby buildings, in back of or surrounding a house in the city. Also includes urban-rooftop, terrace, or balcony gardens.

cladocarpous (klad uh kahr′puhs) *a.* In botany, having the fruit at the end of short side branches.

cladode

cladode (kla′dohd) *n., pl.* **cladodes**. In botany, a leaflike flattened branch growing in the stem of a true leaf, as in *Ruscus* and some species of *Phyllanthus.* Also cladophyll.

cladoptosis (kla dahp toh′sihs) *n.* In botany, the annual falling of leafy twigs instead of individual leaves, such as the process that takes place in many trees of the cypress family.

Cladrastis (kluh dras′tihs) *n.* A genus of 4 species of handsome, slow-growing trees (Leguminosae) with leaves divided into leaflets and large rounded white flowers; the yellowwood. *C. lutea* is cultivated as an ornamental shade tree; it is native to Kentucky, Tennessee, and North Carolina.

clammy locust *n.* A common name for *Robinia viscosa,* a North American tree used as a parent in hybridizing same ornamental *Robinia* such as the cultivars of *R. ambigua.*

Clarkia (klahr′kee uh) *n.* A genus of 33 species of annuals (Onagraceae) native to western North America. They have simple, narrow leaves and showy pink-to-lavender flowers. Used for massing, in borders, or in the wildflower garden. Commonly known as farewell-to-spring, godetia, or mountain garland.

clasping *a.* Wholly or partly surrounding the stem.

classification of plants *n.* Taxonomy; the systematic naming of plants devised by Carl von Linne.

Clausena (klah′see nuh) *n.* A genus of 23 species of tropical trees (Rutaceae). They have alternate, divided leaves, small white or greenish-white flowers, and small round fruits. *C. Lansium* is grown as a fruit tree in the tropics and as an ornamental in warm winter climates. Commonly known as wampi.

clavate (klay′vayt) *a.* Club-shaped; growing gradually thicker toward the far end. Also clavated.

claw *n.* 1. In botany, the narrow base of a petal, especially when it is long, as in pinks and wallflowers. 2. A sharp tool typically having 3 tines, used to weed and cultivate.

clay *n.* 1. A soil class; 2. Soil that contains 10% or more clay; 3. A soil particle less than 0.002 mm in diameter.

clayey soil *n.* Soil made up of fine particles that won't hold much air.

clay loam *n.* A soil containing 27% to 40% clay.

clay mineral *n.* A naturally occurring inorganic crystalline material with particles less than 0.002 mm in diameter.

clay pan *n.* 1. A soil rich in clay; 2. A soil hard when dry, plastic or stiff when wet and it will separate abruptly from overlying soil.

clay pot *n.* A container made of terra-cotta that is used for growing houseplants.

Claytonia (klay toh'nee uh) *n.* A genus of 15 to 20 species of low-growing, succulent, spring-flowering perennials (Portulacaceae) some species native to the Americas. *C. virginica,* native to eastern North America, has a single pairof leaves and a short spike of white or rose flowers. Commonly known as spring beauty.

clean cultivation *n.* Removal of undesirable plants by working the soil around desirable plants.

cleanup bag *n.* A freestanding sack, typically holding 30 gallons or more, used to carry clippings and yard debris.

cleavers *n.* A common name for *Galium aparine.* It has a square, jointed stem, with short reflexed prickles and 8 narrow leaves at each joint. Also known as clivers and goose grass.

cleistogamy (klighs tahg'uh mee) *n.* In botany, when the flowers of a plant have, in addition to the ordinary fully developed flowers, others in which development is arrested in the bud, but which are still fertile and produce an abundance of seed. These latter flowers are nonopening, inconspicuous, and without petals, nectaries, or fragrance. They have small anthers containing few pollen grains and have a much-reduced pistil. They are necessarily self-fertilized, but are always fertile, whereas the more perfect flowers of the same plant are often nearly or completely sterile. Cleistogamy is known to occur in about 60 genera belonging to many very different families, chiefly dicotyledonous. The violet is a familiar instance. Also spelled clistogamy.

Clematis (klehm'uh tihs) *n.* A genus of more than 200 species of mostly deciduous shrubby climbers (Ranunculaceae). The leaves are dark green, often divided into leaflets, and the leaf stalks twist and curl to cling to a support provided for the plant. The flowers are without petals, but the petaloid sepals are often large and brightly colored, creating a spectacular effect. The plumose-tailed, silky seed heads are also ornamental and are particularly effective in dried arrangements. There are many forms in cultivation, with large flowers of various colors, mostly varieties or hybrids that have been obtained from *C. Viticella* of Europe, *C. lanuginosa* of China, and the Japanese species *C. florida* and *C. azurea.* Common names abound: traveler's-joy, virgin's-bower, and old-man's-beard.

Cleome
(spider flower)

Cleome (klee oh'mee) *n.* A large genus of 200 species of tropical and subtropical herbaceous and shrubby plants (Capparaceae). Used as annuals, many of the species have showy flowers; they are useful in the border and as cut flowers. *C. spinosa* is commonly known as spider flower.

Clerodendrum (kler uh dehn'druhm) *n.* A genus of more than 450 species of tropical trees, shrubs, and vines (Verbenaceae). They have opposite leaves and clusters of white, yellow, orange, red, blue, or violet flowers, often showy. They are grown outdoors in warm-region gardens, as indoor/outdoor plants, and as hothouse specimens. Commonly known as bleeding heart, glory-bower, turk's-turban, Kashmir bouquet, pagoda flower, glory tree, and Java glory bean.

Clethra (klee'thruh) *n*. A genus of about 30 shrubs or small trees (Clethraceae), some species native to the Americas. They have alternate finely notched leaves and spikes of many white flowers in terminal racemes. *C. alnifolia*, summersweet or sweet pepperbush, is a handsome shrub with very fragrant flowers. *C. arborea*, the lily-of-the-valley tree, is evergreen, with glossy, bronzy-green leaves and upright clusters of fragrant white flowers that resemble lily-of-the-valley.

Cleyera (klay ayr'a) *n*. A genus of 17 species of tropical and subtropical shrubs and small trees (Theaceae). They have simple, sturdy, glossy, deep green alternate leaves, fragrant, creamy-white, 5-petaled flowers, and a red berrylike fruit.

Clianthus (kligh an'thuhs) *n*. A genus of tender, evergreen shrubs or plants (Leguminosae). They have leaves divided into an odd number of leaflets and large, handsome, white sweet-pea-like flowers. *C. puniceus*, commonly known as parrot's-bill, is an elegant shrub to 8 or 10 feet, with crimson flowers. The genus is commonly known as glory pea.

cliff brake *n*. A common name for ferns of the genus *Pellea*. (See **brake**.)

climate *n*. The characteristic condition of a country or region in respect to the amount or variations of heat and cold, moisture and dryness, wind and calm, etc.; especially, the combined result of all the meteorological phenomena of any region, as affecting its vegetable productions.

climber *n*. In botany, a plant that scrambles upward by attaching itself to other plants or objects (such as a trellis). Climbing plants are distinguished as stem climbers, which, like hops, wind upward around an upright support, and as tendril climbers, which, like grapevines, cling to adjacent objects by slender coiling tendrils. Other plants clamber and cling by means of bristles or spines, or by rootlets.

climbing fern *n*. A common name for *Lygodium*, some species of which are native to tropical America. *L. palmatum* is native to the United States; it is a delicate climbing plant, with sterile fronds that are hand-shaped and lobed and fertile fronds that are forked several times. *L. palmatum* is also called Hartford fern.

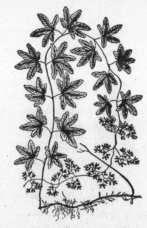

climbing fern or hartford fern

climbing onion *n*. A common name for *Bowiea*, a genus of 2 species of tropical bulbous perennials. It has an exposed bulb to 7 inches across, fleshy, twining, leafless stems to 15 feet long, and small greenish-white flowers. Grown as a novelty in greenhouses. Also called Zulu potato.

climbing-staff tree *n*. A common name for *Celastrus scandens*, a twining woody vine. Also known as climbing bittersweet.

clinandrium (kligh nan'dree uhn) *n., pl.* **clinandria**. In botany, a cavity, at the apex of the column in orchids, in which the anthers rest.

Clintonia (klihn toh'nee uh) *n*. A genus of 6 species of stemless perennials (Liliaceae), some species native to North America. They grow from rhizomes and have basal leaves and large, lily-shaped, white or rose-colored flowers. *C. borealis* (corn lily) and *C. umbellata* (speckled wood lily) are native to eastern North America. *C. Andrewsiana* and *C. uniflora* (bride's bonnet) are native to western North America.

clip-on stake *n*. A device used to support the stems of plants such as tomatoes. The plant is secured to the stake by a piece of plastic, which fits around the stem and through holes in the stake.

Clitoria (kligh toh'ree uh) *n*. A genus of 30 species of tropical and subtropical plants and shrubs (Leguminosae); some species native to the Americas. They are climbing (rarely erect) plants, with alternate leaves divided into leaflets and large blue, white, or red sweet-pea-shaped flowers.

Clivia (kligh′vee uh) *n.* A genus of several bulbs (Amaryllidaceae) with dark green straplike leaves and reddish-yellow or scarlet flowers in a cluster atop a sturdy stalk. Used as a bedding plant or container plant in warm-winter climates and as an indoor/outdoor pot plant elsewhere.

cloche (klohsh) *n.* A bell-shaped cover used to protect a plant from frost or cold; an individual cold frame.

clock vine *n.* A common name for *Thunbergia alata,* a twining perennial vine, sometimes grown as an annual, with triangular leaves and white, creamy-yellow, or orange flowers with a dark center. Also called black-eyed susan vine.

clod *n.* A mass of soil produced by plowing or digging.

clone *n.* A plant that is the result of asexual reproduction and that is genetically identical to the parent. Particularly used where the seedlings tend to be variable, as in citrus and roses. 2. *v.* To propagate a plant by cuttings, budding, and layering in order to obtain a plant identical to the parent.

cloudberry *n.* A species of dwarf berry, *Rubus Chamoemorus,* similar in shape to a raspberry with a creeping root and stems, from 4 to 8 inches high. It is found in arctic and subarctic regions of the Northern Hemisphere. The flowers are large and white, and the berries, which have a smoky taste, are orange-yellow in color and have larger seeds than a raspberry. Also called salmonberry.

cloudberry

cloud grass *n.* (See **Agrotis.**)

clove *n.* A very pungent aromatic spice, the dried flower buds of *Syzygium aromaticum,* (Myrtaceae), cultivated in tropical regions. The tree is a handsome evergreen, from 15 to 30 feet high, with large, elliptic, smooth leaves and numerous purplish flowers on jointed stalks. Every part of the plant abounds in the volatile oil for which the flower buds are prized. 2. One of the small bulbs that make up a mother bulb, as in garlic.

clover *n.* A common name for about 300 various species of the genus *Trifolium* (Leguminosae). They are low-growing plants, usually with a 3-lobed leaf and dense heads or spikes of tiny fragrant flowers. More frequently grown for forage than ornament.

clubroot *n.* A fungal disease causing large swellings in the roots of the cabbage family. To control, avoid planting in previously infected soil or use traditional fungicides.

Clusia (kloo′zhee uh) *n.* A genus of tropical American shrubs or trees (Guttiferae). Many of the species are parasites, and all secrete a milky sap. They have large, thick, wedge-shaped leaves, pink and white flowers 2 inches across, and round, pale green fruit. They tolerate salt spray. Sometimes grown as houseplants.

Cnicus (nigh′kuhs) *n.* A genus of 1 species *C. benedictus* (Compositae), a branching, thistlelike annual 2 feet tall and is slightly hairy, with small yellow flowers.

coalescent (koh uh lehs′ehnt) *a.* Growing together; uniting so as to form 1 body: in botany, properly applied to the organic cohesion of similar parts.

coarse sand *n.* A soil particle that measures between .50 to 1.0 millimeters.

Cobaea
(mexican ivy)

Cobaea (koh bee′uh) *n.* A small genus of about 10 species of fast-growing, tendril-climbing, shrubby vines (Polemoniaceae) native to tropical America. They have alternate, leaves divided into leaflets and large, bell-shaped, violet-to-bright-green flowers. *C. scandens,* from Mexico, has 10-inch long clusters of 2-inch purple or white flowers that bloom from May to October. It is grown as a perennial in warm-winter gardens and as an annual in colder climates. Commonly known as Mexican ivy, monastery bells, or cup-and-saucer vine.

cobnut *n.* A round filbertlike nut; a large hazelnut, the fruit of *Corylus avellana grandis.*

coca (koh′kuh) *n.* 1. A common name for *Erythroxylum Coca* (Erythroxylaceae), a small shrub native to the mountains of Peru and Bolivia but cultivated in other parts of South America; the principal source of the drug cocaine. 2. The dried leaf of *E. Coco.*

cocaine plant *n.* A common name for *Erythroxylum Coca.*

Coccoloba (kuh kahl′uh buh) *n.* A genus of about 150 species of broadleaf evergreen trees, shrubs, or tall woody vines (Polygonaceae) native to tropical and subtropical America. It has large alternate, entire, rounded leaves, 10-inch spikes densely clustered with white flowers, and purple fruit resembling bunches of grapes. *C. uvifera,* the sea grape of the West Indies, grows well in sandy soil and tolerates sea spray.

coccolobis (kuh kahl′uh bihs) *n.* A common name for *Coccoloba.*

Cocculus (kahk′yuh luhs) *n.* A genus of 11 species of tropical twining vines, shrubs, or small trees (Menispermaceae), with shiny, leathery, oblong leaves and clusters of small yellow flowers. *C. carolinus* is a twining vine with 4-inch-long lobed leaves, dense clusters of flowers, and showy bright red fruit. It is native to the southeastern United States and commonly known as Carolina moonseed. Good background plant or espalier.

coccus (kahk′uhs) *n., pl.* **cocci.** In botany, 1 of the separate divisions of a divided seed pod, which splits up into 1-seeded cells.

cocci, showing divisions

cochlear (kohk′lee er) *a.* Shell-shaped.

Cochlearia (kohk lee ar′ee uh) *n.* A genus of 25 species of very hardy maritime plants (Cruciferaceae) found mostly near the seacoast. They have thick leaves, small white flowers, and round seedpods. *C. officinalis,* is commonly known as scurvy grass.

Cochliostema (kohk lee oh stee′muh) *n.* A genus of 2 species of epiphytic tropical plants (Commelinaceae) native to the Americas. They have large leaves in a bromeliadlike rosette and three-petaled flowers. *C. odoratissimum* has 4-foot-long leaves and 1-foot-long stalks of white and blue-violet flowers with yellow filaments. Grown as a greenhouse specimen.

Cochlospermum (kohk luh sper′muhm) *n.* A genus of 15 species of tropical trees or shrubs (Cochlospermaceae). They have hand-shaped lobed leaves, large yellow flowers, and pear-shaped fruits, with numerous seeds covered with a silky down. Grown in warm-winter gardens as a flowering tree. *C. religiosum* is commonly known as silk-cotton tree.

cocklebur *n.* A common name for plants of the genus *Xanthium,* a weed, and for plants of the genus *Agrimonia,* the agrimony.

cockscomb *n.* A name given to flowering plants of various genera but properly confined to *Celosia cristata.* It is also applied to some similar species of *Amarantus.* (See **celosia.**)

cocksfoot orchard grass *n.* (See **Dactylis.**)

cockspur *n.* 1. A common name for *Pisonia aculeata,* a West Indian shrub. 2. A common name for a North American species of thorn, *Crataegus crusgalli,* frequently cultivated as an ornamental shrub.

coco (koh′koh) *n.* A common name for a palm belonging to the genus *Cocos,* which produces the coconut. *C. nucifera* is the coconut palm, which has

cocoa
(coco nut palm)

a cylindrical stem that grows from 60 to 90 feet, with crown of feather-like leaves from 18 to 20 feet long. It has small white flowers, and the fruits, called coconuts, grow in bunches of from 12 to 20. Each seed is enclosed in a very hard shell and is surrounded by a thick fibrous rind, or husk. The meat of the coconut is eaten raw, shredded as a condiment, and pressed for an edible oil. Also called coconut tree. Also spelled cacoa, cocoanut.

coconut *n.* The nut or fruit of the coconut palm, *Cocos nucifera,* grown in Florida, California, and Hawaii. The coconut palm is the source of a wide variety of products from food and oil to cordage. The young leaves yield a material for baskets and mats; the older leaves are used for thatching.

coco plum *n.* A common name for a small spreading tree of tropical America, *Chrysobalanus icaco,* which bears plum-shaped fruit used for making preserves. (See **plum.**)

Cocos (koh′kahs) *n.* A genus of 1 species, *C. nucifera,* the coconut tree. It is a tall palm with long, divided leaves and a large fibrous-coated fruit that encloses a single nut, the coconut. (See **coco.**)

cocozelle (kah kuh zehl′ee) *n.* A variety of summer squash, much like the zucchini.

coddling moth *n.* An insect that, in the larval stage, the main cause of wormy apples and walnuts. The larvae bore into fruit to feed on the pulp, often causing cracked apples. Control with dormant oil sprays and repeated, well-timed applications of *Bacillus thuringiensis* or traditional insecticides. Traps, sanitation, and trichogramma wasps are sometimes effective.

Codiaeum (koh dee ee′uhm) *n.* A genus of 6 species of shrubs and trees (Euphorbiaceae). *C. varieg-atum* is often cultivated in warm-climate gardens, in greenhouses, or as a houseplant for its beautifully variegated foliage. It is commonly known as croton.

codlins-and-cream *n.* A common name for willow herb, *Epilobium hirsutum,* so called from the odor of its bruised leaves, which resembles that of baked apples and cream.

Codonopsis (koh duh nahp′sihs) *n.* A genus of 32 species of annual flowers (Campanulaceae). They have tuberous roots, simple, mostly ovate leaves, and yellowish-green to pale blue bell-shaped flowers, often spotted inside. Commonly known as bonnet bellflower.

Coelogyne (sih lahj′uh nee) *n.* A large genus of 200 species of tropical epiphytic (growing on, but not taking nourishment from a host plant) orchids (Orchidaceae). They have long leaves and sprays of large, handsome flowers. Grown primarily as greenhouse specimens.

Coffea (kahf ee′uh) *n.* A genus of 40 species of tropical shrubs or trees (Rubiaceae). *C. arabica* is the source for coffee. It has glossy, dark green leaves, clusters of fragrant white flowers, and red berries.

coffee *n.* 1. The berry of trees belonging to the genus *Coffea.* Several species, but principally *C. Arabica,* produce the coffee of commerce. It grows to 16 or 18 feet but is kept pruned to 8 or 9 feet, for easy harvesting. It has light brown bark, horizontal, opposite branches, glossy leaves, clusters of fragrant white flowers, and small, red, fleshy fruit that looks like a small cherry. Each berry contains 2 seeds, commonly called coffee beans. Ocassionally grown as a novelty houseplant.

coffee, arabian *n.* A common name for *Coffea arabica,* the coffee tree.

coffee bean *n.* The common term for the seed of the coffee tree.

coffee berry *n.* The fruit of the coffee tree.

coffee fern *n.* A common name for *Pellea andromedifolia,* a small evergreen fern native to California.

coffee nut *n.* The fruit of *Gymnocladus dioica,* the Kentucky coffee tree, the seeds of which have been used as a substitute for coffee beans.

coffee tree *n.* A common name for *Coffea arabica,* and other species that produce the berries from which coffee is derived. (See **coffee**.) California coffee tree, a common name for *Rhamnus californica,* an evergreen shrub native to California; also called coffeeberry. Kentucky coffee tree, a common name for *Gymnocladus dioica,* a large tree native to the United States, the seeds of which have been used as a substitute for coffee.

cohosh (koh'hahsh) *n.* A common name for plants of several species: *Cimicfuga racemosa,* the black cohosh; *Actaea pachypoda* and *A. alba,* respectively, the red and the white cohosh and *Caulophyllum thalictroides,* the blue cohosh.

Coix (koh'ihks) *n.* A genus of about 5 species of annual and perennial grasses (Gramineae). *C. lacryma-jobi* known as Job's tears, is grown as an annual ornamental and for the beadlike balls it produces (actually hardened flower coverings). The beads are white and gray to dark purple and can be strung.

cola nut *n.* A bitter caffeine-containing seed, about the size of a chestnut, produced by a tree, *Cola acuminata* (Sterculiaceae).

Colchicum
(meadow saffron)

Colchicum (kahl'chih kuhm) *n.* 1. A genus of between 60 and 70 species of autumn-blooming bulbs (corms) (Liliaceae), with strap-shaped leaves, generally produced in spring, and crocuslike flowers in autumn. *C. autumnale,* the meadow saffron, grows from a corm with pale lilac, crocus like flowers. The corms are poisonous if eaten.

cold frame *n.* A bottomless box consisting of a wooden or metal frame with a glass or polyethylene top; it is placed on the ground over plants to protect them from cold or frost.

Coleus (koh'lee uhs) *n.* A genus of 150 species of tropical herbs and shrubs (Labiatae). They are grown for their brilliant red, pink, yellow, white, green, or burgundy foliage as summer annuals, houseplants, or greenhouse specimens.

collar *n.* A ring placed loosely around the stem of a plant, especially tomatoes, to prevent cutworm damage.

collard (kahl'erd) *n.* A variety of cabbage with the fleshy leaves scattered upon the stem instead of gathered into a head. Its deep green leaves are considered better flavored after withstanding several frosts.

collenchyma (kuh lehng'kuh muh) *n.* In botany, a layer of tissue immediately beneath the epidermis, having the cells thickened at the angles by a padlike mass, which swells in water. It is found chiefly in the young stems, petioles, and leaf veins of many dicotyledonous plants.

Colletia (kuh lee'shee uh) *n.* A genus of 17 species of stiff, spiny shrubs (Rhamnaceae). It has small leaves, if any, yellow or white tubular flowers, and a leathery, 3-lobed fruit. Grown as a curiosity in tropical gardens or greenhouses.

Collinsia (kuh lihn'zee uh) *n.* A genus of more than 20 species of annuals (Scrophulariaceae) native to North America, chiefly the Pacific coast. They are 1 to 2 feet tall, have opposite or whorled leaves, and handsome, snapdragonlike white-and-rose or white-and-violet flowers. They form a dainty ground cover over bulbs, useful at the edge of borders or under deciduous trees. Commonly known as Chinese-houses.

colloid soil (kah′loyd) *n.* A term for organic or inorganic tiny crystals that are small enough to be easily carried by air or water.

Collomia (kuh loh′mee uh) *n.* A genus of 15 species of low-growing, creeping plants (Polemoniaceae) native to the Americas. They grow from rhizomes and have long, narrow leaves and clusters of pink, scarlet, yellow, white, or purple trumpet-shaped flowers.

colluvium (kuh lyoo′vee uhm) *n.* A deposit of soil at the base of a steep slope.

Colocasia (kahl uh kay′zhee uh) *n.* A genus of 6 species of large perennial plants (Araceae). They have large, dark green, callalike leaves and starchy tubers. *C. esculentum* and its several varieties are cultivated for use as food throughout the tropics. Commonly known as taro.

colonial bent grass *n.* (See **Agrotis**.)

Colorado potato beetle

Colorado potato beetle *n.* A yellow-and-black striped, ladybuglike beetle that eats the foliage of potatoes, tomatoes, and eggplant. Control by handpicking, releasing spined soldier beetles, or by spraying with *Bacillus thuringiensis* var. San Diego, rotenone, or traditional insecticides.

color chart *n.* A variously colored surface that is an aid in identifying colors.

color-in-the-garden *n.* A term used to refer to the use of annuals to give seasonal color when in bloom; for example, impatiens in spring, petunias in summer, and chrysanthemums in fall. Florist-grown plants bought in bloom may be sunk into the garden or placed in cache-pots to create the same effect.

color wheel *n.* A diagrammatic way of showing the basic relationships of colors to one another. Red, red-orange, orange, yellow-orange, and yel

low are considered "warm" colors; green, blue-green, blue, blue-violet, and violet are considered "cool" colors. Although colors are neither warm nor cool in a physical sense, they can impart feelings of warmth or coolness, of passion or tranquility.

coltsfoot *n.* The popular name of the *Tussilago Farfara* (Compositae), naturalized in the United States. Its leaves were once employed in medicine. One of the earliest spring flowers, it can also become invasive.

columbine (kahl′uhm bighn) *n.* The common name for the genus *Aquilegia*. The leaves resemble those of the maidenhair fern, and the multicolored flowers come in nearly every shade. Aquilegia owes its name to the resemblance of its petals and sepals to a flock of doves. They are useful in woodland gardens, in rock gardens,

columbine

along the borders of streams or ponds, or in borders.

column *n.* In botany, a body formed by the union of filaments with one another, as in *Malvaceae,* or of stamens with the style, as in orchids.

Columnea (kah luhm′nee uh) *n.* A genus of 100 species of creeping, climbing, epiphytic (growing on, but not taking nourishment from a host plant) tropical shrubs and vines (Gesneriaceae) native to the Americas. They have opposite, sometimes whorled, leaves and clusters of yellow-to-scarlet tubular flowers. Grown as houseplants or greenhouse specimens for both their flowers and their ornamental foliage.

Colutea (kuh loo′tee uh) *n.* A genus of 25 species of tender shrubs or small trees (Leguminosae) with inflated pods, like small bladders. *C. arborescens,* a deciduous shrub with divided leaves and yellow and red flowers, is grown in mild climates. Commonly known as bladder senna.

coma *n., pl.* **comae** (-mi). In botany: 1. The leafy head of a tree, such as palms, or a tuft of leaves or bracts terminating a stem, such as the leafy top of a pineapple. 2. The silky hairs at the end of some seeds, such as fireweed, *Epilobium*.

coma of willow-herb seed

Combretaceae (kahm bruh tay'see ee) *n. pl.* A family of 15 genera of tropical shrubs or graceful small trees. The prinicipal genera are *Terminalia* and *Combretum.*

comfrey (kuhm'free) *n.* A name given to more than 20 plants of the genus *Symphytum* (Boraginaceae). The root of the common comfrey, *S. officinale,* sometimes cultivated in herb gardens, has large leaves and pale flowers, which are a favorite with bees. The plants grow to more than 4 feet tall and can easily become invasive. For this reason, it is frequently grown at the edge of a field or alongside a barn.

Commelina (kahm uh ligh'nuh) *n.* A genus of about 100 species of tender, creeping perennials (Commelinaceae). They have jointed stems, alternate, entire leaves, and blue, usually three-petaled flowers. Several are cultivated as ground covers or hanging-basket plants for their delicate flowers and graceful habit. Commonly known as wandering jew and spiderwort.

Commelinaceae (kahm uh lih nay'see ee) *n. pl.* A family of perennials, natives mostly of warm climates, recognizable by their three-petaled flowers; the spiderworts. The principal genera are *Tradescantia, Commelina,* and *Cyanotis.* Used as small-scale ground covers in warm-winter gardens or as hanging-basket indoor/outdoor plants anywhere.

commissure (kahm'uh shur) *n.* A joint, seam, suture, or closure; the place where two bodies or parts of a body meet or unite. Specifically, in botany, the face by which 1 carpel or mericarp attaches to another, as in the Umbelliferae.

compact *v.t.* Pressing air out of the soil.

companion planting/cropping *n.* A system of arranging plants in such a manner that a given spe-cies benefits from some characteristic of another. Tomatoes, for example, are thought to be protected from certain insects by the odor of marigolds.

compass plant *n.* A common name for *Silphium laciniatum* (Compositae), a tall, coarse plant native to the western prairies of North America. The leaves are arranged on the stem so as to indicate the cardinal points of the compass, hence the name. Also called rosinweed.

complanate (kohm'pluh nayt) *a.* In botany, lying in one plane; applied to leaves, especially of mosses.

complex soil *n.* 1. A pattern of soil; 2. A mixture of different kinds of soil whose areas are too small to be shown individually.

Compositae (kuhm pahz'uh tee) *n. pl.* The largest family of plants, with more than 950 genera and 20,000 species. They are flowers or, much more rarely, shrubs or, still more rarely trees. The flowers are compound, often with petallike rays around a flat center, like those of daisies, asters, and sunflowers. Chrysanthemums, dahlias and yarrow are also well-known members of the family. A few species are grown for food, such as artichokes, *Cynara,* and lettuces, *Lactuca.* More than 150 species are grown ornamentally.

composite *a.* In botany, belonging to the family Compositae; having the character of this family; as a composite plant; a composite flower. (See **Compositae.**)

compost *n.* The decomposition of a mass of rotted organic matter.

compost activator *n.* A substance, generally bacterial, used to speed the breakdown of organic waste into compost. Also called activator or compost inoculant.

compost aerator (air'ay ter) *n.* Elongated, flanged T-shaped device used to create passages for air and moisture in a compost pile. Also called compost turner.

compost bin *n.* A container to hold decomposing yard and garden wastes, fertilizer, peat, lime, and other substances during the composting process. (See also composter.)

compost bucket *n.* A pail for holding kitchen scraps destined for the compost pile.

compost chopper *n.* A bladed device used to shred yard or garden waste into small pieces that will decompose quickly in a compost pile.

composter *n.* Any of various containers utilizing air, moisture, and solar heat to turn grass clippings, garden refuse, and kitchen scraps into compost. Composters may consist of stacked trays or other chambers arranged to facilitate periodic turning of the mixture.

compost fork *n.* An implement having 4 deeply dished tines that is used to move heaps of compost or manure.

compost inoculant (ihn ahk′yoo lehnt) *n.* A substance which may include bacteria, fungi, enzymes, and hormones that is used to speed the composting process and to improve the quality of the compost. Also called activator or compost activator.

compost tea *n.* A liquid fertilizer made of compost dissolved in water.

compost thermometer *n.* A thermometer having a long probe to measure the temperature in the center of a compost pile.

compost turner *n.* (See **compost aerator.**)

compound *a.* In botany, made up of several similar parts combined into a whole; for example, a compound leaf is a leaf composed of several leaflets.

compound leaf

compressed air sprayer *n.* A misting and spraying device in which air forces water or other liquid through an adjustable nozzle.

compression sprayer *n.* (See **pump sprayer.**)

Comptonia (kahmp toh′nee uh) *n.* A genus of 1 species of deciduous shrub, *C. peregrina* (Myricaceae), native to eastern North America. It is a low shrub with highly aromatic, long, narrow, divided leaves, catkins 1 inch in diameter, and smooth nuts. It is used to cover banks. Commonly called sweet fern.

conceptacle (kuhn sehp′tuh kuhl) *n.* In botany, an organ or a cavity that encloses reproductive bodies in some ferns, fungi, mosses, and algae.

concrescence (kuhn krehs′ehns) *n.* In botany, the union of cell walls by means of a cementing substance formed in process of growth so that they are inseparably grown together. Also called cementation.

concrete *n.* A compact mass of sand, gravel, coarse pebbles, or stone chippings cemented together to form a smooth surface for steps, walkways, or patios.

concretions *n.* Pelletlike grains from concentrations of compounds in soils that cement the soil grains together.

conditioner *n.* A material added to a fertilizer that keeps it flowing free.

conductance *n.* The power to conduct.

conductivity *n.* The physical quantity that measures the readiness with which a medium transmits electricity. Expressed in mhos per centimeter or micromhos per centimeter at 25 degrees C.

Cone of Larch
Cone of Pine

cone *n.* Anything shaped like a cone, as in pinecone. Specifically, in botany, a dry, usually elongated, multiple fruit formed of densely overlapped scales, especially in pined, firs, and spruces, in which a pair of naked seeds is borne upon the upper side of each scale: technically called a strobilus or strobile; in a more general sense, a flower or cluster of flowers having a conelike shape.

coneflower *n.* A name given to certain species of *Rudbeckia* (Compositae), coarse plants with conical centers, especially to *R. laciniata,* whose center is a greenish-yellow oblong disk, and *R. hirta,* in which the conical disk is dark brown. 2. A name given to the purple or hedgehog coneflower, the nearly allied *Echinacea purpurea* and *E. angustifolia,* of the prairies of the western United States.

cone-plant *n.* A common name for small clumping succulent plants of the genus *Conophytum* (Aizoaceae).

conglomerate (kuhn glahm'uh riht) *a.* In botany, densely clustered.

conifer (koh nih fer) *n.* In botany, a plant producing cones; one of the *Coniferae;* a more precise word for so-called "evergreens," such as pines, cypresses, cedars, and junipers, although not all conifers are evergreens, and not all evergreens are conifers.

Coniferae (koh nihf'uh ree) *n. pl.* A family of about 50 genera and about 550 species, mostly evergreen, cone-bearing trees and shrubs; the conifers or evergreens. It is most abundant in temperate and mountainous regions, often forming vast forests in the Northern Hemisphere. The leaves are rigid, needle-shaped, awl-shaped, or scalelike; the flowers are inconspicuous; and the fruit is a dry cone or fleshy and drupelike. The family includes fir, pine, larch, juniper, yew, and cedar.

Conium (kih nee'uhm) *n.* A genus of 2 species of tall biennial plants (Umbelliferae) with finely cut dark green leaves and umbrella-shaped clusters of white flowers. *C. maculatum* is widely naturalized in North America. All parts of the plant are deadly poisonous. *C. maculatum* is commonly known as hemlock, poison hemlock, spotted hemlock, California fern, Nebraska fern, and winter fern.

connate (kah'nayt) *a.* In botany, united congenitally.

connate leaves

Conophytum (kohn oh figh'tuhm) *n.* A genus of small clumping succulents (Aizoaceae). It has nearly stemless, fleshy, cone-shaped, cylindrical foliage and yellow-pink, dandelion-shaped flowers. Grown by collectors as pot plants. Commonly known as cone-plant.

conservation *n.* The act of conserving, guarding, or keeping with care; preservation from loss, decay, injury; the keeping of a thing in a safe or entire state.

consistence *n.* 1. The properties of soil material that determine its ability to change shape; 2. Consistency.

consolidate *v.* To increase the density and reduce pore space in soil.

consumptive use *n.* 1. The water used by plants. 2. Vapor loss. Expressed as equivalent depth of free water per unit of time.

container gardening *n.* Method of growing plants outdoors in barrels, pots, and other containers.

continuous *a.* In botany, not deviating from uniformity; the reverse of interrupted.

contour *n.* An imaginary line connecting points of equal elevation on the soil's surface.

contour basin *n.* A basin made by a levee or border built on a contour.

contour plowing *v.t.* The plowman keeps to a level line at a right angle to the direction of the slope.

contour terrace *n.* Leveling soil out on a slope at a right angle to the direction of the slope.

Convallaria (kahn vuh lar'ee uh) *n.* A genus of 1 to 3 species of flowers (Liliaceae) that grow from rhizomes. *C. majalis,* the lily-of-the-valley, is a stemless perennial with a creeping rootstock, 2 or 3 leaves, and a many-flowered stalk of fragrant white, drooping, bell-shaped flowers. It has naturalized in eastern North America. It is used as a small-scale ground cover in shady places and is often forced from pips in pots indoors for early bloom.

convergent lady beetle *n.* A beneficial insect known as the ladybug or ladybird beetle. Both adults and larvae feed on many pests, especially aphids. They are most effective when they migrate into a yard naturally; releases are of doubtful benefit.

conveyance loss *n.* The loss of water from a conduit due to leakage, seepage or evaporation.

convolute (kahn'vuh loot) *a.* Rolled together, or 1 part over another. In botany, specifically applied to leaves or petals rolled up longitudinally in the bud.

convolute leaf base
crosssection

Convolvulaceae (kuhn vahlv'yuh lay'see ee) *n. pl.* A large family of about 50 genera and 1,200 species, typically twining or trailing vines or shrubs. It includes *Ipomoea* (morning glory), *Convolvulus* (bindweed), and *Cuscuta* (dodder), among others. The family also includes *Ipomoea Batatas* (sweet potato).

Convolvulus (kuhn vahlv'yuh luhs) *n.* 1. A genus of about 225 species of slender, twining vines, with showy, trumpet-shaped flowers (Convolvulaceae). The common species of the fields, such as *C. calystegia sepium* and *C. arvensis,* popularly known as bindweed, are considered noxious weeds. 2. [l.c.] A plant of the genus *Convolvulus.*

coontail *n.* A common name for the genus *Ceratophyllum* (Anthocerotales), a pondweed grown in garden pools. Also known as hornwort.

coontie (koon'tee) *n.* The *Zamia integrifolia* and *Z. pumila,* the arrowroot plant of Florida; also, the arrowroot produced from it. Also spelled coonty and comptie.

Copaifera (koh pay ihf'uh ruh) *n.* A genus of 25 species of tropical trees, some species native to the Americas. They have divided leaves, spikes of white flowers, and 1-seeded pods.

Copernicia (koh per nihsh'ee uh) *n.* A genus of 29 species of tall, handsome fan palms (Palmae) native to tropical America. *C. prunifera,* the young leaves of which are coated with a hard wax, is the carnauba, or wax palm, the source of carnauba wax. Planted ornamentally in tropical and subtropical landscaping. Also known as carnauba palm.

coplant (koh plant') *v.* To plant together or at the same time.

copper *n.* An element used in various forms, including copper sulfate and Bordeaux mixture, to control fungal and bacterial diseases of plants. Also used in strips around tree trunks to act as a barrier to snails.

copperleaf *n.* A common name for the genus *Acalypha,* especially the species *A. Wilkesiana* and the genus *Alternanthera. Acalphya* is grown as a houseplant or greenhouse specimen for its foliage, and *Alternanthera* is grown as a bedding plant, also for its variegated, brightly colored leaves. *Acalypha* is also known as chenille plant; *A. Wilkesiana* is also known as Jacob's-coat, firedragon, beefsteak plant, and match-me-if-you-can. *Alternanthera* is also known as Joseph's-coat.

coppertip *n.* A common name for *Crocosmia Xcrocosmiiflora,* a perennial plant that grows from a corm (bulblike stem swelling) and has narrow leaves and orange-to-crimson flowers.

Coprosma (kuh prahz' muh) *n.* A genus of about 90 species of tender evergreen shrubs or small trees (Rubiaceae). It has opposite, shiny, bright green leaves, inconspicuous white or greenish flowers, and a fleshy yellow or orange fruit. It can be used as a hedge, a screen, a wall shrub, or an espalier. It tolerates wildly varying degrees of moisture, as well as wind, sea spray, and poor soil. *C. repens* is commonly known as mirror plant.

Coptis (kahp'tihs) *n.* A genus of about 10 species (Ranunculaceae), consisting of low, hardy perennials with divided basal leaves, stalks of small white or yellow flowers, and yellow, threadlike rhizomes. Commonly known as goldthread.

coquelicot (kohk′lih koh′) *n.* 1. A common name for the genus *Papaver,* the wild poppy, most often the corn poppy, *P. rhoeas.* 2. Also a common name for *Callirhoe papaver,* a mallow, with poppy-shaped flowers, native to North America.

coquito (koh kee′toh) *n.* A common name for *Jubaea chilensis,* a very beautiful palm, which produces numerous small, edible nuts. The sap, obtained by felling the trees, is boiled down to a sweet syrup, which is sold under the name of palm honey (miel de palma).

coral bean *n.* A common name for *Erythrina corallodendrum,* the coral tree, a spectacular flowering tree that often flowers before the leaves emerge. It has alternate leaves consisting of 3 broad leaflets, showy red or orange flowers, and long, cylindrical pods with shiny red seeds. The seeds, used to make necklaces, are poisonous if eaten.

coralbells *n.* A common name for *Huechera sanguinea,* a low-growing flower with round, scalloped leaves growing from the base of the plant and slim stalks with clusters of nodding, bell-shaped red, white, or coral flowers. Used for edging beds and borders.

coralberry *n.* A common name for *Symphoricarpos orbiculatus,* a shrub with elliptic leaves, small white, bell-shaped flowers, and coral-red berries.

coral drops *n.* A common name for *Bessera elegans,* a Mexican bulb (corm) with 32-inch-long green leaves and short stalks of nodding, bell-shaped scarlet-to-purple flowers striped with green and white.

coral gem *n.* A common name for *Lotus berthelotii,* a many-branched plant with silvery-gray, finely divided leaves and scarlet, curiously shaped flowers. Grown as a small-scale ground cover in warm-winter climates and as a showy indoor/outdoor hanging basket plant anywhere. Also called parrot′s-beak.

Corallorhiza (kor′uh loh righ′zuh) *n.* A genus of 12 species of wild orchids (Orchidaceae), some species native to North America. They are brown or yellowish leafless parasitic plants that grow in shady woods. *C. odontorhiza* and *C. maculata,* which has slim pink stalks of tiny white flowers, are native to North America. Also known as coralroot.

coral pea *n.* A common name for *Kennedia prostrata,* a sprawling shrub with alternate leaves divided into leaflets, scarlet flowers, and long, round pods. Grown in warm-winter climate gardens or as a greenhouse specimen.

coral plant *n.* A common name for *Jatropha multifida* (Euphorbiaceae), a tall shrub frequently cultivated in tropical and subtropical gardens for its clusters of handsome scarlet flowers and deeply cut foliage.

coralroot *n.* A common name for plants of the genus *Corallorhiza.*

coral tree *n.* A common name for shrubs or trees of the genus *Erythrina* (Leguminosae). They have 3-lobed leaves and spikes of showy scarlet flowers, followed by long pods enclosing bright-red seeds. The coral tree of India is *E. variegata;* of the West Indies, *E. corallodendron.*

coralvine *n.* A common name, one of many, for the open and airy subtropical vine *Antigonon leptopus,* which has heart-shaped green leaves and long, trailing sprays of small rosy-pink flowers. Also called rosa de montana, corallita, and queen′s wreath.

coralwort *n.* The common name for plants of the genus *Dentaria.* They grow from fleshy rhizomes; they have compound leaves and stalks with clusters of white, rose or purple flowers. Used in wildflower gardens, rock gardens, or for naturalizing. Also called toothwort or pepperroot.

Corchorus (kor′kuh ruhs) *n.* 1. A genus of tropical plants or small shrubs (Tiliacea) with large alternate, simple leaves and clusters of small yellow flowers. 2. [l.c.] A common name for ornamental shrubby plant, *Kerria Japonica* (Rosaceae), frequently cultivated for its showy, usually double, yellow flowers.

cordate leaf

cordate (kor'dayt) *a.* Heart-shaped, with a sharp tip; having a form like that of the heart on playing cards; for example, a cordate leaf.

cordgrass *n.* (See **Spartina.**)

Cordia (kor'dee uh) *n.* A genus of about 300 tropical deciduous trees or shrubs (Boraginaceae) with alternate simple leaves, clusters of white, yellow, orange, or red flowers, and plumlike fruit. Grown in warm climate gardens or in greenhouses.

cordless hand trimmer *n.* An implement consisting of 2 triangular-toothed metal blades and a rechargeable battery-powered motor used for trimming grass. Also called electric grass shears.

Cordyline (kor duh ligh'nee) *n.* A genus of 20 species of palmlike plants (Agavaceae), some species are native to tropical America. The stem is straight, crowned by a head of long, narrow, drooping leaves and large clusters of small flowers. They are frequently sold under the name *Dracaena.* The more common species, *C. australis* and *C. indivisa,* are used as houseplants. Sometimes called palm lily.

Corema (koh ree'muh) *n.* A genus of 6 or 7 species of heatherlike shrubs (Empetraceae), some species native to the Americas; the crowberry family. They have simple, crowded, alternate leaves, small purplish flowers, and fleshy fruits. Commonly known as crowberry or broom crowberry.

Coreopsis (koh ree ahp'sihs) *n.* A genus of more than 100 species of mostly herbaceous perennials (Compositae), some species native to the Americas. They usually have opposite, divided, or lobed leaves and gold, yellow, orange, maroon, or red flowers. Several of the American species are used in borders or as container plants for their showy, handsome flowers.

coriander (koh ree an'der) *n.* 1. The common name for the herb *Coriandrum sativum.* The fruit (popularly called coriander seeds) is round and nearly smooth, pleasantly aromatic. It is used for flavoring curries, pastry, etc. The leaves are known as cilantro, used fresh in Mexican and Latin American dishes, as well as in Italian cooking.

Coriaria (koh ree a'ree uh) *n.* A genus of 10 to 30 species of shrubs or small trees (Coriariaceae). They have opposite or whorled leaves, spikes of small greenish flowers, and red, black, or purple fruit. The fruit is poisonous.

corkscrew *n.* A common name for *Euphorbia mammillaris,* a spiny, dwarf, cactuslike succulent. Used in rock gardens or as a specimen plant. All species of *Euphorbia* have poisonous, milky sap.

cork tree *n.* 1. A common name for *Quercus Suber,* the outer bark of which is used for making cork. Also called cork oak. 2. A common name for the genus *Phellodendron,* 10 species of very hardy deciduous trees, some with corky bark.

corkwood *n.* Any of several trees with light or porous wood, such as *Erythrina espertilio, Ochroma pyramidale,* and *Leitneria floridana.*

corm (korm) *n.* In botany, a rounded, thick, solid, fleshy, bulblike subterranean stem, producing leaves and buds on the upper surface and roots from the lower, as in the crocus and gladiolus.

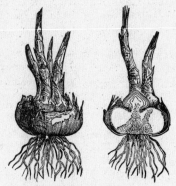

corm of a crocus
entire and crosssection

cormel (kor'mehl) *n.* A smaller, secondary corm produced by an old corm; a bulblet.

corn *n.* 1. The vegetable *Zea mays* in any of its varieties, including sweet corn for table, popcorn, and fodder (for field) corn. 2. The plants that produce corn when growing in the field; the stalks and ears, or the stalks, ears, and seeds after reaping and before threshing, as a field of corn. The plants or stalks are included in the term corn until the seed is separated from the ears. The 3 main types of table corn are yellow, white, and bicolor.

Cornaceae (kor nay'see ee) *n. pl.* A family of 10 genera and 90 species of showy, flowering shrubs or trees. The principal ornamental genera are *Cornus,* the dogwoods, and *Aucuba.* (The best-known species is *A. japonica* 'Variegata', the gold-dust plant.)

cornbind *n.* A common name for bindweed, a species of *Convolvulus.*

cornbottle *n.* A common name for *Centaurea Cyanus.* Also called bluebottle, bachelor's button, or cornflower.

corncob *n.* The elongated, woody, chaff-covered receptacle, which, with the grain embedded in it in rows, constitutes the ear of *Zea mays.*

corn earworm *n.* A moth larva that feeds on developing ears of corn, leaving a brown mush under the husk at the tassel end. It can also attack tomatoes. Many gardeners simply cut off the damaged end of corn before cooking. In severe problems, dabbing mineral oil on emerging tassels may smother the larvae. Repeated sprays of *Bacillus thuringiensis* and releasing trichogramma wasps may also help. Some corn varieties resist infestation; otherwise, traditional insecticides are usually used.

cornel (kor'nuhl) *n.* A common name for species of *Cornus,* the dogwoods.

cornelian cherry (kor neel'yuhn) *n.* A common name for *Cornus mas,* a small tree or shrub with oval leaves, yellow flowers, and edible, dark red fruit. Useful in northern gardens for early spring bloom, fall color, and showy, scarlet fruit.

cornflower *n.* A common name used for any flower growing wild in cornfields, such as the wild poppy; specifically applied to *Centaurea Cyanus.*

corn salad *n.* The common name for *Fedia* or *Valerianella olitoria,* a plant eaten as a salad, found in grain fields in Europe and more recently in America.

cornstalk borers *n. pl.* Several types of moth larvae that bore into the stems and ears of corn, causing reduced production, wilting, broken stems, and/or fallen ears. They also attack other plants including dahlias, gladiolus, beans, peppers, and tomatoes. Difficult to control without using traditional soil insecticides. Repeated applications of *Bacillus thuringiensis* or rotenone and destruction of infested plants may work.

Cornus florida
(dogwood)

Cornus (kor'nuhs) *n.* A genus of about 45 species of lovely, highly valued shrubs and small trees (Cornaceae), some native to the United States. They have simple, entire, usually opposite leaves and are covered in spring with large star-shaped white, greenish-white, or yellow flowers perched like a flock of butterflies on layered branches. They are followed by oval, fleshy, bright red berries that attract birds. *C. florida* (flowering dogwood), native to the eastern United States, is widely planted but is subject to disease. *C. kousa* var. *chinensis* appears to be substantially more disease-resistant. *C. sericea* (*C. stolonifera*), native to North America, is grown for its striking red branches and brilliant scarlet fall color. *C. nuttalli,* native to the Pacific Northwest, is an exquisite woodland tree with showy blossoms that are white, then flushed with pink, but it will not tolerate normal garden watering, fertilizing, and pruning. For best performance, plant it where it has good drainange and leave it alone.

cornute (kor'noot) *a.* Having horns.

Corokia (kor oh'kyuh) *n.* A genus of 4 species of evergreen shrubs (Cornaceae) native to New Zealand. They have intricate zigzag branching patterns, silvery-white new growth, simple, entire, alternate leaves, clusters of starlike yellow flowers, and red or orange berries. Used as a specimen plant in warm-winter gardens or as a container plant.

corolla (kuh rahl′uh) *n.* In botany, the inner set of floral leaves or petals of a flower, within the calyx and immediately surrounding the stamens and pistil. It is delicate in texture and of some color other than green, forming the most conspicuous part of the flower. It is sometimes absent or inconspicuous. It shows an extreme diversity of forms, which are distinguished as either polypetalous (many-petalled) or gamopetalous, as in the morning glory.

corollas of various flowers

corona (kuh roh′nuh) *n., pl.* **coronas**. In botany, a crownlike appendage or series of united appendages on the inner side of a corolla. It often resembles an outgrowth of the perianth, as in the daffodil, or of the staminal circle, as in the milkweed.

Coronilla (kor uh nihl′uh) *n.* A genus of 20 species of mostly hardy shrubs (Leguminosae) the crown vetch. They grow from creeping roots and rhizomes, have odd-numbered, divided leaves and clusters of yellow, white or purple flowers. Grown as ground covers and for erosion control.

coronule (kor′uh nyool′) *n.* In botany, a coronet, or little crown, of a seed; the downy tuft on seeds.

Corozo (kuh roh′soh) *n.* A genus of palms now classified as *Elaeias.*

corpse plant *n.* A common name for the North American saprophyte *Monotropa uniflora;* so called for its pale waxy appearance. Also known as Indian pipe, convulsion root, pinesap, and fitroot (or fitsroot).

Correa (kuh ree′uh) n. A genus of 11 species of tender, winter-flowering shrubs (Rutaceae). They grow to 4 feet, with small, rounded gray-green leaves, densely felted beneath, and tiny white, chartreuse, clear red, pink, or cream-colored fuchsialike flowers. Used as ground covers, on banks or slopes, and as container plants. Commonly known as Australian fuchsia and native fuchsia.

Cortaderia (kor tuh dihr′ee uh) *n.* A genus of about 24 species of vigorous perennial grasses (Gramineae). They grow to 20 feet, with long, narrow, sharply saw-edged leaves and tall stalks topped by creamy, pale tan, or pink feathery plumes. *C. jubata* is a troublesome weed in some mild-winter areas. *C. selloana,* known as pampas grass, is a huge ornamental grown for its tall, feathery, white to pink to purple plumes. Some also have variegated leaves. Used as a lawn ornamental and as a windbreak. Commonly known as pampas grass.

cortex (kor′tehks) *n.* In botany, the cylinder of primary tissue, within the stem of a plant, which extends from the vascular tissue in the center out to the bark, or epidermis. It may function in photosynthesis, food storage, support, and growth of the plant.

cortland *n.* A tangy variety of apple, with red skin and flesh that does not discolor when cut.

Cortusa (kor too′suh) *n.* A genus of 8 species of fairly hardy perennials (Primulaceae). *C. Mathioli* grows to 1 foot, with simple, basal, lobed, long-stemmed leaves and tall clusters of rose or yellow flowers. Used in rock gardens.

Corydalis (kuh rihd′uh lihs) *n.* A genus of 300 species of tender rhizomatous or tuberous perennials (Fumariaceae). They grow to 4 feet, with daintily divided leaves resembling the leaves of bleeding heart or maidenhair fern, and they bear clusters of small spurred yellow flowers. Used in rock gardens, near pools or streams, or in woodland gardens. Useful in moist, shady situations.

Corydalis flower

Corylopsis (kor ih lahp′sihs) *n.* A genus of about 10 species of hardy deciduous shrubs and small trees (Hamamelidaceae). They grow 8 to 10 feet and as wide, with pink new growth maturing into bright green, usually heart-shaped, alternate leaves and pale yellow fragrant flowers that appear before the leaves. Used in shrub borders, at edges of woodland, and in shady locations. Commonly known as winter hazel.

Corylus (kor'ih luhs) *n.* A genus of about 10 species of hardy deciduous shrubs and trees (Betulaceae); the hazelnut. They grow from 10 to 120 feet, with oval, doubly toothed, alternate leaves, catkinlike flowers, and hard-shelled, sweet, edible nuts. Some are grown for their edible nuts, others for ornamental use. Commonly known as filbert, hazel, or hazelnut.

corymb (kor'ihm) *n.* In botany, a short, broad, flat-topped or somewhat convex flower cluster, as in species of the genus *Achillea* (yarrow).

Corynocarpus (kor ihn oh kahr'puhs) *n.* A genus of 4 species of evergreen shrubs and small trees (Corynocarpaceae). *C. laevigata* grows slowly to 50 feet, with big, beautiful, leathery, glossy, oblong dark green leaves, clusters of tiny white flowers, and small, oblong orange fruits that are extremely poisonous if eaten. Used as a container plant, a screen, hedge, or background plant, or in entryways or under overhangs. Commonly known as New Zealand laurel.

Corypha (kor'ih fuh) *n.* A genus of 8 species of very large tropical palms (Palmae). They grow to 80 feet or more, with gigantic, spiny, deeply-divided, fan-shaped leaves on 10-foot-long toothed stems. *C. umbraculifera* has giant 20-foot-long flowers, the largest in the plant kingdom. The trees die after fruiting. Used in the tropics and subtropics as a specimen tree. Also known as talipot palm.

Coryphantha (kor ih fan'thuh) *n.* A genus of 60 species of exceptionally hardy small, round, spiny American cacti (Cactaceae), some of which tolerate temperatures far below 0° F. This genus has been divided into 5 subgenera: *Coryphantha coryphantha, C. Escobaria, C. Glanduligerae, C. Lepidocoryphantha,* and *Coryphantha Pseudocoryphantha.* Grown by collectors.

Cosmos (kahz'muhs) *n.* A genus of about 25 species of self-sowing annuals or perennials (Compositae) native to the Americas. They grow from 2 1/2 to 10 feet with finely cut, bright green opposite leaves and many colors of daisylike flowers that may be single, double, crested or frilled. Used massed in

borders and as a filler among shrubs. They are drought-resistant, and their seeds attract birds.

costmary *n.* A common name for *Chrysanthemum Balsamita,* a coarse, aromatic perennial. It grows to 3 feet, with fragrant leaves and clusters of yellow buttonlike flowers. Traditional in cottage gardens and herb gardens. Also known as alecost, bible leaf, and mint geranium.

Costus (kahs'tuhs) *n.* A genus of 140 species of stout, rhizomatous, tropical perennials (Zingiberaceae). They grow to 10 feet, with spirally arranged leaves on twisted stems and stalks of conelike yellow, red, and white flowers. Used in frost-free gardens. Commonly known as spiral flag.

Cotinus (kaht'uh nuhs) *n.* A genus of 3 species of unusual hardy, woody, deciduous shrubs and trees (Anacardiaceae). *C. coggygria* grows to 25 feet, with roundish, bluish-green leaves that turn yellow to orange red in autumn and with loose clusters of flowers that release dramatic puffs of purple-to-lavender "smoke," followed by long sterile flowers clothed with fuzzy purple hairs. Thrives in difficult situations with poor, rocky soil and little water. Useful as a screen or as a dramatic specimen. The genus is commonly known as smoke tree or smoke bush. *C. coggygria* is commonly known as smoke tree, smoke bush, smoke plant, Venetian sumac, or wig tree.

Cotoneaster (kuh toh'nee as'ter) *n.* A genus of 50 species of woody shrubs and trees (Rosaceae). They grow from a few inches to 20 feet, depending on the species. They have graceful, arching branches, in a fountainlike pattern, with alternate, entire leaves, masses of small pink or white flowers like tiny single roses, and red berries, showy both autumn and winter, that attract birds. Ground cover types are effective erosion control; taller varieties are attractive in the landscape.

cotton seed meal *n.* An organic fertilizer.

cottonweed *n.* A common name for plants of several genera: *Abutilon* and *A. Theophrasti* (Indian mallow), *Anaphalis margaritacea* (pearly everlasting), *Asclepias* (milkweed or butterfly flower), and *Otanthus maritimus.*

cottonwood *n.* A common name for the genus *Populus* (poplar) and, specifically, the hardy North

American species, *P. deltoides,* native from Quebec to Florida and west to Texas. The name refers to the light cottony tuft at the base of the numerous small seeds.

cottonwood, black *n.* A common name for *Populus trichocarpa,* a hardy, slow-growing deciduous tree native to western North America. It grows to 150 to 180 feet at maturity, with furrowed gray bark, heavy limbs, triangular leaves, deep green above and silver below, and drooping catkins that appear before the leaves. Myriads of cottony seeds fall from female trees where male trees are present. Attractive on country properties, away from buildings and water lines; not good in the suburbs because its roots invade water and sewer lines and its large brittle limbs break easily. Also known as Western balsam poplar.

cottonwood, Fremont *n.* A common name for *Populus Fremontii,* a hardy deciduous tree native to California and Arizona. It grows 40 to 60 feet, with broad, triangular, coarsely toothed, glossy yellow-green leaves that turn bright lemon yellow and remain on the tree for a long time and with catkins that appear before the leaves. Plant male trees only; female trees are very messy. Best on country places away from water and sewer lines. Also known as Western cottonwood.

cottonwood, lanceleaf *n.* A common name for *Populus acuminata,* a hardy deciduous tree. It grows to 60 feet with egg-shaped, sharply-pointed glossy green leaves, paler beneath. Best on country places away from water and sewer lines.

cottonwood, narrowleaf *n.* A common name for *Populus angustifolia,* a hardy deciduous tree. It grows to 60 feet, with narrow, glossy dark green leaves, paler beneath. Best on country places away from water and sewer lines.

Cotula (kaht'yuh luh) *n.* A genus of about 60 species of fairly hardy aromatic annuals, biennials, and perennials (Compositae). *C. squalida* grows to a few inches high with soft, hairy, bronzy-green fernlike leaves and clusters of yellow buttonlike flowers. Used as a small-scale ground cover. Commonly known as New Zealand brass buttons.

cotyledon (kaht ih lee'duhn) *n.* In seed plants and ferns, the first leaf or pair or whorl of leaves to appear after sprouting; a seed leaf.

Couropita (koor ahp'ih tuh) *n.* A genus of 20 species of subtropical and tropical trees (Lecythidaceae). *C. guianensis* grows to 50 feet, with simple, alternate leaves, 3-foot-long spikes rising from the trunk or large branches with large, showy, fruit-scented red or yellow flowers, and reddish-brown fruits, 8 inches in diameter, filled with foul-smelling pulp. Grown in subtropical and tropical gardens as a novelty. *C. guianensis* is commonly known as cannonball tree.

coventry bell *n.* A common name for plants of 2 genera: *Campanula Medium* (canterbury bell) and *Anemone pulsatilla* (pasqueflower).

cover crop *n.* Any of various plants, often nitrogen fixing, which are planted with, or in rotation with, edible crops to increase nitrogen, stabilize soil, attract beneficial insects, or to be used as green manure.

cowherb *n.* A common name for *Vaccaria pyramidata,* a weed in crop fields; naturalized in North America. Also known as dairy pink.

cow parsnip *n.* A common name for the genus *Heracleum,* tall biennial and perennial plants native to Eurasia and North America. They have large, deeply cut, toothed leaves and umbrella-shaped clusters of small green, pink, yellow, or white flowers. An impressively large plant, it is usually seen growing wild but is occasionally used in wild gardens or as a specimen plant for its bold effect. The foliage may cause a skin rash.

cowslip *n.* A common name for plants of several genera: *Primula veris, Caltha palustris* (marsh marigold), the genus *Dodacatheon* (American cowslip or shooting star), and *Mertensia virginica* (Virginia cowslip or Virginia bluebells).

crab apple *n.* 1. A common name for the small, tart, and somewhat astringent apples of the crab apple tree. 2. The tree producing the fruit, of the genus *Malus.* Many crab apples are flowering varieties widely grown in the northeastern United States for their masses of white or pink spring blossoms. Used as a lawn tree and street tree. Also called flowering crab and crab tree.

crab tree *n.* The tree that bears the crabs, or crab apples.

crack weeder *n*. A hooked blade for removing grass and weeds growing between slabs, bricks, and stones.

Crambe (kram′bee) *n*. A genus of 20 species of annuals and perennials (Cruciferae). They grow from 3 to 77 feet, depending on the species, with mostly thick, fleshy, large leaves and spikes or clusters of manyy small white flowers. *C. cordifolia* is used in the back of borders. The genus is commonly known as sea kale, a name also used for *C. maritima*.

cranberry *n*. 1. The fruit of several species of *Vaccinium*. The berry, when ripe, is round and dark red and measures little more than 1/4 inch in diameter. The berries make a sauce of fine flavor, and they are much used for tarts. The cranberry grows wild in marshy areas of the eastern United States and is cultivated commercially, especially in Massachusetts. The crowberry, *V. Vitis-Idaea*, is sometimes called the mountain cranberry.

cranberry

cranberry bean *n*. An heirloom variety of bean grown for drying. Its name comes from its deep red markings. Some varieties are also used as shell beans, but they are prized as one of the finest beans for baking. Also called Vermont cranberry bean.

cranberry bush *n*. A common name for several species of *Viburnum*, specifically *V. Opulus* and *V. trilobum*. *V. trilobum*, native to North America, is commonly known as cranberry tree, highbush cranberry, tree cranberry, crampbark, grouseberry, squawbush, summerberry, and pimbina.

cranberry tree *n*. The high or bush cranberry, *Viburnum Opulus*, a shrub of North America and Europe, bearing soft, red, round, acrid berries. The cultivated form, with larger sterile flowers, is known as the snowball or the Guelder rose.

cranesbill *n*. A common name for *Geranium*, a genus of more than 300 species of herbaceous perennials or annuals—rarely subshrubs—(Geraniaceae). They have opposite, lobed leaves, white, pink, rose, blue, or purple flowers, and fruit with long tails, which become spirally twisted. The name derives from the long beak of the fruit, resembling a crane's bill.

crape jasmine (krayp) *n*. A common name for *Tabernaemontana divaricata*, a tropical shrub. It grows to 8 feet or more, with leaves in unequal pairs and with waxy-white flowers that release their fragrance at night. Used in frost-free gardens. Also known as crape gardenia, pinwheel flower, East Indian rosebay, broadleaved rosebay, flowers-of-love, and Adam's apple.

Crassula (kras′yuh luh) *n*. A genus of 300 species of succulent, mostly perennial, plants and shrubs. They have thick, fleshy, opposite leaves and clusters of small white, yellow, or red flowers. Extremely drought-tolerant, they are excellent container plants; used as hedges in mild climates, as houseplants anywhere. *C. argentea* is the popular jade plant or money tree.

Crassulaceae (kras yuh lay′see ee) *n. pl.* A family of about 30 genera and 1,500 species of succulents. The ornamental genera include *Aeonium, Crassula, Dudleya, Echeveria, Kalahchoe, Sedum,* and *Sempervivum*.

Crataegus (kruh tee′guhs) *n*. A genus of approximately 1,000 proposed species of hardy, enthusiastically thorny shrubs and small trees (Rosaceae), many native to North America. They grow from 5 to 40 feet, depending on the species, with alternate leaves, clusters of small white, pink, or red spring- or summer-blooming flowers that attract bees, and showy, bright red winter fruit that attracts birds. Used as street or lawn trees, in informal hedges, and in hedgerows. Commonly known as hawthorn, thorn, red haw, and thorn apple.

crazyweed *n*. A common name for the genus *Oxytropis*. (See **locoweed**.)

creamcups *n.* A common name for *Platystemon californicus,* a pretty poppylike, spring-blooming wildflower native to western North America. It grows to 1 foot and has long, narrow leaves and small cream-colored or yellow flowers. Used in wild gardens or meadow gardens.

creeper *n.* A plant that grows upon the surface of the ground or any other surface, such as a wall or fence, sending out rootlets from the stem, such as ivy, *Hedera;* Virginia creeper, *Parthenocissus quinquefolia;* and the trumpet creeper, *Campsis radicans.*

creeping bent grass *n.* (See **Agrotis.**)

creeping Charlie *n.* A common name for plants of several genera: *Glechoma hederacea* (ground ivy); *Lysimachia Nummularia* (creeping Jennie or moneywort); *Malva sylvestris* (mallow); *Pilea nummulariifolia;* and *Plectranthus* (Swedish ivy).

creeping Jennie *n.* A common name for *Lysimachia Nummularia,* so called from its round leaves. It is a creeping perennial, with long runners that root at the joints, small round leaves, and bright yellow flowers. Used as a small-scale ground cover, near streams, or in hanging baskets. Also called moneywort and herb twopence. 2. A common name for plants of several other genera, including *Echinocystus lobata* (wild cucumber); *Lycopodium clavatum, L. complanatum,* and *L. obscurum* (all mosses known as ground pine); and *Convolvulus arvensis* (field bindweed).

creeping mint *n.* A common name *Meehania cordata,* a fairly hardy, low-growing perennial. It grows to a few inches, spreads by stolons, and has heart-shaped, wrinkled, opposite leaves and spikes of hairy lavender or lilac flowers. Used as a ground cover in shade. Also known as Meehan's mint.

creep soil *n.* The downward slow irregular mass movement of sloping soil.

crenate and doubly crenate leaves

crenate (kree'nayt) *a.* In botany, having the margin cut into even and rounded notches or scallops, as a leaf. When the scallops have smaller ones upon them, the leaf is said to be doubly crenate.

creosote bush (kree'uh soht) *n.* A common name for *Larrea,* tender evergreen North American shrubs. (See **Larrea.**) **Crepis** (kree'pihs) *n.* A genus of about 200 species of annuals, biennials, and perennials (Compositae), some native to North America. Few are grown ornamentally. Commonly known as hawk's-beard.

Crescentia (kruh sehn'shee uh) *n.* A genus of a single species, *C. Cujete* (Bignoniaceae), a tropical tree native to the Americas. It is a broad, spreading tree to 40 feet, with clusters of 6-inch-long leaves, yellow flowers with red or purple veins, and smooth, hard-shelled, 12-inch-long fruit resembling a gourd. Grown in tropical gardens and for the fruit, which is widely used for utensils. Commonly known as calabash or calabash tree.

cress *n.* Watercress, or *Nasturtium officinale,* is used as a salad; the leaves have a moderately pungent taste. It grows on the brinks of streams and in moist grounds. The American watercress is *Cardamine rotundiflora.*

cricket *n.* A small leaping insect that makes a chirping sound by rubbing together its forewings. Most crickets are considered beneficial insects, which only occasionally cause plant damage. (See **mole cricket** for pests of lawns.)

Crinodendron (krigh noh dehn'druhn) *n.* A genus of 3 species of tender trees (Elaeocarpaceae). *C. patagua* grows to 25 feet or more, with simple, toothed dark green leaves, gray-green beneath, masses of waxy-white bell-shaped flowers resembling lilies-of-the valley, and attractive red-and-cream seed capsules. Used as lawn trees in mild-winter climates; useful in moist soils. *C. patagua* is commonly known as lily-of-the-valley tree.

Crinum (krigh'nuhm) *n.* A genus of about 130 species of large tender bulbs (Amaryllidaceae). They grow from 1 to 3 feet, depending on the species, with strap-shaped or sword-shaped leaves and clusters of large, fragrant, lily-shaped white, pink, or red flowers on tall, leafless stalks. Grown in mild-climate gardens, though some species may be planted out in protected spots as far north as New York; good in pots or greenhouses anywhere. Commonly known as crinum lily or spider lily.

Crinum
(spider lily)

crispate (krih'spayt) *a*. Curled or rippled at the margin, as the leaves of *Pittosporum eugenioides*. Also crisped.

Crithmum (krihth'muhm) *n*. A genus of 1 species, *C. maritimum* (Umbelliferae), a hardy coastal perennial. It grows from 1 to 2 feet, with leaves divided into long, fleshy leaflets and with rounded clusters of very small white or yellow flowers. Occasionally used as an ornamental or a salad plant. Commonly known as samfire.

Crocosmia (kroh kohz'mee uh) *n*. A genus of 5 species of tender bulbs (Iridaceae). They grow to 3 to 4, feet with sword-shaped leaves in clumps from the base and spikes with branched stems of bright orange, red, or yellow flowers. Good for naturalizing on slopes or for splashes of garden color in mild winter climates. Excellent as a cut flower. Formerly classified as *Montbretia*, then *Tritonia*, both of which are now used as common names, though montbretia is most frequently used.

Crocus (kroh'kuhs) *n*. 1. A genus of 75 to 80 species of beautiful, brightly colored hardy bulbs (Iridaceae). They grow from fibrous-coated corms, with cup-shaped white, cream, yellow, gold, lavender, and purple flowers, sometimes striped, that appear before the grasslike leaves. Some species bloom in spring, others in fall. The spring-blooming varieties are very widely planted, as they are among the earliest of spring flowers, even blooming through snow. *C. sativus* yields saffron, the dried orange stigma of the flowers, which is used to color and flavor food. 2. A plant of the genus *Crocus*.

crocus, autumn *n*. A common name for *Colchicum* (Liliaceae), a genus of between 60 and 70 species of autumn-blooming perennial plants that grow from bulbs (corms). They have strap-shaped leaves, generally produced in spring, and crocuslike flowers appearing in the autumn. The most familiar is *C. autumnale,* the meadow saffron, which has pale lilac crocuslike flowers. It will bloom on a windowsill without being planted. The corms are poisonous if eaten. Also known as fall crocus, mysteria, and wonder bulb.

crocus, celandine (sehl'an deen) *n*. A common name for *Crocus Korolhowii*, a hardy, fibrous, flattened bulb (corm). It has few leaves and greenish-yellow starlike flowers, densely speckled and often veined. Used in rock gardens.

crocus, Chilean *n*. A common name *for Tecophilaea cyanocrocus,* a tender, fibrous-coated bulb (corm). It grows to 6 inches, with 2 to 3 long, narrow, bright green leaves and deep blue bell-shaped flowers with a white throat.

crocus, Dutch *n*. A common name for *Crocus vernus,* a hardy, fibrous-coated bulb (corm). This is the familiar crocus of early spring, the most widely planted of all crocus. It grows to 6 inches, with narrow, grasslike leaves that appear after the white, yellow, lavender, or purple flowers, which are sometimes feathered, penciled, striped, or streaked. Used in drifts, in pots, and forced for winter bloom.

crocus, iris-flowered *n*. A common name for *Crocus byzantinus*, a hardy, fibrous-coated bulb (corm). It has 2 to 4 leaves; its flowers have white inner segments suffused with lilac and deep purple outer segments. Thrives in the shade and rich organic soil of woodland gardens.

crocus, saffron (saf'ruhn) *n*. A common name for *Crocus sativus,* a hardy, fibrous-coated, flattened bulb (corm). It has many leaves and large fragrant flowers with orange-red stigmas. *C. sativus* yields saffron, the dried orange stigma of the flowers, which is used to color and flavor food. Some sources report that it takes 4,000 stigmas to make 1

saffron crocus

ounce of saffron, which may explain why it is so costly. Grown mostly as a curiosity in the garden; it is more interesting than showy.

crocus, Scotch *n.* A common name for *Crocus biflorus,* a hardy bulb (corm). It blooms in late winter and has white to pale purple flowers.

crocus, tropical *n.* A common name for *Kaempferii rotunda,* a tropical, often stemless, rhizomatous perennial. It grows to 18 inches, with 2 erect leaves, variegated above and purple beneath, and large white flowers, with a lilac lip, that appear before the leaves. Used in mild-climate gardens outdoors, in pots in greenhouses anywhere. Also known as Resurrection lily.

crocus, wild *n.* A common name for a *Anemone nuttalliana,* a hardy perennial native to western North America. It has basal, hand-shaped leaves that appear before the flowers and large, solitary violet-blue flowers, hairy on the outside, and 2 to 3 inches across. Used in wild gardens, rock gardens, and woodland gardens. Also known as pasqueflower, lion's-beard, prairie smoke, and hartshorn plant.

crookneck squash *n.* A variety of yellow summer squash characterized by a long, thin, curving top.

cross *v.* In botany, to produce a hybrid plant by cross-fertilizing individuals of different varieties or species. 2. *n.* A hybrid produced by such cross-fertilization.

Crossandra (krahs an′druh) *n.* A genus of 50 species of tropical flowers or shrubs (Acanthaceae). *C. infundibuliformis* grows to 18 inches, with glossy, very dark green gardenialike leaves and short, full spikes of scarlet-orange or coral-orange flowers. Used most often as a houseplant or grown in greenhouses. The genus is commonly known as firecracker flower.

cross-fertilization *n.* In botany, the fertilization of the ovules of 1 flower by the pollen of another, between plants of the same species, or between individuals of different species, resulting in the production of a hybrid.

cross vine *n.* 1. A common name for *Bignonia capreolata,* a fairly hardy, evergreen climbing woody vine native to the eastern United States. It climbs by tendrils to 50 feet, with leaves divided into long, entire leaflets, yellow or red trumpet-shaped flowers, and seed capsules 7 inches long. Useful to cover walls and in shady, moist situations. Also known as quarter vine and trumpet flower. 2. A common name for *Ampelopsis arborea,* a hardy, bushy, deciduous woody vine native to the eastern United States. It has doubly divided leaves with deeply notched leaflets, loose clusters of greenish flowers, and small, pungent, dark purple berries. Used to cover walls and arbors. Also known as pepper vine. 3. A common name for *Campsis radicans,* a fast-growing, self-clinging, hardy deciduous woody vine native to the eastern United States. It climbs by aerial rootlets to 40 feet or more, with leaves divided into toothed leaflets and clusters of large orange and scarlet flowers 3 inches long and 2 inches wide. Used as a quick summer screen. Also known as trumpet creeper, common trumpet creeper, trumpet vine, cowitch or cowage, and trumpet honeysuckle.

crosswort *n.* A common name for the genus *Crucianella,* 30 or more species of fairly hardy annuals or perennials (Rubiaceae). They grow to 18 inches, with whorls of lower leaves and opposite upper leaves and spikes or clusters of small white, rosy, or blue funnel-shaped flowers. Used in partially shaded sections of rock gardens.

Crotalaria (kroh tuh lar′ee uh) *n.* A genus of more than 500 species of evergreen flowers and shrubs (Leguminosae). *C. agatiflora* is an evergreen shrub that grows quickly to 12 feet and as wide, with pleasing gray-green leaves divided into 3 leaflets and unique flowers that resemble chartreuse birds alight on 14-inch spikes. Usually blooms in summer or fall, but in frost-free gardens may bloom 10 months of the year. Grown for its extraordinary flowers. *C. agatiflora* is commonly known as canary-bird bush. The genus *Crotalaria* is commonly known as rattlebush.

crowbar *n.* A long bar of iron or steel, usually wedge-shaped at 1 end; used to pry and remove large rocks.

crowberry *n.* 1. A common name for the genus *Empetrum. E. nigrum* is a very hardy, heathlike evergreen shrublet native to North America, from the Arctic to New England, Minnesota, and northern California. It is low-growing, with spreading branchlets with tiny oblong leaves, small green or purple flowers, and edible black berries. *E. nigrum* is also known as black crowberry, crake berry, curlew berry, and monox. 2. Also used as a common name for *Arctostaphylos uva-ursa* (bearberry), *Vaccinium macrocarpon* (American cranberry), and *V. Myrtillus* (whortleberry or bilberry).

crown *n*. 1. Same as corona. 2. The point at the base of a plant where stem and root meet. 3. The part of a rhizome containing a large bud and suitable for propagation.

crownbeard *n*. A common name for the genus *Verbesina*, 200 species of flowers, shrubs, and trees native to the Americas. They grow from 3 feet to 9 feet, depending on the species, with mostly long, narrow leaves and yellow daisylike flowers. *V. encelioides* is commonly known as golden crownbeard and butter daisy.

crown daisy *n*. A common name for *Crysanthemum coronarium*, a stout, branched annual. It grows to 4 feet, with leaves divided into sharply toothed segments and masses of yellow or yellowish white edible flowers. Also known as garland chrysanthemum.

crown imperial *n*. A common name for *Fritillaria imperialis*, a hardy bulb. It grows to 3 or 4 feet, with broad, glossy leaves and very unusual long, drooping orange, red, or yellow flowers in clusters at the top of a tall stem topped by a crown of leaves. The bulbs and plants, though ornamental, are notoriously ill-smelling (don't plant them near paths or under windows). Used in borders or in containers.

crown-of-thorns *n*. A common name for *Euphorbia Milii*, a spiny, climbing subtropical shrub. It has stems to 4 feet, with roundish, thin, light green leaves, mostly at the tips of branches, and clustered pairs of bright red flowers. Hybrids may have flowers in yellow, orange, or pink. Used a specimen shrub in warm climates, as an indoor/outdoor plant elsewhere. Also known as Christ plant and Christ's thorn.

crown rot *n*. A fungal disease usually caused by planting too deep, poor soil drainage, or excess moisture around the plant base. It kills many young plants, especially trees. The best solution is to improve drainage or to plant species adapted to wet conditions.

crown vetch (vehch) *n*. A common name for *Coronilla varia*, a hardy, sprawling, tenacious ground cover, useful for controlling erosion. It grows to 2 feet, with leaves divided into many oval leaflets and clusters of lavender-pink flowers. Too invasive for cultivated areas, but excellent on banks and slopes.

Crucianella (kroo'shuh nehl'uh) *n*. A genus of 30 or more species of fairly hardy annuals or perennials (Rubiaceae). Used in partially shaded sections of rock gardens. Commonly known as crosswort.

cruciate flower

cruciate (kroo'shee ayt) *a*. Having leaves or flowers in the form of a cross with equal arms, as certain members of the mustard family.

crucifer (kroo'sih fer) *n*. A plant of the family Cruciferae.

Cruciferae (kroo sihf'er ee) *n*. A family of about 350 genera and 3,200 species of pungent or acrid plants; the mustard family. It includes many edible species including cabbage, broccoli, cauliflower, kale, kohlrabi, turnips, radish, and rutabaga. The edible genera are *Brassica* (cabbage and mustard), *Lepidium* (cress), *Nasturtium* (watercress), *Raphanus* (radish), *Romarmoracia* (horseradish), and *Wasabia* (Japanese horseradish or *wasabe*). The ornamental genera are *Aethionema* (stonecress), *Alyssoides* (bladderpod), *Alyssum* (madwort), *Arabis* (rock cress), *Aubrieta, Aurinia, Brassica* (ornamental kale), *Cardamine, Cheiranthes* (wallflower), *Crambe* (colewort), *Diplotaxis* (rocket), *Draba, Erysimum* (wallflower or blister cress), *Hesperis* (rocket), *Iberis* (candytuft), *Lobularia, Lunaria* (honesty), and *Matthiola* (stock).

crumb structures *n*. The porous granualr structure in soil.

crust *n*. A thin, hard, dry layer of soil that forms on the surface of many soils when they are exposed to excessive heat.

crustaceous (kuhs tay'shuhs) *a*. Having a hard, brittle texture.

Cryptanthus (krihp tan′thuhs) *n.* A genus of about species of terrestrial Brazilian bromeliads (Bromeliaceae). *C. Zonatus* is low-growing, to 18 inches wide, with stiff, wavy brownish-red leaves banded crosswise with green, brown, or white markings. They are grown for their foliage as houseplants or outdoors in warm climates. The genus is commonly known as earth-star; *C. zonatus* is commonly known as zebra plant.

Cryptocoryne (krihp′tuh kor′uh nee) *n.* A genus of 50 species of tropical water plants (Araceae). They have narrow, bladelike simple leaves, the length of which is determined by the depth of the water. Used in aquariums and in water gardens. Commonly known as water-trumpet.

cryptogam (krihp′tuh gam) *n.* A plant, such as a fern, which reproduces by means of spores rather than seeds.

Cryptogramma (krihp′tuh gram′uh) *n.* A genus of 4 species of hardy alpine and boreal ferns (Polypodiaceae). *Cryptogramma crispa* is a small alpine fern with finely divided leaves resembling parsley. Also called European parsley fern and mountain parsley fern. *Cryptogramma* is commonly known as rock brake.

Cryptolaemus beetle (krihp tuh lee′muhs) *n.* A beneficial insect, which is a close relative of the lady beetle. The adults and larvae feed on mealybugs and sometimes aphids. They are most effective in warm, moist weather. The adults are sold through the mail. Also known as mealybug destroyer.

Cryptomeria (krihp tuh mer′ee uh) *n.* A genus of 1 species, *Cryptomeria japonica,* a fast-growing coniferous tree to 150 feet, with soft, needlelike leaves and small, round, reddish-brown cones. The leaves turn red with cold weather. Used as a sentinel tree; grown in groves in Japanese gardens. The dwarf varieties are attractive in containers.

Cryptostegia (krihp tuh stee′jee uh) *n.* A genus of 3 species of vigorous tropical woody vines (Asclepiadaceae). They have opposite, simple leaves and clusters of trumpet-shaped lilac-purple or reddish-purple flowers. Grown in warm climate gardens. Commonly known as rubber vine.

Ctenitis (tehn igh′tihs) *n.* A genus of 150 species of medium-to-large subtropical and tropical ferns

(Polypodiaceae). They have finely cut 24-to-30-inch long fronds, broad at the base. Used for tropical effects in warm climate gardens, in containers, or greenhouses.

Cubanelle (kyoo buh nehl′) *n.* An early-maturing sweet pepper that is bright yellow, turning to deep orange when ripe; an especially good frying pepper.

cucumber *n.* The common name for the *Cucumis sativus,* a popular vining garden vegetable. It has been cultivated for more than 2,000 years. Cucumbers grow in nearly every part of the United States. Seeds of "burpless" and smaller pickling varieties are also readily available.

cucumber beetle *n.* A small greenish-white beetle with black spots or stripes. It feeds on all parts of cucumber, cantaloupe, and melon plants as well as on flowers, including roses and dahlias. It transmits bacterial wilt and cucumber mosaic. Insecticides, including rotenone and pyrethrins, and a good garden cleanup are effective controls.

cucumber root *n.* A common name for *Medeola virginica,* a hardy perennial native to eastern North America, from Nova Scotia to Florida. It grows from an edible rhizome (which tastes like cucumber) to 30 inches, with whorled leaves and clusters of a few dark purple flowers. Also known as Indian cucumber root.

cucumber tree *n.* A common name for any of several American magnolias, especially *M. acuminata,* fairly hardy trees and shrubs. *M. acuminata* is a deciduous tree that grows to 100 feet, with large 10-inch-long leaves, furry beneath, 3-inch-long green or yellow flowers, and 4-inch-long purplish-red fruit.

Cucurbita (kyoo ker′bih tuh) *n.* A genus of more than 20 species of annual or perennial vines (Cucurbitaceae). They are sprawling plants, with simple but variously lobed leaves, yellow flowers, and fleshy, generally very large, fruits. The genus includes pumpkins, squashes, and gourds. Widely grown for their fruit summer vegetable gardens in North America.

Cucurbitaceae (kyoo ker bih tay′see ee) *n. pl.* A family of 114 genera and 500 species of plants, vines, and shrubs. The cultivated genera are *Cucur-*

bita (pumpkins and squash), *Cucumis* (cucumbers and melons), *Citrullus* (watermelon), *Sechium* (chayote), *Luffa* (vegetable sponge), and *Momordica* (bitter melon). Commonly known as the gourd family.

Cudrania (kuh dray'nee uh) *n.* A genus of 5 species of spiny, hardy vines, shrubs, and trees (Moraceae). *C. tricuspidata* is a small tree to 25 feet, with slender thorns, oval leaves, sometimes 3-lobed at the tip, and small, round, edible red fruit. Used for hedges.

cudweed *n.* The common name for species of *Gnaphalium.* The ornamental species have silky or woolly foliage and spikes or clusters of white or yellow flowers. Also called chafeweed or everlasting. Flowers used in dried arrangements. (See also **sea cudweed.**)

cullion (kuhl'yum) *n.* An orchid.

culm (kuhlm) *n.* In botany, the jointed and usually hollow stem of grasses. It is in most cases herbaceous but is woody in the bamboo and some other stout species. The term is also sometimes applied to the solid, jointless stems of sedges.

cultigen (kuhl'tih jehn) *n.* A cultivated plant or group of specific rank for which a wild ancestor is unknown, as in *Zea Mays* (maize).

cultivar (kuhl'tih var) *n.* A horticultural variety, strain, or race that has originated and persisted under cultivation. Cultivars are given a name, usually distinguished by the use of single quotation marks, as in *Zinnia elegans* 'Tom Thumb'.

cultivation *n.* 1. The act or practice of tilling land and preparing it for crops; the agricultural management of land; husbandry in general. 2. The act or process of producing by tillage; as the cultivation of corn or grass. 3. The use of a cultivator upon growing crops.

cultivator *n.* Any of various pronged or bladed long- or short-handled implements pushed or pulled between rows of plants to loosen soil and destroy weeds.

cumin (kuhm'uhn) *n.* 1. A fennellike plant, *Cuminum Cyminum* (Umbelliferae). It is an annual, cultivated for its seed. 2. The fruit of this plant, commonly called cumin seed, is an aromatic used in curries and meat dishes. Also spelled cummin.

Cuminum (koo'mihn uhm) *n.* A genus of 1 species of annual herb, *C. Cyminum* (Umbelliferae). It has finely cut leaves, umbrella-shaped clusters of small rose or white flowers, and aromatic seeds, which provide the culinary flavoring cumin. Commonly known as cumin.

Cunninghamia (kuhn ihng ham'ee uh) *n.* A genus of 3 species of evergreen coniferous trees (Taxodiaceae); the China fir. They have stout, heavy trunks and stiff, pungent, narrow, pointed leaves arranged in spirals. The wood of the Chinese species, *C. lanceolata,* is used for making tea chests.

Cunonia (kyoo noh'nee uh) *n.* A genus of 17 species of trees or shrubs (Cunoniaceae). They have wine-red twigs, opposite, compound leaves, divided into an odd number of leaflets, and dense, spiky clusters of small white flowers in late summer. They are excellent plants for large containers. *C. capensis* is commonly known as African red alder.

Cunonia capensis
(African red elder)

cup-and-saucer *n.* 1. A common name for *Campanula medium,* an herbaceous biennial with blue, pink, or white flowers. 2. Cup-and-saucer vine is a common name for *Cobea scandens,* a tender perennial vine, grown as an annual, with white, violet, or rose-purple flowers.

cup fern *n.* A common name for the genus *Dennstaedtia* (Polypodiaceae), a genus of about 70 species of mostly tropical and subtropical ferns, 1 species of which, *D. punctilobula,* is native to eastern North

America. It has creeping rhizomes and fragrant, 2 1/2-foot-long, pale green fronds; used in woodland or wild gardens. Also known as hay-scented fern.

cupflower *n.* A common name for the genus *Nierembergia,* grown as perennials in borders and rock gardens or as container plants for their showy violet, blue, or white flowers.

Cuphea (kyoo'fee uh) *n.* A genus of about 250 species of herbaceous flowers or small shrubs (Lythraceae). Many have bright-colored flowers, and one, *C. ignea,* is grown as an annual in warm climates or as a houseplant under the name of firecracker plant or cigar flower.

cupid's-dart *n.* A common name for the genus *Catananche,* specifically *C. caerulea,* a perennial with long, narrow leaves and blue, white, or blue-and-white flowers. Used in borders and as an everlasting.

cup-of-gold *n.* A common name for *Solandra guttata,* a woody, heavy tropical vine with large, golden, chalice-shaped flowers that are fragrant at night. Grown in subtropical or tropical climates to cover walls or arbors, or in greenhouses. Also called goldcup or trumpet vine.

cup plant *n.* A common name for *Silphium perfoliatum,* a tall, stout perennial flower (Compositae) native to eastern North America. It has large, coarsely toothed leaves, the upper pairs forming a cup-like cavity; the flowers are large and yellow.

Cupressus (kyoo prehs'uhs) *n.* A genus of 22 species of coniferous trees having small, scalelike, pointed leaves, as in the junipers. The cones are formed of a small number of woody scales, with several small angular seeds to each scale. The common cypress of Europe is *C. sempervirens,* also known as Italian cypress. Useful as a tall, vertical, dark green accent in the landscape, or as a hedge or windbreak, or to line a long driveway. Commonly known as cypress.

cupule (kyoo'pyool) *n.* In botany, a cup-shaped involucre, occurring especially in the oak, beech, chestnut, and hazel, formed by fused bracts.

Curculigo (ker kyool' ih goh) *n.* A genus of 14 or 15 species of tropical stemless plants (Hypoxidaceae). They have long, pleated leaves and dense heads of spikes of small yellow flowers. Grown outdoors in warm climates or in greenhouses as a foliage plant. *C. capitulata* is commonly known as palm grass.

curculio (ker kyoo'lee oh) *n.* Any of various weevils that feed on a variety of fruit and nuts. The adults eat the leaves and flowers and lay their eggs in the fruit, leaving a small crescent-shaped scar. The fruit becomes misshapened and often falls. The larvae eat the fruit. Difficult to control without preventative insecticide sprays. Cleaning up dropped fruit helps.

Curcuma (ker'kyuh muh) *n.* A genus of more than 65 species of robust rhizomatous perennials (Zingiberaceae). *C. Zedoaria,* commonly known as zedoary, has perennial tuberous roots, leaves 2 feet long and 6 inches wide with a purple or chocolate midrib, green bracts, a white calyx, bright yellow flowers, and a terminal purple tuft; it is grown ornamentally. *C. domestica* yields turmeric, a mildly aromatic ingredient used in curry powder. It is grown outdoors in warm climates, in greenhouses anywhere. The genus is commonly known as hidden lily.

currant *n.* 1. A very small kind of raisin or dried grape, imported chiefly from Zante and Cephalonia, and used in cookery. 2. The small, round fruit (a berry) of several species of *Ribes* (Saxifragaceae); the plant producing this fruit. The red currant is *R. rubrum;* the wild black currant, *R. americanum.* The red currant, sharply but pleasantly acid, is much used to make jelly and jam. The black currant, although slightly musky and bitter, makes an agreeable jam.

curry plant *n.* The herb *Helichrysum angustifolium,* so called for pungent scent of its gray-green leaves, but of no real value as a flavoring.

Curtonus (ker tohn'uhs) *n.* A genus of 1 species, *C. paniculatus* (Iridaceae), a corm that produces sword-shaped leaves and a stout, many-flowered panicle of red and yellow flowers.

Cuscuta (kuhs kyoo'tuh) *n.* A genus of widely distributed, slender, leafless, yellow- or orange-colored twining parasitic plants (Convolvulaceae); the dodders. Some are noxious weeds. (See **dodder.**)

Cuscuta
(dodder)

cushaw (koo′shah) *n.* A large, pale green winter squash with darker green stripes. It has a light colored flesh, good for pies when mature or for eating young as a summer squash.

cusp *n.* In botany, a sharp, rigid point.

cuspidate (kuhs′pih dayt) *a.* Terminating in a point, as cuspidate leaves (leaves tipped with a sharp, rigid point or spine, as in thistles). Also cuspidated.

custard apple *n.* The fruit of *Annona reticulata,* a native of the West Indies but cultivated in all tropical countries. It is a large, roundish, dark brown fruit with soft, custardlike flesh. 2. A name sometimes used to describe the cherimoyar.

cut-and-come-again *n.* 1. Any plant, ordinarily a summer annual, that can be cut or sheared after the first flush of bloom and that will bloom again, such as sweet alyssum, pansy, and petunia. 2. Specifically, ten-week stock (Matthiola). *a.* Said of flowers that continue to bloom when blossoms are removed or cut.

cut-and-hold shears *n. pl.* Any of various shears, including scissors, pruners, and loppers, designed to hold a newly cut stem or branch.

cut back *v.* To prune.

cut flowers *n.* Flowers used for ornament, generally indoors, cut at the stem from the rest of the plant, and displayed, usually with other flowers, in a water-filled vase.

Cuthbertia (kuhth ber′tyuh) *n.* A small genus of 3 species of low-growing perennials (Commelinaceae) native to the southeastern United States. They have alternate leaves and small, drooping, bright rose or pink flowers. Grow well in sand and in coastal regions.

cutting *n.* A piece cut off; a slip. Specifically, a small shoot or branch cut from a plant and placed in water, soil, or in some planting medium, to root and form a new plant.

cutting blades *n. pl.* The parts of a lawn mower that trim the grass.

cutting line *n.* The part of a string trimmer, usually monofilament line, that trims grass and weeds.

cuttings *n.pl.* Pieces of stems, leaves, or roots cut from 1 plant and placed in a rooting medium (soil or water) to grow a new plant. (See **cutting**.)

cutworm *n.* A night-feeding moth larva that lives in the ground during the day. It chews at the base of a variety of tender plants, including vegetable seedlings (causing them to fall over like small timbers) and turf grass. Protective collars around the base of seedlings, parasitic nematodes, or soil applications of traditional insecticides are effective controls. *Bacillus thuringiensis* sometimes works.

cutworm

Cyanotis (sigh uh noh′tihs) *n.* A genus of 40 to 50 species of creeping, evergreen perennials (Commelinaceae). They have alternate, sheathing leaves and small, 3-petaled blue or red flowers. They are grown primarily as houseplants. *C. kewensis* is commonly known as teddy bear, and *C. somaliensis* is commonly known as pussy ears.

Cyathea (sigh ath′ee uh) *n.* A genus of about 110 species of tropical and subtropical slender, evergreen tree ferns (Cyatheaceae). Some have short stems; others have stems that reach a height of 40 or 50 feet. The stems are crowned with a beautiful head of large fronds. Used as specimens in greenhouses or grown outdoors in warm winter climates. Commonly known as tree fern. The Australian tree fern, formerly *C. cooperi,* is now classified as *Sphaeropteris cooperi.*

Cyatheaceae (sigh ath ee ay'see ee) *n.* A family of 8 genera and and 650 species of tropical and subtropical ferns with distinct trunks or erect stems; the tree-fern family. Most have large, striking fronds and a treelike trunk.

cyathiform (sigh ath'uh form) *a.* In the shape of a cup.

cyathiform flower of narcissus

cyathium (sigh ath'ee uhm) *n.,pl.* cyathia. In botany, a type of flower characteristic of poinsettia.

cyathus (sigh'uh thuhs) *n.* In botany, a small conical or cup-shaped organ or cavity of a plant.

cycad (sigh'kad) *n.* A common name for any member of the families Cycadaceae, Stangeriaceae, and Zamiaceae. Often grown as ornamentals in warm climates or as houseplants, they resemble palms, with handsome, stiff, pointed, divided leaves and thick, unbranched trunks.

Cycadaceae (sighk uh day'see ee) *n. pl.* A peculiar family of 1 genus, *Cycas,* of primitive, seed-bearing tropical or subtropical plants, similar in many ways to ferns, though some resemble palms in their general appearance. They are long-lived and slow-growing. The stem, which is rarely branched, is elongated by a terminal bud, and it bears a crown of large, rigid, divided leaves. The male flowers form terminal cones. They are grown as houseplants for their curious appearance.

Cycas (sigh'kas) *n.* 1. A genus of 20 species of trees (Cycadaceae). They have simple stems, topped by a crown of crowded frondlike leaves with numerous narrow leaflets. The species most frequently cultivated are *C. revoluta* and *C. circinalis.* Also known as bread palm, funeral palm, sago palm. 2. [l.c.] A plant of the genus *Cycas.*

Cyclamen (sighk'luh muhn) *n.* 1. A small genus of 15 species of low-growing tuberous perennials (Primulaceae). They have attractive, rounded leaves marked with silver and dark green and very handsome, nodding pink, white, red, or magenta reflexed flowers. Grown widely in beds, borders, and as outdoor container plants. The florist's cyclamen, *C. persicum,* is a popular houseplant. Also known as sowbread, persian violet, and alpine violet. 2. [l.c.] A plant of the genus *Cyclamen.*

Cyclanthera (sigh klan ther'uh) *n.* A genus of more than 30 species of fast-growing, tender herbaceous vines (Cucurbitaceae) native to the Americas. They have lobed or compound leaves, small yellow or white flowers, and fleshy fruits. Used for screening.

Cyclanthus (sih klan'thuhs) *n.* A genus of palmlike plants with 1 variable species (Cyclanthaceae) native to tropical America. They are palmlike, with fan-shaped leaves and unisexual flowers arranged in spiral bands.

cycle *n.* In botany, a closed circle or whorl of leaves.

cyclic *a.* Arranged in circles or whorls.

cyclospermous (sigh kloh sper'muhs) *a.* In botany, having the embryo coiled about the central albumen, as the seeds of Caryophyllaceae.

Cydista (sigh dihs'tuh) *n.* A genus of 5 species of showy woody vines (Bignoniaceae) native to tropical America. They have opposite leaves with 2 leaflets, bear spikes of white-to-lavender funnelform flowers, and climb by tendrils. Grown in warm climates as an ornamental. *C. aequinoctialis* is commonly known as garlic vine.

Cydonia (sigh doh'nee uh) *n.* A genus of 2 species of shrubs or small trees (Rosaceae); the quince. They have entire leaves, white to rose-pink 5-petaled flowers, and fragrant fruit resembling yellow apples. The raw fruit is unpalatable; the seeded fruit is used for marmalade and jellies.

Cygon (sigh'gahn) *n.* A systemic synthetic insecticide used to protect plants against a variety of plant pests, including aphids and mites. Applied to leaves or soil.

Cymbalaria (sihm buh lar'ee uh) *n.* A genus of 10 species of creeping perennial ground covers (Scrophulariaceae). They have small, rounded, scalloped leaves and tiny, snapdragonlike blue flowers. Used as small-scale ground covers or in hanging baskets. *C. muralis* is commonly known as Kenilworth ivy, coliseum ivy, and pennywort.

Cymbidium (sihm bihd'ee uhm) *n.* A genus of 40 species of cool-growing epiphytic orchids (Orchidaceae). They have pseudobulbs, long, narrow, straplike leaves, and arching spikes of beautiful flowers in many colors that are often spotted or otherwise marked. Grown primarily as greenhouse plants, they also grow well outdoors in frost-free climates.

Cymbopogon (sihm buh poh'gahn) *n.* A genus of nearly 40 species of perennial grasses (Gramineae) native to warm regions. Grown for aromatic oils contained in the leaves. The most common is *C. citratus,* known as lemon grass, it has lemon-flavored leaves that are widely used as an herb, particularly in Southeast Asian cooking.

cyme (sighm) *n.* In botany, a flower, usually broad and somewhat flat-topped, such as the wood anemone and the buttercup.

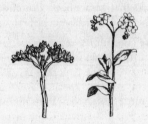

cymes of houseleek and forget-me-not

cymose (sigh'mohs) *a.* Bearing a cyme; composed of cymes; pertaining to or resembling a cyme. Also cymous.

Cynanchum (sih nang'kuhm) *n.* A genus of more than 100 species of climbing, twining vines (Asclepiadaceae) of temperate and tropical regions. They have opposite or whorled leaves, clusters of 5 white-to-deep purple flowers, and long, smooth pods. Commonly called cruel plant, mosquito plant, honey vine, or black swallowwort.

Cynara (sihn'uh ruh) *n.* A small genus of 11 species of tall thistlelike perennials (Compositaceae).

The 2 best-known species are the artichoke, *C. Scolymus,* and the cardoon, *C. cardunculus,* both cultivated as vegetables. They are tall, handsome plants, with large, silvery, deeply cut leaves and striking purple flowers resembling large thistles. The blooms make excellent dried flowers for everlasting bouquets.

Cynodon (sih'noh dahn) *n.* A genus of about 10 species of creeping perennial grasses (Gramineae) native to warm climates. The most common is *C. dactylon* (Bermuda grass), which is widely used as a low-maintenance lawn grass in many mild-winter climates. It is also a troublesome weed in many areas. The hybrid forms do not produce seed and are less invasive.

Cynoglossum (sih noh glahs'uhm) *n.* A genus of between 80 and 90 species of herbaceous flowers (Boraginaceae). The hound's-tongue, *C. officinale,* is now widely naturalized in the United States. It has entire, alternate, hairy leaves, clusters of blue, purple, pink, or white flowers resembling forget-me-nots, and sticky burlike seeds.

Cyperaceae (sih puh ray'see ee) *n. pl.* A family of about 80 genera of grassy or rushlike, mostly perennial plants, with solid and often triangular stems, and leaves with closed sheaths; the sedge family. The small flowers are borne in spikelets. The principal genera are *Carex* and *Cyperus,* which are grown ornamentally in bog gardens, along the sides of streams, or around the edges of ponds.

Cyperus (sigh per'uhs) *n.* A genus of about 600 species of mostly tropical or subtropical annual or perennial plants (Cyperaceae). They have triangular, naked, bamboolike stems with flattened clusters of spiky flowers. Most are bog plants, useful in moist situations for their striking form, interesting silhouette, or shadow pattern. Effective in Oriental gardens, as container plants, or in large flower arrangements. *C. papyrus* is commonly known as papyrus.

Cyphomandra (sigh fuh man'druh) *n.* A genus of about 30 species of shrubs, trees, and plants (Solanaceae) native to tropical America. *C. betacea,* the tree tomato, is cultivated for its large, pear-shaped, orange-colored fruit, which is used in the same way as the tomato. Most often grown as a novelty.

Cyphomandria
(tree tomato)

cypress (sigh'prihs) *n.* 1. The common name of coniferous trees of the genus *Cupressus.* The common cypress of southern Europe is *C. sempervirens. C. macrocarpa,* the Monterey cypress of California, is grown in the West. 2. A name given to other coniferous trees resembling the true cypresses. For example, Lawson's cypress, *Chamaecyparis Lawsoniana,* and Nootka cypress, *C. Nootkatensis,* of the Pacific coast of North America, both grown ornamentally; also, the bald cypress, of the Atlantic states, *Taxodium distichum.* 3. One of several plants that resemble true cypress, as the standing cypress, *Ipomopsis rubra,* a tall, slender plant with divided leaves and scarlet flowers, and the summer cypress, *Kochia scoparia,* a tall, hairy annual, sometimes cultivated, and widely naturalized.

cypress

cypress, bald (sigh'prihs) *n.* A common name for *Taxodium distichum,* a tall tree native to the southeastern United States.

cypress, false (sigh'prihs) *n.* A common name for the genus *Chamaecyparis.*

cypress, mourning (sigh'prihs) *n.* A common name for 2 species of *Chamaecyparis: C. funebris* and *C. Lawsoniana.*

cypress vine (sigh'prihs) *n.* A tropical American vine, *Ipomoea Quamoclit* (Convolvulaceae), which has finely dissected leaves and tubular, bright scarlet flowers. It is widely grown and has naturalized in the southern United States.

Cypripedium (sihp rih pee'dee uhm) *n.* A genus of about 50 species of wild orchids, some species native to North America; the lady's-slipper orchids. Most are rare or endangered in the wild and do not thrive in garden situations. Also known as moccasin flower.

Cyrilla (sih rihl'uh) *n.* A genus of 1 species of evergreen tree or shrub, *C. racemiflora* (Cyrillaceae), native to the coastal plains of the Americas. As a tree, it grows to 30 feet, has oval, entire glossy, leathery leaves, and bears clusters of small fragrant white flowers that attract bees. Commonly known as titi, leatherwood, or he-huckleberry.

Cyrillaceae (sihr uh lay'see ee) *n. pl.* A family of 3 genera and 14 species of small evergreen trees or shrubs, all native to the Americas. *Cyrilla* and *Cliftonia,* each of a single species, are found in the southern United States; they have alternate, simple leaves and spikes of fragrant white or pink flowers that attract bees. Commonly known as ironwood.

Cyrtomium (ser toh'mee uhm) *n.* A genus of about 10 species of ferns (Polypodiaceae); the holly fern. They are 2 to 3 feet tall, with glossy, leathery, toothed dark green leaflets shaped like holly leaves. Grown outdoors in mild climates and as an indoor plant.

Cystopteris (sihs tahp'ter ihs) *n.* A genus of 18 species of delicate rock ferns (Polypodiaceae); the bladder ferns. They are found in cool, damp localities. *C. fragilis,* the brittle fern, is found from within the Arctic Circle to Chile.

Cytisus (siht'ih sihs) *n.* A genus of about 50 species of hardy shrubs (Leguminosae); the broom family. The leaves are usually composed of 3 leaflets, but some species are leafless. The large flowers are typically yellow, occasionally red or white. Some species are common garden plants, such as *C. purpureus,* an elegant procumbent rock-garden specimen. *C. scoparius,* Scotch broom, has naturalized throughout North America. (See **broom**.)

Cytisus
(broom)

cytochrome (sight'uh krohme) *n.* An iron-containing pigment that plays a major role in respiration.

cytology (sigh tahl'uh jee) *n.* The study of cells.

Daboecia (dab ee'she uh) *n.* A genus of 2 species of evergreen shrubs (Ericaceae). They have alternate, simple leaves and spikes of nodding rose, pink, purple, or white flowers. Used on hillsides, in rock gardens, or in wild gardens. *D. cantabrica* is commonly known as Irish heath.

Daconil (dak'oh nihl) *n.* (See **chlorothalonil**.)

Dacrydium (dak rihd'ee uhm) *n.* A genus of 22 species of very tall evergreen coniferous (cone bearing) trees or shrubs (Podocarpaceae) native to the

Southern Hemisphere. Grown in cool, frost-free climates along the Pacific coast of the United States.

Dactylis (dak'tuh lihs) *n.* A genus of grass with a single species, *D. glomerata* (Gramineae). Several varieties are grown as ornamentals for their handsome white- or yellow-striped leaves. Commonly known as cocksfoot orchard grass.

dactyloid (dak'tih loid) *a.* In botany, fingerlike in form or arrangement.

daffodil *n.* A common name for plants of the genus *Narcissus,* especially *N. Pseudonarcissus,* a genus of hardy perennial bulbs. *N. Pseudonarcissus* grows to 18 inches, with long, narrow, blue-green leaves and leafless stalks with often fragrant, distinctively shaped flowers with a circle of flat petals surrounding a central trumpet or cup. Traditionally, they are bright yellow, but hybrids are available in all shades of yellow, red, orange, apricot, pale pink, white, and cream as well as bicolors, in which the corolla (flat petals) are 1 color and the corona (trumpet) is another. Used in beds, borders, under trees and shrubs, under ground covers, naturalized in sweeping drifts in lawns, in pots, and for forcing indoors for winter bloom. They are excellent cut flowers. Also known as daffadilly and daffadowndilly.

daffodil

daffodil, checkered *n.* A common name for *Fritillaria Meleagris,* a very hardy perennial bulb. It grows to 15 inches, with long, alternate leaves and showy bell-shaped flowers intricately patterned in reddish-brown and purple. Used in woodland gardens, rock gardens, or in borders in filtered shade. Also known as snake's-head, checkered lily, or guinea-hen tulip.

daffodil, hoop-petticoat *n.* A common name for *Narcissus Bulbocodium,* a hardy perennial bulb. It grows to 6 inches, with slender, cylindrical leaves and small upward-facing yellow flowers with large trumpets, and small, narrow, pointed petals. Most are true miniatures, best displayed in rock gardens or in containers. also known as petticoat daffodil.

daffodilly, daffodowndilly *n.* (See **daffodil.**)

daffodil, Peruvian *n.* A common name for *Hymenocallis narcissiflora,* a tender summer-blooming bulb native to the Andes of Peru and Bolivia. It grows to 2 feet, with long, straplike leaves and clusters of white, green-striped, spidery flowers with a fringed trumpet. Grown outdoors in mild-winter climates, in pots as an indoor/outdoor plant elsewhere. Also known as basket flower.

daffodil, rush *n.* A common name for *Narcissus Jonquilla,* a tender perennial bulb. It grows to 18 inches, with cylindrical, rushlike leaves and clusters of early, very fragrant golden-yellow flowers with a short cup. Used in borders, rock gardens, and in pots.

daffy *n.* A short form for daffodil.

dagger plant *n.* A name of several cultivated species of *Yucca.* The fiber of this plant is known as dagger-fiber. The name derives from its dagger-shaped leaves.

Dahlia (dal'yuh) *n.* 1. A genus of 27 species of herbaceous, tuberous perennial plants (Compositae). Extensive hybridization has resulted in a multitude of forms, varying in height, in foliage, and especially in the brilliant colors, shapes, and sizes of the flowers. Grown as an annual in cold-winter climates, as a perennial in mild climates. The tubers can be dug up and stored in a dry place for the winter. 2. A plant of the genus *Dahlia.*

Dahlia

dahoon (duh hoon') *n.* A small evergreen tree, *Ilex Cassine,* native to the southern United States. It grows to 40 feet, has leathery, entire, dark green leaves, clusters of yellowish-white flowers, and red, orange, or yellow berries. Commonly called yaupon, cassine, and cassina.

daikon (digh'kahn) *n.* A long, white Asian radish with a crisp texture and mild flavor. They can grow to more than 1 foot without becoming pithy inside. Also called icicle radish.

daisy *n.* A common name applied to plants of many different genera having flowers with a solid central disk surrounded by a circle of many petals, properly called ray flowers. Flowers commonly called daisy are usually members of the Compositae family.

daisy

daisy, African *n.* A common name for several genera including *Arctotis, Dimorphotheca, Osteospermum, Lonas,* and the species *Gerbera jamesonii* (See **daisy, Transvaal**).

daisy, blue *n.* A common name for *Felicia amelloides* (see **marguerite, blue**), the blue species of *Aster* known as Michaelmas daisy (see **daisy, Michaelmas**) and *Cichorium Intybus* (see **chicory**).

daisybush *n.* A common name for the genus *Olearia* (Compositae), shrubby plants with leathery leaves and daisylike flowers in many colors. Grown in warm-winter climates. Also called daisy tree.

daisy, English *n.* A common name for *Bellis perennis,* a low-growing, free-flowering plant mixed with grass in lawns. The larger hybrids are used for edging and as container plants.

daisy, globe *n.* A common name for *Globularia trichosantha* (Globulariaceae), a perennial flower. It grows to 12 inches, with oval leaves and dense, rounded heads of tubular blue flowers. Used in rock gardens.

daisy, oxeye *n.* A common name for *Chrysanthemum Leucanthemum.* Also known as marguerite (See **marguerite**).

daisy, Shasta *n.* A common name for *Chrysanthemum maximum (Leucanthemum maximum).* It has large, lobed leaves and huge, shaggy, white flowers 2 to 4 inches across, sometimes larger.

daisy, Swan River *n.* A common name for *Brachycome iberidifolia,* a neat, mounding plant with finely divided leaves and a profusion of small blue, white, or pink daisylike flowers. Used for edging, raised beds, rock gardens, and in containers.

daisy, Transvaal (tranz'vahl) *n.* A common name for *Gerbera jamesonii.* It is an herbaceous perennial to 2 feet tall, with oblong, deeply lobed, hairy leaves and large cream, yellow, coral, scarlet or orange-red flowers, 4 inches across. Excellent in containers and as a cut flower.

Dalibarda (dal ih bar'duh) *n.* A genus of a single species, *D. repens* (Rosaceae), a creeping, densely tufted perennial native to North America. It has round to heart-shaped leaves and 2 kinds of flowers, both sterile and fertile. The white-petaled sterile flowers are few, and the numerous fertile flowers have no petals. Commonly known as dewdrop, false violet, and Robin runaway.

damask rose *n. Rosa damascema,* a highly fragrant June-blooming rose, long the source of attar of roses.

dame's violet *n.* A common name for the plant *Hesperis matronalis.* It is a much-branched perennial, usually hairy, with long, thin, toothed leaves and small fragrant single or double white, lilac, or lavender flowers. Long cultivated as an ornamental, it has naturalized in North America. Traditional in cottage gardens. Also known as damask violet, dame's rocket and sweet rocket. (See **violet, dame's.**)

dammar pine (dam'er) *n.* A common name for trees of the coniferous genus *Agathis.*

damping off *n.* A common name for a soil disease caused by a number of different organisms. It causes seeds to rot or seedlings to collapse. Best preventative measures: plant in sterile soil, sow seeds treated with a fungicide, or drench soil with fungicide; also, avoid overwatering and planting warm-season vegetables in cold soil.

Danae (da'nee) *n.* A genus of a single species, *D. racemosa* (Liliaceae), an evergreen shrub. It has scalelike, alternate leaves, short terminal clusters of white flowers, and small red fruit. Commonly known as Alexandrian laurel.

dandelion *n.* A well-known plant, *Taraxacum officinale* (Compositae), with 1 large, bright yellow flower, and a tapering, milky, perennial root. It is found under several forms throughout North America. The root has been dried and roasted as a substitute for coffee.

dandelion weeder *n.* An implement for prying and pulling out dandelions and other long-rooted weeds. Also called asparagus knife.

daneflower *n.* The pasqueflower, *Anemone Pulsatilla,* one of the earliest blooms of spring. It has purple blossoms and grows only about 6 inches tall.

Dane's-blood *n.* A common name for 2 different plants, in connection with the legend that they sprang originally from the blood of Danes slain in battle in England. They are the dwarf elder, *Sambucus Ebulus,* and the pasqueflower, *Anemone Pulsatilla.*

Danewort (dayn'wert) *n.* The common name of *Sambucus Ebulus,* the dwarf elder. Also known as Dane's-blood and Daneweed.

dangleberry *n.* A common name for *Gaylussacia frondosa,* the eastern huckleberry. Also known as blue tangle.

Daphne (daf'nee) *n.* 1. A genus of about 50 species of small, hardy, erect or trailing shrubs (Thymeleaceae). They are choice plants, especially the fragrant species. The most widely grown is the winter daphne, *D. odora* 'Marginata', a medium-sized evergreen shrub to 3 feet, with narrow, pointed leaves, bordered with yellow, and nosegay clusters of richly fragrant pinkish-white flowers. 2. A plant of this genus.

Daphniphyllum (daf nih fihl'uhm) *n.* A genus of 25 species of evergreen shrubs and small trees (Daphniphyllaceae). It has alternate or whorled entire leathery leaves, similar to laurel leaves, spikes of inconspicuous flowers, and a 1-seeded fruit. Grows best in warm-winter climates.

Darlingtonia

Darlingtonia (dar lihng toh′nee uh) *n.* A genus of a single species, *D. californica* (Sarraceniaceae), an insect-devouring pitcher-plant native to wet, swampy sites in California and Oregon. The leaves are trumpet-shaped, sometimes 3 feet long, with a vaulted, dilated hood that resembles a cobra's hood. The tube within is lined with rigid hairs that prevent insects from crawling out, and the bottom is filled with a liquid that digests trapped insects.

dasheen (dash een′) *n.* The taro, *Colocasia esculenta.*

Dasylirion (das uh lihr′ee uhn) *n.* A genus of 15 species of stemless or treelike plants similar to yucca (Agavaceae), native to deserts and mountains of the American southwest. They have a dense rosette of rigid, linear, often spiny, leaves and a tall stem bearing a panicle of small white flowers.

dasyphyllous (das ih fihl′uhs) *a.* In botany: 1. Having woolly leaves. 2. Having thickly set leaves.

date *n.* The fruit of the date palm, *Phoenix dactylifera,* used mainly as a confection in North America but extensively as food elsewhere. It is an oblong fruit, which contains a single seed.

date palm *n.* A common name for *Phoenix dactylifera* (Palmae). It grows to 100 feet and is topped by a magnificent crown of large feathery leaves.

Female trees bear large bunches of dates, each bunch weighing from 20 to 25 pounds. The fruit can be eaten fresh or dried. This is the classic palm of desert-movie oases, but it is too large for most home gardens. (See **Phoenix**.)

date palm

date plum *n.* A name for the edible fruit of several species of the genus *Diospyros* and also for the trees.

Datura (duh tu′ruh) *n.* A genus of 8 species of annual or short-lived perennial plants (Solanaceae), some species native to warm regions of the Americas. They have angular-toothed leaves, large funnel-shaped flowers, and prickly, round pods. The leaves and seeds are poisonous. *D. Stramonium* is commonly known as jimsonweed or thorn apple. *D. arborea,* now reclassified as *Brugmansia arborea,* but sold as *B. suaveonlens,* is a shrubby plant, with very large fragrant white blossoms, that is grown ornamentally in warm winter regions. The genus is commonly known as thorn apple.

Daucus (daw′kuhs) *n.* A genus of about 25 species of plants (Umbelliferae) with finely divided leaves and large flattened clusters of tiny white flowers. *D. Carota sativus* is the common carrot. Also known as Queen Anne's lace or wild carrot.

Davallia (duh val′ee uh) *n.* A genus of about 35 species of tropical and subtropical ferns (Polypodiaceae) with furry, creeping rhizomes. The fronds are frequently finely divided and delicately cut into numerous lacy divisions. Some of the species are among the most elegant ferns in cultivation, such as the squirrel's-foot fern, *D. trichomanoides*. Many are popular houseplants.

Davidia (duh vihd'ee uh) *n.* A genus of a single species of flowering tree, *D. involucrata* (Nyssaceae). It grows to 50 or 60 feet and has broad, heart-shaped, toothed leaves, downy beneath. Its white-bracted clusters of flowers give it its common name of dove tree or handkerchief tree.

dawn redwood *n.* A common name for *Metasequoia glyptostroboides,* the only redwood tree not native to North America. It is a deciduous conifer that grows 80 to 90 feet, with soft, light-bright-green leaves and small cones. Grown primarily as a specimen tree or in groves; when young, a good container plant.

dayflower *n.* The popular name for plants of the genus *Commelina*.

daylily *n.* A common name of the genus *Hemerocallis;* so called because each flower blooms for only 1 day.

deadman's hand *n.* 1. A common name for *Dryopteris filix-mas,* from the fact that the young fronds, before they begin to unroll, resemble a closed fist. Also called male fern. 2. The palmately branching seaweed, *Laminaria digitata.* Also called deadman's toe.

dead-men's-fingers *n. pl.* A common name for *Orchis mascula, O. maculata, O. latifolia,* and *O. morio,* so called from their pale, handlike tuberous roots.

dead nettle *n.* The common name of plants of the genus *Lamium* (Labiatae), the leaves of which resemble those of the nettle, though they do not sting.

dealkalization (dee al kuh lih zay'shuhn) *n.* The removal of exchangeable sodium from the soil by a process of leaching or chemically treating the soil.

death camas *n.* A common name for any of several species of the genus *Zigadenus,* known to be poisonous to grazing cattle.

death's-herb *n.* The deadly nightshade, *Atropa Belladonna.*

Debregeasia (dehb reh gee'syuh) *n.* A genus of 5 species of tropical shrubs or small trees (Urticace-

ae). The leaves are alternate and finely toothed, with rounded clusters of flowers, and red, orange, or yellow fruits. It is grown for its attractive foliage and fruit.

Decaisnea (dih kayn'ee uh) *n.* A genus of 2 species of upright shrubs and plants (Lardizabalaceae). They have several erect stalks, divided leaves with entire leaflets, clusters of inconspicuous flowers, and blue fruit that resembles a short cucumber.

decayed organic matter *n.* Decomposed plant or animal matter, used for improving soil.

deciduous (duh sihj'uh wuhs) *a.* Falling or liable to fall, especially after a definite period of time and all at one time; not perennial, persistent or permanent. In botany: 1. Falling off at maturity or at the end of the season, as petals, leaves, fruit, etc.: as distinct from fugacious or caducous organs, which fall soon after their appearance, or from persistent or permanent; not evergreen. 2. Losing the foliage every year; made up of or having deciduous parts: as, deciduous trees.

declinate (dehk'lih nayt) *a.* In botany, bent or curved downward or forward.

Decodon (dehk'oh dahn) *n.* A genus of a single species of pondweed, *D. verticillatus* (Lythraceae) native to the United States. It has woody or corky arching stems, opposite or whorled leaves, and clusters of purple flowers. Commonly known as swamp loosestrife, water willow, or water oleander. Grown on the margins of garden ponds or in bog gardens.

decollate snail (dehk'ah layt) *n.* A predator of the common garden snail; released as a biological control.

decompose *v.* To release chemicals from organic matter by means of bacterial action.

decompound *a.* In botany, divided into a number of compound divisions, such as a leaf divided into leaflets or a cluster of flowers divided into many branchlets. Also decomposite.

Decumaria (dehk yuh mar'ee uh) *n.* A genus of 2 species of woody vines (Saxifragaceae) native to China and North America. They have opposite, entire leaves, small white flowers, and a ribbed seed capsule shaped like a top. *D. barbara* climbs to 30 feet; also known as wood-vamp and climbing hydrangea.

decumbent (duh kuhm′behnt) *a*. In botany, a plant that has its base laying on the fround, and a stem that grows upward.

decurrent (duh kur′ehnt) *a*. In botany, extending downward beyond the place of insertion: as, a decurrent leaf, i.e., a leaf with a base that extends downward along the stem.

decussate (dehk′uh sayt) *a*. In botany, arranged in pairs alternately crossing each other at right angles.

deep percolation *n*. The downward movement of water into the soil beyond the reach of a plant's roots.

deep soil *n*. Soil that is deeper than 40 inches that continues until it becomes rock or another strongly contrasting material.

deer *n*. A large mammal that feeds on many garden plants. Usually a problem in many rural and suburban areas. Planting deer-resistant plants or enclosing the garden with a tall fence are the most reliable control measures.

deer-foot *n*. A common name for *Achlys triphylla,* a perennial plant of the barberry family with fan-shaped leaves, with 3 leaflets, and spikes of small flowers; native to the Pacific coast of North America. Sometimes planted in rock gardens or wild gardens. Also known as vanilla leaf.

deer grass *n*. A common name for species of *Rhexia,* especially the common meadow beauty, *R. virginica,* native to North America. It grows from tubers (potatoe-like growths) to 1½ feet tall and has long, narrow leaves and clusters of rose-purple flowers. It is grown in moist locations, in borders, and in rock gardens.

deer repellent *n*. Any of various substances applied to foliage to discourage deer from feeding on garden plants.

deflocculate (dee flahk′yuh layt) *v*. To break up the soil aggregates into individual particles.

defluent (deh′floo ehnt) *a*. In botany, running downward; decurrent.

defluvium (dee floo′vee uhm) *n*. A falling off, such as the bark of a tree, from disease.

defoil *v*. To strip a plant of leaves.

defoliate *v*. To deprive of leaves; to cut or pick off the leaves of a plant, especially prematurely.

defoliation *n*. The loss of leaves, as by the depredations of insects; specifically, the fall of leaves in autumn.

defoliator *n*. That which defoliates or strips of verdure; specifically, in entomology, any insect that destroys the leaves of trees.

deforest *v*. To deprive of forests; to cut down and clear away the forests.

deforestation *n*. The act of cutting down and clearing away the forests of a region or a tract of land.

degradation *n*. The change of 1 kind of soil to a more highly leached soil.

dehisce (dih′hihs) *v*. In botany, to open, such as the seed capsules or pods of plants.

dehiscence (dih hihs′ihns) *n*. In botany, the bursting open of a capsule or pod for the discharge of the seeds, or of an anther to set free the pollen.

dehiscent (dih hihs′ehnt) *a*. Opening, such as the seed pod of a plant.

dehydration *n*. The loss of water.

Delonix (dih loh′niks) *n*. A genus of 3 species of tropical trees (Leguminosae). The leaves are alternate and divided, with clusters of flamboyantly showy bright red flowers. Widely grown in tropics and subtropics as a spectacular flowering tree. Commonly known as royal poinciana, flamboyant, or peacock flower.

deltoid (dehl′toid) *a*. In botany, triangular and attached to the stem at the broad end: such as, a deltoid leaf.

Dendrobium (dehn droh′bee uhm) *n*. An extensive genus of 900 species of epiphytic (living on a host but not taking nourishment from it) orchids (Orchidaceae). They are widely variable in appearance and growth habit, but many species are grown in greenhouses for their unusual flowers.

Dendrobium

Dendrochilum (dehn drahk ee luhm) *n.* A genus of 100 species of epiphytic orchids (Orchidaceae) native to southeast Asia and the Malay archipelago. They grow from a pseudobulb and have 1 narrow leaf and tall spikes of many small flowers. Commonly known as chain orchid.

dendroid (dehn′droid) *a.* Treelike; dendriform; arborescent; branching like a tree.

Dendromecon (dehn droh mee′kahn) *n.* A genus of 1 or 2 variable species of perennial evergreen shrubs (Papaveraceae) native to California (including northern Baja) and the Channel Islands. It is a much-branched shrub with simple, entire, leathery leaves and 2-inch-wide, poppylike, bright yellow flowers. Drought-tolerant, it is used on banks, roadsides, and in native plant gardens. Commonly known as bush poppy.

denitrification *n.* The process by which bacterial action reduces nitrates in the soil to ammonia or free nitrogen that can escape into the air.

Dennstaedtia (dehn stehd′ee uh) *n.* A genus of about 70 species of mostly tropical and subtropical ferns (Polypodiaceae), 1 species of which, *D. punctilobula,* is native to eastern North America. It has creeping rhizomes and 2½-foot-long fragrant pale green fronds. Used in woodland or wild gardens. Commonly known as cup fern or hay-scented fern.

denshire (dehn′sher) *v.* To improve land by burning piles of earth, turf, and stubble and then spreading the ashes over the ground as compost. Also densher.

Dentaria (dehn tar′ee uh) *n.* A genus of 10 species of hardy plants (Cruciferae). They have scaly creeping or tuberous roots, deeply cut leaves, and large white or light-purple flowers. Commonly known as toothwort and pepperroot.

dentate (dehn′tayt) *a.* In botany, having acute teeth that project outward: Such as, a dentate leaf; or having toothlike projections: such as, a dentate root.

denticulate (dehn tihk′yoo layt) *a.* Finely dentate; edged with minute toothlike projections: such as, a denticulate leaf, calyx, etc.

deodar (dee′uh dahr) *n.* A common name for *Cedrus deodara,* a coniferous tree. Also called East Indian cedar.

Derris (der′ihs) *n.* A genus of 70 to 80 species of woody lianas and trees (Leguminosae). They have alternate, divided leaves and spikes or clusters of showy white, yellow, or purple flowers. The roots of *D. elliptica, D. uliginosa,* and *D. malaccensis* are a source of the natural pesticide rotenone.

desalinization *n.* The removal of salts from saline soil.

Deschampsia (dih shamp′see uh) *n.* A genus of 40 to 50 species of annual and perennial grasses (Gramineae) native to temperate areas. A few are grown as ornamentals. The most common is *D. caespitosa* (tufted hair grass), prized for it delicate flower spikes in shades of silver, yellow, gold, green, and sometimes purple.

desert candle *n.* A common name for the genus *Eremurus* (Liliaceae). It has thick roots, narrow leaves in tufts or rosettes, and tall spikes of flowers, sometimes as tall as 9 feet. Also known as foxtail lily and king's spear.

desert soil *n.* A light-colored surface soil that develops in warm- to-cool arid climates.

desert willow *n.* A common name for *Chilopsis linearis,* a large shrub or small tree native to Mexico and the southwestern United States. It has long, narrow, simple leaves and spikes of yellow-striped, bell-shaped flowers in white, pink, lilac, lavender, or purple. Also known as flowering willow.

desilting area *n.* An area used to remove sediment from flowing water.

desorption *n.* The removal of absorbed materials from surfaces.

detailed soil map *n.* A map showing the different classifications of soil in a designated area.

Deutzia (doit'see uh) *n.* A genus of about 40 species of handsome flowering shrubs (Saxifragaceae), some species native to the mountains of Central America. They have opposite, serrate leaves and bear clusters of white, pink, or lavender flowers so numerous that they nearly obscure the foliage.

devil's-claw, common *n.* A purple-flowered herb, *Probiscidea jussieui,* grown for the young fruit and the dried seedpods, which have a clawlike shape.

devil's club *n.* A common name for the prickly plant *Oplopanax horridus,* native to northwestern North America.

devil's milk *n.* The white, milky, poisonous sap juice of various common plants, particularly those of the genus *Euphorbia.*

devil's paintbrush *n.* A common name for plants of 3 genera—*Hieracium, Picris,* and *Erechtites*—naturalized as weeds throughout the northeastern United States. Also called hawkweeds.

devil's shoestring *n.* A common name for *Tephrosia virginiana,* so called from its tough, slender roots; native to the United States. Also known as goat's-rue.

devil's-tongue *n.* A common name for the cactus *Opuntia humifusa.* It has flattened joints edged with spines, large yellow flowers 4 inches in diameter, and green to purple fruit.

devil's-walking-stick *n.* A common name for *Zanthoxylum clava-Herculis,* a tall shrub or small tree with 1-foot-long leaves divided into many leaflets and covered with thorns and clusters of flowers; native to the United States. Also known as Hercules'-club, pepperwood, and southern prickly ash.

devilwood *n.* The common name for *Osmanthus americanus,* a small tree native to the southern United States and Mexico. It grows to 45 feet, has glossy, entire, pointed leaves and clusters of small, fragrant creamy-white flowers.

dewberry (dyoo'ber ee) *n.* The popular name for the *Rubus macropetalus,* a bramble that grows in woods and the borders of fields. The fruit is bluish-black, with an agreeable acid taste, much like the flavor of a blackberry.

dew plant *n.* A common name for *Drosera rotundifolia,* an insect-devouring plant native to moist situations. Occasionally grown in the bog garden or under glass as a novelty. Also called sundew.

dextrorse (dehk'strors) *a.* Twining spirally upward around an axis, as in the hop or morning glory.

dhak (dahk) *n.* A handsome flowering tree, *Butea monosperma* (Leguminosae), native to India. It grows to 50 feet, with a crooked trunk, leaves divided into leaflets, showy orange-red flowers, and silvery-gray fruit. Commonly known as flame-of-the-forest. (See **Butea.**)

dhauri (daw'ree) *n.* A common name for the tropical shrub *Woodfordia fruticosa* (Lythraceae). Its long, spreading branches are covered with black-dotted leaves and brilliant red flowers.

di- A combining form, similar to bi- and meaning two, twofold, or double, as in dicotyledon, which means having two seed leaves.

diadelphous (digh uh dehl'fuhs) *a.* In botany, having stamens united in two sets by their filaments: as, diadelphous stamens. In the flowers of most beans and peas, nine out of ten stamens are often united, while one is by itself.

diageotropic (digh uh jee oh troh'pihk) *a.* In botany, growing at right angles to the direction of gravity.

diageotropism (digh uh jee oh troh'pihz uhm) *n.* In botany, a turning of roots, branches, or rhizomes in a direction at right angles to that of gravity.

diaheliotropic (digh uh hee'lee oh troh'pihk) *a.* In botany, the turning of the upper surfaces of a plant's leaves toward the sunlight; pertaining to diaheliotropism.

diaheliotropism (digh uh hee lee oh troh'pihz uhm) *n.* In botany, the tendency of a plant to turn the upper surfaces of its leaves toward the light.

dialycarpous (digh uh lih kar'puhs) *a.* In botany, bearing fruit composed of separate carpels. Also apocarpous.

dialypetalous (digh uh lih peht′uh luhs) *a*. In botany, plants that have the corolla of the flower divided into distinct petals; also polypetalous.

dialyphyllous (digh uh lih fihl′uhs) *a*. In botany, made of separate leaves: applied to a calyx formed from several sepals or a corolla formed by several petals.

dialysepalous (digh uh lih sehp′uh luhs) *a*. In botany, having a calyx made of separate sepals; polysepalous.

diamond flower *n*. A common name for the genus *Ionopsidium*, slender annuals. *I. acaule* is a creeping plant with round leaves and white, lilac, or purple flowers. Used in rock gardens and cool greenhouses.

diandrous (digh an′druhs) *n*. In botany, a flower with two stamens.

diandrous varieties
a China pink *b* clove pink

Diapensia (digh uh pehn′see uh) *n*. A genus of 4 species of evergreen tufted evergreen perennials (Diapensiaceae), some species native to North America. *D. lapponica* forms dense cushions to 4 inches high, with thick, leathery, narrow leaves and erect white flowers. It is used in rock or alpine gardens but is hard to grow at low elevations.

Diapensiaceae (digh uh pehn see ay′see ee) *n. pl.* A small order of 6 genera and 10 species of evergreen shrublets or perennials. The cultivated genera include *Diapensia*, *Pysidanthera*, *Shortia*, and *Galax*, all of which are small plants suitable for the rock garden or alpine garden.

Diascia (digh ash′ee uh) *n*. A genus of 50 species of low-growing slender plants (Scrophulariaceae). The plants form mats or clumps and have salmon or coral-pink double-spurred flowers. Commonly known as twinspur.

diatomaceous earth (digh uh tuh may′shuhs) *n*. A material composed of skeletal remains of diatoms (single-celled algae); used as an insecticide. The sharp edges of the diatoms lacerate soft-bodied insects like aphids and ants. Usually used as a barrier but can be applied to foliage. Most effective in hot, dry weather.

diazinon (digh az′ih nahn) *n*. A synthetic insecticide widely used against many soil pests, particularly in lawns. Very toxic to birds.

dibble *n*. A pointed instrument used to make holes in the ground for seeds or seedlings.

Dicentra (digh sehn′truh) *n*. A genus of about 19 species of delicate perennial herbs (Fumariaceae), some species native to North America. They have attractive, dissected leaves and arching stalks of heart-shaped or two-spurred, nodding pink and white flowers. Commonly known as bleeding heart.

dichasial (digh kay′zee uhl) *a*. In botany, pertaining to or resembling a dichasium, a flower cluster with two main stalks within the cluster.

dichasium (digh kay′zee uhm) *n*. In botany, a flower cluster with two main stalks or branchlets within the cluster.

dichlamydeous (digh kluh mihd′ee uhs) *a*. In botany, having both a calyx and a corolla.

dichogamous (digh kahg′uh muhs) *a*. In botany, exhibiting or characterized by dichogamy. Also dichogamic.

dichogamy (digh kahg′uh mee) *n*. In botany, a provision in hermaphroditic flowers to ensure cross-fertilization (and prevent self-fertilization) by a difference in the time of maturity of the anthers and stigma.

Dichondra (digh kahn′druh) *n*. A genus of 9 species of perennial herbs (Convolvulaceae) native to mostly mild-weather climates. *D micanthra*, commonly known as dicondra, creates a lush cover of small round leaves. It is widely grown as a water-loving ground cover and a lawn substitute in mild-winter climates of the United States. It can also become a weed.

Dichorisandra (digh kor ih san′druh) *n.* A genus of about 30 species of tropical perennials (Commelinaceae) native to the Americas. The leaves are large, alternate, and sheathing, with blue or purple flowers on erect stems. Grown outdoors in warm-winter climates or as houseplants anywhere. *D. thyrsiflora,* which has flower clusters 6 inches long, is commonly known as blue ginger.

dichotomy (digh kaht′uh mee) *n.* In botany, a mode of branching by repeated forking, as is shown in some stems, the veining of some leaves, etc.

Dicksonia (dihk sohn′ee uh) *n.* A genus of 30 species of tree ferns (Dicksoniaceae) with large, much-divided fronds and short trunks, usually several feet high. *D. antarctica* is one of the most ornamental tree ferns in cultivation. Useful in moist situations in warm-winter climates; excellent container plants. Commonly known as Tasmanian tree fern.

diclinism (digh kligh′nihz uhm) *n.* In botany, the state of having stamens or pistils in separate flowers; the state of being diclinous.

diclinous (digh kligh′nuhs) *a.* In botany, having stamens or pistils in separate flowers.

dicoccous (digh kahk′uhs) *a.* In botany, formed of two one-seeded carpels.

dicotyledon (digh kaht ihl ee′dihn) *n.* A plant that produces a newly emerged seedling with two seed leaves before it produces mature leaves. Monocotyledons produce a newly emerged seedling with only one leaf. (See **Dicotyledoneae**.)

Dicotyledoneae (digh kahd ihl uh doh′nee ee) *n.* One of two major classes of plants, the other being Monocotyledonae. Dicotyledons have two seed leaves; the mature leaves branching, netlike veins, and the flowers have five, or sometimes, four parts. They include deciduous trees, such as maples and lilacs; broadleaf evergreens, such as magnolias and live oaks; flowering perennials, such as roses and geraniums; most vegetables, including tomatoes; and weeds, such as dandelions and hawkweeds. Commonly called dicots.

dicotyledonous (digh kaht ihl ee′dihn uhs) *a.* In botany, having two seed leaves: as dicotyledonous embryo, seed, or plant.

Dictamnus (dihk tam′nuhs) *n.* 1. A genus of 1 extremely variable species, *D. albus* (Rutaceae). It has long, oval, serrate leaves and showy white flowers, which are of various colors. The whole plant is covered with glands that secrete a strong-smelling oil so volatile that, in hot weather, the air around the plant becomes flammable. If a lighted match is held near the flowers on warm, still evenings, volatile oils exuded from glands on that part of the plant will ignite and burn briefly, hence its common names of gas plant and burning bush. It is traditional in country-cottage gardens. Also known as fraxinella or dittany. 2. A plant of the genus *Dictamnus*.

dictyogen (dihk′tee uh jehn) *n.* A monocotyledon having net-veined leaves.

dictyogenous (dihk tee ahj′uh nuhs) *a.* In botany, having the character of a dictyogen; having the general character of an endogen, but with netted leaf-veins.

Dictyosperma (dihk tee uh sper′muh) *n.* A genus of 2 species of tropical palms (Palmae). *D. album* is an elegant, fast-growing feather palm that attains a height of 45 feet or more. It has 12- foot-long finely cut fronds, a dark gray or black trunk, and reddish-yellow fruit. Nearly extinct where native, it is found in tropical gardens where cultivated. Also known as common princess palm.

didymous (dihd′ih muhs) *a.* In botany, twofold; twin; growing double, such as the fruits of umbelliferous plants or the tubers of some orchids.

didynamous (digh dihn′uh muhs) *a.* In botany, having four stamens in two unequal pairs, such as most mints.

didynamy (digh′dihn′uh mee) *n.* In botany, the condition of being in two unequal pairs, such as stamens.

dieback *n.* A malady characterized by the dying of individual limbs or sections of plants. It can be caused by a number of different insects, diseases, or cultural practices, including root rots, borers, or extreme cold.

Dieffenbachia (dee fehn bak'ee uh) *n*. A genus of about 30 species of plants (Araceae) native to tropical America. Many fancy-leaved hybrids have been developed from *D. Seguine* and *D. maculata*. They have canelike stems and large, broad leaves, often spectacularly marked with white. Dieffenbachia is extremely poisonous when eaten; the acrid sap burns the mouth and throat and may paralyze the vocal cords, hence its common name of dumb cane. Widely grown as houseplants and greenhouse specimens.

Dierama (digh er'ah muh) *n*. A genus of 25 species of summer-blooming corms (Iridaceae). They have slender, tough leaves and 4-to-7 foot tall arching stems with pendulous, bell-shaped, mauve, purple, or white flowers. Useful in moist situations, especially where arching stems can be reflected in water. Commonly known as wandflower, fairy wand, or angel's-fishing-rods.

Diervilla (dihr vihl'uh) *n*. A genus of 3 species of small, deciduous shrubs (Caprifoliaceae) native to eastern North America. They have opposite, simple leaves and clusters of small yellow flowers. Useful for holding steep slopes, as a background planting, or as a tall ground cover. Commonly known as bush honeysuckle.

Diervilla
(bush honeysuckle)

Dietes (digh ay'teez) *n*. A genus of 5 species of tender perennials (Iridaceae). They have stout, creeping rhizomes, narrow, swordlike leaves, and branched stalks of white or yellow flowers resembling miniature Japanese iris. They are long-blooming, drought-tolerant, and accepting of many soils. Often used in public plantings; excellent in perennial borders, beds, and containers. Commonly known as African iris and fortnight lily.

diffuse (dihf yoos') *a*. In botany, spreading widely and loosely; extended; dispersed; scattered.

dig *v*. To break up and turn over piecemeal, as a portion of ground; for example, to dig a garden with a spade.

digging *n*. The act of excavating; plowing or turning soil over with a spade or shovel or by hand.

digging fork *n*. A 4-tined implement used for soil preparation and planting shrubs.

digging spade *n*. A D-handled shovel designed to be pushed into the ground with the foot; used in soil preparation and in planting shrubs.

Digitalis (didj ih tahl is) *n*. A genus of 19 species of biennials or faily hardy perennials (Scrophulariaceae). They grow from 2 feet to 8 feet with hariy, gray-green leaves in basal rosettes and tall spikes of tubular white, yellow, pink, rose, and purple flowers, often spotted. The flowers attract hummingbirds. The leaves are poisonous. Traditional in cottage gardens, herb gardens, and English borders. Commonly known as foxglove.

digitate (dihj'uh tayt) *a*. In botany, having deep radiating divisions, like fingers; especially applied to compound leaflets that grow from the top of the leaf stem.

dill *n*. A name given to *Anethum graveolens* (Umbelliferae), an erect annual plant, with feathery leaves, yellow flowers, and an aromatic seed. A native of the Mediterranean, it is cultivated in herb gardens for both its foliage and seeds (dillweed and seeds). The seeds are used in breads and pickling; the leaves are used in cheese blends and with fish.

Dilleniaceae (dih lee nee ay'see ee) *n. pl*. A family of 11 genera and 275 species of mostly tropical flowers, trees, and shrubs. The leaves are alternate; the flowers are yellow, white, or, occasionally, red. Two genera are planted ornamentally, *Dillenia* and *Hibbertia*.

dillweed *n*. (See **dill**.)

dilly *n.* 1. A common name for a small tree, *Mimusops emarginata* (Sapotaceae), native to the Florida keys and the West Indies. Commonly known as the wild dilly or wild sapodilla. 2. Same as daffodil.

dimerous *a.* In botany, having two parts in each whorl of flowers.

dimidiate (dih mihd′ee uht) *a.* In botany, having one part so much smaller than the other as to appear to be missing, or almost so.

dimorphism (digh mor′fihz uhm) *n.* In botany, the occurrence of two distinct forms of flowers, leaves, or othe parts on the same plant, or on plants of the same species, as in some *Eucalyptus.*

Dimorphotheca (digh mor fuh thee′kuh) *n.* A genus of about 7 species of plants (Compositae). They are low-growing, clumping plants with alternate, simple, coarsely lobed leaves and daisylike white, purple, orange, or yellow flowers. Used as a ground cover and as a border. Commonly known as African daisy or cape marigold.

dimorphous (digh mor′fuhs) *a.* Existing in two forms of leaf or flower or other part on the same plant or on plants of the same species. (See **dimorphism**.)

dindle *n.* 1. The common corn sow-thistle; also, sow-thistle, *Sonchus.* 2. Hawkweed: *Hieracium, Picris, Erechtites.* Most of these are weeds of European origin, now naturalized throughout the world.

dioecian (digh oh ee′shuhn) *a.* (See **dioecious**.)

dioeciopolygamous (digh ee′shee oh puh lihg′uh muhs) *a.* In botany, polygamous with a tendency to dioeciousness, or to the prevalence of flowers of one sex on individual plants, such as a plant with mostly female flowers.

dioecious (digh ee′shuhs) *a.* In botany, unisexual, with male and female flowers on separate plants, such as in holly and willow. Also dioecian.

Dionaea (digh uh nee′uh) *n.* A genus of 1 species of carnivorous plant, the Venus-flytrap, *Dmuscipula muscipula* (Droseraceae), native to bogs of North and South Carolina. It has a rosette of leaves growing from the base of the plant and a stalk topped by a cluster of rather large white flowers. The leaves have a 2-lobed appendage with 3 very delicate hairs and a fringe of stout, marginal bristles on each lobe.

The hairs are remarkably sensitive, and when touched by a fly or other insect, the lobes of the leaf suddenly close on the insect and trap it. The capture is followed by the copious secretion of an acid liquid that digests the prey. This process may be repeated several times by the same leaf.

Dioon (digh oh ahn′) *n.* A genus of 4 or 5 species of tropical cycads (Zamiaceae) native to Mexico and Central America. The trunk is very short and stout, with a crown of large, rigid, and spine-tipped divided leaves. It bears both male and female cones, the female cones becoming very large. Grown ornamentally in subtropical and tropical gardens and in greenhouses.

Dioscorea (digh uh skoh′ree uh) *n.* A large genus of about 500 species of twining vines (Dioscoreaceae). They have fleshy, tuberous roots, and several species are widely grown for food. The principal species is *D. Batatas.* Commonly known as yam. (See **yam**.)

Dioscoreaceae (digh uh skoh ree ay′see ee) *n. pl.* A family of 9 to 10 genera of plants distinguished by their ribbed, veined leaves, tuberous roots, twining stems, and inconspicuous flowers. Only *Dioscorea* is cultivated.

Diosma (digh ahz muh) *n.* A genus of 12 to 15 species of heatherlike plants (Rutaceae). The fragrant foliage is dotted with glands, and the flowers are white or pinkish. Grown in warm-winter climates for their flowers. Commonly known as buchu or breath-of-heaven.

Diospyros (digh uh spigh′ruhs) *n.* A large genus of nearly 200 species of trees and shrubs (Ebenaceae). *D. virginiana* and *D. Kaki* are grown for their edible fruit and ornamental value. Commonly known as persimmon.

Dipelta (digh pehl′tuh) *n.* A genus of 4 species of hardy, deciduous flowering shrubs (Caprifoliaceae). The leaves are opposite and simple, with stalks of bell-shaped or tubular pink or purple flowers enclosed by large, showy bracts.

dipetalous (digh peht′uh luhs) *a.* In botany, having two petals.

diphyllous (digh fihl′uhs) *a.* In botany, having two leaves.

Diplazium (digh play′zee uhm) *n.* A genus of more than 300 species of tropical ferns (Polypodiaceae). Sometimes combined with *Athyrium.* They have simple, divided leaves ranging from 2 to 5 feet long.

diplotegia (dihp luh tee′jee uh) *n.* In botany, a seed capsule that develops from the ovary in some plants such as the iris, in which the ovary is situated below the floral envelopes.

Dipsacaceae (dihp suh kay′see ee) *n. pl.* A family of 9 genera and about 160 species of tall plants, with opposite leaves and small flowers in heads; native to Europe, Asia, and Africa. Major genera include *Dipsacus,* the teasel, and *Scabiosa,* the pincushion flower, which is grown ornamentally.

dipsacaceous (dihp suh kay′shuhs) *a.* Belonging to or having the characteristics of the family *Dipsacaceae.* Also dipsaceous.

Dipsacus (dihp′suh kuhs) *n.* A small genus of prickly biennial plants of about 15 species (Dipsacaceae). *D.sativus,* the fuller's teasel, has prickly flowerheads, which were once used to raise the nap on wool. (See **teasel.**)

Dipsacus
(teazel)

dipterous (dihp′tuh ruhs) *a.* In botany, having two winglike appendages.

Dirca (der′kuh) *n.* A genus of 2 species of deciduous shrubs (Thymelaeaceae) native to North America. Both *D. palustris,* of the Atlantic states, and *D. occidentalis* of California are known as leatherwood, from their very tough, fibrous inner bark. Drooping clusters of yellow flowers precede the leaves and are followed by small red-greenish fruit.

dis- A prefix meaning two. (See **di-.**)

Disa (digh′suh) *n.* A genus of 130 species of tropical terrestrial orchids (Orchidaceae). They have tuberous roots, dark green leaves, and stalks of showy striped-red flowers to 4 inches across.

Disanthus (dihs an′thuhs) *n.* A genus of 1 species of large deciduous shrub (Hamamelidaceae). It grows to 24 feet, has long, oval, alternate leaves, which color red to orange in autumn, and tiny, dark purple flowers. Grown for its fall color.

disboscation (dihs bahs kay′shuhn) *n.* The act of disforesting; the act of converting woodland into farm land.

disbud *v.* To remove buds or shoots; to remove the unnecessary buds of a tree or vine to fulfill the needs of training, in order to allow more space and nourishment for the development of the remaining buds.

disbudding *n.* The act of removing some buds from flower plants to encourage other buds of the same plant to form larger flowers. Also called pinching back.

disc *n.* (See **disk.**)

Dischidia (dihs kihd ee uh) *n.* A genus of about 80 species of fleshy, twining, tropical and subtropical herbaceous, epiphytic vines (Asclepiadaceae). They root and climb on trees and have fleshy leaves and small white, violet, or red flowers.

Dischidia

discoid (dihs′koid) *a.* In botany: 1. In the flower of plants of the *Compositae* (sunflower or daisly family), pertaining to the buttonlike central part. 2. In such plants, having only the central part and not the outer petallike parts of the flower, such as in tansy.

dish garden *n.* A collection of plants, generally relatively small ornamentals, grown together in 1 container.

disinfection *n.* Purification from infectious matter; the destruction of germs of infectious diseases.

disk *n.* In botany: 1. Any flattened circular organ of a plant, such as the adhesive ends of the tendrils of the Virginia creeper. 2. In plants such as asters and sunflowers, the buttonlike center of the flower. 3. A fleshy enlargement of the receptacle in some flowers.

disk flower *n. pl.* In the *Compositae,* one of the minute tubular components of the central area of the flower head.

dispermous (digh sper'muhs) *a.* In botany, having two seeds.

dispersion of soil (dihs per zhuhn uhv soil) *n.* The breaking up of soil into very fine particles and its suspension in water.

Disporum (digh spor'uhm) *n.* A genus of 15 species of woodland flowers (Liliaceae), some species native to North America. They grow from rhizomes, have alternate, oval, pointed leaves, small creamy-white to greenish-white flowers, and red fruit. Commonly known as fairy bells.

dissected *a.* In botany, deeply cut into numerous narrow segments: applied to leaves, etc.

dissepiment (dih sehp'uh muhnt) *n.* In botany, a partition within an organ of a plant; for example, the membrane that separates sections of the orange and other citrus fruits.

dissepimental (dih sehp uh mehn'tuhl) *a.* Pertaining to or of the nature of a dissepiment.

dissilient (dih sihl'yuhnt) *a.* Bursting open with some force, as the pod or capsule of *Impatiens.*

distichous (dihs'tih kuhs) *a.* In botany, arranged in two vertical rows.

Distictis (dihs tihk'tuhs) *n.* A genus of 9 species of woody vines (Bignoniaceae) native to the West In-

dies. They have leaves divided into 3 leaflets, terminating in a tendril, and clusters of tubular purple, pink, red, or white flowers. Grown in warm-winter climates.

Disyston (digh'sihs tahn) *n.* A synthetic, systemic insecticide (chemical name: disulfoton) applied to the soil.

ditch fern (dihch fern) *n.* A common name for *Osmunda regalis.* Also called royal fern.

dittany (diht'uh nee) *n.* 1. A common name for the plant *Dictamnus albus.* 2. *Cunila Origanoides,* a fragrant labiate of the Atlantic states. 3. A labiate, *Origanum Dictamnus,* called dittany of Crete.

divaricate (digh var'uh kuht) *a.* In botany, spreading widely apart, as a divaricate branch. Also divaricated.

divarication (digh var uh kay'shuhn) *n.* In botany, the act of branching off or diverging; separation into branches.

divided *a.* Separated to the base or midrib, as the leaves of palms and clover.

division *n.* In botany: 1. A method of propagation in which mature plants are separated at the roots to make 2 or more new plants. 2. A major primary category in the hierarchy of plant classification, ranking below the subkingdom and above the class.

Dizygotheca (digh zih goh'thuh kuh) *n.* A genus of 15 species of tropical or subtropical shrubs or small trees (Araliaceae). They have lacy, finely divided leaves, which are dark green above and reddish beneath, with large clusters of flowers, which are rarely seen in cultivation. Used primarily as a houseplant. Commonly known as false aralia.

D layer *n.* A stratum underlying the soil profile that is unlike the material from which the soil was formed.

dock *n.* The common name for those species of *Rumex* that are characterized by little or no acidity and have leaves that are not arrowhead-shaped. They are coarse herbs, mostly perennials, with thickened rootstocks. Some are troublesome weeds and widely naturalized. Some varieties are grown in herb gardens, including Western dock, *R. crispus;* patience dock, *R. Patientia;* sour dock, *R. Acetosa;* and water dock, *R. hydrolapathum.*

dockmackie *n.* A common name for *Viburnum acerifolium,* a shrub with maplelike leaves that color red in autumn and with broad clusters of white flowers. Also known as maple-leaved viburnum.

dodder *n.* The common name of plants of the genus *Cuscuta* (Convolvulaceae), a group of stringlike, branched, twining, leafless, yellowish or reddish annual parasites. (See **Cuscuta**.)

dodecamerous (doh duh kam'uh ruhs) *a.* In botany, having the whorls of the flower (petals, sepals, etc.) in twelves. Also written 12- merous.

Dodecatheon (doh duh kath'ee uhn) *n.* A genus of about 14 species of low-growing perennial flowers (Primulaceae), mostly native to North America. They resemble miniature cyclamen, with a rosette of rounded leaves and an upright stalk bearing several handsome purple or white nodding flowers with reflexed petals. Commonly known as shooting star. Used in wildflower gardens or in rock gardens.

Dodonaea (doh duh nee'uh) *n.* A genus of about 50 species of mostly tropical and subtropical shrubs (Sapindaceae). They grow to 15 feet tall and have willowlike leaves and attractive creamy-to-pinkish winged fruit. *D. viscosa* 'Purpurea', native to Arizona, has rich bronzy-purple leaves. Used as an espalier, a hedge, or an informal screen.

dogbane *n.* A common name for *Apocynum androsaemifolium,* a 2-foot- tall native American wildflower with opposite, oval leaves and clusters of tiny pink bell-shaped flowers. Sometimes used in the hardy perennial border. Also called dog's bane. (See **Apocynum**.)

dogbane family *n.* The common name for the family Apocynaceae.

dogberry *n.* Any of certain small, inedible fruits generally considered unfit for human consumption, such as chokeberry, prickly wild gooseberry, rose hips, or the fruit of the mountain ash, *Sorbus americana.*

dogberry tree *n.* A common name for *Cornus sanguinea.* Also known as dogwood.

dog rose *n.* The *Rosa canina* (Rosaceae), or wild brier. It is a common British plant, growing in thickets and hedges. The fruit, known as the hip is rich in vitamin C.

dog's bane *n.* (See **dogbane**.)

dogtooth violet *n.* A common name for *Erythronium Dens-canis,* a low-growing plant with oblong leaves, mottled with reddish-brown, and with white and rose-to-purple flowers.

dog tree *n.* A common name for trees of several different genera: *Cornus, Euonymous, Sambucus, Alnus,* and *Viburnum.*

dogwood *n.* A common name for the trees of the genus *Cornus,* such as the flowering dogwood, *C. florida,* a highly ornamental tree, covered in May or early June with a profusion of large white or pale pink flowers; the mountain dogwood, *C. Nuttallii;* and the red osier dogwood, *C. sericea.* (See **Cornus**.)

dogwood family *n.* A common name for the family Cornaceae.

dolabriform (doh lab'ruh form) *a.* Having the form of an axhead.

Dolichos (dahl'ih kahs) *n.* A genus of 60 species of twining herbaceous vines (Leguminosae). *D. Lablab,* often called the Egyptian or hyacinth bean, is grown for food in warm regions and as an ornamental annual elsewhere. It grows from 10 to 30 feet. It has leaves with 3 leaflets, purple or white flowers, and velvety pods containing white and black edible beans.

dolomitic limestone (doh luh miht'ihk) *n.* A fertilizer that contains magnesium.

Dombeya (dahm bay'uh) *n.* A genus of 200 species of handsome tropical shrubs and small trees (Bittneriaceae). They have large, simple, alternate, and tropical-looking leaves and clusters of rose, pink, or white hydrangealike flowers. Used to create tropical effects or as an espalier.

Doodia (doo'dee uh) *n.* A small genus of 11 species of dwarf tropical ferns (Polypodiaceae). They have divided fronds from 6 to 18 inches long. Grown in warm, protected places outdoors or in greenhouses.

doom palm *n.* A common name for *Hyphaene thebaica* (Palmae), a palm remarkable for its repeatedly branched stem, each branch terminating in a tuft of large fan-shaped leaves. The fruit is about the size of an apple; it has a fibrous, mealy rind, which tastes like gingerbread. Also spelled doum palm. Also known as gingerbread tree.

doom palm

Doritis (dor igh′tuhs) *n.* A genus of 2 species of tropical epiphytic orchids (Orchidaceae). They are similar to *Phalenopsis,* with few basal, fleshy leaves and, usually, many-flowered stalks of white to amethyst-purple flowers.

dormancy *n.* The state of being dormant; a resting phase for plants, during which they may have no leaves or flowers.

dormant spray *n.* Any type of pesticide applied to dormant, usually leafless, plants to control a number of insects and diseases. (See **lime sulfur** and **horticultural oil.**)

Doronicum (duh rahn′ih kuhm) *n.* A genus of about 30 species of perennial flowers (Compositae). *D. cordatum* and *D. Pardalianches,* commonly known as leopard's-bane, are cultivated for their flowers. They have basal leaves and showy, daisy-like yellow flowers. Used in borders.

Dorotheanus (dor uh thee an′uhs) *n.* A genus of 10 species of dwarf, succulent annuals (Aizoaceae). It has leaves that form rosettes on short branches and ice-plantlike white, pink, orange, or red flowers. It is used as a temporary ground cover in difficult, dry soils. Commonly known as Livingstone daisy.

dorsal *a.* Pertaining to or attached to the back of a plant or plant part; facing away from or situated outside the axis of a plant.

dorsifixed (dor′sih fihkst) *a.* In botany, attached at the back of a plant or plant part, such as the anthers of lilies.

dorsiventral (dor sih vehn′truhl) *a.* In botany, flattened and having a definite front and back surface, such as a blade of grass.

Dorstenia (dor stee′nee uh) *n.* A genus of about 170 herbaceous plants and shrubs (Moraceae), some species native to tropical America. The leaves are basal and very variable, with curiously shaped flowers. Grown as a novelty.

Dorstenia flower

Doryanthes (dor ee an′theez) *n.* A genus of 2 species of enormous succulents (Agavaceae). They form a gigantic cluster of a hundred or so leaves, 6 inches wide and 8 feet long. They have a flower stalk that towers 15 feet high and reddish-brown flowers in long clusters up to six feet long. They require a substantial area; not for the small garden.

Dorycnium (doh rihk′nee uhm) *n.* A genus of about 10 to 15 species of cloverlike plants (Leguminosae) native to the Mediterranean region and the Canary Islands. They have leaves divided into 5 leaflets and butterflylike white, rose, and purple flowers.

Doryopteris (doh ree ahp′tuh rihs) *n.* A genus of 25 species of small tropical ferns (Polypodiaceae) with black, glossy stems and highly variable fronds.

double *a.* In botany, having the number of petals largely increased, as in forms of camellias, chrysanthemums, zinnias, and many other flowers.

douglas fir *n.* A common name for *Pseudotsuga menziesii,* native to North America. The common name is in honor of the renowned plant hunter David Douglas.

Douglasia (duhg las′ee uh) *n.* A genus of 6 species of alpine perennials, some species native to the mountains of North America. They have leaves in rosettes and red, yellow, or purple tubular flowers. Used in rock gardens and alpine collections.

doum palm *n.* (See **doom palm**.)

doveflower *n.* A common name for *Peristeria elata,* an orchid native to Central America; so called from the resemblance of the flower to a white dove with expanded wings. Also called Holy Ghost flower.

dove's-foot *n.* The common name for *Geranium molle,* so called from the shape of its leaf.

dove tree *n.* A common name for *Davidia involucrata.* It grows to 50 or 60 feet; it has broad, heart-shaped, toothed leaves that are downy beneath and white-bracted clusters of flowers. Commonly known as dove tree or handkerchief tree.

Dovyalis (doh vee al′ihs) *n.* A genus of 22 species of subtropical shrubs or small trees (Flacourtiaceae). They have simple, entire, alternate leaves, inconspicuous flowers, and an edible pale orange or yellow berry. Commonly known as kei apple and umkokolo.

Downingia *n.* A small genus of 11 species of low-growing annuals (Lobeliaceae) native to the Americas. They have simple, entire leaves and showy blue or white flowers.

down tree *n.* The common name for the fast-growing tropical tree Ochroma pyramidale, native to South America; so called from the downy covering of the seeds. Also known as balsa.

downy mildew *n.* A fungal disease thriving in cool, damp weather. It causes brown spots on older leaves, particularly of melons and cucumbers, and the leaves eventually dry and drop. Controls include traditional fungicides, planting resistant varieties, pruning to increase air circulation, and planting in warm locations.

Draba (dray′bah) *n.* A genus of about 250 species of very hardy, low herbaceous perennials, or rarely annuals (Cruciferae), mostly native to cold mountainous regions and the Arctic. They have simple leaves in a basal rosette, and clusters of small, dainty white, yellow, rose, or purple flowers.

Dracaena (druh see′nuh) *n.* 1. A genus of 40 species of tropical shrubs or trees (Agavaceae). The leaves are large and entire, often somewhat fleshy, and grow in tufts at the ends of the branches. The flowers are small. Various species are grown as houseplants though some that are known under the name belong to the related genus *Cordyline.* 2. Dracena is a common name for *Cordyline.*

Dracaena
(dragon tree)

Dracocephalum (dray koh sehf′uh luhm) *n.* A genus of 45 species of small plants or subshrubs (Labiate). They have opposite, simple, and entire leaves and clusters of tubular, 2-lipped, intense blue or violet flowers. A common name for the genus is dragon's-head or dragonhead, a translation from Latin of the genus name.

Dracunculus (druh kuhng kyuh luhs) *n.* A genus of 2 species of herbaceous plants (Araceae). *D. vulgaris* has long, narrow, white-spotted leaves forming a fan-shape, and large, stinky, callalike flowers, green on the outside, reddish-purple within. Commonly known as green dragon.

dragonhead *n.* (See **Dracocephalum**.)

dragonroot *n.* A common name for *Arisaema Dracontium* and for the root of the jack-in-the-pulpit, *Arisaema triphyllum.*

dragon's-head *n.* (See **Dracocephalum**.)

dragon tree *n.* The common name for *Dracaena Draco.* (See **Dracaena.**)

drain *v.* To remove water from the soil by artificial means, such as drainage ditches, buried perforated plastic pipes, or a gravel sump. Also to amend heavy clay soils with sand or organic material.

drainage *n.* 1. The removal of excess water from the soil. 2. water moving down in the soil. 4. A system of conduits, channels, or passages by means of which something is drained.

drain-well *n.* A pit sunk through an impervious layer of earth or stone to a porous layer, to draw off water.

draw hoe *n.* A traditional hoe, with a long handle attached to a transverse blade, used for cultivating and weeding.

drepaniform (druh pan'uh form) *n.* In botany, sickle-shaped.

dried blood *n.* An organic fertilizer that leaves an acid reaction.

dried flowers *n. pl.* Blossoms that have been dehydrated but have retained a natural shape and color.

drift *n.* Soil material deposited by geological process in 1 place after having been removed from another place.

drill *n.* 1. In agriculture, a machine for planting seeds, as of grasses, wheat, oats, corn, etc., by dropping them in rows and covering them with earth. 2. A row of seeds deposited in the earth; the trench or channel in which the seeds are deposited. *v.* In agriculture: 1. To sow in rows, drills, or channels, as to drill wheat. 2. To sow with seed in rows; for example, the field was drilled, not sown broadcast (scattered).

drill-harrow *n.* A small harrow employed to remove weeds and to pulverize the earth between rows of plants.

drill-plow *n.* A plow for sowing grain in rows.

Drimys (drigh'mihs) *n.* A genus of aromatic evergreen shrubs or small trees (Winteraceae), some species native to the Americas. *D. Winteri* has alternate, leathery, aromatic evergreen leaves and clusters of creamy-white jasmine-scented flowers. Commonly known as winter's bark.

Drimys winteri
(winter's bark)

drip irrigation *n.* A system of watering by which moisture running through a porous hose is slowly released through tiny holes, or emitters, to the root zone of plants.

drop spreader *n.* A trough-shaped container mounted on wheels through which seed, fertilizer, lime, or other bulk material drops at a set rate through an adjustable slit in the bottom.

dropwort *n.* A common name for *Filipendula vulgaris,* (Rosaceae), a plant with alternate leaves divided into many leaflets and tall, plumelike flowers on 3-foot-tall stems.

Drosanthemum (droh san'thuh muhm) *n.* A genus of 95 species of succulent perennials (Aizoaceae). It has fleshy leaves, with glistening dots as though flecked with ice crystals, and free-flowering orange, yellow, pale pink, or purple typical iceplant flowers with many narrow petals. Used to create sheets of color in difficult situations, including poor soil, limited moisture, and steep slopes. Controls erosion and can be fire-retardant.

Drosera (drahs'uh ruh) *n.* A genus of carniverous plants (Droseraceae) found in bogs. Their leaves are covered with glandular hairs, which exude drops of a clear, glutinous fluid that glitter in the sun; hence the name sundew. These glandular hairs capture small insects and trigger secretion of a digestive fluid. Grown as a curiosity. Commonly known as sundew.

Drosera
(sundew)

Droseraceae (drahs uh ray′see ee) *n. pl.* A family of 4 genera and 90 to 100 species of insectivorous plants found in marshes; the sundew family. The genera include *Drosera, Dionoea, Drosophyllum,* and *Aldrovanda.*

drought-tolerant plants *n.* Plants that can survive periods of time with little or no water. Also spelled drouth-tolerant.

drowning *n.* A surplus of water that drowns plant roots by eliminating oxygen from the soil.

drumstick tree *n.* A common name for the flowering tree *Cassia fistula,* so called from the shape of its 2-foot-long pods. It grows to 30 feet and has leaves divided into large leaflets and pale yellow flowers that appear before the leaves.

drupaceous (droo pay′shuhs) *a.* Pertaining to or producing drupes.

drupe (droop) *n.* In botany, a stone-fruit having a hard, nutlike inner part surrounded by a fleshy or fibrous outer layer, such as the peach, cherry, olive, and walnut.

drupelet (droo′pluht) *n.* A small drupe, especially as applied to the individual components of aggregate fruits such as blackberries and raspberries, which consist of many seeds, each surrounded by its own fleshy layer. Also drupel.

druxy (druhk′see) *a.* Pertaining to a tree or tim-

ber, having decayed spots or streaks in the heartwood.

Drynaria (drigh nar′ee uh) *n.* A genus of about 20 species of tropical epiphytic ferns (Polypodiaceae). They have erect, short, broad sterile leaves and long, deeply divided fertile fronds to 6 feet long.

Dryopteris (drigh ahp′tuh rihs) *n.* A genus of 150 species of terrestrial woodland ferns (Polypodiaceae), some species native to the Americas and Hawaii. They often have finely cut leaves and are usually drought-tolerant. Useful in the woodland garden. Commonly known as wood fern or shield fern.

dry sand *n.* A sandy deposit with low water-holding capacity.

Duchesnea (doo kay′nee uh) *n.* A genus of 2 species of low-growing perennial ground cover (Rosaceae) native to southern Asia. It has rounded, finely notched leaflets, small yellow flowers resembling strawberry blossoms, and red, many-seeded fruit. Commonly called mock strawberry. Used as a small-scale ground cover.

Dudleya (duhd′lee uh) *n.* A genus of about 40 species of mostly perennial succulents (Crassulaceae) native to the American West. They have smooth, fleshy, light green leaves, often in a rosette, and stalks of small starlike flowers.

duff *n.* The partly decomposed organic surface layer of forested soil.

dulcamara
(bittersweet)

dulcamara (duhl kuh mah′ruh) *n.* A name for the bittersweet, *Solanum Dulcamara,* a common hedge plant native throughout Europe, particularly the

Mediterranean region, and naturalized in the United States. All parts are poisonous.

dumb cane *n.* A common name for *Dieffenbachia,* so called because its acrid sap will burn the mouth and throat and, may paralyze the vocal chords, destroying the power of speech when chewed. (See **Dieffenbachia**.)

dune *n.* A mound of loose sand piled up by wind.

Duranta (dyuh ran'tuh) *n.* A genus of about 30 evergreen shrubs (Verbenaceae) native to subtropical and tropical America. They have pairs of glossy green leaves and bear a great profusion of white, lilac, violet-blue, or purple flowers, which attract butterflies. Grown outdoors in warm winter climates or in greenhouses elsewhere.

Dursban (ders ban') *n.* A common synthetic insecticide (chemical name: chlorpyrifos) used to control a variety of pests or trees, lawns, and ornamentals. Effective against ants and many soil-dwelling insects.

dust/dusting *n.* Method of pesticide control in which a dry substance (dust) is applied by spraying (dusting).

duster *n.* A device consisting of a bin, a wand with a nozzle, and a crank mechanism; used for applying dust or powder to plants.

dusting equipment *n.* Any of various combinations of containers and tubes or hoses used for holding and applying dusts. (See **sprayer**.)

dust mulch *n.* A dry, loose surface layer of a cultivated soil, effective in reducing water loss from the underlying soil.

dusty miller *n.* The *Centaurea cineraria* and the *Senecio Cineraria,* common cultivated foliage plants that are covered with white tomentum (tiny hairs), which gives the plant a silvery, ashy-gray appearance.

Dutch bulbs *n.* A common term for spring-blooming bulbs grown in Holland. They are planted out in fall for bloom the following spring. Examples include tulips, daffodils, and hyacinths. Used in early borders, for massing in beds, and in containers.

Dutch elm disease *n.* A devastating fungal disease of American elms *(Ulmus americana)* and some related species, spread by the bark beetle. It causes dieback and eventual death of the tree. Control is difficult and best handled by an arborist. For assistance, contact local forestry officials.

Dutch hoe *n.* (See **scuffle hoe**.)

Dutchman's-breeches *n.* A common name for *Dicentra Cucullaria,* so called from its broad, double-spurred flowers.

Dutchman's-pipe *n.* The common name for *Aristolochia durior,* a woody vine with broad, handsome leaves, so called from its curiously shaped flowers. (See cut under **Aristolochia**.) Useful as a screen for porches or as a wall cover.

dwarf fruit tree *n.* 1. A small fruit tree reaching a height at maturity of as little as 4 or 5 feet and bearing early, but normal fruit.

dwarf plants *n. pl.* Plants of genetically small size or those dwarfed by grafting (such as dwarf apple trees) or by pruning and restricted root growth (such as bonsai).

dwarf shrubs *n.* Shrubs that are selected or hybridized that are typically shorter and more compact than the species; for example, *Nandina domestica* 'Nana' grows to only 1 foot high where the species grows to 6 to 8 feet.

Dyckia (dihk'yuh) *n.* A genus of 103 species of succulent or tufted perennials (Bromeliaceae) native to South America. They have spiny-edged leaves in basal rosettes and stalks of yellow, orange, or red tubular flowers. They form large clumps, which makes them useful bedding plants in warm climates.

dyeing flowers *n. pl.* Blossoms capable of producing dyes.

dyer's-broom *n.* The plant *Genista tinctoria,* used to make a yellow dye.

dyer's-weed *n.* Same as dyer's woad.

dyer's woad (wohdd) *n.* The woad, or yellow-weed, *Isatis tinctoria,* which affords a yellow dye. Also called dyer's- weed.

E

e- a prefix meaning 1. not, as edentate, not dentate; 2. without, as ebracteate, without bracts, or 3. beyond, out, outward, as exogenous, growing from the outside. Also ex-.

eared *a.* Having ears or awns, such as in corn or wheat.

eardrop *n.* A common name for the genus *Dicentra*. Golden eardrop is common name for *Dicentra chrysantha,* so called for its dangling, golden flowers. Lady's eardrop is a common name for *Fuschia,* so called from the dangling, pendantlike flowers.

earsh (ersh) *n.* (See **eddish.**)

earth auger (aw'ger) *n.* (See **auger.**)

earth-ball *n.* A common name for the truffle *Tuber melanosporum,* which grows underground on the roots of oaks, beech, and hazel. Considered the choicest of all edible mushrooms.

earthnut *n.* A common name for the peanut, *Arachis hypogaea.* Also called groundnut.

earth staple *n.* A u-shaped wire for securing row covers or plastic mulches to soil.

earthworm *n.* A common name for several species of soil-dwelling worms. Extremely beneficial, they loosen and aerate the soil, and help break down organic matter.

earwig *n.* A night-feeding insect with threatening-looking pinchers at its posterior end. It is actually quite harmless, feeding primarily on decaying organic matter and other insects, including aphids. However, they also eat soft plant parts, such as flowers, and are usually considered a pest. Control measures include trapping at night in rolled-up newspapers, eliminating hiding places through garden cleanup and using pesticidal baits.

Easter flower *n.* 1. A common name for *Anemone pulsatilla,* also called pasqueflower. 2. A common name for *Narcissus,* also called daffodil. (See **daffodil** and **Narcissus.**)

Easter-herald's-trumpet *n.* A common name for *Beaumontia grandiflora,* a woody evergreen vine with long, oval leaves and fragrant, trumpet-shaped white trumpet-shaped flowers 5 inches long and 4 inches across. Also called herald's-trumpet or Easter-lily vine.

Ebenaceae (ehb uh nay'see ee) *n. pl.* A family of 6 genera of shrubs or trees. The ornamental genera include *Diospyros,* the persimmon, *Maba,* and *Royena.* (See cut under **Diospyros.**)

ebony *n.* A name given to various woods distinguished in general by their dark color and hardness; extensively used for carving, ornamental cabinetwork, instruments, canes, etc. The most valuable is *Diospyros Ebenum,* which grows in Sri Lanka. The most usual color is black. Mountain ebony, of the East Indies, is the wood of *Bauhinia variegata.*

ebracteate (ee brack'tee ayt) *a.* In botany, without bracts.

ebracteolate (ee brak'tee uh layt) *a.* In botany, without small bracts (bracteoles).

ecalcarate (ee kal'kuh rayt) *a.* In botany, having no spur.

ecarinate (ee kar'uh nayt) *a.* In botany, without a carina or keel.

ecaudate (ee kaw'dayt) *a.* In botany, without a tail.

Ecballium
(squirting cucumber)

Ecballium (ehk bal'ee uhm) *n.* A genus of 1 species, *E. Elaterium* (Cucurbitaceae), the squirting cucumber. It is so named because the fruit, when ripe, separates suddenly from its stalk and, at the same moment, shoots the seeds and juice from the hole left by the stalk.

Eccremocarpus (ehk′ruh moh kar′puhs) *n.* A genus of 3 or 4 climbing vines (Bignoniaceae) native to South America. They have leaves divided into pairs of small leaflets and 5-lobed scarlet, orange, or yellow flowers. Commonly known as glory flower. Grown as a perennial in warm-winter climates, as an annual elsewhere.

Echeveria (ehch′uh vuh ree′uh) *n.* A genus of about 100 species of succulents (Crassulaceae) native to the Americas. Commonly called hen and chickens. They have thick, fleshy leaves, mostly in rosettes, and stalks of 5 bell-shapped, nodding pink, red, or yellow flowers, which rise out of the rosette.

Echinacea (ehk uh nay′shee uh) *n.* A genus of 3 species of coarse, stiff plants (Compositae) native to the prairies of North America. They have large, alternate, oblong leaves and showy flower heads with drooping purple rays and dark purple centers. Used in perennial borders and prairie gardens.

echinate (ee kigh′nayt) *a.* Prickly; covered with stiff pines or bristles.

Echinocactus (ih kigh′nuh kak′tuhs) *n.* A genus of about 16 species of cactus (Cactaceae) native to Mexico and the southwestern United States. They are globose or oval, strongly ribbed, and spiny; they have large and showy yellow flowers. Commonly known as barrel cactus.

Echinocereus (ih kigh′noh sihr′ee uhs) *n.* A genus of 35 species of low-growing, usually spiny, ribbed cactus (Cactaceae) native to Mexico and the southwestern United States. The bell-shaped or tubular red, purple, yellow, or white flowers burst through the surface above the spines, open during the day, and close at night. Commonly known as hedgehog cactus or pitaya. Grown mainly by collectors.

Echinocystis (ehk ih noh sihs′tihs) *n.* A genus of a single species of annual vine, *E. lobata* (Cucurbitaceae), native to North America. It climbs by tendrils, has numerous white flowers, and an oval, prickly fruit, which becomes a papery, inflated pod.

Commonly known as wild balsam apple or prickly cucumber.

Echinodorus (ehk ih nahd′uh ruhs) *n.* A genus of about 30 species of aquatic plants (Alismataceae), some species native to the Americas. They often have spotted leaves, usually submerged; pretty, long-stemmed white flowers; and clusters of spiny, beaked fruit. Commonly known as burhead.

Echinopsis (ehk ih nahp′sihs) *n.* A genus of 30 species of small ribbed cactus (Cactaceae) native to South America. They are round to oblong, straight ribbed, with night-blooming tubular pink or white flowers. Commonly known as sea-urchin cactus.

Echioides (ehk ee oi′deez) *n.* A genus of a single species, *E.longifliorum* (Boraginaceae), an erect herbaceous perennial. It has basal leaves and clusters of yellow, purple-spotted flowers. Commonly known as prophet flower. Used in borders or in rock gardens.

Echium (ehk′ee uhm) *n.* A genus of 35 species of tall, hairy, somewhat shrubby, plants (Boraginaceae). They have simple, alternate leaves and clusters of blue, purple, red, pink, or white flowers. *E. vulgare,* the common viper's bugloss, or blueweed, with showy blue flowers, has become naturalized in some parts of the United States. The genus is commonly known as viper's bugloss.

ecology *n.* The study of the interrelationships of plants, animals, and their environment.

eddish (ehd′ihsh) *n.* Stubble; a stubble field. Also called earsh and ersh.

edelweiss

edelweiss (ayd′uhl wighs) *n*. A common name for *Leondontopodium alpinum,* native to high mountains. It is a low, herbaceous perennial with woolly, white leaves and dense clusters of tubular white flowers. Grown by alpine collectors.

edge *v*. To provide with an edge, fringe, or border, as, to edge a flower bed with dwarf boxwood.

edger *n*. (See **edging tool**.)

edging *n*. 1. Any nonbiodegradable material, typically plastic or metal, installed in the ground to separate flower beds from lawn or other landscape areas. 2. A border; a skirting; specifically, in horticulture, a row of plants set along the border of a flower-bed; as an edging of dwarf boxwood.

edging knife *n*. (See **edging tool**.)

edging shears *n. pl*. Shears used to cut the edges of grass along walks, around garden beds, etc. The blades are often set at an angle and fitted to long handles so that the operator can work in a standing position.

edging tile *n*. Decorative cast-concrete border used to contain gravel on paths, define the boundaries of beds, or separate adjacent plantings.

edging tool *n*. A long-handled, sharp-edged device used to slice sod. Designed to be pushed into the ground with the foot, an edging tool is used to make a crisp line between landscape features, as between lawn and flower beds or paths.

Edraianthus (ehd ray an′thuhs) *n*. A genus of about 12 species of tufted perennials (Campanulaceae). They have long, slim leaves and showy clusters of bell-shaped purple, violet, blue, or white flowers. Commonly known as grassy-bells. Used in the rock garden.

efflorescence (ef luh rehs′ihnts) *n*. In botany, the time or state of flowering; anthesis.

efflorescent (ef luh rehs′ihnt) *a*. Blooming or flowering.

eggplant *n*. The aubergine, *Solanum Melongena* var. *esculentum,* cultivated for its large oblong fruit, of a dark purple color or sometimes white or yellow. The pulp is soft, with a slightly bitter juice that is usually removed before cooking by sprinkling the cut pulp with salt and squeezing out the juice thus produced.

eggplant

eglantine (ehg′luhn tighn) *n*. The common name for *Rosa Eglanteria;* also called sweetbrier. 2. The wild rose or dogrose, *Rosa canina.*

Egyptian onion *n*. A variety of *Allium cepa* that bears clusters of tiny bulblets on top of 2- or 3-foot-long stems. The weight of the bulblets bends the stem, and the bulblets fall to the ground where they take root and form new plants. The bulblets are mild flavored and used in cooking much like shallots. Also known as circle onion or walking onion.

Ehretia (eh reesh′ee uh) *n*. A genus of 50 species of tropical and subtropical shrubs or trees (Boraginaceae). They have simple, alternate, wavy, finely notched leaves and clusters of white, blue, and mauve flowers.

Eichhornia (ighk hor′nee uh) *n*. A genus of 6 or 7 rhizomaceous aquatic plants (Pontederiaceae) native to tropical America. They have floating or submerged leaves and spikes of showy lavender-blue, violet, or pale violet flowers. *E. crassipes* is the common water hyacinth, a serious pest in natural waterways in warm regions. *Eichhornia* spp. may be used in garden pools and ponds, but it can become a pernicious weed in warm climates.

Elaeagnaceae (ehl′ee ag nay′see ee) *n. pl*. A small family of 3 genera and 45 species of hardy shrubs or trees. The 3 genera are *Elaeagnus, Hippopha,* and *Shepherdia.* Commonly known as the oleaster family.

Elaeagnus (ehl ee ag′nuhs) *n*. A genus of about 40 species of hardy shrubs or small trees (Elaeagnaceae). *E. angustifolia* is a very hardy tree that grows to 20 feet, with attractive silvery leaves and fragrant, summer-blooming flowers. Commonly known as oleaster, Russian olive, silverberry, and wild olive.

Elaeagnus angustifolia
(oleaster)

Elaeocarpaceae (ih lee oh kahr pay'see ee) *n.* A family of 8 to 12 genera and 350 to 400 species. They are tropical and subtropical trees and shrubs with simple leaves and clusters or spikes of showy flowers. The genera cultivated in warm climates of the United States include *Aristotelia, Crinodendron, Elaeocarpus,* and *Muntingia.* Commonly known as the Elaeocarpus family.

Elaeocarpus (ih lee oh kahr'puhs) *n.* A genus of more than 60 species of tropical and subtropical trees and shrubs (Elaeocarpaceae). They have simple leaves and spikes of small flowers. The fruit is oblong or round, consisting of a rough, bony nut surrounded by a fleshy pulp.

Elaeocarpus family (ih lee oh kahr'puhs fam'uh lee) *n.* (See **Elaeocarpaceae**.)

Elaphoglossum (ehl'uh foh glahs'uhm) *n.* A genus of more than 400 species of tropical epiphytic ferns native to the Americas. They have thick, tongue-shaped leaves to 2 feet long and 10 inches wide. *E. crinitum* is commonly known as elephant-ear fern. Usually grown as a hothouse specimen.

Elatinaceae (ih lat'uhn ay'see ee) *n. pl.* A family of 2 genera and 40 to 50 species of small water

plants with opposite leaves and axillary flowers; the waterworts. (See **Elatine**.)

Elatine (ih lat'uh nee) *n.* A genus of 10 to 20 species of small annual water plants (Elatinaceae) growing in wetlands. Commonly known as waterwort. Sometimes used as aquarium plants.

elder *n.* The common name for species of *Sambucus.* The ordinary elder of North America is *S. Canadensis* with black-purple berries, is well-known as a shrub of rapid growth; the stems contain an unusual amount of pith. The red-berried elder is *S. racemosa,* and the dwarf or ground elder is *S. Ebulus.* **Box-elder,** the *Acer Negundo,* is a North American tree often cultivated for shade.

elecampane (ehl'ih kam payn) *n.* The common name of *Inula Helenium,* a robust stout plant (Compositae) widely naturalized in the United States. It has hairy stems; large, irregularly toothed leaves, which are velvety beneath; and daisylike yellow flowers.

elecampane

electric fence *n.* An electrified wire exclosure, which, when touched by deer or other animals that might enter a garden, discourages them by delivering a nonlethal shock.

electric grass shears *n.* (See **cordless hand trimmer**.)

electric hotbed *n.* A cold frame used for extending the growing season. Once heated by the decomposition of cow or horse manure, hotbeds are now usually heated by an electrical mat or heating element.

Eleocharis (ehl ee ahk'uh rihs) *n.* A genus of about 160 species of rushes (Cyperaceae) that grow in wetlands. They are characterized by mostly cylindrical, bamboolike stems and by bisexual flowers appearing between closely overlapping scales. Commonly known as spike rush. *E. dulcis,* commonly known as Chinese water chestnut, is grown for its edible tubers. Other species are used as aquarium plants.

elephant creeper *n.* The common name for *Argyreia nervosa* (Convolvulaceae), a woody climber that reaches the tops of the tallest trees. It has heart-shaped leaves to 1-foot across and are woolly white beneath and clusters of large, deep rose flowers. Also known as woolly morning glory.

elephant ear *n.* A common name for 2 different genera, *Alocasia* and *Colocasia. Alocasia* is a tropical perennial with large, leathery, arrow-shaped leaves and a callalike flower. *Colocasia* is a tropical perennial with tuberous roots and mammoth, heart-shaped gray-green leaves; commonly known as taro. (See **elephant's ear**.)

elephant-ear fern *n.* A common name for *Elaphoglossum crinitum,* a tropical epiphytic fern native to the Americas. It has thick, tongue-shaped leaves to 2 feet long and 10 inches wide. Usually grown as a hothouse specimen.

elephant garlic *n.* A large-podded variety of *Allium sativum,* with a slightly milder flavor than the smaller-podded variety.

elephant's ear *n.* A common name for plants of several genera: *Begonia,* from the 1-sided form of their leaves; *Caladium,* for their large, attractive leaves; and *Enterlobium cyclocarpum,* an ornamental tropical tree. (See **elephant ear**.)

elephant's foot *n.* A common name for *Dioscorea elephantipes,* a twining vine that has pointed leaves and that grows from a tuber; a member of the yam family. Also known as Hottentot bread.

Elettaria (ehl uh tar′ee uh) *n.* An genus of possibly 6 species of tropical perennial plants (Zingiberaceae). *E. Cardamomum* furnishes the spice cardamom. Also spelled cardamon or cardamum.

elk tree *n.* A common name *Oxydendrum arboreum,* a slow-growing tree native to the eastern United States; grown for its scarlet leaves in autumn. Also called elkwood, sourwood, or sorrel tree.

Elliottia (ehl ee aht′ee uh) *n.* A genus of a single species of deciduous shrubs (Ericaceae) native to

eastern Georgia and southern South Carolina. It has simple, alternate leaves and many clusters of white flowers.

elm *n.* The common name for the genus *Ulmus,* mostly large trees, with wide-spreading and gracefully curving branches. Of the European species, the common English elm is *U. procera. U. glabra,* the Scotch elm, or wych elm, is a smaller tree than the English elm. The American species, *U. americana,* has been decimated throughout the United States by the Dutch elm disease; it is also called American elm, white elm, or water elm. *U. crassifolia* is the cedar elm of the southern United States and northern Mexico; *U. Thomasii* is commonly known as the cork elm, or rock elm. *U. rubra* is commonly known as the red elm or slippery elm. *U. alata,* with corky-winged branches, is commonly known as winged elm, small-leaved elm, or wahoo elm. (See also **Ulmus**.)

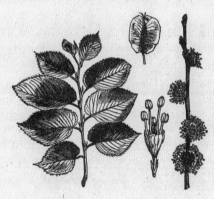

elm leaves, with flower and fruit on a larger scale

elm family *n.* The common name for Ulmaceae. (See **elm**.)

elm leaf beetle *n.* A devastating pest of elm trees. The adults, but especially the wormlike larvae, feed on foliage, eating just between the leaf veins. Trees eventually look hazy brown, with the entire canopy skeletonized. Repeated infestations can eventually kill the tree. Traditional pesticides and banding can be effective, but the help of an arborist is usually required.

Elodea (ehl uh dee′uh) *n.* A genus of about 12 species of waterweeds (Hydrocharitaceae) native to the Americas. They have whorls of slim leaves and flowers in long spathes. Grown as pondweeds in aquariums and ponds, they have naturalized and have become a noxious weed throughout much of Europe and parts of North America.

Elsholtzia (ehl shohlt'see uh) *n.* A genus of about 30 species of aromatic annual plants and subshrubs (Labiatae). They are attractive, late-blooming plants with opposite, finely toothed leaves and spikes of purple or blue flowers. *E. Stauntonii* is commonly known as mintshrub.

eluviation (ee loo vee ay'shuhn) *n.* The movement of moisture and nutrients from 1 place to another in the soil.

Elymus (ehl'uh muhs) *n.* A genus of about 150 mostly perennial grasses (Gramineae). Several are grown as ornamentals for their brilliant blue foliage. Commonly known as blue wild ryegrass.

emarginate (ee mar'juh nayt) *a.* In botany, having a shallow notch at the tip, for example, on a leaf.

emargination (ee mar juh nay'shuhn) *n.* A notching of the margin, for example, along the edge of a leaf.

Embothrium (ehm bahth'ree uhn) *n.* A genus of 8 species of tropical evergreen trees (Proteaceae), native the central and southern Andes. They have long, willowy branches, alternate, entire, leathery leaves, and showy scarlet flowers to 2 inches long. Grown in warm-winter climates as a specimen flowering tree. *E. coccineum* is commonly known as Chilean fire tree.

embryo (ehm'bree oh) *n.* In botany, the developing rudimentary plant contained in the seed of flowering plants prior to germination and growth.

embryotega (ehm bree oht'uh guh) *n.* In botany, a small circular thickening near the seed scar on the seeds of some plants, such as members of the spiderwort family.

emersed (ee muhrst') *a.* Rising above the water, such as the leaves of many water plants.

Emilia (ih meel yuh) *n.* A genus of 20 species of tropical herbaceous flowers (Compositae). They are erect, slender plants to 2 feet tall and have alternate leaves and flat-topped clusters of red, yellow, rose, or purple flowers. *E. javanica* is commonly known as tassel flower or Flora's-paintbrush.

Emmenanthe (ehm uh nan'thee) *n.* A genus of a single species, *E. penduliflora* (Hydrophyllaceae), native to western North America. It has finely divided oblong leaves with clusters of many small, nodding, pale yellow or light pink flowers. Commonly known as yellow bells, golden bells, or whispering bells.

Empetraceae (ehm puh tray'see ee) *n. pl.* A family of 3 genera and 6 or 7 species. They are low, shrubby, heathlike evergreens, with small flowers without petals and drupelike fruit. The ornamental genera include *Empetrum, Corema,* and *Ceratiola.* Commonly known as the crowberry family.

Empetrum (ehm'puh truhm) *n.* A genus of 3 or 4 species of low, heathlike shrubs; the crowberry. Some species are native to North America. They have narrow, whorled leaves and small greenish or purplish flowers. *E. nigrum,* the crakeberry, has edible black berries.

empress tree *n.* A common name for *Paulownia tomentosa,* a fast-growing tree with showy clusters of fragrant, trumpet-shaped lilac-blue flowers, named for the great ballerina Anna Pavlova.

enantioblastic (ihn ant'ee uh blas'tihk) *a.* Pertaining to a plant embryo, originating at the end directly opposite the hilum (seed scar).

enation (ih nay'shuhn) *n.* An outgrowth from the surface of a leaf or other plant part.

Encarsia wasp (ehn kar'see uh) *n.* A beneficial insect, harmless to humans, that preys on the larvae of some species of whitefly. Most effective in greenhouses. Sold through the mail. Also known as whitefly parasite.

Encelia (ehn seel'yuh) *n.* A genus of about 14 species of low-branching shrubs or perennial plants (Compositae) native to the Americas. They have alternate, entire, or toothed leaves and daisylike yellow or purple flowers.

Encephalartos (ihn sehf'uh lahr tuhs) *n.* A genus of about 20 species of palmlike plants (Zamiaceae) having short cylindrical or spherical trunks, with a crown of stiff, divided leaves, which often have spiny leaflets. Grown outdoors in warm-winter climates or in conservatories for their ornamental leaves.

encino (ehn see'noh) *n.* The common name for *Quercus agrifolia,* the coast live-oak, native to California. It is a large evergreen tree, with spiny, hollylike leaves. Becoming rare due to development, it is now a much-valued native oak.

endemic (ehn'dehm'ihk) *a.* Native to, naturally restricted to, or found only in a particular area or region.

endive (ehn'dighv) *n. Cichorium Endivia* (Compositae), distinguished from the chicory, *C. Intybus,* by its annual root and less bitter taste. It has long been in cultivation and is in common use as a salad.

endocarp (ehn'duh karp) *n.* In fruits whose pericarp consists of dissimilar layers, the innermost layer. It may be hard and stony, such as the pit of a plum or peach, membranous as the core of an apple, or fleshy, such as the pulp of an orange,

endogen (ehn'duh jehn) *n.* A plant that develops from or on the inside, as most monocots.

endogenous (ehn dahj'uh nuhs) *a.* In botany: 1. Of or pertaining to endogens; as, endogenous plants; 2. proceeding from within: as, endogenous growth.

endostome (ehn'duh stohm) *n.* In botany; the opening in the inner covering of the ovule.

endosulfan (ehn'doh suhl'fan) *n.* A broad-spectrum, synthetic insecticide used to control many plant pests, including whiteflies and thrips. Common trade name: Thiodan.

Endymion (ehn dihm'ee uhn) *n.* A genus of 3 or 4 species of perennial bulbs (Liliaceae). They have narrow, basal leaves and spikes of fragrant blue, pink, or white flowers. Commonly known as wood hyacinth. Used in woodland gardens or in drifts under deciduous trees or low-growing perennials.

English hanging basket *n.* A hanging planter made of wire and generally lined with moss; used for growing draping or trailing plants.

English Hawthorn *n.* A common name for *Cra-*

taegus laevigata, a thorny shrub or small tree, much used in hedges. (See **hawthorn** and **Crataegus.**)

English pea *n.* A term used to distinguish peas that are shelled before eating from edible podded varieties or, especially in the southern states, from the so-called black-eyed pea, which is a bean variety.

English planter *n.* Any of variously shaped metal frames, which, when lined with sphagnum moss or dark plastic, is used for growing ornamental plants.

English wall basket (ihng'lihsh wahl bas'kiht) *n.* A half-round wire frame, generally lined with moss, mounted on a wall; used for growing ornamental plants.

Enkianthus (ehn kee an'thuhs) *n.* A genus of 10 species of hardy, deciduous shrubs (Ericaceae). They have simple, alternate leaves, which are crowded at the ends of the branches, and clusters of drooping, nodding, bell-shaped red or white flowers. Useful in shaded locations with acid soil.

ensiform (ehn'suh form) *a.* Sword-shaped; long, narrow, flat, and tapering to a point, as the leaves of many species of iris.

Entada (ehn tah'duh) *n.* A genus of about 30 species of woody vines or small trees (Leguminosae), some species native to tropical America. They have alternate leaves divided into many small long leaflets, clusters of flowers, and, often, large striking pods.

Entelea (ehn tee'lee uh) *n.* A genus of 1 species of shrub or small tree (Tiliaceae). It has heart-shaped leaves and clusters of white flowers.

Enterolobium (ehn ter oh loh'bee uhm) *n.* A genus of 5 or more species of tropical trees (Leguminosae) native to the Americas. They have pairs of alternate leaves and white flowers. Commonly known as elephant's-ear.

entire *a.* Having an unborken margin, without lobes or indentations, such as the leaves of boxwood or privet.

entomophilous (ehn toh mahf'uh luhs) *a.* Literally, insect-loving; applied to flowers whose structure ordinarily requires insects to pollinate them so that seeds can form.

Eomecon (ee ahm ih kahn) *n.* A genus of a single species of herbaceous perennial, *E. chionantha* (Papaveraceae). It grows from a spreading rhizome and has a branched stem, tufted, basal leaves, and short-lived, spring-blooming clusters of poppylike white flowers 2 inches across. Commonly known as snow poppy.

Epacridaceae (ehp uh krih day'see ee) *n. pl.* A family 30 genera of shrubs and small trees, mostly native to heaths and bogs. The ornamental species include *Astroloma, Cyathodes, Dracophyllum, Leucopogon, Pentachondra,* and *Styphelia.*

epappose (ee pap'ohs) *a.* In botany, having no tuft of bristles (pappus), a fetaure often found on seeds that are dispersed by the wind, such as those of dandelion.

epazote (ehp'uh zoht) *n.* An annual herb, *Chenopodium ambrosoides;* related to the common pigweed, grown for its strong-flavored leaves, which are used in Mexican and Central American dishes, especially with beans, where they are thought to counteract the gasiness of beans. It is easy to grow from seed.

Ephedra (ehf'uh druh) *n.* A genus of 40 species of clumping, low-growing desert shrubs (Ephedraceae) found in desert or alkaline regions. They are nearly leafless, with numerous branches, and have triangular cones, which grow at the nodes. Used as a ground cover in desert gardens.

epicalyx (ehp ih kay'lihks) *n.* In botany, a calyxlike involucre of bracts below the true calyx, as in the mallow, or of sepals, as in the potentilla.

epicarp (ehp'ih karp) *n.* In botany, the outer skin of fruits.

epichilium (ehp ih kihl'ee uhm) *n.* In botany, the terminal part of the lip of some orchids. Also epichil or epichile.

epicotyl (ehp'ih kaht ihl) *n.* in botany, the part of a plant embryo or seedling above the cotyledons.

epicotyledonary (ehp ih kaht ihl eed'ihn eh ree) *a.* In botany, pertainng to the epicotyl; situated above the seed leaves (cotyledons)

Epidendrum (ehp uh den'druhm) *n.* A large genus of more than 1,000 species of mostly epiphytic orchids (Orchidaceae) native to tropical and sub-tropical America. They vary much in form, but the stems are often pseudobulbs, bearing strap-shaped, leathery leaves. There are many species in cultivation for their handsome flowers. Commonly known as buttonhole orchid.

Epigaea (ehp uh jee'uh) *n.* A genus of plants of 2 species (Ericaceae); one, *E. repens,* the well-known mayflower, or trailing arbutus, native to the United States. They are prostrate or creeping evergreens, with fragrant rose-colored or white flowers appearing in early spring. Used as a choice woodland ground cover, particularly under pines.

Epigaea
(mayflower or trailing arbutus)

epigeal (ehp ih jee'uhl) *a.* 1. Of a plant, growing above the surface of the ground, as most pants in the garden; 2. Of a cotyledon, forced above the ground in the process of germination, as in beans, morning glories, and many other plants; 3. Of plants gemination, typified by cotyledons that appear above the ground. Also epigeous, epigean, epigaean, or epigeic.

epigenous (eh pihj'uh nuhd) *n.* In botany, growing on the surface of a leaf or other plant organ, for example, many fungi grow on the surface of leaves; mildew is a specific example.

epigynous (ih pihj'uh nuhs) *a.* In botany, referring to calyx, corolla, and stamens: appearing to grow from the top of the ovary, but actually fused to it, as in the cranberry.

Epilobium (ehp uh loh'bee uhm) *n.* A genus about 200 very hardy herbaceous plants or subshrubs (Onagraceae) widely distributed through temperate and arctic regions. The flowers are pink or purple, or rarely yellow, and the seeds are crowned with a tuft of long, silky hairs. The name willow herb is given to the more common species, of which the most conspicuous is *E. angustifolium,* a tall perennial with a simple stem bearing long spikes of large purple flowers and willowlike leaves. Both the genus and *E. angustifolium* are commonly known as fireweed.

Epimedium (ehp uh mee′dee uhm) *n.* A small genus of 21 species of low-growing, rhizomatous perennial herbs (Berberidaceae). They have leaves divided into 3 heart-shaped leaflets and spikes of waxy-textured white, pink, red, or yellow flowers. Several species are grown ornamentally, especially *E. alpinum* and *E. grandiflorum.* Used in rock gardens and woodland gardens and as a ground cover in shady locations.

Epipactis (ehp uh pak tihs) *n.* A genus of about 24 species of terrestrial orchids (Orchidaceae), some species native to North America. They grow from rhizomes and have erect, stout, leafy stems and a spike of purplish-brown or whitish flowers. Commonly known as helleborine.

epipetalous (ehp uh peht′uh luhs) *a.* Borne on the petals or the corolla of a flower: applied to stamens, and to plants whose stamens are attached to the corolla.

Epiphyllum (ehp uh fihl′uhm) *n.* A genus of 16 species of mostly epiphytic cactus (Cactaceae) native to tropical America. They have numerous branches formed of short, flattened, bright green joints, and they have large, showy, often fragrant, flowers. Commonly known as orchid cactus or pond-lily cactus.

epiphyte (ehp′uh fight) *n.* In botany, a plant that grows on another plant but does not derive its nourishment from it, such as many ferns, orchids, and bromeliads.

epiphytic (ehp uh fiht′ihk) *a.* Pertaining to or having the nature of an epiphyte.

Epipremnum (ehp uh prehm′nuhm) *n.* A genus of 10 species of trailing vines (Araceae). *E. aureum*

has glossy green, heart-shaped juvenile leaves, marbled with white. The mature leaves grow to 30 inches long, are divided, and are heavily marked with white or yellow. Commonly known as pothos or devil's ivy. Widely grown as a houseplant in its juvenile form.

Episcia (ih pihsh′ee uh) *n.* A genus of about 10 species of showy, low-growing creeper (Gesneriaceae) native to tropical America. The leaves are opposite, oval, velvety, and beautifully colored; the flowers resemble African violets. Grown as a houseplant or a greenhouse specimen, often in hanging baskets.

episepalous (ehp uh sehp′uh luhs) *a.* In botany, growing on or fused with a sepal; applied to stamens.

episperm (ehp′uh sperm) *n.* In botany, the hard external covering of a seed.

epispore (ehp′uh spor) *n.* In botany, the outer coat or membrane of a spore.

epithet (ehp′uh theht) *n.* In botany, the part of the scientific Latin name of a plant which follows the name of the genus and identifies the species, variety, or other sub-unit. In the name of the moss rose *Rosa centifolia muscosa, centifolia* is the specific epithet, and *muscosa* is the varietal epithet.

epixylous (ehp uh zigh′luhs) *a.* In botany, growing on wood.

epruinose (ee proo′uh nohs) *a.* In botany, having no bloom or powdering coating upon the surface of the leaf, stem or other plant part; not pruinose.

Equisetaceae (ehk wuh suh tay′see ee) *n. pl.* A distinct, primitive family of 1 genus, *Equisetum;* the horsetail family. Found all over the world in wetlands, bogs, marshes, and roadside ditches. They are perennial plants with spreading rootstocks and jointed, upright, hollow stems with grooves containing substantial amounts of silica. They are primitive in that they reproduce by spores rather than seeds.

equisetaceous (ehk wuh sih tay′shuhs) *a.* In botany, pertaining to the *Equisetaceae* (the horsetail family).

Equisetum (ehk wuh see'tuhm) *n.* A genus of 35 species (Equisetaceae). *Equisetum hyemale,* the scouring rush, contains silica; because silica is abrasive, the stems are used for polishing wood and metal. *Equisetum* is commonly known as horsetail. Useful in containers as a specimen; inclined to be invasive in moist locations.

Equisetum
(horsetail)

equitant (ehk'wuh tihnt) *a.* Leaves that overlap each other to form a fan, such as in many species of *Iris*.

Eragrostis (er uh grahs'tihs) *n.* A large varied genus of nearly 350 species of annual and perennial grasses (Gramineae) native to warm climates. Several are grown as ornamentals for their beautiful, fine-textured flower heads. Commonly called love grass.

Eranthemum (ih ran'thuh muhm) *n.* A tropical genus of about 30 species of plants and shrubs (Acanthaceae). They have pairs of oval dark green oval leaves, which are prominently veined, and spikes of tubular deep blue or rose flowers. Used as a container plant in protected areas or as a greenhouse specimen.

Eranthis (ih ran'thihs) *n.* A genus of 7 species of spring-flowering dwarf flowers (Ranunculceae). They grow from tubers. The leaves, which are bright green and deeply lobed, form a ruff at the base of each bright yellow or white buttercuplike flower; the basal leaves appear after the flowers. Commonly known as winter aconite. Grown in beds with other early-blooming small bulbs.

Eranthis
(winter aconite)

Eremochloa (er uh moh kloh'uh) *n.* A genus of about 10 species of perennial grasses (Gramineae). *E. ophiurides* (centipede grass) is used as a fine-textured lawn grass in the southeastern United States.

Eremurus (er uh myoo'ruhs) *n.* A genus of 35 to 40 species of perennials (Liliaceae). The roots are thick; the bright green leaves are narrow, forming tufts or rosettes; and the white, pink, yellow, or orange flowers occur on long spikes, some as tall as 9 feet. Also known as foxtail lily, desert candle, and king's spear. Magnificent in large borders as background plants.

Erica (ih righ'kuh) *n.* A large genus of about 500 species of branched, rigid shrubs (Ericaceae); the heaths or heather. The leaves are very small, narrow, and rigid, with spikes of white, yellow, green, rose, or purple urn-shaped or bell-shaped flowers. Useful on slopes, as ground covers, and in rock gardens; the taller varieties can be used as screens. All attract bees.

Erica cinerea
(heather)

Ericaceae (er uh kay'see ee) *n. pl.* A family of 70 genera and more than 1,900 species of mostly evergreen shrubs and small trees. The major ornamental genera include *Andromeda, Arbutus, Erica, Kalmia, Pieris,* and *Rhododendron.* Commonly known as the heath family.

ericaceous (ehr uh kay'shuhs) *a.* Of or pertaining to heath or to the *Ericaceae;* resembling or consisting of heaths.

ericetal (ehruh see'tuhl) *a.* Composed of or containing heaths.

Erigenia (er ih jeen'yuh) *n.* A genus of a single species, *E. bulbosa* (Umbelliferae), a tuberous, nearly stemless perennial native to North America. It grows to 9 inches tall and has leaves divided into 3s and clusters of small white flowers. It is one of the first plants to bloom in spring.

Erigeron (ih rihj'uh ruhn) *n.* A genus of about 200 species of small, low-growing flowers (Compositae) native to North America but widely naturalized around the world. They have alternate, toothed leaves and multitudes of small, daisylike white, pink, lavender, or violet flowers with yellow centers. Used in rock gardens, in wild gardens, in borders, or on stone walls. Commonly known as fleabane.

Eriobotrya (er ee oh bah'tree uh) *n.* A genus of several species of shrubs or small trees (Rosaceae).

They have large, simple, sharply toothed leaves, clusters of white flowers, and small, sweet, fragrant fruits. Used as a fruit tree or an espalier. Commonly known as loquat.

Eriodictyon (er ee oh dihk'tee ahn) *n.* A small genus of 8 species of low, resinous, evergreen shrubs (Hydrophyllaceae) native to the American Southwest and Mexico. They have alternate, simple, hairy, and sticky leaves and curved clusters of white, purple, or blue tubular flowers. Commonly known as yerba santa.

Eriogonum (er ee ohg'uh nuhm) *n.* A large genus of 150 species of perennials and shrubs (Polygonaceae) native to the western and southeastern United States and Mexico. They are mostly low herbs or woody-based perennials, many with leaves in basal rosettes and domed or rounded clusters of small white, yellow, or red flowers. Used on dry banks, massed, or in rock gardens. Commonly known as wild buckwheat.

Eriophyllum (er ee oh fihl'uhm) *n.* A genus of 13 species of flowers and subshrubs (Compositae) native to western North America. They have alternate, entire, furry white leaves and sunflowerlike yellow flowers. A drought-tolerant plant useful in dry gardens. Commonly known as woolly sunflower.

Eritrichium (er uh trihk'ee uhm) *n.* A genus of 30 species of very hardy woolly alpine plants (Boraginaceae), some species native to North America. They are low-growing, hairy perennials with simple, alternate leaves and clusters of blue flowers. Used in rock gardens. Commonly known as alpine forget-me-not.

erodible (ih rohd'uh buhl) *a.* A term used to describe a soil that is vulnerable to erosion.

Erodium (ih roh'dee uhm) *n.* A genus of 60 species of plants (Geraniaceae). They form clumps 1-foot across and have round dark green leaves with scalloped edges and multitudes of cup-shaped rose-pink or white flowers. Used as small-scale ground covers and in borders or rock gardens. Commonly known as heron's bill, crane's bill, or stork's bill.

erose (ih rohs') *a.* Having an irregularly jagged margin, as if gnawed: applied to a leaf or other plant part.

erosion *n.* The wearing away of the land through the action of moving water, wind, or other geological agents.

erosion, showing the wearing away of soil layers

erosive *a.* A term used in reference to water having the sufficient velocity to cause erosion.

Eryngium (ih rihn′jee uhm) *n.* A genus of about 200 species of thistlelike perennial plants (Umbelliferae). They resemble a thistle and have stiff, dusty blue leaves, variously lobed and spiny toothed. The flowers are white or a striking steel-blue or amethyst, surrounded by spiny blue bracts. Commonly known as eryngo or sea holly.

ersh (ersh) *n.* (See **eddish**.)

Erysimum (ih rihs′uh muhm) *n.* A genus of 80 species of plants (Cruciferae), some species native to North America. They have curly, narrow, entire leaves and dense, showy spikes of fragrant yellow, orange, red, or purple flowers. *E. asperum,* the western wallflower, is cultivated for its large, showy orange or yellow flowers. Useful in cottage gardens, in beds and borders.

Erythrina (er uh three′nuh) *n.* A genus of 100 species of shrubs or trees (Leguminosae), mostly tropical, with 3-part leaves and spikes of large butterflylike flowers, usually blood-red or orange. They are commonly known as coral trees. *E. herbacea,* commonly known as coral bean or Cherokee bean, is common through the southeastern part of the United States.

Erythronium (er uh throh′nee uhm) *n.* A genus of 25 species of hardy spring-blooming perennial flowers (Liliaceae). They are low and nearly stemless plants, with a solid scaly corm, 2 smooth leaves, which are often mottled, and a scape bearing 1 or several large, nodding, lilylike yellow, pink, purple, rose, or white flowers. Used in the wild garden, the rock garden, or in shady locations. Commonly known as the dogtooth violet.

Erythrophleum (ih rihth′ruh flee′uhm) *n.* A genus of 10 species of large tropical trees (Leguminosae). They have leaves divided into pairs of leaflets and dense spikes of small green, yellow, cream, or red flowers.

Erythroxylum
(coca)

Erythroxylum (er uh thrahks′uh luhm) *n.* A genus of 200 species, native mainly to tropical America. They have dense, alternate, simple leaves and small, five-petalled yellowish white, and a fleshy red fruit. The best-known species, *E. Coca,* of Bolivia and Peru, yields the drug cocaine. Used ornamentally as a hedge. Commonly known as coca or cocaine plant.

Escallonia

Escallonia (ehs kuh loh′nee uh) *n.* A genus of 39 species of fast-growing evergreen shrubs or small trees (Saxifragaceae). They have simple, entire leaves and bear clusters of rose-red or white, sometimes fragrant, late autumn flowers. Used as espaliers, hedges, or specimen shrubs.

escape *n.* In botany, a plant that has escaped from cultivation, and naturalized, more or less permanantly. For example, Queen Anne's lace is an escaped carrot.

escarole (ehs'kuh rohl) *n.* (See **endive**.)

Eschscholtzia (eh shohlt'see uh) *n.* A small genus of 8 to 10 perennial herbs (Papaveraceae) native to California and the adjacent region. They have delicate, finely divided, blue-green leaves and bright yellow, cream, or orange flowers. *E. californica,* the California poppy, is widely grown. Used on dry slopes; usually grown as an annual.

espalier (ih spal'yer) *n.* 1. A trelliswork of various forms on which the branches of fruit trees or fruit bushes are extended horizontally, in fan shape, etc., in a single plane, with the object of securing freer circulation of air for the plant, as well as better exposure to the sun. 2. A tree or plant trained on such a trellis or system. Trees trained as espaliers are not subjected to such abrupt variations of temperature as are wall trees. 3. *v.* To train on or protect by an espalier, as a tree or trees.

espathate (ee spay'thayt) *a.* In botany, lacking a spathe.

esquamulose (ee sway'myuh lohs) *a.* In botany, lacking minute scales; not squamulose.

etagere (ay tah zhair') *n.* A series of open shelves for growing and displaying plants; a tiered plant stand.

ethion (eh thigh'ahn) *n.* A synthetic insecticide effective against sucking and chewing insects, particularly mites and whiteflies.

etiolate (ee'tee uh layt) *vt.* To blanch or whiten a plant or part of a plant by exclusion of sunlight. It is often done with cauliflower, endive, and celery.

etiolation (ee tee uh lay'shuhn) *n.* 1. The process (often associated with celery) of causing a plant to whiten by excluding sunlight.

eucalypt (yoo'kuh lihpt) *n.* A tree or shrub belonging to the genus *Eucalyptus.*

Eucalyptus (yoo kuh lihp'tuhs) *n.* A genus of 522 species of tender, fast-growing, long-lived,

broadleaf evergreen trees and shrubs (Myrtaceae). The leaves are leathery and smooth and have a strong, distinctive odor. The flowers are usually in clusters of 3 or more, with a firm, capsulelike calyx, no petals, and many stamens. The fruit is a capsule, often hard and woody. Many of the trees are very tall; and some, as *E. globulus* and *E. diversicolor,* reach a height of more than 400 feet. Many species exude a gum, whence the common name of gum tree. Used as screens, windbreaks, and specimen trees. Eucalypts have naturalized in many places around the world.

Eucalyptus globulus
(gum tree)

Eucharis (yoo'kah rihs) *n.* A genus of several species of bulbs (Amaryllidaceae) native to Central and South America. *E. grandiflora* has broad, straplike leaves and clusters of large, pure white, and very fragrant flowers, 3 inches across, borne at the end of a sturdy 2-foot stalk. Grown mainly as a greenhouse plant. Commonly known as Amazon lily.

Eucnide (yook'nih dee) *n.* A genus of about 8 species of plants (Loasaceae) native to the southwestern United States and Mexico. *E. bartonoides* is a low, spreading, much-branched plant with showy bright yellow flowers. Commonly known as rock nettle.

Eucomis (yoo'kuh mihs) *n.* A genus of 10 species of perennial bulbs (Liliaceae). The wavy-edged leaves form basal rosettes. Small green-and-purple flowers, topped by a crown of green bracts resembling the top of a pineapple, appear at the ends of thick, 2-to-3-foot stalks. Used as a container plant;

grown outdoors in warm climates, in greenhouses elsewhere. Commonly known as pineapple lily.

Eucommia (yoo kahm'ee uh) *n.* A genus of 1 species of hardy deciduous tree, *E. ulmoides* (Eucommiaceae). It grows to 60 feet and has alternate, simple, elmlike leaves.

Eucryphia (yoo krihf'ee uh) *n.* A genus of 4 or 5 species of broadleaf evergreen trees or shrubs (Eucryphiaceae). They have opposite, leathery leaves and large, 2½-inch-long, 4-petaled white flowers with tufts of yellow stamens. Used as large specimen trees or shrubs.

eucyclic (yoo sihk'lihk) *a.* In botany, having a regualr alternation of parts: applied to flowers in which the petals, stamens, etc., are equal in number in each whorl, and alternate with one another.

Eugenia (yoo jee'nee uh) *n.* A genus of about 1,000 species of slow-growing broadleaf evergreen shrubs and trees (Myrtaceae) mostly native to tropical America. They have opposite, simple, firm, glossy leaves and spikes of flowers with many stamens, which are followed by a fleshy fruit. Used as a specimen shrub or hedge.

eulalia grass (yoo lay'lee uh) *n.* (See **Miscanthus.**)

Euonymus (yoo ahn'ih muhs) *n.* A genus of 170 species of shrubs and small trees (Celastraceae). They grow from 3 feet to 25 feet, depending on the species, with opposite, simple leaves, clusters of small green or yellow flowers, and showy pink, red, or yellow seed capsules that splite to show orange-red seeds. Some deciduous species, such as *E. alata* (winged spindle tree), *E. europaea* (European spindle tree), and *E. atropurpurea* (burning bush) color beautifully in autumn. Used as a screen, an unclipped hedge, or grown as small trees for their excellent fall color. *E. Fortunei,* and evergreen vine or shrub, is useful for erosion control. Commonly known as spindle tree. (See cut under **burning bush**.)

Euphorbia (yoo for'bee uh) *n.* 1. A genus of more than 1,600 species of plants, shrubs, or trees (Euphorbiaceae) found worldwide. The genus is extremely variable, but its members are characterized by a milky sap that, in some species, is caustic and can cause severe skin rashes. They vary greatly in habit, especially the tropical species, which are sometimes shrubs or trees. Many African species have succulent, leafless, spiny, and angled stems, resembling those of a cactus. The true flowers are inconspicuous; what appear to be the flowers are actually colored bracts. Many species are cultivated for ornament, such as poinsettia, *E. pulcherrima,* for its bright-colored floral bracts; snow-on-the-mountain, *E. marginata,* for its white-striped leaves; and *E. angularis* for its cactuslike form. The genus is commonly known as spurge. 2. [l.c.] A plant of this genus.

Euphorbia
(spurge)

Euphorbiaceae (yoo for bee ay'see ee) *n. pl.* An important family of 283 genera and more than 7,300 species, mostly tropical. They are plants, shrubs, or trees with an acrid milky sap, and some are poisonous. The major genera include *Euphorbia, Croton, Ricinus, Phyllanthus,* and *Acalypha.* Commonly known as the spurge family.

euphorbiaceous (yoo for bee ay'shuhs) *a.* Pertaining to or having the characteristics of the Euphorbiaceae (the spurge family).

euphorbium (yoo for'bee uhm) *n.* A gum or resin derived from *Euphorbia resinifera* and other species. Used in veterinary medicine.

euphrasy (yoo'fruh see) *n.* The eyebright, *Euphrasia officianalis.*

Euptelea (yoop tehl'ee uh) *n.* A genus of 3 species of trees and shrubs (Eupteleaceae). They have alternate, finely notched leaves and attractive flowers with no petals but many dark red stamens which sometimes appear before the leaves. Used in moist locations.

European corn borer *n.* (See **cornstalk borers**.)

Eurya (yoo′ree uh) *n.* A genus of about 70 species of tropical and subtropical broadleaf evergreen shrubs and small trees (Theaceae). They have alternate, scalloped, serrate leaves and inconspicuous flowers. The shrubs are grown for their refined foliage.

Euryale (you ree′uh lee) *n.* A genus of 1 species of prickly waterlily, *E. ferox* (Nymphaceae). It has round, flat leaves and small, day-blooming flowers. Used in garden pools and ponds. Commonly known as prickly waterlily or gorgon.

Euryops (yoo′ree ahps) *n.* A genus of 50 species of long-blooming evergreen shrubs (Compositae). They have dark green or gray-green finely divided leaves and bright yellow daisylike flowers. Used in mild climates in borders, beds, clumps, containers, or as a low hedge.

Eustoma (yoo stoh′muh) *n.* A genus of 3 species of flowers (Gentianaceae) native to the Americas. They have opposite, gray-green leaves and tall stems of blue, pink, or white tulip-shaped flowers. Used in pots, borders, or cutting gardens. Commonly known as Texas bluebell, prairie gentian, or Lisianthus.

Eustrephus (yoo stree′fuhs) *n.* A genus of 1 species, *E. latifolius* (Liliaceae), a climbing, woody perennial vine. It has smooth, long, narrow, alternate leaves and clusters of small white, light blue, pale pink, or purple flowers. Grown outdoors in warm climates, in greenhouses elsewhere.

Euterpe (yoo ter′pee) *n.* A genus of 20 species of palms (Palmae) native to tropical America. They have slender, cylindrical trunks, sometimes nearly 100 feet in height, crowned by a tuft of divided leaves. They are the source of hearts of palm. *E. oleracea* and *E. edulis* are commonly known as cabbage palm or assai palm.

evapotranspiration (ih vap′ah tranz puh ray′shuh) *n.* 1. The loss of water from the soil by evaporation and plant transpiration. 2. Water on the surface taken away by water, wind, air, and elements.

evening primrose *n.* A common name for the genus *Oenothera.* (See **Oenothera**.)

everbloomer *n.* A plant that blooms continously throughout the growing season.

evergreen *n.* and *a.* A plant that retains its green growth through more than one growing season. Evergreen is often used as a synonym for conifers, such as firs and pines, which remain green throughout the winter. It also refers to broadleaf evergreens such as holly, ivy, rhododendron, and many others. Evergreens shed their old leaves in the spring or summer, after the new foliage had been formed, and consequently are green throughout the year.

evergreens, broad-leaved *n. pl.* A term used to distinguish all plants that do *not* lose their leaves in autumn from conifers. Conifers tend to have needlelike leaves. The term includes such familiar garden ornamentals as *Buxus* (boxwood), *Camellia, Rhododendron,* and *Hedera* (ivy). Also called broadleaf evergreens.

evergreens, dwarf *n. pl.* A term used to describe conifers that are naturally dwarf or hybridized for small size; for example, Tom Thumb arborvitae, *Thuja occidentalis* 'Little Gem'.

everlasting flowers *n. pl.* (See **everlastings**.)

everlasting, pearly *n.* A common name for the flower *Anaphalis margaritacea,* widespread along roadsides in North America and prized for its small, pure white flowers, which retain their shape when dried.

everlastings *n. pl.* A common name for plants whose flowers retain their form, color, and brightness long after being gathered. It is applied to species of *Gnaphalium, Anaphalis, Helichrysum, Xeranthemum,* etc. Also called immortelle.

everlasting, winged *n. Ammobium alatum,* a perennial, but usually grown as an annual, valued in dried arrangements for its 1-inch flowers, which retain their shape and color when dried.

Evodia (ih voh′dee uh) *n.* A genus of 50 or more species of tropical and subtropical shrubs or trees (Rutaceae). They have opposite leaves and clusters of small pink, white, or greenish-white flowers.

Evonymus (ih vahn′uh muhs) *n.* A synonym for *Euonymus.*

ex- See **e-**.

Exacum (ehks'uh kuhm) *n*. A genus of 20 to 30 flowers (Gentianaceae). They have small, opposite, simple, glossy leaves and clusters of blue or white flowers. Grown as a summer-flowering annual or houseplant.

exalate (ehks ay'layt) *a*. In botany, lacking wings or winglike appendages; not alate.

exalbuminous (ehks al byoo'muh nuhs) *a*. In botany, without endosperm: applied to seeds. also exendospermous, exendospermic.

exanthem *n*. 1. In botany, a blotch on the surface of a leaf, etc. 2. A copper-deficiency disease of plants, prevalent in citurs and olive, and characterized by dieback and blotches on leaves and fruit.

exchangeable *a*. A term used to describe ions in the absorbing complex of soil that can be exchanged with other ions.

exchangeable sodium *n*. Sodium that is attached to the surface of soil particles and that can be exchanged with other positively charged ions in the soil solution.

exfoliate (ehks foh'lee ayt) *v*. To peel off in layers or flakes, as the bark of certain trees.

exocarp (ehk'soh karp) *n*. In botany, the outer layer of the covering of a fruit when it consists of two dissimilar layers.

Exochorda (ehk soh kor'duh) *n*. A genus of a few species of deciduous shrubs (Rosaceae). *E. racemosa* is a beautiful loose, open, slender shrub with densely flowered spikes of large white flowers. Commonly known as pearlbush.

exogen (ehk'soh jehn) *n*. In botany, a plant in which the growth of the stem is in successive concentric layers, such as most trees.

exogenous (ehk sahj'uh nuhs) *a*. Growing by additions on the outside, such as the rings of a tree trunk.

exotic *a*. and *n*. Of foreign origin or character; introduced from a foreign country or a different region. An exotic plant is one not native to the place where it is growing, such as Japanese honeysuckle, which has naturalized in the northeastern states, or eucalyptus trees, which have naturalized on the west coast.

exsuccous (ehk suhk'hs) *a*. Dry, without juice, sap, or moisture; withered.

extrafloral *a*. Of a plant part that does not form part of a flower.

extrorse (ehk strors') *a*. In botany, facing away from the direction of the growth (in reference to the anther of a flower).

eye *n*. 1. An undeveloped bud on a tuber, as on a potato; 2. a cutting with a single bud; 3. the center of a flower when differently colored than the petals, as in many hibiscus.

Fabaceae (fuh bay'see ee) *n*. *pl*. A synonym for Leguminosae.

Fabiana (fuh bee an'uh) *n*. A small genus of 25 shrubs (Solanaceae) native to South America. *F. imbricata* is an heathlike evergreen shrub, with small crowded leaves and a profusion of pure white flowers. Commonly known as false heather.

Fagaceae (fuh gay'see ee) *n*. A family of 6 genera and 600 species of deciduous trees and shrubs. They have alternate, simple leaves and male flowers in catkins; the fruit is a nut enclosed in a bur. The major ornamental genera are *Castenea* (chestnut), *Fagus* (beech), and *Quercus* (oak).

Fagus (fay'gus) *n*. A genus of 10 species of hardy trees (Fagaceae); the beech. The common or European beech, *F. sylvatica,* grows to 80 feet, with smooth bark and branches forming a beautiful head with thick foliage. Ornamental cultivars are grown, such as the copper beech (*F.s.*'Atropurpurea') with wine-colored leaves, the weeping beech (*F.s.* 'Pendula'), and the fern-leafed beech (*F.s.*'Laciniata') with divided leaves. The American beech, *F. grandiflora,* is similar to the European Beech and grows to 100 feet, with large oval leaves that turn yellow in autumn.

fair-maids-of-February *n.* A common name for *Galanthus nivalis,* a hardy perennial bulb with 2 to 3 basal leaves and dainty, nodding, bell-shaped white flowers. Also known as common snowdrop.

fair-maids-of-France *n.* A common name for several double-flowered varieties of garden flowers, including *Ranunculus aconitifolius* and *Saxifraga granulata.*

fairy ring *n.* A fungal disease of lawns usually caused by decaying organic matter (wood debris or dead tree roots) below ground. Dark green rings of grass, surrounded by lighter colored or dead turf and the presence of mushrooms are symptomatic. Chemical control is usually not very effective; instead, aerate the lawn and keep it well-watered and fertilized.

falcate (fal′kayt) *a.* Hooked; curved like a scythe or sickle; falciform.

falciform (fal′ sih form) *a.* Sickle-shaped; falcate.

fallow *a.* Plowed and left unseeded; left for a considerable time unworked or unseeded after tillage; untilled; uncultivated; neglected, said of land; often used figuratively. *v.* To render fallow; put (land) into the condition of a fallow, namely, by plowing, harrowing, and breaking it without seeding, for the purpose of destroying weeds and insects.

Fallugia (fuh loo′jee uh) *n.* A genus of 1 species, *F. paradoxa* (Rosaceae), native to the southwestern United States and northern Mexico. It grows to 8 feet and has small, clustered, lobed dark green leaves, rusty beneath, and white flowers resembling roses on long stems. The fruit develops feathery purplish plumes, is green at first, then turns pink or red. Tolerant of heat and drought and useful for erosion control. Commonly known as Apache plume.

fall webworm *n.* A fuzzy, pale green or yellow caterpillar that feeds on the foliage of fruit and shade trees and some shrubs. It forms large silken nests in tree branches. Control by pruning out nests, banding, releasing trichogramma wasps, or spraying *Bacillus thruringiensis.*

false acacia (uh kay′shee uh) *n.* A common name for *Robinia Pseudoacacia,* a large thorny tree with fragrant white flowers.

false aralia (uh ray′lee uh) *n.* A common name for the genus *Dizygotheca,* tall, slender houseplants with palmate leaves.

false arborvitae (ahr ber hight′ee) *n.* A common name for *Thujopsis dolabrata,* a coniferous evergreen shrub. Also known as hiba cedar.

false cypress *n.* A common name for the genus *Chamaecyparis,* a genus of coniferous evergreen trees.

false dragonhead *n.* A common name for the genus *Physostegia,* a perennial with narrow green leaves and spikes of small snapdragonlike flowers. Also known as obedient plant.

false heather *n.* A common name for *Fabiana imbricata,* a heathlike evergreen plant.

false spirea (spigh ree′uh) *n.* A common name for the genus *Sorbaria,* large deciduous shrubs with clusters of white flowers.

fameflower *n.* A common name for the genus *Talinum,* semisucculent plants with clusters of showy flowers.

family *n.* In the system of botanical classification, a group of related plants below the category of order above the category of genus. It consists of genera that resemble one another in certain broad characteristics, not always immediately apparent. Though usually made up of several or many genera, some families may consist of only a single genus. The family name is usually—but not always—recognized by the ending *-aceae;* some major familes have the ending *-ae,* such as Compositae and Leguminosae. (See **classification of plants**.)

fan palm *n.* Any palm having fan-shaped leaves, in distinction from those with divided leaves. A common name for palms of several genera including *Sabal, Trachycarpus, Chamaerops,* and *Washingtonia.*

fan-shaped *a.* Resembling a fan in shape or form; flabellate.

fan spray *n.* A nozzle that breaks a stream of water into fine particles and blows it through the air in an arc like that of an open fan. Also called fan sprayer or flaring rose.

fan-training *n.* In horticulture, a method of training a tree or vine on a wall or trellis in such a manner that the branches radiate from the trunk at regular intervals and at continually smaller angles, the lower branch on each side being approximately horizontal. Half fan-training is a method of training similar to fan-training, but in which the lower branches rise obliquely from the trunk.

fanwort (fan'wert) *n.* A common name for the genus *Cabomba,* aquatic plants with floating leaves and small flowers.

farewell-to-spring *n.* A common name for the genus *Clarkia,* a North American native with tapered leaves and delicate pink flowers splotched with red. Also known as godetia.

farinose (far'uh nohs) *a.* In botany, covered with a mealy powder, as the leaves of *Primula farinosa* and other plants.

farkleberry *n.* A common name for *Vaccinium arboreum,* a shrub or small tree of the southern United States. It bears a small, black, many-seeded berry with a dry and rather astringent pulp. Also known as sparkleberry and whortleberry.

fasciate (fash'ee ayt) *a.* In botany, banded or compacted together; exhibiting fasciation. Also fasciated.

fasciation (fash ee ay'shuhn) *n.* In botany, a malformation in plants, in which a stem or branch becomes expanded into a flat, ribbonlike shape, as if several stems were joined together lengthwise; a similar malformation involving 2 or more stems.

fascicle (fas ih kuhl) *n.* In botany, a close cluster or bundle, as of leaves, stems, or flowers. Sometimes limited in use to a compacted cyme.

fascicle of the mallow flower

fastigiate (fas tihj'ee iht) *a.* In botany, having clustered and erect branches, as in the Lombardy poplar. Also fastigiated.

fastigiate trees (fas tihj'ee iht treez) *n. pl.* Trees grown for their narrow, columnar shape.

Fatshedera (fats hehd'uh ruh) *n.* A genus of 1 species (Araliaceae), a bigeneric hybrid, a cross between *Hedera helix* (English ivy) and *Fatsia japonica* (Formosa rice tree). It is an evergreen shrub with large hand-shaped leaves and large clusters of small creamy-white flowers. Commonly known as aralia ivy, ivy tree, or botanical-wonder.

Fatsia (fat'see uh) *n.* A genus of 1 species of broadleaf evergreen shrub or tree, *F. japonica* (Araliaceae). It has big, glossy, fanlike dark green leaves to 16 inches wide and many rounded clusters of whitish flowers. Commonly known as Formosa rice plant or Japanese fatsia.

Faucaria (fow kar'ee uh) *n.* A genus of 33 species of perennial succulents (Aizoaceae). They form clumps of fleshy, spotted, semicylindrical basal leaves and yellow flowers that open in the afternoon. Commonly known as tiger's-jaw.

fava bean *n.* A broad bean popular in the cooking of southern Europe and the Middle East, not commonly grown in American gardens. It is among the meatiest and largest of beans and is used fresh or dried. Most varieties thrive best in a moderately cool, moist climate, but heat-tolerant varieties are available.

faveolate (fuh vee'uh liht) *a.* Honeycombed; alveolate. In botany, also favose.

feather-fleece *n.* A common name for *Stenanthium gramineum* var. *robustum,* a bulb with grasslike leaves and clusters of green, white, or purple flowers. Also known as feather bell. Used in borders and wild gardens.

featherfoil *n.* A common name for the genus *Hottonia,* so called from its finely divided leaves. Also known as water violet.

Felicia (fih lihsh'ee uh) *n.* A genus of 83 species of plants, subshrubs, and shrubs (Compositae). *F. amelliodes* has oval, slightly aromatic foliage and masses of sky-blue, yellow-centered daisylike flowers. Used in borders, beds, and as a container plant. Commonly known as blue marguerite.

felonwort (fehl'uhn wert) *n.* A common name for *Solanum Dulcamara.* It is a shrubby, climbing vine with oval leaves, long, stalked clusters of violet and green flowers, and red fruit. It has naturalized in America. Also called bittersweet, celandine, herb Robert, or deadly nightshade. All parts of the plant are poisonous.

feltwort (fehlt'wert) *n.* A common name for *Verbascum Thapsus,* so called from its thick, felty leaves. It is a large plant with large, soft furry leaves and tall spikes of yellow flowers. Also known as mullein. It is an attractive pasture or roadside weed.

female *n.* In botany, a plant that produces fruit; that plant that bears the pistil and receives the pollen or fertilizing element of the male plant, or the analagous organ in cryptogams. *a.* In botany, pertaining to the kind of plants that produce fruit; pistil-bearing; pistillate; producing pistillate flowers.

fence *n.* An enclosure around a yard, field, or other tract of ground, or around or along the sides of any open space. Specifically, a fence for land is understood, especially in the United States, to be a line of posts and rails or wire, or of boards or pickets; but the term is applicable to a wall, hedge, ditch or trench, bank, or anything that serves to guard against unrestricted entry or exit, to obstruct the view, or merely as a tangible dividing line.

Fendlera (fehnd'ler ruh) *n.* A genus of 2 or 3 species of intricately branched shrubs (Saxifragaceae) native to southwestern United States. They have opposite, entire leaves and large, showy white flowers.

fennel *n.* 1. An aromatic plant, *Faeniculum vulgare* (Umbelliferae), a native of southern Europe and common in cultivation. It is a tall, herb with feathery leaves, yellow flowers, an agreeable odor, and a sweet aromatic taste. Several varieties are cultivated in America for their seeds, which are used in cooking.

fennel-flower *n.* A common name for *Nigella damascena,* a much-branched plant with finely cut threadlike leaves, large white, rose, or light blue flowers, and curious papery horned seed capsules used in dried bouquets. Has been used medicinally. Traditional in cottage gardens. Also known as love-in-a-mist.

fenugreek (fehn'yih greek) *n.* A common name for *Trigonella Foenum-graecum* (Leguminosae), an annual plant indigenous to western Asia, but widely naturalized and extensively cultivated in Asia, Africa, and some parts of Europe. The sticky seeds are used as food and also in medicine. Also spelled foenugreek.

fern *n.* One of a large group of spore-producing perennial plants. About 10,000 species of ferns are known, the greaatest concentration of which are found in the mountains in the tropics. They are typically low-growing plants with leafy fronds, though a few species are shrubby or treelike. Most have fibrous roots, but some grow from creeping rhizomes. They reproduce asexually by means of spores produced on the backs or edges of the fronds. Some species have both fertile fronds, which produce spores, and sterile fronds, which do not. The germinating spores produce a small, green, flat shieldlike phase that looks nothing like the mature fern. After fertilization, a frond-bearing plant develops that is recognizable as a fern. Ferns are distinguished from most other plants primarily by the fact that they do not produce either flowers or seeds.

fern

fern, basket *n.* A common name for *Nephrolepis pectinata,* a compact fern with fronds divided into grayish-green leaflets.

fern, Boston *n.* A common name for *Nephrolepis exaltta* 'Bostoniensis', the classic Victorian parlor fern. It has spreading, arching fronds divided into small, narrow leaflets; the fronds can grow to 5 feet long. Often grown in hanging baskets or placed on a fern stand as a houseplant, or grown as an indoor/outdoor plant.

fern, cinnamon *n.* A common name for *Osmunda cinnamonea,* a large fern with rust-colored hairs on juvenile fronds, and mature fronds to 5 feet long.

fern, cliff-brake *n.* A common name for the genus *Pellea.*

fern, cloak *n.* A common name for *Notholaena,* a genus of 60 species of small drought-tolerant ferns found in dry rocky places, some species native to western North America. They have finely cut fronds that are typically mealy, chaffy, or hairy.

fern, crested *n.* A common name for *Dryopteris cristata,* with fronds 2½ feet long.

fern, deer *n.* A common name for *Blechnum spicant,* a large fern that produces both sterile and fertile fronds. The fertile fronds are erect, stiff, and narrow with widely spaced leaflets, and the sterile fronds are glossy-green and spreading.

fernery (fern'uh ree) *n.* A place where ferns are growing, often in a greenhouse; a plantation of ferns.

fern, felt *n.* A common name for the genus *pyrrosia,* climbing epiphytic ferns with long, simple, entire leathery leaves, furry beneath.

fern, flowering *n.* A common name for the genus *Osmunda,* some species native to North and South America. They are mostly hardy large ferns with divided fronds to 5 or 6 feet long. No true ferns flower, but the spore cases of this fern resemble flowers.

fern, Hartford *n.* A common name for *Lygodium palmatum,* a climbing fern with hand-shaped sterile fronds and much-forked fertile fronds.

fern, hart's-tongue *n.* A common name for *Phyllitis scolopendrium,* a small fern with simple, strap-shaped fronds.

fern, holly *n.* A common name for *Polystichum Lonchitis,* which has leathery evergreen fronds to 2 feet long.

fern, maidenhair *n.* A common name for the genus *Adiantumn* exquisitely fragile ferns with glossy black stems and fronds divided into fan-shaped leaflets. A choice garden plant in moist soils. A few species are hardy; some are native to North America.

fern, mother *n.* A common name for *Asplenium bulbiferum,* a fern with lacy, arching fronds on which develop small bulbils. The bulbils will grow into new plants where they touch or fall to the soil; hence, the name mother fern.

fern, ostrich *n.* A common name for large, hardy striking ferns of the genus *Matteuccia,* ferns that have both fertile and sterile fronds; the fertile fronds are in the center, and the sterile fronds form a crown around them. (See **Mateuccia.**)

fern, royal *n.* A common name for *Osmunda regalis,* a large, handsome, very hardy North American fern with double-divided fronds to 6 feet long. It thrives in moist, shady situations.

fern, tree *n.* A common name for ferns in several genera, including *Blechnum, Cibotium, Cyathea,* and *Dicksonia.* They are characterized by slim, hairy trunks topped by a crown of long, arching fronds. Most are subtropical or tropical.

fern, Venus's-hair *n.* A common name for *Adiantum capillus-veneris,* an exquisite tender or tropical maidenhair fern. It grows to 2 feet tall with delicate, fragile, doubly-divided frons with fan shaped leaflets. Grown as a houseplant, greenhouse specimen, or outdoors in shady, moist, protects parts of mild climate gardens. Also known as southern maidenhair, Venus's-hair, and dudder grass.

fern, walking *n.* A common name for both the genus *Camptosorus* and the species *C. rhizophyllous.* They have long, narrow, tapering fronds with a little tail at the end that can start new plants where it touches the soil.

Ferocactus (fer uh kak'tuhs) *n.* A genus of 25 species of fiercely spiny globular cacti (Cactaceae) native to the southwestern United States. They are strongly ribbed, cylindrical-to-round cacti, with red-to-yellow flowers that last several days, and they bear oblong, fleshy fruit. Commonly known as barrel cactus.

Feronia (fuh roh'nee uh) *n.* A genus of tropical trees of a single species, *F. limonia* (Rutaceae). It is a thorny tree with divided leaves, dull-red flowers, and with an edible acid fruit, which is known as elephant apple or wood apple. Citrus can be grafted onto the rootstock.

ferric iron (fer'ihk) *n.* An oxidized or high-volence form of iron.

ferrous iron (fer'uhs) *n.* A reduced or low-volence form of iron.

fertile *a.* 1. Bearing or producing abundantly, as of vegetable growth; capable of sustaining abundant growth, as fertile soil. 2. In botany: a. Fruiting, or capable of producing fruit; having a functional pistil, as a fertile flower; bearing functional pollen, as fertile stamens. b. Capable of fertilizing, as an anther with well-developed pollen.

fertility *n.* The quality of soil that enables it to provide compounds in adequate amounts and in proper balance for the growth of specified plants.

fertilization *n.* 1. The act or process of rendering land fertile, fruitful, or productive; the application of fertilizer. 2. In botany, the process by which pollen reaches and acts upon the ovules and assures the production of fruit; also, the analogous process in cryptogams.

fertilizer *n.* A natural or manufactured material added to soil to supply nutrients to plants.

fertilizer grade *n.* An expression that indicates the percentage of plant nutrients in a fertilizer.

fertilizer injector *n.* A device connected to the faucet end of a garden hose; it contains about 1 pint of liquid or water soluble fertilizer and mixes it at a predetermined rate with water flowing through the hose.

Ferula (fer'uh luh) *n.* A genus of more than 100 species of thick-rooted perennials (Umbelliferae). They are generally tall, bold plants with dissected leaves and large rounded clusters of small yellow or green flowers. Some species, such as *F. communis,* the giant fennel, and *F. tingitana* are cultivated as ornamental foliage plants.

fescue (fehs'kyoo) *n.* (See **Festuca**.)

Festuca (fehs too'kuh) *n.* A genus of about 400 species of mostly perennial grasses (Gramineae) na-

tive to temperate areas. Called fescues, it includes valuable ornamentals, such as the low-growing, silvery-blue-foliaged *F. ovina glauca* (blue fescue), and several ground-cover or lawn grasses, such as *F. elatior* (tall fescue) and *F. rubra* (red fescue).

feterita (feht uh ree'tuh) *n.* A common name for *Sorghum bicolor.*

fetterbush (feht'er bush) *n.* A common name for a compact, rounded broadleaf evergreen shrub, *Pieris floribunda,* (Ericaceae), native to the southern United States. It has simple, leathery, elliptical leaves and bears numerous clusters of fragrant white flowers. Used in shady, moist situations. Also known as mountain pieris.

feverfew *n.* 1. A common name for *Chrysanthemum Parthenium,* a European species naturalized in the United States, formerly cultivated as a medicinal herb. Some ornamental varieties are common in gardens. Rarely and improperly called wild chamomile because of its small flowers and yellow centers.

feverroot (fee'ver root) *n.* A common name for a weedy perennial, *Triosteum perfoliatum,* native to the United States. Also called wild coffee and tinker's weed.

fever tree *n.* A common name for *Pinckneya pubens* (Rubiaceae), native to the southeastern United States. Commonly known as Georgia bark or fever bark.

fevertwig (fee'ver twihg) *n.* A common name for *Celastrus scandens.* Also known as bittersweet. (See **bittersweet**.)

feverweed *n.* A common name for several plants of the widely distributed genus *Eryngium.*

feverwort (fee'ver wert) *n.* Same as feverroot. A common name for 2 different plants, *Triosteum perfoliatum* and *Eupatorium perfoliatum.*

fibril (figh'bruhl) *n.* 1. A small fiber. 2. In botany, a root hair.

fibrillose (figh'bruh lohs) *a.* In botany, furnished with or made up of fibrils.

Ficus (figh'kuhs) *n.* A genus of 800 trees or shrubs (Moraceae) characterized by bearing minute flowers within a nearly closed round or pear-shaped fruit; the fig. The genus is remarkable for the peculiar arrangement by which cross-fertilization occurs through the agency of fig wasps (*Blastophaga*, etc.), a process called caprification. The genus includes the edible fig, *F. carica;* the banyan, *F. benghalensis;* and the bo tree, *F. religiosa,* under which Gautama Buddha received enlightenment. Several tropical species are widely grown as houseplants, particularly weeping fig, *F. benjamina;* rubber plant, *F. elastica;* and fiddle-leaf fig, *F. lyrata.*

fiddlehead *n.* The common name for the tightly curled fronds of certain ferns, which are gathered in the early spring and cooked as a vegetable.

field capacity *n.* The highest amount of moisture remaining in a soil after free water has been allowed to drain away. Expressed as a percentage of oven-dry weight of soil or other convenient unit.

field moisture *n.* The water that soil contains under field conditions.

fiesta flower *n.* A common name for *Pholistoma auritum,* a small scrambling annual vine, native to California, with hand-shaped leaves and clusters of lavender-to-blue or -violet flowers.

Ficus carica
(fig)

fig *n.* The common name for species of the genus *Ficus* and for their fruit. The common fig, *F. Carica,* is a native of the Mediterranean region; it has been cultivated from a very early date and is now found in most warm temperate countries. It is a small tree, with large, rough, deciduous leaves and a small fruit, which varies much in size, color, and flavor, and of which 2 crops are usually borne each season.

fig banana *n.* A small variety of the banana, common in the West Indies.

fig tree *n.* A common name for trees of the genus *Ficus,* but most often for the edible fig, *F. carica.* (See **Ficus.**)

figwort (fihg'wert) *n.* The common name for the genus *Scrophularia,* rarely planted ornamentally.

figwort family (fihg'wert) *n.* A common name for the family *Scrophularaceae,* which includes the ornamental genera *Antirrhinum* (snapdragon), *Digitalis* (foxglove), and *Penstemon* (beard-tongue).

filament *n.* In botany, the threadlike stalk of a stamen that bears the anther.

filbert *n.* 1. A common name for deciduous nut trees of the genus *Corylus.* 2. A common name for the fruit of the cultivated variety of the European hazelnut, *Corylus Avellana.* The Turkish filbert is the fruit of *C. Colurna.* (See **Corylus.**) 3. The shrub that bears the nut. Also called hazelnut.

filiciform (fih lihs'uh form) *a.* In the shape of a fern or fern frond.

Filipendula (fihl uh pehn'juh luh) *n.* A small genus of hardy perennials (Rosaceae), some species native to North America. They have alternate, divided, fernlike leaves and showy plumes of small flowers. *Filipendula rubra* is commonly known as queen-of-the-prairie and is useful in meadow gardens or at the back of the border. The genus is commonly known as meadowsweet.

film water *n.* Water held on the surface of soil particles that does not drain away.

fimble *n.* The male hemp plant or the fiber made from it. Also called fimble hemp.

fimbria (fihm'bree uh) *n., pl.* **fimbriae** In botany, a fringelike border; the peristome of a moss.

fimbriate petals
of *Dianthus*

fimbriate (fihm'bree iht) *a.* In botany, fringed; bordered with hairs or with slender processes, as a fimbriate petal. Also fimbriated.

fine sand *n.* Soil particles measuring from .10 to .25 millimeter.

fine-textured soil *n.* A clayey soil containing 35% or more clay.

finger fern *n.* A common name for any of the ferns in the genus *Asplenium*.

fingerflower *n.* An old name for the foxglove, *Digitalis purpurea*.

finocchio (fih nohk yoh) *n.* The Florence fennel, an anise-flavored vegetable with a bulbous base. (See **Florence fennel**.)

fir *n.* A common name for coniferous trees of the genus *Abies*, a genus of about 40 hardy, evergreen trees (Pinaceae); the true fir. It is distinguished from spruce and pine by its erect female cones. Included in this genus are *A. alba* (silver fir) and *A. procera* (noble fir).

fir cone *n.* The cone-shaped fruit of the fir.

fire blight *n.* A bacterial disease that kills branches and limbs of members of the rose family, including apples, pears, and quince. The dead branches retain leaves, looking as if they were scorched by fire. The disease is spread through wounds and from blossom to blossom, usually in wet spring weather. To control, use sterile pruning shears to cut out dead wood, making sure to cut into healthy tissue at least 6 inches below the dead parts. To prevent infection, spray with copper fungicide during bloom.

firebrush, Chilean *n.* A common name for *Embothrium coccineum*, a small flowering tree with long leaves and spikes of showy scarlet flowers; native to the central and southern Andes.

firecracker flower *n.* 1. A common name for *Dichelostemma ida-maia*, which grows from a corm and has narrow, grasslike leaves and clusters of pendulous, tubular scarlet flowers tipped with green. Useful in dry woodland gardens. 2. A common name for the genus *Crossandra*, subtropical shrubs with oval leaves and spikes of showy, tubular bright orange flowers.

fire-retardant plants *n.* A common term for plants that do not burn easily, such as ice plant (*Carpobrotus, Delosperma, Drosanthemum*, etc.) or redwood trees *(Sequoia sempervirens)*. They are used as barrier plantings around houses in areas where wildfires threaten homes in the dry season.

firethorn *n.* A common name for the genus *Pyracantha*, evergreen thorny shrubs with masses of small white flowers and red winter berries, which attract birds.

fire tree *n.* A common name for *Metrosideros excelsus*, a large tree with oblong leaves, furry beneath, and dense clusters of showy, brilliant red flowers.

fireweed *n.* A common name for any of several species of pioneer plants, which are among the first to colonize burned-over areas. These include *Erechthites hireacifolia, Epilobium angustifolium,* and *Latuca canadensis.*

fire-wheel tree *n.* A common name for the genus *Stenocarpus*, slow-growing trees with deeply lobed, shiny juvenile leaves and smaller, entire mature leaves. The tubular scarlet or yellow flowers occur in clusters like the spokes of a wheel and sometimes grow out of the bark of the trunk. Used in warm climates as a specimen tree.

fir family *n.* A common name for the genus *Abies*, the true firs, tall coniferous evergreen trees.

Firmiana (fer mee a'nuh) *n.* A genus of 10 species of deciduous trees (Sterculiaceae) native to China. They have large, alternate, lobed, tropical-looking leaves, each stem looking like a parasol. They have large, loose, upright clusters of greenish-white flowers at the ends of branches. Commonly known as Chinese parasol tree.

firming *n.* A term to indicate light-packing of soil around roots.

first bottom *n.* The normal flood plain of a stream.

fir tree *n.* A common name for trees of the genus *Abies*, the true firs. Sometimes also applied to other coniferous evergreen trees of the genera *Picea* (spruce) and *Pinus* (pine).

fishhook cactus *n.* A common name for *Ferocactus wislizenii*, a tall, thick-ribbed cactus with spines to

2 inches long and large, tubular orange-red or yellow flowers.

fish meal *n.* An organic fertilizer made of fish.

fishtail palm *n.* A common name for the genus *Caryota,* a small genus of tropical palms with bipinnate leaves and wedge-shaped leaflets, strongly toothed at the ends. Grown outdoors in warm-winter climates and a choice houseplant or greenhouse specimen anywhere.

fishtail weeder *n.* An instrument having a bladed notch resembling the tail of a fish; used in removing weeds. Also called asparagus knife.

fitroot *n.* A common name for *Monotropa uniflora,* a waxy, white leafless saprophytic plant shaped like a peace pipe. Also known as Indian pipe.

Fittonia (fih toh′nee uh) *n.* A genus of 2 species of ornamental, low, creeping plants (Acanthaceae). They have handsome, oval dark green leaves conspicuously veined with white. They are grown for their foliage as houseplants.

five-finger *n.* 1. A common name for the genus *Potentilla,* the plants of which have leaves with 5 leaflets. The marsh-five-finger is *P. palustris.* Also called cinquefoil. 2. Five-fingers is a common name for *Syngonium auritum,* a tropical plant with 5-parted leaves, usually grown as a houseplant.

five-leaf *n.* A synonym for cinquefoil, the genus *Potentilla.*

five-spot *n.* A common name for *Nemophila maculata,* a low-growing annual with rounded lobed leaves and white flowers with 4 small spots and 1 large one. Used in beds as an overplanting for spring bulbs.

fixation *n.* The conversion of a soluble material form to a relatively insoluble form.

flabellate (fluh behl′iht) *a.* In botany, fan-shaped. Also flabelliform.

flaccid (flak′sihd) *a.* Limp; lacking in strength; weak.

Flacourtia (fluh kort′ee uh) *n.* A genus of 15 species of tropical and subtropical evergreen shrubs or small trees (Flacourtiaceae). They have alternate, simple leaves, flowers without petals, and a fleshy, edible, berrylike fruit. *F. indica,* the Madagascar plum, is used in warm-winter gardens for hedges.

Flacourtiaceae (fluh kort′ee ay′see ee) *n.* An order of 84 genera and 850 species of tropical and subtropical evergreen trees and shrubs. They have alternate, simple, leathery leaves, flowers sometimes without petals, and a fleshy, berrylike fruit. The major ornamental genera are *Azara, Idesia, Olmediella,* and *Xylosma.*

flag *n.* A common name for any of several genera of plants with sword-shaped leaves, mostly growing in moist places; particularly, various species of *Iris,* such as *I. germanica* (fleur-de-lis) Cattail flag is the common name for the genus *Typha;* Corn flag is the common name for the genus *Gladiolus* and the species *G. Segetum;* sweet flag is *Acorus Calammus.*

flag, blue *n.* A common name for *Iris versicolor.* It is a hardy perennial native to Eastern North America; it grows to 3 feet, with narrow, sword shaped leaves and tall stalks of showy blue, blue- violet, red-violet, lavender, or, occasionally, white flowers. Also known as poison flag.

flag, cattail *n.* A common name for *Typha,* a genus of water-loving cattails, some pecies native to North America. They are hardy perennials with long, narrow, tough leaves and cattails that grow from 6 to 10 feet tall. Used in bog gardens and at the edges of garden pools. May be invasive. Cattails are striking in flower arrangements.

flag, corn *n.* A common name for the genus *Gladiolus* (see **Gladiolus**), especially *Gladiolus segetum.* *G. segetum* is a tender perennial bulb (corm) that grows to 2 feet, with sword-shaped leaves and tall stalks with 6 to 10 flaring, bright purple flowers.

flagellum (fluh jehl′uhm) *n., pl.* **flagella** In botany: 1. A runner or stolon of a plant, rooting and forming new plants at the nodes, as in the strawberry. 2. A twig or young shoot.

flagellum of strawberry plant

flageolet (flaj uh lay') *n.* A variety of bean, popular in French cooking for its creamy texture and ability to blend with other flavors. Although usually found in its pale green color, there are darker types ranging to a deep red.

flag, slender blue *n.* A common name for *Iris prismatica,* a hardy perennial native to eastern North America. It grows to 2½ feet, with erect, long, narrow leaves and blue or blue-violet flowers.

flag, sweet *n.* A common name for *Acorus calamus,* It is a hardy perennial that grows to 6 feet, with long, narrow leaves, a 4-inch- long spadix (petallike sheath), and a thick, pink, aromatic root. used in bog gardens.

flag, water *n.* A common name for *Iris Pseudacorus.* Also known as yellow flag. (See **flag, yellow.**)

flag, Western blue *n.* A common name for *Iris missouriensis,* a hardy, drought-tolerant perennial native to western North America. It grows to 2 feet, with long, narrow leaves and large, pale lavender-blue or white flowers with purple veins.

flag, yellow *n.* A common name for *Iris Pseudacorus.* It is a hardy, self-sowing perennial that grows to 5 feet, with sword-shaped leaves and clusters of yellow to almost orange flowers on tall stalks. Thrives in moist, shady situations; useful along streams, at edges of pools, or in bog gardens. Can become invasive. Also known as water flag and yellow water iris.

flamboyant *n.* A common name for *Delonix regia,* a tropical tree with masses of brilliant scarlet flowers. Used to line avenues or as a striking specimen tree in southern Florida, Hawaii, Puerto Rico, and the U.S. Virgin Islands.

flameflower *n.* A name of species of *Pyrostegia venusta,* a tropical evergreen climbing vine with oval leaflets, tendrils, and orange trumpet-shaped flowers that give a brilliant show in fall and early winter in warm-winter climates. Also known as flaming trumpet, flame vine, or golden shower.

flame-of-the-forest *n.* A common name for tropical trees of 2 different genera, *Butea monosperma* and *Spathodea campanulata. B. monosperma,* a tree that grows to 50 feet, has a crooked trunk, leaves divided into leaflets, showy orange-red flowers,

and silvery-gray fruit. *S. campanulata,* a tree that grows to 70 feet, has glossy leaves divided into oval leaflets and clusters of tulip-shaped orange-red flowers edged with yellow, which may appear in any season.

flame-of-the-woods *n.* A common name for *Ixora coccinea* (Rubiaceae), a tropical evergreen shrub grown in warm-climate gardens for its large clusters of scarlet flowers. Also known as jungle-flame or jungle geranium.

flame tree *n.* A common name for 2 species of Australian trees, *Brachychiton australis* and *B. acerifolius,* briefly deciduous trees that flower, while leafless, with spectacular red flowers.

flamingo flower *n.* A common name for *Anthurium Scherzeranum,* a slow-growing compact plant with long, oblong, dark green leaves and unusual waxy, bright scarlet, rose, salmon, or white flowers. Grown as houseplants or greenhouse specimens.

flamingo plant *n.* 1. A common name for *Hypoestes phyllostachya,* a low-growing houseplant grown for its pink-spotted foliage. Also known as freckleface and pink polka-dot plant. 2. Also a common name for *Justicia carnea,* an erect evergreen shrub with heavily veined leaves and dense clusters of pink-to-crimson tubular flowers; grown outdoors in warm-winter climates, as a houseplant or greenhouse specimen anywhere.

flannelbush *n.* A common name for the genus *Fremontodendron,* a genus of evergreen shrubs or small trees native to California and Arizona. They have alternate, leathery leaves, felty beneath, and large, showy, bright yellow flowers. Drought-tolerant, but look best with regular watering.

flannelflower *n.* 1. A common name for *Actinotus helianthi,* an erect, furry perennial with large, divided leaves and woolly, petallike bracts. Grown as an annual in cold climates.

flaring rose *n.* A broad, perforated nozzle used to cast a soft spray on seedlings or other delicate plants. Also called fan spray.

flash tape *n.* A breeze-activated, metalized plastic tape that produces bursts of light in response to breezes; suspended over crops to scare away birds.

flat *n.* A container for holding packs of plant starter cells. Also called seed flat.

flax *n.* The common name for plants of the genus *Linum* and for the fiber obtained from the stems of *L. usitatissimum.* This species, of unknown origin, has been in cultivation from antiquity; it yields a vegetable fiber in popular use over a large part of the Old World. The plant is an annual, with slender stems about 2 feet tall, which by various processes are separated from all useless matter, leaving the elongated soft, silky fiber, which is spun into thread.

flax

flax family *n.* A common name for the order Linaceae.

flaxseed *n.* The seed of flax; linseed. Used to make linseed oil.

flaxweed *n.* A common name for *Linaria vulgaris.* Also called toadflax or spurred snapdragon.

fleabane *n.* One of several composite plants, so called from their supposed power of driving away fleas.

flea beetle *n.* A tiny, hopping insect (there are many kinds) that attacks a variety of plants, including vegetables and dicondra lawns. They usually start by eating small holes in leaves; the plants then wither or look scalded. They are very destructive to dicondra lawns and often transmit harmful viruses to vegetable plants. Control with sanitation, row covers, rotenone or pyrethrin sprays on vegetables, or traditional insecticides.

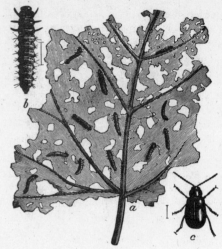

flea beetle
a grape leaf, showing damage *b* larva *c* beetle

fleaseed *n.* Same as fleawort.

fleawort *n.* A common name for *Plantago Psyllium,* named for the shape of its seeds. Also called fleaseed.

fleeceflower (flees'flow er) *n.* A common name for the genus *Polygonum,* a genus of plants and vines with open sprays of small white or pink flowers. Also called knotweed and smartweed.

fleecevine, silver (flees'vighn) *n.* A common name for *Polygonum Aubertii,* a fast-growing vine with heart-shaped leaves and a frothy mass of creamy-white flowers from spring through fall. Also called silver-lace vine and China fleecevine.

fleur-de-lis (fler duh lee') *n., pl.* **fleurs-de-lis** (fler duh lee'). A common name for *Iris × germanica,* the iris chosen for the royal emblem of France. Also fleur-de-lys, fleur-de-luce.

flintwood *n.* A common name for *Eucalyptus pilularis,* a tall, straight tree with glossy, sickle-shaped leaves and clusters of flowers.

floating heart *n.* A name given to the genus *Nymphoides,* from their floating, heart-shaped leaves. Used in garden pools, ponds, and tubs for their attractive foliage.

floating row cover *n.* Lightweight fiber sheet, water and air permeable, placed over a row of plants for protection from insects, heat, or cold.

floccose (flah'kohs) *a.* Having tufts of soft, woolly hairs.

flocculate (flahk'yuh layt) *v.* To clump together individual tiny soil particles.

flocculose (flahk'yuh lohs) *a.* In botany, finely floccose. Also flocculous.

floccus (flahk'uhs) *n., pl.* **flocci** In botany: a small tuft of woolly hairs.

flood irrigation *n.* A shallow flood of water over level soil.

flora (flohruh) *n., pl.* **floras** (floh'ruhz) or **florae** (floh'ree) In botany: 1. A book that systematically describes the plants of a particular country, region, or geological period. 2 a. Plant life in general, often in contrast to fauna. b. The plants native to or adapted to a particular country, region, habitat, or belonging to a particular period, as the Australasian flora or the flora of the Carboniferous period. c. Plant life of a particular kind, as parasitic flora.

floral *a.* Containing, belonging to, or relating to a flower; pertaining to flowers in general; made of flowers, as a floral bud, a floral leaf, or floral ornaments.

floral envelope *n.* The perianth of a flower.

Florence fennel *n.* A variety of *Foeniculum vulgare,* grown for its thick, overlapping leafstalks, which swell above ground level to form a tender, white head. Its slightly anise flavor and crisp texture make it useful in salads, or it can also be steamed as a hot vegetable. It differs from the herb fennel, which has thin, tough stems and grows much taller. It is rich in vitamin A. Also known as finocchio.

florescence (floh rehs'ehns) *n.* Blooming; the unfolding of a flower; the state of being in bloom.

florescent (floh rehs'ehnt) *a.* Being at the point or stage of florescence.

floret *n.* A small flower, especially when in a cluster or in a multiple-flowered inflorescence, as in the flowers of the Compositae or in the Gramineae.

floribunda (floh'ruh buhn'duh) *n.* The name for roses derived from crosses of polyantha and hybrid tea roses, resulting in vigorous and bushy plants that produce numerous open clusters of large roses, such as 'Iceberg', 'Simplicity', and 'Angel Face'.

floriculture (floh'ruh kuhl cher) *n.* The cultivation of flowers or of flowering plants, usually commercially.

floriculturist (floh ruh kuhl'cher ihst) *n.* A person who specializes in working with or growing flowers.

floriferous (flo-rif'e-rus) *a.* Producing many flowers.

floriform (floh'ruh form) *a.* In the form of a flower.

floriparous (floh rihp'uh ruhs) *a.* In plants that normally bear fruits, producing secondary flowers instead of fruits.

florist *n.* One whose business is the sale of flowers and ornamentals.

florist's flower vase *n.* A tapered metal bucket, slightly flared toward the top, used to hold cut flowers.

floscular (flahs'kyh ler) *a.* In botany, same as discoid, as applied to disk flowers in the Compositae; composed of florets. Also flosculous, flosculose.

flossflower *n.* A common name for the genus *Ageratum,* low-growing annuals with toothed leaves and numerous dense clusters of tassellike blue, lavender, white, or pink flowers. Used in borders, beds, and pots.

floss-silk tree *n.* A common name for *Chorisia speciosa,* a fall-flowering tree with a spiny trunk, hand-shaped leaves, and large, showy pink, rose, or burgundy flowers shaped like narrow-petaled hibiscus. Grown in mild climates as a specimen tree.

flow regulator *n.* A device for governing the rate at which water flows through a hose.

flower *n.* 1. In botany, that part of a seed plant that usually bears the reproductive organs, especially when brightly colored or otherwise conspicuous. When the stem of a flower bears only pistils, it is a female, or pistillate, flower. When it bears only stamens, it is male, or staminate. If bearing both, it is termed a bisexual, or perfect, flower; if, in turn, it has 2 floral envelopes—the corolla and calyx—it is called a complete flower. 2. In popular language: a. Any blossom or inflorescence. b. Any plant considered with reference to its blossom, or of which the blossom is the essential feature; a plant cultivated for its floral beauty. *v.* To blossom; bloom; produce flowers.

flower arrangement *n.* A combination of individual cut flowers to create an aesthetically pleasing whole.

flowering plant *n.* A plant that produces flowers, fruit, and seeds.

flower-de-luce (flow′er duh loos′) *n.* A name for *Iris* ×*germanica,* the French fleur-de-lis.

floweret *n.* A floret; sometimes, 1 of the segments of a cauliflower head.

flower-fence *n.* A common name for the *Caesalpinia pulcherrima,* a prickly, subtropical evergreen shrub bearing showy large red flowers with yellow edges. Used in warm-winter gardens, for hedges or as single shrubs. Also called pride-of-Barbados, dwarf poinciana, and Barbados-pride.

flower gatherer *n.* Scissors mounted on a tube, typically 2 to 3 feet long, used for cutting and holding flower stems.

flower head *n.* In botany, a form of inflorescence giving the effect of a single flower, consisting of a dense cluster of florets sessile upon the shortened summit of the axis, as in the Compositae.

flowering maple *n.* A common name for *Abutilon,* a viny, broadleaf, evergreen shrub with maple-like leaves and curious drooping flowers. Used as an open, spreading shrub, an espalier, or as a houseplant in cold climates. Also called Chinese bellflower, Chinese lantern, and parlor maple.

flowering rush *n.* A common name for *Butomus umbellatus,* an erect aquatic plant growing from rhizomes with tufts of long, narrow leaves and showy clusters of rosy-pink flowers. Used in large garden pools and ponds.

flowering stones *n.* A common name for odd dwarf succulents of 2 different genera, *Lithops* and *Dinteranthus.* Both are mimicry plants, looking like small stones cleft in the center, out of which a many-petaled flower appears. Grown primarily by collectors.

flowerless *a.* Having no flowers.

flower-of-an-hour *n.* A common name for *Hibiscus Trionum,* the flower of which is open only in midday. It has lobed leaves and white, cream, or yellow flowers with a dark red eye. Has naturalized in warm regions worldwide.

flowerpot *n.* A pot in which flowering plants or shrubs may be grown; generally made of unglazed clay, tapered toward the bottom, and perforated with 1 or more holes for drainage.

flower press *n.* A device in which flowers may be dried and preserved. A flower press consists of layers of cardboard and blotting paper sandwiched between 2 wooden boards, which are held together in the corners by adjustable screws.

flower ring *n.* A wire loop supported by stakes to prop and contain a cluster of weak-stemmed flowers such as bachelor buttons or campanulas.

flowers, fragrant *n.* Any flowers that have an attractive smell, such as roses, jasmine, daphne, citrus, and honeysuckle.

flower shows *n.* Any organized display of flowers, whether of living plants or cut flowers. Many are organized by specialty plant societies for a particular kind of flower, such as orchids, rhododendrons, daffodils, geraniums, or roses. The entries are typically judged and awarded ribbons based on color, shape, and quality of bloom.

flowers, state *n.* Flowering plants designated as motifs or used in state insignias.

flower stalk *n.* In botany, a peduncle or pedicel; the usually leafless part of a stem or branch that bears a flower cluster or a single flower.

flower support *n.* A stake, typically of plastic-coated wire, to prop or brace a single weak-stemmed plant such as lily or gladiolus. Also called loop stake.

fluellen (floo ehl′ihn) *n.* A common name for 2 different species of *Veronica, V. officinalis* and *V. Chamaedrys.*

fluorescent-light gardening (floo rehs′ehnt) *n.* The process of growing plants under artificial lights.

fluorescent tube (floo rehs′ehnt) *n.* A type of light bulb that emits ultraviolet light. Fluorescent lamps are used to start and maintain plants indoors.

fly honeysuckle *n.* A common name given to 2 species of *Lonicera, L. canadensis* and *L. Xylosteum.*

fly orchid *n.* The common name of *Ophrys insectifera,* from the resemblance of the flowers to flies, complete with 2 glossy, eyelike knobs at the base of the flower. Sometimes planted in wildflower gardens.

fly poison *n.* A common name for *Amianthium muscitoxicum,* a bulb native to eastern North America. It has a single stem to 4 feet tall, with long, narrow leaves and spikes of many small white flowers. The bulb is poisonous when eaten.

foalfoot *n.* A common name for *Tussilago Farfara,* so called from the shape of the leaves. It has very early spring flowers but can become a pernicious weed. Widely naturalized in eastern North America. Also called coltsfoot.

foamflower *n.* A common name for *Tiarella cordifolia,* a low-growing plant with heart-shaped leaves and stalks of small white flowers. Grown in the wild garden, rock garden, or woodland garden for the bronze fall color of the foliage.

Foeniculum (fee nihk yuh luhm) *n.* A small genus of 2 or 3 species of plants (Umbelliferae). They have finely divided, fernlike aromatic leaves and rounded clusters of yellow flowers. *F. vulgare,* the common fennel, has a thickened base, which is edible, and edible seeds that taste like licorice. It attracts birds and has naturalized on the West Coast of the United States.

foenugreek (fehn'yih greek) *n.* (See **fenugreek**.)

fog nozzle *n.* A sprayer for applying a fine mist to plants.

folding saw *n.* An instrument used for pruning that folds in half so that when the tool is not in use, the teeth of the blade are stored and protected in a groove within the tool handle.

foliaceous (foh lee ay'shuhs) *a.* Being or resembling a leaf. In botany, having the texture or form of a leaf, as a foliaceous sepal or bract.

foliage *n.* The mass of growing plant leaves in their natural form and condition, or a cluster of same; leafage.

foliage plant *n.* A plant conspicuous for its attractive foliage rather than for its flowers, as the various kinds of *Coleus* and *Philodendron.*

foliar *a.* Consisting of or pertaining to leaves.

foliar diagnosis *n.* A chemical analysis to estimate the plant-nutrient status of plant-nutrient requirement of the soil.

foliar feeding *n.* The feeding of plants by spraying plant food on their leaves.

foliate *a.* In botany, leafy; furnished with leaves or leaflets, as a foliate stalk.

foliation *n.* The leafing of plants; vernation, the disposition of the nascent leaves within the bud.

foliicolous (foh lee ihk uh luhs) *a.* Growing upon leaves; parasitic on leaves, as many fungi.

foliolate (foh'lee uh layt) *a.* In botany, of or pertaining to, consisting of, or having leaflets. Used in combination, as bifoliolate, having two leaflets.

foliole *n.* In botany, a leaflet; a small part resembling a leaf.

foliose *a.* Leafy or resembling a leaf. Also folious.

follicle *n.* In botany: a dry, 1-celled seed vessel consisting of a single carpel, and dehiscent only by the ventral suture, as in the milkweed and larkspur.

follicle of larkspur
fruit

Fontanesia (fahn tuh nee'zhee uh) *n.* A genus of 2 species of deciduous privetlike shrubs (Oleaceae). They have opposite, entire leaves and leafy clusters of small white flowers.

fool's-stones *n.* A common name for several species of European wild orchids of the genus *Orchis.*

footstalk *n.* In botany, the stalk, or petiole, of a leaf or the peduncle of a flower.

forcing *n*. In horticulture, the art or practice of raising plants by artificial heat, at a season earlier than the natural one.

forcing house *n*. In horticulture, a hothouse for forcing plants.

forcing pit *n*. A pit of wood or masonry, sunk in the earth, for containing fermenting materials to produce bottom heat in forcing plants.

Forestiera (for ehs tee ihr'uh) *n*. A genus of 20 species of fast-growing shrubs or trees (Oleaceae) native to the Americas. *F. neomexicana* has opposite, smooth medium-green leaves, clusters of small yellow flowers, and black or purple olive-like fruit. Used as a fast-growing, drought-tolerant screen. Also known as Mexican privet or desert olive.

forget-me-not *n*. 1. A common name for the genus *Myosotis,* especially *M. scorpioides* (Boraginaceae). It has circular clusters of sky-blue flowers with a yellow center. Traditionally considered the emblem of friendship. Often grown in cottage gardens or in combination with spring-blooming bulbs. 2. Creeping forget-me-not is a common name for *Omphalodes verna,* a spring-blooming perennial. It has oval leaves and blue or white flowers and spreads by runners.

forget-me-not, Chinese *n*. A common name for *Cynoglossum amabile,* a biennial to 2 feet tall with large, soft, hairy gray-green leaves and loose sprays of rich blue, pink, or white flowers. Used in beds, borders, and the wild garden.

forget-me-not, true *n*. A common name for the genus *Myosotis.* (See **forget-me-not**.)

fork *n*. A short-handled, 3-tined implement similar in design to a table fork; used to loosen small areas of soil.

form *n*. A botanical category below a variety in rank and differing only trivially from other related forms, such as in flower color. Also forma, *pl.* formae.

form genus *n*. In biology, a taxonomic category artificially created for organisms whose development, life history, structure, or relationships are obscure.

form species *n*. In biology, a species placed in a form genus.

fornicate *a*. In botany, overarched with fornices, as the throat of the corolla of the forget-me-not. Also forniciform.

fornix *n., pl.* **fornices** In botany, a small arching scale or appendage in the throat of the corolla of some plants, as in the forget-me-not.

Forsythia (for sih'thee uh) *n*. 1. A genus of 6 or 7 species of hardy, early-blooming, fountain-shaped deciduous shrubs (Oleaceae). They bear numerous showy yellow flowers on bare branches in early spring. Their medium-green foliage blends well with other shrubs. Used as a screen, espalier, bank cover, or with other shrubs. 2. [l.c.] A plant of this genus.

Fortunella (for chuh nehl'uh) *n*. A genus of 4 or 5 species of evergreen shrubs or trees (Rutaceae); the kumquats. They are similar to citrus and have alternate leaves, richly fragrant white flowers, and round, fleshy, thick-skinned bright orange fruit with edible rind.

Fothergilla (fahth'er gihl'uh) *n*. A genus of 4 or 5 species of deciduous shrubs (Hamamelidaceae) native to the southeastern United States. They have alternate, simple, coarsely toothed leaves and small brushlike white flowers. The leaves turn scarlet, crimson, or purplish red in fall, and they are grown primarily for fall color. Commonly known as witch alder.

foundation planting *n*. Plants placed around the base of a building.

fountain *n*. An artificial basin or tank for receiving a flow of living water, from which it may be drawn for any use, or from which, by the force of its own pressure, it may rise or spout in jets, sprays, or showers.

fountain grass *n*. (See **Pennisetum**.)

Fouquieria (foo kee ihr'ee uh) *n*. A genus of about 9 species of curiously spiny shrubs or small trees (Fouquieriaceae) native to the deserts of the American Southwest. They have long, stiff, whiplike gray branches covered with thorns. The branches are usually leafless, but after the rains, small, fleshy round leaves appear briefly, as do foot-long clusters of brilliant crimson, pale purple, or white tubular flowers. *F. splendens* is commonly known as ocotillo, coachwhip, vine cactus, and Jacob's staff.

Fouquieriaceae (foo kee ihr ay'see ee) *n.* A family of 2 genera of spiny shrubs and trees, *Fouquieria* and *Idira,* native to southwestern North America; the candlewood family.

four-o'clock *n.* A common name for *Mirabilis jalapa,* so called from the fact that its flowers open in the afternoon. It is an erect, many-branched perennial that forms mounded clumps, 3 to 4 feet high and wide, with trumpet-shaped red, yellow, or white flowers. Also called marvel-of-Peru and beauty-of-the-night.

four-o'clock family *n.* A common name for *Nyctaginaceae,* which includes the genera *Mirabilis, Bougainvillea,* and *Pisonia.*

foxbane *n.* A common name for *Aconitum Lycoctonum,* a tall perennial with rounded leaves and spikes of purple-lilac monk's-hood-shaped flowers. Many *Aconitum* species are poisonous.

foxberry *n.* A common name for *Arctostaphylos Uva-ursi,* a ground cover with leathery, glossy, bright green leaves, small white or pink flowers, and pink or red winter berries. Also known as bearberry.

foxglove *n.* 1. A common name for *Digitalis purpurea,* one of the most stately ornamental flowering plants. It has large tubular flowers in groups at the end of long, upright stems. The flowers are purple or sometimes white or rose-colored. Traditional in cottage gardens.

foxglove family *n.* A common name for the genus *Digitalis.*

fox grape *n.* The common name of several species of small North American wild grapes, especially *Vitis Labrusca* of the northern and western United States.

foxtail *n.* (See **Alopecurus**.)

fox-tail barley *n.* (See **Hordeum**.)

fragipans (fraj'ih panz) *n.* The dense and brittle layers in soil that roots and water cannot penetrate and that owe their hardness to density or compactness.

frame *n.* (See **cold frame** and **electric hotbed**.)

Francoa (frang koh'uh) *n.* A genus of 4 or 5 species of stemless perennials (Saxifragaceae) native to Chile. They form spreading clumps, with large, wavy-margined leaves and gracefully arching stems of pure white or pink flowers. Commonly known as maiden's wreath.

frangipani (fran jih pan'ee) *n.* 1. A common name of the genus *Plumeria,* flowering tropical trees famous for their fragrance, as well as the species *Plumeria rubra.* Also called red jasmine. 2. A perfume made from the flowers of *Plumeria rubra.*

Frankenia (frang kee'nee uh) *n.* A genus of about 25 species of low, heathlike perennials or undershrubs (Frankeniaceae) widely distributed in warm, dry regions but mostly found near the sea or in saline soils.

Frankeniaceae (frang kee nee ay'see ee) *n. pl.* A family of shrubs represented by the genus *Frankenia.*

Franklinia (frangk lihn'ee uh) *n.* A genus of a single species of hardy, fall-blooming deciduous shrub or small tree (Theaceae) native to North America. It has alternate, simple, spoon-shaped bright green leaves, which turn scarlet in fall, and large white flowers with many yellow stamens that sometimes coincide with fall foliage. Commonly known as Franklin tree.

Franklin tree *n.* (See **Franklinia**.)

Frasera (fray'zer uh) *n.* 1. A genus of mostly biennial plants (Gentianaceae) native to North America. They have a single, erect stem growing from a thick root; mostly basal, simple, entire leaves; and rounded clusters of white, yellow, or blue flowers. Commonly known as green gentian and columbo.

fraxinella (frak'suh nehl'uh) *n.* A common name *Dictamnus albus,* a large back-of-the-border perennial. Also known as gas plant, dittany, and burning bush.

Fraxinus (frak'sih nuhs) *n.* A genus of about 65 species of deciduous trees (Oleaceae); the ash family. They are mostly large, fast-growing trees with opposite leaves divided into leaflets, clusters of inconspicuous flowers, and maplelike seeds. They are used as shade trees, lawn trees, and street trees. (See **ash**.)

freckleface *n.* A common name for *Hypoestes phyllostachya,* and indoor plant grown for its pink-spotted leaves. (See **flamingo plant**.)

free *a.* A term used to describe the condition of a substance within a mixture when it is not chemically combined with other components of the mixture.

Freesia (free'zhee uh) *n.* A genus of 19 species of fragrant flowering perennial bulbs (Iridaceae). They have swordlike leaves and long stalks with numerous, powerfully fragrant tubular flowers in a wide range of colors: yellow, white, pink, red, orange, gold, lavender, or blue.

Fremontia (free mahn'tee uh) *n.* A common name for *Fremontodendron,* named for John Charles Fremont (1830-1890), who explored the American West with Kit Carson as his guide. (See **Fremontodendron**.)

Fremontodendron (free mahn'toh dehn'druhn) *n.* A genus of 2 species or more or less evergreen shrubs native to California and Arizona. They have lobed, leathery leaves with a feltlike coating beneath and conspicuous, saucerlike bright yellow flowers. Commonly known as Fremontia or flannelbush.

French honeysuckle *n.* A common name for plants of 2 different species, *Hedysarum coronarium* and *Centranthus ruber. H. coronarium* is a 4-foot-tall perennial with leaves divided into several pairs of leaflets and stalks crowded with fragrant deep red flowers. *C. ruber* is a drought-tolerant, self-sowing, bushy perennial with 4- inch-long bluish-green leaves and dense terminal clusters of tiny pale pink, rose, red or white flowers; it has naturalized widely throughout the American West.

Freycinetia (fray suh neesh'ee uh) *n.* A genus of about 65 species of climbing vines (Pandanaceae). They have stems with aerial props and long, narrow leaves forming a crown at the ends of branches. The flowers are surrounded by colored bracts in white or pale lilac. They are grown outdoors in tropical, rainy climates, in greenhouses elsewhere.

friable *a.* Used to describe rich loamy soils that are loose and easy to work.

friar's-cap *n.* The wolf's-bane, *Aconitum Napellus,* so called from its hooded sepals. (See **Aconitum**.)

frijole (free hoh'lee) *n.* The common name in Spanish for the cultivated bean that forms an important staple of food.

frijolillo (free hoh leel'yoh) *n.* A common name for *Erythrina corallodendron* (Leguminosae), a West Indian tree with 3-part leaves and with spikes of large butterflylike flowers, usually blood-red or orange. It is also known as coral bean.

fringe cups *n.* A common name for *Tellima grandiflora,* a drought-tolerant perennial native to western North America. It has rounded, lobed leaves and tall, slender stalks of small, urn-shaped deep red flowers. A choice subject in a shady spot in the rock garden or with ferns in the woodland garden.

fringed orchid, large purple *n.* A common name for *Habenaria psycodes* var. *grandiflora,* which has a 3-foot-long leafy stem with long, narrow leaves and dense stalks of showy, fragrant purple, lilac, or white flowers. A hardy wild orchid native to eastern North America.

fringepod *n.* A common name for the genus *Thysanocarpus* (Cruciferae), a genus of plants with round, flattened, winged pods, the edges of which are fringed. Also called lacepod.

fringe tree *n.* A common name for *Chionanthus virginicus,* a small tree or airy shrub found on riverbanks in the United States, from Pennsylvania to Texas. It bears loose, drooping clusters of white flowers, the long narrow petals of which suggest the name. Purple fringe tree is a common name for *Cotinus Coggygria,* also called smoke tree.

Fritillaria imperialis
(crown fritillary)

Fritillaria (friht uh lar'ee uh) *n.* A genus of about 100 species of perennial bulbs (Liliaceae), some species native to North America. They have leafy stems and large, drooping, bell-shaped red or yellow flowers. *F. imperialis,* the crown imperial or crown fritillary, is striking in appearance, but both bulbs and flowers have a skunklike odor. Excellent in borders and containers. *F. Meleagris,* the checkered lily or snake's-head, is used in wild or woodland gardens.

fritillary (friht'uh ler ee) *n.* The common name of plants of the genus *Fritillaria.*

frogbit (frahg'biht) *n.* 1. A common name for *Hydrocharis Morsus-ranae,* a floating aquatic plant, with rounded, heart-shaped leaves and small white flowers. 2. The *Limnobium Spongia,* an aquatic plant with rounded leaves native to the United States. Also known as frog's-bit.

frond *n.* In botany, a leaf of a palm or fern.

frondage *n.* Fronds collectively.

frondent *a.* Leafy.

frondescence *n.* In botany: The period or state of coming into leaf; leafage; foliage.

frondescent *a.* Coming into leaf.

frondiferous *a.* Producing fronds or leaves.

frondlet *n.* A small frond.

frondose *a.* Bearing or resembling fronds.

frost *n.* 1. That state or temperature of the air that occasions freezing or the congelation of water; severe cold or freezing weather. 2. The state or condition of being frozen; said of the surface of the ground when frost extends to a depth of 10 inches.

frost control *v.* The act of minimizing frost damage to plants by covering them, watering them lightly, or placing them in a protected area.

frost-free days *n. pl.* The number of days in a growing season in any given area.

frostroot *n.* The common fleabane of North America. (See **Erigeron**.)

frostweed *n.* A common name for *Helianthemum canadense,* so called from the crystals of ice that shoot from the bursting bark toward the base of the

stem during freezing weather in autumn; native the eastern United States. Also called frostwo rockrose, or sunrose.

frostwort *n.* (See **frostweed**.)

fructescence (fruhk tehs'ehns) *n.* The time of maturing of fruit.

fructiferous (fruhk tihf'uh ruhs) *a.* Bearing or producing fruit.

fructification *n.* 1. The act of forming or producing fruit. 2. Specifically, in botany: a. The production of fruit by a plant; fruiting. b. The ripened ovary and its appendages; the fruit of a plant.

fructify *v.* To bear or produce fruit; to make fruitful.

fruit *n.* 1. In common usage, any product of vegetable growth useful to humans or animals, as grapes, figs, corn, cotton, flax, and all cultivated plants. 2. In a more limited sense, the reproductive product of a tree or other plant; the seed of plants, or the part that contains the seeds, as wheat, rye, oats, apples, pears, nuts, etc. 3. In a still more limited sense, an edible, succulent product of a plant, normally covering and including the seeds, as the apple, orange, lemon, peach, pear, plum, a berry, a melon, etc. 4. In botany, the matured ovary of a plant, consisting of the seeds and their pericarp (coating), and including whatever may be incorporated with it; also, the spores of cryptogams and the organs accessory to them. The kinds of fruit are very numerous and differ greatly in character and degree of complexity. *v.* To produce fruit; to come into bearing.

fruit, compound *n.* A fruit that consists of several ovaries.

fruit dot *n.* In botany, the sorus of ferns.

fruit fly *n.* A tiny fly that lays eggs on many types of fruit, including apples, citrus, cherries, and walnuts. The larvae (maggots) bore into ripe fruit, disfiguring or causing rotting. There are many types, including ones that can devastate agricultural crops. Sanitation, sticky traps, and properly timed sprays of traditional insecticides are the most effective control measures. Small red balls coated with sticky material can be effective traps in apple trees.

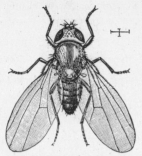

fruit fly (cross shows natural size)

fruit-gatherer *n.* A device for gathering fruit from trees, as a pair of shears attached to the end of a pole and operated by means of a cord. In this device, a bag or basket is commonly fastened to the pole below the shears, to catch the fruit as it falls. Also called fruit-picker.

fruiting body *n.* A specialized organ for producing spores, as in mushrooms and mosses.

fruitlet *n.* 1. A small fruit. 2. A unit of a collective fruit.

fruit-picker *n.* Same as fruit-gatherer.

fruits, small *n. pl.* Fruits raised in market gardens, such as strawberries, raspberries, and currants.

fruit tree *n.* A tree cultivated for its fruit, or a tree whose principal value consists in the fruit it produces, as the cherry tree, apple tree, or pear tree.

fruit trees, dwarf *n.* A term used to describe both genetic dwarf trees and trees grafted onto dwarf rootstock. For example, peaches that are genetic dwarfs produce full-sized fruit on trees that rarely grow more than 3 feet tall. Fruits grafted onto dwarf rootstock, such as citrus or apples, produce normal fruit on trees that grow to no more than 8 feet tall. Many grafted fruit trees are also sold as semidwarf, growing to approximately 10 feet tall. All the dwarf fruit are excellent in suburban yards, small-space situations, and in containers.

frumentaceous (froo mehn tay'shuhs) *a.* Having the character of or resembling wheat or other cereal.

frutescent *a.* In botany, having the appearance or habit of a shrub; shrubby, as a frutescent stem.

fruticose *a.* 1. Resembling a shrub; shrubby, as a fruticose stem.

fruticulose (froo tihk'yuh lohs) *a.* Resembling a small shrub.

Fuchsia (fyoo'shuh) *n.* 1. A genus of about 600 to 700 species of highly ornamental shrubs and small trees (Onagraceae) mostly native to the Americas. They have opposite leaves, many brightly colored, dangling, reflexed tubular flowers that attract hummingbirds, and a fleshy fruit. Extremely useful as shrubs in the garden or as spectacular hanging-basket plants in bright, protected areas. Often grown under lath. 2. [l.c.] A plant of this genus.

fuller's herb *n.* The soapwort, *Saponaria officinalis,* so called from its use in removing stains from cloth.

fuller's teasel *n.* The teasel, *Dipsacus sativus.* Also known as **fuller's thistle** and **fuller's weed.**

Fumariaceae (fyoo ma ree ay'see ee) *n. pl.* A family of 19 genera and 425 species; the fumitory family. The ornamental genera are *Adlumia, Corydalis, Rupicapnos,* and *Dicentra.*

fumariaceous (fyoo ma ree ay'shuhs) *a.* Belonging to or resembling the Fumariaceae.

fumewort *n.* A plant of the order Fumariaceae.

fumitory *n.* The common name for species of the obsolete genus *Fumaria,* previously classified under Fumariaceae. Climbing fumitory is a common name for *Adlumia fungosa,* an herbaceous vine with feathery, fernlike leaves and white or pink flowers that resemble *Dicentra,* commonly called bleeding heart.

fumitory or bleeding heart family *n.* A common name for Fumariaceae.

fungal *a.* In botany, pertaining to, characteristic of, or consisting of a fungus or fungi. Also fungous. *n.* A fungus.

Fungales (fuhng gay'leez) *n. pl.* (See **Fungi.**)

Fungi *n. pl.* A division of diverse plants that lack chlorophyll and, therefore, do not photosynthesize. They include mushrooms, molds, smuts, rusts, and yeasts. A few are edible, such as *Boletus;* many more are plant diseases, such as powdery mildew. Also called Fungales.

fungicide (fuhn jih sighd) *n.* An agent that destroys fungi; specifically, a material used to control fungal disease on plants, plant parts, and soil.

Funginex (fuhn'jih neks) *n.* (See **triforine**.)

fungus *n., pl.* **fungi** A plant classified under the division Fungi.

funiculus of a *Lunaria*
seed pod, showing
funiculi marked *a*

funiculus (fyoo nihk'yuh luhs) *n., pl.* **funiculi** In botany, the stalk of an ovule (the stem of a seed or its case). Also funicle.

Funkia (fuhng'kee uh) *n.* An obsolete term for plants now classified as *Hosta.*

funnelform *a.* Having the form of a funnel; specifically, in botany, applied to a corolla of a flower in which the tube enlarges gradually from below, as the morning glory; infundibuliform.

funnelform corolla
of a flower

furcate (fer'kayt) *a.* Forked.

Furcraea (fer kree'uh) *n.* A genus of 20 species of slow-growing, succulent perennial plants (Agavaceae) native to tropical America. They have sword-shaped basal rosettes of thick, fleshy leaves and flowers clustered on very tall stalks.

furfuraceous (fer fyuh ray'shuhs) *a.* In botany, coated with branlike flaky particles; scurfy.

furrow *n.* A trench in the earth, especially that made by a plow. *v.* To cut a furrow in; make furrows in; plow.

furrowed *a.* Having longitudinal channels, ridges, or grooves, as a furrowed stem.

furrow weed *n.* A weed growing on plowed land.

furze *n.* A common name for any of several species of *Ulex* or *Genista,* much-branched, and sometimes spiny, shrubs with clusters of yellow flowers. Some species of both genera are grown ornamentally. Also called gorse and whin. Needle furze is a common name for *Genista anglica,* which has slender, finely pointed spines.

fusarium wilt (fyoo sair'ee uhm wihlt) *n.* A soil-borne disease that infects the roots or seeds of many plants, causing wilting or dieback. It often kills young seedlings (see **damping-off**) and infects lawns (causing irregular or circular dead patches) and tomatoes. Control by careful watering, planting resistant species or varieties, and using sterile soil and fungicide-treated seed. Traditional fungicides can also be effective.

fuscous (fuhs'kuhs) *a.* Brown; brown tinged with gray.

fusiform (fyoo'zuh form) *a.* Tapering both ways from the middle like a spindle, as the radish. Also fusate.

Gaillardia (guh lahr'dee uh) *n.* A genus of 14 species of handsome annual, biennial, or perennial herbaceous flowers (Compositae) native to the Americas. The plants are 2 to 4 feet tall with rough, gray-green leaves and large, showy, daisylike red, yellow, maroon, or bicolored flowers. Commonly known as blanketflower.

Galanthus (guh lan'thuhs) *n.* A small genus of 12 species of early-blooming perennial bulbs (Amaryllidaceae). They have narrow leaves and nodding, bell-shaped white flowers with a dot of green on each petal. Also known as snowdrop.

Galax (gay′laks) *n.* A genus of a single species of evergreen perennial flower, *Galax urceolata* (Diapensiaceae), native to open woods from Virginia to Georgia. It has rounded, heart-shaped leaves and tall, wandlike stems bearing numerous small white flowers. Grown as a slow-spreading ground cover in woodland gardens or as a specimen in rock gardens. Commonly known as wandflower, galaxy, and coltsfoot.

galbulus (gal byuh luhs) *n.*, *pl.* **galbuli** In botany, a spherical cone formed of thick scales with a narrow base, as in the cypress, or berrylike with fleshy scales, as in the juniper.

galea (gay′lee uh) *n.*, *pl.* **galeae** In botany, a helmet-shaped part of a calyx or corolla, as the upper lip of a ringent or labiate corolla.

Galeandra (gal ee an′druh) *n.* A genus of 20 species of terrestrial or epiphytic orchids (Orchidaceae) native to Central and South America and the West Indies. They grow from a pseudobulb and have more or less deciduous, pleated leaves and large, showy yellow, dark purple, or olive-green flowers, often streaked or blotched with violet or purple. *G. lacustris* is commonly known as helmet orchid.

galeate (gay′lee ayt) *a.* 1. In botany, having a galea. 2. Helmet-shaped, for example, the helmet-shaped upper sepal of monkshood.

Galega (guh lee′guh) *n.* A genus of 6 to 8 species of tall perennials (Leguminosae). They have divided leaves and stalks of butterfly-shaped blue or white flowers. *G. officinalis* is commonly known as goat's rue.

galeiform (guh lee′uh form) *a.* Helmet-shaped.

Galium (gay′lee uhm) *n.* 1. A large genus of 300 species of low-growing herbs (Rubiaceae). They have square, slender stems, whorls of aromatic leaves, and clusters of tiny white flowers. The stems and fruit are frequently armed with minute, hooked prickles. *G. odorata* is the aromatic herb commonly known as sweet woodruff, traditionally used in making May wine. The genus is commonly known as bedstraw or cleavers. 2. [l.c.] A plant of the genus *Galium*.

gall *n.* An abnormal plant growth on foliage, branches, or roots caused by irritation from an insect, a fungus or a virus.

gall on oak leaf, showing interior

gallica rose (gal′ih kuh) *n.* A common name for *Rosa gallica,* an antique rose with prickly, bristly stems, smooth, dark green leaves, and pink, purple, or dark red fragrant flowers 2½ inches across. Some, like 'Rosa Mundi', are striped red on white. Also called French rose.

Galphimia (gal fihm′yuh) *n.* A genus of 12 species of shrubs or small trees (Malpighiaceae) native to tropical America. They have opposite, simple leaves and clusters or spikes of 5-petaled yellow flowers. Grown outdoors in warm winter gardens, in greenhouses elsewhere.

Galtonia (gahl tohn′ee uh) *n.* A genus of 3 species of summer- or fall-blooming perennial bulbs (Liliaceae). They have basal, fleshy, straplike leaves with stalks of nodding, funnel-shaped, fragrant white flowers. Also known as summer hyacinth.

gamete *n.* A mature sex cell (as a sperm or an egg) possessing a haploid chromosome set and capable of developing into a new individual by fusion with another gamete.

gametophyte (guh meed′uh fight) *n.* The generation or stage of a plant producing gametes, existing only as a rudimentary structure in seed plants and as distinguished from the sporophyte, or asexual form.

Gamolepis (guh mahl′uh pihs) *n.* A genus of 15 species of small shrubs and plants (Compositae). They have alternate leaves and daisylike yellow or orange flowers.

gamopetalous (gam uh peht′uh luhs) *a.* In botany, having the petals joined at the base; belonging to the Metachlamydeae. Also monopetalous.

gamophyllous (gam uh fihl′uhs) *a*. In botany, having united leaves or leaflike organs.

gamosepalous (gam oh sehp′uh luhs) *a*. In botany, having the sepals united. Also monosepalous.

garbanzo *n*. (See **chick-pea**.)

Garcinia (gahr sihn′ee uh) *n*. A genus of 200 tropical trees or shrubs (Guttiferae). They have opposite, simple, usually thick leaves and a fleshy fruit with a thick rind. *G. Mangostana*, commonly known as mangosteen, is an excellent tropical fruit, but it does not fruit outside the tropics.

garden balm *n*. A common name for the herb *Melissa officinalis*; also called lemon balm.

garden balsam *n*. A common name for *Impatiens Balsimina*, a branching annual with alternate, long, narrow leaves and white, yellow, or dark red flowers, often spotted. Also known as rose balsam.

garden clogs *n*. Thick-soled, brightly colored, molded plastic shoes shaped like Dutch wooden shoes.

garden compost *n*. An organic matter such as well-decayed leaves, grass clippings, and vegetable waste, added to the soil as an amendment to improve its texture and drainage and to enrich it with nutrients.

gardener's-garters *n*. (See **Phalaris**.)

garden fence *n*. An exclosure, often temporary and made of mesh supported by wood or metal stakes; used to keep animals—dogs, deer, rabbit, etc—out of a garden.

garden frame *n*. A structure, typically of metal, which holds the glass or acrylic sheets of a cold frame. May also include shelves and a mist-irrigation system.

garden-gate *n*. A common name for several species of *Viola*, including *V. arvensis* and *V. ocellata*, also known as the pansy; an abbreviation of the common name kiss-behind-the-garden- gate. 2. A common name for *Geranium robertianum*, also called herb Robert.

garden gloves *n*. Sturdy gloves, often having a double-layered palm and thumb; used to protect gardeners' hands from blisters and scratches.

garden hose *n*. (See **hose**.)

Gardenia (gahr deen′yuh) *n*. A genus of 200 species of small tropical and subtropical trees and shrubs (Rubiaceae). They have opposite or whorled glossy, dark green leaves and large, handsome white or cream-colored flowers, which are often deliciously fragrant. *G. jasminoides*, commonly known as Cape jasmine, is grown in frost-free climates outdoors, as an indoor/outdoor plant in cold climates.

garden seat *n*. A low, padded bench on wheels; used while sowing, weeding, or harvesting to prevent stiff knees and aching back.

garland flower *n*. A common name for plants of several different species, including *Daphne Cneorum*, *Erica persoluta*, and *Hedychium coronarium*. *D. Cneorum* is a creeping shrub with small, narrow leaves and numerous rose-red, pink, or white fragrant flowers. *E. persoluta* is a heatherlike plant with stalks of many tiny rosy-red flowers. *H. coronarium* is a tropical plant, related to ginger, with stalks of very fragrant white flowers.

garlic *n*. 1. A bulbous plant, *Allium sativum*, a relative of the onion in use since ancient times. It is used as a flavor in cooking. It has a very strong odor and a pungent taste. Each bulb is composed of several lesser bulbs, called cloves of garlic, enclosed in a papery coat and easily separable.

garlic chive *n*. A garlic-flavored green of the onion family, *Allium tuberosum*. It is similar to the common chive, but its leaves are not tubular; instead, they are flat with a foldlike keel. The leaves are used raw or cooked, as a mild garlic flavoring.

garlic shrub *n*. A common name for *Adenocalymna alliacea*, a shrubby tropical American vine (Bignoniaceae) with shiny leaves, which smell like garlic when bruised, and showy, bright yellow flowers.

garlic vine *n*. A common name for *Cydista aequinoctialis*, a shrubby subtropical vine that climbs by tendrils, and has opposite leaves and stalks of streaked white to lavender tubular flowers.

Garrya (gar′ee uh) *n*. A genus of about 15 species of evergreen shrubs (Garryaceae) native to western North America. They have opposite, simple, leathery leaves and catkinlike flowers. Used as a display shrub, as a screen, or an informal hedge. Commonly known as silk-tassel or silk-tassel bush.

Garryaceae (gar ee ay'see ee) *n.* A family of a single genus, *Garrya,* of evergreen shrubs. Commonly known as the silk-tassel family.

gas plant *n.* A common name for *Dictamnus albus,* so called from the flammable vapor it gives off, which can be ignited with a match into a little puff of flame on still summer evenings. Also called fraxinella.

Gasteria (ga stihr'ee uh) *n.* A genus of about 50 species of succulent perennials (Liliaceae). They form clumps of thick, fleshy, spotted, flat leaves in a basal rosette and have long stalks of loose clusters of red, green-tipped flowers. Commonly called lawyer's-tongue, mother-in-law's-tongue, or oxtongue.

Gaultheria (gahl thihr'ee uh) *n.* A large genus of 100 species of aromatic evergreen shrubs or almost herbaceous plants (Ericaceae) mostly native to the Americas. They have glossy or leathery oval leaves with nodding, urn-shaped flowers and fleshy, aromatic, red or black fruit. *G. procumbens,* commonly known as wintergreen or checkerberry, is a small creeping plant with aromatic, edible red berries; native to eastern North America. (See **wintergreen**.) *G. Shallon,* the salal, is a small shrub that bears black edible berries, which attract birds; native to Oregon and California.

Gaura (gah'ruh) *n.* An genus of 18 species of erect perennials (Onagraceae) native to the southwestern United States and northern Mexico. They have alternate, simple leaves and arching, wandlike stalks of delicate white or pink flowers. *G. Lindheimeri* is a long-lived, drought-tolerant perennial, useful in dry-climate gardens.

gayfeather *n.* A common name for *Liatris spicata,* a perennial native to North America that grows to 5 feet tall with simple, long, narrow leaves and many showy purple plumes. Excellent in the back of the border or in meadow or prairie gardens. Also called blazing star or button snakeroot.

Gaylussacia (gay luh saysh'ee uh) *n.* A genus of about 40 species of creeping shrubs (Ericaceae) native to North and South America. They have alternate, simple leaves, spikes of small white, pink, or red flowers, and black, glossy fruit. The fruit of some species is edible and is usually known as the huckleberry. (See **Vaccinium**.)

Gazania (guh zay'nee uh) *n.* A genus of 16 species of herbaceous perennials and subshrubs (Compositae). Some species clump, whereas others creep; both have large, showy daisylike multicolored flowers in dazzling colors with dark eyes, which open only in sunny weather. The creeping sorts make good ground covers; the clumping kinds are excellent massed in beds or used as edging for the border.

gazebo *n.* A decorative garden structure, akin to a freestanding porch, which may contain benches or statuary.

geiger tree *n.* A common name for *Cordia Sebestena,* a subtropical evergreen shrub or small tree (Boraginaceae) grown in warm-winter gardens. It has thick, rough, hairy oval leaves and large open clusters of orange or scarlet flowers.

geitonogamy (gigh uhn ahg'uh mee) *n.* In botany, the pollination of a pistil by pollen from another flower of the same plant.

Gelsemium (jehl see'mee uhm) *n.* A genus of 3 species of twining vines (Loganiaceae), some native to North America. They have opposite, entire evergreen leaves and fragrant yellow flowers. *G. sempervirens,* commonly known as yellow jessamine, is native to the southern United States and Central America; all parts of the plant are poisonous. Can be used as a ground cover or trained on a trellis.

Gelsemium sempervirens
(yellow jessamine)

geminate *a.* Twin; combined in pairs; binate.

geminiflorous (jehm uh nee floh′ruhs) *a.* Having flowers in pairs.

gemma (jehm′uh) *n., pl.* **gemmae** 1. Broadly, a bud. 2. In botany, in some cryptogams, an asexual, budlike reproductive body.

gemmaceous (jeh may′shuhs) *a.* Of or relating to gemmae.

gemmate (jehm′ayt) *a.* 1. Having gemmae. 2. In botany, reproducing by buds.

gemmation (jeh may′shuhn) *n.* In botany, the act of budding; asexual reproduction in which a new organism originates locally within the body or on the surface of the parent. Also gemmulation.

gemmiform (jehm′uh form) *a.* Resembling a gemma.

gemmoid (jehm′oid) *a.* Having the nature or form of a gemma.

gemmule (jeh′myool) *n.* In botany, a small bud or gemma.

gene *n.* In botany, the parts of the chromosomes of the cells of plants that determine inherited traits. For every trait or characteristic (for example, flower color), a plant generally receives 1 gene from each parent.

generic *a.* 1. Pertaining to, of the nature of, or forming a mark of a genus, or a kind or group of similar things; comprehending a number of like things, without specifying them: opposed to specific. (See **genus**.) 2. Specifically, in botany, having the taxonomic rank or classificatory value of a genus; for example, a generic name or description, generic characters or differences, generic identity. In the botanic classification of *Genipa Americana,* for example, Genipa is the generic name of over 75 trees with similar characteristics, differing from other genera or groups of plants. 3. Distinctly characteristic; so marked as to constitute or denote a distinct kind.

generic agreement/identity *n.* The agreement of objects that belong to the same genus.

generic area *n.* The region to which the members of a genus are limited in distribution. (The place in a generic area where the genus is most numerously represented by species or individuals is known as its metropolis.)

generic description/diagnosis *n.* A description or characterization of a genus in botany.

generic difference *n.* The distinctions between objects that belong to different genera; a characteristic of a being or an object that differentiates it generically from another or others. For example, one genus may have lilylike flowers, another daisylike flowers.

generic diversity *n.* The differences between individuals of different genera.

generic name *n.* The denomination that comprehends all the species, as of a group of animals, plants, or fossils, which have generic characters in common. (See **genus**.)

genesis *n.* The means of development and origin of soil.

geniculate (jih nihk′yuh liht) *a.* Bent at an abrupt angle, like a knee. Also geniculated.

Genipa (jih nee′puh) *n.* A genus of 6 species of broadleaf evergreen trees (Rubiaceae) native to tropical America. They have large, leathery, opposite leaves, clusters of big white or pale yellow flowers, and dark-colored, succulent fruit with a thick rind, which is sometimes edible, as in the case of the genipap.

genipap or marmalade box

genipap (jehn′uh pap) *n.* The fruit of *Genipa Americana,* native to the West Indies and South America. It is about the size of an orange and has a pleasant vinous flavor. Also called marmalade box.

Genista (jih nihs'tuh) *n.* A large genus of 75 to 90 species of often spiny shrubs (Leguminosae). They are leafless or have small, simple leaves and yellow sweet-pealike flowers. They are drought-tolerant and useful in hillside plantings in Mediterranean climates. Commonly known as broom. The woadwaxen or dyer's greenweed, *G. tinctoria,* is a dye plant, giving a bright yellow color.

Genista tinctoria
(woadwaxen)

gentian (jehn'chuhn) *n.* The common name for species of the genus *Gentiana.* They are flowers with small, opposite leaves and white, yellow, red, purple, or blue flowers, often spotted. They are prized specimens in rock gardens or alpine collections.

Gentiana (jehn chee an'uh) *n.* A genus of about 200 to 350 species of annual, biennial, or perennial flowers. Many species are hardy or very hardy, some being native to the arctic. They have smooth, opposite, entire leaves and usually showy, white, yellow, red, purple, or blue flowers, often spotted. (See **gentian**.)

Gentianaceae (jehn chee uh nay'see ee) *n. pl.* A family of about 70 genera and 800 widely distributed species. They have smooth, opposite, entire leaves, typically showy, white, yellow, red, purple, or blue flowers, and a usually 1-celled capsule with numerous small seeds. The ornamental genera include *Gentiana, Lisianthus, Centaurium, Swertia,* *Eustoma, Sabbatia,* and *Frasera.* Commonly known as the gentian family.

gentianaceous (jehn chee uh nay'shuhs) *a.* Pertaining or belonging to the *Gentianaceae.*

gentianella (jehn chuh nehl'uh) *n.* A common name for *Gentiana acaulis,* a dwarf perennial species of the Alps, bearing large, beautiful, intensely blue flowers.

gentian family (jehn'chuhn) *n.* A common name for *Gentianaceae.*

gentian, fringed (jehn'chuhn) *n.* (See **Gentianopsis**.)

Gentianopsis (jehn'chuh nahp'sihs) *n.* A genus of 15 species of plants (Gentianaceae). They have opposite leaves and showy purple or blue (rarely white) flowers. Commonly known as fringed gentian.

gentian, spurred (jehn'chuhn) *n.* A common name for the genus *Halenia.*

genus *n., pl.* **genera**, rarely **genuses**. A kind; a sort; a class. In botany, a classification above the species, containing a group of species (sometimes a single species), all of which have certain structural characters different from those of other plants. It is entirely a matter of expert opinion or current usage what characteristics are considered to constitute a genus; and genera are constantly modified and shifted by taxonomists. The correct name of any genus is the one that was published first, if it has been accurately described, and is not the same as the name of some other genus. The names of the genus and the species together form the scientific name of a plant. In writing the technical name of any animal or plant, the generic term always precedes the specific and begins with a capital letter, as *Camellia japonica,* where *Camellia* is the genus, and *japonica* is the species.

Geonoma (jee ahn'uh muh) *n.* A genus of 75 or more species of small, slender, graceful, shade-tolerant palms native to the forests of tropical America. Used in warm-winter gardens or grown in greenhouses.

geotropic (jee uh trahp'ihk) *a.* Of or pertaining to, or exhibiting, geotropism.

geotropism (jee aht′ruh pihzm) *n.* 1. Tropism in which gravity is the orienting factor, up or down. 2. In botany, tropism in which growth is toward the earth. Also geotropy.

Geraniaceae (juh ray nee ay′see ee) *n. pl.* A family of 11 genera. The major ornamental genera are *Monsonia, Pelargonium, Geranium, Erodium,* and *Sarcocaulon.* Commonly known as the geranium family.

geraniaceous (juh ray nee ay′shuhs) *a.* Pertaining or belonging to the family Geraniaceae.

Geranium (juh ray′nee uhm) *n.* 1. A genus of more than 300 species of herbaceous perennials or annuals, rarely subshrubs (Geraniaceae). They have opposite, lobed leaves; white, pink, rose, blue, or purple flowers; and fruit with long tails, which become spirally twisted. From the long beak of the fruit, the common species have received the name cranesbill. 2. [l.c.] A plant of the genus *Geranium.* 3.[l.c.] A plant of the genus *Pelargonium,* which includes, for example, common geranium, *P. hortorum;* Martha Washington geranium, *P. domesticum;* and ivy geranium, *P. peltatum.* 4. [l.c.] A common name for *Saxifraga stolonifera,* strawberry geranium, a trailing houseplant, with heart-shaped leaves, that spreads by runners.

geranium, ivy (juh ray′nee uhm) *n.* A common name for *Pelargonium peltatum,* a trailing perennial that has semisucculent, glossy, bright green leaves with pointed lobes and clusters of white, pink, rose, red, or lavender flowers. Used in window boxes and hanging baskets in warm climates, as an indoor/outdoor plant in cold climates.

Gerbera (ger′buh ruh) *n.* A genus of 70 species of herbaceous perennials (Compositae). They have leaves in a basal rosette and large showy single flowers on tall stalks in brilliant colors of red, yellow, coral, and flame. Excellent in containers; superb cut flowers. Commonly known as Transvaal daisy.

German ivy *n.* A common name for *Senecio mikanioides,* a tall, twining perennial vine with ivylike leaves. Used in window boxes or as a hanging basket plant. Has naturalized in coastal California.

germander (jer man′der) *n.* A common name for plants of the genus *Teucrium,* especially for *T. Cha-*

maedrys, having purple flowers, common in England. The germander of the United States is *T. Canadense,* a compact, low-growing herb with small, glossy, dark green leaves, often used as a border for its tidy shape.

germinate *v.* To cause to grow or sprout; to begin to grow; sprout.

germination *n.* The act, process, or result of germinating; the development of a seed. Specifically, in botany: 1. The process of development of a seed into a plant. The conditions necessary for germination are moisture, oxygen, and warmth. Moisture softens the seed, relaxes the tissues of the embryo, and dissolves nutrients in the seed, such as sugar or dextrine, to be absorbed by the embryo. The absorption of oxygen is necessary for the chemical changes that accompany growth. The degree of warmth needed to begin the growth process varies in different species; some seeds, as those of wheat, are capable of germinating upon melting ice, whereas others require a temperature

germinating seeds, with central figure showing seedling

higher than 60°F. As an immediate result of the growing process, a root is produced, which strikes downward, fixing itself in the soil and beginning to absorb nourishment for the new plant. At the same time, the growth is directed upward to develop a stem and leaves. 2. The similar development of a plant from the spore in cryptogams such as ferns. 3. The early period of growth in a bud, as of a bulb or of a rhizome. 4. The protrusion and growth of the pollen tube from the pollen grain.

germinative *a.* Pertaining to germination; capable of germination.

germ tube *n.* In botany, a tubular, threadlike growth first formed by most spores in germination.

Gesneraceae (gehs nih ray′see ee) *n. pl.* A family 120 genera, natives of tropical or subtropical regions. They are plants or shrubs, with usually opposite, hairy leaves and with large, showy, and often very handsome flowers. Among the major ornamental genera are *Gesneria, Gloxinia, Saint-paulia, Columnea, Aeschynanthus, Streptocarpus,* and *Achimenes,* many species of which are grown as choice houseplants, including African violets.

gesneraceous (gehs nuh ray'shuhs) *a.* Belonging or pertaining to the family Gesneraceae.

Gesneria (gehs nihr'ee uh) *n.* A genus of about 60 species of perennial plants or shrubs (Gesneraceae) native to the West Indies and northern South America. They have alternate leaves and red, yellow, or green tubular flowers.

Geum (je'uhm) *n.* A genus of 50 species of perennials (Rosaceae), some of which are hardy or very hardy. They are evergreen except in the coldest climates. They have basal leaves and white, yellow, or red 5-petaled flowers on tall stems. *G.rivale* is commonly known as chocolate-root and Indian chocolate.

gherkin *n.* A small-fruited variety of the cucumber, or simply a young green cucumber of an ordinary variety, used for pickling.

ghost plant *n.* A common name for *Graptopetalum paraguayense,* a succulent with rosettes of small, thick, luminous white leaves with a pink cast. Grown for its curiously colored and interestingly shaped foliage. Used as a small-scale ground cover and in containers. Also called mother-of-pearl plant.

giant daisy *n.* A common name for the genus *Wytheia* and *Chrysanthemum serotinum. Wytheia* is a tap-rooted perennial with large yellow or white flowers 3 to 4 inches across. *C. serotinum* is an erect perennial from 4 to 7 feet tall with long, narrow leaves and daisylike white flowers, with yellow centers, that grow to 3 inches across.

giant reed *n.* A common name for *Arundo donax,* a tall European grass, with woody stems, that grows to 20 feet tall. It is similar to bamboo, with flat, 2-foot-long leaves and flowers in 2-foot-high, narrow, erect clusters.

giant sunflower *n.* A common name for *Helianthus giganteus,* a perennial that grows to 10 feet; it has rough, hairy leaves and daisylike flowers 3 inches across.

Gilia (jihl'ee uh) *n.* A large genus of between 20 and 30 species of flowers (Polemoniaceae) mostly

to western North America. The leaves are alternate, sometimes in a basal rosette, with showy bell- or funnel-shaped blue, pink, red, yellow, or white flowers. Useful and colorful in wild gardens or in borders.

Gillenia (jih lee'nee uh) *n.* A genus of 2 species of tall perennials (Rosaceae) native to North America. They have 3-part leaves and white flowers loosely clustered on the slender branches. Commonly known as American ipecac, Indian physic, or bowman's root.

Gillenia
(bowman's root)

gill-over-the-ground *n.* A common name for *Glechoma hederacea,* a creeping perennial with neat pairs of round, scalloped, bright green leaves and small trumpet-shaped blue flowers. Used as a small-scale ground cover or as a hanging-basket plant. Can be a serious pest in lawns and gardens. Also called ground ivy and run- away-robin.

gillyflower (jihl'ee flow er) *n.* 1. The clove pink or carnation, *Dianthus caryophyllus,* especially one of the smaller varieties. The name gillyflower was used by Chaucer, Spenser, Shakespeare, and other writers of former times. Also distinguished as the clove gillyflower. Also known as gilliflower. 2. The stock, *Matthiola incana,* although less commonly.

ginger *n.* The rhizome (swollen root section) of *Zingiber officinalis,* a reedlike perennial plant, with annual leafy stems 3 or 4 feet high and with flowers in conical spikes growing on leafless stems. The rhizome has an aromatic odor and a pungent taste and has been dried and used as a spice from the remotest times. It is used fresh in Asian and Caribbean dishes and also crystallized as a candy.

ginger

ginseng (jihn'sehng) *n.* A plant of the genus *Panax;* the root of which is highly valued as a tonic and stimulant in Asia, where it is ascribed almost miraculous powers. Ginseng is a native of Asia and of the eastern United States. Dwarf gingseng, *Panax trifolius,* is a low species of the United States, with a thick pungent root. American ginseng is a common name for *Panax quinquefolius,* a variety with similar characteristics, native to the United States.

ginseng

gingerbread tree *n.* A common name for the palm *Hyphaene thebaica* (Palmae), remarkable among palms for its repeatedly branched stem, each branch terminating in a tuft of large fan-shaped leaves. The fruit is about the size of an apple and has a fibrous, mealy rind, which tastes like gingerbread.

ginger family *n.* A common name for Zingiberaceae, a family of tropical and subtropical clumping perennials with fleshy rhizomes, canelike stems, large leaves, and stalks of showy, fragrant flowers.

ginger, wild *n.* A common name for *Asarum caudatum,* a remarkably handsome perennial ground cover with heart-shaped leaves and inconspicuous flowers hidden under the leaves; good in shady situations.

Ginkgo (gihng'koh) *n.* A genus of a single species of deciduous tree, *Ginkgo biloba* (Ginkgoaceae). It is a graceful, hardy tree with distinctive, fan-shaped light green leaves (similar to the leaflets of maidenhair fern) that turn clear yellow in fall. Plant only male trees for ornamental use, as female trees produce quantities of nasty-smelling fruit. Also called maidenhair tree. Also spelled gingko.

gipsywort *n.* A common name for *Lycopus europaeus,* a creeping perennial with opposite leaves and small white flowers dotted purple. Used in bog gardens and wild gardens. Has naturalized widely in North America. Also spelled gypsywort.

glabrescent (glay brehs'uhnt) *a.* Becoming glabrous.

glabrous (glay'bruhs) *a.* Smooth; having a surface devoid of hair or down, as a glabrous leaf. Also glabrate.

gladiate (glad'ee ayt) *a.* Sword-shaped; ensiform.

gladiole (glad''ee ohl) *n.* A gladiolus.

Gladiolus (glad ee oh'luhs) *n., pl.* **gladioli** (-li) 1. A genus of 250 to 300 species of very beautiful tender, perennial bulbs (Iridaceae). They grow from flattened corms and have sword-shaped leaves and erect leafy stems bearing a spike of large, brilliantly colored flowers. Used in the back of borders, in beds, or in containers; excellent cut flowers. 2. A plant of the genus *Gladiolus;* also called swordlily.

gland *n.* In botany, any of the secreting organs of plants or of glandlike bodies.

glandular *a.* 1. Pertaining to or resembling a gland. 2. Bearing glands. 3. Derived from glands. Also glandulous.

glans (glanz) *n.*, *pl.* **glandes** A nut seated in or enclosed by an involucre.

Glastonbury thorn *n.* A common name for the hawthorn *Crataegus monogyna* cv. 'Praecox', a tree with thorns, deeply lobed leaves, and masses of early spring flowers.

glaucescent (glah sehs'uhnt) *a.* Becoming glaucous; faintly glaucous.

Glaucium (glah'see uhm) *n.* A genus of 20 to 25 species of flowers (Papaveraceae). They have gray-green leaves, yellow or red poppylike flowers, and a copper-colored juice. *G. flavum,* commonly known as yellow horn-poppy, is naturalized in the eastern United States. Fairly drought-tolerant, *Glaucium* combines well with succulents. Usually grown as an annual.

glaucous (glah'kuhs) *a.* 1. Of a pale, yellow-green color; of a bluish-gray or bluish-white color. 2. Having a waxy or powdery, frosty-looking bloom that tends to rub off, as glaucous grapes or plums.

Glechoma (glee koh'muh) *n.* A genus of 10 species of low, creeping plants (Labiatae). *Glechoma hederacea* is a creeping perennial with neat pairs of round, scalloped, bright green leaves and small trumpet-shaped blue flowers. Used as a small-scale ground cover or as a hanging-basket plant. Can be a serious pest in lawns and gardens. Also called ground ivy and run-away-robin.

Gleditsia
(honey locust), with pod

Gleditsia (gluh diht'see uh) *n.* A genus of 12 species of fast-growing, deciduous, formidably thorny trees (Leguminosae); the honey locust. They have alternate leaves divided into leaflets, inconspicuous greenish flowers, and twisted flat pods 12-to-18 inches long. *G. triacanthos,* the honey locust, is a large tree, native to the eastern United States, useful as a specimen tree, particularly in desert gardens.

Gleichenaceae (gligh kee nay'see ee) *n. pl.* A family of 5 genera and 150 species of ferns. (See **Gleichenia**.)

Gleichenia (gligh kee nee uh) *n.* A genus of 10 species of thicket-forming, sun-loving tropical ferns *(Gleichenaceae)* native to the islands of the South Pacific and Australia. They have continuously branching fronds, much divided, and wide-spreading. Some species are grown ornamentally in subtropical gardens.

gley soil (glay) *n.* A soil layer that waterlogging and lack of oxygen have caused to turn gray.

Gliricidia (glihr uh sihd'ee uh) *n.* A genus of 6 to 10 species of small deciduous trees and shrubs (Leguminosae) native to tropical America. They have alternate, divided leaves, spikes of mostly pink, butterflylike flowers, and long flat pods. *G. sepium* is widely planted in warm winter climates as a shade tree and as a flowering fence. All parts of the plant are poisonous.

globe amaranth (am'uh ranth) *n.* The plant *Gomphrena globosa* (Amaranthaeae), well known for its abundant round heads of flowers. The flowers are very durable after cutting, which makes them useful as everlastings. Colors range from creamy white, through pink, to a deep magenta, as well as bright orange-red.

globeflower

globeflower *n.* A common name for *Trollius Europaeus* (Ranunculaceae), native to swampy or moist places of the north temperate zone. It has shiny, deeply lobed leaves and yellow-to- orange flowers. The conspicuous colored petals are incurved, giving the flowers a globular form. Useful for bright color in shade, near garden pools, in borders, and in rock gardens.

globe thistle *n.* The common name for *Echinops* species, grown as ornamentals for their bright blue globes of thorny seeds. The foliage is pale green, stiff, and prickly, but the plant is attractive, even when not in bloom. The globes can be picked while immature and dried with some success, although they more often fall apart on drying.

Globularia (glahb yuh la′ree uh) *n.* A genus of 20 species of plants or small shrubs (Globulariaceae). They have alternate, simple, shiny leaves, often in basal rosettes, and round heads of small blue flowers.

glochidiate (gloh kihd′ee iht) *a.* In botany, barbed at the tip. Also glochideous.

glomerate (glahm uh riht) *a.* In botany, compactly clustered.

glomerulate (glah mer′uh liht) *a.* Arranged in small, compact clusters. Also glomerulose.

glomerule (glahm uh rool) *n.* In botany, a dense flower cluster that forms a head, as in the flowering dogwood, *Cornus florida.*

Gloriosa (gloh ree oh suh) *n.* A genus of 5 or 6 species of tuberous-rooted climbing vines (Liliaceae). *G. rothschildiana* has opposite or whorled leaves, terminating in tendrils by which it climbs, and large, beautiful lilylike red flowers edged with yellow. Grown as a houseplant, in containers as an indoor/outdoor plant, or in greenhouses.

glory-bower *n.* A common name for *Clerodendron,* a genus of tropical trees, shrubs, and vines. It has opposite or whorled leaves and clusters of often showy flowers, resembling bleeding heart. Grown as a shrubby vine in warm-region gardens, as an indoor/outdoor plant elsewhere, as a greenhouse plant anywhere.

glory-bush, Brazilian *n.* A common name for *Tibouchina Urvilleana,* a large shrub with oval or oblong ribbed leaves, edged with red and velvety beneath, and large, showy, brilliant royal-purple flowers 3 inches across.

glory-flower, Chilean *n.* A common name for the genus *Mocarpus,* climbing vines with opposite, 2-part leaves and clusters of tubular yellow, orange, or scarlet flowers. A tender perennial, it is grown as an annual in cold climates.

glory-of-the-snow *n.* A common name for the genus *Chionodoxa,* perennial early spring-blooming perennial bulbs, with narrow basal leaves and spikes of loose clusters of intensely blue or white tubular flowers. Used in beds, borders, in woodland gardens, or in containers.

glory-of-the-sun *n.* A common name for *Leucocoryne ixioides,* a perennial bulb with basal leaves and rounded clusters of white or pale blue fragrant flowers. Used to naturalize in dry-summer areas, combined with other bulbs, or in pots.

glory vine, crimson *n.* A common name for *Vitis Coignetiae,* a stout, woody vine with heavy foliage that turns a magnificent scarlet in autumn. The leaves are heart-shaped and 1-foot across, velvety gray or rust beneath. Best grown on a sturdy arbor or pergola.

Glottiphyllum (glaht uh fihl′uhm) *n.* A genus of 58 species of free-flowering dwarf, perennial succulents (Aizoaceae); the tongueleaf. They have crowded, tongue-shaped or cylindrical, soft leaves and masses of yellow flowers. Grown in pots in succulent collections.

Gloxinia (glahk sihn′ee uh) *n.* 1. A genus of a few species of semisucculent perennials (Gesneraceae) native to Central and South America. They are low and almost stemless, with creeping rhizomes, opposite, toothed leaves, and large, nodding, bell-shaped blue, lavender, pink or white flowers. Commonly grown as houseplants or in greenhouses. 2. [l.c.] A plant of this genus. 3. The common name of tuberous-rooted plants of the genus *Sinningia.*

gloxinia, common (glahk sihn′ee uh) *n.* The common name for tuberous-rooted, semisucculent plants of the genus *Sinningia.* They are hairy perennials, with large, soft, mostly basal leaves and rose, red, white, and violet flowers that are very showy.

glumaceous (gloo may'shuhs) *a*. Glumelike; having glumes; chaffy.

glume (gloom) *n*. A chaffy bract, as in the Gramineae and related plants; especially an empty bract at the base of a grass spikelet.

glumiferous (gloo mihf'uh ruhs) *a*. In botany, having glumes.

gnaphalioid (nuh fay'lee oid) *a*. In botany, belonging or relating to the genus *Gnaphalium*.

Gnaphalium (nuh fay'lee uhm) *n*. 1. A genus of 120 species of woolly herbs (Compositae). It has alternate, simple, entire woolly leaves and small clusters of yellow or white flowers. Commonly known as everlasting. 2. [l.c.] A plant of this genus.

gnatflower *n*. A common name for the North American wildflowers *Cleome serrulata* and *C. lutea*. Also bee orchis.

goatsbeard *n*. 1. A common name for *Aruncus*, a small genus of 4- to 7-foot-tall North American perennials with airy, plumelike flowers that grow well in moist, shaded locations. An excellent back-of-the-border plant. 2. The genus *Tragopogon*, a genus of tap-rooted biennial and perennial plants with long, coarse, plumose bristles attached to the seed. 3. False goatsbeard is a common name for *Astilbe biternata*, which is very similar in appearance to *Aruncus*.

goatsfoot *n*. A common name for *Oxalis caprina*, which has leaves divided into leaflets and with violet flowers.

goatskin gloves *n*. Flexible, medium-weight gloves for garden work.

goat's rue *n*. A common name for *Galega officinalis*, which grows to 5 feet, has leaflets in 5 to 8 pairs, and white, lilac, or pink butterflylike flowers.

goatweed *n*. A common name for *Aegopodium Podagraria*, a fast-spreading, vigorous ground cover used in shaded areas. The cultivar 'Variegatum' with white-margined leaves is most widely planted. Can easily become a weed; has naturalized in parts of United States. Also called goutweed and bishop's-weed.

goggles *n*. Protective eyeglasses worn while operating power garden tools.

goldcup *n*. 1. A common name for the wildflower *Caltha palustris*, also called marsh marigold or king cup. 2. A common name for various wildflower species of *Ranunculus*, especially *R. acris* and *R. bulbosus*. Also called buttercup.

gold-dust plant *n*. A common name for *Acuba japonica*, so called from its yellow-speckled leaves. *A. serratifolia* is called gold-dust tree.

golden chain *n*. A common name for trees of the genus *Laburnum*, so called from their long clusters of yellow flowers. *L. anagyroides* is known as golden chain.

golden club *n*. A common name for *Orontium aquaticum*, a North American aquatic plant with floating or aerial leaves up to 1 foot long and a club-shaped yellow spadix.

golden cup *n*. A common name for *Hunnemannia fumarifolia*, a bushy perennial native to Mexico with finely cut, gray-green foliage and cup-shaped, poppylike, foliage and flowers.

golden dewdrop *n*. A common name for *Duranta repens*, a creeping, woolly evergreen shrub or tree that forms multistemmed clumps with drooping, vinelike branches. It has oval leaves, blue-violet tubular flowers, and yellow berries.

golden eardrops *n*. A common name for *Dicentra chrysantha*, a bushy perennial with graceful, finely cut, fernlike blue-gray foliage and arching sprays of golden-yellow flowers.

golden flower *n*. A common name for *Chrysanthemum segetum*. Also called corn marigold. (See **Chrysanthemum**.)

golden glow *n*. A common name for *Rudbeckia lacinata* 'Hortensia', a tall, bushy perennial that spreads by underground stems. It has deeply lobed light green leaves and bright yellow, double flowers with drooping petals. Useful at the back of the border; can be invasive.

golden marguerite *n*. A common name for *Anthemis tinctoria*, a bushy biennial or short-lived perennial with finely divided light green leaves, woolly white beneath, and golden-yellow daisylike flowers. Used in the summer border. Also called yellow chamomile.

goldenpert *n.* A common name for *Gratiola aurea,* a low-growing North American plant with small golden-yellow flowers.

goldenrain tree *n.* A common name for deciduous trees of the genus *Koelreuteria.* Also a common name for *K. paniculata,* an open-branching tree with leaves divided into many leaflets and showy large, loose clusters of small yellow fragrant flowers that attract bees.

goldenrod *n.* A common name for plants of the genus *Solidago,* the species of which are tall, bushy perennials with plumes of numerous small golden flowers; mostly native to North America. Its pollen is often blamed for hay-fever misery, which should more properly be attributed to ragweed, which blooms at the same time. (See **Solidago**.)

goldenrod, hybrid *n.* A common name for cultivars of *Solidago,* which are hybridized for ornamental use; for example, *S.* 'Golden Mosa', which has very pale yellow flowers.

goldenseal *n.* A common name for *Hydrastis canadensis,* native to eastern North America, which grows from a thick yellow rhizome, has rounded, basal, lobed leaves and greenish-white flowers. Also called yellow puccoon or orangeroot.

golden shower *n.* A common name for 2 different species, *Cassia fistula* and *Pyrostegia venusta.* *C. fistula* is a deciduous flowering tropical tree with large leaves divided into several pairs of leaflets and long clusters of pale yellow flowers, which appear before the leaves. *P. venusta* is a tropical evergreen climbing vine with oval leaflets, tendrils, and orange trumpet-shaped flowers that give a brilliant show in fall and early winter in warm winter climates. Also known as flaming trumpet, flame vine, or flameflower.

golden spoon *n.* A common name for the tropical American tree *Byrsonima crassifolia* (Malpighiaceae), which takes its common name from the shape and color of its petals. It has oblong leaves and clusters of clawed yellow or orange flowers. It is grown for its edible yellow fruit.

golden saxifrage (sak'suh frihj) *n.* A common name for the genus *Chrysosplenium,* small semi-aquatic creeping plants with rounded leaves and small green and yellow flowers. Useful as a ground cover in moist situations, in bog gardens, and at pool margins.

golden stars *n.* A common name for the genus *Bloomeria.* Also for the species *B. crocea,* a summer-blooming bulb with basal, grasslike leaves and clusters of tiny wheel-shaped orange flowers; native to California.

golden tuft *n.* A common name for plants of 2 species, *Helichrysum orientale* and *Aurinia saxatile.* *H. orientale* is a perennial with downy leaves and clusters of yellow everlasting flowers; also called goldflower. *A. saxatile* is a perennial with gray leaves and masses of yellow flowers; usually grown on stone walls and in rock gardens; also called basket-of-gold.

golden wood millet *n.* (See **Milium**.)

golden yarrow (yar'oh) *n.* A common name for *Achillea millefolium.* (See **yarrow**.)

gold fern *n.* A common name for ferns in which the lower surface of the frond is covered with bright yellow powder, giving a golden color. This occurs in many species of *Pityrogramma* and *Notholaena.* *P. chrysophylla* is commonly known as goldfern.

gold fields *n.* A common name for *Lasthenia chrysotoma,* a much-branched North American annual with simple, hairy leaves and small yellow flowers.

goldflower *n.* A common name for plants of several different species, including *Helichrysum orientale,* *Hypericum* × *moseranum,* and *Hymenoxys Cooperi.* *H. orientale* is a perennial with downy leaves and clusters of yellow everlasting flowers. *H.* × *Moseranum* is a small shrub with oval leaves and bright yellow cup-shaped flowers. *H. Cooperi* is a leafy perennial or biennial with soft divided leaves and clusters of yellow flowers.

goldilocks *n.* 1. A common name for the genus *Chrysocoma,* composite small plants or shrubs with heads of yellow flowers. 2. A common name for *Aster linosyris,* an erect, bushy perennial with long, narrow leaves and bright yellow flower without petals. Also spelled goldylocks.

gold of pleasure *n.* A common name for *Camelina sativa,* a European annual widely naturalized in North America, a weed in crop fields.

goldthread *n.* A common name for the genus *Coptis*, evergreen perennials with basal evergreen leaves divided into 3 with stalks of small white or yellow flowers; so called from its fibrous yellow roots. Useful in moist situations and in the border and rock garden. (See **Coptis**.)

goldylocks *n.* (See **goldilocks**.)

Gomphrena (gahm free'nuh) *n.* A genus of more than 100 species of flowers (Amarantaceae), some species native to tropical America. They have oblong leaves and round heads of small purple, white, or yellow flowers, which retain their form and color after drying. Also known as globe amaranth. Grown as everlastings for dried bouquets; used as edging or bedding plants or as container plants.

gomuti (goh moo'tee) *n.* A common name for *Arenga pinnata*, a tropical palm. The trunk produces a considerable amount of good sago, a dry granulated or powdered starch; the juice from the flower sheaths is collected as a sweet syrup and for fermentation into toddy. Also called sago palm. Also spelled gomuto.

Gongora (gahng'guh ruh) *n.* A genus of 20 species of epiphytic orchids (Orchidaceae) native to tropical America. They have large pleated leaves and drooping clusters of fragrant flowers.

Gonolobus (goh nahl'uh buhs) *n.* A genus of 100 species of twining or trailing perennial woody vines (Asclepiadaceae), all native to the Americas. They have mostly heart-shaped, opposite leaves and clusters of 5 dull or dark-colored flowers. Also known as anglepod.

Goodeniaceae (gu dee'nee ay'see ee) *n. pl.* An family of 13 genera of herbaceous plants or shrubs. The ornamental genera include *Scaevola* and *Dampiera*, both perennial ground covers. Commonly known as the Goodenia family.

good-king-henry *n.* A common name for *Chenopodium Bonus-Henricus*, a European herb naturalized in the United States, which is used as a pot herb. Also known as good-king-harry.

Goodyera (gud'yuh ruh) *n.* A genus of 40 species of low terrestrial orchids (Orchidaceae) found throughout the world. They have a creeping rootstock and a tuft of basal leaves, usually prettily marked with white veins, and a spike of small white flowers. Commonly known as rattlesnake plantain or latticeleaf.

gooseberry *n.* The berry or fruit of the plant *Ribes uva-crispa*. It is a thorny or prickly shrub, and the fruit is usually studded with small, flexible spikes. Cultivated extensively in northern Europe, it succeeds only moderately in America. Many varieties have been produced, the fruit differing in size, color, and quality, as well as degree of smoothness. The wild gooseberries of North America include several species, the fruit of which is rarely eaten. Barbados gooseberry *Pereskia aculeata*, is a cactaceous shrub bearing an edible berry. Cape gooseberry, *Physalis Peruviana*, is a native of tropical America, cultivated for the fruit, which is sometimes made into a preserve.

gooseberry tree *n.* A common name for *Phyllanthus acidus*, a tree with oval leaves, clusters of tiny red flowers, and small fruits; it has naturalized in southern Florida and the West Indies.

goosefoot *n.* A common name for the genus *Chenopodium*, so called from the shape of the leaves. They are mostly weeds, though *C. album*, known as lamb's-quarters, and *C. Bonus-Henricus*, known as good-king-henry, are used as edible greens. *C. Quinoa*, known as quinoa or quinua, produces a highly nutritious flour. Also called pigweed.

goosefoot family *n.* A common name for *Chenopodiaceae*.

goose grass *n.* 1. A common name for *Potentilla Anserina*; also known as silverweed and goose tansy. 2. A common name for the grass *Bromus mollis*; also known as soft chess. *B. mollis* has naturalized in North America.

goosetongue *n.* 1. A common name for *Achillea Ptarmica*, also known as sneezewort. 2. A common name for *Galium*, also called cleavers.

gopher *n.* A difficult-to-control mammal that burrows below ground, devouring roots, bulbs, and sometimes whole plants. It is best controlled with traps, poisonous baits, or screen barriers around the roots of valuable plants.

gopher barrier *n.* (See **gopher basket**.)

gopher basket *n.* A wire container installed around plant roots to protect against gophers. Also called gopher barrier.

gopher trap *n.* Any of various devices used to lure and hold gophers. Some traps are designed to kill, others to hold live for release elsewhere.

gopherwood *n.* A common name for *Cladrastis lutea,* a flowering tree with divided bright green leaves that turn yellow in fall, and, at maturity, clusters of fragrant white flowers resembling wisteria blossoms; native to the southeastern United States. Used as a terrace, patio, or lawn tree.

Gordonia (gor doh′nee uh) *n.* A genus of 30 species of very ornamental evergreen shrubs or small trees (Theaceae) with large white flowers some species native to the southern United States. *G. Lasianthus* is found near the coast from North Carolina to Mississippi; also known as loblolly bay.

Gordonia
(loblolly bay)

gorse (gors) *n.* A common name for *Ulex Europaeus,* a much-branched and spiny shrub with clusters of yellow flowers. Also called furze or whin.

gorsy (gor′see) *a.* Abounding in gorse; relating to gorse; resembling gorse.

Gossypium (gah sihp′ee uhm) *n.* A genus of 32 species of tender plants and shrubs (Malvaceae); cotton. They have usually 3- to 5-lobed leaves, white-to-yellow or purple-red flowers surrounded by 3 large bracts, and a 3- to 5-celled seed pod, the seeds densely covered by long, woolly hairs.

gourd *n.* 1. The fruit of *Cucurbita,* varieties that are not used for food, forming hard-shelled outer walls. 2. The fruit of *Lagenaria vulgaris,* varying greatly in form, but usually club-shaped, or enlarged at one end; its hard rind is used for bottles, dippers, etc. Different varieties are known as bottle gourd, club gourd, or trumpet gourd, or calabash.

goutweed *n.* A common name for *Aegopodium Podagraria,* a fast-spreading, vigorous ground cover used in shaded areas. The cultivar 'Variegatum' with white-margined leaves is most widely planted.

Can easily become a weed; has naturalized in parts of United States. Also called goatweed and bishop's-weed.

governor's plum *n.* A common name for *Flacourtia indica,* a small evergreen tree with alternate simple leaves, flowers without petals, and a fleshy, edible, berrylike fruit. Also called Madagascar plum. Used in warm-winter gardens for hedges.

graft *n.* 1. A method of plant propagation. 2. The point where a scion is inserted in the stock. *v.* To attach a scion to stock for the purpose of propagation.

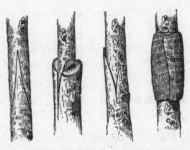

grafts
a saddle graft *b* cleft graft *c* whip graft *d* taped
graft

graft hybrid *n.* A hybrid produced by grafting a branch of 1 species (scion) onto another (rootstock), in which the 2 grow together to form a single plant or tree.

grafting tape *n.* A kind of tape backed with biodegradable cloth; used in budding and grafting operations and in banding tree wounds. Also called nurseryman's tape.

grafting thread *n.* Fine waxed string used in budding and grafting operations.

grafting wax *n.* A waxy substance used to hold and seal tree or rose grafts.

grain *n.* 1. The unhusked or threshed seed of 1 of the cereal plants: wheat, rye, oats, barley, maize, or millet; a corn. 2. Collectively, corn in general; the gathered seeds of cereal plants in mass.

gramineous (gruh mihn′ee uhs) *a.* Grasslike; belonging or pertaining to the family Gramineae. Also gramineous, gramineal.

Grammatophyllum (gram′uh tuh fihl′uhm) *n.* A genus of about 10 species of tropical epiphytic orchids (Orchidaceae). They have pseudobulbs with canelike stems, long, narrow leaves, and arching flower clusters to 6 feet long.

granadilla (gran uh dihl'uh) *n*. The fruit of *Passiflora quadrangularis,* which is sometimes as large as a coconut, and is much esteemed in tropical countries as a pleasant dessert fruit. It is a principal component to grenadine.

grandiflora (granf'uh flor'uh) *n*. A bush rose that is a cross of floribunda and hybrid tea roses, producing both clusters and single blossoms on the same plant. The flowers are quite large.

graniform (gran'uh form) *a*. Having the form of a grain or seed.

granular *a*. Composed of, containing, bearing, or resembling grains or granules. Covered with small grains or granules. Also granulose, granulous.

granular fertilizer *n*. A fertiiizer made up of particles 0.1 inch in diamter.

granulate *v*. 1. To form into granules; make rough on the surface. 2. To become formed into grains; become granular. *a*. Consisting of or resembling grains or granules. Also granulated.

granulation *n*. In botany: 1. The process of granulating. 2. One of the little elevations in a granulated surface.

granule *n*. A little grain; a fine particle.

grape *n*. 1. A pulpy edible fruit or berry growing in clusters on vines of the genus *Vitis*. 2. The vine that produces this fruit; the grapevine. The cultivated grape of Europe, whether it be for wine or for table use, is the *Vitis vinifera,* of which there are hundreds of varieties, ranging in color from pale green to reddish- purple to very dark blue or purple.

grape arbor *n*. An arched-shaped latticework trellis to support grape vines.

grape fern *n*. A common name for the genus *Botrychium*, a genus of fleshy ferns, so called because the spore cases somewhat resemble a cluster of grapes.

grapefruit *n*. The pomelo, a smaller variety of the shaddock, *Citrus maxima*. It is successfully cultivated in Florida.

grape hyacinth (high'uh sihnth) *n*. A common name for the small purple spring-flowering bulb *Muscari botryoides*. (See **hyacinth**.)

grape ivy *n*. A common name for the genus *Cissus* and the species *C. rhombifolia,* a tropical vine, with dark green leaves, that climbs by tendrils. Widely grown as a houseplant or hanging-basket plant; can be grown outdoors trained on a trellis or pergola in warm- winter climates.

grapevine *n*. The vine that bears grapes, often used ornamentally in making wreath bases. (See **Vitis**.)

grass catcher *n*. A container mounted either behind or on the side of a lawn mower to hold grass clipplings.

grasshopper *n*. A hopping and flying insect that feeds on many types of plant foliage. The population size varies year to year. In bad years, it can do devastating damage. It is best controlled with traditional pesticides. In large areas (measured in acres), it can be controlled biologically with grasshopper spore. Also called locust.

grasshopper spore *n*. A naturally occurring disease, *Nosema locustae,* used as a biological control of grasshoppers. Most effective on large acreages.

grass shears *n*. Long-bladed scissors, either short- or long- handled; used to trim the grass around trees, shrubs, stone walls, and walkways.

grass trimmer *n*. A battery-powered, multibladed machine for cutting grass in places inaccessible to a lawn mower, primarily edges.

grass tree *n*. A common name for Australian treelike plants (Liliaceae). They have a stout, trunklike caudex, topped by a tuft of long, grasslike, wiry foliage and a tall flower-stalk with a dense, cylindrical spike of small white flowers.

gravel plant *n*. A common name for *Epigaea repens,* a creeping evergreen shrub some species native to North America. It has oval or rounded bright green leaves and white-to-pink fragrant flowers. Also called trailing arbutus or mayflower.

gravelroot *n*. 1. A common name for *Eupatorium purpureum,* a tall, stout North American perennial with large, whorled, vanilla-scented leaves and clusters of purple or pink flowers; also called Joe-

Pye weed. 2. A common name for *Collinsonia canadensis,* an erect aromatic plant, growing from rhizomes, with lemon-scented leaves and flowers; native to North America; also called horse balm or richweed.

gravitational water *n.* The water, in large pores of the soil, that drains away under the force of gravity.

greasewood *n.* One of various low shrubs prevalent in saline and alkaline soils in the dry valleys of the western United States; desert scrub brush. They are mostly of the goosefoot family, for example, *Sarcobatus* and *Atriplex.*

great northern *n.* A fast-cooking bean variety grown for drying.

great soil group *n.* Any 1 of several broad groups of soil with fundamental characteristics in common.

greenbrier *n.* A common name for the genus *Smilax,* especially *S. rotundifolia,* a greenish-yellow North American climbing vine with tendrils, prickly stems, thick, alternate leaves, clusters of small greenish flowers, and blue-black fruit.

green broom *n.* The dyer's broom, *Genista tinctoria.* Also called greening-weed, green-weed. (See **Genista.**)

greenhouse *n.* A building of glass or, now more commonly, plastic, used to grow and protect tender plants.

greening-weed *n.* Same as green broom.

green manure *n.* An organic crop material, turned under the soil, to be used as a fertilizer to add nitrogen to the soil.

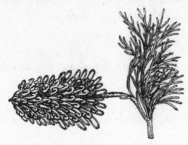

Grevillea, flowering branch

Grevillea (gruh vihl′ee uh) *n.* A large genus of 250 tender broadleaf evergreen trees and shrubs (Proteaceae), very variable in size and appearance. *G. robusta,* the silky oak, is a large tree that grows to 150 feet. It has fernlike leaves—golden above, silvery beneath—and large clusters of bright golden-orange flowers in early spring. Used as a specimen or street tree in warm-weather climates.

Grewia (groo′yuh) *n.* A genus of 150 species of tender vines, shrubs, and trees (Tiliaceae). *G. occidentalis* is a free-branching evergreen shrub with oblong, deep green leaves and clusters of small, starlike lavender, pink, or white flowers. Used in warm- climate gardens as a bank cover, an espalier, a hedge, or a screen. *G. occidentalis* is commonly known as lavender starflower.

grim-the-collier (kahl′yer) *n.* A common name for *Hieracium aurantiacum,* a European species of hawkweed now naturalized in the United States; so called from its black smutty whorls of small leaves just below the flowers.

Grindelia (grihn deel′yuh) *n.* A genus of between 50 and 60 species of coarse, mostly perennial, taprooted plants or subshrubs (Compositae) native to the Americas. They have alternate leaves and heads of asterlike yellow flowers, often sweet-smelling and sticky. Used in rock gardens, meadow gardens, and wildflower gardens. Commonly known as tarweed, rosinweed, gum plant, gumweed, and sticky-heads.

gripgrass *n.* A common name for plants of the genus *Galium;* low-growing herbs with square, slender stems, whorls of aromatic leaves, and clusters of tiny white flowers. The stems and fruit are frequently armed with minute, hooked prickles. Also known as cleavers.

Griselinia (grih zuh lihn′ee uh) *n.* A genus of 6 species of tender, broadleaf, evergreen trees or shrubs (Cornaceae), some native to Chile. They are upright, with thick, leathery, lustrous, alternate leaves that always look well-groomed. Used as specimens in warm- winter gardens, as an espalier, or in containers.

gromwell (grahm′wehl) *n.* The common name for the genus *Lithospermum,* hairy perennials with simple, alternate, entire leaves and clusters of white, yellow, or orange flowers. Used in rock gardens and borders.

ground ash *n.* An ash sapling of a few years' growth.

ground cedar *n.* A common name for *Juniperus communis,* an evergreen shrub or small tree with long, sharp-pointed leaves and hard, berrylike cones. The cones provide the flavor for gin. Widely used for foundation plantings.

ground-cherry *n.* An American plant of the genus *Physalis.*

ground cover *n.* A planting of low-growing or trailing plants used to carpet the ground, as an underplanting under trees or as an overplanting for bulbs.

ground hemlock *n.* A creeping variety of the American yew, *Taxus canadensis,* a coniferous evergreen native to North America. It is a low, spreading shrub with pointed yellow-green leaves.

groundnut *n.* The peanut, the pod of *Arachis hypogaea.*

ground pine *n.* A common name for several species of *Lycopodium,* or club moss, especially *L. clavatum,* the common club moss, a long, creeping evergreen moss native to North America and elsewhere. It is also called running pine. Another species is *L. obscurum,* a graceful, tree-shaped evergreen plant, about 8 inches high, native to North America. Used as a small-scale ground cover in moist, shady places such as a woodland garden.

ground pink *n.* A common name for *Phlox subulata,* a mat-forming evergreen perennial with stiff, needlelike leaves and masses of small pink, rose, lavender-blue, or white flowers. Fairly drought-tolerant, it is used as a small-scale ground cover. Also known as moss pink, moss phlox, and mountain phlox.

ground plum *n.* A common name for *Astragalus crassicarpus,* a creeping perennial, native to North America, which grows from rhizomes. It has alternate, divided leaves; violet-purple butterflylike flowers; and thick, corky pods resembling a plum in shape and size.

groundsel (grownd'suhl) *n.* A common name for the genus *Senecio,* 1 of the largest genera of flowering plants, with more than 2,000 species.

groundsel tree (grownd'suhl) *n.* A common name for *Baccharis halimifolia,* a shrub native to the coastal marshes of North and Central America. It has oblong, gray-green leaves, somewhat resembling those of the groundsel, and clusters of white or yellow tubular flowers. Also called groundsel bush. Resistant to salt spray, it is useful for seaside plantings. (See **Baccharis.**)

ground squirrel *n.* An underground-dwelling mammal that can become a pest by chewing on plant foliage, eating bulbs, and burrowing aggressively. Control with baits, traps, or barriers.

ground water *n.* 1. Water that fills all unblocked pores of underlying material below the water table 2. The upper limit of saturation.

grow light *n.* A broad-spectrum fluorescent light used to grow plants indoors.

growing tray *n.* A compartmentalized tray, like an ice-cube tray, used for starting seeds. Also called cell tray.

growth form *n.* The form of a plant; also called growth habit or, simply, habit. Shrub and vine are growth forms.

growth ring *n.* The layer of wood developed in 1 growth season of a tree, usually 1 year; annular ring.

grub *n.* A wormlike larva of many kinds of beetles. It usually lives underground, often eating plant roots. It can be a serious pest, especially of lawns. Control with parasitic nematodes, pyrethrum, or traditional pesticides.

grugru (groo'groo) *n.* A common name for subtropical palms of the genus *Acrocomia.* They are water-loving palms with a tall trunk, sometimes covered with 3-inch-long black spines, and have divided, prickly leaves. Grown in warm-climate gardens.

grumose (groo'mohs) *a.* In botany, formed of clustered, coarse grains or granules. Also grumous.

Guadalupe palm (gwah duh loo'pee) *n.* A common name for *Brahea edulis,* a slow-growing tropical palm with a stout trunk, spiny-stemmed, 6-foot-wide leaves and a fleshy, edible fruit. Used in warm climates as a garden tree or street tree.

Guaiacum (gwigh'uh kuhm) *n.* A genus of about 6 species of tropical and subtropical evergreen trees and shrubs (Zygophyllaceae) native to dry regions of the Americas. They have opposite, leathery, divided leaves; white, blue, or purple flowers; and very hard resinous wood. Grown ornamentally in warm-winter climates for their attractive flowers and foliage. Useful in seaside plantings; resistant to salt spray. Commonly known as lignum vitae.

Guaiacum
(lignum vitae)

guango (gwahng'goh) *n.* A common name for *Samanea Saman,* a broadleaf evergreen tree (Leguminosae) native to tropical America. It has large leaves divided into leaflets, velvety beneath, with dense clusters of yellow flowers. Used as a shade tree in parks and large gardens. Also known as rain tree.

guano (gwah'noh) *n.* A strong organic fertilizer composed of bird droppings.

guarabu (gwah ruh boo') *n.* A common name for several species of *Astronium* (Anacardiaceae), a genus of large tropical hardwood trees native to the Americas.

guava (gwah'vuh) *n.* One of several species of *Psidium,* a genus of tropical America, especially *P. Guayava,* which is now cultivated and naturalized in most tropical countries. There are 2 varieties of the fruit, known as the red or apple-shaped and the white or pear-shaped guava. The pulp has an agreeable acid flavor and is made into jelly.

guelder rose (gehl'der) *n.* A common name for *Viburnum Opulus,* especially *V. Opulus* 'Roseum'; the snowball bush. It is a large deciduous shrub with maplelike leaves that color brilliant red in fall; large, round, dense clusters of white flowers; and scarlet fruit. (See **Viburnum** and **cranberry bush**.)

guinea-hen *n.* A common name for *Fritillaria Meleagris,* the petals of which are spotted like the feathers of guinea fowl. It is a perennial bulb (Liliaceae) with leafy stems and large, drooping, bell-shaped flowers in early spring. Also called guinea-hen flower, checkered lily, or snake's-head. Used in wild or woodland gardens.

gum *n.* A common name for various species of trees, especially of the genera *Eucalyptus,* of Australia, and *Nyssa* and *Liquidambar* of the United States. For trees of the genus *Eucalyptus,* gum refers specifically to those species with smooth, peeling bark. Of the eucalypts, the blue gum is *E. Globulus* (see **blue gum tree**); the cider gum, *E. Gunnii;* the scarlet-flowering gum, *E. ficifolia;* the gimlet gum, *E. salubris;* the spotted gum, *E. maculata;* the manna gum, *E. viminalis;* the red gum, *E. calophylla;* the Murray red gum or river red gum, *E. camaldulensis;* the salmon gum, *E. salmonophloia;* and the scarlet gum, *E. phoenicia.* Others include lemon-scented gum, *E. citriodora;* sugar gum, *E. cladocalyx;* Mindanao gum, *E. deglupta;* red-cap gum, *E. erythrocorys;* large-fruited red-flowering gum, *E. leucoxylon macrocapa* 'Rosea'; red-spotted gum, *E. mannifera maculosa;* snow gum, *E. niphophila;* ghost gum, *E. papuana* and *E. pauciflora;* round-leafed snow gum, *E. perriniana;* silver-dollar gum, *E. polyanthemos;* silver-mountain gum, *E. pulverulenta;* flooded gum, *E. rudis;* Sydney blue gum, *E. saligna;* coral gum, *E. torquata;* and lemon-flowered gum, *E. woodwardii.* In the United States, the sour gum is *Nyssa sylvatica;* the sweet gum, *Liquidambar Styraciflua.* (See **Eucalyptus**.)

gumbo *n.* The pod of *Abelmoschus esculentus,* also called okra, a vegetable that thrives in southern gardens. The pod is small, about 4 inches long, and contains a gelatinous pulp used to thicken stews.

gumbo-limbo *n.* A common name for *Bursera Simaruba,* a subtropical deciduous tree with peeling, birchlike bark, leaves divided into leaflets, and dense spikes of flowers. Also called West Indian birch.

gumbo soil *n.* 1. Adobe soil 2. An alkaline soil found in the West and Southwest of the United

States that has sufficient nutrients for plant growth but is too closely packed in texture for most gardening purposes.

gummiferous (guh mihf'uh ruhs) *a.* Producing or bearing gum.

gum plant *n.* A common name for the genus *Grindelia,* so called from the sticky secretion that covers them. A genus of coarse, tap-rooted, mostly perennial plants or subshrubs native to the Americas. They have alternate leaves and heads of asterlike yellow flowers, often sweet-smelling and sticky. Used in rock gardens, meadow gardens, and wildflower gardens. Also known as tarweed, rosinweed, gumweed, and sticky-heads.

gum tree *n.* (See **gum**.)

gumweed *n.* (See **gum plant**.)

gumwood *n.* A common name for *Commidendron rugosum* (Compositae), a rare, treelike shrub found only on the island of St. Helena.

Gunnera (guh nihr'uh) *n.* A genus of 35 species of marsh plants (Gunneraceae). They have gigantic, awe-inspiring, lobed, frilled leaves, 5 to 9 feet across, in basal rosettes that grow from a stout rootstock, and corncoblike spikes of minute flowers. Grown in moist situations for their dramatic foliage.

Gunnera

Gutierrezia (goo tee uh reezh'uh) *n.* A genus of 25 species of sticky perennial flowers (Compositae) native to western North and South America. They are low-growing plants with long, narrow, sometimes threadlike, leaves and many clusters of small asterlike yellow flowers. Also known as matchweed, matchbrush, snakeweed, resinweed, broomweed, and turpentine weed.

guttate (guht ayt) *a.* In botany, spotted, as if by drops. Also guttated.

Guttiferae (guh tihf'uh ree) *n. pl.* A family of 40 genera and 1,000 species of tropical trees and shrubs. They have resinous juice, opposite, leathery, evergreen leaves, and clusters of flowers with many stamens. The family includes some edible fruits, as the mangosteen and mammee apple. The major cultivated genera are *Garcinia, Clusia, Calophyllum,* and *Mammea.*

guttiferous (guh tihf'uh ruhs) *a.* Yielding gum or resinous substances; specifically, belonging or pertaining to the family Guttiferae.

Guzmania (gooz man'ee uh) *n.* A genus of 126 species of terrestrial or epiphytic bromeliads (Bromeliaceae) native to damp jungles of tropical America. They have stiff, entire leaves in basal rosettes and spikes of yellow or white flowers with showy red, orange, or yellow bracts. Grown as houseplants or as indoor/outdoor plants in warm climates.

Gymnocalycium (jihm noh kuh lihs'ee uhm) *n.* A genus of 40 species of round, ribbed cacti (Cactaceae) native to South America. They are small, round, spiny cacti with showy, long tubular white, red, pink, and occasionally yellow or chartreuse flowers. Usually grown as houseplants. Commonly known as chin cactus.

gymnocarpous (jihm nuh kahr'puhs) *a.* In botany, having a naked fruit, especially in lichens.

Gymnocladus dioica
(Kentucky coffee trade)

Gymnocladus (jihm nahk'luh duhs) *n.* A genus of 3 species of deciduous trees (Leguminosae) native to the eastern United States and eastern Asia. They are large ornamental trees with stout branches, doubly divided leaves that turn yellow in autumn, and clusters of small greenish-white flowers, followed by long, hard pods enclosing several large seeds. *G. dioica,* the fast-growing Kentucky coffee tree, has an interesting winter silhouette; it tolerates poor soil, extremes of heat and cold, and some drought. Useful in harsh climates and difficult soils.

gymnogynous (jihm nahj′uh nuhs) *a.* In botany, having a naked ovary.

gymnosperm (jihm′nuh sperm) *n.* A plant belonging to the Gymnospermae, characterized by naked seeds, as in the conifers.

Gymnospermae (jihm nuh sper′mee) *n. pl.* One of the two main divisions of seed plants. The class includes gingko, conifers, and cycads. All are trees or shrubs, mostly evergreen and all have naked seeds, usually in a cone.

gymnospermous (jihm nuh sper′muhs) *a.* In botany, of, pertaining to, or resembling the class Gymnospermae; having naked seeds: opposed to angiospermous. Also gymnogenous, gymnospermal, gymnospermic.

gymnospore (jihm′nuh spor) *n.* A naked spore.

gymnosporous (jihm nahs′puh ruhs) *a.* In botany, having naked spores.

Gynandria (jih nan′dree uh) *n. pl.* A class made up of plants with gynandrous flowers.

gynandrous (jih nan′druhs) *a.* In botany, having the stamens adnate to and apparently borne upon the pistil, as in all orchids.

gynandrous flower

gynantherous (jih nan′thuh ruhs) *a.* In botany, having stamens converted into pistils.

gyno- *comb. form* In botany, pistil or ovary.

gynobase (jih′noh bays) *n.* In botany, a prolongation or enlargement of the receptacle of a flower, bearing the gynoecium.

cross section of a gynobase flower

gynodioecious (jih′noh digh ee′shuhs) *a.* In botany, having perfect and female flowers upon separate plants. (See **dioecious**.)

gynoecium (jih nee′see uhm) *n., pl.* **gynoecia** (jih nee′see uh) The pistil or collective pistils of a flower; the female portion of a flower as a whole: correlative to androecium. Also gynecium, gynaeceum.

gynomonoecious (jih′noh moh nee′shuhs) *a.* In botany, having both female and perfect flowers upon the same plant.

gynophore (jihn′uh for) *n.* In botany, an elongation of the receptacle of a flower, bearing the gynoecium at its apex, as in some Capparidaceae.

gynophorous flower

gynostegium (jih noh stee′jee uhm) *n., pl.* **gynostegia** In botany, a covering of the gynoecium.

gynostemium (jih noh stee′mee uhm) *n., pl.*

gynostemia The column of an orchid, formed by the union of the androecium and gynoecium.

Gynura (jih noo′ruh) *n.* A genus of about 100 species of tropical plants and subshrubs (Compositae). They have long, narrow, toothed leaves with soft, velvety purple hairs and small, ill-smelling yellow-orange flowers. Grown as houseplants for their striking purple foliage. Commonly known as velvet plant.

Gypsophila (jihp sahf′uh luh) *n.* A genus of about 125 species of slender, graceful plants. They are airy, open plants with small, sparse, narrow blue-green leaves and masses of tiny flowers in delicate clusters. *G. paniculata* and *G. elegans* are commonly known as baby's breath. Used in borders, rock gardens, or on dry stone walls. An exceptionally long-lasting cut flower, lovely in bouquets.

gypsum (jihp′suhm) *n.* 1. Calcium sulfate. 2. A fertilizer used on alkaline soil to allow calcium to be readily available to plants.

gypsy moth *n.* An imported insect whose larva is a voracious eating caterpillar, feeding on the foliage of many types of trees. A very serious pest in many parts of the United States. Best controlled with the biological insecticide *Bacillus thuringiensis*. Sticky bands around tree trunks can also trap migrating caterpillars. For large trees, consult an arborist for help.

gypsyweed *n.* A common name for *Veronica officionalis.* (See **Veronica**.)

gyroma (ji roh′muh) *n., pl.* **gyromata** In botany: 1. The annulus of a fern. 2. The shield of some lichens.

habanero (hab buh ner′ah) *n.* An extremely hot variety of peppers, growing in a nearly round shape with a pointed end. The peppers have light green wrinkled skins that turn orange as they mature. Also known as Scotch bonnetts.

Habenaria (hay buh na′ree uh) *n.* A large genus of about 100 species of terrestrial, tuberous-rooted orchids (Orchidaceae). It consists of leafy plants with narrow leaves and spikes of often fringed flowers. *Habenaria psycodes* var. *grandiflora,* native to eastern North America and the showiest of the beautiful fringed orchids, is commonly called large purple-fringed orchid, large butterfly orchid, or plume-royal. The genus is commonly known as fringed orchid or rein orchid.

Habenaria
(fringed orchid)
a entire plant *b* flower stalk

Haberlea (hay ber′lee uh) *n.* A genus of 2 species of perennial plants (Gesneriaceae). They have oval, scalloped leaves and stalks of nodding, tubular, pale lilac flowers. Used in rock gardens.

habit *n.* The general characteristic appearance of a plant; for example, a weeping habit describes plants with drooping branches.

habitat *n.* The type of place in which a plant grows naturally.

Habranthus (huh bran′thuhs) *n.* A genus of 10 species of perennial bulbs (Amaryllidaceae) native to the Americas. They have long, narrow leaves and stalks of pink, yellow, or red flowers.

hackberry *n.* 1. A common name for the North American tree *Celtis occidentalis*. The leaves are alternate and elmlike, the flowers small, with dark purple or red fruit. The trees are deep-rooted and, once established, will tolerate drought, wind, heat, and alkaline soil. Often used near paved areas, as their roots do not disturb the surface. Also called nettle tree, hoop ash, false elm, beaverwood, manyberry, and sugarberry. 2. A common name for *C. australis,* the European hackberry or nettle tree. Also called hagberry and bird cherry.

hackberry leaves and fruit

hackia (hak′ee uh) *n.* A common name for the genus *Tabebuia,* shrubs or trees native to tropical America. They have opposite, hand-shaped leaves and spikes or clusters of showy yellow, white, pink, red or purple flowers. Useful in warm winter climates as spectacular flowering specimens or street trees.

hackmatack *n.* A common name for *Larix laricina,* also called American larch, black larch, and tamarack. (See **larch**.)

haekaro (hee′kuh roh) *n.* A common name for *Pittosporum umbellatum,* an evergreen tree. It grows to 30 or 40 feet and has leathery leaves and clusters of many small, red flowers. Used in warm climate gardens.

Haemanthus (hee man′thuhs) *n.* A genus of about 60 species of low-growing bulbs (Amaryllidaceae). They have broad basal leaves, stalks of dense clusters of red or white summer- or fall-blooming flowers, and colorful berries. Commonly known as African blood lily or blood lily.

Haemaria (hee ma′ree uh) *n.* A genus of a single species of tropical orchid, *H. discolor* (Orchidaceae). It is grown for its attractive foliage: It has purple leaves with red or gold veins or black-green leaves with pale green veins. Commonly known as gold-lace orchid.

Haematoxylum (heem uh takh′suh lahn) *n.* A genus of 3 species of spiny shrubs or trees (Leguminosae), some native to tropical America. They have divided leaves, short, loose, showy clusters of small, yellow flowers, and long, flat pods. Grown in warm-climate gardens for their showy flowers.

Haemodoraceae (heem′uh doh ray′see uh) *n. pl.* A family of about 16 genera of perennials. They have long, basal leaves and spikes or clusters of dense flowers with long, soft, shaggy hairs. Ornamental genera include *Anigozanthos, Conostylis,* and *Lachnanthes.* Commonly known as bloodwort.

hagberry *n.* A common name for a species of cherry, *Prunus Padus.* Also called bird cherry.

ha-ha *n.* A sunken fence formed by a ditch between slopes. Also spelled haw-haw.

hair grass *n.* (See **Koeleria** and **Deschampsia**.)

hair-trigger flower *n.* An Australian plant of the genus *Stylidium,* especially *S. graminifolium,* in which the stamens spring instantly from 1 side to the other of the flower when touched.

hairy mellic (mehl′ihk) *n.* (See **Melica**.)

Hakea (hah′kee uh) *n.* A genus of about 100 species of evergreen shrubs or small trees (Proteaceae). They have alternate, leathery leaves, sometimes needlelike or prickly, and spikes or clusters of showy, fluffy flowers. Commonly known as pincushion tree. They are tough plants, useful in difficult situations in warm-winter regions since they tolerate poor soil, drought, and some frost.

Hakonechloa (hahk uh nehk loh′uh) *n.* A genus with 1 species, *H. macra* (Gramineae), a perennial grass. Grown as an ornamental for its elegant leaves and yellow-green airy blooms. Varieties are available with white or yellow variegated leaves.

Halenia (huh lee′nee uh) *n.* A genus of more than 70 species of annuals, biennials, and perennials (Gentianaceae), some species native to North America. *H. cornulata* is an annual or biennial that grows to 2 feet, with oblong or oval leaves and small pale yellow flowers. Commonly known as spurred gentian.

Halesia (huh lee′zee uh) *n.* A genus of 5 species of deciduous trees or shrubs (Styraceae), some native to eastern North America. They are handsome shrubs or small trees, with alternate, toothed leaves and nodding, white, bell-shaped flowers, appearing in spring before the leaves and usually borne on slender branches, forming arches or rows of bells along the underside, giving to the whole plant a beautiful appearance. *H. diptera* and *H. carolina* are both native to the South and Midwest; *H. diptera* is hardy to Zone 8, *H. carolina* hardy to Zone 5. Commonly known as snowdrop tree or silver-bell tree.

Halesia
(snowdrop tree)

half-hardy annuals *n. pl.* A term used to describe plants that will tolerate some frost, but not a long freeze, such as China asters or zinnias.

Halimodendron (ha lih moh dehn'druhn) *n.* A genus of a single species, *H. halodendron* (Leguminosae), a hardy, deciduous, spiny shrub. It has divided leaves with gray-downy leaflets and clusters of butterflylike, pale purple flowers. Useful in saline soils. Commonly known as salt tree.

Halleria (huh lair'ee uh) *n.* A genus of 5 species of shrubs or trees (Scrophulariaceae). They have simple, opposite leaves, clusters of red flowers, and a berrylike fruit.

halophilous (hal ahf'uh lous) *a.* In botany, preferring, or habitually growing in salty soil as maritime plants.

halophyte (hal'uh fight) *n.* The saltwort, a plant, such as those of certain genera in the families Chenopodiaceae, Compositae, or Plumbaginaceae, that are adapted to saline soils and inhabit salt marshes and seacoasts.

Haloragaceae (hal'uh ruh gay'see uh) *n. pl.* An order of 6 genera and 125 species of aquatic plants; the water-milfoil family. The cultivated genera are *Myriophyllum* and *Proserpinaca.*

Hamamelidaceae (ham uh mehl uh day'see ee) *n. pl.* A family of 23 genera of trees or shrubs. The cultivated genera include *Corylopsis* (winter hazel), *Hamamelis* (witch hazel), *Liquidamber* (sweet gum), and *Parrotia.*

Hamamelis (ham uh mehl'uhs) *n.* A genus of 6 species of deciduous shrubs or small trees (Hamamelidaceae), some native to temperate eastern North America. They have simple, toothed leaves and clusters of nodding, fragrant yellow flowers with crumpled-looking petals. Commonly known as witch hazel.

hamate (hay'mayt) *a.* In botany, curved at the tip, like a hook.

Hamburg (*n.* A black variety of the *Vitis vinifera,* or European grape. The berries are oblong and have a peculiarly delicate and refreshing flavor.

Hamelia (huh mee'lee uh) *n.* A genus of 40 species of deciduous tropical or subtropical shrubs (Rubiaceae) native to the Americas. They have opposite or whorled entire leaves and clusters of small red or yellow flowers. *H. patens* is a small flowering tree with long, elliptical leaves and handsome scarlet or orange flowers. It is commonly known as scarlet bush or fire bush. It is grown in warm-winter regions.

hammock *n.* A body-length swing of insect-penetrable mesh hung between 2 trees or on a frame to entice, but seldom rest, the body of a gardener.

hammock fern *n.* A common name for *Blechnum occidentale,* a tropical American fern with creeping rhizomes and divided, sharply pointed leaves to 18 inches long.

handpicking *n.* A pest-control technique whereby the pest is physically removed from the plant by hand. Can be very effective with some larger insects, including tomato hornworms and snails.

hand planter *n.* A hand machine for planting seeds.

hand rake *n.* A miniature, short-handled leaf rake used to tidy garden beds.

hand sprayer *n.* A pump-action, hand-held device consisting of a tube attached to a container; used to apply pesticides, herbicides, fertilizers, or other liquids to plants. Also called can sprayer.

hanging basket *n.* A container on a cord or rope suspended from a brace, tree, or other structure; used for growing decorative plants. A hanging basket may serve as a planter or hold another planter. Also called a hanging planter.

hanging moss *n.* A name for certain lichens of the genera *Usnea* and *Ramalina,* particularly *Usnea,* from their habit of hanging in long fringes from the branches of trees, etc. (See **Usnea**.) The name is also sometimes given to the bromeliad *Tillandsia usneoides;* also known as Spanish moss or graybeard, which has a similar habit. (See **Tillandsia**.)

hanging plant rotator *n.* A device that rotates a hanging plant a precise number of degrees (usually 90°) to ensure even lighting.

haploid (hap'loid) *a.* Having the number of chromosomes characteristic of the germ cells, or half the number present in the body cells.

Haplopappus (hap loh pahp'uhs) *n.* A genus of 150 species of tap-rooted plants and shrubs (Compositae) chiefly native to southern and western North America. They have alternate leaves and large, many-flowered heads of yellow flowers.

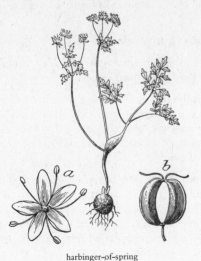

harbinger-of-spring
a flower *b* fruit

harbinger-of-spring *n.* A common name for *Erigenia bulbosa* (*Umbelliferae*), a small, tuberous, early-blooming hardy perennial, with leaves divided into

many leaflets and small white flowers. It is native to eastern North America from southern Ontario, Canada, south to Alabama, and west to Kansas. Also known as pepper-and-salt.

Hardenbergia (har dihn ber'jee uh) *n.* A genus of 3 species of evergreen twining vines and sub-shrubs (Leguminosae). They have alternate, divided leaves and a profusion of long, dangling clusters of small butterflylike violet flowers. Useful for creating delicate tracery on walls, covering a trellis, or as a ground cover.

hardening off *v.* The process of gradually acclimatizing greenhouse- or hotbed-grown plants to outdoor growing conditions.

hard fern *n.* A common name for several species of ferns of the genus *Blechnum*, particularly *B. Spicant.*

hardiness *n.* The capability of a plant to withstand low temperatures without artificial protection.

hardiness zones *n. pl.* Areas classified by climate and temperature range for the purpose of determining which plants will succeed or fail within a given region. Most commonly used are those published by the U.S. Department of Agriculture, which divides the United States into 11 zones, 1 being the coldest and 11 the warmest. Plants living in Zones 1 through 4 are considered to be very hardy; those in Zones 5 through 7 are hardy; those in Zones 8 through 9 are fairly hardy; in Zone 10, plants are described as tender (most will not survive freezing); and those in Zone 11, which is frost- free, are considered subtropical or tropical. The USDA Zones are classified by average low temperature. Specifically, Zone 1 has an average low temperature of -50 F; Zone 2, -50 to -40 F; Zone 3, -40 to -30 F; Zone 4, -30 to -20 F; Zone 5, -20 to -10 F; Zone 6, -10 to 0 F; Zone 7, 0 to 10 F; Zone 8, 10 to 20 F; Zone 9, 20 to 30 F; Zone 10, 30 to 40 F; and in Zone 11, average low temperatures do not fall below 40 F. Freezing is 32 F.

hardock *n.* A common name for any plant of the genus *Arctium;* the burdock. It is a tall, tap-rooted plant with very large leaves. It has naturalized in North America. Generally regarded as a weed.

hardpan *n.* A hard or cementlike soil or soil layer.

hardwood *n.* The wood from trees with encapsulated seeds (that is, nuts or fruits), as distinguished from a conifer or cone-bearing tree, which has naked seeds. Oak, maple, and walnut are all hardwoods. Pine and fir are softwoods.

hardy orange *n.* A common name for *Poncirus trifoliata,* a deciduous citrus tree with stiff, angled, thorny branches, oval leaves divided into 3 leaflets, large, white, powerfully fragrant flowers that appear before the leaves, and fragrant but hard, bitter, and inedible fruit. Useful as an impenetrable hedge as far north as Zone 8. Also known as trifoliate orange.

hardy plants *n.* A term used to describe plants that thrive in cold- winter regions, for example, *Forsythia, Spirea, Viburnum,* and *Paeonia* (peonies). Some plants require winter chill to flower or fruit well, such as lilacs *(Syringa)* and many apples *(Malus).*

harebell *n.* A common name for *Campanula rotundifolia,* the well-known bluebell of Scotland. It is a mat-forming perennial with long, slim leaves on the stems and a rosette of rounded, heart-shaped leaves at the base. It has delicate, nodding, bell-shaped blue flowers. Useful in borders, woodland gardens, rock gardens, or naturalized under deciduous trees. 2. A common name for *Endymion nonscriptus,* also called wood hyacinth.

harebell or bluebell

harefoot *n.* A common name for *Trifolium arvense,* a clover naturalized in the United States. Same as hare's-foot.

hare's-bane *n.* A common name for *Aconitum lycoctonum,* a poisonous species of monkshood that has broadly lobed leaves and tall spikes of purple flowers. Also called wolf's-bane.

hare's-beard *n.* A common name for *Verbascum Thapsus,* an attractive roadside weed. Also called common mullein, velvet plant, or flannel plant.

hare's-ear *n.* A common name for *Bupleurum rotundifolium* (Umbelliferae). It has alternate perfoliate leaves and rounded clusters of yellowish-green flowers.

hare's-foot *n.* A common name for *Trifolium arvense,* a clover widely naturalized in the United States. (See **harefoot**.)

haricot bean (har'uh koh) *n.* The kidney bean.

harlequin bug *n.* (See **stinkbugs**.)

harlock *n.* A common name for *Arctium Lappa,* also known as burdock, a tall growing weed noted for its large leaves.

Harpephyllum (har puh fihl'uhm) *n.* A genus of a single species, *H. caffrum,* a tender, fast-growing broadleaf evergreen tree (Anacardiaceae). It has alternate, divided, leathery, glossy leaves, clusters of small white flowers, and tart, edible, dark red fruit. Useful against high walls for its interesting silhouette.

harpula (harp'yuh luh)

n. A common name for the tree *Harpullia cupanioides.* (See **Harpullia**.)

Harpullia (har puhl'ee uh) *n.* A genus of about 35 species of deciduous trees (Sapindaceae). They are erect trees with alternate, divided, leaves, clusters or spikes of green flowers, and red- or orange-colored fruit.

Harrisia (huh'rihs ee uh) *n.* A genus of 20 species of vinelike cacti (Cactaceae) native to tropical America. They are slender, spiny, ribbed cacti, with knobby, sprawling stems, needlelike spines, tubular white nocturnal flowers, and red, orange, or yellow fruit.

harrow *n.* A rake-like implement drawn over plowed soil to prepare it for planting. *v.* To draw a harrow over soil; to break or tear with a harrow, as to harrow land or ground.

Hartford fern *n*. A common name for the genus *Lygodium*, a genus of unusual tropical and temperate ferns, some species native to America; specifically used for *L.japonicum*. Also known as climbing-fern.

hart's-eye *n*. A common name for *Origanum dictamnus*, an aromatic perennial herb with thick, round, woolly white leaves and spikelets of small pink or purple flowers. Also known as Crete dittany. Used in rock gardens, herb gardens, window boxes, hanging baskets, and containers.

hart's-thorn *n*. A common name for *Rhamnus cathartica*, a shrub or tree with spine-tipped twigs, leathery, toothed, glossy green leaves that turn yellow in autumn, clusters of flowers, and black fruit. Also known as buckthorn. Useful as a hedge or tree in difficult situations since it tolerates cold, drought, poor soil, and wind.

hart's-tongue *n*. A common name for 2 different ferns; *Phyllitis Scolopendrium*, which has long simple fronds, and, less often, the tropical American fern *Polybotria cervina*.

harvest-apple *n*. A small, early variety of apple, ripening in August.

hashish *n*. A common name for the tops and tender parts of *Cannabis sativa*, a tall plant with long, toothed, hand-shaped leaves and spikes or panicles of flowers. Best known for its hallucinatory properties, it is illegal to grow in the United States. Commonly known as pot, marijuana, ganjah, bhang, or Indian hemp. Also spelled hasheesh.

hastate (has'tayt) *a*. Of a leaf, shaped like an arrowhead, but with the basal lobes turned outward.

haw *n*. 1. A yard or piece of enclosed land. 2. A name for the fruit of any *Viburnum*, specifically *V. nudum*. (See **Viburnum**.) 3. Any berry.

hawk's-beard *n*. A common name for any plant of the genus *Crepis*, a few species of which, such as *Crepis rubra*, are cultivated. (See **Crepis**.)

hawkweed *n*. A common name for any plant of the genus *Hieracium* (Compositae). They are perennial plants growing from runners, with leaves in a basal rosette and clusters of orange, white, or yellow flowers. Used in rock gardens; may become a pest.

Haworthia (hay wer'thee uh) *n*. A genus of about 160 species of perennial succulents (Liliaceae). They are clump-forming plants with thick, fleshy leaves shaped like long, narrow triangles, often interestingly patterned, and clusters of small, white, striped flowers borne at the ends of tall stalks arising from the center of the plant. Commonly known as star cactus, wart plant, or cushion aloe.

hawthorn *n*. A common name for *Crataegus laevigata*, a thorny shrub or small tree, much used in hedges. It has stiff branches bearing strong thorns, small, deeply lobed or cut leaves, masses of white or pink flowers in spring, and red berries in winter. The fruit is the haw, which attracts birds. The name is also applied to the genus *Crataegus* in general. (See **Crataegus**.)

hawthorn
a branch with fruit *b* branch with flowers

hay-scented fern *n*. A common name for the North American fern *Dennstaedtia punctilobula*, so called on account of the fragrance of its fronds. It grows from slender rhizomes forming large clumps with narrowly triangular leaves on 30-inch-long fronds.

hazel *n*. A common name for deciduous shrubs or small trees of the genus *Corylus*. They have alternate, oval, doubly-toothed leaves, drooping catkins, and clusters of small, edible nuts. (See **Corylus**.)

hazel

hazel, European *n.* A common name for *Corylus Avellana,* a hardy, deciduous shrub that grows to 15 feet. It has broad, rounded, downy leaves that turn yellow in fall; attractive yellow catkins that hang on all winter; and tasty, round, edible nuts. Also called European filbert.

hazelnut *n.* 1. The nut of the hazel. It consists of a hard, round shell enclosing a single seed composed of 2 equal, thick, fleshy parts. The nuts are usually clustered but sometimes solitary. The nutritious and edible part, or "meat," of the nut is pleasantly flavored. 2. The plant that bears the hazelnut. (See **hazel**.)

hazelwort *n.* A common name for *Asarum europaeum,* a low-growing, evergreen, perennial ground cover with lustrous green leaves and tiny greenish-purple or brown flowers. Also known as asarabacca and wild ginger. (See **Asarum**.)

head *n.* 1. In botany, the top of a plant consisting of a dense mass of leaves, as a head of lettuce. 2. A short, compact cluster of flowers. *v.* 1. To form a head, as a cabbage. 2. To cut back the shoots of plants in order to induce lateral growth.

head betony *n.* A common name for *Pedicularis canadensis,* better known as the wood betony or lousewort. It is a perennial herb with large, divided leaves and red or yellow flowers.

heal-all *n.* A common name for any of several plants supposed to possess great healing virtues, especially *Prunella vulgaris,* more commonly called self-heal. Among the other plants sometimes called by this name are *Habenaria orbiculata, Collinsonia canadensis* (horse-balm), and *Sedum Rosea* (rose-root).

healing herb *n.* A plant, *Symphytum officinale,* generally called comfrey.

heart liverleaf *n.* A common name for *Hepatica americana* and *H. nobilis.* They are small, hardy, low-growing perennials with kidney-shaped leaves and tiny lavender-blue, rose, or white flowers. (See **liverleaf**.)

heartnut *n.* A common name for *Juglans ailanthifolia* var. *cordiformis.* It is a tall tree with leaves divided into many leaflets, downy beneath, with heart-shaped, pointed, and thin-shelled nuts. Used as a rootstock for commercially grown walnuts. Also known as Japanese walnut.

heart-of-the-earth *n.* The planet self-heal, *Prunella vulgaris.* (See **heal-all**.)

heartpea *n.* A common name for *Cardiospermum Halicacabum,* a fast-growing subtropical or tropical climbing perennial woody vine with smooth, alternate, toothed leaves, small white flowers, and curious inflated, bladderlike fruits. Also known as balloon vine. Widely naturalized throughout the world. Grown from seed as an annual in cold weather climates and as a perennial in mild-winter regions. Used to cover a trellis or fence.

heartsease *n.* A popular and poetic name for plants of the genus *Viola,* especially *V.* × *wittrockiana.* Also known as pansy.

heartseed *n.* A common name for plants of the genus *Cardiospermum* (of which name it is a literal translation), but especially of *C. Halicacabum,* a beautiful vine also known as balloon vine, from its large, triangular, inflated fruit. Also known as heartpea and wintercherry. (See **heartpea**.)

heart snakeroot *n.* A common name for *Asarum canadense,* a low-growing, deciduous perennial native to North America from New Brunswick to North Carolina. It has large, downy green leaves and small brownish-purple flowers. Also known as asarabacca, snakeroot, and wild ginger.

heartwood *n.* The older, nonliving central wood in a tree.

heath *n.* A common name for the genus *Erica,* a large genus of about 500 species of branched rigid shrubs (Ericaceae); the heaths or heather. The leaves are very small, narrow, and rigid, with spikes of white, yellow, green, rose, or purple urn-shaped or bell-shaped flowers. Useful on slopes, as ground covers, and in rock gardens; the taller varieties can be used as screens. All attract bees.

heather *n.* A common name for any heath, especially *Calluna vulgaris,* the Scotch heather. It is an evergreen shrub with tiny, dense, scalelike dark-green leaves and 1-sided spikes of rosy-pink bell-shaped flowers. (See **Calluna**.)

heather bell *n.* A common name for *Erica cinerea,* a small, hardy European shrub to 2 feet tall with small, shiny leaves and spikes or clusters of purple flowers that fade to blue. It has naturalized on Nantucket Island.

heathery *a.* Of, pertaining to, or resembling heather; abounding with heather; heathy.

heath family *n.* A common name for plants of the family *Ericaceae,* which has 17 genera and 1,900 species of shrubs or small trees, mostly native to temperate zones and moist, acid soils. The leaves are very small, narrow, and rigid, with spikes of white, yellow, green, rose, or purple urn-shaped or bell-shaped flowers that are often showy.

heathwort *n.* A common name for any plant of the genera *Erica* and *Calluna;* a heath or heather. (See cut under **Ericaceae**.)

heathy *a.* Of, pertaining to, or characteristic of heath; covered or abounding with heath.

heating cable *n.* An electric device used to heat soil in a greenhouse or cold frame.

heating system *n.* A unit consisting of an adjustable temperature controller and a heat mat; used to maintain soil temperature during germination and seedling development or during root growth of cuttings.

heat mat *n.* A low-voltage heater used to warm soil during seed germination, seedling development, and root growth of cuttings.

heavenly bamboo *n.* A common name for *Nandina domestica,* an airy, delicate shrub that looks like bamboo but is actually related to the barberry family (Berberidaceae). It has small, narrow, pointed, bamboolike soft green leaves that turn red with cold but do not drop, delicate clusters of tiny white flowers, and bright red berries through winter. Will not tolerate severe winters. Extremely useful for hedges, screening, Oriental effects, or in containers.

heaving *n.* The pushing of plants out from the soil as a result of alternate freezing and thawing action.

heavy pine *n.* A common name for *Pinus ponderosa,* a huge, attractive pine to 200 feet or more, but often smaller, with needlelike leaves in bundles of 3 and prickly, oblong reddish-brown cones 3 to 8 inches long. It is native to the American West from British Colimbia to Mexico. Excellent in containers, from bonsai to barrels; otherwise, only for ranches or estates. (See **pine**.)

heavy soil *n.* A term to indicate a clayish fine-textured soil.

Hebe (hee′bee) *n.* A genus of between 70 and 80 species of tender shrubs and trees (Scrophulariaceae). They have opposite, simple, leathery leaves and dense spikes of white, pink, blue, or purple flowers. Useful in mild climates as foundation plants, hedges, or as specimen shrubs or in seaside plantings, as they tolerate salt spray.

Hebenstretia (hehb ehn stree′shuh) *n.* A genus of about 30 species of tender plants or shrubs (Scrophulariaceae). Most have alternate, narrow, simple leaves and terminal spikes of white or yellow flowers. They are grown as annuals in cold climates.

Hechtia (hehk′tee uh) *n.* A genus of 45 species of succulent, terrestrial bromeliads (Bromeliaceae) native to the southern United States, Mexico, and Central America. They have long, stiff, spiny-toothed leaves in dense rosettes and clusters of small white or rose flowers in colorful bracts.

Hedeoma pulegioides
(American pennyroyal)

Hedeoma (heed ee oh'muh) *n.* A genus of 30 species of low, aromatic, herbaceous plants (Labiatae) native to the Americas. The best-known species is *H. pulegioides,* native to eastern North America, which has hairy stems, elliptic, fragrant leaves, and clusters of bluish-purple flowers on a slim spike. Also known as American pennyroyal.

Hedera (hehd'uh ruh) *n.* A genus of 5 species of self-clinging evergreen woody vines (Araliaceae), which climb by aerial rootlets; the ivy. They have simple, hand-shaped, shiny, green leaves and, on mature growth, rounded clusters of small yellowish-white flowers. *H. Helix,* known as English ivy, is useful as a ground cover, on walls, fences, or in pots. *H. canariensis,* known as Algerian ivy, is useful in mild-climate public plantings, such as along the steep banks of freeways, as a ground cover, and on fences, walls, and buildings. English ivy is significantly hardier than Algerian ivy. It has many named cultivars, often grown as foliage plants in hanging baskets and as houseplants.

hedge *n.* A barrier or fence formed by bushes or small trees growing together; a closely planted row of shrubbery. *v.* To enclose or fence with a hedge; to separate by a hedge.

hedge binding *n.* Something used to bind together the bushes composing a hedge.

hedge bindweed *n.* A common name for the weed *Calystegia sepium,* a perennial herbaceous vine with triangular leaves and white trumpet-shaped flowers. It grows on hedges and fences and is considered a noxious weed. Also known as wild morning glory, bindweed, and Rutland beauty.

hedge knife *n.* An implement for trimming hedges.

hedge pink *n.* The soapwort, *Saponaria officinalis.*

hedge planter *n.* A frame for holding young hedge plants in position while being set out in a furrow to form a hedge.

hedgerow *n.* A row of shrubs or trees planted to enclose or separate fields.

hedge scissors *n. pl.* A large, crooked kind of scissors or shears for trimming hedges.

hedge shears *n.* A long-bladed scissors for trimming hedges.

hedging *n.* The process or work of making or trimming hedges.

Hedycarya (hehd ih kar'ee uh) *n.* A genus of 20 species of tender trees and shrubs (Monimiaceae). They have opposite leaves, clusters of inconspicuous flowers, and bright red fruit. Used in warm climate gardens.

Hedychium (hee dihk'ee uhm) *n.* A genus of 50 species of robust, tropical perennial flowers (Zingiberaceae); ginger lily. The plants grow from a horizontal tuberous rhizome; the stem is erect and leafy; the leaves are opposite and handsome. The flowers are generally large, showy, and fragrant, ranging in color from white to yellow to red. H. coronarium, with white, powerfully fragrant flowers, is commonly known as garland flower. Grown in subtropical or tropical gardens outdoors, in hothouses elsewhere.

Hedyotis (hehd ih oh'tihs) *n.* A genus of 400 species of shrubs (Rubiaceae). Most have narrow, opposite leaves and clusters of small white or blue flowers. *H. caerulea* is a delicate perennial native to eastern North America; it forms dense tufts from 2 to 4 inches high; commonly known as bluets, Quaker-ladies, or innocence. Used in wildflower or native plant gardens.

Hedysarum boreale
a flower *b* fruit

Hedysarum (hee dihs'uh ruhm) *n.* A genus of 100 to 150 species of perennial plants or small shrubs (Leguminosae). They have alternate, divided leaves and spikes of showy, butterflylike purple, red, or white flowers. *H. boreale* grows to 2 feet tall, with red flowers, and is very hardy; native from Saskatchewan, Canada, and North Dakota to Oklahoma.

Hedyscepe (hehd ih seep') *n.* A genus of a single species, *H. Canterburyana* (Palmae), a slow-growing, slender palm. It has a very narrow, green trunk, long, divided leaves, and deep red fruit. It is grown as a specimen in warm-winter areas, elsewhere in containers as an indoor/outdoor plant, or as a greenhouse specimen. Commonly known as umbrella palm.

heel *n.* In propagation, the base of a cutting, tuber, or other plant part along with a piece of the stem of a parent plant.

heeling in *n.* The process of temporarily covering the base of a plant, especially a dormant plant, with soil for a short period.

Helenium autumnale
(sneezeweed)

Helenium (hih lee'nee uhm) *n.* A genus of 40 species of plants (Compositae) native to the Americas; sneezeweed. They have alternate, entire, drooping leaves and clusters of yellow flowers. The best-known species, *H. autumnale,* grows as a wildflower from Quebec, Canada, south to Florida and Arizona, west to British Columbia, Canada; it is

called sneezeweed from its ability to produce violent sneezing. Used as a perennial at the back of borders or in wildflower gardens. Will tolerate drought, heat, and benign neglect.

helianthaceous (hee lee an thay'shuhs) *a.* In botany, related to *Helianthus.*

Helianthella (hee lee an thehl'uh) *n.* A genus of 8 species of rough, hairy perennials (Compositae) native to the mountains of western North America. They have erect, leafy stems, simple, entire leaves, and yellow daisylike flowers.

Helianthemum (hee lee an'thuh muhm) *n.* A genus of 110 species of low-growing flowers or subshrubs (Cistaceae), some species native to North and South America. *H. nummularium* has small, narrow, opposite leaves and masses of 5-petaled flame-red, apricot, peach, orange, rose, salmon, pink, or white flowers that open only in sunshine. *H. canadense,* commonly known as frostweed, is native to the eastern United States; it has large yellow flowers. Commonly known as sun rose or rock rose.

Helianthus
(sunflower)

Helianthus (hee lee an'thuhs) *n.* A genus of about 150 species of tall, leafy flowers (Compositae) native to the Americas; sunflower. They have simple leaves and individual, sunflowerlike yellow, red, or purple flowers, sometimes with a center of a contrasting color. Used in meadow or prairie gardens or grown for their seeds, which attract birds. Commonly known as sunflower.

Helichrysum (hehl uh krigh′suhm) *n.* A large genus of between 300 and 500 species of flowers, subshrubs, or shrubs (Compositae). They are characterized by flowers that dry well, retaining their bright colors. They are also known as everlasting or immortelle, and are widely used for dried bouquets and wreaths. *H. bracteatum* is grown for its red, yellow, orange, pink, or white flowers; it is commonly known as strawflower.

Helicodiceros (heh lih koh dihs′uh ruhs) *n.* A genus of a single species, *H. muscivorus* (Araceae), a tender perennial. It grows to 2 feet, has lobed leaves, and ill-smelling dark green callalike flowers spotted with brown or purple. Commonly known as twist arum.

Heliconia (hehl uh kah′nee uh) *n.* A genus of 150 species of tropical bananalike plants (Heliconiaceae), some species native to tropical America. They have broad, bananalike leaves and arching spikes of brilliant scarlet, red, orange, yellow, or white lobster-claw-shaped bracts. They are striking specimens in tropical gardens or greenhouses. They are long-lasting cut flowers. Commonly known as lobster-claw or false bird of paradise.

Helicteres (heh lihk tihr′eez) *n.* A genus of 40 species of small trees and shrubs (Byttneriaceae), some species native to tropical America. They have alternate simple leaves, tubular, clawed flowers, generally in clusters, and twisted fruit.

Helictotrichon (hih lih tuh trigh′kahn) *n.* A genus of about 100 species of perennial grasses (Gramineae). Several are used as ornamental grasses. The most notable is *H. sempervirens* (blue oat grass), grown for its striking blue, ribbed foliage and arching blue blooms, which gradually turn light brown.

Heliocarpus (hee′lee uh kar′puhs) *n.* A genus of 22 species of trees and shrubs (Tiliaceae) native to tropical America. They have simple lobed leaves, clusters of small flowers, and seeds with a halo of feathery fringe resembling the sun.

Heliocereus (hee lee oh sehr′ee uhs) *n.* A genus of about 5 species of slender cacti (Cactaceae) native to Mexico and Central America. They have slim stems, few ribs, short, needlelike spines, and showy, tubular scarlet flowers, sometimes 6 inches across.

Heliophila (hee lee ahf′uh luh) *n.* A genus of more than 100 species of annuals or tender shrubs (Cruciferae). They have long, narrow, entire leaves, long spikes of yellow, white, pink, or blue flowers, and pendulous pods.

heliophilous (hee lee ahf′uh luhs) *a.* Fond of the sun; attracted by or becoming most active in sunlight.

heliophobic (hee lee ahf′uh luh) *a.* Shunning sunlight; shade-loving.

Heliopsis (hee lee ahp′sihs) *n.* A genus of 12 species of tall flowers (Compositae) native to the Americas. They have oval, opposite leaves and showy, daisylike yellow, orange, or purple flowers with yellow, brown, purple, or red centers. *H. helianthoides,* native to the eastern and midwestern United States, is commonly known as oxeye. Used in borders, meadow gardens, and prairie gardens.

heliotrope (hee′lee uh trohp) *n.* 1. A common name for plants of the genus *Heliotropium. Heliotropium* consists of herbs or shrubs with hairy, alternate, simple leaves and clusters of small blue, purple, pink, or white flowers. *H. arborescens,* common heliotrope, grows to 4 feet, and has long been a favorite garden plant, cherished for the sweet fragrance of its flowers. Traditional in cottage gardens. 2. A common name for *Valeriana officinalis,* which grows to 4 feet, with light green leaves divided into leaflets and rounded clusters of tiny fragrant white, pink, red, or lavender-blue flowers. Used in herb gardens or borders; can become invasive. 3. The bluish-purple or pinkish-lilac color of some flowers of the heliotrope.

heliotropic (hee lee uh trohp′ihk) *a.* Turning or tending to turn toward the sun, as leaves or flowers.

heliotropism (hee lee ah′truh pihz uhm) *n.* In botany, the tendency of plant organs such as leaves, stems, or flowers to orient themselves according to the direction in which sunlight strikes them.

Heliotropium (hee lee uh troh′pee uhm) *n.* A genus of 250 species of tender plants and shrubs (Boraginaceae). They have simple, alternate leaves and clusters of small blue, purple, pink, or white flowers. *H. arborescens* is common heliotrope, long a favorite garden plant, much loved for the fragrance of its flowers. (See **heliotrope**.)

Helipterum (hih lihp'tuh ruhm) *n.* A genus of between 60 and 90 species of flowers, subshrubs, or shrubs (Compositae). They have alternate, entire leaves and clusters of flowers with petallike bracts. They dry well and are frequently used in dried arrangements. Commonly known as everlasting, strawflower, and immortelle.

hellebore (hehl'uh bor) *n.* 1. A common name for plants of the genus *Helleborus* (Ranunculaceae). They are long-lived, early-blooming evergreen perennials with deeply lobed leaves and long-lasting green, white, rose, or purple flowers. *H. niger,* commonly known as black hellebore or Christmas rose, blooms in winter. *H. orientale* is commonly known as the Lenten Rose. *H. viridis,* the green hellebore, has naturalized in the eastern United States. Hellebores are choice garden plants for moist shady situations. Used in perennial borders and in woodland gardens under high-branching trees. Difficult to establish, hellebores hate to be transplanted or otherwise disturbed. All hellebores are poisonous. 2. A common name for similar plants of other genera. The genus *Veratrum* (Liliaceae) is known as false hellebore. *V. viride,* is also known as American white hellebore, itchweed, and Indian poke. 3. A term used for a natural insecticide made from *V. viride.*

hellebore, false *n.* A common name for the genus *Veratrum* (Liliaceae), a genus of hardy perennials that grow from rhizomes, some species native to North America. They grow from 2 to 7 feet, depending on species with alternate, pleated leaves and clusters of white, green, brown, maroon, or purple flowers. Used in borders and in the wild garden. (See **hellebore**.)

helleborine (hehl'uh buh righn) *n.* 1. A common name for orchids of the genus *Epipactis* (Orchidaceae). They are perennials with creeping rhizomes, fibrous roots, leafy stems, and loose spikes of dull-colored flowers. 2. A common name for the genus *Cephalanthera,* a genus of European orchids.

Helleborus (heh lehb'uh ruhs) *n.* A genus of 20 species of evergreen perennials (Ranunculaceae); hellebore. They are long-lived, erect plants with

deeply cut leaves and white, green, rosy-pink, or purple flowers. *H. niger* is commonly known as Christmas rose or black hellebore. (See **hellebore**.)

Helleborus niger
(Christmas rose)

hellweed *n.* A common name for *Cucutus* (dodder), *Convolvulus,* (bindweed), and *Ranunculus arvensis,* (corn crowfoot). All are considered noxious weeds.

helmetflower *n.* 1. A common name for *Aconitum Napellus,* also known as wolf's-bane or monkshood. 2. A common name for *Scutellaria,* also known as skullcap. 3. A common name for an epiphytic South American orchid of the genus *Coryanthes,* so called from its helmet-shaped lip.

helobious (heh loh'bee uhs) *a.* Living in swamps or marshes.

Helonias (hih loh'nee uhs) *n.* A genus of a single species, *Helonias bullata* (Liliaceae), a spring-blooming perennial, native to wet places from New Jersey to northwestern Georgia. It is a very handsome plant that grows from tuberous rhizomes. It has oblong basal leaves and a hollow, densely flowered, 3-foot stalk covered with tiny pink or purple fragrant flowers. Commonly known as swamp pink.

Helwingia (hel wihn'jee ah) *n.* A genus of 3 species of deciduous shrubs (Cornaceae). They are smooth shrubs with alternate, simple, toothed leaves and clusters of small flowers borne on the upper surface of the leaves. Grown mostly as a curiosity.

Hemerocallis (hehm uh roh kal'uhs) *n.* 1. A genus of 15 species of hardy, long-lived, clump-forming perennials (Liliaceae). They have long, narrow, arching leaves and large lilylike flowers in a cluster at the top of leafless stems that stand well above the foliage. They are tough, adaptable, and virtually pest-free, a very nearly flawless plant; they will survive even the most casual gardener. Used in beds and borders, usually massed; also used in containers. The dwarf varieties are effective as edgings or in rock gardens. Commonly known as daylily. 2. [l.c.] A plant of this genus.

Hemiptelea (hih mihp tee'lee uh) *n.* A genus of a single species, *H. Davidii* (Ulmaceae), a small hardy deciduous tree. It has elliptic, finely toothed, elmlike leaves and intimidating spines to 4 inches long. Sometimes used as a hedge.

hemlock *n.* A common name for *Conium maculatum* (Umbelliferae), a lethally poisonous plant. It is a tall, erect, branching biennial, with a smooth, shiny, hollow stem (usually marked with purplish spots), elegant fernlike leaves, and white flowers in rounded clusters resembling Queen Anne's lace. It is widely naturalized in the Americas. The poison is the alkaloid conine.

hemlock spruce *n.* A common name for the genus *Tsuga;* also called hemlock. It is a genus of evergreen coniferous trees with slender horizontal branches, white-banded, flattened needles, and small brown cones that hang down from the branches. *T. Mertensiana* is commonly known as mountain hemlock; *T. Caroliniana* is commonly known as Carolina hemlock. Used as a background, screen, or hedge.

hemp *n.* 1. A common name for the genus *Cannabis,* an annual herbaceous plant, the fiber of which constitutes the hemp of commerce. Native to central Asia, it is now widely grown throughout the world. It is illegal to grow here in the United States without a government permit, as it is also the source of the recreational drug marijuana. 2. The tough, strong fiber of this plant, which is useful in making coarse fabrics, such as sailcloth, and in making ropes and cables.

hemp agrimony *n.* A common name for the genus *Eupatorium,* especially *E. cannabinum.* It is a downy perennial, 4 feet tall, with long, basal leaves and dense clusters of red, mauve, or white flowers. Also known as boneset and thoroughwort. Traditional in herb gardens, cottage gardens, and also used in borders and wild gardens.

hemp family *n.* A common name for *Cannabaceae,* a family of 2 genera, *Cannabis* (marijuana) and *Humulus* (hops).

hemp nettle *n.* A common name for the genus *Galeopsis.* They are erect, coarse, bristly annual weeds resembling hemp somewhat in appearance, with stiff hairs reminding one of nettle. Widely naturalized in the United States.

hemp palm *n.* A common name for the palm *Chamaerops humilis.* It is a tender, clump-forming dwarf palm with fan-shaped leaves borne on prickly stems and a small berrylike fruit. Commonly known as fan palm, dwarf palm, or palmetto. 2. A common name for *Rhapis excelsa,* a short, clumping palm with a fiber-covered trunk and fan-shaped leaves. Also called bamboo palm, slender-lady palm, miniature fan palm, and fern rhapis.

hemp tree *n.* A common name for *Vitex Agnus-castus,* also known as chaste tree, native to southern Europe and naturalized in the southern United States as well as the warmer parts of the world. It is a deciduous aromatic shrub or small tree with dark green fanlike leaves, with long narrow leaflets, and spikes of lavender-blue flowers in summer and fall. It grows to 20 feet in low deserts, to 6 feet in coastal areas, and blooms best with summer heat. Also called monk's pepper tree, sage tree, Indian-spice tree, and wild pepper. (See **Vitex.**)

hempweed *n.* A common name for *Eupatorium cannabinum,* also called hemp agrimony. Climbing hempweed, *Mikania scandens,* is a climbing vine with clusters of lilac or purple flowers, native to the United States and tropical America.

hen and chickens *n.* A common name for plants of several genera, including *Bellis perennis,* a small plant with daisylike flowers; *Sempervivum montanum,* a succulent also called houseleek; the genus *Echeveria,* a genus of succulents; and *Glechoma hederacea,* also called ground ivy.

henbane

Hepatica
(liverleaf)

henbane *n.* A common name for the poisonous weed *Hyoscyamus niger* (Solanaceae), also called common henbane. It is widely naturalized in the United States. It is a coarse, erect biennial herb, having soft, clammy, hairy foliage of a disagreeable odor and pale yellowish-brown flowers streaked with purple veins. It yields the drug hyoscyamine. Also called black henbane, stinking nightshade, and hog's-bean or hog-bean.

henequen (hehn'ih kuhn) *n.* 1. A strong fiber, similar to sisal, which is produced from the leaves of a Central American agave and used mainly for making twine. 2. The plant from which this fiber is made. Also spelled heniquen.

henna (hehn'uh) *n.* The Egyptian privet or mignonette trees, *Lawsonia inermis,* a shrub bearing leaves in opposite pairs and numerous small and fragrant white flowers. The powdered leaves are used as a dye, producing a reddish-brown color.

he-oak *n.* A common name for the genus *Casuarina,* a genus of somber-looking evergreen Australian trees, having long, thin, threadlike, jointed, furrowed, drooping branches that look like pine needles. Useful in warm coastal climates and desert climates as it tolerates salt spray, salinity, dry or wet soil, heat, and wind. Used as a sentinel tree for its interesting silhouette, as a windbreak, as a specimen tree, or as a street tree. Also known as she-oak, beefwood, and Australian pine.

Hepatica (hih pat'ih kuh) *n.* A genus of 10 species of small, hardy, hairy evergreen perennials (Ra-

nunculaceae); the liverleaf. They have lobed, long-stemmed, thick leaves and stalks of white, purple, or blue flowers. Useful for naturalizing in woodland gardens.

Heracleum (her uh klee'uhm) *n.* A genus of 60 species of tall biennial and perennial plants (Umbelliferae), some species native to North America; cow parsnip. They have large, deeply cut, toothed leaves and umbrella-shaped clusters of small green, pink, yellow, or white flowers. An impressively large plant, it is usually seen growing wild but is occasionally used in wild gardens or as a specimen plant for its bold effect. The foliage may cause a skin rash.

Heracleum
(cow parsnip)

herb *n.* 1. A plant without woody, persistent stems above ground, as distinguished from a shrub or tree. 2. A plant used for its medicinal, aromatic, or savory qualities.

herbaceous (her bay′shuhs) *a*. 1. Not woody, pertaining to a plant or stem: dying to the ground each year, usually in winter, for example, peonies. 2. Leaflike in color texture.

herbage *n*. 1. Leafy vegetation. 2. The herbaceous parts of a plant.

herbal *a*. Pertaining to or consisting of herbs. *n*. 1. A book in which plants are classified and described; a treatise on the kinds, qualities, uses, etc., of plants; a book of systematic and medicinal botany. 2. An herbarium.

herbalism *n*. The knowledge of herbs.

herbalist *n*. 1. A person who is skilled in the knowledge of plants or makes collections of them. 2. A dealer in medicinal plants, or a person who treats disease with botanical remedies only.

herbarium *n*. A collection of dried plants systematically arranged. The plants are attached to sheets of paper, either by small gummed strips of paper or by gluing 1 side of the specimen.

herb Barbara *n*. A common name for *Barbarea vulgaris*, a winter cress native to both Europe and America.

herb Bennet *n*. A common name for the European plant *Geum urbanum*, also known as avens. It is aromatic and astringent, and it has been used in medicine.

herb carpenter *n*. The self-heal or heal-all, *Prunella vulgaris*.

herb Christopher *n*. A common name of several different plants, including *Osmunda regalis* (royal flowering fern), *Filipendula ulmaria* (meadowsweet), and *Stachys officinalis* (betony).

herb Gerard *n*. A common name for *Aegopodium Podagraria*, an invasive ground cover that often crosses the line between a vigorous ornamental and a troublesome weed. It is a fast-growing perennial that spreads by creeping rootstocks. It has light green divided leaves and small white or yellow flowers. *A. Podagraria* and its varigated form, *A.P. Cv. 'Varigatum'*, are both used as ground covers and edgings. Also called bishop's-weed, goutweed, ashweed, ground ash, and ground elder.

herb-grace *n*. (See **rue**.)

herb Louisa *n*. The lemon verbena, *Aloysia triphylla*, a shrub from Chile with lemon-scented leaves.

herb Margaret *n*. The English daisy, *Bellis perennis*.

herb-of-grace *n*. The common rue, *Ruta graveolens*. Also called herb-grace, herb-of-repentance, and herb-repentance.

herborist *n*. An herbalist.

herborization *n*. An excursion for studying or collecting plants.

herb-repentance *n*. Same as herb-of-gracxe, or rue. (See **rue**.)

herb Robert *n*. A common name for *Geranium Robertianum*, native to North America in woods or damp places. Also known as garden-gate and red robin.

herb robert
a fruit

herb trinity *n*. A common name for *Viola tricolor*, so called in reference to the 3 colors in 1 flower. Also known as pansy and Johnny-jump-up. 2. A common name for *Hepatica americana* and *H. nobilis*, so called in reference to the 3 leaves or lobes in 1 leaf. (See **Hepatica**.)

hercogamous (her kagh′uh muhs) *a*. Incapable of self-pollination.

hercogamy (her kahg′uh mee) *n.* A condition in which structural obstacles within a flower make self-pollination impossible.

Hercules'-club *n.* A common name for *Aralia spinosa* (Araliaceae), native to the United States. It is a small, clump-forming tree, to 30 feet high, with huge, divided leaves, dense, stout thorns, and clusters of small white or greenish flowers. The foliage gives a subtropical effect. Also called angelica tree, and devil's-walking-stick.

Heritiera (hehr uh tihr′uh) *n.* A genus of about 30 species of tropical trees (Sterculiaceae). They are handsome trees of considerable size, with alternate, simple leaves and clusters of small flowers.

Hermannia (her man′ee uh) *n.* A genus of more than 100 species of plants and small shrubs (Byttneriaceae). They have alternate, simple leaves and clusters of 5-petaled, nodding, fragrant yellow flowers. *H. verticillatais* commonly known as honey bells.

hermaphrodite (her maf′ruh dight) *n.* In botany, a flower that exhibits the characteristics of both sexes; specifically, having fully developed stamens and pistils within the same flower. (See **perfect**.) *a.* Same as hermaphroditic.

hermaphroditic (her maf′ruh diht ihk) *a.* Bisexual; exhibiting the characteristics of both sexes; specifically, having fully developed stamens and pistils within the same flower. Same as hemaphrodite.

Hernandia (huhr nan′dee ah) *n.* A genus of 14 species of tropical trees (Hernandiaceae). It has large, alternate, heart-shaped leaves and clusters of small greenish-yellow flowers.

Hernandia
flower and leaf

Hernandiaceae (huhr nan dee ay′shee ee) *n. pl.* A family of plants, of 4 tropical genera, typified by the genus *Hernandia*.

Herniaria (huhr nee a′ree uh) *n.* A genus of 35 species of small prostrate plants (Caryophyllaceae). They have small entire leaves and clusters of minute flowers. *H. glabra* is commonly known as rupturewort. Used in rock gardens or on rock walls.

heron's-bill *n.* A common name for the genus *Erodium* (Geraniaceae), from the supposed resemblance of the long-beaked fruit to the head and beak of a heron. They have round, scalloped leaves and clusters of 5-petaled purple, violet, rose, white, or yellow flowers. Used in sunny borders or rock gardens or as a small-scale ground cover; some species are weeds. Also called heronbill or stork's-bill.

Hesperaloe (hehs′per ah loh) *n.* A genus of 3 species of evergreen perennials (Agavaceae) native to northern Mexico and adjacent United States. They have narrow, fibrous, basal leaves, to 6 feet long, which form grasslike clumps, and very tall stalks of bell-shaped green, lavender, pink, or red flowers, some to 8 feet. Grown as a specimen plant with other desert plants or as a container plant. Tolerates drought and desert sun.

hesperidium (heh spuh rihd′ee uhm) *n., pl.* **hesperidia** (uh) In botany, a fruit with a leathery rind, such as an orange.

Hesperis (hehs′puh rihs) *n.* A genus of 24 species of biennial or perennial erect, much-branched flowers (Cruciferae); rocket. They have narrow, mostly entire leaves, and showy, large, loose spikes of white, rose, mauve, or purple flowers, sometimes fragrant. *H. matronalis* is commonly known as dame's rocket, dame's violet, or sweet rocket. Traditional in cottage gardens, it has naturalized in North America.

Heteranthera (hehd uh ran′thuh ruh) *n.* A genus of 10 species of aquatic herbs (Pontederiaceae), native mostly to North and South America; mud plantain. They grow in mud or shallow water, have submerged or floating leaves, which may be rounded or narrow, and blue, white, or yellow flowers. Used chiefly in aquariums.

heterauxesis (hehd′uh awk see′suhs) *n.* In botany, the irregular growth of a plant due to unequal rates of growth in its parts.

heterodromous (hehd uh rahd′ruh muhs) *a.* Having the genetic spiral of the branches different from that of the main stem, affecting, for example, the way in which leaves are arranged around a stem.

heterodromy (hehd uh rahd'ruh mee) *n*. In botany, a difference in direction of the genetic spiral in the branch and the main stem.

heterogamous (hehd uh rahg'uh muhs) *a*. In botany, bearing 2 kinds of flowers in which the sexual parts are different.

heterogamy (hehd uh rahg'uh mee) *n*. The condition of being heterogamous.

Heteromeles (hehd uh ruh mehl'eez) *n*. A genus of a single species, *Heteromeles arbutifolia* (Rosaceae), native to California and Baja California and common in the coastal ranges of California from Mendocino Country south to Mexico and east to the Sierra Nevada. It is a shrub or small tree, with simple, dark, shiny, evergreen, sharply toothed leaves, and flat clusters of small white flowers, and bright red fruit that attracts birds. The contrast between the clusters of bright red fruit and the dark, shiny foliage is strikingly ornamental. Commonly known as toyon and California holly.

heteromerous (hehd uh rahm'uh ruhs) *a*. In botany, of flowers, having the parts of adjoining whorls different in number.

heteromorphic (hehd uh ruh mor'fihk) *a*. Having irregular, abnormal, or unusual structure, as the leaves of a young plant. Also heteromorphous.

heteromorphism (hehd uh ruh mor'fihz uhm) *n*. The condition of being heteromorphic.

heterophyllous (hehd uh roh fihl'uhs) *a*. In botany, having 2 different kinds of leaves on the same stem.

heterophylly (hehd uh roh fihl'ee) *n*. In botany, the condition of being heterophyllous.

heterosporous (hehd uh ruh spor'uhs) *a*. Having more than 1 kind of asexually produced spores (applied to ferns).

heterostyled (hehd uh roh stigh'uhld) *a*. Having the styles of the flower of 2 or more different forms.

heterotactic (hehd uh roh tak'tihk) *a*. Characterized by heterotaxis. Also heterotactous.

heterotaxis (hehd uh roh tak'sihs) *n*. Abnormal arrangement of parts or organs as compared to a normal type.

Heuchera (hyoo'kuh ruh) *n*. A genus of 35 to 50 perennial flowers (Saxifragaceae), native mostly to western North America; coralbells or alumroot. They are low-growing flowers with rounded, heart-shaped, scalloped basal leaves and slim stalks with clusters of nodding, bell-shaped red, white, or coral flowers. Used for edging, beds, and borders.

Heuchera
(coralbells)
a flower stalk *b* root and leaves

Hevea (hee'vee uh) *n*. A genus of 9 species of tropical trees (Euphorbiaceae) native to South America. They secrete a milky juice and have 3-part leaves and loose clusters of small white flowers without petals. Formerly, the best source for natural rubber.

hexapetaloid (hehk suh peht'uh loid) *a*. Of a flower, having 6 petals. Also hexapetalous.

Hibbertia (hih buhr'shuh) *n*. A genus of about 100 species of erect or sprawling shrubs and vines (Dilleniaceae). They are small- to medium-sized shrubs with slender trailing or climbing stems, alternate, simple leaves, and clusters of showy yellow flowers. Useful in warm-winter climates.

Hibbertia
flowering branch

hibernaculum (high buhr nak'yuh luhm) *n.*, *pl.* **hibernacula** (-la) In botany, the part of a plant that is dormant in winter, as a bud or bulb.

Hibiscus moscheutos
(rose mallow)

Hibiscus (high bihs'kuhs) *n.* 1. A genus of 250 species of flowers, shrubs, or trees (Malvaceae) native to tropical and warm temperate regions. They have simple or lobed leaves and very large, bell-shaped red, purple, yellow, or white flowers, usually with a dark-colored eye. *H. rosa-sinensis* has toothed, glossy green leaves and large, handsome white, red, yellow, or apricot flowers; there are many cultivars. It is commonly known as Hawaiian hibiscus, Chinese hibiscus, China rose, rose-of-China, and blackening plant. *Hibiscus syriacus,* commonly known as rose-of-Sharon, or althea, is a shrub or small tree with small triangular, deeply lobed leaves and with white, red, purple, or blue-lavender flowers with a red eye. *H. Moscheutos,* native to the midwestern and eastern United States, is

commonly known as common rose mallow, mallow rose, swamp rose mallow, and wild cotton. It grows to 8 feet tall, with huge—up to 1 foot across—lobed leaves, which are green above and downy white beneath, and pink, rose, or white flowers with a crimson eye. 2. [l.c.] A plant of this genus.

hickory *n.* 1. A common name for deciduous nut trees of the North American genus *Carya* (Juglandaceae). It has alternate, divided leaves, drooping catkins, and nuts encased in a thick green husk, the meats of which are particularly sweet. (See **Carya.**) Grown both for its nuts and for use as a summer shade tree. 2. The wood of this tree, which is heavy, strong, and flexible.

hickory
a nuts

hickory acacia (uh kay'shuh) *n.* A common name for a tall tender shrub or small tree, *Acacia leprosa* (Leguminosae). It has drooping branchlets, long, narrow, leaflike stems, and clusters of yellow flowers.

hickory elm *n.* A common name for *Ulmus Thomasii,* native to the eastern and midwestern United States. A large, hardy, column-shaped tree with ridged, corky branches, furry buds, and large, toothed leaves to 6 inches long that are smooth on top and downy beneath. Also called rock elm and cork elm.

hickory nut *n.* The small, hard-shelled, sweet-flavored nut of the North American hickory tree. The hickory nut is enclosed in a thick firm husk, which at maturity splits open spontaneously at 4 seams. The meat yields a large amount of excellent

213

oil. Grown both for its nuts and its use as a summer shade tree.

hickory pine *n.* A common name for *Pinus aristata,* native to the mountains of California and Colorado; also called bristlecone pine. In the eastern United States, hickory pine refers to *P. pungens,* also called table-mountain pine. (See **Pinus.**)

hickory, shagbark *n.* A common name for *Carya ovata,* the most prized of the hickory nuts other than pecan. It has a shaggy bark, grows to 120 feet tall, and has elliptic, 6-inch long leaves and white-husked nuts. Also known as shellbark hickory.

Hieracium (high uh ray'see uhm) *n.* A genus of between 700 and 1,000 species of perennials (rarely annuals) (Compositae); hawkweed. The leaves are often toothed, and the cylindrical or bell-shaped flowers are generally in loose clusters. *H. venosum,* a native of the eastern United States, is called rattlesnake weed. *H. aurantiacum,* native to Europe, is known as orange hawkweed, king-devil, or grim-the-collier, on account of the black hairs on the flower stalk. *H. pilosella* is commonly known as mouse-ear. Some hawkweeds are grown in rock gardens; others, such as *H. aurantiacum,* are troublesome weeds.

Hieracium venosum
(rattlesnake weed)
a leaf rosette withroot *b* flower stalk

high mallow *n.* A common name for *Malva sylvestris,* a European plant, now naturalized in the eastern United States. It is a fast-growing, erect, bushy biennial, usually grown as an annual, with rough, coarse hairs on the stems, heart-shaped or rounded leaves, and large, pale lavender-pink flowers with dark purple veins. Used for fast, tall edgings or in borders.

high-wheel cultivator *n.* A machine composed of 2 handles attached to a wheel, behind which are mounted tines for loosening soil and destroying weeds.

hilar *a.* In botany, belonging to the hilum, or scar, on a seed produced by the attachment to the pod, as with beans.

hill *n.* 1. A small raised mound or raised row with a cluster of cultivated plants, as a hill of potatoes. 2. A group of vining plants or others planted in a cluster instead of a row, such as a hill of squash or pumpkin, even if the soil is not mounded above the level of the garden.

hillock tree *n.* A common name for the evergreen shrub *Melaleuca hypericifolia.* It grows from 6 to 10 feet, has small opposite, coppery-green leaves, and dense clusters of bright orange-red flowers. Tolerates wind and drought.

hills-of-snow *n.* A common name for the North American species *Hydrangea arborescens,* a much-branched shrub from four to ten feet with oval gray-green leaves, downy beneath, and large rounded clusters of small white flowers, some with a lace-cap effect. Also called smooth hydrangea, wild hydrangea, and seven-bark.

hillwort *n.* The pennyroyal, *Mentha pulegium.*

hilum (high'luhm) *n., pl.* **hila** (-luh) In botany, the scar on a seed marking its point of attachment, as with beans or peas.

hinau tree (hee'now) *n.* A common name for *Elaeocarpus dentatus,* a tall tree native to New Zealand. It grows to 60 feet, has long, narrow or oblong leaves, clusters of small white flowers, and little purplish-gray fruits. Grown in warm-winter gardens.

hip *n.* The fruit of the dogrose or wild brier, *Rosa canina* or *R. Eglanteria,* high in vitamin C. The dried hip is commonly used as tea, and the ripe hip is made into jelly.

hipberry *n.* The hip or fruit of the rose. (See **hip**.)

Hippeastrum (hihp ee as'truhm) *n.* A genus of 75 species of perennial bulbs (Amaryllidaceae) native mostly to tropical America. They grow from large bulbs, with strap-shaped basal leaves and tall, sturdy stalks with showy clusters of large red, pink, white, salmon, and apricot trumpet-shaped flowers. Grown mainly as container plants; must be lifted in cold- or wet-winter climates. Commonly known as amaryllis or barbados lily.

Hippobroma (hihp uh broh'muh) *n.* A genus of a single species, *H. longiflora* (Lobeliaceae), native to the West Indies. It is a poisonous herbaceous perennial with long, simple, alternate leaves and small tubular white flowers. It has become a weed in the tropics.

Hippocastanaceae (hihp uh kas tuh nay'see ee) *n. pl.* An order of 2 genera and 15 species native to the Northern Hemisphere; the horse-chestnut family. Most species are trees with alternate leaves divided fan-wise into large, toothed leaflets and with showy red, white, or yellow flowers that attract hummingbirds. The fruits are a leathery, warty, or smooth capsule enclosing a large, rich-brown nut, commonly known as a buckeye. The only genus grown ornamentally is *Aesculus,* the horse-chestnut tree. Several species are magnificent flowering shade trees.

Hippocrepis (hihp uh kreep'uhs) *n.* A genus of 12 species of tender trailing or shrubby perennials (Leguminosae); the horseshoe vetch. They have alternate leaves divided into many small leaflets, clusters of sweet pea-shaped yellow flowers, and crooked pods. *H. comosa,* the common horseshoe vetch, is used as a small-scale lawn substitute, as a ground cover on steep banks, or in rock gardens.

Hippophae (hih pah'fee ee) *n.* A genus of 2 species of spiny shrubs or trees (Elaeagnaceae). *H. rhamnoides* is a thorny shrub with long narrow, willowlike silvery leaves and masses of bright yellow berries, which are tart and edible. Commonly known as sea buckthorn.

Hippuris (hih pyoo'ruhs) *n.* A genus of a single species, *H. vulgaris* (Hippuridaceae), a marsh or aquatic plant. It is an erect herb, with crowded whorls of narrow, hairlike leaves and inconspicuous flowers, which are also whorled. Occasionally grown in bog gardens or ponds. Commonly called mare's tail.

Hiptage (hihp tay'jee) *n.* A small genus of 25 species of tropical shrubs and vines (Malpighiaceae). *H. bengalensis* has opposite, simple, leathery leaves and spikes of 5-petaled, fragrant white flowers. Grown in tropical gardens for its fragrant flowers.

hirse (hers) *n.* The broomcorn, *Sorghum bicolor.*

hirsute (huhr soot') *a.* Having coarse, rough hairs.

hispid (hihs'puhd) *a.* Having stiff, bristly hairs or tiny spines.

hispidity (hihs pihd'uh tee) *n.* The state of being hispid.

hispidulous (hihs pihd'yoo luhs) *a.* In botany, somewhat hispid.

Histiopteris (hihs tee ahp'tuh ruhs) *n.* A genus of 10 species of tropical terrestrial ferns (Polypodiaceae) with long, creeping, furry rhizomes. *H. incisa* has huge, shiny, climbing leaves to 10 feet long on 6-foot stems.

hive vine *n.* A common name for the genus *Mitchella,* particularly *M. repens,* hardy evergreen trailing perennials native to North America. It has tiny, glossy dark green leaves, small white flowers, and little red berries, which are edible but tasteless. Also called partridgeberry, two-eye berry, running box, and twinberry. Used in rock gardens or as a ground cover under trees.

hoary *a.* Covered with white or grayish down or hairs, as a leaf.

hobblebush

hobblebush *n.* A common name for *Viburnum alnifolium,* a vert hardy deciduous shrub native to North America from New Brunswick to Michigan and North Carolina. It has rounded, heart-shaped leaves, broad, flat clusters of handsome, white flowers, followed by clusters of brilliantly colored

red fruit that turns purple-black. The leaves turn claret in fall, and the fruit attracts birds. Also known as American wayfaring tree, devil's shoe-strings, dogberry, dog hobble, moosewood, moosebush, mooseberry, tanglefoot, tangle-legs, trip-toe, White Mountain dogwood, and witch hobble.

hoe *n.* Any of various implements having a long handle attached to a transverse blade; used for cultivating and weeding. *v.* 1. To cut, dig, scrape, or clean with a hoe; to clear from weeds or cultivate with a hoe, as to hoe turnips or cabbages; the breaking up of the soil crust to ½ to 1 inch deep by hand. 2. To use a hoe.

hoe

hog bean *n.* A common name for the poisonous weed *Hyoscyamus niger (Solanaceae),* also called hog's-bean. (See **henbane**.)

hognut *n.* A common name for *Carya glabra,* also called pignut or broom hickory.

hog peanut *n.* A common name for the genus *Amphicarpaea* (Leguminosae), a genus of twining herbaceous vines. *A. bracteata,* native to North America, has purplish flowers at the top, which seldom produce fruit, and others at the base, which produce fleshy, 1-seeded pods that ripen underground or on the ground under fallen leaves.

hog plum *n.* A common name for *Prunus angustifolia,* native to the the eastern United States; also called Chickasaw plum. Also a common name for *Spondias Mombin* (Anacardiaceae).

Hoheria (hoh hee′ree uh) *n.* A genus of 2 to 5 species of tender small trees and shrubs (Malvaceae). They have leathery, toothed bright green leaves and clusters of pure white flowers. Some, such as *H. populnea,* commonly known as lacebark, have interesting bark texture. Useful as graceful, summer-flowering trees, they are especially attractive when planted in clumps, like birch, or in woodland plantings. *H. glabrata* is commonly known as mountain ribbonwood.

Holboellia (hohl bul′ee uh) *n.* A genus of 10 species of hardy twining vines (Lardizabalaceae). They have alternate, long-stemmed leaves divided into a fan of leaflets and bear spikes or clusters of purple, white, or greenish flowers.

Holcus (hahl′kuhs) *n.* A genus of 6 to 8 species of annual or perennial grasses (Gramineae). The best-known species is *H. mollis,* which can be a very invasive weed; however, *H.m.* 'Albo-variegatus' is more restrained, has leaves with green and white striping, and is a more worthy garden subject. Commonly known as velvet grass.

holly *n.* 1. A common name for plants of the genus *Ilex,* particularly *I. Aquifolium,* a hardy evergreen shrub or tree also known as English holly. *I. opaca* and *I. cassine* are hollies native to the United States. They are evergreen trees, similar in appearance to English holly. (See **Ilex** and **holly, English**.)

holly
a female flower *b* male flower

holly, box *n.* A common name for *Ruscus aculeatus,* a tender evergreen shrub with small, stiff, spiny-pointed, dark green leaves and red or yellow berries. Used by florists for winter decorations and grown in mild-winter climates. Also called butcher's-broom.

holly, California *n.* A common name for *Heteromeles arbutifolia,* an evergreen shrub or small tree native to Western North America. (See **Heteromeles**.)

holly, English *n.* A common name for *I. Aquifolium.* It grows from 20 to 40 feet tall, with prickly, thick, leathery, dark green, glossy leaves and clusters of small, white flowers followed by shiny, red, round berries. The species has been much hybridized, and there are many cultivars, some with a blue cast to the leaves, some variegated with white or yellow, some quite dwarf. It is widely used as a specimen shrub and as a clipped hedge; the smaller varieties are useful in containers. The branches and berries are traditional winter-holiday decorations.

holly family *n*. A common name for Aquifoliaceae.

holly fern *n*. A common name for the ferns *Cyrtomium falcatum* and *Polystichum Lonchitis,* which have leaflets shaped rather like holly leaves; *Arachniodes aristata* is the East Indian holly fern.

hollygrape *n*. A common name for the genus *Mahonia.* They are shrubs with long, holly-shaped leaves, spiky clusters of yellow flowers, and blue-purple berries in grapelike clusters. The new, young leaves are reddish, turning green at maturity, and bronzy or purplish in cold weather. Also called Oregon grape.

hollyhock *n*. A common name for the genus *Alcea* (Malvaceae). There are many varieties, with large single and double flowers, characterized by the tints of white, yellow, red, purple, and dark purple approaching to black. Old-fashioned hollyhocks grow to 9 feet; newer hybrids are 5 to 6 feet tall. Traditional in cottage gardens, at the back of the border, and to create a nostalgic effect.

hollyhock-rose *n*. A common name for *Selaginella lepidophylla,* a dense, stiff, densely tufted moss that dries up and turns brown in drought and turns green and resumes growth with the application of water; native to the Americas. Also called resurrection plant.

holly laurel *n*. A common name for *Prunus ilicifolia,* native to California. It is a dense, evergreen shrub or small tree with shiny, leathery, oval or round leaves with spiny teeth, spikes of tiny white flowers, and small red fruits. Also called holly-leaved cherry and islay.

holly rose *n*. A common name for *Turnera ulmifolia,* a West Indian shrub with downy stems, long, toothed leaves, and yellow flowers that open only in the morning. Also called yellow alder.

holly, sea *n*. A common name for *Eryngium maritimum,* a perennial with stiff, dusty-blue leaves and striking steel-blue or amethyst flowers, surrounded by spiny blue bracts. Also known as eryngo. (See **Eryngium**.)

holm *n*. A common name for *Quercus Ilex,* an evergreen oak. Same as holly oak and holm oak.

holm oak *n*. A common name for *Quercus Ilex,* an evergreen oak. Same as holly oak.

Holmskioldia (hohm shohl dee′uh) *n*. A genus of 10 species of tropical shrubs (Verbenaceae). *H. sanguinea* has opposite, simple leaves and clusters or spikes of large, showy brick-red or orange flowers. Also called Chinese hat plant, Mandarin's-hat, and cup-and-saucer plant. Grown in warm-winter climates.

Holodiscus (hahl oh dihs′kuhs) *n*. A genus of a few species of deciduous shrubs or small trees (Rosaceae) native to western North America. They have simple, alternate, toothed leaves and nodding, branched clusters of small, creamy-white flowers that attract birds. Useful in woodland gardens. *H. discolor* is commonly known as ocean spray and creambush; *H. dumosus* is also called mountain spray or rock spirea.

holster *n*. A case, typically of leather, attached to the belt at the hip; used for carrying a tool, such as a pruner.

Holy-Ghost *n*. The wild angelica of Europe, *Angelica sylvestris.*

Holy Ghost flower *n*. A common name for *Peristeria elata,* an epiphytic orchid native to tropical America. It has long, narrow leaves to 3 feet long and spikes of 10 to 15 waxy, fragrant white flowers resembling a flock of doves in flight. This is the national flower of Panama. Also called doveflower and dove orchid. Same as dove plant.

holy herb *n*. A former name for *Verbena officinalis* (vervain).

Homalocladium (hoh mahl uh klay′dee uhm) *n*. A genus of 1 species *H. platycladum* (Polygonaceae), a tropical deciduous shrub. It has flat, articulated, striped conelike stems that are leafless during flowering; the greenish flowers are in small clusters at alternate joints. The narrow leaves appear after the plant has bloomed. Commonly known as centipede plant, tapeworm plant, and ribbonbush.

Homalomena (hoh mahl uh mee′nuh) *n*. A genus of 130 species of tropical flowers (Araceae), some species native to tropical America. They have entire leaves and anthuriumlike green, white, or red spathes. Grown in hothouses.

homogamous (hoh mahg′uh muhs) *a*. In botany: 1. Of a plant, having all the flowers alike. 2. Of a flower, having the stamens and pistils maturing at the same period.

homogamy (hoh mahg'uh mee) *n.* The state of being homogamous.

homogonous (hoh mahg'uh nuhs) *a.* In botany, having stamens and pistils of the same height in members of the same species.

homogony (hoh mahg'uh nee) *n.* The state of being homogonous.

homomallous (hoh muh mal'uhs) *a.* In botany, referring to the leaves of mosses, curving to one side.

homopetalous (hoh muh peht'uh luhs) *a.* In botany, having all the petals formed alike.

homosporous (hoh muh spor'uhs) *a.* Producing only 1 kind of spore.

homostyled (hoh'muh stigh uhld) *a.* In botany, of a flower, having all styles of 1 length.

honesty *n.* In botany, a name for several plants, especially for the small plant *Lunaria annua* (Cruciferae), so called from the transparency of its round, flat seed coverings. The perennial honesty is *L. rediviva.*

honewort *n.* A common name for several herbs, such as *Cryptotaenia canadensis,* also called white chervil, and *Sison amomum,* also called stone parsley.

honey bell *n.* A common name for *Hermannia verticillata (Byttneriaceae),* a low-growing subshrub. It has alternate, simple leaves and clusters of nodding, 5-petaled, fragrant yellow flowers.

honeyberry *n.* A common name for *Celtis australis,* a tall, tender tree with long, narrow leaves, inconspicuous flowers, and dark purple berries that attract birds. Also known as Mediterranean hackberry, European hackberry, European nettle tree, and lote tree.

honeybloom *n.* A common name for *Apcynum androsaemifolium,* a hardy perennial native to North America. It grows to 2 feet and has opposite, entire, oval leaves and small, bell-shaped pink flowers. Also known as spreading dogbane. Used in the perennial border.

honey bread *n.* A common name for *Ceratonia siliqua,* a small drought-tolerant and fire-retardant evergreen tree (Leguminosae) native to the eastern Mediterranean. The dense, dark green leaves are alternate and divided into round leaflets; the small red flowers bloom in spring. The pods, often called locust beans, contain a sweet pulp used as a substitute for chocolate. Also known as the carob tree and Saint-John's-bread.

honeybush *n.* A common name for *Melianthus,* a genus of adaptable, fast-growing, tender evergreen shrubs. They have striking foliage—1-foot-long gray-green leaves divided into strongly toothed leaflets—and, in late winter or early spring, tall spikes of showy dark red flowers, which attract bees. Grown in mild-winter climates for their interesting silhouette, sprawling over a wall, or in containers.

honeybush, large *n.* A common name for *Melianthus major.* It is an adaptable, fast-growing, tender evergreen shrub with striking foliage—1-foot-long gray-green leaves divided into strongly toothed leaflets—and tall spikes of showy, dark red flowers in late winter or early spring. Attracts bees. The foliage smells bad when bruised. Also known as honeyflower.

honeydew *n.* 1. A sweet substance found on the leaves of trees and other plants in small drops, like dew. There are 2 kinds, 1 secreted from the plants and the other by plant lice, bark lice, and leaf hoppers. The name is properly applied to the sugary secretion from the leaves of plants, occurring most frequently in hot weather. It usually appears as small glistening drops, but if particularly abundant, it may drip from the leaves in considerable quantity, when it has been called manna. The manna ash, *Fraxinus Ornus,* exhibits this phenomenon, as does *Carduus arctiodes.* 2. A variety of smooth-skinned melon, *Cucumis melo.*

honeydew *n.* A sweetish secretion exuded by many insects, including aphids, mealybugs, scale, and whiteflies. The secretion attracts ants, which harvest the honeydew and protect the pests from natural predators. It also develops a blackish mold, known as sooty mold. Heavily infested plants, especially trees, drip honeydew, staining anything underneath, often cars. The best control is to exclude ants (banding with sticky materials is effective) from the plant and then try to control the source pest. Insecticidal soaps will help clean the foliage.

honeydewed *a.* Covered with honeydew, usually referring to foliage and buds.

honeyflower *n.* A common name for *Melianthus major,* a tender ornamental shrub, the flowers of which yield much honey. (See **honeybush** and **honeybush, large.**) It is also a common name for *Lambertia formosa,* a tall Australian shrub with long, narrow leaves and clusters of red or yellow flowers; also called mountain devil. Also, a name for *Protea mellifera,* a South African shrub with shiny, narrow, oblong leaves and 5-inch heads of white-to-red flowers that attract bees. Also called sugarbush.

honey locust *n.* A common name for the genus *Gleditsia,* ornamental North American trees. They are fast-growing deciduous trees, usually covered with stout spines, with spreading, arching branches, much-divided leaves with oval leaflets, inconspicuous flowers, and dramatic 18-inch pods filled with sweet pulp. Exceedingly adaptable, they tolerate cold, heat, wind, drought, and any soil from acid to alkaline; they will thrive even in the most desolate site.

honey mesquite *n.* A common name for *Prosopis juliflora,* a small, spiny, deep-rooted tree or shrub of the southwestern United States and Mexico. It forms large thickets and has pods that are rich in sugar. Also called honeypod, algarrobo, or mesquite.

honeypod *n.* Same as honey mesquite.

honeysuckle *n.* 1. A common name for the genus *Lonicera* (Caprifoliaceae), upright or twining, sometimes deciduous, vines or shrubs. They have simple, opposite leaves, and often fragrant white, red, or yellow flowers, which are succeeded by sweetish red berries. The common honeysuckle, *L. Periclymenum,* is also known as woodbine. *L. sempervirens* (trumpet or coral honeysuckle), native to North America, is cultivated for the beauty of its large, unscented flowers, which are red outside and yellow inside. *L. canadensis* is the American fly honeysuckle; it has a honey-yellow corolla slightly tinged with red. *L. Tatarica,* the Tatarian honeysuckle, is a dense, upright shrub with small pink or rose flowers and bright red winter berries. Honey-

suckles often attract hummingbirds to their tubular flowers and other birds to their berries. 2. A plant of some other genus. The name honeysuckle is often applied to the genus *Aquilegia* (Columbine), particularly to the native wild columbine, *A. canadensis.* Also to *Rhododendron prinophyllum* (Ericaceae); the purple honeysuckle, *R. periclymenoides;* and the swamp honeysuckle, *R. viscosum.* Honeysuckle is also used as a common name for *Justicia californica,* a small desert shrub, often leafless, with arched branches and short spikes of tubular red flowers. (See **Lonicera**, **Justicia**, and **Rhododendron.**) 3. The flower of any of the above plants.

trumpet honeysuckle

honeysuckle clover *n.* A common name for any clover rich in nectar. Such clovers attract bees.

honeysuckled *a.* Covered with honeysuckles.

honeysuckle family *n.* A common name for Caprifoliaceae.

honeywort *n.* A common name for plants of the genus *Cerinthe* (Boraginaceae). *C. major* is a European annual, 1 to 2 feet high, with heart-shaped leaves and yellow and purple flowers that secrete much honey.

Hoodia *n.* A genus of 16 species of leafless perennial succulents (Asclepiadaceae). They have many-angled, spiny stems and clusters of cup-shaped light yellow flowers 3 inches across.

hook climber *n.* A plant that climbs by the aid of hooks or prickles, such as certain types of roses.

hookweed *n.* A common name for the mint *Prunella vulgaris* (Labiatae), also called heal-all or self-heal. It is a creeping plant with long stems, oval leaves, and deep violet-blue or white flowers. Traditional in herb gardens and cottage gardens; also used in rock gardens and shady borders.

hoop ash *n.* 1. A common name for the tree *Fraxinus sambucifolia,* a species of ash. Also called black ash and ground ash.

hoop-petticoat daffodil *n.* A common name for the miniature daffodil *Narcissus Bulbocodium,* so called from the unusual shape of its yellow flowers. (See **Narcissus.**)

hoop pine *n.* A common name for *Araucaria Cunninghamii,* a large tender, coniferous tree. Grown for its striking silhouette of upturned branches, it can tower to more than 100 feet at maturity, a size that makes it best suited to parklands and great estates. Also called the Moreton Bay pine.

hoops *n.* Riblike structures, generally of wire, used to support fabric, such as plastic or mesh, covering a row of plants.

hop *n.* A perennial vine, *Humulus Lupulus,* with long twining stems and abundant 3- to 5-lobed leaves. The female flowers, which grow in catkins, are used to flavor malt liquors and to preserve them from fermentation, their active properties depending on the presence of an aromatic and mildy narcotic resin, called lupulin, secreted by the scales and fruit.

hopbine *n.* The climbing or twining stem of the hop plant. Same as hopbind.

hopbush *n.* A common name for the shrubs *Dodonaea viscosa* and *D. cuneata* (Sapindaceae). *D. viscosa* is native to the southwestern United States and Central America. *D. cuneata* grows to 15 feet tall and has willowlike leaves and attractive creamy-to-pinkish winged fruit. *D. viscosa* cv. 'Purpurea' has rich bronzy-purple leaves. Used as an espalier, a hedge, or an informal screen.

hop frame *n.* A trellis or frame of poles or wires, on which growing hopvines may be supported.

hop hornbeam *n.* A common name for *Ostrya,* a genus of hardy trees. They grow to 60 feet, have alternate, toothed leaves, flowers in catkins, and clusters of nuts resembling hops.

hop marjoram (mahr′juh ruhm) *n.* A amall herb, *Origanum Dictamnus,* more commonly known as dittany of Crete. The reference to hops derives from its small flowers, which resemble hops blossoms.

hopper *n.* A tray or basket in which a sower carries seed; a seed basket.

hopper spreader *n.* A 2-wheeled machine composed of a cylinder mounted on an axle. The rotating blades of a hopper spreader distribute seed, fertilizer, lime, or other bulk material in an even pattern, adjustable from wide to narrow, at a uniform rate.

hop picker *n.* 1. One who picks hops. 2. A contrivance for picking hops; specifically, a combined mill and cleaning machine for stripping hops from the vines, sorting them, and freeing the catkins from the leaves and stems.

hop pole *n.* A slender pole, from 18 to 25 feet in height, used to support a hop vine.

hop tree *n.* A common name for *Ptelea trifoliata,* a North American shrub or small tree. It has 3-part leaves and small clusters greenish-white flowers. The winged fruit is bitter and is used as a substitute for hops. Also called wafer ash.

hop tree
a male flower *b* female flower *c* fruit

hop trefoil *n.* A common name for *Trifolium procumbens* (Leguminosae), a European clover, naturalized in the United States. Also called yellow clover.

hopvine *n.* The climbing stem or vine of the hop plant, *Humulus Lupulus.*

hopyard (hahp'yahrd) _n._ A field or an enclosure where hops are raised.

Hordeum (hor'dee uhm) _n._ A genus of about 30 species of annual and perennial grasses (Gramineae) native to temperate regions. It includes _H. vulgare_ (the cereal crop, barley) and _H. jubatum_ (the ornamental foxtail or squirreltail barley). Foxtail barley is an exceptionally beautiful grass, with soft, fluffy, arching seed heads that resemble a fox's tail.

horehound _n._ The popular name of the common or white horehound, _Marrubium vulgare,_ naturalized in North America. It is an erect, branched herb, covered with cottony white hairs; the flowers are small and almost white, and the leaves are plae green. The black horehound is _Ballota nigra._ The water horehound is 1 of the various species of _Lycopus._

horizon soil _n._ A layer of soil approximately parallel to the soil surface.

Horminum (hor migh'nuhm) _n._ A genus of a single species, _H. pyrenaicum_ (Labiatae), a perennial that grows from rhizomes. It has basal, heart-shaped, scalloped leaves and showy violet-blue or white flowers. Used in rock gardens; particularly well adapted to lime soils. Commonly known as dragon-mouth.

hormone _n._ Any of certain chemical substances that are produced by living cells in 1 part of the plant and initiate cellular activity (such as growth or flowering) in a distant part of the plant.

hornbeam _n._ A common name for the genus _Carpinus,_ small or medium-sized hardy, deciduous trees; ironwood. _C. Caroliniana,_ the American hornbeam, is also called blue beech and water beech. It is a shrub or small tree, 10 to 20 feet high, with alternate, toothed leaves, flowers in catkins, and nutlike fruits. (See **Carpinus.**)

horn-of-plenty _n._ A common name for _Fedia cornucopiae,_ grown for both its flowers and for use as a salad plant. It has large, opposite, simple leaves and clusters of white-to-red flowers. Also called African valerian.

hornwort _n._ A common name for the genus _Ceratophyllum,_ aquatic plants used in garden pools and streams. They have floating, leafy branches with threadlike leaves and inconspicuous flowers. (See **Ceratophyllaceae.**)

horse-balm _n._ A strong-scented plant of the American genus _Collinsonia,_ having large leaves and yellowish flowers. _C. Canadensis_ is the best-known species, also known as richweed or stoneroot.

horse balm _n._ A common name for _Collinnsinia,_ a strong-scented perennial native to eastern North America. It has large, aromatic leaves and yellowish flowers. _C. Canadensis,_ the best-known species, is also known as the richweed or stoneroot. Also known as horseweed.

horsebean _n._ A common name for _Vicia Fava,_ so called from being fed to horses, or from its large size. It grows to 6 feet tall, has divided leaves with pairs of oblong leaflets, white pealike flowers with a purple blotch, and 12-inch pods containing edible beans. Some people of Mediterranean descent are severely allergic to the beans and the pollen. It is a true bean, but a vetch, an ancient Old World food dating back thousands of years. Sometimes planted as a cool-growing cover crop in vegetable plots as it enriches the soil with nitrogen. Also called fava bean or broad bean.

horse brier _n._ A common name for _Smilax rotundifolia,_ a prickly deciduous vine with glossy leaves and blue-black berries; native to North America. Also known as common greenbrier, bullbrier, or common catbrier.

horse chestnut _n._ 1. A common name for hardy deciduous trees of the genus _Aesculus,_ the horse chestnut. Most species are trees with alternate leaves divided fan-wise into large, toothed leaflets and with showy red, white, or yellow flowers that attract hummingbirds. The fruits are a leathery, warty, or smooth capsule enclosing a large, rich-brown nut, commonly known as a buckeye. Several species are magnificent flowering shade trees. (See **Aesculus** and **buckeye.**) 2. The nut or fruit of the horse-chestnut tree.

horse-chestnut family _n._ A common name for the family Hippocastenaceae, of which only _Aesculus,_ the horse-chestnut tree, is grown ornamentally.

horse daisy _n._ A common name for _Chrysanthemum Leucanthemum,_ a slender, erect perennial, that grows to 3 feet tall, with tonguelike basal leaves

221

and single, daisylike white flowers with yellow centers. Naturalized in North America. Also called oxeye daisy.

horse elder *n.* The common name of *Inula Helenium*, a robust, stout plant (Compositae), widely naturalized in the United States. It has hairy stems, large, irregularly toothed leaves, velvety beneath, and yellow daisylike flowers. Also called elecampane. Traditional in cottage gardens and herb gardens. Same as horseheal.

horsefly weed *n.* A common name for *Baptisia tinctoria* (Leguminosae), native to the northeastern and midwestern United States. It is a bushy perennial that grows to 4 feet, with leaves divided into 3-part leaflets and tall spikes of bright yellow flowers. Useful in the perennial border, the meadow garden, and the wild garden. Also known wild indigo or rattleweed.

horsefoot *n.* A common name for *Tussilago Farfara*, a perennial which has long-stemmed, heart-shaped leaves 4 to 8 inches wide and early-blooming, daisylike yellow flowers. Widely naturalized in eastern North America, it can become a pernicious weed in the garden. Also known as coltsfoot and horsehoof.

horse gentian *n.* A common name for the genus *Triosteum*, a hardy perennial wildflower with simple, opposite, entire leaves and clusters of yellow or purple flowers. Not widely grown, as it is inclined to be weedy; sometimes included in herb gardens. (See **Triosteum**.)

horse gowan *n.* A common name for several wildflowers, including *Chrysanthemum Leucanthemum* (oxeye daisy), *Matricaria recutita* (sweet false chamomile), *Taraxacum officinale* (dandelion), *Crepis,* and *Hypochoeris.*

horseheal *n.* A common name for *Inula Helenium,* a robust, stout plant (Compositae), widely naturalized in the United States. Also called elecampane, horseheel, and horse elder. (See **horse elder**.)

horsehoof *n.* A common name for *Tussilago Farfara,* a perennial widely naturalized in Eastern North America. Also known as coltsfoot and horsefoot. (See **horsefoot**.)

horse knob *n.* A common name for the flower head of *Centaurea nigra,* a European flower naturalized in the northeastern United States. It is a perennial with large, hairy leaves and rose-purple flowers. Also known as knapweed, horse knop, black knapweed, Spanish buttons, and hard heads.

horsemint *n.* An American plant, *Monarda punctata.*

horse nettle *n.* A common name for *Solanum carolinense,* a wildflower common in the southern United States. It has long, toothed, wavy-edged leaves, prickly beneath, and clusters of violet-to-white flowers.

horse parsley *n.* A common name for *Smyrnium Olusatrum* (Umbelliferae), so called from its height of 4 feet and its large leaves. Also known as alexanders.

horseradish *n.* A cultivated plant, *Armoracia rusticana* (Cruciferae), originally a native of middle Europe and western Asia, and also its root, which has a sharp, pungent taste, and is used grated fresh as a condiment.

horseradish

horseradish tree *n.* A common name for *Moringa pterygosperma,* a deciduous tropical tree grown for its edible fruit. It has divided leaves, clusters of fragrant white flowers, and long, 3-part, podlike capsules. The fresh root has a pungent odor and a warm taste, much like those of the horseradish.

horseshoe vetch *n.* A common name for the genus *Hippocrepis* (Leguminosae). *H. comosa* is a perennial ground cover, which forms a 3-inch-high mat and has divided leaves with tiny leaflets, clusters of yellow sweet pea-shaped flowers, and horseshoe-shaped marks on its pods. It is drought-resistant, tolerates poor soils, and helps prevent erosion on steep banks. Used as a ground cover and in rock gardens.

horse sorrel *n*. A common name for *Rumex hydrolapathum,* a tall perennial that grows to 6 feet, with long, narrow leaves and large clusters of small green or reddish flowers. Used at pond margins and along streams. Also known as giant water dock.

horse sugar *n*. A common name for the genus Symplocos, a genus of tender trees or shrubs. Also known as sweetleaf.

horsetail *n*. A common name for the genus *Equisetum,* a very distinct, primitive family found in wetlands, bogs, marshes, and roadside ditches. They are perennial plants with spreading rootstocks and jointed, upright, hollow stems with grooves containing substantial amounts of silica. They are primitive in that they reproduce by spores rather than seeds. May be invasive in moist soils. (See **Equisetaceae.**)

horsetail tree *n*. A common name for *Casuarina equisetifolia,* a fast-growing tender tree, 40 to 70 feet in height. It has naturalized in Florida. Its common name derives from the leafless, wiry branches, which closely resemble the stems of *Equisetum.*

horse violet *n*. A common name for *Viola pedata,* a North American wildflower native to the eastern United States. It has dainty leaves, divided into 3 to 5 segments, and dark purple and light lilac flowers. Used in the wildflower or woodland garden. Also called bird-foot violet.

horticultural *a*. Pertaining to horticulture.

horticultural bean *n*. A type of shell bean highly favored for baked beans.

horticultural oil *n*. A refined oil sprayed on plants to control a variety of insect pests. It kills by smothering pests and eggs, or by disrupting membrane functions. It may also prevent some fungal diseases. Highly refined types are called summer, superior, or verdant oils and can be used during the growing season as long as temperatures are below 90 F. Heavier types are called dormant oils and are used on dormant deciduous plants.

horticulture *n*. The cultivation of a garden, an orchard, or a nursery; the art and science of cultivating flowers, fruits, vegetables, and ornamental plants.

horticulturist *n*. A person who specializes in horticulture.

hortus siccus (hor'tuhs sihk'uhs) *n*. A collection of specimens of plants carefully dried and preserved for botanical purposes; and herbarium.

hose *n*. A flexible pipe, typically of plastic or rubber, used to carry water from faucet to garden.

hose adapter *n*. A threaded device through which 2 incompatible hose endings may be connected to each other.

hose bracket *n*. An L-shaped, wall-mounted device used to hold coiled garden hose.

hose cassette *n*. A retractable hose reel.

hose-end sprayer *n*. A bottle or jar that attaches to the nozzle end of a garden hose and contains fertilizer, pesticide, herbicide, or other substances. The bottle contents are mixed with water at a predetermined rate before the substance is sprayed through the nozzle.

hose extender *n*. (See **watering wand**.)

hose grabber *n*. (See **hose holder**.)

hose guides *n. pl.* Devices, anchored by stakes, used to route a garden hose above or around plants. The notched, or open-loop-top, type is used to route hose above or around plants. The spool type is used to guide hose around corners.

hose hanger *n*. A freestanding, generally staked, device used to support coiled garden hose.

hose holder *n*. A clamp mounted on a stake, typically 14 to 30 inches high, to support and aim the flow of water from a hose. Also called hose grabber.

hose mender *n*. A coupler used to reconnect the 2 ends of a broken garden hose.

hose-in-hose *n*. A flower that appears to have a double corolla, 1 within another, as in certain azaleas.

hose reel *n.* A freestanding cylindrical device on which a garden hose may be wound and stored.

hose saver *n.* A steel spring device attached at the faucet end of a garden hose to prevent the hose from kinking and cracking.

hose swivel *n.* A rotatable metal connector installed between a faucet and a hose to prevent a garden hose from kinking.

host *n.* A plant that supports a parasite habitually dwelling in or upon it.

Hosta (hah'stuh) *n.* A genus of 40 species of choice, hardy, long- lived, shade-loving perennials (Liliaceae). They grow from short rhizomes and have large, handsome, oval or heart-shaped basal leaves with summer- or fall-blooming spikes of delicate white, blue, lilac, or violet lilylike flowers that stand well above the leaves. Some species have fragrant flowers. They are used in shady borders, in woodland gardens, and in containers. They must be protected from slugs and snails. Also called daylily and plantain lily. Previously classified as *Funkia* and sometimes still called by that name.

hotbed *n.* A bed of earth heated by fermenting substances and covered with glass to defend it from the cold air; intended for raising early plants or for protecting tender exotics.

hotbed, electric *n.* (See **electric hotbed**.)

hotbed weeder *n.* A hook-shaped tool used to remove unwanted plants.

hotcap *n.* An individual, conically shaped plant cover used to protect against frost, sun, birds, and insects.

hothouse *n.* A structure kept artificially heated for the growth of tender exotic plants or subtropical plants, or for the production of native fruits, flowers, etc., out of season. In degree of temperature, strictly, the hothouse stands between the greenhouse and the stove-house, or orchid-house.

Hottentot fig *n.* A common name for *Carpobrotus edulis* and *C. acinaciformis.* They are tender succulent sub-shrubs with thick, fleshy leaves and brilliant pink, yellow, or purple flowers that grow to 4 and 5 inches across. Tolerant of sandy soil, salt spray, drought, and neglect, they are also somewhat fire-retardant. Used as ground covers on steep banks and as freeway plantings. Also known as ice plant.

Hottentot bread *n.* A common name for *Dioscorea elephantipes.* It grows from a woody-looking tuber and has long, thin, twining stems with round or kidney-shaped, sharply pointed leaves. Grown as a curiosity in desert gardens or in the greenhouse. Also known as elephant's foot.

Hottonia (hah toh'nee uh) *n.* A genus of 2 species of floating aquatic perennial plants (Primulaceae) some species native to North America; water violet or featherfoil. They have finely divided leaves and hollow, almost leafless, flower stalks, with whorls of white or lilac flowers. Sometimes used as an aquarium plant.

hound's-tongue *n.* A common name for the genus *Cynoglossum;* beggar's-lice. It has large, broad, flat leaves, clusters of small, bright blue, purple, pink, or white flowers, and wretchedly sticky burs. Used in woodland gardens and shady borders.

hound's-tongue

houseleek *n.* The common name of the plants of the genus *Sempervivum* (Crassulaceae). The common houseleek, *S. tectorum,* is a perennial succulent with a rosette of very thick, fleshy leaves and slender stalks of small pink flowers; it is very tenacious. Also known as common houseleek, hen and chickens, roof houseleek, and old-man-and-woman. Used in rock gardens, as edging in beds, in borders, and in containers.

houseleek
a fruit

houseplant *n*. Any of many plants adaptable to the light, heat, and moisture conditions of a house and thus able to be grown indoors.

Hovea (hoh'vee uh) *n*. A small genus of 12 species of tender variable shrubs (Leguminosae). They have alternate, simple leaves, clusters or spikes of blue or purple butterflylike flowers, and short pods. Used in mild-climate gardens.

Hovenia (hoh vee'nee uh) *n*. A genus of 2 species of very hardy deciduous trees or shrubs. They have alternate, long-stemmed leaves, clusters of small purplish flowers, and little fruits. *H. dulcis*, the Japanese raisin tree, which is very hardy, has greenish flowers and edible fruit stalks.

Howea (how'ee uh) *n*. A genus of 2 species of tropical feather palms (Palmae). They are slowing-growing palms with clean green trunks; as old leaves shed, they leave marks on the trunk. The leaves may be 7 to 9 feet in length. These are the *Kentia* palms of florists; also that Victorian classic, the parlor palm. They still make excellent houseplants. Also known as Belmore sentry palm, curly palm, Foster sentry palm, Kentia palm, thatch palm.

Hoya (hoy'uh) *n*. A large genus of 200 species of climbing, twining vines of shrubs (Asclepiadaceae). They are herbaceous plants, with twining or climb-ing stems, opposite, simple, entire, fleshy or leathery evergreen leaves, and rounded clusters of waxy pink and white flowers. They are excellent houseplants. Commonly known as wax plant, wax flower, wax vine, and porcelain flower.

huckleberry *n*. A name for the different species of *Gaylussacia* and for some of the species of *Vaccinium,* also for their fruit. The name is properly restricted to the species of *Gaylussacia*. They are shrubs with either evergreen or deciduous alternate leaves. *G. baccata* is the common black huckleberry; *G. frondosa* is the bluetangle or blue huckleberry. For the huckleberries of the genus *Vaccinium,* See **blueberry,** their more appropriate name.

Hudsonia (huhd soh'nee uh) *n*. A genus of 3 species of short-lived, heathlike shrubs or subshrubs (Cistaceae) native to eastern North America. They have white scalelike or needlelike leaves and individual bright yellow flowers. Useful in dry, sandy soil or seaside plantings. Commonly known as beach heather.

Huernia (hoo er'nee uh) *n*. A genus of 60 species of tender dwarf, leafless, succulent perennial plants (Ascleiadaceae). They have toothed, angled stems and clusters of yellow bell-shaped flowers, often spotted with crimson or mottled with purple. Commonly known as dragon flower.

hull *n*. The outer covering of a nut, seed, or fruit. *v*. To remove the hull of.

hulver *n*. A common name for *Ilex Aquifolium;* also called English holly.

humble plant *n*. A common name for *Mimosa pudica,* a tender perennial, generally grown as a houseplant, with finely cut leaves, which fold when touched, and small, fluffy, pink blossoms. Also called sensitive plant.

Humea (hyoo mee'uh) *n*. A genus of about 7 species of plants and shrubs (Compositae) native to southern Australia and Madagascar. They have alternate, entire leaves and clusters of small, sweet-scented purple, red, rose, or pink flowers. The leaves of *H. elegans* can cause a rash. Used as indoor/outdoor plants.

humid acids *n. pl.* 1. A term sometimes interchangeable for humus. 2. The alkali-soluble end products of the decomposition of organic matter in mineral soils.

humidity meter *n.* An instrument for measuring the relative amount of moisture in house or greenhouse air.

humming line *n.* A ribbon suspended over crops, that emits an ultrasonic sound to discourage birds.

Humulus (hyoo'myuh luhs) *n.* A genus of 2 species of rough-stemmed, twining perennial vines (Cannabaceae). They have mostly opposite, deeply lobed, hand-shaped leaves and bear flowers in both clusters and catkins. *H. lupulus,* the common hop, is grown as an ornamental vine and for its female flowers which are used to flavor beer.

humus *n.* The well-decomposed, stable part of organic matter in mineral soils.

Hungarian wax *n.* A bright yellow hot pepper variety that turns bright red when ripe. It is about 8 inches long and 2 inches across.

Hunnemannia (huhn uh man'ee uh) *n.* A genus of a single species, *H. fumariifolia* (Papaveraceae), native to Mexico. It is a tender perennial with smoky-gray, finely cut leaves and large, cup-shaped, clear yellow flowers 3 inches across. Excellent in dry, sunny borders. Commonly known as Mexican tulip poppy or golden cup.

huntsman's-cup *n.* A common name for the genus *Sarracenia,* particularly *S. purpurea,* carnivorous wildflowers found in bogs or swamps of the eastern and Gulf coastal regions of North America. They grow from creeping rhizomes and look like hollow tubes or pitchers. Grown as a novelty in terrariums or as a houseplant. Also known as pitcher plant or sidesaddle flower.

huntsman's-horn *n.* A common name for *Sarracenia flava,* carnivorous pitcher plants native to the southern Atlantic states. It has erect, trumpet-shaped, red-veined leaves, 2 to 4 feet long, and large yellow flowers on tall stalks. Also known as yellow pitcher plant, trumpets, trumpet leaf, or umbrella-trumpets.

Hura (hyuhr'uh) *n.* A genus of 2 species of tropical trees (Euphorbeaceae) native to the Americas. *H. crepitans,* the sandbox tree, is remarkable for the loud report with which its seed capsules burst; it is

often called the monkey's dinner-bell or monkey-pistol. It is a large branching tree with glossy, poplarlike leaves, inconspicuous flowers, and ribbed, roundish fruits the size of an orange. Grown in tropical gardens or greenhouses. The milky juice may be irritating to the skin and eyes.

Hura
(sandbox tree)

hurr-bur *n.* A common name for *Arctium Lappa,* a tall, stout, large-leaved perennial, generally regarded as a weed. Also called burdock. (See **burdock.**)

hurtleberry *n.* A former name for huckleberry.

husk *n.* An outer covering of the fruit of a plant, as in corn husks. *v.* To remove the husk of.

husks on corn, stripped down

Hutchinsia (huh chihn'zee uh) *n.* A genus of 2 or 3 species of small perennial and annual alpines (Cruciferae). They have hairy divided or entire leaves and spikes of small white flowers. They are grown in alpine gardens, rock gardens, and on stone walls.

hyacinth (high'uh sihnth) *n.* 1. A common name for hardy bulbs of the genus *Hyacinthus* (Liliaceae), specifically, *H. orientalis,* the common hyacinth. They have narrow, bright green, basal leaves and spikes of numerous, fragrant, often drooping, bell-shaped white, yellow, pink, red, or blue flowers. Hyacinths, like tulips, bloom best in cold-winter climates. Just as gardeners in cold-winter climates can lift (dig up) tender bulbs and store them in a dry, warm place over winter, mild-climate gardeners can lift hyacinths and other bulbs that require winter chilling and store them in the refrigerator for 6 to 8 weeks. In both cases, dig in fall and replant in spring. 2. A common name for flowers of other genera of spring-blooming bulbs, particularly: *Scilla, Muscari,* and *Camassia.*

Hyacinth orientalis
(common hyacinth)

hyacinth, grape (high'uh sihnth) *n.* A common name for *Muscari,* a genus of long-lived, hardy bulbs. It grows from 6 to 18 inches, depending on the species, with fleshy, narrow, grasslike leaves and dense spikes of small, urn-shaped blue or white flowers in early spring. Used for naturalizing in drifts, massed under shrubs or trees, in rock gardens, as edging for beds or borders, and in containers. Useful planted with other bulbs because the leaves come up in fall, indicating where other spring bulbs, such as daffodils, jonquils, and tulips, are located. Grape hyacinths are dormant in summer, requiring little or no water.

hyacinth, musk (high'uh sihnth) *n.* A common name for *Muscari racemosum,* a hardy, spring-flowering bulb. It grows to 10 inches with basal leaves 1 foot long and densely flowered spikes of 20 to 50 musk-scented purple flowers that age to yellow. Also known as nutmeg hyacinth.

hyacinth, nutmeg (high'uh sihnth) *n.* A common name for *Muscari racemosum,* a hardy, spring-flowering bulb. (See **hyacinth, musk**.)

hyacinth, Peruvian (high'uh sihnth) *n.* A common name for *Scilla peruuviana,* a tender perennial bulb native to the Mediterranean, its botanical and common names notwithstanding. It grows to 2 feet, with long, floppy, straplike leaves and 12-inch stalks topped by a large dome-shaped cluster of 50 or more blue-purple, starlike flowers. Grown outdoors in mild climates, in pots elswhere. Also known as hyacinth-of-Peru, Cuban lily, and Peruvian jacinth.

hyacinth pot (high'uh sihnth) *n.* A container for forcing a hyacinth. A collar fits inside the top of the pot, supporting the bulb above a reservoir of water.

hyacinth, scilla, large (high'uh sihnth) *n.* A common name for *Scilla hyacinthoides,* a long-lived. hardy, perennial, spring- blooming bulb. It grows to 3 feet, with basal leaves tapered at both ends and loose, many flowered spikes of violet-blue, bell-shaped flowers.

hyacinth, star (high'uh sihnth) *n.* A common name for *Scilla amoena,* a long-lived, hardy perennial, spring-blooming bulb. It grows to 6 inches, with floppy, basal, strap-shaped leaves and spikes of blue star-like flowers.

hyacinth, starry (high'uh sihnth) *n.* A common name for *Scilla autumnalis,* a long-lived, hardy perennial, fall-blooming bulb. It grows to 6 inches, with long, narrow, partly cylindrical, basal leaves and spiikes of purple starlike flowers. Also known as large autumn scilla.

hyacinth, tassel (high'uh sihnth) *n.* A common name for *Muscari comosum,* a hardy bulb. It grows from 12 to 18 inches, with long, green basal leaves, 1 inch wide, and spikes of curious, shredded- looking flowers; the fertile flowers are green-brown, the sterile flowers blue-purple. Also known as fringe hyacinth. *M.c* 'Monstrosum', the feathered or plume hyacinth, has sterile violet- blue to red-purple flowers with finely cut, twisted petals.

Hyacinthus (high'uh sihn'thuhs) *n*. A genus of a single species of bulb, *H. orientalis* (Liliaceae). It has narrow, basal leaves and stalks of fragrant, bell-shaped white, yellow, pink, red, or blue flowers. Used massed in beds, in borders, in containers, and forced indoors for early bloom. (See **hyacinth**.)

hyacinth, wild (high'uh sihnth) *n*. A common name for *Camassia scilloides,* a hardy bulb native to eastern North America. It has long, narrow leaves and stalks with many small white, blue, or blue-violet flowers. Used in perennial borders, wood-land gardens, and wildflower gardens. Also called meadow hyacinth, indigo squill, and eastern camassia.

hyacinth, wood (high'uh sihnth) *n*. A common name for *Endymion,* a genus of long-lived, hardy, perennial, spring blooming bulbs. Specifically, a common name for *E. non-scriptus,* also called hare-bell and English bluebell. *E. non-scriptus* is a hardy, spring- blooming bulb resembling common hya-cinth, with narrow, basal leaves and 1-foot stalks of nodding, bell-like blue flowers. *Endymion* is often sold as *Scilla*. (See **Endymion** and **harebell**.)

hybrid *n*. The offspring of 2 plants of different varieties, species, or genera. Also used as an adjective.

hybridity *n*. The state of being hybrid.

hybridizable *a*. Capable of producing hybrid off-spring by crossing with another variety, species, or genus.

hybridization *n*. The process of producing hy-brid offspring, or the state of being crossbred.

hybridize *v*. To produce or cause to produce a hybrid.

hybridizer *n*. A person who hybridizes plants.

hybrid musk rose *n*. A common name for hy-brids of *Rosa moschata,* a vigorous deciduous shrub with clusters of heavily fragrant ivory-white flow-ers. The hybrids have large clusters of almost ever-blooming red, pink, buff, yellow, or white roses and ornamental red or orange hips. Useful in rose gardens, cottage gardens, or grown on walls or fences.

hybrid perpetual rose *n*. Prior to the advent of hybrid tea roses, hybrid perpetual roses were the most popular garden roses. They are large, hardy, vigorous roses that bloom repeatedly, which is how they got the name perpetual. The red-to-pink flow-ers tend to be large, up to 7 inches across, opulent, and richly fragrant. 'American Beauty' is a classic hybrid perpetual rose.

hybrid rugosa rose *n*. Hybrid rugosa roses are extremely vigorous and hardy deciduous shrubs with very prickly stems, glossy green crinkly leaves, white, yellow, pink, and red flowers, and bright red, tomato-shaped fruit. These are tough plants, enduring cold, wind, drought, and salt spray. In addition, they prevent erosion and are virtually free of pests and diseases. 'Blanc Double de Coubert' is a classic hybrid rugosa rose. Used as hedges and in seaside plantings

hybrid tea rose *n*. Hybrid tea roses are the most popular of all varieties of roses, typified by their long stems and slim, elegant buds. The class was introduced in 1867, and thousands of varieties have been hybridized since that time. The bushes range from 2 feet to 6 feet tall, with red, pink, orange, yellow, white, lavender, and multicolored flowers. The best known hybrid tea rose is the pink and yellow 'Peace', introduced at the end of World War II.

Hydnocarpus (hihd nuh kar'puhs) *n*. A genus of 40 species of tropical trees or shrubs (Flacourtiace-ae). They have alternate, entire leaves and flowers that grow singly or in clusters.

Hydrangea (high drayn'juh) *n*. 1. A genus of 23 species of erect or climbing shrubs (Saxifragaceae), some species native to the Americas. *H. macro-phylla,* the French hydrangea, is a large shrub; it is grown for the beauty and size of its flowers, which form immense globular clusters of blue or pink. The flower color is determined by the acidity or alkalinity of the soil in which the plant is grown: The flowers are blue or purple in acid soils, pink in alkaline soils. (Adding aluminum sulfate to the soil will make it more acid; lime or superphosphate will make it more alkaline.) *H. arborescens,* the wild hydrangea, is native to the mountains of the eastern United States. *H. quercifolia,* the oakleaf hydrangea, is native to the southeastern United States. *H. anomala petolaris,* the climbing hydrangea, is a self-clinging vine with large, flat, lace-cap clusters of white flowers. 2. [l.c.] A plant of this genus.

Hydrangea arborescens
(wild hydrangea)

hydrangea vine, Japanese *n.* A common name for *Schizophragma hydrangeoides,* a self-clinging vine with broadly oval, toothed leaves and large, showy, lace-cap clusters of white flowers.

Hydrastis (high dras′tuhs) *n.* A genus of 2 species of low-growing perennials (Ranunculaceae), 1 native to North America. *H. canadensis,* a small perennial herb, has a thick, knotted, yellow rhizome, basal, lobed, notched leaves, and a small greenish-white flower. It is sometimes used in dyeing, and gives a beautiful yellow color from which it derives the common names yellowroot, orangeroot, goldenseal, and yellow puccoon.

Hydriastele (high drigh′uh stehl) *n.* A genus of 9 species of tall, clumping, slender, tropical palms (Palma). Used in tropical gardens.

Hydrocharis (high drahk′uh ruhs) *n.* A genus of 2 species of floating aquatic plants (Hydrocharitaceae). *H. Morsus-ranae* is commonly known as frogbit. Used in aquariums.

Hydrocleys (high′droh klays) *n.* A genus of 4 species of floating aquatic plants (Butomaceae) native to tropical America. *H. nymphoides* with broadly heart-shaped floating leaves and showy clusters of yellow flowers, is commonly known as water poppy. Used in garden pools and tubs.

Hydrocotyle (high druh kahd′ih lee) *n.* A genus of 50 to 60 perennials (Umbelliferae). They are usually small, creeping plants that root at the nodes. They have creeping stems, round, crinkly leaves, and clusters of small white flowers. Commonly known as water pennywort and navelwort. Used as a ground cover in moist or wet locations.

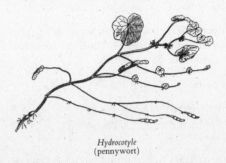

Hydrocotyle
(pennywort)

hydrogen *n.* An element, found in the soil, that is needed by plants to grow.

hydrophilous (high druh fihl′uhs) *a.* In botany, pollinated by the agency of water.

Hydrophyllaceae (high druh fuh las′ee ee) *n. pl.* A family of 25 genera and about 300 species, most of which are native to western North America; the waterleaf family. It consists mostly of plants, or rarely shrubs, with hairy stems, variable leaves, and white or blue flowers. wild gardens.

Hydrophyllum
(waterleaf)
a flower *b* fruit

Hydrophyllum (high druh fihl′uhm) *n.* A genus of 8 species of moisture-loving perennial or biennial plants (Hydrophyllaceae) native to North America; waterleaf. They have widely variable leaves and clusters of bell-shaped white, pale blue, purple, and green flowers. Used in bog gardens or

hydrophyte (high′druh fight) *n.* A plant that grows in water or waterlogged soil.

hydroponics *n.* A method of growing plants in water rather than soil. The plants' roots are suspended in a nutrient solution.

hydrous *a.* Containing water.

hydroxyapatite (hy-drak′-se-ap-a-tit) *n.* A member of the apatite groups or mineral rich in the hydroxyl groups.

Hygrophila (high grahf′ihl uh) *n.* A genus of 100 species of tropical waterweeds (Acanthaceae), found in bogs and wet places. They have opposite, variable, entire leaves at the surface and divided leaves below the surface, and they bear clusters of pale violet, pale blue, or white flowers. Grown as submerged plants in aquariums.

hygrophyte (high′gruh fight) *n.* A plant growing in wet places.

Hylocereus (high loh sihr′ee uhs) *n.* A genus of 18 species of climbing cacti (Cactaceae) native to tropical America. They have 3-angled, spiny stems, which climb by aerial roots, and large night-blooming, often fragrant, white or red flowers. *H. undatus* is commonly known as queen-of-the-night.

Hymenanthera (high muh nan′thuh ruh) *n.* A genus of 7 species of tender, stiff shrubs or small trees (Violaceae). They have small alternate leaves, often clustered, clusters of small flowers, and white or purple berries. Grown in warm-winter climates.

Hymenopappus (high mehn oh pahp′uhs) *n.* A genus of 10 species of herbaceous biennials or perennials (Compositae) native to the United States and Mexico. They have basal rosettes of leaves and alternate, divided leaves on the stems, and they bear clusters of daisylike white flowers with yellow, reddish-purple, or white centers. Grown in the hardy perennial border, the prairie garden, or the

wild garden. *H. scabiosaeus* var. *corymbosus* is commonly known as the old plainsman.

Hymenoxys (high muh nahk′sihs) *n.* A genus of 20 species of small annuals and perennials (Compositae) native to western North America and South America. They have basal or alternate leaves, variously shaped, and daisylike yellow flowers.

Hyoscyamus (high uh sigh′uh muhs) *n.* A genus of 15 species of low-growing annuals and perennials (Solanaceae). They have alternate, coarsely toothed or divided leaves, with leafy spikes of tubular white or yellow flowers. *H. niger,* widely naturalized in the United States, is commonly known as henbane or black henbane. (See **henbane**.)

hypanthial (high pan′thee uhl) *a.* Pertaining to, or resembling, a hypanthium.

hypanthium (high pan′thee uhm) *n., pl.* **hypanthia** (-a) In botany, the part of certain flowers (roses, for example) usually formed by the fusion of the lower portions of their petals, sepals, and stamens.

Hypericaceae (high pehr uh kay′see ee) *n. pl.* A family of 8 genera and 350 species of herbs, shrubs, or, rarely, trees. They have simple, opposite (rarely whorled) entire leaves, often dotted with resinous glands, and yellow flowers with numerous stamens.

Hypericum
(St. John's-wort)

Hypericum (high pehr′uh kuhm) *n.* 1. A large genus of 300 species of plants, shurbs, or subshrubs, widely distributed throughout the temperate regions of the world; St.-John's-wort. They are herbs or shrubs with simple, opposite (rarely whorled) entire leaves, often black dotted, and 5-petaled yellow flowers with many stamens. *H. calycinum* is a low-growing, drought-resistant species grown as a ground cover. 2. [l.c.] A plant of this genus.

hypertrophy *n.* In botany, excessive growth or overdevelopment of the organs of plants.

Hyphaene (high fee′nee) *n.* A genus of fewer than 30 species of tropical palms (Palmae); gingerbread palm. They have short, branching trunks, each branch terminating in a tuft of large fan-shaped leaves with sharp-toothed stems. The branching, catkinlike spikes of flowers are produced between the leaves; individual trees are either male or female. The oblong fruit has a thick, fibrous rind with a smooth polished skin, enclosing a single hollow seed. *H. thebaica* is the gingerbread palm or doom or Egyptian down palm. (See **doom palm**.)

Hypochoeris (high poh keh′ruhg) *n.* A genus of about 70 species of yellow-flowered plants (Compositae), some species native to South America; cat's-ear. They have a basal rosette of soft, woolly leaves and yellow or white narrow, flat flowers. *H. radicata,* the spotted cat's-ear, has naturalized in North America. Grown in the wild garden.

hypocotyl (high puh kaht′ihl) *n.* In botany, the part of the stem of a plant embryo or seedling that is below the seed leaves.

hypocotyledonary (high′puh kaht ih lee′duh na ree) *a.* Located below the seed leaves.

hypogenous (high pah′juh nuhs) *a.* Growing on the under surface, especially pertaining to a fungus on the underside of a leaf.

hypogynous (high pah′juh nuhs) *a.* In botany, having the sepals, petals, and stamens arising from the portion of a flower situated below the ovary.

hypogyny (high pah′juh nee) *n.* In botany, the state of being hypogynous.

Hypolepis (high pohl′uh puhs) *n.* A genus of 45 species of tropical and subtropical terrestrial ferns (Polypodiaceae). The fronds are from 3 to 8 feet long and much divided. Grown in greenhouses.

hypophyllous (high puh fihl′uhs) *a.* Situated on the underside of a leaf.

Hypoxidaceae (high pahk sih day′see ee) *n. pl.* A family of 6 genera of plants growing from tuberous rhizomes or corms; the star-grass family. They

have mostly basal, grasslike, or broad leaves and spikes of flowers. The ornamental genera are *Curculigo, Hypoxis,* and *Rhodohypoxis.*

Hypoxis (high pahk′sihs) *n.* A genus of 110 bulbs (Hypoxidaceae); most are native to the Southern Hemisphere. They are herbaceous plants with usually narrow, sometimes grasslike leaves; they have pretty white or yellow star-shaped flowers, either single or in spikes. *H. hirsuta,* a yellow-flowered species native to the United States, is commonly known as star grass.

hypsophyll (hihp′suh fihl) *n.* A leaf located underneath spore-bearing leaves.

hypsophyllary (hihp suh fihl′uh ree) *a.* Pertaining to the hypsophyll.

Hyptis (hihp′tihs) *n.* A genus of 400 species of plants or shrubs (Labiatae) native to warm regions of the Americas. They have opposite, often toothed, leaves and spikes of tubular flowers.

hyssop (hihs′uhp) *n.* A small bushy herb of the genus *Hyssopus. H. officinalis,* common is gardens, is mildly aromatic. Anise hyssop, *Agastache Foeniculum,* is a fragrant herb, often grown to attract bees.

hyssop

Hyssopus (hih soh′puhs) *n.* A genus of 5 species of perennials (Labiatae). They are perennial herbs to 2 feet tall with wandlike branches; long, narrow, pungent, entire dark green leaves; and spikes of densely clustered white, pink, or blue-purple flowers. *H. officinalis* is commonly known as hyssop. Traditional in herb gardens and cottage gardens.

Hystrix (hihs'trihks) *n.* A genus of about 7 species of perennial grasses (Gramineae). *H. patula* (bottlebrush grass) is a valuable ornamental grown for its unusual stiff, pink flower spike that resembles a bottlebrush.

Iberis (igh beh'ruhs) *n.* A genus of 30 species of annuals and perennials (Cruciferae); candytuft. They have narrow leaves and clusters or spikes of white, pink, red, or purple flowers. Some kinds are fragrant, such as *I. amara.* Used in beds, borders, rock gardens, or containers and as small-scale ground covers.

Iberis
(candytuft)
a flower *b* fruit *c* seed

Iboza (ee boh'zah) *n.* A genus of 12 species of plants or shrubs (Labiatae). They have opposite, often toothed, aromatic leaves and clusters of small, fragrant flowers. Grown in warm-climate gardens.

icaco (ih kak'oh) *n.* A common name for *Chrysobalanus Icaco* native to Florida and the West Indies. It is an evergreen shrub, to 30 feet high, with broad, leathery leaves, small clusters of white flowers, and fruit about the size of a plum, which is edible but insipid. Also known as coco plum.

iceberg lettuce *n.* A closely compacted, crisp, white lettuce variety rarely grown by home gardeners. It is usually considered difficult to grow outside California, where most of the commercial crop is grown, but seeds are available and some gardeners are raising it successfully.

ice plant *n.* A common name for plants of the family Aizoaceae, including the genera *Aptenia, Carpobrotus, Cephalophyllum, Delosperma, Drosanthemum, Lampranthus, Malephora, Mesembryanthemum,* and *Oscularia.* The leaves are covered with tiny transparent blisters that glisten like flecks of ice. They are widely cultivated as fire-retardant, erosion-retardant, and drought-resistant ground covers in warm climates. Also known as dew plant.

icterus (ihk'tuh ruhs) *n.* In botany, jaundice.

igneous rock (ihg'nee uhs) *n.* A rock produced through the cooling of melted mineral matter.

Ilex (igh'lehks) *n.* 1. A genus of 400 species of trees and shrubs (Aquifoliaceae), some species native to the Americas; holly. Hollies have alternate, often spiny and often evergreen leaves, white flowers, and bright red winter berries. Evergreen hollies are grown in moderate-winter climates to Zone 7; deciduous hollies are hardier. The branches are often cut for winter-holiday decoration. 2. [l.c.] A tree or shrub of this genus.

Illiciaceae (ihl'ihs ee uh see e) *n. pl.* A family of 1 genus and 42 species, some native to North America. They are broadleaf evergreen shrubs or small trees with aromatic leaves, small clusters of white or red-purple flowers, and star-shaped fruit called star anise.

Illicium
(star anise)
a fruit

Illicium (uh lihs'ee uhm) *n.* A genus of 42 species of aromatic evergreen shrubs or small trees (Illici-

232

aceae), some native to North America; anise trees. The fruit is called star anise and the seeds are used to flavor the liqueur anisette. *I. floridanum*, native from Florida to Louisiana, is an evergreen shrub, 6 to 10 feet high, with 6-inch aromatic leaves and large red-purple flowers with nodding, overlapping petals.

illuvial horizon (ih loo′vee uhl) *n.* An accumulation of material in the B horizon (subsoil) that moved into it from the A horizon (topsoil).

imbricate (ihm′bruh kayt) *a.* Overlapping in regular order, as the scales on the leaf buds of plants.

Imbricate scales of a
hemlock cone

immarginate (ihm mahr′jihn ayt) *a.* Having no margin.

immature soil *n.* A soil that lacks clear individual horizons.

immortelle (ihm or tehl′) *n.* Any one of the flowers commonly called everlasting. From their papery texture, these flowers retain their natural color and appearance after drying and are therefore much used for wreaths and other ornamental purposes.

immortelle, mountain (ihm or tehl′) *n.* A common name for *Erythrina Poeppigiana*, a tree often planted to shade coffee trees.

Imperata (ihm puh rah′tuh) *n.* A genus of 8 species of perennial grasses (Gramineae) native to warm regions. *I. cylindrica* (Japanese blood grass) is a valuable ornamental grown for its deep burgundy-red foliage.

impulse sprinkler *n.* A hose attachment used to spray bursts of water over all or part of a circle of lawn or garden. The area of spray is adjustable.

imou pine (ee′moo) *n.* A common name for the tree *Dacrydium cupressinum*, a tender, evergreen, coniferous tree. It grows to 100 feet, has tiny scalelike leaves, and tiny cones. Grown in cool, frost-free areas along the Pacific coast. Also called rimu.

imparipinnate (ihm pahr′ih pihn ayt) *a.* In botany, odd-pinnate, having pairs of leaves opposite along a central stem, with a single leaf at the end.

Imparipinnate
leaf

Impatiens (ihm pay′shuhnz) *n.* A genus of 500 species of flowers or shrubs (Balsaminaceae), a few species native to North America; balsam. They have succulent stems and simple leaves. Some having 5-petaled flowers; others have clusters of curiously shaped (almost orchidlike) blossoms. The pods have 5 segments, which coil elastically and eject the seeds by popping open violently. This is the origin of the common names snapweed and touch-me-not; it is also known as balsam and jewelweed. The American species, commonly called jewelweed, are *I. pallida*, the pale touch-me-not, and *I. capensis*, the spotted touch-me-not or lady's-earrings. They attract hummingbirds. (See **balsam**.) The most commonly grown garden species is busy Lizzy, *I. wallerana*, which has been much hybridized.

imperfect *a.* Diclinous; having the pistils and stamens in separate flowers.

impervious soil *n.* A soil through which water, air, or roots penetrate very slowly or not at all.

inarable (ihn ar′uh buhl) *a.* Not arable; not capable of being plowed or tilled.

inarch *v.* To graft by uniting a scion to the stock, without separating the scion from its parent tree.

inarching *n.* The method of grafting new plant growth onto a stronger root system by establishing young plants near an existing tree and removing matching areas of bark to bind growing branches of the younger tree to branches of the old until they grow together and can be separated with the new branches attached to the older rootstock.

inarching

inbreed *v.* To subject to inbreeding; to breed from individuals of the same parentage or otherwise closely related.

inbreeding *n.* Deliberate self-pollination of a plant by transferring pollen from 1 of its flowers to the stigma of the same flower or to another flower of the same plant. Repeating this process for several generations ensures that the line will breed true.

incanous (ihn kay'nuhs) *a.* Hoary; grayish or whitish.

Incarvillea (ihn kar vihl'ee uh) *n.* A genus of 14 species of mostly tender perennials (Bignoniaceae). They have basal or alternate, leaves divided into leaflets and clusters or spikes of red, rose, pink, white, yellow, or purple tubular flowers. Grown in warm- winter climates; the tuberous roots must be lifted in cold climates. Used in rock gardens or greenhouses.

incense cedar *n.* A common name for *Calocedrus decurrens,* a large, symmetrical, pleasantly aromatic coniferous tree native to the mountains of the Pacific coast of the United States from Oregon south to Baja California. The open cones look like ducks' bills. Also known as California incense cedar. Once established, tolerates heat, poor soil, and drought. Used as a windbreak, high screen, or green wall.

incised *a.* In botany, having a sharp, deeply and irregularly notched margin, as an incised leaf.

included *a.* Not sticking out or projecting, as when pistils are included in the corolla.

incubous (ing'kyoo buhs) *a.* In botany, overlapping, like shingles.

incumbent (ihn kuhm'buhnt) *a.* In botany, lying on another organ, as an incumbent anther lying against a filament.

indeciduous (ihn duh sihd'yoo uhs) *a.* Not deciduous; not losing its leaves annually; evergreen, as trees.

indehiscence (ihn dih hihs'ihns) *a.* In botany, the property of not remaining closed or sealed, but opening spontaneously, such as a seed capsule bursting open to scatter seeds.

indehiscent (ihn dih hihs'ehnt) *a.* In botany, not popping or splitting open spontaneously when mature, as a capsule or an anther.

indeterminate *a.* Said of a plant part that continues to grow while flowering, such as indeterminate tomatoes, which continue to grow until they die, or a flower spike that continues to elongate even as the lower blossoms open.

Indian apple *n.* A common name for *Podophyllum peltatum,* native to North America. It is a rhizomatous perennial to 18 inches, with large lobed leaves to 1 foot across, white flowers 2 inches or more in diameter, and yellow or red edible fruit. Also known as May- apple, mandrake, wild lemon, raccoon-berry, and wild jalap. Used in shady places in the wild garden.

Indian arrow *n.* A common name for *Euonymus atropurpurea,* a small deciduous North American shrub or small tree. It grows to 25 feet, with elliptic leaves that are furry beneath, clusters of purple flowers, and crimson seed capsules. Also known as burning bush or wahoo.

Indian balm *n.* A common name for *Trillium erectum* and *T. recurvatum,* both native to North America. They are spring-blooming perennial wildflowers with erect purple flowers arising out of the center of a 3-leaved whorl. Also called purple trillium or birthroot. (See **Trillium**.)

Indian bean *n.* A common name for trees of the genus *Catalpa,* as well as two North American species *C. bignonioides* and *C. speciosa. Catalpa* trees have large, simple leaves, showy spikes of white, pink, or yellow flowers, and long, dark brown pods. Also called Western catalpa, cigar tree, and catawba. Grown as a street tree or lawn tree.

Indian cherry *n.* A common name for the genus *Amelanchier* and *Rhamnus caroliniana. R. caroliniana,* native to the United States, is a deciduous tree, that grows to 30 feet, with elliptic 6-inch leaves, clusters of small, greenish flowers, and red fruit that turns black when ripe; also called buckthorn. Grown for their showy fruits. *Amelanchier* is a genus of 25 species of shrubs and small trees, several native to North America, with alternate, toothed leaves, spikes of early-blooming white flowers, and dark purple fruits; also called serviceberry, shadbush, juneberry, and sugarplum. The fruits of both attract birds. Used as specimen trees or shrubs for their spring flowers and fall color.

Indian corn *n*. A variety of the native American plant *Zea Mays*.

Indian cress (in'de-an kres) *n*. A common name for *Tropaeolum majus,* also known as nasturtium. It is a low-growing annual flower or vine with round, scalloped gray-green leaves and broad, long-spurred brilliant yellow, orange, gold, or red flowers. They are grown as bedding plants, as edging for borders, in window boxes, or as companion plants in the vegetable garden. Both the leaves and the flowers are used in salads.

Indian cucumber *n*. A common name for *Medeola virginica,* native to eastern North America. It is a perennial that grows from a rhizome with leaves in whorls, clusters of greenish-yellow small flowers, and dark purple fruit. The edible rhizomes taste like cucumber. Same as Indian cucumber root.

Indian cup *n*. A common name for the genus *Sarracenia,* particularly *S. purpurea,* carnivorous wildflowers found in bogs or swamps of the eastern and Gulf coastal regions of North America. They grow from creeping rhizomes and look like hollow tubes, cups, or pitchers. Grown as a novelty in terrariums or as a houseplant. Also known as pitcher plant, huntsman's-cup, and sidesaddle flower.

Indian elm *n*. A common name for the North American tree *Ulmus rubra,* also known as slippery elm or red elm. It is a small- or medium-sized tree with a broad, open crown, spreading branches, and long oval leaves that turn yellow in autumn.

Indian fig *n*. A common name for *Opuntia Ficus-indica,* a nearly spineless, bushy, or treelike cactus that grows to 18 feet. It has large yellow flowers 4 inches across and red, edible, fleshy fruit.

Indian hemp *n*. A common name for *Apocynum cannabinum,* a North American perennial that grows to 4 feet with opposite 6-inch leaves and clusters of white-to-green flowers. The milky juice is poisonous. Grown in the hardy border. Also called hemp dogbane.

Indian ginger *n*. Same as wild ginger. (See **ginger.**)

Indian-paintbrush *n*. A common name for the North American perennial wildflowers *Castilleja californica* and *C. coccinea.* Not often grown in gardens; where they volunteer, they should be cherished for their showy red spikes of early spring flowers.

Indian pipe *n*. A common name for *Monotropa uniflora,* from the resemblance of the plant when in flower to a white clay pipe. A saprophyte that grows in heavy woodland duff rather than in soil, it is also called corpse plant or pine sap. (See **Monotropa.**)

Indian plum family *n*. A common name for Flacourtiaceae, a family of 84 genera and 850 species of tropical and sub tropical trees and shrubs. (See **Flacourtiaceae.**)

Indian poke *n*. A common name for *Veratrum viride,* a poisonous North American perennial from which a natural pesticide is made. It grows to 7 feet tall, has oval leaves 12 inches long, and bears clusters of small yellow-green flowers. Also called American white hellebore, itchweed, and false hellebore. (See **Veratrum.**)

Indian root *n*. A common name for 2 plants native to North America, *Aralia racemosa* and *Gillenia trifoliata. A. racemosa* is a perennial that grows from rhizomes to 6 feet tall, has huge, 30-inch leaves divided into leaflets, and bears clusters or spikes of small white or greenish flowers. Also known as American spikenard. *G. trifoliata* is a perennial with leaves divided into three leaflets and clusters of white or pink 5-petaled flowers. Grown in wild or rock gardens. Also called bowman's-root and Indian physic.

Indian's-dream *n*. A common name for the North American fern *Pellaea atropurpurea.* It has tufted, leathery leaves, 12 inches long and 6 inches wide and dark purple stems. Also known as purple cliff brake. Grown in rock gardens.

Indian shoe *n*. A common name for hardy woodland orchids of the genus *Cypripedium,* from the resemblance of the inflated lip to an Indian moccasin. Many species are native to North America. Do not collect these in the wild, as many species are endangered and few survive transplanting. Also called moccasin flower and lady's slipper.

Indian shot *n.* A common name for the genus *Canna,* particularly *C. indica,* so called from the hard, shotlike seeds, of which there are several in the pod. It is a tender perennial that grows to 4 feet tall, with large, 18-inch leaves and showy red, yellow, or orange summer flowers. Grown in mild-climate gardens, usually in beds. (See **Canna.**)

Indian tobacco *n.* A common name for *Lobelia inflata,* a hairy annual native to North America. It grows to 3 feet and has narrow leaves and spikes of blue-violet or white flowers. The stems and leaves are poisonous; the poison is the alkaloid lobeline.

Indian turnip *n.* A common name for *Arisaema triphyllum,* a North American perennial that has a root resembling a small turnip, 1 or 2 large oval leaves, divided into 3 leaflets, and calla lily-like flowers. Also called dragonroot and jack-in-the-pulpit.

Indian turnip

India-rubber plant *n.* A common name for *Ficus elastica,* a tropical tree with large, simple, glossy leaves. Grown outdoors in subtropical gardens, as a popular houseplant anywhere.

India wheat *n.* A common name for *Fagopyrum tataricum,* a buckwheat grown as a cover crop in orchards to attract bees. Also known as Tartarian buckwheat.

indigenous (ihn dihj'uh nuhs) *a.* Native; not exotic.

indigo (ihn'dih goh) *n.* A substance obtained in the form of a blue powder from dried plants of the genus *Indigofera* (Leguminosae) and used as a blue dye (see **indigo plant**). Indigo is produced by the decomposition of a substance called indican. The plant is bruised and fermented in vats of water, depositing the blue substance, which is collected and dried. False indigo is an American plant, *Baptisia australis* (Leguminosae), also called blue false indigo and wild indigo.

indigo
a flower *b* fruit

indigo broom (ihn'dih goh) *n.* The wild indigo, *Baptisia australis.*

Indigofera (ihn dih'johf eh ruh) *n.* A genus of 800 species of perennials and shrubs (Leguminosae). They have divided leaves and spikes of small red or purple flowers. Some of the species yield the dark blue dye indigo.

indigo plant (ihn'dih go) *n.* A plant of the genus *Indigofera,* from which indigo is obtained.

indigo weed (ihn'dih go) *n.* The wild or false indigo. (See **Baptisia.**)

indigo, wild (ihn′dih goh) *n.* (See **Baptisia**.)

indoor gardening *n.* The art of growing plants indoors using natural and/or artificial light.

indumentum (ihn doo mehn′tuhm) *n.* In botany, any hairy covering or pubescence that forms a coating, as on a leaf. Also indument.

induplicate *a.* Rolled inward, as the leaves in a bud.

indusium (ihn doo′zee uhm) *n. pl.* **indusia** (-a). In botany, a small flap covering the sori, or fruit dots, in ferns; a collection of hairs united so as to form a sort of cup and enclosing the stigma of a flower.

inferior *a.* Below; beneath; lower.

inferior ovary *n.* A basal, ovule-bearing part of a pistil borne below the point of attachment of the perianth and stamens.

infiltration rate *n.* The rate of water controlled by surface conditions that enters the soil.

inflated *a.* Enlarged or swelled out, as an inflated perianth.

inflorescences of various plants

inflorescence *n.* The flowering part of a plant; the arrangement of flowers on a plant; the process of coming into bloom; blossoming.

infrafoliar (ihn frah foh′lee ar) *a.* Below the leaves, as infrafoliar flowers.

infrared mulch *n.* A plastic sheet placed around plants to warm the soil by infrared radiation and to inhibit weed growth by blocking most visible radiation.

infraspecific *a.* Referring to categories of classification below that of species, such as subspecies.

infructescence (ihn fruhk tehs′ehns) *n.* The fruiting stage of a plant.

infundibuliform (ihn fuhn dihb′yoo lee form) *a.* Having the form of a funnel.

infundibuliform
flower of datura

ingraft *v.* To insert, as a scion of 1 tree or plant into another, for propagation. Also spelled engraft.

inkberry *n.* A common name for *Ilex glabra,* a hardy, elegant evergreen shrub native to North America. It grows from 2 to 10 feet high, has slender, flexible branches, leathery glossy leaves, clusters of small white flowers that attract bees, and small black berries.

ink plant *n.* A common name for *Coriaria myrtifolia,* formerly used to make a black dye.

inorganic *a.* 1. Not natural; not organic; artificial. 2. Composed of other than animal or plant matter; mineral.

inorganic fertilizer *n.* A chemical fertilizer that quickly releases nitrogen into the soil.

inorganic nitrogen *n.* The element nitrogen in combination with other mineral elements.

insecticidal soap *n.* A low-toxicity pesticide made from the salts of fatty acids. It kills soft-bodied insects, like aphids, spider mites, thrips, and whiteflies, by disrupting cell membranes. (Make your own by mixing 2 tablespoons dishwashing detergent in 1 gallon of water.) It may burn foliage in hot weather. It is sometimes combined with other materials, such as citrus oil or sulfur, to increase efficiency. Complete coverage of the plant is essential to control.

insecticide *n.* An agent that kills insects; specifically, that which kills insect pests of plants and humans.

insectivorous *a.* Feeding or depending on insects, as an animal or a plant such as *Dionaea.*

inserted *a.* In botany, attached, as a stamen on a corolla.

insertion *n.* The place or manner of attachment, as the insertion of petals.

intake rate *n.* The rate at which rain or water enters the soil. Expressed in inches per hour.

Italian grape hoe *n.* A hoe with a sharp blade and a curved handle; used for chopping weeds, breaking up compacted soil, cutting roots, digging trenches, and building raised beds.

integrated pest management *n.* An approach to pest control that strives to manage pests at acceptable levels instead of completely eliminating them. It begins with techniques that are least disruptive, such as planting resistant varieties, using biological controls, less toxic sprays and appropriate cultural techniques, and only using traditional synthetic pesticides as a last resort.

integument (ihn tehg'yoo mehnt) *n.* The outer envelope of an ovule, which, with other parts, forms the seed coat.

inter- *prefix.* Between or among.

interaxillary (ihn ter ak'sih la ree) *a.* In botany, situated between or within the axils of leaves.

interfoliaceous (ihn ter foh'lee ay shee uhs) *a.* In botany, situated between the leaves, especialy opposite leaves. Also interfoliar.

internode *n.* A part or space between 2 nodes.

internode on a portion of stem *a*

interrupted fern *n.* A common name for *Osmunda Claytoniana,* a hardy North American fern with divided fronds to 4 feet long, sterile fronds on the outside, fertile fronds in the center. Used in moist, shady wild or woodland gardens.

intra- *prefix.* Within or inside.

intrazonal *a.* A term used to describe a soil group with characteristics determined by local factors, such as parent material.

introrse (ihn trohrs') *a.* Turned or facing inward, such as an introrse anther facing toward the center of the flower.

introrse anthers (with parts of flower removed to show interior)

Inula (in'yoo lah) *n.* A genus of more than 100 species of hardy plants (Compositae). They have basal or alternate leaves and heads of yellow flowers. *I. Helenium,* the elecampane, elf dock, horseheal, horse elder, or scabwort, is naturalized in England, North America, western Asia, and Japan. Has been used medicinally. (See **elecampane**.) Used in borders and traditional in cottage and herb gardens.

inverted *a.* Upside down.

involucel (ihn vohl'oo sehl) *n.* In botany, a secondary involucre in a compound cluster of flowers, as in many of the Umbelliferae. *a.* **involucellate** (in-vol-u-sel'at).

involucra (ihn'voh loo kruh) *n.pl.* The plural form of involucrum.

involucral (ihn'voh loo kral) *a.* Pertaining to an involucre.

involucrate (ihn'voh loo krayt) *a.* Having an involucre. Also involucred.

involucre (ihn'voh loo ker) *n.* In botany, any collection of whorls of small leaves or bracts beneath a flower or an inflorescence.

involucre of leaves below dogwood flower

involucriform (ihn voh loo'krih form) *a.* Resembling an involucre.

involucrum (ihn voh loo'kruhm) *n. pl.* **involucra** (-kra). In botany, same as involucre.

involute (ihn voh loot) *a.* Specifically, in botany, rolled inward, as the margin of a leaf.

Ionopsidium (igh a nohp sihd'ee um) *n.* A genus of 5 species of annual flowers (Cruciferae). They have rosettes of basal leaves and white, purple, or pink flowers on leafy stalks. Commonly known as diamond flower.

Ipheion (ihf ee igh'ahn) *n.* A small genus of bulbs (Amaryllidaceae) native to South America. They have long, narrow, basal leaves, which smell like onion when bruised, and pale blue, dark blue, or white starlike flowers. Used as a easy-to-grow ground cover in shaded, moist situations or as an edging in beds and borders.

Ipomoea (ihp oh'mee uh) *n.* A genus of 500 species of tender and tropical herbaceous vines (Convolvulaceae); morning glory. They have twining stems, alternate, usually entire leaves, and bell-shaped or trumpet-shaped flowers. Sweet potatoes are the root of *I. Batatas.* Morning glories are traditionally used over arches in cottage gardens, over gates, or on trellises, fences, and walls.

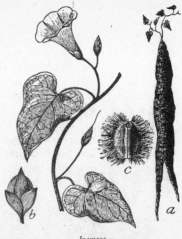

Ipomoea
(morning glory)
a root *b* fruit *c* seed

Ipomopsis (ihp oh mahp'sihs) *n.* A genus of 24 species of mostly perennial or biennial flowers (Polemoniaceae) most native to North America. They have leafy stems, hairy, alternate leaves, and clusters of red, gold, yellow, blue, white, scarlet, or cream tubular flowers. *I. aggregata* is commonly known as scarlet gilia or skyrocket. Best massed in beds, borders, or containers; also useful in the wild garden.

Iresine (igh ruh see'nee) *n.* A genus of 70 species of tropical and tender perennials or small shrubs (Amarantaceae); bloodleaf. They have opposite leaves, often purple-red or yellow-veined, and clusters or spikes of minute white flowers. Grown for their foliage as annuals or as indoor/outdoor plants in containers.

Iridaceae (ihr ihd uh'see ee) *n. pl.* A family of 60 genera and 800 or more species, widely distributed throughout the temperate or warm regions of the world; the iris family. They are perennial flowers, with mostly basal, sword-shaped leaves and spectacularly showy flowers. The ornamental genera include *Iris, Ixia, Crocus, Gladiolus, Dietes, Freesia,* among others. (See **Crocus** and **Iris**.)

iridaceous (ihr ih day'shee uhs) *a.* Resembling or pertaining to plants of the family Iridaceae, especially the *Iris.*

Iris *n.* 1. A genus of 200 or more hardy perennials (Iridaceae) that grow from rhizomes or bulbs. They have sword-shaped or grasslike leaves and generally large, showy purple, yellow, white, or multicolored flowers. They have been much categorized and hybridized, the major categories being bearded iris (German iris, *I. × germanica*), crested iris, beardless iris (Japanese iris and Siberian iris), Aril iris, and bulbous iris (English, Spanish, and Dutch iris). The bearded iris is commonly known as fleur-de-lis or flower-de-luce. Several are native to North America, including *I. versicolor*, blue flag; *I. virginica*, southern blue flag; *I. verna*, dwarf iris; *I. cristata*, crested dwarf iris; and *I. Douglasiana*, the Douglas iris. Used in beds, borders, and in containers; native species are superb in the wild garden. 2. [l.c.] Any plant of this genus.

Iris
a flower and bud b rhizome and leaves

iris borer *n*. A moth or beetle larva that bores into the foliage and eventually the rhizome of iris. It causes secondary rotting of rhizome. Usually controlled with traditional insecticides. Parasitic nematodes may also work.

Iris family *n*. A common name for Iridaceae.

irisroot (igh′rihs root) *n*. Same as orrisroot.

Irish cobbler *n*. A variety of potato popular since the late 1800s for its ability to perform well in all climates. White, oblong, and with a fine-flavored, mealy flesh, it is favored for mashing.

Irish furze *n*. A common name for *Ulex europaeus strictus*, a narrow, compact shrub with few-flowers.

Irish heath *n*. A common name for *Daboecia cantabrica*, an erect, slightly spreading European shrub with slender dark green leaves, whitish below, and clusters of small, egg-shaped pink or purple flowers. Grown as a specimen shrub.

Irish moss *n*. A common name for *Sagina subulata*, a dense, compact, small-scale ground cover. As *Sagina* is not a true moss, it will not grow under the damp, heavily shaded conditions true mosses re-

quire; it needs partial sun and good drainage to thrive. Suited to rock or wall gardens or between paving. (See **moss**.)

iron *n*. A soil nutrient required by plants to manufacture chlorophyll. In dry, alkaline soils, plants may not be able to absorb iron from the soil, which causes the leaves to turn yellow with green veins. Products containing iron chelates may be added to the soil or sprayed on foliage to make iron available to the roots and leaves.

ironbark tree *n*. A common name for any of several trees of the genus *Eucalyptus*, having solid bark and extremely heavy, hard, durable wood. The gray ironbark tree is *E. paniculata*; the white ironbark tree is *E. Leucoxylon*.

iron chelate (kee′layt) *n*. A form of iron that is readily available to plants when iron in the soil is not available to the roots. Commercial products containing iron chelates may be sprayed on the leaves or put on the soil. Iron is essential to chlorophyll formation, the process that makes leaves green and allows photosynthesis to take place.

ironheads *n.pl*. A common name for *Centaurea nigra*, so called in reference to the hard, knobby bracts beneath the flowers. Also called knapweed.

iron oak *n*. A common name for any of several North American oaks such as *Quercus stellata*. Also known as post oak.

irontree *n*. A common name for the genus *Metasideros*, tender or tropical broadleaf evergreen vines, shrubs, or trees. They have simple, opposite leaves and clusters or spikes of red or white flowers, often showy.

ironweed *n*. A common name for the genus *Vernonia*, tender perennial vines, subshrubs, shrubs, and trees some species native to the Americas. They have alternate leaves and purple flowers, either single or in clusters. Grown in borders or in wild gardens for their late summer and autumn bloom.

ironwood *n*. A common name for any of numerous species of especially hard-wooded trees, belonging to many genera. In North America, the name commonly denotes the genus *Carpinus*, *Bumelia lycioides*, *Cliftonia monophylla*, *Cyrilla racemiflora*, *Eugenia confusa*, *Mesua ferrea*, and *Ostrya virginiana*.

ironwort *n.* A common name for the genus *Sideritis,* a genus of shrubby or low-growing mints.

irregular *a.* In botany, not having all the members of the same part alike; assymetrical; lacking uniformity, said of flowers.

irrigate *v.* 1. To pass a liquid over or through; moisten by a flow of water or other liquid. 2. Specifically, to water, as land, by causing a stream or streams to be distributed over it. (See **irrigation**.)

irrigation *n.* The act of watering or moistening; the covering of anything with water or other liquid for the purpose of making or keeping it moist, especially, the distribution of water over the surface of land to promote the growth of plants.

isadelphous (igh suh del'fuhs) *a.* In botany, having the separate bundles of stamens equal in number, as in the flowers of beans.

isandrous (igh san'druhs) *a.* In botany, having the stamens similar and equal in number to the divisions of the corolla.

isanthous (igh san'thuhs) *n.* In botany, having regular flowers.

Isatis (igh'suh tuhs) *n.* A genus of 30 species of annual or hardy perennial plants (Cruciferae). They have simple leaves and clusters or spikes of small yellow flowers. The leaves of *I. tinctoria,* called dyer's woad or asp-of-Jerusalem, were used by the ancient Britons to stain their skin blue.

Isertia (igh sur'tee uh) *n.* A genus of about 25 species of shrubs or trees (Rubiaceae) native to the West Indies and tropical America. They have large, leathery leaves and many showy scarlet, white, or yellow tubular flowers.

isogynous (igh soh jihn uhs) *a.* In botany, having the pistils, or the carpels of which the single pistil is composed, equal in number to the sepals.

isomerous (igh sohm'uh ruhs) *a.* In botany, composed each of an equal number of parts, as the members of the several circles of a flower; exhibiting isomerism.

Isoplexis (igh soh plek'sihs) *n.* A genus of 3 species of tender subshrubs (Scrophulariaceae). They have alternate leaves and densely flowered spikes of showy yellow flowers.

Isopyrum (igh soh pigh'ruhm) *n.* A genus of 30 species of small, slender, delicate perennials (Ranunculaceae). They have 2-part or 3-part columbinelike leaves and solitary or loose clusters of white flowers. May be naturalized in wild gardens.

isostemonous (igh soh stehm'oh nuhs) *a.* In botany, having the stamens equal in number to the sepals or petals.

isostemony (igh soh'stehm'oh nee) *n.* The state or condition of being isostemonous.

Isotoma (igh soh toh'muh) *n.* A genus of herbaceous plants now classified as *Laurentia.*

ita palm (ee'tuh) *n.* A common name for *Mauritia flexuosa* (Palmae) native to tropical America. It is a tall palm that grows along the Amazon River in marshes and floodplains. It grows to 100 feet, has long-stemmed, deeply divided leaves, and 4-foot long flower clusters.

itchweed *n.* A common name for Veratrum viride, a poisonous North American perennial from which a natural pesticide is made. It grows to 7 feet tall, has oval leaves 12 inches long, and bears clusters of small yellow-green flowers. Also known as American false hellebore. (See **Veratrum** and **hellebore, false.**)

Itea virginica
(Virginia willow)

Itea (ih tee'uh) *n.* A genus of 10 species of tender or tropical trees or shrubs (Saxifragaceae). They have alternate, simple leaves and spikes of small, handsome, sometimes fragrant, white flowers. *I. virginica,* called the Virginia willow, the only North

American species, is native to the eastern United States from New Jersey southward. It is hardy and deciduous, the leaves turning a brilliant red in autumn. *I. ilicifolia,* commonly known as hollyleaf sweetspire, is grown throughout the West; it is a graceful evergreen shrub used near pools or silhouetted against walls.

Ithuriel's spear (ihth′yer ee uhlz) *n.* A common name for *Triteleia laxa,* a spring-blooming bulb native to California and southwestern Oregon. It has slim basal leaves and stalks with clusters of small, nodding, trumpet-shaped purple-blue flowers. The name comes from a character, the Spirit Ithuriel, in John Milton's *Paradise Lost.* Formerly classified as *Brodiaea.*

ivory nut *n.* The seed of *Phytelephas macrocarpa,* a low- growing palm native to South America. The seeds are produced, 4 to 9 together, in hard, clustered capsules, each head weighing about 25 pounds when ripe. Each seed is about as large as a hen's egg; the albumen is close-grained and very hard, resembling the finest ivory in texture and color; for this reason, it is called vegetable ivory and is often in ornamental work, including inlay and scrimshaw. It is also known *nas corozo.*

ivory palm *n.* A common name for *Phytelephas macrocarpa,* the tree that bears the ivory nut. The nuts, called vegetable ivory, are produced in 25-pound clusters, and are used as a substitute for ivory. The harvested nuts are an environmentally sound use of a South American rainforest tree. Also known as tagua nut.

ivory tree *n.* A common name for *Wrightia tinctoria,* a tropical small tree, with elliptical leaves and large clusters of white flowers.

ivy *n.* A common name for handsome broadleaf evergreen vines of the genus *Hedera* (Araliaceae). The leaves of *H. Helix,* English ivy, are smooth and shiny, varying in form, from oval entire to 3- and 5-lobed. The inconspicuous greenish flowers grow in round clusters and are succeeded by deep-green or almost black berries. *H. h.* 'Hibernica', commonly known as Irish ivy, is grown for its large leaves and rapid growth. *H. canariensis,* the Algerian ivy, is ubiquitous on the West Coast, where it is considered to be the workhorse of California landscaping. Ivy attains a great age, the

shaggy stem ultimately becoming several inches thick and capable of supporting the weight of the plant. It has been celebrated from remote antiquity, and it was held sacred in some countries, such as Greece and Egypt.

English ivy
a flower *b* fruit

ivy-tod *n.* A common name for a clump of ivy.

ivy tree *n.* A common name for *Neopanax arboreus,* a tender, broadleaf evergreen tree, that grows to 25 feet. It has hand-shaped leaves, clusters of 5 flowers, and black-purple berries. Grown in warm-winter regions.

Ixia (eek′see uh) *n.* A genus of 30 species of tender bulbs (corms) (Iridaceae). They have narrow, sword-shaped leaves and long, wiry stems, bearing spikes of large, showy, cup-shaped cream, yellow, orange, red, or pink flowers with dark centers. Excellent cut flowers, they are grown in beds in warm climates, in pots in cold climates. Also known as African corn lily.

Ixiolirion (eek′see oh lihr′ee ahn) *n.* A genus of three species of bulbs (Amaryllidaceae). They have onionlike bulbs, simple, erect stems, and clusters of pretty blue or violet trumpet-shaped flowers. Also known as lily-of-the-Altai.

Ixora (eek′suh ruh) *n.* 1. A genus of 400 species of tropical broadleaf evergreen shrubs and small trees (Rubiaceae). They have opposite or whorled, leathery leaves and clusters of white, yellow, orange, pink, or red long, tubular flowers. Many species are cultivated for the elegance and, in some cases, the fragrance of their flowers. 2. [l.c.] A plant of this genus.

jaboticaba (zhuh boot ih kahb′uh) *n*. A common name for *Myrciaria cauliflora* a tender, medium-sized Brazilian tree with narrow leaves, clusters of white flowers growing out of the trunk and branches, and a small, edible white-to-purple fruit. Requires frost-free winters and cool, humid summers.

Jacaranda (jak uh ran′duh) *n*. A genus of 50 species of trees *Bignoniaceae* native to tropical America. They are tall, elegant trees, with much divided, fernlike leaves, and large, showy clusters of blue, violet, white, or pink flowers. A beautiful street tree or specimen tree in mild-winter climates.

jacinth (jays′ihnth) *n*. A common name for *Hyacinthus,* a spring-blooming bulb. Same as hyacinth.

jackfruit *n*. A common name for the large tropical tree *Artocarpus heterophyllus,* with long, stiff, glossy oval leaves, 4 spikes of flowers growing from the trunk and branches, and 2-foot-long, greenish-yellow, spike-studded edible fruit. Also known as jack tree.

jack-in-the-bush *n*. A common name for the succulent *Umbilicus rupestris* (Crassulaceae), with round basal leaves and tall spikes of tiny yellow flowers.

jack-in-the-pulpit *n*. A common name for *Arisaema triphyllum:* so called from its upright, fleshy flower spike surrounded and overarched by a large, leaflike structure. Also called Indian turnip and dragonroot. (See **Araceae**.)

Jacob's ladder *n*. A common name for the genus *Polemonium* (Polemoniaceae), as well as the species *P. caeruleum* so called from the ladderlike arrangement of its leaves and leaflets. It grows tall and erect to 1 foot, with lush rosettes of finely divided, fernlike, bright green leaves and large clusters of bell-shaped blue, purple, yellow, or white flowers. Traditional in cottage gardens.

Jacob's ladder
a stem and roots *b*
flower cluster

Jacquemontia (jah kwee mohn′tee ah) *n*. A genus of about 120 species of herbaceous, twining vines (Convolvulaceae); natives mostly of tropical and subtropical America. They have heart-shaped entire leaves and small morning-glory blue or white flowers.

Jacquinia (jah kween′ee ah) *n*. A genus of 25 species of trees or shrubs (Theophrastaceae) native to dry tropical America. They have thick, leathery leaves, sometimes spine-tipped, and clusters or spikes of small red, yellow, or white flowers.

jade plant *n*. A common name for *Crassula arborescens,* a treelike succulent with thick, fleshy, often red-rimmed, leaves and clusters of pink starry flowers. Used as a pot plant, a drought-tolerant hedge, or a specimen in warm-climate areas, as a houseplant anywhere.

jaggery palm *n*. A common name for *Caryota urens,* a single-stemmed palm with attractive, finely divided, dark green leaves, the ends split like fishtails. Unlikely to fruit, but if it should, handling the fruit can cause a virulently itchy rash. Also called fishtail palm. Grown mostly as a houseplant or greenhouse specimen.

jalapeño (hahl uh payn′yoh) *n*. A hot pepper variety, of a color ranging from green to red, red being the hottest.

jambolana (jam buh la′nuh) *n*. A common name for *Syzygium cumini,* a slow-growing East Indian

243

tree with long, oval leaves, clusters of white flowers, and purplish-red, edible, berrylike fruit. Closely related to *Eugenia* and often sold under that name. Grown in mild-winter climates. Also called jambolan.

jambu (jam′boo) *n.* A common name for *Syzygium cumini.* Also called jambolana.

Jamesia (jaym′zee uh) *n.* A genus of a single species, *J. americana,* native to western North America. It is a hardy, deciduous shrub to 6 feet, with flaking bark, oval or rounded serrate, fuzzy, green leaves, gray beneath, and clusters of small white or pink flowers.

Jamestown weed *n.* A common name for *Datura Stramonium,* a North American annual that grows to 5 feet, with long, oval, toothed or lobed leaves and trumpet-shaped flowers. A common roadside weed, it is extremely poisonous, and the source of the drug hyoscyamine. Same as Jimsonweed.

jamrosade (jam′roh zayd) *n.* A common name for the fruit of *Syzygium Jambos,* also called the rose apple, which has a mild flavor and the fragrance of rose water. Prized for use in making jellies and confections.

Japan clover *n.* A common name for *Lespedeza striata* (Leguminosae), widely naturalized throughout the southeastern United States. It has many, small 3-part leaves and tiny pink to lavender flowers. Grown as a forage plant.

Japanese anemone (uh nehm′oh nee) *n.* A common name for *Anemone xhybrida,* a clumping herbaceous perennial with soft, maplelike leaves and tall stalks of white, silvery-pink, or rose flowers that bloom in late summer and autumn. Useful in the perennial border, a classic in old-fashioned gardens. Also called Japanese windflower.

Japanese angelica tree *n.* A common name for *Aralia elata,* a hardy shrub or tree to 45 feet tall, with thorny stems, bold, striking leaves divided into fuzzy, oval leaflets, and large clusters of small white or greenish flowers.

Japanese apricot *n.* A common name for *Prunus Mume,* a winter- flowering apricot with oval, pointed leaves and masses of small spicily fragrant white or dark red flowers. Also called Japanese flowering plum. (See **Japanese flowering plum**.)

Japanese arborvitae (ar′ber vee′tee) *n.* A common name for *Thuja Standishii,* a fairly hardy, slow-growing, evergreen, pyramidal coniferous tree to 50 feet, with sprays of scalelike or needlelike leaves and small, erect cones. Used as a screening plant.

Japanese artichoke *n.* A common name for *Stachys affinis,* an erect, hairy plant with white or light red flowers; grown for its edible tubers.

Japanese ash *n.* A common name for *Fraxinus manchurica,* a hardy deciduous tree to 100 feet, with opposite, divided leaves.

Japanese ashberry *n.* A common name for *Mahonia japonica,* a shrub that grows to 7 feet, with oval, spiny-edged leaves divided into paired leaflets and long, drooping spikes of yellow flowers. Used in Japanese gardens.

Japanese aspen *n.* A common name for *Populus Sieboldii,* a fairly hardy deciduous tree to 60 feet, with drooping catkins and rounded, pointed leaves.

Japanese azalea *n.* A common name for any of several species of *Rhododendron,* particularly *R. japonicum,* a fairly hardy shrub to 6 feet, with long, oval leaves and clusters of large, trumpet-shaped, yellow, orange, or brick-red flowers.

Japanese banana *n.* A common name for *Musa Basjoo,* a tender perennial to 8 feet, grown for its foliage, having leaves 4 to 5 feet long, clusters of yellow-green or brown flowers, and small, narrow, 2½ inch-long bananalike greenish-yellow fruit. A prized ornamental in Japanese gardens.

Japanese barberry *n.* A common name for *Berberis Thunbergii,* a dense, compact, hardy, deciduous shrub to 5 feet, with graceful, slender, arching branches, small yellow-green to red variegated leaves, clusters of red flowers, and red, lustrous fruit. Excellent fall color. Used as a specimen shrub or hedge.

Japanese beautyberry *n.* A common name for *Callicarpa japonica,* a hardy shrub to 5 feet tall, with long finely toothed, oval leaves, clusters of white-to-pink flowers, and violet berries.

Japanese beech *n.* A common name for *Fagus crenata,* a hardy deciduous tree to 90 feet, with a rounded crown, oval leaves, and hard-shelled nuts.

Japanese beetle *n.* A very destructive pest introduced from Japan. The adult beetles feed voraciously on the foliage of many plants, especially deciduous trees. The grubs feed on roots and are serious pests of lawns. The beetles can be controlled somewhat with pheromone traps; the grubs can be effectively killed using *Bacillus popillea* or parasitic nematodes. Traditional pesticides are also effective.

Japanese beetle trap *n.* A container baited with floral and/or sex scents to capture the voracious, garden-consuming Japanese beetle.

Japanese bittersweet *n.* A common name for *Celastrus orbiculatus,* a hardy, deciduous, twining vine with large, nearly round, leaves and yellow-to-orange fruit capsules that split open to reveal scarlet seeds. Grows best in cold-winter regions. Grown for winter color and for use in dried arrangements.

Japanese black pine *n.* A common name for *Pinus Thunbergiana,* a hardy evergreen conifer to 130 feet, often much smaller, with spreading branches and an asymmetrical shape at maturity. It has long, stiff, bright green needles in pairs and brown, oval, 3-inch-long cones. Unlike many conifers, it responds well to pruning and shearing. Used as a specimen tree, or, heavily pruned, in Oriental gardens, and for bonsai.

Japanese cherry *n.* A common name for *Prunus serrulata,* a much-hybridized species famous for its masses of spring flowers. It grows to 30 feet, has long, smooth, oval, finely toothed leaves, and white or pink, often double, flowers in lavish profusion. Grown as specimen trees, in clumps, or to line an avenue. Also called Japanese flowering cherry.

Japanese chestnut *n.* A common name for *Castanea crenata,* a hardy deciduous tree to 30 feet, with long, oblong, finely toothed, fuzzy leaves, catkins, and shiny brown nuts. Resistant to chestnut blight. Grown as a shade tree.

Japanese cedar *n.* A common name for *Cryptomeria japonica,* a fast-growing coniferous tree to 150 feet with soft, needlelike leaves and small, round, reddish-brown cones. The leaves turn red with cold weather. Used as a sentinel tree; grown in groves in Japanese gardens. Dwarf varieties are attractive in containers.

Japanese climbing fern *n.* A common name for *Lygodium japonicum,* a vining fern with finely di-

vided triangular leaves. Grown outdoors in mild climates on trellises or in hanging baskets, as a greenhouse plant anywhere.

Japanese cornel dogwood *n.* A common name for *Cornus officinalis,* a hardy, deciduous, small tree or shrub with elliptic, pale green leaves, small clusters of yellow flowers, and round red fruit. Useful as a single specimen or in shrub borders. Also known as Japanese cornel and Japanese carnelian cherry.

Japanese cypress *n.* A common name for *Chamaecyparis obtusa,* a mostly hardy coniferous tree with reddish-brown bark, glossy leaves in flattened, frondlike, drooping branchlets, and tiny cones. The Dwarf cultivars are less hardy than the species. Also called hinoki cypress.

Japanese elm *n.* A common name for *Ulmus Davidiana* var. *japonica,* a broad-crowned deciduous tree to 90 feet, with oval leaves. Same as keaki.

Japanese farmer's weeder *n.* A knife-shaped tool for pulling, piercing, cutting, and prying weeds.

Japanese flowering plum *n.* A common name for *Prunus Mume,* a winter-flowering plum with oval, pointed leaves and masses of small, spicily fragrant white or dark red flowers. It is considered the longest-lived of all flowering fruit trees, becoming eventually a gnarled, picturesque, round-crowned tree 20 to 30 feet tall. Much used as a flowering tree, Japanese gardens, as well as for bonsai.

Japanese garden *n.* A garden in the Japanese style, which strives to recreate nature on a microcosmic scale. It suggests the wildness of nature by asymmetry and odd-numbered grouping of trees, plants, stones, etc. It builds the concept of time into the garden by emphasizing the beauty of each season; spring bloom, fall color, winter silhouette. Change is demonstrated by motion as well, for example, a rushing stream contrasted by a stable stone. In general, the color palette of a Japanese garden is all the shades and tones of green. A plant's shape, rather than its flowers, is emphasized. Straight lines, rigid geometric patterns, and a single view are generally avoided. Winding paths open up a different view, a new perspective, around each curve. In addition to the aesthetic principles, Japanese gardens typically incorporate Shinto or Zen elements as well, for example, 5 large stones to represent the 5 Virtues.

The purpose of a Japanese garden is to evoke a sense of the beauty of nature and to leave the viewer feeling serene and composed.

Japanese hawthorn *n.* A common name for *Rhaphiolepis umbellata,* a rounded, broadleaf evergreen shrub to 10 feet, with oval leaves, clusters of small white flowers, and small black berries. Used as an informal hedge or a background plant.

Japanese hazel *n.* A common name for *Corylus Sieboldiana,* a shrub to 15 feet, with oval, hairy leaves, flowers in catkins, and small brown nuts with a bristly husk.

Japanese hemlock *n.* A common name for *Tsuga diversifolia,* a fairly hardy evergreen conifer with small, delicate leaves and small cones. Also *T. Sieboldii,* a fairly hardy evergreen conifer with entire leaves banded in white. Useful as a lawn tree.

Japanese holly *n.* A common name for *Ilex crenata,* a fairly hardy shrub or small tree to 15 feet, with lustrous, deep green, oval leaves with wavy edges, white flowers, and small black berries. Looks more like a boxwood than a holly and is used, like box, for edgings and hedges.

Japanese honeysuckle *n.* A common name for *Lonicera japonica,* a semievergreen twining vine with oval leaves, highly fragrant white or purplish flowers, and shiny black winter berries. A useful, fragrant vine or ground cover in the West, it has become a pest in the Northeast.

Japanese hop *n.* A common name for *Humulus japonicus,* an ornamental twining vine with deeply lobed serrate leaves, sometimes variegated with white, and flowers in greenish clusters that look like little pinecones. Grown as an annual on porches and over pergolas.

Japanese iris *n.* A common name for *Iris ensata,* a graceful, upright, beardless iris, with sword-shaped leaves and stems to 4 feet tall, bearing exquisite, flat, spreading violet, pink, rose, red, or white flowers. Superior in moist borders, on stream banks, at edges of pools, or in containers.

Japanese knotweed *n.* A common name for *Polygonum cuspidatum,* a perennial growing from rhizomes and forming large clumps of jointed, red-brown stems with heart-shaped leaves and clusters of small greenish-white flowers. Grown as a ground cover in wild gardens, it is extremely invasive. Also called bamboo or Mexican bamboo.

Japanese ivy *n.* A common name for *Parthenocissus tricuspidata,* a dense, fast-growing, self-clinging vine with simple leaves, famous for their brilliant scarlet fall color. Grown on brick or stone walls, this is the ivy of the Ivy League.

Japanese lantern plant *n.* A common name for plants of 2 different species, *Hibiscus schizopetalus* and *Physalis alkekengi. H. schizopetalus* is a shrub to 9 feet, with slender, drooping branches, oval leaves, and delicate, pendant flowers, streaked with pink or red that dangle from a long stem. *P. alkekengi* is a perennial with angular branches, entire light green leaves, nodding white flowers, and fruits that look like paper lanterns. The stalks are excellent to use in dried arrangements.

Japanese laurel *n.* 1. A common name for *Aucuba japonica* (Cornaceae). *A. japonica* is an evergreen branching shrub, with smooth opposite leaves and small, unisexual flowers. It is prized for its mass of glossy, leathery, oval-toothed green leaves, splotched with yellow, and its coral-red berries. 2. Also a common name for *Crassula argentea,* a perennial succulent shrub to 10 feet, with small, fleshy, oval green leaves, often red-margined, and clusters of white or pink flowers. Used as a houseplant anywhere, in containers, or as a shrub or hedge in mild climates.

Japanese lilac *n.* 1. A common name for *Syringa villosa,* native to China, a very hardy deciduous shrub with large, oblong leaves and 1-foot-long clusters of lilac or pinkish-white fragrant flowers. Used as a specimen shrub in cold climates. 2. A common name for *S. reticulata,* native to Manchuria, a hardy, very large shrub, easily trained to tree shape, with showy, oddly fragrant white flowers. Also called Japanese tree lilac.

Japanese linden *n.* A common name for *Tilia japonica,* a hardy deciduous tree to 65 feet, with small, alternate leaves and clusters of yellowish or white fragrant flowers that attract bees.

Japanese mint *n.* A common name for *Mentha arvensis piperescens,* an erect, hairy perennial to 3 feet. It has oval, toothed, aromatic leaves and lilac, pink, or white flowers.

Japanese oak *n.* A common name for *Lithocarpus glaber* (Fagaceae), a perennial broadleaf evergreen shrub or tree to 30 feet, with elliptic or oblong leathery, alternate leaves, catkins, and acorns. Grown in the South and in California.

Japanese pagoda tree *n.* A common name for *Sophora japonica,* a round-headed, deciduous tree to 80 feet, with leaves divided into small leaflets and long, loose clusters of yellowish-white flowers. Also known as Chinese scholar tree.

Japanese parasol fir *n.* A common name for *Sciadopitys verticillata,* a slow-growing evergreen conifer to 40 feet, in cultivation, with small, scale-like leaves along the branches and whorls of needles that look like the spokes of an umbrella at the tips of the branches. Also called Japanese umbrella pine. A choice specimen tree; superb in containers.

Japanese pear *n.* A common name for *Pyrus pyrifolia,* a hardy deciduous tree to 50 feet, with glossy, leathery, ovate leaves that color brilliant burgundy in fall, white 5-petaled flowers, and hard, brown, apple-shaped gritty fruit. *P.p. culta* has sweet, juicy, edible round fruit called Asian pear.

Japanese persimmon *n.* A common name for *Diospyros Kaki,* a tree to 40 feet, with large ovate leaves, yellowish-white flowers, and reddish-to-orange fruit with orange flesh. The slightly pointed oval fruit of 'Hachiya' is astringent until mushy ripe; 'Fuyu', shaped like a flattened tomato, can be eaten while still firm.

Japanese pink *n.* A common name for *Dianthus chinensis* 'Heddewigii', has small, narrow leaves and loose clusters of small rosy-lilac flowers with a purple eye. Grows from 6 to 30 inches. Used in borders, flower beds, and rock gardens.

Japanese pittosporum (pih tahs'puhr uhm) *n.* A common name for *Pittosporum Tobira,* an evergreen shrub with dense, leathery, dark green leaves and clusters of small creamy-white fragrant flowers, with a fragrance like orange blossoms. Does best in mild-winter climates. Used massed, as a screen, as a foundation plant, and in containers.

Japanese plum *n.* 1. A common name for *Prunus salicina,* a small tree to 25 feet, with oblong, pointed, usually shiny, leaves, small 5-petaled white flowers, and edible, medium-to-large yellow or light red plums. Parent to many edible plum cultivars. 2. A common name for *Eriobotrya japonica,* a tree with large, oval, strongly-veined leaves, small yellow flowers, and small golden-yellow edible fruits. Also called loquat. Grown for fruit and to create subtropical effects in mild temperate climates.

Japanese privet (prihv'uht) *n.* A common name for *Ligustrum lucidum* and *L. japonicum. L. lucidum* is a fast-growing broadleaf evergreen tree, which grows to 35 to 40 feet, with glossy, pointed, leathery medium-to-dark-green leaves, large feathery clusters of white flowers, and masses of blue-black berries. Used as a street tree, a windbreak, screen, a lawn tree, and in containers. *L. japonicum* is a compact, dense broadleaf evergreen shrub to 10 feet, with thick, glossy, dark green oval leaves, paler beneath, sprays of tiny white oddly fragrant flowers that attract bees, and clusters of blue-black berries that attract birds. Used for clipped hedges, screening, and topiary.

Japanese quince *n.* A common name for *Chaenomeles speciosa,* a hardy deciduous or semievergreen shrub with alternate, toothed, shiny green leaves tinged with red and many early-blooming, large red, rose, pink, or white flowers. They are picturesque and practically indestructible, tolerating extremes of cold and heat as well as light to heavy soils. The flowers attract birds. There are many hybrids available. This is the traditional flower used to symbolize and celebrate the Chinese New Year. Used for hedges, barriers, and for bonsai. Also known as flowering quince and japonica.

Japanese raisin tree *n.* A common name for *Hovenia dulcis,* a hardy deciduous tree to 30 feet, with toothed, ovate leaves, spikes of small greenish flowers, and small red fruit. The fruit stalks are edible.

Japanese red pine *n.* A common name for *Pinus densiflora,* a hardy fast-growing evergreen conifer to 100 feet, but usually much less. It has pairs of 5-inch-long bright blue-green or yellow-green needles and 2-inch-long, oval, tawny brown cones. At maturity, it is asymmetric, and it may grow multiple trunks. Useful for an informal effect.

Japanese rose *n.* A common name for the genus *Kerria,* large deciduous shrubs with arching branches covered with small yellow, roselike flowers. Also called Japan globeflower. Grown as a specimen plant.

Japanese rubber plant *n.* A common name for *Crassula argentea,* a perennial succulent shrub to 10 feet, with small fleshy, oval green leaves, often red-margined, and clusters of white or pink flowers. Used as a houseplant anywhere, in containers, or as a shrub or hedge in mild climates.

Japanese silver grass *n.* (See **Miscanthus**.)

Japanese snowball *n.* A common name for *Viburnum plicatum,* a choice, hardy deciduous shrub with oval, toothed, soft dark green leaves, rounded clusters 2 to 3 inches across of white sterile blossoms, and spectacular purple-red color in autumn. Used as a specimen shrub.

Japanese snowbell *n.* A common name for *Styrax japonicus,* a hardy deciduous tree with alternate, simple, shiny leaves that turn red or yellow in fall and drooping spikes of fragrant white flowers in early summer. Used as a shade tree or patio tree. Also called Japanese storax.

Japanese snowflower *n.* A common name for *Deutzia gracilis,* a hardy deciduous flowering shrub to 6 feet, with bright green sharply toothed leaves and clusters of snowy white flowers on slender, arched branches. Used as a specimen shrub; best against an evergreen background.

Japanese spruce *n.* 1. A common name for *Abies Mariesii,* a hardy evergreen conifer to 75 feet, with short, bluish-green grooved needles and oval 3-inch-long dark purple cones. Grown as a specimen tree. 2. A common name for *Picea jezoensis,* a hardy evergreen conifer to 150 feet, with short silvery-green needles, dark green beneath, and 3½-inch-long cones. Also called Yeddo spruce.

Japanese spurge *n.* A common name for *Pachysandra terminalis,* a hardy evergreen ground cover with small, toothed dark green leaves and spikes of white flowers. Extremely useful as a ground cover in shady areas.

Japanese star anise *n.* A common name for *Allicium anisatum,* a broadleaf evergreen tree to 25 feet, with oval, aromatic leaves that give off an aniselike odor when bruised, and white-to-yellow flowers. Cut branches are a traditional decoration on Buddhist graves.

Japanese storax (stoh′raks) *n.* A common name for *Styrax japonicus,* a hardy deciduous tree with alternate, simple, shiny leaves that turn red or yellow in fall and drooping spikes of fragrant white flowers in early summer. Used as a shade tree or patio tree. Also called Japanese snowbell.

Japanese tree lilac *n.* A common name for the *Syringa reticulata,* native to Manchuria, a hardy, very large shrub, easily trained to tree shape, with showy, oddly fragrant white flowers. Also called Japanese lilac.

Japanese umbrella pine *n.* A common name for *Sciadopitys verticillata,* a slow-growing evergreen conifer to 40 feet, in cultivation, with small, scale-like leaves along the branches and whorls of needles that look like the spokes of an umbrella at the tips of the branches. A choice specimen tree; superb in containers. Also called Japanese parasol fir. 2. A common name for *Pinus densiflora* 'Umbraculifera', a dwarf hardy evergreen conifer with pairs of 5-inch-long bright blue-green or yellow-green needles and 2-inch-long, oval, tawny brown cones. At maturity, it is broader than high and it may grow multiple trunks. Used in rock gardens and containers.

Japanese walnut *n.* A common name for *Juglans ailantifolia,* a tree to 60 feet, with much-divided leaves, downy beneath, and a small, sticky, round fruit containing a thick-shelled, edible nut.

Japanese white pine *n.* A common name for *Pinus parviflora,* a hardy evergreen conifer to 50 feet, often much less, forming a broad pyramid at maturity. It has needles in bundles of 5 and 2 to 3-inch-long oval, reddish-brown cones. Used as a broad shade tree, as a container plant, and for bonsai.

Japanese windflower *n.* A common name for *Anemone* x*hybrida,* a clumping herbaceous perennial with soft, maplelike leaves and tall stalks of white, silvery-pink, or rose flowers that bloom in late summer and autumn. Useful in the perennial border, a classic in old-fashioned gardens. Also called Japanese anemone.

Japanese wisteria (wihs tihr′ee uh) *n.* A common name for *Wisteria floribunda,* a long-lived woody vine to 35 feet or more, with long leaves divided into small leaflets and showy violet, violet-blue, red, or pink flowers in long clusters. *W.f.* cv.

'Longissima' has flower clusters 3 feet long. Used to cover arbors and porches; grown along the eaves of a sun-room or house. Requires sturdy support.

Japanese witch hazel *n.* A common name for *Hamamelis japonica,* a hardy shrub or tree to 30 feet, with oval, pointed leaves and clusters of small, yellow fragrant flowers with narrow, crumpled-looking petals. Treasured for its early bloom, and attractive winter silhouette.

Japanese yew *n.* A common name for *Taxus cuspidata,* a hardy evergreen conifer to 50 feet, usually smaller, with compact, dark green needles in flat sprays and fleshy red or yellow fruit. Used as clipped formal hedges and screens, particularly in shady areas with moist soil.

Japan globeflower *n.* A common name for the genus *Kerria,* large deciduous shrubs with arching branches covered with small yellow roselike flowers. Also called Japanese rose. Grown as a specimen plant.

japonica (juh pahn'ih kuh) *n.* 1. A common name for *Camellia japonica,* the camellia, a choice, slow-growing, flowering shrub to 45 feet at maturity, with showy red, pink, white, or variegated flowers. 2. A common name for *Chaenomeles speciosa,* a hardy deciduous or semievergreen shrub with alternate, toothed, shiny green leaves tinged with red and many early-blooming, large, red, rose, pink or white flowers. 3. A common name for *Lagerstroemia indica,* crape myrtle, a small, drought-and-heat resistant deciduous shrub or tree to 30 feet, with small, rounded, alternate leaves and spectacular masses of fluffy red, pink, purple, and white flowers throughout summer.

jardiniere stand (jahrd'ihn ihr) *n.* An ornamental structure for holding plants.

jarool (juh rool') *n.* A common name for *Lagerstroemia speciosa,* a deciduous tree to 80 feet, with clusters of showy purple or white flowers. (See **myrtle, queen's crape**.)

Jasione (jay see'oh nee) *n.* A genus of 10 species of herbaceous flowers (Campanulaceae). They have simple basal leaves and long, partially leafy stems with dense terminal clusters of blue or white flowers.

jasmine *n.* 1. A common name for plants of the genus *Jasminum.* 2. A common name for plants of other species that have heavily fragrant flowers, such as *Trachelospermum jasminoides* (star jasmine), and *Cestrum nocturnum* (night-blooming jasmine). 3. A synonym for jessamine. Also spelled jasmin.

jasmine
a flower

jasmine, bastard *n.* A common name for plants of the genus *Cestrum* (Solanaceae), a genus of about 150 species of fast-growing vines, shrubs, and trees, native to tropical America. They have clusters of richly fragrant, funnel-shaped red, yellow, white, or greenish flowers. Used on trellises or as an espalier in mild-winter climates. The flowers and fruit attract birds.

jasmine, Cape *n.* A common name for *Gardenia jasminoides,* a tender evergreen shrub to 6 feet, with dense, glossy, dark green leaves and extraordinarily fragrant white flowers. There are many named cultivars. Excellent in containers and in raised beds, as espaliers, or as specimen plants.

jasmine, Carolina *n.* A common name for *Gelsemium sempervirens,* a heat-loving evergreen twining vine, native to areas from Virginia to Texas and Central America, with glossy, narrow leaves and masses of fragrant bright yellow flowers. All parts of the plant are poisonous. Grown on porches, trellises, fences, and over walls. Also known as Carolina jessamine or yellow jasmine.

jasmine, Chilean *n.* A common name for *Mandevilla laxa,* a deciduous vine to 15 feet or more, with long, oval leaves and showy, large, powerfully fragrant white flowers. Grown on trellises and fences in mild climates.

jasmin, night *n.* A common name for *Nyctanthes arbor-tristis,* a shrub or small tree with heart-shaped leaves and fragrant, tubular, orange flowers, which open at night. Grown in mild climates for its heavily perfumed flowers.

jasmine, red *n.* A common name for the tropical tree *Plumeria rubra,* which grows to 25 feet, with long, heavily veined leaves and clusters of sweetly fragrant red, purple, pink, yellow, or white flowers. Grown as a lawn tree and does well in containers in warm climates, such as southern California and Hawaii. Also known as frangipani.

Jasminum (jaz'mih nuhm) *n.* A genus of about 200 species of tender and tropical shrubs and vines (Oleaceae). They have much-divided leaves and white, yellow, or pink tubular, often sweetly fragrant, flowers. Well-known species include *J. officinale* (common white jasmine or poet's jasmine), *J. grandiflorum* (Spanish jasmine), and *J. Sambac* (Arabian jasmine or pikake), all of which are used in perfumes. Many other species are prized for their elegance and fragrance.

jaundice-berry *n.* A common name for *Berberis vulgaris,* a deciduous shrub with small, spiny oval leaves, short spikes of yellow-to-red flowers, and red, oblong berries. Also called jaundice tree and barberry.

Jeffersonia (jehf uhr soh'nee uh) *n.* A genus of 2 species of herbaceous perennials (Berberidaceae) 1 native to eastern North America, the other to eastern China. The plants have a perennial rhizome, with basal leaf blades and solitary white or blue flowers on slender, leafless stalks. The seed capsule opens near the top, as if by a lid. *J. diphylla,* commonly known as twinleaf, is native to the eastern United States, its white, inch-wide blossoms appearing in April or May.

jellico (jehl'ih koh) *n.* The plant *Angelica sylvestris.*

Jersey tea *n.* A common name for *Ceanothus americanus,* an ornamented plant often cultivated after transplanting from the wild.

Jerusalem artichoke (ahr'tuh chohk) *n.* A species of sunflower, *Helianthus tuberosus,* also called the girasole and, more recently for commerce, the sun-

choke. This sturdy perennial grows 10 feet tall and produces a crisp, potatolike tuber. The daisy-shaped flowers are brilliant orange.

Jerusalem cherry *n.* A common name for *Solanum Pseudocapscium,* an ornamental plant, popular for its showy fruit, which is poisonous.

Jerusalem thorn *n.* A common name for *Parkinsonia aculeata,* a deciduous, sparsely-leaved shrub or small tree to 20 feet, with spiny twigs, leaves divided into many small leaflets, and clusters of many yellow flowers that bloom in spring and intermittently throughout the year. Tolerant of drought and alkaline soil, it is useful in desert gardens.

jessamine, jessamin (jehs'uh muhn) *n.* Same as jasmine.

jessamine, Carolina (jehs'uh muhn) *n.* (See **jasmine, Carolina.**)

jessamine, willow-leaved (jehs'uh muhn) *n.* A common name for *Cestrum parqui,* a many-branched broadleaf evergreen shrub with dense, narrow, willowlike leaves, clusters of small, powerfully fragrant greenish-yellow flowers in summer, and dark violet-brown berries. The flowers and fruit attract birds; the foliage is poisonous to livestock. Grows best in mild-winter climates in protected spots where summer fragrance can be enjoyed.

jetbead *n.* A common name for *Rhodotypos scandens,* a hardy deciduous shrub 3 to 6 feet tall, with oval, pointed, shiny, toothed leaves, large, white 4-petaled flowers, and shiny, black pea-sized berries.

jet stream sprayer *n.* A nozzle with a single, small opening attached to a garden hose to produce a strong, narrow flow of water.

jewelweed *n.* 1. A common name for *Impatiens pallida* and *I. capensis,* both wildflowers native to eastern North America. They are annuals to 5 feet, with shiny, oval, pointed, toothed leaves and spikes of nodding orange-yellow or canary-yellow flowers on slender stalks. They attract hummingbirds. Also known as balsam, touch-me-not, and snapweed. 2. A common name for the genus *Impatiens.* (See **balsam** and **Impatiens.**)

jewelweed family *n.* A common name for *Balsaminaceae,* a family of 2 genera and more than 500 species of flowers or subshrubs, most native to tropical and subtropical Asia and Africa. They have succulent stems, simple leaves, 5-petaled flowers, and elastic seedpods that explode open to spread the seeds. *Impatiens* is the only cultivated genus. Also known as the balsam, touch-me-not, or snapweed family.

Jew's mallow *n.* A common name for *Corchorus olitorius* (Tiliaceae), an erect, much-branched tropical annual to 12 feet and more, with large oval, pointed leaves and deep-yellow flowers. Also known as tossa jute.

Jew's myrtle *n.* A common name for *Ruscus aculeatus,* a prickly-leafed evergreen shrub to 3 feet, with greenish flowers and red or yellow berries. Flattened leaflike branches bear flowers and fruit in the center of the leaf and are used in everlasting arrangements. Tolerates drought, heavy moisture, and competition from tree roots; can be grown as a houseplant. Also known as box holly and butcher's-broom. (See **holly, box.**)

Jew's thorn *n.* 1. A common name for *Paliurus Spina-Christi,* a spiny tree to 20 feet, with small oval, pointed leaves and greenish-yellow flowers; hardy to Zone 7. Also known as Christ's-thorn and Jerusalem thorn. 2. A common name for *Ziziphus Jujuba,* a hardy deciduous spiny tree or large shrub to 40 feet, with oval, pointed, prickly leaves that turn yellow in fall, clusters of small, late-blooming green, yellow, or white flowers, and edible, date-like, apple-flavored fruits. Tolerates heat, drought, saline and alkaline soils, and is generally pest-free. Grown for its fruit, fall color, and winter silhouette. Also called common jujube and Chinese date.

jicama (hee'kuh muh) *n.* A vining plant, *Pachyrhizus erosus or P. tuberosus,* grown in the Southwest for its underground tuber (potatolike root), which is edible. The roots have a creamy- white, crisp flesh that is eaten raw or cooked. Jicama is low in calories and contains potassium and vitamin C.

jimsonweed *n.* A common name for the poisonous North American plant *Datura Stramonium,* which has angular-toothed leaves, large, funnel-shaped white flowers, and prickly, round pods. It has naturalized worldwide. Also known as jimson, jimpson, jimpson-weed; also called thorn apple.

Joannesia *n.* A genus of 2 species, of which only *J. principes* (Euphorbiaceae), native to Brazil, is cul-

tivated. It is a handsome tropical tree, with leaves divided into 3 to 7 leaflets, clusters of yellow flowers, and a warty, fleshy fruit. Used in tropical gardens.

Job's tears *n.* A species of grass, *Coix Lacryma,* or the beads made of its fruit. (See **Coix.**)

Joe-Pye weed *n.* 1. A common name for *Eupatorium purpureum,* native to eastern North America, a tall perennial to 10 feet, with open clusters of pink or purple flowers. Also known as sweet Joe-Pye weed and green-stem Joe-Pye-weed. 2. A common name for *E. maculatum,* which grows to 2 to 6 feet, with large, whorled leaves and clusters of purple flowers; native to damp areas of eastern North America. Also known as smokeweed.

joewood *n.* A common name for *Jacquinia Barbasco,* a subtropical American shrub or small tree to 15 feet, with clusters of oval, pointed, fleshy, four-inch-long leaves, spikes of small, fragrant, white 5-petaled flowers, and small orange berries. Grown in Florida and the West Indies. Also known as barbasco.

John-go-to-bed-at-noon *n.* A common name for *Tragopogon pratensis,* a hardy perennial to 3 feet, with yellow flowers. It has naturalized throughout the United States.

Johnny-jump-up *n.* 1. A common name for *Viola tricolor,* a low-growing annual or short-lived perennial flower with rounded, scalloped leaves and cheerful purple, yellow, and white flowers. It has been widely hybridized in other colors, including mauve, lavender, apricot, and red. Used in edging borders, massed in small areas, or in containers. 2. A common name for any of several North American wild violets such as *V. pedata* (bird-foot violet) and *V. pedunculata* (California golden violet). (See **violet, California golden.**)

John's-wort *n.* Same as St.-John's-wort. (See **Hypericum.**)

jointed *a.* With nodes, as the joints of a grass stem.

joint fir *n.* A common name for the genus *Ephedra,* 40 species of clumping, low-growing desert shrubs (Ephedraceae) some species native to desert or alkaline regions of South America. They are nearly leafless, with numerous branches, and triangular cones, which grow at the nodes. Used as a ground cover in desert gardens.

jointweed _n._ A common name for the genus _Polygonella,_ native to eastern North America, the species of which have jointed stems, clublike leaves, and spikes of small pink, white, or green flowers.

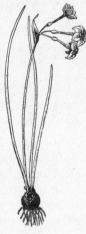

jonquil

jonquil (jahn'kwuhl) _n._ A common name for _Narcissus Jonquilla_ (Amaryllidaceae), an early-blooming bulb with narrow, rushike leaves to 18 inches, clusters of small, fragrant, pale yellow flowers on leafless stems. _N. odorus_ is called campernelle jonquil.

Joseph-and-Mary _n._ A common name for _Pulmonaria officinalis,_ a rough, hairy perennial to 12 inches, with white-spotted basal leaves and clusters of small rose-violet-to-blue flowers. Used in borders, beds, and cottage gardens and as a ground cover in shady areas. Also known as lungwort.

Joseph's coat _n._ A common name for _Amaranthus tricolor,_ an erect, many-branched annual to 4 feet, with oval leaves blotched with shades of red, yellow, and green, and inconspicuous flowers. Grown for its brightly colored foliage, and its edible leaves which can be eaten like spinach.

Joshua tree _n._ A common name for _Yucca brevifolia,_ a slow-growing small tree native to elevated desert regions of the western United States. It grows to 15 to 30 feet, with short, broad, sword-shaped leaves and 20-inch spikes of yellow to

cream-colored flowers. Tolerates drought and heat. Useful in desert gardens.

joss flower _n._ A common name for _Narcissus Tazetta orientalis,_ a bulb with long, narrow leaves and small clusters of early-blooming fragrant flowers with yellow petals and short orange trumpets at the top of leafless stems. Used in borders, beds, window boxes, and other containers; naturalized in lawns. Can be forced indoors for winter bloom.

Jove's-fruit _n._ A common name for _Lindera melissaefolia,_ a deciduous shrub native to wet places of the southeastern United States. It grows to 6 feet, has downy branches, large, oval, aromatic leaves, small yellow flowers, and red berries. Useful in moist soils.

Jubaea (joo bay'ah) _n._ A genus of a single species of palm, _J. chilensis_ (Palmae), native to coastal Chile. It is a huge, slow-growing palm to 50 feet, with a wide trunk and divided, feathery silver-green leaves, sharply curved at the tip. Grown outdoors in Mediterranean climates, as an indoor/outdoor plant elsewhere. Also known as Chilean wine palm, honey palm, syrup palm, coquito palm, and little cokernut palm.

Jubaeopsis (joo bay ahp'sihs) _n._ A genus of a single species of palm, _J. caffra_ (Palmae). It is a palm to 20 feet with divided 15 foot long leaves with a prominent midrib. Grown in mild winter climates.

Judas tree
_a_ flower cluster _b_ branch with
fruit _c_ flower

Judas tree _n._ 1: A common name for _Cercis Siliquastrum,_ a hardy tree to 40 feet with heart-shaped leaves, clusters of handsome purple flowers, and 4-inch long pods. 2. A common name for the genus *Cercis,* also known as redbud.

Juglandaceae (juh glan day'see ee) *n. pl.* The walnut family, consisting of 6 genera and 60 species of hardy trees. They have alternate, divided leaves with odd-numbered leaflets; sterile flowers in catkins, fertile flowers, either solitary or in small, erect spikes; and dry-hulled nuts. The important genera are *Juglans* (walnut) and *Carya* (hickory). They are grown for shade, beauty, and for their edible nuts. (See **hickory** and **walnut.**)

Juglans (juh'glanz) *n.* A genus of about 20 species of large, hardy, handsome, nut-bearing trees (Juglandaceae) some species native to the Americas; the walnut. They are large, spreading trees with alternate leaves divided into odd-numbered leaflets, male flowers in drooping catkins, and nuts ridged with a thick, fleshy, closely adhering husk. *J. regia* is commonly known as English walnut. *J. nigra* is the black walnut, native to eastern North America. *J. cinerea* is commonly known as butternut. *J. regia* (English walnut) and *J. californica* (southern California black walnut) are susceptible to aphids. (See **walnut.**)

jugum (joo'guhm) *n., pl,* **juga** (guh) In botany: 1. A pair of opposite leaflets in a pinnate leaf. 2. A ridge on the fruits of the family Ammiaceae.

jujube (joo'joob) *n.* 1. The name of several species of tree or shrub of the genus *Zizyphus.* 2. The edible fruit of these plants.

jumping bean *n.* The seed of any Mexican shrubs of the *Sebastiania* and *Sapium* genera, which, when infested by the larva of a small moth, *Carpocapsa saltitans,* makes tumbling and jumping movements. Also jumping seed.

Juncaceae (juhng kay'see ee) *n., pl.* A family of 8 or 9 genera of water-loving plants found worldwide; the true rushes. The ornamental genera, *Juncus* and *Luzula* (the wood rush), prefer shady, wet ground and temperate climates. They have cylindrical, stiff leaves, resembling grasses and sedges. (See **Juncus.**)

juncaceous (juhng kay'shuhs) *a.* In botany, pertaining to or resembling the Juncaceae.

Juncaginaceae (juhng kah juhn'uh see ee) *n., pl.* A family of 4 genera and 16 species of erect, wetland

plants, native to cool temperate regions. They grow from rhizomes, have long, basal, rushlike leaves, and spikes of inconspicuous flowers. The only cultivated genus is *Triglochin.*

Juncus, two varieties

Juncus (juhng'kuhs) *n.* A genus of 240 species of rushes (Juncaceae) native mostly to temperate regions. They are erect plants, with stiff, smooth, simple, slender, hollow or pithy stems and small heads of greenish or brownish flowers. Used in moist, shady locations as a ground cover or a novelty; also useful for controlling erosion along streams and on riverbanks.

Juneberry *n.* 1. The shadbush or serviceberry of North America, *Amelanchier alnifolia,* and other species. It is a bush or small tree, sometimes attaining the height of 30 feet, covered in spring with graceful white flower clusters, and yielding later a small berrylike fruit of a deep purple color and pleasant, tart flavor.

June bug *n.* A common name for several night-flying beetles, which usually emerge in June. The adults feed on the foliage of a variety of plants, usually deciduous trees. The grubs are serious pests of lawns. Control is the same as for the Japanese beetle: pheromone traps, *Bacillus popillae,* or traditional insecticides.

juniper *n.* A common name for plants of the genus *Juniperus,* dense, coniferous evergreen shrubs or trees. There are 70 species and hundreds of cultivars, in every possible height, width, foliage color, and picturesque shape. Tough, durable plants, they tolerate neglect, drought, and a wide variety of soils, they will grow in full sun or light shade. Used as ground covers, erosion control on hillsides, screens, windbreaks, specimens, and as container plants. The most widely grown woody plant in the West, junipers are susceptible to root rot in waterlogged soils, aphids, spider mites, twig borers, and juniper blight. Otherwise, they will endure to the Apocalypse and beyond.

juniper

Juniperus (joo nuh per'uhs) *n.* A genus of 70 species of coniferous shrubs or trees; the true junipers. The leaves are either scalelike or needlelike, the female fruit resembles a fleshy berry.

jupiter's-beard *n.* 1. A common name for *Sempervivum tectorum,* a succulent also known as houseleek. 2. A common name for the genus *Anthyllis,* annuals, perennials, and shrubs with dense, cloverlike purple, pink, yellow, or white flowers and long pods.

Justicia (juhs tihsh'uh) *n.* A genus of 300 species of erect evergreen, tropical perennials and shrubs (Acanthaceae). They have downy stems, opposite, entire leaves, and clusters of white, violet, pink, or red flowers that vary widely in shape from 1 species to the next. Grown in warm climate gardens or in greenhouses.

jute *n.* A common name for plants of the fiber-producing genus *Corchorus* (Tiliaceae); chiefly, 1 of 2 species, *C. capsularis* and *C. olitorius,* which furnish the glossy fiber for jute, used to make twine and burlap.

K

Kadsura (kahd'suh ruh) *n.* A genus of 22 species of fast-growing, moderately hardy or tropical evergreen twining vines (Schisandraceae). They have slender leaves, pink or white cup-shaped flowers, and showy bright red berries.

Kaempferia (kehmp fuh'ree uh) *n.* A genus of 50 species of nearly stemless tropical plants (Zingiberaceae). They have thick, aromatic rhizomes, leaves clustered at the base, and spikes or heads of white, yellow, violet, or purple flowers. Grown in greenhouses or warm-climate gardens.

kaffir boom (kaf'uh bohme) *n.* A common name for *Erythrina caffra,* a tender semievergreen tree, with large, broadly oval, pointed leaves, vermilion, yellow, or white flowers with a deep keel, and long, woody pods. Used in mild-winter climates as a flowering and shade tree. Also known as coral tree.

kaffir plum (kaf'uh) *n.* A common name for *Harpephyllum caffrum,* a tender tree to 30 feet, with leaves divided into long, slender leaflets, tight clusters of very small white or green flowers, and small, dark red, tart, edible fruit. Grown in mild-winter climates as a specimen.

Kageneckia (kaj uh nek'ee uh) *n.* A genus of small broadleaf evergreen South American trees (Rosaceae) native to Chile. They have coarse, leathery, sharp-toothed, oval, pointed leaves and small, 5-petaled white flowers.

kahikatea (kigh'kee tee uh) *n.* A common name for *Podocarpus dacrydioides,* a tender coniferous tree. It grows to the height of 100 feet or more, with overlapping, spreading, reddish new foliage and scalelike mature leaves, and yellow male catkins. Grown in warm-winter climates. Also called white pine, red pine, and kahika.

Kai apple (kigh) *n.* A common name for *Dovyalis caffra,* a subtropical shrub or small tree to 20 feet with stiff, sharp spines, oval, pointed, leaves at the base of the spines, inconspicuous flowers, and edible, smooth, yellow berries. Also called Kei apple, taking its name from the Kei River.

kainite (kigh'night) *n.* A natural salt contained in a fertilzer that is used as a source of potash (14% k).

kaki (kay'kee) *n.* The persimmon of Japan, or Chinese date, *Diospyros Kaki,* or its fruit.

Kalanchoe (kal uhn koh'ee) *n.* 1. A genus of 125 species of perennial tropical succulents or shrubs (Crassulaceae). They have opposite, entire, lobed, fleshy leaves, sometimes felty, and clusters of large white, yellow, red, orange, or salmon bell-shaped flowers. Grown mainly as houseplants or indoor/outdoor plants. Also known as Palm-Beach-bells. 2. [l.c.] A plant of this genus.

kale *n.* A variety of cabbage, *Brassica oleracea,* with curled or wrinkled leaves not forming compact heads like the common cabbage, nor yielding a fleshy, edible bloom like the cauliflower and broccoli, and usually having a long stalk. Kale is a cool-weather crop; the flavor of its leaves is enhanced by frost. It is rich in vitamin A. Also known as borecole. The ornamental kale is used as a bedding plant, for its rosettes of white, cream, pink, and purple leaves.

kale, Indian *n.* 1.A common name for *Colocasia esculenta,* a large perennial plant with big, dark green, callalike leaves and starchy edible tubers. Also known as taro, it has long been cultivated for food, particularly in the Pacific Islands. 2. A common name for *Xanthosoma sagittifolium,* a perennial with edible tubers, large, broad, arrow-shaped leaves and greenish-white callalike flowers. Also known as yautia, malanga, tannia, and ocumo. Both are used in warm-climate gardens to create a tropical effect, grown as houseplants elsewhere.

kale-turnip *n.* Same as kohlrabi, of which it is merely an English translation from German.

kale, wild *n.* A common name for the roadside weed *Brassica Kaber,* an annual to 3 feet, with hairy stems, lobed leaves, and clusters of small bright yellow flowers. Often seen growing in fields and orchards.

Kalmia (kal'mee uh) *n.* A genus of 6 species of very hardy broadleaf evergreen shrubs (Ericaceae) native to North America. They are handsome shrubs, with shining, simple leaves and clusters of showy white, pink, or purple flowers. Also known as laurel or American laurel. Grown in woodland gardens, as a foundation plant, or as a specimen in filtered light.

*Kalmia
(laurel)
a flower*

Kalmiopsis (kal mee ohp'sis) *n.* A genus of a single species, *K. Leachiana* (Ericaceae), a hardy, low-growing broadleaf evergreen shrub native to the Siskiyou Mountains of southwestern Oregon. It has alternate, simple, leathery, dark green leaves and abundant leafy clusters of small, rosy, bell-shaped flowers. Good in woodland situations with filtered light and in moist, acid soils, as a companion to *Rhododendron, Kalmia,* etc.

Kalopanax (kuh lap'uh naks) *n.* A genus of a single species, *K. pictus,* a hardy deciduous tree (Araliaceae). It grows to 80 feet, with large, shiny, lobed leaves, dark green above and light green below, and large clusters 5-petaled white flowers.

kangaroo apple *n.* 1. A common name *Solanum aviculare,* a tender fast-growing broadleaf evergreen shrub to 10 feet, with smooth, deeply cut leaves to 12 inches long, clusters of purple flowers, and an edible, yellow fruit. Grown in mild-winter climates as a specimen. 2. The edible, egg-shaped, yellow berry of *S. aviculare.*

kangaroo grape *n.* A common name for *Cissus antarctica,* a trailing vine, climbing by tendrils, with red, furry new growth and with leaves divided into 3 shiny, toothed leaflets. Widely grown as a houseplant or an indoor/outdoor plant in hanging baskets. Also known as kangaroo vine.

kangaroo thorn *n.* A common name for *Acacia armata,* a tender spiny, bushy evergreen shrub to 15 feet tall. It has waxy, semioval, light green leaves, short, sharp spines, and early-blooming, ball-shaped yellow flowers. Used as a pot plant in cold climates and as a hedge, thorny barrier, and to bind sand in warmer climates. Tolerates drought, sandy soils, extremes of heat and cold, and temperatures to 10°F. Also called kangaroo acacia.

kangaroo vine *n.* A common name for *Cissus antarctica,* a trailing vine. (See **kangaroo grape**.)

kaoliang (kow′lee ahng) *n.* A common name for *Sorghum bicolor,* grown for forage and for use in making syrup.

kaolin minerals (kay′uh lihn) *n. pl.* A group of nonswelling clay minerals in which 1 layer of silicon and oxygen alternates with a layer made up of aluminum, oxygen, and hydrogen.

kapok (kay′pak) *n.* A common name for *Ceiba pentandra,* a deciduous tropical tree to 150 feet or more, with spreading branches, a thick, buttressed trunk covered with thorns, leaves divided into narrow leaflets, showy yellow, rose, or white flowers, and large seedpods filled with white cottonlike fibers. From the abundant cottony covering of the seeds, *C. pentandra* is known as silk-cotton tree. Grown ornamentally in tropical gardens.

karo (kay′roh) *n.* A common name for *Pittosporum crassifolium,* a dense shrub or small broadleaf evergreen tree to 25 feet, though usually clipped much lower. It has gray-green oblong leathery leaves, clusters of small maroon flowers in late spring, and conspicuous round, fuzzy, gray seed capsules. Tolerates neglect, some drought, wind, salt air, and a wide variety of soils. Widely used in mild climates as a foundation plant, hedge, windbreak, seaside planting, and general all-purpose shrub.

katsura tree (kat′suh ruh) *n.* A common name for *Cercidiphyllum Japonicum,* a hardy tree with dainty, heart-shaped, blue-green leaves that color beautifully in red or yellow in autumn. The flowers are inconspicuous. Grown in parks or gardens as a specimen tree.

kauri pine (kow′ree) *n.* The common name for *Agathis,* a genus of tall tender evergreen coniferous trees (Araucariaceae). They have broad, entire, glossy, leathery leaves, with both male and female cones. Used in mild climates as a sentinel or skyline tree.

kava (kav′uh) *n.* 1. A common name for *Piper methysticum,* a tropical shrub of the pepper family. It is an erect, soft-stemmed shrub 8 to 20 feet, which grows from a thick rhizome and has rounded, oval, pointed dark green leaves. 2. The beverage derived from the root of this plant.

kawakawa (ka′wuh ka′wuh) *n.* A common name for *Macropiper excelsum,* an ornamental, tropical aromatic shrub or small tree to 20 feet, native to New Zealand. It has rounded, oval, pointed leaves, spikes of very small red flowers, and clusters of oval yellow-to-orange fruit. Used in gardens of the wet tropics.

keel *n.* In botany: 1. A central ridge along the back of any organ of a plant. 2. The fused, lowermost petals of a butterfly-shaped flower.

Kei apple (kay) *n.* 1. A common name for *Dovyalis caffra,* a sub-tropical shrub or small tree. It can be used for hedges, and it yields an edible fruit. 2. The fruit of this shrub, which resembles a small yellowish apple. It serves for a pickle when green, and when ripe it can be made into a preserve. Also spelled kai apple. (See **Kai apple**.)

Kelthane (kehl thayn′) *n.* A synthetic insecticide (chemical name: dicofol) used primarily for control of spider mites.

kenaf (kuh′naf) *n.* A common name for *Hibiscus cannabinus,* a prickly, shiny-leaved annual to 6 feet tall, with variable leaves and single or clustered yellow or purple flowers with a dark purple eye. Used in the back of borders.

Kenilworth ivy *n.* A common name for *Cymbelaria muralis,* a dainty, charming, creeping perennial with small, round scalloped leaves and tiny blue-and-white snapdragon-shaped flowers. Excellent on rock walls, in hanging baskets and as a small-scale ground cover in moist shade. Spreads easily.

Kennebec (kehn′uh behk) *n.* An all-purpose potato variety originating in the Kennebec Valley of Maine. It has smooth skin and white flesh and is a favorite of home gardeners.

Kennedya (kuh nee′dee uh) *n*. A genus of 15 species of tender showy perennial twining vines (Leguminosae). They have alternate, 3-part leaves, sometimes downy leaves, showy, butterflylike dark red to nearly black flowers, and long, narrow seedpods. Commonly known as coral pea.

Kentucky bluegrass *n*. (See **Poa**.)

Kentucky coffee tree *n*. A common name for *Gymnocladus dioica,* a fast-growing tree to 100 feet, with 2-part deep-green leaves that color yellow in autumn, and 6- to 10-inch reddish-brown pods. It has an interesting winter silhouette and tolerates poor soil, extremes of heat and cold, and some drought. Useful in harsh climates and difficult soils.

Kentucky wonder *n*. A snap bean variety that is popular with home gardeners for its flavor and suitability for freezing.

kernel *n*. 1. The inner portion of a seed, usually applied to an edible seed or the central part of a nut or fruit seed. 2. The whole seed of a cereal such as corn or wheat. *v*. To form kernels.

Kerria (ker′ee uh) *n*. A genus of a single species of shrub, *K. japonica* a flowering shrub (Rosaceae). It is an open, airy, graceful deciduous shrub with long, slender branches, entire, toothed, bright green leaves that color yellow in fall, and masses of large, solitary, yellow roselike flowers. Commonly known as Japanese rose or Japan globeflower.

Keteleeria (ked uhl ih′ree uh) *n*. A genus of 9 species of very tall, tender evergreen conifers (Pinaceae). They grow to 100 feet or more, with long, glossy needles and large, erect, woody cones.

keyaki (kee ya′kee) *n*. A common name for *Zelkova serrata,* a hardy, pest-resistant, wide-spreading tree to 60 feet or more, with smooth, gray bark and elmlike leaves that color yellow or red in fall. Its wood is prized for making the Japanese cabinets called *tansu.* Used as a shade tree, street tree, or as a substitute for elms where Dutch elm disease is a problem.

key fruit *n*. A common name for dry, windborne, winged seedpods, such as those of maple or elm. Same as samara.

khair (kigh′uhr) *n*. A common name for *Acacia Catechu.* It has short, hooked, 5-inch-long spines, 2-part leaves, and dark yellow flowers. It yields the brown dye used to make khaki.

khat (kat) *n*. A common name for *Katha edulis,* a tender broadleaf evergreen spreading shrub with red bark, red stems, and bronzy green, shiny, oval leaves, which take on reddish tints through fall and winter. It has very small white flowers. It tolerates drought, poor soil, and coastal winds. Used in public plantings because it endures all privation.

Khaya (kigh′uh) *n*. A genus of 10 species of tall, buttressed tropical trees (Meliaceae). They are tall trees, with wood resembling mahogany, leaves divided into leaflets, and clusters of white flowers.

ki (kigh) *n*. A plant, *Cordyline terminalis* (Agavaceae) of Asia and the Pacific Islands. Its root is baked and eaten, and it is widely grown as an ornamental. Also known as ti.

kiabooca (kigh uh boo′kuh) *n*. A common name for *Pterocarpus indicus* (Leguminosae), a tropical tree that produces the wood called Burmese rosewood. Also called amboyna and padauk.

kidney bean *n*. A plant of the genus *Phaseolus* (Leguminosae), especially *Phaseolus vulgaris,* the common twining kidney bean of vegetable gardens, so called from the shape of the seeds. The green pods of the common kidney bean, with their contents, are eaten as a snap bean, or the dry seeds are baked or boiled. Also called French bean and haricot.

kidneyroot *n*. The Joe-Pye-weed, *Eupatorium purpureum.*

kidney-shaped *a*. Having the shape or form of a kidney; reniform. A kidney-shaped leaf is a leaf wider than it is long, with an indentation at the base.

kidney-shaped leaf

kidney vetch *n*. A common name for *Anthyllis Vulneraria,* an annual, biennial or perennial that grows up to to 1 foot tall. It has dense, cloverlike yellow to dark red or white flowers and long pods. Sometimes grown in an herb garden or in a collection of medicinal plants. Also known as lady's-fingers and woundwort.

kidneywort *n.* 1. A common name for *Umbilicus rupestris* (Crassulaceae), a succulent perennial with fleshy, rounded leaves and yellow or green flowers on long stalks. Also called pennywort and navelwort. 2. A common name for *Baccharis pilularis*, a dense, billowy, matlike broadleaf evergreen shrub, native to California, with small, rounded, oval dark green leaves, clusters of little white flowers, and seed heads with fluffy white bristles. Tolerates a wide range of moisture, from swamp to desert. Often planted as a ground cover. Also called coyote bush.

Kigelia (kigh jee'lee uh) *n.* A genus of about 10 species of large flowering tropical trees (Bignoniaceae). *K. pinnata* has whitish bark and spreading branches, that grow to 50 feet, large, divided alternate leaves, loose, drooping clusters of showy orange-to-red flowers, and bizarre-looking seedpods that resemble huge salamis. The fruit is often 2 feet or more in length, hanging from a long stalk. Grown as a novelty. Commonly known as sausage tree.

Kiggelaria (kihj uh lair'ee uh) *n.* A genus of 4 species of tender shrubs or small trees (Flacourtiaceae). They have elliptic, entire or serrate leaves and clusters of 5-petaled male flowers and solitary female flowers. Grown in warm-winter climates.

kikar (kee kuhr) *n.* A common name for *Acacia nilotica*, a tropical tree to 75 feet, with 3-inch-long spines, 2-part leaves, clusters of yellow flowers, and 6-inch-long pods.

king-apple *n.* An old variety of large apple, red in color.

kingcup *n.* A common name for several different *Ranunculus* species, including *R. bulbosus*, *R. acris*, and *R. repens*, as well as *Caltha palustris*, all of which are wildflowers with bright yellow flowers. The *Ranunculus* are European species naturalized in the United States; *C. palustris* is native to the eastern United States; *R. repens* is the only one grown ornamentally. It has rounded, glossy, deeply cut leaves and bright yellow buttonlike flowers on 1- to

2-foot stems. Useful as a ground cover in moist situations; may become invasive. The *Ranunculus* species are commonly known as buttercup; the *Caltha* is also called marsh marigold.

king devil *n.* A common name for *Hieracium aurantiacum*, a troublesome European weed widely naturalized in the United States. It is a perennial that spreads by stolons, forming a continuous mat of pale green leaves, lying flat on the ground. Also known as hawkweed.

king fern *n.* A common name for *Osmunda regalis*, a very hardy, widely adapted perennial American fern, native from Newfoundland and Saskatchewan to South America. It is an extremely handsome fern, with twice-cut fronds to 6 feet long. Useful in moist, shady locations. Also known as royal or flowering fern.

kingfisher daisy *n.* A common name for *Felicia Bergeriana*, a low-growing, bushy annual with wiry stems, opposite, oval leaves, and blue daisylike flowers on long stems.

king nut *n.* 1. A common name used for *Carya laciniosa*, a hardy deciduous tree native to the eastern United States. It grows to 120 feet, has large divided leaves with long oval leaflets, downy beneath, and round yellow or red nuts. Also called shellbark hickory, and big shellbark. 2. Also, the nut.

king palm *n.* A common name for the genus *Archontophoenix*, a genus of 2 species of tender, slender Australian palms, 50 feet tall, with a 10- to 15-foot spread. They have feathery, divided leaves 8 to 10 feet long. Grown outdoors in warm-climate gardens or as a houseplant anywhere.

king's spear *n.* A common name for *Asphodeline lutea*, a hardy perennial to 4 feet tall, with leafy stems, long, narrow leaves, and spikes of fragrant yellow flowers. Useful in perennial borders or in the wild garden. Also known as asphodel.

kink-free hose *n.* A garden hose that allows water to flow freely, even when bent.

kinnikinnick (kihn'uh kuh nik') *n.* 1. A common name for *Arctostaphylos Uva-ursi*, a very hardy, prostrate, creeping evergreen perennial, with small, round, shiny, dark green leaves, tiny white or pink flowers, and small red berries. Also called bearberry, sandberry, hog cranberry, and mealberry. 2. *Cornus sericea (C. stolonifera),* a widely adaptable North American shrub to 10 feet, with dark red branches, pointed oval leaves that color brilliant red in fall, clusters of large white flowers, and white or blue fruit. Also known as red osier dogwood. Useful in moist situations for its spring bloom, fall color, and bright red winter silhouette. 3. *Rhus virens,* a broadleaf evergreen shrub native to the southwestern United States. It has compound leaves with diamond-shaped leaflets, clusters of white flowers, and small fruits. Also known as evergreen sumac, lintisco, or tobacco sumac. Also spelled kinnikinic.

kiss-me *n.* 1. A common name for *Viola tricolor,* the pansy. Also called kisses. 2. *Saxifraga umbrosa,* also called London pride. 3. *Geranium robertianum,* also called herb Robert.

Kitaibelia (kit ai buh'lee uh) *n.* A genus of 1 species, *K. vitifolia* (Malvaceae), a tall, robust, many-stemmed perennial. It grows to 5 feet or more, with white, downy new growth, simple, lobed, grapelike leaves, and white-to-rose 5-petaled flowers.

kitchen garden *n.* A garden or a piece of ground usually near the house used to raise vegetables and herbs for the table.

kittul (kuh tool') *n.* A common name for *Caryota urens,* a tender tropical Asian palm with leaves divided into wedge-shaped leaflets, strongly toothed at the ends. Grown outdoors in warm-winter climates and as a choice houseplant or greenhouse specimen anywhere. Also known as fishtail palm.

kiwi *n.* A common name for *Actinidia chinensis,* an oval edible fruit of Asian origin, now grown commercially in New Zealand and California. Its bright green interior is juicy, tart, and wholly edible. The brown skin is very thin and slightly furry. Kiwi grows on a vine in sunny or partially shaded locations. Also known as kiwifruit and Chinese gooseberry, although it is not related to the gooseberry.

Kleinhovia (klighn hoh'vee uh) *n.* A genus of a single species of *K. hospita,* a tropical tree. It has very large oval pointed alternate leaves, and big loose clusters of red flowers, which are succeeded by curious, top-shaped, bladderlike, five-winged fruits. Grown ornamentally in frost-free gardens.

knackaway (nak'uh way) *n.* A common name for *Ehretia Anacua,* a deciduous North American shrub or tree with rough-surfaced, 2-inch-long, pointed leaves, clusters of fragrant white flowers, and small, round yellow fruit. Commonly called anaqua or anacua. Also spelled knockaway.

knapsack sprayer *n.* A device worn on the back consisting of a container plus a perforated nozzle mounted on a wand; used for spraying, misting, foliar feeding, or as a portable watering device. Also called backpack sprayer.

Knapweed
lower stem with root

knapweed *n.* A common name for the genus *Centaurea,* a genus of annuals and herbaceous plants (Compositae). They have alternate leaves and flowers with single heads, all the florets of which are tubular. Some annuals, such as *C. cyanus* (cornflowers or bachelor's buttons) and *C. moschata* (sweet sultan), are grown in borders and cottage gardens. Several perennials, commonly known as dusty miller, are grown for their silvery-gray or nearly white foliage, for example, *C. cineraria.* Also known as knobweed and horse balm.

knawel (naw'uhl) *n.* A common name for any small weed of the genus *Scleranthus.* They have opposite leaves, flowers with no petals, and seeds contained in a nutlet. Occasionally used in rock gardens.

knee *n.* 1. A sharp bend in a tree branch. 2. A protruding enlargement of the roots at the base of certain swamp-growing trees.

kneeler *n.* A device to help gardeners lower themselves down or push themselves up from a kneeling position. A kneeler typically has handholds several feet high attached to a cushioned platform. The device may be reversible for use as a garden bench.

kneeling pad *n.* A mat, generally rectangular and impervious to water, for cushioning the knees while gardening.

kneepads *n., pl.* Cushions strapped behind the knees to protect the kneecaps while kneeling or crawling.

Knightia (nighd'ee uh) *n.* A genus of 3 species of tender trees or shrubs (Proteaceae). They have alternate, entire, leathery leaves, dense spikes of brown furry flowers, and hard fruit pods.

knight's-spur *n.* A common name for the genus *Delphinium,* widely grown flowers with maplelike leaves and showy spikes of blue, pink, white, red, or yellow blooms characterized by long spurs. Also called larkspur.

Kniphofia (nip hoh'fee uh) *n.* A genus of about 60 to 70 species of large, handsome, showy tender perennials (Liliaceae). They have long, narrow leaves and dense spikes of yellow or scarlet drooping, tubular flowers on tall, leafless stalks. They are hardy with protection, or the roots may be lifted in cold climates. Fairly drought tolerant. Used in specimen clumps and in large borders. Commonly known as red-hot poker, torch lily, poker plant, and tritoma; tritoma is the former genus.

knobweed *n.* Same as knapweed.

knockaway *n.* (See **knackaway**.)

knot *n.* A lump or swelling in or on a part of a plant, such as the node of a grass, or the dense part of the wood of a tree where a branch grows out of the trunk.

knot garden *n.* A formal bed of compact ornamentals or herbs planted in intertwining patterns to resemble a knot. These were popular in Elizabethan England and are found in period restorations of the American colonial period.

knotweed *n.* A common name for both weeds and ornamentals of the genus *Polygonum.*

knurl *n.* A dense, contorted knot in wood.

koa (koh'uh) *n.* A common name for *Acacia Koa,* a Hawaiian tree, to 60 feet, with blade-shaped leaves, short spikes of yellow flowers, and a 6-inch-long narrow pod.

Kochia (koh'kee uh) *n.* A genus of 80 species of plants and subshrubs (Chenopodiaceae). Only *K. scoparia* is cultivated; it is a softly rounded, dense, hairy, much-branched annual to 5 feet, with 3-inch-long needlelike leaves and inconspicuous flowers. It is commonly known as summer cypress and belvedere. *K.s. trichophylla* colors reddish purple in fall and is commonly known as Mexican fire bush or burning bush. Grown for its foliage as a specimen or as a temporary hedge in short- summer regions.

Koeleria (kehl air'ee uh) *n.* A genus of about 35 species of perennial grasses (Gramineae). A few are grown as ornamentals for their neat, tufted, blue foliage and shiny flower heads. Commonly known as hair grass.

Koelreuteria paniculata
(Chinese flame tree)

Koelreuteria (kehl roi tih'ree uh) *n.* A genus of 4 species of ornamental, flowering deciduous trees (Sapindaceae). They have divided leaves, large clusters of fragrant yellow flowers with crimson appendages, and fat, papery capsules like a cluster of little Japanese lanterns. The pods are used in dried arrangements. The flowers attract bees. *K. paniculata* is the most widely planted species. It is very hardy, and tolerates cold, heat, drought, wind, and alkaline soil. It is much used in difficult soils and climates as a street tree, park tree, and lawn tree. Commonly known as golden rain tree or varnish tree. *K. bipinnata* is hardy and has large, divided leaves that turn yellow in December, clusters of yellow flowers, and orange-, red- or salmon-colored fruit much used in dried arrangements. Commonly known as Chinese flame tree.

kohlrabi (kohl ra′bee) *n.* The stem turnip, *Brassica oleraceae* (Cruciferae). It is a frequently cultivated variety of the cabbage plant, in which the stem above the ground swells into a large bulblike formation, which is similar in texture to a white turnip, but has a milder flavor.

kola nut *n.* A bitter, caffein-containing seed, about the size of a chestnut, produced by a tree of western tropical Africa, *Cola acuminata* (Sterculiaceae). Also spelled cola nut.

Kolkwitzia (kohl kwit′see uh) *n.* A genus of a single species, *K. amabilis* (Caprifoliaceae). It grows to 10 to 15 feet, with graceful, arching stems, oval, opposite gray-green leaves, and clusters of small pink, yellow-throated flowers followed by conspicuous pinkish-brown bristly fruit. Commonly known as beautybush.

Kopsia (kop′see uh) *n.* A genus of 30 species of tropical trees and shrubs (Apocynaceae). They have milky sap, opposite, entire leaves, and short clusters of white, yellow, or pink, sometimes fragrant, flowers.

Korean grass *n.* (See **Zoysia**.)

Kosteletzkya (kahs tuh lets′kee uh) *n.* A genus of 25 species of plants and subshrubs (Malvaceae), some species native to North and South America. *K. virginica,* native to salt marshes from New York to Louisiana, is a tall hardy perennial to 4 or 5 feet, with ample, heart-shaped or halberd-shaped 3-lobed leaves and large, pink hibiscuslike flowers, often 2½ inches across. Commonly known as seashore mallow.

Krigia (krihg′ee uh) *n.* A genus of eight species of small dandelionlike flowers (Compositae) native to North America. They are low-growing plants with milky juice, leaves in a basal rosette, yellow or orange many-petaled flowers on leafless stems, and a fluffy seed head. Commonly known as dwarf dandelion and generally regarded as more of a weed than an ornamental.

kudzu (kuhd′zoo) *n.* A common name for *Pueraria lobata,* a fast-growing vigorous perennial vine introduced to the southeastern United States from China and Japan for fodder and erosion control. It is a somewhat woody, hairy vine to 60 feet, with wide oval or diamond-shaped leaves, fragrant reddish-purple flowers, and hairy 4-inch-long pods. It has become a rampant weed in many areas. Also known as kudzu vine.

Kuhnia (kyoo′nee uh) *n.* A genus of 6 species of perennials (Compositae) native to the United States and Mexico. *K. eupatorioides* is an erect perennial to 4 feet, with long, narrow leaves and clusters of cream or yellow daisylike flowers.

kumquat (kuhm′kwaht) *n.* A small, oblong citrus fruit of the genus *Fortunella.* The fruit resembles the orange and is grown for use in preserves or is eaten raw. It is a popular evergreen container plant. It grows wherever citrus thrives.

labellum (lah behl′luhm) *n., pl.* **labella** (la-bel′la) A lip, particularly the lip of an orchid.

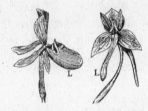

labella of different species of orchids (labeled L)

Labiatae (lay bee ay′tee) *n., pl.* A family of 180 genera and 3,500 species of plants, subshrubs, and shrubs; the mint family. This family usually has square stems, opposite or whorled leaves, and spikelike clusters of whorled flowers. Mints are grown for many reasons: ornamentally, as flavorful herbs, and for the essential oils of perfumes. The widely grown genera include *Coleus, Lavandula* (lavender), *Melissa* (lemon balm), *Mentha* (mint), *Ocimum* (sweet basil), *Origanum* (oregano), *Perovskia* (Russian sage), *Rosmarinus* (rosemary), *Salvia* (sage), *Satureja* (savory), *Stachys* (lamb's ears), and *Thymus* (thyme). *Lamiaceae* is a synonym for the genus.

labiate (lah'bee uht) *a.* In botany: 1. 2-lipped, as a calyx or corolla divided into 2 unequal parts, like the lips of a mouth. 2. Pertaining to the Labiatae. *n.* A plant of the family Labiatae.

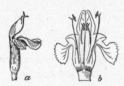

labiate corolla
a side view *b* cross section

labium (lah'bee uhm) *n., pl.* **labia** (-a) In botany, the lower lip of a a flower with 2 lips.

Labrador tea *n.* An evergreen shrub, *Ledum groenlandicum,* native to cold regions of North America. The cultivar 'compactus' is a dwarf form.

Laburnocytisus (laah bur noh sigh tee'suhs) *n.* A small tree, *L. Adamii,* called a graft chimera, the result of grafting the shrub *Cytisus purpureus* (broom) on the tree *Laburnum anagyroides* (golden chain tree). The grafted plant has 3-part leaves and nodding clusters of dull purple flowers. Occasionally, the tree may produce branches with yellow flowers.

Laburnum (lah ber'nuhm) *n.* A genus of 4 species of fairly hardy flowering trees and shrubs (Leguminosae). They have 3-part, alternate leaves, drooping, wisterialike clusters of yellow, butterfly-shaped flowers, and pealike pods. Used as a lawn tree, in clumps, or in double rows to line a driveway. Also grown as a multistemmed shrub in a shrub border with lilacs and rhododendrons. It is poisonous if eaten, particularly the seeds. Commonly known as golden chain tree and bean tree.

laccate (lahk'ayt) *a.* In botany, appearing as if varnished.

lacebark *n.* 1. A common name for *Brachychiton acerifolius,* a briefly deciduous, drought-tolerant tender tree to 20 to 60 feet, with large, glossy, bright green, fanlike leaves, loose clusters of bell-shaped scarlet flowers that bloom on bare branches, and canoe-shaped woody fruits used in dried arrangements. Also known as flame tree. A spectac-

ular flowering tree in mild-climate gardens. 2. Also, *B. discolor,* a tender tree to 100 feet, briefly deciduous in cooler climates, with large lobed leaves, pale beneath, and clusters of pink or red bell-shaped flowers. Commonly known as Queensland lacebark.

lace bug *n.* A small, lacy-winged insect that sucks juices from the foliage of many plants, particularly broadleaf evergreens like azaleas and rhododendrons. The infested leaves often turn whitish, then brown, then drop. Do not confuse with lacewings, beneficial insects. Usually controlled with insecticidal soaps, horticultural oil, pyrethrum, or traditional pesticides.

lace fern *n.* A common name for *Cheilanthes gracillima,* a small, elegant North American fern, with 2-part, divided, foot-long fronds, densely woolly on the underside. It is native in dry, rocky places from British Columbia to California. Used in woodland and wild gardens.

lace flower, blue *n.* A common name used for *Trachymene coerulea,* an annual to 2 feet tall, with compound leaves and flat-topped, lacelike clusters of small lavender blue flowers. Used massed in beds.

laceleaf *n.* A common name for *Aponogeton madagascariensis,* an aquarium plant. (See **latticeleaf.**)

lacerate *a.* Having the apex or margin torn or irregularly cut. Also lacerated.

lacewing *n.* A beneficial insect. The adults and larvae feed on a variety of plant pests including aphids, mites, and thrips. Common in most gardens, but can be purchased through the mail.

Lachenalia (laash uh nay'lee uh) *n.* A genus of 50 species of tender bulbs plants (Liliaceae). They have straplike succulent, brown-spotted leaves and spikes of pendulous white, yellow, blue, or red tubular flowers on a thick stalk. Commonly known as Cape cowslip and leopard lily.

Lachnanthes (lak nan'theez) *n.* A genus of a single species of rhizomatous perennial, *L. caroliana,* native to swamps of eastern North America and Cuba. It grows to 2½ feet, with long, narrow leaves and clusters of yellow flowers 5 inches across. Used in moist situations and bog gardens. Also known as redroot, dye root, and paint root.

lacinia (lah sihn′ee uh) *n., pl.* **laciniae** (-e). In botany, a long slash or incision in a leaf, petal, or similar organ; also, one of the narrow lobes resulting from such cuts.

laciniate (lah sihn′ee ayt) *a.* In botany, irregularly cut into narrow, usually pointed lobes; jagged; fringed; said of leaves, petals, bracts, etc. Also laciniated, laciniose.

lacinate leaf

lacinula (lah sihn′yoo luh) *n., pl.* **lacinulae** (-le). In botany, a small narrow lobe or fringe.

lacinulate (lah sihn′yoo layt) *a.* In botany, having small finely cut leaves or petals.

lacrimiform (lak′rih mih form) *a.* In botany, teardrop-shaped.

Lactuca (lak too′kuh) *a.* A genus of between 50 and 90 species of annuals (Compositae); lettuce. They have milky juice, typically edible leaves in a basal rosette, and small clusters of pale yellow or blue flowers on tall stalks. Most are grown as a popular salad vegetable. Commonly known as lettuce.

Lacuna (la koo′nuh) *n., pl.* **lacunae** (-ne) A gap, hole, or cavity.

lacunulose (la koo′noo lohs) *a.* In botany, having tiny holes.

lacustrine deposit (luh kuhs′streen) *n.* Material deposited from lake waters.

ladder *n.* Any of variously mounted steps used to reach high branches while pruning or while picking fruit.

ladies′ bedstraw *n.* Same as lady's bedstraw.

ladies′-tresses (lay′deez tresses′) *n.* A common name for *Spiranthes,* a genus of orchids. (See **lady's-tresses.**)

lad's-love *n.* A common name of the southernwood, *Artemisia Abrotanum.*

ladybells *n.* A common name for the genus *Adenophora,* hardy, summer-blooming perennials (Campanulaceae). They grow to 3 to 4 feet, often with toothed leaves, and with clusters of blue, bell-shaped flowers on tall stalks.

ladybug *n.* (See **convergent lady beetle**.)

lady fern *n.* A common name for *Athyrium Filix-femina,* a hardy, vigorous, elegant fern native to North America. It has doubly divided, bright green fronds up to 3 feet long. There are numerous ornamental varieties and many cultivars. Used in woodland gardens and shady, moist situations.

ladyfinger *n.* 1. A common name for *Digitalis purpurea.* Also known as foxglove. (See **Digitalis** and **foxglove.**) 2. A gold-skinned potato variety, with an exceptionally high sugar content.

lady-of-the-night *n.* A common name for *Brunfelsia americana,* a subtropical shrub or small tree, native to the West Indies, with oval leaves and fragrant, night-blooming, tubular white flowers. Grown in moist situations in warm-climate gardens.

lady's bedstraw *n.* Our lady's bedstraw, *Galium verum.*

lady's bower *n.* A common name for *Clematis Vitalba.* Also called traveler's-joy.

lady's-delight *n.* A common name for *Viola tricolor.* Also known as pansy.

lady's-eardrops *n.* A common name for *Fuchsia,* a genus of subtropical trees, shrubs, and hanging-basket plants with alternate, opposite, or whorled leaves and curiously shaped, often showy, pendulous brightly colored flowers in shades of red, pink, purple, and white. Used as specimen shrubs, in containers, and in hanging baskets.

lady's-finger *n.* 1. A common name for *Anthyllis Vulneraria;* also called kidney vetch. 2. A common name for *Abelmoschus esculentus;* also known as okra. 3. A finger-shaped variety of the potato, formerly common; it is small, white, and has a delicate flavor.

lady's-glove *n.* A common name for *Digitalis purpurea;* also called purple foxglove.

lady's-mantle *n.* An herb, *Alchemilla vulgaris* (Rosaceae). Its leaves are deeply pleated and are known for their ability to hold droplets of dew in their folds. Grown as an ornamental for its rich green foliage.

lady's slipper *n.* 1. A common name for *Cypripedium,* a genus of about 50 species of wild orchids some species native to North America. Most are rare or endangered in the wild and do not thrive in garden situations. Also known as lady-slipper and moccasin flower. 2. *Impatiens balsamina,* a branching annual with alternate, long, narrow leaves and white, yellow, or dark red flowers, often spotted. Also known as garden balsam and rose balsam.

lady's-smock *n.* A common name for *Cardamine pratensis,* an erect perennial to 20 inches, with divided leaves and white or rose colored 4-petaled flowers. Traditional in cottage gardens; also used in cool, moist borders and rock gardens. Commonly called cuckooflower, lady smock, ladies'-smocks, lady smocks, mayflower, meadow cress, and bitter cress.

lady's tresses *n.* A common name for the genus *Spiranthes.* These orchids, some native to North America, are low-growing plants with spikes of spirally arranged white flowers. Also called lady-tresses, ladies' tresses, and lady's traces.

Laelia (lee′lee uh) *n.* A genus of 30 species of epiphytic orchids (Orchidaceae) native to Central and South America. They have pseudobulbs, fleshy, leathery leaves, and spikes with clusters of large, showy white, pink, lavender, and purple flowers. A few have red, yellow, or orange flowers. Grown primarily as houseplants or greenhouse specimens.

Lagenaria (laj uh na′ree uh) *n.* A genus of plants of 6 species of tender, mostly annual vines (Cucurbitaceae) some species native to South America. They are climbing vines, with broad leaves, large white flowers, and gourds that are extremely variable in color, size, and shape. The gourds may be round, crooknecked, coiled, or shaped like bottles, dumbbells, or spoons. Grown as a novelty and for Thanksgiving table decorations.

Lagerstroemia (lay ger stree′mee uh) *n.* A genus of 55 species of subtropical and tropical trees and shrubs (Lythraceae). They have mostly opposite leaves and masses of large, showy, rounded clusters of white, red, or purple flowers. The most widely grown is *L. indica,* also known as crape myrtle, which is used in warm climates as a deciduous lawn tree, specimen tree, or street tree. (See **myrtle, crape**.)

Lagunaria (lah goon ahr′ee uh) *n.* A genus of a single species, *L. Patersonii,* (Malvaceae), a tender broadleaf evergreen tree. It grows to 20 to 50 feet, has thick, oval olive-green leaves, 2-inch-wide hibiscuslike pink-to-rose flowers, and brown seed capsules which are often used in flower arrangements, even though they have fibers that may irritate skin. It is tolerant of a variety of soils, heat, drought, wind, and salt spray. Grown especially in seaside gardens, as a showy windbreak, screen, specimen tree, or in clumps. Commonly known as primrose tree and cow itch tree.

Lagurus (luh gyoo′ruhs) *n.* A genus of 1 species of annual grass, *L. ovatus* (Gramineae). Grown for its beautiful, fuzzy flower spikes, which are also excellent for use in dried arrangements. Commonly called hare's-tail grass.

lambkill *n.* A common name for *Kalmia angustifolia,* a very hardy, slender shrub, native to eastern North America. It grows to 3 feet, with opposite, narrow, oval leaves and small clusters of purple-to-crimson flowers. The leaves are poisonous if eaten. Also known as sheep laurel, pig laurel, and wicky.

lamb's ears *n.* A common name for the ornamental herb *Stachys officinalis,* grown for its soft, furry pale green leaves, which are used in dried arrangements and herbal wreaths. The leaves are about 4 inches long and grow in a rosette close to the ground. The flower stalk rises above the leaves to as tall as 2 feet, bearing a long cluster of small pink flowers.

lamb's-quarters *n.* A common name for *Chenopodium album,* a common annual North American weed. It grows to 10 feet, with oval, pointed leaves and small flowers. The leaves can be cooked, like spinach. Also known as pigweed and white goosefoot.

lamella (lah mehl′luh) *n., pl.* **lamellae** (-e). A thin plate, or an organ or part resembling one. Also lamel.

lamellate (lahm′uh layt) *a.* Composed of or having lamellae. Also lamellar.

Lamiaceae (lay mee ay'see ee) *n., pl.* An alternative classification for Labiatae, the mint family.

Lamiastrum (lay mee ays'truhm) *n.* A genus of 1 species, *L. galeobdolon* (Labiatae), a hardy perennial ground cover. It grows to 2 feet, with rounded, oval, pointed leaves and spikes of snapdragonlike yellow flowers. Commonly known as yellow archangel.

lamina (lahm'ih nuh) *n., pl.* **laminae** (-ne). A thin plate or scale. Specifically, in botany, the blade or expanded portion of a leaf or petal.

Lamium (lay'mee uhn) *n.* A genus of 40 species of hardy annual and perennial trailing, sprawling ground covers (Labiatae). They grow from 1 to 2 feet, with pairs of heart-shaped, opposite leaves, often variegated with silver, and short spikes of hooded pink or white flowers. Used as a small space ground cover in shade, in rock gardens, and in hanging baskets. Commonly known as dead nettle.

Lampranthus (lam pran'thuhs) *n.* A genus of 160 species of creeping, spreading tender perennial succulents (Aizoaceae). They grow 1 to 2 feet, with thick, fleshy, opposite leaves and masses of large, showy, brilliant white, pink, red purple, or yellow- to- orange flowers that attract bees. Used in seaside gardens, pots, or baskets. Extremely drought-tolerant. Commonly known as ice plant.

lanate (lan'ayt) *a.* Woolly; covered with long, fine, curly hairs.

lance-linear *a.* In botany, long, narrow, and pointed such as a leaf.

lanceolate leaves

lanceolate (lan'see oh layt) *a.* Shaped like a lance head; in botany, tapering from a rounded base toward the apex, or sometimes tapering in both directions, as a lanceolate leaf. Also lanceolated, lanceolar, lanciform.

lancepod *n.* A common name for the genus *Lonchocarpus,* mostly a genus of tropical trees. They grow to 50 feet, with alternate, divided leaves, spikes of very showy white or violet flowers, and long, flat seedpods. Also known as bloody bark.

lanciform (lan'sih form) *a.* Lance-shaped; long, narrow, and pointed, sometimes broader at the base than at the tip.

land *n.* 1. A term that describes the solid surface of the earth. 2. A broad term that includes soil, surface soil, mineral deposits, and water supplies in a certain area.

land-capability classification *n.* Soil that is grouped into special units, subclasses, and/or classes according to their capability for intense use and treatments that are required for sustained use.

landform *n.* A geomorphological term used to express earthly surface formations.

landscape *n.* A view or prospect of rural scenery, more or less extensive, such as is seen from a single point of view.

landscape architect *n.* A person who designs and often supervises the placement of elements (plants, walkways, and other structures) in an outdoor setting.

landscape fabric *n.* Any of various porous organic or inorganic cloths or mats used to discourage weeds from growing. Also called weed mat.

Landscape-gardening *n.* The art of laying out grounds and arranging trees, shrubs, flowers, paths, fountains, etc., to produce pleasant and attractive effects.

lanose (la'nohs) *a.* Woolly; lanate.

Lantana (lan tah'nuh) *n.* A genus of 155 species of fast-growing tropical and subtropical flowering shrubs (Verbenaceae), sometimes grown as annuals. They grow to 4 feet, with opposite or whorled, wrinkled-looking, aromatic leaves, masses of multicolored yellow, orange, red, white, purple, or lilac flowers in small rounded clusters, and black fruit that attracts birds. Used as foundation shrubs, in beds, in containers, spilling over walls, in window boxes, and in hanging baskets; the low, spreading types are used for erosion-control on steep banks. Commonly known as shrub verbena.

Lantana
(shrub verbena)

lanuginous (la noo′jih nuhs) *a*. Downy; covered with soft fine hairs, like down. Also lanuginose.

lanugo (la noo goh) *n*. In botany, a soft, dense cottony or downy growth.

Lapageria (la puh′jihr ee uh) *n*. A genus of 1 species, *L. rosea* (Liliaceae), a showy, subtropical, evergreen, woody, twining vine; the national flower of Chile. It grows from 10 to 20 feet with oval, glossy, leathery, alternate leaves and showy, bell-shaped, rose to rose-crimson flowers. Grown outdoors in mild climates or as a greenhouse specimen. Commonly known as Chilean bellflower and Chile-bells.

Lapeyrousia (lap uh roo′zee uh) *n*. A genus of about 50 species of hardy (with winter protection) summer-blooming bulbs (corms) (Iridaceae). They grow from 3 to 18 inches high, with narrow, basal leaves and blue, violet, lilac, red, pink, or white flowers on tall stalks. Grown in greenhouses for spring bloom or outdoors in borders.

Lapidaria (lap ih dar′ee uh) *n*. A genus of 1 species, *L. margaretae* (Aizoaceae), of stemless, perennial succulent that looks like a pile of pale green stones. It forms clumps 2 inches high, with thick, fleshy leaves and large golden-yellow flowers, the

petals reddish below. Commonly known as Karoo rose.

larch *n*. A common name for the genus *Larix,* a hardy to very hardy elegant, conical, deciduous, coniferous tree. It grows to 50 feet or taller, with soft tufts of short, narrow needles and round, woody cones. The new leaves are pale green in spring and color bright yellow or orange in fall. They have an interesting winter silhouette and grow best in cold climates and moist soils. They attract birds.

larch, American *n*. A common name for *Larix larusina,* a very hardy tall deciduous coniferous tree native to North America. It grows to 60 feet and has light blue-green needles that turn a lovely yellow in autumn and small, shiny, scaly cones. Also known as black larch.

American larch
a branch with leaves *b* branch with cones

larch, Chinese *n*. A common name for *Larix Potaninii,* a hardy deciduous coniferous tree. It grows to 60 feet and more with short gray-green needles and small oval cones.

larch, Dahurian *n*. A common name for *Larix Gmelinii,* a very hardy tall deciduous coniferous tree. It has hairy branchlets, bright green needles and shiny oval cones.

larch, Dunkeld *n*. A common name for *Larix Eurolepis,* a hardy deciduous coniferous tree, a hybrid between European larch *(L. decidua)* and Japanese larch *(L. Kaempferi).* It closely resembles Japanese larch, but has smaller soft blue-green needles. A fast growing tree that can be effectively dwarfed in containers.

larchen *a.* Of, pertaining to, or of the nature of larches.

larch, European *n.* A common name for *Larix decidua,* a very hardy tall deciduous coniferous tree. It grows to 60 feet or more with grass green needles that turn yellow or orange in fall and fuzzy, oval cones.

larch, golden *n.* A common name for *Pseudolarix Kaempferi,* a hardy deciduous coniferous tree. It grows to 130 feet, with clusters of bright green leaves that color yellow in autumn and 3-inch cones that hang down. Will not grow in limestone soils.

larch, Japanese *n.* A common name for *Larix Kaempferei,* a fast growing deciduous coniferous tree that grows to 60 feet with short bluish-green needles and small woody brightly-colored red-purple cones. The leaves turn brilliant yellow in fall. Attractive to birds. Excellent as a background tree with evergreen conifers or near water for reflection.

larch, Western *n.* A common name for *Larix occidentalis,* a hardy deciduous coniferous tree. It grows to 150 feet in the wild, between 30 and 50 feet in cultivation. It has stiff, sharp needles and small, hairy scaled cones. Also known as tamarack.

Lardizabalaceae (lahr dih zab uh lay′cee ee) *n., pl.* A family of 7 genera of woody, twining vines. They have alternate leaves divided into leaflets, flowers with petallike sepals, and berrylike fruit. The cultivated genera are *Akebia, Decaisnea, Holboella, Lardizabala, Sinofranchetia,* and *Stauntonia.*

Larix (la′rihks) *n.* A genus of 10 species of hardy to very hardy tall, deciduous, coniferous trees (Pinaceae). They grow from 50 to 180 feet, with soft tufts of short, narrow needles and round, woody cones. The new leaves are pale green in spring and color bright yellow or orange in the fall. They attract birds. Commonly known as larch. (See **larch.**)

larkspur *n.* A common name for the genus *Delphinium,* a genus of hardy herbaceous perennials. They grow from 12 inches to 8 feet tall, depending on the species, with lobed, fanlike leaves, variously cut and divided, and with spirelike stalks of blue, lavender, purple, pink, red, yellow, or white flowers. Superb in borders and excellent cut flowers. The flowers attract birds.

Larrea (lar′ree uh) *n.* A genus of 4 species of tender evergreen resinous shrubs (Zygophyllaceae) native to dry regions of southwestern North America, Mexico, and South America. They grow to 4 to 10 feet with opposite, divided, leathery leaves that are covered with a gummy secretion that smells like creosote. They bear 5-petaled yellow flowers and round, furry fruit. Used as a wind or privacy screen and as a clipped hedge. Although they are heat-and drought-tolerant, they look best with moderate water. Commonly known as creosote bush.

larva (lar′vuh) *n., pl.* **larvae** (lar′vee) The first stage of an insect after leaving the egg. A caterpillar is a larva of a moth or butterfly. Often the larva can be a more serious plant pest than the adult.

Lasthenia (las theen′ee) *n.* A genus of 16 species of annuals or tender perennials usually grown as annuals; (Compositae), native mostly to the west coast of North America. They grow to 2 feet, with opposite leaves and yellow daisylike flowers. *L. chrysostoma* is commonly known as gold fields.

Latania (lah tay′nee uh) *n.* A genus of 3 species of ornamental subtropical fan palms (Palmae). They grow to 50 feet, with spiny-stemmed, fan-shaped leaves. Commonly known as latan palm.

Latania
(latan palm)

lateral *a.* On, toward, or from the side, as a lateral branch.

latex *n.* A milky, usually white or yellowish fluid produced by such plants as *Euphorbia* and *Asclepias*.

lath house *n.* A framework of widely spaced narrow boards used to protect plants from the sun by providing partial shade.

Lathyrus (lath'ih ruhs) *n.* A genus of more than 100 species of annual or perennial climbing vines that cling by tendrils (Legumiosae). They grow from 4 to 9 feet, with alternate, gray-green leaves, clusters of showy, sometimes sweetly fragrant, pastel pink, lavender, white, or magenta flowers, and long, narrow pods. *L. odorata* is commonly known as sweet pea.

laticiferous (lad ih sihf'uh ruhs) *a.* In botany, bearing, containing, or secreting latex.

latticeleaf *n.* A common name for *Aponogeton madagascariensis,* an aquarium plant with broadly oval submerged leaves with a lacelike network of veins. Also called laceleaf and lattice plant.

latticeleaf

Lauraceae (law'ruh 'see ee) *n., pl.* A family of 47 genera and 2,500 species, widely distributed; the laurel family. They are mostly broadleaf evergreen trees and shrubs, with leathery alternate leaves, inconspicuous flowers, and green, yellow-green, or red berries. The cultivated genera include *Cinnamomum* (cinnamon), *Laurus* (sweet bay), *Persea* (avocado), *Sassafras*, and *Umbellularia*.

lauraceous (law ray'shuhs) *a.* Of or pertaining to the Lauraceae.

laurel *n.* 1. The bay tree or bay laurel, *Laurus nobilis.* 2. Any one of many diverse plants whose leaves suggest those of the true laurel, such as *Prunus Laurocerasus* (English laurel), *Kalmia* (American laurel), and *Rhododendron maximum* (great laurel).

Laurus nobilis
(bay)

laurel cherry *n.* A common name for *Prunus Laurocerasus* (Rosaceae), a very tender shrub or small tree. It grows to 30 feet, with dense, broad, oval, leathery, glossy, light green leaves, inconspicuous white flowers, and small black fruit. Often used as a large clipped hedge but better used as a tall, unclipped screen or as a spreading shade tree. It is commonly known as laurel but must not be confused with the culinary laurel, or sweet bay, *Laurus nobilis.* Also known as English laurel and cherry laurel.

laurel family *n.* A common name for Lauraceae.

Laurus (law'ruhs) *n.* A genus of 1 or 2 species of tender shrubs and trees (Lauraceae). *L. nobilis,* the culinary bay, grows 12 to 40 feet, with oval, pointed, leathery, aromatic leaves, small yellow flowers, and small black or dark purple fruit. This is the bay leaf of great soups, stews, and spaghetti sauce, as well as the crowns of laurels with which ancient Greek athletes were crowned (and, on which one should not rest too long). Grown as a background shrub, screen, and classic, formal container plant; also, traditionally clipped as topiary. Commonly known as bay, sweet bay, and Grecian laurel.

laurustinus (law ruhs tee'nuhs) *n.* A common name for *Viburnum Tinus,* a hardy broadleaf evergreen shrub or small tree. It grows to 6 to 12 feet, with oval, leathery, dark green leaves, tight clusters of fragrant white flowers, and clusters of bright metallic-blue fruit. Used for hedges, screens, and topiary. Also known as laurustine.

Lavandula *n.* A genus of 20 species of drought tolerant richly aromatic perennial herbs and shrubs

(Labiatae). They grow to 1 to 3 feet, with narrow gray-green aromatic leaves and spikes of small lavender-to-purple fragrant flowers. Grown as low hedges or edgings, traditional in herb gardens and cottage gardens, and excellent in the sunny border. Commonly known as lavender.

Lavatera (lah vah'teh ruh) *n.* A genus of 25 species of tender flowers and large shrubs (Malvaceae). They grow to 15 feet, depending on the species, with maplelike leaves and large white or rose-purple hibiscuslike flowers nearly year-round. Takes full sun, most soils, drought, wind, and salt spray. Used as a specimen shrub or as a hedge; particularly useful in coastal gardens. Commonly known as tree mallow.

lavender *n.* A common name for any of several aromatic plants of the genus *Lavandula,* especially *L. vera,* the true lavender, which is used in the making of perfume. The plant is a woody perennial, hardy to southern New England, with pale green, fragrant leaves. The flowers, which are borne at the ends of thin stems, are tiny, purple, and intensely fragrant. The fragrance remains after the plant is dried, making it a popular plant for potpourri. French lavender is *Lavandula Spica;* sea lavender, the plant *Limonium latifolium.* (See **sea lavender**.)

lavender
a stem with leaves *b* flower spike

lavender cotton *n.* A common name used for a branched, low evergreen shrub, *Santolina chamaecyparissus.* Its silvery-gray foliage is sometimes used in knot gardens, where it contrasts nicely with deeper shadows of green. The flowers are small and yellow.

lavender mist *n.* Meadow rue, of the genus *Thalictrum;* grown in masses, especially in wild gardens.

lavender thrift *n.* The sea-lavender, *Limonium latifolium.*

lawn *n.* Space, usually level, covered with grass, and kept smoothly mown, as near a house or in a public park. The front lawn is the most universal feature of American residential landscaping.

lawn-and-leaf bag *n.* (See **leaf bag.**)

lawn coring tool *n.* A step-on implement used to aerate turf by removing plugs of sod.

lawn edger *n.* (See **edging tool.**)

lawn mower *n.* A machine for cutting grass. May be hand-, gasoline-, or electric-powered and either rotary or reel type.

lawn rake *n.* (See **leaf rake.**)

lawn shears *n.* (See **grass shears.**)

lawn tractor *n.* A gasoline-powered vehicle with rotary blades for cutting grass.

Lawsonia (law soh'nee uh) *n.* A genus of 1 species, *L. inermis,* a large tender shrub (Lythraceae). It grows to 20 feet, with small oval leaves and fragrant clusters of small white, rose, or cinnabar-red flowers. The leaves are the source of henna, an orange dye. Grown as an ornamental in warm regions. Commonly known as henna and migonette tree.

Lawson's cypress *n.* A common name for *Chamaecyparis Lawsoniana,* a large, hardy, evergreen coniferous timber tree. It has scalelike leaves in flattened sprays and round cones. Excellent as a large specimen tree, a hedge, a screen, or as a container plant; sometimes used for bonsai. Also known as Port Orford cedar and mourning cypress.

lax *a.* Scattered; widely spaced, as a lax cluster of flowers.

269

layer *v*. In horticulture, to propagate by bending and pegging the shoot of a living stem to the soil, the shoot striking root while still attached to the parent plant. Once the root is established, the shoot is cut from the mother plant, and potted up as a separate plant.

layering *n*. The operation of propagating plants by layers. (See **layer.**) The illustration shows the layered shoot bent down and held to the ground by a hooked peg, the young rootlets, and a thick stake supporting the extremity of the shoot in an upright position.

layering

Layia (lay′ee uh) *n*. A genus of 15 species of low-growing annuals (Compositae). They grow 5 to 16 inches high, with entire, toothed, or lobed leaves and yellow daisylike flowers with white-tipped petals. Used in the flower garden as a bedding plant or in containers. Commonly known as tidytips.

lazybed *n*. A bed for growing potatoes, in which the potatoes are laid on the surface of the soil and covered with earth taken out from trenches on both sides. This way of planting potatoes is now rarely used.

LD-50 *n*. A test measurement to provide the relative toxicity, usually oral, of a pesticide to mammals (at this concentration, the material killed half the test animals): the higher the number, the less toxic the material. LD-50 does not, however, represent a complete picture of the danger a pesticide presents. Carefully research the toxic properties of any pesticide, organic or chemical, before applying. (See **pesticide toxicity**.)

leach *v*. 1. To wash or drain by percolation of water; to treat by downward drainage, as rain washing away nutrients from the soil.

leaching *n*. The process of losing nutrients or salts from the soil through percolation or treating by downward drainage.

leaded wall nail *n*. A hardened-steel nail, about 1 inch long, driven into wood or masonry to train young vines and secure mature ones. A pliable lead strip attached to the nailhead holds the stem or branch in place. (See also **plant trainer**.)

leader *n*. In botany, the primary or terminal shoot of a plant, such as the topmost point of a fir or larch tree, or the strongest shoot of a young fruit tree.

lead plant *n*. A common name for *Amorpha canescens*, a hardy deciduous North American shrub with dense white hairs. It grows to 4 feet, with alternate, divided leaves, spikes of blue or white flowers, and beanlike pods.

lead tree *n*. A common name for *Leucaena glauca*, a subtropical American shrub or small tree, widely naturalized in Southern Florida. It grows to 30 feet, with leaves divided into tiny leaflets, pale beneath, clusters of white flowers, and long fuzzy pods with attractive seeds. Grown ornamentally in subtropical gardens. Also known as white popinac.

leadwort *n*. A common name for the genus *Plumbago*, tender perennial flowers, sprawling sub-shrubs, and climbing vines. They have alternate, simple, entire leaves and loose clusters of baby-blue, white, or red flowers.

leadwort, Cape *n*. A common name used for *P. Capensis* (*P. auriculata*), a tender shrub or vine. It grows to 12 feet or more, with fresh-looking, light to medium green leaves, phloxlike clusters of baby-blue or white flowers. Also known as Cape plumbago.

leadwort, Ceylon *n*. A common name for *P. zeylanica*, a much-branched tropical shrub. It has pointed, oval leaves and dense spikes of white flowers. Also known as white-flowered plumbago.

leadwort family *n*. A common name for Plumbaginaceae.

leaf *n*. The part of a plant that grows along the sides of stems or branches, or in clumps at the base of the plant. Most are green and contain chlorophyll. Ordinarily, leaves are the part of a plant that performs photosynthesis, the process of converting sunlight and carbon dioxide into energy for the plant to grow. It is common for leaves to grow, fall off, and be replaced. Plants entering dormancy may lose all their leaves, for example maples which lose their leaves in fall, are leafless in the winter, and replace them in spring and summer. Leaves come in many shapes and sizes, and most are arranged in a consistent manner along the stem, either directly opposite each other or alternating, one leaf on one side, the next leaf on the other side of the stem.

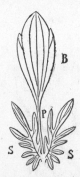

leaf showing parts, labeled
B blade *P* petiole *S* stipules

leafage *n*. Leaves collectively; foliage.

leaf bag *n*. A plastic or biodegradable plastic bag, usually 30- gallon capacity, used to contain leaves, grass clippings, or other garden debris for disposal. Also called lawn-and-leaf bag.

leaf blower *n*. A machine, consisting of a tube through which air is blown by a gas or electric motor, used to move leaves or debris from a lawn or driveway. Also called power blower.

leaf bud *n*. A bud producing a stem with leaves only, as distinguished from a flower bud.

leaf-cutting bee *n*. A plant pest that cuts small sections of leaves or flower petals to use to line its nest. To protect this valuable pollinator, control measures are not recommended as damage is usually minor.

leafed *n*. Having leaves; used frequently in combination, as broad-leafed thin-leafed, etc.

leafhopper *n*. A tiny, grasshopper-looking insect that sucks juices from the leaves of many kinds of plants. In the process, it distorts the foliage and transmits plant-damaging viruses. Stippled, light colored, or distorted foliage is one of the first signs of infestation. Many types of vegetables and berries are severely damaged. Horticultural oils, insecticidal soaps, floating row covers, and good garden cleanup may help. Botanical and traditional insecticides are most effective.

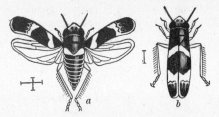

leafhopper
a wings extended *b* wings closed (lines show actual size)

leaflet *n*. A little leaf; in botany, 1 of the divisions of a compound leaf; a foliole.

leaf miner *n*. A larva of various moths, beetles, and flies. It burrows in leaf tissue, resulting in light-colored or transparent, meandering tunnels in leaves. It also can distort the foliage and cause leaf drop. The damage, mostly cosmetic, can be very unsightly. Timing is critical for control with traditional pesticides. Floating row covers can exclude pests from vegetables.

leaf mold *n*. A compost of decayed leaves. It can be used, alone or mixed with earth or other substances, as a soil for growing plants.

leaf plant *n*. A foliage plant, grown for decoration.

leaf rake *n*. A tool, having springy metal, bamboo, or flexible plastic tines, used for removing autumn leaves from lawn and garden.

leaf roller *n*. The larva of various types of caterpillars that rolls leaves around itself as it feeds. It infests a variety of plants but usually does the most damage on fruit trees, where it also feeds on small fruit. Control by handpicking or spraying with *Bacillus thuringiensis*.

leaf scar *n*. The mark left on a stem where a leaf has been lost or removed. Easily seen on palms where old leaves have shed.

leaf shredder *n*. A device for cutting leaves, twigs, and other small debris into small pieces. A leaf shredder may come as a stand-alone device or as an attachment to a power lawn mower or garden tractor.

leaf spot *n*. A general term used to describe various types of foliage diseases that usually result in circular spots on leaves. It can also infect fruit. Usually controlled with well-timed fungicidal sprays. (See **anthracnose, black spot,** and **scab**.)

leafstalk *n*. The stalk that attaches the leaf to the stem or branch; the petiole.

leafy *a*. 1. Having many leaves, usually used in reference to broadleaved trees, such as oaks, rather than needle-like leaves, as on firs.

leather fern *n*. 1. A common name used for *Acrostichum aureum,* a subtropical fern. The thick, leathery, divided fronds grow from 3 to 9 feet. Grows well in wet coastal gardens of warm regions. Also known as golden fern. 2. A common name for *Rumohra adantiaformis,* a tropical terrestrial or epiphytic fern. It has broadly triangular lacy fronds 3 feet long. Widely used by florists for cut foliage. Also known as ten-day fern, iron fern, and leatherleaf fern.

leatherflower *n*. A common name for the genus *Clematis.* Also a common name for the North American species *C. versicolor, C. virginiana,* and *C. Viorna.* They are hardy climbing vines that grow from 10 to 20 feet, with leaves divided into leaflets and showy masses of creamy-white, purple, or bluish-lavender flowers.

leatherleaf *n*. 1. A common name for *Polypodium Scouleri,* a North American fern native to the West Coast. It has leathery, divided leaves 18 inches long. Used in woodland gardens. Also known as leathery polypody. 2. A common name for *Chamaedaphne calyculata,* a very hardy evergreen shrub native to bogs. It grows to 5 feet, with narrow, oval leaves, rusty beneath, and short spikes of tiny white flowers. Also known as cassandra.

leatherwood *n*. A common name for *Ceratopetalum apetalum,* a tender Australian tree. It grows to 60 feet and has silver bark, oval, pointed, toothed leaves, and clusters of small white or rose flowers. Also known as coachwood. 2. A common name for *Cyrilla racemiflora,* a tender shrub or small tree native to the Americas. It grows to 30 feet or more, with glossy, leathery, narrow, oval leaves and spikes of small white flowers, which attract bees. Also known as titi, red titi, black titi, white titi, huckleberry, ironwood, and myrtle. 3. A common name for *Eucryphia lucida,* a tender broadleaf evergreen tree. It grows from 25 to 40 feet, with glossy, narrow, oval leaves and large, fragrant white flow-

ers. 4. A common name for the genus *Dirca,* a genus of 2 species of North American shrubs.

leatherwood
(*Dirca* genus)
a branch with flowers *b* branch with fruit and leaves

Lecythidaceae (leh sih thuh day'see ee) *n. pl.* A family of 15 genera of trees native to tropical America. They have alternate, simple leaves and clusters of asymmetrical flowers with many stamens. The ornamental species are *Bertholletia, Couroupita, Gustavia,* and *Lecythis.*

Lecythis (lehs'ih thuhs) *n*. A genus of 50 species of tall tropical trees (Lecythidaceae) native to the Americas. They grow to 80 feet, with alternate, simple, leathery leaves, clusters of sulfur yellow, white, violet, and rose flowers, and woody pods that open with a lidlike top. Commonly known as monkey pot.

Ledum (lee'duhm) *n*. A genus of 4 species of hardy to very hardy evergreen shrubs (Ericaceae), several native to arctic bogs. They grow to 6 feet, with alternate, simple, entire, leathery leaves and dense clusters of small white 5-petaled flowers. *L. groenlandicum* is commonly known as Labrador tea. Useful in evergreen borders in moist soils.

Leea (lee'uh) *n*. A genus of 70 species of subtropical and tropical shrubs and small trees (Leeaceae). They grow from 6 to 20 feet, depending on the species, with fernlike, lacy, glossy leaves divided into many leaflets. Popular as a houseplant for its foliage and used in frost-free gardens for a lush tropical effect.

leek *n.* One of several species of the genus Allium; especially, a biennial culinary plant, *Allium Ampeloprasum.* It is distinguished from the onion by having a cylindrical base instead of a spherical bulb, by its flat leaves, and by its milder flavor. It was probably cultivated in ancient Egypt, and, according to Pliny, it was made prominent among the Romans by Nero.

Legousia (leh gooz'ee uh) *n.* A genus of 15 species of annual flowers (Campanulaceae). They grow from 6 to 18 inches, depending on the species, with simple, alternate leaves and clusters of small blue or white flowers. Used as edging in flower beds and in rock gardens.

legume (leh'goom) *n.* 1. A plant of the Leguminosae (the legume family), the fruit or seed of which is used for food (such as beans and peas), or as a soil-improving cover crop or for animal feed (such as clover and alfalfa); pulse. 2. The seed pod of such a plant. 3. A table vegetable from such a plant—the term used mainly in menus.

legumen (leh goo'mehn) *n.* Same as legume.

Leguminosae (leh gyoo'mih noh'see) *n., pl.* A family of 600 genera and 1,200 species of flowers, vines, shrubs, and trees. A few of the ornamental genera include *Acacia, Albizia* (albizzia), *Cassia* (senna or shower tree), *Cercis* (redbud or Judas tree), *Cytisus* (broom), *Erythrina* (coral tree), *Gleditsia* (honey locust), *Laburnum* (bean tree), *Lathyrus* (vetchling or wild pea), *Mimosa, Phaseolus* (bean), *Pisum* (pea), *Robinia* (locust), *Tamarindus,* and *Wisteria.* Commonly known as the pea or pulse family.

leguminous (leh goo mih nuhs) *a.* Pertaining to plants that bear legumes, such as peas; specifically, of or pertaining to, the Leguminosae.

Leiophyllum (lee o figh'luhm) *n.* A genus of 1 species of hardy evergreen shrub, *L. buxifolium* (Ericaceae), native to eastern North America. It grows to 3 feet, with tiny, simple, entire, boxlike leaves and clusters of white-to-pink flowers. Used in borders and rock gardens. Commonly known as box sand myrtle.

Leitneria (light neh'ree uh) *n.* A genus of 1 species, *L. floridana* (Leitneriaceae), a hardy deciduous shrub or small tree native from Florida west to Texas. It grows to 25 feet, with long, narrow leaves, silky beneath, and woolly catkins that appear before the leaves. Useful in moist, shady places. Commonly known as corkwood.

Leitneriaceae (light neh ree ay'see ee) *n., pl.* A family of 1 genus and 1 species of shrub or small trees native to North America. The ornamental genus is *Leitneria.* Commonly known as the corkwood family.

Lemaireocereus (luh mehr ee of see'ree uhs) *n.* A genus of 26 species of large, spiny-ribbed, cylindrical cacti (Cactaceae) native to North and South America, from Arizona to Peru. They are simple to treelike, some branched, with bell-shaped or trumpet-shaped white, yellow-green, yellow, rose, pink, or purple flowers and spiny red fruit. They make dramatic specimens in desert gardens. *L. marginatus* is known as organ-pipe cactus.

Lemna (lehm'nuh) *n.* A genus of 9 species of hardy minute floating aquatic plants (Lemnaceae). Their tiny leaves, with threadlike rootlets, spread rapidly on the surface of pools and ponds, but rarely flower. Sometimes grown as food for fish or waterfowl, less often as an ornamental. Commonly known as duckweed, duck's-meat and frog's-buttons.

Lemnaceae (lehm nay'see ee) *n. pl.* A family of 6 genera and 30 species of minute, floating perennial water plants. The ornamental genera are *Lemna, Spirodela, Wolffia,* and *Wolffiella.* Commonly known as the duckweed family.

lemnad (lehm'nahd) *n.* A plant of the genus *Lemna,* also known as duckweed.

lemon *n.* 1. The fruit of the tree *Citrus Limon.* It is botanically a berry of elliptical shape, knobbed at the top, with a pale yellow rind whose outer layer is charged with a fragrant oil, and a light-colored pulp, full of an acid, well-flavored juice. 2. The tree that yields this fruit.

lemon balm *n.* A garden herb, *Melissa officinalis,* also known as Melissa. It is grown for its fragrant foliage, which, when fresh, gives off a strong lemon scent when touched. The scent and flavor do not last when the herb is dried.

lemon cucumber *n.* A yellow-skinned variety of cucumber, the shape and size of a lemon.

lemongrass *n.* A sweet-scented tropical grass, *Cymbopogon citratus.* It is used in cooking, and its fragrant oil is used in perfumes. (See **Cymbopogon.**)

lemon thyme (tighm) *n.* A lemon-scented garden herb, *Thymus Serpyllum.* It is rarer than common thyme, *Thymus vulgaris,* and not as hardy.

lemon verbena (ver bee'nuh) *n.* A garden shrub, *Aloysia triphilla,* related to the verbena. Its leaves have a strong lemon fragrance, which lasts after they have been dried. The durability of its fragrance makes it a favored ingredient in potpourri. It is frequently grown in greenhouses, but in its native South America, it may reach 10 feet in height. As a houseplant, it has the habit of dropping all its leaves in midwinter and looking quite dead before sprouting new growth.

lemon walnut *n.* A common name for *Juglans cinerea,* a very hardy, large, spreading North American tree, native from New Brunswick to Arkansas. It grows from 50 to 60 feet, taller in its native habitat, with leaves divided into many narrow, fuzzy leaflets, and with sweet, edible, hard-shelled nuts inside a sticky husk. Used as a spreading shade tree, and also grown for its excellent nuts. Also known as butternut or white walnut.

Lens *n.* A genus of 6 species of annual sprawling plants (Leguminosae). *L. culinarus* grows to 18 inches, having alternate leaves divided into many leaflets with a tendril at the end, small, pea-like white flowers and flat, square pods with seeds known as lentils. Grown for its seeds, which are usually dried. Commonly known as lentil.

Lenten rose *n.* A common name for *Helleborus orientalis,* a choice, long-lived, hardy evergreen perennial that blooms early and long in winter and spring. It grows in clumps to 2 feet tall, with handsome, glossy leaves, 16 inches across and divided into toothed leaflets, and green, purple, or rose cuplike flowers, prettily spotted or speckled. It is very poisonous. Used in the shady perennial border or massed under high-branching trees. Resents tranplanting.

Lentibulariaceae (lehn tihb yih lar ee ay'see ee) *n.* A family of 5 genera of mostly carnivorous small water plants. The ornamental genera are *Pinquicula* and *Utricularia.* Commonly known as the bladderwort family.

lenticel (lehn'tih suhl) *n.* In botany, a lens-shaped body of cells, formed on the outside of a woody plant stem, which serve in the exchange of gases between the stem and the outer air.

lenticellate (lehn tih sehl'ayt) *a.* Pertaining to or having lenticels.

lenticular (lehn tihk'yoo lar) *a.* Resembling a lentil or a double-convex lens, as some seeds.

lentiginous (lehn tihj'ih nuhs) *a.* In botany, covered with minute dots; freckled; speckled. Also lentiginose.

lentil (lehn'tuhl) *n.* The annual plant Lens culinaris (Leguminosae) or its seeds. It is widely cultivated in the Mediterranean region and the Orient, having been in use in Egypt and the East from antiquity. The small, flattened seeds furnish a nutritious food, simlar to peas and beans, and are cooked whole or split or ground into meal. The leafy stems of the lentil serve as fodder, and when in blossom, the plant is a good source of honey.

lentiscus (lehn tihs'kuhs) *n.* A common name for *Pistacia Lentiscus,* a tender shrub. It grows to 15 feet, with leaves divided into oval leaflets and reddish fruits that turn black. Also known as lentisk and mastic tree.

Leonotis (lee oh noh'duhs) *n.* A genus of 30 species of annuals, perennials, and shrubs (Labiatae). They grow from 1 to 8 feet, depending on the species, have opposite and usually toothed leaves, and bear whorled spikes of large, showy, yellow, orange, red, or white tubular flowers. Commonly known as lion's-tail and lion's-ear.

Leontopodium (lee ahn tuh poh'dee uhm) *n.* A genus of hardy low, tufted, and woolly perennials (Compositae). *L. alpinum,* a short-lived, white, woolly perennial, the edelweiss, grows from 4 to 12 inches tall, with slender white leaves, which radiate like the arms of a starfish, and small crowded heads of white flowers. Used in rock gardens, indoors in pots, or as part of an alpine collection.

Leonurus (lee ahn noo'ruh) *n.* A genus of 4 species of biennials or hardy perennials (Labiatae). They grow from 4 to 6 feet, with opposite leaves and with spikes of white, pale pink, or rose-pink flowers in whorls. Used in borders. Commonly known as motherwort.

leopard flower *n.* A common name used for *Belamcanda chinensis,* a hardy perennial. (See **lily, blackberry.**)

leopard plant *n.* A common name for *Ligularia tussilaginea,* a tender perennial bog plant. It forms a mound 1 to 2 feet high, with long-stemmed, thick, leathery leaves, speckled and blotched with cream or yellow, and yellow daisylike flowers. Used in shady beds, entryways, or containers.

leopard's bane *n.* A common name for the genus *Doronicum,* particularly *D. cordatum* and *D. Pardalianches.* They are perennials with basal leaves and showy, daisylike yellow flowers. Used in borders.

Lepechinia (lehp eh kihn′ee uh) *n.* A genus of 40 aromatic plants or shrubs (Labiatae) native to the Americas, from California to Argentina, and in Hawaii as well. *L. calycina* grows to 4 feet, with fragrant oval, pointed leaves and spikes of whorled white or pink flowers, blotched or veined with purple.

Lepidium (leh pihd′ee uhm) *n.* A genus of 100 species of annuals, perennials, and subshrubs (Cruciferae). *L. sativum* grows to 2 feet, with edible leaves and with spikes of very small green or white flowers. Used as a piquant salad vegetable. It has naturalized in North America. The genus is commonly known as peppergrass, pepperwort, and tongue grass; *L. sativum* is commonly known as garden cress.

lepidote (lehp′ih doht) *a.* In botany, covered with dry scales or scaly spots.

leprose (lehp′rohs) *a.* In botany, having scaly or dry scales. Also leprous.

Leptodactylon (lehp toh dak′tih lahn) *n.* A genus of 5 species of shrubs and subshrubs (Polemoniaceae) native to western North America. They grow to 3 feet, with fan-shaped leaves and trumpet-shaped white, pink, lilac, or yellow flowers.

Leptodermis *n.* A genus of 30 species of hardy deciduous shrubs (Rubiaceae). *L. oblonga* grows to 4 feet tall, with small, oblong leaves and ½ inch-long funnel-shaped violet-purple flowers.

Leptopteris (lehp tahp′ter ihs) *n.* A genus of 7 species of subtropical ferns (Osmundaceae). They grow to 4 feet, with very thin, finely-divided, dark green, leaves clustered at the top of stout rhizome. Grown in warm-climate gardens or as greenhouse plant. *L. superba* is commonly known as Prince-of-Wales fern or Prince-of-Wales plume.

Leptospermum (lehp toh sper′muhm) *n.* A genus of 40 species of tender evergreen shrubs and small trees (Myrtaceae). They grow to 30 feet, with alternate, entire leaves and white, pink, or red flowers. Used as a specimen tree in the landscape for its graceful branching habit and spring flowers. Commonly known as tea tree because Captain Cook brewed tea from the leaves of *L. scoparium* to prevent scurvy among the members of his crew. The leaves of *L. petersonii* are lemon-scented.

leptosporangiate (lehp toh spoh rahn′jee ayt) *a.* In botany, having each spore case formed from a single cell, as in certain ferns.

Lespedeza (lehs puh dee′zuh) *n.* A genus of 120 species of hardy perennial plants and low shrubs (Leguminosae). They grow from 12 inches to 10 feet, depending on the species, with cloverlike leaves, spikes of small butterfly-shaped flowers. Commonly known as bush clover.

lesser celandine (sehl′an deen) *n.* A common name for *Ranunculus Ficaria,* a hardy perennial that grows from a fleshy tuber. It grows to 12 inches, with branching stems and fleshy, rounded, 2-inch-long leaves and golden-yellow inch- wide flowers. Naturalized in North America. Also known as small celandine and pilewort.

lettuce *n.* A salad green, *Lactuca sativa,* a hardy annual, extensively cultivated. There are many varieties of the garden plant, which may be grouped as head lettuces, low forms with depressed cabbagelike heads, and Cos lettuces, erect-growing varieties with long heads that taper downward.

lettuce, Indian *n.* 1. A common name for the genus *Montia* (Portulacaceae), a genus of about 50 species of annual or perennial plants. They grow to 15 inches or less, with fleshy, alternate basal leaves, often edible, and spikes of small white or pink flowers. Useful in moist soils and near water. Also known as miner's lettuce. 2. A common name for *Frasera carolinensis,* a hardy North American plant,

7 feet tall, with 2-foot-long clusters of yellowish-white flowers spotted with purple. 3. A common name for *Pyrola rotundifolia,* a very hardy evergreen perennial to 12 inches tall, with small glossy leaves and spikes of white fragrant flowers. Also called round-leaf wintergreen, false wintergreen, wild lettuce, and wild lily-of-the-valley.

lettuce, lamb's *n.* A common name for *Valerianella,* a genus of annuals and biennials some species native to North America. They have simple, opposite, succulent leaves and headlike clusters of white, red, or blue tubelike flowers. Grown mostly for salad greens, useful in the vegetable plot or for edible landscaping. Also known as cornsalad.

Leucaena (loo see'nuh) *n.* A genus of 50 species of mostly tropical shrubs and trees (Leguminosae), most native to tropical America. They grow from 25 feet to 60 feet, depending on the species, with alternate, finely divided leaves and clusters of 5-petaled flowers.

Leucanthemum (loo kahn'thuh nuhm) *n.* A genus undergoing reclassification. *Chrysanthemum maximum,* the Shasta daisy, has been reclassified as *Leucanthemum maximum,* but the name is not yet widely accepted. Most Shasta daisies are still labeled *Chrysanthemum maximum* in nurseries and catalogs.

Leuchtenbergia (look tehn berg'ee uh) *n.* A genus of 1 species, *L. principis* (Cactaceae), a small cactus with long, weak spines native to Mexico. It grows to 2 feet, sometimes branched, with huge, fragrant, yellow funnel-shaped or bell-shaped flowers, 4 inches across. Grown by collectors. Commonly known as agave cactus and prism cactus.

Leucocoryne (loo koh kor'ee ee) *n.* A genus of 4 to 6 species of tender bulbs (Amaryllidaceae) native to Chile. *L. ixioides* grows to 18 inches with narrow, grasslike leaves and clusters of fragrant lavender-blue flowers with white centers. Used in rock gardens, dry summer areas of mild-climate gardens, or in pots. Commonly known as glory-of-the-sun.

Leucocrinum (loo koh krigh'nuhm) *n.* A genus of 1 species, *L. montanum* (Liliaceae), of hardy stemless rhizomatous flowers native to the American West, from Oregon east to South Dakota and south to New Mexico. It has narrow, 5-inch-long leaves

and clusters of spring-blooming, fragrant, pure-white flowers with yellow anthers. Commonly known as mountain lily, star lily, and sand lily.

Leucodendron (loo koh dehn'druhn) *n.* A genus of 60 species of tender shrubs and trees (Proteaceae). They grow from 1 foot to 40 feet, depending on the species, with entire, leathery leaves, showy male flowers resembling daisies, and cone-like female flowers. *L. argenteum* is commonly known as silver tree. Used in mild climate coastal gardens.

Leucojum (loo'koh juhm) *n.* A genus of 9 species of hardy bulbs (Amaryllidaceae). They grow to about 12 inches, with strap-shaped leaves and nodding, bell-shaped white flowers, each segment tipped with green. Easy to grow and permanent, they are used under deciduous trees, under shrubs, in cool borders, or on slopes. Commonly known as snowflake.

Leucophyllum (loo koh figh'luhm) *n.* A genus of 12 species of shrubs (Scrophulariaceae), native to the American Southwest, (including Texas and New Mexico) and Mexico. *L. frutescens* grows from 5 to 12 feet tall, with small, silvery, felty leaves and bell-shaped rose-purple flowers that bloom in summer. Used in desert gardens where it forms a round mass, or it can be clipped as a hedge. Tolerates high heat and dry soil. *L. frutescens* is commonly known as Texas ranger, barometer bush, and ceniza.

Leucospermum (loo koh sper'muhm) *n.* A genus of 40 species of tender erect or sprawling shrubs (Proteaceae). They grow from 4 to 12 feet, depending on the species, with narrow, leathery, hairy, oval leaves crowded along the stems and spectacular clusters of huge, shaggy, thistlelike flowers in combinations of orange, rose, red, or coral. Superb cut flowers that dry well; a superior specimen in mild-winter coastal climates. Commonly known as pincushion.

Leucothoe (loo koth'uh wee) *n.* A genus of 50 species of hardy to tender shrubs (Ericaceae), some native to the Americas. They grow from 3 feet to 12 feet, depending on the species, with alternate, simple, leathery leaves, which are tinted bronze in winter, and graceful, waxy, urn-shaped white or pink flowers similar to lily-of-the-valley. Used in woodland gardens or massed under broadleaf evergreens. Commonly known as fetterbush.

level *v.* To carefully rake soil to prepare for planting.

level terrace *n.* An embankment, constructed on a contour, which cuts horizontally across the slope. A means of creating a level area on hillsides or slopes.

leverwood *n.* A common name for the genus *Ostrya,* especially *O. virginiana,* a hardy deciduous tree native to eastern North America. It grows to 60 feet, with alternate, toothed, oval leaves, catkins, and small nuts. Also known as American hop hornbeam.

Levisticum (luh vihs′tuh kuhm) *n.* A genus of 1 species, *L. officinale* (Umbelliferae), a hardy perennial. It grows to 6 feet, with glossy, 3-part celery-like leaves, rounded clusters of small greenish-yellow flowers, and celery-flavored seeds. Traditional in herb gardens and cottage gardens; useful in the edible landscape (the leaves, stems, and seeds are all edible). Commonly known as lovage.

Lewisia (loo′ihzh′ee uh) *n.* A genus of 20 species of very hardy low-growing perennials (Portulacaceae) native to North America. They have fleshy evergreen leaves in basal rosettes and exquisite, large white, rose, or red flowers, some resembling waterlilies. Choice plants for the rock garden or alpine collection. Considered difficult to grow, they require perfect drainage.

Leycesteria (ligh sehs ter′ee uh) *n.* A genus of 6 species of hardy to tender deciduous shrubs (Caprifoliaceae). *L. formosa* grows to 6 feet, with large heart-shaped-to-oval pointed leaves, some as much as 7 inches long, and drooping spikes of small trumpet-shaped purple flowers that bloom in fall. *L. formosa* is commonly known as Himalayan honeysuckle.

liana (lee an′uh) *n.* A climbing and twining, usually woody plant, found mostly in tropical rainforests, which may climb to the level of the tree canopy. Also liane.

Liatris (lee′uh trihs) *n.* A genus of 40 species of hardy North American perennials (Compositae) native from Ontario to Florida and west to Alberta and New Mexico. They grow from 1 to 6 feet, depending on the species, with basal tufts of narrow, grassy leaves and narrow plumes of magenta flowers. Extremely tolerant of heat, cold, drought, and poor soil. Useful in perennial borders mixed with whites and pale pinks. Commonly known as gayfeather, blazingstar, and button snakeroot.

Libertia (lih ber′shuh) *n.* A genus of 20 species of fibrous-rooted plants (Iridaceae), some native to South America. They grow from 10 inches to nearly 5 feet, depending on the species, with long, narrow leaves and clusters of small white or blue flowers.

Libocedrus (ligh boh see′druhs) *n.* A former genus, now classified as *Calocedrus* (Cupressaceae), a genus of 3 species of evergreen conifers, some native to North America. They are symmetrical trees to as much as 90 feet tall, with rich green foliage in flat sprays, which give off a pungent fragrance in warm weather. They have reddish-brown bark and unusual cones that look like ducks'-bills and open on the tree. Commonly known as incense cedar.

lichen (ligh′kehn) *n.* A complex plant that consists of fungi growing in partnership with algae. Not ordinarily cultivated, these plants can be interestingly decorative in gardens when they grow naturally on surfaces such as rocks or tree trunks.

lichens

lichenism (ligh′kehn ihzm) *n.* The symbiosis between some fungi and algae that creates lichens.

lichenoid (ligh′kehn oid) *a.* In botany, resembling lichen.

lichenous (ligh′kehn uhs) *a.* Relating to, resembling, or covered with lichens. Also lichenose.

Licuala (lih kyoo ah′luh) *n.* A genus of more than 100 species of small, attractive, tropical Old World palms (Palmae), some of which grow in clusters. They grow from 5 feet to 20 feet, depending on the species, with fan-shaped leaves on spiny stems and orange or red fruit. Used in warm-climate gardens or as potted plants indoors.

lid *n.* In botany, the cap of a boxlike seed capsule.

life plant *n.* A common name for 2 different plants, *Biophytum sensitivum* and *Kalanchoe pinnata.*

liferoot *n.* A common name for *Senecio aureus,* a very hardy perennial flower native to North America, from Newfoundland to Florida and Texas. It grows to 30 inches, with heart-shaped basal leaves, tinged purple beneath, and clusters of small yellow daisylike flowers. Also known as golden ragwort and golden groundsel.

light soil *n.* A term used to indicate a sandy or coarse- textured soil that drains rapidy. It also may lack important plant nutrients.

lightwood *n.* A common name used for *Acacia melanoxylon,* a tender fast-growing, densely leaved tree. It grows to 40 feet, with long, oblong dark green leaves and puffy clusters of creamy or straw-colored flowers that bloom in early spring. The roots are invasive, the branches are brittle, and it litters all over, but it tolerates high heat and provides quick shade in hot climates. Also known as blackwood and black acacia.

ligneous (lihg′nee uhs) *a.* In botany, consisting of or resembling wood; woody, as distinguished from herbaceous.

lignescent (lihg nehs′ehnt) *a.* Tending to be or become ligneous or woody; somewhat woody.

lignify (lig′nih figh) *v.* To convert into or become wood or woody.

ligniperdous (lihg nih per′duhs) *a.* Destructive of wood.

lignum (lihg′nuhm) *n.* Woody tissue, as contrasted with soft tissue or with bark.

lignum vitae (lig′nuhm vigh′dee) *n.* A common name for trees and shrubs of the genus *Guaiacum,* and for species of several different genera of trees, including *Metrosideros, Acacia, Eucalyptus,* and *Vitex.*

ligula (lihg′yoo luh) *n., pl.* **ligulae** In botany, same as ligule.

Ligularia (lihg′yoo lahr ee uh) *n.* A genus of 50 to 150 much-debated species of tall, bold, showy perennials (Compositae), some very hardy. They grow from 3 to 6 feet, depending on the species, with big leaves, some as much as a foot wide, and showy spikes or clusters of yellow or orange flowers. Useful in moist soils.

ligulate (lihg′yoo layt) *a.* In botany: 1. Strap-shaped, such as a corolla, leaf, or petal. 2. Furnished with a ligule, as a ligulate grass. Also ligulated, ligular.

ligule (lihg′yool) *n.* In botany, a strap-shaped plant part; the blade formed by the corolla in some or all the florets of many members of the daisy family (Compositae). The strap- shaped part that sticks up from the top of the sheath in many grasses, palms, and some other plants.

liguliflorous (lihg′yoo lih floh ruhs) *a.* In botany, having heads composed exclusively of strap-shaped florets.

Ligusticum (lih guhs′tih kuhm) *n.* A genus of 40 to 50 species of hardy perennials (Umbelliferae). *L. lucidum* grows to 4 feet tall, with divided leaves and large clusters of white flowers. Used in perennial borders.

Ligustrum (lih guhs′truhm) *n.* A genus of 50 species of fast-growing, hardy to tender deciduous or evergreen shrubs and small trees (Oleaceae). They grow from 6 feet to 40 feet, depending on the species, with opposite, entire, oval, pointed leaves, abundant, showy clusters of oddly-scented small white flowers that attract bees, and black berries that attract birds. Used as clipped hedges, informal screens, in tubs or large pots, as windbreaks, or street trees. The many advantages are offset by as many disadvantages: The fruit stains concrete; bird-planted volunteers sprout everywhere; and bare fruiting clusters are brown, unattractive, and long-lasting. Commonly known as privet and hedge plant.

lilac *n.* A common name for shrubs of the genus *Syringa,* as well as for *Melia Azederach* and *Ceanothus thyrsiflorus. Syringa* is a widely grown hardy spring-blooming shrub, much cherished for the sweet fragrance of its lilac, lavender, purple, or white flowers, which attract bees. (*M. Azederach,* see **lilac, Indian.**)

lilac, Australian *n.* A common name for *Hardenbergia violacea,* a tender evergreen vine. It has glossy, oval, dark green leaves and long, drooping clusters of small sweet pea-like rose, violet, or white flowers. Used on low walls, fences arbors, and trellises or pegged to the ground as a ground cover. Also known as vine lilac or coral pea.

lilac, German *n.* A common name for *Centranthus ruber,* a tender perennial with long, narrow, opposite leaves and spikes of fluffy, fragrant, red, pink, or white flowers. It is self-sowing, drought-tolerant, tolerates poor soil, and attracts hummingbirds and butterflies. It has naturalized in northern California. Used on slopes, banks, and walls. Also known as red valerian or Jupiter's-beard.

lilac, Hungarian *n.* A common name for *Syringa Josikaea,* a very hardy deciduous shrub. It grows to 12 feet with glossy, oval, 5 inch-long leaves and 7-inch clusters of lilac flowers. Used as a specimen shrub in harsh-winter climates.

lilac, Indian *n.* A common name for *Melia Azedarach,* a tender deciduous large shrub or tree. It is a round-headed, densly-branched tree to 40 feet or more, with 3-foot-long leaves, many leaflets that turn clear yellow in fall; it bears clusters of fragrant purple flowers and small, yellow, egg-shaped fruit remains on the tree after the leaves fall. The fruit attracts birds. Used in warm-climate gardens; survives light frost. Tolerates heat and drought. Also known as chinaberry, China tree, pride-of-India, pride of China, Persian lilac, paradise tree, bead tree, margosa, Syrian bead tree, and Japanese bead tree. 2. A common name for *Lagerstroemia indica,* a small, deciduous, drought-and-heat resistant shrub or tree to 30 feet, with small, rounded, alternate leaves and spectacular masses of fluffy red, pink, purple, and white flowers throughout the summer. Excellent as a lawn tree, patio tree, and street tree. Also known as crape myrtle.

Liliaceae (lihl ee ay'see ee) *n., pl.* A family of about 240 genera and 3,000 species of mostly perennial flowers, many of which grow from bulbs, corms, rhizomes, or tubers. The ornamental genera include *Aloe, Asparagus, Asphodelus* (asphodel), *Aspidistra, Alstroemeria* (Peruvian lily), *Calochortus* (mariposa lily), *Camassia* (camass), *Chlorophytum* (St. Bernard's lily), *Colchicum, Convallaria* (lily-of-the-valley), *Endymion* (wood hyacinth), *Eremurus* (desert candle), *Erythronium* (trout lily or fawn lily), *Eucomis* (pineapple lily), *Fritillaria* (fritillary),

Haworthia (star cactus or cushion aloe), *Hemerocallis* (daylily), *Hosta* (plantain lily), *Hyacinthus* (hyacinth), *Kniphofia* (torch lily or red-hot poker plant), *Lachenalia* (Cape cowslip), *Lapageria* (Chilean bellflower), *Lilium* (lily), *Liriope* (lily turf), *Muscari* (grape hyacinth), *Ophiopogon* (mondo grass), *Polygonatum* (Solomon's seal), *Scilla* (squill), *Smilax* (greenbrier), *Tricyrtis* (toad lily), *Trillium* (wakerobin), *Tulipa* (tulip), and *Zigadenus* (death camas).

liliaceous (lihl ee ay'shius) *a.* Pertaining to or characteristic of lilies or of plants of the order Liliaceae; lilylike.

Lilium (lihl'ee uhm) *n.* A genus of 80 to 90 species of perennial bulbs, many of them hardy (Liliaceae). They grow from 10 inches to 8 feet, depending on the species, with unbranched leafy stems, alternate or whorled leaves, and trumpet-shaped or bell-like flowers, sometimes fragrant, in every color but blue. Much hybridization has taken place, and the most widely grown cultivars are the Asiatic, Aurelian, American, Candidum, and Oriental hybrids. Many species are still choice selections in the garden, including *Lilium auratum* 'Platyphyllum', (gold-band lily), *L. candidum* (Madonna lily), *L. longiflorum* (Easter lily), and *L. regale* (regal lily). Grown in borders, beds, and containers. Commonly known as lily.

lillypilly *n.* A common name for *Acmena Smithii,* a large tender evergreen flowering shrub or small tree. It grows from 10 to 25 feet, with shiny pinkish-green or green leaves, abundant clusters of small white flowers, and white-to-purple edible berries. A rangy shrub that needs pruning. Also known as lillypilly tree.

lily *n.* 1. A plant of the genus *Lilium,* or its flower. 2. Any one of many plants resembling the lily.

lily, adobe *n.* A common name for *Fritillaria pluriflora,* a tender bulb with narrow leaves and clusters of pink-to-purple bell-shaped flowers; native to northern California. The name comes from the thick clay soil in which it typically grows. Also known as pink fritillary.

lily, African *n.* A common name for *Agapanthus africanus,* a tender evergreen perennial. It has fleshy roots and grows to 18 inches, with strap-like leaves and tall stalks with clusters of many blue or white funnellike flowers. Used in warm climates, in large clumps, in beds and borders, as well as in containers and as a specimen. Magnificent cut flowers. Extraordinarily tolerant of difficult conditions, they appear to tolerate everything but freezing and foot traffic, enduring smog, poor soil, heat, and drought once established. Also known as blue agapanthus and lily-of-the-Nile.

lily, African blood *n.* A common name for the genus *Haemanthus* (Amaryllidaceae), a genus of about 60 species of low-growing tender bulbs. They have broad basal leaves, stalks of dense clusters of red or white summer- or fall-blooming flowers, and colorful berries. Also known as blood lily.

lily, African corn *n.* A common name for the genus *Ixia,* a genus of 30 species of tender bulbs (corms) (Iridaceae). They have narrow, sword-shaped leaves and long, wiry stems, bearing spikes of large, showy, cup-shaped cream, yellow, orange, red, or pink flowers with dark centers. Excellent cut flowers, they are grown in beds in warm climates, in pots in cold climates.

lily, alligator *n.* A common name for *Hymenocallis Palmeri,* a tender bulb native to Florida. It grows to 16 inches, with long, narrow leaves and large, solitary, slightly fragrant white flowers, 3 inches long and 2 inches across. Grown outdoors in mild climates, in pots anywhere.

lily, alp *n.* A common name for the genus *Lloydia* (Liliaceae), 12 species of hardy alpine perennial bulbs, some native to western North America. *L. serotina* grows to 6 inches, with grasslike leaves and tiny (5/6-inch) yellow-white flowers with purple veins. Used in alpine gardens and collections.

lily, alpine *n.* A common name for *Lilium parvum,* a hardy perennial bulb native to stream banks and wet meadows in the mountains of southern Oregon and central California. It grows to 5 feet, with narrow, whorled leaves, and spikes of tiny, bell-shaped orange to dark red flowers with purplish-brown spots. Useful in moist, cool soils. Also known as Sierra lily and small tiger lily.

lily, Amazon *n.* A common name for *Eucharis grandiflora,* native to the Andes of Colombia and Peru. It has broad, straplike leaves and clusters of large, pure white, and very fragrant flowers, 3 inches across, borne at the end of a sturdy 2-foot tall stalk. Grown mainly as a greenhouse plant. Also known as Eucharist lily, Madonna lily, and lily-of-the-Amazon.

lily, Amazon water *n.* A common name for *Victoria amazonica,* a tender South American water lily. It has huge floating leaves, 3 to 6 feet across, with turned-up edges like a griddle, heavily ridged beneath, and with fragrant flowers that open white and then turn to pink or red. Used on very large ponds or lakes in frost-free climates or grows as an annual. Also known as royal water lily, water maize, and Amazon water-platter.

lily, American Turk's-cap *n.* A common name for *Lilium superbum,* a hardy bulb native to wet soils of the eastern United States, from New Hampshire to Georgia and Alabama. It grows to 8 feet, with narrow, whorled leaves and clusters of large, nodding orange-scarlet flowers spotted with purplish brown. Useful massed in the back of moist borders. Also known as Turk's-cap lily, lily-royal, swamp lily, and Turk's-cap.

American Turk's cap lily
1 plant 2 roots and bulbs

lily, arum *n.* A common name for *Zantedeschia aethiopica,* a tender rhizomatous perennial. It grows to 3 feet or more in clumps of broad, entire, arrow-shaped leaves and very large white calla-shaped flowers with a yellow spike in the middle. Used in borders and beds with moist soil, along streams, around ponds, and in bog gardens. Also known as florist's calla, garden calla, common calla, calla lily, pig lily, and trumpet lily.

lily, Atamasco *n.* A common name for *Zephyranthes Atamasco,* a fairly hardy perennial bulb native to the southeastern United States, from Virginia to Florida and Alabama. It grows to 12 inches, with narrow, sharp-edged, grasslike leaves and large, solitary white flowers tinged with purple. Blooms a few days after rain. Used in woodland gardens, wild gardens, native plant collections, rock gardens, in the foreground of borders, or in pots.

lily, Australian water *n.* A common name for *Nymphaea gigantea,* a tender, day-blooming, tuber-bearing water lily. It has green leaves, purple beneath and fragrant, soft purplish-blue or white flowers. Used in ponds and pools.

lily, avalanche *n.* A common name for *Erythronium grandiflorum,* a hardy bulb native to the mountains of western North America, from British Columbia east to Montana and south to Utah. It grows from 12 to 24 inches, with 2 basal unspotted leaves and spikes of bright golden-yellow flowers. Used in shady wild gardens or rock gardens; difficult to grow at low elevations.

lily, Aztec *n.* A common name for *Sprekelia formosissima* (Amaryllidaceae), a Mexican bulb with narrow, sword-shaped leaves and with a stalk bearing one large, crimson, curiously shaped blossom. Used outdoors in warm climates, in pots or massed, and in greenhouses anywhere. Also known as jacobean lily, St. James's lily and orchid amaryllis.

lily, Backhouse hybrid *n.* A common name for *Lilium* ×*Backhousei,* a hardy perennial bulb. It grows to 6 feet, with whorled leaves and stalks of 20 to 30 cream, yellow, pink, or burgundy flowers with dark spots. Used on borders and beds for summer bloom.

lily, barbados *n.* A common name for the genus *Hippeastrum* (Amaryllidaceae), a genus of 75 species of perennial bulbs native mostly to tropical America. They grow from large bulbs, with basal strap-shaped leaves and tall, sturdy stalks with showy clusters of large red, pink, white, salmon, and apricot trumpet-shaped flowers. Grown mainly as container plants; must be lifted in cold- or wet-winter climates. Also known as amaryllis.

lily, bell *n.* A common name for *Lilium Grayi,* a hardy perennial that spreads by stolons, native to the southeastern United States, from Virginia to North Carolina and west to Tennessee. It grows to 4 feet, with narrow, pointed, sometimes whorled leaves and small, nodding, bell-shaped reddish-orange flowers with purple-brown spots. Used in wild gardens. Also known as orange-bell lily, Gray's lily, and roan lily.

lily, belladonna *n.* A common name for *Amaryllis belladonna,* a very long-lived tender perennial bulb. It forms clumps of strap-shaped leaves that appear in winter and die back in summer, when tall, brown, leafless stalks of many fragrant, pale pink trumpet-shaped flowers appear, usually in August. It has naturalized along the West Coast of the United States. Useful in perennial borders. Resents transplanting and may not bloom for several years if moved any time except just after bloom. Also known as Cape belladonna and naked-lady lily.

lily, Bellingham hybrid *n.* A common name for *Lilium* ×*pardaboldtii,* a perennial bulb. It grows to 5 feet, with whorled leaves and tall stalks of many red-orange spotted flowers, with petals bent sharply backward. Used in beds and borders.

lily, Bermuda Easter *n.* A common name for *Lilium longiflora eximium,* a perennial bulb. It grows to 3 feet or more, with many long, narrow alternate leaves and fragrant trumpet-shaped white flowers more than 7 inches long. Grown in pots indoors for holiday bloom. Also known as Easter lily and Bermuda lily.

lily, blackberry *n.* A common name for *Belamcanda chinensis,* a hardy perennial. It grows to 3 to 4 feet, with 10-inch-long irislike leaves, orange flowers dotted with red, and a seed capsule that resembles a blackberry. The curious seed capsules are used in flower arrangements. Used in clumps in borders. Also known as leopard lily and leopard flower.

lily, blood *n.* A common name for *Haemanthus,* a genus of tender low-growing bulbs.

lily, blue funnel *n.* A common name for *Androstephium coeruleum,* a hardy fibrous-coated corm native to the central United States, from Kansas to Texas. It grows to 8 inches, with basal, grasslike leaves and stalks with clusters of blue flowers. Used in wild gardens.

lily, blue bead *n.* A common name for *Clintonia borealis,* a hardy rhizomatous perennial native to eastern North America. It grows to 18 inches, with a few leaves 12 inches long, clusters of small, nodding greenish-yellow flowers, and blue berries that give the plant its common name. Useful in moist, shady places; does well in the woodland garden. Also known as corn lily.

lily, boat *n.* A common name for *Rhoeo spathaceae,* a low-growing, subtropical, succulent perennial. It has stems to 8 inches, with dense, dark green leaves, purple beneath, and curious 3-petaled white flowers borne in boat-shaped bracts. Used as a houseplant or in hanging baskets; in subtropical climates, as a small-scale ground cover. Also known as purple-leaved spiderwort, oyster plant, Moses-on-a-raft, Moses-in-a-boat, Moses-in-the-cradle, Moses-in-the-bulrushes, man-in-a-boat, two-men-in-a-boat, and three-men-in-a-boat.

lily, bugle *n.* A common name for the genus *Watsonia,* a tender bulb (corm). It grows 3 to 6 feet, depending on the species, with narrow, rigid, sword-shaped leaves and tall stalks of peach, pink, lavender, red, scarlet, or white flowers resembling gladiolus. Used in borders, beds, and pots. Good cut flowers.

lily, butterfly *n.* A common name for *Hedychium coronarium,* a robust perennial to 6 feet, with large, broad leaves and dense spikes of richly fragrant white flowers. Grown in warm winter climates outdoors, in greenhouses elsewhere. Useful in water gardens, near pools, for tropical effects, and excellent in containers. Also known as garland flower, butterfly ginger, white ginger, ginger lily, and cinnamon jasmine.

lily, calla *n.* A common name for *Zantedeschia aethiopica,* a tender rhizomatous perennial. It grows to 3 feet or more, in clumps of broad, entire arrow-shaped leaves and has very large, calla-shaped white flowers with a yellow spike in the middle. Used in borders and beds with moist soil, along streams, around ponds, and in the bog garden. Also known as arum lily, florist's calla, garden calla, common calla, pig lily, and trumpet lily.

lily, Canada *n.* A common name for *Lilium canadense,* a hardy perennial bulb native to eastern and central North America, from Nova Scotia to Virginia and west to Ohio and Kentucky. It grows to 5 feet, with long, whorled leaves and tall stalks with large, nodding, orange-yellow to red spotted flowers to 3 inches across. Used in the wild garden or meadow garden. Also known as wild yellow lily, meadow lily, yellow-bell lily, and yellow lily.

lily, candlestick *n.* A common name for *Lilium* × *hollandicum* and *L. pensylvanicum. L. xhollandicum* is a hybrid perennial bulb that grows to 30 inches and has spikes of red, yellow, or orange flowers. *L. pensylvanicum* which spreads by stolons, is native to northeast Asia despite its misleading latin name. It grows to 3 feet, with long, alternate leaves and very large red or scarlet flowers, yellow at the base and spotted purplish-black.

lily, Cape blue water *n.* A common name for *Nymphaea capensis,* a tender, day-blooming water lily. It has large floating leaves 16 inches in diameter and showy sky-blue flowers 6 to 8 inches across. Used in water gardens and garden pools.

lily, Cape Cod pink water *n.* A common name for *Nymphaea odorata rosea,* a hardy, day-blooming water lily. It has thick, entire, dull green leaves, purplish beneath, and fragrant, deep pink flowers, 4 inches across, that open in the morning. Used in water gardens and in garden pools.

lily, Carolina *n.* A common name for *Lilium Michauxii,* a hardy perennial bulb. It grows to 4 feet, with fleshy, whorled leaves and large, nodding fragrant orange-scarlet spotted flowers 4 inches long. Used in wild gardens, and in borders. Also known as Turk's-cap lily.

lily, Caucasian *n.* A common name for *Lilium monadelphum,* a hardy perennial bulb. It grows to 5 feet, with many long, narrow, alternate leaves and numerous, large, nodding, fragrant golden-yellow flowers 5 inches across.

lily, celestial *n.* A common name for the genus *Nemastylis,* a tender bulb native to North and South America. *N. acuta* grows from 6 to 18 inches, with leaves 12 inches long and blue flowers almost 3 inches across that bloom in early morning. *N. acuta* is also known as prairie iris.

lily, chamise *n.* A common name for *Lilium rubescens,* a hardy perennial bulb native to the coastal ranges of the western United States from southern Oregon to central California. It grows to 6 feet, with whorled leaves 4 inches long and spikes of many white or pale lilac flowers with purple spots. Also known as chaparral lily and redwood lily.

lily, checker *n.* A common name for *Fritillaria lanceolata,* a hardy perennial bulb native to western North America, from British Columbia to southern California and east to Idaho. It grows 3 to 4 feet, with long, narrow, whorled leaves and attractive bowl-shaped purple-brown flowers mottled with greenish-yellow. Easily grown in the wild garden. Also known as narrow-leaved fritillaria.

lily, checkered *n.* A common name for *Fritillaria Meleagris,* a very hardy perennial bulb. It grows to 15 inches, with long, alternate leaves and showy bell-shaped flowers intricately patterned in reddish-brown and purple. Used in woodland gardens, rock gardens, or in borders in filtered shade. Also known as snake's-head or guinea-hen tulip.

lily, Chinese lantern *n.* A common name for *Sandersonia aurantiaca,* a tuberous-rooted perennial. It grows to 2 feet, with long, narrow leaves and slender, drooping stalks of bell-shaped orange flowers. Grown in greenhouses. Also known as Christmas bells.

lily, Chinese sacred *n.* A common name for *Narcissus tazetta* var. *orientalis,* a tender perennial bulb. It grows to 18 inches, with long, narrow basal leaves and leafless stalks topped by clusters of sweetly fragrant, jonquillike yellow flowers. Used under trees, in borders, in containers, and often forced for winter bloom.

lily, Chinese white *n.* A common name for *Lilium leucanthum,* a hardy perennial bulb. It grows to 4 feet, with many, long, narrow, alternate leaves and stalks of fragrant, drooping, trumpet-shaped greenish-white flowers flushed pale yellow on the inside.

lily, climbing *n.* A common name for *Gloriosa,* a genus of tropical vines. (See **lily, gloriosa.**)

lily, coast *n.* A common name for *Lilium maritimum,* a tender perennial bulb native to coastal Cal-

ifornia. It grows to 4 feet, with long, narrow, mostly alternate leaves and with stalks of several small, bell-shaped, dark red flowers spotted with maroon.

lily, cobra *n.* 1. A common name for the genus *Darlingtonia,* a remarkable genus of a single carnivorous species, *D. californica,* an insect-devouring pitcher plant native to wet, swampy sites in California and Oregon. The leaves are trumpet-shaped, sometimes 3 feet long, with a spreading hood, that looks like a cobra's hood. The inside of the tube is covered with rigid hairs directed downward, and the bottom is filled with a liquid that digests trapped insects. 2. A common name for *Arisaema speciosum,* a tuberous-rooted flower with large pointed leaves and a flower closely resembling its cousin *A. triphyllum* (jack-in-the-pulpit), with a long tail. Grown ornamentally for its curious flowers, handsome summer foliage, and colorful fruit.

lily, Columbia *n.* A common name for *Lilium columbianum,* a hardy perennial bulb native to western North America, from British Columbia to California and east to Idaho. It grows to 5 feet or more, with long, narrow, whorled leaves and spikes of dainty, nodding, yellow, golden, or red flowers spotted with maroon. Also known as Oregon lily.

lily, corn *n.* A common name for flowers of several different genera, including the genus *Ixia* (African corn lily), *Clintonia borealis* (blue bead lily), and *Veratrum californicum* (skunk cabbage).

lily, cow *n.* 1. A common name for *Caltha palustris,* a golden-flowered bog plant with stout, creeping rootstocks, lush green, rounded heart-shaped leaves, and showy yellow flowers having sepals, but not petals. Used in moist soils and in bog gardens. Also known as cowslip, marsh marigold, meadow bright, kingcup, and May blob. 2. A common name for *Nuphar,* a genus of water plants also known as spatterdock, yellow pond lily, water collard, and marsh collard.

lily, crane *n.* A common name for *Strelitzia reginae,* a dramatic subtropical perennial flower. It grows to 3 feet or more, with large, broad, long-stemmed leaves and strikingly dramatic orange, blue, and white flowers on long, stiff stems. Magnificent in warm-climate gardens or in greenhouses; excellent exotic cut flowers. Its large leaves are easily tattered by wind. Also known as bird-of-paradise, queen's bird-of-paradise, and crane flower.

lily, Crinum *n.* A common name for *Crinum,* a genus of tender perennial bulbs. (See **Crinum.**)

lily, Cuban *n.* A common name for *Scilla peruviana,* a long-lived tender bulb native to the Mediteranean, despite its inappropriate English and latin names. It grows 18 inches or more with strap-shaped leaves 1 foot long and spikes of 50 to 100 small blue-violet, purple, or white flowers. Grown outdoors in mild climates, in greenhouses, and in pots. Also known as Peruvian jacinth or hyacinth-of-Peru.

lily, desert *n.* A common name for *Hesperocallis undulata,* a tender bulb native to southern California and western Arizona. It grows to 2 feet, with narrow, strongly crisped, white-margined leaves 2 feet long and fragrant, trumpet-shaped white flowers with a broad green stripe on the back.

lily, dwarf ginger *n.* A common name for *Kaempferia Roscoana,* a tropical perennial. It grows from a rhizome, with dark green leaves marked by pale bands and short spikes of white flowers. Grown outdoors in warm-climate gardens, as indoor/outdoor plants in pots, or in the greenhouses. Also known as peacock lily.

lily, Easter *n.* A common name for *Lilium longiflora eximium,* a perennial bulb. It grows to 3 feet or more, with many long, narrow alternate leaves and fragrant, trumpet-shaped white flowers more than 7 inches long. Grown in pots indoors for holiday bloom. (Do not plant forced Easter lilies out in the garden with other lilies, as they may carry a virus that can infect other lilies.) Also known as Bermuda Easter lily and Bermuda lily.

lily, Egyptian water *n.* A common name for *Nymphaea caerulea* and *N. Lotus,* both tender water lilies. *N. caerulea* is a day-blooming water lily, which has light blue flowers 3 to 6 inches across. *N. Lotus* is a tender, night-blooming, white water lily, blushed pink, 5 to 10 inches across, that opens at night and remains open until noon the following day. These 2 water lilies are the lotus depicted in ancient Egyptian art. *N. caerulea* is also known as blue lotus. *N. Lotus* is also known as Egyptian water lotus, lotus, Egyptian lotus, and white lotus.

lily, Eucharist *n.* A common name for *Eucharis grandiflora,* a tender bulb. (See **lily, Amazon.**)

lily, Eureka *n.* A common name for *Lilium occidentale,* a tender perennial rhizome native to coastal California and Oregon. It grows to 6 feet, with long leaves and stalks of nodding orange flowers with maroon dots, green centers, and purple anthers. Also known as Western lily.

lily, European white water *n.* A common name for *Nymphaea alba,* a vigorous, hardy, day-blooming water lily. It has leaves 12 inches in diameter, red when young, and white flowers 4 to 5 inches across with yellow stigmas. Also known as platter dock.

lily, fairy *n.* A common name for the genus *Zephyranthes,* a genus of low-growing tender bulbs, some native to the Americas. They grow from a few inches to 2 feet, depending on the species, with narrow, grasslike leaves and white, pink, red, or yellow trumpet-shaped flowers. The flowers appear a few days after rain in the wild. Used in rock gardens, at the front of borders, or in pots. Also known as zephyr lily or rain lily.

lily, fairy water *n.* A common name for *Nymphoides aquatica,* a hardy water lily native to the United States, from New Jersey south to Florida and west to Texas. It has round to kidney-shaped leaves, purple beneath, and summer-blooming clusters of small white flowers. Used in water gardens, ponds, and tubs. Also known as banana plant and aquatic banana plant.

lily family *n.* A common name for *Liliaceae.*

lily, fawn *n.* A common name for *Erythronium californicum,* a tender bulb native to the coastal ranges of northern California. It grows from 4 to 14 inches, with 6-inch-long leaves mottled with brown spots and small cream to white flowers, banded wih yellow, orange, or brown inside. Used in wild gardens or as a choice specimen in rock gardens. 2. A common name for the genus *Erythronium.*

lily, fire *n.* A common name for plants of 3 different genera, including the genus *Cyrtanthus,* as well as for *Xerophyllum tenax,* and *Zephyranthes tubiflora.* (See **Xerophyllum,** and **Zephyranthes.**)

lily, flamingo *n.* A common name for *Anthurium andraeanum,*, a tropical American jungle flower. It grows to several feet, with large, oblong, dark green leaves and striking waxy red, rose, pink, or white flowers. Used as a houseplant. It will bloom continuously in a warm (80 to 90o F) greenhouse. An excellent and exceptionally long-lasting cut flower. Also known as flamingo plant or oilcloth flower.

lily, flax *n.* A common name for 2 genera, *Dianella* and *Phormium. Dianella* is a genus of tropical rhizomatous plants with grass like leaves, loose clusters of nodding, blue or white flowers, and a blue berry. *Phormium* is a large perennial growing from 7 to 15 feet, depending on the species, with basal, sword-shaped leaves and leafless stalks topped by clusters of dull red or yellow flowers.

lily, fragrant plantain *n.* A common name for *Hosta plantanginea,* a long-lived, hardy perennial grown primarily for its handsome foliage. It forms large, leafy clumps of attractive glossy, bright yellow-green leaves and spikes of pretty, fragrant, white funnel-shaped flowers in late summer and autumn. Used in shady borders and beds and in containers.

lily, fragrant water *n.* A common name for *Nymphaea odorata,* a hardy day-blooming water lily native to the eastern United States. It has thick, entire, dull green leaves, purplish beneath, and fragrant white flowers (pink in the variety *N. o. rosea*) 3 to 5 inches across that open in the morning. Used in water gardens and in garden pools. Also known as white water lily and pond lily.

lily, garland *n.* A common name for the genus *Hedychium,* a genus of robust perennials growing from rhizomes, with handsome large, broad leaves and dense spikes of richly fragrant white flowers. Grown in warm winter climates outdoors or in greenhouses anywhere. Useful in water gardens, near pools, in frost-free gardens for tropical effects, and excellent in containers. Also known as ginger lily.

lily, giant *n.* A common name for *Doryanthes excelsa,* an Australian succulent that grows to 18 feet. It has 4-foot-long, curved leaves, many dark red bracts, and flowers in a round ball at the top of a 12-foot stalk. (See **Doryanthes**.) 2. A common name for *Cardiocrinum gigantum,* a tall Asiatic summer lily with leaves in a basal rosette and large fragrant white flowers, striped with red or purple, on a 12-foot stem.

lily, giant water *n.* A common name for *Victoria,* a genus of tender South American water lilies. They have huge floating circular leaves, up to 6 feet across with edges 3 to 8 inches high, heavily ridged beneath, and fragrant floating flowers that open white and then turn to pink or red. Used on very large ponds or lakes in frost-free climates or grown as annuals. Also known as water-platter.

lily, ginger *n.* A common name for the genus *Hedychium,* robust perennials with dense spikes of richly fragrant white, yellow, red, or orange flowers with red or pink stamens. Also a common name for *H. coronarium.* Grown in warm-winter climates outdoors, in greenhouses elsewhere. Useful near pools, for tropical effects, and excellent in containers. (See **Hedychium; lily, garland;** and **lily, butterfly**.)

lily, globe *n.* A common name for *Calochortus albus,* a tender perennial bulb native to the mountains of California. It grows to 30 inches, with basal leaves to 2 feet long and stalks bearing lovely small, nodding, white globular flowers in spring. A beautiful plant grown primarily by collectors; requires summer dormancy. Also known as fairy lantern.

lily, globe spear *n.* A common name for *Doryanthes excelsa,* a gigantic tender succulent. It grows to 18 feet, with masses of 100 or more leaves, 8 feet in length in basal rosettes, and 12-foot spikes topped by 12-inch round clusters of bright red flowers, each flower is 4 inches long. Used in large gardens where they are strikingly dramatic.

lily, gloriosa (glohr′ee oh suh) *n.* A common name for *Gloriosa* (Liliaceae), a genus of 5 or 6 species of tuberous-rooted climbing tropical vines. *G. rothschildiana* has opposite or whorled leaves, terminating in tendrils by which it climbs, and extraordinary, large, red lilylike flowers edged with yellow. Grown as a houseplant, in containers as an indoor/outdoor plant, or in greenhouses. Also known as glory lily and climbing lily.

lily, gold-banded *n.* A common name for *Lilium auratum,* a hardy perennial bulb. It grows to 4 to 8 feet, with long, narrow leaves and magnificent sweetly fragrant, waxy white flowers spotted with crimson and banded with gold. 'Platyphyllum' has flowers a foot wide. Used in borders and beds. Needs staking. Also known as gold-band lily and golden-rayed lily.

lily, golden hurricane *n.* A common name for *Lycoris africana,* a fairly hardy perennial bulb native from China to Burma, despite its misleading name. It grows to 18 inches, with narrow leaves and summer-blooming golden-yellow flowers with petals bent backward. Used in rock gardens and at the front of borders; needs winter protection. Also known as golden spider lily.

lily, golden-rayed *n.* (See **lily, gold-banded.**)

lily, golden spider *n.* (See **lily, golden hurricane.**)

lily , Gray's *n.* (See **lily, bell.**)

lily, Guernsey *n.* A common name for *Nerine sarniensis,* a tender perennial bulb. It grows to 18 inches, with clusters of crimson funnel-shaped flowers and with long, narrow leaves, which appear after blooming. Grown outdoors in mild winter climates, in pots as indoor/outdoor plants, and in greenhouses.

lily, herb *n.* A common name for *Alstroemeria haemantha,* a tender subtropical perennial bulb native to Chile. It grows to 3 feet, with long, narrow leaves and deep red flowers streaked with yellow. Used in warm-climate gardens or in pots as an indoor/outdoor plant.

lily, hidden *n.* A common name for *Curcuma,* a genus of robust tropical rhizomatous perennials. *C. petiolata* has long, broad leaves and spikes of green bracts with rose-pink edges surrounding yellowish white flowers; also known as queen lily. Grown in frost-free gardens or in greenhouses.

lily, Humboldt *n.* A common name for *Lilium Humboldtii,* a fairly hardy perennial bulb native to the Sierra Nevada range of California. It grows 3 to 6 feet, with long, narrow, whorled leaves and nodding, recurved, bright orange flowers, dotted with maroon that bloom in early summer.

lily, India red water *n.* A common name used for *Nymphaea rubra,* a tender, night-blooming water lily. It has bronzy-red floating leaves that darken to

green, hairy beneath, and deep purple-red flowers, 6 to 10 inches across, that remain open until noon. Used in water gardens.

lily, infafa (ihn fah'fah) *n.* A common name used for 2 different species, *Cyrtanthus mackenii* and *C. ochroleucus,* tender bulbs that grow to 12 inches, with narrow leaves and loose clusters of white tubular flowers on *C. mackenii* and yellow tubular flowers on *C. ochroleucus.* Used in mild-climate gardens in partial shade or in pots as indoor/outdoor plants.

lily, jacobean *n.* A common name for *Sprekelia formosissima* (Amaryllidaceae) a Mexican bulb with narrow, sword-shaped leaves and a stalk bearing one large, crimson, curiously shaped blossom. Used outdoors in warm climates massed or in pots, and in greenhouses anywhere.

lily, Japanese *n.* A common name for *Lilium japonicum,* a perennial bulb. It grows to 3 feet, with firm, alternate, dark green leaves and fragrant, rose-pink trumpet-shaped flowers. Used in beds and borders.

lily, Japanese Turk's-cap *n.* A common name for *Lilium Hansonii,* a very hardy perennial bulb. It grows to 5 feet, with whorled leaves and spikes of nodding, fragrant, orange-yellow flowers with purple-brown spots. Grows best in light shade; highly resistant to virus diseases.

lily, Josephine's *n.* A common name for *Brunsvigia Josephinae,* a tender perennial bulb. It grows to 18 inches, with long, straplike leaves and clusters of many large, bright red flowers. Used in sunny borders in mild climates.

lily, kaffir (kahf'fihr) *n.* A common name for the genus *Clivia,* a tender evergreen perennial with tuberous roots, broad, strap-shaped leaves, and clusters of winter-blooming, trumpet-shaped orange flowers followed by attractive red berries. Tolerates deep shade and some drought. Excellent as a specimen, massed as a ground cover, in shady borders, and in containers.

lily, Kamchatka (kahm chaht'kuh) *n.* A common name for *Fritillaria chamschatcensis,* a very hardy perennial bulb. It grows to 2 feet, with long, narrow, whorled leaves and several small purple-black bell-shaped flowers. Used in rock gardens and alpine collections.

lily, knight's-star *n.* (See **lily, Barbados.**)

lily, lavender globe *n.* A common name for *Allium tanguticum,* a hardy perennial bulb. It grows to 16 inches, with long, narrow, leaves and many-flowered clusters of purple flowers. Used in rock gardens.

lily, lemon *n.* A common name for plants of 2 genera, *Hemerocallis Lilioasphodelus* and *Lilium Parryi. H. Lilioasphodelus* is a very hardy daylily to 3 feet, with fragrant yellow flowers 4 inches long. *L. Parryi* is a lily that grows to 6 feet, with alternate leaves and 1 to 25 large, fragrant clear lemon-yellow flowers.

lily, Lent *n.* A common name for the genus *Narcissus* (daffodil) as well as for *Lilium candidum* (Madonna lily).

lily, leopard *n.* A common name for *Lilium Catesbaei; L. pardalinum; Lachenalia bulbiferum; Belamcanda chinensis* (blackberry lily); and the genus *Sansevieria* (bowstring hemp or devil's-tongue). *L. Catesbaei,* native to the southeastern United States, grows to 2 feet, with long, narrow, basal leaves and large, single, cup-shaped red flowers 5 inches long; also known as pine lily, southern red lily, and tiger lily. *L. pardalinum,* native to the West Coast of the United States, grows to 8 feet, with whorled leaves and nodding, orange-red flowers 4 inches across; also known as panther lily. (See **Belamcanda** and **lily, blackberry.** Also see **Lachenalia** and **Sansevieria.**)

lily, lesser Turk's-cap *n.* A common name for *Lilium pomponium,* a perennial bulb. It grows to 3 feet, with long, alternate leaves with silvery edges and 1 to 10 nodding, brilliant scarlet, purple-spotted flowers that smell awful. Also known as little Turk's-cap lily, minor Turk's-cap lily, and turban lily.

lily, little Turk's-cap *n.* (See **lily, lesser Turk's-cap.**)

lily, Long's red *n.* A common name for *Lilium Catesbaei longii,* closely resembling *L. Catesbaei* (leopard lily), but having no basal leaves, broader stem leaves, and without long recurving tips on the flowers. (See **lily, leopard.**)

lily, Madonna *n.* 1. A common name for *Lilium candidum,* a tender perennial bulb. It grows to 6 feet, with long, basal leaves and 5 to 20 sweetly fragrant, clear waxy-white flowers. Used in borders, clumps, beds, and pots. 2. A common name for *Eucharis grandiflora.* (See **lily, Amazon.**)

lily, magic *n.* A common name for *Lycoris squamigera,* a fairly hardy perennial bulb. It grows to 2 feet, with straplike leaves and leafless stalks topped by clusters of pink or rosy-lilac spidery-looking flowers with petals curved backward. Used outdoors in mild climates, in colder climates with protection, and in pots. Also known as Resurrection lily.

lily, magnolia water *n.* A common name for *Nymphaea tuberosa,* a hardy North American water lily. It has round leaves, 15 inches across, and pure white, lightly fragrant flowers, 4 to 9 inches across, that are open until noon. Used in water gardens and garden pools. Also known as tuberous water lily.

lily, marhan (mahr'han) *n.* A common name for *Lilium* ×*Backhousei.* (See **lily, Backhouse hybrid.**)

lily, mariposa (mahr'ih poh suh) *n.* A common name for the genus *Calochortus* (Liliaceae), a genus of about 60 species of perennial bulbs native to the western United States and to Mexico. The leaves are basal and the flowers are large and showy and very variously colored. Also known as mariposa, sego lily, globe tulip, star tulip, and butterfly tulip.

lily, Martagon *n.* A common name for *Lilium Martagon,* a long-lived, hardy perennial bulb that forms large clumps. It grows to 6 feet, with purplish, sometimes hairy stems, narrow, whorled leaves, and spikes of 3 to 50 purplish-pink black-spotted flowers. Used in beds, borders, or as individual clumps. Also known as Turk's-cap, Turk's-cap lily, and turban lily.

lily, meadow *n.* A common name for *Lilium canadense,* a hardy North American bulb. (See **lily, Canada.**)

lily, Michigan *n.* A common name for *Lilium michiganense,* a hardy perennial bulb native to North America, from Ontario to Manitoba south to Tennessee, Arkansas, and Kansas. It grows to 5 feet, with narrow, whorled leaves and clusters of nodding orange-red flowers spotted with orange-maroon.

lily, milk-and-wine *n*. A common name for *Crinum latifolium zeylanicum*, a tropical perennial bulb. It grows from a huge bulb, 8 inches in diameter, with many strap-shaped leaves and clusters of 10 to 20 trumpet-shaped white and dark purple flowers. Used in mild-climate gardens (may need protection), in pots as an indoor/outdoor plant, as a houseplant, or in the greenhouse to create tropical effects.

lily, minor Turk's-cap *n*. A common nane for *Lilium pomponium*. (See **lily, lesser Turk's cap**.)

lily, mountain *n*. A common name for plants of 2 genera; *Leucocrinum montanum* (See **Leucocrinum**) and *Lilium auratum* (See **lily, gold-banded**).

lily, naked-lady *n*. A common name for × *Amarygia*, (a cross between *Amaryllis Belladonna* and *Brunsvigia Josephinae*), a tender perennial bulb. It has clear deep rose flowers suffused with carmine.

lily, Nankeen *n*. A common name for *Lilium xtestaceum*, a cross between *L. candidum* (Madonna lily) and *L. chalcedonicum* (scarlet turk's-cap-lily). It has purplish stems to 6 feet, with many, long, narrow alternate leaves and spikes of 1 to 12 fragrant, nodding, apricot or Nankeen-yellow flowers 3 inches across.

lily, narrow-leaved plantain *n*. A common name for *Hosta lancifolia*, a long-lived hardy perennial. It grows in leafy clumps to 2 feet, with attractive narrow, glossy, oval, pointed, dark green leaves and spikes of funnel-shaped pale lavender flowers each 2 inches long. Grown primarily for its foliage; the flowers are a lovely bonus.

lily, Natal *n*. A common name for *Dietes*, a genus of tender perennials. They form thick clumps from 1 foot to 4 feet, depending on the species, with narrow, stiff, gray-green irislike leaves and spikes of multicolored flowers resembling miniature Japanese iris. Individual flowers last only a day, but bursts of bloom come every 2 weeks spring through fall. Used in individual clumps, in containers, or in sunny borders. Also known as fortnight lily, butterfly iris, and African iris.

lily-of-China *n*. A common name for *Rohdea japonica*, a tender rhizomatous perennial. It forms leafy, evergreen clumps of large, arching, strap-shaped leaves and thick, short spikes of cream-colored flowers followed by dense clusters of red berries. It is a tough, sturdy houseplant or an outdoor plant in mild climates. Also known as sacred-lily-of-China.

lily-of-the-Altai *n*. A common name for the genus *Ixiolirion*, a genus of 3 species of fairly hardy onionlike bulbs, with simple, erect stems and clusters of pretty blue or violet trumpet-shaped flowers.

lily-of-the-Amazon *n*. (See **lily, Amazon**.)

lily-of-the-field *n*. A common name for the genus *Anemone* (windflower) and for *Sternbergia lutea*. *S. lutea* is a hardy bulb, with narrow, 12-inch-long basal leaves and golden-yellow flowers, resembling crocuses, on long stems; also called winter daffodil. Used in rock gardens, near pools, in borders, and for cut flowers.

lily-of-the-Incas *n*. (See **Alstroemeria**.)

lily-of-the-Nile *n*. See **lily, African**.)

lily-of-the palace *n*. A common name for *Hippeastrum aulicum*, a tropical perennial bulb. It grows to 2 feet, with bright green leaves and 6-inch-long red flowers with a green throat. Used in mild-climate gardens or as a houseplant.

lily-of-the-valley *n*. (See **Convallaria**.)

lily-of-the-valley bush *n*. A common name for *Pieris japonica*, a hardy shrub. It grows to 10 feet, with bronzy-pink or brilliant scarlet new leaves, which mature to glossy, dark green, and clusters of small white, pink, or red flowers resembling lily-of-the-valley. Used as a specimen shrub, in Oriental gardens, in woodland gardens, in entryways, and in containers. Also known as lily-of-the-valley shrub.

lily-of-the-valley, false *n*. A common name for the genus *Maianthemum* (Liliaceae), a genus of 3 species of hardy to very hardy low-growing bulbs. *M. canadense* and *M. kamtschaticum* are native as far north as the Aleutians and the Northwest Territories. They grow from 6 inches to 14 inches, with rounded, pointed leaves and spikes of white flowers, sometimes fragrant. Used to naturalize in moist, shady places.

lily, of-the-valley, star-flowered *n*. A common name for *Smilacina stellata*, a perennial. It grows from a rhizome to 2 feet, with narrow leaves, usually folded lengthwise, and spikes of white flowers. Useful in woodland gardens and moist, shady beds and borders. Also known as starflower.

lily-of-the-valley, wild *n.* 1. A common name for *Mianthemum canadense.* (See **lily-of-the-valley, false.**) 2. A common name for *Pyrola elliptica,* an evergreen North American perennial to 12 inches, with oval leaves and spikes of white or creamy flowers. Also called shinleaf. 3. A common name for *Pyrola rotundifolia,* a very hardy evergreen North American perennial to 12 inches tall, with small, glossy leaves and spikes of white fragrant flowers. Also called round-leaf wintergreen, false wintergreen, wild lettuce, and Indian lettuce.

lily, one-day *n.* A common name for the genus *Tigridia,* a tender perennial bulb native to Mexico, Guatemala, and the Andes of Peru and Chile. *T. Pavonia* grows to 30 inches, with narrow, ribbed, swordlike leaves and showy triangular orange, red, pink, yellow, or white flowers spotted or blotched with darker colors. Used in pots and sunny or partly shady borders. Also known as Mexican shellflower, shellflower, and tigerflower.

lily, orange *n.* A common name for *Lilium bulbiferum,* a hardy perennial bulb. It grows to 4 feet, with many narrow, alternate leaves and spikes of 1 to 20 orange-red cup-shaped flowers 4 inches across.

lily, orange-bell *n.* A common name for *Lilium Grayi.* (See **lily, bell.**)

lily, orange-cup *n.* A common name for *Lilium philadelphicum,* a hardy perennial bulb native to North America, from Maine and Ontario south to North Carolina and Kentucky. It grows to 3 feet, with narrow, whorled leaves and cup-shaped orange to orange-red flowers with purple spots. Used in wild gardens and woodland gardens. Also known as wood lily and wild orange-red lily.

lily, Oregon *n.* A commom name for *Lilium columbianum.* (See **lily, Columbia.**)

lily pad *n.* The broad, floating leaf of a water lily, especially as it lies upon the water where it is growing.

lily, palm *n.* 1. A common name for *Cordyline australis,* a tender treelike plant which grows to 40 feet, with narrow, swordlike leaves and long, branching clusters of small fragrant white flowers. Grown outdoors in warm winter climates as a specimen plant. Also known as giant dracena, fountain dracena, cabbage tree, and grass palm. 2. A common name for *Yucca gloriosa,* a multitrunked shrub or small tree native from North Carolina to Florida. It grows to 10 feet, with tufts of sword-shaped leaves and large, erect clusters of white flowers. Easy to grow in sunny borders or as a specimen. Also known as Spanish dagger, Roman candle, soft-tip yucca, and Lord's-candlestick.

lily, Palmer spear *n.* A common name for *Doryanthes Palmerii,* an enormous tender succulent. It forms a gigantic cluster of 100 or more leaves 8 feet long and a 6-to-15 foot tall flower stalk with clusters, up to 6 feet long, of reddish-brown flowers. Used as a dramatic specimen in large mild-climate gardens and in containers. Also known as spear lily.

lily, panther *n.* A common name for *Lilium pardalinum.* (See **lily, leopard.**)

lily, paradise *n.* A common name for *Paradisea Liliastrum,* a hardy perennial. It grows from a rhizome to 2 feet, with long, very narrow leaves and spikes of showy, trumpet-shaped white flowers. Used in the foreground of the hardy border. Also known as St.-Bruno's-lily.

lily, perfumed fairy *n.* A common name for *Chlidanthus fragrans,* a fairly hardy with protection perennial bulb. It grows to 10 inches, with basal, straplike leaves and fragrant, tubular yellow flowers 3 inches long.

lily, Peruvian *n.* (See **Alstroemeria.**)

lily, pig *n.* A common name for *Zantedeschia aethiopica.* (See **lily, arum.**)

lily, pine *n.* A common name for *Lilium Catesbaei.* (See **lily, leopard.**)

lily, pineapple *n.* Also known as pineapple flower. (See **Eucomis.**)

lily, pinewoods *n.* A common name for *Eustylis purpurea,* a North American perennial bulb native to the sandy pinewoods of Louisiana and Texas. It grows to 18 inches, with long, narrow, pleated leaves and spikes of red-purple to violet flowers that bloom in early summer and again in fall. Used in woodland gardens and shady borders. Also known as propeller flower and purple pleatleaf.

lily, pink Easter *n*. A common name for *Echinopsis multiplex,* a small, stubby, spiny Brazilian cactus. It grows to 8 inches, with yellow spines to 1 inch long and rose-red flowers to 10 inches long. Grown by collectors. Also known as barrel cactus and Easter lily cactus.

lily, pink porcelain *n*. A common name for *Alpinia Zerumbet,* a tropical perennial. It grows to 12 feet, with attractive shiny leaves, 2 feet long and 5 inches wide, and showy, fragrant waxy-white flowers marked with red, purple, and brown. The best of the gingers, its roots are hardy to 15° F., but it does best in warm- winter climates or in greenhouses where it is evergreen. Used to create tropical effects in shaded, moist, protected places. Also known as shell ginger and shellflower.

lily, plantain *n*. A common name for hardy perennials of the genus *Hosta,* in the lily family. (See **Hosta**.)

lily, pond *n*. 1. A common name for any plant of the family *Nymphaeaceae,* most often used for *Nymphaea odorata.* (See **lily, fragrant water**.) 2. A common name for the 25 species of *Nuphar,* especially *N. advenum,* very hardy aquatic perennial plants. They grow from rhizomes in the muddy bottoms of ponds or sluggish streams. They have roundish, glossy 12- to 16-inch leaves that float on the water and cup-shaped 2- to 2½-inch-wide yellow flowers. Rarely planted as an ornamental. Also known as spatterdock and cowlily.

lily, pot-of-gold *n*. A common name for *Lilium iridollae,* a tender perennial bulb native to northwestern Florida and southern Alabama. It grows to 5 feet, with whorled leaves and spikes of 1 to 8 nodding, slightly fragrant, golden-yellow flowers with brown spots. Used in moist soils.

lily, prickly water *n*. A common name used for *Euryale ferox,* a very prickly perennial aquatic plant. It has large, (4 feet in diameter) spiny-ribbed, dark grenn leaves, purple beneath, with day-blooming purple flowers that are prickly on the outside. Used in water gardens or large pools. Also known as gorgon.

lily, pygmy water *n*. A common name used for *Nymphaea tetragona,* a very hardy day-blooming perennial water lily, native in North America from Ontario to northern Idaho and from Siberia to Japan. It has oval leaves 3 to 4 inches across and small white flowers that open in the afternoon. The smallest species of water lily in cultivation, it is used in water gardens and tubs.

lily, queen *n*. A common name for *Curcuma petiolata.* It has long, broad leaves and spikes of green bracts with rose-pink edges surrounding yellowish-white flowers. Grown in frost-free gardens or in greenhouses.

lily, rain *n*. (See **lily, fairy**.) A common name for *Zephyranthes,* a genus of 40 species in the amaryllis family. They are small bulbous plants, with rush-like leaves and long-stemmed flowers resembling crocuses. *Z. atamasco* and *Z. candida* have white flowers tinged pink, *Z. citrina* has yellow flowers, and *Z. grandiflora* has pink flowers. Hybrids come in many shades. They takje their name from their habit of blooming after rain following a dry spell. Often called fairy lilies or zephyr lilies. (See **lily, fairy**.)

lily, red ginger *n*. A common name used for *Hedychium coccineum,* a subtropical and tropical perennial. It grows to 6 feet, with long, narrow leaves and spikes of fragrant, waxy red flowers. Used to create tropical effects in frost-free gardens, in large containers, and in greenhouses. Also known as scarlet ginger lily.

lily, red spider *n*. A common name for *Lycoris radiata,* a tender perennial bulb. It grows to 18 inches, with narrow, straplike leaves and clusters of spidery, coral-red flowers. Used in beds and borders or as potted plants. Also known as spider lily.

lily, redwood *n*. A common name for *Lilium rubescens.* (See **lily, chamise**.)

lily, regal *n*. A common name for *Lilium regale,* a hardy perennial bulb. It grows to 6 feet, with many alternate leaves and big, beautiful fragrant trumpet-shaped flowers, pure white on the inside, burgundy on the outside. Easy to grow in beds, borders, or in large clumps. Also known as royal lily.

lily, Resurrection *n*. 1. A common name for *Kaempferia rotunda,* a tender perennial. It grows from a rhizome to 18 inches tall, with 2 long, narrow, erect basal leaves and spikes of white flowers with a lilac lip. Grown in warm winter gardens or in greenhouses. Also known as tropical crocus. 2. A common name for *Lycoris squamigera.* (See **lily, magic.**)

lily, roan *n.* A common name for *Lilium Grayi.* (See **lily, bell.**)

lily, rock *n.* A common name for *Dendrobium speciosum,* a subtropical and tropical epiphytic orchid. It grows to 30 inches, with leafy stems and long dense spikes of many small yellow flowers marked with red or violet. Grown in greenhouses.

lily, royal *n.* A common name for *Lilium superbum.* (See **lily, American Turk's-cap**) and for *Lilium regale* (See **lily, regal**).

lily, royal water *n.* (See **lily, Amazon water.**) *Nymphaea amazonica.*

lily, sand *n.* A common name for *Leucocrinum,* a hardy North American perennial. (See **Leucocrinum.**)

lily, Santa Cruz water *n.* A common name for *Victoria Cruziana,* a tropical water lily native to South America. It has large soft, circular, floating leaves with upturned edges and fragrant white flowers that change to pink or red on the second day. Used in garden pools and ponds. Also known as Santa Cruz water-platter.

lily, Scarborough *n.* A common name for *Vallota speciosa,* a tender perennial bulb. It grows to 2 feet, with straplike leaves up to 2 feet long and clusters of bright scarlet funnel-shaped flowers. Grown in frost-free gardens or in small pots; blooms best when the roots are crowded.

lily, scarlet ginger *n.* A common name for *Hedychium coccineum,* a tropical perennial. (See **lily, red ginger.**)

lily, scarlet Turk's-cap *n.* A common name for *Lilium chalcedonicum,* a perennial bulb. It grows to nearly 5 feet with many narrow, alternate leaves, with silver margins, and with spikes of 1 to 10 sweet-scented, nodding vermilion-scarlet flowers with strongly recurved petals. It is now rare.

lily, seersucker plantain *n.* A common name for *Hosta seiboldii,* a hardy perennial. It forms 30-inch tall leafy clumps of narrow leaves, with white or yellow margins, and has spikes of many violet funnel-shaped flowers. Grown primarily as a foliage plant; the pretty flowers are a bonus.

lily, sego *n.* A common name for *Calochortus nuttallii,* a hardy perennial bulb native to South Dakota, south to Arizona, New Mexico, and Nevada. It grows to 18 inches, with narrow leaves and tuliplike white flowers tinged with lilac and yellow at the base. It is the state flower of Utah. Used in borders and rock gardens. (See **lily, mariposa.**)

lily, Shasta *n.* A common name for *Lilium Washingtonianum minus,* a hardy perennial bulb native to California. It grows to 6 feet, with narrow, whorled leaves and spikes of fragrant, trumpet-shaped white flowers with red spots. Used in wild gardens and in woodland gardens with acid soil and fast drainage.

lily, showy Japanese *n.* A common name for *Lilium speciosum,* a perennial bulb. It grows to 5 feet, with leathery, alternate leaves, and has spikes with clusters of many large, nodding, fragrant white flowers suffused with rose-pink, that bloom in late summer and early fall. Used in woodland gardens and partially shady borders. Also known as showy lily and Japanese lily.

lily, Siberian *n.* A common name for *Ixiolirion tatarica,* a fairly hardy perennial bulb. It grows to 16 inches, with narrow, greenish-gray leaves and wiry stems topped by loose clusters of small violet-blue trumpet-shaped flowers. Used in woodland gardens and wild gardens where fallen leaves provide a natural mulch. Also known as Tartar lily.

lily, Sierra *n.* (See **lily, alpine.**)

lily, small tiger *n.* (See **lily, alpine.**)

lily, snake *n.* A common name for *Dichelostemma volubile,* a hardy perennial bulb (corm) native to California. It grows to 5 feet, with 2 to 5 grasslike leaves and with twisted stalks topped by clusters of small, narrow, tubular pale pink to rose flowers. Used in dry woodland gardens, wild gardens, or on sunny banks. Does well in poor, dry soils. Also known as twining brodiaea.

lily, Solomon's *n.* A common name for *Arum palaestinum,* a tender perennial bulb. It grows to 2 feet with long-stemmed, arrow-shaped leaves and callalike green flowers, dark purple inside, with a dark purple spike. Used in shady borders or as an indoor/outdoor plant in cold-winter climates. Also known as black calla.

lily, southern red *n.* A common name for *Lilium Catesbaci.* (See **lily, leopard**.)

lily, spear *n.* A common name for *Doryanthes,* a genus of 2 species of gigantic succulents. (See **lily, globe spear** and **lily, Palmer spear**.)

lily, speckled wood *n.* A common name for *Clintonia umbellulata,* a hardy perennial native to the eastern United States, from New York to Tennessee and Georgia. It grows from a rhizome to 18 inches, with narrow, oval, basal leaves and many-flowered clusters of tiny white flowers spotted with green and purple. Used in woodland gardens or moist, shady borders.

lily, spider *n.* A common name for *Crinum, Hymenocallis,* and *Lycoris radiata.* (See **lily, crinum** and **lily, red spider**.)

lily, St.-Bernard's- *n.* 1. A common name for *Anthericum Liliago,* a tender perennial. It grows from tuberous roots to 3 feet, with long, narrow basal leaves and slender spikes of white flowers. Used in borders in mild-winter climates or grown in cool greenhouses. Also known as spider plant. 2. A common name for *Chlorophytum,* which is also known as spider plant. (See **Chlorophytum**.)

lily, St.-Bruno's- *n.* (See **lily, paradise**.)

lily, St.-James's- *n.* (See **lily, Aztec**.)

lily, St.-Joseph's- *n.* A common name for a cross between *Hippeastrum reginae* and *H. vittatum,* now largely superseded in gardens by more recent hybrids.

lily, star *n.* A common name for plants of several genera, including *Leucocrinum, Lilium concolor,* and *Zigadenus Fremontii. Lilium concolor* is a perennial bulb that grows to 3 feet and has long, narrow, alternate leaves and spikes with clusters of glossy, scarlet star-shaped flowers. *Zigadenus Fremontii* is a perennial bulb native from southern Oregon to northern Baja California; it grows to 3 feet, with very long narrow basal leaves and tiny yellowish-white flowers. (See also **Leucocrinum**.)

lily, sunset *n.* A common name for what is probably a cross between *Lilium pardalinum* and *L. Humbodldtii.* Its yellow flowers are tipped bright red and spotted with red. (See **lily, leopard** and **lily, Humboldt.**)

lily, swamp *n.* A common name for two different plants: *Lilium superbum* (See **lily, American Turk's-cap.**) and *Saururus cernuus* (see **lizard's-tail**).

lily, sword *n.* (See **Gladiolus**.)

lily, Tartar *n.* (See **lily, Siberian**.)

lily, thimble *n.* A common name for *Lilium Bolanderi,* a perennial bulb native to northern California and southern Oregon. It grows to nearly 4 feet, with whorled leaves and spikes of small, funnel-shaped, deep crimson flowers spotted with purple.

lily, tiger *n.* A common name for *Lilium Catesbaei* (leopard lily) and *L. lancifolium. L. lancifolium* is a perennial bulb that grows to 6 feet, with many, long, narrow alternate leaves and spikes of large orange or salmon-red flowers spotted with purple-black. (See **lily, leopard**.)

lily, toad *n.* A common name for *Tricyrtis,* a genus of moderately hardy perennials. It grows from a rhizome to 3 feet, with narrow, oval, pointed leaves and small flowers that are not showy, but are wonderfully complex on close examination. Used in shady, moist situations with rich soil.

lily, toad-cup *n.* A common name for *Neomarica,* a genus of tender perennials. It grows from a rhizome to 3 feet, with sword-shaped, many-veined leaves and clusters of large, beautiful irislike blue, white, or yellow flowers. Grown outdoors in frost-free gardens, in mild-winter climates with protection, and as houseplants. It propagates by small plantlets, which form at the top of the flower spikes, that bend to the ground and root, hence the common name walking iris. Also known as fan iris, house iris, twelve-apostles, and false flag.

lily, torch *n.* A common name for *Kniphofia,* a marginally hardy perennial. (See **Kniphofia**.)

lily, triplet *n.* A common name for *Triteleia laxa,* a hardy perennial bulb (corm) native to western North America. It grows to 3 feet, sometimes less, with 1 to 2 long, narrow leaves and spikes with clusters of violet-blue funnel-shaped flowers. Used in wild gardens or on sunny banks. Also known as grassnut.

lily, trout *n.* A common name for the genus *Erythronium,* particularly *E. americanum,* a hardy perennial bulb (corm) native from Nova Scotia west to Minnesota and south to Alabama. It grows to 12 inches, with oval, mottled basal leaves and nodding, single yellow flowers 2 inches long. Used in wild or woodland gardens or in shady situations. Also known as yellow adder's tongue and amber bell. (See also **Erythronium.**)

lily, trumpet *n.* A common name for *Lilium longiflorum,* a perennial bulb that grows to 3 feet or more, with many long, narrow alternate leaves and fragrant trumpet-shaped white flowers more than 7 inches long. Also known as white trumpet lily. 2. A common name for *Zantedeschia aethiopica,* also known as arum lily. (See **lily, arum** and **Zantedeschia.**)

lily, tuberous water *n.* (See **lily, magnolia water.**)

lily, turban *n.* A common name for both *Lilium Martagon* (martagon lily) and *L. pomponium* (lesser Turk's-cap lily).

lilyturf *n.* A common name for 2 different genera, *Liriope* and *Ophiopogon,* both clump-forming ground covers with white, lilac-blue, or pale purple flowers. *Ophiopogon* is also known as mondo grass.

lilyturf, big blue *n.* A common name for *Liriope muscari,* a tender perennial evergreen ground cover that grows to 18 inches, with grasslike leaves 2 feet long and dense spikes of dark purple flowers that resemble grape hyacinth.

lilyturf, creeping *n.* A common name for *Liriope spicata,* a moderately hardy evergreen perennial ground cover that spreads by underground stems, grows to 9 inches, has grasslike leaves, and bears spikes of pale lilac to white flowers.

lilyturf, dwarf *n.* A common name for *Ophiopogon japonicus,* an evergreen perennial hardy to 10° F. It forms dense clumps that spread slowly by underground stems. It has dark green grasslike leaves and short spikes of light lilac flowers virtually hidden by leaves.

lilyturf, white *n.* A common name for *Ophiopogon jaburan,* an evergreen perennial that forms large clumps to 2 feet, with long, arching grasslike leaves and short spikes with nodding clusters of chalk-white flowers.

lily, Turk's-cap *n.* A common name for several different species of lily, including *Lilium Martagon* (see **lily, Martagon**), *L. Michauxii* (see **lily, Carolina**), and *L. superbum* (see **lily, American Turk's-cap**).

lily, Victoria water *n.* A common name for *Victoria regia,* a tropical water lily relative with floating leaves to 6 feet across, with rims turned upwards several inches, and large flowers opening white and aging pink to red.

lily, voodoo *n.* A common name for *Sauromatum venosum.* (See **monarch-of-the-East.**)

lily, Washington *n.* A common name for *Lilium Washingtonianum,* a hardy perennial bulb native to the mountains of northern to central California. It grows to 6 feet, with narrow, whorled leaves and spikes of fragrant, trumpet-shaped white flowers with red spots. Used in wild gardens and in woodland gardens with acid soil and fast drainage.

lily, water *n.* A common name for plants in the genus *Nymphaea* (Nymphaeaceae), or a plant in the same family. All have floating leaves arising from a submerged rootstock and large, many-petaled flowers that float or rise above the surface. *Nymphaea* had many hybrids, generally classified into hardy and tender, the latter divided in turn into day- and night-blooming kinds.

lily, wester *n.* A common name for *Lilium occidentale.* (See **lily, Eureka.**)

lily, wheeled *n.* A common name for *Lilium medeoloides,* a perennial bulb. It grows to 30 inches, with narow, pointed leaves and clusters of nodding apricot-to-scarlet flowers spotted with black.

lily, white trumpet *n.* A common name for *Lilium longiflorum.* (See **lily, trumpet.**)

lily, white water *n.* A common name for *Nymphaea odorata.* (See **lily, fragrant water.**)

lily, wild orange-red *n.* A common name for *Lilium philadelphicum.* (See **lily, orange-cup.**)

lily, wild yellow *n.* A common name for *Lilium canadense.* (See **lily, Canada.**)

lily, wood *n.* A common name for *Lilium philadelphicum.* (See **lily, orange-cup.**)

lily, yellow *n.* A common name for *Lilium canadense.* (See **lily, Canada.**)

lily, yellow pond *n.* A common name for *Nuphar,* a genus of water plants. (See **lily, cow.**)

lily, yellow Turk's-cap *n.* A common name for *Lilium pyrenaicum,* a perennial bulb. It grows to 4 feet, with dense, narrow, pointed, alternate leaves and spikes of nodding, ill-smelling, sulphur-yellow flowers spotted with purplish-black.

lily, yellow water *n.* A common name for *Nuphar luteum,* a hardy perennial floating aquatic plant native to eastern North America and elsewhere. It has large, leathery, floating leaves, 16 inches long and 12 inches wide, and many-petaled yellow flowers almost 3 inches across. Used in water gardens. 2. A common name for *Nymphaea mexicana,* a tender perennial floating aquatic plant. It grows from a rhizome and has floating, mottled leaves 4 to 8 inches across and bright yellow flowers 4 inches across. Used in mild-climate water gardens.

lily, yellow-bell *n.* A common name for *Lilium canadense.* (See **lily, Canada.**)

lily, zephyr *n.* A common name for the genus *Zephyranthes.* (See **lily, fairy.**)

limb *n.* 1. A primary branch of a tree. 2. The expanded, flat portion of a plant part, such as the upper portion of a petal.

limbate (lihm'bayt) *a.* In botany, bordered: said especially of a flower in which 1 color is surrounded by an edging of another color.

lime *n.* A common name for *Tilia,* a genus of large, hardy trees, some species native to North America. They grow from 35 feet to 100 feet or more, depending on the species, with pairs of alternate, heart-shaped leaves and drooping clusters of fragrant white flowers. The tree bears a globose fruit, smaller than the lemon, with a thin rind that yields a pleasant-tasting, highly acid juice. Used as a street, park, or shade tree. Also known as lime tree.

lime *n.* 1. A term used for all limestone or agricultural lime. 2. A material used to neutralize acid soil. 3. Ground limestone (calcium carbonate), hydrate lime (calcium hydroxide), or burnt lime (calcium oxide) (CaO).

lime requirement *n.* The amount of standard ground limestone required to bring a layer of an acre of acid soil (6.6 pH) to some specific lesser degree of acidity. Expressed in tons per acre of nearly pure limestone.

limestone *n.* A material worked into the soil to raise the pH from an acid pH to an alkaline pH.

lime sulfur *n.* A caustic pesticide made from calcium polysulfide. Usually used as a dormant spray to control various diseases, including leaf spot, peach leaf curl, and powdery mildew. Also effective against mites, scale, and some other insects.

lime, wild *n.* A common name for *Zanthoxylum Fagara,* a tender evergreen shrub or small tree native to southwestern Texas and to Florida south to the West Indies and South America. It grows to 30 feet, with divided leaves with small, oval leaflets and spikes of small flowers.

Limnanthes (lihm nahn'thhez) *n.* A genus of 7 species of small annuals (Limnanthaceae). They grow to 12 inches or more, with alternate, divided leaves and single yellow, white, or pink 5-petaled flowers. Used in flower beds, where they make sheets of early spring color. Commonly known as meadow foam.

Limnocharis (lihm noh'kah rihs) *n.* A genus of 2 species of tropical erect aquatic plants (Butomaceae). They grow to 2 feet or more, with long-stemmed, tufted leaves and clusters of 3-petaled yellow flowers. Used in water gardens, in shallow-water pools, or in tubs.

Limonium (lih mo'nee uhm) *n.* A genus of 150 species of fairly hardy, mostly perennial, low-growing flowers (Plumbaginaceae). They grow from 6 inches to 3 feet, depending on the species, usually with leaves in a basal rosette, and have tall, slender spikes of yellow, blue, or white flowers. Grown in rock gardens, sunny borders, and for long lasting cut flowers or everlasting bouquets. Commonly known as sea lavender, marsh rosemary and statice.

Linaceae (lih nay'see ee) *n., pl.* A family of 14 genera and 275 species of annuals, perennials, and shrubs. They have alternate, simple, entire leaves and clusters of scarlet, yellow, or blue flowers. Commonly known as the flax family.

linaceous (lih nay'shiuhs) *a.* Of or pertaining to the family Linaceae.

Linanthus (lih nahn'thuhs) *n.* A genus of 35 species of mostly annuals (Polemoniaceae), native chiefly to western North America. They are low-growing flowers, typically with opposite, hand-shaped leaves and clusters of yellow, blue, or white bell-shaped or funnel-shaped flowers. Useful in sunny locations.

Linaria (lih nah'ree uh) *n.* A genus of 100 species of mostly Mediterranean annuals and perennials (Scrophulariaceae). They grow from 6 inches to 4 feet, depending on the species, with opposite or whorled leaves and with spikes of yellow, blue, purple, or violet flowers. Best massed in beds or borders. Commonly known as toadflax and spurred snapdragon.

lincoln *n.* A small pea variety, good for freezing and with a sweet flavor.

lindane *n.* A very toxic pesticide, which has lost its registration for most home uses. Can be used against borers in some areas.

linden *n.* A tree of the genus *Tilia;* the lime tree. An oil, used by perfumers, is distilled from its flowers. The American linden is *T. Americana,* and is called basswood and bee tree, among other names.

Lindera (lihn'der uh) *n.* A genus of 100 species of mostly deciduous aromatic shrubs and trees (Lauraceae), 2 of which are native to eastern North America; *L. Benzoin* (spicebush or Benjamin bush) and *L. melissifolia* (Jove's fruit). They grow 15 to 30 feet, with alternate aromatic leaves, clusters of small yellow flowers, and, often, showy red berries.

linear *a.* In botany, like a line; long and slender, as a linear leaf. Used in combination, as a linear-lanceolate leaf, a long, narrow leaf pointed like a lance.

lineate *a.* Marked with lines. Also lineated, lined.

line marker *n.* A device used to make straight garden rows. Twine from a reel mounted on top of 1 of 2 stakes is stretched over the soil.

lineolate (lihn'ee oh layt) *a.* In botany, marked with fine lines. Also lineolated.

ling *n.* A common name for *Calluna vulgaris,* a hardy shrub. It has opposite, 4-ranked leaves and spikes of tiny flowers in white, pink, deep pink, lavender, or purple. Also known as heather. 2. A common name for *Trapa bicornis,* an aquatic plant with edible seeds. It has glossy, bladelike, floating leaves and small white flowers. Also known as water chestnut. 3. A common name for *Eleocharis dulcis,* a tender aquatic perennial with edible tubers. It has sheathlike basal leaves and dense spikes of straw-colored flowers. Also known as Chinese water chestnut.

lingberry *n.* A common name used for *Vaccinium Vitis-idaea minus,* a hardy, low-growing evergreen shrub native to North America. It grows to 12 inches with small, glossy, leathery, rounded, oval dark green leaves, drooping spikes of pink-to-red bell-shaped flowers and small, sour, edible, dark red, fruit. Used in wild gardens, as a small-scale ground cover, in boggy situations, and as an attractive container plant. Also known as lingonberry, mountain cranberry, and rock cranberry.

lingy *a.* Abounding in heaths; heathy; heathery.

link stake *n.* Same as linking stake.

linking stake *n.* An L-shaped stake, part of a modular system, used to form rings, squares, lines, or irregular units to support perennials. Linking stakes may range from about 12 to 40 inches in height. Also called link stake.

Linnaea (lihn nee'uh) *n.* A genus of one species, *L. borealis* (Caprifoliaceae), a very hardy trailing evergreen subshrub native to North America. It has opposite, simple, rounded leaves and oddly-shaped rose or white double flowers. Used in the wild garden or woodland garden as a small-scale ground cover; a choice collector's rarity. Commonly known as twinflower.

Linnaean (lihn nee'uhn) *a.* Pertaining to, or relating to the method of Carl von Linne (Linnaeus), the celebrated Swedish botanist (1707-1778) who introduced the system of binomial nomenclature. Also Linnean. (See **binomial**.)

Linum (lih'nuhm) *n*. A genus of 200 species of drought-resistant, sun-loving annual or perennial flowers (Linaceae). They grow from 4 inches to 3 feet, depending on the species, with narrow, simple, alternate, entire leaves and delicate clusters of red, yellow, blue, or white 5-petaled flowers. Used in borders. Commonly known as flax.

lion's-ear *n*. 1. A common name for *Leonotis.* Also known as lion's-tail. (See **Leonotis**.) 2. A common name for *Leonurus Cardiaca,* an herbaceous perennial. It grows to 5 feet tall, with opposite lobed leaves and spikes of whorled white or pale pink bell-shaped flowers. Also known as motherwort.

lion's foot *n*. A common name for *Prenanthes,* a genus of erect perennials, some native to North America. They grow to 6 feet, with large pawlike leaves and clusters of white-to-purple flowers. Also known as rattlesnake root. 2. A common name for *Leontopodium alpinum,* a very hardy, mat-forming, tufted perennial native to the mountains of Europe. It forms loose tufts and has white, woolly leaves and masses of star-shaped white flowers. A choice rock-garden plant. Also known as edelweiss.

lion's-heart *n*. 1. A common name for *Physostegia,* a hardy perennial flower native to eastern North America. It grows to 4 feet or more, with opposite and often toothed leaves, and bears small, snapdragonlike white, purple, or pink flowers that can be twisted to point in any direction and will then hold that position. Used in borders or in wild gardens. *Physostegia* is also known as false dragonhead and obedience plant. 2. A common name for *Dracocephalum,* a genus of annuals and hardy perennials, some species native to North America. They grow from 4 inches to 3 feet, with opposite and often toothed leaves, and bear clusters of small, snapdragon-like blue, white, violet, or rose-red flowers. Used in moist, shady situations. *Dracocephalum* is also known dragonhead.

lion's-mouth *n*. 1. A common name for *Antirrhinum,* a genus of annual and perennial flowers, some native to western North America. They grow from 12 inches to 5 feet, depending on the species, with small, simple, entire leaves and 2-lipped flowers.

Used in beds and borders, and wonderful in children's gardens; the smaller hybrids are useful in pots and window boxes. Also known as snapdragon. 2. A common name for *Digitalis,* a hardy perennial or biennial flower, 1 species native to North America. It grows from 3 to 6 feet, with alternate, simple leaves in basal rosettes and tall spikes of bell-shaped purple, yellow, brownish, or white flowers, often spotted or streaked. Used in borders, woodland gardens, wild gardens, and traditional in cottage gardens. Also known as foxglove. 3. A common name for *Linaria,* a genus of annuals and hardy perennial flowers. They grow from 6 inches to 4 feet, with opposite, whorled leaves and blue, purple, violet, or yellow snapdragonlike flowers. Best used in masses; otherwise wispy. Also known as toadflax.

lion's-tail *n*. A common name for *Leonotis Leonurus,* a drought-resistant, sun-loving shrub. It grows 3 to 6 feet, with long, oval leaves and summer-to-fall-blooming spikes of whorled clusters of large showy orange tubular furry flowers. Used as a specimen plant. Also known as lion's-ear. 2. A common name for *Leonurus Cardiaca,* an herbaceous perennial. It grows to 5 feet tall, with opposite lobed leaves, spikes of whorled white or pale pink bell-shaped flowers. Also known as motherwort and lion's-ear.

lion's-tooth *n*. A common name for *Taraxacum,* the common dandelion, generally regarded as a weed. It has narrow, toothed leaves in a basal rosette, bright yellow flowers, and fluffy seed heads. Also known as blowballs.

lip *n*. In botany: 1. Either of the divisions of a 2-lipped (bilabiate) flower. 2. In orchids, 1 of the 3 petals that differs from the other 2 in shape.

Liparis (lihp'uh rihs) *n*. A genus of 250 species of orchids (Orchidaceae) found worldwide, some native to North America. They grow from 9 inches to 2 feet, with 1 or more fleshy basal leaves and spikes of flowers in a wide variety of colors. Commonly known as twayblade.

lip fern *n*. A common name for *Cheilanthes* (Polypodiaceae), a genus of 180 species of ferns widely distributed in tropical and temperate regions. They have hairy, woolly or scaly fronds with leaves divided into leaflets. Sometimes grown in greenhouses.

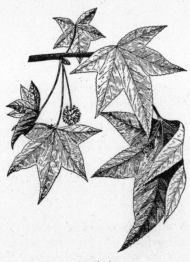

Liquidambar
(sweet gum)

Liquidambar (lihk'wihd ahmb uhr) *n.* A genus of 4 species of deciduous trees (Hamamelidaceae), of which *L. Styraciflua* is native to the Americas. They grow to 120 feet, with maplelike leaves that color beautifully even in warm–climate regions and with spiny, round brown fruits used in dried arrangements. Used as a street tree, shade tree, or lawn tree. Commonly known as sweet gum. 2. [l.c.] A tree of this genus.

Liriodendron
(tulip tree)

Liriodendron (lihr'ee uh dehn drohn) *n.* 1. A genus of 2 species of hardy deciduous trees (Magnoliaceae), of which *L. tulipifera* is native to the eastern United States. They grow to 60 feet and taller, with 4-lobed, lyre-shaped leaves that color yellow and reddish-brown in fall, even in mild-winter regions; tulip-shaped flowers striped with zigzag patterns of apple green, cream, and pale orange; and conelike fruit. Used as a street tree, lawn tree, and shade tree. Commonly known as tulip tree, tulip poplar, yellow poplar, and whitewood. 2. [l.c.] A tree of this genus.

Liriope (lih righ'uh pee) *n.* A genus of 5 species of hardy, low-growing, evergreen perennial ground covers (Liliaceae). They have grasslike leaves, spikes of small white or lilac-blue flowers, and black berrylike fruit. Used as small-scale ground covers, in moist rock gardens, along streams, around pools, or in containers as a houseplant. Commonly known as lilyturf.

Lisianthus (lihs ee ahn'thuhs) *n.* A genus of 15 species of subtropical and tropical annual and perennial flowers (Gentianaceae). *L. nigrescens* grows to 6 feet, with narrow leaves and clusters of large purplish-black flowers. *L. Russellianus* is now classified as *Eustoma grandiflorum*.

Listera (lihs'teh ruh) *n.* A genus of 30 species of hardy to very hardy wild orchids (Orchidaceae), some species native to North America. They grow to 18 inches, with pointed, oval leaves and spikes of small green or purple flowers. Commonly known as twayblade.

Litchi (ligh'chee) *n.* A genus of several species of broadleaf evergreen subtropical and tropical trees (Sapindaceae). They grow to 40 feet, have divided leaves with 3 to 9 leathery leaflets that are coppery red when young, later turning dark green. They bear inconspicuous flowers and a red, fleshy, edible fruit. Used in frost-free gardens, but it only fruits under hot, humid conditions. Commonly known as litchi or litchi nut.

Lithocarpus (lihth uh kar'puhs) *n.* A genus of 275 species of broadleaf evergreen oaklike shrubs or trees (Fagaceae). One species, *L. densiflorus*, is native to western North America. It grows to 150 feet, with leathery, sharply toothed leaves, smooth above, and gray-green beneath, clusters of tiny white flowers, and acornlike fruit. Used as a street or lawn tree. Commonly known as tanbark oak.

Lithodora (lihth uh dor'uh) *n.* A genus of 7 species of low-growing subshrubs or shrubs (Boraginaceae). They grow to 12 inches, with small, soft, narrow leaves and bright blue or purple tubular flowers. Used as small-space ground cover, in rock gardens, and over walls.

lithophyte (lihth'oh fight) *n.* A plant that grows on the surface of rocks, getting its nourishment from the air, as some orchids.

lithosol (lihth'uh sohl) *n.* A shallow soil consisting of imperfectly weathered rock fragments or nearly all barren rock.

Lithospermum (lihth oh sper'muhm) *n.* A genus of 44 species of widely distributed hairy perennial flowers (Boraginaceae). They grow to 3 feet tall, with simple, alternate leaves and clusters of white, yellow, or orange flowers. Used in rock gardens and borders. Commonly known as gromwell and puccoon. Many plants once classified as *Lithospermum* are now classifed as *Lithodora, Moltkia,* or *Buglossoides.*

litre (leet'ray) *n.* A common name for *Lithrea caustica,* a small broadleaf evergreen tree native to Chile. It grows to 20 feet, with small oval, pointed leaves, clusters of small creamy-yellow flowers, lustrous white fruit, and poisonous sap that causes a painful skin rash. Used in mild climates.

Litsea (liht'see uh) *n.* A genus of about 400 species of tropical and subtropical shrubs and trees (Laureaceae). The most widely grown is *L. aestivalis,* native to the southeastern United States. It is a deciduous shrub to 9 feet, with small narrow, oval leaves, clusters of yellow flowers that appear before the leaves, and small round, red fruit. Commonly known as pondspice.

little bluestem *n.* (See **Andropogon.**)

little-pickles *n.* A common name for *Othonna capensis,* a perennial ground cover. It has trailing, slender branches with small cylindrical, fleshy, pale green leaves and yellow daisylike flowers. Used as a ground cover in frost-free climates.

Littonia (lih tohn'ee uh) *n.* A genus of 7 species of tender perennial flowers (Liliaceae). *L. modesta* grows from rhizomes to 6 feet tall, with narrow or oval pointed leaves and clusters of orange bell-shaped flowers.

littoral (lihd'uh rahl) *a.* Of or pertaining to a shore, especially of the sea; growing on or near the shore.

Littorella (lihd oh rehl'luh) *n.* A genus of 2 species of perennial aquatic plants (Plantaginaceae). They have creeping stems, with rosettes of leaves at each node, and single flowers on short stems. Used as an aquarium plant.

lituate (liht'yoo ayt) *a.* In botany, forked, with the points turned outward.

liturate (liht'yoo rayt) *a.* Spotted.

live animal trap *n.* Variously sized containers used to capture and keep a live animal such as a skunk, opposum, woodchuck, squirrel, or raccoon until it can be transported and released in a remote area. Also called *live trap.*

live-oak *n.* A common name for any of several broadleaf evergreen oaks, native mostly to North America. These include *Quercus agrifolia* (coast live oak or California live oak); *Q. chrysolepis* (canyon live oak); *Q. myrsinifolia* (Japanese live oak); *Q. virginiana* (southern live oak); *Q. Wislizeni* (interior live oak). They have elliptic, sometimes spiny leaves, catkins, and acorns. Used as spreading shade trees. Also live-oak.

liverleaf *n.* A common name for the genus *Hepatica,* a small hardy, rather hairy perennial flower. It grows to 9 inches, with long-stemmed, heart-shaped, thick, lobed evergreen leaves and solitary white, purple, or blue flowers on hairy stems. Used in moist soils in the woodland gardens, where they may naturalize. Also known as liverwort.

liverwort, noble *n.* A common name for *Hepatica nobilis,* a hardy, low-growing, rhizomatous perennial flower. It grows to 6 inches, with 3-lobed heart-shaped leaves, purplish and silky beneath, and solitary white, purple or blue flowers 1 inch or more across. Used in woodland gardens.

live trap *n.* (See **live animal trap.**)

Livistona (lihv ihs toh'nuh) *n.* A genus of 30 species of tall slow-growing, subtropical and tropical fan palms (Palmae). They grow from 20 to 100 feet, depending on the species, with spiny stems, and fan-shaped leaves split at the edges. Used as houseplants in temperate climates, as ornamental trees in subtropical and tropical climates. Also known as Australian cabbage palm, cabbage palm, chinese fan palm, chinese fountain palm, Gippsland palm.

lizard's-tail *n.* 1. A common name for the genus *Saururus,* a genus of erect perennial bog plants. 2. A common name for *Saururus cernuus,* an erect perennial North American bog plant. It grows from an aromatic, creeping rhizome to 3 to 5 feet, with oval, pointed leaves and slender, drooping spikes of tiny white flowers. Used in moist, shady locations. Also known as lizardtail, water dragon, and swamp lily.

Loam *n.* 1. The textural class named for soil containing 7% to 22% clay, 28% to 50% silt, and less than 52% sand. 2. A term referring to a mellow soil rich in organic matter.

loamy soil *n.* A general term for a soil of intermediate texture.

Loasa (loh'ah suh) *n.* A genus of 105 species of subtropical and tropical annuals and subshrubs (Loasaceae). They grow to 18 inches, with opposite leaves and curious yellow, red, or white flowers with sacklike or hooded petals. Some species have stinging hairs. Grown in warm-climate gardens.

Loasaceae (loh uh say'see ee) *n., pl.* A family of 13 genera and 250 species of flowers native to the Americas. They are rough, bristly plants, often with stinging hairs, variously shaped leaves and 4-to-5-petaled flowers. The ornamental genera are *Blumenbachia, Cagophora, Eucnide, Loasa,* and *Mentzelia.*

loasaceous (loh uhl say'shiuhs) *a.* Pertaining to or having the characters of the family Loasaceae.

lobate (loh'bayt) *a.* 1. Having a lobe or lobes, such as a lobate leaf. Also lobated.

lobe *n.* In botany, usually a major projection, segment, or division halfway to the middle or less of a leaf, fruit, or other organ of a plant.

lobed *a.* Having a lobe or lobes; lobate.

lobelet *a.* In botany, a little lobe; a lobule.

Lobelia (loh bee'lee uh) *n.* A genus of 375 species of annuals and perennials (Lobeliaceae), many native to North America. They grow from 6 inches to 3 feet, depending on the species, with alternate, simple leaves and white, yellow, violet, dark blue, or pale blue flowers. *L. Erinus* is used as a hanging-basket plant, for edging, on walls, or in rock gardens. *L. Cardinalis* is a superb 3-foot-tall erect pe-

rennial with brilliant scarlet flowers; used in moist soils. Commonly known as cardinal flower. 2. [l.c.] A plant of this genus.

Lobelia cardinalis
(cardinal flower)
a flower spike *b* lower stem with roots

Lobeliaceae (loh bee lee ay'see ee) *n., pl.* A family of 25 genera of flowers, sometimes shrubs or trees. They have alternate leaves and irregular-shaped flowers. The ornamental genera are *Centropogon, Downingia, Hippobroma, Hypsela, Laurentia, Lobelia, Monopsis,* and *Pratia.*

lobeliaceous (loh bee lee ay'shiuhs) *a.* Pertaining to or resembling the Lobeliaceae.

lobelia family (loh bee'lee uh) *n.* A common name for Lobeliaceae.

Lobivia (loh bihv'ee uh) *n.* A genus of 70 species of low-growing, spiny, ribbed cacti (Cactaceae) native to South America. They are thick, fleshy, cylindrical or globular cacti, rarely taller than 12 inches, with large, showy red, yellow, pink, orange, purple, or lilac flowers, sometimes as large as the plant. Used as potted plants. Commonly known as cob cactus.

loblolly bay (lahb'lah lee) *n.* A common name for *Gordonia Lasianthus,* a fairly hardy tree native to the southern United States. It grows to 90 feet, with glossy, narrow, oval, dark green leaves and large white flowers. Used as an elegant flowering ornamental tree. Also known as black laurel.

loblolly pine (lahb'luh lee) *n*. A common name for *Pinus Taeda*, a tall, hardy coniferous tree native to eastern and southeastern North America. It grows to 100 feet, with clusters of 9-inch-long needlelike leaves and oval cones up to 5 inches long. Also known as frankincense pine and old-field pine.

loblolly tree (lahb'lah lee) *n*. A common name for *Cordia dentata*, a large evergreen shrub or small tree native to tropical America. It grows to 30 feet, with broad, rough, toothed leaves, large clusters of small yellow or white flowers, and white oblong fruit. Used as an oramental in warm-climate gardens. Also known as jackwood.

lobster-claw *n*. A common name for the genus *Heleconia*, a tropical perennial. It grows to 10 feet, depending on the species, with large, broad banan-alike leaves and large, showy, curiously shaped brightly colored flowers in drooping clusters. Used as greenhouse plants in cold climates, as outdoor plants in warm-climate gardens. Also known as false bird-of-paradise.

lobster-claws *n*. 1. A common name used for *Cheiridopsis Pillansii*, a dwarf clump-forming succulent. It has very short stems, with thick, fleshy, opposite leaves, whitish gray with dark dots, and large bright yellow flowers. Grown by collectors as a potted plant. 2. A common name for *Vriesea carinata*, a tropical epiphytic bromeliad. It grows to 12 inches, with narrow green leaves and spikes of yellow flowers. Used as a houseplant or grown in greenhouses.

Lobularia (lahb uh lah'ree uh) *n*. A genus of 5 species of Mediterranean annuals and perennials (Cruciferae). *L. maritima* is a low-growing perennial, often grown as an annual, with small, narrow, entire leaves and masses of tiny white, pink, and reddish-purple fragrant flowers that attract bees. Used as an edging, carpeting, and bulb cover; also used in window boxes, on walls, and tumbling over the edges of pots. Reseeds prolifically. Commonly known as sweet alyssum.

Lockhartia (lahk har'tee uh) *n*. A genus of 25 species of tropical epiphytic orchids (Orchidaceae) native to Central and South America. They have

stems nearly 2 feet tall, virtually concealed by many 2-ranked leaves, and small multicolored flowers.

locoweed *n*. A common name for the genus *Oxytropis*, a perennial weed; some species are native to North America. They have divided leaves, spikes of white, yellow, purple, and pink pealike flowers, and beanlike pods. Sometimes grown ornamentally, but better known as poisonous to cattle. Also called crazyweed. 2. Also *Cicuta* (water hemlock), 1 of the most violently poisonous plants of the northern temperate region; *Eupatorium rugosum* (white snakeroot); *Haplopappus* (rayless goldenrod); and *Chrysothamnus* (rabbitbrush).

locust *n*. A common name for several trees of the family *Leguminosae*, including *Ceratonia siliqua* (carob), the North American genus *Robinia* and *R. Pseudoacacia* (black or yellow locust or false acacia). *Robinia* consists of hardy deciduous shrubs and trees, usually with thorny branches, feathery, divided leaves with round leaflets, showy clusters of fragrant white, pink, or purple flowers that attract bees, and long, flat pods. Tolerates heat, drought, poor soil, and a wide range of temperatures. Also known as locust tree.

locust bean *n*. The fruit of the carob tree. (See **Ceratonia**.)

locust, bristly *n*. A common name for *Robinia hispida*, a hardy deciduous shrub native to the southeastern United States. It grows to 7 feet, with hairy leaves, spikes of butterflylike rose or pale purple flowers, and short, hairy pods. Also known as moss locust.

locust, clammy *n*. A common name for *Robinia viscosa*, a deciduous tree native to the southeastern United States. It grows to 40 feet, with branches that ooze a sticky secretion, leaves divided into oval, pointed leaflets, 3-inch spikes of dark red and pink flowers, and hairy pods.

locust, honey *n*. 1. A common name for *Gleditsia*, a genus of fast-growing, deciduous, formidably thorny trees (Leguminosae) widely distributed throughout the world. They have alternate leaves divided into leaflets, inconspicuous greenish flowers, and twisted flat pods 12 to 18 inches long. 2. *Gleditsia triacanthos*, the honey locust, is a large tree native to the eastern United States; useful as a specimen tree, particularly in desert gardens.

locust, water *n*. A common name for *Gleditsia aquatica,* a deciduous tree native to the southeastern United States. It grows to 60 feet, with divided leaves, short spikes of small, greenish flowers, and thin, oval pods. Also known as swamp locust.

lodicule (lahd'uh kyool) *n*. In botany, 1 of the 2 or 3 delicate scales that occur in the flowers of some grasses, at the base of the ovary and below the stamens.

Lodoicea (lahd oh ihs'ee uh) *n*. A genus of 1 species of slow-growing tropical fan palm, *L. maldivica* (Palmae). It grows to 100 feet, with 20-foot long and 12-foot wide fan like leaves that are split at the edges, and with 20-inch-long seeds that are the largest in the plant kingdom. Commonly known as double coconut, Seychelles nut, and coco-de-mer.

loess (loh'uhs) *n*. A geological deposit of fine material, mostly silt, transported by wind.

loganberry *n*. A dark purple, fleshy berry, a cultivar of *Rubus ursinus*. Loganberries resemble blackberries in their culture and are widely grown in the Pacific states.

Logania (loh gay'nee uh) *n*. A genus of 30 species of tender shrubs and trees (Loganiaceae). *L. vaginalis* grows to 6 feet or more, with narrow, opposite leaves and clusters of small white flowers. Used in mild-climate gardens.

Loganiaceae (loh'gay nee ay see ee) *n., pl*. A family of 32 genera and 800 species of flowers, vines, shrubs, and trees. They have opposite, simple leaves and clusters of regular flowers. Several genera produce poisons and drugs. The ornamental genera include *Buddleia, Gelsemium,* and *Logania*.

Lolium (loh'lee uhm) *n*. A genus of about 8 species of annual and perennial grasses (Gramineae). Several are useful lawn grasses, stabilizing ground covers, or pasture grasses. Most often used is the lawn grass *L. perenne,* commonly known as perennial ryegrass.

Lomatia (loh may'shee uh) *n*. A genus of 12 species of tender shrubs and trees (Proteaceae). They grow to 20 feet, with alternate leaves and loose spikes of flowers. Grown outdoors in frost-free gardens; in greenhouses elsewhere.

Lomatium (loh may'shee uhm) *n*. A genus of 70 species of hardy perennials (Umbelliferae), native mostly to western North America. They grow from 4 inches to 30 inches, depending on the species, often with dissected leaves, and with clusters of small yellow, white, or purple flowers. Sometimes planted in wildflower gardens. *L. utriculatum* is commonly known as spring gold.

Lombardy poplar *n*. A common name for *Populus nigra* 'Italica', a fast-growing hardy deciduous tree. It grows to 90 feet, with triangular leaves that color butter yellow in autumn and with flowers in drooping catkins. Used in rural areas where fast growth, low maintenance, and toughness are valued; effective in lining long driveways or avenues and useful as a windbreak.

loment (loh'mehnt) *n*. In botany, a leguminous fruit, as the tick trefoil, which breaks up into numerous dry, 1-seeded, pieces when ripe. Also lomentum, *pl*. **lomenta**.

Lonas (lohn'ahs) *n*. A genus of 1 species, *L. annua* (Compositae), an annual flower. It grows to 12 inches, with alternate, finely divided leaves and dense clusters of rayless flowers. Used as a bedding plant. Tolerates coastal fog and wind. Commonly known as African daisy and yellow ageratum.

Lonchocarpus (lahng kuh kar'puhs) *n*. A genus of 100 species of mostly tropical trees (Leguminosae). They grow to 50 feet, with alternate, divided leaves, showy spikes of white-to-violet flowers and flat, dry pods. Grown in subtropical and tropical gardens for their flowers. Commonly known as lancepod.

London pride *n*. 1. A common name for *Saxifraga umbrosa,* a hardy perennial flower. It grows to 18 inches, with basal rosettes of small, shiny tongue-shaped leaves, open clusters of pink flowers on wine-red flower stalks. Used in moist, shady situations; traditional in cottage gardens. 2. A common name for *Dianthus barbatus,* a vigorous biennial flower, often grown as an annual. It grows to 18 inches, with narrow, pointed leaves and flat-topped clusters of white, pink, rose, red, purple, violet, or bicolored flowers. Used as an edging or massed in beds; traditional in cottage gardens. Also known as Sweet William. 3. A common name for *Lychnis chalcedonica,* a very hardy perennial flower. It grows to 24 inches, with soft, furry, oval, pointed leaves and dense clusters of scarlet flowers with deeply cut petals. Used in borders. Also known as Maltese cross.

longan (lahng′gahn) *n*. 1. A common name for *Euphoria Longan,* a tender broadleaf evergreen tree. It grows to 40 feet, with leaves a foot long divided into leaflets, yellowish-white flowers, and small, yellow-brown, juicy, edible fruit. Grown as a fruit tree in frost-free climates. Also known as lungan. 2. The fruit itself.

long-day plant *n*. Any plant which requires long hours of sunlight to set bloom; ordinarily, plants that are native to latitudes greater than 60° both north and south of the equator. Long-day plants flower in late spring and early summer. Lettuce is a long-day plant, flowering when days exceed 17 hours of light per day. Chrysanthemums and pointsettias are short-day plants. Growers give such plants long hours of artificial light in greenhouses to force them into out-of-season bloom.

long-handled lopper *n*. Short-bladed, heavy duty scissors with long handles; used to prune branches up to about 1½ inces in diameter.

long moss *n*. A common name for *Tillandsia usneoides,* an epiphytic plant, with gray threadlike stems and leaves, forming dense pendulous tufts, which drape the trees in the forests of the Americas. (See **Tillandsia.**) Also called Spanish moss and graybeard.

long purples *n*. A common name for *Lythrum Salicaria,* an erect perennial flower. (See **loosestrife, purple.**)

long reach pruner *n*. An implement consisting of runing shear blades attached to a long tube, typically 4 to 6 feet; used to cut hard-to-reach branches.

Lonicera (loh′nih seh ruh) *n*. A genus of more than 150 species of upright or twining, sometimes deciduous, vines or shrubs (Caprifoliaceae), some species native to North America. They have simple, opposite leaves and white, red, or yellow flowers, often fragrant, which are succeeded by sweetish red berries. The common honeysuckle, *L. Periclymenum,* a native of central and western Europe, cultivated in the United States, is also known as woodbine. *L. sempervirens* (trumpet or coral honeysuckle), native to North America, is cultivated for the beauty of its large, unscented flowers, which

are red on the outside and yellow within. *L. canadensis* is the American fly honeysuckle; it has a honey-yellow corolla slightly tinged with red. *L. Tatarica,* the Tatarian honeysuckle, is a hardy dense upright shrub with small pink or rose flowers and bright red winter berries. In the Americas, honeysuckles often attract hummingbirds to their tubular flowers; other birds are attracted to their berries. Commonly known as honeysuckle.

looking-glass plant *n*. A common name for *Coprosma repens,* a tender prostrate shrub or small tree. It grows to 10 feet as a shrub, to 25 feet as a tree, with shiny, glossy, oval leaves, inconspicuous flowers, and orange or yellow fruit. Used as a clipped shrub or hedge. Also known as mirror plant.

loop stake *n*. (See **flower support.**)

loosestrife *n*. A common name for plants of 2 genera, *Lysimachia* and *Lythrum.*

loosestrife family *n*. A common name for Lythraceae.

loosestrife, purple *n*. A common name for *Lythrum Salicaria,* an erect perennial flower naturalized in North America. It grows to 6 feet, with long, narrow, pointed, downy leaves and with spikes of whorled clusters of purple flowers; it is considered an invasive weed where it has naturalized. Also known as long purples and spiked loosestrife.

Lopezia (loh pee′zee uh) *n*. A genus of 18 species of subtropical flowers and shrubs (Onagraceae). They grow from 3 to 6 feet, with long, narrow, pointed leaves and spikes of many small, curiously shaped 4-petaled rose, pink, or lilac-pink flowers. Used in frost-free gardens or grown in greenhouses.

Lophocereus (lahf uh ser′ee uhs) *n*. A genus of 2 variable species of treelike, spiny, ribbed cacti (Cactaceae) native to southern Arizona and Baja California. They grow from 10 to 15 feet, with clusters of night-blooming pink flowers.

lopper *n*. Short bladed, heavy-duty scissors used to prune branches up to about 1½ inches in diameter. Branches with smaller diameters may be cut with pruners. (See also **ratchet lopper.**)

lopping *n*. 1. The procedure by which all the branches of a tree, except the crop or leading shoot, are cut off for the sake of the profit to be derived from them, as contrasted with pruning, by which some of the branches are cut off for the sake of the tree. 2. That which is cut off; severed branches (commonly used in the plural).

lopping ax *n*. A small, light ax used for trimming trees.

lopping shears *n*. Long-handled, heavy-duty scissors used to cut twigs, branches, or roots. Lopping shears cut branches with larger diameters than those cut with pruning shears.

loquat (loh′kwaht) *n*. 1. An evergreen shrub or tree, *Eriobotrya japonica,* native to China and Japan, and commonly introduced in warm temperate climates. It is an ornamental plant, with leaves nearly a foot long, and yields a fruit of a yellow color, resembling a small apple. 2. The fruit of this tree.

Loranthaceae (loh ran thay′see ee) *n., pl.* A family of 20 genera of mostly parasitic plants; the mistletoe family. They have broad, entire, leathery, opposite leaves, green, yellow, or red flowers, and fleshy fruit that attracts birds. Those species that are parasitic on deciduous trees should be removed before they weaken the health of the host tree. Traditionally hung from doorjambs during the holidays, at which time the unwary may find themselves the recipient of an unexpected kiss.

lords-and-ladies *n*. A common name for *Arum maculatum,* a hardy perennial flower. It grows to 8 inches, with bladelike leaves, often spotted with black or purple, and callalike flowers. Used in cottage gardens. Also known as cuckoopint and Adam-and-Eve.

lorette pruning (lor eht′) *n*. A type of pruning, developed and primarily used in France, to train espaliered fruit trees.

Loropetalum (lohr uh peht′uh luhm) *n*. A genus of 1 species, *L. chinense* (Hamamelidaceae), a subtly beautiful, tender broadleaf evergreen shrub or small tree. It grow 3 to 5 feet tall, to 12 feet in great age, with soft, round, light green leaves and clusters of white flowers with twisted petals. The flowers may appear at any time of year, and individual leaves may turn red or yellow at any season. Used as a shrub, ground cover, or hanging-basket plant.

lotus *n*. A common name for *Nymphaea* and *Nelumbo,* 2 genera of water lilies.

Lotus *n*. A genus of about 100 species of trailing, prostrate plants and subshrubs (Leguminosae), found mostly in the temperate zone. They grow from 2 to 4 feet, depending on the species, with leaves divided into leaflets, pealike red or yellow flowers, and narrow pods. Used as a ground cover or hanging-basket plants.

lotus, blue *n*. A common name for *Nymphaea caerulea* and *N. stellata,* both blue-flowered water lilies.

lotus, Egyptian *n*. A common name for *Nymphaea caerulea* and *N. Lotus,* both tender water lilies. *N. caerulea* is a day-blooming waterlily; *N. Lotus* blooms at night.

lotus tree *n*. A common name for *Celtis australis.* It grows from 40 to 80 feet, with coarsely toothed, sharply pointed dark green leaves and round, dark purple fruit that attracts birds. Useful in difficult situations: tolerates wind, heat, drought, and alkaline soil. Also known as European nettle tree, Mediterranean hackberry, lote tree, and honeyberry. 2. A common name for *Diospyros Lotus* and *D. virginiana,* both deciduous trees, the hardiest of the persimmons. They grow to 45 feet, with simple, glossy, alternate, dark green leaves, and red, green, or yellow-green flowers. *D. Lotus* is used primarily as rootstalk for the edible persimmon, *D. Kaki. D. virginiana* has small, yellow-to-orange edible fruit, astringent until fully ripe. Also known as date plum.

louseberry (lows′behr ree) *n*. A common name for *Euonymus europaea,* a hardy deciduous large shrub or small tree. It grows to 25 feet, usually much less, with medium-green scalloped leaves that turn rose-pink in fall, inconspicuous flowers, and showy pink-to-red fruit, which splits to show bright orange seeds that attract birds. Used as a landscape-structure plant with showy fruit. Also known as European spindle tree.

lovage (luv′aj) *n*. 1. The plant *Levisticum officinale* (Umbelliferae), a native of the mountains of central Europe, cultivated in herb gardens. It is sometimes called Italian lovage or garden lovage. Its leaves and stems resemble celery in both flavor and appearance, although the stalks are thinner and tougher.

love apple *n*. An old name for the common tomato.

love grass *n*. (See **Eragrostis**.)

love-in-a-mist *n.* 1. A common name for *Nigella damascena,* a self-sowing, spring-blooming annual. It grows to 30 inches, with threadlike leaves that form a collar under blue, white, or rose flowers and with seed capsules that are decorative in everlasting bouquets. The seeds, called black cumin, are used for flavoring in cooking. Traditional in cottage gardens and herb gardens. Also known as fennel-flower. 2. A common name for *Passiflora foetida,* a tropical vine native to the Americas. It has ill-smelling leaves, white, pink, lilac, or purple curiously shaped flowers, and red or yellow edible fruit. Also known as running pop and wild water lemon. 3. A common name for *Cerastium tomentosum,* a low-growing, widely adapted, short-lived hardy perennial ground cover. It grows from 6 to 8 inches, with small silvery-gray leaves that form dense, tufted mats and with masses of white summer-blooming flowers. Prefers dry soils; needs good drainage. Used to cascade over walls, in rock gardens, between stepping-stones, and as edging. Also known as snow-in-summer. 4. A common name for *Clematis Viorna,* native to eastern and central United States. It climbs to 10 feet, has bright green leaves, purple bell-shaped flowers, and fluffy white seed heads. Also known as snow-in-summer, leatherflower, and vase vine.

love-in-idleness *n.* A common name for *Viola tricolor.* Also known as Johnny-jump-up, wild pansy and heartsease.

love-lies-bleeding *n.* A common name for *Amaranthus caudatus,,* a large, vigorous, much-branched annual flower. It grows 3 to 8 feet, with large leaves to 10 inches long and red flowers in drooping, tassellike clusters. Grown mainly as a novelty. Also known as tassel flower. 2. A common name for the genus *Dicentra,* also known as bleeding heart. 3. A common name for *Adonis annua,* an annual to 16 inches, with divided leaves and small green-and-red or purple-and-red flowers with a dark basal spot.

loveman *n.* A common name for the prickly weed *Galium.* Also known as bedstraw, goosegrass, or cleavers.

love plant *n.* A common name for *Anacampseros telephiastrum,* a prostrate, succulent, mat-forming ground cover. It has small, thick, fleshy leaves that form a basal rosette and reddish flowers on 6 inch-long stems. Also known as copper leaves and sand rose.

love plant, Mexican *n.* A common name for *Kalanchoe pinnata,* a perennial succulent. It grows from 2 to 3 feet, with fleshy, scalloped leaves that form plantlets in the notches of the scallops. The plantlets will grow into separate plants if they fall on soil. Grown as a novelty. Also known as air plant, life plant, floppers, curtain plant, mother-in-law, good-luck leaf, miracle leaf, and sprouting leaf.

love tree *n.* A common name for *Cercis Siliquastrum,* a hardy deciduous flowering tree. It grows to 40 feet, with rounded or heart-shaped leaves, clusters of small purplish-rose flowers that appear before the leaves, sometimes growing out of the trunk, and 4-inch-long pods. Grown for early blooming flowers, summer shade, and good fall color. Also known as Judas tree.

low maintenance plants *n., pl.* Plants requiring minimal care or tending.

Luculia (loo koo'lee uh) *n.* A genus of 5 species of tender shrubs (Rubiaceae). They grow from 6 to 20 feet, depending on the species, with leathery, opposed leaves and clusters of white or pink flowers. Grown in frost-free gardens outdoors or in greenhouses anywhere.

Ludwigia (luhd wihj'ee uh) *n.* A genus of 75 species of water or bog plants (Onagraceae), many native to the Americas. They have simple leaves and yellow or white summer-blooming flowers. The aquatic forms used in aquariaums; the other forms in moist soils. Commonly known as false loosestrife.

luffa (loof'uh) *n.* A genus of the order Cucurbitaceae, the gourd family, characterized by large fruits, which are dry and fibrous. They are climbing plants, with white flowers. The fruit is dry and oblong or cylindrical in shape and dried for use as a bath sponge.

Lunaria (loo nah'ree uh) *n.* A genus of 2 or 3 species of erect, branching biennial or perennial flowers (Cruciferae). They grow to 4 feet, with broad, simple, toothed leaves, clusters of white-to-purple flowers, and satiny, flat, round pods, often used in dried bouquets. Commonly known as honesty, money plant, moonwort, and satinflower.

lunate (loo′nayt) *a.* Crescent-shaped.

lungwort *n.* A common name for plants of several genera including *Hellebore, Hieracium, Mertensia, Pulmonaria,* and *Verbascum,* all formerly thought to be useful in curing lung diseases.

lupine (loo′pihn) *n.* A common name for the genus *Lupinus.*

lupine

Lupinus (loo pigh′nuhs) *n.* A genus of 200 species of annual and perennial flowers and subshrubs (Leguminosae). They grow from a few inches to 6 feet, depending on the species, with hand-shaped leaves and very showy spikes of blue, white, pink, and yellow flowers. There are many hybrids, most of which are useful in the perennial border. Commonly known as lupine.

lustwort *n.* A common name for *Drosera rotundifolia,* a carnivorous bog plant. It has rounded leaves, in basal rosettes, that have sticky hairs to trap insects, which the plant then devours, and it bears small white, pink, or purple flowers. Grown mainly as a curiosity, occasionally in the bog garden. Also known as round-leafed sundew.

Luzula (loo′zoo luh) *n.* A genus of about 40 species of grasslike perennial plants (Juncaceae) native to temperate regions. They have stems growing in tufts, with flat, pliant, grasslike leaves and white, yellow, or brown flowers. Several are grown as ornamentals or ground covers in woody areas. Commonly called wood rush.

Lycaste (ligh′kas′tee) *n.* A genus of 40 species of epiphytic orchids (Orchidaceae) native to tropical America. They grow from 6 to 30 inches, with 1 to 3 pleated leaves emerging from a pseudobulb, and bear showy, multicolored flowers on leafless stalks. *L. virginalis* has been much hybridized. Grown in warm greenhouses.

Lychnis (lihk′nihs) *n.* A genus of 35 species of annual or hardy perennial flowers (Caryophyllaceae). They grow from 20 inches to 3 feet, depending on the species, with opposite leaves and clusters of white, scarlet pink, or purple flowers. Used in borders; the smaller species used in rock gardens. Commonly known as campion and catchfly.

Lycium (lihsh′ee uhm) *n.* A genus of about 100 species of tender or tropical, erect or clambering, sometimes spiny, woody shrubs (Solanaceae). They grow from 7 to 10 feet, depending on the species, with clustered, narrow, entire, alternate leaves, solitary or clustered narrow, bell-shaped green, white, or purple flowers, and scarlet berries. Grown in warm-climate gardens; tolerate a wide variety of soils. Commonly known as matrimony vine and boxthorn.

Lycopersicon (ligh kah per′see kahn) *n.* A genus of about 7 species of subtropical and tropical weak-stemmed plants (Solanaceae). They grow to 10 feet, with divided, roughly toothed leaves, loose clusters of small flowers, and round, pulpy red or yellow fruit. The most widely grown species, *L. lycopersicum,* is the common garden tomato. There are many cultivars. Commonly known as tomato.

lycopod (ligh′koh pahd) *n.* A plant of the genus *Lycopodium* or of the family Lycopodiaceae.

Lycopodiaceae (ligh′koh poh dee uh′see ee) *n., pl.* A family of 2 genera and 450 species of spore-bearing, vascular fern allies; the club-moss family or lycopodium family. They have many scalelike or needlelike leaves and spikelike cones with spores. The ornamental genus is *Lycopodium.*

Lycopodium (ligh koh poh′dee uhm) *n.* A genus of 450 species of low-growing evergreen perennial plants (Lycopodiaceae). They have many scalelike or needlelike leaves and spikelike cones filled with spores. Grown in moist, shady places or in hanging baskets in greenhouses. Commonly known as club moss.

Lycopodium
(club moss)

lycopodium family (ligh koh poh dee uhm) *n.* A common name for Lycopodiaceae.

Lycopus (ligh'koh puhs) *n.* A genus of 4 species of hardy perennials (Labiatae) that spread by stolons. They grow to 3 feet, with square stems, opposite leaves, and spikes of small flowers in whorls. Used in wildflower gardens and in moist soils. *L. americanus* is native to North America; *L. europaeus* has naturalized throughout North America: Both are common roadside weeds. Commonly known as bugleweed, gypsywort, and water horehound.

Lycoris (ligh koh'ruhs) *n.* A genus of 11 or more species of bulbs (Amaryllidaceae). They grow to 2 feet, with straplike leaves that die before the flowers develop and have tall, leafless stalks topped by clusters of pink, white, red, or yellow flowers, which are sometimes fragrant. Grown under glass or planted deep in cold climates. Commonly known as spider lily.

Lygodium (ligh goh'dee uhm) *n.* A genus of 40 species of climbing ferns (Schizaeaceae). They grow to 8 feet, with delicate, lacy, light green leaves, and they climb by twining stems. *L. japonicum* is grown outdoors in mild-winter climates; in cool greenhouses anywhere. Commonly known as climbing fern.

Lyonia (lee oh'nee uh) *n.* A genus of 40 to 50 species of mostly subtropical shrubs or small trees (Ericaceae). They grow from 6 to 15 feet, occasionally much larger, with simple, alternate leaves and clusters or spikes of white to pink flowers. Useful in moist soils.

lyrate leaf

lyrate (ligh'rayt) *a.* Resembling a lyre; for example, in botany, a lyrate leaf is a leaf that is divided into several lobes, which increase in size toward 1 large terminal lobe. Also lyrated, lyriform.

Lysichiton (ligh see kih'tahn) *n.* A genus of 2 species of robust stemless hardy perennials (Araceae) native to swamps of western North America and to Asia. They grow from thick rhizomes, with huge bright green leaves, 5 feet long and 1 foot wide, and bright yellow, partially inflated, callalike flowers. They are ill-scented when bruised. Interesting in bog gardens or along streams and pools. Commonly known as skunk cabbage.

Lysiloma (ligh suh loh'muh) *n.* A genus of 30 to 35 species of shrubs and trees (Leguminosae) native to the Americas. *L. Thornberi,* native to the Rincon Mountains of Arizona, grows to 12 feet, with finely cut, bright green acacialike leaves, heads of tiny white flowers, and long, flat, ridged pods. Best grown in frost-free gardens, but will come back from root after a light frost. Good informal shrub, patio tree, or transition plant between garden and desert. Tolerates heat and drought. Commonly known as fern-of-the-desert and feather bush.

Lysimachia (ligh suh'mahk ee uh) *n.* A genus of about 165 species of flowers and rarely, shrubs (Primulaceae). They grow to 4 feet, with simple leaves, often dotted with glands, and with yellow, white, pink, purple, or blue bell-shaped flowers. Used in moist situations. *L. vulgaris* has naturalized in North America; it is considered an invasive weed where it has naturalized. Commonly known as loosestrife.

Lythraceae (ligh thray′see ee) *n., pl.* A family of 22 genera of flowers, shrubs, and trees; the loose-strife family. They have opposed or whorled entire leaves and, typically, spikes of many small flowers. The ornamental genera are *Cuphea, Lagerstroemia,* and *Lythrum.*

lythraceous (ligh thray′shuhs) *a.* Pertaining to the Lythraceae, or resembling them.

Lythrum (ligh′thruhm) *n.* A genus of 30 species of annual or perennial flowers (Lythraceae), some native to North America. They grow to 6 feet, with angled or winged stems, entire leaves, and pairs or clusters of purple or white flowers that bloom in late summer or fall. Used in borders, wild gardens, and moist situations. An excellent cut flower. Commonly known as loosestrife.

 **M**

Maackia (mak′kee uh) *n.* A genus of 6 to 12 spe-cies of deciduous trees (Leguminosae). They grow from 40 to 70 feet, depending on the species, with alternate leaves divided into opposite leaflets, clus-ters of white butterfly-shaped flowers, and flat pods.

Maba (mah′buh) *n.* A genus of about 70 species of tender evergreen shrubs and trees (Ebenaceae). They grow to 20 feet and have alternate, entire leaves, silky flowers, either solitary or in clusters, and small round berries. Grown ornamentally in mild- winter climates.

Macadamia (mak uh day′mee uh) *n.* A genus of about 10 species of subtropical shrubs and trees (Proteaceae); the macadamia nut. *M. integrifolia* grows to 60 feet tall and 50 wide with large leaves in whorls of 3 or 4 and with densely flowered spikes of white blooms, each having from 100 to 300 flow-ers and fruit that yields the sweet, edible macad-amia nut.

macaw palm (muh′kaw) *n.* A common name for any of several species of *Acrocomia,* fast-growing, sometimes spiny, deciduous tropical palms, native to Central and South America. They grow from 25 to 50 feet, depending on species, with divided, pointed leaves, flowers in sets of 3, and fibrous round fruit. Used in warm-winter climates. Also known as macaw tree and grugru.

Macfadyena (mahk fahd yay′nuh) *n.* A genus of 3 or 4 species of fast-growing, self-clinging woody vines (Bignoniaceae) native to tropical America. *M. unguis-cati* grows to 40 feet, has leaves divided into 2 leaflets with a terminal, clawlike, forked ten-dril. It bears bright yellow trumpet-shaped flowers. Used in frost-free climates; clings to any support. Commonly known as cat's-claw, cat's-claw trum-pet, funnel creeper, cat's-claw creeper, and yellow trumpet vine.

Machaeranthera (mahk uh rahn′thuh ruh) *n.* A genus of 25 to 30 species of flowers or shrubs (Compositae) native to western North America. They grow to 3 feet with alternate, often divided, leaves and asterlike flowers with yellow centers and blue or white petals.

machete (muh shehd′ee) *n.* A large, heavy knife used to cut brush.

Mackaya (muh kay′uh) *n.* A genus of 1 species, *M. bella,* of tender shrub (Acanthaceae). It grows to 5 feet with glossy, dark green opposite leaves and long clusters of pale lavender flowers, streaked with purple. Used in warm-climate gardens in shade, even dense shade.

Macleaya (meh klay′uh) *n.* A genus of 2 species of large, stately, hardy perennials (Papaveraceae). *M. cordata* has branching stems to 8 feet, with deeply lobed gray-green leaves 10 inches wide and tall stalks with clouds of tiny pink flowers that look like plumes. Plant as a specimen or in clumps; they may crowd out smaller, more delicate plants. Com-monly known as plume poppy.

Maclura (meh kloo′ruh) *n.* A genus of 1 species, *M. pomifera* (Moraceae), of thorny tree, native to south-central North America. A spreading tree that grows to 60 feet, it is often multitrunked, with formidable 4-inch-long thorns, handsome, shiny, oval leaves, large heads (female) and spikes (male) of flowers, and fruit that looks like a warty green orange. Useful as a big, tough, rough-looking hedge, screen, or hedgerow. They endure all privation, tolerating heat, cold, wind, drought, poor soil, and some alkalinity. Commonly known as Osage orange, hedge apple, and bowwood.

Maclura
(Osage orange)

Macodes (mah koh'deez) *n.* A genus of 10 species of tropical terrestrial orchids (Orchidaceae). *M. petola* has variegated leaves and long spikes of as many as 15 small, red-brown flowers with a white lip. Grown primarily by collectors.

Macradenia (mak rad uh'nee uh) *n.* A genus of 8 species of epiphytic tropical American orchids (Orchidaceae). They have a single leaf emerging from a pseudobulb and an arching stem with small, rich brown or yellow flowers. Grown in warm greenhouses.

Macrocarpaea (mak ruh kahr'pee ee) *n.* A genus of 30 species of tall, rather woody, perennial plants and shrubs (Gentianaceae) native to Colombia. *M. glabra* is a shrub that grows to 7 feet and has leafy branches with elliptic to long, narrow leaves and slim clusters of yellow or green flowers. Used as a specimen shrub.

macrophyllous (mak roh figh'luhs) *a.* In botany, having large leaves, usually with many veins.

Macropiper *n.* A genus of about 6 species of shrubs and trees (Piperaceae). *M. excelsum,* the aromatic New Zealand pepper tree, grows to 20 feet; it has smooth, shiny, rounded or oval, pointed, wavy-edged leaves; and it bears reddish spikes of small flowers and yellow to orange berries. Commonly known as kawa-kawa.

Macroplectrum (mak roh plehk'truhm) *n.* A genus of 4 species of robust, tropical, epiphytic or-

chids (Orchidaceae). *M. sesquipedale* has stems to 3 feet; fleshy, straplike leaves that completely enclose the stem; and foot-long stalks of white star-shaped flowers 7 inches across. Grown in warm greenhouses.

macropodous (mak rahp'uh duhs) *a.* In botany, of a plant or plant part, having a long stem or stalk; of a plant embryo, having a large or long hypocotyl.

macropore *n.* A large, non-capillary pore found in soil through which water drains by gravity.

Macrosiphonia (mak roh sihf oh'nee uh) *n.* A genus of 10 species of western North American perennials and subshrubs (Apocynaceae). They grow to 12 inches, with furry, oval-to-rounded opposite leaves and large, soft, white flowers 4 inches long and 2 inches across.

Macrozamia (mak roh zay'mee uh) *n.* A genus of 14 species of palmlike plants (Zamiaceae) of Australia, similar to cycads in appearance and culture. They grow from 6 inches to 6 feet, depending on the species, with crowns of deeply and finely divided leaves resembling those of tree ferns, sometimes on twisted stems, and with large cones on stalks with red or yellow seeds. Grown in warm-winter climates.

macular (mak'yuh luhr) *a.* Spotted.

madder *n.* A plant of the genus *Rubia.* The ordinary dyer's madder is *R. tinctorum;* a climbing, herbaceous, or, at the base, somewhat shrubby plant, with whorls of dark green leaves and small yellowish flowers; native to the Mediterranean region.

madder family *n.* A common name for Rubiaceae.

madderwort *n.* Any plant of the madder family, *Rubiaceae,* which includes such ornamental plants as *Gardenia, Coprosma,* and *Ixora,* as well as plants of economic importance such as coffee and quinine.

Madeira vine (muh dih'ruh) *n.* A common name for *Anredera cordifolia,* a fast-growing South American twining vine. It grows to 20 feet, with fleshy leaves that have small aerial tubers between the stem and leaf and with long clusters of fragrant, white flowers. Usually used in tropical gardens. Also known as mignonette vine.

Madia (mah'dee uh) *n.* A genus of 17 or 18 species of heavy-scented, sticky, hairy flowers (Compositae) native to western North American and Chile; the tarweeds. They grow from a few inches to 4 feet with sticky, richly aromatic leaves and small, yellow daisylike flowers that close at midday in most species. This is a drought-tolerant western wildflower that might be used in a meadow garden. Commonly known as tarweed.

madrone (muh droh'nuh) *n.* A common name for *Arbutus menziesii,* a strikingly handsome and picturesque tree that grows to 100 feet; native to western North America. It has a peeling bark that exposes orange branches, leathery elliptical, pointed leaves — shiny dark green above and dull green beneath — clusters of white-to-pink flowers that attract bees and hummingbirds, and clusters of brilliant red or orange winter berries that attract birds. Difficult to grow outside its native range; much to be cherished if already growing in the garden. Also known as madrona and madrono.

madwort *n.* A common name for the genus *Alyssum.*

madwort, rock *n.* A common name for *Aurinia saxatilis,* a perennial with gray leaves and masses of tiny golden-yellow flowers. It is used in borders, rock gardens, and on stone walls. Also known as basket-of-gold, golden tuft, madwort, golden-tuft alyssum, and gold dust.

Maesa (muh'suh) *n.* A genus of about 100 species of evergreen erect or straggling shrubs and small trees (Myrsinaceae). They grow to 30 feet and have alternate, simple leaves with translucent dots and spikes of small, white flowers.

maggot *n.* A fly larva. As garden pests, maggots burrow through stems, roots, and fruit, stunting or killing plants, or rendering edible parts inedible. They commonly infest the roots of members of the onion and cabbage family (see **cabbage maggot**) and corn. Control with floating row covers, diatomaceous earth, or traditional pesticides; predatory nematodes may also be effective.

magic flower *n.* A common name for *Cantua buxifolia,* a tender shrub native to Peru, Bolivia, and northern Chile. It grows to 10 feet, with small, boxlike leaves and small clusters of spectacular pink and red flowers with purple pollen sacs. Grown outdoors in mild climates; in greenhouses anywhere. Also known as magic tree, sacred-flower-of-the-Incas, magic-flower-of-the-Incas, and sacred-flower-of-Peru.

magic weeder *n.* A 3-tined, claw-shaped tool used for hand weeding and cultivating.

magnesium (magne'zeam) *n.* An element found in combination in minerals; in plants, located either in the seeds or in the chlorophyll.

Magnolia (mag noh'lyuh) *n.* A genus of 85 or more species of handsome, often spectacular, deciduous and evergreen shrubs and trees (Magnoliaceae) native to Asia and the Americas. They grow from 6 feet to 80 feet, depending on the species. They have alternate, entire, often leathery, leaves; large, solitary white, pink, purple, or yellow flowers, often showy, sometimes very fragrant; and conelike fruit with shiny red or orange seeds. The evergreen species are not hardy. Magnolias have been much hybridized, and there are many cultivars. Some of the most ornamental magnolias are *M. grandiflora,* a large, handsome tree with huge, fragrant white flowers, the scent of the South; *M. × soulagiana,* a lovely spreading tree with large white, pink, or wine-colored flowers that appear before the leaves; *M. stellata,* a large deciduous shrub bearing very early unusual flowers with strap-shaped petals and yellow fall color. *M. sargentiana robusta* is a deciduous tree to 35 feet and has dinner-plate-sized pink or mauve flowers 8 to 12 inches across, one of the most spectacular of flowering plants.

Magnolia grandiflora
(magnolia)
a flowering branch *b* cone

Magnoliaceae (mag noh lee ay'see ee) *n. pl.* A family of about 12 genera and more than 200 species of evergreen or deciduous shrubs and trees. They have alternate, simple, usually entire, leaves and usually large, showy, sometimes fragrant, flowers and conelike or winged fruit. The ornamental genera are *Alcimandra, Liriodendron, Magnolia, Michelia,* and *Talauma.*

magnoliaceous (mag noh lee ay'shuhs) *a.* Of or pertaining to plants of the family Magnoliaceae; resembling the magnolia.

magnolia family (mag noh'lyuh) *n.* A common name for Magnoliaceae.

maguey (muh gay') *n.* The common name for any of several fleshy-leaved agaves, such as *Agave decumbre* and *Agave americana.*

mahoe (muh hoh') *n.* A common name for several different trees or shrubs, including *Hibiscus elatus, H. tiliaceus, Melicythus ramiflorus,* and *Thespesia populnea.* All these trees produce fibers. *H. elatus* is the blue mahoe, the national tree of Jamaica. Also known as maho.

mahogany (muh hahg'uh nee) *n.* A common name for the wood of many different trees that produce a desirable timber. Among these are *Swietenia Mahagoni* and *S. macrophylla,* both of which are no longer available due to excessive cutting.

mahogany birch (muh hahg'uh nee) *n.* A common name for *Betula lenta,* a source of wintergreen. Also known as cherry birch, sweet birch, black birch, and mountain mahogany.

mahogany family (muh hahg'uh nee) *n.* A common name for Meliaceae.

mahogany, swamp (muh hahg'uh nee) *n.* A common name for *Eucalyptus robusta,* a tall, big, strong tree. It grows to 90 feet, with rough, red-brown stringy bark, leathery, shiny, dark green leaves, masses of pink-tinted creamy-white flowers all year round, blooming most heavily in winter, and clusters of small, cylindrical seed capsules. Used as a screen or windbreak. Tolerates wind, sand, and saline soils.

mahogany, West Indies (muh hahg'uh nee) *n.* A common name for *Swietenia Mahagoni,* a tree much valued for its wood, but no longer available due to excessive cutting.

Mahonia (muh hoh'nee uh) *n.* A genus of more than 100 species of broadleaf evergreen shrubs (Berberidaceae), many species native to the Americas. They grow from 2 feet to 12 feet, depending on the species, with alternate leaves divided into an odd number of spiny-toothed, hollylike leaflets and with dense clusters of yellow flowers and clusters of blue, black, or red berries that attract birds. Useful in dry, shady situations. Used as specimen shrubs, foundation plantings, barrier or screen plantings, in Oriental gardens, and in containers. Commonly known as Oregon grape or holly grape.

Maianthemum (may an'thuh muhm) *n.* A genus of 3 species of hardy to very hardy low-growing bulbs (Liliaceae). *M. canadense* and *M. kamtschaticum* are native as far north as the Aleutians and the Northwest Territories. They grow from 6 inches to 14 inches, with rounded, pointed leaves and spikes of white flowers, sometimes fragrant. Used to naturalize in moist, shady places. Commonly known as false lily-of-the-valley.

Maianthemum
(false lily-of-the-valley)
a flower *b* fruit

maidenhair *n.* A common name for *Adiantum,* a large genus of 200 or more species of ferns, widely distributed, and great favorites in greenhouses on account of their delicate, lacy fronds. It includes the common maidenhair ferns, *A. Capillus-Veneris* and *A. pedatum,* the latter native to North America. They thrive best in temperatures between 60 and 65 F.

maidenhair tree *n.* A common name for *Ginkgo biloba,* a deciduous tree native to China. It is a graceful, hardy tree with distinctive, fan-shaped, light green leaves (similar to the leaflets of the maidenhair fern) that turn clear yellow in fall. The female trees produce quantities of nasty-smelling fruit; plant only male trees for ornamental use. Also called ginkgo. (See **Ginkgo**.)

leaf of maidenhair tree or *Ginkgo*

maiden pink *n.* A common name for *Dianthus deltoides,* a low-growing, hardy perennial flower. It forms mats of short leaves and has small scarlet, rose, pink, white, purple, or variegated flowers with sharply toothed petals that bloom in summer and often in fall as well. Used in flower beds.

maize (mayz) *n.* Corn, the plant *Zea Mays* of the grass family.

Malabar spinach (mal'uh bahr) *n.* A climbing vine, *Basella alba,* with fleshy leaves which can be cooked like spinach. The flavor is milder and because the leaves grow high above the ground, there is no sand clinging to them, as there often is to spinach. It is a tender annual that thrives in warm climates, but it can be grown in the north by starting the seeds indoors. The leaves are rich in vitamins A and C, as well as in iron and calcium.

Malachra (mal ah'kruh) *n.* A genus of 9 species of coarse, hairy, subtropical and tropical American annuals and perennials (Malvaceae). *M. radiata* grows to 8 feet, with deeply lobed leaves and heads of tiny pink flowers. Grown as a tender annual.

Malacothamnus (mal ah koh thahm'nuhs) *n.* A genus of 20 species of low, woody shrubs (Malvaceae) native to California and northern Baja California. They grow from 6 to 9 feet, depending on the species, with deeply lobed leaves and clusters of spikes of many-white-to-deep-mauve flowers.

Grown in mild climates. Commonly known as chaparral mallow.

Malacothrix (mal ah koh'thrihks) *n.* A genus of about 15 species of western North American woody plants (Compositae). *M. californica* grows to 12 inches, with woolly, finely divided basal leaves and stalks of small, solitary, pale yellow flowers with straplike petals.

malanga (muh lahn'guh) *n.* A common name for the genus *Xanthosoma* and *Colocasia esculenta*. Both are tropical plants grown primarily for their edible tuberous roots. Also grown ornamentally for their large, dramatic foliage.

malathion (mal uh thigh'ahn) *n.* A broad-spectrum, synthetic insecticide effective against a wide range of garden pests, including aphids, mites, and scale.

Malaxis (muh lak'sehs) *n.* A genus of about 300 species of terrestrial wild orchids (Orchidaceae). They have swollen bulbs at the base, 1 to 5 leaves, and spikes or clusters of small green flowers. Used in wild gardens. Commonly known as adder's mouth.

Malay apple (muh'lay) *n.* A common name for *Syzygium jambos* and *S. malaccensis,* both medium-sized tropical trees that produce edible fruit. *S. jambos* has long, narrow, glossy, dark green leaves, clusters of large greenish-white flowers with a long, showy stamen and fragrant, creamy-yellow, oval edible fruit used for jellies and confections. Also known as rose apple and Malabar plum. *S. malaccensis* has leathery, glossy, dark green leaves, clusters of showy, purplish-red flowers, and edible, pear-shaped brown fruit eaten raw or cooked. Considered one of the most beautiful of tropical trees. Also known as rose apple, large-fruited rose apple, pomerac jambos.

Malcolmia (mah kohl'mee uh) *n.* A genus of 25 to 30 species of Mediterranean annual and perennial flowers (Cruciferae). *M. maritima,* also known as virginian stock, is a summer annual that grows to 15 inches, with soft, bluish, oblong leaves and lightly fragrant, 4-petaled white, yellow, pink, lilac, and magenta flowers. Used as a bulb cover or in beds. Commonly known as malcolm stock.

male *a.* In botany, having flowers that have stamens only and do not produce fruit or seed.

maleberry *n.* A common name for *Lyonia ligust-rina,* a tender deciduous shrub native to southeastern North America. It grows to 12 feet or less, with widely variable leaves and clusters of white flowers. Useful in moist, shady situations; grown mainly in shrub collections. Also known as he-huckleberry and male blueberry.

male fern *n.* A common name for *Dryopteris Filix-mas,* a large, elegant, nearly evergreen fern with fronds growing in a crown. It has finely divided fronds 4 feet long, and some varieties are crested, crisped, forked, or dwarf.

mallow *n.* A common name for any plant of the genus *Malva,* or of the order Malvaceae, the mallow family.

mallow, curled *n.* A common name for *M. ver-ticillata,* a Eurasian plant with strongly crisped leaves, naturalized in the United States.

mallow family *n.* A common name for *Malvaceae.*

mallow, glade *n.* A common name for *Napaea dioica,* a coarse perennial with white flowers, often seen as a roadside weed in the Midwest.

mallow, globe *n.* A common name for the genus *Sphaeralcea,* perennial plants and small shrubs native to arid regions of the Americas. Also known as false mallow.

mallow, high *n.* A common name for *Malva sylvestris,* a European flower naturalized in the United States. Also known as cheeses.

mallow, marsh *n.* A common name for *Althaea officinalis,* a tall, erect, gray, velvety perennial wild-flower native to coastal marshes of the eastern United States. Also called white mallow.

mallow, musk *n.* A common name for *Malva mo-schata,* a leafy-branched, hairy perennial to 3 feet, with divided leaves and white or rose mauve flowers 1 to 2 inches across.

mallow, prairie *n.* A common name for *Sphaer-alcea coccinea,* a sprawling, hardy perennial native to North America, a wildflower from Manitoba to Texas and Arizona. It has gray-to-white furry leaves and short spikes of red-to-orange flowers. Also known as red false mallow.

mallow, rose *n.* A common name for the genus *Hibiscus,* especially *H. Moscheutos. H. Moscheutos* is a hardy perennial to 8 feet, with oval, toothed, deep green leaves, whitish beneath, and huge flowers up to 1 foot across in red, white, pink, or rose, often with a deep red eye. It has the largest flower of all hibiscus. The flowers need protection from wind. *H. Moscheutos* is also known as perennial hibiscus, swamp rose mallow, mallow rose, marsh mallow, and wild cotton.

mallow, tree *n.* A common name for *Lavatera ar-borea,* a biennial that often flowers the first year. It grows to 10 feet, with large, broad-lobed leaves, 9 inches long and as wide, and clusters of purple-red flowers with dark veins. Naturalized in coastal California.

mallow, Venice *n.* A common name for *Hibiscus Trionum,* an erect or straggling flower to 4 feet, with lobed leaves and white, cream, or yellow flowers with purple veins. It has naturalized in North America. Also known as flower-of-an-hour.

Malope (mal'uh pee) *n.* 1. A genus of 3 species of Mediterranean annuals (Malvaceae). *M. trifida* grows to 3 feet, with simple, rounded, typically 3-lobed leaves and large, showy white, rose, or purple flowers with a dark center. 2. [l.c.] A plant of this genus.

Malpighia (mal pihg'ee uh) *n.* A genus of 30 species of broadleaf evergreen tropical American shrubs and trees (Malpighiaceae). They grow to 10 feet, depending on the species, with opposite, simple leaves, sometimes covered with stinging hairs; clusters of white, rose, or red clawed flowers; and red, orange, scarlet, or purple fruit. Grown as ornamentals in tropical gardens. *M. glabra,* the Barbados cherry, is grown for its fruit.

Malpighiaceae (mal pihg ee ay'see ee) *n., pl* A family of 60 genera and 850 species of tropical vines, shrubs, and trees. The ornamental genera are *Bunchosia, Byrsonima, Galphimia, Gaudichaudia, Hiptage, Lophanthera, Malpighia, Mascagnia, Sphedamnocarpus, Stigmaphyllon,* and *Tirstellateia.*

Maltese cross *n.* A common name for *Lychnis chalcedonica,* a perennial that grows to 3 feet, with soft, furry leaves and stems and clusters of scarlet flowers with deeply cut petals.

Malus (may'luhs) _n._ A genus of about 25 species of small, much-branched, hardy deciduous shrubs and trees (Rosaceae); the apple and crabapple. They grow to 50 feet (most smaller), with soft, toothed leaves, masses of white flowers in clusters, and round, firm, red, yellow, or green edible apples or crabapples. In horticulture, _Malus_ usually refers to flowering crabapple, and apple refers to apple trees grown for their fruit. Grown for spring bloom, summer shade, fall fruit, autumn color, or all of the above. Commonly known as apple or crabapple trees.

Malva (mal'vuh) _n._ A genus of about 30 species of annual, biennial, or short-lived perennial plants (Malvaceae). They grow to 4 feet, with small, round, hollyhocklike leaves and white, pink, or purple saucerlike flowers. Used in the perennial border. Commonly known as mallow and musk mallow.

Malvaceae (mal vay'see ee) _n. pl._ A family of 95 genera of flowers, shrubs, and trees. Cotton (_Gossypium_), belongs to this order, as do also the hollyhock, the hibiscus, the abutilon, and nearly all the plants called mallows. Major genera include _Abelmoschus, Abutilon, Alcea_ (hollyhock), _Althea, Alogyne_ (blue hibiscus), _Anisodontea, Callirhoe, Gossypium_ (cotton), _Hibiscus, Hoheria, Iliamna, Lavatera, Malva,_ and _Sidalcea._

malvaceous (mal vay'shuhs) _a._ Pertaining or belonging to Malvaceae, the mallow family.

Malvaviscus (mal vav vihs'kuhs) _n._ A genus of 3 species of subtropical and tropical American vines, shrubs, and trees (Malvaceae). They have simple or lobed leaves and bright red tubular or trumpet-shaped flowers. Used as ornamentals, some of which have naturalized in Old World tropics and subtropics. Commonly known as sleepy mallow or wax mallow.

Mammea (muh mee'uh) _n._ A genus of 50 species of subtropical trees (Guttiferae). _M. Americana,_ native to the West Indies, is a tall tree, to 60 feet, with a thick, spreading head, opposite, simple leaves, showy, sweet-scented white flowers 1 inch across, and rough, russet-colored fruit with edible yellow flesh. The seeds are toxic. Grown in subtropical gardens for its fruit; in the French Antilles, a liqueur is distilled from the flowers. Commonly known as mamey, mammee, mammee apple, and South American apricot.

mammee sapota (suh poh'duh) _n._ A common name for _Pouteria sapota,_ a tropical tree grown for its edible fruit. Also known as sapota, sapote, mamey sapota, mamey colorado, marmalade plum, marmalade tree, and marmalade fruit.

Mammillaria (mam uh lah'ree uh) _n._ A genus of 150 species of low-growing, round-to-oblong, spiny cacti (Cactaceae), most native to Mexico. They grow to a few inches tall, with small, day-blooming, bell-shaped flowers in many colors including white-to-cream, reds, pinks, and yellows. Some varieties are woolly. This genus has received substantial taxonomic attention and currently consists of 6 subgenera and 6 sections. Widely collected, it is used in desert gardens, and in containers. Commonly known as pincushion or strawberry cactus.

mammillate (mam'uh layt) _a._ In botany, having nipple-shaped protuberances.

mammillation (mam uh lay'shuhn) _n._ 1. In botany, the state of having nipple-shaped protuberances. 2. A nipple-shaped protuberance.

mamoncillo (mahm uhn see'yoh) _n._ A common name for _Melicoccus bijugatus,_ a slow-growing tropical fruit tree. It grows to 60 feet, with divided, 6-inch long alternate leaves, small fragrant flowers, and small, round green edible fruit with a leathery rind. Used as a dooryard tree in South Florida and tropical gardens. Also known as Spanish lime, genip, genipe, and honeyberry.

mandarin orange (man'duh rihn) _n._ A common name for fruit varieties of _Citrus reticulata,_ including tangerines and Satsuma oranges; grown in Florida and the Gulf States and less in California.

Mandevilla (man duh vihl'uh) _n._ A genus of about 100 species of tropical vines and flowers with milky sap (Apocynaceae). They have opposite or whorled entire, sometimes sticky, leaves and spikes of day-blooming trumpet-shaped flowers. _M. splendens_ 'Alice du Pont' is a beautiful, tender, twining vine to 30 feet, with big, glossy, oval leaves and clusters of large, hot-pink, trumpet-shaped flowers that bloom spring through fall. Used in warm-climate gardens or in greenhouses anywhere.

Mandragora (man drag′uh ruh) *n.* A genus of 6 species of hardy perennial plants and vines (Solanaceae) with thick or tuberous roots; the mandrake. *M. officinarum* grows to 12 inches, with often branching roots, large oval leaves, and small greenish-yellow flowers. Once believed to have magical properties, the roots contain the poison hyoscyamine. Commonly known as mandrake.

Mandragora
(mandrake)

mandrake (man′drayk) *n.* A common name for the plant *Mandragora officinarum,* which has been regarded as an aphrodisiac and a medicinal plant for centuries.

manetti (manet′ee) *n.* In horticulture, a variety of rose used as a grafting understock, specifically *Rosa chinensis.* The name comes from Saverio Manetti (1784), an Italian botanist.

Manettia (muh nehd′ee uh) *n.* A genus of more than 100 species of flowers and twining vines (Rubiaceae) native to tropical America. They have opposite, notched or fringed leaves and bright red, yellow, or white firecracker-shaped flowers. Used as an indoor/outdoor plant or in greenhouses.

Manfreda (man free′duh) *n.* A genus of fewer than 20 species of low-growing American succulents (Agavaceae) native to the southwestern United States and to Mexico. They grow from a rhizome and have 1 or more rosettes of thick, fleshy leaves and tall spikes of large pink, red, white, or yellow flowers; some species are fragrant. Commonly known as false aloe.

mangel-wurzel (mang′guhl wer′zuhl) *n.* A variety of beet, *Beta vulgaris,* producing a larger and coarser root than the garden beet; it is extensively cultivated as food for cattle.

manger basket *n.* A trough-shaped wire frame, generally lined with moss, used for growing decorative plants.

Mangifera (man jihf′uh ruh) *n.* A genus of about 40 species of subtropical trees (Anacardiaceae); the mango. *M. indica* is a handsome tree that grows to

90 feet and spreads to 125 feet. It has stiff, long, narrow, pointed leaves, clusters of small pinkish-white or reddish-yellow flowers, and fragrant, edible, tough-skinned fruit that is variable in shape, size, and color — usually oval, 3 to 5 inches, and red, green, or yellow. In the tropics, it is a prodigious producer of fruit; in subtropical frost-free climates, the size of the tree and the fruit crop are much diminished. Commonly known as mango.

Mangifera indica
(mango)
a flowering branch *b* fruit

mango *n.* 1. The juicy, sweet, and slightly acid fruit of the mango tree. 2. The tree that produces mangos.

mangosteen (man′goh steen) *n.* A common name for an important tropical fruit tree, *Garcinia Mangostana,* native to Malay. It has opposite, simple, usually thick leaves and a fleshy, edible fruit with a thick rind. It does not fruit outside the tropics. The term is used for the fruit as well, which is also called mangostine.

mangrove (man′grohv) *n.* A common name for *Rhizophora Mangle,* a subtropical tree native to South Florida and tropical America. It grows along seashores, in salty or brackish water, to 40 feet and has blunt oval or elliptic opposite leaves, large, leathery, yellow flowers, and small fruit. It is unusual in its development of many adventitious roots, which arch out from the lower part of the trunk and hang down from the branches; it is also curious in that its seed germinates in the fruit, sending down a long root into the mud, sometimes a distance of several feet, before dropping from the parent tree. Used to stabilize shorelines; ecologically critical as a habitat for birds, fish, and crustaceans. Also known as American mangrove.

mangrove

mangrove, button (man'grohv) *n.* A common name for the genus *Conocarpus,* tropical trees that grow in mangrove swamps of North and South America and Africa. They have alternate, simple, leathery leaves and conelike heads of minute flowers.

Manihot (man'uh haht) *n.* A genus of about 160 species of plants, shrubs, and trees (Euphorbiaceae) native to North and South America. *M. esculenta* is a shrub to 9 feet, with milky sap, deeply lobed leaves, and small, 6-angled, winged fruit. The roots, which are the source of tapioca, are poisonous until cooked. *M. esculent* is commonly known as tapioca, cassava, manioc, bitter cassava, sweet-potato tree, and yucca.

Manilkara (man uh kar'ruh) *n.* A genus of 85 species of tropical broadleaf evergreen trees with milky sap (Sapotaceae). They grow to 100 feet or more, with thick, alternate leaves, small, whitish flowers, and large-seeded fruit. *M. zapota,* also known as sapodilla, is an attractive ornamental, widely grown in the tropics for its edible fruit; its milky sap is chicle, the original base for chewing gum.

manioc (man'ee ahk) *n.* The cassava plant or its product. The manioc, or cassava, is a very important food staple in tropical America.

manjack *n.* A large West Indian tree of the species *Cordia elliptica* or *C. macrophylla.*

manna gum (mah'nuh) *n.* A common name for *Eucalyptus viminalis,* a tender Australian tree. It grows to 150 feet, with a white trunk, peeling bark, drooping, willowlike branches with long, narrow, light green leaves, flowers that bloom year-round (usually too high to be seen), and pea-sized, roundish seed capsules. Best used as a sentinel tree, on large ranches, along highways, or in parks; not for small gardens or for planting close to your house, as it exudes a gummy secretion that is extremely deleterious to the finish on cars.

manroot *n.* A common name for *Ipomoea leptophylla,* a North American morning glory with an immense tuberous root (resembling a man in shape), native to dry areas of Nebraska and Wyoming, south to Texas and New Mexico. It grows to 4 feet, with long, narrow, entire leaves and large pink or purple flowers to 3 inches across. Also known as bush morning glory, bush moonflower, man-of-the-earth, and wild potato-vine.

manure fork (muh nyoo'uhr) *n.* A 4- to 10-tined fork similar to a pitchfork; useful in moving heavy loads, as in a compost pile. The tines of a manure fork are longer, finer, and more closely spaced than those of a pitchfork. (See also **pitchfork** and **spading fork**.)

manzanita (man zuh need'uh) *n.* A common name for the genus *Arctostaphylos,* as well as many of its species, native to the western United States. Also a common name for *A. Manzanita,* a shrub or small tree to 12 feet and taller, with shiny, broadly oval leaves, open, drooping clusters of white-to-pink flowers, and red berrylike fruit. Grown in loose, well-drained soil in woodland or wild gardens. Also known as bearberry.

maple *n.* A common name for trees of the genus *Acer,* about 200 species of mostly deciduous trees and shrubs native to northern temperate regions. Maples have opposite, usually palmate, leaves, inconspicuous flowers, and double-winged seed capsules. Many maples are widely cultivated for shade and ornament, and others are valuable for their timber. Among the most useful in the garden are the *A. palmatum* (Japanese maple), *A. circinatum* (vine maple), and *A. rubrum* (scarlet maple). Maple syrup and maple sugar are made in North America from the sap of *A. saccharum,* the native sugar maple.

maple, Amur (ah mwa'uhr) *n.* A common name for *Acer Ginnala,* a hardy deciduous shrub or small tree, usually multitrunked. It grows to 20 feet, with 3-lobed, toothed leaves, which turn a striking scarlet in autumn, and clusters of small, yellow, fragrant flowers, followed by handsome, bright red, winged fruit. Used as a multitrunked tree that does best with winter cold.

maple, ash-leaved *n.* A common name for *Acer Negundo,* a widely cultivated, much hybridized, hardy North American deciduous tree to 50 or 70 feet, with light green or variegated leaves that turn brilliant yellow in autumn. Native from Saskatchewan to California and south to Guatemala, from New England south to Florida, it is widely naturalized in Quebec and the Maritime Provinces of Canada. Commonly known as box elder. Despite its wide adaptation, other maples are preferable in the garden, as *A. Negundo* self-sows prolifically, hosts box-elder bugs, suckers badly, and breaks easily.

maple, big-leaf *n.* A common name for *Acer macrophyllum,* a fine species native from California to southeast Alaska. It grows to 100 feet, with large, deeply lobed leaves, to 15 inches wide, that turn a clear yellow in autumn. Too large for small gardens or as a street tree; excellent in moist soils of large woodland gardens or along streams.

maple, coliseum red *n.* A common name for *Acer cappadocicum* 'Rubrum', a hardy deciduous tree with a compact, rounded crown. It grows to 70 feet, usually much less, with bright red spring foliage, that turns rich, dark green in summer.

maple, David's *n.* A common name for *Acer Davidii,* a hardy deciduous tree. It grows from 20 to 50 feet and has pointed oval-to-oblong leaves that turn bright orange, yellow, or purple in fall and showy clusters of greenish-yellow flowers in spring.

maple, evergreen *n.* A common name for *Acer oblongum,* a hardy deciduous tree, evergreen in mild-winter climates. It grows from 20 to 50 feet, with bronzy-pink new growth and long, narrow, shiny, deep green oval leaves.

maple family *n.* A common name for *Aceraceae.*

maple, flowering *n.* A common name for *Abutilon,* a genus of flowering shrubs. (See **Abutilon**.)

maple, Formosan (fawr moh'suhn) *n.* A common name for *A. morrisonense,* a fast-growing, upright deciduous tree. It grows to 30 or 40 feet, with greenish bark striped with white and large 3-lobed leaves that emerge red in spring, turn light green in summer, and bright red in autumn. Used as a specimen tree. Will not tolerate high heat, dry soil, or wind. Also known as Mt. Morrison maple.

maple, full-moon (ma'pl, ful-mune') *n.* A common name for *Acer japonicum,* a small, slow-growing, shrublike tree with nearly round 2-to-5-inch-long many-lobed leaves. *A.j.* 'Acontifolium', the fernleaf full-moon maple, has deeply cut leaves with toothed lobes and good fall color. *A.j.* 'Aureum', golden full-moon maple, has pale gold new leaves that become a delicate chartreuse in summer.

maple, hedge *n.* A common name for *Acer campestre,* a deciduous shrub or round-headed tree to 35 feet or more, with corky twigs and lobed leaves that turn clear yellow in fall. There are several cultivars. Grows best in high-rainfall climates, such as those of England and the Pacific Northwest. Also known as field maple.

maple, Japanese *n.* A common name for two small species; including *Acer japonicum* and *A. palmatum. A. palmatum,* the most widely grown, has hundreds of superb cultivars. It is a very hardy, slow-growing, deciduous tree to 20 feet, often multistemmed. The most airy and delicate of all maples, it is a choice garden tree, with excellent shape, silhouette, and fall color. The new growth is glowing red, the summer leaves are soft green, and the fall foliage is scarlet, orange, or yellow. Its slender red or green branches make a lovely winter pattern. Will tolerate cold, but not wind or saline soils. Essential in Oriental gardens, superb in containers, the most frequently grown bonsai subject—an all-around wonderful tree.

maple, Norway *n.* A common name for *Acer platanoides,* a very adaptable, widely grown, hardy large tree, to 60 feet or more, with many cultivars. It has glossy, 5-lobed, sharply pointed leaves, showy upright clusters of flowers that appear in spring before the leaves, and bright yellow fall color. It has voracious roots, both deep and surface, and it attracts aphids, which lead to honeydew drip and sooty mold.

maple, paperbark *n.* A common name for *Acer griseum,* a slow-growing, hardy deciduous tree. It grows to 20 feet or more, with attractive, cinnamon-brown peeling bark, leaves divided into 3 small, coarsely toothed leaflets that turn bright red and orange in autumn, and showy winged seeds. Grown as a specimen for its unusual and appealing bark and striking winter silhouette.

maple, red *n.* A common name for *Acer rubrum,* a hardy deciduous North American tree, native from Newfoundland to Florida, west to Minnesota and Texas. It grows to 120 feet, usually much less, with 3- to 5-lobed leaves that turn brilliant scarlet in autumn. Used as a lawn, park, or street tree. Also known as scarlet maple, swamp maple, or soft maple.

maple, rock *n.* A common name for *Acer saccharum,* a hardy North American tree native to the United States and Canada east of the Rockies. It grows to 130 feet, usually much smaller, with 5-lobed, hand-shaped leaves that turn yellow and red in fall, which are spectacular in cold regions. Used as a lawn, park, street, or shade tree. In the northeast, it is tapped for maple sap that is made into maple syrup and maple sugar. Also known as sugar maple and hard maple.

maple, Rocky Mountain *n.* A common name for *Acer glabrum,* a hardy deciduous shrub or small tree native to the western United States from southeast Alaska east to South Dakota, south to California and New Mexico. It grows to 30 feet, often less, with dark red twigs and 3- to 5-lobed leaves, or leaves divided into 3 leaflets, that turn yellow in fall. Grows best in the mountains; generally forms a multistemmed clump.

maple, silver *n.* A common name for *Acer saccharinum,* a hardy deciduous North American tree. It is a graceful, fast-growing, open tree from 40 to 130 feet with equal spread. It has sharply cut leaves, silvery beneath, that in autumn turn red, orange, and yellow, sometimes in the same leaf. It has problems in the garden, developing chlorosis in alkaline soils, attracting aphids, which subsequently cause honeydew drip and sooty mold, and it breaks easily. Also known as white maple, soft maple, and river maple.

maple, soft *n.* A common name for both *Acer rubrum* (red maple) and *A. saccharinum* (silver maple).

maple, Southern sugar *n.* A common name for *Acer barbatum,* a hardy North American tree native from Virginia to Florida and west to Texas. It grows to 50 feet, with gray or purple twigs and small 3- to 5-lobed leaves. Also known as sugar tree and Florida maple.

maple, striped *n.* A common name for *Acer pensylvanicum,* a very hardy small, slender tree, native to the eastern United States and southeastern Canada. It grows from 15 to 35 feet, with light green bark conspicuously striped with white lines, and large, rounded, 3- lobed leaves that turn clear yellow in fall. Also known as moosewood, whistlewood, and Pennsylvania maple.

maple, sugar *n.* A common name for *Acer saccharum,* a hardy North American tree of noble appearance, native to the United States and Canada east of the Rockies. It grows to 130 feet, usually much smaller, with 5-lobed, hand-shaped leaves that turn spectacular shades of gold, orange, scarlet, or crimson in autumn. Used as a lawn, park, street, or shade tree. In the northeast, it is tapped for maple sap that is made into richly flavored maple syrup and maple sugar. Also known as rock maple and hard maple. *A.s. grandidentatum,* native from the mountains of Montana and Wyoming to northern Mexico, is known as bigtooth maple.

maple, swamp *n.* Same as red maple, a common name for *Acer rubrum.*

maple, sycamore (sihk′uh moh uhr) *n.* A common name for *Acer pseudo-platanus,* a hardy deciduous tree. It grows to 100 feet, with large, 5-lobed yellow-green leaves that are undistinguished in fall color. Numerous cultivars offer a wide variety of summer leaf colors and patterns including stripes, spots, dots, and blotches in several shades of green, yellow, pink, and red. Also known as mock plane and sycamore.

maple, trident *n.* A common name for *Acer Buergeranum,* a hardy, deciduous, low, spreading tree. It grows to 50 feet, often much less, with glossy, 3-lobed leaves, pale beneath, that usually turn red, sometimes orange or yellow in fall. Used as a patio tree and a much-favored bonsai subject.

maple, vine *n.* A common name for *Acer circinatum,* a hardy small, slender, sprawling, airy, delicate-looking deciduous shrub or tree native to western North America from British Columbia to northern California. It grows to 35 feet, with 5-

to 11-lobed leaves that turn orange, scarlet, or yellow in fall. Untrimmed, it forms natural bowers and creates a woodland effect; trained, it can be espaliered against a shady wall. In open, sunny situations, it loses its vinelike characteristics. Also known as Canada moonseed.

maqui (mah kee′) *n.* A common name for *Aristotelia chilensis,* a broadleaf evergreen shrub. It grows to 7 feet, with shiny, toothed, sometimes variegated, leaves, small green flowers, and berrylike edible fruit. Used as in mild-winter gardens.

Maranta (muh ran′tuh) *n.* A genus of 20 tropical American perennials (Marantaceae). They are clump-forming plants that grow from 15 inches to 6 feet, depending on the species, with variably shaped, sometimes spotted, leaves that fold upward at night and with inconspicuous flowers and fruit. Used primarily as houseplants.

marasca (muh ras′kuh) *n.* A small black wild cherry, a variety of *Prunus avium,* from which the liquer maraschino is distilled.

Marattia (muh rad′ee uh) *n.* A genus of 60 species of large tropical and temperate ferns *(Marattiaceae).* They have thick, short stems and glossy, dark-green fronds that grow from 4 to 15 feet long, depending on species, divided 2 or 3 times into leaflets. Not generally available in nurseries, but sometimes grown ornamentally in Hawaii.

marcescent (mahr sehs′uhnt) *a.* Of a plant part, withering but not falling off.

Marcgravia (mahrk gray′vee uh) *n.* A genus of 45 species of mostly epiphytic, tropical American climbing vines (Marcgraviaceae) native to the West Indies. *M. rectiflora* grows to 40 feet, with oblong, pointed leaves and clusters of small flowers. Commonly known as shingle plant.

Marcgraviaceae (mahrk gray vee ay′see ee) *n. pl.* A family of 5 genera of climbing, often epiphytic, vines. The only genus grown ornamentally is *Marcgravia.*

mare's tail *n.* A common name for *Hippuris vulgaris,* a rarely grown bog plant that thrives only in deep or running water. It has whorled, long, narrow, entire, firm leaves above water and larger, flaccid, submerged leaves and bears flowers on stalks up to several feet long.

mare's tail, flowering branch

marginal farmland *n.* 1. Surface soil only a few inches deep. 2. Land repeatedly farmed without benefit of humus or chemical replacements.

margosa (mahr goh′suh) *n.* A common name for *Melia Azedarach,* a tender deciduous large shrub or tree. (See **Melia.**)

marguerite (mahr′gyuh reet) *n.* 1. A common name for *Chrysanthemum frutescens,* a bushy, woody-based perennial, grown as an annual in cold climates. It grows to 3 feet, with coarsely divided, bright green leaves and an abundance of white, yellow, or pink daisylike flowers 2 inches across. Used in borders, massed in beds, and excellent in containers. Also known as Paris daisy. 2. A common name for *C. Leucanthemum,* a slender, erect perennial that has naturalized as a weed in the United States. It grows to 3 feet, with white daisylike flowers on long stems. Also known as oxeye daisy, white daisy, and whiteweed. 3. A common name for *Bellis perennis,* a low-growing perennial flower, often grown as an annual. Formerly grown mainly in lawns, it has been hybridized into fully double varieties that form clumps, with many-petaled pink, rose, red, or white flowers on 6-inch stems. Used for edging, low bedding, or in meadow gardens. Does not tolerate poor soil, hot sun, or dry conditions. Also known as English daisy.

marguerite, blue (mahr′gyuh reet) *n.* A common name for *Felicia amelloides,* a somewhat rangy annual. It grows to 3 feet, with entire, opposite leaves and masses of small, blue daisylike flowers. Used in borders, beds, and in containers. Also known as blue daisy.

marguerite, golden (mahr′gyuh reet) *n.* A common name for *Anthemis tinctoria,* a bushy biennial or short-lived perennial. It grows to 3 feet, with downy, erect angular stems, finely divided leaves, which are smooth above, white and woolly beneath, and golden-yellow daisylike flowers 2 inches across. Used in the summer border and in traditional cottage and herb gardens. Also known as dog fennel and chamomile.

Margyricarpus (mahr jigh rih kar′puhs) *n.* A genus of 10 species of evergreen South American shrubs (Rosaceae) native to the Andes. *M. setosus* grows to 12 inches, with small, narrow, alternate leaves and small, green flowers with dark red anthers and small, white berrylike fruit. Used in rock gardens in mild-winter climates. Commonly known as pearl fruit, pear fruit, pearlberry.

marigold (mar′uh gohld) *n.* 1. A common name for the genus *Tagetes,* annual or perennial flowers native to the Americas. They have divided leaves and many-petaled yellow, orange, or red-brown flowers. The short French marigold (*T. patula* hybrids) grows to 18 inches and is widely used as an edging plant or in containers. African marigolds (*T. erecta* hybrids) grow to 3 or 4 feet and are used in borders, beds, or in containers. Both French and African marigolds are grown with vegetables as companion plants to discourage nematodes. African marigold is also known as Aztec marigold and American marigold. 2. A common name for *Calendula officinalis,* an annual self-sowing flower that grows to 2 feet, with long, narrow, sticky, aromatic leaves and double daisylike yellow, orange, apricot, and cream-colored flowers. Used in borders, beds, and containers; traditional in cottage gardens. Blooms from fall to spring in mild-winter climates; otherwise, summer through fall. Also known as pot marigold.

marigold, corn (mar′uh gohld) *n.* A common name for *Chrysanthemum segetum,* an erect annual that has naturalized in the United States and South America. It grows to 2 feet, with oval, finely divided leaves and golden-yellow flowers more than 2 inches across. Also known as corn chrysanthemum.

marigold, fetid (mar′uh gohld) *n.* A common name for the genus *Dyssodia,* strongly scented annual or perennial flowers and subshrubs native to the southwestern United States and to Mexico. *D. tenuiloba* is the only species grown ornamentally. It is a spreading, bushy, self-sowing annual or perennial that grows to 12 inches, with sticky, divided, threadlike leaves and daisylike golden-orange flowers with yellow centers. Used as a bedding plant for its long season of bloom. It is widely naturalized in warm climates. Also known as Dahlberg daisy and golden-fleece.

marigold, fig (mar′uh gohld) *n.* (See **Mesembryanthemum**.)

marigold, pot (mar′uh gohld) *n.* A common name for *Calendula officinalis.* (See **marigold**.)

marigold, signet (mar′uh gohld, sihg′neht) *n.* A common name for *Tagetes tenuifolia,* a slender annual flower. It grows to 2 feet, with leaves divided into narrow, pointed leaflets and with masses of small yellow flowers.

marigold, sweet-scented (mar′uh gohld) *n.* A common name for *Tagetes lucida,* a perennial usually grown as an annual. It grows to 30 inches, with long, narrow, simple leaves and clusters of many small yellow flowers. Also known as sweet mace.

marijuana (mar uh wahn′uh) *n.* A common name for *Cannabis sativa,* an erect shrub with long, toothed leaves and spikes or panicles of flowers. Best known for its hallucinatory properties, it is illegal to grow in the United States. Commonly known as pot, bhang, and hemp.

marine ivy *n.* A common name for *Cissus incisus,* a stout North American scrambling or climbing semideciduous or evergreen vine. It grows enthusiastically, with 3-lobed or trifoliate leaves divided into oval leaflets, rounded clusters of flowers, and small black fruit. Used as a ground cover or to cover latticework in frost-free climates: the Boston ivy of subtropical gardens. Also known as marine vine and possum grape.

marjoram (mahr′juh ruhm) *n.* A plant of the genus *Origanum,* of several species, belonging to the same family as mint. Sweet marjoram, *O. Majorana,* a perennial plant with small white blossoms, is peculiarly aromatic and flavorful, and is much used in cookery. Common or wild marjoram, *O. vulgare,* also a perennial plant, has small pink flowers. Nurseries commonly confuse the 2 varieties.

market garden *n.* A garden in which vegetables and fruits are raised for the market.

market gardener *n.* One who raises vegetables and fruits for sale.

marking plow *n.* In agriculture, a plow used for making small furrows to serve as guides in various operations, as in plowed land for planting corn, or in a field to be marked out for planting an orchard.

marl (mahrl) *n.* An earthy deposit consisting mainly of calcium carbonate; used for liming acid soil.

marlberry (mahrl beh'ree) *n.* A common name for *Ardisia escallonoides,* a large shrub or small tree native to south Florida, the West Indies, and Mexico. It grows to 20 feet, with large, pointed leaves, white flowers, and small black, glossy fruit.

marmalade plum *n.* A common name for *Pouteria sapota,* a tropical tree grown for its edible fruit. Also known as sapota, sapote, mamey sapota, mamey colorado, mammee sapota, marmalade tree, and marmalade fruit. Also, the name for the fruit.

marrow *n.* 1. The pith of plants. 2. The pulp of fruits. 3. In England, the name for a zucchini; also called vegetable marrow.

Marrubium (muh roo'bee uhm) *n.* A genus of 30 species of whitish, woolly, bitter, aromatic herbs (Labiatae); hoarhound. They have square stems branching from the base to 18 inches. *M. vulgare,* common hoarhound, has broadly rounded oval wrinkled leaves and small white flowers in whorled clusters on stalks. Naturalized in North America. Traditional in cottage and herb gardens; formerly used in medicine and old-fashioned candies. Commonly known as white hoarhound.

Marsdenia (mahrz dee'nee uh) *n.* A genus of more than 100 species of subtropical twining vines (Asclepiadaceae). *M. roylei* has soft, downy new growth with heart-shaped pointed leaves, often downy beneath, and small clusters of bell-shaped flowers and fruit.

marsh bellflower *n.* A common name for *Campanula aparinoides,* a North American wildflower found in bogs and wet meadows. It has small blue or white bell-shaped flowers and is rather weedy in appearance.

marsh cinquefoil (sihngk'fawl) *n.* The common name for *Potentilla palustris,* a hardy perennial North American and Eurasian wildflower. It has creeping stems, with leaves divided into notched leaflets, often hairy beneath, and loose clusters of red-to-purple flowers. Also called marsh five-finger.

marsh elder *n.* A common name for *Viburnum Opulus,* a very hardy deciduous large shrub. It grows to 20 feet, with large, soft, maplelike dark green leaves that turn a beautiful red in autumn; clusters, 4 inches in diameter, of white flowers, with sterile flowers creating a lace-cap effect; and large red, showy fruit. *V.O.* 'Roseum', the common snowball bush, is a sterile hybrid. Used as a specimen shrub in cold-winter regions. Also known as Guelder rose, European cranberry, cranberry bush, and whitten tree.

marsh fern *n.* A common name for *Rumohra adantiaformis,* a tropical terrestrial or epiphytic fern. It has broadly triangular lacy fronds 3 feet long. Widely used by florists for cut foliage. Also known as ten-day fern, iron fern, and leatherleaf fern.

marsh five-finger *n.* A commone name for *Pontentilla palustris,* a hardy perennial North American wildflower. (See **marsh cinquefoil**.)

marsh-mallow *n.* A common name for *Hibiscus moscheutos palustris,* a hardy perennial. (See **mallow, rose**.)

marsh-mallow

marsh marigold (mar'uh gohld) *n.* A common name for *Caltha palustris,* a golden-flowered bog plant with stout, creeping rootstocks, lush green, rounded, heart-shaped leaves, and showy yellow flowers, having sepals but not petals. Used in moist soils and in bog gardens. Also known as cowslip.

marsh pennywort *n.* A common name for *Hydrocotyle vulgaris,* a creeping ground cover with round, wrinkled leaves and rounded clusters of 3 to 5 purplish-green flowers. Used as a ground cover in moist situations. Also known as water pennywort and navelwort.

marsh tea *n.* A common name for *Ledum palustre,* a very hardy evergreen shrub. It grows to 3 feet, with small, entire, leathery, alternate leaves, rusty and furry beneath. Useful in cold-climate evergreen borders; does well in sandy or peaty moist soils. Also known as crystal tea and wild rosemary.

marsh trefoil (tree'foil) *n.* The common name of the *Menyanthes trifoliata* (Gentianaceae, Menyanthaceae), a bog plant native to the more temperate parts of the Northern Hemisphere. Used in bog gardens. Also called buckbean.

Marsilea (mahr sihl'ee uh) *n.* A genus of about 65 species of aquatic ferns (Marsilaceae). They grow from rhizomes on land or in water, with leaves that look like 4-leaf clover. In water, the leaves float; on land, they are erect. Used in water gardens, as pot plants, and in greenhouses. Commonly known as pepperwort and water clover.

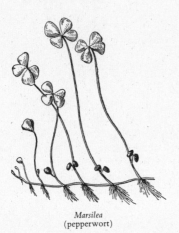

Marsilea
(pepperwort)

Marsileaceae (mahr sihl ee ay'see ee) *n. pl.* A family of 3 genera and 70 species of aquatic or amphibious herbaceous ferns that grow from rhizomes. They have 2- or 4-parted leaves on long, threadlike stems. The ornamental genera are *Marsilea* and *Pilularia.*

marvel-of-Peru *n.* A common name for *Mirabilis Jalapa,* a shrubby, tuberous, perennial native to tropical America, grown as an annual in cold climates. It grows to 3 feet high and as wide, with deep green, oval leaves and red, white, yellow, or variegated funnel-shaped flowers that open only toward evening or on cloudy, overcast days. Also known as four-o'clock and beauty-of-the-night.

marygold (meh'ree gohld) *n.* An alternative spelling of marigold. (See **marigold**.)

Mary Washington *n.* A hardy disease-resistant variety of asparagus.

Masdevallia (mas duh val'ee uh) *n.* A genus of 300 species of tropical American epiphytic orchids (Orchidaceae). They have 1 long, leathery, narrow leaf and spikes of 1 or many loosely clustered flowers, which are of medium size, have very small petals, and are beautifully marked and colored. Grown in cool greenhouses, mostly by collectors.

mask-flower *n.* A common name for the genus *Alonsoa,* tropical American annual or perennial flowers or shrubs. They grow to 3 feet, have 4-sided stems, leaves opposite or in threes, and spikes of showy, deep orange, red, or scarlet flowers with a black or dark purple throat. Grown as annuals in summer, as houseplants in winter.

masterwort *n.* 1. A common name for *Heracleum Sphondylium,* a tall biennial or perennial plant (Umbelliferae) native to North America; American cow parsnip. It has large, deeply cut, toothed leaves, often downy beneath, and umbrella-shaped clusters of small green, pink, yellow, or white flowers. An impressively large plant, growing to 9 feet, it is usually seen growing wild but is occasionally used in wild gardens or as a specimen plant for its bold effect. The foliage may cause a skin rash. 2. A common name for *Archangelica atropurpurea,* which grows to 6 feet, with dark purple stems, 3-part leaves, and rounded clusters, 10 inches across, of white flowers. Formerly grown in cottage and herb gardens. Also known as great angelica and alexanders.

Matricaria (mat ruh kah'ree uh) *n*. A genus of 35 species of annual, biennial, or perennial flowers (Compositae), often aromatic. *M. recutita*, commonly known as chamomile, grows to 30 inches, with finely cut, rather fernlike leaves and small, daisylike white and yellow flowers. The dried flowers are used to make a soothing herbal tea. Traditional in herb gardens and cottage gardens. The genus is commonly known as matricary. The plants, sold in nurseries as *Mat-*

Matricaria
(chamomile)

ricaria 'White Stars', 'Golden Ball', and 'Snowball', are varieties of *Chrysanthemum parthenium*. The chamomile sold as an aromatic ground cover is *Chamaemelum nobile (Anthemis nobilis)*; its flowers yield a rather bitter tea.

matrimony vine *n*. A common name for *Lycium*, a genus of tender or tropical, erect or clambering, sometimes spiny, woody vines (Solanaceae). They grow from 7 to 10 feet, depending on the species, with clustered, narrow, entire, alternate leaves, narrow, bell-shaped, green, white, or purple flowers, and scarlet berries. Grown in warm-climate gardens; they tolerate a wide variety of soils. Also known as box thorn.

matrimony-vine, common *n*. A common name for *Lycium halimifolium*, a hardy, generally woody, vine with arching or spreading branches that has naturalized in eastern North America. It grows to 10 feet long with small, narrow leaves and small, dull lilac-purple flowers.

Matteuccia (mad ee ooch'ee uh) *n*. A genus of 3 species of large, bold, hardy ferns (Polypodiaceae). They have fronds 6 to 9 feet long that are long and sterile, making a vaselike crown around the shorter, inner fertile fronds. Used as a striking specimen or in the wild garden. Commonly known as ostrich fern.

Matthiola (muh thigh'uh luh) *n*. A genus of 50 species of annuals, perennials, or subshrubs (Cruciferae). They grow to 30 inches, with soft, gray, long, narrow, variably shaped leaves and with spikes of clusters of lilac, purple, or white flowers. *M. longipetala bicornis*, evening scented stock, is wonderfully fragrant at night. Used in beds and borders. A long-lasting cut flower. Commonly known as stock.

mattock *n*. A pickaxlike tool used to loosen soil, pull up rocks, or remove deep-rooted weeds.

mature soil *n*. Any soil with well-developed soil horizons.

Mauritia (mawr rihsh'ee uh) *n*. A genus of 16 species of tropical American fan palms (Palmae) bearing a crown of enormous fan-shaped leaves that grow in standing water or where there is a high water table. *M. flexuosa* grows to 100 feet; it has leaves to 20 feet long, cylindrical leaf stems to 13 feet long and blades to 6 feet long, 4-foot long flowers, and fruit 2 inches around. *M. flexuosa* is commonly known as tree-of-life, ita palm, morichi palm, or miriti palm.

Maxillaria (mak suh lah'ree uh) *n*. A genus of about 400 species of tropical American epiphytic orchids (Orchidaceae). They are extremely variable in size, shape, and flower form. Grown in a shaded greenhouse.

maximum-minimum thermometer *n*. An instrument used to measure and record the high and low temperatures each day.

Mayapple

may apple *n*. A common name for *Podophyllum peltatum*, a hardy North American perennial, native from Quebec to Florida and Texas. It grows from creeping rhizomes to 18 inches, with 5- to 9-lobed leaves, 1 foot across, large, waxy, white flowers, and red or yellow edible fruit. Used in shady places in the wild garden. Also known as Mayapple, mandrake, wild lemon, raccoonberry, and wild jalap.

May blob *n.* A common name for *Caltha palustris,* a golden-flowered bog plant with stout, creeping rootstocks, lush green, rounded, heart-shaped leaves, and showy yellow flowers, having sepals but no petals. Used in moist soils and in bog gardens. Also known as cowslip and marsh marigold.

Maybloom *n.* A common name for the genus *Crataegus,* thorny shrubs or small trees, much used in hedges. They have stiff branches bearing strong thorns, small, deeply lobed or cut leaves, masses of white or pink flowers in spring, and red berries in winter. The fruit is the haw, which attracts birds. Also known as hawthorn, Maythorn, and maybush. (See **Crataegus**.)

May blossom *n.* A common name for *Convallaria majalis,* the lily-of-the-valley, a perennial stemless herb, with a creeping rootstock, 2 or 3 leaves, and a many-flowered stalk of fragrant white, drooping, bell-shaped flowers. It has naturalized in eastern North America. Ornamentally, it is used as a small-scale ground cover in shady places and forced from pips in pots for early bloom. Also called may lily.

maybush *n.* The hawthorn or whitethorn.

May cherry *n.* A common name for *Amelanchier,* a genus of small trees and shrubs native to northern temperate zones, having clusters of showy white flowers, alternate, toothed leaves, and small dark purple or black fruits. Commonly known as serviceberry, shadblow, and Mayduke.

Mayduke *n.* A variety of sour cherry.

Mayflower *n.* A name for any of several flowers that bloom in May, including hawthorn (*Crataegus*), cuckooflower (*Cardamine pratensis*), marsh marigold (*Caltha palustris*), and trailing arbutus (*Epigaea repens*).

mayflower, Canada *n.* A common name for *Maianthemum canadense,* native as far north as the MacKenzie River region of the Northwest Territories. It grows from 6 inches to 14 inches, with rounded, pointed leaves and with spikes of white flowers, sometimes fragrant. Used to naturalize in moist, shady places. Commonly known as false lily-of-the-valley.

Mayhaw *n.* A small tree, *Crataegus,* of the United States, frequently transported from the wild. Its fruit is used for preserves, jellies, etc. Also called apple haw.

maypop *n.* A common name for *Passiflora incarnata,* the passionflower, or its fruit. The fruit, which is the size of a hen's egg, is edible but insipid.

mayten (migh'tehn) *n.* A common name for *Maytenus Boaria,* a dainty, graceful evergreen tree with long, draping branchlets, resembling a small-scale weeping willow; native to Chile. It grows slowly to 50 feet, with small, neat leaves, clusters of greenish flowers, and a red-netted seed. Superb as a lawn tree, patio tree, and street tree.

Maytenus (migh tee'nuhs) *n.* A genus of about 200 species of subtropical and tropical shrubs and trees (Celastraceae). *M. serratus* is a shrub to 6 feet; *M. Boaria* is a tree to 50 feet (see **mayten**).

Maythorn *n.* A common name for *Crataegus,* a genus of thorny shrubs or small trees. Same as Maybloom. (See **Crataegus**.)

mazer tree (may'zuhr) *n.* A common name for *Acer campestre,* a deciduous shrub or round-headed tree to 35 feet or more, with corky twigs and lobed leaves that turn clear yellow in fall. There are several cultivars. Grows best in high-rainfall climates, such as those of England and the Pacific Northwest. Also known as field maple or hedge maple.

Mazus (may'zuhs) *n.* A genus of about 30 species of tender perennial ground covers (Scrophulariaceae). *M. reptans* is a creeping ground cover with leafy branches, small, toothed, bright green leaves, and clusters of small purplish-blue flowers marked with white and yellow, resembling monkey flower. Used as small-scale ground cover or in rock gardens.

meadow *n.* 1. A piece of moist, low-lying land often used as pastureland or for raising hay. 2. An upland area covered with grass and generally surrounded by woodlands.

meadow beauty *n.* A common name for plants of the genus *Rhexia,* a genus of hardy, low-growing North American perennials and ground covers. Also called deer grass.

meadow-beauty family *n.* A common name for Melastomaceae.

meadow bright *n.* A common name for *Caltha palustris.* Also called marsh marigold.

meadow campion (kamp′ee uhn) *n.* A common name for *Lychnis Flos-cuculi.* It has naturalized in North America from Quebec to Pennsylvania. Also known as cuckooflower and ragged robin.

meadow cress *n.* A common name for *Cardamine pratensis,* an erect perennial to 20 inches, with divided leaves and white or rose-colored 4-petaled flowers. Traditional in cottage gardens; also used in cool, moist borders and rock gardens. Commonly called cuckooflower, lady smock, ladies′-smocks, lady smocks, mayflower, and bitter cress.

meadow fern *n.* 1. A common name for *Polypodium vulgare,* which has 3-foot-long fronds 5 inches wide. There are many cultivars, and it is widely grown ornamentally in woodland gardens or shady situations. 2. A common name for species of *Dryopteris,* terrestrial temperate-zone ferns, many native to North America. 3. A common name for *Myrica Gale,* a hardy deciduous North American and Eurasian shrub that grows to 5 feet, with alternate, simple leaves, catkins, and small waxy, yellow fruits.

meadow foam *n.* A common name for *Limnanthes,* small annual wildflowers native to the west coast of North America. *L. Douglasii* grows to 1 foot or more, with shiny yellow-green, doubly-divided, parsleylike leaves and masses of fragrant 5-petaled yellow, white, and pink flowers that make sheets of color on low ground in early spring. Used in moist situations.

meadow foxtail *n.* (See **Alopecurus.**)

meadow parsnip *n.* A common name for the genus *Heracleum.* Also called cow parsnip.

meadow pea *n.* A common name for *Lathyrus pratensis,* a perennial plant to 3 feet, with narrow, pointed leaflets in pairs, showy spikes of yellow sweet pea-shaped flowers, and black pods.

meadow pine *n.* A common name for 2 species of pines, *Pinus caribaea* and *P. Taeda.*

meadow pink *n.* 1. A common name for *Lychnis Flos-cuculi,* which has naturalized in southern Canada and northeastern United States. It is a perennial to 3 feet, with narrow, clasping stem leaves and clusters of small rose-red or white flowers. Also known as ragged robin. 2. A common name for *Dianthus deltoides,* a vigorous, low-growing perennial with narrow, soft, gray-green leaves and pink, white, or red flowers. Used in rock gardens. Also known as maiden pink. 3. A common name for *Habenaria,* a large genus of terrestrial tuberous-rooted orchids (Orchidaceae). They are leafy plants with narrow leaves and spikes of often fringed flowers. *H. psycodes* var. *grandiflora,* native to eastern North America and showiest of the beautiful fringed orchids, is also called large purple fringed orchid, large butterfly orchid, or plume-royal. The genus is commonly known as fringed orchid or rein orchid.

meadow queen *n.* A common name for plants of 2 different genera, *Filipendula* and *Spirea.*

meadow rue *n.* A common name for the genus *Thalictrum,* open, airy perennials, some native to the United States. They grow from 10 inches to 6 feet, with delicate columbinelike leaves and spikes or clusters of small white, lilac, purple, or yellow flowers with many stamens but no petals. Useful in protected, moist, shady situations. Lovely in the wild garden or around pools and streams.

meadow rue

meadow saffron *n.* Most properly, the plant *Colchicum autumnale,* from its resemblance to the true saffron, *Crocus sativa.* The name is often extended to the genus *Colchicum.*

meadow sage *n.* A common name for *Salvia pratensis,* an aromatic perennial that grows to 3 feet tall, with oval, pointed, or oblong leaves and spikes of white, violet-blue, or pinkish-white flowers in whorled clusters.

meadow saxifrage (saks'uh frihj) *n.* A common name for *Saxifraga granulata,* a perennial that grows to 20 inches, with small, kidney-shaped leaves and clusters of white single or double flowers. Grown in rock gardens or at the front of the perennial border. Also called fair-maids-of-France.

meadowsweet *n.* A common name for plants of 3 different genera: *Astilbe, Filipendula,* and *Spirea.*

mealybug *n.* A small, white, cottony-looking insect that infests many houseplants but can also be a pest outdoors. Control indoors by daubing the pests with a cottony swab dipped in rubbing alcohol or by spraying with insecticidal soap. Outdoors, many beneficial insects, including the mealybug destroyer, provide control. Horticultural oils and traditional pesticides are also effective. You may also have to control ants, which cultivate mealybugs to harvest their sugary secretions (see **honeydew**).

mealybug destroyer *n.* (See **Cryptolaemus beetle**.)

mealy tree *n.* A common name for the genus *Viburnum,* hardy upright flowering shrubs or small trees. Also known as arrowwood.

mechanical analysis *n.* The physical analysis of soil material to determine its grain-size fraction.

mechanical stability *n.* The resistance of soil broken down by mechanical forces like tillage or abrasion.

Meconopsis (mehk uh nahp'sehs) *n.* A genus of 45 species of hardy or semihardy perennial flowers (Papaveraceae). *M. betonicifolia,* the blue poppy, grows to 6 feet, has oval, pointed leaves, gray-green beneath, and showy clusters of drooping buds that open into blue-violet or purple flowers 2 inches across. Grows well with rhododendrons and azaleas; likes cool, moist, acid soil and summer water. Commonly known as Asiatic poppy.

Medeola (muh dee'oh luh) *n.* A genus of a single species, *M. virginica* (Liliaceae); native to eastern North America from Nova Scotia to Florida, Alabama, and Louisiana. It grows from a crisp, edible rhizome, has 2 whorls of leaves, clusters of small greenish-yellow flowers, and dark purple berries. Also called Indian cucumber root.

Medeola
(Indian cucumber root)

medicinal plants *n. pl.* Plants that are or have been used medicinally.

Medinilla (med uh nihl'uh) *n.* A genus of 150 species of tropical shrubs, some epiphytic (Melastomaceae). They grow to 8 feet or less, depending on the species, with simple, entire leaves and long clusters of white, pink, coral-red, or red flowers. Grown as hedges or foundation plants in the tropics or as greenhouse plants anywhere.

medium sand *n.* Soil particles measuring between 0.25 to 0.50 millimeters.

medlar (mehd'luhr) *n.* 1. A common name for *Mespilus germanica,* a small deciduous tree with brown fruit that ripens only after frost. 2. A common name for *Vangueria infausta,* a tropical shrub to 10 feet, with brown fruit.

Medusa's head *n.* A common name for *Euphorbia Caput-Medusae,* a slim, cylindrical, many-branched, trailing succulent that looks remarkably like mythological Medusa's hair of snakes.

megaspore (meg'a-spor) *n.* The larger type of spore produced by plants that produce 2 types.

325

meiosis (migh oh'sehs) *n.* In flowering plants, a process occurring during pollination by which the chromosomes of the male and female gametes line up together and then divide so as to form new gametes having half the number of chromosomes as the somatic cells of the plant. This process assures that, as traits from both parents are passed on to succeeding generations, the offspring will exhibit some individual variation from either parent.

Melaleuca (mehl uh loo'kuh) *n.* A genus of more than 100 species of tender evergreen shrubs and small trees (Myrtaceae), most native to Australia. They grow from 5 feet to 40 feet, depending on the species, with narrow, sometimes needlelike, leaves, and white, yellow, orange-red, red, pink, lilac, or purple flowers resembling bottlebrush. Many species have attractive bark that peels in thick, papery layers. Tolerates heat, wind, poor soil, and salt air. Used in mild-climate areas as lawn trees, park trees, street trees, shade trees, as screening plants, or in coastal gardens. Commonly known as bottlebrush or honey myrtle.

Melampodium (mehl ahm poh'dee uhm) *n.* A genus of 12 species of hardy perennials (Compositae) native to the southwestern United States, the West Indies, and Central and South America. They grow to 12 inches, with opposite, entire or divided leaves and daisylike white flowers with yellow centers. Used in rock gardens.

melancholy thistle *n.* A common name for *Cirsium heterophyllum,* a large, bold, Old World thistle used in the border for striking effects. It grows to 4 feet, with soft-prickled leaves, felty beneath, and large red, purple, or white flowers.

Melanthium (meh lan'thee uhm) *n.* A genus of 4 species of hardy perennials (Liliaceae) native to eastern North America. They grow from creeping rhizomes to 5 feet or less, depending on the species, with narrow to oval pointed leaves and large clusters of green or white flowers. Used in moist situations in bog gardens or wild gardens. *M. virginicum* of the United States is commonly known as bunchflower.

Melastoma (meh las'tuh muh) *n.* A genus of 70 species of tropical flowering shrubs and small trees (Melastomataceae). They grow from 8 to 20 feet, depending on the species, with opposite, entire

leaves and large, showy white, pink, or purple flowers 1 to 3 inches across. Used in warm climates and in greenhouses anywhere. *M. malabathricum* is commonly known as Indian rhododendron.

Melastomataceae (meh las tuh muh tay'see ee) *n. pl.* A family of 240 genera and 3,000 species of mostly tropical plants, shrubs, and trees. They have simple, opposite or whorled leaves, regular flowers, and berrylike or capsulelike fruit. The ornamental genera include *Melastoma* and *Tibouchina.*

Melastomaceous (meh las tuh may'shuhs) *a.* Belonging to or resembling plants in the family *Melastomaceae.*

Melia (me'li-a) *n.* A genus of 10 species of tender shrubs and trees (Meliaceae). *Melia Azedarach,* a tender, deciduous large shrub or tree. It is round headed and dense branched, growing up to 40 feet or more, with 3-foot-long, twice-divided leaves with many leaflets that turn clear yellow in fall. It bears clusters of fragrant purple flowers, and small, yellow, egg-shaped fruits, which are attractive to birds and remain on the tree after the leaves fall. Used in warm-climate gardens; survives light frost and tolerates heat and drought. Also known as chinaberry, China tree, margosa, pride-of-India, pride of China, Persian lilac, Indian lilac, paradise tree, bead tree, Syrian bead tree, and Japanese bead tree.

Melia
(chinaberry)

Meliaceae (mee lee ay'see ee) *n. pl.* A family of 50 genera and 1,400 species of tropical shrubs and trees; the mahogany family. The ornamental genera include *Cedrela, Melia,* and *Swietenia.*

meliaceous (mee lee ay'shuhs) *a.* Belonging to or resembling plants in the family Meliaceae.

Melianthaceae (mee lee an thay'see ee) *n. pl.* A family of 3 genera of perennial plants, shrubs, and trees. They have opposite, simple or compound leaves, often large, and typically showy flowers, usually in spikes. The ornamental genera are *Greyia* and *Melianthus*.

Melianthus (mee lee an'thuhs) *n.* A genus of 6 species of shrubby tender perennials (Melianthaceae). They grow to 12 to 14 feet, with large, striking grayish-green leaves divided into 9 to 11 strongly-toothed leaflets and 12-inch spikes of small reddish-brown flowers. Used to sprawl over walls, in containers, or combined with succulents. Commonly known as honeybush.

Melica (mehl'ih kuh) *n.* A genus of about 80 species of perennial grasses (Gramineae) native to temperate regions. A few are grown as ornamentals for the light, airy appearance of their flower spikes. The most common is *M. ciliata* (hairy mellic), which has blue-green foliage and hairy spikes.

Melicoccus (mehl uh kahk'uhs) *n.* A genus of 2 species of subtropical trees (Sapindaceae) native to the West Indies and South America. *Melicoccus bijugatus,* a slow-growing tropical fruit tree, grows to 60 feet, with divided 6-inch-long alternate leaves, many-flowered clusters of small fragrant flowers, and small, round green edible fruit with a leathery rind. Used as a dooryard tree in southern Florida and tropical gardens. Also known as Spanish lime, genip, genipe, and honeyberry.

melilot (mel'ilot) *n.* A common name for *Melilotus,* a genus of fragrant herbs. (See **Melilotus**.)

Melilotus (mehl uh loh'duhs) *n.* A genus of 20 species of annual or biennial plants (Leguminosae); sweet clover. They grow from a few inches to 10 feet, depending on the species, with leaves divided into 3 leaflets and slender spikes of small butterfly-shaped white or yellow flowers that attract bees. Widely naturalized in North America. Commonly known as sweet clover and melilot.

Melissa *n.* A genus of about 3 species of perennial herbs (Labiatae). They grow to 2 feet or more, with opposite, toothed leaves and spikes with whorled clusters of white bell-shaped flowers. Traditional in herb gardens and cottage gardens; the leaves are used as a culinary herb to flavor fish, salads, and cold drinks. Commonly known as balm.

Melissa oil *n.* A volatile oil obtained from *Melissa officinalis,* (balm), which gives to the plant its aromatic, lemonlike odor.

Melocactus (mehl uh kak'tuhs) *n.* A genus of 36 species of slow-maturing, spiny, strongly ribbed, oval cacti (Cactaceae) native to the Americas. They have woolly hairs, tiny red or pink day-blooming flowers, and red club-shaped fruit. Some species take from 5 to 20 years to bloom. Grown by collectors and in warm-climate gardens.

melocoton (mehl'uh kuh tohn) *n.* 1. The quince tree or its fruit. 2. A large kind of peach. Also spelled melocotoon.

melon *n.* A trailing, annual, succulent herbaceous plant, *Cucumis Melo,* or its fruit. It has been cultivated from earliest times in the hot countries of the East, the melons of Persia being especially celebrated; it is now planted wherever there is sufficient summer heat to mature its fruit. The term is also used in a general sense for all melons, including the watermelon.

melon cactus *n.* A common name for *Melocactus communis,* a Jamaican cactus that grows to 3 feet tall and 1 foot thick, with stout spines to 2 inches long.

melon tree *n.* The papaya, *Carica Papaya*.

Melothria (me loth'ri a) *n.* A genus of 85 species of climbing or creeping vines (Cucurbitaceae), a few species native to North America. They have entire or lobed leaves, small, inconspicuous flowers, and small fruit.

melting out *n.* A term referring to leaf-spotting diseases of lawns. It is common in cool, wet weather, when it causes long, irregular dark spots of grass blades. Control by mowing grass at the proper height, aerating, improving drainage, increasing sunlight, or spraying with traditional fungicides.

membranaceous (mehm bruh nay'shuhs) *a.* Resembling a membrane; soft, thin, and translucent.

Memecylon (muh mehs'uh lawn) *n.* A genus of 150 species of tropical shrubs and trees (Melastomataceae). They grow from 10 feet to 25 feet, with opposite leaves and flat or rounded clusters of 4-petaled white or blue flowers.

Mendel's laws *n. pl.* The basic patterns of genetic inheritance, as determined experimentally by Gregor Mendel in the 19th century. They establish that each gamete receives 1 complete set of genes after meiotic division, that the genes contributed by both parents to the offspring result in hybrids with characteristics of both parents but identical to neither, and they determine the relationship of dominant and recessive genes.

Menispermaceae (mehn uh spuhr may′see ee) *n. pl.* A family of 65 genera of mostly tropical twining woody vines, some native to North America. The ornamental genera are *Coccolulus* and *Menispermum,* some species of which contain alkaloids that are poisonous if eaten. Commonly known as the moonseed family.

menispermaceous (mehn uh spuhr may′shuhs) *a.* Pertaining to or resembling plants of the family Menispermaceae.

Menispermum (mehn uh spuhr′muhm) *n.* A genus of 2 species of very hardy woody vines (Menispermaceae). *M. canadense,* native to eastern North America, grows to 12 feet, with 8-inch-long rounded leaves, fuzzy beneath when young, and clusters of small white or yellow flowers. Grown over arbors for its attractive foliage. Commonly known as yellow parilla.

Menispermum
(yellow parilla)

Mentha (mehn′thuh) *n.* A genus of 25 species of erect or creeping aromatic perennial herbs (Labiatae) that hybridize freely among themselves: As many as 600 species have been identified, but these have been reclassified into a well-defined 25. They grow from 1 foot to 3 feet tall, with mostly opposite, entire, sweetly fragrant leaves and spikes with dense clusters of white or lavender flowers in whorls. Traditional in herb gardens and cottage gardens for use as culinary herbs in teas and cold drinks. They become weedy without regular trimming and can be invasive in moist soils, spreading by runners. Commonly known as mint.

Mentzelia (mehnt see′lee uh) *n.* A genus of 60 species of flowers and shrubs (Loasaceae) native to the Americas. The shrubby types often have interesting, shredding bark. *M. laevicaulis,* commonly known as blazing star, is a biennial that grows to almost 4 feet, with shiny white stems, wavy-toothed leaves, and very showy large, yellow star-shaped flowers 4 inches across. Useful in dry situations.

Menyanthes (mehn ee an′theez) *n.* A genus of a single species, *Menyanthes trifoliata* (Gentianaceae, Menyanthaceae), a circumboreal perennial bog plant native to wetlands of the Northern Hemisphere. It grows from a creeping rhizome to 1 foot, with oval, alternate leaves divided into 3 leaflets and with spikes of 10 to 20 white to purple funnelform flowers, each 1 inch across. Used in bog gardens. Also called bogbean, buckbean and marsh trefoil.

Menziesia (mehn zigh ee′see uh) *n.* A genus of 6 or 7 species of hardy, sometimes sprawling, deciduous shrubs (Ericaceae), some species native to North America. They grow from 6 to 15 feet, depending on the species, with alternate, simple leaves and clusters of small yellow-green, yellow-red, white, pink, and bright red bell-shaped flowers. Used in rock gardens. Commonly known as mock azalea.

mericarp (mehr′uh kahrp) *n.* One of the halves of the fruit of certain plants, such as the maple, whose fruits split into halves.

Merlin's-grass *n.* A common name for *Isoetes lacustris,* an aquarium plant. Commonly known as quillwort.

mermaid weed *n.* A common name for the genus *Proserpinaca,* which consists of 4 perennial aquatic plants native to the Americas. They have long, narrow, alternate leaves, some floating, some submerged, and inconspicuous flowers. Sometimes grown in pools and aquariums.

Merremia (mehr ehm'ee uh) *n.* A genus of 80 species of vigorous twining perennial vines (Convolvulaceae). *M. dissecta* is native to the southeastern United States. *M. tuberosa* is commonly known as Hawaiian wood rose, wood rose, yellow morning glory, Ceylon merrimia, and Spanish woodbine; its flowers are widely used in dried arrangements. They have highly variable leaves and morning glorylike white or yellow flowers.

merrybells *n.* A common name for the genus *Uvularia*, hardy rhizomatous perennials. They grow to 2 1/2 feet tall, with alternate, simple leaves and nodding bell-shaped yellow flowers. Useful in shady locations and in the wild garden. Also known as bellwort, haybells, and cowbells.

Mertensia (muhr tehnch'ee uh) *n.* A genus of 45 species of hardy perennials (Boraginaceae), some species native to North America. They grow from a few inches to 4 feet, depending on the species, with simple, alternate, entire leaves and loose clusters of gracefully nodding blue, purple, or white flowers resembling giant forget-me-nots. Used in moist, shady places, the woodland garden, and in borders with ferns or drifts of daffodils. *M. virginica* is commonly known as Virginia bluebells, though cultivars are available in both pink and white. The genus is commonly known as lungwort.

mescal bean (meh'skal) *n.* A common name for *Sophora secundiflora*, a slow-growing, usually multistemmed, broadleaf evergreen summer-flowering tree. It grows to 25 feet or more, with silky, soft leaves divided into leaflets, showy clusters of fragrant butterfly-shaped violet-blue flowers, and woody pods with bright red seeds used in making necklaces. The seeds are poisonous if eaten. Grown as a showy tree in desert areas, as a choice small lawn, patio, or street tree, or as a tall screen or thicket. Thrives in hot sun and alkaline soil. Also known as Texas mountain laurel and frijolito.

mesclun (mehs'kluhn) *n.* A mixture of early tender greens grown for salads. Although nearly any young green can be used, many seed houses sell packets of mixed seeds to provide an interesting variety in small gardens.

Mesembryanthemum (meh zehm bree an'thuhm muhm) *n.* A genus of 74 species of tender annual or biennial succulent ground covers. *M. crystallinum* grows to a few inches high and several feet wide, with fleshy leaves to 4 inches long that are covered with tiny transparent blisters, which glisten in sunlight like flecks of ice; it bears white or pink daisylike flowers. It grows wild in coastal California. Used as a drought-tolerant, fire-retardant ground cover. This is the least ornamental of the plants commonly called *Mesembryanthemum*, now reclassified as *Carpobrotus, Cephalophyllum, Delosperma, Dorotheanthus, Drosanthemum, Lampranthus, Malephora,* and *Oscularia*. Also known as ice plant, icicle plant, and pebble plant, and fig marigold.

mesocarp (meh'zoh kahrp) *n.* In botany, the central portion of the ripened wall of a fruit.

mesochil (meh'zoh kihl) *n.* The middle part of the lip in certain orchids that have this organ divided into 3 parts.

Mespilus (mehs puh'luhs) *n.* A genus of a single species, *M. germanica*, a small, hardy deciduous, sometimes thorny, fruit tree (Rosaceae); the medlar. It grows to 20 feet with large, oblong leaves, white flowers 2 inches across, and apple-shaped brown fruit, about 2 inches around, which is inedible until after frost. The fruit is used for preserves. Commonly known as medlar.

mesquite (muh skeet') *n.* A common name for the genus *Prosopis*, spiny, drought-tolerant deciduous large shrubs or trees native to warm regions of the Americas. *P. glandulosa torreyana*, the western honey mesquite, grows to 30 feet tall and 40 feet wide, with leaves divided into tiny bright green leaflets, spikes of small greenish-yellow flowers that attract bees, and long, flat seedpods. Used as a desert shade tree. Also spelled mesquit.

mesquite bean (muh skeet') *n.* The fruit of *Prosopis juliflora*, native to Mexico, the West Indies, Colombia, and Venezuela. Plants called *P. juliflora* in the United States are more likely to be *P. glandulosa*.

mesquite gum (muh skeet') *n.* A gum exuded by the fruit of mesquite, similar to gum arabic.

mesquite, screw-pod (muh skeet') *n.* A common name for *Prosopis pubescens*, a large shrub or small tree native from California east to southern Utah and south to Mexico. It grows from 6 to 32 feet, with leaves divided into soft, furry leaflets and with fruit tightly curled into a cylinder. Also known as screw bean and tornillo.

Mesua (meh'shuh wuh) *n.* A genus of 3 species of medium-sized tropical trees (Guttiferae). They have long, narrow, leathery leaves and large, showy, fragrant white flowers 3 inches across.

Mesurol (mehs'yoo rawl) *n.* A synthetic pesticide (chemical name: methiocarb) used to control slugs and snails on ornamental plants.

metaldehyde (meht al'duh highd) *n.* A synthetic pesticide commonly used in snail and slug baits.

Metasequoia (mehd uh seh kwoi'yuh) *n.* A genus of 1 species, *M. glyptostroboides,* a hardy deciduous conifer (Taxodiaceae); the dawn redwood. It grows to 100 feet, with light-bright green soft new leaves that turn light bronze in fall. Best grown as a grove, bringing the beauty of redwoods to cold regions.

methoxychlor (mehth ahks'uh klor) *n.* A broad-spectrum synthetic pesticide usually used to control insect pests of fruit trees.

Metrosideros (mee troh seh dih'ruhs) *n.* A genus of 60 species of tender, broadleaf evergreen woody vines, shrubs, and trees (Myrtaceae). They grow from 30 to 60 feet, depending on the species, with firm, leathery, dense, opposite, simple leaves and clusters of red, white, or yellow flowers. Used in coastal gardens, tolerating wind and salt spray; also as a lawn tree or street tree. Commonly known as bottlebrush and iron tree.

Metrosideros
(bottlebrush or iron tree)

Meum (mee'uhm) *n.* A genus of 1 species, *M. athamanticum,* an aromatic hardy perennial (Umbelliferae). It grows to 2 feet, with divided leaves in a basal rosette and clusters of white-to-pink flowers.

Mexican bamboo *n.* A common name for *Polygonum cuspidatum,* a perennial growing from rhizomes and forming large clumps of jointed, red-brown stems with heart-shaped leaves and clusters of small greenish-white flowers. Grown as a ground cover in wild gardens, it is extremely invasive. Also called bamboo or Japanese knotweed.

Mexican bean beetle *n.* A small copper-colored beetle with black spots. It feeds on the foliage of beans and some peas, turning them to lace. Control by planting resistant varieties early in the season; releasing spined soldier bugs, good garden cleanup, hand-picking, and floating row covers also help. Pyrethrins, rotenone, and traditional pesticides are effective controls.

Mexican breadfruit *n.* A common name for *Monstera deliciosa,* a stout, sturdy tropical perennial epiphytic climber. It grows to 30 feet or more, with huge, 3-foot wide, deeply lobed leaves, large, boat-shaped, cream-colored flowers, and edible fruit. Used primarily as a houseplant in containers and for a tropical effect in warm-winter climates. Also known as split-leaf philodendron, Swiss cheese plant, breadfruit vine, hurricane plant, fruit-salad plant, and window plant.

Mexican buckeye *n.* A common name for *Ungnadia speciosa,* a deciduous shrubby tree native to the southwestern United States and northern Mexico. It grows to 30 feet, with leaves divided into long, narrow leaflets and with clusters of fragrant, rose-colored flowers, 1 inch across, that appear before the leaves in spring. Also known as Texan buckeye, Spanish buckeye, and false buckeye.

Mexican cypress (sigh'prehs) *n.* A common name for *Cupressus lusitanica,* a tender conifer native to Central America. It grows to 75 feet, with drooping branchlets, scalelike gray-green leaves and tiny grayish cones. Also known as Portuguese cedar and cedar-of-Goa.

Mexican fireweed *n.* A common name for the summer annual *Kochia scoparia.* Grown for its foliage, it is widely naturalized in the United States. Also called belvedere and summer cypress.

Mexican jumping bean *n.* The seed of any Mexican shrubs of the *Sebastiania* and *Sapium* genera, which, when infested by the larvae of a small moth, *Carpocapsa saltitans,* makes tumbling and jumping movements. Also jumping bean and jumping seed.

Mexican orange *n.* A common name for *Choisya ternata,* a tender, subtropical, broadleaf evergreen shrub. It grows to 8 feet, with lustrous, yellow-green, 3-part, fan-shaped leaves and clusters of sweetly fragrant, orange blossomlike white flowers that attract bees. Used as an attractive informal screen or hedge, as a specimen, and in containers.

Mexican persimmon (puhr sihm′uhn) *n.* A common name for *Diospyros texana,* a North American tree. It grows to 40 feet, with small, oval leaves, 5-petaled flowers, and small round, black fruit. Also known as black persimmon.

Mexican piñon pine (peen yohn′) *n.* A common name for *Pinus cembroides,* a small, fairly hardy, drought-tolerant, coniferous tree native to the southwestern United States and Mexico. It grows to 25 feet tall, with short, stiff, curved needles, usually in bunches of 3, and small, round yellow or reddish-brown cones. Also spelled pinyon. Also known as Mexican stone pine.

Mexican poppy *n.* A common name for *Argemone mexicana,* a drought-tolerant annual flower. It grows to 3 feet, with prickly leaves and large, showy, clear yellow or orange poppylike flowers. Grown as a summer annual in dry soils. Also known as prickly poppy.

Mexican rose *n.* A common name for *Portulaca grandiflora,* a drought-tolerant prostrate annual. It grows to a few inches, with fleshy cylindrical leaves and lustrous red, cerise, rose-pink, orange, yellow, white, or pastel roselike flowers, often striped, and 1 inch or more across. Used on hot, dry banks, in rock gardens, as edging in borders, and in shallow containers and hanging baskets; useful in hot, dry, sunny situations. Also known as rose moss.

Mexican scammony (skam′muh nee) *n.* A common name for *Ipomoea orizabensis,* a twining vine.

Mexican star *n.* A common name for *Milla biflora,* a tender North American bulb. (See **Milla**.)

Mexican stone pine *n.* A common name for *Pinus cembroides,* a short-needled, round-topped small pine of desert mountains of the Southwest. Also called Mexican pion.

Mexican sunflower *n.* A common name for the genus *Tithonia,* 10 species of stout annual or perennial flowers. *T. rotundifolia* grows to 6 feet, with velvety green, oval-pointed leaves and large spectacular flowers with red-orange petals and yellow centers. Used in the back of the border; lower growing varieties used as a low summer hedge.

Mexican tea *n.* A common name for *Chenopodium ambrosioides,* an annual or perennial strong-scented herb that grows to 3 1/2 feet with long oblong leaves and spikes or clusters of small flowers. It has naturalized in North America. Also known as Spanish tea, wormseed, and American wormseed.

Mexican tulip poppy *n.* A common name for *Hunnemania fumariifolia,* a tender, bushy perennial native to Mexico. It grows to 2 feet, with delicate, finely divided, blue-green leaves and large, soft yellow flowers 3 inches across with crinkled petals. Used in dry, sunny borders. Also known as golden cup.

Mexican white pine *n.* A common name for *Pinus ayacahuite,* a coniferous tree native to the mountains of Mexico and Guatemala. It grows to 100 feet, with bluish-green needles in bundles of 5 and large cylindrical cones 15 inches long.

mezereon (meh zihr′ee uhn) *n.* A common name for *Daphne mezereum,* a hardy deciduous shrub. It grows to 5 feet, with oval leaves, clusters of early-blooming, fragrant, lilac-purple, reddish-purple, or white flowers that appear before the leaves, and red fruit. All parts of the plant are poisonous. Tends to be gawky, so best planted in clumps. Also known as February daphne.

mezereum family (meh zihr′ee uhn) *n.* A common name for Thymelaeaceae, a family of 40 genera and 50 species, including *Daphne.* Also mezereon family.

mezquite (muhz keet′) *n.* (See **mesquite**.)

mice *n. pl.* Small rodents that sometimes become pests by chewing on tree trunks or eating ripening vegetables like melons. Some types are called voles. Protective collars, fencing, keeping mulches at least 3 inches away from tree trunks, cats, traps, and poisonous baits are effective controls.

Michaelmas daisy (mihk′uhl muhs) *n.* A common name for hybrids of *Aster novae-angliae* and *A. novi-belgii,* tall, graceful, branching perennial flowers. They grow from 3 to 4 feet, with clusters of bright blue-violet, purple, rose-red, and white daisylike flowers. Dwarf varieties are available. Used in perennial borders; smaller varieties used as edging, in beds, in rock gardens, and in containers.

Michelia (migh kee′lee uh) *n.* A genus of 50 species of tender shrubs and trees (Magnoliaceae). *M. figo,* the banana shrub, is a slow-growing shrub to 15 feet, with dense, glossy, medium-green leaves and clusters of small, creamy, magnolialike flowers with a powerful banana fragrance. A choice plant for entryways, patios, or near windows where the fragrance can be enjoyed.

michihli (mih′kih lee) *n.* A leafy, upright variety of *Brassica rapa,* of the Pekinensis group, with large green leaves around a yellow heart. Loosely classed in grocery stores as Chinese cabbage, it is used in stir-fry and other Asian dishes.

Miconia (migh koh′nee uh) *n.* A genus of 1,000 species of tropical shrubs and trees (Melastomataceae) native to tropical America. *M. calvescens* grows to 15 feet, with large, broadly oval, wavy-edged leaves that have white or pale green veins and are reddish-bronze beneath. It bears clusters of white, rose, purple, or yellow flowers and edible fruit.

micro *a.* Very small. (*comb. form,* **micro-**).

microclimate *n.* The climate of a small area, as the sunny or shady or moist part of a garden.

Microcoelum (migh kroh seel′uhm) *n.* A genus of 2 species of slender Brazilian palms (Palmae). *M. weddellianum* grows to 10 feet, with 4-foot-long leaves, divided into 50 to 60 blades, and red-black scales along the leaf stems; it has 3-foot-long, flower spikes and small fruit. Widely grown in subtropical and tropical gardens, including Southern Florida. Commonly known as Weddell palm.

Microgramma *n.* This genus is now classified as *Polypodium,* a genus of rhizomatous ferns.

Micromeria (migh kroh muh′ree uh) *n.* A genus of 70 species of low-growing perennial plants and shrubs (Labiatae). They grow to a few inches, with aromatic, opposite, often entire leaves and spikes with whorled clusters of small white to pale violet or purple tubular flowers. Used in rock gardens; traditional in herb gardens and cottage gardens. Commonly known as savory.

micro nutrients *n. pl.* Very small amounts of nutrients needed by plants.

microphyllous (migh kroh figh′luhs) *a.* 1. In botany, having small leaves. 2. Having leaves with only 1 unbranched vein.

microsporangium (migh kroh spuh ranj′ee uhm) *n. pl.* In plants that produce 2 types of spores, the receptacle that contains only the smaller type; analogous to the pollen sac of the anther in a seed plant.

microspore *n.* In botany, the smaller type of spore produced by those plants that have 2 types.

microstylous (migh kroh stigh′luhs) *a.* Of a flower, having short styles.

midrib *n.* In botany, the central vein of a leaf or leaflike part.

midribbed *a.* Possessing a midrib.

mignonette (mih nyuh neht′) *n.* A common name for the genus *Reseda,* particularly *R. odorata,* a summer annual grown for its sweet fragrance. Traditional in cottage gardens; also used massed in beds, or in containers.

mignonette, common (mih nyuh neht′) *n.* A common name for *Reseda odorata.* (See **mignonette.**)

mignonette, Jamaica (mih nyuh neht′) *n.* A common name for *Lawsonia inermis* (Lythraceae), a large tender shrub . It grows to 20 feet, with small oval leaves and fragrant clusters of small white, rose, or cinnabar-red flowers. The leaves are the source of henna, an orange dye. Grown as an ornamental in warm regions. Also known as henna and migonette tree.

mignonette family (mih nyuh neht′) *n.* A common name for Resedaceae.

mignonette tree (mih nyuh neht′) *n.* A common name for *Lawsonia inermis,* also known as Jamaica mignonette and henna.

mignonette vine (mih nyuh neht′) *n.* A common name for *Anredera cordifolia,* a fast-growing South

American twining vine. It grows to 20 feet, with fleshy leaves that have small aerial tubers between the stem and leaf and with long clusters of fragrant, white flowers. Used in tropical gardens, but the tuberous roots will survive light frost. Also known as Madeira vine.

Mikania (muh kay'nee uh) *n.* A genus of about 150 species of mostly tropical climbing or twining vines and, rarely, erect shrubs (Compositae) native to North and South America. They grow to 15 feet, with opposite leaves and clusters of small pink, white, or greenish-yellow flowers. Used in wild gardens; some species used in hanging baskets. Commonly known as climbing hempweed.

mildew *n.* 1. A growth, usually whitish in color, produced on living plants by fungus. 2. A fungus that causes such growth.

milfoil (mihl'foil) *n.* A composite herb, *Achillea Millefolium,* also called yarrow. (See **yarrow**.)

milfoil water family (mihl'foil) *n.* A common name for *Haloragaceae,* a family of water or marsh plants used in pools or aquariums.

Milium (mihl'ee uhm) *n.* A genus of 4 species of annual and perennial grasses (Gramineae) native to temperate regions. *M. effusum* 'Aureum' is grown as an ornamental for its yellowish foliage and ability to grow in shade; commonly known as Bowles' golden grass or golden wood millet.

milk thistle *n.* A common name for *Silybum Marianum,* a European thistle that has spiny, lobed leaves marbled with white. It has naturalized as a weed in the United States. Also known as St. Mary's thistle, blessed thistle, and holy thistle.

milk tree *n.* A common name for the genus *Mimusops,* tropical evergreen shrubs or small trees of the Old World.

milk vetch (milk'vech) *n.* A common name for the genus *Astragalus.*

milkweed *n.* A common name for *Asclepias,* a genus of perennials, many native to North America. They have hairy, lance-shaped, dark green leaves and clusters of brilliant orange-red flowers, followed by seeds tufted with long silky hairs. Used in meadow gardens, wild gardens, and often seen growing wild. Also known as butterfly weed; attracts monarch butterflies.

milkweed family *n.* A common name for Asclepiadaceae, a family of about 130 genera and 2,000 species of perennial plants, shrubs, and vines, mostly succulent with milky sap. It includes milkweed *(Asclepias),* carrion flower *(Stapelia),* and wax plant *(Hoya).*

milkwort *n.* A common name for 2 genera, *Polygala* and *Campanula.*

milky spore *n.* (See **Bacillus**.)

Milla (mih'luh) *n.* A genus of 6 or 7 species of tender bulbs (Amarylidaceae) native to the southwestern United States, Mexico, and Guatemala. *Milla biflora,* native to Arizona, New Mexico, and northern Mexico, grows to 18 inches, with grasslike basal leaves and clusters of green-striped buds that open into fragrant, starry white flowers, green on the outside. Used in rock gardens, as edging, in pots, or in sunny borders. Must be mulched or lifted in cold climates. Also called Mexican star-of-Bethlehem.

Millingtonia (mih lihng toh'nee uh) *n.* A genus of 1 species, *M. hortensis,* a tall, tropical, broadleaf evergreen tree (Bignoniaceae) widely naturalized in central India. It grows to 80 feet, with drooping branchlets, corky bark, divided leaves with narrow, oval pointed leaflets, clusters of fragrant, handsome, trumpet-shaped white flowers 3 inches long, and narrow fruit 12 inches long.

millipede (mihl'uh peed) *n.* A hard-shelled, wormlike creature with many small legs. It is slow moving, compared with the quicker centipede. It feeds mostly on decaying organic matter and is not usually considered a garden pest. It sometimes feeds on below- ground vegetables, or ones, like cabbage, that touch the ground, or seeds. The best control is to clean up organic matter.

Miltonia (mihl toh'nee uh) *n.* A genus of 25 species of epiphytic tropical orchids (Orchidaceae) native to the highlands of Central and South America. They grow from pseudobulbs to 2 1/2 feet, often less, with long, graceful, light green leaves, exquisite multicolored flowers that look like large pansies and last a month or more on the plant. Grown by collectors as houseplants or in a cool greenhouse. Commonly known as pansy orchid.

Mimosa (meh moh'suh) *n.* 1. A genus of 500 species of plants, vines, shrubs, and trees (Leguminosae), sometimes spiny. Widely variable in height and habit, they have alternate, doubly divided leaves, clusters or spikes of powderpufflike flowers, and long, flat, woody pods. In some species, the leaves are sensitive, folding closed when touched. 2. [l.c.] A plant of this genus.

Mimulus (mihm′yuh luhs) *n.* A genus of 150 species of annual and perennial flowers and shrubs (Scrophulariaceae), many native to western North America. They grow from 8 inches to 5 feet, depending on the species, with opposite, simple leaves, often sticky, and yellow, orange, red, blue, violet, or purple flowers. Used in woodland gardens, some in bog gardens, in borders, in pots, or as specimen shrubs. Commonly known as monkey flower.

Mimusops (meh myoo′sahps) *n.* A genus of 20 species of tropical evergreen shrubs and trees (Sapotaceae). They grow to 30 feet or more, with oval, pointed leaves and clusters of white flowers. Commonly known as milk tree.

Mina (mihn′uh) *n.* A genus of 1 species, *M. lobata* (Convolvulaceae), a fast-growing tender perennial vine, sometimes grown as an annual, native to Central and South America. It grows 15 to 20 feet, with 3-lobed leaves 3 inches across, and long slender garlands of small crimson flowers that fade to yellow and white. Used as a fast-growing vine, going to 20 feet in its first season. Commonly known as Spanish flag.

mineral *n.* 1. An inorganic substance. 2. The solid homogeneous crystalline chemical element that results from the inorganic process of nature.

mineralization *n.* The release of mineral matter from organic matter.

mineral soil *n.* A general term for soil composed chiefly of mineral matter.

miniature rose *n.* A term for true roses 6 to 12 inches or slightly taller, with miniature canes, leaves, and tiny white, pink, red, or yellow flowers. Often hybridized from *Rosa chinensis minima.* Most often grown in pots, window boxes, rock gardens, or as houseplants.

mint *n.* Any of various plants of the genus *Mentha.* The most familiar species are *M. piperita* (peppermint), and *M. spicata* (spearmint), well known

as flavoring for candies and condiments. The corn mint is *M. arvensis.* The pennyroyal mint, or pennyroyal, is *M. Pulegium. M. requienii* is the tiny Corsican mint. Mints are easily grown in gardens, and tolerate wetter soils than most herbs. Some varieties tend to be invasive.

Mentha piperita
(peppermint)

mintbush *n.* A common name for the genus *Prostanthera,* strongly aromatic, profusely flowering evergreen shrubs or subshrubs native to Australia.

mint family *n.* A common name for Labiatae. A synonym for Labiatae is Lamiaceae.

Mirabilis (meh rab′uh lehs) *n.* A genus of 60 or more species of very bushy annuals and perennials (Nyctaginaceae), many tuberous-rooted, most native to warm regions of the Americas. They grow to 3 feet or more, with opposite leaves and clusters of pink, yellow, purple, or white flowers, sometimes striped. Most widely grown is *M. Jalapa,* a tuberous-rooted, bushy, tender perennial, known as four-o'clock, marvel-of-Peru, and beauty-of-the-night; its tubers can weigh up to 40 pounds. Grown massed in beds, in perennial borders in warm climates, or as annuals in cold climates. The genus is commonly known as umbrellawort.

miriti palm (mihr′uh dee) *n.* A common name for *Mauritia flexuosa (Palmae),* a tall palm native to tropical America and along the Amazon. (See **Mauritia.**)

Miscanthus (mihs kan'thuhs) *n.* A genus of about 20 species of perennial grasses (Gramineae). Several species and their many varieties rank among the most beautiful and useful ornamental grasses. Grown for their feathery plumes and colorful foliage, ranging from red to purple and yellow to silver and white. The most common is *M. sinensis* and its varieties, many of which get quite large; known as eulalia grass or Japanese silver grass.

mistflower *n.* A common name for *Eupatorium coelestinum,* a hardy perennial native to the eastern United States and the West Indies. It grows to 3 feet, with triangular, coarsely toothed leaves 3 inches long and dense clusters of many bright blue to violet flowers. Used in borders. Also known as hardy ageratum.

mistflower

mistletoe *n.* 1. A European shrub, *Viscum album,* growing parasitically on various trees. It has oblong leaves and small yellowish-green flowers; in winter it is covered with small white berries. It is found on a great variety of trees, especially apple trees. Mistletoe was consecrated to religious purposes by the ancient Celtic people of Europe. 2. The plant *Phoradendron serotinum,* commonly used in holiday decoration in North America.

Mitchella (mihch ehl'uh) *n.* A genus of 2 species of hardy, low-growing, trailing, evergreen perennial plants (Rubiaceae) native to eastern North America from Nova Scotia south to eastern Mexico. They grow to 12 inches long, with glossy, dark green, opposite leaves, little funnel-shaped white flowers in pairs, and scarlet or white berries, which are edible but bland. Used as a ground cover under trees, or in rock gardens. Commonly known as partridgeberry.

mite *n.* A tiny spiderlike insect. Many are plant pests and are often referred to as spider mites. Others are beneficial insects (see **predatory mites**). These pest types feed on many plants, leaving the foliage silvery or minutely speckled. They can also leave a fine webbing on the undersides of leaves. They are hard to control with traditional pesticides; in fact, such sprays often result in increased populations. The best control is to encourage or release beneficial insects, including predatory mites, keep foliage clean, water regularly, or spray with insecticidal soap, sulfur, or horticultural oil.

Mitella (meh tehl'uh) *n.* A genus of 12 species of hardy perennials (Saxifragaceae), many species native to western North America from Alberta west to Alaska, south to central California. They grow from a few inches to 2 feet, with mostly basal, heart-shaped leaves and spikes of small, delicately lacy, white, greenish, or yellowish flowers and fruit. Used in rock gardens and wild gardens. Commonly known as miterwort, mitrewort, or bishop's-cap.

miterwort (migh'duhr wort) *n.* A common name for the genus *Mitella.* Also spelled mitrewort.

miterwort, false (migh'duhr wort) *n.* A common name for the genus *Tiarella,* rhizomatous perennials, most native to North America. The leaves are either heart-shaped or divided into 3 leaflets; the 5-petaled white or red flowers are borne in spikes. Useful in shady locations, the woodland garden, or rock garden; grown for the brilliant fall color of the foliage.

miticide (might'ih sighd) *n.* Any material used to control or kill mites.

mitosis (migh toh'sehs) *n., pl.* **mitoses** (-seez) Cell division such as occurs after fertilization of the female germ cell by the male. It is usually preceded by halving and differentiation of the chromosomes within the nucleus. Cell division is the process by which plants grow.

mitrewort (migh'duhr wort) *n.* A common name for *Mitella,* a genus of hardy North American perennials. (See **miterwort**.)

mitriform (migh'truh form) *a*. In botany, having a hollow conical shape, resembling a bishop's miter.

mitriform capsule

moccasin flower *n*. A common name for *Cypripedium,* a genus of about 50 species of wild orchids native to North America and Eurasia; the lady's-slipper orchids. Most are rare or endangered in the wild and do not thrive in garden situations. Also known as Indian shoe.

mock apple *n*. A common name for *Echinocystis lobata,* an annual North American vine that climbs by tendrils and has a round, prickly fruit. Also called wild balsam apple, wild mock cucumber, mock cucumber, and prickly cucumber. Planted to cover arbors and fences.

mockernut *n*. A common name for *Carya tomentosa,* a slow-growing, hardy, deciduous North American nut tree. It grows to 90 feet, with leaves divided into long leaflets and with sweet, thick-shelled nuts. Also known as white-heart hickory, mockernut hickory, and squarenut.

mock orange *n*. A common name for shrubs of many genera, including all species of *Philadelphus,* as well as *Prunus caroliniana, Prunus laurocerasus, Styrax americanus, Maclura pomifera, Bumelia lycioides, Pittosporum tobira,* and *Pittosporum undulatum.* All these have sweet-scented flowers with a fragrance reminiscent of orange blossoms.

mock strawberry *n*. A common name for a fairly hardy, creeping ground cover. It grows nearly flat, with bright green leaves in 3 finely notched leaflets, bright yellow 5-petaled flowers, and soft, round red fruit, edible but bland, that attracts birds. Used as a small-scale ground cover under open shrubs or small trees. Can become invasive in moist soils. Also known as Indian strawberry or Indian mock strawberry.

moisture tension *n*. The force at which water is held by soil. Expressed as the equivalent of a unit column of water in centimeters.

mole *n*. A small burrowing mammal that feeds primarily on soil insects, such as earthworms. Moles become pests when their vigorous burrowing makes a mess of lawns or occasionally damages plants. Traps are the most effective means of control.

mole plant *n*. A common name for *Euphorbia Lathyris,* an annual or biennial to 3 feet, with long, narrow, pointed leaves and a large cluster of yellow flowers at the top of the stem. It has a caustic, poisonous milky juice reputed to discourage moles and gophers. Also known as gopher plant, caper spurge, and myrtle spurge.

mole trap *n*. Any of various skewer- or scissors-type devices used to trap and kill moles.

molecule *n*. A group of atoms bonded together.

Molinia (moh leen'ee uh) *n*. A genus of 2 species of perennial grasses (Gramineae) native to wet areas. *M. caerulea* (purple moor grass), as well as its many varieties, is a popular ornamental grown for its colorful, often variegated foliage and loose flower heads. It is also a host for the fungus that causes ergot of rye, rendering the grain unfit for use.

Moltkia (mohlt'kee uh) *n*. A genus of 6 species of perennial flowers and small shrubs (Boraginaceae). They grow to 18 inches, with simple, entire, alternate leaves and clusters of small blue, purple, or yellow 5-petaled flowers. Used in rock gardens.

Molucca balm (muh luhk'uh) *n*. A common name for *Moluccella laevis,* an annual flower. Also known as bells of Ireland and shellflower. (See **Moluccella.**)

Moluccella (moh luhk sehl'uh) *n*. A genus of 4 species of annuals (Labiatae). *M. laevis* grows to 3 feet, with opposite, oval or triangular leaves and spikes of bell-shaped green flowers. Used in borders; an excellent, long-lasting cut flower; also used in dried arrangements. Commonly known as Molucca balm.

molybdenum (muh lihb'duh nuhm) *n*. A trace element present in most soils and plants.

Momordica (muh maw′deh keh) *n.* A genus of 42 species of fast-growing tropical vines (Cucurbitaceae). They have deeply lobed or compound leaves, rather showy, open or bell-shaped white or yellow flowers, and small, warty, bitter fruit of a red or orange color. The immature fruits of *Momordica balsamina* are the cherished bitter melon of Oriental cooking. The mature fruits make interesting arrangements.

monadelphous (mahn uh dehl′fuhs) *a.* Of the stamens of a flower, united into 1 group, as can be seen in *Hibiscus*.

monadelphous flower

monander (muh nan′duhr) *n.* In botany, a plant having only 1 stamen, such as certain orchids.

monandrous (muh nan′druhs) *a.* In botany, having a single stamen.

monandrous flower

monarch-of-the-East *n.* A common name for *Sauromatum guttatum,* a tender tuberous perennial. It grows to 3 feet, with large, deeply lobed, fanlike leaves and foul-smelling callalike flowers with a red-spotted green callalike flower and a black-purple central spike to 3 feet long. Grown as a novelty or houseplant. Large tubers will bloom, without planting, on windowsills. Also known as voodoo lily or red calla.

Monarda (muh nahr′duh) *n.* A genus of 12 species of annual or perennial aromatic plants (Labiatae),

with a fragrance between that of mint and basil. They form bushy, leafy clumps from 12 inches to 4 feet, depending on the species. They have opposite, entire or toothed leaves and spikes of whorled clusters of white, pink, salmon pink, scarlet, or purple flowers that attract bees and hummingbirds. Used in masses in borders, in the wild garden, and traditional in cottage gardens and herb gardens. Commonly known as bee balm, oswego tea, wild bergamot, or horsemint.

Monarda
(beebalm)

Monardella (mahn uhr dehl′uh) *n.* A genus of 20 species of aromatic annual or perennial plants (Labiatae) native to western North America. They grow to 18 inches, with small, opposite leaves and spikes of whorled clusters of rose-purple or scarlet flowers. Used in rock gardens.

Moneses (moh nuh′seez) *n.* A genus of 1 species, *M. uniflora,* of hardy rhizomatous perennials (Pyrolaceae) native to North America. They have round, wavy-toothed leaves and solitary, fragrant white or pink flowers. Used in woodlands or wild gardens. Commonly known as one-flowered pyrola or one-flowered shinleaf.

money-flower *n.* The common honesty, *Lunaria annua.*

money plant *n.* The common honesty, *Lunaria annua.*

moneywort *n.* A common name for *Lysimachia Nummularia,* so called from its round leaves. It is a creeping perennial with long runners that root at the joints, small, round leaves, and bright yellow flowers. Used as a small-scale ground cover, near streams, or in hanging baskets. Also called creeping Jenny and herb twopence.

moniliform (muh nihl′uh form) *a.* Constricted at intervals and resembling a string of beads, as certain pods, roots, and stems.

Monimiaceae (muh nihm ee ay′see ee) *n. pl.* A family of 30 genera of tropical and subtropical shrubs and trees. They have aromatic, opposite leaves and inconspicuous flowers. The ornamental genera are *Hedycarya, Laurelia,* and *Pumus.*

monkey apple *n.* A common name for *Clusia rosea,* a subtropical West Indian tree with thick, leathery leaves, large pinkish-white flowers 2 inches across, and round greenish-white inedible fruit. Grown in warm-climate gardens; sometimes as a houseplant. Also called Scotch attorney, balsam apple, cupey, and copey.

monkey bread (mung′ki bred) *n.* A common name for the baobab tree; also, the fruit of the baobab tree. The fruit is a large woody capsule with numerous seeds embedded in a fibrous pulp; used to make a lemonade.

monkey bread fruit and flower

monkey flower *n.* A common name for *Mimulus,* a genus of annual and perennial flowers and shrubs. (See **Mimulus.**)

monkey pot *n.* A common name for *Lecythis,* a genus of 50 species of lofty tropical trees (Lecythidaceae) native to the Americas and its fruit. They grow to 80 feet, with alternate, simple, leathery leaves, clusters of sulfur yellow, white, violet, and rose flowers, and woody pods that open with a lidlike top.

monkey puzzle tree *n.* A common name for *Araucaria araucana,* a slow-growing, fairly hardy South American tree. It grows from 70 to 90 feet and has closely overlapping, leathery, sharp-pointed leaves and large cones. Juvenile trees are grown as pot plants. Mature trees drop branchlets of painfully spiky leaves, and huge cones come down with a crash. Grown as a novelty, but not a wonderful lawn tree. Also known as Chilean pine.

monkshood *n.* A plant of the genus *Aconitum,* especially *A. Napellus.* Also called friar's-cap, foxbane, helmetflower, and wolf's-bane.

monkshood-vine *n.* A common name for *Ampelosis aconitifolia,* a hardy vine. It has long-stemmed, deeply cut, hand-shaped leaves similar to those of monkshood *(Aconitum)* and small orange, yellow, or blue fruit. Used as a cover for walls and arbors.

mono- *comb. form* One or single.

monocarp (moh′noh kahrp) *n.* In botany, a plant that bears fruit once and then dies.

monocarpellary (moh noh karh′puh lehr ee) *a.* Of a flower, consisting of only 1 carpel.

monocarpic (moh noh kahr′pihk) *a.* Bearing fruit once and then dying, as annual plants.

monocarpous (moh noh kahr′puhs) *a.* In botany: 1. Of a flower, having a single ovary, whether simple or compound. 2. Monocarpellary.

monoclinous (moh′noh kligh nuhs) *a.* In botany, having the stamens and pistils in the same flower.

monocotyledon (moh noh kahd uh lee′duhn) *n.* A monocotyledonous plant; that is, one having a single seed leaf. (See **Monocotyledonae,** and **endogen.**)

Monocotyledonae (moh noh kahd uh lee′doh nee) *n. pl.* A subclass of flowering plants having a single seed leaf. The parts of the flowers are in threes (not in fives, as in dicotyledons), the first leaves are alternate, and the leaf veins are parallel. The class has 50,000 species, among which are the orchids, grasses, lilies, palms, amaryllis, iris, banana, pineapple, arum, rush, and sedge families. Commonly known as monocots.

monocotyledonous (moh noh kahd uh lee′doh nuhs) *a.* In botany, of or resembling plants of the subclass Monocotyledoneae, as in having only 1 seed leaf.

Monodora (moh noh doh′ruh) *n.* A genus of 15 species of tropical shrubs and trees (Annonaceae). *M. myristica* grows to 100 feet, with long; broad, drooping leaves to 20 inches long, large, pendulous, long-stemmed, white-to-yellow flowers spotted with red; and fruit, 6 inches in diameter, with aromatic seeds that are sometimes used like nutmeg. Commonly known as Africa nutmeg and Jamaica nutmeg.

monoecious (muh nee′shuhs) *a.* In botany, having male and female flowers on the same plant. Also spelled monecious.

monoecism (muh nee′sihz uhm) *n.* The condition of being monoecious. Also spelled monecism.

monogynoecial (moh noh jeh nee′shuhl) *a.* In botany, formed from a single pistil of a flower, as certain fruits.

monomerous (muh nahm′uhr uhs) *a.* In botany: 1. Having only 1 member in each whorl (pistil, stamen, petal, or sepal), said of a flower. 2. Monocarpellary.

monopetalous (moh noh pehd′uh luhs) *a.* In botany: 1. Having only 1 petal. 2. Having the petals united into 1 piece by their edges or at the base.

monopodial (moh noh poh′dee uhl) *a.* Having growth of the stem or rhizome continuing in the same direction indefinitely.

monopodium (moh noh poh′dee uhm) *n., pl.* **monopodia** (-a). In botany, an axis of growth that extends in the direction of previous growth, with lateral branches being produced beneath it, for example, as in certain coniferous trees.

monosepalous (moh noh sehp′uh luhs) *a.* In botany: 1. Having the sepals united. 2. Having only 1 sepal.

monosperm *n.* A plant that produces only 1 seed.

monospermous *a.* In botany, having only 1 seed.

monosporous (moh′noh spohr uhs) *a.* Having only 1 spore.

monostichous (muh nahs′teh kuhs) *a.* Arranged in a single row along a stem, as certain flowers.

monostylous (moh′noh stigh luhs) *a.* In botany, having only 1 style.

monosymmetrical *a.* In botany, capable of being bisected into similar halves with reference to a single plane; bilaterally symmetrical, as the flower of the sweet pea.

monotocous (muh nahd′uh kuhs) *a.* In botany, producing fruit only once, as annuals.

Monotropa (muh naht′ruh puh) *n.* A genus of 6 species of saprophytic fleshy plants (Pyrolaceae), some native to North America. They have white, red, or tawny stems and grow from 12 to 16 inches tall, with alternate, bractlike leaves and white, red, or pink flowers. *M. uniflora* is commonly known as Indian pipe, corpse plant, fitroot or fitsroot, pinesap, and convulsion root.

Monotropa
(Indian pipe)

monotypic *a.* Of a genus, consisting of a single species.

monovalent cations (kad′igh uhn) *n. pl.* Ions having a single positive charge.

Monstera (mahn′ztuhr uh) *n.* A genus of 12 species of epiphytic tropical climbing vines (Araceae). They grow very tall, frequently climbing to the tops of trees, with large, leathery, often perforated, leaves and short-lived, boat-shaped flowers; some species have edible fruit. Used primarily as houseplants; as outdoor vines in tropical or subtropical regions. Commonly known as windowleaf.

Monstera
(windowleaf)
a spadix and spathe

Montanoa (mahn tuh noh'uh) *n*. A genus of between 30 and 50 species of evergreen shrubs and small trees (Compositae) native to Central and South America. They grow from 10 to 20 feet, depending on the species, with opposite leaves and clusters of white, rose, or purple flowers. *M. grandiflora* grows to 12 feet, with large, deeply cut leaves and daisylike flowers, 3 inches across, with a fragrance like that of freshly baked cookies. Useful for tropical effects, as a winter flower, or as a background plant in mild-winter climates. Commonly known as daisy tree.

Montbretia (mahnt bree'shee uh) *n*. A former genus, the plants of which are now classified as *Tritonia* and *Crocosmia*. Now used as a common name for *Crocosmia*.

Monterey cypress (sigh'prehs) *n*. A common name for *Cupressus macrocarpa*, a beautiful, tender, coniferous evergreen tree, native to coastal California, picturesque in old age. It grows to 40 feet and more, with small scalelike pointed leaves and small cones. Used as an attractive, fast-growing windbreak along the coast, but subject to many diseases elsewhere.

Monterey pine *n*. A common name for *Pinus radiata*, a fast-growing, tender, evergreen coniferous tree. It grows from 80 to 100 feet, with 3- to 7-inch needles, in bundles of threes or twos, and clusters of lopsided cones 3-to-6-inches long. Used as a windbreak and fast-growing screen.

Montia (mahn'tee uh) *n*. A genus of about 50 species of annual or perennial plants (Portulaceae). They grow to 15 inches or less, with fleshy, alternate basal leaves, often edible, and spikes of small white or pink flowers. Useful in moist soils and near water. Commonly known as miner's lettuce.

moon daisy *n*. A common name for *Chrysanthemum Leucanthemum*, an erect, rhizomatous perennial flower. It grows to 3 feet, with long, toothed leaves and daisylike flowers with yellow centers and white petals. Has naturalized as a weed in North America. Also known as oxeye daisy, moonpenny, and moonflower.

moon fern *n*. A common name for *Botrychium Lunaria*, a small fern native to North and South America as well as the Old World. Also known as moonwort.

moonflower *n*. 1. A common name for *Ipomoea alba*, a tropical climbing vine with large fragrant night-blooming white flowers. 2. A common name for *Chrysanthemum Leucanthemum*, a naturalized weed with white daisylike flowers. Also known as moonpenny and oxeye daisy. 3. A common name for *Anemone nemorosa*, a low-growing woodland perennial with white flowers.

moonseed *n*. A common name for *Menispermum*, a genus of 2 species of very hardy woody vines, some species of which contain alkaloids and are poisonous.

moonseed, Canadian *n*. A common name for *Menispermum canadense*, a woody vine native to eastern North America. It grows to 12 feet, with 8-inch-long rounded leaves, fuzzy beneath when young, and clusters of small white or yellow flowers. Grown over arbors for its attractive foliage. Also known as yellow parilla.

moonseed, Carolina *n*. A common name for *Cocculus carolinus*, a twining vine with 4-inch-long lobed leaves, dense clusters of flowers, and bright red fruit; native to the southeastern United States. Good background plant or espalier.

moonseed family *n*. A common name for Menispermaceae, a family of 65 genera of mostly tropical twining woody vines, some native to North America. The ornamental genera are *Coccolulus* and *Menispermum*, some species of which contain alkaloids that are poisonous if eaten.

moonwort *n.* A common name for *Botrychium Lunaria,* a small fern native to North and South America as well as the Old World. Also known as moon fern. (See **Botrychium.**)

moor *n.* A tract of open, untilled, and more or less elevated land, often overrun with heath.

moor grass *n.* (See **Molinia.**)

moorwort *n.* A common name for *Andromeda,* a genus of small shrubs, several of which are native to North America. Also known as bog rosemary.

moose elm *n.* A common name for *Ulmus rubra,* a small- to medium-sized deciduous tree native to eastern and southeastern North America and west to Texas. Also called slippery elm.

moosewood *n.* 1. A common name for *Acer pensylvanicum,* a very hardy small, slender tree. (See **maple, striped.**) 2. A common name for *Dirca palustris,* a hardy deciduous shrub native to eastern North America. Also known as wicopy and ropebark. 3. A common name for *Viburnum alnifolium,* a hardy deciduous shrub native to eastern and central North America. Also known as hobblebush, American wayfaring tree, devil's shoestring, dogberry, dog hobble, moosebush, mooseberry, tanglefoot, tangle-legs, trip-toe, White Mountain dogwood, witch hobble, and witch hopple.

Moraceae (muh ray'see ee) *n.* A family of 53 to 75 genera and 1,400 to 1,850 species of vines, shrubs, and trees. The ornamental genera include *Cecropia, Ficus* (fig), *Maclura* (osage orange), and *Morus* (mulberry).

Moraea (muh ree'uh) *n.* A genus of 100 species of tender bulbs (corms) (Iridaceae). They grow 4 feet or less, with sword-shaped leaves and clusters of multicolored irislike flowers, each of which blooms for a single day. Used in perennial borders, beds, and containers. Commonly known as butterfly iris and Natal lily.

Morchella (mawr kehl'uh) *n.* A genus of edible wild mushrooms; the morels. They are conical, heavily pitted, and typically appear in May in many regions of the United States. Much prized in French cuisine. Also known as morel.

morel (muh rehl') *n.* A common name for the genus *Morchella,* an edible wild mushroom. (See **Morchella.**)

morello (muh reh'loh) *n.* A cherry with a dark red skin, becoming nearly black if allowed to hang long. The deep purplish-red flesh is tender, juicy, and acid. It is a standard cherry, often used in cooking and preserved in brandy.

Moreton Bay chestnut (mohr'tuhn) *n.* A name given to *Castanospermum australe,* also called bean tree or black bean.

Moreton Bay fig (mohr'tuhn) *n.* A common name for *Ficus macrophylla,* a large subtropical and tropical tree. It grows to 50 feet in cultivation, to 200 feet in the wild, with large, glossy, oval, pointed leaves, silvery or rusty-dotted below, and small, round reddish-brown-to-purple fruit. Also known as Australian banyan.

Moreton Bay pine (mohr'tuhn) *n.* A common name for *Araucaria cunninghamii,* a large tender coniferous tree. Grown for its striking silhouette of upturned branches, it can tower to well over 100 feet at maturity, a size that makes it best suited to parklands and great estates. Also called hoop pine.

Morinda (muh rihn'duh) *n.* A genus of approximately 80 species of tropical vines, shrubs, and trees (Rubiaceae). *M. citrifolia,* the Indian mulberry or awl tree, is a small tree with entire leaves, small white flowers, and fleshy, yellow, poisonous fruit.

Moringa (muh rihnj'guh) *n.* A genus of 3 or more species of deciduous trees (Moringaceae). They grow to 30 feet, with large leaves to 2 feet long divided into small leaflets, white fragrant flowers to 1 inch across, and long, narrow, pendulous edible fruit. Grown as an ornamental in tropical gardens.

Moringaceae (moh rihnj gay'see ee) *n. pl.* A common name for the moringa family.

morning flower *n.* A common name for the genus *Orthrosanthus,* perennial flowers native to tropical America. It grows from 18 inches to 3 feet, with basal, grasslike leaves and clusters of violet-blue flowers. Also known as morning flag.

morning glory *n.* A common name for plants of the genera *Ipomoea, Convolvulus, Calystegia, Merremia,* and *Argyreia.* Also a common name for the species *I. nil* and *I. tricolor.*

morning glory, beach *n.* A common name for *Ipomoea Pes-capra,* a creeping vine to 60 feet used for binding sand dunes. Also known as railroad vine.

morning glory, Brazilian *n.* A common name for *Ipomoea setosa,* a tropical perennial twining vine with 3-lobed grapelike leaves and rose-purple flowers to 3 inches long.

morning glory, bush *n.* A common name for *Convolvulus cneorum,* a small, fast-growing tender shrub. It grows from 2 to 4 feet, with silky, silvery round-to-oval leaves and white or pink flowers with yellow throats opening from pink buds. Used in rock gardens or as a bank cover. It is fire-retardant when given adequate water. Also known as silverbush.

morning glory, Ceylon (say'lawn) *n.* A common name for *Merremia tuberosa,* a tropical perennial twining vine. It has variable, 7-parted leaves, with the middle segment longer than those on the sides, yellow flowers to 2 inches long, and round fruit. Also known as wood rose, Hawaiian wood rose, yellow morning glory, and Spanish woodbine.

morning glory, common *n.* A common name for *Ipomoea purpurea,* a fast-growing annual twining vine, naturalized in North America. It has hairy stems, large leaves, either entire or lobed, and purple, blue, or pink flowers. Used to cover fences, arbors, sun porches, or gazebos.

morning glory, dwarf *n.* A common name for *Convolvulus tricolor,* a bushy, trailing summer annual. It grows to 12 inches high and 24 inches wide, with small, narrow leaves and white-margined blue flowers with yellow throats. Used as edging, to tumble over walls, in pots, and in hanging baskets.

morning glory family *n.* A common name for *Convolvulaceae,* a family of 50 genera and 1,200 species of vines, shrubs, and trees. It includes *Ipomoea* (morning glory), *Convolvulus* (bindweed), and *Cuscuta* (dodder), among others. The principal food product of the family is the sweet potato, *Ipomoea Batatas.*

morning glory, ground *n.* A common name for *Convolvulus mauritanicus,* a tender evergreen perennial. It grows 1 to 2 feet tall, with trailing branches to 3 feet or more, and has soft, round, furry, gray-green leaves and clusters of blue or violet-purple flowers to 2 inches across. Used on banks, as a ground cover, as a cascade over walls, in window boxes, or in hanging baskets.

morning glory, Imperial Japanese *n.* A common name for *Ipomoea Nil,* a fast-growing summer annual or perennial twining vine. It has heart-shaped or oval, lobed leaves and very showy violet, purple, rose, or blue flowers, which may be fringed, fluted, or double. Grown over fences, up posts, and on arbors or gazebos.

morning glory, red *n.* A common name for *Ipomoea coccinea,* a fast-growing annual twining vine native to the eastern and southeastern United States. It grows to 10 feet, with heart-shaped-to-oval leaves and scarlet flowers with a yellow throat. Also known as star ipomoea.

morning glory, silver *n.* A common name for *Argyrea splendens,* a tall, tropical climbing vine. It has long, elliptic leaves, white and silky beneath, and long-stemmed, rose-colored flowers. Used in warm-climate gardens.

morning glory, wild *n.* A common name for *Calystegia sepium,* a twining perennial vine native to North America. It has oval-to-triangular, long-stemmed leaves and rose-colored flowers. Naturalized in the United States and widely considered a noxious weed. Also known as bindweed, hedge bindweed, and Rutland beauty. 2. The common name for *Convolvulus arvensis,* popularly known as bindweed, and considered a noxious weed.

morning glory, woolly *n.* A common name for *Argyrea nervosa,* a large tropical climbing vine. It has large oval-to-heart-shaped leaves 12 inches across, furry beneath, with large, long-stemmed, rose-colored flowers. It has naturalized in Florida.

morning glory, yellow *n.* A common aname for *Merremia tuberosa,* a tropical perennial twining vine. (See **morning glory, Ceylon.**)

morphology *n.* The science of the form and structure of animals and plants and of their organs.

Morus (moh'ruhs) *n.* A genus of about 10 species of deciduous trees (Moraceae), some species native to the Americas. They grow to 80 feet or less, depending on the species, with simple, alternate, wrinkled leaves, often lobed, and flowering catkins. The edible fruit, which resembles a blackberry, attracts birds, the foliage is food for silkworms. Commonly known as mulberry.

mosaic (moh zay'ihk) *n.* Unusual mottling, streaking, or veining, often very colorful, in the leaves of a plant. Often caused by a virus.

moss *n.* A common name for low-growing, non-flowering, rootless plants, without a vascular (circulatory) system, of the class Musci. Some are grown ornamentally, for example, *Sagina* (Irish moss). Other genera are called mosses, such as *Lycopodium* (club moss) and *Selaginella* (little club moss or spike moss), but these are not true mosses since they have vascular systems.

mossberry *n.* (See **cranberry**.)

moss campion (kam'pee uhn) *n.* A common name for *Silene acaulis,* a hardy, dwarf, tufted, mosslike plant, with purple flowers 1/2-inch across; native to the mountains of western North America. Used in rock gardens and in alpine collections. Also known as cushion pink and carpet pink.

moss, flowering *n.* 1. A common name for *Pyxidanthera barbulata,* a low-growing, creeping evergreen plant native to the eastern United States, with small bright green leaves and numerous tiny white or rose-colored flowers. Used in rock gardens, but difficult. Also known as pyxie and pine-barren-beauty. 2. A common name for *Sedum pulchellum,* a biennial succulent native to the eastern United States with small, blunt, cylindrical, fleshy leaves and clusters of rosy-purple flowers on stalks to 12 inches tall.

moss locust *n.* A common name for *Robinia hispida,* a deciduous shrub native to the southeastern United States. It spreads by stolons and grows to 7 feet, with leaves having several pairs of very small dark green leaflets, clusters of small rose or pale purple flowers, and hairy fruit 3 inches long. Grown as a specimen shrub. Also known as rose acacia, bristly locust, and mossy locust.

moss pink *n.* A common name for *Phlox subulata,* a low-growing hardy perennial native to the rocky hills of the eastern and central United States. It grows to 6 inches, with needlelike leaves on creeping stems and masses of rose, pink, white or lavender-blue flowers. A choice rock-garden plant. Also known as moss phlox and mountain phlox.

moss rose *n.* A common name for *Rosa centifolia muscosa,* a hardy fragrant rose noted for the moss-like growth on its buds and calyx. It is believed to be a mutation of *R. centifolia,* probably in the 1700s. *R. centifolia* is also known as the cabbage rose or Provence rose.

mother-of-thousands *n.* A common name for plants of several genera, including *Cymbelaria muralis* (Kenilworth ivy, pennywort, or colosseum ivy), *Saxifraga stolonifera* (strawberry geranium), *Bellis perennis* (English daisy), *Chrysanthemum Leucanthemum* (oxeye daisy), *Brachycome iberidifolia* (Swan River daisy), any plant of the genus *Vittadinia,* and any of the wildflowers of the genera *Aster* and *Erigeron* (fleabane).

mother-of-thyme *n.* The wild thyme, *Thymus Serpyllum.* A low, woody variety with hairy leaves.

motherwort *n.* A common name for plants of several genera: *Leonurus, Artemisia* (mugwort, sagebrush or wormwood), *Chrysanthemum parthenium* (feverfew), *Eupatorium purpureum* (Joe-Pye weed), and *Lysimachia nummularia* (moneywort or creeping Jenny).

moth mullein (muh'lehn) *n.* A common name for *Verbascum Blattaria,* the parent of several garden hybrids. It is a tall biennial that grows to 6 feet from a rosette of basal leaves, with smooth, dark green cut or toothed leaves and tall spikes of yellow or white flowers with purple stamens. It has naturalized in North America. Used in sunny borders.

moth orchid *n.* A common name for *Phalaenopsis,* a genus of epiphytic tropical orchids. They are low-growing orchids, with thick, broad, leathery leaves and tall, slender spikes of large, showy, exquisite white, pale yellow, pink, or lavender flowers 3 to 6 inches across. The flower sprays may reach 3 to 5 feet in length. Used as long-blooming houseplants or grown in greenhouses with 60° to 70° F night temperatures. Also known as moth plant.

moth plant *n.* A plant of the genus *Phalaenopsis.* Also known as moth orchid.

moth trap *n.* A pheromone-baited device used to lure and capture moths.

mottled leaf (mahd'uhld) *n.* 1. A disease caused by a zinc deficiency that reduces the size of leaves and fruits in citrus plants. 2. A disease that causes the leaves of cherry to pucker and wrinkle.

mountain ash *n.* A common name for trees of several genera: *Sorbus, Eucalyptus Sieberi* (black mountain ash) and *E. regnans* (giant gum), and *Fraxinus texensis* (Texas ash).

mountain avens (av'ehnz) *n.* A common name for *Dryas octopetala,* a very hardy, small, prostrate shrub native to alpine and arctic regions of North America, specifically from Alaska to Greenland. It has large white strawberrylike flowers, followed by a number of seeds with long, feathery silver-white tails. Choice subjects for the rock garden or alpine collection.

mountain balm *n.* A common name for a tender evergreen shrub, *Eriodictyon californicum,* native to California and Oregon. It has narrow, sticky leaves, with white hairs between the veins, and clusters of purple-to-white flowers. The genus is commonly known as yerba santa.

mountain cranberry *n.* A common name for *Vaccinium Vitis-Idaea* var. *minus,* a very hardy dwarf evergreen shrub native to North America. It forms dense mats with creeping rhizomes, and it has small, glossy, dark green leaves, clusters of pink-to-red flowers, and sour, edible red berries resembling cranberries. The berries are prized for use in preserves and syrups. Used as an attractive container plant or as a small-scale ground cover in moist soils. Commonly known as rock cranberry, lingberry, lingenberry, and lingonberry.

mountain damson *n.* A common name for *Simarouba glauca,* a tropical tree native from southern Florida to the West Indies, west to Mexico, and south to Costa Rica. It grows to 50 feet, with long leaves divided into many oblong or narrowly oval leaflets, clusters of scarlet or purple flowers, and fleshy, elliptical fruit. Also known as paradise tree, bitterwood, and aceituno.

mountain fern *n.* A common name for *Thelypteris Oreopteris (Polystichum montanum)* and *T. phegopteris,* hardy ferns. *T. Oreopteris* is native from Washington to Alaska; it has long, narrow, divided fronds 3 feet long and 8 inches wide. Also known as mountain wood fern. *T. phegopteris (Polypodium phegopteris)* has finely divided fronds 9 inches long and 8 inches wide. Both can be used in the woodland garden. Also known as long beech fern and narrow beech fern.

mountain fringe (moun'tan frinj) *n.* A common name for *Adlumia fungosa,* a hardy, high-climbing perennial vine native to eastern North America. It climbs by its leaf stems and has delicate, fernlike leaves and clusters of white-to-purple flowers resembling a bleeding heart. Useful in shady situations and cool, moist soils, in woodland gardens, and in places protected from wind. Also known as climbing fumitory, mountain fringe, and Allegheny vine.

mountain heath *n.* A common name for *Phyllodoche caerulea,* a very hardy dwarf evergreen heathlike shrublet native to arctic and subarctic regions, south to Maine and New Hampshire. It grows to 6 inches, with tiny leaves and purple urn-shaped flowers. Used in rock gardens in moist, peaty soil. Also known as mountain heather.

mountain holly *n.* 1. A common name for *Nemopanthes mucronatus,* a hardy shrub native to eastern North America, from Newfoundland west to Indiana and south to Virginia. It grows to 10 feet, spreading by stolons, with smooth, fibrous bluish-green leaves that turn yellow in autumn, yellow 4- or 5-petaled flowers, and dark red fruit. The new growth has purple branches, which turn ash-gray at maturity. Grown for its attractive fruit and colorful fall foliage. Also known as catberry and Canadian holly. 2. A common name for *Ilex ambigua* var. *montana,* a hardy deciduous shrub or small tree native to the United States, from Massachusetts to Alabama and Georgia. It has large, dull green leaves, slightly wrinkled beneath, and round red, translucent fruit. Also known as large-leafed holly and mountain winterberry. 3. A common name for *Prunus ilicifolia,* a dense evergreen shrub or small tree native from California to northern Baja California. It grows from 3 to 25 feet with shiny, leathery, crisped leaves, small creamy-white flowers, and small red or yellow fruit. Used as a small tree, tall screen, or formal clipped hedge. Also known as holly-leaved cherry, hollyleaf cherry, evergreen cherry, wild cherry, and islay.

mountain laurel *n.* A common name for plants of 2 genera: *Kalmia latifolia* (calico bush, ivy, ivybush, and spoonwood) and *Umbellularia californica* (bay tree, California bay, California laurel, California olive, myrtle, Oregon myrtle, and pepperwood).

mountain lover *n.* A common name for *Paxistima Canbyi,* a dwarf evergreen shrub native to the mountains of Virginia and West Virginia. It grows to 16 inches, with long, blunt leaves and small reddish-brown flowers. Used in the border, wild garden, or rock garden. Also known as cliff-green. 2. A common name for *P. Myrsinites,* a prostrate, spreading evergreen shrub native to North America, from British Columbia east to Montana and south to California and Mexico. It has tiny, finely notched, dark green glossy leaves and small reddish-brown flowers. Used in the rock garden. Also known as Oregon boxwood.

mountain magnolia (mag noh'lyuh) *n.* A common name for *Magnolia acuminata* and *M. fraserii,* deciduous trees native to North America. *M. acuminata* is a hardy tree, native from southern Ontario to Louisiana, that grows from 60 to 80 feet, with large leaves to 10 inches long, hairy beneath, small greenish-yellow flowers, and handsome reddish seed capsules with red seeds. Used as a shade or lawn tree. Also known as cucumber tree. *M. fraserii* is a fairly hardy tree native to the South from Virginia to northern Alabama. It grows to 50 feet, with large leaves to 18 inches long, looking like parasols at the end of the branches, showy, fragrant white or pale yellow flowers to 10 inches across, and showy rose-red seed capsules in summer. Used as a lawn tree or woodland tree. Also known as ear-leaved umbrella tree.

mountain mahoe (muh hoh') *n.* A common name for *Hibiscus tiliaceus,* a tropical spreading evergreen shrub or small tree. It grows to 20 feet or more, with leathery leaves, green above and white below, and clusters of yellow or white flowers with red eyes that fade to orange-yellow to deep red. Also known as mahoe.

mountain mahogany *n.* 1. A common name for *Betula lenta,* a deciduous tree native to North America, from Maine to Alabama. Its aromatic twigs and bark are the main source of wintergreen. Also known as cherry birch, sweet birch, mahogany birch, and black birch. 2. A common name for *Taxus brevifolia,* a slow-growing evergreen coniferous tree native to western North America, from Alaska to California and east to Montana. Also known as western yew.

mountain maple *n.* A common name for *Acer spicatum,* a very hardy North American shrub or small tree native from Newfoundland south to Georgia, west to Minnesota. It grows to 30 feet and has gray, downy twigs and 3- to 5-lobed leaves, light green above and furry below, that turn orange, scarlet, or yellow in autumn. 2. A common name for *Acer glabrum douglasii* var. *Torreyi,* a hardy deciduous shrub or small tree native to the Sierra Nevada of California. It grows to 30 feet, often less, with dark red twigs and 3- to 5-lobed leaves that turn yellow in fall. Grows best in the mountains; generally forms a multistemmed clump. Also known as Sierra maple. 3. A common name for *Acer circinatum,* the vine maple, a hardy small, slender, sprawling, airy, delicate-looking deciduous shrub or tree native to western North America, from British Columbia to northern California. It grows to 35 feet, with 5- to 11-lobed leaves that turn orange, scarlet, or yellow in fall. Untrimmed, it forms natural bowers, creates a woodland effect; or it can be trained as an espalier against a shady wall. It loses its vinelike characteristics in open, sunny situations. 4. A common name for *Alnus rhombifolia,* a hardy fast-growing deciduous tree native to western North America. It grows from 50 to 100 feet, with a 40-foot spread, depending on conditions, with coarsely toothed dark green leaves, pale green beneath. The seeds attract birds. Used in moist soils, especially near streams. Also known as white alder.

mountain mint *n.* A common name for aromatic plants of several genera, including the North American genus *Pycnanthemum; P. virginianum, Satureja* (savory), *Calamintha* (calamint), and *Monarda didyma* (bee balm).

mountain parsley *n.* A common name for *Cryptogramma crispa,* a small alpine or woodland fern with finely divided leaves resembling parsley. Also called European parsley fern and mountain parsley fern.

mountain pride *n.* A common name for *Penstemon Newberryi,* a mat-forming, woody-based perennial native to California and Nevada. It grows to 20 inches, with small, thick, roundish leaves and rose-red summer flowers that attract hummingbirds. Used in rock gardens.

mountain rhubarb (roo'bahrb) *n.* A common name for *Rumex alpinus,* for the most part a road-side weed; however, dried flowers of *Rumex* are gathered for dried-flower arrangements. The young leaves of *R. alpinus* are edible. Also known as monk's rhubarb.

mountain rose *n.* A common name for plants of several genera: *Rosa pendulina* (alpine rose), *Antigonon leptopus* (chain-of-love vine, love vine, queen's wreath, queen's jewels, Mexican creeper, corallita, rosa de montana, Confederate vine, pink vine, and coral vine), and *Rhododendron catawbiense* (catawba rose, mountain rosebay, and purple laurel).

mountain sandwort *n.* A common name for *Arenaria groenlandica,* a very hardy North American mat-forming perennial native from Greenland south to Tennessee. It grows to 6 inches and has tiny, narrow leaves and clusters of white flowers. Used in rock gardens or grown over walls. Also known as mountain daisy.

mountain sorrel (saw'ruhl) *n.* A common name for the genus *Oxyria,* a very hardy perennial native to alpine and arctic regions. It has basal, kidney-shaped leaves, clusters of small, green flowers, and red, broadly-winged fruit. Used in moist rock gardens.

mountain spinach *n.* A common name for a tall erect plant, *Atriplex hortensis,* so called for its large succulent leaves, which are used as spinach. It is cultivated in France, under the name *arroche.* Also called garden orache.

mountain-sweet *n.* New Jersey tea. (See **Ceanothus**.)

mountain tea *n.* The American wintergreen, (See *Gaultheria procumbens.*)

mourning bride *n.* A common name for *Scabiosa atropurpurea;* a self-sowing annual, which may persist in mild-winter climates. It grows to 3 feet and has coarsely toothed, oblong leaves, with many long, wiry stemmed clusters of dark purple, lilac, rose, pink, or white flowers. It has naturalized in California. Also known as pincushions and sweet scabious.

mouse-ear *n.* A common name for plants of several genera: *Hieracium Pilosella* (mouse-ear hawkweed and felon herb), *Antennaria plantaginifolia* (mouse-ear everlasting, mouse-ear plantain, and cat's-foot), *Myosotis* (forget-me-not and scorpion grass), *Cerastium* (mouse-ear chickweed and clammy chickweed), and *Arabidopsis Thaliana* (mouse-ear cress). Most of these are weeds, with the exception of *Myosotis.*

mouse plant *n.* A common name for *Arisarem proboscideum,* a Mediterranean rhizomatous creeping perennial. It has long, narrow leaves and curiously shaped olive-green hooded flowers with a deep purple mouth and a green taillike tip 4 to 6 inches long. Useful in partly shaded situations.

mouse trap *n.* Any of various devices for luring and trapping mice. Spring traps kill; live traps do not.

mow *n.* A heap or pile of hay, or of sheaves of grain, deposited in a barn; also, in the west of England, a rick or stack of hay or grain. *v.* 1. To cut down (grass or grain) with a sharp implement; cut with a scythe or (in recent use) a mowing machine; to cut down in general. 2. To cut the grass from, as to mow a meadow.

mower-mulcher *n.* A machine for simultaneously mowing grass and recutting the clippings, which are then spread on the lawn as mulch. Also called mulching mower.

mucro (myoo'kroh) *n., pl.* **mucrones** (myoo kroh'neez). In botany, a short, sharp spur, as on the tip of a leaf.

mucronate (myoo'kruh nayt) *a.* Having a short, sharp point or tip.

mucronulate (myoo kruh'nuh layt) *a.* Having a very small mucro.

mucronulate leaf

Mucuna (myoo kyoo'nuh) *n.* A genus of more than 100 species of tropical climbing or creeping vines (Leguminosae). They climb to 60 feet, with alternate leaves divided into 3 leaflets and showy, draping clusters of orange, red, scarlet or multi-colored butterflylike flowers. The fruit is a thick, leathery, beanlike pod often covered with stinging hairs. Grown in tropical gardens or in warm greenhouses.

mudar (muh dahr´) *n.* A common name for the genus *Calotropis*, especially *C. gigantea* and *C. procera*, both grown as greenhouse specimens. Also called madar.

mud plantain (plan´tuhn) *n.* A common name for *Heteranthera*, a genus of tender North American water plants. Grown in pools or ponds. 2. A common name for the genus *Alisma*, widely distributed marsh or water plants, some species native to North America. Grown in ponds or bogs for both its foliage and its many white or rose-tinged flowers.

Muehlenbeckia (myoo luhn behk´ee uh) *n.* A genus of about 20 species of unusual tender, evergreen, climbing, woody vines, (Polygonaceae) with thin wirelike black or brown stems, forming a dense tangle. *M. complexa* grows from 20 to 30 feet, with tiny round leaves and inconspicuous white flowers. Used to cover anything unsightly: rock piles, old stumps, etc; also useful as as a beach plant. The genus is commonly known as wire vine or wire plant; *M.complexa* is known as maidenhair vine, necklace vine, horsehair vine, or mattress vine.

mugwort *n.* The plant *Artemisia vulgaris.* The leaves are pale green and furry beneath.

mulberry *n.* The berrylike fruit of the mulberry tree. The black mulberry, *M. nigra*, yields a pleasant, dark-colored fruit, and its leaves were formerly in extensive use for feeding silkworms. The white mulberry, *M. alba,* has almost superseded the black mulberry in silkworm culture. The red or American mulberry, *M. rubra,* a native of the United States, is the largest species of the genus.

mulberry

mulberry, French *n.* A common name for *Callicarpa americana,* a shrub native to North America, from Virginia to Texas and the West Indies. It grows to 6 feet, has long, toothed leaves, rusty and furry beneath, and bears clusters of blue flowers and abundant violet-colored berries. Also called beautyberry.

mulberry, Indian *n.* A common name for *Morinda citrifolia*, a small tropical tree with entire leaves, small, white flowers and fleshy, yellow, poisonous fruit. Also known as the awl tree.

mulberry or fig family *n.* A common name for *Moraceae*, a family of 53 to 75 genera and 1,400 to 1,850 species of vines, shrubs, and trees. The ornamental genera include *Cecropia*, *Ficus* (fig), *Maclura* (Osage orange), and *Morus* (mulberry).

mulberry tree *n.* (See **mulberry**.)

mulch (muhlch) *n.* Any of various organic or inorganic materials, such as leaves, hay, straw, manure, or black plastic, spread around plants to prevent moisture loss and discourage weed growth. *v.* To spread mulch.

mulching blade (mulhch´ihng) *n.* A lawn mower blade that cuts grass, redirects the clippings back into the path of the blade, chops them finely, and redeposits them as mulch on the lawn.

mulching mower (muhlch´ihng) *n.* (See **mower-mulcher**.)

mulching paper (muhlch´ihng) *n.* A biodegradable sheet made of peat; used to reduce water use and discourage weeds.

mule *n.* A plant hybrid that is self-sterile and usually cross-sterile due to infertile pollen or undeveloped pistils.

mull *n.* A humus-rich layer of forested soils consisting of mixed organic and mineral matter.

mullein (muh´lehn) *n.* A common name for the genus *Verbascum*, biennial or short-lived perennial flowers. *V. olympicum* grows to 5 feet, with a basal rosette of soft, furry, almost white leaves and a tall stalk of showy yellow flowers. Grown for its foliage the first year, for its flowers thereafter. Used in the border and the wild garden. Also known as Adam's flannel, blanket leaf, blanket plant, candlewick mullen feltwort, flannelflower, hare's-beard, hare's-beards, hag-taper, hag's-taper. An alternate spelling is mullen.

mullein
a flower spike *b* single leaf

mullein pink (muh′lehn) *n.* A common name for *Lychnis Coronaria,* a self-sowing annual, biennial, or perennial. It grows to 3 feet, with attractive, silky white leaves and tall stalks of magenta-to-crimson flowers. Best used massed. Also known as crown-pink, rose campion and dusty miller.

multi- *comb. form* Many.

multicarpellate (muhl teh kahr′puh layt) *a.* Having a compound pistil or ovary formed by the joining of several carpels.

multiple fruit *n.* A fruit such as the pineapple, which is actually the fruits of several flowers that have formed in a single cluster.

mung bean (muhng′) *n.* A tiny green Asian bean variety used to make bean sprouts.

Munstead lavender (muhn′stehd) *n.* A strain of *Lavandula angustifolia,* dwarf in growth and blooming earlier than the other English lavenders. It blooms profusely with deep purple flowers, which are highly fragrant and retain the scent well on drying.

Muntingia (muhn tinj′ee uh) *n.* A genus of 1 species, *M. Calabura,* of tropical American tree (Elaeocarpaceae). It grows to 30 feet, with asymmetrical, alternate leaves, single or clustered white flowers, and small white fruit. Also known as calabur.

muriate of potash (myoo′ree ayth uhv pahd′ash) *n.* A slow-acting fertilizer that adds oxide of potassium to the soil. Same as potassium chloride.

muricate (myoo′ruh kayt) *a.* Having a rough surface due to the presence of many tiny sharp points.

Murraya (muh′ree uh) *n.* A genus of 4 species of subtropical shrubs or small trees (Rutaceae). *M. paniculata* is a fast-growing shrub or small tree to 12 feet, with glossy, dark green leaves divided into leaflets and small, bell-shaped, jasmine-scented flowers that bloom several times a year and attract bees. Used as a hedge, for topiary, or as a background shrub. The genus is commonly known as mock orange. *M. paniculata* is commonly known as orange jessamine, orange jasmine, satinwood, cosmetic-bark tree, and Chinese box.

Musa (myoo′zuh) *n.* A genus of 25 giant subtropical treelike plants (Musaceae), the largest herbaceous plants known; the banana. They grow from 2 feet to 30 feet, with huge, broad leaves to 9 feet long, enormous flower stalks with red, reddish-purple, or yellow flowers, and edible bananas in colors ranging from yellow to red to velvety pink. Grown for the bananas and for the tropical effect of the massive leaves and exotic flowers. Commonly known as banana or plantain.

Musaceae (myoo zay′see ee) *n. pl.* A common name for the banana family, a family of 2 genera and 42 species of huge herbaceous plants. The ornamental genera are *Ensete* and *Musa.*

musaceous (myoo zay′shuhs) *a.* In botany, pertaining to or resembling the family Musaceae.

Muscari (muhs kay′righ) *n.* A genus of 40 species of spring-flowering bulbs (Liliaceae). They grow to 18 inches, with narrow, grassy, fleshy leaves and stalks of small, urn-shaped blue, white, or, rarely, yellow flowers. Used to naturalize in drifts, in woodland gardens, massed under trees and shrubs, as edging, in rock gardens, and in containers. Commonly known as grape hyacinth.

muscat (muhs′kat) *n.* One of several varieties of grape, mostly white, used in wine making.

Musci (muh′sigh) *n. pl.* A large class of cryptogamous plants; the mosses. They are low, tufted plants, a few inches in height, always with a stem and distinct leaves, producing spore cases (sporangia), which usually open by a terminal lid and contain simple spores. (See cut under **moss**.)

musciform (muhs′uh form) *a.* In botany, relating to or resembling moss.

mushquash root (muh′skwash) *n.* A common name for the North American plant *Cicuta maculata,* a bog plant that grows to 6 feet, with purple-mottled stems, much-divided leaves, and large rounded clusters of small white flowers. It is poisonous. Sometimes grown in the bog garden. Also known as spotted cowbane and beaver poison.

mushroom (mush′rume) *n.* A common name for the fruiting body of fungi. Mushrooms are found in all parts of the world and are usually of very rapid growth. Some mushrooms are edible and much prized, including the morel *(Morchella esculenta)* and the king bolete *(Boletus edulis),* also known as *cep, porcini,* and *steinpilz.*

muskflower *n.* A common name for plants of several different genera: *Mimulus* (monkey flower), especially *M. moschatus* (musk plant); *Erodium* (crane's-bill), especially *E. moschatum* (musk clover or white-stemmed filaree); *Muscari* (grape hyacinth), especially *M. racemosum* (musk hyacinth or nutmeg hyacinth); and *Malva* (mallow), especially *M. moschata* (musk mallow). Also known as musk plant and musk.

musk mallow *n.* 1. A common name for *Malva moschata,* a leafy-branched, hairy perennial to 3 feet, with divided leaves and white or rose-mauve flowers 1 to 2 inches across. Also known as musk rose.

muskmellon *n.* A well-known plant, *Cucumis Melo,* and its fruit, more often known as cantaloupe.

musk rose *n.* A common name for *Rosa moschata,* a species of rose, so called from its fragrance. It is a tall rose with arching or overhanging canes and fragrant white flowers 1 to 2 inches across. It has naturalized in North America. 2. Also a common name for *Malva moschata* (musk mallow).

musk seed *n.* A common name for the seed of *Hibiscus moschatus,* used for perfume and to flavor coffee. Also known as abelmosk and amber seed.

mustard *n.* A plant of the genus *Brassica.* The ordinary species are *B. nigra* (black mustard), and *B. alba* (white mustard). The black and white mustards are largely cultivated in Europe and America for their seeds which are crushed and sifted and then mixed with other ingredients as a condiment.

mustard family *n.* A common name for Cruciferae, a family of about 350 genera and 3,200 spe-

mustard
1 flower stalk 2 single leaf

cies of pungent or acrid plants. It includes many edible species, including cabbage, broccoli, cauliflower, kale, kohlrabi, turnips, radish, and rutabaga. The edible genera are *Brassica* (cabbage and mustard), *Lepidium* (cress), *Nasturtium* (watercress), *Raphanus* (radish), *Romarmoracia* (horseradish), and *Wasabia* (Japanese horseradish, or *wasabe*). The ornamental genera are *Aethionema* (stonecress), *Alyssoides* (bladderpod), *Alyssum* (madwort), *Arabis* (rock cress), *Aubrieta, Aurinia, Brassica* (ornamental kale), *Cardamine, Cheiranthes* (wallflower), *Crambe* (colewort), *Diplotaxis* (rocket), *Draba, Erysimum* (wallflower, or blister cress), *Hesperis* (rocket), *Iberis* (candytuft), *Lobularia, Lunaria* (honesty), and *Matthiola* (stock). Brassicaceae is a synonym for Cruciferae.

mustard, mithridate (mihth′ruh dayt) *n.* A common name for *Thlaspi arvense,* a rather weedy, erect, ill-smelling annual that has naturalized in North America. It is of interest for its flat, short-winged pods. Also known as pennycress, field pennycress, French weed, fanweed, and stinkweed.

mustard, tower *n.* A common name for *Arabis glabra,* a stiff, erect biennial to 4 feet, with oblong, notched leaves and spikes of small yellowish-white flowers. It has naturalized in North America.

mustard, wild *n.* A common name for *Brassica Kabe,* a troublesome yellow-flowered weed in fields. Also known as charlock and California rape.

mustard, wormseed *n.* A common name for *Erysimum cheiranthoides,* a slender, yellow-flowered mustard considered a troublesome weed.

mutation *n.* An alteration in genetic material caused by an actual physical change within the genes of a cell. When such changes occur in the germ cells, they are able to be passed on to the offspring as inherited traits, producing such effects as a leaf shape or flower color different from that of the parent.

Mutisia (myoo tihz'hee uh) *n.* A genus of 60 species of tender erect shrubs or climbing vines (Compositae) native to South America. They grow to 20 feet, with alternate leaves, many terminating in a tendril by which it climbs, and large purple, scarlet, rose, pink, orange, or yellow flowers. Used in mild-climate areas.

mycelial (migh see'lee uhl) *a.* Of or pertaining to mycelium.

mycelioid (migh see'lee oid) *a.* In botany, resembling mycelium.

mycelium (migh see'lee uhm) *n.* The mass of filaments that form the rootlike part of fungi.

mycology (migh kah'luh jee) *n.* The science of fungi; the study of mushrooms.

Mylar tape (migh'lahr) *n.* A mirrorlike tape used to frighten birds. Cut into streamers, Mylar tape frightens by both sound and reflection.

Myoporaceae (migh ahp uh ray'see ee) *n. pl.* A family of 5 genera and 180 species of shrubs and trees. The ornamental genera are *Bontia, Eremophila,* and *Myoporum.*

Myoporum (migh ahp'uh ruhm) *n.* A genus of 30 species of fairly tender shrubs and trees (Myoporaceae). They grow from 3 inches to 30 feet, depending on the species, with shiny, alternate, dark green leaves and clusters of bell-shaped white flowers. Used for hedges and windbreaks. They are also fire-retardant.

Myosotidium (migh uh soh tih'dee uhm) *n.* A genus of 1 species, *M. Hortensia* (Boraginaceae), a bushy perennial. They grow to 2 feet, with large, glossy, fleshy leaves and large, dense clusters of dark blue flowers.

Myosotis (migh uh soh'dehs) *n.* A genus of 50 species of annual, biennial, or perennial flowers (Boraginaceae). They grow from a few inches to 2 feet, with simple, entire basal leaves and clusters of exquisite, tiny blue, pink, or white flowers. Tradi-tional in cottage gardens; used as a small-scale ground cover, as a bulb cover, or massed in beds. Self-sows in moist, shady situations. Commonly known as forget-me-not and scorpion grass.

Myrcianthes (muhrsh ee uhn'theez) *n.* A genus of 50 species of subtropical evergreen shrubs and trees (Myrtaceae) native from Florida to South America. They grow to 60 feet, with opposite, simple, aromatic leaves, which smell like nutmeg, and clusters of white flowers.

Myrciaria (muhrsh ee ahr'ee uh) *n.* A genus of 40 species of tropical evergreen shrubs and trees (Myrtaceae) native to tropical America. They grow to 40 feet, with narrow, simple, opposite leaves, clusters of white flowers, some that bloom from the branches and trunk, and round berries, edible in some species.

Myrica (meh righ'kuh) *n.* A genus of 50 species of deciduous or evergreen shrubs and trees (Myricaceae), some native to North America. They grow from 5 feet to 60 feet, depending on the species, with simple, alternate, glossy, dark green leaves, inconspicuous flowers, and waxy-crusted gray or purple fruit, sometimes edible. *M. pensylvanica* is commonly known as bayberry; *M. californica* is commonly known as California wax myrtle. Used for screening plants or clipped hedges.

Myrica
(California wax myrtle)

Myricaceae (meh righ'kuh see ee) *n. pl.* A family of 2 genera of shrubs and trees. The ornamental genera are *Myrica* and *Comptonia.* Also known as the bayberry family.

Myricaria (meh righ kay'ree uh) *n.* A genus of 10 species of deciduous shrubs (Tamaricaceae). *M. germanica* grows to 6 feet, with alternate, scalelike leaves and clusters of white or pink flowers. The genus is commonly known as false tamarisk.

Myriophyllum (mihr ee oh fih'luhm) *n.* A genus of 45 species of mostly aquatic or bog plants (Haloragaceae). They grow from 3 to 8 feet, depending on the species, with feathery, plumelike leaves, the submerged leaves often differing in shape from the surface leaves, and spikes of small flowers. Used in pools. Commonly known as milfoil or water milfoil.

Myristica (meh rih'steh kuh) *n.* A genus of 80 species of sub-tropical evergreen trees (Myristicaceae). *M. fragrans* grows to 70 feet, with narrow, pointed, oblong leaves and clusters of pale yellow flowers. The seeds are the spice nutmeg; the scarlet netting (aril) around the seed is the spice mace. Grown in hot, moist climates as a novelty. *M. fragrans* is commonly known as nutmeg.

Myristica fragrans
(nutmeg)

Myristicaceae (meh rihs tuh kay'see ee) *n. pl.* A family of 15 genera of tropical evergreen trees. The cultivated genus is *Myrica.*

Myrrhis (mih'rehs) *n.* A genus of one species *M. odorata* (Umbelliferae), a fairly hardy perennial. They grow from 2 to 3 feet, with lacy, delicate, fernlike leaves and airy clusters of tiny white flowers. The spicy green seeds flavor salads, and the edible roots that can be eaten raw or cooked. Traditional in cottage gardens and herb gardens. Commonly known as anise, myrrh, sweet cicely, or sweet chervil.

Myrsinaceae (muhr suh nay'see ee) *n. pl.* A family of 32 genera and 1,000 species of tropical and subtropical evergreen shrubs and trees. The ornamental genera are *Ardisia, Maesa, Myrsine,* and *Suttonia.*

myrsinaceous (muhr suh nay'shuhs) *a.* Belonging to, resembling, or pertaining to the family Myrsinaceae.

Myrsine (muhr'suh nee) *n.* A genus of 5 species of dwarf evergreen shrubs and trees (Myrsinaceae). *M. africana* grows to 6 feet, with dark red vertical stems, very dark green, small, rounded, glossy leaves, and inconspicuous flowers. Used for low, clipped hedges, foundation plantings, narrow beds, containers, and topiary. It is smog-resistant and drought-tolerant. *M. africana* is commonly known as African boxwood and Cape myrtle.

Myrtaceae (muhr tay'see ee) *n. pl.* A family of 80 genera and 3,000 species of shrubs and trees, many tropical or subtropical; the myrtle family. The family is important for fruits, such as guava and rose apple, and spices, including allspice, clove, and oil of bay, as well as for ornamental use. The ornamental genera include *Callistemon* (bottlebrush), *Eucalyptus* (eucalypt or gum), *Eugenia, Feijoa* (pineapple guava), *Leptospermum, Melaleuca* (honey myrtle and bottlebrush), *Myrtus* (myrtle), *Psidium* (guava), *Syzygium, Tristania,* and *Ugni.*

myrtaceous (muhr tay'shuhs) *a.* In botany, of, resembling, or pertaining to the family Myrtaceae.

myrtle (muhr'duhl) *n.* A common name for plants of several different genera: the genus *Myrtus,* especially *M. communis* (Greek myrtle); *Cyrilla racemiflora* (leatherwood), *Umbellularia californica* (bay tree), and *Vinca minor* (common periwinkle).

Greek myrtle
a branch with flowers *b* branch with fruit

myrtle, Australian willow (muhr′duhl) *n.* A common name for *Agonis flexuosa,* a tender tree native to western Australia. It grows to 25 to 35 feet, with draping, pendulous branches, willowlike aromatic leaves that smell like peppermint when bruised, and white flowers in spring and summer. A superb small tree for frost-free gardens; it freezes to ground at 25° F. Used as a lawn tree, as an espalier, or as a tub plant. Also known as peppermint tree and willow myrtle.

myrtle, blue (muhr′duhl) *n.* A common name for both *Ceanothus thyrsiflorus,* a blue-flowered shrub native to California and Oregon, and *Vinca minor,* a small-leaved, blue-flowered ground cover.

myrtle, bog (muhr′duhl) *n.* A common name for *Myrica Gale,* a hardy deciduous North American shrub that grows to 5 feet, with alternate, simple leaves, catkins, and small, waxy, yellow fruits. Also known as Dutch myrtle, meadow fern and sweet gale.

myrtle, bracelet honey (muhr′duhl) *n.* A common name for *Melaleuca armillaris,* an evergreen shrub or small tree. It grows to 30 feet, with drooping branches, peeling bark, prickly, light green, needlelike leaves, and spikes of fluffy white flowers. Useful as a clipped hedge or an informal screen; becomes picturesque with age. Tolerates seashore conditions, including wind. Also known as drooping melaleuca.

myrtle, California wax (muhr′duhl) *n.* A common name for *Myrica californica,* a tender shrub or small tree. It grows to 30 feet, with simple, glossy, dark green leaves, inconspicuous flowers, and waxy-crusted purple fruit, attractive to birds. Used as a screen or an informal hedge. Also known as Pacific wax myrtle and California bayberry.

myrtle, candleberry (muhr′duhl) *n.* A common name for several different species, including *Myrica cerifera* (candleberry), *M. Faya,* and *M. pensylvanica* (bayberry).

myrtle, Cape (muhr′duhl) *n.* A common name for *Myrsine africana,* a tender dwarf evergreen shrub. (See **Myrsine**.)

myrtle, classic (muhr′duhl) *n.* A common name for *Myrtus communis,* a tender evergreen shrub. (See **Myrtus**.)

myrtle, crape (muhr′duhl) *n.* A common name for *Lagerstroemia indica,* a small deciduous drought- and-heat resistant shrub or tree. It grows to 30 feet, with small, rounded, alternate leaves and spectacular masses of fluffy red, pink, purple, and white flowers throughout the summer. Excellent as a lawn tree, patio tree, and street tree. Crepe myrtle is an alternate spelling.

myrtle, downy (muhr′duhl) *n.* A common name for *Rhodomyrtus tomentosa,* a subtropical shrub. It grows to 5 feet, with small, green, opposite, simple, leaves, densely downy beneath, large rose-pink flowers, and dark-purple, aromatic, edible, sweet berries. The fruit is eaten raw or made into jams. Also known as hill goosebery and hill guava.

myrtle, Dutch (muhr′duhl) *n.* A common name for *Myrica gale,* a hardy deciduous North American shrub. Same as bog myrtle. (See **myrtle, bog**.)

myrtle, dwarf (muhr′duhl) *n.* A common name for *Myrtus communis* 'Microphylla', a tender dwarf shrub. It has tiny, close-set, overlapping aromatic leaves, sweet-scented white flowers with many stamens, and bluish-black berries. Also known as German myrtle and Polish myrtle.

myrtle family (muhr′duhl) *n.* A common name for Myrtaceae. (See **Myrtaceae**.)

myrtle, flag (muhr′duhl) *n.* A common name for *Acorus calamus,* a bog-loving rhizomatous perennial. It grows from a fragrant rhizome with long, grasslike leaves and irislike yellow flowers. Used in bog gardens, water gardens, and along the edges of pools or streams. Also known as calamus and sweet flag.

myrtle, German (muhr'duhl) *n.* (See **myrtle, dwarf.**)

myrtle, Greek (muhr'duhl) *n.* A common name for *Myrtus communis,* a tender evergreen shrub. (See **Myrtus.**)

myrtle, gum (muhr'duhl) *n.* A common name for the genus *Angophora,* evergreen shrubs and trees native to eastern Australia. *A. costata* grows 40 to 50 feet, with equal spread; it has a beautiful smooth trunk in tones of cream, rose, and mauve, shiny red new growth maturing into thick, glossy, eucalyptuslike leaves, and clusters of white summer-blooming flowers. Used as a skyline tree. Needs room, but otherwise is as tough and tolerant as its *Eucalyptus* cousins.

myrtle, honey (muhr'duhl) *n.* A common name for the genus *Melaleuca,* and particularly *M. Huegelii,* shrubs and trees native to Australia. *M. Huegelii* grows to 10 feet, with pale bark, dense thorns to 5 inches long, whipcord branches, alternate, spirally arranged, overlapping oval, pointed leaves, and flowers that are pink in the bud, white when open.

myrtle, Oregon (muhr'duhl) *n.* A common name for *Umbellularia californica,* a broadleaf evergreen tree native to California and Oregon. It grows to 80 feet tall and more than 100 feet wide in its native habitat, with long, narrow, pointed, aromatic, dark green leaves, inconspicuous yellowish flowers, and an olivelike, inedible green fruit. Often multitrunked, they make an excellent screen or background; the leaves are fragrant after rains. Also known as California bay, California laurel, California olive, bay tree, mountain laurel, and pepperwood.

myrtle, Polish (muhr'duhl) *n.* A common name for *Myrtus communis* 'Microphylla', a tender dwarf shrub. Same as dwarf myrtle. (See **myrtle, dwarf.**)

myrtle, queen's crape (muhr'duhl) *n.* A common name for *Lagerstroemia speciosa,* a deciduous flowering tree. It grows to 80 feet, with large, leath-ery leaves to 1 foot long and large clusters of showymauve, pink, purple, or white flowers with many stamens that appear before the leaves. Grown in mild climates as a flowering tree for its showy flowers. Also known as pride-of-India and jarool.

myrtle, running (muhr'duhl) *n.* A common name for *Vinca minor,* a small-leaved, blue-flowered ground cover. Also known as myrtle and common periwinkle.

myrtle, sand (muhr'duhl) *n.* A common name for the genus *Leiophyllum,* dwarf evergreen shrubs native to the eastern United States. Used in the border and rock gardens. *L. buxifolium* is commonly known as box sand myrtle; *L.b.* var. *prostratum* is known as Allegheny sand myrtle.

myrtle, sand-verbena (muhr'duhl, sand vuhr bee'nuh) *n.* A common name for *Backhousia,* a genus of tender evergreen shrubs and trees. They grow to 50 feet, with aromatic, opposite leaves and rounded clusters of fragrant white flowers. Grown in frost-free gardens.

myrtle, scent (muhr'duhl) *n.* A common name for *Darwinia,* a genus of tender, evergreen, heathlike shrubs. They grow from 2 to 4 feet, with long, narrow, opposite leaves and clusters of white flowers with red anthers.

myrtle, sea (muhr'duhl) *n.* A common name for *Baccharis halimifolia,* a hardy semievergreen shrub native to the coastal marshes of North and South America. It grows to 12 feet, with small gray-green leaves and clusters of white or yellow tubular flowers that bloom in autumn. Used in seashore gardens; resistant to salt spray. Also known as groundsel tree, groundselbush, consumption weed, and silverling.

myrtle, Swedish (muhr'duhl) *n.* A common name for *Myrtus communis,* a tender evergreen shrub. (See **Myrtus.**)

myrtle, wax (muhr'duhl) *n.* A common name for *Myrica cerifera,* a North American tree found from New Jersey to Florida and west to Texas. It grows to 35 feet, has evergreen pointed leaves with tiny grayish-white fruit that yields a wax used in making candles. Also known as candleberry myrtle, candleberry, and waxberry.

myrtle, Western tea (muhr'duhl) *n*. A common name for *Melaleuca nesophylla,* a tender evergreen shrub or small tree native to western Australia. It grows to 20 feet or more and has thick, spongy, peeling bark, thick, round, gray-green leaves and clusters of showy lavender, rose-pink, or mauve flowers. Useful in seaside and desert gardens. Tough and tolerant, it thrives despite sea spray, poor, rocky soil, abundant moisture or very little moisture, and desert heat. Unpruned, it is picturesque in old age. Also known as pink melaleuca.

Myrtus (muhr'duhs) *n*. A genus of 16 species of evergreen shrubs and small trees (Myrtaceae). *M. communis* is a tender evergreen shrub to 15 feet, with dense, small, pointed, bright green leaves, pleasantly aromatic when touched, sweet-scented white flowers with many stamens, and small bluish-black berries. Used as a formal or an informal hedge or screen; old plants have a lovely branching pattern. Also known as common myrtle, true myrtle, classic myrtle, Greek myrtle, and Swedish myrtle.

naiad (nay'uhd) *n*. In botany, a plant of the genus *Najas* or any plant of the family Najadaceae.

naiadaceous (nay uh day'shuhs) *a*. In botany, of, pertaining to, or of the nature of the Naiadaceae.

Naiadaceae (nay uh day'see ee) *n. pl*. A family of 1 genus and 35 species of aquatic annuals; the naiad family. They have narrow, opposite leaves and inconspicuous flowers. The ornamental genus is *Najas.*

Najas (nay'uhs) *n*. A genus of 35 species of aquatic annuals (Naiadaceae). They grow in shallow water to 18 inches, with narrow, opposite leaves and inconspicuous flowers. Sometimes grown in aquariums. Commonly known as naiad and water nymph.

naked *a*. In botany, lacking an enveloping structure, as a naked bud; lacking pubescence.

naked flower *n*. A flower lacking petals, sepals, or bracts.

naked lady *n*. 1. A common name for *Colchicum autumnale,* from the fact that the flower appears without any leaf. (See also **autumn crocus**.) 2. A common name for *Amaryllis belladonna*. (See also **lily, belladonna**.)

nakedwood *n*. A common name for the genera *Colubrina* and *Canella. Colubrina* is a genus of trees or shrubs, native mostly to Central and South America, 1 species of which, *C. arborescens,* is known as wild coffee. *Canella* is a genus of 1 species, *C. Winterana,* a subtropical aromatic evergreen tree native to the West Indies and Florida. Commonly known as wild cinnamon.

Namaqualand daisy (nuh mahk'wuh lahnd) *n*. A common name for *Venidium,* a genus of annuals or tender perennials. It grows from 2 to 3 feet, with alternate leaves, usually woolly, and large, solitary golden yellow or bright orange flowers up to 6 inches across. Usually grown as an annual.

nandin (nahn'dehn) *n*. A common name for *Nandina domestica*. Also known as sacred bamboo. (See **bamboo**.)

Nandina (nahn dighn'uh) *n*. A genus of 1 species, *Nandina domestica* (Berberidaceae), of tender evergreen shrubs. It grows to 6 to 8 feet, with bamboolike leaves that turn red in cold weather but do not fall, and airy sprays of tiny white flowers, followed by attractive clusters of red winter berries. Used as specimen plants, as an informal screen or hedge, to create Oriental effects, and in pots. It loses its leaves at 10° F and is killed to the ground at 5° F. Commonly known as heavenly bamboo, sacred bamboo, and nandin.

nannyberry *n*. A common name for *Viburnum Lentago,* a very hardy, massive, deciduous shrub or small tree. It grows to 30 feet as a single-trunked tree or somewhat less as a shrub. It has finely toothed oval leaves that turn purplish-red in fall, flat clusters of creamy white flowers 2 to 4 inches across, and edible bluish-black winter berries. Also known as sheepberry, black haw, cowberry, nanny plum, sweetberry, tea plant, wild raisin, and sweet viburnum.

Napa cabbage (nahp'uh) *n*. Any of several varieties of *Brassica rapa* of the Chinensis group, commonly called Chinese cabbage in grocery stores. Napa types are those that grow in tightly compacted long heads, as opposed to the leafy, looser varieties.

Napaea dioica
(glade mallow)

Napaea (nah pee'uh) *n.* A genus of 1 species, *Napaea dioica* (Malvaceae), a very hardy perennial native to the eastern and central United States from Ohio west to Illinois and Minnesota. It grows from 4 to 8 feet, with big, bold maplelike leaves 2 feet long and as wide and with clusters of small white flowers. Generally seen as a roadside weed in the Midwest. Commonly known as glade mallow.

nap-at-noon *n.* A common name for plants of 2 genera, *Tragopogon pratensis* and *Ornithogalum umbellatum* (star-of-Bethlehem and summer snowflake), both of which have naturalized as weeds in North America. Both species close their flowers by midday, hence their common name. Also called noon-flower.

napiform (nay'puh form) *a.* Having the shape of a turnip, as a napiform root.

Narcissus (nahr sihs'uhs) *n.* 1. A genus of 26 species of hardy perennial bulbs (Amaryllidaceae). They grow from a few inches to 30 inches, depending on the species, with long, narrow leaves and lovely, often fragrant flowers with a ring of petals surrounding a trumpet or cup. They come in a multitude of colors, most commonly, bright yellow and white. The larger species are used for bedding, naturalized in lawns or woodland gardens, under deciduous trees, in borders, in containers, or forced for winter bloom. The smaller species are choice selections in rock gardens or tucked in stone walls.

Commonly known as daffodil. 2. [l.c.] A plant of the genus *Narcissus.*

nardine (nahr'dehn) *a.* Pertaining to nard; having the qualities of spikenard.

Narthecium (nahr theesh'ee uhm) *n.* A genus of 6 species of hardy perennial bog plants (Liliaceae), some species native to North America. They grow from rhizomes, with basal, grasslike leaves and greenish-yellow flowers in terminal clusters. Commonly known as bog asphodel.

naseberry *n.* A common name for *Manilkara zapota,* a tropical evergreen tree. It grows to 100 feet or more, with thick, alternate leaves, small, whitish flowers, and large-seeded fruit. *M. zapota,* also known as sapodilla, is an attractive ornamental, widely grown in the tropics for its edible fruit; its milky sap is chicle, the original base for chewing gum.

Nasturtium officinale
(watercress)

Nasturtium (nuh stuhr'shuhm) *n.* 1. A genus of 6 species of smooth, succulent perennial plants (Cruciferae) that grow in running water; watercress. *N. officinale* has floating leaves divided into fleshy, rounded leaflets and tiny white flowers. Used as as a pungent addition to salads and essential to watercress tea sandwiches. (See also **watercress**.) 2. A common name for *Tropaeolum tuberosum,* a showy annual plant with round, flat leaves and large yellow, orange, or red blossoms. The fruits are pickled and used in the place of capers, and the leaves and flowers serve for a salad, where they add a peppery flavor. The plants, which are used as annuals in window boxes, and in hanging pots, grow especially well near the seashore. Once planted, they do not transplant well.

Natal plum *n.* A common name for *Carissa grandiflora (C. macrocarpa),* a fast-growing, tender, evergreen spiny shrub. It grows from 5 to 7 feet, occasionally much taller, with lustrous, leathery, rich-green oval leaves, large, sweetly scented, white star-shaped flowers, and red plumlike fruit. Used as a specimen shrub, as a screen or clipped hedge in mild climates, or as an indoor plant in cold climates. Also known as amatungulu.

native *a.* Of indigenous origin or growth; not exotic or of foreign origin; for example, the California poppy is native to California.

naturalize *v.* To cause to adapt, grow, and spread as though it were native, such as a naturalized flower. For example, Queen Anne's lace has naturalized in North America.

navelwort *n.* A common name for plants of 3 different genera, including *Hydrocotyle* (water pennywort), *Omphalodes* (navelseed), and *Umbilicus rupestris* (pennywort).

navicular (nuh vihk'yuh luh) *a.* Having the shape of a boat, as the chaffy bracts at the base of the spikelet of most grasses.

necklace poplar (pahp'luhr) *n.* 1. A common name for *Populus balsamifera,* a hardy, fast-growing, deciduous North American tree. It grows to 75 to 100 feet, with thick, smooth, triangular leaves, whitish beneath. Also known as balsam poplar, balm of Gilead, hackmatack, and tacamahac. Because its roots are inclined to invade water and sewer lines in small city and suburban gardens, it is best used on large country properties away from water and sewer pipes. 2. A common name for *P. deltoides,* a hardy North American tree native from Quebec to Florida and west to Texas. (See also **cottonwood**.)

necklace tree *n.* A common name for *Ormosia,* a genus of tropical trees. They grow 50 to 75 feet, with alternate leaves divided into leathery leaflets,

clusters of butterfly-shaped purple flowers, and flat pods with ornamental red or red-and-black seeds used as beads.

necklace vine *n.* A common name for *Crassula rupestris* and *Muehlenbeckia complexa. C. rupestris* is a succulent, slender, spreading subshrub with thick, triangular leaves and clusters of pink flowers. Grown as a houseplant anywhere. Commonly known as buttons-on-a-string, rosary vine, bead vine, and rosary plant. *M. complexa* grows from 20 to 30 feet, with tiny round leaves and inconspicuous white flowers. Used to cover anything unsightly—rock piles, old stump, etc; also useful as a beach plant. *M. complexa* is known as maidenhair vine, necklace vine, horsehair vine, or mattress vine.

nectarine (nehk tuh'reen) *n.* A variety of the common peach, from which its fruit differs by having a smooth skin instead of a downy one and a firmer pulp. (See **peach**.)

nectary (nehk'tuhr ee) *n.* In botany, a gland of a plant that secretes nectar.

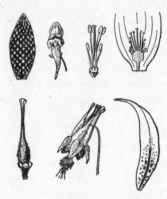

nectaries of various plants

neem *n.* A broad-spectrum, nontoxic, botanical insecticide derived from the neem tree, *Azadirachta indica.* Because it has a short residual, it must be applied often to be effective. Azadirachtin is the active ingredient.

Neillia (nee ihl'ee uh) *n.* A genus of about 10 species of very hardy deciduous spirealike shrubs (Rosaceae). They grow to 10 feet, with alternate leaves and clusters of pink or white flowers. Used as a shrub in cold-winter climates.

Neillia
a flower *b* fruit *c* leaf

Nelumbo (neh luhm'boh) *n.* 1. A genus of 2 species of large hardy water lilies (Nymphaeaceae). *N. nucifera* has large round leaves 1 to 3 feet or more in diameter and very fragrant pink, rose, or white flowers 4 to 10 inches across; the seedpods are used in dried arrangements. *N. nucifera* is also known as sacred lotus and East Indian lotus. *N. lutea,* native to North America, has somewhat smaller leaves and yellow flowers. *N. lutea* is also known as American lotus, water chinquapin, yanquapin, wonka-

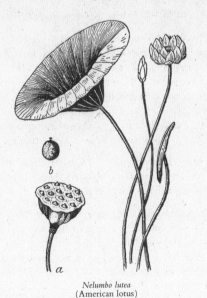

Nelumbo lutea
(American lotus)
a seedpod *b* seed

pin, yellow nelumbo, and pond nuts. Grown for their spectacular flowers, ornamental seedpods, and edible roots, known as lotus root. The genus is commonly known as lotus, water lotus, and sacred bean. *N. nucifera* is held sacred by Buddhists and is frequently depicted in Oriental art. 2. [l.c.] A plant of this genus.

Nemastylis (nehm uh stigh'lehs) *n.* A genus of 25 species of tender perennial bulbs (Iridaceae) native to North and South America. *N. floridana* grows from 6 inches to 4 1/2 feet, depending on the species, with narrow leaves and violet flowers, with a white eye, that bloom in early autumn. *N. acuta* grows from 6 to 18 inches, with leaves 12 inches long and blue flowers, almost 3 inches across, that bloom in early morning. *N. acuta* is also known as prairie iris. Commonly known as celestial lily.

Nematanthus (neh muh tahn'thuhs) *n.* A genus of more than 30 species of South American epiphytic shrubs (Gesneriaceae). They have opposite leaves in pairs and curiously shaped multicolored flowers, often red and yellow, and variously spotted, striped, and streaked. Used as houseplants or in greenhouses.

nematocide (nehm'uhd uh sighd) *n.* Any substance that can be used to kill nematodes.

nematode (nehm'uh tohd) *n.* A microscopic worm. Some are plant pests, infesting mostly roots but sometimes foliage; others are beneficial insects (see **parasitic nematode**), preying on soil pests. Nematode problems are difficult to identify because the pest is small and the symptoms are similar to soil-borne diseases: lack of vigor, wilting or dieback, and yellowing foliage. Soil types also often cause small knotty growths or spots on the roots. If you suspect nematodes, contact your cooperative extension office for proper identification. To avoid further problems, buy healthy plants, keep them growing vigorously, rotate crops, and carefully dispose of infested plants. Chitin and soil sterilization are also effective controls.

Nemesia (neh mee'zhee uh) *n.* A genus of 50 species of annuals and tender perennials (Scrophulariaceae). They grow to 2 feet, with opposite leaves and spikes of variously colored flowers. Grown as annuals in beds, as a bulb cover, in pots, and hanging baskets.

Nemopanthus (neh moh pahn′thuhs) *n.* A genus of 1 species, *N. mucronatus* (Aquifoliaceae), a hardy shrub native to eastern North America, from Newfoundland west to Indiana and south to Virginia. It grows to 10 feet, spreading by stolons; it has smooth, fibrous, bluish-green leaves that turn yellow in autumn, yellow 4- or 5-petaled flowers, and dark red fruit. The new growth has purple branches, which turn ash-gray at maturity. Grown for its attractive fruit and colorful fall foliage. Commonly known as mountain holly, catberry, and Canadian holly.

Nemophila (neh mahf′uh luh) *n.* A genus of 11 species of delicate annuals (Hydrophyllaceae) native to North America. They grow to 12 inches, with finely divided leaves and white or blue flowers. Used in beds, as a bulb cover, and in pots.

nemoral (nehm′uh ruhl) *a.* In botany, growing in groves or woodland.

nenuphar (nehn′yuh fahr) *n.* A common name for 2 water lilies, *Nymphaea alba* (European white water lily) and *Nuphar luteum* (yellow water lily). (See **lily**.)

Neomarica (nee oh muh righ′kuh) *n.* A genus of 15 species of tender perennials (Iridaceae). They grow from rhizomes to 3 feet, with sword-shaped, many-veined leaves and clusters of large, beautiful, irislike blue, white, or yellow flowers. Grown outdoors in frost-free gardens, in mild-winter climates with protection, and as houseplants. They propagate by small plantlets that form at the top of flower spikes, which bend to the ground and root, hence the common name walking iris. Also known as toad-cup lily, fan iris, house iris, twelve-apostles, false flag, and walking iris.

Neoregelia (nee oh ruh gay′lee uh) *n.* A genus of 52 species of colorful subtropical epiphytic bromeliads (Bromeliaceae). They grow to 24 inches, with brightly colored, boldly patterned rigid leaves in basal rosettes and inconspicuous flowers inside colored bracts. Used as houseplants; grown for their foliage.

Nepenthaceae (neh puhn thay′see ee) *n. pl.* A family of 2 genera of carnivorous plants. The cultivated genus is *Nepenthes*.

Nepenthes (neh pehn′theez) *n.* A genus of 70 species of carnivorous tropical plants (Nepenthaceae). They have leaves that form a hollow tube containing liquid, which traps and digests insects. Grown as a novelty houseplant. Commonly known as pitcher plant.

Nepenthes
(pitcher plant)
pitcher-shaped leaf

Nepeta (nehp′uhd uh) *n.* A genus of 250 species of hardy perennial herbs (Labiatae). They grow from 8 inches to 4 feet, depending on the species, with opposite, often aromatic, gray-green leaves and loose spikes of lavender, blue, or white flowers. Traditional in herb gardens and cottage gardens. Attractive to cats, who delight in rolling and sleeping in it, to the serious detriment of the plant's ornamental effect. The genus is commonly known as catmint; *N. cataria* is commonly known as catnip.

nephroid (neh′froid) *a.* Kidney-shaped; reniform.

Nephrolepis (neh frahl′uh pehs) *n.* A genus of 30 species of subtropical and tropical sword ferns (Polypodiaceae), some species native to the Americas. They grow from rhizomes, with finely divided fronds to 5 feet long. Used in shady beds in mild climates and as hanging-basket plants, houseplants, indoor/outdoor plants, and in greenhouses anywhere. Commonly known as sword fern.

Nephthytis (nehf thigh′dehs) *n.* A genus of 4 species (Araceae), rarely cultivated. Houseplants sold as *Nephthytis* are usually *Syngonium*.

Nerine (neh righ′nee) *n.* A genus of 20 or more species of autumn-flowering tender perennial bulbs (Amaryllidaceae). They grow to 2 to 3 feet, with strap-shaped leaves and rounded clusters of red, white, orange, or pink funnel-shaped flowers that bloom August through January. Grown in mild climates outdoors or in pots in greenhouses.

Nerium (nih'ree uhm) *n*. A genus of 2 species of long-flowering, tender, evergreen shrubs (Apocynaceae). They grow from 3 to 20 feet, with long, narrow, pointed, dark green leaves, attractive in all seasons, and abundant clusters of showy red, pink, salmon, or white flowers. One of the few truly deer-resistant plants, it is also tolerant of all sorts of difficult conditions including poor soil, desert heat, drought, smog, wind, and blazing sun. Essential to Mediterranean gardens. Used for practically everything: as specimen shrubs, hedges, screens, windbreaks, and in containers. All parts of the plant are poisonous if eaten; smoke from burning branches can cause irritation. Commonly known as oleander.

nervation *n*. The arrangement or distribution of nerves. Often: venation. Also nervature.

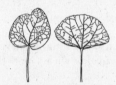

leaves showing nervation

nerved *a*. In botany, veined; ribbed; nervose.

netting *n*. Nylon or plastic mesh used as a drape to keep birds out of fruit trees, berry patches, or vegetable gardens. Netting may also be attached to a frame to form a trellis. (See also **protective netting**.)

nettle, dead *n*. Also known as dumb nettle and white dead nettle. (See **Lamium**.)

nettle, false *n*. A common name for the genus *Boehmeria*, of which only 1 species is grown ornamentally for its foliage.

nettle, flame *n*. A common name for the genus *Coleus*. (See **Coleus**.)

nettle tree *n*. A common name for *Celtis occidentalis*, also known as western redbud. (See **Celtis**.)

neuter *a*. In botany, sexless; having neither stamens nor pistils, as the ray flowers of many Compositae, the marginal flowers of *Hydrangea*, and the upper florets of many grasses. Also neutral.

neuter flowers of viburnum

neutral soil *n*. 1. A soil that is neither significantly acid nor alkaline. 2. A soil with a pH of 7.0., 3. A soil with a pH of between 6.6 and 7.3.

Neviusia (nehv uh yoo'see uh) *n*. A genus of 1 species, *N. alabamensis,* a tender, deciduous shrub (Rosaceae) native to Alabama. It grows to 6 feet, with sharply pointed, simple leaves and an abundance of short, open clusters of feathery, white flowers. Commonly known as snow wreath.

New York fern *n*. A common name for *Thelypteris noveboracensis,* a hardy fern native to eastern North America. It has finely divided pale green fronds to 2 feet long and 7 inches wide. Used in cold-climate gardens.

New Zealand Christmas tree *n*. A common name for 2 species of *Metrosideros; M. excelsis* and *M. robustus.* They are large broadleaf evergreen shrubs or trees. Both have large clusters of scarlet flowers from May to July in the Northern Hemisphere, in December in the Southern Hemisphere, the season and the combination of red and green giving it its common name of Christmas tree. Used as lawn and street trees in mild climates.

New Zealand laurel *n*. A common name for *Corynocarpus laevigata,* a tender, handsome, slow-growing evergreen shrub or small tree. It grows 20 to 40 feet with beautiful glossy, leathery, dark green, oblong leaves, clusters of tiny white flowers, and extremely poisonous orange oblong fruit. Used as a screen, hedge, background plant, or in containers.

nibung (nee'buhng) *n*. A common name for *Oncosperma tigillarium,* a magnificent massive, spiny, tropical palm. It grows in multistemmed clusters to 60 feet, with elegant leaves to 20 feet and fragrant yellow flowers. Used in tropical gardens or in greenhouses.

Nicandra (nigh kahn′druh) *n.* A genus of 1 species of annual flower (Solanaceae). It grows from 3 to 8 feet, with large oval, pointed leaves, 12 inches long and solitary blue or violet and white bell-shaped flowers. Grown as an annual, it has escaped in the warmer regions of the United States. Commonly known as apple of Peru and shoo-fly plant.

nicker tree *n.* A common name for trees of 2 genera, specifically *Gymnocladus dioica* (Kentucky coffee tree) and several species of *Caesalpinia.* (See **Gymnocladus** and **Caesalpinia.**)

Nicotiana (nih koh shee ahn′uh) *n.* A genus of 70 species of annual or tender perennials and, rarely, shrubs (Solanaceae), some species native to the warm regions of the Americas. They grow from 18 inches to 30 feet, depending on the species, with alternate, simple, entire leaves and clusters of fragrant, tubular white, yellow, green, purple, or red flowers. Used in borders and beds as well as in pots; grown for their sweet evening perfume. This is the tobacco genus; *N. tabacum* is tobacco.

Nicotiana tabacum
(tobacco)
a flower stalk *b* leaf

nicotine sulfate *n.* A broad-spectrum, botanical pesticide derived from the tobacco plant. Because it is very toxic to humans, its use is restricted in many areas and availability is limited.

Nidularium (nihj uh lah′ee uhm) *n.* A genus of 23 species of subtropical epiphytic bromeliads (Bromeliaceae). They grow from 1 to 4 feet, with long, narrow, straplike leaves, in dense basal rosettes, and a central spike of red, purple, or white flowers surrounded by colored bracts. Grown as houseplants in pots in warm, shady, humid situations such as a bathroom or greenhouse.

Nierembergia (nihr uhm buhr′jee uh) *n.* A genus of 30 species of tender perennial flowers (Solanaceae) native to Central and South America, with *N. hippomanica violacea* naturalized in warm regions of the United States. They grow from 4 inches to 3 feet, with stiff, very narrow, bright green alternate leaves and white, blue, or purple cuplike flowers. Used in borders, rock gardens, or as pot plants. Commonly known as cupflower.

Nigella (nigh jehl′uh) *n.* A genus of 20 species of annuals (Ranunculaceae). They grow to 18 inches, with long, narrow, finely divided, often threadlike leaves, showy white, blue, or yellow flowers, and papery, horned seed capsules. Used in borders and excellent as a cut or dried flower. Seeds of several species, known as black cumin, have been used as a spice. Commonly known as fennel-flower and wild fennel.

Nigella
(fennel-flower)

night-blooming *a.* Blooming or blossoming at night.

night-blooming cereus (sih′ree uhs) *n.* A common name for several night-blooming cacti, including *Hylocereus undatus, Nyctocereus serpentinus, Selenocereus,* and *S. grandiflorus,* all of which have large fragrant flowers that open nocturnally. (See **cactus** and **Cereus.**)

night-blooming plants *n.* Plants that bloom at night; often sweetly fragrant to attract nocturnal pollinators such as moths and bats.

night jasmine (jahz'mehn) *n.* A common name for 2 subtropical shrubs, *Cestrum nocturnum* and *Nyctanthes arbor-tristis.* Both have white flowers that are extemely fragrant at night. (See **Nyctanthes**.) Grown in warm climates or in greenhouses for their fragrance. *C. nocturnum* has white berries that attract birds, and is also known as night jessamine.

nightshade *n.* 1. A plant of the genus *Solanum,* or of the Solanaceae, or night-shade family. Chiefly, *S. nigrum,* the common or black nightshade, a weed of shady places, or *S. dulcamara,* the bittersweet, or poisonous nightshade. (See **bittersweet**.) Also, the belladonna, or deadly nightshade (See **Atropa**.) and the henbane, or stinking nightshade, *Hyoscyamus.* 2. The common name of a few plants of other orders, including three-leafed nightshade, a plant of the genus *Trillium.*

nightshade

ninebark *n.* A common name for *Physocarpus,* a genus of hardy, deciduous, spirealike shrubs with peeling, layered bark, several species native to North America. It grows from 3 to 10 feet, with simple, alternate leaves (with brilliant fall color in some species) and rounded clusters of tiny white or pink flowers in spring or early summer. Used as a specimen shrub.

Nippon-bells (nihp uhn') *n.* A common name for *Shortia uniflora,* a hardy, low-growing perennial. It grows to 8 inches, in clumps of oval, glossy, green leaves, with wavy edges, and masses of nodding white bell-like flowers, 1 inch wide. Useful in shady, moist, acid soils such as in woodland gardens and under azaleas and rhododendrons; also used in pots or as houseplants.

Nitella (nigh tehl'uh) *n.* A genus of 100 species of fragile water plants (Characeae), several species of which are native to North America. They have threadlike branches with leaflike branchlets. Used in aquariums. Commonly known as stonewort.

nitrate of soda *n.* An inorgnic fertilizer that leaves an alkaline reaction.

nitrification (nigh truh feh kay'shuhn) *n.* The formation of nitrates and nitrites from ammonia.

nitrogen *n.* An element heavily drawn upon by plant crops; usually the first element in the soil to be depleted.

nitta tree (nihd'uh) *n.* A common name for several species of *Parkia,* especially *P. biglobosa* (African locust) and *P. filicoidea* (African locust bean), tropical flowering trees with orange, red, or rose flowers and long pods. Grown in warm climates.

nocturnal *a.* Active at night; said of flowers that bloom at night. (See **night-blooming**.)

node (nohd) *n.* In botany, the often swollen or modified part of a stem that normally bears a leaf or a whorl of leaves.

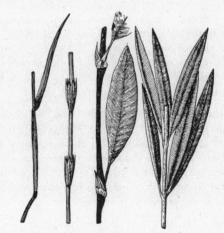

nodes of various plants

nodiferous (noh dihf'uh ruhs) *a.* In botany, bearing or producing nodes.

nodose (noh'dohs) *a.* In botany, having numerous knotty or knobby nodes.

nodulated (nah'duh layd ehd) *a.* 1. Having nodules. 2. In leguminous plants, having symbiotic bacteria-containing nodules on the roots.

nodule (nah'jool) *n., pl.* **noduli** (-ih) 1. A little knot or lump. 2. In botany, a plant bud; a swelling containing symbiotic bacteria on the root of a leguminous plant. Also nodulus.

nodulose (nah'juh lohs) *a*. In botany, having tiny nodules. Also nodulous.

noisette (nwuh zeht') *n*. A common name for a hybrid rose, a cross between *R. chinensis* (China rose) and *R. moschata* (musk rose). The first off-spring were notable for their repeat bloom and yellow flowers; later crossed with *R. chinensis,* it produced repeat bloomers in white and pink as well as yellow; crossed with tea roses, it produced larger flowers. Collected by rose growers as an antique or old rose. Excellent in cottage gardens, English-style gardens, and collections of old roses.

Nolana (noh lay'nuh) *n*. A genus of 60 species of tender, low-growing perennials *(Nolanaceae)* native to semidesert regions of Chile and Peru. They have trailing branches, small, oval, pointed leaves and bright blue petunialike flowers with white throats. Used as an edging in flower beds or in hanging baskets.

nomenclature *n*. 1. A system of naming things; specifically, the names of plants; terminology. 2. The international vocabulary of Latin names for kinds of plants, standardized by commissions set up by the appropriate taxonomic experts. (See **binomial**.)

Nolina (noh ligh'nuh) *n*. A genus of 25 species of tender perennials (Agavaceae). They grow from 6 to 10 feet, with tough, stiff, grasslike leaves and insignificant small, white flowers. Over time, they form a thick trunk topped by a fountain of grasslike leaves. Used in dry landscape or desert gardens. Commonly known as bear grass.

nonporous subsoil (nahn poh'ruhs) *n*. 1. Hardpan. 2. Soil through which water will not drain.

noonflower *n*. A common name for *Tragopogon pratensis*. (See **nap-at-noon**.)

nopal (noh'puhl) *n*. A common name for the genus *Opuntia* (prickly pear) and the genus *Nopalea,* both large cacti that grow to shrub- or tree-size. *Opuntia* is native from Massachusetts to the Strait of Magellan; *Nopalea* is native to Mexico and Central America.

Nopalea (noh pay'lee uh) *n*. A genus of 10 species of large, long-lived, sometimes spiny cacti (Cactaceae) that grow to shrub- or tree-size. They grow from 6 to 35 feet, depending on the species, with a cylindrical trunk, flattened joints, small, deciduous leaves, red or pink flowers with many stamens, and a red, juicy fruit. Used in desert gardens.

Nopalxochia (noh puhlks'oh shee uh) *n*. A genus of 4 species of small epiphytic cacti (Cactaceae) native to southern Mexico. They have long, narrow, flat branches, sometimes spiny, and pink or red funnel-shaped flowers that last several days. Grown by collectors.

Norfolk Island pine *n*. A common name for *A. heterophylla,* a tender tree. It grows to 200 feet at maturity, but is usually seen in its juvenile form as a houseplant. It has firm, overlapping, scalelike leaves. Used as an indoor/outdoor plant or a houseplant. Also known as house pine and Australian pine.

Norway pine *n*. A common name for *Pinus resinosa,* a very hardy North American evergreen conifer, native from Newfoundland to Pennsylvania and Minnesota. It grows to 90 feet, with glossy, needlelike leaves, in bunches of 2 and small cones. Used in severe- winter climates. Also known as red pine.

Norway spruce *n*. A common name for *Picea abies,* a very hardy evergreen tree, 1 of the most widely planted conifers in North America. It grows to 150 feet, with short, dark green, needlelike leaves and large, 7-inch-long cones that hang down. There are a great many cultivars from which to choose. Used as a windbreak in extremely cold areas.

nosegay *n*. A common name for *Plumeria rubra,* a subtropical flowering tree. It is a handsome, rounded tree to 25 feet, with leathery, pointed leaves, clustered at the tips of its branches, and masses of clusters of showy, waxy, sweetly fragrant red, purple, pink, yellow, or white flowers that bloom June to November. Used as a spectacular specimen tree in warm climates, as a container plant, or as an indoor/outdoor plant. Also known as frangipani and plumeria.

Nosema locustae (noh see'muh loh'kuhs tee) *n*. (See **grasshopper spore**.)

Notholaena (nahth'uh lee nuh) *n*. A genus of 60 species of tender to tropical small ferns (Polypodiaceae), most native to the dry regions of the Americas. They grow to 14 inches, with lacy, finely divided fronds. Used in rock gardens; remarkably drought-tolerant for ferns. Commonly known as cloak fern.

Notholaena
(cloak fern)

Nothoscordum (nahth uh shawr'duhm) *n*. A genus of 20 species of tender American bulbs (Amaryllidaceae), similar to onions without the pungent smell. They are native from Virginia to Mexico. They grow to 2 feet, with long, narrow, basal leaves and clusters of yellow or white flowers, sometimes fragrant. Commonly known as false garlic and grace garlic.

Notocactus (noh doh kahk'tuhs) *n*. A genus of 25 species of unbranched, spiny, tender South American cacti (Cactaceae). They grow from 3 inches to 6 feet depending on the species, and are round or cylindrical in shape, with yellow, orange, or red flowers to 3 inches across. An easy-to-grow cactus for desert gardens or collectors. Commonly known as ball cactus.

nozzle *n*. Any of variously designed spouts on a hose or watering can, which pattern and direct the flow of water.

nucament (nyoo'kuh muhnt) *n*. In botany, a catkin; an ament.

nuciform (nyoo'suh form) *a*. In botany, nutshaped.

nuculanium (nyoo kyuh lay'nee uhm) *n*., *pl.* **nuculania** (-a) In botany, a fleshy fruit, containing 2 or more cells and several seeds, as the grape. Also nuculane.

Nuphar (nyoo'fuhr) *n*. A genus of 25 species of hardy water lilies (Nymphaeaceae). They have long, flat, thick, oval leaves, to 16 inches, and yellow or purple many-petaled flowers that stand above the water. Used in garden pools and ponds. Commonly known as spatterdock, cow lily, yellow pond lily, water collard, and marsh collard.

nurseryman's tape *n*. (See **grafting tape**.)

nut *n*. 1. The fruit of certain trees and shrubs that have the seed enclosed in a bony, woody, or leathery covering that does not open when ripe. Specifically, a hard, dry, 1-celled and 1-seeded fruit, such as the nuts of the hazel, beech, oak, and chestnut. In the walnut (*Juglans*) and hickory (*Carya*), the fruit is seemingly intermediate between a stone fruit and a nut. 2. Loosely, a similar vegetable product, as a tuberous root (earthnut, groundnut), leguminous pod (peanut), or seed (physic nut).

nutgall *n*. A gall, chiefly of the oak.

nut, Jesuits' *n*. A common name for *Trapa natans*. Used in water gardens. Also known as trapa nut, water caltrop, saligot, and ling. (See **ling**.)

nut, Madeira (muh dih'ruh) *n*. A common name for *Juglans regia*. Also called English walnut. (See **walnut, English**.)

nutmeg *n*. 1. The kernel of the fruit of the nutmeg tree, *Myristica fragrans*. The fruit, with some resemblance to a peach, has a fleshy, edible exterior, which splits in 2, releasing the seed, enveloped in a fibrous substance that is known as the spice mace.

nutmeg flower *n*. A common name for *Nigella sativa*, an annual flower. It grows to 18 inches, with finely divided leaves, blue flowers, and aromatic seeds that can be used as a spice. Traditional in cottage and herb gardens. Also known as black cumin and Roman coriander. (See **Nigella**.)

nut, Queensland *n.* (See **Macadamia**.)

nut rush *n.* A common name for *Cyperus esculentus,* a subtropical or tropical perennial marsh plant. It grows from edible tubers to 2 feet, with long, narrow leaves and inconspicuous brownish flowers. Used in tub water gardens; otherwise, often considered a troublesome weed. Also known as nut grass, nut sedge, yellow nut grass and yellow nut sedge.

nut, Spanish *n.* A common name for *Gynadriris Sisyrinchium,* a tender perennial bulb (corm). It grows to 18 inches, with long, narrow leaves and clusters of lavender, lilac, or blue-purple flowers with white and yellow markings.

nut tree *n.* Any tree that bears nuts; specifically, the hazel.

nut tree, Australian *n.* A common name for *Macadamia.* Also known as Queensland nut tree. (See **Macadamia**.)

nutrient *n.* Any essential element taken in by a plant needed for growth.

Nyctaginaceae (nihk tuh juh nay'see ee) *n. pl.* A family of 32 genera and 300 species of flowers, shrubs, and trees; the four-o'clock family. The ornamental genera are *Abronia* (sand verbena), *Bougainvillea,* *Mirabilis* (four-o'clock), *Nyctaginia* (scarlet musk flower), and *Pisonia.*

Nyctaginia (nihk tuh juh'nee uh) *n.* A genus of 1 species of tender perennial (Nyctaginaceae) native to the Southwest and Mexico. It grows to 16 inches, with oval or triangular leaves and scarlet, funnel-shaped flowers. Commonly known as scarlet musk flower.

Nyctanthes (nihk tahn'thuhs) *n.* A genus of 1 or 2 species of subtropical shrubs and trees (Verbenaceae or Oleaceae). *N. arbor-tristis* has oval to heart-shaped leaves and clusters of richly fragrant, night-blooming, white flowers. Grown for its fragrance in warm-climate gardens or in greenhouses. Commonly known as night jasmine or tree-of-sadness.

nyctitropic (nihk tuh trap'ihk) *a.* In botany, exhibiting nyctitropism.

nyctitropism (nihk tih'truh pihz uhm) *n.* In botany, the sleep movement of certain plants or parts of plants whereby they assume at nightfall, or just before, certain positions unlike those that they have maintained during the day.

Nyctocereus (nihk toh sih'ree uhs) *n.* A genus of 6 species of slender, ribbed, branched, spiny cacti (Cactaceae) native to Mexico and Central America. They grow to 10 feet, sometimes trailing rather than erect, and have night-blooming, white, funnel-shaped flowers, sometimes fragrant, and round, red fruit. Easy to grow in desert gardens, as a houseplant, or in cactus collections.

Nymphaeaceae (nihm fee ay'see ee) *n. pl.* A family of 8 genera of perennial water lilies. The ornamental genera are *Nymphaea* (water lily), *Nelumbo* (lotus), and *Victoria* (giant water lily).

Nymphoides (nihm foi'deez) *n.* A genus of 20 species of perennial water plants (Gentianaceae or Menyanthaceae), some native to North America. They have long-stemmed, heart-shaped floating leaves, 8 inches across, and clusters of white, cream, or bright yellow flowers. Used in garden ponds and tubs. Commonly known as floating heart.

Nyssa (nihs'uh) *n.* A genus of 6 or 7 species of hardy deciduous trees (Nyssaceae), native mostly to North America. *N. sylvatica* (sour gum, pepperidge, black gum, or upland tupelo) grows slowly to 50 feet, with alternate, simple, oval leaves that turn hot, coppery red in autumn, tiny greenish-white flowers, and small olivelike black fruit that attracts birds. Used as a lawn tree; has brilliant fall color and dramatic winter silhouette. Tolerates poor drainage, a wide variety of soils, and occasional drought. Commonly known as tupelo.

oak *n.* A common name for *Quercus,* a genus of handsome, spreading, long-lived hardwood trees, some species native to North America. They grow from 5 to 120 feet, depending on the species, with characteristically lobed, alternate leaves, sometimes spiny-tipped, and acorns of varying sizes that attract squirrels and many species of birds, including jays and acorn woodpeckers. Used in several ways:

as magnificent specimen trees, shade trees, lawn trees, street trees, and climbing trees, depending on the species.

oak, Austrian turkey *n.* A common name for *Quercus cerris austriaca,* a hardy deciduous tree. It grows to 10 feet, with lobed leaves 5 inches long and a mossy cup enclosing about half the acorn.

oak, ballota (buh loh′duh) *n.* A common name for *Quercus ilex rotundifolia,* a tender evergreen tree, a subspecies of the holm or holly oak. It grows to 60 feet, with glossy, dark green, rounded leaves and edible acorns. Used as a street or lawn treen or may be clipped as a hedge. Tolerates salt air and wind. Also known as balloot and bellote.

oak, barren *n.* A common name for *Quercus marilandica,* a hardy deciduous tree native to the United States, from New York to Florida, west to Nebraska and Texas. It grows to 50 feet, usually less, with lobed, alternate leaves fruit. Also known as blackjack oak, blackjack, and jack oak. 2. A common name for *Quercus ilicifolia,* a hardy, deciduous, much-branched shrub native from Maine to Virginia and Kentucky. It grows to 10 feet or more, with large, lobed, spiny leaves 4 inches long, powdery white beneath, and acorns with the cup covering half the nut. Also known as scrub oak and bear oak.

oak, Bartram (bahr′truhm) *n.* A common name for *Quercus Xheterophylla,* a cross between *Q. phellos* (willow oak) and *Q. rubra* (northern red oak). It is a hardy, deciduous tree native to the eastern United States. It grows to 80 feet, with oblong, lobed, spiny-tipped leaves.

oak, basket *n.* 1. A common name for *Quercus prinus,* a hardy, deciduous North American tree native from Delaware to Florida and Texas. It grows to 100 feet, with shiny, bright green, coarsely toothed leaves and acorns. Also known as chestnut oak, swamp chestnut oak, rock chestnut oak. 2. A common name for *Q. Michauxii,* a round-headed, hardy, deciduous tree native to the eastern United States. It grows to 100 feet, with roughly triangular bright green leaves, rich autumn color, and oval acorns on stalks. Useful in moist soils. Also known as cow oak, swamp white oak, and swamp chestnut oak.

oak, bear *n.* A common name for *Quercus ilicifolia.* (See **oak, barren**.)

oak, black *n.* A common name for *Quercus velutina,* a hardy deciduous tree native to the eastern United States, from Maine to Florida and Texas. It grows to 100 feet or more, with large, lobed leaves to 10 inches long and acorns topped by a fringed, furry cup. Also known as yellow-barked oak and quercitron. (See **quercitron**.)

oak, blackjack *n.* (See **oak, barren**.)

oak, blue *n.* A common name for *Quercus Douglasii,* a hardy deciduous tree native to the foothills and mountains of central California. It grows to 50 feet, with bluish-green, shallowly lobed, almost square leaves, which turn pastel pink, yellow, and orange in autumn, and oval acorns with a shallow cup. Useful in hot, dry situations.

oak, bluejack *n.* A common name for *Quercus incana,* a tender deciduous shrub or low tree native to southeastern United States. It grows to 25 feet with mostly entire, narrow, fuzzy leaves and round acorns with a shallow cup. Also known as turkey oak, high-ground willow oak, and sandjack.

oak, bur *n.* A common name for *Quercus macrocarpa,* a hardy, fast-growing, deciduous tree native to North America, from Nova Scotia to Pennsylvania and Texas. It grows to 80 feet, with large, deeply lobed leaves, 10 inches long, and large, round acorns with a mossy cup. Useful in moist soils and difficult conditions. Also known as mossy-cup oak.

oak, California black *n.* A common name for *Quercus Kelloggii,* a tender deciduous tree with stout, spreading branches. It grows to 70 feet or more, with pale pink new growth that matures into glossy, bright green, deeply lobed leaves, with bristly points, that turn yellow or yellow-orange in autumn. It has long, narrow acorns. The name black oak comes from the dark, furrowed, checkered bark. A good moderate-sized tree for shade and fall color, with an excellent winter silhouette. Tolerates dry, sandy soils. Also known as Kellogg oak.

oak, California live *n.* A common name for *Quercus agrifolia,* a round-headed, wide-spreading tender evergreen tree native to the coastal ranges of California. It grows to 20 to 70 feet in cultivation, to 100 feet in the wild, with, rounded hollylike, spiny leaves, glossy above, and long, pointed acorns. Used as a shade tree or lawn tree. Also known as California field oak.

oak, California scrub *n.* A common name for *Quercus dumosa,* a tender evergreen shrub native to California. It grows to 8 feet, with small, oval, spiny-toothed leaves and acorns. Useful for erosion control; extremely drought-tolerant.

oak, California white *n.* A common name for *Quercus lobata,* a large, wide-spreading, fairly hardy deciduous tree. It grows to 70 feet or more with massive trunk and limbs, deeply lobed oval leaves and long, pointed acorns. The name white oak comes from the pale ash-colored, distinctly checkered bark. Useful as a huge shade tree on parks, ranches, or estates. Also known as valley oak.

oak, canyon *n.* A common name for *Quercus chrysolepis,* a handsome, round-headed, tender evergreen tree native to the slopes and canyons of California and southern Oregon. It grows from 20 to 60 feet, with oval, spiny-toothed, downy-yellow leaves and oval acorns with turban-shaped golden, fuzzy cups. Also known as canyon live oak.

oak, Catesby (kayt′bee) *n.* A common name for *Quercus laevis,* a tender deciduous tree native to the United States, from North Carolina to Louisiana. It grows to 50 feet, with shiny, deeply lobed leaves and acorns with a deep, scaly cup. Also known as turkey oak.

oak, chestnut *n.* A common name for *Quercus Muehlenbergii,* and *Q. prinus* (basket oak). *Q. Muehlenbergii* is a hardy deciduous tree native to the United States, from New England to Florida, west to Minnesota and Texas. It grows to 100 feet or more, with oval, toothed, yellow-green leaves, pale and downy beneath, with rich fall color and small, round acorns. Also known as yellow chestnut oak and yellow oak. (See **oak, basket**.)

oak chestnut *n.* A shrub or tree of the genus *Castanopsis* (chinquapin).

oak, chinquapin (chihng′kuh pin) *n.* A common name for *Quercus prinoides,* a hardy deciduous shrub native from Maine to Alabama and Texas. It grows to 6 feet, with oval leaves, 5 inches long, and acorns half-covered by the cup. Also known as dwarf chestnut oak.

oak, cork *n.* A common name for *Quercus Suber,* a large, wide-spreading, tender evergreen tree with thick, corky bark from which corks are made. It grows from 70 to 100 feet, with shiny, dark green, oval leaves, gray beneath, and acorns. Used as a shade tree, park tree, and street tree, but the easy-to-carve bark is painfully vulnerable to vandalism. Useful in the desert; drought-tolerant once established.

oak, cow *n.* A common name for *Quercus Michauxii.* (See **oak, basket**.)

oak, Daimyo (digh′mee oh) *n.* A common name for *Quercus dentata,* a hardy deciduous tree. It grows to 80 feet, with large, lobed leaves to 12 inches long, fuzzy beneath, and small, round acorns.

oak, Darlington *n.* A common name for *Quercus laurifolia,* a round-headed, tender deciduous or semievergreen tree native to the United States, from Virginia to Florida and Louisiana. It grows to 60 feet, with oval leaves, sometimes slightly lobed, and small acorns on a short stalk. Also known as laurel oak and laurel-leaved oak.

oak, deer *n.* A common name for *Quercus Sadlerana,* an evergreen shrub native to California. It grows to 8 feet, with chestnutlike oval leaves, with prominent veins and acorns with a shallow cup.

oak, durmast *n.* A common name for *Quercus petraea,* a hardy deciduous tree. It grows to 80 feet, with lobed leaves 5 inches long.

oak, dwarf chestnut *n.* A common name for *Quercus prinoides.* (See **oak, chinquapin**.)

oak, Emory *n.* A common name for *Quercus Emoryi,* a handsome, tender evergreen tree native to the Southwest, from Arizona to New Mexico, Texas, and northern Mexico. It grows to 60 feet, usually smaller in gardens, with leathery oval leaves that turn golden in late spring, just before the new growth. Useful in desert areas, but needs occasional deep soaking in summer.

oak, Engelmann *n.* A common name for *Quercus Engelmannii,* a wide-spreading, tender evergreen tree native to southern California and northern Mexico. It grows to 60 feet, with oval, smooth-edged leaves. Also known as mesa oak.

oak, English *n.* A common name for *Quercus rober,* a fairly fast-growing, spreading, open, short-trunked, hardy deciduous tree. It grows to 100 feet, with lobed leaves that drop in autumn without much change in color. Used as a lawn tree and shade tree. Also known as truffle oak.

oak, flowering *n.* A common name for *Chorizema cordatum,* a tender, trailing evergreen shrub. It grows from 3 to 5 feet or more, with small, oval, prickly, dark green leaves and sweet-pea shaped orange and purple flowers from February through June. Used on banks, spilling over a wall, or in hanging baskets. Also known as Australian flame tree.

oak, gambel (gahm′buhl) *n.* A common name for *Quercus Gambelii,* a hardy deciduous shrub native to the United States, from Colorado to New Mexico. It grows 20 to 30 feet, with lobed dark green leaves that turn yellow, orange, or red in fall. It often forms colonies from its underground root system. Also known as Rocky Mountain white oak.

oak, Gander *n.* A common name for *Quercus* × *Ganderii,* a cross between *Q. agrifolia* and *Q. Kelloggii.*

oak, Havard *n.* A common name for *Quercus Havardii,* a low-growing, hardy deciduous shrub native to Texas and New Mexico. It grows to 2 1/2 feet, with lobed dark green leaves, fuzzy beneath. Also known as shinnery oak.

oak, high-ground willow *n.* A common name for *Quercus incana.* (See **oak, bluejack**.)

oak, holly *n.* A common name for *Quercus ilex,* a dense, wide-spreading, marginally hardy evergreen tree. It grows from 40 to 70 feet, with glossy, dark green, oval, pointed leaves. Used as a lawn tree, shade tree, or street tree. Will tolerate severe clipping into formal shapes, salt spray, and wind. Also known as holm oak.

oak, huckleberry *n.* A common name for *Quercus vacciniifolia,* a marginally hardy sprawling evergreen shrub. It grows to 2 feet or more, with small, oval, entire gray-green leaves. Used in large rock gardens, mountain gardens, and wild gardens.

oak, Indian *n.* A common name for *Barringtonia acutangula,* a tender evergreen tree. It grows to 40 feet, with oval, pointed leaves and long, drooping spikes of small 4-petaled red flowers. Used for seaside gardens in mild climates.

oak, interior live *n.* A common name for *Quercus Wislizenii,* a dense, tender evergreen tree, often wider than high, native to central California and the Sierra foothills. It grows from 30 to 70 feet, with glossy oval leaves, yellowish beneath. Used as lawn trees in large lawns and in parks. Awkward in youth and adolescence, it is an arborescent ugly duckling, which matures into a handsome adult tree.

oak, island *n.* A common name for *Quercus tomentella,* a tender evergreen tree native to the coastal islands of California and Baja California. It grows to 35 feet, with narrow leaves to 3 inches long.

oak, Italian *n.* A common name for *Quercus Frainetto,* a little-known attractive, erect, shapely, hardy deciduous tree. It grows to 120 feet, with glossy, dark green, deeply lobed leaves 8 inches long. It is drought-tolerant once established. Also known as Hungarian oak.

oak, jack *n.* A common name for *Quercus marilandica* (barren oak) and *Q. ellipsoidalis.* (See **oak, barren**.) *Q. ellipsoidalis* is a very hardy deciduous North American tree native from Manitoba to Michigan and Iowa. It grows to 80 feet or more, with oval, narrowly lobed leaves, the lobes having pointed teeth. Also known as northern pin oak.

oak, Japanese evergreen *n.* A common name for *Quercus acuta,* a small, bushy, hardy evergreen tree. It grows to 40 feet, with oval, wavy-margined leaves and clustered acorns with downy cups. Also known as Japanese red oak.

oak, Jerusalem *n.* A common name for *Chenopodium Botrys,* an aromatic annual. It grows to 2 feet, with large, lobed leaves, 4 inches long, and spikes of small flowers. It has naturalized in North America. Also known as feather geranium.

oak, Kellogg *n.* A common name for *Quercus Kelloggii.* (See **oak, California black**.)

oak, konara (koh nahr′uh) *n.* A common name for *Quercus glandulifera,* a hardy deciduous tree. It grows to 50 feet, with shiny, toothed leaves, grayish and fuzzy beneath.

oak, laurel *n.* 1. A common name for *Quercus imbricaria,* a slow-growing hardy deciduous tree native to the eastern United States, from Pennsylvania to Arkansas. It grows from 60 to 100 feet, with shiny, dark green, narrow, tapering leaves, downy beneath, that turn rich autumn colors, and small acorns. Also known as shingle oak. 2. A common name for *Quercus laurifolia*. (See **oak, Darlington**.)

oak, leather *n*. A common name for *Quercus durata*, a spreading evergreen shrub native to California. It grows to 5 feet, with small, dark green, leathery, oval leaves, with sharp teeth, and small round acorns with deep cups.

oak, Lebanon *n*. A common name for *Quercus libani*, a hardy deciduous tree. It grows to 30 feet, with long, narrow, lightly downy leaves, with bristles at the ends of the veins, and acorns nearly enclosed by a scaly cup.

oak, live *n*. A common name for *Quercus virginiana*, a moderate to fast-growing tender evergreen or semievergreen tree native to the eastern United States, from Virginia to Florida and Mexico. It grows to 60 feet, with a spreading crown, heavy limbs, shiny, dark green, smooth-edged leaves, whitish beneath, and small oval acorns. Useful as a lawn tree in low-desert gardens; thrives on ample water. Also known as southern live oak.

oak, maul *n*. A common name for *Quercus chrysolepis*. (See **oak, canyon**.)

oak, McDonald *n*. A common name for *Quercus Macdonaldii*, a small tender deciduous tree native to southern California. It grows to 45 feet, with lobed, bristle-tipped leaves. Sometimes considered a form of *Q. dumosa*.

oak, Mongolian *n*. A common name for *Quercus mongolica*, a hardy deciduous tree. It grows to 100 feet, with large, oval leaves, clustered at the ends of its branches, and acorns with a thick, scaly cup.

oak, mossy-cup *n*. A common name for *Quercus macrocarpa*. (See **oak, bur**.)

oak moth *n*. A pest of western oaks. The larvae feed on foliage, defoliating trees in bad years. Small green pellets (larvae droppings) under trees are the first signs of infestation. Control measures are usually necessary only in bad years. The young larvae can be controlled with *Bacillus thuringiensis*. Traditional pesticides are also effective but usually need to be applied by an arborist.

oak, northern pin *n*. A common name for *Quercus ellipsoidalis*. (See **oak, jack**.)

oak, northern red *n*. A common name for *Quercus rubra*, a round-topped, wide-spreading, fast-growing hardy deciduous tree. It grows to 80 feet or more, with red new growth that matures into lobed, spiny leaves, 5 to 8 inches long, that color dark red or orange in fall. Used in parks, on large lawns, or to line avenues and boulevards. Also known as red oak.

oak, Oregon *n*. A common name for *Quercus Garryana*, a round-headed tender deciduous tree, often with twisted branches. It grows to 100 feet, with grayish, scaly, checkered bark and glossy, green, leathery, lobed leaves, often rusty beneath. Used as a shade tree or to provide dappled shade for rhododendrons. Also known as Garry oak, Oregon white oak, and western oak.

oak, Oriental white *n*. A common name for *Quercus aleina*, a hardy deciduous tree. It grows to 70 feet, with large, green, oval leaves, downy beneath, and acorns with a gray, downy cup.

oak, overcup *n*. A common name for *Quercus lyrata*, a hardy deciduous tree native to the eastern United States, from New Jersey to Florida and Texas. It grows to 100 feet, with deeply lobed leaves and an acorn nearly enclosed by the cup. Useful in wet soils. Also known as swamp post oak.

oak, pin *n*. A common name for *Quercus palustris*, a round-headed, wide-spreading hardy deciduous tree native to the eastern United States, from Massachusetts to Delaware and Arkansas. It grows to 80 feet, with dark green, deeply cut, bristle-pointed lobed leaves that turn red, yellow, or russet brown in autumn. Used as a lawn tree; the lower branches drape attractively. Also known as Spanish oak.

oak, poison *n*. A common name for three species: *Rhus diversiloba, R. radicans,* and *R. toxicodendron. R. radicans* and *R. toxicodendron* are also known as poison ivy. These are all deciduous plants, native to North America, that cause long-lasting itchy skin rashes when touched. *R. diversiloba* and *R. radicans* can assume a variety of growth habits, from ground cover to shrub to vine to tree. *Rhus diversiloba* has leaves divided into 3, lobed, oaklike leaflets. *R. radicans* and *R. toxicodendron* have leaves divided into 3 ivylike leaflets. The leaves tend to be shiny dark green in spring and summer and to color beautifully in fall. *R. diversiloba* does not grow east of the Rocky Mountains. *R. radicans* grows as far west as eastern Oregon and eastern Washington. *R. toxicodendron* does not occur west of the Rocky Mountains. Despite their adaptability to a wide variety of soils, light levels, and moisture levels, and despite their attractive fall color, poison oak and poison ivy are not grown ornamentally and are best avoided in the wild. The rule for identifying all of them is: Leaflets three, let it be. Burning the leaves and branches can release the irritating oils into the air; don't do it. Spray with herbicide to remove from garden areas.

oak, possum *n.* A common name for *Quercus nigra,* a semievergreen hardy tree native to the eastern United States, from Delaware to Florida to Texas. It grows to 80 feet, with fine-textured, roughly triangular shiny green leaves and small acorns. Useful in moist soils. Also known as water oak.

oak, post *n.* A common name for *Quercus stellata,* a hardy deciduous tree native to the eastern United States, from Massachusetts to Florida, west to Kansas and Texas. It grows to 100 feet, usually much less, with large, lobed dark green leaves, pale beneath, and acorns with downy cups.

oak, red *n.* A common name for *Quercus rubra.* (See **oak, northern red.**)

oak, ring-cupped *n.* A common name for *Quercus glauca,* a tender evergreen tree or bushy shrub. It grows to 50 feet, with oval leaves, gray and silky beneath when young, and acorns with a furry cup.

oak, rock chestnut *n.* A common name for *Quercus prinus.* (See **oak, basket.**)

oak, Rocky Mountain scrub *n.* A common name for *Quercus undulata,* a hardy deciduous tree native from Colorado to Texas and Northern Mexico. It grows to 30 feet, with bluish-green, hairy, oval leaves.

oak root fungus *n.* A soil-borne disease common in parts of the dry-summer western United States. It infects the roots of many plants, causing gradual decline, yellowing foliage, wilting, and dieback. Light brown mushrooms around the base of plants and fan-shaped whitish mold under the bark are sure signs of infection. Infected plants are hard to save. For problems in large trees, consult an arborist; otherwise, the method of control is to plant resistant species. Also called *Armillaria* root rot.

oak, scarlet *n.* A common name for *Quercus coccinea,* an open, high-branching, hardy deciduous tree native to the eastern United States, from Maine to Florida west to Kansas. It grows from 60 to 80 feet, with bright green deeply lobed leaves, with pointed lobes, that turn brilliant scarlet in autumn if nights are cold enough. Used as a street tree and lawn tree.

oak, scrub *n.* A common name for *Quercus ilicifolia.* (See **oak, bear.**)

oak, she- *n.* A common name for *Casuarina.* (See **Casuarina.**)

oak, shingle *n.* A common name for *Quercus imbricaria.* (See **oak, laurel.**)

oak, shinnery (shihn'uh ree) *n.* A common name for *Quercus Havardii.* (See **oak, Havard.**)

oak, Shumard's red (shoo'mahrdz) *n.* A common name for *Quercus Shumardii,* a hardy deciduous tree native to the southeastern United States. It grows to 75 feet or more, with glossy, dark green, prickly lobed leaves that turn red or red-brown in fall. Used as a street or lawn tree.

oak, silk *n.* A common name for *Grevillea robusta,* a fast-growing tender evergreen tree. It grows to 150 feet, with finely textured leaves and with spikes of clusters of bright golden-orange feathery flowers in early spring. Used as a quick screen, shade tree, and street tree. Drought-tolerant, it thrives in desert heat and poor soil, but does not take wind. Also known as silky oak.

oak, Southern live *n.* A common name for *Quercus virginiana.* (See **oak, live.**)

oak, Spanish *n.* 1. A common name for *Quercus falcata,* a hardy deciduous tree native to the eastern United States, from New Jersey to Florida and Texas. It grows to 80 feet, with large, lobed leaves, fuzzy beneath. Also known as Spanish red oak. 2. A common name for *Quercus palustris.* (See **oak, pin.**)

oak, swamp chestnut *n.* A common name for *Quercus Michauxii* and *Q. prinus,* both of which are also called basket oak. (See **oak, basket.**)

oak, swamp post *n.* A common name for *Quercus lyrata* (see **oak, overcup**) and *Q. Michauxii* (see **oak, basket.**)

oak, swamp white *n.* 1. A common name for *Quercus bicolor,* a very hardy deciduous tree native to North America, from Quebec to Georgia and Arkansas. It grows to 70 feet, with scaling, flaky bark and shiny dark green leaves with shallow lobes or scallops, silver white beneath. Useful in wet soils. 2. A common name for *Q. Michauxii,* also called basket oak. (See **oak, basket.**)

oak, tanbark *n.* A common name for *Lithocarpus densiflorus,* a handsome tender tree native to the western United States. Also known as tan oak. (See **Lithocarpus.**)

oak, Texas red *n.* A common name for *Quercus texana,* a marginally hardy deciduous tree native to Texas. It grows to 35 feet, with lobed leaves with 5 sharp points.

oak, truffle *n.* A common name for *Quercus rober.* Also called English oak. (See **oak, English.**)

oak, turkey *n.* A common name for *Quercus incana* (see **oak, bluejack**) and *Q. laevis* (See **oak, Catesby**).

oak, Turner *n.* A common name for *Quercus Turnerii,* a possible hybrid between *Q. ilex* and *Q. rober.* It is a semievergreen tree that grows to 50 feet, with lobed leaves 4 inches long.

oak, ubame (oo bah′mee) *n.* A common name for *Quercus phillyraeoides,* a marginally hardy evergreen tree. It grows to 30 feet, with wavy-edged, oval leaves.

oak, valley *n.* A common name for *Quercus lobata.* Also called California white oak. (See **oak, California white.**)

oak, water *n.* A common name for *Quercus nigra.* Also called possum oak. (See **oak, possum.**)

oak, western *n.* A common name for *Quercus Garryana.* Also known as Oregon oak. (See **oak, Oregon.**)

oak, white *n.* A common name for *Quercus alba,* a very hardy round-headed, wide-spreading deciduous tree native to the United States, from Maine to Florida and Texas. It grows to 100 feet, with pale gray fissured bark, and large, lobed soft-green leaves that turn purple-crimson in fall.

Quercus alba
(white oak)

oak, willow *n.* A common name for *Quercus phellos,* a round-headed hardy deciduous tree native to the eastern United States, from New York to Florida and Texas. It grows from 50 to 90 feet, with drooping lower branches and long, narrow, willowlike leaves that color yellow in fall. Used as a lawn tree.

oak, yellow *n.* A common name for *Quercus Muehlenbergii.* Also known as chestnut oak. (See **oak, chestnut.**)

oak, yellow-barked *n.* A common name for *Quercus velutina.* Also known as black oak. (See **oak, black.**)

oak, yellow chestnut *n.* A common name for *Quercus Muehlenbergii.* Also known as chestnut oak. (See **oak, chestnut.**)

oat grass *n.* (See **Arrhenathrum.**)

obcordate (ahb kor′dayt) *a.* In botany, inversely heart-shaped, with the broader end and its strong notch at the top instead of the bottom.

obcordate leaf

obdeltoid (ahb dehl′toid) *a.* In botany, inversely deltoid; triangular with the apex downward.

obdiplostemonous (ahb dihp loh stee′muh nuhs) *a.* In botany, having the stamens in two whorls, those of the outer whorl being opposite the petals.

obdiplostemony (ahb dihp loh stee′muh nee) *n.* In botany, the condition of being obdiplostemonous.

obedient plant *n.* A common name for *Physostegia.* (See **false dragonhead** and **Physostegia.**)

oblanceolate (ahb lahn′see uh leht) *a.* In botany, inversely lanceolate; shaped like a lance-point reversed, with the tapering point next to the leafstalk.

oblique *a.* In botany, slanting with unequal sides.

oblong *a.* Specifically, in botany, longer than broad, and mostly parallel-sided.

oblong leaf

obovate (ahb oh′vayt) *a.* In botany, inversely ovate; having the broad end upward or toward the apex, as in many leaves.

obovate leaf

obovoid (ahb oh′void) *a.* In botany, shaped like an egg, with the narrow end forming the base, as an obovoid fruit; inversely ovoid.

obrotund *a.* In botany, approaching a round form.

obtuse leaf

obtuse *a.* In botany, blunt, or rounded at the extremity, as an obtuse leaf, sepal, or petal.

Ochna (ahk′nuh) *n.* A genus of 90 species of tropical shrubs and trees (Ochnaceae). *O. serrulata* is a shrub to 5 feet, with small, narrow, oval leaves with sharp teeth, yellow-green flowers the size of buttercups in early summer, and glossy jet-black seeds with a red center. Used as a specimen shrub in warm climates; in containers, in greenhouses, or as a houseplant anywhere. Commonly known as Mickey Mouse plant.

Ochnaceae (ahk nay′see ee) *n. pl.* A family of 20 genera of flowers, shrubs, and trees. The ornamental genera are *Ochna* and *Ouratea.*

Ochroma (ahk roh′muh) *n.* A genus of 1 variable species, *O. pyramidale,* a fast-growing pioneer tree (Bombacaceae) of lowland tropics, native to the American tropics. Commonly known as balsa, this is the source of balsa wood.

Ocimum (ahs′uh muhn) *n.* A genus of 150 species of tender herbs or shrubs (Labiatae); basil. They grow from 5 inches to 6 feet, depending on the species, with opposite, oval, pointed aromatic leaves and spikes of whorled white, yellow, pink, or purple flowers. Traditional in herb gardens as culinary herbs, particularly *O. basilicum* (sweet basil), the essence of pesto. Commonly known as basil.

Ocimum basilicum
(sweet basil)

Oconee bells (uh koh′nee) *n.* A common name for *Shortia galicifolia,* a hardy stemless perennial, native to mountains from Virginia to Georgia. It grows to 8 inches, spreading by creeping root-stocks, with glossy, spiny-toothed round or oval basal leaves and white, pink, or blue bell-shaped flowers. Used in wild gardens, rock gardens, or shady places.

ocotillo (oh koh tihl′oh) *n*. A common name for *Fouguieria splendens,* a curious tender spiny shrub, native to the Mojave and Colorado deserts from New Mexico west to Southern California into Baja, California and east to Texas and Mexico. It has many stiff whiplike gray stems 8 to 25 feet high covered with stout thorns with small, fleshy, rounded leaves that appear briefly after rains and then drop. Clusters of tubular red flowers also appear after rains. Used in desert gardens, as a screen, as an impenetrable hedge, or for its strange silhouette. Also known as coach-whip, Jacob's-staff, and vine cactus.

ocrea of *Polygonum*

ocrea (ahk′ree uh) *n*., *pl*. **ocreae** (-e). In botany, a sheathing stipule, or a pair of stipules united into a tubular sheath around the stem, as in *Polygonum.*

octandrian (ahk tahn′dree uhn) *a*. Having the characteristics of the class Octandria; having 8 distinct stamens. Also octandrious.

octopus tree *n*. A common name for *Schefflera actinophylla.* (See **umbrella tree, Queensland**.)

odd-pinnate *a*. In botany, pinnate (leaves with opposite pairs) with a terminal odd leaflet, as in the rose. (see under **imparipinnate**.)

Odontoglossum (oh dahnt′uh glahs uhm) *n*. A genus of 250 species of extemely handsome, highly variable, epiphytic orchids (Orchidaceae) native to the cool highlands of tropical America. They grow from 1 to 3 feet, with leaves folded lengthwise and spikes of showy, long-lasting, multicolored flowers, attractively splotched and spotted. Widely grown by collectors, as a winter houseplant, or in cool greenhouses.

Odontonema (oh dahnt′oh nee muh) *n*. A genus of 40 species of mostly shrubs (Acanthaceae), native to Mexico and Central America. They grow from 5 to 15 feet, with opposite, entire leaves and spikes of red or pink tubular flowers. Grown in the South or in greenhouses.

odoriferous (oh duh rihf′uh ruhs) *a*. Giving odor or scent, usually sweet; diffusing fragrance; fragrant, as odoriferous flowers.

Oenanthe (ee nahn′thee) *n*. A genus of 30 species of perennial wildflowers (Umbelliferae), some species native to the coastal marshes of North America. *O. sarmentosa* grows to 5 feet, with leaves divided into toothed leaflets and rounded clusters of white flowers.

Oenothera (ee nuh thihr′uh) *n*. A genus of 80 species of annuals and perennials (Onagraceae), many species native to North America. They grow from a few inches to 2 feet, with alternate leaves and rose, pink, yellow, or white flowers, the color deepening in age on some species. Used in beds and borders, low-growing species in rock gardens or as a small-scale groundcover. Commonly known as evening primrose and sundrops.

Oenothera
(evening primrose)
a flower stalk *b* plant with roots

offset *n*. 1. An offshoot; specifically, in botany, a short lateral shoot by which certain plants such as the houseleek, *Sempervivum tectorum,* are propagated. 2. A small bulb at the base of a mother bulb.

oil spray *n*. (See **horticultural oil**.)

okra *n.* The vegetable *Abelmoschus esculentus,* cultivated in the East and West Indies and the United States, where it is especially popular in the South. The long, ridged pods are filled with a jellylike substance that thickens soups, stews, and other dishes to which it is added. It is rich in vitamin C. Formerly classed as *Hibiscus;* it is also known as gumbo.

Oldenlandia (ohl duhn lahn′dee uh) *n.* A genus of 300 species of subtropical perennials and shrubs (Rubiaceae). *O. natalensis* is a shrublet that grows to 12 inches, with narrow, pointed leaves and clusters of tubular lavender flowers. Used in frost-free gardens or as an indoor/outdoor plant.

old maid *n.* A common name for 2 annual flowers, *Catharanthus rosea* (Madagascar periwinkle and rose periwinkle) and *Zinnia elegans* (zinnia and youth-in-old-age). (See **Catharanthus** and **Zinnia**.)

old-man-of-the-Andes *n.* A common name for *Borzicactus Trollii,* a slow-growing slender, ribbed, erect, cylindrical, spiny cactus covered with long white hairs. It grows to 2 feet, with spines 2 inches long and rose-colored flowers. Grown by collectors or as a houseplant.

old-man's-beard *n.* 1. A common name for 2 species of *Clematis: C. virginiana,* virgin's bower or leatherflower (see **leatherflower**) and *C. vitalba,* traveler's-joy (see **traveler's-joy**). 2. A common name for *Chionanthus virginicus,* fringe tree (see **fringe tree**).

Olea (oh′lee uh) *n.* A genus of 20 species of tender broadleaf evergreen shrubs and trees (Oleaceae). *O. europea,* the olive, is a very long-lived tree, enduring a century or more, that grows to 30 feet, with small, willowlike, silvery leaves, clusters of small yellowish flowers, and olives. Old, gnarled olive trees have tremendous character. Used as street trees, lawn trees, and specimen trees. Useful in desert gardens and in poor soil; essential to a Mediterranean effect. Commonly known as olive.

Oleaceae (oh lee ay′see ee) *n. pl.* A family of 29 genera and about 600 species of vines, shrubs, and trees. The ornamental genera include *Chionanthus* (fringe tree), *Forsythia* (golden bells), *Fraxinus* (ash), *Jasminus* (jasmine or jessamine), *Ligustrum* (privet), *Olea* (olive), *Osmanthus,* and *Syringa* (lilac).

oleander (oh lee ahn′duhr) *n.* A common name for the genus *Nerium,* an erect, tender evergreen shrub. It grows from 8 to 15 feet, and as wide, with narrow, pointed, leathery dark green leaves, attractive in all seasons, and masses of clusters of showy white, pink, salmon, rose, red, or magenta flowers, sometimes fragrant, and long, narrow pods with feathery seeds. Used for everything: hedges, screens, specimen shrubs, container plants, and freeway plantings in mild-winter climates; essential to a Mediterranean effect. A tough plant that endures all privation: drought, poor soil, alkaline soil, heat, wind, and neglect, on top of which it is deer-proof. All parts of the plants are poisonous. Do not burn branches or leaves or use the branches as barbecue skewers.

oleander, common (oh lee ahn′duhr) *n.* A common name for *Nerium oleander,* a tender evergreen shrub. Also known as rosebay. (See **oleander**.)

Olearia (oh lee ah′ree uh) *n.* A genus of 130 species of tender evergreen shrubs and trees (Compositae). They grow from 3 to 20 feet, depending on the species, with leathery leaves and white, blue, or purple daisylike flowers with white, yellow, purple, or dark red centers and fruit. Used as a specimen shrub in mild-winter climates. Commonly known as daisybush and tree aster.

oleaster (oh lee ahs′tuhr) *n.* A common name for *Elaeagnus,* fast-growing, dense, full, firm, tough large shrubs or small trees of varying degrees of hardiness, 1 species native to North America, *E. commutata* (silverberry). They grow from 6 to 20 feet, depending on the species, with alternate leaves covered with silvery or brown scales that make evergreen species sparkle in the sunlight, small, fragrant flowers, and decorative red fruit, which in some species attracts birds and in others is edible. Drought-tolerant once established. Used for screening, hedges, bank covers, or as background shrubs; useful in seaside gardens.

oleaster family (oh lee ahs′tuhr) *n.* A common name for Elaeagnaceae. (See **Elaeagnaceae**.)

oleraceous (ahl uh ray′shuhs) *a.* In botany, of the nature of a potherb; fit for kitchen use.

olericulture (ahl'uh ruh kuh chur) *n*. In horticulture, the growing, storing, processing, and marketing of vegetables.

olig-/oligo- *comb. form* Few; deficiency; little.

olivaceous (ahl uh vay'shuhs) *a*. Of an olive-green color; like an olive.

olive *n*. 1. The oil-tree, *Olea Europaea,* cultivated from the earliest times. Now grown in southern California. It grows to about 40 feet tall, with a rounded top; the trunk and branches are apt to be gnarled in shape, and the leaves are small and lance-shaped, dull green above and silvery beneath. It is an evergreen, of great longevity, and it thrives in poor and dry sandy soils. 2. The fruit of the common olive tree: small, oval, and bluish-black in color when fully ripe. It is the source of olive oil and is also eaten brined or pickled.

olive
a branch with fruit *b* flower cluster

olive family *n*. A common name for Oleaceae. (See **Oleaceae**.)

olive plum *n*. A common name for *Cassine*. (See **Cassine**.)

olive wood *n*. A common name for *Cassine*. (See **Cassine**.)

Omphalodes (ahm fay lohdz') *n*. A genus of 24 species of annuals and perennials (Boraginaceae). They grow from 8 inches to 2 feet, depending on the species, with simple, alternate, basal leaves and loose spikes of small white or blue flowers. Useful

in moist soils and in wild and woodland gardens. Commonly known as navelwort and navelseed.

Onagraceae (ahn uh gray'see ee) *n. pl*. A family of 21 genera and 600 to 700 species of annuals, perennials, shrubs, or trees, some growing on land, others in water. The ornamental genera include *Clarkia* (farewell-to-spring or godetia), *Epilobium* (fireweed), *Fuchsia* (lady's eardrops), *Gaura, Oenothera* (evening primrose), and *Zauschneria* (California fuchsia and hummingbird flower).

Oncidium (ahn sihd'ee uhm) *n*. A genus of about 400 species of small epiphytic orchids (Orchidaceae) native to tropical America. They grow from pseudobulbs to several inches tall, with fleshy, flat leaves and spikes, as much as 5 feet long, of clusters of multicolored flowers, showy in some species. Grown by collectors in warm or cool greenhouses, depending on the species. Commonly known as dancing-lady orchid.

Oncosperma (ahng koh sper'muh) *n*. A genus of a few species of tropical, spiny palms (Palmae). They grow from 20 to 50 feet, depending on the species, sometimes in clumps, with long, divided leaves. Used in moist soils in tropical gardens. Also known as nibung palm.

one-berry *n*. A common name for the genus *Celtis* (hackberry) and *Mitchella repens* (partridgeberry). (See **Celtis**, **hackberry**, and **Mitchella**.)

onion *n*. The garden vegetable *Allium Cepa* (see **Allium**), especially its bulbous root, the part chiefly used as food. It is a biennial plant, with long tubular leaves and a swelling, pithy stalk. The bulb is composed of closely concentric layers and varies much in size and color, which runs from dark red to white, and in the degree of pungency. It endures tropical heat and the coolest temperate climate. Its numerous varieties include Bermuda onion, a superior mild-flavored quality of onion; pearl onion, a variety of onion with small bulbs; bunching or green onions, also called scallions, grown for their green tops; and top onion, or Egyptian onion (of Canadian origin), which produces at the summit of the stem, instead of flowers and seeds, a cluster of bulbs, which are used for pickles and as sets for new plants.

onion, sea *n*. A common name for *Ornithogalum caudatum* (pregnant onion), *Scilla verna* (spring squill), and *Urginea maritima* (see **Urginea**). *O. caudatum* grows from a shiny, above-ground bulb, with floppy, strap-shaped leaves and tall spikes of small starlike white flowers. The bulblets form under the skin, like a marsupial in a pouch, and grow to marble size before emerging. Hardy to 25° F. *S. verna* is a moderately hardy perennial bulb that grows to 6 inches, with narrow, grasslike leaves and violet-blue flowers. Also known as spring squill.

onion, wild *n.* A common name for *Allium cernuum* and *A. canadense,* both perennial bulbs native to North America. *A. cernuum,* native from New York to South Carolina, west to British Columbia and California, grows to 2 feet, with flat, long, narrow leaves, which smell strongly of onion when bruised and stalks topped by clusters of many nodding, rose or white flowers. Also called nodding onion and lady's leek. *A. canadense,* native to eastern North America, grows to 12 inches, with narrow leaves, which smell strongly of onion when bruised, and stalks topped by pink or white flowers. Grown in wild gardens, native-plant gardens, or rock gardens. Also known as wild garlic, meadow leek, and rose leek.

Onobrychis (ahn uh brigh'kehs) *n.* A genus of 100 species of perennials or spiny shrubs (Leguminosae). *O. arenaria* is a perennial that grows to 2 feet, with pairs of leaves divided into oval or narrow leaflets and slender spikes of small pink or white sweet-pea-shaped flowers.

Onoclea sensibilis
(sensitive fern)

Onoclea (ahn uh klee'uh) *n.* A genus of 1 species, *O. sensibilis,* a large, hardy fern (Polypodiaceae). It has sterile fronds 4 1/2 feet long and fertile fronds 2 feet long, both finely divided. Grows enthusiastically; may be invasive in wet, rich soils. Commonly known as sensitive fern because it is damaged by frost.

Ononis (oh noh'nehs) *n.* A genus of 70 species of perennials and subshrubs (Leguminosae). They grow from a few inches to 2 feet, depending on the species, with leaves divided into 3 leaflets and long stems with small clusters of rose, pink, or white sweet-pea-shaped flowers. Commonly known as restharrow.

Onopordum

Onopordum (ahn uh pawr'duhm) *n.* A genus of 25 species of woolly, thistlelike biennial plants (Compositae). They grow from 15 inches to 9 feet, depending on the species, with large, alternate, prickly leaves, sometimes lobed, and large, bristly, purple, violet, or white flowers. Some species have naturalized in parts of North and South America.

Onosma (ahn uhz'muh) *n.* A genus of 125 to 130 species of hairy annuals, perennials, and subshrubs (Boraginaceae). They grow from a few inches to 2 feet, with alternate, entire, mostly basal leaves and clusters of yellow, blue, or red tubular flowers, sometimes fragrant. Used in borders and rock gardens.

oogamous (oh ah'gah muhs) *a.* In botany, being reproduced by the fusion of a small mobile male gamete with a large immobile female gamete.

open-pollinated *a.* Pollinated by wind or insects, not by human intervention.

Ophioglossaceae (ah fee oh glah say'see ee) *n. pl.* A family of 3 genera and 60 species of ferns. The ornamental genera are *Botrychium* (grape fern or moonwort) and *Ophioglossum* (adder's-tongue or adder's-tongue fern).

Ophioglossum
(adder's tongue)

Ophioglossum (ah fee oh glahs'uhm) *n.* A genus of 30 to 50 species of fleshy ferns (Ophioglossaceae), some species native to the Americas. They grow fronds from 2 inches to 5 feet long, depending on the species. Commonly known as adder's-tongue or adder's-tongue fern.

Ophiopogon (ah fee oh poh'gahn) *n.* A genus of 10 species of tender, clump-forming ground covers (Liliaceae). They grow to 12 inches, with narrow, grasslike leaves and spikes of small white, lilac-blue, or pale purple flowers. Used as a small-scale ground cover, as an indoor/outdoor plant, or in rock gardens and containers. Commonly known as lilyturf and mondo grass.

Ophrys (ah'frehs) *n.* A genus of 35 species of terrestrial orchids (Orchidaceae). They grow to 2 feet, with mostly basal leaves and spikes of brightly colored flowers that mimic insects like bees, flies, and spiders. Sometimes planted in wild gardens.

opium *n.* (See **poppy, opium**.)

Oplopanax (uh plahp'uh naks) *n.* A genus of 2 species of magnificent, hardy, spiny shrubs (Araliaceae). *O. horridus* is native from Michigan to Oregon and north to Alaska. It grows to 10 feet, with spiny stems, densely studded with half-inch thorns, large leaves 10 inches wide, prickly on both sides, spikes of greenish-white flowers, and fleshy red fruit. A native plant, but not usually grown ornamentally. Commonly known as devil's club.

opposite leaves

opposite *a.* In botany: 1. situated on opposite sides of an axis, as leaves when there are 2 on 1 node; 2. having a position between an organ and the axis on which it is borne, as a stamen when it is opposite a sepal or petal.

Opuntia (oh puhnch'ee uh) *n.* A genus of about 300 species of sprawling-to-treelike spiny jointed cacti (Cactaceae) native to the Americas, from British Columbia to the Strait of Magellan. They have fleshy, flattened, paddlelike or cylindrical joints, large, showy white, yellow, orange, red, rose, cerise, or pink flowers, and fruit, often fleshy, sometimes edible. Used on exposed, rocky banks, in desert gardens, to create a desert effect, or grown by collectors. They enjoy heat, drought, and sandy soils. Commonly known as prickly pear.

Opuntia
(prickly pear)

orache (ahr'uhk) *n.* A tall, hardy annual herb, *Atriplex hortensis,* grown since ancient times for its thick leaves, which are cooked like spinach. Commonly grown in gardens in North America until the 19th century, it is a hardy substitute for spinach in areas where true spinach runs to seed before producing a crop of leaves. It grows well in the shade and will withstand highly alkaline soils. Also spelled orach. Also called mountain spinach.

orange *n.* A common name for *Citrus sinensis,* a tender tree. It grows from 20 to 40 feet, with glossy, oval, pointed yellow-green leaves, masses of small white, sweetly fragrant flowers, and round, orange, edible winter fruit. There are also dwarf forms that grow to no more than 8 feet. Unusual in that the tree fruits and flowers simultaneously. Used as specimen trees in mild-winter climates, as lawn trees, near patios, and as indoor/outdoor plants anywhere; traditional in containers and tubs. It is now cultivated in nearly all tropical and subtropical lands, including the southern parts of the United States, having become wild in Florida. Its flowers are prized when fresh (see **orange blossoms**), and (chiefly those of the bitter orange) yield neroli oil and orange-flower water. The trees are grown as much for their ornamental value and fragrance as for their fruit. 2. The fruit of the orange tree, a round, large fruit of 8 or 10 divisions, containing pulp and an acidic, refreshing juice. Oranges are especially rich in vitamin C. There are 3 principal varieties of the orange: the sweet orange, including the ordinary market sorts; the bitter or Seville orange or bigarade, used for making marmalade; and the bergamot orange, subspecies *Bergamia.*

orange flower *n.* 1. A common name for *Trillium erectum,* a very hardy perennial wildflower native to North America, from Ontario to Illinois east to Georgia and North Carolina. It grows to 2 feet, with big, diamond-shaped leaves and white, yellow, or purple flowers on 4-inch stalks. Used in wild gardens or in moist, shady locations. Also known as purple trillium. 2. A common name for *Choisya ternata.* Also called Mexican orange. (See **Mexican orange**.) 3. A synonym for many plants called mock orange. (See **mock orange**.)

orange flower, Mexican *n.* A common name for *Choisya ternata.* Also called Mexican orange. (See **Mexican orange**.)

orange grass *n.* A common name for *Hypericum gentianoides,* a low-growing annual wildflower native to eastern North America. It grows to 18 inches, with wiry stems and minute, scalelike leaves and tiny yellow flowers. Also known as pineweed.

orange jessamine (jehs'uh mehm) *n.* A common name for *Murraya paniculata.* (See **Murraya**.)

orange, mandarin *n.* A small, flattened variety of orange in which the rind separates very readily from the pulp, the latter sweet and deliciously flavored. (See **tangerine**.)

orange, native *n.* A common name for *Microcitrus australasica,* a tender, spiny, broadleaf evergreen tree. It grows from 30 to 40 feet, with oval pointed or diamond-shaped leaves, solitary flowers, and long, narrow, juicy, acid, greenish-yellow fruit. Used as a parent in hybridizing citrus or as rootstock for grafted citrus. Also known as Australian finger lime.

orange, navel *n.* A very large, sweet, and usually seedless variety of orange, so called from a navel-like formation at the end.

orange, Osage (oh'sayj) *n.* A common name for *Maclura pomifera,* a tree native to Arkansas and Texas and naturalized throughout the eastern United States. (See **Maclura**.)

orangeroot *n.* A common name for the genus *Hydrastis,* particularly *Hydrastis canadensis* (goldenseal). (See **Hydrastis** and **goldenseal**.)

orange, wild *n.* A common name for several trees: *Poncirus trifoliata,* hardy orange (see **hardy orange**); *Zanthoxylum clava-Herculis,* Hercules'-club (see **Hercules'-club**); and *Prunus caroliniana,* cherry laurel. *P. caroliniana* is a hardy broadleaf evergreen tree, native to the United States from North Carolina to Texas, that grows to 40 feet or less, with glossy narrow, oval, pointed leaves, dense spikes of white flowers with a sweet fragrance like orange blossoms, and dry, black fruits.

orbicular (awr bihk'yuh luhr) *a.* Nearly or completely circular, as an orbicular leaf. Also orbiculate.

orbicular leaf

orchard *n*. 1. A garden. 2. A piece of ground, usually enclosed, devoted to the culture of fruit trees, especially apple, pear, peach, plum, and cherry trees; a collection of cultivated fruit trees.

orchard ladder *n*. A tripod ladder used to access fruit trees.

orchid *n*. A common name for any plant of the family Orchidaceae, one of the largest plant families in the world, with an estimated 600 to 800 genera and 17,000 to 30,000 species, found all over the world except in deserts. (See **Orchidaceae**.)

Orchidaceae (awr kuh day'see ee) *n. pl*. A family of 600 to 800 genera and 17,000 to 30,000 species of flowers found all over the world except in deserts. The ornamental genera include *Bletilla, Calypso, Cattleya, Corallorhiza* (coralroot), *Cymbidium, Cypripedium* (ladyslipper orchid), *Dendrobium, Epidendrum* (buttonhole orchid), *Miltonia* (pansy orchid), *Orchis, Paphiopedilum* (ladyslipper orchid), *Phalaenopsis* (moth orchid), *Pleione, Vanda,* and *Vanilla*.

orchidaceous (awr kuh day'shuhs) *a*. Pertaining to, or resembling the orchids; belonging to the family Orchidaceae.

orchid, buttonhole *n*. A common name for *Epidendrum*. (See **Epidendrum**.)

orchid cactus *n*. A common name for the genus *Epiphyllum*. (See **Epiphyllum**.)

orchid, cranefly *n*. A common name for *Tipularia discolor,* a hardy terrestrial orchid native to the eastern United States, from New Jersey to South Carolina. It grows to 2 feet, with dull green heart-shaped leaves, blotched with purple above, and small, nodding green, yellow, rust-bronze, or purple flowers. Used in shaded woodland gardens. Also known as elfin-spur, crippled-cranefly, and mottled-cranefly.

orchid, dancing-lady *n*. A common name for *Oncidium*. (See **Oncidium**.)

orchid, fen *n*. A common name for *Liparis Loeselii,* a hardy terrestrial orchid native to North America. It grows to 10 inches, with 2 fleshy, oval leaves, 7 inches long, and spikes of tiny white or chartreuse flowers. Used in moist places in wild gardens. Also known as bog twayblade, yellow twayblade, Loesel's twayblade, olive scutcheon, and russet-witch. (See **Liparis**.)

orchid, fringed *n*. A common name for the genus *Habenaria*. (See **Habenaria**.)

orchid, ladyslipper *n*. A common name for *Cypripedium* and *Paphiopedilum*. (See **Cypripedium** and **Paphiopedilum**.)

orchid, moth *n*. A common name for *Phalaenopsis*. (See **Phalaenopsis**.)

orchidologist (awr keh dahl'uh jehst) *n*. An orchid specialist.

orchidology (awr keh dahl'uh jee) *n*. The special branch of botany or of horticulture that relates to orchids.

orchid, pansy *n*. A common name for *Miltonia*. (See **Miltonia**.)

orchid, ragged *n*. A common name for *Habenaria lacera,* a hardy terrestrial orchid native to eastern North America. It grows to 2 1/2 feet, with narrow leaves, 8 inches long, and spikes of yellowish-green or whitish-green flowers. Also known as green fringed orchid and ragged fringed orchid.

orchid, rein *n*. A common name for the genus *Habenaria*. (See **Habenaria**.)

orchid tree *n*. A common name for 2 species of *Bauhinia; B. purpurea* and *B. variegata*. They are subtropical (hardy to 22° F) deciduous trees that grow from 20 to 35 feet, with light green lobed leaves, masses of showy light-pink-to-purple 3-inch wide orchidlike flowers, and long, flat pods. They make spectacular street trees, lawn trees, or specimen trees in mild-winter/warm-spring climates. *B. variegata* is also known as mountain ebony; *B.purpurea* is also known as butterfly tree.

orchid, vanda (vahnd'uh) *n*. A common name for the genus *Vanda*. (See **Vanda**.)

showy orchis

Orchis (awr′kehs) *n.* A genus of 50 species of hardy terrestrial orchids (Orchidaceae), some species native to North America. They grow to 12 inches, with basal leaves, leafy stems, and spikes of rose, red-purple, mauve, and pure yellow, multicolored, curiously shaped flowers. Used in moist locations in wild gardens.

order *n.* The level of botanical classification between family and class. The names of orders usually end in *-ales.* For example, the cabbage rose is *Rosa centifolia. Rosa* is the genus; *centifolia* is the species. It is in the family Rosaceae, the order Rosales, and the class Dicotyledonae.

order of bloom *n.* The sequence of blooming times of plants in a garden.

Origanum vulgare
(oregano)

oregano (or ehg′uh noh) *n.* A flavorful herb grown for its small oval leaves, or, as in the less flavorful wild oregano (also known as pot marjoram), for its pink flowers, which attract bees and dry well for winter arrangements. There is no botanical distinction between the herbs commonly known as oregano and marjoram, but in culinary use, oregano describes the plants whose leaves have a stronger, peppery flavor. It is most commonly used with tomatoes, in tomato sauces, and on pizza. It is a perennial, sometimes grown as an annual in a cool climate.

Oregon grape *n.* A common name for the genus *Mahonia,* especially *M. Aquifolium* and *M. nervosa. M. Aquifolium* is a hardy broadleaf evergreen shrub native to northwestern North America, from British Columbia to northern California. It grows to 6 feet or more, with oval, spiny-toothed, hollylike leaves, clusters of yellow flowers, and edible blue-black fruit. Used as a specimen shrub, low screen, foundation or background shrub, or in containers. Also known as mountain grape, holly mahonia, holly barberry, and blue barberry. *M. nervosa* is a low-growing hardy broadleaf evergreen shrub native to northwestern North America, from British Columbia to northern California. It grows to 2 feet, with leaves divided into glossy, bristle-toothed green leaflets, upright clusters of yellow flowers, and blue berries. Used as a ground cover, it gives the impression of a stiff, leathery fern. Also known as longleaf mahonia.

organic *n.* A term referring to any material that is derived directly from plants or animals. *a.* 1. A term used to describe fertilizer that releases nitrogen slowly into the soil. 2. Relating to living organisms. 3. Derived from living organisms. 4. Containing carbon compounds.

organic gardening *n.* A method of gardening utilizing only organic materials, such as manure, peat moss, and compost, and rejecting inorganic materials, such as rock phosphate, ammonium, insecticides, and pesticides.

organic soil *n.* A term applied to soil that consists primarily of organic matter like peat or muck.

oriental fruit moth *n.* A moth whose pinkish larvae bore into the stem end or near the pit of peaches and nectarines, ruining the fruit. They sometimes bore into twigs and branches. Control with *Bacillus thuringiensis* or traditional pesticides.

Oriental pear *n.* A fruit, *Pyrus pyrifolia,* with golden- to russet-brown skin and a firm, applelike texture. It is aromatic in flavor, and juicy, even after storage. The trees are dwarf, growing to about 15 feet, and hardy in Zones 5 to 8.

Origanum (uh rihg′uh nuhm) *n.* A genus of 15 to 20 species of annual, perennial, and shrubby herbs (Labiatae); marjoram. They are weedy, sprawling, aromatic culinary herbs, including *O. vulgare* (oregano) and *O. Majorana* (sweet marjoram). Traditional in herb gardens and cottage gardens; excellent in window boxes and pots. They must be trimmed regularly to be ornamental. Used in tomato-based sauces for pasta and pizza. Commonly known as marjoram.

Orixa (oh rihks′uh) *n.* A genus of 1 species, *O. japonica* (Rutaceae), a hardy deciduous shrub. It grows to 10 feet, with glossy, oval, pointed leaves and greenish, solitary, 4-petaled flowers.

Ormosia (awr mo′zhee uh) *n.* A genus of more than 50 species of tropical trees (Leguminosae), some species native to tropical America. They grow to 75 feet or less, with alternate, leathery, divided leaves, clusters of small butterfly-shaped purple flowers, and long pods with red or black seeds used to make necklaces. Commonly known as necklace tree.

ornamental grasses *n.* Varieties of grass grown for their showy seed heads, many of which are dried for winter arrangements.

Ornithogalum

Ornithogalum (awr nuh thahg′uh luhm) *n.* A genus of about 100 species of perennial bulbs *(Liliaceae)* of varying degrees of hardiness. They grow from a few inches to 3 feet, with narrow, basal leaves and often showy clusters of white, yellow, or orange-red flowers, mostly spring-blooming. Used in borders, beds, and pots. Some are excellent cut flowers.

Orontium (awr awn′shuhm) *n.* A genus of 1 species, *O. aquaticum* (Araceae), a hardy perennial water plant native to the eastern United States, from Massachusetts to Florida and Louisiana. It has many tufted leaves that grow from a thick rhizome, a bright yellow spike, 4 inches long, on a white stalk, 3 feet long, and blue-green berries. Used in sunny bogs or water gardens. Commonly known as golden club.

orpine (awr′pehn) *n.* A common name for the genus *Sedum.* (See **Sedum.**)

orpine, evergreen (awr′pehn) *n.* A common name for *Sedum Anacampseros,* a low-growing succulent with creeping stems. It has small, grayish, rounded, fleshy leaves and 6-to-10-inch stems topped with clusters of tiny purple flowers. Used in rock gardens, for edging, and in pots.

orpine family (awr′pehn) *n.* A common name for Crassulaceae. (See **Crassulaceae.**)

orris (or′ihs) *n.* Any of several iris varieties, from which orrisroot is obtained. In potpourri making, orrisroot is an ingredient that fixes or holds the scents of other flowers and leaves.

orth-/ortho- *comb. form* In botany, upright or vertical.

Orthene (or′theen) *n.* (See **acephate.**)

Orthocarpus (awr thuh kahr′puhs) *n.* A genus of 25 species of annual wildflowers (Scrophulariaceae) native to western North and South America. They grow to 15 inches, with alternate leaves and spikes of yellow, cream-colored, crimson, or purple cloverlike flowers. Used in meadow gardens or wild gardens. Commonly known as owl's clover.

orthostichous (awr′thahs tuh kuhs) *a.* In botany, exhibiting orthostichy; arranged in vertical ranks.

orthostichy (awr thahs′stuh kee) *n.* In botany, a vertical rank; an arrangement of leaves or scales at different heights on an axis so that their median planes coincide, as the vertical ranks of leaves on a stem.

orthotropic (awr thuh trahp′ihk) *a.* In botany, of or pertaining to or exhibiting orthotropism; growing more or less vertically.

orthotropism (awr′thuh′truh pihz uhm) *n.* In botany, vertical growth; the tendency of plants to grow more or less vertically.

orthotropous (awr thuh′truh puhs) *a.* In botany, a term describing a condition in which all parts of a seed grow in a straight line.

Orthrosanthus (awr throh sahn′thuhs) *n.* A genus of 8 or 9 species of perennial flowers (iris) (Iridaceae). *O. chimboracensis* grows 18 inches to 3 feet, with grasslike basal leaves and light violet-blue open-faced flowers. Used in beds and borders with other bulbs. Commonly known as morning flag or morning flower.

oscillating hoe *n.* A tool with a long handle attached to a rounded transverse blade; used for cultivating and weeding. Unlike a draw hoe, an oscillating hoe works on both the push and pull strokes. Also called push-pull hoe or a stirrup hoe.

oscillating sprinkler *n.* A hose attachment used to spray water back and forth over an arc. Typically adjustable to cover 180°, 90°, or 45°.

osier (oh′zhuhr) *n.* A common name for *Salix viminalis*, a very hardy large shrub or small tree. It grows to 30 feet, with pussy willow-like silver buds and narrow, 10-inch long, willowlike silvery-white leaves, silky beneath. Useful in moist soils or along streams; the branches are used in making baskets. Also known as basket willow.

osier, red (oh′zhuhr) *n.* A common name for *Cornus sericea* (*C. stolonifera*), native to North America, a hardy, deciduous, shrubby dogwood grown for its striking red branches and brilliant scarlet fall color. Used as a specimen plant or in shrub borders. Also known as American dogwood and redtwig dogwood.

Osmanthus (ahz mahn′thuhs) *n.* A genus of 30 to 40 species of marginally hardy, mostly slow-growing, evergreen shrubs and trees (Oleaceae), a

few species native to North America and Hawaii. They grow from 6 to 45 feet, depending on the species, with attractive, clean, leathery leaves and inconspicuous but sweetly fragrant flowers. Used as foundation shrubs, for massing, as background plants, for screening, or in containers. Commonly known as devilwood.

Osmorhiza
(sweet cicily)

Osmorhiza (ahz muh righ′zuh) *n.* A genus of 11 species of hardy perennials (Umbelliferae), some species native to eastern North America. They grow to 3 feet, with delicately cut, lacy, fernlike leaves and flat-topped clusters of tiny white or yellow flowers. Traditional in cottage gardens. Commonly known as sweet cicely.

osmosis (ahz moh′sehs) *n.* The diffusion of fluids through a semipermeable membrane, as in a living cell. Also osmose.

osmund (ahz′muhnd) *n.* A common name for the genus *Osmunda*. (See **Osmunda**.)

Osmunda (ahz muhnd′uh) *n.* A genus of 10 species of large ferns (Osmundaceae), some species native to North America. They have much-divided fronds from 4 to 6 feet long, depending on the species. Used in wild gardens and in moist, shady places. The fronds die to the ground in winter. Commonly known as flowering fern.

Osmundaceae (ahz muhn day′see ee) *n. pl.* A family of 3 genera and 17 species of ferns. The ornamental genera are *Leptopteris, Osmunda,* and *Todea.*

osmundaceous (ahz muhn day'shuhs) *a.* In botany, pertaining to or resembling the family Osmundaceae.

osoberry (oh'suh behr ee) *n.* A common name for *Oemleria cerasiformis,* a very hardy deciduous shrub native from British Columbia to California. It grows to 15 feet, with simple, oval leaves, spikes of small, white, fragrant flowers, and blue-black berries. Also known as Indian plum.

ostrich fern *n.* A common name for large, hardy, striking ferns of the genus *Matteuccia.* (See **Matteuccia.**)

Ostrya (ahs'tree uh) *n.* A genus of 10 species of hardy deciduous trees. They grow to 60 feet, with alternate, toothed leaves that turn yellow in the fall, flowers in catkins, and clusters of light tan nuts resembling hops. Commonly known as hop hornbeam.

Ostrya
(hop hornbeam)

Oswego tea (ah swee'goh) *n.* Another name for bee balm, referring to its use as a tea leaf.

Othonna (oh thahn'uh) *n.* A genus of 150 species of tender perennials and shrubs (Compositae). *O. carnosa* is a shrubby plant that grows to 9 inches, with fleshy, cylindrical leaves crowded at the tips of the branches and clusters of small daisylike yellow flowers. Useful in fast-draining soils. *O. capensis* is a ground cover commonly known as little-pickles. (See **little-pickles.**)

Ouratea (oo rah'tee uh) *n.* A genus of 200 species of tropical deciduous shrubs and trees (Ochnaceae) native to the West Indies. *O. littoralis* is a shrub or small tree that grows to 20 feet, with oval leaves and clusters or spikes of fragrant yellow flowers with 5 fan-shaped petals.

outgrowth *n.* That which grows out of something else; an offshoot.

ovary *n.* In botany, the enlarged, rounded, usually basal, ovule-bearing part of a pistil, ultimately becoming the fruit.

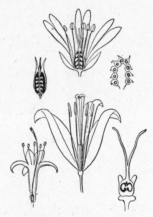

ovaries, with ovules, of various flowers

ovate *a.* Egg-shaped; having a figure like the longitudinal section of a hen's egg; oval, but broader at the basal end, as ovate leaves.

ovate leaf

overplant *v.* To plant too abundantly.

overwater *v.* To water too much.

ovule *n.* In botany, an outgrowth of the ovary, which upon fertilization, becomes the seed.

Oxalidaceae (ahk sal uh day'see ee) *n. pl.* A family of 7 genera and over 1,000 species of flowers, shrubs, or, rarely, trees. The ornamental genera are *Averrhoa, Oxalis,* and *Biophytum.*

Oxalis (ahk'sah lihs) *n.* A genus of 850 species of mostly tender, low-growing perennials (Oxalidaceae) that typically grow from bulblets, tubers, or rhizomes. They grow to a few inches tall, with cloverlike leaves and flowers in every color but blue. Most are small, delightful, easy-to-grow flowers, but *O. corniculata* (red oxalis) is a pestiferous weed. Used in woodland gardens and rock gardens, on stone walls, in pots and hanging baskets, or as cheerful little houseplants. Commonly known as wood sorrel or lady's-sorrel.

Oxalis
(wood sorrel)

Oxera (ahk′suh ruh) *n.* A genus of 20 species of tender evergreen climbing vines or shrubs (Verbenaceae). *O. pulchella* has a refined apearance, growing to 6 feet, with glossy, leathery, very dark green oval leaves and clusters of waxy, white trumpet-shaped flowers. Useful in high shade or cool, sunny spots. Commonly known as royal climber.

oxeye *n.* A common name for *Chysanthemum Leucanthemum* (see **marguerite**), plants of the genus *Buphthalum* (see **Buphthalum**), *Rudbeckia hirta* (see **black-eyed Susan**), and plants of the genus *Heliopsis* (see **Heliopsis**). *C. Leucanthemum* is also called oxeye daisy.

oxeye, creeping *n.* A common name for *Wedelia trilobata,* a tender, trailing, perennial ground cover that spreads by creeping, rooting stems. It spreads to 6 feet or more, with 3-lobed leaves and small yellow flowers resembling zinnias or marigolds. Used as a fast-covering ground cover. Also known as wedelia.

oxeye daisy *n.* A common name for *Chrysanthemum Leucanthemum.* Also called marguerite. (See **marguerite**.)

oxeye or oxeye daisy
a flower and upper stem *b* lower stem and roots

oxeye, yellow *n.* A common name for *Rudbeckia hirta* (see **black-eyed Susan**) and *Chrysanthemum segetum* (see **marigold, corn**).

oxidation *n.* A chemical change involving the addition of oxygen.

oxide *n.* A compound of any element mixed with oxygen alone.

oxlip *n.* A common name for *Primula elatior,* a hardy perennial. It grows to 12 inches, with long, oval leaves, downy beneath, and clusters of sulfur-yellow funnel-shaped flowers. Used in beds and borders.

oxtongue *n.* A common name for *Anchusa,* especially *A. officinalis Picris* and *Gasteria* (see **Gasteria**).

Oxydendrum (ahk see dehn′druhm) *n.* A genus of 1 species, *O. arboreum,* a slow-growing hardy deciduous tree (Ericaceae) native to the eastern United States. It grows 50 to 80 feet, with narrow, pointed leaves, which color scarlet and orange in autumn, and long, drooping, 10-inch clusters of tiny creamy-white bell-shaped flowers that attract bees. Grown for its excellent fall color. Used as a patio tree, shade tree, or in containers when young. Commonly known as sourwood, sorrel tree, or titi.

oxygen *n.* An element found in the soil needed by plants for growth.

Oxyria (ahk sihr′ee uh) *n.* A genus of 2 species of very hardy, low-growing, alpine perennials (Polygonaceae). They grow to 2 feet, with small round or kidney-shaped leaves, clusters of many small greenish flowers, and red fruit. Used in moist rock gardens; grown mainly by collectors. Commonly known as mountain sorrel.

Oxytropis (ak sih'truh pehs) *n.* A genus of about 300 species of low-growing, often hardy perennials (Leguminosae), some species native to North America. They have divided leaves, spikes of white, yellow, purple, and pink pealike flowers, and beanlike pods. Sometimes grown ornamentally, but generally considered a weed; best known as poisonous to cattle. Commonly known as locoweed or crazyweed. (See **crazyweed**)

Oxytropis
(locoweed)

own-root *a.* In horticulture, grown upon its own root, without grafting or budding; applied to many plants, as roses.

oyster plant *n.* A common name for *Tragopogon porrifolius* (salsify), *Mertensia maritima,* and *Rhoeo spathacea. T. porrifolius* is an edible root vegetable, a hardy tap-rooted biennial. *M. maritima* is a hardy perennial that grows to 2 feet, with small, narrow leaves and clusters of tiny pink flowers that fade to blue and pink. *R. spathacea* is a tropical foliage plant, often grown as a houseplant or as a ground cover in frost-free climates. Also known as boat lily. (See **lily, boat**.)

Pachira (puh chuh'ruh) *n.* A genus of large tropical trees (Bombacaceae). They have glossy leaves, divided handwise into long-oval leaflets, and large flowers, with a prominent brush of stamens, white to pink or red. *P. aquatica* is known as shaving-brush tree and water chestnut. Seedlings with heavy trunks are occasionally sold as novelty bonsai.

Pachistima (puh kihs'tuh muh) *n.* (See **Paxistima**.)

pachy- *comb. form. Thick.*

Pachyphytum (pak eh figh'tuhm) *n.* A genus of 12 species of succulent perennials (Crassulaceae). They are notable chiefly for crowded, 1- to 2-inch thick, nearly round leaves. *P. oviferum* (moonstone) has grayish, lavender-toned leaves.

Pachypodium (pak eh poh'dee uhm) *n.* A genus of 17 species of succulent tropical plants (Apocynaceae). They have heavy trunks, leathery leaves, and saucer-shaped flowers. Desert plants, they are leafless during dry periods. The species commonly seen as a house plant is *P. lamerei,* with a tapered trunk crowned with long, narrow leaves, spines, and white flowers, 4 inches wide. Sometimes called Madagascar palm.

Pachyrhizus (pak eh righ'zuhs) *n.* A genus of 2 species of tuberous-rooted, twining tropical vines (Leguminosae). They twine to 20 feet, with 3-parted leaves and short clusters of blue or white flowers, followed by pods filled with seeds (poisonous when mature). The heavy, turnip-shaped, brown-skinned, white-fleshed tubers are crisp, juicy, and somewhat sweet. *P. erosus* is called yam bean or, more frequently in markets, jicama.

Pachysandra (pak eh san'druh) *n.* A genus of 4 or 5 species of hardy evergreen shrubs (Buxaceae). They have creeping underground rootstocks and erect stems, with leaves clustered at the ends, and clusters of small white flowers. *P. terminalis,* often called Japanese spurge, is widely used as a ground cover in shady situations; the 8-inch stems bear strongly toothed 3- to 4-inch-long leaves. 'Variegata' has leaves with white markings. The native *P.*

procumbens is more clumping in habit and has leaves with brownish markings. It is sometimes called Allegheny spurge.

Pachystachys (pak eh stah′kuhs) *n.* A genus of 12 species of large tropical perennials or shrubs (Acanthaceae). They have long, narrow, heavily-veined leaves and 3- to 6-foot-long stems topped by 6-inch spikes of brilliant flowers. *P. coccinea,* with red flowers, is called cardinal's guard. *P. lutea,* with yellow flowers, is golden candle or lollipop flower.

Pachyveria (pak eh vuh′ree uh) *n.* Succulent perennials, hybrids between *Pachyphytum* and *Echeveria.* The many species have thick, fleshy leaves, usually with a bluish or lavender powdery finish. Used in dish gardens, or in warm-winter regions, in bedding or rock gardens.

Paeonia (pee oh′nee uh) *n.* A genus of 33 species of large, long-lived hardy perennials or shrubs, some species native to the Northern Hemisphere; peonies. They have heavy, tuberous roots, divided (sometimes almost fernlike) foliage, and large flowers, borne singly or a few to a stem, at the ends of the branches. A few species are in widespread garden use. (See **peony.**)

Paeoniaceae (pee oh nee ay′see ee) *n.* The peony family, including *Paeonia* and *Glaucidium.*

pagoda tree *n.* A common name given to several trees because of their form or their supposed association with temples. Chinese or Japanese pagoda tree is *Sophora japonica,* also sometimes called Chinese scholar tree. The name is also applied to *Plumeria* (frangipani) and to *Ficus benghalensis, F. indica* (banyan).

paintbrush, scarlet *n.* Same as Indian paintbrush.

painted cup *n.* A common name for species of *Castilleja.*

painted lady *n.* A common name for *Lathyrus odoratus* (sweet pea) and for *Echeveria derenbergii.*

pakchoi (bahk choi′) *n.* A vegetable with long white stalks and dark green leaves; common in Chinese cooking. Also spelled pak-choy. (See **Bok choy.**)

palas tree (puh lahsh′) *n.* A common name for *Butea monosperma,* a tropical tree growing to 45 feet, with divided leaves, leathery leaflets, and showy flame-colored flowers. Yields a gum called Bengal kino. Also called flame-of-the-forest.

pale *n.* In botany, the palea of a grass.

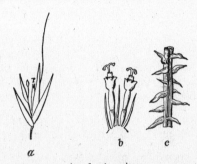

palae of various plants
a in a flowering plume of oats *b* in yarrow *c* on a fern stem

palea (pay′lee uh) *n.* 1. In botany: 1. One of the chafflike bracts or scales under the individual flowers in the heads of many Compositae, as in the sunflower. 2. The upper bract that encloses, with the lemma, the flower in grasses. Also palet. 3. The scales on the stems of certain ferns; ramentum.

paleaceous (pay lee ay′shuhs) *a.* In botany, chaffy or chafflike; covered with chaffy scales.

Palisota (puh luh soh′duh) *n.* A genus of tropical perennials (Commelinaceae). They have large, broad leaves (18 to 36 inches long, 6 to 8 inches wide) in rosettes or on short stems and a profusion of small white-to-pinkish flowers, followed by masses of showy, fleshy orange, red, or purple fruits. *P. barteri* and *P. mannii* are sometimes seen as greenhouse plants.

Paliurus (pal ee yoo′ruhs) *n.* A genus of 12 species of deciduous semihardy spiny shrubs (Rhamnaceae). They have small, alternate, oval leaves, yellowish flowers, and inch-wide, dry, brownish-yellow fruit. *P. spina-christii* is planted sometimes as a protective hedge. Commonly known as Christ thorn, Christ's thorn, or Jerusalem thorn.

palm *n.* 1. An evergreen, woody-stemmed tree, shrub, or vine in the palm family (Palmae or Arecaceae). They are nearly always single-stemmed, with very large divided leaves, spirally arranged, clustered in a rosette at the top of the stem, generally small flowers, clustered in many branchlets on large inflorescences, and a berrylike fruit often hard and nutlike, sometimes brightly colored. Palms are highly valuable for food, fiber, oil, wood, sugar, timber, and wax. Most are also highly attractive as landscape or houseplants. 2. A plant with a real or fancied resemblance to a palm, such as sago palm, *Cycas revoluta* which is not a true palm. In some tropical or semitropical regions landscape architects consider palm-like plants as palms for design purposes. *Yucca, Cordyline, Beaucarnea,* and banana are examples. 3. A plant used as a substitute for palm in Palm Sunday church usage. Willow, yew, holly, olive, box, and hemlock (*Tsuga*) are examples.

palmaceous (pal may′shuhs) *a.* Of, pertaining to, or resembling the Palmae, or palm family.

palma christi (pal muh krihs′tee) *n.* A common name for the castor-oil plant, *Ricinus communis.*

Palmae (pal may′) *n. pl.* The palm family, also known as Arecaceae. (See **Palm**.)

palmate (pal′mayt) *a.* In botany, having 3 or more lobes, leaflets, or nerves radiating from a common point.

palmate leaf of a maple

palmatifid (pal mad′uh fihd) *a.* In botany, divided in a palmate manner about halfway to the base.

palmatisect (pal mad uh′sehkt) *a.* In botany, cleft in a palmate manner, usually more than halfway to the base.

palm, betel (beed′uhl) *n.* Also known as betel-nut palm. (See **Areca**.)

palm cabbage *n.* The edible bud of a number of palm species known as cabbage palms.

palmery (pahm′uh ree) *n., pl.* **palmeries** A palm-house.

palmetto (pal mehd′oh) *n.* A name applied to a number of palm species, especially those in the genus *Sabal.* The most common is cabbage or blue palmetto (Sabal palmetto) of the southeastern United States, a tree to 35 feet. Dwarf species from the same region are porcupine palmetto or needle palm, *Rhapidophyllum hystrix;* dwarf palmetto, *Sa-*

bal minor; and saw palmetto, *Serenoa repens.* Taller species of *Sabal* (50 to 60 feet or more) grown in the United States are Puerto Rican hat palm, *S. causiarum* often sold as *S. blackburniana* or *S. umbraculifera* and Mexican palmetto, *S. mexicana.* Saw palmetto is one of the many names of *Acoelorrhaphe wrightii;* others are Everglades palm, silver saw palm, and saw cabbage palm.

palm house *n.* A glass house for growing palms and other tropical plants.

palm, peach *n.* A common name for *Bactris gasipaes (Gulielma gasipaes),* a tropical tree. It has several spiny stems to 60 feet, carrying many spines and crowns of 12-foot-long leaves and heavily bearing red, orange, or yellow 2-inch edible fruits.

palm, pindo (pihn′doh) *n.* A common name for *Butea capitata.* (See **Butea**.)

palmyrae (pal migh′ruh) *n.* A common name for *Borassus flabellifer,* an East Indian palm to 80 feet or more, with a head of 8- to 10-foot-long fan-shaped leaves. Also known as palmyra palm and palmyra tree.

pampas grass (pam′puhs) *n.* A name applied to 2 tender grasses in the genus *Cortaderia. C. selloana* growss to 10 feet or more in clumps of slender, arching leaves topped by 1- to 3-foot-long plumes of silver or pink. A desirable ornamental in southern or western gardens, where space is adequate. *C. jubata,* with shorter leaves and plumes at the top of long, naked stalks, is attractive but is a vicious weed. (See **Cortaderia**.)

pampas-rice (pam′puhs righs) *n.* A variety of the common sorghum, *Sorghum vulgare,* with a drooping panicle; grown to some extent in the southern United States.

panamiga (pan′uh mee guh) *n.* A common name for *Pilea involucrata,* in the nettle family. It has prostrate or somewhat erect stems, with oval, round-tipped, 1½-inch leaves of bronzy green with crinkled surface, purple beneath. Grown as houseplants. Also sometimes known as friendship plant. Also spelled panamigo.

Panax (pay′naks) *n.* A genus of about 6 species of hardy perennials (Araliaceae); ginseng. They have 1- to 2 foot-long stems and leaves of 5 leaflets. The rhizomes of the Asiatic *P. pseudoginseng* and American *P. quinquefolius,* both known as ginseng, have legendary medicinal qualities.

Pancratium (pan kray′shee uhm) *n.* A genus of 4 species of tender, summer-flowering bulbs with strap-shaped basal leaves and white flowers with a corona like that of a daffodil. *P. maritima* is evergreen, with 2½ foot stems topped by a cluster of white, very fragrant 3-inch flowers.

Pancratium
1 bulb with young leaves *2* flowers

Pandanaceae (pan duh nay′se ee) *n. pl.* A family of 3 or 4 genera and several hundred tropical shrubs, trees, and vines; the screw-pine family. All have leathery, strap-shaped leaves, crowded toward the ends of the branches, clustered small flowers, and fleshy fruits sometimes gathered into a single fleshy mass. The genera *Freycinetia* and *Pandanus* are cultivated.

Pandanus (pan day′nuhs) *n.* A genus of more than 650 species of tropical shrubs or trees, with single or branched trunks, stilt roots to help support them, and leathery, often spine-edged leaves. *P. veitchii* is a common houseplant, with 2- to 3-foot long leathery, narrow, spine-edged leaves with longitudinal white or cream stripes. Commonly known as screw pines, so named for their spirally arranged leaves.

panda plant *n.* 1. A common name for *Kalanchoe tomentosa,* a succulent houseplant to 1½ feet, with thick, fleshy 2-inch-long leaves densely coated with white fuzz and strongly marked at the tips with brown. 2. Less commonly, a name applied to the horsehead or fiddle-leaf philodendron, *P. bipennifolium,* which was once known as *P. panduriforme.*

Pandorea (pan doh′ree uh) *n.* A genus of 7 or 8 tender woody vines in the bignonia family (Bignoniaceae). The bower plant, *B. jasminoides,* has glossy leaves, with 5 to 9 leaflets, and loose clusters of trumpet-shaped, 2-inch flowers with deep pink throats (white in the variety 'Alba', pink in 'Rosea'). *P. pandorana* wonga-wonga vine has many-flowered clusters of smaller, cream flowers, streaked with purple.

panicle (pan′eh kuhl) *n.* A loosely branched, pyramidal flower cluster.

panicle of flowers

panicled (pan′eh kuhld) *a.* Furnished with or arranged in branched clusters.

paniculate (puh nihk′yuh leht) *a.* In botany, arranged in branched clusters. Also panicled.

Panicum (pan′ih kuhm) *n.* A diverse genus of about 450 species of annual and perennial grasses (Gramineae) of wide distribution. *P. virgatum* (switch grass) is a popular ornamental grown for its loose, feathery plume and colorful foliage, mostly in shades of red and blue, depending on the variety.

pannose (pa′nohs) *a.* Having the appearance or texture of felt or woolen cloth.

pansy *n.* The common name for *Viola* x*wittrockiana,* a hybrid involving several species of *Viola.* They are hardy annuals or short-lived perennials, leafy and freely branching, with large (to 5-inch) flowers in a wide range of colors, usually marked with contrasting centers. (Formerly known as *V.*

387

tricolor, a name properly applied to Johnny-jump-up, an ancestor of the garden pansy.) Also known as heart's-ease.

pansy, wild *n.* A common name occasionally given to *Viola pedunculata,* also known as wild Johnny-jump-up and California golden violet.

Papaver (puh pay'uhr) *n.* A genus of about 50 species of generally hardy or semihardy annuals and perennials (Papaveraceae); poppies. They have blue-gray hairy leaves (divided or cut), milky sap, showy flowers with 2 sepals and 4 petals, and roundish seed capsules that shed seed through a series of pores beneath a terminal disk.

Papaveraceae (puh pay uhr ay'see ee) *n.* A family of about 25 genera of annuals and perennials (rarely shrubs); the poppy family. They usually have showy flowers, borne singly on stems, and a seed-bearing capsule that opens by pores at the top. Some of the more important genera are *Argemone, Dendromecon, Eschscholzia, Glaucium, Hunnemannia, Meconopsis, Papaver, Romneya,* and *Sanguinaria.* The fumitory family (Fumariaceae) is sometimes included here.

papaveraceous (puh pav uh ray'shuhs) *a.* Pertaining to the Papaveraceae or to the poppy family.

papaya (puh pigh'yuh) *n.* 1. The fruit of the papaya tree, *Carica papaya* (Papayaceae), an evergreen tree or shrub in the papaya family widely grown in tropical and mild subtropical climates. The fruit is very sweet, pear-shaped, and filled with small black seeds in the center. Rarely grown *C. pubescens* (mountain papaya) is a hardier plant but with inferior fruit. The babaco or bush melon of the Andes is *P. heilbornii,* sometimes sold as *P. pentagona.*

Papayaceae (pap uh yay'see ee) *n. pl.* An outdated name for Caricaceae, the papaya family.

paperbark *n.* A common name applied to a number of trees, notably *Melaleuca quinquenervia* (often sold as *M. leucadendron,* which it is not), a tropical tree widely planted in California and a naturalized pest in Florida. It grows to 25 feet or more, with narrow evergreen leaves and 3-inch spikes of fluffy white flowers. The pale, thick, spongy bark separates in thin layers, hence the name. Also known as punk tree and swamp tea tree. Other paperbarks

are *M. ericifolia* and *M. rhaphiophylla,* both known as swamp paperbark.

paper birch *n.* A common name for *Betula papyrifera.*

paper mulberry *n.* A common name for *Broussonetia papyrifera,* a hardy deciduous tree in the mulberry family (Moraceae). It has unlobed or deeply lobed leaves, rough to the touch. In the tropics, the fibrous inner bark is used in making tapa cloth. Also known as paper tree.

paper mulch *n.* A biodegradable sheet of peat moss and cardboard placed around plants to protect them from temperature extremes, to hold moisture, and to keep them clean.

paper reed *n.* A common name for *Cyperus papyrus,* a tender aquatic perennial; papyrus. It grows to 10 feet or more, with green stems topped with roundish clusters of threadlike rays. The pith of the stems was rolled to make papyrus, a writing material used by the ancient Egyptians. The plant is used in water gardens for a tropical effect.

paper rush *n.* Same as paper reed.

paper-shrub *n.* A common name for *Daphne bholua* (formerly *D. cannabina*), a tender evergreen or deciduous shrub. It grows to 7 feet or more, with clustered, fragrant, purplish-pink and white flowers. The bark is sometimes used as papermaking material.

Paphiopedilum (paf ee oh pehd'uh luhm) *n.* A genus of about 60 species of tropical ground-dwelling (usually) orchids with fans of thick leaves on short stems. The flowers have an enlarged upper sepal, the 2 lateral sepals fused together, and 1 of the petals (the lip) folded into a pouch that contains the pistils and stigma. The flowers are large and showy, with colors that range from white through green and yellow to pink, red, brown, and purple, often marked with contrasting flushes, warts, or hairs. Widely grown in greenhouses by orchid fanciers, who usually call them lady's slippers, paphs, or cyps (sips), an abbreviation of the name *Cypripedium,* now applied only to the hardy lady's slippers.

papilionaceous (puh pihl ee uh nay'shuhs) *a.* Butterfly-shaped, as the flowers of peas, beans, and many other plants of the Leguminosae.

papilionaceous flower of the common bean, one side removed to show center

papilla (puh pihl'uh) *n., pl.* **papillae** (ih). In botany, a small nipple-shaped protuberance.

papillary (pap'uh leh ree) *a.* Pertaining to or resembling a papilla. Also papillar; papillose; papillate.

papillate (pap'uh layt) *a.* Formed into, resembling, bearing, or ending in a papilla. Also papillated; papillose.

papilliferous (pap uh lihf'uh ruhs) *a.* In botany, bearing nipple-shaped protuberances. Also papillate.

papilliform (puh pihl'uh form) *a.* Resembling a nipple-shaped protuberance.

papoose root (pa poos') *n.* A common name for *Caulophyllum thalictroides,* a hardy perennial in the barberry family (Berberidaceae). It grows to 3 feet, with finely divided leaves, small white flowers, and small blue fruits. Occasionally grown in shady gardens. Also known as blue cohosh.

pappose (pa'pohs) *a.* Having or resembling the type of bristly or feathery perianth of composite plants such as thistles and dandelions. Also pappous.

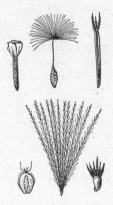

pappus of various plants

pappus (pa'puhs) *n.* A bristly, feathery, or fluffy perianth whorl crowning the ovary or fruit in the Compositae, adapted for the dispersal of the fruit by the wind or other means.

papyraceous (pap uh ray'shuhs) *a.* Made of or resembling papyrus or paper.

papyrus (puh pigh'ruhs) *n.* The paper reed or paper rush, *Cyperus papyrus.* (See **paper reed**.)

papyrus, dwarf or **miniature** (puh pigh'ruhs) *n.* A common name for *Cyperus isocladus,* (also known as *C. haspan*), a miniature of *C. papyrus*. It grows only 1 to 2 feet tall, with a head of threadlike rays 2 to 8 inches across. Used as an aquarium or pot plant.

Paradisea (par'uh digh see uh) *n.* A genus of 2 perennials in the lily family (Liliaceae). The hardy *P. liliastrum* (formerly known as *Anthericum liliastrum*) has clumps of strap-shaped leaves that spring from fleshy rootstocks and 2-inch lilylike white flowers that appear in a 1-sided array on a 2-foot stalk. Commonly known as paradise lily or St.-Bruno's-lily. (See **lily, paradise**)

paradise apple *n.* A dwarf variety of *Malus pumila paradisiaca,* an apple tree with pink flowers and tiny fruit. Used as grafting understock for dwarfing.

paradise-stock *n.* A horticulturist's name for certain hardy slow-growing apple-stocks, upon which more thrifty-growing varieties are grafted, the result being a dwarfing of the graft.

paradise tree *n.* A common name sometimes used for *Melia azedarach* (Chinaberry tree), and for *Simarouba glauca,* a tropical tree. It grows to 50 feet, with 16-inch leaves divided featherwise into many leaflets, clustered small pale yellow flowers and small red or purple fruits.

Parahebe (par uh hee'bee) *n.* A genus of 30 mostly evergreen subshrubs or perennials (Scrophulariaceae) related to *Hebe* and *Veronica*. They have small, opposite leaves and elongated clusters of blue, pink, or white flowers. *P. catarractae,* with trailing stems to 12 inches, has white flowers veined with pink or purple. Named varieties are pure white or blue. Used in rock gardens.

parallel-veined *a.* In botany, having veins quite or nearly parallel, as the leaves of *Tibouchina urvilleana.*

paraphysate (puh raf'uh seht) *a.* In botany, having or marked by paraphyses.

paraphysis (puh raf'uh sehs) *n., pl.* **paraphyses.** One of the erect, slender, sterile filaments accompanying the spore-bearing or sexual organs of spore-bearing plants such as ferns.

parasite *n.* An organism that grows in or on another plant or animal, getting all or part of its nutrients from it, and usually showing a degree of adaptive structural modification.

parasitic nematode (par uh siht'ihk neem'uh tohd) *n.* A beneficial insect applied to the soil to control soil pests, including weevils, armyworms, and cutworms. Several species are sold through the mail.

parasol fir *n.* 1. A common name for *Sciadopitys verticillata* (Taxodiaceae) an attractive, hardy evergreen conifer. A choice landscape plant. More commonly known as umbrella pine or Japanese umbrella pine. 2. A name sometimes applied to *Pinus pinea,* more often called Italian stone pine; and to *Pinus densiflora umbraculifera,* more often called umbrella pine.

parasol tree *n.* A common name for *Firmiana simplex,* a tender deciduous tree. It grows to 60 feet, with foot-wide leaves, with 3 to 5 lobes at the end of long stalks, clustered small yellow flowers, and canoe-shaped seed vessels to 5 inches long. Sometimes used for tropical effects in the South and in California. Also called Chinese parasol tree, Chinese bottle tree, and phoenix tree.

Parathelypteris (par uh theh lihp teh'rihs) *n.* An alternate name for some species of *Thelypteris,* including *T. nevadensis* (Sierra water fern) and *T. noveboracensis* (New York fern).

Pardanthus (par dan thuhs) *n.* A synonym for *Belamcanda chinensis,* a hardy irislike plant. It has 2-inch orange or yellow flowers, spotted dark red, and showy, shiny-black roundish fruits (resembling blackberries) crowded along a central axis. Commonly known as blackberry lily or leopard flower.

parenchyma (puh rehng'kuh muh) *n.* In botany, the plant tissue consisting of undifferentiated thin-walled cells capable of division even when mature, and which manufacture and store food, make up the pulp of fruits and much of leaves, roots, and parts of stems.

parenchymal (puh rehng'kuh muhl) *a.* Pertaining to or of the nature of parenchyma.

Paris *n.* A genus of perennials (Liliaceae) growing from underground rhizomes (not swellings). They have erect, unbranched stems that carry whorls of leaves, topped by a single flower with threadlike petals of yellow, surrounded by broad green sepals. They resemble trilliums, but with 4 flower parts instead of 3. *P. polyphylla* and *P. quadrifolia* (herb paris) are occasionally seen in gardens. The red or black seeds of the latter are poisonous.

Paris Quadrifolia
(herb Paris)

Paris daisy *n.* A common name for *Argyranthemum frutescens* (formerly *Chrysanthemum frutescens*). Also known as marguerite.

Parkia (pahr'kee uh) *n.* A genus of 40 species of tropical evergreen trees (Leguminosae). *P. javanica* grows to 140 feet, with finely divided yellowish-white small flowers in tight clusters on long stalks, followed by large bean-shaped seedpods. Sometimes planted as an ornamental in large parks.

Parkinsonia (pahr kuhn soh'nee uh) *n.* A genus of 12 or more woody, usually spiny, plants (Leguminosae). The tree *P. aculeata* is widely grown in warm-winter regions everywhere, especially in desert and near-desert conditions. It grows to 30 feet, with green bark, spiny branches, and clusters of nearly 1-inch yellow flowers. It has twice divided leaves, with tiny leaflets that soon fall, leaving a light shade cast by green stems and midribs. Commonly known as Jerusalem thorn or Mexican palo verde. Tolerates drought, wind, and alkaline soil.

parmeliaceous (pahr mee lee ay'shuhs) *a*. In botany, belonging to or having the characters of the genus *Parmelia* or the family Parmeliaceae.

parmelioid (pahr mee'lee oid) *a*. In botany, resembling or belonging to the genus *Parmelia*.

Parmentiera (pahr muhn tih'ruh) *n*. A genus of 9 species of trees or shrubs (Bignoniaceae). They have opposite leaves, usually divided into 3 leaflets, and large flowers, followed by long, candle-shaped fruits. *P. cereifera* has white flowers 3 inches long, followed by whitish or yellowish fruits that can reach 4 feet. Sometimes grown in tropical landscapes. Commonly called candle tree.

Parnassia (pahr nas'ee uh) *n*. A genus of 15 species of hardy, usually evergreen perennials (Saxifragaceae). They have leaves clustered in rosettes and white or yellowish rounded flowers borne singly on stalks to 6 inches or more, depending on the species. All require moisture and thrive in bogs. *P. palustris* is sometimes grown in wet areas of rock gardens. Commonly known as grass-of-Parnassus or bog stars.

Parodia (par uh'dee uh) *n*. A genus of possibly 50 species of small cacti. They have round or cylindrical spiny bodies, single or clustered, usually ridged or knobbed and funnel-shaped brightly colored flowers. Extremely popular for house or greenhouse culture because of their flowers and attractively shaped bodies and spine patterns.

Paronychia
(whitlowwort)

Paronychia (par uh nihk'ee uh) *n*. A genus of 40 or more species of small annual or perennial plants (Caryophyllaceae). They have tiny and inconspicuous flowers, often hidden by attractive silvery bracts. Some species are grown in rock gardens. Commonly known as nailwort or whitlowwort.

parrot's beak *n*. 1. A common name for *Clianthus puniceus* (Leguminosae), a tender evergreen climbing shrub. It has leaves composed of many small leaflets and 3-inch scarlet flowers with beak-shaped keel. Sometimes grown in greenhouses or outdoors in mild-winter climates. Also known as red kowhai or glory pea, the latter a name also used for *Clianthus formosus*, the Sturt Desert pea of Australia. 2. A common name sometimes applied to *Lotus berthelotii*, a tender trailing member of the pea family with finely cut silvery foliage and bright orange-red flowers, a favored hanging-basket plant in mild-winter climates.

parrot's-feather *n*. A common name for *Myriophyllum aquaticum (M. proserpinacoides)*, an aquatic plant. Its stems can grow to 6 feet, with dense, very finely cut foliage. Sometimes grown in aquariums. Also known as milfoil or water milfoil.

parrot's-flower *n*. A common name for *Heliconia psittacorum*, a tropical giant perennial. Its stems grow to 6 feet or more, with 18-inch-long leaves, and upright clusters of green, orange, and red flowers resembling long beaks.

parsley *n*. A biennial garden herb, *Petroselinum crispum*, a native of the eastern Mediterranean region, now widely cultivated and sometimes running wild. Its aromatic leaves are used to flavor soups and other dishes; also used as a garnish, for its curly green leaves. The variety *neapolitanum* is flat, finely cut, and of finer flavor than common curly parsley and is preferred for culinary use. Another variety, the Hamburg parsley, is grown for its large root, which is used in soups, etc., or as a separate dish. Parsely leaves are often chewed to neutralize the after-taste of garlic.

parsley fern *n*. 1. A common name for a number of ferns: *Cryptogramma crispa*, a European fern to 8 inches, and *C. acrostichoides*, an American fern to 12 inches, both are also known as rock brakes: *Asplenium bulbiferum*, a tender fern to 4 feet with finely divided leaves more commonly known as mother fern (for the tiny plantlets that form on the fronds).

2. A common name for *Tanacetum vulgare,* not a true fern, but a flower commonly known as tansy, which is widely naturalized in North America. (See **tansy.**)

parsley haw *n.* A common name occasionally applied to *Crataegus marshallii (C. apiifolia),* a small deciduous tree in the rose family native to the southeastern United States. It has deeply cut leaves and white flowers, followed by bright red fruit.

parsley piert (peert) *n.* A common name for *Alchemilla microcarpa,* a 4-inch annual with rounded, deeply cut leaves and inconspicuous flowers.

parsnip *n.* A biennial plant, *Pastinaca sativum,* widely cultivated in gardens. It is an erect plant, with a taproot resembling a pale yellow carrot. It has been used as food from ancient times. In the garden, parsnips are left in the ground all winter, to be dug as soon as the ground thaws in the spring. They have a sweet, nutty flavor and are an excellent source of vitamin C.

parted *a.* In botany, divided nearly to the base, as leaves. Also partite.

Parthenium (pahr thee′nee uhm) *n.* A genus of 16 species of shrubs and herbs (Compositae), most species native to desert or semidesert conditions. They are not especially attractive. *P. argentatum* (guayule) has periodically attracted attention as a source of latex that can be processed into rubber.

Parthenocissus (pahr thuh noh sihs′uhs) *n.* A genus of 10 to 15 species of hardy deciduous vines that climb (usually) by tendrils. Leaves are either lobed or divided into leaflets and inconspicuous flowers, followed by dark blue or black clustered berries. *P. henryana* has bronzy green leaves, turning bright red in fall, with 5-toothed leaflets veined in ivory, purple beneath. *P. quinquefolia,* (Virginia creeper) has similar leaves of dark green, which turn red in autumn. It climbs by adhesive disks at the ends of forked tendrils and is sometimes called woodbine. *P. inserta* is similar in appearance but has less attractive fall color. *P. tricuspidata* (Boston ivy), has 3-lobed leaves with striking orange to red to scarlet fall color. It and its small-leafed variety 'Lowii' are familiar covers on brick or stone walls.

parthenogenesis (pahr′thuh noh jehn uh sihs) *n.* In botany, the reproduction of offspring from an egg cell without fertilization.

partridgeberry *n.* A common name for *Mitchella repens,* a hardy trailing evergreen perennial in the madder family. It has small, shiny, opposite leaves and ½-inch white flowers in pairs on short stems, followed by bright red paired berries-edible but insipid. Sometimes used in woodland gardens. Also known as twinberry, squawberry, running box, squaw vine, and two-eyed berry.

partridgeberry

partridge pea *n.* A common name for *Cassia fasciculata (Chamaecrista fasciculata),* a yellow-flowered annual native to much of the eastern United States. Better known as prairie senna or golden cassia.

Paspalum (pas′puh luhm) *n.* A genus of at least 330 species of annual and perennial grasses (Gramineae) native mostly to tropical areas of the New World. Two species, *P. notatum* (bahia grass) and *P. vaginatum* (seashore paspalum), are sometimes used as lawn grasses in mild-winter climates.

pasqueflower
1 flowering plant 2 single leaf

pasqueflower *n.* 1. A garden flower, *Anemone Pulsatilla.* It is a low herb, with a woody rootstock, 3 deeply cut leaves, and violet-purple flowers. Also called daneflower. Its name derives from its being one of the spring's earliest flowers, often in bloom by Easter. 2. A common name for a group of plants considered to be either in the genus *Pulsatilla* or *Anemone.*

Passiflora (pas uh floh'ruh) *n.* A genus of about 400 mostly tropical vines (Passifloraceae); the passionflowers. They climb by tendrils, with alternate leaves, either lobed or simple, and with flowers of unusual and generally attractive appearance, often with a showy, fringelike crown of slender tendrils inside the sepals and petals. The fruit is a many-seeded berry, edible in some species. *P. incarnata* (maypop) is native to Kansas and Pennsylvania. *P. edulis* is grown for its purple or yellow aromatic fruit, passion fruit. Others are grown for ornament in warm-winter gardens or in houses or greenhouses.

Passifloraceae (pas uh fluh ray'see ee) *n. pl.* A family of 12 genera; the passionflower family. The only genus much cultivated is *Passiflora.*

passionflower *n.* A common name for a member of the genus *Passiflora.* Well-known garden examples include *P. caerulea,* blue passionflower; *P.* x *alatocaerulea (P. pfordtii),* the best-known kind in gardens; *P. mollissima,* pink-flowered banana passion fruit; and *P. quadrangularis,* granadilla.

passionflower
a fruit

passion vine *n.* Same as passionflower.

Patersonia (pad uhr soh'nee uh) *n.* A genus of 18 to 20 species of tender perennials (Iridaceae). They have short rhizomes, swordlike leaves, and generally blue flowers (rarely yellow or white) with 3 prominent outer segments, the inner small or absent. Individual flowers are short-lived, but large clumps give a good show.

path *n.* A walkway through a garden constructed of stone, brick, concrete, bark chips, or other moisture-resistant material.

patience *n.* A common name for *Rumex patientia,* a 6-foot dockweed sometimes grown in gardens. Also known as patience dock, patience plant and rhubarb dock.

patience plant *n.* A common name occasionally used for *Impatiens wallerana,* which is also sometimes called patient Lucy. (See also **patience**.)

patio *n.* A court or enclosure connected with a house, and open to the sky.

pattypan *n.* A flattened variety of summer squash, with creamy flesh and a cream-colored smooth skin. They are easier to stuff than other summer squash varieties, because of their round shape and flat bottom. Also known as scallopini, for the scalloped edges of the squash.

pauci- (paw'see) *comb. form* Few, as paucifoliate, few-leaved.

Paulownia
(princess tree)
flowering tree

Paulownia (paw loh'nee uh) *n.* A genus of 6 deciduous trees (Bignoniaceae). The best known is *P. tomentosa (P. imperialis),* which grows to 60 feet, with large simple or 3-lobed leaves (leaves on young plants may be even larger). The flowers which appear before the leaves expand, are in a foot-long pyramidal cluster; individual flowers are 2 inches long, tubular and flaring, pale purple in color, and fragrant. Not reliably hardy where temperatures dip to 0°. Commonly called princess tree or empress tree.

Paurotis (paw roh duhs) *n*. A synonym for the genus *Acoelorrhaphe*.

Pavetta (pah vehd'uh) *n*. A genus of aout 400 species of tropical shrubs or trees (Rubiaceae). The flowers are usually small, long-tubed, clustered, and white to greenish or red.

Pavonia (puh voh'nee uh) n. A genus of tender perennials or shrubs (Malvaceae). *P. multiflora*, sometimes known as *Tripochlamys multiflora*, a 6-foot evergreen shrub, has unusual flowers: the calyx and outer bracts are red, the petals purple, and the anthers blue. Sometimes grown as a greenhouse novelty. *P. hastata*, with 2-inch pink or white flowers, and *P. spinifex*, with 3-inch yellow flowers, have escaped from cultivation in the Southeast.

pawpaw (puh paw') *n*. The tree *Asimina triloba*, native to the United States, or its fruit. It is a small tree, with showy purple flowers which have thin oval leaves. The smooth, oblong fruit is 3 or 4 inches long, filled with a sweet pulp, in which are embedded the beanlike seeds. The pulp has a rich, custardlike flavor. The tree is ornamental, turning yellow in autumn. Also written papaw.

Paxistima (paks uh stigh'muh) *n*. A genus of 2 species of small evergreen shrubs (Celastraceae). They have opposite, leathery, inch-long leaves and inconspicuous flowers and fruit. Sometimes used in shade or rock gardens as a ground cover. *P. canbyi*, commonly called cliff-green or mountain-lover, grows to 16 inches; *P. myrsinites*, Oregon boxwood, is low-growing, spreading to 40 inches.

pea *n*. The seed of an annual hardy vine, *Pisum sativum* (Leguminosae); also, the vine itself. The pea is marked by its climbing habit with a branching tendril and its large flowers, which are followed by hanging pods containing sweet nutritious seeds. Peas were known to the ancient Greeks and Romans, and their cultivation is now general. In the so-called English pea, only the seeds are edible, but the pods of the sugar pea or snow pea, common in Asian cooking, are eaten. The seeds are now mostly eaten when young and tender, but they are also split when ripe, then dried and used in soups.

pea, Angola *n*. A common name for *Cajanus cajan*, a shrubby member of the pea family. Its seeds are used as food under the names cajan, catjang, pigeon pea, Congo pea, Angola pea, no-eye pea, red gram, dahl, and dhal. Also used as a cover crop and for green manure.

pea, beach *n*. A common name for *Lathyrus japonicus*, a trailing hardy perennial in the pea family. It has stems to 2 feet and clusters of purple flowers. Also known as seaside pea and sea pea.

pea bean *n*. A small white bean variety popular in baked beans.

pea, black-eyed *n*. A twining plant, *Vigna unguiculata*, has long pods and seeds, which are used for human and livestock food. This is an important crop in the southern United States. Also called cowpea.

pea, butterfly *n*. 1. A common name for *Centrosema virginianum*, a tropical trailing or climbing perennial in the pea family. It has large flowers, ranging from pink and white to purple. Also known as spurred butterfly pea. 2. A common name for *Clitoria*, a genus of 30 species of mostly tender climbing perennials in the pea family. *C. ternatea*, with 2-inch bright blue flowers, is frequently cultivated as a house or greenhouse plant.

peach *n*. 1. The fleshy fruit of the tree *Prunus Persica*. 2. A garden and orchard tree, *Prunus (Amygdalus) Persica*. The peach is a rather weak, irregular tree, 15 or 20 feet high, with shiny narrow leaves. The roundish fruit is 3 or 4 inches in diameter and covered with down; when ripe, the color is whitish or yellow, beautifully flushed with red; its juicy flesh is a source of potassium and vitamin A. The peach is closely related to the almond. It is now widely cultivated in the United States, especially on the shores of Chesapeake Bay and Lake Michigan and in California. Peaches are eaten raw and canned, as well as dried, like apricots.

peach, desert *n*. A common name for *Prunus andersonii*, a deciduous desert shrub. It grows 3 to 4 feet, with small, bundled leaves, ½-inch rose-colored flowers, and ½-inch fuzzy fruit with scant, dry flesh. Sometimes planted in desert gardens for minimum maintenance.

peach-house *n.* In horticulture, a house in which peach trees are grown, for the purpose either of forcing the fruit out of season or of producing it in a climate unsuitable for its culture in the open air.

peach leaf curl *n.* A fungus that infects peach and nectarine leaves, causing distorted, multicolored (red, orange, and yellow) new growth. Spread by winter rains. Control with multiple dormant sprays of fixed copper or lime sulfur.

peach oak *n.* A common name sometimes given to *Quercus phellos (willow oak).*

peach, wild *n.* A common anme for *Prunus fasciculata,* a 3- to 8-foot dense, tangled deciduous shrub, similar to desert peach. Also known as desert almond or wild almond.

peacock flower *n.* A common name for *Delonix regia,* a tree in the pea family. Better known as flamboyant or royal poinciana. (See **Delonix.**)

peacock iris *n.* A common name for *Moraea neopavonia (M. pavonia),* a tender perennial in the iris family. It grows from corms that produce a single leaf and a 1- to 2-foot-long stalk bearing an orange-red flower marked with blue-black or greenish black.

pea, Congo *n.* (See **pea, Angola.**)

pea family *n.* The Leguminosae, a huge family of 657 genera and more than 16,000 species of annuals, perennials, shrubs, vines, and trees. The flowers of many are irregular, with keels, wings, and standards in sweet-pea fashion. This group is the Papilionaceae, sometimes known as Fabaceae. Others, with more regular-appearing flowers, are known as Caesalpiniaceae. A third group has small flowers borne in tight clusters (the family Mimosaceae). All bear seeds in a pod, which splits along the margins. The family is alternatively known as Fabaceae.

pea, glory *n.* A common name for either of 2 species of *Clianthus. C. formosus (C. dampieri)* is a tender annual or perennial with 3-inch scarlet flowers, often marked with black; also known as Sturt's desert pea. *C. puniceus* is a climbing shrubby perennial with bright red flowers; also known as

parrot's-beak or parrot's-bill. Grow as an espalier or on a trellis for best display.

pea, hoary (hoh′ree) *n.* A common name for *Tephrosia,* a genus of 300-400 species of perennials or shrubs of the pea family. *P. virginiana,* a 2-foot perennial native to the eastern and southern parts of the United States, has silky-furry new growth and 2-inch clusters of yellowish and purplish flowers. Also known as goat's rue, catgut, and rabbit's pea.

pea, Lord Anson's blue *n.* A common name for *Lathyrus nervosus,* a perennial to 2 feet, with clusters of inch-wide blue flowers.

peanut *n.* 1. One of the edible fruits of *Arachis hypogaea,* not a true nut. 2. The plant that bears these fruits, a vine spreading 3 to 4 feet across. The seedpods grow underground, each with 1 to 3 fruits, usually. 2. Peanuts are an important crop in the southeastern United States, but can be grown wherever there are 4 to 5 frost-free months, as far north as New York. Peanuts are a source of protein.

pea, perennial *n.* 1. A common name for *Lathyrus latifolius,* a common perennial pea with broad bluish-green leaflets and clusters of large pink, white, or rose flowers. 2. A common name for *Lathyrus sylvestris,* a perennial with narrower leaflets and smaller flowers. Also known as flat pea, everlasting pea, and narrow-leafed perennial pea.

pea, pigeon *n.* Same as Angola pea (*Cajanus cajan*).

pear *n.* 1. The fruit of the pear tree. 2. The tree *Pyrus communis.* Though close to the apple botanically, it differs in its more upright habit, smooth, shiny leaves, pure-white flowers, the granular texture of the fruit, and the shape of the fruit, which tapers toward the base and has no depression around the stem. The tree is long-lived, specimens existing that are 200 or 300 years old. It is a highly successful fruit in the United States. There are thousands of varieties of pear, but only a few are really important: the Seckel is an American variety with small fruit, often pickled or preserved whole; the Bartlett, a juicy fruit, is the most commonly grown; Bose and D'Anjou are finer and crisper. Although an excellent source of fiber, pears contain only small amounts of vitamins and minerals. Dwarf pears (those grafted or budded on quince stocks) are more convenient for gardens; standard pears (those grafted or budded on seedling pear stocks) are more productive.

pear, alligator *n.* An old-fashioned common name for *Persea americana* (avocado).

pear, garlic *n.* A common name for Crateva religiosa, a tropical tree. It grows to 45 feet, with white-spotted bark, leaves with 3 leaflets, and white flowers, followed by large white-to-green fruits with yellow pulp. Also known as temple plant.

pear haw *n.* A common name for *Crataegus calpodendron* (C. *tomentosa*), a hardy deciduous tree, also called blackthorn. (See **haw, hawthorn,** and **Crataegus.**)

pearl barley *n.* (See **barley.**)

pearl-berry *n.* A common name for *Margyricarpus setosus*, a tender evergreen shrub. It has tiny leaves divided into narrow leaflets, inconspicuous flowers, and pearl-white fruits a little more than ¼ inch in size. Occasionally seen in rock gardens or collections of oddities. Also known as pearl fruit.

pearlbush *n.* A common name for *Exochorda* (Rosaceae), a genus of 4 species of tall, hardy deciduous shrubs. They have attractive white flowers in long clusters. The best known is a hybrid, *E.* x*macrantha* 'The Bride'. It grows to 6 feet, with dense clusters of mildly fragrant 1½-inch flowers.

pearl fruit *n.* (See **pearl-berry**.)

pearl plant *n.* A common name for *Haworthia margaritifera,* a tender succulent, with 6-inch rosettes of fleshy triangular leaves carrying pearly-white small bumps.

pearlwort *n.* A common name for a member of *Sagina* (Caryophyllaceae), a genus of 25 species of annuals or perennials. *S. subulata,* the best known, is a low-growing, dense, mosslike plant with creeping, rooting stems and a small show of small white flowers on short stems. It is better known as Irish moss; a yellow form, 'Aurea', is Scotch moss. Both are sometimes called *Arenaria verna,* which is a similar plant.

pearlwort, Corsican *n.* Probably a misnomer for Corsican sandwort, *Arenaria balearica,* a creeping, tiny-leafed, flat perennial with ½-inch white flow-

ers. An aggressive ground cover in damp, shady places.

pearly everlasting *n.* (See **everlasting, pearly.**)

pea, rosary *n.* A common name for *Abrus precatorius,* a tropical vine with purplish or pinkish-to-white flowers, followed by pods containing hard, glossy scarlet seeds with a black marking. The seeds are deadly poisonous. Also known as love pea, Indian licorice, wild licorice, licorice vine, weather plant, prayer-beads, coral-bead plant, red-bead vine, and crab's eye.

pear slug *n.* A slimy-looking fly larva that feeds on a variety of fruit-tree foliage, including that of pears and cherries. It leaves lacy patches on the leaves. Usually controlled with well-timed sprays of traditional pesticides. Cultivating around trees also helps kill emerging adults.

pear thorn *n.* (See **pear haw**.)

pea, sweet *n.* a common name for *Lathyrus odoratus,* a familiar climbing annual pea. It climbs to 6 feet or more, with large, clustered flowers with sweet perfume. Dwarf strains exist.

pea, Tangier (tan jee'uhr) *n.* A common name for *Lathyrus tingitanus,* an annual vine in the pea family with stems to nearly 4 feet, and 1 to 3 rose pink flowers in a cluster.

pea tree *n.* A common name for 60 or so species of hardy trees or shrubs of the genus *Caragana* (Leguminosae). All have leaves divided into leaflets, spines, and yellow pea-shaped flowers. The one most grown is *C. arborescens,* Siberian pea tree which grows to 20 feet and is exceptionally hardy to cold and wind. It has dwarf and weeping varieties. *C. frutex,* which grows to 10 feet, is occasionally grown. Also known as pea shrub.

peat pellet *n.* A small ball or disk made of sphagnum moss, used for starting plants from seed.

peat pot *n.* A container made of sphagnum moss, typically 2 to 3 inches in diameter, used for starting seeds. Because peat pots are biodegradable, they are transplanted along with the plant into the soil.

pea, tuberous *n.* *Lathyrus tuberosus,* a perennial pea with pink flowers and edible tuberous roots. Also called earthnut pea, Dutch-mice, and tuberous vetch.

pecan *n.* A common name for *Carya illinoensis* (*C. pecan*), a large deciduous tree related to the walnut (Juglandaceae), native to the southern and central United States. It grows to 70 feet, with leaves divided into 5 to 8 pairs of narrow leaflets, inconspicuous flowers, and oval nuts an inch or more in length. It is much cultivated for its nuts wherever summers are hot and winters not intensely cold.

pecan
a flowing branch *b* nut

Pecteilis (pehk tigh′lihs) *n.* A genus of 4 species of subtropical or tropical terrestrial orchids. From tiny tubes, they produce erect, few-leafed, 12-inch stems, topped by 1 to 6 white 1½ to 2-inch flowers with lacy, deeply cut lips. Species sold as *P. radiata* may be the similar *P. susannae*. Sometimes called *Habenaria*. Both are occasionally sold as egret flowers or egret orchids.

pectinate (pehk′tuh nayt) *a.* In botany, resembling a comb; divided nearly to the base with narrow, close segments, as the leaves of some ferns.

Pedaliaceae (puh day lee ay′see ee) *n. pl.* A family of 18 genera and 95 species of annuals, perennials, or shrubs; the sesame family. *Sesamum indicum* is important for seed and oil. *Martynia* and *Proboscidea* are occasionally grown.

pedate leaves

pedate (peh′dayt) *a.* In botany, palmate, with the 2 lateral lobes divided into smaller segments, as the leaf of *Helleborus foetidus*.

pedati- *comb. form* Pedate; pedately.

pedicel (pehd′uh sehl) *n.* In botany, the stalk of a flower. Also pedicle.

pedicels on a flower cluster
a single flower enlarged, showing pedicel

pedicellate (pehd uh sehl′leht) *a.* Having or attached by a pedicel or pedicels. Also pedicelled; pedicellated.

pedicelliform (pehd uh sehl′uh form) *a.* Having the form of a pedicel.

pediculate (peh dihk′yuh layt) *a.* Having a pedicel or pedicels. Also pedicellate; pediculated; pedunculate.

Pedicularis (peh dihk yuh lahr′ehs) *n.* A genus of 350 species of annuals, biennials, and perennials (Scrophulariaceae). They have toothed, lobed, or finely cut leaves and white, yellow, pink, red, or purple flowers in showy elongated clusters with many bracts. Although attractive, they are difficult to grow, many being partially parasitic on the roots of other plants. *P. canadensis* (common lousewort) grows to 1½ feet, with yellowish or reddish flowers. *P. densiflora* (Indian warrior) has red flowers. *P. groenlandica*, elephant-heads, has small red or purple flowers, with a long curved beak like an elephant's trunk.

Pedilanthus (pehd uh lan′thuhs) *n.* A genus of succulent shrubs (Euphorbiaceae). *P. tithymaloides* has fleshy stems that grow to 6 feet (usually much less), with a broad, 4-inch-long leaf at each node, and red or purple flowers and surrounding bracts.

The variety 'Variegata', has zigzag stems to 1½ feet and leaves variegated with white and pink. Often called devil's backbone or Jacob's ladder.

Pediocactus (pehd ee uh kahk′tuhs) *n.* A genus of 7 species of small, hardy, globular or cylindrical cacti native to the western United States. They have single or clustered stems and many-petaled bell-shaped flowers. *P. papyracanthus (Sclerocactus p.)* grows to 3 inches, with inch-wide white flowers and long, flattened, paperlike spines. *P. simpsonii* gows to 5 inches, with pink or yellow 2-inch flowers, and a profusion of white spines; also known as snowball cactus.

peduncle (pee′duhng kuhl) *n.* In botany, a stalk supporting a solitary flower or flower cluster.

pedunculate (pee duhng′kyuh layt) *a.* In botany, having a peduncle; growing on or from a peduncle. Also peduncled; pedunculated.

Pelargonium (pehl ahr goh′nee uhm) *n.* A genus of 250 or more species of annuals, perennials, or shrubs in the geranium family (Geraniaceae). The genus includes many scented geraniums, the florists' so-called geraniums so familiar as house or outdoor summer bedding plants (*P. xhortorum*), ivy geraniums *(P. peltatum)*, and the show, regal, or Martha Washington geraniums (*P. xdomesticum*), which are commonly called pelargoniums. All differ from the true hardy perennial geraniums (Geranium) by having irregular rather than symmetrical flowers.

pelican flower *n.* A common name for *Aristolochia grandiflora,* a tropical vine with large (to 2 feet or more), smelly, greenish and purple flowers shaped like a pelican's pouch and beak.

Pellaea (puh lee′uh) A genus of 80 species of small to middle-sized ferns, often growing among rocks in many regions of the world, hence called cliffbrake. *P. andromedifolia* (coffee fern of California) grows to 2½ feet and tolerates summer drought by going dormant. *P. rotundifolia* (button fern), a common houseplant, has 1-foot fronds with short (¾-inch), nearly round leaflets.

Pellionia (puh lee oh′nee uh) *n.* A genus of about 50 species of tropical perennials or shrubs (Urticaceae). *P. repens,* often sold as P. *daveauana* or *P. argentea,* is the familiar houseplant known as water-melon begonia or trailing watermelon begonia, with trailing stems and smooth olive-green leaves, marked with silver and purple beneath.

pellitory (pehl′uh tor ee) *n.* 1. A perennial weed, *Parietaria officinalis;* specifically, the wall-pellitory, a small bushy plant growing on old walls, etc. The name is extended to all the species of the genus; *P. Pennsylvanica* is the American pellitory. 2. The feverfew, *Chrysanthemum Parthenium;* also, the other chrysanthemums of the group often classed as *Pyrethrum.*

Peltandra virginica
(arrow arum)

Peltandra (pehl tan′druh) *n.* A genus of 2 species of hardy aquatic perennials (Araceae). They have arrow-shaped 15-inch-long leaves on 3-foot stems that arise from thick rhizomes and green callalike flowers—inconspicuous in *P. virginica,* white and showy in *P. sagittifolia.* Occasionally grown in ponds or boggy gardens. Commonly known as arrow arum.

peltate (pehl′tayt) *a.* In botany, having the stem inserted into the under surface not far from the center, as in the leaves of *Tropaeolum majus.*

petate leaf

Peltophorum (pehlt uh′faw ruhm) *n.* A genus of 15 evergreen tropical trees (Leguminosae). They have leaves that are twice divided into many leaflets and large clusters of golden-yellow flowers. Much planted for ornament in tropical regions. *P. ptero-carpum* is known as yellow poinciana or yellow-flame.

pencil tree *n.* A common name for *Euphorbia tir-ucalli,* a shrub or tree in the Spurge family, so called because its thin, leafless stems resemble green pencils. Also known as pencil bush or milkbush.

pendent (pehn'duhnt) *a.* Hanging or supported from above; drooping. Also pendulous. Also spelled pendant.

Pennisetum (pehn uh seet'uhm) *n.* A genus of 120 species of annual and perennial grasses (Gramineae) native to tropical and warm temperate areas. Several are grown as ornamentals. The most common is *P. setaceum* 'Cupreum' (purple fountain grass), which has purplish-brown foliage and arching, reddish-brown plumes.

penta- *comb. form.* Five.

pentadelphous (pehn tuh dehlf'uhs) *a.* In botany, grouped together in 5 sets, as the stamens of the linden, which are in bunches of 5 united by their filaments.

pentamerous (pehn tam'uh ruhs) *a.* Consisting of 5 sets of parts, as in flowers such as many of the rose family, which have calyx lobes, petals, stamens, and other flower parts in 5s, or multiples of 5.

pentandrous (pehn tan'druhs) *a.* Pertaining to a flower, having 5 stamens.

pentastichous (pehn tas'teh kuhs) *a.* In botany, describing an arrangement of leaves upon the stem in 5 vertical rows or ranks, as in the apple tree.

Pennisetum (pehn uh see'duhm) *n.* A genus of about 80 species of annual or perennial grasses, mostly tropical. *P. americanum,* pearl millet, is a food crop. Several are ornamentals. Perennial *P. alopecuroides* grows to 3½ feet, with 6-inch-long silvery pink plumes; named varieties come in many sizes and colors, including the black-tasseled 'Moudry'. *P. setaceum* (*P. ruppellii*), fountain grass, has purplish-pink tassels and can become a weed in mild-winter climates; its purplish and red varieties are not so aggressive. *P. villosum,* feathertop, has silvery or tawny tassels.

penny cress *n.* A common name for *Thlaspi,* a genus of 60 species of annuals or perennials, so named because the winged seedpods are flat and round. *T. arvense,* naturalized in the United States, is also called field penny cress, penny grass, Frenchweed, fanweed, stinkweed, and mithridate mustard.

pennyflower *n.* Another name for money plant, *Lunaria annua,* a well-known biennial, so named for its round, flat silvery seed pods. Also called honesty, moonwort, satin flower, silver dollar, and bolbonac.

pennygrass *n.* 1. Same as penny cress. 2. A common name for *Rhinanthus crista-galli,* an annual in the figwort family. Rarely planted, it has yellow flowers and flat, round seeds. Also called yellow rattle and rattlebox.

pennyroyal *n.* 1. A branched, low-growing perennial herb, related to spearmint and peppermint, *Mentha Pulegium.* The leaves are small, and the flowers grow in dense clusters. Although it is intensely fragrant, its scent is not useful in food or perfume, as with the other mints. 2. A plant of the genus *Hedeoma;* the American pennyroyal.

pennyroyal, American *n.* A comon name for *Hedeoma pulegioides,* an annual in the mint family. Also called mock pennyroyal or pudding grass.

pennyroyal, bastard *n.* A common name for *Trichostema dichotomum,* an annual in the mint family.

pennywinkle *n.* A variant of periwinkle. (See **Vinca** and **Catharanthus**.)

pennywort *n.* A common name for a number of plants with small, round leaves; *Umbilicus rupestris* (*Cotyledon umbilicus*), a small perennial also called navelwort; many species of marsh- or water-pennywort, members of the genus *Hydrocotyle* in the parsley family, especially *H. vulgaris.* Also called navelwort; and *Linaria cymbalaria,* the Kenilworth ivy, a creeping perennial.

Penstemon (pehn stee'muhn) *n.* A genus of about 250 species of perennials and small shrubs (Scrophulariaceae), most native to western North America. They have opposite or whorled leaves and flowers in erect elongated or rounded clusters; both the leaves and flowers are variable in size. The individual flowers have a long tube and are two-lipped in appearance, in colors ranging from white through cream to pink, blue, red, and purple. Many species are grown, nearly all are fine garden plants, especially when grown near their native range. Named garden hybrids are common. The best known are the seed-grown bedding plants sold as *P. gloxinioides* (actually, probably hybrids involving *P. hartwegii*), but selections of *P. barbatus* are popular: these have names like 'Firebird', 'Prairie Fire', 'Prairie Dusk', and 'Rose Elf'. A few are dwarf, shrubby rockgarden plants (*P. barrettiae, P. davidsonii, P. pinifolius,* and *P. rupicola.*)

Pentapterygium (pehn tap tuh'ruh jee uhm) *n.* A synonym for *Agapetes.*

Pentas (pehn'yuhs) *n.* A genus of 30 or 40 species of tropical perennials or shrubs (Rubiaceae). *P. lanceolata* is a shrubby perennial to (rarely) 6 feet, with opposite, oval, roughish leaves and rounded clusters of star-shaped, ½-inch flowers in pink, lavender, red, or white. Grown as a houseplant or outdoors in frost-free climates. Commonly called star-cluster or Egyptian star-cluster.

peony (pee'uh nee) *n.* A common name for a perennial or shrub in the genus *Paeonia,* numbering 33. Most commonly grown are selections of *P. lactiflora,* the common or Chinese peony. They are extremely hardy perennials, with tuberous roots, much divided leaves, and very large (to 6 inches or more) single, semidouble, or fully double flowers in shades of white, pink, and red. Scores of named varieties are in nurseries, and hybridization with other species is continuing, with wider color range. Shrubby tree peonies (*P. moutan*) have permanent woody stems to 6 feet, with very large single to double flowers in pink, purple, red, and white. Hybrids of these and *P. lutea,* another woody peony, have produced a range of yellow to salmon to deep red tree peonies sometimes defined by botanists as *P. lemoinei.*

Peperomia (pehp uhr oh'mee uh) *n.* A genus of 1,000 or so small, generally fleshy tropical perennials (Piperaceae). Many species are grown as houseplants for their shiny, fleshy, sometimes colorfully marked leaves (their flowers are tiny, borne on spikes that may in themselves be conspicuous). *P. argyreia* is the common green and silvery watermelon begonia. *P. caperata,* with dark seersucker-like blistered leaves, is known as emerald ripple or

green ripple. *P. rotundifolia (P. nummulariifolia),* a trailing plant, with tiny round leaves, is sometimes called yerba linda or creeping Charley.

Peplis (pehp'lehs) *n.* A genus of 8 species of annuals (Lythraceae). They grow in water or wet places. *P. diandra,* water purslane, with 16-inch stems, very narrow leaves, and inconspicuous flowers, is sometimes grown in ponds or aquariums.

pepo (pee'poh) *n.* 1. In botany, the many-seeded, hard-rinded, fleshy fruit of the Cucurbitaceae family. Examples are the pumpkin, gourd, squash, cucumber, and melon. 2. The dried ripe seed of the pumpkin.

pepper *n.* Peppers are grown on small, compact plants and require moderately warm temperatures in order for the blossoms to develop fruit. They are grown throughout the United States. Bell peppers are the mild, chunky-shaped varieties. Both green and red peppers of the hot and sweet types are rich in vitamins A and C.

pepper-bush, sweet *n.* A common name for *Clethra alnifolia,* a hardy deciduous shrub. It grows to 10 feet, with 4-inch-long toothed leaves and erect spikelike clusters of white (rarely pink) fragrant flowers in summer.

pepper, Celebes (sehl uh'beez) *n.* A common name for *Piper ornatum,* an ornamental tropical vine with dark green leaves, heavily spotted with pink.

pepper, chili *n.* A hot *Capsicum* variety, often dried and ground as seasoning.

pepper, Chinese *n.* A common name for *Zanthoxylum piperitum,* a shrub or tree in the rue family. The dried fruit is powdered into a pungent, aromatic spice; the leaves are also used as seasoning and decoration under the name *sansho.* Also known as Japanese pepper, Japan pepper, and Szechwan pepper.

pepper family *n.* A common name for Piperaceae, a family of 14 genera and nearly 2,000 species of mostly tropical vines, shrubs, small trees, or succulent perennials. They have tiny flowers on fleshy spikes, followed by fleshy fruits. *Piper nigrum* is the pepper of commerce; *Macropiper,* some species of *Piper,* and *Peperomia* have ornamental value.

peppergrass *n.* A common name for the genus *Lepidium*. Also known as pepper cress and peppermint.

pepperidge *n.* A common name for *Nyssa sylvatica*. Also known as black gum, sour gum, or tupelo.

pepper, Malabar (maluh bahr) *n.* The common peppercorns produced in Malabar, among the best quality.

peppermint *n.* The herb *Mentha piperita,* naturalized in many parts of the United States and often cultivated. The plants grow to a height of about 12 inches and spread via runners (stems that grow along the top of the ground and take root). The peppermint is not as invasive as spearmint and is more popular in herb gardens. Its aromatic and pungent leaves produce an oil, which is often used in candy making. (See **Mentha.**)

peppermint tree *n.* A common name for *Agonis flexuosa,* a tender tropical evergreen with weeping branches. It grows to 35 feet, with narrow leaves that smell like mint when crushed. Occasionally planted where winter temperatures do not fall below 25 to 27° F.

pepper, poor man's *n.* A common name for *Lepidium sativum,* an annual in the cress family. Also known as garden cress, peppergrass or pepperwort.

pepper-root *n.* Any member of the genus *Dentaria,* fleshy perennials in the cress family. Also called toothwort; *D. californica,* is also called milkmaids.

pepper tree *n.* A common name for trees or shrubs in *Schinus,* a genus in the Cashew family. *S. molle,* California pepper tree, is a fast-growing evergreen with a rugged trunk, gracefully weeping branches clad in leaves that are divided into many narrow leaflets, and drooping clusters of tiny whitish flowers, followed by strings of small, dry, deep pink berries. Native to Peru, it has long been planted in California and Arizona. The pink berries are sometimes employed as pink peppercorns; some people may be allergic to them. *S. terebinthifolius,* Brazilian pepper, is a dense, round-headed tree with darker green, broader leaflets and showy red berries. A choice plant in milder California gardens, it has escaped to become a weed on Florida, where it is sometimes called Florida holly.

pepper vine *n.* 1. A common name for *Piper nigrum.* 2. A common name for *Ampelopsis arborea,* a deciduous vine in the grape family native to the United States. It bears small dark purple fruits that resemble pepper berries.

pepper, white *n.* A hulled form of *Piper negrum.*

pepper, wild *n.* A common name for *Vitex agnuscastus,* a shrub or tree in the verbena family (Verbenaceae). Also known as monk's pepper tree, chaste tree, hemp tree, sage tree, and Indian spice.

pepperwood *n.* 1. One of the toothache trees or prickly ashes, especially *Zanthoxylum clava-herculis,* also known as Hercules'-club and southern prickly ash. 2. A common name for *Umbellularia californica,* a tree with pungently aromatic leaves. Also known as California laurel, bay laurel, California bay, myrtle, and Oregon myrtle.

percurrent *a.* In botany, running through the entire length from base to tip, as the midrib of a leaf.

peregrina (pehr uh gree'nuh) *n.* A common name for *Jatropha integerrima,* a tropical shrub or small tree. Its leaves are highly variable in shape, and its inch-wide flowers are red. Also called spicy jatropha.

perennate (per'uh nayt) *v.* In botany, to live perennially from 1 year to another.

perennation (per uh nay'shuhn) *n.* In botany, the tendency of a plant to live for more than 2 growing seasons.

perennial (puh rehn'ee uhl) *a.* In botany, continuing more than 2 years; used specifically of a plant that dies back seasonally, but produces new growth from a persisting part, as a perennial herb. *n.* In botany, a plant that renews its top growth seasonally and that lives year after year.

perennial marker *n.* A large label, typically of metal, mounted at an angle on a long stake or stakes, used to identify perennial plants. Perennial markers are shorter than rose markers and taller than plant markers.

perennial ryegrass (puh rehn'ee uhl righ'gras) *n.* (See **Lolium.**)

Pereskia (puh rehs'kee uh) *n.* A genus of tropical trees, shrubs, and vines (Cactaceae). The flowers are generally showy, and the fruit of some species is edible. They are remarkable for having true leaves, unusual for cacti. *P. aculeata* is a vine with 3-inch-long leaves, white, yellow, or pink flowers, 1½ inches or more in width, and spiny yellow edible (but acid) fruit. The varieties 'Godseffiana' and 'Rubescens' are grown for their variegated foliage. Commonly known as Barbados gooseberry or lemon vine.

perfect *a.* In botany, having both stamens and pistils; hermaphroditic: said of a flower, also of a whole plant whose flowers have both male and female parts.

perfect flower *n.* A flower that contains complete sets of both male and female reproductive parts.

perfoliate leaves

perfoliate (puhr foh′lee ayt) *a.* In botany, having a stem that seems to pass through the blade, said of a leaf, such as those of many honeysuckles.

pergola (puhr′goh luh) *n.* An arbor formed of a horizontal trellis supported by columns or posts; also, a platform or balcony so protected; hence, an architectural construction resembling such an arbor. Also spelled pergula.

perianth (peh′ree anth) *n.* In botany, the floral envelope, especially when it is not clearly differentiated into calyx and corolla, as in the tulip.

pericarp (peh′ruh kahrp) *n.* In botany, the wall of a fruit that is fleshy, as in berries, or hard, as in nuts. Also pericarpium.

pericarpial (peh′ruh kahr′pee uhl) *a.* In botany, of or relating to the wall of a fruit. Also pericarpic.

pericarpoidal (peh ruh kahr′poi duhl) *a.* In botany, resembling a pericarp.

perigynium (puh ruh jih′nee uhm) *n.* In botany, the saclike bract that surrounds the pistil in the sedges of the genus *Carex.*

perigynous (puh rihj′uh nuhs) *a.* In botany, surrounding the pistil of a flower.

perigyny (puh rihj′uh nee) *n.* In botany, the state or condition of being perigynous.

Perilla (puh rihl′uh) *n.* A genus of 6 species of annuals (Labiatae). *P. frutescens (P. nankinensis)* is widely grown as an ornamental, especially in its purple-leafed (Atropurpurea) and curly-leafed (Crispa) varieties. Growing to 3 feet, the plants resemble *Coleus,* with 5-inch-long, deeply toothed purple or green leaves. The leaves are strongly aromatic, and are used as flavoring and food coloring under the name *shiso,* and the tops are pickled. It is a tender annual, quite sensitive to frost. Can prove weedy if allowed to seed. Sometimes called beefsteak plant.

Periploca (puh rihp′luh kuh) *n.* A genus of 11 species of shrubs or vines (Asclepiadeceae). *P. graeca* is a deciduous vine with dark, glossy foliage and clusters of greenish and purple flowers followed by yellow fruits. The fruits and the sap are poisonous. Commonly called silk vine.

Peristeria (puh rihs stuh′ree uh) *n.* A genus of 9 tropical orchids. *P. elata* has 3-foot leaves and 10 to 15 white, waxy, fragrant flowers on a 4-foot-long elongated cluster. The national flower of Panama, it is called Holy Ghost flower, dove flower, or dove orchid, from the dovelike appearance of the flower lip.

Peristrophe (puh rih′strohph) *n.* A genus of 15 species of evergreen tropical perennials or subshrubs (Acanthaceae). *P. hyssopifolia* grows to 2 feet, with 3-inch-long dark green leaves and small clusters of deep pink to red flowers. Its yellow-marked variety 'Aureo-variegata' is known as marbleleaf.

periwinkle *n.* 1. A common name for *Vinca major* and *Vinca minor,* familiar evergreen ground cover plants with blue (rarely pink or white) flowers. 2. The name periwinkle or Madagascar periwinkle is applied to *Catharanthus roseus,* formerly called *Vinca rosea,* and is still widely sold under that name.

branch of periwinkle, showing a single-flower peduncle

Perovskia (puh rahvz'skee uh) *n.* A genus of 7 species of perennials or shrubby perennials (Labiatae). They have finely cut gray-green leaves on stiff, erect stems, topped by large, branched, somewhat open clusters of fuzzy blue flowers. *P. abrotanoides* and *P. atriplicifolia* are much advertised, but plants most often sold are hybrids of the two. 'Blue Spire' is one of the latter. Valuable for late-summer bloom and drought-tolerance.

Persea (puhr'see uh) *n.* A genus of about 150 species of evergreen trees (Lauraceae). *P. americana (P. gratissima),* the best known, is the familiar avocado or alligator pear. *P. borbonia,* native to the southeastern United States, grows 30 to 40 feet, with 6-inch-long leaves and ½-inch dark blue fruit. It is sometimes planted as an ornamental tree and is commonly called red bay, swamp red bay, sweet bay, laurel tree, tisswood, and Florida mahogany. *P. indica* is similar and is likewise rarely planted.

Persicaria (puhr suhl kah'ree uh) *n.* A name formerly applied to many species of *Polygonum.*

persimmon (puhr sihm'uhn) *n.* A common name for several trees in the genus *Diospyros,* also the name given to the fruit of these trees. *D. virginiana* is the familiar hardy native persimmon, a 40-foot tree with 1- to 2-inch orange fruit that is sweet and edible when thoroughly ripe, intolerably puckery until then. *D. kaki,* Japanese persimmon, is much cultivated in many varieties for its large orange or orange-red fruits. *D. texana,* black persimmon, native to Texas and Mexico, has small, nearly black fruit. The persimmon is rich in vitamin A and *D. Virginiana* is rich in vitamin C, as well.

persistent *a.* In botany, of leaves or flower petals that remain attached to the plant rather than falling off.

Persoonia (puhr soon'ee uh) *n.* A genus of about 60 species of tropical trees or shrubs (Proteaceae). All have leathery evergreen leaves and yellow, white or greenish flowers. The Australian species, mostly shrubby, are known by the euphonious names of geebung and snottygobble.

pest *n.* Any very noxious, mischievous, or destructive insect or animal in a garden.

pest-free plants *n.* Plants resistant to insects.

pesticide *n.* Any substance used to kill, repel, prevent, destroy, or mitigate a pest problem. They include fungicides, insecticides, herbicides, and bactericides.

pesticide labeling *n.* The instructions on how a pesticide is to be used according to the law. They include information on what pest and plant the material can be used on, how it should be applied, and at what concentrations. It is very important to read labels carefully and follow them to the letter. Doing otherwise is not only dangerous, it is against the law.

pesticide registration *n.* The process by which a pesticide is approved for specific uses by the Environmental Protection Agency or state agencies. These uses are listed on the pesticide label. It is unlawful to use the product in any other way.

pesticide toxicity (tahk sihs'ih tee) *n.* The relative hazard of a pesticide as a poison to humans, animals, and the environment. It is scientifically evaluated on many levels, including danger when inhaled, ingested, or contacted by humans, toxicity to wildlife, and persistence in the environment. For gardeners, a general guide is provided by warning words on pesticide labels. Although all pesticides can be dangerous, the word *danger* on the label indicates the greatest hazard, the word *warning* means a moderate hazard, and *caution* means slightly hazardous. Carefully research the toxic properties of any pesticide, organic or chemical, before applying it in a garden. (See **LD-50.**)

pest netting *n.* A lightweight net draped over fruit trees, berries, or row crops to protect them from birds, rabbits, and deer.

petal *n.* In botany, one of the individual, usually colored parts of the corolla of a flower.

403

petaline (pehd′uh lighn) *a.* In botany, pertaining to, attached to, or resembling a petal in form or color, as the calyx lobes of the passionflower.

petaloid (pehd′uh loid) *a.* Resembling a flower petal in form, texture, and color, as the bracts of *Poinsettia* and *Bougainvillea.*

petalous (pehd′uh luhs) *a.* Having petals.

Petasites (pehd uh sighd′eez) *n.* A genus of about 15 species of perennial herbaceous plants (Compositae). Most have large basal leaves and flowers that appear early in spring, before the foliage. All like moisture and can become invasive, but may be useful ground cover in wet places. *P. fragrans,* winter heliotrope, has strongly vanilla-scented flowers in midwinter. *P. hybridus,* butterbur or bog rhubarb, has 2-foot-long roundish leaves on tall stalks. *P. japonicus* has 32-inch-long leaves; its form *giganteus* has leaves that can reach nearly 5 feet, on 6-foot stalks.

petiolar (pehd′ee oh luhr) *a.* In botany, pertaining to, growing on, or supported by the stem of a leaf. Also petiolary.

petiolate (pehd′ee oh layt) *a.* In botany, having a petiole or stalk, as an oak or birch leaf. Also petioled.

petiole (pehd′ee ohl) *n.* In botany, the stalk or support that attaches the blade of a leaf to the stem.

petiolule (pehd′ee uh lool) *n.* In botany, the stalk of a leaflet of a compound leaf, such as that of the locust or rose.

petits pois (puh tee′pwah) *n.* A variety of very small peas that are sweet, tender, and flavorful. They are popular in France, and seed is available for home gardeners in the United States.

Petrea (pee′tree uh) *n.* A genus of 30 species of tropical vines, trees, and shrubs (Verbenaceae). All have dark green, rough-surfaced leaves and blue flowers. *P. volubilis,* queen's wreath, is widely grown in warm regions, including Florida and Southern California. A vine to 35 feet, it has drooping clusters of blue-to-purple flowers in clusters to a foot long. Also known as sandpaper vine.

Petrophila (peh trahf′igh luh) *n.* A genus of 40 species of low-to- medium-sized evergreen shrubs (Proteaceae). They have stiff leaves, often lobed or divided, and dense spikes or cones of yellow or white flowers.

Petrophytum (peh trahf′igh tuhm) *n.* A genus of 3 species of very small evergreen shrubs (Rosaceae) native to the mountains of the western United States. They form dense evergreen cushions of tiny leaves and have white flowers resembling short, dense, furry spiraea clusters. *P. caespitosum* and *P. hendersonii* are sometimes grown in rock gardens on walls.

Petrorhagia (peh traw ah′jee uh) *n.* A genus of about 25 annuals or perennials (Cruciferae). *P. saxifraga,* makes a mat of very narrow foliage, covered with pink flowers. Grown in rock gardens. White and pink single and double forms exist.

Petroselinum (peht roh suh ligh′nuhm) *n.* A genus of 3 species of (Umbelliferae). *P. crispum* is common parsley.

Petunia (peh too′nyuh) *n.* A genus of 35 species (Solanaceae), closely related to *Nicotiana.* Short-lived perennials, they are usually grown as annuals for bedding out. Garden petunias are *P. xhybrida;* they come in a dazzling range of colors, from white through yellow to red and in every shade of pink and rose to deep purple. Many are bicolored, and double forms are common.

peyote (pay oh′dee) *n.* 1. A drug derived from the dried bodies of the cactus *Lophophora williamsii,* native to Texas, widely known as a hallucinogen. 2. The active ingredient in the cacti, also known as mescaline. The cactus plants, living or dried, are also known as mescal buttons.

pH *n.* A numerical designation of acidity and alkalinity in soils and other biological systems. A pH of 7.0 indicates precise neutrality, higher values indicate alkalinity, and lower values indicate acidity.

Phacelia (fuh see′lee uh) *n.* A genus of 150 to 200 species of annuals and perennials (Hydrophyllaceae), most species are native to the western United States. The leaves are usually hairy or furry, and the blue or white flowers are borne in long, coiled fiddleneck clusters. *P. campanularia,* California bluebell, a desert annual to 20 inches, has intensely bright blue flowers. It is sometimes grown from seed in wild or drought-tolerant gardens. Others, though attractive, are rarely grown.

Phaedranassa (fee druh nahs'uh) *n.* A genus of 6 species of tropical American bulbous perennials (Amaryllidaceae). They have large, stalked basal leaves that occur with the flowers, which appear 6 to 10 in a cluster atop a 2½-foot stalk. The drooping flowers have long red tubes, flaring into green or yellowish-green tips.

Phaius/Phajus (figh'uhs) *n.* A genus of 30 terrestrial orchids (Orchidaceae). The only species grown outside specialists' collections is *P. tankervilliae* (*P. grandifolius*), a large terrestrial orchid with leaves up to 3 feet long and spikes, to 6 feet, of 4- to 5-inch flowers of brown, yellow, and white; often called nun's orchid.

Phalaenopsis (fahl uh nahp'sehs) *n.* A genus of 40 to 55 species of tropical epiphytic (growing on, but not taking nourishment from a host plant) orchids (Orchidaceae). The plants are monopodial (having a single stem or growth axis), with a fan of thick, glossy dark green leaves on a short stem and an erect or arching flower stem bearing several flowers, small to large, thin to fleshy, and ranging from white to yellow, pink, purple, and green, all with small, brightly colored lips. The flowers of some are barred or spotted with contrasting colors. Most species in cultivation are hybrids, with large whites being favored. Among the most beautiful and popular of orchids, they are widely grown in greenhouses and are generally successful house plants, given some care. Often called moth orchids.

Phalaris (fal'uh rehs) *n.* A genus of about 15 annual and perennial species of grasses (Graminae). *P. canariensis,* canary or birdseed grass, is grown for birdseed. *P. tuberosa stenoptera,* Harding grass, is grown for forage. *P. arundinacea,* reed canary grass, a hardy perennial to 5 feet tall, is grown as an ornamental, especially in the variety *picta,* a white-striped form known as gardener's-garters and ribbon grass.

phanerogam (fan'uh roh gam) *n.* A seed plant or flowering plant, such as a pine tree, bamboo, or poppy, as opposed to a cryptogam or spore-bearing plant, such as a fern or mushroom.

phanerogamic (fan'uh roh gam'ihk) *a.* In botany, belonging to the Phanerogamia; flowering, seed-bearing. Also phanerogamian, phanerogamous.

phaseolus (fuh see'uhl luhs) *n.* A genus of 20 or so species of mostly climbing annuals or perennials (Leguminosae). It includes many of the edible beans: *P. acutifolius,* Southwestern tepary bean; *P. coccineus,* scarlet runner bean, grown for its red or white flowers as well as its beans; *P. lunatus,* lima bean; and *P. vulgaris,* kidney bean, green or snap bean, haricot, French bean, runner bean, or wax bean. The ornamental vine sold as *Phaseolus caracalla* or *P. gigantea,* the snail vine, is *Vigna caracalla.*

pheasant's-eye *n.* 1. A common name for species of the genus *Adonis* in the buttercup family, annuals or perennials with very early-blooming solitary flowers of yellow, white, or red. 2. A common name for *Narcissus poeticus,* a narcissus, generally white, with a short cup of red or orange red.

Phegopteris (fuh gahp'tuh rehs) *n.* A genus of 3 species of creeping, spreading hardy ferns (Thelypteriaceae or Polypodiaceae). They seldom grow more than a foot tall, with finely twice-divided, rather thin fronds. Sometimes used as a ground cover in shaded areas. *P. connectilis* is the beech fern, northern beech fern, long (or narrow) beech fern; *P. hexagonoptera* the southern beech fern or broad beech fern.

Phellodendron (fehl uh dehn'druhn) *n.* A genus of 10 species of hardy deciduous trees (Rutaceae). They have compound leaves, having 5 to 13 leaflets, inconspicuous clustered flowers, and small berrylike fruit. The leaves turn bright yellow in fall. *P. amurense,* which grows to 50 feet, with corky bark, is occasionally planted as a shade tree. All are commonly known as cork trees.

phenology (feh nahl'uh jee) *n.* The branch of science concerned with the influence of climate on periodic biological phenomena, such as the flowering of plants.

phenotype (fee'nuh tighp) *n.* In botany, the outward form, appearance, and characteristics of a plant, produced by the interaction of environmental and situational factors upon the traits dictated by the plant's genes.

pheromone (fair'uh mohn) *n.* A chemical released by insects that attracts members of the same species. Pheremones are usually sexual in nature and are used to lure insects for trapping, monitoring populations, or to disrupt mating.

pheromone trap (feh′ruh mohn) *n.* Any of various containers baited with sexual scent, used to lure and entrap garden pests.

Philadelphus (fihl uh dehl′fuhs) *n.* A genus of 60 species of mostly hardy shrubs (Philadelphaceae). Most are deciduous, all have opposite leaves and 4-petaled flowers, usually fragrant and usually white. *P. lewisii* is the state flower of Idaho. Most garden examples are complex hybrids with clustered single or double white flowers. Some have purple-centered flowers. All are called mock orange, a name they share with several other shrubs, and occasionally syringa, a name that properly belongs to the lilac.

Philodendron (fihl uh dehn′druhn) *n.* A genus of more than 350 species of tropical or subtropical evergreen climbers, shrubs, or small trees (Araceae). They have leathery, glossy leaves, sometimes deeply cut and divided and small flowers borne on a club-shaped spike surrounded by a large leaflike spathe (the calla represents this type of flower). Some have short stems and large leaves in rosette form (self-heading or bird's nest philodendrons); some have erect stems crowned by huge, deeply cut or divided leaves; others are climbers, often with trailing aerial roots. Many of these shade-tolerant plants are trained on stakes as houseplants.

philodendron, bird's-nest (fihl uh dehn′druhn) *n.* A common name for short-stemmed plants, with rosettes of large leaves. *P. cannifolium* and *P. wendlandii* are among these, along with many hybrids such as 'Lynette' *P. bipinnatifidum*; they have 6-foot stems, marked by leaf scars, crowned by yard-long, deeply-cut leaves. The common subtropical plant known as *P. selloum* belongs here, along with a number of varieties.

philodendron, dubia (fihl uh dehn′druhn, dyoo′bee uh) *n.* A common name for *Philodendron radiatum,* a climber, with leaves deeply cut into very narrow segments.

philodendron, 'Emerald Queen' (deep green) **'Royal Queen'** (deep red) (fihl uh dehn′druhn) *n.* Climbing plants with foot-long arrow-shaped leaves, these are probably hybrids between *P. domesticum* and *P. erubescens.*

philodendron, fiddle-leaf (fihl uh dehn′druhn) *n.* A climbing plant with 16-inch-long leaves,

oddly lobed to resemble a violin or (some think) a horse's head. Also called horsehead philodendron.

philodendron, heart-leaf (fihl uh dehn′druhn) *n.* A common name for *Philodendron scandens,* a slender, trailing or climbing plant with leaves 3 to 5 inches long, 1 of the most familiar houseplants. In the open ground or in a greenhouse, the leaves can reach 1 foot. Often sold as *P. oxycardium.*

philodendron, red-leaf (fihl uh dehn′druhn) *n.* A common name for *Philodenron erubescens,* climbing, with deep red stems and 16-inch-long leaves, tinged dark red.

philodendron, spade-leaf (fihl uh dehn′druhn) *n.* A common name for *Philodendron domesticum,* a climber with arrow-shaped dark green leaves to 2 feet long. Often sold as *P. hastatum.*

philodendron, split-leaf (fihl uh dehn′druhn) *n.* A common name for *Monstera deliciosa,* although sometimes called *P. pertusum.*

Phlomis (floh′mehs) *n.* A genus of about 100 species of perennials or shrubs (Labiatae). The leaves are usually roughish or woolly, and the yellow, pink, purple, or white flowers occur in tiers around erect stalks that stand above the foliage. *P. fruticosa,* a shrub to nearly 5 feet, has gray woolly leaves and tiers of bright yellow flowers. Commonly called Jerusalem sage. *P. lanata* has yellowish woolly leaves and 18-inch spikes of yellow flowers. *P. russeliana* has spires of yellow flowers above spreading mats of woolly gray foliage.

Phlox (flahks) *n.* A genus of more than 60 species of annuals and generally hardy perennials (Polemoniaceae), nearly all native to North America. The leaves are usually opposite, and the clustered flowers are roundish and divided into 5 lobes. *P. bifida* (sand phlox) is a tufted low plant with needle-like leaves and lavender flowers with notched lobes; a rock-garden plant. *P. carolina* (thick-leaved phlox) is a perennial to 4 feet tall, with a pyramidal cluster of purplish to pink flowers. 'Miss Lingard' is a white selection. This species is noted for resistance to mildew. *P. divaricata* (wild Sweet William or blue phlox), a slowly spreading woodland perennial to 18 inches tall, has pale blue flowers. *P. drummondii* (Drummond or annual phlox) grows to 18 inches or more (dwarf forms exist) and has dense clusters of round or fringed flowers in pink, white, rose, red, buff, and purple. Relatively rare *P. mesoleuca* is dwarf and spreading, with flowers of purplish-pink, red, yellow, orange, or white. *P. nivalis* (creeping phlox) has flowers of purple to white. Its choice variety 'Camla' is salmon pink. *P. paniculata* (perennial phlox, summer phlox, or fall phlox) is the familiar tall (to 5 or 6 feet) perennial with large terminal clusters of white, pink, lavender, purple, pink, or red, often with contrasting eyes. *P. subulata* (moss pink, moss phlox, or mountain phlox) is a dwarf cushion-forming, spreading plant with needlelike leaves, often used as a ground cover or rock-garden plant. White, pink, red, and lilac-blue forms exist.

phlox family (flahks) *n.* The Polemoniaceae, a family of 18 genera and more than 300 species of annuals, perennials, shrubs, vines, or (rarely) trees. The important genera are *Cantua, Cobaea, Gilia, Phlox,* and *Polemonium.*

Phoenix *n.* A genus of 17 species of tropical or subtropical feather-leafed palms. They are called date palms, although only 1 species produces dates of commercial value. *P. canariensis* (Canary Island date palm) is the hardiest of the species, thriving well into northern California. A widely planted ornamental, its heavy (3-foot-thick) trunk can reach 50 feet and carries a huge head of 20-foot-long fronds. *P. dactylifera* (date), is taller, more slender, and produces secondary trunks as suckers from the base. It produces edible dates, provided it has a hot, dry climate and adequate water at the root. *P. reclinata* (Senegal date palm) has clustered trunks to 20 feet or more crowned by 9-foot-long leaves; it is a valued ornamental, and is sometimes sold as *P. paludosa. P. roebelenii* (miniature or pygmy date palm or Roebelin palm) has a slender stem to 6 feet, with a crown of 4-foot-long leaves. A choice landscaping or houseplant. *P. rupicola* (cliff date palm) grows to 20-feet, with 9-foot-long leaves. *P. sylvestris* (wild date palm or India date) reaches 50 feet, with a relatively slender trunk and 15-foot-long leaves.

Phoradendron (foh ruh dehn′druhn) *n.* A genus of about 200 species of (Loranthaceae). The American mistletoes are parasites on trees, although they possess chlorophyll. Heavy infestations can damage or kill trees. Some have minute, scalelike leaves; others have 2-inch- long leaves. The twigs, espe-

cially those bearing the white, translucent fruit, are gathered and sold as Christmas decorations. The berries are poisonous.

Phormium (fawr′mee uhm) *n.* A genus of 2 species of large perennials (Agavaceae). They have tough, leathery, swordlike leaves, arranged fanwise, and tall, striking lilylike brownish-red or yellow flowers. *P. colensoi* (mountain flax) has 5-foot leaves and 7-foot flower clusters, wheareas *P. tenax* (New Zealand flax or New Zealand hemp) has leaves that can reach 9 feet, with flower stalks to 15 feet. A number of named varieties exist, including dwarfs; bronze, red-leafed kinds, and yellow-striped varieties; and a host of multicolored varieties with names like 'Maori Queen', 'Apricot Queen', and 'Maori Sunrise'.

phosphorus *n.* An element used by plants to promote root and tuber growth, and the production of flowers and seeds. In a commercial fertilizer, its proportion is represented by the second of 3 numbers; 5-10-5 fertilizer, therefore, contains twice as much phosphorus as nitrogen or potassium.

Photinia (foh tihn′ee uh) *n.* A genus of 60 species of deciduous or evergreen shrubs (Rosaceae). All have alternate leaves, smooth-edged or saw-toothed, small white flowers in large clusters, and clustered berrylike fruit. The most widely planted is the evergreen hybrid *P.* x*fraseri,* best known for its variety 'Birmingham', a shrub or tree to 15 feet, with 2- to 5-inch-long glossy, bright green leaves that are a fine coppery red when expanding. The white flower clusters are showy, but fruit does not form. Can be trained as a small tree, but most frequent use is as a hedge or screen. Other species are *P. glabra* (Japanese photinia) an evergreen shrub to 10 feet, with 3-inch-long shiny evergreen leaves, 4-inch flower clusters, and red berries turning black; *P. serrulata* (Chinese photinia) a broad shrub or tree to 30 feet or more, usually kept smaller by pruning, with 8-inch-long narrow, spiny-edged leaves (bright reddish bronze on expanding), 6-inch flower clusters, and red berries; and *P. villosa,* deciduous and hardy, with good red fall color. The plant sold as *P. arbutifolia* is *Heteromeles arbutifolia,* the toyon.

photoperiod *n.* The relative lengths of alternating periods of light and darkness affecting the growth and maturity of an organism, as flowering, or the dropping of leaves of deciduous plants.

407

photoperiodism *n.* The ability to respond to the lengths of alternating periods of light and darkness.

photosynthesis *n.* The chemical reaction, powered by energy from light, by which carbon dioxide from the atmosphere combines with water to produce free oxygen and the sugars that the plant uses to provide energy for its growth, reproduction, and tissue repair. Photosynthesis takes place mainly within the leaves and is normally mediated by light-sensitive pigments known as chlorophylls.

phototactic *a.* In botany, pertaining to, characteristic of, or exhibiting phototaxis.

phototaxis *n.* In botany, the orientation of a plant or plant part(s) with reference to the direction of the source of light. Also phototaxy.

Phragmipedium (frag muh pee'dee uhm) *n.* A genus of 20 tropical orchids, some of which are occasionally seen in collections. The lip is a pouch, as in *Cypripedium* and *Paphiopedilum,* and, like these, *Phragmipedium* is often called lady's slipper. *P. caudatum* is remarkable for its long (to 30 inches), twisted petals.

pH test kit *n.* (See **soil test kit**.)

Phygelius (figh jeel'ee uhs) *n.* A genus of 2 species of shrubby perennials (Scrophulariaceae). Both are called, along with their hybrids, Cape fuchsia. *P. aequalis,* to 3 feet, has pinkish-orange long-tubed flowers in close clusters; its variety 'Yellow Trumpet' has bright yellow flowers. *P. capensis,* a sprawling shrub to a possible 9 feet, has looser clusters of deep red flowers. Hybrids in a wide range of colors from pink and yellow through orange-red to red are superior to the parents. Shrubby in mild winters, they die back to the ground in prolonged frost or hard freeze.

Phyla (figh'luh) *n.* A genus of 15 species of creeping perennial herbs in the verbena family (Verbenaceae). *P. nodifera* (or *P. nodiflora*), is sometimes used as a lawn substitute in warm regions. A flat grower, it has generally grayish-green leaves and small, flat heads of white or lilac flowers. It withstands foot traffic and needs little water. Frequently known as *Lippia nodiflora.*

phyllade (fih'layd) *n.* In botany, 1 of the small imperfect leaves in *Isoetes.*

Phyllanthus (feh lahn'thuhs) *n.* A genus of about 650 species of perennials, shrubs, and trees (Euphorbiaceae). A few are grown for their odd branching habit, in which opposite pairs of leaves along branchlets give the appearance of compound leaves. When the flowers appear, they seem to be borne on the leaves. These are called foliage flowers. More important are *P. acidus* (Otaheite gooseberry or gooseberry tree), with edible acid fruit; and *P. emblica* (emblic or myrobalan), a tree to 50 feet, which produces tannin and edible fruit.

phyllary (fih'uh ree) *n.* In botany, 1 of the bracts forming the involucre of flowers of the Compositae.

Phyllitis (feh ligh'dehs) *n.* *P. scolopendrium* is another name for *Asplenium scolopendrium,* hart's-tongue fern, a hardy evergreen fern with long, narrow, undivided leaves to 18 inches. It is also sometimes called deer-tongue fern.

phylloclade (fih'uh klayd) *n.* In botany, a flattened stem or branch that assumes the functions of foliage, as the broad, succulent stems of the Cactaceae. Also phylloclad; phyllocladium.

Phyllocladus (feh lahk'luh duhs) *n.* A genus of 5 species of coniferous trees or large shrubs in its own family (Phyllocladaceae) or in the podocarpus family (Podocarpaceae). The cones are reduced to a few scales, and the leaves are also reduced to scales, with flattened, chlorophyll-bearing branchlets taking their place. *P. trichomanoides* is the most widely planted of these rare trees. Commonly called celery pines from the odd appearance of the "foliage." Also known as tanekaha.

phyllode (fih'lohd) *n.* In botany, a flat, expanded petiole that usurps the form and function of a leaf blade, as in many species of *Acacia.* Also phyllodium.

phyllodineous (fhl uh dihn'ee uhs) *a.* In botany, having or relating to phyllodes. Also phyllodinous.

phyllodium (fih'loh dee uhm) *n.* Same as phyllode.

Phyllodoce (fih'oh dohs) *n.* A genus of 8 species of small evergreen shrubs (Ericaceae), all from northern latitudes or high mountains. They have tiny, crowded needlelike leaves and a profusion of small bell-shaped or urn-shaped flowers in clusters at the stem tips. *P. breweri* (red heather or mountain heather) and *P. empetriformis* (pink mountain heather), native to western mountains, are sometimes grown, but with difficulty.

phyllody (fihl'uh dee) *n.* In botany, the metamorphosis of a plant organ, such as the corolla of a flower, into a green leaf.

phyllogenetic (fihl'oh juh neh tihk) *a.* Concerned with or relating to the development of leaves.

phylloid (fil'oid) *a.* Leaflike.

phyllomania (fih'luh may nee uh) *n.* In botany, the production of leaves in unusual numbers or in unusual places.

phyllome (fih'lohm) *n.* In botany, a leaf or a plant part that is genetically derived from a leaf.

phyllomic (feh lahm'ihk) *a.* Pertaining to or resembling a phyllome.

phyllophore (fihl'uh foh uhr) *n.* In botany, the top of a palm stem.

phyllotaxy (fihl uh tak'see) *n.* In botany, the distribution or arrangement of leaves on a stem; also, the genetically determined laws that govern such distribution. Also known as phyllotaxis.

phylum (figh'luhm) *n.* In botany, a primary division of the plant kingdom. This is a rather nonspecific term, which does not denote a particular level in the hierarchy of plant classification, such as the order or genus, but instead refers to any major division.

Phyllostachys (feh lahs'tuh kehs) *n.* A genus of 80 species of bamboos, which are giant grasses (Graminae), native to temperate or warm-temperate climates. They form groves by spreading underground rhizomes (root swellings), which give rise to woody stems that may, in some species, reach 70 feet. Only a few are widely distributed. Among the hardiest are *P. aureosulcata* (forage bamboo), to 30 feet; and *P. nigra* (black bamboo), to 30 feet, with black stems. The largest are *P. bambusoides* (timber bamboo), to 70 feet with stems to nearly 6 inches thick; and *P. pubescens* (moso bamboo), equally tall and with even heavier stems. The most widely planted is probably *P. aurea* (golden bamboo), to 20 feet, with yellow stems.

Physalis (figh'suh lehs) *n.* A genus of about 80 annual and perennial plants (Solanaceae). All have small white to yellow or purple flowers with large calyces that further enlarge to surround the berry-like fruit with a papery husk, like a bag or lantern. Some are used as food: *P. ixocarpa* (tomatillo) has 2-inch fruit that is harvested as an ingredient in Latin American sauces. Ripe fruit is yellow or purple and sweet. *P. peruviana* (ground cherry, Cape gooseberry, or poha) bears a smaller, sweet yellow fruit used for pies. *P. alkekengi (P. franchetii)* (Japanese lantern or Chinese lantern), grown for ornament, has a large red papery husk surrounding a small red fruit.

Physaria (figh sah'ree uh) *n.* A genus of 14 perennials (Cruciferae) native to western North America. They are low, dense-growing plants, with somewhat furry leaves and elongated clusters of yellow flowers that are replaced by inflated seedpods. *P. didymocarpa* and *D. geyeri* are occasionally grown in rock gardens.

Physocarpus (figh suh kahr'puhs) *n.* A genus of 10 or more species of hardy deciduous shrubs (Rosaceae). They somewhat resemble spireas, with lobed, sometimes heavily veined leaves and clusters of white or pink-tinged flowers at the branch tips. *P. opulifolius*, to 10 feet, has flowers that are conspicuous for the number of white stamens. 'Luteus' and 'Dart's Gold' have attractive yellow foliage. Commonly known as ninebark, a name derived from the bark, which peels from the stems in strips or sheets.

Physostegia (figh suh stee'jee uh) *n.* A genus of 15 or so species of perennials (Labiatae). They have smooth, bright green leaves and 2-lipped white to pink or purplish flowers in a narrow spike at the top of the stems. *P. virginiana*, the principal variety, grows to 4 feet, with long spikes of white to pink or nearly red 2-inch flowers. There are many named varieties. Commonly called obedient or obedience plant because the flowers can be moved around the stalks and will hold their positions.

Phyteuma (figh too'muh) *n.* A genus of 40 species of hardy perennials (Campanulaceae). They have clustered blue to white flowers, often with elongated lobes that give them the common name horned rampion. *P. comosum* has clusters of remarkably elongated, narrow flowers that resemble pincushions. It is a difficult rock garden plant and is rarely grown in the United States. *P. spicatum* is known as the spiked rampion.

Phytolacca (figh duh lahk'uh) *n.* A genus of about 25 species of large perennials, shrubs, or trees (Phytolaccaceae). The plants have large leaves, long clusters of small white or purplish flowers, and berrylike fruit. One species is significant: *P. americana* (**P. decandra**) grows from a large (and poisonous) root, sending up annual shoots to 10 or 12 feet, with 6- to 12-inch-long leaves and drooping 6-inch-long clusters of flowers that turn into purplish-black berries with a red, staining juice. Commonly known as poke, pokeweed, scoke, garget, pocan, or pigeon berry.

Phytolaccaceae (figh duh lah kay'see ee) *n. pl.* A family of 18 to 20 genera and 65 species of herbs, vines, shrubs, and trees; the pokeweed family. *Phytolacca* is the only species of great horticultural significance.

Picea (pihs'ee uh) *n.* A genus of 35 to 45 species of coniferous trees. They have needlelike leaves on persistent bases, which remain after needles fall, and drooping cones. Valuable timber and ornamental trees. Commonly called spruces.

piceous (pihs'ee uhs) *a.* In botany, pitch-black; glossy brownish- black.

pick *n.* A hammerlike tool used for breaking up rocks or loosening soil. Also called pickax.

pickaback plant *n.* Common name for *Tolmiea menziesii*. It has soft, somewhat furry, 5-inch-long leaves that produce miniature plantlets where they join the leaf stalk. Although hardy to considerable cold, it is also widely used as a houseplant or hanging-basket plant. Also called piggyback plant, thousand mothers, and youth-on-age.

pickax *n.* A tool having a sharp point on one side of the head and a broad blade on the other. The pointed end is used for loosening hard soil and the blade for cutting roots.

pickerelweed *n.* 1. A common name for any plant of the genus *Pontederia*, especially *P. cordata*, an aquatic plant native to North America. Its arrow-shaped leaves and spike of blue flowers spring from a root that grows in shallow water.

pickerelweed family *n.* The Pontederiaceae, 6 genera of aquatic plants sometimes grown in ponds or aquariums. *Pontederia* and *Eichhornia* (water hyacinths) are well known.

pickleweed *n.* A common name for plants in the genus *Salicornia*, succulent, apparently leafless plants of salt marshes and tidal flats. The stems, which resemble strings of pickles joined end to end, are edible but rarely used in salads. Also known as pigeonfoot, samphire, and glasswort.

Pieris (pigh'uhr ehs) *n.* A genus of 7 or 8 species of evergreen shrubs or small trees (Ericaceae). They have leathery leaves, which often display brilliant shades of copper and red on expanding, and long clusters of white (rarely pink or red) flowers in the leaf joints or at branch ends. The individual flowers are small, urn-shaped, and waxy in texture. All are acid-soil plants. *P. japonica* is the most widely grown and 1 of the hardiest; it grows to 10 feet or more and has 6-inch-long drooping clusters of white (or pink in some named varieties) flowers. *P. floribunda (Andromeda floribunda)* (fetterbush or mountain pieris), native to the mountains of the southeastern United States, has dull green leaves and upright flower clusters. *P. formosa* and *P. f. forrestii* have exceptionally brilliant expanding foliage and heavy flower clusters, as does *P.* 'Forest Flame', a hybrid between *P. japonica* and *P. formosa.*

pigeonberry *n.* 1. A common name for poke or pokeweed (*Phytolacca americana*). 2. A common name for *Duranta repens*, also known as sky flower and golden dewdrop.

pigeonfoot *n.* A common name for *Salicornia europaea*, a salt-marsh plant. Also called glasswort, samphire, and pickleweed. (See **pickleweed**.)

pigeon plum *n.* A common name for *Coccoloba diversifolia*, a small tree in the buckwheat family native to the Caribbean and south Florida. It has small edible fruits.

pigeon-wings *n. pl.* A common name for species of *Clitoria*, blue-flowered plants better known as butterfly pea.

piggyback plant *n.* Same as pickaback plant, *Tolmiea menziesii.*

pignut *n.* 1. Common name for *Carya cordiformis*, a large deciduous tree in the Walnut family. Also called bitternut or swamp hickory. 2. A common name for the related *Carya glabra,* also known as pignut hickory, small-fruited hickory, and broom hickory.

pig's-face *n.* A common name for *Carpobrotus aequilaterus,* a succulent perennial, also the fruit of this plant. Also known as pigface. The plant sold under this name is likely to be *Carpobrotus chilensis,* the sea fig, commonly called ice plant.

pigweed *n.* 1. A common name for *Chenopodium album,* a weed sometimes cooked as food. 2. A common name for *Amaranthus retroflexus,* a weed in the same family, also known as redroot, redroot pigweed, green amaranth, and wild beet. 3. A name loosely applied to purslane, *Portulaca oleracea.*

Pilea (pigh'lee uh) *n.* A genus of more than 200 species of annuals or perennials (Urticaceae). They have insignificant flowers, but many species have attractive leaves. These species are common houseplants. *P. cadierei* (aluminum plant or watermelon pilea) has 3-inch-long leaves strikingly marked with silver. *P. involucrata* (panamiga or friendship plant) has dark green, crinkled leaves with purplish undersurfaces. *P. microphylla* (artillery plant) is erect, to 1 foot tall, with tiny leaves crowded on the branches in a somewhat fernlike effect. It 'shoots' its pollen, hence the name. *P. nummulariifolia* is a trailing plant with tiny round leaves. Commonly known as creeping Charlie.

pileate (pigh'lee eht) *a.* In botany, having a pileus, or cap, like a mushroom.

pileolus (pigh lee'uh luhs) *n.* In botany, a small pileus.

Pileostegia (pigh lee oh stee'gee uh) *n.* A genus of 4 species of plants (Hydrangeaceae or Saxifragaceae). *P. viburnoides* is sometimes seen in mild-winter climates. It is an evergreen vine, clinging by holdfasts to tree bark or other rough surfaces, with oval dark green leaves, to 6 inches long, and small white flowers, borne in 6-inch-wide clusters.

pileus (pigh'lee uhs) *n.* In botany, the expanded umbrellalike cap of a mushroom.

pilewort *n.* A common name for *Ranunculus ficaria* buttercup, also known as lesser celandine and small celandine.

pill bug *n.* A small, multilegged, crustaceanlike insect that rolls up into a ball when disturbed. It feeds mainly on decaying organic matter but may occasionally damage young seedlings or ripening vegetables in contact with the ground. Cleaning up organic matter and letting soil dry out will discourage their presence.

pillwort *n.* A plant in the genus *Pilularia,* especially *P. globulifera,* so called from the pelletlike fruiting bodies.

pilose (pigh'lohs) *a.* Covered with hair, especially with fine or soft hair. Also pilous.

pilosity (pigh lahs'uh dee) *n.* The state of being pilose.

pilous (pi'lus) *a.* Same as pilose.

Pilularia (pihl yuh lah'ree uh) *n.* A genus of 6 species of semiaquatic or aquatic ferns. They grow submerged or at the water's edge, with grasslike leaves, and pelletlike fruiting bodies (sporocarps). Commonly called peppergrass or pillwort.

Pimelea (peh mee'lyuh) *n.* A genus of 80 species of tender shrubs (Thymeleaceae). They have evergreen, usually stalkless leaves, and usually in opposite pairs, each pair at right angles with the next. *P. ferruginea,* to 3 feet, has crowded narrow leaves and clusters of pink-to-red flowers at the branch ends. *P. prostrata* (often sold as *P. coarctata*) is a trailing plant with gray-blue leaves and tiny white flower clusters; sometimes seen in rock gardens. Commonly called rice flowers.

Pimenta (peh mehn'tuh) *n.* A genus of 2 (possibly 5) species of tropical aromatic, evergreen trees (Myrtaceae). *P. dioica,* a 40-foot tree with 6-inch leathery leaves, is the source of allspice, which is the dried unripe fruit. *P. racemosa* is the bay or bay-rum tree, the source of an aromatic oil used in perfumery.

pimento (pih mehn'toh) *n.* 1. Allspice, the berry of *Pimenta officinalis (Eugenia Pimenta)*, a tree native to the West Indies, but cultivated almost exclusively in Jamaica. 2. The tree yielding this spice, a beautiful much-branching evergreen, 30 feet in height.

pimiento (pih myehn'toh) *n.* Any of various sweet red peppers cut into strips and preserved by brining or pickling as a garnish or as a stuffing for green olives.

pimpernel (pihm'puhr nehl) *n.* A common name for annuals and perennials in the genus *Anagallis* in the primrose family. *A. arvensis* is a common annual weed with tiny round red flowers; it is called scarlet pimpernel, poor man's weatherglass, or shepherd's clock. The perennial *A. monellii,* its variety *linifolia,* and its cultivated variety 'Phillipsii' have blue flowers with a tiny red eye.

Pimpinella (pihm puh nehl'uh) *n.* A genus of about 150 species of (Umbelliferae). They have finely divided leaves and broad, flat clusters of white, yellowish white, or pinkish flowers. *P. anisum,* an an annual to 18 inches tall, is important as anise or aniseed, grown for flavoring. The perennials *P. major* (greater burnet saxifrage) and *P. saxifraga* (burnet saxifrage) grow to 3 feet and have pinkish flowers.

Pinaceae (pigh nay'see ee) *n. pl.* A family of 9 genera and about 200 species of mostly evergreen cone-bearing trees; the pine family. They all have needlelike leaves in whorls or bundles. The genera are *Abies, Cedrus, Keteleeria, Larix, Picea, Pinus, Pseudolarix, Pseudotsuga* and *Tsuga.* Extremely important horticulturally and economically.

Pinanga (peh nang'uh) *n.* A genus of more than 100 small to intermediate tropical trees (Palmae). They are suitable only for humid tropical gardens or hothouses.

pinaster (pigh nas'tuhr) *n.* Another common name for *Pinus pinaster,* also known as cluster pine, French turpentine pine, or maritime pine.

pin cherry *n.* A common name for *Prunus pensylvanica,* a small tree with clusters of small acid fruits, sometimes used for jelly making. Also known as wild red cherry, bird cherry, and fire cherry.

pinching *n.* A method of pruning plants by removing new leaves or buds to encourage fuller growth.

pin clover *n.* A common name for *Erodium cicutarium,* also called alfilaria, red-stemmed filaree, wild musk, stork's-bill, and pin grass.

pincushion cactus *n.* A common name for the genus *Mammillaria,* about 150 species of low-growing cacti. They are also called strawberry cacti, from the small red fruits.

pincushion flower *n.* 1. A common name for the genus *Scabiosa,* 80 or so annuals and perennials in the teasel family. 2. A common name for the genus *Leucospermum,* 40 species of evergreen shrubs. Both are so named for a resemblance of their prominently protruding flower parts and a pincushion.

pine *n.* 1. Strictly, a common name for any member of the genus *Pinus.* In combination with other words, a plant with a real or fancied resemblance to a pine, for example, Amboina pine for *Agathis dammara.* (See **Pinus.**)

pine, Afghan *n.* A common name for *Pinus eldarica.* Possibly a race of *P. brutia* or *P. halepensis brutia,* this is one of the most popular pines for desert regions.

pine, African fern *n.* A common name for *Podocarpus gracilior,* a tender tree with long, narrow, light green leaves. The plant has a soft, billowing look. Much used for landscaping where winters are mild.

pine, air *n.* A common name for *Aechmea,* a genus of epiphytes (growing on, but not taking nourishment from most plants) in the pineapple family (Bromeliaceae).

pine, Aleppo (uh leh'poh) *n.* A common name for *Pinus halepensis,* a light green pine with an irregular form. A rugged, tough tree for hot, dry locations. Also known as Jerusalem pine.

pineapple *n.* 1. The fruit of *Ananas comosus,* so called from its faint resemblance to a pinecone. The fruit consists of a matured head of flowers, consolidated in 1 compact, juicy mass. They are grown commercially in Hawaii but will grow throughout the southern United States. 2. The plant *Ananas comosus,* widely cultivated and naturalized throughout the tropics. Its short stem rises from a cluster of rigid leaves, like those of the aloe, but thinner. The leaves, some 3 feet long, yield a strong fiber, which in the Philippine Islands and elsewhere is woven into fabric. So-called pineapple-cloths are also made from the fiber of other species of Bromeliaceae, such as *Bromelia Pinguin,* the wild pineapple.

pineapple family *n.* A family of 45 genera and about 2,000 species of perennials or subshrubs, mostly epiphytes (air plants), but with some terrestrial and even a few desert plants; the Bromeliaceae, also called the Bromelia family. The leaves are usually stiff and in rosettes or cups, with a central inflorescence, simple or branched, with colorful bracts and often brilliantly colored flowers. The flowering rosettes usually die, but the offsets carry on, and some species form huge clumps. The pineapple is the only commercially important member, but hundreds of ornamentals are grown.

pineapple flower *n.* A common name for 10 species of bulbous plants of the genus *Eucomis*. They range from 1 to 6 feet in height and have a basal rosette of leaves, from which springs a stalk, topped by a heavy cluster of greenish or whitish flowers, topped in turn by a smaller rosette of leaves in pineapple fashion. Used as houseplants or grown outdoors in mild-winter climates. Also known as pineapple lily.

pineapple guava (gwah′vuh) *n.* A common name for *Feijoa sellowiana*, an evergreen shrub or small tree. It has leathery, green foliage, gray underneath, purplish-white flowers with a prominent cluster of dark red stamens. The flower petals are fleshy, sweet and edible, and the gray-green 3-inch fruits that follow are delicious. Markets sell them as *feijoas*. Named varieties of high fruit quality are available. An outstanding ornamental plant in mild-winter climates; useful for hedges, screens, and as single specimens.

pine, Australian *n.* A common name for *Araucaria heterophylla, Casuarina. Casuarina* is a genus of trees that superficially resembles pines. Long, thin, jointed green branches look like long pine needles. It is very drought-resistant and will tolerate saline soils. It is often used as a seaside tree. They are better known as she oaks or beefwoods. *A. heterophylla* is better known as Norfolk Island pine.

pine, Austrian *n.* A common name for *Pinus nigra*, a dense, dark green pine to 40 feet or more. Especially useful in cold, windy sites as a windbreak.

pine barren *n.* A sandy or peaty expanse of land covered sparsely with longleaf or pitch pine trees.

pine, beach *n.* A common name for *Pinus contorta*, a short-needled pine of moderate size and picturesque form, native to the Pacific coast.

pine, Bhutan (boo tan′) *n.* A common name for *Pinus wallichiana*, a tall tree with bluish green or grayish needles. Also known as Himalayan white pine, and blue pine.

pine, big-cone *n.* A common name for *P. coulteri*, a spreading, open tree with long, deep green needles and huge, foot-thick cones. Also known as Coulter pine.

pine, bishop *n.* A common name for *Pinus muricata*, a rugged, wind-tolerant pine from the California coast.

pine, black cypress (sigh′prehs) *n.* A common name for *Callitris endlicheri*, a conifer with scalelike leaves rather than needles. Also known as red cypress pine.

pine, Bosnian (bahz′nee uhn) *n.* A common name for *Pinus leucodermis*, a compact, shapely pine with pale bark and dark blue cones.

pine, bristlecone *n.* A common name for *Pinus aristata*, a slow-growing tree, from high western mountains, with rugged, picturesque form. Also known as hickory pine.

pine, Buddhist *n.* A common name for *Podocarpus macrophyllus*, a tree that resembles a large-needled yew with 4-inch-long leaves.

pine, Canary Island *n.* common name for *Pinus canariensis*, a tall, slender, fast-growing, long-needled pine for mild-winter climates.

pine, cedar *n.* A common name for *Pinus glabra*, a dark green, short-needled pine of the South. Also known as spruce pine.

pine, celery *n.* A common name for *Phyllocladus trichomanoides*, an unusual conifer with flattened branchlets that resemble finely cut leaves.

pine, Chilean *n.* A common name for *Araucaria araucana*, a picturesque tree with spine-tipped, broad scalelike leaves and heavy cones. Better known as monkey puzzle

pine, Chilghoza (chihl goh′zuh) *n.* A common name for *Pinus gerardiana*, a bluish-green pine with edible nuts. Also known as Gerard's pine and Nepal nut pine.

pine, Chinese *n.* A common name for *Pinus tabuliformis, Crassula tetragona.* *P. tabuliformis* may be either tall and slender or short and flat-topped, with long, drooping needles. *C. tetragona* is a small succulent houseplant that has a fancied resemblance to a pine.

pine, Chinese water *n.* A common name for *Glyptostrobus lineatus,* a deciduous conifer resembling the American bald cypress.

pine, Chinese white *n.* A common name for *Pinus armandii,* an ornamental pine with drooping blue-green needles.

pine chir (chihr) *n.* A common name for *Pinus roxburghii,* a tall pine with foot-long, drooping, light green needles. Also known as Indian longleaf pine and Emodi pine.

pine, cluster *n.* A common name for *Pinus pinaster,* a tall pine with deeply fissured bark and stiff, shiny green needles. Also known as French turpentine pine and maritime pine.

pine, common screw *n.* A common name for *Pandanus utilis,* better known as screw palm, but actually neither pine or palm but a tropical tree with long (6-foot) leaves much used for mats and thatch. Also known as screw pine.

pine, cow's-tail *n.* A common name for *Cephalotaxus harringtoniana drupacea,* a large shrub or small tree resembling a yew *(Taxus),* but with a plumlike fruit.

pine, cypress (sigh'prehs) *n.* A common name for 16 species of trees of the genus *Callitris,* conifers whose leaves are scales, not needles.

pine, dammar (dam'uhr) *n.* A common name for 20 species of 20 tropical or subtropical trees of the genus *Agathis,* conifers with broad, leathery leaves.

pine, digger *n.* A common name for *Pinus sabiniana,* a tall, gaunt, open, often multitrunked pine from California's arid foothills.

pine, dwarf Siberian *n.* A common name for *Pinus pumila,* a prostrate or shrubby (to 9 feet) pine. Also known as dwarf stone pine.

pine, dwarf white *n.* A common name for *Pinus strobus* 'Nana,' a dwarf form of white pine for rock garden use.

pine, eastern white *n.* A common name for *Pinus strobus.* A valuable tall timber tree with soft blue-green needles. There are many horticultural varieties. Also known as white pine.

pine family *n.* (See **Pinaceae**.)

pine, Formosa (fawr moh'suh) *n.* A common name for *Pinus taiwanensis,* a tender pine from the island of Taiwan.

pine, foxtail *n.* A common name for *Pinus balfouriana,* a small pine from California mountains with short, dark green needles in dense tufts.

pine, frankincense *n.* A common name for *Pinus taeda,* a valuable southern timber pine with bright green needles. Also known as loblolly pine and old-field pine.

pine, Georgia *n.* A common name for *Pinus palustris,* a southern timber, pulp, and turpentine tree with long, deep green needles.

(See pine, chilghoza.)

pine, giant *n.* A common name for *Pinus lambertiana,* A western mountain pine to more than 200 feet, with long (to 20-inch) cones. Also known as sugar pine.

pine, gray *n.* A common name for *Pinus banksiana,* a northern pine adapted to cold and poor soils; often shrubby. Also known as jack pine and scrub pine.

pine, house *n.* A common name for *Araucaria heterophylla,* a large tree with symmetrical branch whorls and dark green, short needles. A familiar houseplant as a juvenile. Usually called star pine or Norfolk Island pine.

pine, imou (ee'moo) *n.* A common name for *Dacrydium cupressinum,* a tree of slow growth to 100 feet, with attractive drooping branchlets on young trees. Also known as red pine.

pine, Italian stone *n.* A common name for *Pinus pinea,* flat-topped in maturity, with edible seeds known as pignola nuts. Also known as stone pine and umbrella pine.

pine, Jeffrey *n.* A common name for *Pinus jeffreyi,* a tall pine of the Sierra Nevada and southern Oregon.

pine, Jelecote (jeh'luh coht) *n*. A common name for *Pinus patula*, a Mexican pine with long, drooping, bright green needles. Also known as Mexican yellow pine.

pine, Jersey *n*. A common name for *Pinus virginiana*, a small to medium-sized pine of the eastern United States. Thrives on poor soil. Also known as scrub pine and spruce pine.

pine, jointed *n*. A common name for *Polypodium subauriculatum*, a tropical fern (not a pine).

pine, knobcone *n*. A common name for *Pinus attenuata*, an open, irregular pine with yellowish green needles. Tolerates poor soil and drought.

pine, Korean *n*. A common name for *Pinus koraiensis*, a dark green pine to 100 feet.

pine, lacebark *n*. A common name for *Pinus bungeana*, an open, picturesque pine with light green needles, and bark that flakes to reveal white new bark beneath.

pine, limber *n*. A common name for *Pinus flexilis*, a slow-growing pine to 50 to 60 feet, with limber branches that droop.

pine, lodgepole *n*. A common name for *Pinus contorta latifolia*, a taller, more symmetrical, lighter green version of beach pine from high elevations.

pine, longleaf *n*. A common name for *Pinus palustris* and *P. oocarpa*. The first is the same as Georgia pine; also known as southern yellow pine and yellow pine. The second is a Mexican pine with foot-long, drooping, bright green needles.

pine, long-tag *n*. A common name for *Pinus echinata*, a tall pine of the eastern United States, with 5-inch-long dark green needles. Also known as shortleaf pine.

pine, Macedonian *n*. A common name for *Pinus peuce*, a medium-large tree of dense habit and dark blue-green color.

pine, mahogany (muh hahg'uh nee) *n*. A common name for *Podocarpus totara*, a tree to 100 feet, with blunt, dull green, 1-inch-long needles and small red fruits. Also known as totara pine.

pine, mountain *n*. A common name for *Pinus mugo*, a shrub or small tree of irregular growth pattern, with short, crowded needles. The form com-

monly seen is *P. m. mugo*, a broad, dense shrub. Also known as mugho or mugo pine and Swiss mountain pine.

pine-needle mulch *n*. A soil surface cover of pine needles.

pine, New Caledonian *n*. A common name for *Araucaria columnaris*, a tall tropical tree with symmetrical branches clad with short, scalelike overlapping leaves. Older trees become broad-topped, with many short branches along the lower trunk.

pine, Norway *n*. A common name for *Pinus resinosa*, a tall tree of the eastern United States, with shiny green leaves and heavy plates of rust-red bark. Also known as red pine.

pine, nut *n*. A common name for *Pinus edulis* and *P. monophylla*. Both are pinons, nut-bearing pines of the Southwest. The first has needles in bundles of 2, the second has single needles. Both are low, flat, and round in habit when mature, symmetrical and slow-growing while young. Extremely heat- and drought-tolerant. *P. edulis* is also known as two-leaved nut pine. *P. monophylla* is also known as stone pine.

pine nut *n*. The edible seed of several species of pine, such as the Italian stone pine.

pine, pinon (peen yohn') *n*. A common name for *Pinus quadrifolia*, a tree similar to nut pines, except for having needles in bundles of 4. Also spelled pinyon.

pine, pitch *n*. A common name for *Pinus rigida*, a pine of the eastern United States to 60 feet, with dark green needles.

pine, Port Jackson *n*. A common name for *Callitris rhomboidea*. (See **Oyster Bay pine**.)

pine, poverty *n*. A common name for *Pinus virginiana*, a mountain tree of the eastern United States. It grows 30 to 50 feet, with twisted dark green needles. Tolerates poor soil.

pine, prickly *n*. A common name for *Pinus pungens*, a pine to 50 feet, with dark green, stiff, twisted needles. Also known as yellow pine and table mountain pine.

pine, prince's *n*. A common name for *Chimaphila umbellata cisatlantica*, a hardy herb or subshrub native to eastern North America. It grows to 10 inches, with smooth, evergreen leaves to 2 or more inches and small clusters of small pink flowers. Used as an understory plant in woodland gardens. Also known as pipsissewa.

pine, princess *n.* A common name for *Crassula pseudolycopodioides*, and *Lycopodium obscurum*. The first is a small succulent houseplant with a fancied resemblance to a pine. The second is a club moss, a distant relative of the ferns.

pine, Rocky Mountain yellow *n.* A common name for *Pinus ponderosa scopulorum*, the eastern race of western yellow pine, somewhat smaller and with shorter leaves.

pine, rough-barked Mexican *n.* A common name for *Pinus montezumae*, a 70-foot tree, with foot-long, stiff, bluish-green needles.

pine, running *n.* A common name for *Lycopodium clavatum*, a club moss, a primitive plant distantly related to ferns.

pine, sand *n.* A common name for *Pinus clausa*, a shrub or small tree with thin, dark green needles. Native to Florida.

pinesap *n.* A common name for several saprophytic plants (plants without chlorophyll that subsist on decaying vegetation). The most common is *Monotropa uniflora*, a dead-white, leafless plant with a nodding white flower; found wild in deep woodlands. Better known as Indian pipe or corpse plant.

pine, Scotch *n.* A common name for *Pinus sylvestris*, a hardy pine to 100 feet, with stiff, twisted, bluish-green needles. Valuable for timber and for Christmas-tree farming. Also known as Scots pine and Scots fir.

pine, slash *n.* A common name for *Pinus elliottii*, a fast-growing pine to 100 feet or more, native to the southern United States. Valuable for timber, pulpwood, and turpentine.

pine, Soledad (sahl'uh dad) *n.* A common name for *Pinus torreyana*, a large, heavy-branching pine native to a very restricted site in San Diego County, California. Also known as Torrey pine.

pine, Swiss stone *n.* A common name for *Pinus cembra*, a slow- growing, dense pine with a symmetrical cone shape in youth.

pine, tanyosho (tahn yoh'soh) *n.* A common name for *Pinus densiflora* 'Umbraculifera', a slow-growing pine, but early to assume its mature flat-topped shape and early to bear cones. A variety of Japanese red pine.

pine, thatch screw *n.* A common name for *Pandanus tectorius*, not a pine, but a 20-foot member of the screw-pine family (Pandanaceae) with spine-edged leaves 3 to 5 feet long.

pine tree *n.* A plant in the genus *Pinus*.

pine tree, miniature *n.* A common name for *Crassula tetragona*, a small succulent. Sometimes used to create a miniature dish landscape. Also known as baby pine of China and Chinese pine.

pine, twisted-leaf *n.* A common name for *Pinus teocote*, a Mexican pine to 90 feet, with thick, furrowed bark and stiff, spreading, dark green needles.

pine, Veitch screw (vehch) *n.* A common name for *Pandanus veitchii*, a houseplant with long, narrow, spine-edged, white-striped leaves. (See also **Pandanus**.)

pineweed *n.* A common name for *Hypericum gentianoides*, an annual with scalelike leaves and small yellow flowers. Also known as orange grass.

pine, western white *n.* A common name for *Pinus monticola*, a valuable timber tree of western mountains. It grows to 200 feet, with bluish-green needles.

pine, western yellow *n.* A common name for *Pinus ponderosa*, chief timber pine of the western United States, a possible 200-footer of great bulk, with orange-brown checkered bark and long, stiff, dark green needles.

pine, white bark *n.* A common name for *Pinus albicaulis*, a shrub or small tree of high western mountains, often nearly prostrate from wind and snow, with stiff, dark green needles.

pin grass *n.* A common name for *Erodium cicutarium*. Also known as alfilaria, filaree, red-stemmed filaree, wild musk, pin clover, stork's-bill, and pink needle.

Pinguicula (pihng gwaihk'yuh luh) *n.* A genus of 46 species of stemless perennials (Lentibulariaceae).

They have smooth shiny leaves that grow from a basal rosette; sticky with glands, the leaves trap and digest small insects. The inch-wide flowers occur singly or a few together at the top of long stalks and somewhat resemble purple, pink, yellow, or white violets. Sometimes grown by hobbyists in terrariums. Some are hardy to light frost. Commonly known as butterwort.

pink *n*. 1. A common name for a plant in *Dianthus*, a genus in the pink family with 300 species, which include the common garden pinks and carnations. 2. Any of several plants that bear a real or fancied resemblance to a pink.

pink, California Indian *n*. A common name for *Silene californica*, a 2- to 4-foot perennial with fringed scarlet 2-inch flowers.

pink, Cheddar *n*. A common name for *Dianthus gratianopolis (D. caesius)*, a small cushion plant with gray foliage and small fringed pink flowers.

pink, clove *n*. A common name for *Dianthus caryophyllus*, better known as carnation.

pink, cluster-head *n*. A common name for *Dianthus carthusianorum*, a 2-foot perennial with clustered pink to purple or white 1½-inch flowers.

pink, cottage *n*. A common name for *Dianthus plumarius*, which forms a 12- to 16-inch cushion, with narrow blue-gray leaves and fragrant, fringed flowers in white, pink, rose, or red.

pink, cushion *n*. A common name for *Silene acaulis*, a dwarf (to 4 inches) plant with mosslike foliage and small pink, purple, or white flowers.

pink, Deptford *n*. A common name for *Dianthus armeria*, an annual or biennial pink with small, clustered reddish flowers on 16-inch stems.

pink, fire *n*. A common name for *Silene virginica*, a 2- to 3-foot perennial with fringed scarlet flowers.

pink, grass *n*. Another common name for cottage pink. Also, the common name for a small hardy terrestrial orchid, *Calopogon pulchellus*.

pink, Indian *n*. A common name for *Spigelia marilandica*, a 2-foot perennial with red flowers lined with yellow; better known as pinkroot or wormgrass. Also, another name for cardinal flower, *Lobelia cardinalis*.

pinna (pihn′uh) *n*. In botany, 1 of the primary divisions or leaflets of a divided leaf or frond, such as in ferns and palms.

pinnate (pih′nayt) *a*. In botany, resembling a feather in structure, with the parts arranged on both sides of an axis. Used especially of compound leaves, such as those of the palm and locust. Also pennate.

pinnatifid (peh nad′uh fihd) *a*. In botany, cut or sectioned to form a feather shape, as the fronds of many ferns.

pinnation (peh nay′shuhn) *n*. In botany, the state or condition of being pinnate.

pinnatisect (peh nad′uh sehkt) *a*. In botany, cut to the midrib in a pinnate manner.

pinnulate (pihn′yuh layt) *a*. In botany, having divided segments that are themselves further divided, as the leaves of some acacias. Also pinnulated.

pinnule (pihn′yool) *n*. In botany, a secondary pinna; one of the ultimate divisions of a doubly divided leaf. Also pinnula.

pinon (peen yohn′) *n*. Any of several nut-bearing pines of the Southwest and Mexico. Name is also used for the nut. Also spelled pinyon. (See **pine, nut**) and **pine, pinon**.)

pinto bean *n*. A medium-sized bush bean grown for drying. The beans are used in soups for their slightly spicy flavor and are a basic ingredient in Mexican dishes.

Pinus *n*. A genus of 110 species of evergeen trees (rarely shrubs) with needlelike leaves borne in bundles of from 1 to 5 or more and cones with woody scales; the pines. Most are from temperate or cold climates, although a few are tropical. Important for timber, turpentine, resin, shade, and ornament.

pinwheel *n*. A common name for *Aeonium haworthii*, a tender succulent shrub with dense growth to 1 or 2 feet, and 2-inch rosettes of fat, blue-green leaves at the end of each branch. The leaves are sometimes red-edged, and the clustered flowers are cream-colored.

pinxter flower *n*. A common name for *Rhododendron periclymenoides (R. nudiflorum)*, a hardy deciduous rhododendron or azalea native to the eastern

United States. It grows to 9 feet, with clusters of long-tubed 1½-inch pink, rarely white, flowers with a sweet fragrance. It is also known as pinkster flower, pinxterbloom, and, most commonly, honeysuckle.

pipal tree *n.* A common name for *Ficus religiosa,* a tender deciduous fig tree (Moraceae). This tender fig is briefly deciduous in spring. It has thin, roundish leaves with a long, pointed 'tail.' The foliage is open, shade comparatively light, and the leaves flutter in the lightest breeze. Also spelled pipul, peepul, or peepal.

Piper *n.* A genus of 1000 or so tropical shrubs or small trees, some climbing. They have smooth, simple leaves and tiny flowers on fleshy spikes, followed by a berrylike fruit with a thin flesh. The genus includes pepper and a number of other economic or ornamental plants. *P. nigrum* furnishes black and white pepper. *P. ornatum* (Celebes pepper) and *P. porphyrophyllum* are ornamental greenhouse vines.

Piperaceae (pigh puh ray'see ee) *n.* A family of 9 genera and more than 1,000 species; the pepper family. *Piper* (pepper) and *Peperomia* are horticulturally important. *Macropiper* is sometimes grown as an ornamental in cool, mild climates.

piperaceous (pihp uh ray'shuhs) *a.* Pertaining to or belonging to the *Piperaceae.*

pipe vine *n.* A common name for *Aristolochia durior (A. macrophylla)* and *A. californica,* vines so called from the resemblance of the flower to a curved tobacco pipe. Also called Dutchman's pipe or, in the case of *A. californica* birthwort.

pipewort *n.* Any plant in *Eriocaulon,* a genus of 1000 or so species in the pipewort family. They are small, rushlike plants of wet places with dense heads of tiny flowers. *E. decangulare* is rarely cultivated in bog gardens.

pippin (pihp'ihn) *n.* A variety of apple.

pipsissewa (pihp sihs'uh wuh) *n.* A common name for *Chimaphila umbellata,* a small evergreen subshrub in the wintergreen family. Also known as prince's pine.

Piptanthus (pihp tan'thuhs) *n.* A genus of 8 or 9 species of shrubs (Leguminosae). *P. nepalensis* is a 10-foot shrub, with leaves divided into 3 leaflets and 1-inch pea-shaped flowers in dense 6-inch clusters. Tender in severe cold.

Piqueria (peh kih'ree uh) *n.* A genus of 20 species of annuals, perennials, or shrubs (Compositae). *P. trinervia,* a tender 3-foot plant with small, white, very fragrant flowers, is the plant grown by florists as *Stevia.*

Pisonia (peh soh'nee uh) *n.* A genus of about 50 species of tropical trees and shrubs (Nyctaginaceae). *P. umbellifera (P. Brunoniana)* is rarely grown, but its variety 'Variegata', with 5- to 6-inch leaves strongly marked with white and pink, is sometimes grown as a houseplant or tub plant.

pistache, Chinese (puh stash') *n.* A common name for *Pistacia chinensis,* a large deciduous shade tree with leaves divided into many leaflets. It is noted for brilliant fall color and is a favored ornamental and street tree.

pistachio (peh stash'ee oh) *n.* The nut of *Pistacia vera,* a pistachio nut.

Pistacia (peh stash'ee uh) *n.* A genus of 10 species of trees and shrubs (Anacardiaceae). (See **pistache, chinese** and **pistachio**.)

Pistia (pihs'tee uh) *n.* A genus of 1 species, *P. stratiotes* (Araceae), water lettuce, a tender floating plant with a leaf rosette resembling a floating lettuce plant. Sometimes used in ponds or aquariums.

pistil *n.* In botany, the female or ovule-bearing organ of a flower. A complete pistil consists of three parts: ovary, style (when present), and stigma.

pistillate *a.* 1. In botany, having a pistil. 2. Having pistils but no functional stamens.

pistilline *a.* In botany, relating or belonging to the pistil.

pistillode *n.* A rudimentary or vestigial pistil.

pistol grip nozzle *n.* A watering device mounted on a hose, which turns on or off by squeezing a trigger. Also called trigger nozzle.

Pisum (pigh'suhm) *n.* A genus of 6 species (Leguminosae). *P. sativum,* the garden pea, green pea, English pea, or common pea, is the chief species.

pitahaya (pihd uh high'uh) *n.* 1. The name for any of several large cacti bearing edible fruit, also the fruit itself. 2. A common name for small cacti in the genus *Echinocereus*. Also spelled pitaya.

Pitcairnia (piht kahr'nee uh) *n.* A genus of more than 250 species of perennials or subshrubs (Bromeliaceae). Most have rosettes of spiny-edged leaves and simple or branched spikes of yellow or red flowers.

pitcher *n.* In botany, a specially adapted tubular or cup-shaped modification of the leaf of certain plants, particularly of the genera *Nepenthes* and *Sarracenia* (pitcher plants).

pitcher plant *n.* Any plant with leaves modified into pitcher-shaped hollow receptacles to hold liquid, which traps and digests insects. Hardy eastern and southern pitcher plants are in the genus *Sarracenia*. Tropical epiphytic pitcher plants are in the genus *Nepenthes*. California pitcher plant, *Darlingtonia californica*, has 1- to 2-foot erect, hollow, hooded leaves and large green and purple flowers on tall (to 4-feet) stalks. Also known as cobra lily.

pitchfork *n.* A 3- to 5-tined, long-handled fork for lifting and moving soil. The tines of a pitchfork are shorter, more rounded, and broader than those of a manure fork. (See also **manure fork** and **spading fork**.)

Pithecellobium (pihth uh sehl oh'bee uhm) *n.* A genus of 100 to 200 species of tropical trees or shrubs (Leguminosae). They have twice-divided spiny leaves with relatively few, small leaflets and balls of fluffy white or yellow flowers. *P. flexicaule* (Texas ebony) is an elegant, slow-growing tree with fine-textured foliage and fragrant flowers—a good tree for desert landscapes.

Pittosporaceae (pihd uh spuh ray'see ee) *n.* A family of 9 genera and 200 species of trees, shrubs, and climbers, mostly from tropical or warm temperate regions; the pittosporum family. *Hymenosporum*, *Pittosporum*, and *Sollya* are important genera.

Pittosporum (peh tahs'puh ruhm) *n.* A genus of about 100 species of evergreen shrubs and trees (Pittosporaceae). They have simple, smooth-edged, alternate or whorled leaves and solitary or clustered flowers, often fragrant. *P. tobira* (often called tobira or mock orange) grows to 18 feet with fragrant

clustered white flowers that turn to buff. It is a favorite shrub in California and the deep South. *P. crassifolium*, *P. eugenioides*, and *P. tenuifolium* (*P. nigricans*) are favored hedge subjects in mild climates, and *P. undulatum*, *P. viridiflorum*, and *P. rhombifolium* reach large tree size.

Pityrogramma (pihd uh roh gram'uh) *n.* A genus of 15 species of ferns (Polypodiaceae) grown for the yellow or white, waxy undersurfaces of their fronds. Most are greenhouse plants, but *P. triangularis* (goldback fern) grows wild from Canada to Baja California along the coast. Commonly known as gold or silver ferns.

placenta *n.* In botany, the part of the carpel of flowering plants that bears the ovules.

plane tree *n.* A common name for a tree in the genus *Platanus*. The most widely planted is London plane, the hybrid *P. xacerifolia*. The American plane, also called sycamore or buttonwood, a tall, bulky tree native to the eastern, southern, and midwestern United States, is *P. occidentalis*. The California plane tree is *P. racemosa*, the Arizona plane *P. wrightii*. All have light brown bark that flakes off in large pieces to reveal very pale, smooth bark beneath, and all have large, lobed maplelike leaves. The true Oriental plane, *P. orientalis*, with leaves deeply cut into narrow segments, is seldom seen.

Plantaginaceae (plan tuh juh nay'see ee) *n. pl.* The plantain family.

Plantago *n.* A genus of annuals or perennials (Plantaginaceae) with tiny flowers tightly packed in close spikes. *P. lanceolata*, with narrow, ribbed leaves and little oval heads on long stalks, is a common weed, usually called buckhorn plantain, ribgrass, ripple grass, English plantain, or narrow-leaved plantain. *P. major* has broad, oval, bright green leaves and tall, thin spikes of green. Usually called common plantain, it is also known as whiteman's-foot, and cart-track plant. 'Atropurpurea', with purple leaves, is sometimes grown in gardens.

plantain (plant'uhn) *n.* 1. A tropical plant, *Musa paradisiaca*, or its fruit. The plantain closely resembles the banana, of which it is a variety. It is distinguished in appearance by purple spots on the stem and by its longer fruit. The plantain is commonly eaten cooked before fully mature, whereas the banana is mostly eaten fresh when ripe. The fresh fruit is comparable chemically with the potato, although less nutritious. 2. Common name of any member of the genus *Plantago.* (See **Plantago**.)

plantain, rattlesnake (plan'tuhn) *n.* A common name for any of several species of *Goodyera,* a genus of 40 small terrestrial orchids. *G. pubescens* and *G. repens* have oval leaves marked with white veins.

plant breeding *n.* The propagation of selected plants to develop distinctive qualities, such as brighter blooms or disease resistance.

plant caddy *n.* (See **plant dolly**.)

plant dolly *n.* A small, wheeled platform to hold and move large indoor or patio plants. Also called plant caddy.

planter *n.* Any of various rot-resistant containers for growing and displaying flowers, herbs, ornamental grasses, or trees. Planters may be made of such materials as cedar, redwood, teak, or polyethylene.

planter pulley *n.* A device used to lower and raise hanging plants for watering and tending.

plant feeder *n.* A device that holds and distributes plant food. A hose-end plant feeder mixes fertilizer with water at the end of a garden hose.

planting *n.* 1. The act or art of inserting plants in the soil. 2. A planted place; a grove; a plantation.

planting terrace *n.* A series of 3 or more tiers containing soil or other growing medium supported by frames, used to grow strawberries or to make floral displays.

plant marker *n.* A label on a stake, used to denote location of plants. Labels may be made of wood, metal, or plastic and may be preprinted or handwritten. Also called plant label or pot stake.

plant mister *n.* A bottle with a trigger spray head, used for spraying or misting plants. Also called plant sprayer.

plant patent *n.* The proprietary right in the genetic material and propagation of a particular plant, limiting its use by others.

plant saucer *n.* A shallow dish placed under a potted plant to protect floors and furniture by catching excess water.

plant sprayer *n.* (See **plant mister**.)

plant tag *n.* A metal marker, similar to the tag on a Christmas package, attached to a plant stem with wire.

plant tie *n.* A strip of material used to tether plants to a stake or lattice. Among materials used for plant ties are string, paper string, plastic, and covered wire. Also called garden tie.

plant trainer *n.* A flat nail with an eye in 1 end through which wire is threaded to create a support system for training wall plants against a brick, stone, or wooden wall. (See also **leaded wall nail**.)

Platanaceae (plat uh nay'see ee) *n. pl.* A family of 1 genus, *Platanus;* the plane tree or sycamore family

Platycerium (plad ee sih'ree uhm) *n.* A genus of 17 epiphytic (growing on, but not taking nourishment from host plants) tropical ferns (Polypodiaceae). They support themselves on trees by broad, shield-shaped sterile fronds, which are green, aging to brown. The fertile leaves are forked like deer or moose antlers. They are popular greenhouse plants except in mildest winter climates. Commonly known as staghorn or elkhorn ferns.

Platycladus (plad'ee klah duhs) *n.* A genus of a single species *P. orientalis* (Cupressaceae), nearly always sold as *Thuja* (or *Thuya*) *orientalis.* The basic species is a tree to 40 feet, with scalelike leaves and branchlets arranged in flat vertical planes. Many selections exist, including dwarfs, columns, globes, and cones, and foliage color can be green, golden, blue-green, or variegated. Commonly known as Oriental arborvitae.

Platycodon (plad'ee koh dahn) *n.* A genus of a single species, *P. grandiflorus* (Campanulaceae), a hardy perennial. It grows to 2½ feet, with narrow, deep green leaves and open clusters of 2- to 3-inch blue flowers (rarely white or pink), which open from round balloonlike buds into shallow cups with pointed lobes. Commonly known as balloon flower.

Platylobium (plad'ee loh bee uhm) *n.* A genus of 4 species of shrubs (Leguminosae). *P. formosum* and *P. obtusangulum,* 3-foot evergreen shrubs with yellow and red pea-shaped flowers, are grown ornamentally.

Platystemon (plad′ee stee muhn) *n.* A genus of 1 species, *P. californicus* (Papaveraceae), an annual poppy. It grows to 1 foot, with inch-wide cream-to-yellow flowers. Commonly known as cream-cups.

pleach *v.* To unite (the branches of shrubs, vines, etc.) by plaiting, weaving, or braiding them together.

Plectostachys (plehk toh stak′uhs) *n.* A genus of 2 species of subshrubs (Compositae). *P. serpyllifolia* is a sprawling plant with crowded tiny furry-white leaves. It is sometimes sold as a dwarf form of *Helichrysum petiolare,* which it resembles on a reduced scale.

Plectranthus (plehk tran′thuhs) *n.* A large genus of about 350 species of annuals, perennials, and subshrubs (Labiatae). The commonly cultivated kinds are trailing plants with opposite, toothed leaves and clusters of 2-lipped bluish or purplish flowers. Commonly known as Swedish ivy, Swedish begonia, or spur flower. *P. nummularius* has smooth, fleshy, nearly round, toothed leaves; it is often sold as *P. australis,* a different plant. *P. oertendahlii* is similar, but its leaves are heavily veined and purple beneath.

Pleioblastus (pligh oh blahs′tuhs) *n.* A genus of 20 or so dwarf to medium-sized bamboos in the grass family (Graminae). *P. humilis* (to 3 feet) and *P. pygmaeus* (to 1 foot) are used as coarse ground covers, as are the white-variegated *P. argenteostriatus* and *P. variegatus.* All these are aggressive spreaders by underground rhizomes. *P. auricoma* is a handsome foliage plant of 3 to 6 feet, with golden-green leaves striped bright yellow. *P. simonii* can reach 24 feet; it has a variegated form, 'Variegatus'. All may be sold under the name *Arundinaria.*

Pleione (pligh oh′nee) n. A genus of 16 species of generally terrestrial orchids. They grow from pseudobulbs, with thin-textured, often pleated, leaves and attractive flowers, which resemble small cattleya orchids, usually in shades of pink or purplish, often with white and yellow touches. Among the hardiest of orchids, they thrive in cool, moist gardens along the Pacific coast in California and Oregon. *P. formosana* and P. *bulbocodioides* are the most widely distributed.

Pleiospilos (pligh aws′pigh lohs) *n.* A small genus of 4 species of small succulent (fleshy) perennials (Aizoaceae). A pair of fleshy leaves sit on the ground, looking like pebbles or small rocks. One or more many-petaled flowers emerge from the cleft between the leaves. As the old leaves die off, a new pair emerges. Much grown by succulent fanciers in pots or dish gardens. *P. bolusii* and *P. nelii* are the most widely grown. Commonly known as splitrocks or mimicry plants.

pleurisy root (plu′ruh see) *n.* A common name for *Asclepias tuberosa,* a plant of the milkweed family, so named from its former medicinal use. Also called butterfly weed.

pleurisy root
1 flowering stem *2* root with lower leaves

plicate (pligh′kayt) *a.* In botany, folded lengthwise like a fan; pleated. Also plicated.

plicate leaf

plow *v.* 1. To turn up with a plow; till. 2. To make furrows, grooves, or ridges in, as with a plow; furrow; figuratively, to move through like a plow; make one's way through. Sometimes spelled plough.

plow layer *n.* Surface soil.

plum *n.* 1. A fruit of any of the trees called plums, specifically, the fruit of a tree of the genus *Prunus,* distinguished from the peach and apricot by its smooth surface, smaller size, and unwrinkled stone, as well as from the cherry by the bloom (dusty look) on its surface and commonly larger size. Plums are eaten fresh or cooked as a dessert fruit, as well as a dried fruit in the form of prunes. 2. One of several small trees of the genus *Prunus*. The numerous varieties of the common edible plum are classed as *P. domestica*. The Japanese plum, *P. Japonica*, is grown in California and the southern United States.

Plumbaginaceae (pluhm baj uh nay'see ee) *n.* A family of 22 genera and 440 species of perennials, shrubs, and vines; the plumbago or leadwort family. The important genera are *Acantholimon*, *Armeria*, *Ceratostigma*, *Goniolimon*, *Limonium*, *Plumbago*, and *Psylliostachys*.

Plumbago (pluhm bay'goh) *n.* A genus of 15 species of shrubs and perennials (Plumbaginaceae). *P. auriculata* (Cape plumbago) is a sprawling shrub or climber to 12 feet, with light green leaves and phloxlike round clusters of pale blue (rarely white) flowers, widely used in mild-winter climates. It is often sold as *P. capensis. P. indica* has long clusers of red flowers and is more purely tropical.

plum, beach *n.* A common name for *Prunus maritima*, a straggling bush on the coast from Maine to Mexico, with a rather pleasant red or purple fruit, often preserved. It grows in poor soils and withstands weather extremes.

plum, cherry *n.* A cherrylike form of the common plum, the variety *cerasifera*, also called myrobalan plum.

plum, Chickasaw (chihk'uh saw) *n.* A common name for *Prunus angustifolia*, a native species now naturalized widely from New Jersey to Texas and south to Florida. It bears a thin-skinned, globose red or yellow fruit which has pleasant flavor. It is often cultivated.

plumcot (pluhm'kaht) *n.* A hybrid between the plum and the apricot, which never achieved popularity.

plume flower *n.* A common name for *Justicia carnea (Jacobinia carnea)*, a 4- to 6-foot subshrub. It is a dark green, rounded shrub, with each stem ending in a rounded, tightly-packed cluster of rose-pink 2-inch flowers. Grown as a greenhouse plant except in mildest winter climates. Usually called

Brazilian plume flower; also known as flamingo plant, paradise plant, and king's crown.

Plumeria (ploo mih'ree uh) *n.* A genus of 8 species of small deciduous (but becoming evergreen in mild, moist climates) trees or shrubs (Apocynaceae). They have thick, fleshy branches with terminal clusters of long, narrow, shiny leaves and open clusters of extremely fragrant white, pink, yellow, or red flowers to 4 inches wide. *P. rubra* is the most widely grown. *P. obtusa*, Singapore plumeria, is more nearly evergreen and has smaller (2-inch) white flowers. Grown as greenhouse plants except in mildest winter climates, and a favorite flower for Hawaiian leis. Commonly known as frangipani, plumeria, nosegay, temple tree, or pagoda tree.

plum fir *n.* A common name for *Podocarpus andinus*.

plum, greengage *n.* A large, firm-fleshed, green variety.

plum juniper (joo'nuh puhr) *n.* A common name for *Juniperus drupacea*, a 60-foot tree in the cypress family. Its cones have been modified into a 1-inch fleshy, edible fruit, with the seeds forming a central stone. Also called Syrian juniper or habbel.

plumose (ploo'mohs) *a.* Feathery or plumelike, with fine hairs on opposite sides, as in the pappus of some Compositae.

plumosity (ploo mahs'uh dee) *n.* The state of being plumose. Also plumoseness.

plum-yew *n.* A common name for plants in the genus *Cephalotaxus*. They resemble yews (*Taxus*), but their cones are fleshy, resembling small plums.

plum, wild *n.* Any undomesticated plum, specifically: (a) the *Prunus spinosa;* (b) in eastern North America, the wild yellow or red plum, or Canada plum, *P. Americana*, which has a well-colored fruit with pleasant pulp, but tough acidic skin; common along streams, etc., and sometimes planted; (c) in western North America, *P. subcordata*, whose red fruit, which is large and edible, is often gathered.

Poa (poh'uh) *n.* A genus of 300 to 500 species of annual and perennial grasses (Gramineae) native to a wide range of mostly cool or cold-winter climates. *P. pratensis*, known as Kentucky bluegrass, is one of the most widely grown lawn grasses. Others are sometimes weeds or rarely used as lawn grasses. Also known as bluegrass.

pod *n.* In botany, a dry fruit or seed vessel that pops open when mature and is more or less elongated and cylindrical or flattened, as of the pea, bean, or catalpa.

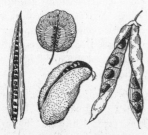

pods of various plants

Podalyria (poh duh lah′ree uh) *n.* A genus of 20 species of tender shrubs (Leguminosae). *P. calyptrata,* to 9 feet, has short clusters of pink, ¾-inch, pea-shaped flowers. *P. sericea,* to 2 feet, has silvery, silky foliage and small pink, pea-shaped flowers, borne singly.

Podocarpaceae (poh doh kahr pay′see ee) *n.* A family of evergreen trees and shrubs with needle-like, scalelike, or broad, leathery leaves. They differ from conifers in having cones modified into a structure in which a single seed rests on, or is enclosed by, a fleshy body called an aril, which may look like a swollen stalk or a fleshy fruit.

Podocarpus (poh′doh kahr puhs) *n.* A genus of about 100 species of evergreen trees and shrubs (Podocarpaceae), a few hardy in the United States. The most widely grown are the Chinese and Japanese *P. macrophyllus* (southern yew, Japanese yew, Buddhist pine), a 45-foot tree with dark green leaves to 4 inches long, and ⅜-inch wide; and its shrubby variety *maki,* a dense, erect shrub. Common in mild-winter areas is *P. gracilior* (fern pine), a light green, billowy-looking tree to 75 feet, but supple enough in youth to use as a vine or an espalier. It is sometimes sold as *P. elongatus. P. henkelii* is similar, but with larger, darker green, drooping leaves. *P. dacrydioides* (kahika, white pine, red pine) and *P. totara* (totara pine, mahogany pine), are important New Zealand timber trees. Broad-leafed *P. nagi* is properly *Nageia nagi.*

Podophyllum (pahd uh figh′luhm) *n.* A genus of 5 species of hardy perennials (Berberidaceae). All have broad, shield-shaped lobed leaves that rise directly from underground rhizomes; the flowering stalks have 2 or more leaves, with the flower or flowers in the joint between. *P. peltatum* (May apple or wild mandrake) is a common woodland plant in the eastern United States. The flowering stems have 2 leaves, with a 2-inch white, waxy flower between, followed by a yellow 2-inch berry. (Most parts of the plant are poisonous.) Unflowered stems have a single, deeply lobed, foot-wide leaf. *P. hexandrum (P. emodi),* has leaves, spotted with brown, white or pink flowers, and red berries.

Podranea (poh dray′nee uh) *n.* A genus of 2 species of shrubby tropical vines (Bignoniaceae). The leaves are divided into 4 or 5 pairs of leaflets, with an additional pair at the tip, and funnel-shaped flowers in clusters. *P. brycei,* (Queen of Sheba vine) has pink flowers marked with red and yellow. *P. ricasoliana* (pink trumpet vine) has pale pink flowers striped with red.

podzolization (pahd zahl eh zay′shuhn) *n.* The process by which soils are depleted of alkaline material and become more acid.

Pogonia
ophiogles-soides (rose Pogonia)

423

Pogonia (puh goh'nyuh) *n.* A genus of small terrestrial perennial orchids (Orchidaceae). The only species grown is *P. ophioglossoides,* a 2½-foot plant of peaty, boggy soil, with 1- to 2-inch-wide pink or white fragrant flowers. Commonly known as rose pogonia, snake-mouth, or adder's mouth.

Poinciana, dwarf *n.* A common name for *Caesalpinia pulcherrima.* (See **Caesalpinia**.)

Poinciana, royal *n.* A common name for *Delonix regia.* (See **Delonix**.)

poinsettia (poin sehd'uh) *n.* A common name for *Euphorbia pulcherrima,* the well-known Christmas plant, with scarlet or white leaflike bracts surrounding the clustered small yellow true flowers.

poinsettia, annual (poin sehd'uh) *n.* A common name for an annual usually called *Euphorbia heterophylla,* but which is probably *E. cyathophora,* with red markings on its upper leaves. Also known as Mexican fire plant.

poisonberry *n.* A common name for *Solanum nigrum,* a shrub or vine in the nightshade family (Solanaceae). Better known as black or common nightshade

poison bulb *n.* A common name for *Crinum asiaticum,* a large bulbous perennial in the lily family.

poison hemlock *n.* A common name for 2 plants in the parsley family; *Cicuta maculata,* also called water hemlock; and *Conium maculatum,* also called hemlock and spotted hemlock. Both are deadly poisonous when eaten.

poison ivy *n.* A common name for *Toxicodendron radicans,* formerly *Rhus toxicodendron,* a deciduous vine. Contact with any part of the plant can cause a severe rash in sensitized people. (See **oak, poison**.)

poison tree *n.* A common name for about 15 species of the genus *Acokanthera,* in the dogbane family. *A. oblongifolia* and *A. oppositifolia* are tropical shrubs with attractive dark green to purplish evergreen leaves and white or pinkish fragrant flowers. All parts of the plant are poisonous.

pokeberry *n.* The fruit of the pokeweed.

poker plant *n.* A common name for 60 or 70 species of *Kniphofia (Tritoma),* perennials in the lily family. They form thick clumps of grasslike leaves,

from which spring tall stems, topped with long, tight clusters of tubular flowers, usually orange-red or yellow. Also known as red hot poker, tritoma, and torch lily.

pokeweed *n.* A common name for a plant of the genus *Phytolacca,* especially *P. americana* of eastern North America. This is a strong-growing, branching herb, bearing clusters of white flowers and deep purple, juicy berries. The young shoots are boiled like asparagus, although other parts of the plant are poisonous. Also called poke, inkberry-weed, and pigeonberry. (See **Phytolacca**.)

Polanisia (pahl uh nihz'ee uh) *n.* A genus of 6 species of annuals (Capparaceae). They somewhat resemble *Cleome* (spider flowers), having white to purplish or pink flowers with clusters of long stamens.

Polanisia

pole bean *n.* Any one of the twining varieties of the common garden bean, requiring the support of a pole.

polecat weed *n.* An alternate name for the skunk cabbages, eastern *Symploccarpus foetidus* and western *Lysichiton camtschatcense* and *L. americanum,* stout perennials in the arum family, with a faint scent of skunk.

Polemoniaceae (pahl uh moh nee ay'see ee) *n.* A family of 18 genera and more than 300 species of annuals or perennials, rarely shrubs or vines; the phlox family. The important cultivated genera are *Cantua, Gilia, Ipomopsis, Leptodactylon, Linanthus, Phlox,* and *Polemonium.*

Polemonium (pahl uh moh'nee uhm) *n.* A genus of 25 species of annuals or perennials (Polemoniaceae), with leaves divided into many leaflets and, usually, clustered blue flowers. *P. caeruleum* (Jacob's ladder or Greek valerian) is a 3-foot perennial with inch-wide clustered flowers. *P. reptans* is a somewhat smaller plant, and *P. carneum* has salmon pink flowers.

Polianthes (pahlee an'thhez) *n.* A genus of 2 species of perennials (Agavaceae). They grow from heavy, short, bulblike rhizomes, with tufted grasslike leaves, and flowers in clusters at the top of naked stalks. *P. tuberosa* is the familiar tuberose, with single or double waxy-white, powerfully fragrant flowers, widely grown in gardens and the florist trade. *P. geminiflora (Bravoa geminiflora)* has pairs of red-orange, downward-facing flowers along its blooming stalk.

pollard (pah'lurd) *n.* A tree cut back nearly to the trunk, and thus caused to form a dense head of spreading branches, which are in turn cut for basket-making and kindling. Willows and poplars especially are pollarded.

pollen *n.* The mass of microspores or grains located on the anthers of seed plants and containing the male gametophytes.

pollenation *n.* Same as pollenization, pollination.

pollen tube *n.* In seed plants, the tube that develops from the wall of the pollen grain, providing a passage for male gametophytes to reach the embryo sac for fertilization.

pollinate *v.* In botany, to convey pollen to the stigma of a plant. Also pollenize.

pollinated *a.* Supplied with pollen.

pollination *n.* In botany, the fertilization of a flowering plant by the transfer of pollen from an anther of a flower to a stigma prepared to receive it.

poly- *comb. form* Many.

polyadelphous stamens

polyadelphous (pahl ee uh dehlf'uhs) *a.* In botany, having the stamens united in 3 or more bundles, as in some species of *Hypericum*.

Polyalthia (pah lee al thee'uh) *n.* A genus of more than 100 species of tropical trees and shrubs (Annonaceae), with thick, leathery-petaled, greenish or reddish brown flowers.

polyandrous (pahl ee an'druhs) *a.* In botany, having many stamens.

polycarpellary (pahl ee kahr'puh leh ree) *a.* In botany, composed of several carpels.

polycarpic (pahl ee kahr'pihk) *a.* In botany, producing fruit many times or indefinitely; having a gynoecium forming 2 or more distinct ovaries or carpels. Also polycarpous.

polycotyledon (pahl ee kahd uh lee'duhn) *n.* A plant having more than 2 cotyledons or seed-leaves, as is normally the case with pines and most conifers.

polycotyledonous *a.* Having more than 2 cotyledons.

polycotyledony (pahl ee kahd uh lee'don nee) *n.* In botany, an aberrant increase in the number of cotyledons, as in *Cola acuminata,* where they vary from 2 to 5.

polyethylene film, air layering with *n.* A method of vegetative propagation in which new roots are encouraged to form around a sliver cut from a plant's stem. Polyethylene film replaces the moist moss traditionally wrapped around a wound to keep it moist.

Polygala (puh lih'guh luh) *n.* A genus of about 500 species of annuals, perennials, and shrubs, rarely trees (Polygalaceae). They have irregularly-shaped, sometimes showy flowers. *P. calcarea,* to 8 inches, with bright, blue flowers, is a rock-garden shrublet, as is *P. chamaebuxus,* with purple and yellow flowers. *P. cowellii* (violeta, violet tree, or tortuguera) is a tropical deciduous tree with showy violet flowers. Tender *P. xdalmaisiana* is a thin, upright shrub with a nearly continuous production of rosy-purplish flowers. *P. paucifolia* is a native wildflower 6 or 7 inches tall, with rosy-purple flowers. Commonly known as milkworts.

Polygalaceae (puh lihg uh lay'see ee) *n. pl.* A family of 10 genera and 1,000 species; the milkwort family. Only *Polygala* is much cultivated.

polygalaceous (puh lihg uh lay'shuhs) *a.* Of or pertaining to the Polygalaceae.

polygamodioecious (puh lihg uh moh digh ee-'shuhs) *a*. Essentially dioecious, but also having some bisexual flowers present in some or all plants.

polygamous (puh lihg'uh muhs) *a*. In botany, bearing both unisexual and bisexual flowers on the same plant or on plants of the same species.

Polygonaceae (puh lihg uh lay'see ee) *n*. A family of 40 genera and about 800 species of annuals, perennials, shrubs, trees, and vines; the buckwheat family. The flowers are without petals, but the sepals may be petallike; the fruit is a small nutlike seed (achene). The important genera are *Eriogonum*, *Fagopyrum*, *Homalocladium*, *Muehlenbeckia*, *Polygonus*, *Rheum*, and *Rumex*.

polygonaceous (pluh lihg uh nay'shuhs) *a*. In botany, pertaining to or belonging to the Polygonaceae.

Polygonatum (pahl ee gahn'uh duhm) *n*. A genus of perennials (Liliaceae). The stems arise from a thickened rootstock and are erect or leaning, with neatly arranged stalkless leaves at regular intervals; in the axils of the upper leaves are nodding, small, white, bell-like flowers in pairs or in larger clusters. *P. biflorum* grows to 3 feet, *P. commutatum* to 6 feet. *P. odoratum thunbergii* 'Variegatum' has leaves bordered with white. The plants are shapely rather than showy, and are good woodland accents. Commonly known as Solomon's-seals.

Polygonum (puh lihg'uh nuhm) *n*. A genus of about 150 species of annuals and perennials (Polygonaceae). The stems appear jointed because of swelling at the leaf nodes; the flowers, usually pink, red, or greenish white, are in drooping clusters or tight heads. *P. affine* is an evergreen ground cover plant to 1½ feet, with 2- to 3-inch spikes of bright rose flowers. *P. amplexicaule* (mountain fleece) is a 3-foot plant, with 6-inch clusters of rose-red or white flowers. *P. aubertii* (silver-lace vine) and *P. baldschuanicum* (Bokhara fleece-vine) are vines; *P. aubertii* has erect clusters of fragrant white flowers, whereas *P. baldschuanicum* has pink clusters. *P. capitatum* is a ground cover for mild climates, with ground-hugging branches topped by round, cloverlike pink flower heads. *P. cuspidatum compactum*, often sold as *P. reynoutria*, is an aggressive ground cover, with reddish-pink flowers. *P. cuspidatum* (Japanese knotweed or Mexican bamboo) is an

8-foot perennial, with 5-inch leaves and small white flowers. *P. orientale* (prince's feather or kiss-me-over-the-garden-gate) is a 6-foot annual, with drooping 3 ½-inch pink flower clusters. *P. sachalinense* (sacaline) is a giant perennial to 12 feet tall, sometimes grown for forage or as a screen; it can become an ineradicable weed. *P. vacciniifolium* is a neat evergreen ground cover with round ¾-inch-long leaves and 3-inch pink flower clusters. Commonly known as knotweed or smartweed.

polygynoecial (pah lee jeh nee'shee uhl) *a*. In botany, having a number of pistils joined together, as in aggregate fruits such as the raspberry.

polygynous (puh lihj'uh nuhs) *a*. In botany, having many styles.

polynutrient fertilizer *n*. A fertilizer that contains more than 1 major plant nutrient.

polymorphic *a*. Occurring in several distinct forms, as leaves on the same plant that have different shapes; polymorphous.

polymorphism *n*. In botany, the capability or tendency to have wide variation in form. Also polymorphy.

polymorphous *a*. Having or assuming many forms. Also polymorphic.

polymorphy *n*. Same as polymorphism.

polypetalous *a*. In botany, having 2 or more separate petals.

Polypodiaceae (pahl ee poh'dee ay see ee) *n. pl*. A family of numbering 180 genera and about 7,000 species of ferns; the polypody family. Most of the well-known temperate ferns are included here, as well as many less familiar tropical genera.

polypodiaceous (pahl ee poh dee ay'shuhs) *a*. Of or pertaining to the Polypodiaceae.

Polypodium (pahl ee poh'dee uhm) *n*. A large genus of tropical and temperate ferns (Polypodiaceae) with creeping, branching rhizomes and stalked fronds that may be simple (tongue- or strap-shaped) or much divided. The best known are the hardy polypodies, soil-, rock-, or tree-dwelling ferns with creeping rhizomes and once-divided evergreen fronds of thickish texture. *P. virginianum* (rock polypody or American wall fern) common in the eastern United States, has 10-inch fronds. *P. californicum, P. glycyrrhiza* (licorice fern) and *P. scouleri* (leathery polypody) are found on the West Coast. Among tropicals, *P. aureum* (rabbit's-foot, hare's-foot, or golden polypody) is a familiar hanging-basket plant, with heavy, brown, surface-creeping rhizomes and coarsely cut fronds, to 4 feet. *P. subauriculatum*, with trailing, finely cut 3-foot fronds has the odd name of jointed pine.

Polypodium vulgare
(polypody)

polypody (pahl'ee poh dee) *n.* A common name for any fern in the genus *Polypodium*, especially *P. vulgare*, the European polypody, wall fern, or adder's fern.

Polypogon (pahl ih poh'gahn) *n.* A genus of 15 to 20 annual and perennial grasses (Gramineae) native to warm temperate regions. *P. monspeliensis* (annual beard grass) is a handsome ornamental grown for its silky flower heads.

Polyscias (pahl ee see'ahs) *n.* A genus of tropical shrubs and trees (Araliaceae). All have divided leaves, some finely divided. *P. balfouriana* (Balfour aralia) to 25 feet but usually much less, has green-and-gray speckled erect stems and leaves with 3 leaflets edged with white. *A. filicifolia* (fern leaf aralia) to 8 feet, has divided leaves with odd shapes, varying from broad to nearly threadlike; it also has white-marked varieties. *P. fruticosa* (Ming aralia) to 8 feet, has its leaves divided and divided again into very narrow segments. *P. guilfoylei* (geranium leaf aralia, wild coffee, or coffee tree) has coarser leaves, the leaflets usually edged white. Generally seen as

large house or tub plants, they survive in the warmest U.S. climates, where they may be used as hedges.

polysporangium (pahl ee spuh ranj'ee uhm) *n., pl.* **sporangia** In botany, a sporangium containing many spores.

polystemonous (pahl ee stee'muh nuhs) *a.* Having many stamens; polyandrous.

Polystichum (puh lihs'teh kuhm) *n.* A genus of 120 species of ferns (Polypodiaceae). The shield ferns include many familiar hardy ferns. *P. acrostichoides* is the familar Christmas fern of the eastern United States. *P. aculeatum* (prickly shield fern or hedge fern) has finely divided leaves. *P. munitum* (western sword fern) is an evergreen to nearly 6 feet tall. The stiff-leaved holly ferns include *P. andersonii, P. braunii, P. dudleyi, P. lonchitis,* and *P. scopulinum. P. setiferum* (hedge fern or English fern) has many named forms.

polytomous (pahl ee duh'muhs) *a.* 1. In botany, divided into more than 2 subordinate parts or branches; pinnatifid.

polytomy (pahl ee duh'mee) *n.* The state of being divided into more than 2 parts.

pomaceous (poh may'shuhs) a. 1. Of, relating to, or typical of apples. 2. Belonging to the family Malaceae. 3. Having the characteristics of a pome.

Pomaderris (poh muh deh'rehs) *n.* A genus of 40 species of tender subtropical shrubs and trees. They grow to 10 to 20 feet, with evergreen, generally downy leaves and greenish-white or (usually) yellow flowers and fruit. Used as ornamentals.

pome (pohm) *n.* The typical fruit of species of *Pyrus, Crataegus,* and certain other members of the rose family. It consists of a fleshy layer surrounding a core containing (usually) 5 seeds within a papery capsule.

pomegranate (pahm'uh gran iht) *n.* 1. The fruit of the tree *Punica Granatum*. It is of the size of an orange and has 6 rounded angles and a hard rind filled with numerous seeds, each enclosed in a layer of red pulp with a pleasant, slightly acid taste. This seed covering is the edible part of the fruit. 2. The tree *Punica Granatum*, which produces the fruit pomegranate. It is now widely cultivated and naturalized in subtropical regions. It grows 15 or 20 feet high, with numerous slender branches, some of them thorny, and with lance-shaped leaves. It is a fine ornamental plant; the flowers are scarlet, large, and sometimes doubled. It thrives in the southern United States and can be grown with moderate protection even in the climate of the middle Atlantic states.

pomegranate

pomiferous (poh mihf′uh ruhs) *a.* Producing pomes.

pomme blanche (pahm blahnsh) *n.* A common name for *Psoralea esculenta,* a very hardy perennial herb. It grows to 1½ feet, with divided leaves and short, dense spikes of yellowish to bluish flowers. Also known as breadroot, Indian turnip, and prairie potato.

pomologist (poh mahl′uh jehst) *n.* A person who is versed in pomology; a cultivator of fruit trees.

pomology (poh mahl′uh jee) *n.* 1. A department of knowledge that deals with fruits; a branch of gardening that embraces the cultivation of fruit trees or fruit-bearing shrubs. Also pomalology.

Poncirus (pahn sigh′ruhs) *n.* A genus with a single species, *P. trifoliata* (Rutaceae), a hardy shrub or small tree. It grows 10 to 12 feet, with thorny branches, leaves of three leaflets, fragrant white flowers, and 2-inch yellow fruit so acid as to be inedible. Used as an impenetrable hedge, as a parent in breeding hardy citrus varieties, or as a rootstock for dwarf citrus. Commonly known as trifoliate orange or hardy orange.

pond apple *n.* A common name for *Annona glabra* (*A. laurifolia*), a tender tropical tree. It grows to 40 feet, with evergreen 7-inch oval leaves and fragrant yellowish flowers marked with red. The large (to

6-inch) fruit is fragrant but of poor quality. Used as rootstock for grafting.

pond dogwood *n.* A common name for a hardy deciduous North American shrub, *Cephalanthus occidentalis.* It grows to 20 feet, with glossy 6-inch leaves and small white flowers in crowded inch-wide clusters. Used as a shrub in landscaping wet places. Also known as buttonbush.

pond spice *n.* A common name for a hardy deciduous shrub, *Litsea aestivalis (L. geniculata).* It grows to 9 feet, with zigzag branching and 2-inch narrow, leathery leaves and inconspicuous yellow flowers, followed by small red fruits. Occasionally used in native shrub plantings.

pondweed *n.* A common name for a variety of hardy aquatic perennials with submerged or floating leaves and (usually) inconspicuous flowers. Many are in the genus *Potamogeton*; *P. natans* is found floating or immersed in ponds and ditches in most parts of the world.

pondweed, Cape *n.* A common name for *Aponogeton distachyus,* a desirable aquarium plant. It has fragrant flowers in forked clusters in the midst of bright green, narrowly oval floating leaves. Also known as water hawthorn.

pondweed, choke *n.* A common name for *Elodea (Anacharis) canadensis,* a freshwater plant native to North America; often an obstruction to boats.

pondweed, horned *n.* A common name for *Zannichellia palustris,* a slender submerged plant widely distributed over the world. So called from the pointed nutlets of the fruit.

pondweed, tassel *n.* A common name for *Ruppia.* Also known as ditch grass.

Pongamia (pahng uh′mee uh) *n.* A genus with 1 species, *P. pinnata (P. glabra)* (Leguminosae), a tropical evergreen tree. It grows to 40 feet, with glossy, aromatic leaves divided into 5 to 7 leaflets and showy cream to purplish pink flowers in 5-inch clusters, followed by woody pods. Used as a street or garden tree. Commonly known as karum tree, poonga-oil tree, or Indian beech.

Pontederia (pahn tuh dih′ree uh) *n.* A genus of several species of hardy aquatic perennials. They grow in shallow water, with long-stalked narrow leaves that rise above the water and blue flowers atop stems that can reach 4 feet. Used as ornamentals in water gardens. Commonly known as pickerel weed.

Pontederiaceae (pahnt uh dih ree ay′see ee) *n. pl.* A family of 6 genera and several species of aquatic or wet-growing herbs. They have oval or roundish leaves and blue, purple, or white flowers. The ornamental genera are *Eichhornia, Heteranthera,* and *Pontederia.*

pool *n.* A small body of water, which may be a focal point in a landscape design and which is the essential element in water gardening.

popcorn *n.* 1. One of several varieties of Indian corn suitable for "popping." They have small ears and kernels, the latter white, yellow, or red, sharp-pointed or not. Popcorn abounds in oil, the expansion of which under heat causes an explosion, in which the contents of the kernel become puffed out, nearly hiding the seed coat, and becoming a pure-white color. 2. Corn thus prepared; popped corn.

poplar (pahp′luhr) *n.* A common name for a number of hardy to very hardy trees in the genus *Populus.* It is also applied loosely to some unrelated plants. Trees of the genus *Populus* are deciduous, with broadly triangular leaves, inconspicuous flowers, and fluffy seeds. Most have brilliant yellow fall color. They grow fast to moderate or great size, producing light, soft wood. Much of the wood is converted into pulp for papermaking. Various species are planted for shade and ornament. The aspens and cottonwoods are true poplars, though not often called by that name.

poplar, balsam (pahp′luhr) *n.* A common name for *Populus balsamifera,* the tacamahack. Also called (especially the variety *candicans*) balm of Gilead.

poplar birch (pahp′luhr) *n.* A common name for *Betula pendula* (B. alba), European white birch.

poplar, Carolina (pahp′luhr) *n.* A common name for *Populus deltoides* 'Carolina', a variety of the eastern cottonwood.

poplar, downy (pahp′luhr) *n.* A common name for *Populus heterophylla,* river- or swamp-cottonwood, a moderate-sized tree of the eastern and southeastern United States.

poplar, silver (pahp′luhr) *n.* A common name for *Populus alba,* white poplar.

poplar, weeping (pahp′luhr) *n.* A common name for the variety *pendula* of *Populus grandidentata,* large-toothed aspen. Both species and variety are used ornamentally.

poppy *n.* 1. A common name for many plants, mostly annuals and perennials but including a few shrubs. 2. A plant of the genus *Papaver.* The poppies are showy herbs, cultivated chiefly in gardens. The opium poppy, *P. somniferum,* is the source of opium, of edible seeds, and of a valuable oil. The opium poppy is a blue-gray, 4-foot-tall plant with wavy leaves. The flowers of garden strains are single or double, to 4 inches wide, and white, pink, red, or purple. The common red poppy, corn poppy, or Flanders poppy is *P. rhoeas.* The petals are deep red or scarlet with a dark eye, or, when doubled, varying in color. The long-headed poppy, *P. dubium,* has smaller flowers of a lighter red, with an elongated capsule. The Iceland poppy, *P. nudicaule,* is a popular perennial much used in mild-winter areas as a winter or early-spring bedding plant. The perennial Oriental poppy, *P. orientale,* the most showy species, has a very large, deep red, pink, salmon, or white flower on a tall stem. 3. Any of several plants belonging to other genera.

poppy
a flowering stem *b* root and lower leaf *c* fruit

poppy, celandine (sehl′uhn dign) *n.* A common name for *Stylophorum diphyllum,* a hardy perennial. It grows to 1½ feet, with lobed leaves and yellow 2-inch flowers. Used in wild or woodland gardens.

poppy, garden *n.* Specifically, the opium poppy.

poppy, horned *n*. A common name for *Claucium*, a genus of annuals, biennials, and perennials. They have finely divided gray-green leaves in a basal rosette and large, single yellow or red flowers with a black blotch at the base of the petals. Usually grown as drought-tolerant annuals. Also known as sea poppy.

poppy mallow *n*. A common name for members of *Callirhoe*, perennials of the mallow family, especially *C. involucrata*, the purple poppy mallow, with stems spreading on the ground, roundish leaves, and purplish-red flowers.

poppy opium *n*. A common name for *Papaver somniferum*, a showy annual. It grows to 4 feet, with coarsely lobed or toothed leaves and large, poppy-like white, red, pink, or purple flowers 4 inches across. The milky sap is the source of the drug opium, and cultivation in the United States in strictly controlled.

poppy, prickly *n*. A common name for *Argemone mexicana*, now widely diffused, often a weed. The pods and leaves are prickly, the latter blotched with white; the flowers are yellow or white. Also commonly known as Mexican poppy. (See **Argemone**.)

poppy, Shirley *n*. A garden strain of *Papaver rhoeas*.

poppy, Welsh *n*. A common name for *Meconopsis cambrica*, a branching perennial (*Papaveraceae*) that grows to 2 feet. The leaves are deeply cut and the 3-inch flowers are yellow or orange. (See **Meconopsis**.)

Populus (pahp′yoo luhs) *n*. A genus of 35 species of hardy to very hardy trees. They grow from 40 to 100 feet or more, with generally triangular leaves, inconspicuous flowers, and small seeds, often tufted with cottony hairs. Used as shade trees, screens and barriers. Commonly known as poplar, aspen, or cottonwood.

pop-up sprinkler heads *n*. Nozzle parts of an irrigation system which are buried in the lawn until the system is turned on and water pressure forces them to rise slightly above the surface.

Porana (poh ran′uh) *n*. A genus of 25 species of tropical vines in the morning-glory family (Convolvulaceae). *P. paniculata* grows to 30 feet, with heart-shaped leaves and small white funnel-shaped flowers in large branching clusters. Used as an ornamental vine. Commonly known as bridal bouquet.

pore *n*. A small, usually circular opening, as in the surface of a leaf.

pore space *n*. The total space within soils that is not occupied by soil particles.

porosity (puh rahs′uh dee) *n*. The degree to which soil mass is permeated with pores or cavities.

porous subsoil (poh′ruhs) *n*. A subsoil in which air between its particles allows water to drain through easily.

Portia tree (por′shuh) *n*. A common name for *Thespesia populnea* (Malvaceae), a tropical tree in the mallow family. It grows to 60 feet, with evergreen heart-shaped leaves and 2-inch yellow flowers, marked with red and fading to orange-yellow. Used as an ornamental tree.

Port Orford cedar *n*. A common name for *Chamaecyparis lawsoniana*, a hardy tree native to northern California and southern Oregon. It grows to more than 100 feet, with tiny scalelike leaves in flattened sprays. Many horticultural varieties are grown. Also sometimes known as Lawson cypress and ginger pine.

Portulaca (por chuh lak′uh) *n*. 1. A genus of 100 or so species of tender annual plants (Portulacaceae) with thick, fleshy leaves and colorful flowers. Used as ornamental bedding plants. *P. oleracea* (purslane), a weed widely scattered throughout temperate regions, is edible and sometimes cultivated as a potherb. 2. A common name for *Portulaca grandiflora*, also called sunplant or rose moss, a popular ornamental with yellow, red, or purple flowers, often very bright and showy. They thrive in bright sunshine. A garden strain offered as Wildfire, with small but brightly colored flowers, is actually *P. umbraticola*.

Portulacaceae (por chuh luh kay′see ee) *n. pl*. A family of 16 genera and 500 species of annuals and perennials (1 shrub) the purslane family. They usually have fleshy leaves and showy flowers.

Portulacaria (por chuh lak′ah ree uh) *n*. A genus of 1 species, *P. afra*, tender subtropical shrub. Widely used outdoors in warm-winter regions, as a houseplant elsewhere. It is sometimes called miniature jade tree because of its small, thick leaves. Also known as purslane tree.

possum haw *n*. (See **Ilex** and **Viburnum**.)

post-hole digger *n*. An implement, often shaped and hinged like a clamshell, which is attached to a long T-handle used to dig small, deep holes for fence posts.

Potamogeton (pahd uh moh jee'tahn) *n*. A genus of 80 to 100 species of hardy water plants. They grow from a few inches to 20 feet, with leaves mostly submerged and inconspicuous flowers and fruit. Used as aquarium or pool plants. Commonly known as pondweed.

potassium *n*. An element used by plants for growth, often present in soil but not in the right form to be absorbed by plant roots unless humus (decayed organic matter) is present.

potato *n*. The tubers (swollen root growths) of the plant *Solanum tuberosum* or the plant itself. The potato is a native of the Andes, particularly in Chile and Peru, and was probably first introduced into Europe by the Spaniards, about the middle of the 16th century. Its progress in Europe was slow, its culture, even in Ireland, not becoming general till the middle of the 18th century; nevertheless, it is now a staple food in most temperate climates. The fruit of the potato plant is a worthless green berry; the plant's useful product is the undergroud tubers, which become much enlarged under cultivation. These tubers, which are of a roundish or oblong shape, sometimes flattish, are set with "eyes," really the beginnings of leaves, containing ordinarily several buds; it is by means of these that the plant is usually propagated. The food value of the potato lies mostly in starch, of which it contains from 15 to 20 or 25%. The tops, called vines, contain a poisonous alkaloid, solanin, absent in the tubers except when exposed to the sun, when they turn green and should not be eaten. To distinguish it from the yellow sweet potato, this plant is sometimes called white potato or Irish potato.

potato hook *n*. A hand tool with bent forklike tines, used for digging potatoes from the ground.

potato planter *n*. An implement for planting seed potatoes and covering them with soil. A planting-share plows a furrow, into which the potatoes are dropped by an automatic device, and a following covering-share turns the soil over them.

potato scoop *n*. A hand-screen in the form of a grated shovel for taking up potatoes that have been dug by a potato digger. The soil sifts through the grating-bars, which detain the tubers.

potato tree *n*. A common name for *Solanum macranthum,* a tender subtropical shrub in the nightshade family.

pot-bound *a*. Said of a plant having an overly extensive system of roots in a too-small pot.

Potentilla (poh tuhn tihl'uh) *n*. A genus of 500 or so species of hardy perennials, annuals, and shrubs (Rosaceae). They have small, roundish flowers, usually yellow or white, a few pink, orange, or red. Many brilliant-flowered perennial or shrubby species are found in cultivation, under the name potentilla. Also known as five-finger or cinquefoil.

Potentilla
(cinquefoil)

Poterium (poh tih'ree uhm) *n*. A genus of about 25 species perennials or small shrubs (Rosaceae), now transferred into *Sanguisorba.* Commonly known as burnet.

pot feet *n. pl*. Small supports placed under pots and planters to raise them off the ground for better drainage and air circulation.

potherb *n*. Any herb or leafy green prepared for food use by boiling or steaming in a pot; particularly, one of which the tops or the whole plant is used.

pot-holder ring *n.* A round metal band, which, when attached to a wall or other structure, holds and supports a clay pot.

Pothos (poh'thahs) *n.* The common or florists' name for *Epipremnum aureum,* a common houseplant with glossy deep green leaves, variegated with yellow. The plant is also known as *Scindapsus aureus* or *Rhaphidophora aurea.*

pot plant *n.* Any plant grown in a pot.

pot stake *n.* (See **plant marker.**)

potted plant *n.* Any plant grown in a container.

potting *n.* In horticulture, the transfer of plants from beds or benches to flowerpots, or from 1 pot to another.

potting bench *n.* A work surface, usually with a storage shelf, used for indoor garden tasks such as seeding and transplanting.

potting shed *n.* A shed or structure in which plants are potted.

potting tray *n.* A low-rimmed, flat container used to hold soil, water, tools, and other materials for planting or transplanting.

pot waterer *n.* An L-shaped wand, with a shut-off valve, which attaches to a hose and is used for misting or watering plants in containers.

poverty plant *n.* A common name for *Hudsonia tomentosa,* a very hardy subshrub. It grows to 8 inches, with tiny scalelike leaves and tiny yellow flowers. Used in dry, sandy places or near the shore. Also known as beach heather.

povertyweed *n.* 1. A common name for *Anaphalis margaritacea,* better known as pearly everlasting. It is attractive in dry roadside or meadow plantings. 2. A common name for *Iva hayesiana,* used in Southern California as a ground cover in dry, difficult situations.

powdery mildew *n.* A fungal disease that causes white or grayish spots or powderylike threads on the new growth of many plants, including roses, photinia, and euonymus. Traditional fungicidal sprays are the most effective controls. Antitranspirant sprays may also help prevent infection.

power mower *n.* (See **rotary lawn mower.**)

power reel mower *n.* A machine for cutting grass. The reel, a cylinder formed of blades mounted on an axis, is powered by a gasoline engine.

power trimmer *n.* A long-bladed electric- or gasoline-powered tool used for cutting hedges or for pruning.

powitch (pow'ihch) *n.* A common name for *Malus fusca,* a hardy ornamental tree to 30 feet, with toothed, sometimes lobed leaves, white flowers, and ½-inch blackish fruit. Also known as Oregon crab apple.

prairie dock *n.* A common name for *Silphium terebinthinaceum,* a coarse, hardy perennial native to the central states, from Canada to the Gulf of Mexico. It grows to 10 feet, with 2-foot-long leaves and yellow daisylike 3-inch flower heads. Also known as prairie burdock.

prairie gentian (jehn'chuhn) *n.* A common name for *Eustoma grandiflorum (Lisianthus),* a hardy annual or biennial flower. It grows to 3 feet, with gray-green leaves and cup-shaped 2-inch flowers of purplish blue. Improved garden strains have larger flowers on shorter plants. Double-flowering forms are now available, as well as pink, white, yellow, and red colors. Excellent cut flowers, but not easy to grow, they are nearly always called lisianthus.

prairie rose *n.* A common name for the native *Rosa setigera,* a very hardy vine. It trails or climbs 6 to 15 feet, with leaves of 3 to 5 leaflets, and clustered 1½ to 3-inch-wide flowers, pink fading to white. Used as a parent to bring cold-hardiness to climbing roses. Also known as Michigan rose.

Pratia (prah'shuh) *n.* A genus of 20 species of low, creeping perennial plants with tiny leaves and 2-lipped flowers in white or blue. *P. angulata* is grown as a ground cover in mild-winter regions; it needs ample moisture and shade in hot summers.

prayer plant *n.* (See **Maranta.**)

praying mantis *n.* A voracious feeding insect that eats many types of insects, both pests and beneficials. It has limited value as a beneficial insect, although its egg casings are sold as such in nurseries and through the mail.

predatory mites *n. pl.* Several species of beneficial insects used to control spider mites and thrips. Harmless to plants. Sold through the mail.

premorse (pree mawrs') *a.* Appearing to be broken off at the end, as a root or stem.

Prenanthes (pree nan'theez) *n.* A genus of 1 species of hardy perennials. It grows to 6 feet, with finely divided leaves and clusters of drooping purple flowers. It is often called rattlesnake root, a name more properly used for *Nabalus serpentaria.*

pretty face *n.* A common name for *Triteleia ixioides (Brodiaea i.),* a semihardy flowering bulb native to California. It has 1 or 2 narrow, grasslike leaves and 2-foot stems bearing a cluster of golden-yellow flowers, striped faintly with brown. Also known as golden brodiaea.

pricking off *n.* A method of transplanting very small seedlings. The blade of a pocket knife or a plant marker is used to remove each tiny plant from 1 spot and to transplant it to another.

pricking out *n.* A method of thinning seedlings by clipping them off at the soil level so as not to disturb the roots of adjoining plants.

prickle *n.* A small spinelike point arising from the bark or epidermis of a plant, rather than from the wood.

prickly *a.* Covered with prickles.

prickly ash *n.* A common name for *Zanthoxylum americanum,* a shrub or small tree, with ashlike leaves, and branches armed with strong prickles. *Z. clava-herculis* (also called prickly ash) is similar.

prickly broom *n.* (See **Ulex.**)

prickly cedar *n.* (See **Juniperus.**)

prickly palm *n.* Same as prickly pole.

prickly pear *n.* The fruit of several species of cacti in the genus *Opuntia,* armed with prickles or nearly smooth. The best fruits come from *O. ficus-indica;* they are roughly egg-shaped, greenish to red and yellow in color, and filled with sweet pulp and many seeds. Also known as Indian fig and, in Spanish-speaking regions, as *tuna.*

prickly pole *n.* A common name for *Bactris guineensis,* a tropical tree to 12 feet, with 3-foot divided leaves on fiercely spiny stalks and small black edible fruit. Also known as Tobago cane.

prickly thrift *n.* A common name for hardy perennials the genus *Acantholimon* in the plumbago family. They grow to under a foot in height, with long, narrow, often spiny, leaves and sprays of pink (rarely white) flowers. Used as rock-garden plants.

pride of Barbados *n.* A common name for *Caesalpinia pulcherrima (Poinciana pulcherrima),* a subtropical or tropical shrub. It grows to 10 feet, with finely divided leaves and large clusters of red and yellow flowers. Used as an ornamental shrub or screening plant. Also known as flower fence and dwarf poinciana.

pride of California *n.* A common name for *Lathyrus splendens,* a tender perennial vine native to extreme southern California. It grows to 10 feet, climbing by tendrils, with divided leaves and showy, 1-inch sweet-pea-shaped flowers in clusters. Sometimes grown in dry landscapes in mild-winter climates.

pride of China *n.* (See **Melia.**)

pride of Ohio *n.* (See **Dodecatheon.**)

primrose *n.* 1. A plant of the genus *Primula,* especially *Primula vulgaris,* in which the flowers appear as if on separate flower stalks. Several other species bear different names, such as auricula, cowslip, oxlip, and polyanthus. 2. Any of several other plants with some resemblance to the primrose.

primrose, bird's-eye *n.* A common name for *Primula farinosa, P. laurentiana,* and *P. mistassinica,* all with silvery leaves and small, yellow-eyed pink or lilac flowers in small clusters.

primrose, Chinese *n.* A common name for *Primula sinensis,* a familiar houseplant.

primrose, drumstick *n.* A common name for *Primula denticulata (P. cashmeriana),* a primrose with dense heads of small purplish, pink (rarely white) flowers.

primrose, English *n.* A common name for *Primula xpolyantha,* widely grown primrose with broad clusters of flowers in white, yellow, orange, pink, red, or blue. Also known as polyanthus.

433

primrose, evening *n.* (See **Oenothera**.)

primrose, fairy *n.* A common name for *Primula malacoides,* a short-lived perennial with white, pink, or purplish flowers on 18-inch stalks. Widely used as a bedding plant in mild-winter regions.

primrose, Himalayan *n.* A common name for *Primula sikkimensis,* a tall (to 3 feet) species, with nodding fragrant yellow flowers.

primrose, Japanese *n.* A common name for *Primula Japonica,* one of the handsomest species, with purplish red, pink, or white flowers unfolding in successive whorls on tall (to 2½-feet) stems.

primrose peerless *n.* A common name for *N. xmedioluteus (N. biflorus)* a narcissus.

Primula (prihm′yuh luh) *n.* A genus of about 130 species of beautiful low-growing perennials (Primulaceae). The leaves form a rosette and the flowers are white, pink, purple, or yellow, usually grouped in clusters or whorls. The common name for several species is primrose.

Primulaceae (prihm′yuh luh see ee) *n. pl.* A family of 20 to 28 genera and 800 to 1,000 species of perennials and annuals. The ornamental genera are *Anagallis, Androsace Cyclamen, Dodecatheon, Primula, Lysimachia,* and *Soldanella.*

primulaceous (prihm yuh lay′shuhs) *a.* Pertaining to or resembling the primrose family, Primulaceae.

prince's-feather *n.* 1. A common name for *Amaranthus hybridus erythrostachys (A. hypochondriacus),* a showy garden annual from tropical America, sometimes 6 feet tall, bearing thick, crowded spikes of small red flowers. The leaves of many garden varieties are intensely colored in shades of yellow, orange, and red. The name sometimes extends to other species of the genus. Also known as Prince-of-Wales'-feather. 2. A common name for *Polygonum orientale,* a 6-foot-tall garden annual with 3-inch spikes of pink flowers. Also called kiss-me-over-the-garden-gate and princess feather.

prince's-plume *n.* A common name for *Stanleya pinnata,* a hardy shrubby perennial. It grows to 5 feet, with narrow leaves and 1-foot-long dense, narrow clusters of yellow flowers. Used as an ornamental in desert regions. Also known as desert plume.

Prinsepia (prihn see′pee yuh) *n.* A genus of 3 or 4 species of very hardy deciduous shrubs related to *Prunus* (Rosaceae). They grow to 6 feet, with spiny stems, oval leaves, small yellow or white blossoms, and a cherrylike fruit. Used occasionally as ornamentals.

Pritchardia (prihch ahr′dee uh) *n.* A genus of 36 species of tropical palms (Palmae). They grow from 15 to 60 feet, according to species, with crowns of large, fan-shaped leaves. Used as landscape plants in tropical regions.

privet *n.* 1. A common name for hardy shrubs or trees in the genus *Ligustrum.* 2. A shrub, *Ligustrum vulgare,* of northern Europe, planted and somewhat naturalized in North America; the common or garden privet, also known as prim.

privet, Amur (ah moo′uhr) *n.* (See **Ligustrum**.)

privet, California *n.* (See **Ligustrum**.)

privet, swamp *n.* (See **Forestiera**.)

privet, Texas *n.* A common name for *Ligustrum japonicum,* often sold as *L. texanum.*

privet, waxleaf *n.* A common name for *Ligustrum japonicum.*

Proboscidea (proh buh sihd′ee uh) *n.* A genus of 9 species of tender annuals (Martyniaceae). *P. louisianica* is the species commonly grown. They grow to 2 feet tall, with roundish leaves up to a foot wide. The 2-inch flowers are white to violet, and the fruit is a capsule with a long beak, which splits on drying. The young, fleshy fruits are pickled like cucumbers; the dry, mature pods are used in decorative dried arrangements. Commonly known as unicorn plant or proboscis flower.

process *n.* In botany, an organic structure arising from the surface of a plant or plant part, as a spine on a stem.

procumbent *a.* In botany, trailing or lying flat without taking root

productivity *n.* The present capability of a kind of soil for producing a specified kind of plant.

profile *n.* A vertical section of the soil through all its layers.

propagating bench *n.* In horticulture, a stationary shallow box, usually filled with fine sand, but sometimes with earth, which is kept moist, and into which cuttings or slips are inserted until they have taken root. A propagating bench is usually placed so that heat can be applied beneath it.

propagating box *n.* In horticulture, a shallow wooden box or pan, properly movable (compare propagating bench), for holding slips and cuttings in sand. It is usually placed over the hot flues or water pipes in a shady part of a plant house, or on the sand bed in a propagating house. Sometimes the cuttings in the box are covered with a propagating glass.

propagating glass *n.* In horticulture, a bell glass used to cover cuttings or seedlings in a hotbed, nursery, or garden.

propagating house *n.* In horticulture, any greenhouse especially adapted or used for the propagation or increase of plants from cuttings, or for growing them from the seeds.

propagation *n.* The act of propagating; the multiplication or continuance of the kind or species by natural generation or reproduction, as the propagation of plants or animals. In the greater number of flowering plants propagation is effected naturally by means of seeds, but many plants are also propagated by the production of runners or lateral shoots, which spread along the surface of the soil and root at the joints, from which they send up new stems. Plants are also propagated by suckers rising from rootstocks and by various other natural means. Propagation may be effected artificially by cuttings, grafting, budding, inarching, etc.

propagation chamber *n.* (See **propagator**.)

propagator *n.* A compartment consisting of a tray and clear top, similar to a miniature greenhouse, designed to provide proper light and humidity for starting seedlings, rooting leaves or stem cuttings, starting tubers, and handling transplants. Also known as a propagation chamber.

propagule (prah puh'gyool) *n.* In botany, a shoot, such as a runner or sucker, which may be used for propagation.

prophet flower *n.* A common name for *Arnebia griffithii, A. echioides,* and *Echioides longiflorum.* (See **Arnebia**.)

prophyllum (proh fihl'uhm) *n.* 1. A secondary bract on a flower stalk. 2. A 2-edged initial bract on the flowering part of a plant.

propoxur (proh pahks'er) *n.* A broad-spectrum insecticide (common trade name: Baygon) used against many household pests and some garden pests, including earwigs.

Proserpinaca (proh suhr puh nay'kuh) *n.* A genus of about 4 species of tender aquatic perennials (Haloragaceae). They grow to 2 or 3 feet, with insignificant flowers. *P. palustris* and *P. pectinata* are sometimes used as aquarium or pool plants. Commonly known as mermaid weed.

Prosopis (pruh soh'pehs) *n.* A genus of about 25 species of hardy or semihardy shrubs and trees (Mimosoicdeae). They grow to 30 feet, with leaves twice divided into tiny leaflets and abundant small yellow flowers in tight clusters. Used as a shade or landscape tree in desert regions and as range food for animals. Commonly known as mesquite.

Prosopis
(mesquite)
a flowering branch and leaves *b* pod

Prostanthera (pruh stan'thuh ruh) *n.* A genus of more than 50 species of tender subtropical shrubs (Labiatae). They grow from 2 to 30 feet or more, according to species, with small, usually highly aromatic leaves and a profusion of 2-lipped flowers in white, shades of blue or purple, rarely red or yellow. Used as landscape plants in warm-winter regions, especially the purple (rarely pink) *P. rotundifolia.* Commonly known as mintbush.

prostrate *a.* Lying flat on the ground.

Protea (proh'dee uh) *n.* A genus of about 100 species of subtropical shrubs (Proteaceae). Some are low prostrate, whereas others grow to 20 feet or more, with leathery evergreen leaves and threadlike flowers, but crowded into dense heads surrounded by showy colored bracts, somewhat resembling giant thistles. Used as ornamental shrubs in warm-winter regions; flower heads are common as cut flowers. *P. cynaroides* (king protea), with 8-inch pink to red flower heads, and *P. grandiceps* (peach protea), with 6-inch peach pink to red heads, are the best known.

Protea

Proteaceae (proh dee ay'see ee) *n. pl.* A family of 55 genera and about 1,200 species of shrubs and trees. They have usually alternate leaves and flowers in clusters, sometimes in tightly clustered heads. The many ornamental genera include *Banksia, Embothrium, Grevillea, Hakea, Leucodendron, Leucospermum, Macadamia, Protea,* and *Telopea.*

protective collar *n.* Some type of physical devise that encircles the trunk or stem of a plant to exclude pests.

protective netting *n.* A mesh material used to discourage birds and other animals from harming berries, bushes, trees, shrubs, and vines or used as a winter wrap over a trellis.

proteranthous (prah duh ran'thuhs) *a.* Having flowers that appear before the leaves of a deciduous plant, as in *Jacaranda mimosifolia* and many species of *Prunus.*

prothallium (proh thal'ee uhm) *n., pl.* **prothallia.** The gametophyte stage of ferns and certain other related plants, consisting of a small structure attached to the soil and containing the sexual organs.

protogynous (prohd uh jigh'nuhs) *a.* Of a flower, having the stigma mature before the anthers.

protogyny (proh tah'juh nee) *n.* The condition of having the stigma mature before the anthers.

Provence rose *n.* A common name for *Rosa centifolia* and its descendants, hardy shrubs with divided leaves and (usually) double, fragrant flowers in pink, red, and white. Also spelled Provins rose. They are also known as cabbage roses or Centifolia roses, and include also the moss roses.

pruinose (proo'uh nohs) *a.* Having a frosty appearance due to a bloom or powder on the surface; said of certain plant surfaces, such as the undersides of leaves, or the surface of grapes or blueberries.

prune *n.* 1. A plum suitable to be dried. 2. The dried fruit of 1 of several varieties of the common plum tree. There is a large production of prunes in California. Prunes are often stewed as a sauce and are valued for their nutritious (a source of iron) and laxative properties.

Prunella (proo nehl'uh) *n.* A genus of 4 species of sprawling perennials (Labiatae). They have erect flowering stems, and spread by tough underground rootstocks. They have simple or deeply cut leaves and flowers that are crowded in a dense spike. The names are often confused by commercial growers. *P. vulgaris* is the common wild plant with deep purple flowers. *P. grandiflora* has purple flowers in 2-inch spikes; there are also pink and white forms, sometimes offered as *P. webbiana.* A plant sold as *P. laciniata* is probably *P. grandiflora* 'Pinnatifida', used in rock gardens, as foreground perennials, or as a ground cover. Also known as self-heal.

pruner *n.* Any of various heavy-duty scissors for lopping or cutting off stems or small branches up to ¾ inch in diameter. Loppers are used to cut larger-diameter branches.

prune tree *n*. A common name for a plum tree that bears fruit sufficiently high in sugar to dry without spoiling.

pruning *n*. The act of trimming or lopping off what is superfluous; specifically, the act of cutting off branches or parts of trees and shrubs with a view to strengthening those that remain or to bringing the tree or plant into a desired shape. Root pruning is also practiced with a spade or otherwise in order to control size, promote fruitfulness, or secure a growth of fibrous roots near the stem prior to transplanting.

pruning chisel *n*. A chisel used for pruning trees. It is often made with a concave cutting edge, as a safeguard against slipping.

pruning hook *n*. A knife with a hooked blade, used for pruning trees, vines, etc.

pruning knife *n*. A knife used for pruning; a cutting tool with a curved blade for pruning; a pruning hook.

pruning saw *n*. An implement having a toothed, curved blade, used for cutting branches.

pruning seal *n*. (See **tree paint**.)

pruning shears *n*. Heavy-duty scissors used to cut unwanted twigs, branches, or roots. Pruning shears cut smaller diameter branches, typically up to ¾ inch; lopping shears cut larger branches.

Prunus (proo'nuhs) *n*. A genus of more than 400 species of trees and shrubs (Rosaceae), mainly natives of north temperate regions. They are usually small trees, sometimes shrubs, with white, pink, or rose-colored (generally showy) flowers, in clusters or sometimes singly, and fleshy fruit containing a single hard seed or stone. Many of the most valuable fruit trees belong here, including the peach, apricot, cherry, almond, and plum. Nearly all parts contain the elements of prussic acid, rendering the kernels and bark (and the wilted leaves of some species) poisonous if eaten freely.

Pseuderanthemum (soo duh ran'thuh muhm) *n*. A genus of 60 species of tropical perennials or shrubs (Acanthaceae). *P. atropurpureum* grows to 4 feet, with 6-inch purple or metallic-green leaves and 6-inch spikes of white flowers. Used as a houseplant or conservatory plant. Commonly known as purple false eranthemum.

pseudobulb *n*. A fleshy enlargement resembling a bulb at the base of the stem, as in many epiphytic orchids.

pseudocarp (soo'doh kahrp) *n*. A fruit, such as an apple or a strawberry, which consists largely of tissue other than the ripened ovary.

pseudocarpous (soo'doh kahrp'uhs) *a*. In botany, producing pseudocarps.

Pseudolarix (soo doh'lah rihks) *n*. A genus of a single species *P. kaempferi (P. amabilis, Chrysolarix)* (Pinaceae) a hardy tree. It grows to more than 100 feet, with clustered soft, needlelike, bright green leaves that turn to yellow before dropping in the fall and 3-inch-long drooping cones. Used as an ornamental tree. Commonly known as golden larch.

Pseudopanax (soo doh pay'naks) *n*. A genus of about 10 species of tender subtropical shrubs or small trees (Araliaceae). They have evergreen leaves, often displaying remarkably different forms during different life stages, large clusters of flowers, and small black drupelike (berrylike, with a single seed) fruits. Grown in California as container or garden plants.

Pseudosasa (soo doh sah'suh) *n*. A genus of 3 species (Gramineae). *P. japonica*, a running bamboo of moderate spreading habit, grows to 15 feet, with stems to ¾ inch in diameter and evergreen leaves to 13 inches long, 1½ inches wide. One of the hardier bamboos, it grows as far north as New York. Commonly known as arrow bamboo.

pseudospermium (soo doh spuhr'mee uhm) *n*. In botany, any 1-seeded fruit that is whole at maturity, as in the sunflower.

pseudospermous *a*. Pertaining to or resembling a pseudospermium.

Pseudotsuga (soo doht soo'guh) *n*. A genus of 5 species of hardy pine trees (Pinaceae). They have flattened, needlelike leaves, about 1 inch long. Used as timber trees, occasionally as park or ornamental trees. *P. macrocarpa* (big cone spruce), is a 70-foot tree native to the mountains of southern California. *P. menziesii* (Douglas fir) is widely distributed throughout the West; it grows to nearly 300 feet and is 1 of the most important timber trees of North America.

Psidium (sihd'ee uhm) *n*. A genus of about 100 species of subtropical and tropical shrubs and trees (Myrtaceae). They grow 25 to 30 feet, with simple-oval or long-oval evergreen leaves and white flowers. The best-known species have edible fruit known as guavas. *P. guajava* (common guava) has fruit to 4 inches long, with pink or yellow flesh. *P. litorale* has 2 varieties, yellow guava and strawberry guava, with red fruits. These are somewhat hardier than *P. guajava*.

Psoralea (suh ray'lee uh) *n*. A genus of 130 or so species of hardy or tender perennials or shrubs (Leguminosae). The leaves are divided into leaflets, the flowers are usually clustered, and the fruits are 1-seeded pods. *P. esculenta* (pomme-de-prairie, pomme blanche, prairie turnip, and prairie apple) is a perennial 1½ feet, with yellowish to bluish flowers and an edible tuberous (potatolike) root. *P. pinnata* is a tender shrub to 12 feet with very narrow evergreen leaflets and clusters of blue and white flowers. The plant looks like a small pine tree, and the flowers smell like grape soda. Some species are commonly known as scurfy peas.

Psychotria (sigh koh'tree uh) *n*. A genus of about 700 species of tropical shrubs (Rubiaceae). They have evergreen leaves and clustered white, yellow, or red flowers. Commonly known as wild coffee.

psyllid (sihl'ihd) *n*. A small flylike insect that feeds on the foliage and buds of a variety of plants, causing distorted, cupped foliage and leaf drop. The pear psyllid is one of the most damaging, releasing a toxin or virus, while feeding, which can kill plants. Sometimes accompanied by honeydew and sooty mold or leaf galls. Dormant oil sprays, sulfur, and insecticidal soaps are effective controls on fruit trees; otherwise, traditional pesticides are used.

Psylliostachys (sihl ee oh stahk'uhs) *n*. A genus of 7 or 8 species of annuals (Plumbaginaceae), with a rosette of leaves growing close to the ground, and long (to 1½ feet), thin spikes of tiny pink flowers. The spikes are useful for cutting and drying. Also sold as *Limonium* or *Statice suworowii*.

Pteles (tehl'eez) *n*. A genus of 3 species of hardy trees (Rutaceae). They grow 20 to 25 feet, with aromatic, deciduous leaves of 3 leaflets and inconspicuous flowers followed by clusters of dry, flat, winged fruits. Sometimes used as ornamental trees in shady places. *P. trifoliata* is commonly known as stinking ash, water ash, or hop tree.

pteridologist (tehr uh dahl'uh jehst) *n*. A person who is versed in the study of ferns.

pteridology (tehr uh dahl'uh jee) *n*. The science of ferns; a treatise on ferns.

pteridophyte (tuh rihd'uh fight) *n*. A fern or fern ally such as plants of the genus *Equisetum*.

Pteris (teh'rehs) *n*. A genus of 250 or more species of hardy to tender perennial ferns (Polypodiaceae). The most common are *P. cretica* (Cretan brake), which grows to 1½ feet, and has many varieties, some variegated or crested; and *P. tremula* (Australian brake), which grows to 6 feet and is occasionally grown in mild-winter gardens. Many are used as ornamentals in the landscape or as houseplants. Commonly known as brakes.

Pteris
(brake fern)

pterocarpous (tehr uh kahr'puhs) *a*. In botany, having winged fruit.

Pterocarpus (teh ruh kahr'puhs) *n*. A genus of 100 or so species of tropical trees (Leguminosae). They grow from 40 to 80 feet, with finely divided leaves, showy flowers, and flat pods. *P. indicus* (Padauk or Burmese rosewood) is an 80-foot tree with red, black-striped wood; *P. santalinus* (red sandalwood) has fragrant red wood. Used as timber or as a source of dye. Commonly known as padauk or rosewood.

Pterocarya (teh ruh kah′ree uh) *n.* A genus of 10 species of deciduous hardy trees. They grow to 100 feet, with divided leaves, inconspicuous flowers, and long (to 1½ foot) strings of winged nutlets. Used as shade or landscape trees. Commonly called wingnut.

Pterocephalus (teh′ruh sehl uh luhs) *n.* A genus of 20 species of hardy perennials (Dipsaceae). *P. parnassii* grows to 3 or 4 inches, with tufts of 1½-inch leaves and tight clusters of purplish-pink flowers.

Pterospermum (teh′ruh spuhr′muhm) *n.* A genus of 25 species of tropical trees (Byttneriaceae). *P. acerifolium* grows to 100 feet, with roundish leaves a foot or more across, and large white solitary flowers. Sometimes used as an ornamental tree.

Ptychosperma (tigh koh spuhr′muh) *n.* A genus of tropical trees (Palmae or Arecaeae). *P. elegans* (Alexander or solitaire palm) grows to 36 feet with 7- to 8-foot-long feathery divided leaves. *P. macarthurii* is a slender, smooth-stemmed palm to 20 feet, with arched, feathery fronds to 6 feet. All are elegant palms used as ornamentals in tropical and subtropical regions.

puberulent (pyoo ber′yuh luhnt) *a.* In botany, covered with fine, short down.

pubescence *n.* In botany: 1. A covering of down or hair, as on the surface of a leaf. 2. The state of having such a covering.

pubescent *a.* In botany, fuzzy; covered with down or hairs, as the leaves of the African violet.

puccoon (puh koon′) *n.* A common name for *Sanguinaria canadensis:* bloodroot, also called red puccoon. (See **bloodroot**.) 2. A common name for 1 of 3 or 4 American species of *Lithospermum*, with bright golden-yellow flowers. (See **Lithospermum**.)

puddled soil *n.* Dense, massive soil, artificially compacted when wet, a common result of tillage of clayey soil when it is wet.

Pulmonaria (puhl muh nah′ree uh) *n.* A genus of 12 species of hardy perennials (Boraginaceae). They grow from creeping rhizomes, with basal leaves, often spotted or hairy, small stem leaves and flowers in slender clusters. *P. angustifolia* grows to 1 foot, with green leaves and blue (rarely pink or white) flowers. *P. montana* has purple or reddish flowers; *P. officinalis* has white-spotted leaves and blue or violet flowers. Used as garden perennials in shady places. Commonly known as lungwort or Jerusalem sage.

Pulsatilla (puhl suh tihl′uh) *n.* A genus of 30 species of hardy perennials (Ranunculaceae), often grouped with *Anemone*. They spring from a woody rootstock, with a rosette of hairy, finely cut leaves immediately below the large flowers, which ripen into seeds crowned with feathery tufts. Many species bloom in early spring in the mountains or plains. The most common is *P. vulgaris*, with 3-inch flowers of violet to white. All are commonly known as pasqueflower.

pulse *n.* 1. The edible seeds of cultivated leguminous plants such as peas, beans, and lentils. 2. Any of the various plants that produce pulse.

Pultenaea (puhl tuh′nee ee) *n.* A genus of about 100 species of tender sub-tropical or tropical shrubs (Leguminosae). They grow to 6 feet, with small, narrow evergreen leaves and clustered yellow or yellow-and-red pea-shaped flowers. Grown as ornamental shrubs in subtropical climates. Often known as bacon-and-eggs.

pulverant (puhl′vuhr uhnt) *n.* A term applied to ungranulated fertilizers that are largely powdered.

pulvinate (puhl′vuh nayt) *a.* In botany, cushion-shaped.

pummelo (puh′muhl oh) *n.* A common name for *Citrus maxima (C. grandis)*, a subtropical or tropical tree. It grows to 30 feet, with glossy evergreen leaves and fragrant white flowers, followed by large, thick-skinned, yellow, edible fruit. It is an ancestor of the grapefruit. Used as a fruit tree in mild-winter regions. Also known as pomelo, pumelo, or shaddock.

pumpkin *n.* The fruit of varieties of 3 species of *Cucurbita;* also, the plant that produces it. The plant is a coarse vine, often many feet long; the leaves are heart-shaped and nearly 1 foot across, and rough and almost prickly, as are also their hollow stalks. The fruit is nearly globular or somewhat oblong, flattened at the ends, 1 foot or more in length, and of a deep orange-yellow color when ripe. Inside, it is partly filled with a dryish, stringy pulp containing the seeds; the fleshy layer, 1 or 2 inches thick, is beneath the rind. It is thought to have been known to the native Americans and to have been planted by them among their maize. It is grown for table use, especially in pumpkin pie, and for ornamental use, especially for carved jack-o'-lanterns.

pump sprayer *n.* A device for applying pesticides, herbicides, fertilizers, or other liquids to plants. It consists of a 1- to 2- foot-tall tank and a wand with a nozzle. After the liquid is mixed in the tank, air is pumped into it. Also called a compression sprayer.

punctate *a.* In botany, having the surface marked with dots, points, or pits.

Punica (pyoo'neh kuh) *n.* A genus of 1 species, *P. granatum,* a deciduous small tree or large shrub with orange-scarlet flowers and edible, leathery-skinned fruit, full of seeds encased in bright red, juicy, flavorful acid pulp. Several varieties are grown for fruit, wheareas others are purely ornamental, including dwarf and double-flowering kinds and at least 1 with yellow and red double flowers, 'Mme. Legrelle'. Commonly known as pomegranate

Punicaceae (pyoo nuh kay'see) *n.* A family of 1 genus and 1 species, *Punica granatum,* the pomegranate family.

punk oak *n.* (See **Quercus**.)

punk tree *n.* (See **Melaleuca**.)

purging cassia (kash'uh) *n.* A common name for *Cassia fistula* or its fruit. (See **Cassia**.)

purple moor grass *n.* (See **Molinia**.)

purple wreath *n.* (See **Petrea**.)

Purshia (puhr'shee uh) *n.* A genus of 2 species of very hardy shrubs (Rosaceae). They grow 10 to 12 feet with small, crowded 3-sectioned leaves, and small cream-to-yellow flowers. Useful as browse in arid western states. Commonly known as antelope bush.

purslane (pers'layn) *n.* A common name for *Portulaca oleracea,* a wild herb (rarely cultivated), widely distributed through warm and temperate climates. It is a low-growing annual of a reddish-green color, with fleshy stems and leaves and with small yellow flowers. Purslane is used, now less than formerly, as a potherb and is cultivated in Europe in several varieties for this purpose. In America, it is regarded chiefly as a weed and is rather troublesome in gardens because of its abundance and persistence.

purslane family (puhrs'layn) *n.* A common name for Portulacaceae, a family of 16 genera and 500 species of annuals, perennials, or subshrubs, often with fleshy leaves and attractive flowers. Some ornamental genera are *Calandrinia, Claytonia, Lewisia, Portulaca, Portulacaria,* and *Talinum.*

Puschkinia (push kihn'ee uh) *n.* A genus of 1 species, *P. scilloides* (Liliaceae), a very hardy flowering bulb with 2 or 3 narrow, strap-shaped basal leaves and pale blue flowers, striped deeper blue, in slender, 8-inch clusters.

push lawn mower *n.* A hand-powered machine, generally of the reel type, used for cutting grass.

push-pull hoe *n.* (See **oscillating hoe**.)

pussy-ears *n.* A common name for *Calochortus tolmiei, Cyanotis somaliensis,* and *Kalanchoe tomentosa.*

pussy willow *n.* A common name for *Salix discolor.* The name is also applied to other species of *Salix* with furry catkins. (See **Salix**.)

pustular (pus'tu lar) *a.* In botany, having bumps, as though blistered.

pustule (pus'tyul) *n.* A raised area or bump.

Putoria (pyoo toh'ree uh) *n.* A genus of 3 species of small shrubs (Rubiaceae). *P. calabrica* grows to 8 inches, with narrow ½-inch- long leaves and dense clusters of pink flowers at the ends of sprawling branches. Sometimes grown in rock gardens where frosts are not severe.

puttyroot *n.* A common name for *Aplectrum hiemale.* (See **Aplectrum**.)

Puya (poo'yuh) *n.* A genus of 168 species of subtropical or tropical perennials (Bromeliaceae). Unlike most bromeliads, they are terrestrial, and most grow in dry climates. Some are of huge size, with rosettes of spine-edged leaves and showy flowers in spikes or spikelike clusters. *P. berteroniana* has 6-foot spikes of greenish blue flowers. Occasionally planted in parks or botanic gardens in mild climates.

Pycnanthemum (pihk-nan'the mum) n. A genus of 20 species of hardy perennials in the Mint family (Labiatae). They grow to 3 feet, with aromatic leaves and whitish or purplish flowers. Commonly known as mountain mint.

Pycnostachys (pihk noh stah'kuhs) n. A genus of 35 species of tropical perennials (Labiatae). They grow to 6 feet, with narrow, usually toothed leaves and spikes of bright blue flowers. Grown in greenhouses or tropical gardens.

Pyracantha (pigh ruh kan'thuh) n. A genus of 6 species of hardy shrubs (Rosaceae). They grow to 15 feet, with thorny branches, evergreen leaves, clustered white flowers, and a profusion of red or orange-red (rarely yellow) fruit. Many named varieties are in the nursery trade; some are low enough to be used as ground covers, whereas others are tall. Their spines make them a useful barrier, and their fruits are showy well into winter.

pyrene (pigh'reen) n. A nutlet within a drupe, such as the seed of a peach enclosed in its pit.

pyrenocarp (pi re'no karp) n. In botany, a stone fruit, or drupe, such as the peach or cherry.

pyrethrins (pigh reeth'rihnz) n. pl. Naturally occurring chemicals extracted from seeds of the pyrethrum daisy, *Tanacetum cinerariifolium,* and used in various insecticides.

pyrethroids (pigh reeth'roidz) n. pl. Synthetic pyrethrins.

Pyrethropsis (pigh ree thrahp'suhs) n. A genus of 10 or so perennials or small shrubs (Compositae). They have finely divided, silvery leaves and daisy-like pinkish, purplish, yellow, or white flowers. *P. gayana,* to 18 inches, has white daisies with pink undersides; *P. hosmariense* has white flowers. Used in rock gardens or perennial borders where winters are mild.

pyrethrum (pigh ree'thruhm) n. 1. An insecticide prepared from the powdered flowers of *Tanacetum cinerariifolium,* formerly *Chrysanthemum* or *Pyrethrum.* Relatively nontoxic to humans. 2. Any plant in the former genus *Pyrethrum,* now merged into other genera. The most commonly known by that name was the painted daisy, formerly *Pyrethrum coccineum,* now *Tanacetum coccineum.*

pyriform (pigh rih'form) a. Pear-shaped.

Pyrola (pigh roh'luh) n. A genus of 15 species of hardy perennials (Pyrolaceae). They are creeping evergreen plants, with erect stems to 1 to 1½ feet tall, with shiny leaves and small white or pink flowers. Woodland plants, they are difficult to grow and propagate. Commonly known as wintergreen and shinleaf.

Pyrolaceae (pigh roh lay'see ee) n. A family of 10 or 12 genera and 40 species of woodland perennial plants; the wintergreen family (sometimes included in the heath family, Ericaceae). The ornamental genera are *Chimaphila, Moneses,* and *Pyrola.*

Pyrrosia (pih roh'see uh) n. A genus of 100 or so species of mostly tropical epiphytic ferns with undivided leathery fronds. *P. lingua* (Japanese felt fern) is hardy out of doors in California and similar climates. It has creeping rhizomes (swollen root growths) and erect, leathery fronds to 15 inches long. Used as a pot or hanging-basket plant (especially in its crested or monstrose forms), rarely as a ground cover.

Pyrus (pigh'ruhs) n. A genus of about 20 species of hardy trees (Rosaceae). It includes the fruiting pears (*P. communis* and hybrids of this and *P. pyrifolia*); Asian pears (*P. pyrifolia*); and several species grown as ornamental trees. All have glossy foliage and masses of white flowers. *P. kawakamii* (evergreen pear) is evergreen in most winters in mild climates and blooms in or around midwinter. *P. calleryana* (callery pear) is a favored street tree, especially in its named varieties 'Aristocrat', 'Bradford', 'Capital', and 'Whitehouse'. It has white flowers followed by shiny, leathery foliage that turns purplish-red before falling. *P. salicifolia* (willow-leafed pear) has narrow, silvery leaves; a weeping form, 'Pendula', is a handsome yard tree.

pyxidate (pihks'uh dayt) a. In botany, having the characteristics of a pyxis.

pyxis (pihks'ehs) n., pl. **pyxides** In botany, a fruit, usually a capsule, whose top pops off at maturity and falls away like a lid, as in the common purslane.

quail bush *n.* A common name for *Atriplex lentiformis,* a tender, spreading, sometimes spiny, shrub native to southwestern North America. It grows to 3 to 10 feet high and 6 to 12 feet wide, with small oval blue or silvery leaves and flowers and seeds that attract birds. Used in desert gardens and seashore gardens as a hedge or windbreak. Tolerates salt air and alkaline soils and is fire-retardant. Also known as white thistle and lens-scale.

Quaker-ladies *n.* A common name for 2 different plants, *Centaurea cyanis* (cornflower) and *Hedyotis caerulea* (bluets). (See **Centaurea** and **Hedyotis**.)

quamash (kwuh mahsh') *n.* (See **camas** and **Camassia**.)

quarantine *n.* 1. A restraint placed upon the transport of plants or plant products suspected of harboring diseases or pests. 2. A place where imported plants suspected of carrying diseases are held.

quartervine *n.* A common name for *Bignonia capreolata,* a fairly hardy climbing evergreen vine native to the eastern United States. It grows to 50 feet, with oval, pointed, entire leaves, some with terminal tendrils, and clusters of yellow-to-red trumpet-shaped flowers 2 inches long. Used as a wall cover. Also known as crossvine and trumpet flower.

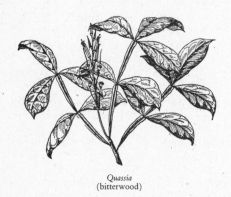

Quassia
(bitterwood)

Quassia (kwahsh'ee uh) *n.* A genus of 1 species, *Q. amara* (Simaroubaceae), a tropical American shrub or small tree. It grows to 25 feet, with alternate leaves divided into oval leaflets and showy spikes of crimson flowers 2 inches long. Used in frost-free gardens. Commonly known as bitterwood and Surinam quassia.

quebracho (kay bra'choh) *n.* A common name for *Pithecellobium arboreum,* a tropical tree native to Mexico, Central America, and the West Indies. It grows to 60 feet, with leaves divided into many leaflets and with spikes of small white flowers and red cylindrical pods. Used in frost-free gardens.

Queen Anne's lace *n.* A common name for *Daucus carota carota,* a hardy biennial flower (actually a wild carrot escaped in North America from colonist's vegetable gardens). It grows to 3 feet, with finely cut fernlike leaves and large clusters of tiny white flowers, giving the effect of a delicate lace. Considered a wildflower, it self-sows too readily to be welcome except in very large meadow gardens - and maybe not even there. Also known as wild carrot, queen's-lace, and devil's-plague.

queen of the meadow *n.* A common name for several different plants including the genus *Spirea* (See **bridal wreath**), *Eupatorium purpureum* (See **Joe-Pye weed**) and *Filipendula ulmaria. F. Ulmaria* is a hardy perennial flower that has naturalized in eastern North America. It grows to 6 feet, with huge (8 feet long) alternate fernlike leaves divided into oval, pointed leaflets and a 3-lobed terminal leaflet. It has feathery, plumelike clusters of tiny white flowers. Useful in the hardy border.

queen of the night *n.* A common name for *Selenicereus grandiflorus,* a spiny West Indian climbing cactus with 1-inch wide stems. It climbs or drapes to 15 feet, with needlelike spines and large night-blooming white flowers 7 to 10 inches across. Easy to grow in hanging baskets in frost-free gardens.

queen of the prairie *n.* A common name for *Filipendula rubra,* native to the eastern United States. It grows to 8 feet, has alternate, divided fernlike leaves, and showy plumes of deep peach-blossom-pink flowers. It is useful in meadow gardens or at the back of borders.

queen's-delight *n.* A common name for *Stillingia sylvatica,* a fairly hardy subshrub native to the eastern United States. It grows from a woody rhizome to 2 feet, with oval, alternate green or red leaves and spikes of yellow flowers without petals. Also known as queen's-root.

queen's-flower *n.* A common name for *Lagerstroemia speciosa,* a tender deciduous flowering tree. It grows to 80 feet, with oval leaves and clusters of white or purple flowers. Grown for its showy masses of bloom in frost-free gardens. Also known as pride-of-India.

Queensland nut *n.* A common name for the tropical edible nut macadamia. (See **Macadamia**.)

Queensland pittosporum (peh thas'puh ruhm) *n.* A common name for *Pittosporum rhombifolium,* a tender shrub or tree. It grows 15 to 35 feet, with glossy, nearly diamond-shaped rich green, leaves, clusters of small white flowers, and clusters of yellow-to-orange fruit. Used as a patio or lawn tree or as an informal screen.

quercitron (kwuhr'sih truhn) *n.* A common name for *Quercus velutina,* a very hardy deciduous tree native to the eastern United States, from Maine to Texas. It grows to 100 feet, with large, lobed dark green leaves, catkins, and acorns. Also known as black oak and yellow-barked oak.

Quercus (kwuhr'kuhs) *n.* A genus of 450 species of deciduous or evergreen trees (Fagaceae); the oaks. They grow from scrubsize to handsome, spreading trees, depending on the species, typically with lobed or toothed leaves, catkins, and acorns. The deciduous varieties often provide brilliant fall color. Used as shade trees, specimen trees, and street trees. Commonly known as oak.

quick-acting fertilizer *n.* A fertilizer that forces plants into quick growing spurts.

quickbeam *n.* A common name for *Sorbus Aucuparia,* a very hardy deciduous tree. It grows to 60 feet, with long, fernlike leaves divided into oval, finely toothed leaflets that turn yellow, orange, or red in autumn; it bears clusters of small white flowers and large bunches of round, scarlet berries that attract birds all through winter. A good small garden or street tree, it tolerates extremes of temperature, strong winds, and low humidity. Also known as European mountain ash and rowan tree.

quick-connect hose system *n.* (See **snap adapter**.)

quick-in-the-hand *n.* A common name for *Impatiens pallida,* an annual wildflower native to North America, from Newfoundland to Saskatchewan south to Georgia and Kansas. It grows to 5 feet, with oval leaves, canary-yellow flowers, and smooth seed capsules that explode when touched. It takes its name from the sudden bursting of its seed capsule when touched. Also called jewelweed, pale touch-me-not, and pale snapweed.

quick test *n.* A simple, rapid test of soil designed to give approximation of the nutrients available to plants.

quillaja (kwih lay'uh) *n.* A common name for *Quillaja Saponaria,* a tender tree, native to Chile. It grows to 25 to 30 feet or more, with drooping branchlets, leathery oval leaves, clusters of white 5-petaled flowers, and handsome small brown fruit that opens into the shape of a star. Tends to be multitrunked. Used as a narrow screening tree or trimmed into a tall hedge. Also known as soapbark tree.

Quillaja (kwih lay'uh) *n.* A genus of 4 species of tender broadleaf evergreen trees (Rosaceae), native to South America. They have simple, thick, leathery, alternate leaves and small clusters of hairy, 5-petaled flowers.

quillwort *n.* A common name for *Isoetes,* a genus of aquatic perennial plants. They grow from an underwater rhizome to 14 inches, with narrow, hollow, quilllike leaves; they propagate by spores. Used in aquariums.

quinate (kwigh'nayt) *a.* In botany, having an arrangement of 5 similar parts together, especially used to describe leaflets.

quince (kwihnts) *n.* 1. The fruit of the tree *Cydonia oblonga,* the true quince. It is pear-shaped, or in 1 variety apple-shaped, large, sometimes weighing 1 pound, of a golden-yellow color when ripe, and very fragrant. Although it is too hard and acid for eating raw, it is largely used for jelly, preserves, and marmalade because of its high pectin content, which makes preserves jell better. The quince is a small hardy tree, usually dwarfed, but sometimes reaching 15 or 20 feet in height, having crooked, spreading branches, which produce the flowers singly at their ends. Besides bearing fruit, the quince often serves as a stock for dwarfing the pear tree.

Although it can be grown throughout temperate zones, it thrives in the central band of states from Pennsylvania to California. 2. Shrubs and trees of the genus *Chaenomeles,* which are grown for their white to brilliant pink spring blossoms. *C. speciosa,* known as Japanese flowering quince, is a favorite of bonsai growers.

quince

quinoa (kee noh'uh) *n.* An annual herb, *Chenopodium quinoa,* native to Peru, Chile, etc., much cultivated in these areas for its seeds, which are ground into grain, a valuable food source of protein. When cooked, the grain resembles wild rice. The plant has large seed heads, much like those of amaranth, and triangular, spinachlike leaves; it resembles some common species of goosefoot or pigweed. Although unknown in North America until recently, it is now available as a cereal and may soon be available as a seed for home gardeners. It grows best in high altitudes and has suceeded in tests in Colorado, but it grows also at lower elevations in the northwestern United States.

quinquefoliolate (kwihn kweh foh'lee ayt) *a.* In botany, having 5 leaflets.

Quisqualis (kweh skwahl'ehs) *n.* A genus of 4 species of tropical vines (Combretaceae). *Q. indica,* the Rangoon creeper, grows to 30 feet, with large, opposite, simple leaves and spikes of fragrant tubular flowers that bloom white and fade to pink and red. Used in frost-free gardens or in greenhouses.

quiver tree *n.* A common name for *Aloe dichotoma,* a tender treelike succulent. It grows to 30 feet, with many forking branches, long, narrow, fleshy gray-green leaves with brownish-yellow

teeth, and 12-inch-long clusters of bright canary-yellow flowers.

rabbit *n.* A common mammal, which becomes a garden pest in many rural areas by chewing on the foliage and bark of many plants. The best control is to build fences or sink soil barriers to keep them out of the garden. (Ironically, rabbit sculptures are in some places favored garden ornaments.)

rabbitberry *n.* A common name for *Shepherdia argentea.* (See **buffalo berry.**)

rabbit brush *n.* A common name for *Chrysothamnus nauseosus,* a shrub native to dry regions in the Southwest, where it covers large areas of semidesert; related to the sunflower. It grows to 6 feet, with grayish foliage and clusters of yellow flowers. Often used in landscaping where water is scarce.

rabbit brush

rabbit-ears *n.* A common name for the cactus *Opuntia microdasys,* so called because small new pads atop older ones suggest ears. Also called bunny-ears.

rabbit repellent *n.* Any of various substances applied to foliage to discourage rabbits from eating garden vegetables and ornamental plants.

rabbit's-foot fern *n.* A common name for several ferns, including *Humata tyermannii*, many species of *Davallia*, and *Polypodium aureum*. *Humata* and *Davallis* ferne have very finely divided fronds and slender, furry above-ground creeping rhizomes (sprouting root growths). *P. aureum* is a large fern with heavy brown creeping rhizomes. All are sometimes called hare's-foot or bear's-foot ferns, and all are used as hanging-basket or pot plants.

rabbit tracks *n.* A common name for *Maranta leuconeura kerchovianat*. It has 7- to 8-inch oval leaves with a series of brown markings at the margin, hence the name. Used as a houseplant. Also called prayer plant (for its leaves, which fold in pairs at night resembling praying hands).

raccoon-berry *n.* Common name for *Podophyllum peltatum*. It is also called May apple mandrake, wild lemon, and wild jalap. (See **May apple.**)

raceme (ray seem') *n.* In botany, a spikelike stalk upon which numerous flowers are borne on individual stems, such as in the lily-of- the-valley and *Wisteria*.

racemed (ray seemd') *a.* In botany, having or forming a raceme.

racemiferous (ras uh mihl'uh ruhs) *a.* Bearing racemes.

racemiform (ray see'muh form) *a.* In botany, shaped like a raceme.

racemose (ras'uh mohs) *a.* In botany: 1. Having the character or appearance of a raceme. 2. Arranged in racemes or racemelike flower spikes. Also racemous.

rachidian (ruh kihd'ee uhn) *a.* Of or pertaining to a rachis. Also rachial; rachidial.

rachilla (ruh kihl'uh) *n.* In botany, a secondary stem or axis of a spikelet in grasses and sedges.

rachis of rye grass

rachis (ray'kehs) *n.* In botany, the elongated stem or axis of flower stalk or of the stem of a leaf that is composed of multiple leaflets.

Radermachera (rahd'uhr mahk uh ruh) *n.* A genus of 15 tropical trees or shrubs (Bignoniaceae). *R. sinica* has bright green, finely divided leaves. In the open ground in mild-winter climates, it may grow to tree size and produce clusters of bright yellow trumpet-shaped flowers. Usually sold as a houseplant under the name of China doll.

radiate *a.* In botany: 1. Spreading outward in a wheel shape from the center, as leaves around a stem. 2. Bearing ray flowers, as do many members of the family Compositae, such as daisies.

radical *a.* In botany, pertaining to or growing from the root.

radicate *v.* 1. To take root. 2. To cause to take root; to plant deeply and firmly.

radicate (rad'uh kayt) *a.* In botany, rooted. Also radicated.

radication (rad uh kay'shuhn) *n.* The process of taking root or of causing to take root.

radicchio (rad deek'yoh) *n.* A red variety of chicory, which grows in small, upright heads. It is used raw in salads, where it adds a pleasantly bitter flavor. Also known as red Verona, for the area where it originated in Italy.

radicicolous (rad uh sihk'uh luhs) *a.* Living upon or in roots. Also radicolous.

radicle *n.* In botany, the rudimentary root of an embryo or seedling.

radicolous (ra dihk'uh luhs) *a.* Same as radicicolous.

radicular (ra dihk'yuh luhr) *a.* In botany, of or relating to the radicle or root.

radiculose (ra dihk'yuh lohs) *a.* In botany, producing numerous rootlets.

radish *n.* A plant, *Raphanus sativus,* cultivated for its edible root. It has been grown since ancient times in Egypt for its crisp, fleshy root, which, although not very nutritious, is pleasantly pungent; it is usually eaten raw as a relish or in salads. The radish is

445

generally used young and fresh, but some varieties are grown for winter use. The root varies greatly in size, in form (long and tapering, turnip-shaped, olive-shaped, etc.), and also in color (white, scarlet, pink, reddish-purple, yellowish, or brown). Radish is a cool-weather crop, quick to grow, but going quickly to seed in hot weather. The long white varieties are often called icicle radishes, and the long hot Japanese varieties are known as daikon. (See also **horseradish tree.**)

radix (ray′dihks) *n.* The root of a plant.

raffia (raf′ee uh) *n.* 1. A common name for the palm, *Raphia farinifera* (R. ruffia). The fronds may reach 60 feet in length. The cuticle of the leaf stalks is the source of a fiber used in basketry and for plant ties. 2. The prepared fiber.

ragged robin *n.* A common name for *Lychnis flos-cuculi,* a hardy perennial naturalized in the eastern United States. It grows to 3 feet, with rose-red or white flowers. Also called cuckooflower.

ragged robin

ragweed *n.* A common name for any plant in the genus *Ambrosia.* The weedy *A. artemisiifolia,* common ragweed, and *A. trifida,* giant ragweed, are notorious for their pollen, which is considered a source of hay fever. The genus now embraces plants formerly called *Franseria* or bur sage. The latter are generally beach or desert plants of the West.

ragwort *n.* A common name for many groundsels, members of the genus *Senecio. S. jacobaea* is the common weedy ragwort of Europe, now naturalized in North America.

ragwort, golden *n.* A common name for *Senecio aureus.* Also known as golden groundsel.

ragwort, purple. *n.* A common name for *S. elegans,* a tender annual that has escaped to the wild in California. It grows to 2 feet, with purple flowers.

ragwort, sea *n.* A common name for *Senecio cineraria* or *S. vira-vira,* tender woolly leaved perennials often grown as annuals. Better known as dusty miller.

railing hanger *n.* A device that clamps onto a railing to support flower baskets or bird feeders.

rainfall *n.* The amount of water, coming down as rain. The rainfall is measured by means of the pluviometer or rain-gauge. The average rainfall of a particular region includes the snow, if any, reduced to its equivalent in water.

rain gauge *n.* A calibrated tube held by a stake, used for measuring the amount of rain that falls at a given place. Also called sprinkler gauge.

rain lily *n.* A common name for *Zephyranthes,* a genus of 40 species in the amaryllis family. They are small bulbous plants, with rushlike leaves and long-stemmed flowers resembling crocuses. *Z. atamasco* and *Z. candida* have white flowers tinged pink, *Z. citrina* has yellow flowers, and *Z. grandiflora* has pink flowers. Hybrids come in many shades. They take their name from their habit of blooming after rain following a dry spell. Often called fairy lilies or zephyr lilies.

rain tree *n.* A common name for *Samanea saman* (*Pithecellobium saman*), a large fast-growing tropical tree. It grows to 80 feet with a 100-foot spread, with leaves divided into many 2-inch leaflets, inconspicuous fluffy pink flowers, and large pods. Also known as saman or monkey pod.

raised bed *n.* An area for growing plants, typically enclosed by landscape timbers, in which the growing medium can be precisely determined. Raised beds are particularly useful to physically challenged and elderly gardeners.

raised bed builder *n.* A hoe-shaped implement used to spread soil, compost, or sand in a raised garden bed.

raisin *n.* A dried grape of certain sweet varieties. In the United States, most raisins are produced in California.

raisin tree *n.* A common name for *Hovenia dulcis*, a small deciduous tree in the buckthorn family. The greenish fruit is held on curiously swollen, fleshy reddish stalks, which are edible and faintly sweet. Also called Japanese raisin tree.

rake *n.* Any of various implements having pegs or prongs of metal or rubber mounted on a transverse bar, used for gathering leaves or spreading soil.

rake, garden *n.* A long-handled tool having numerous short, still metal prongs mounted transversely on a bar; used for spreading and combining soil, fertilizer, lime, compost, and other materials in the garden.

rake, leaf *n.* A leaf rake has long, flexible prongs, often of bamboo, spread in a fanlike arrangement and slightly bent at the ends.

ramentaceous (ram uhn tay′shuhs) *a.* In botany, covered with, consisting of, or resembling ramentum.

ramentum (ruh mehn′tuhm) *n., pl.* **ramenya**. In botany, a thin, brownish, fringed scale that appears on the young shoots or leaves of many ferns. Also rament; palea.

ramie (raym′ee) *n.* A common name for *Boehmeria nivea*, a perennial plant in the nettle family. It grows to 5 feet or more, with coarse 6-inch-long oval leaves and inconspicuous flowers. It is grown for its fine, strong fiber, used in clothing. Also known as China grass and China silk plant.

Ramonda (ruh mohn′duh) *n.* A genus of 3 species of hardy perennial plants (Gesneriaceae). *R. myconii, R. nathaliae,* and *R. serbica* are similar, all resembling African violets (*Saintpaulia*), having rosettes of furry leaves and erect stalks bearing purple, pink, or white flowers. Although hardy nearly to 0°, they are not easy to grow, needing shade, rich soil, and excellent drainage.

ramose (ray′mohs) *a.* Branched; having many branches. Also ramous.

rampion (ram′pee uhn) *n.* a common name for *Campanula rapunculus*, a biennial bellflower formerly widely cultivated for its fleshy white edible roots, which were used in salads. (The German name is Rapunzel.)

rampion, German (ram′pee uhn) *n.* A common name for *Oenothera biennis*, a weedy biennial evening primrose. It grows 1 to 6 feet, with yellow flowers. The roots and young foliage are sometimes eaten.

rampion, horned (ram′pee uhn) *n.* A common name for members of the genus *Phyteuma*. They have tightly clustered flowers, which open from long, slender buds, and long, protruding styles.

ram's-head *n.* A common name for *Cypripedium arietinum*, a small lady's slipper or moccasin flower. It has purplish-brown flowers with an oddly-shaped white lip. Also known as ram's-head orchid.

ramtil (ram′tihl) *n.* A common name for *Guizotia abyssinica*, an annual. It grows to 3 feet, and has oily black seeds, a source of a valuable oil. The seeds appear in birdseed mixtures and sometimes sprout from spilled seed. Also called ramtilla and niger seed.

ramuliferous (ram yuh lihf′uh ruhs) *a.* In botany, having many small branches. Also ramulose; ramulous.

ramulose (ram′yuh lohs) *a.* Same as ramuliferous.

ramulus (ram′yuh luhs) *n.* In botany, a small branch or branchlet.

Randia (ran′dee uh) *n.* A genus of 200 shrubs or trees (Rubiaceae). *R. formosa* is a 12-foot evergreen shrub, with hanging tubular white flowers 6 inches long. Grown in tropical climates or in greenhouses.

Rangoon creeper (ran′goon) *n.* A common name for *Quisqualis indica* (Combretaceae), a tropical vine. It grows to 30 feet, with spikes of fragrant white flowers that age to pink and red. Popular in greenhouses or outdoors in the mildest subtropical climates.

Ranunculaceae (ruh nuhng kyuh lay′see ee) *n.* A family of 58 genera and 1,750 species of chiefly of herbaceous plants, with a few shrubs and vines; the buttercup or crowfoot family. Among the many ornamental genera are *Aconitum, Anemone, Aquilegia, Clematis, Delphinium, Helleborus, Ranunculus, Thalictrum,* and *Trollius.*

ranunculaceous (ruh nuhng kyuh lay'shuhs) *a.* Of or pertaining to the Ranunculaceae.

Ranunculus (ruh nuhng kyuh luhs) *n.* A genus of about 400 species of annuals, biennials, or perennials, some aquatic, widely distributed in the colder regions of the world (Ranunculaceae). The flowers, many known as buttercups, are usually yellow, but some species are white, pink, or red. The best known in gardens is *R. asiaticus,* the Persian or turban ranunculus, a tuberous plant to 1½ feet, with fernlike foliage and a profusion of semidouble to fully double flowers in yellow, orange, pink, red, and white. *R. repens,* creeping buttercup, is a yellow-flowered lawn weed, but a double-flowered form ('Flore Pleno') is sometimes used as a ground cover in damp soils. A few buttercups are choice and rather difficult rock garden plants (*R. glacialis,* for instance). Many are common meadow or pasture weeds.

Raoulia (ray oo'lee uh) *n.* A genus of low-growing, mossy-appearing plants (Compositae). *R. australis* makes tight gray mats with scattered pale yellow flowers. *R. tenuicaulis* is even flatter in growth. Sometimes grown in rock gardens for their flat, dense carpets of tiny leaves and spanglings of tiny yellow flowers.

rape *n.* A common name for *Brassica napus,* an annual or biennial plant. It resembles mustard in appearance and is grown primarily as a source of oil from its seeds (canola oil) as well as for stock feed and as green manure.

Raphanus (raf'uh nuhs) *n.* A genus of plants (Cruciferae) including *R. sativus* (common radish) and *R. caudatus* (rat-tail radish) grown for its long, slender, edible seed capsules.

raphe (ray'fee) *n.* In botany, the part of the supporting stalk of an ovule that is fused to its outer covering. It is usually shaped like a ridge.

raspberry *n.* 1. The fruit of several plants of the genus *Rubus,* consisting of many small juice-covered seeds in clusters, which, unlike those of the blackberry, separate from the white fleshy core together when ripe, thus giving the fruit the shape of a thimble. Besides its extensive use as a dessert fruit, the raspberry is used for jellies and jams, and its juice is used for flavoring. 2. The plant that produces the raspberry. The common garden raspberry is *Rubus Idaeus,* a shrub with perennial creeping rootstock, nearly erect, prickly, biennial stems, and a red pleasant fruit. The wild red raspberry of North America is the same species, but not quite so tall, the leaves being thinner and the fruit not so firm, large, or highly flavored; it is common in the northern states, especially on newly cleared grounds. The black raspberry, thimbleberry, or blackcap is the American *R. occidentalis,* a shrub with long, recurved biennial stems and a black fruit. It is very productive with little care, and affords good garden varieties. The flowering raspberry, an American species, *Rubus odoratus,* is an ornamental shrub of the eastern United States, with large leaves and showy purple or pink flowers blooming all summer; the fruit is of little value.

raspberry, flowering *n.* A common name for *Rubus odoratus,* a 9-foot thornless shrub with pinkish purple 2-inch flowers. Also called purple flowering raspberry.

raspberry, Rocky Mountain *n.* A common name for *Rubus deliciosus,* a tall thornless shrub with 2-inch white flowers. Also called Rocky Mountain flowering raspberry. *R. trilobus* is similar, and there is a hybrid between the 2 called *R.* 'Tridel'.

rasp fern *n.* A common name for ferns of the genus *Doodia. D. aspera* is called prickly rasp fern or hacksaw fern because of its rough foliage. *D. caudata* (small rasp fern) and *D. media* (common rasp fern) are also occasionally grown. Although they are not hardy, they are easy to grow and attractive. Grown indoors in pots or outdoors in the mildest climates.

ratchet lopper *n.* A long-handled, heavy-duty scissors and ratchet mechanism used to cut twigs, branches, or roots up to 1¼ inches in diameter. The ratchet increases hand power.

ratchet pruner *n.* Shears for cutting tree branches or shrubs. A ratchet mechanism, operating on the principle of the lever, increases hand power.

Ratibida (ruh tihb'uh duh) *n.* A genus of 5 species of perennials or biennials (Compositae). The flower heads resemble those of *Rudbeckia* (black-eyed Susan), but the central disk is columnar rather than flat. *R. columnifera* and *R. f. pulcherrima* have white, yellow, or purplish red ray flowers, all with brown central columns. *R. pinnata* has yellow ray flowers. Commonly known as coneflower or prairie coneflower.

rat-poison plant *n.* A common name for *Hamelia patens,* also known as firebush or scarlet bush.

rattan (ra tan') *n.* 1. A common name for palms in the genera *Calamus* and *Daemonorops.* Many are climbing, reaching great length by clinging to trees by means of hooked spines. The stems are important as the source of canes for furniture construction. 2. A common name for *Rhapis humilis* (slender lady palm) a clumping palm grown as an ornamental plant. 3. The canes provided by the stems of these palms.

rattlebox *n.* A common name for any of the species of *Crotalaria,* the seeds of which rattle in their pods. The name is also used for species of *Rhinanthus, Halesia carolina* (the silver bell tree) and for *Silene vulgaris* (bladder campion).

rattlebox
(*Crotalaria* species)

rattlebush *n.* A common name for any of the species of *Crotalaria,* as well as *Baptisia tinctoria* (wild indigo).

rattlesnake fern *n.* A common name for *Botrychium virginianum,* a member of the grape ferns or

moonworts, or ferns in the adder's-tongue family. A deciduous fern with broadly triangular fronds to 30 inches long. (See **fern, rattlesnake.**)

rattlesnake master *n.* A name applied to several plants alleged to be cures for snake bites. *Eryngium yuccaefolium, Liatris* species, and *Manfreda virginica (Agave v.)* all bear the name. The first 2 are also called button snakeroot.

rattlesnake root *n.* A common name for species of *Prenanthes,* perennials in the sunflower family; for *Polygala senega,* also known as senega root; and for *Cimicifuga racemosa,* also known as black cohosh and black snakeroot.

rattlesnake weed *n.* A common name for the hawkweed *Hieracium venosum,* a yellow-flowered perennial; also for species of *Liatris, Eryngium yuccaefolium,* and species of *Goodyera.*

rattle-top *n.* A common name for species of *Cimicifuga,* the bugbanes.

rattleweed *n.* A common name for plants in the genera *Astragalus, Crotalaria, Oxytropis,* and to bladder campion *(Silene vulgaris).* It is also sometimes applied to the bugbanes *(Cimicifuga).*

rattrap *n.* Any of various devices for luring and trapping rats. Spring traps kill; live traps do not.

Rauwolfia (row ool'fee uh) *n.* A genus of trees and shrubs (Apocynaceae). An evergreen tree rarely seen in Southern California and usually called *Alstonia scholaris* is probably *R. samarensis* or *R. javanica.*

Ravenala (rav uh nay'luh) *n.* A giant tropical treelike perennial (Strelitziaceae). *R. madagascariensis* is commonly known as traveler's tree because its leaf stalks hold a large amount of liquid sometimes used to slake the thirst of travelers. Large (to 12 feet long) bananalike leaves arise in fan shape from the top of a trunk which can reach 30 feet.

ray *n.* In botany: 1. One of the flower stems in an umbel, a flower cluster in which all such stems arise from the same point. 2. A daisylike or ray flower.

ray flower *n.* One of the petallike parts of the flowers of many of the Compositae, such as the sunflower and aster.

reaction *n.* The degree of acidity or alkalinity of a soil mass expressed in pH.

Rebutia (ree boo'tee uh) *n.* A genus of 40 species and countless varieties of small perennial cactus (Cactaceae). Stems are globular or cylindrical, single or clustered, usually knobbed or ribbed. Profuse bloomers, with flowers ranging from white through yellow and orange to red and purple. Many are known as crown cactus.

receptacle *n.* In botany: the enlarged end of the stem of a flower upon which the reproductive organs of the flower are borne.

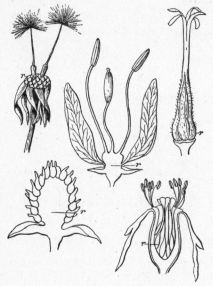

receptacles of various flowers

receptacular *a.* In botany, of or pertaining to a receptacle.

recurvate (reh kuhr'vayt) *a.* Same as recurved.

recurved *a.* In botany, curved downward or backward, as the petals of most species of *Cyclamen*.

redberry *n.* 1. A common name for *Rhamnus crocea*, an evergreen shrub native to California.

redbud *n.* A common name for the American species of *Cercis*, sometimes also known as Judas tree or flowering Judas.

red cedar *n.* 1. A common name for *Juniperus virginiana*. 2. A name sometimes applied to *Thuja plicata*, more commonly known as giant arborvitae, giant cedar, canoe cedar, or western red cedar. 3. A

name sometimes applied to incense cedar, *Calocedrus decurrens*.

red gum *n.* A common name for *Eucalyptus camaldulensis*, a large tree also known as Murray red gum; *E. calophylla*, also known as marri.

red-ink plant *n.* A common name for *Phytolacca americana*, the pokeweed or poke.

red oak *n.* A common name for *Quercus rubra (Q. borealis)*, also known as northern red oak. (See **oak, Northern red**.)

red oak, Japanese *n.* (See **oak Japanese evergreen** and **Quercus**.)

red oak, Shumard's *n.* (See **oak, Shumard's red** and **Quercus**.)

red oak, Spanish *n.* (See **oak, Spanish** and **Quercus**.)

red ribbons *n.* A common name for *Clarkia concinna*, an annual with bright pink flowers with ribbon-shaped petals.

redroot *n.* A common name for *Lachnanthes caroliana*, an herbaceous perennial related to the bloodroot. It is also known as paint root or dye root. The name is also sometimes applied to *Ceanothus americanus*, the New Jersey tea.

redshanks *n.* A common name for *Adenostoma sparsifolium*, an evergreen shrub in the rose family, so named for its peeling reddish bark.

red thread *n.* A fungal disease that first results in red or pink threadlike strands on grass leaf blades. Eventually the turf looks soggy, then turns brown. Common in humid climates and under-fertilized lawns. To control, increase nitrogen fertilization, and, if necessary, adjust pH. Traditional fungicides can also be helpful.

redwood *n.* A common name for *Sequoia sempervirens*, the coast redwood. It is a gigantic, fast-growing evergreen conifer that soars to 300 feet. Native to the Western North America, it is one of the world's largest trees. It has an immense reddish-brown trunk, scale-like leaves, and small cones. It is a valuable timber tree.

redwood branch with cones

redwood, giant *n*. A common name for *Sequoiadendron giganteum*. It grows to 250 feet with a huge trunk many feet in diameter, bark to 20 inches thick, and elliptical female cones. Also known as big tree and giant sequoia.

redwood, dawn *n*. A common name for *Metasequoia glyptostroboides*, a deciduous relative of the sequoias well established in temperate areas. (See **Metasequoia**.)

reel mower *n*. A machine for cutting grass composed of a cylinder formed of blades mounted on an axis. Hand powered mowers are of the reel type; power mowers may have either reel or rotary blades.

reflexed *a*. In botany, bent or recurved backward or downward; applied to petals, sepals, leaf-veins, etc.

registration of plant names *n*. Term for the concept of naming all new cultivated varieties of plants according to rules promulgated by International Horticultural Congresses.

regolith (rehg'uh lihth) *n*. 1. The unconsolidated nature of loose earth materials (soil, sand, loose rock, etc.) above the solid rock on the earth's surface.

regular *a*. In botany, having the members of each whorl of floral organs arranged in a symmetrical shape, as in the rose and petunia.

Rehderodendron (ray'dehr oh dehn'druhn) *n*. A genus of 9 species of deciduous trees or shrubs (Styracaceae). *R. macrocarpum* has fragrant white flowers and attractive red fruits. Though rare, it is attractive and hardy to around 15°.

Rehmannia (ruh mayn'ee uh) *n*. A genus of 9 species of semi-hardy herbaceous perennials (Gesneriaceae). *R. elata* grows to 5 feet, bearing long, narrow clusters of purplish rose foxglove-shaped flowers with yellow throats and red spots. Grows well in moist, rich soils and filtered light.

Reineckea (righ nehck'ee uh) *n*. A low perennial ground cover plant (Liliaceae). It much resembles mondo grass *(Ophiopogon)*, but has pink flowers. Grown as a pot plant and in mild climate gardens.

Reinhardtia (righn hart'ee uh) *n*. A genus of 6 species of small tropical palms occasionally grown as greenhouse or house plants. *R. gracilis*, to 8 feet, and *R. simplex*, to 5 feet, are sometimes offered by nursries.

rein orchis (rayn or'kuhs) *n*. A common name for *Habenaria*, a genus of 100 or so species of terrestrial perennial Orchids (Orchidaceae). They are also called fringed orchids.

Reinwardtia (rihn war'tee uh) *n*. A genus of 1 or 2 species of tender evergreen shrubs (Linaceae). *R. indica* grows to 2½ feet tall with clusters of bright yellow 2-inch flowers produced almost continuously in warm weather. Commonly called yellow flax. (Sometimes confused with *Linum flavum*, also called yellow flax.)

Renanthera (reh nan'thuh ruh) *n*. A genus of 15 species of tropical perennial epiphytes (growing on hosts but not taking nourishment from them) in the (Orchidaceae). The red, orange, or yellow flowers come in dense, often branched clusters and are extremely showy. Grown in hot, humid climates or in greenhouses anywhere.

reniform (ren'uh form) *a*. In botany, kidney-shaped; bean-shaped.

repellent *n*. Any of various substances applied around plants or to foliage to discourage animals from entering or eating a garden.

replum (rehp'luhm) *n*. In botany, the framework that divides the various sections of certain seed cases, which break open when mature, and that remains when the sections fall away.

repot *v.t.* To shift plants in pots from one pot to another, usually of a larger size, or to remove from the pot and replace the old soil with fresh earth.

Reseda (reh seh'duh) *n.* A genus of 55 species of annuals or perennials (Resedaceae). Most widely used is *R. odorata,* the mignonette, a low-growing annual with inconspicuous whitish, greenish, or yellowish flowers with a powerful, sweet fragrance. Traditional in cottage gardens.

residue: *n.* The amount of an inorganic fertilizer, pesticide, or herbicide which remains in plants, soils, or groundwater after the growing season in which it was applied. Such residues may damage future crops, render vegetables toxic, and pollute groundwater and nearby streams.

residual *n.* The length of time a pesticide remains active after it has been applied.

residual fertilizer *n.* The amount of fertilizer that remains in the soil after one or more planting seasons.

resmethrin (rehz mehth'rihn) *n.* A synthetic pyrethrin used as an insecticide.

respirator *n.* A device covering the nose and/or mouth to prevent inhalation of noxious substances such as pesticides and dusting powders.

rest-harrow *n.* A common name for *Ononis,* a genus of perennials and shrubs in the Pea family, especially *O. spinosa (O. arvensis). O. spinosa* is a perennial, sometimes spiny, that grows to 2 feet with leaves divided into leaflets and pairs of pink sweet pea-shaped flowers.

rest period *n.* A period of dormancy induced by withholding water during part of the year, needed by some plants, such as *Zantedeschia Rehmannii* (red calla), in order to bring about bloom in the coming season.

resurrection fern *n.* A common name for *Polypodium polypodioides,* a creeping epiphytic evergreen fern with leathery fronds that are gray and scaly beneath. Capable of extreme dormancy in drought, reviving with favorable growing conditions. (See **fern, resurrection.**)

resurrection plant *n.* A name given to several plants that shrivel and curl up in drought and expand again when wet, such as *Anastatica hierochuntica,* an annual in the Cress family (Cruciferae). It is also called rose-of-Jericho. Best known is perennial *Selaginella lepidophylla,* a dense tufted moss.

Retama (reh tam'uh) *n.* A genus of 4 species of essentially leafless shrubs (Leguminosae). The green branches bear sweetly scented white or yellow pea flowers. *R. monosperma,* bridal veil broom, is sometimes classified as *Genista monosperma.*

reticulate (reh tihk'yuh leht) *a.* In botany, netlike; resembling netting. Also reticular; reticulated; retiform.

reticulum (reh tihk'yuh luhm) *n., pl.* **reticula.** In botany, any plant structure with a netlike form.

retiform (rehd'uh form) *a.* Same as reticulate.

retrorse (reh traw'uhrs) *a.* In botany, turned backward or downward.

retuse (reh toos') *a.* In botany, blunt at the tip, with a slight notch.

revolute (rehv'uh loot) *a.* Rolled or curled backward or downward, as the margins of the leaves of *Pittosporum Tobira.*

revolute leaf

revolving sprinkler *n.* (See **whirling sprinkler.**)

Rhamnaceae (ram nay'see uh) *n.* A family of over 50 genera and 875 species of trees and shrubs (rarely vines) usually with inconspicuous flowers and fruits that are either drupes (like a date), or capsules. Important genera are *Ceanothus, Pomaderris, Rhamnus,* and *Ziziphus.* Commonly called the Buckthorn family.

rhamnaceous (ram nay'shuhs) *a.* Of or pertaining to the family Rhamnaceae.

Rhamnus (ram'nuhs) *n.* A genus of of over 100 species of evergreen or deciduous shrubs known as the buckthorns. They have inconspicuous flowers and berrylike fruits. Deciduous *R. frangula* (alder buckthorn) and evergreen *R. alaternus* (Italian buckthorn) are useful as hedges or screens. Two evergreens, *R. crocea* (redberry) and its form *ilicifolia* (hollyleaf redberry) are useful in mild, dry climates. *R. californica* is similarly useful. It has black berries.

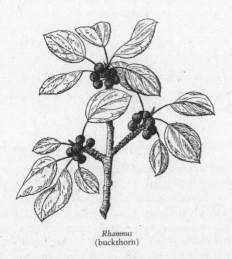

Rhamnus
(buckthorn)

Rhaphidophora (raf'ee dahf'or uh) *n.* A synonym for *Epipremnum aureum,* a popular trailing house plant commonly sold as Pothos. It has slender stems, and glossy oral to heartshaped leaves variegated with yellow or white. (See **Epipremnum.**)

Rhaphiolepis (raf ee ol'uh pihs) *n.* A genus of 15 or so species of evergreen shrubs or small trees (Rosaceae). *R. indica,* its many named varieties, and the hybrid *R.* x *delacouri* are commonly called India hawthorn. Compact shrubs to 6 feet (usually less), they freely produce terminal clusters of white or pink flowers. Dark blue berries follow. Extremely popular where winters are not severe. *R. umbellata* (*R. ovata*), can reach 10 feet and has white flowers. Treelike 'Majestic Beauty' can reach 15 feet; it may be a hybrid with *Eriobotrya,* the loquat.

Rhapidophyllum (raf ee doh fighl'um) *n.* A genus of 1 species, *R. hystria,* a low-growing spiny fan palm. It is native to the southern United States, and one of the hardiest palms. Commonly known as needle palm.

Rhapis (ray'pihs) *n.* A genus of 12 species of cluster palms with slender stems and fan-shaped leaves. *R. excelsa,* to 12 feet tall, usually much less, is a favored palm for containers or for landscaping in subtropical climates. It is called lady palm, bamboo palm, or ground rattan. *R. humilis,* to 18 feet is larger and has larger leaves than *R. excelsa.* It is called slender lady palm or rattan palm.

Rheum (ree'uhm) *n.* A genus of 50 species of perennials (Polygonaceae), with large, bold leaves and tall, slender flower clusters with many small whitish, greenish, or reddish flowers. *R. xcultorum* is the garden rhubarb, grown for edible leaf stalks. *R. palmatum,* with huge leaves and deep red flowers, is sometimes grown in large borders.

Rhexia (reks'ee uh) *n.* A genus of 10 species of perennials (Melastomataceae). *R. virginica,* meadow beauty or deer grass, grows to 1½ feet tall, and has rose-purple 2 inch flowers in branching clusters.

Rhexia virginica
(meadow beauty)

Rhinanthus (righ nan'thuhs) *n.* A genus of 45 species of annual, semi-parasitic annuals (Scrophulariaceae). They are weeds in pastures, 18 inches tall, with small yellow or brown flowers. Commonly known as yellow rattle, rattle, or rattlebox.

rhipidium (rih pihd'ee uhm) *n., pl.* **rhipidiumd.** In botany, a fan-shaped flower cluster.

Rhipsalidopsis (rihp'sal ih dohp'sihs) *n.* A genus of 2 species of epiphytic cactus (Cactaceae). They have jointed stems terminated by long-tubed, many-petaled flowers. *R. gaertneri,* the Easter cactus, has red 3-inch flowers. *R. rosea* has rose-pink flowers 1½ inches wide.

Rhipsalis (rihp'say lihs) *n.* A genus of about 50 species of epiphytic perennial cactus (Cactaceae). They are leafless, with green cylindrical or jointed branches, small white flowers, and small juicy fruits, usually white. Many resemble mistletoe, growing on trees and bearing white berries. Often called mistletoe cactus.

rhizanthous (righ zan'thuhs) *a.* Appearing to flower from the root of the plant.

rhizina (reh zigh'nuh) *a.* Same as rhizoid. Also rhizine.

rhizinous (reh zigh'nuhs) *a.* In botany, having rhizoids.

rhizocarpous (righ zoh kahr'puhs) *a.* In botany, having the stems and foliage annual but the underground parts perennial, as in *Iris* and *Gladiolus.* Also rhizocarpic.

rhizogenic (righ zuh jehn'ihk) *a.* Producing roots. Also rhizogenetic; rhizogenous.

rhizoid (righ'zoid) *n.* In botany, a plant structure that resembles a root in function and overall appearance, but not in its internal structure.

rhizoidal (righ'zoid'uhl) *a.* In botany, pertaining to, resembling, or characteristic of a rhizoid.

rhizomatous (righ zahm'uh duhs) *a.* Producing, possessing, or resembling a rhizome.

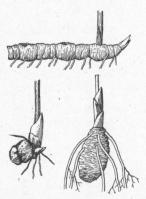

rhizomes of various plants

rhizome (righ'zohm) *n.* In botany, a thickened, modified stem lying on or under the ground, bearing scalelike leaves, and usually producing shoots above and roots below. Rhizomes may be long and slender, as in mints and some lawn grasses, or thickened with deposits of reserve food material, as in species of *Iris* and Solomon's-seal. Also rootstock.

rhizomorphous (righ'zuh mor fuhs) *a.* Rootlike in form. Also rhizomorphic.

Rhizophora (rih zahf oh ruh) *n.* A genus of 3 species of tropical broadleaf evergreen trees (Rhizophoraceae). *R. mangle,* the American mangrove, grows along tidal shores and marshes in Florida. It has prominent stilt roots.

rhizophoraceous (righ zahf uh ray'shuhs) *n.* Of or pertaining to Rhizophoraceae, the mangrove family.

Rhodanthe (roh dan'thuh) *n.* A former genus now classified as *Helipterum.* (See **Helipterum.**)

Rhodiola (roh'dee oh luh) *n.* A genus of about 50 species of perennials (Saxifragaceae). They have thick, fleshy roots and annual flowering stems bearing clusters of white, green, yellow, or red flowers. They resemble large, coarse sedums and are sometimes included in that genus. *R. rosea,* the roseroot, is found throughout the northern hemisphere. It is also known as *Sedum rosea.*

Rhodochiton (roh doh kigh'tahn) *n.* A genus of 3 species of tender perennial vines (Scrophulariaceae). *R. atrosanguineum (R. volubile)* can grow to 10 feet, with a profusion of hanging, deep red, bell-shaped flowers set in pink saucer-shaped calyces. It may be grown in pots indoors, or outdoors as an annual.

Rhododendron (roh duh den'druhn) *n.* A genus of perhaps 800 species (and innumerable hybrids) of trees or shrubs (Ericaceae). All have simple leaves clustered toward branch tips and nearly all have clustered flowers; most are evergreen. *R. catawbiense,* from the Appalachians, has rose-purple flowers and is the parent of many garden hybrids. It is also called Catawba rhododendron, mountain rosebay, and purple laurel. *R. carolinianum,* Carolina rhododendron, is a smaller plant with lighter pink flowers; it also has white-flowered varieties.

R. maximum, great laurel or rosebay, can grow to 30 feet; it has rose-pink flowers. *R. macrophyllum (R. californicum),* grows near the West Coast and has rose-colored flowers. *R. occidentale,* with white and yellow, pink-flushed flowers, grows on the West Coast. *R. canadense,* the rhodora, is a deciduous rhododendron notable for having 2-lipped rose-purple flowers. Most garden rhododendrons and azaleas are hybrids of complex origin.

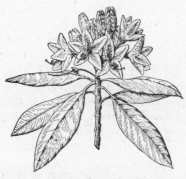

Rhododendron maximum
(great laurel)

Rhodohypoxis (roh duh high poks′uhs) *n.* A genus of 6 species of near-bulbous plants (Hypoxidaceae). *R. baurii* is among the smallest of bulbous or tuberous-rooted plants. Clumps of grassy leaves to 4 inches long are studded with small six-petaled white, pink, or red flowers. They are hardy to around 20°, but must be dry in winter.

Rhodophiala (roh duh figh ahl′uh) *n.* A genus of 30 or so species of bulbous plants (Amaryllidaceae). They resemble smaller amaryllis *(Hippeastrum)* with yellow, pink, or red flowers. *R. advena* and *R. pratensis* are hardy where freezes are rare.

Rhodora (roh dor′uh) *n.* A synonym for *Rhododendron canadense.*

rhubarb (roo′bahrb) *n.* 1. A common garden plant, *Rheum Rhabarbarum,* grown for its tender leafstalks, which are a spring substitute for fruit in making tarts, pies, etc. Rhubarb is a perennial and is usually planted along a garden edge or elsewhere out of the way of annual garden plowing. The leaves are quite large and should not be eaten because of the toxic amounts of oxalic acid they contain. It thrives in northern regions with cool, moist summers and winters with frost to a depth of several inches. Rhubarb is also known as pieplant.

Rhus (ruhs) *n.* A genus of 200 species of evergreen or deciduous shrubs or trees (Anacardiaceae). Although some have simple leaves, most have divided foliage, that of the deciduous kinds often showing brilliant fall colors. Tightly clustered tiny flowers produce clusters of berrylike fruit. They are commonly called sumac. *R. copallina* (shining sumac), *R. glabra* (smooth sumac), and *R. typhina* (staghorn sumac) are chiefly grown for fall color. *R. succedanea,* the wax tree, produces wax from its fruits while the sap furnishes lacquer. *R. verniciflua,* the varnish tree, is a chief souce of lacquer; its leaves are poisonous to the touch, as are those of *R. toxicodendron* and *R. diversilobum,* poison ivy and poison oak. (The last two named are now classified as *Toxicodendron radicans* and *T. diversilobum.*) *R. lancea* (African sumac) is an evergreen shade tree for warm, dry climates. *R. integrifolia* (lemonade berry) and *R. ovata* (sugar bush) are evergreen shrubs with leathery simple leaves; they are much used in California landscapes. *R. laurina,* now called *Malosma laurina,* is another evergreen for mildest climates. *R. aromatica* (fragrant sumac), and *R. trilobata* (skunk bush) are hardy deciduous shrubs used for coarse ground cover.

Rhus toxicodenron
(poison ivy)

Rhynchelytrum (rihnk′ee ligh′truhm) *n.* A genus of 14 species of annuals and perennials (Gramineae), only *R. repens (R. roseum),* ruby grass, is grown as an ornamental. It has 8-inch loose, silky, purplish-to-red blossoms.

Rhyncholaelia (rihnk′oh leh lee uh) *n.* A genus of 2 tropical epiphytic perennial orchids (Orchidaceae). They were formerly named *Brassavola. R. dig-byana* has greenish–white 6-inch flowers with a wildly fringed white lip. It is the parent of innumerable orchid hybrids. *R. glauca* has white, green, or lavender 5-inch flowers with white or yellowish lips marked rose or purple. Both are fragrant.

Rhynchostylis (rink'oh stigh lihs) *n.* A genus of 15 species of tropical epiphytic orchids with densely clustered flowers. *R. coelestis* has white flowers marked blue. *R. gigantea* and *R.retusa* have spikes of white flowers marked purple. All are known as foxtail orchids.

rib *n.* In botany, 1 of the primary veins of a leaf or other plant organ.

ribbon bush *n.* A common name for *Homalocladium platycladium,* a leafless climbing shrub with flat green jointed stems. Also known as centipede plant.

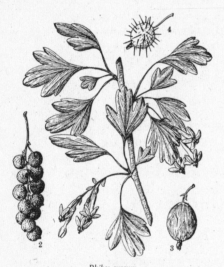

Rhibes aureum
(golden currant)
also, fruits of *2* red currant *3* English gooseberry *4* wild gooseberry

Ribes (righ'behz) *n.* A genus of about 150 species of shrubs, the currants and gooseberries (Grossulariaceae). Species with thorny or prickly stems and fruit and with flowers carried singly or a few together are called gooseberries; those with smooth stems and flowers in elongated clusters are called currants. Common gooseberry is *R. uva-crispa (R. grossularia).* Red currant is *R. silvestre* and *R. spicatum,* both formerly called *R. rubrum.* Black currant is *R. nigrum.* Among ornamental species are scarlet

R. speciosum, fuchsia–flowered gooseberry; *R. sanguineum,* winter currant, with long clusters of pink, white, or red flowers ; spicily fragrant *R. aureum* and *R. odoratum,* golden, buffalo, or Missouri currants; and the evergreen *R. laurifolium* and *R. viburnifolium.,* the Catalina currant.

ribgrass, ribwort *n.* A common name for the genus *Plantago,* the plantains, especially *P. lanceolata.*

riceflower *n.* A common name for plants in the genus *Pimelea. P. ferruginea* is a 3-foot shrub with tightly clustered pink flowers. *P. prostrata (P. coarctata),* is a low, spreading shrub with grayish foliage and tiny clusters of white flowers. It is sometimes seen in rock gardens.

rice paper plant *n.* A common name for *Tetrapanax papyriferus,* a large, hardy shrub. The pith of the stems is used for making rice paper. The plant is an evergreen shrub or small tree to 20 feet with leaves 1 to 2 feet wide. Also know as rice paper tree.

richweed *n.* 1. A common name for horse balm, horseweed, citronella, or stoneroot (*Collinsonia canadensis*), a lemon-scented perennial in the mint family (Labiatae). 2. A common name for *Pilea fontana* and *P. pumila,* also called clearweed and coolwort, weeds in the Nettle family (Urticaceae).

Ricinus (righ sih'nuhs) *n.* A genus of 1 species *R. communis* is a shrub or small tree. Commonly grown as an annual in cold–winter climates; it becomes a tree where frosts are light or infrequent. Plants can reach 12 feet in one season from seed, with 2-foot-wide lobed leaves and terminal clusters of flowers that turn to smooth or spiny capsules containing large mottled seeds. The seeds are extremely poisonous, although they are the source of castor oil. Many horticultural varieties have bronzy or red leaves or stems. Commonly called castor oil plant, castor oil tree, or palma Christi.

riddle *n.* A coarse sieve for sifting soil or compost and for winnowing beans or seeds. Also known as a soil sieve.

riding mower *n.* A vehicle for cutting grass consisting of a rotary blade, gasoline powered engine, and operator seat and controls.

Riga fir *n.* A common name for *Pinus sylvestris rigensis,* a variety of Scotch pine. It is a very hardy evergreen coniferous tree with stiff, blue-green needles in pairs and gray to reddish brown cones.

It has a straight trunk with reddish bark, and grows from 70 to 100 feet. Popular as a Christmas tree. Also known as Riga pine.

riparian (reh peh′ree uhn) *a.* Living or growing along the banks of a river or other watercourse. Also riparial; riparious.

ripple-grass *n.* A common name for *Plantago lanceolata,* a perennial with heavily ribbed narrow, pointed basal leaves. It is a common lawn weed. Also known as ribgrass, harrow-leaved plantain, and buckhorn.

river birch *n.* A common name for *Betula nigra,* a tree of stream sides and bottom lands. Also called black birch or red birch.

Rivina (rih vee′nuh) *n.* A genus of 3 species of perennials (Phytolaccaceae). *R. humilis,* the rouge plant, blood berry, or baby pepper is sometimes grown as a houseplant or greenhouse plant. It grows to 4 feet, with 4-inch leaves and drooping clusters of red berries which follow small greenish to pink flowers.

rivulose (rihv′yuh lohs) *a.* In botany, marked with irregular, crooked, or wavy lines.

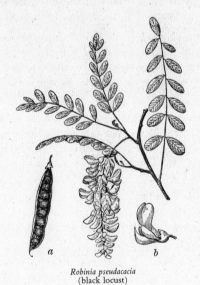

Robinia pseudacacia
(black locust)
a pod *b* flower

Robinia (roh bee′nee uh) *n.* A genus of about 20 species (and some hybrids) of trees and shrubs (Leguminosae). All have leaves divided into leaflets

and clusters of white or pink flowers. *R. pseudoacacia,* the black or yellow locust, is a tree that can reach 90 feet, with dangling 8-inch clusters of white fragrant, flowers. It has many named varieties, of which the yellow-leaved 'Frisia' is best known. The hybrid *R. xambigua* has several named varieties with pink flowers, 'Decaisneana' and Idahoensis being best known. Shrubby locusts with pink flowers are *R. hispida,* rose acacia, bristly locust, or moss locust; *R. kelseyi,* Allegheny moss; *R. viscosa,* clammy locust; and *R. neomexicana.*

robin's plantain *n.* A common name for *Erigeron pulchellus,* a hairy rhizomatous perennial (Compositae) native to the United States from Maine to Texas. It grows to 2 feet tall, with clusters of blue, pink, or white daisylike flowers. Also known as Poor Robin's plantain.

roble (roh′bluh) *n.* A Spanish word for a deciduous oak tree. In California, it is a common name for *Quercus lobata,* the California white oak or valley oak. (See **oak, California white.**)

rocambole (rahk′uhm bohl) *n.* A variety of garlic, *Allium sativum,* also called serpent garlic. Its flavor and culture are the same as garlic. *Allium Scorodoprasum* is sometimes incorrectly called rocambole, and Egyptian onion, 1 of the many varieties of *A. cepa,* is sometimes called garden rocambole.

Rochea (roh shee′uh) *n.* An obsolete name for 3 species of *Crassula.* The plant commonly sold as *R. coccinea* is a 1- to 2-foot succulent, with fleshy leaves packed on the stems, giving a squarish look. Bright red clustered flowers top each stem.

rock brake *n.* A common name for ferns in the genus *Cryptogramma.* The name is also sometimes applied to other small ferns, such as the cliff brakes *Pellaea.*

rock cotoneaster *n.* A common name for *Cotoneaster horizontalis,* a deciduous sprawling shrub (Rosaceae) with small, round glossy bright green leaves that color orange and red in autumn. It has small white or pink flowers followed by showy bright red berries. Useful on banks to control erosion. Also known as rock spray.

rockcress *n.* The common name *Arabis,* a genus of low-growing annuals, biennials, and perennials

457

(Cruciferae), many species native to North America. They have spikes of white pink or purple flowers and thrive in full sun.

rockcress, mountain *n.* A common name for *Arabis alpina,* a perennial with leaves in basal rosettes and white flowers. Plants grown under this name are often the closely-related *A. cavcasica.*

rockcress, California *n.* A common name for *Arabis blepharophylla,* a perennial that grows to 8 inches with oblong leaves and fragrant rose-purple flowers. It is native to central California. Also known as purple rockcress.

rockcress, wall *n.* A common name for *Arabis caucasica (A. albaa),* a perennial with soft, furry white leaves in tufted rosettes and spikes of fragrant white flowers.

rockcress, purple *n.* A common name for *Arabis blepharophylla.* (See **rockcress, California.**)

rock elm *n.* A common name for *Ulmus thomasii* (*U. racemosa*), a very hardy decidous tree native to eastern North America from Quebec to Nebraska. It has large leaves, notched on the edges, and downy beneath. The branches are heavily ridged. Also known as cork elm.

rockery *n., pl.* An artificial mound formed of rocks, the spaces between them filled with earth. Often used for planting small choice plants that require fast drainage, such as ferns or alpines.

rocker bottom *n.* A tool having a curved blade shaped like the rocker of a rocking chair. Used to remove weeds with deep tap roots from hard ground.

rockery trowel *n.* A narrow tool for weeding and planting in rock gardens and other tight spots.

rocket *n.* A common name for *Eruca vesicaria (E. sativa),* an annual widely used as a salad herb. Also known as rocket, roquette, arugula, and rucola. The name is also sometimes applied to *Barbarea vulgaris,* also called winter cress, and to species of *Diplotaxis.*

rocket, dame's *n.* A common name for *Hesperis matronalis,* a biennial or perennial grown for its fragrant lilac, purple, or white flowers. It is also known as dame's violet and white rocket.

rocket

rocket, dyer's *n.* A common name for *Reseda luteola,* a biennial that grows to 5 feet with leaves divided into leaflets and short spikes of greenish-yellow flowers. Also known as weld.

rocket larkspur *n.* A common name for *Consolida ambigua (Delphinium consolidda).* Also known as larkspur. (See **larkspur.**)

rock garden *n.* A rocky area, natural or constructed, where alpine and other small plants are grown.

rock plant *n.* A plant that grows on or among rocks in its native habitat, such as many small ferns.

rock purslane (pers'layn) *n.* A common name for *Calandinia,* a genus of fleshy low perennials (Porlulacaceae) with narrow basal or alternate leaves and clusters of red or rose flowers. used in borders and rock gardens.

rockrose *n.* A common name for *Cistus,* a genus of evergreen shrubs. They are drought tolerant and will survive light frost. All have showy white, pink, or reddish purple flowers, and some have fragrant foliage.

rockrose family *n.* A common name for the family Cistaceae, which includes *Cistus, Halimium, Halimiocistus,* and *Helianthemum* (the sunroses).

rock spiraea (spigh ree'uh) *n.* A common name for *Petrophytum,* 3 species of low, mat-forming plants (Rosaceae) with feathery white flower spikes that rise a few inches above mats of tiny evergreen leaves. It is used in rock gardens.

Rodgersia (rod jers'ee uh) *n.* A genus of 6 species of large perennial herbs (Saxifragaceae). They grow to 5 or 6 feet tall, with large leaves divided into leaflets or deeply lobed. Small astilbelike flowers are less important than the foliage. All like much moisture and rich soil. *R. aesculifolia, R. pinnata,* and *R. podophylla* are useful in bog or waterside gardens. *R. tabularis,* with round, shield-shaped leaves, is now classified as *Astilboides tabularis.*

Rodriguezia (rahd ree geez'ee uh) *n.* A genus of 35 epiphytic perennial orchids (Orchidaceae) native to tropical America. It has clusters of showy, fragrant, white, cream, yellow, or red flowers, often with contrasting markings. Grown in greenhouses.

Roemeria (roh'mar ee uh) *n.* A genus of 6 species of slender annuals (Papaveraceae). They have finely divided leaves and showy short-lived poppy-like red or purple flowers. Also called purple horned poppy or wind rose.

rogue *n.* A plant that falls short of a standard of horticultural quality required by nurserymen, gardeners, etc. *v.* To uproot or destroy, as plants which do not conform to a desired standard.

Rohdea (roh'dee uh) *n.* A genus of 2 or three species of rhizomatous perennials (Liliaceae), *R. japonica* is an evergreen perennial (Liliaceae) that grows from a stout rhizome. It has fans of leathery, deep green leaves and inconspicuous flowers in a short dense spike that are followed by bright red fruits. Forms with white-variegated or crested leaves are much cherished by collectors.

roller *n.* A metal, water-filled drum mounted on an axle used for smoothing and tamping soil and turf.

romaine lettuce (roh mayn') *n.* A tall-growing variety of lettuce, whose firm leafstalks remain straight instead of curving around the crown at the top to form a sphere. It has frilly, dark outer leaves and a crisp, light green heart.

romano (roh mahn'oh) *n.* A flat-podded variety of green bean, available in either pole or bush plants.

roma tomato (roh'mah) *n.* A small, egg-shaped variety of tomato, with thick flesh and less juice than slicing tomatoes. They are favored for making tomato sauces and other cooking uses, because they are drier and meatier. Also called Italian tomato or plum tomato.

Romneya (rohm'nee uh) *n.* A genus of 1, possibly 2, large shrubby perennials (Papaveraceae). *R. coulteri,* the matilija or matilija poppy, is an 8-foot plant with gray green leaves and white, yellow-centered poppy flowers to 9 inches across. It spreads freely by underground rhizomes. For best appearance, it should be cut back to short stubs in winter, and mulched heavily where frosts are severe. *R. trichocalyx* is probably a minor variant of *R. coulteri.*

Rondeletia (ran'deh leh'shuh) *n.* A genus of 150 tropical shrubs or trees (Rubiaceae) native to the Americas. All have evergreen foliage and clustered flowers at the branch tips. *R. amoena,* grows to 15 feet, with salmon pink flowers with yellow throats. *R. cordata* is similar, with red buds opening to salmon flowers.

roof garden *n.* An urban garden on the flat roof of a building in which plants are grown in containers or, occasionally, raised beds.

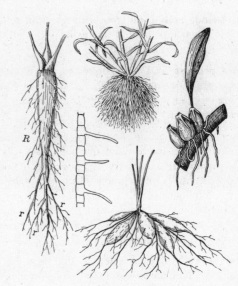

roots of various plants

root *n.* In botany, the part of a plant that typically grows downward into the soil and serves to anchor the plant, as well as to absorb water and minerals needed by the plant for its growth and other functions. The root systems of plants vary greatly in size and shape, depending on the species and growing conditions, from taproots reaching deep underground to spreading fibrous masses consisting of many rootlets; they are often deeper and/or broader than the above-ground height and spread of the plant.

rooter *n*. A tool similar to a mattock having a bladed end for digging small holes for bulbs or plants and a toothed end to chop and pry weeds from the soil.

root grafting *n*. In horticulture, the process of grafting scions (shoots) directly on a small part of the root of some appropriate stock, the grafted root being then potted.

rooting compound *n*. A powdery substance into which fresh cuttings are dipped before inserting in soil or medium, containing hormones to promote the formation of roots.

root irrigator *n*. A sprinkler which produces surges of water to force moisture deep into the ground. Especially useful for trees and shrubs growing in heavy or compacted soil.

root-knot nematode (root′naht neem′uh tohd) *n*. Any nematode that causes swollen growths on plant roots. (See **nematode**.)

root pruning *v*. The act of cutting the roots of large plants, primarily shrubs or trees, to force more vigorous growth or to prepare the plant for transplantation.

root rot *n*. A name used to describe a disease caused by soil-borne fungi that kill plant roots. Such fungi thrive in overly wet or poorly drained soil with insufficient aeration. Plants turn yellow, individual branches wilt or die back, and the entire plant may die. The best control is to improve drainage and cut back on watering. Very few fungicides provide effective control.

root weevils *n. pl.* A group of flightless insects that attack both the leaves and roots of many plants. The adult beetles chew notches in leaves. The larvae feed on roots, causing plants to wilt or die. Control with floating row covers, hand-picking, sticky barriers on trunks, parasitic nematodes, pyrethrum, rotenone, or traditional insecticides.

root zone *n*. The part of the soil in which plant roots grow.

Rosa *n*. A genus of 100 to 150 species of erect or climbing shrubs, the roses (Rosaceae). They have compound leaves, stems that are often thorny or prickly, and 5-petaled red, pink, white, or yellow flowers with many stamens. Many roses are known by their common name (see **rose**). Others are known generally by their scientific names. *R. ecae*, a 3-foot rose with yellow flowers, is a parent of some shrub roses. *R. filipes* is a climber with clustered small white flowers. *R. xfortuniana* is a tender evergreen rose with double white flowers; it is used as an understock in mild climates. *R. gigantea* is a huge climber with 6-inch pale yellow to cream flowers; it is a parent of 'Belle of Portugal,' a large pink double rose. *R. moyesii* is a 10-foot shrub with deep red flowers. *R. omeiensis pteracantha* is notable chiefly for its huge, soft, blood-red prickles. *R. primula* resembles *R. ecae,* but is taller. Aso important to this genus are the thousands of named hybrids that have appeared over the centuries.

Rosaceae (roh zay′see ee) *n*. The rose family, with 107 genera and 3,100 species, includes trees, shrubs, and herbaceous plants. The family includes most of the temperate-climate fruits and a very large number of ornamental trees, shrubs, and flower garden plants. Widely planted genera include *Amelanchier* (service berry), *Crataegus* (hawthorne), *Mahs* (apple), *Prunus* (cherry or plum), *Pyrus* (pear), *Rosa* (rose), and many others.

rosarian (roh zah′ree uhn) *n*. A cultivator of roses; a rose- grower; a rose-fancier.

rose *n*. 1. A common name for *Rosa,* a genus of erect, climbing, evergreen or (usually) deciduous flowering shrubs. They are among the best loved and most widely planted of all garden shrubs. 2. A perforated nozzle attached to the spout of a watering can or to a wand to break water or other liquid into fine particles and blow it through the air. Roses are made in differing sizes to produce spray ranging from extra fine to coarse.

rose acacia (uh kay′shuh) *n*. A common name for *Robinia hispida,* also known as bristly locust or moss locust, a hardy deciduous shrub or small tree with divided leaves and drooping clusters of pea-shaped purplish rose flowers.

rose, Alpine *n*. A common name for *Rose pendulina,* a fairly hardy, nearly thornless rose that grows to 4 feet, with red, rose, or purple 1½-inch flowers and somewhat furry leaves.

rose, apothecary *n*. A common name for *Rose gallica.*

rose apple *n*. A common name for the tropical evergreen tree, *Syzygium jambos (Eugenia jambos)* that grows to 40 feet, with attractive glossy leaves and white flowers. The 1½-inch pale yellow fragrant fruit that is bland, but useful for preserves.

rose arch *n*. A structure which supports climbing roses or other vines or shrubs which is used to span an opening, as the entrance or passage to a garden.

rose, Austrian brier *n*. A common name for *Rosa foetida,* a hardy deciduous prickly shrub which has oddly-scented single yellow flowers 2 to 3 inches across. It is a slender shrub that has cones 5 to 10 feet long.

rose, Austrian copper *n*. A common name for *Rose foetida,* 'Bicolor'. It resembles Austrian brier rose, but the single flowers are scarlet inside, yellow outside. It is an important ancestor of modern hybrid teas.

rose, baby *n*. A common name for *Rosa multiflora,* a vigorous hardy deciduous climber to 10 feet and as wide. It has clusters of small white flowers, followed by profusion of red fruit which attracts birds. Can be either thorny or thornless. Best on large properties; the spiny form makes a good barrier hedge.

rose, Banksia (bangk'see uh) *n*. A common name for *R. Banksiae,* an evergreen thornless climbing rose with single or double white or yellow flowers. Also known as Lady Banks' rose and Banksian rose.

rosebay *n*. 1. A common name for *Rhododendron maximum,* a very hardy evergreen shrub or tree native to the Appalachian region of the United States. It grows 15 to 30 feet with long oblong leaves and clusters of rose pink flowers. Also known as great laurel. 2. A common name for *Nerium oleander,* also known as oleander. (See **oleander.**)

rosebay, Lapland *n*. A common name for *Rhododendron lapponicum,* a very hardy dwarf shrub natove to the Arctic. It grows to 12 inches with tiny oblong leaves and small purplish-pink flowers.

rose, Bengal *n*. (See **rose, China.**)

rose, Bourbon *n*. A common name for *Rose* ×*borboniana,* a group of hybrid roses of much debated parentage. Suggested parents include *R. odorata* (Tea rose), *R. chinensis* (China rose), and *R. damascena bifera* (Autum Damask rose). Bourbon roses are hardy, deciduous shrubs or climbers with very fragrant white pink or red flowers. Extremely popular from 1820 to 1870, they are now cherished as antique roses. Best known varieties include 'La Reine Victoria' and 'Souvenir de la Malmaison'.

rose bower *n*. An arch-shaped latticework trellis used to support roses.

rose, brier *n*. A common name for *Rose canina,* a very hardy, very prickly shrub that grows up to 10-feet tall, with arching canes and clusters of white or pink flowers followed by bright red fruit. Also called dog rose and dog brier.

rose, burnet *n*. A common name for *Rose pimpinellifolia (R. spinosissima),* a hardy 3-foot prickly shrub with white, yellow or rarely pink flowers. Also called Scotch rose.

rose, cabbage *n*. A common name for *Rosa centifolia,* a hardy, prickly, deciduous, large shrub to 6 feet with very fragrant, double pink flowers. A source of attar of roses. Also called Provence rose, Provins rose, and hundred-leaved rose. A favorite old rose, the best varieties for small gardens are 'Rose de Meaux' and 'Petite de Hollande'. This is the rose of the Dutch Masters.

rose, California *n*. A common name for *Rosa californica,* a hardy, prickly large shrub to 10 feet with single pink flowers that is native to California.

rose campion (kam'pee uhn) *n*. A common name for *Lychnis coronaria,* a perennial (Caryophyllaceae). It is a self-sowing woolly-white, branching plant with magenta-red flowers. White- and pink-flowered forms exist. It is also called mullein pink and dusty-miller.

rose chafer (chay'fer) *n*. A type of scarab beetle that damages many plants, including roses and other flowers, lawns, and vegetables. The damage is similar to that done by the Japanese beetle: lacy patches on the foliage and deformed blossoms. To control, cultivate around plants to destroy overwintering grubs; release parasitic nematodes, use row covers, or spray with rotenone, pyrethrum, or traditional insecticides.

rose, Cherokee *n.* A common name for *Rosa laevigata*, a hardy, prickly evergreen climbing rose to 15 feet with large white fragrant single flowers followed by orange fruit. It has naturalized in the United States.

rose, chestnut *n.* A common name for *Rosa roxburghii*, a prickly shrub to 8 feet with prickly buds opening to fragrant double, bright pink fowers. Also known as chinquapin rose.

rose, China *n.* A common name for *Rosa chinensis*, a fairly hardy nearly thornless low-growing evergreen rose with clusters of pink flowers. Its variety 'Minima' (*R. roulettii*), is an ancestor of the miniature roses. China roses were crossed with Autumn Damask roses (*R. damaseena bifera*) to produce modern repeat-blooming roses.

rose, Christmas *n.* A common name for *Helleborus niger*, a hardy, evergreen perennial in the buttercup family (Ranunculaceae) that blooms in the winter. See Christmas rose under Christmas, hellebore, and *Helleborus*.

rose, cinnamon *n.* A common name for *Rosa cinnamomea*, a hardy, prickly thicket-forming rose that grows to 6 feet, with slim, red, flexible cones and 2-inch purplish-pink flowers followed by scarlet fruit.

rose, climbing *n.* A common name for *Rosa setigera*, a hardy, prickly vigorous garden rose that grows from 3 feet to 6 feet, with clustered pink flowers that fade to white. Native to North America from Ontario to Florida, it is used in breeding roses for hardiness. Also called prairie rose.

rose, cluster *n.* A common name for *Rosa pisocarpa*, a hardy, nearly thornless rose that grows to 6 feet tall, with 1-inch pink flowers. It is native to North America from British Columbia to California.

rose, damask (dam'uhsk) *n.* A common name for *Rosa damascena*, a large, hardy old rose that grows up to 8 feet, with very fragrant double pink to red flowers. R.d. 'Versicolor', is the celebrated York and Lancaster rose, with pure white, pure pink, and variegated pink and white bloom on a single bush. Other excellent varieties are 'Celsiana' with blush pink blooms and 'Madame Hardy', white with green center. *R.d. bifera* (Autumn Damask) is the "Rose of Castile" of Spanash missions.

rose, dog *n.* (See **rose, brier**.)

rose, eglantine (ehg'luhn tighn) *n.* A common name for *Rosa eglanteria*, a hardy, deciduous, vigorous shrub or climber to 6 feet with fragrant foliage and bright pink flowers. The leaves smell like apples, especially after rain. Also called sweetbrier and eglantine.

rose, evergreen *n.* A common name for *Rosa sempervirens*, a tall hardy, prickly, climbing evergreen rose to 16 feet with fragrant single white flowers followed by orange-red fruits.

rose, fairy *n.* A common name for *Rosa chinensis minima* (*R. rouletti*,) a hardy dwarf rose to 18 inches with small single or double rose-red flowers. The parent of the miniature roses.

rose family *n.* A common name for Rosaceae. (See **Rosaceae**.)

rose, Father Hugo's *n.* A common name for *Rosa hugonis*, a dense, hardy, prickly deciduous shrub with arching branches to 8 feet covered with lightly fragrant bright yellow 2-inch flowers followed by dark red fruit.

rose, French *n.* A common name for *Rosa gallica*, a hardy, thorny, deciduous shrub to 5 feet with pink, slate blue, purple or red flowers that have traditional old rose fragrance. *R.g.* 'Officinalis' is the apothecary rose which grows to 30 inches tall with semidouble, very fragrant flowers. It is also known as the red rose of Lancaster. The petals of French roses are dried for potpourri. It has naturalized in eastern North America.

rose geranium (juh ray'nee uhm) *n.* The common name of *Pelargonium graveolens*, a popular houseplant or tender garden plant with fragrant foliage and small purplish-pink flowers. There are many named varieties.

rose, ground *n.* A common name for *Rosa spithamea*, a prickly low-growing single pink rose native to California that spreads by creepy rootstocks.

rose, guelder (gehld'uhr) *n.* A comon name for *Viburnum opulus*, a shrub in the honeysuckle family (Caprifoliaceae). (See **guelder rose**.)

rose, Harison's yellow *n.* A common name for *Rosa ✕ harisonii*, a vigorous, hardy, thorny, deciduous low-rowing rose with fragrant, semi-double bright yellow flowers and show fruit. An old rose that is disease-free and resistant to drought once established.

rose, Himalayan musk *n*. A common name for *Rosa Brunonii,* a very hardy, very thorny deciduous tall climber with many fragrant white flowers.

rose, hip *n*. A common name for the fruit of roses.

rose, hundred-leafed *n*. (See **rose, cabbage.**)

rose, Japanese *n*. A common name for *Rosa rugosa,* a prickly, vigorous exceptionally hardy rose that grows from 3 to 8 feet. It has handsome, crinkly leaves and single pink fragrant flowers followed by large red fruits. Also known as sea tomato and ramanas rose.

rose, Lady Penzance *n*. A common name for *Rosa* × *penzanceana,* a thorny climber with pink or amber yellow-centered flowers. It is a hybrid of sweetbrier and Austrian brier.

roselle (roh zehl) *n*. A common name for *Hibiscus sabdariffa,* an annual or perennial plant that grows to 6 feet tall. It has yellow flowers with bracts and bright red fruit. The acid fruit is used in making refreshing drinks and jellies. It is an ingredient in herb teas under the name Jamaica or Jamaica sorrel. It is also called Indian or red sorrel in the West Indies.

rose, Macartney *n*. A common name for *Rosa bracteata,* a hardy, prickly tall climbing evergreen rose to 20 feet with large, fragrant white flowers followed by bright orange fruit. It has naturalized in the United States.

rose mallow *n*. 1. A common name loosely applied to any member of the genus *Hibiscus*. 2. More specifically, *H. moscheutos,* a perennial that grows to 8 feet, with 6- to 8-inch white, pink, or red flowers.. It is also called common rose mallow. (See **Hibiscus**.)

rose mallow, great *n*. A common name for *Hibiscus grandiflorus,* a tender evergreen perennial shrub native to the south-eastern United States. It grows to 8 feet with large leaves and huge white, pink, or purple-rose flowers with a red center.

rose mallow, soldier *n*. A common name for *Hibiscus militaris,* a hardy evergreen perennial shrub. It grows from 3 to 7 feet, triangular leaves, and pink white flowers, crimson at the center. It is native to the United States from Pennsylvania and Minnesota to Texas and Florida. Also called halberd-leaved rose mallow.

rose marker *n*. A large label, typically of metal, mounted at an angle on a long stake or stakes, used to identify roses.

rosemary *n*. A woody evergreen shrub, *Rosmarinus officinalis,* widely cultivated in herb gardens. A trailing variety is called prostrate or bonsai rosemary. The leaves have a fragrant smell and a warm, pungent taste; it is used to flavor meat dishes, especially lamb and chicken. Its aromatic leaves are long and needlelike, its flowers white to pale blue and very small. The shrub grows to 8 feet in height in southern climates. In gardens north of Connecticut, it is brought indoors in pots for the winter.

rosemary
1 flower 2 leaf

rosemary, bog *n*. A common name for *Andromeda polifolia,* a very hardy dwarf, creeping North American shrub with gray-green narrow leaves and clusters of small pale pink flowers at the branch tips. Also a common name for the genus. (See **bog, rosemary**.)

rosemary, wild *n*. A common name for *Ledum palustre,* a 3-foot shrub with narrow evergreen leaves and densely clustered small white flowers.

rose, memorial *n*. A common name for *Rosa wichuraiana,* a hardy evergreen or semi-evergreen trailer or climber with white flowers.

rose moss *n*. A common name for *Portulaca grandiflora,* a showy succulent annual in the purslane family (Portulacaceae). Usually called Portulaca.

rose, moss *n.* A common name for *Rosa centifolia,* 'Muscosa', a hardy, prickly deciduous shrub with stems and buds that are covered with a mossy fringe of stout green hairs. A Victorian favorite, and a cherished old rose, it grows to 6 feet with very fragrant, double pink flowers.

rose, musk *n.* A common name for *Rosa moschata,* a vigorous, prickly, hardy deciduous shrub. It grows to 8 feet with clusters of ivory white flowers of musky fragrance on arching branches.

rose, Noisette *n.* A common name for *Rosa* × *noisettiana,* a tender, deciduous shrubby climbing rose, a hybrid between musk and China roses. Noisette roses bloom repeatedly with clusters of white, pink, or red flowers.

rose, Nootka *n.* A common name for *Rosa nutkana,* a hardy, prickly, deciduous shrub to 6 feet with pink flowers and red fruit. It is native from California to Alaska.

rose-of-heaven *n.* A common name for *Lychnis coeli-rosa,* a freely branching annual. It bears a profusion of inch-wide flowers in pink, red, or lavender-blue. An excellent cut flower, it is sometimes sold as *Viscaria, Agrostemma,* or *Silene.*

rose-of-Sharon *n.* 1. A common name for *Hibiscus syriacus,* a hardy deciduous shrub that grows to 10 feet or more. It bears single or double white, pink, red, or purplish-blue flowers 3 inches wide. It is also called althaea or shrub althaea. 2. *Hypericum calycinum,* a shrubby ground cover plant in the St.-John's-wort family (Hypericaceae). It is better known as Aaron's-beard or creeping St.-John's-wort.

rose-of-Venezuela *n.* A common name for *Brownea grandiceps,* a tropical evergreen tree with coarse, divided foliage and 8- to 9-inch tight, round, clusters of bright red flowers.

rose, pasture *n.* A commonn name for *Rosa carolina,* a very hardy wild rose to 3 feet with pink flowers. It is native from Nova Scotia and Minnesota to Nebraska and Florida.

rose, Persian yellow *n.* A common name for *Rosa foetida* 'Persiana', a variety of Austrian brier with bright yellow double flowers that don't smell good.

rose, polyantha (pahl ee an'thuh) *n.* A common namme for *Rosa rehderana,* a low, spreading bush with white flowers in large clusters.

rosery *n.* A place where roses grow; a nursery of rose-bushes; a rosary.

rose-scented geranium (juh ray'nee uhm) *n.* A common name for *Pelargonium capitatum,* a scented-leaf geranium with many named varieties.

rose, swamp *n.* A common name for *Rosa palustris,* a thicket-forming rose that grows up to 7 feet, with 2-inch pink flowers.

rose, tea *n.* A common name for *Rosa odorata,* a fairly hardy evergreen shrub or climber with white, pink, or yellow flowers. These are the florist's roses with large blooms, long stems, and not much fragrance. Subject to nearly innumerable pests and diseases.

rose tree *n.* A standard (pruned and trained to grow on a single trunk in a topiary) rose; a rose-bush.

rosetum (roh zeh'tuhm) *n., pl.* **rosetums, roseta.** A garden or border devoted to the cultivation of roses.

rose, Turkestan *n.* (See **rose, Japanese.**)

rose, wood *n.* A common name for *Rosa gymnocarpa,* an 8-foot shrub of the West Coast of North America, with 1-inch flowers.

rosin plant
(*Silphium* species)

rosin plant (rahz'uhn) *n.* 1. Plants in the genus *Silphium,* large perennials, especially *S. laciniatum,*

western United States. Its roots are a source of tannin and yellow dye. *R. acetosella,* sheep sorrel, red sorrel, or common sorrel, is a common weed of roadsides and gardens.

Rumex acetosella
(sheep sorrel)

Rumohra (roo maw'ruh) *n.* A name for *R. adiantiformis,* a tropical or subtropical evergreen fern with finely cut fronds of durable texture. It is widely used in the florist trade and for landscaping. Also known as leather fern, leatherleaf fern, or iron fern,

rupturewort *n.* A common name for plants of the genus *Herniaria,* annual or perennial plants in the pink family. *H. glabra* is used in rock gardens or as a low groundcover. A flat, spreading grower, it is densely clad with tiny roundish green leaves that take on reddish tones in cold weather.

Ruschia (roosh'ee uh) *n.* A genus of about 350 species of small succulent shrubs or perennials (Aizoaceae). They have thick, triangular, blue-green leaves and white or pink flowers that resemblance daisies. Grown as houseplants or greenhouse plants.

Ruscus (ruhs'kuhs) *n.* A genus of 3 species of evergreen shrubby plants (Liliaceae). All have minute leaves and leathery, deep green leaflike branches. Male and female flowers are borne on the pseudo-

leaf surfaces, and if both sexes are present the females produce bright red globular fruits. *R. aculeatus* is commonly called butcher's broom. Its branches are stiff and spine-pointed. *R. hypoglossum* is similar, but more rounded in growth habit and not spiny.

rush *n.* Any plant in the genus *Juncus,* plants with roundish, generally erect green stems. Leaves are sometimes present. Most are found in wet ground. Flowers are clustered at stem tops and are generally inconspicuous. A few are grown for their odd form. The name is also occasionally applied to plants with similar form.

rush, flowering *n.* A common name for *Butomus umbellatus* (Butomaceae), a water-loving hardy perennial. It has rushlike leaves, and open clusters of pink flowers on 4½-foot stems. Also known as water gladiole.

rush, soft *n.* A common name for *Juncus effusus,* a hardy perennial that grows from 1- to 6- feet tall.

rush, spiral *n.* A common name for *Junas effusus (Spiralis),* a variety of the soft rush that has spirally twisted stems.

rush, zebra *n.* A common name for *Junas effusus (Vittatus)* and *J. effusus (Zebrinus).* These have stems horizontally banded with white and green.

rush nut *n.* A common name for *Cyperus esculentus,* a hardy perennial plant that grows from 6 to 24 inches tall and has roots bearing small brown tubers. It is commonly called nutsedge or nut grass. A nearly ineradicable lawn weed. The variety 'Sativus' has larger tubers which are edible. Also called chufa or earth almond.

Russelia (ruh see'lee uh) *n.* A genus of 50 species of tender shrubs or subshrubs (Scrophulariaceae). *R. equisetiformis* has trailing or climbing bright green branches to 4 feet long, with small leaves that drop soon. It bears a profusion of red firecracker-shaped flowers nearly throughout the year in mild climates. An excellent hanging basket plant. Common names are coral plant, fountain plant, or fountain bush.

russet (ruhs'iht) *n.* A brown-skinned baking potato with flaky white flesh.

Russian olive *n.* A common name for *Elaeagnus angustifolia,* a hardy deciduous tree. Growing to 20 feet or more, it has narrow leaves, silvery beneath, tiny yellow fragrant flowers, and small yellow and silvery inedible fruit. It is widely planted in harsh climates for its resistance to cold, drought, and wind, and for its fruit which is eaten by birds.

Russian statice (stat'ihs) *n.* An annual plant, *Phylliostachys Suworowii,* grown for its long spikes of tiny bright pink flowers, which dry very well for winter arrangements. Also known as pink pokers, they are usually sold under the incorrect classification of the related genus *Limonium.*

rust *n.* A fungal disease that forms small pustules of red-brown (sometimes purple) spores on the undersides of leaves, which eventually turn yellow and die. It infects many plants, including roses, hollyhocks, snapdragons, and some lawn grasses. Warm days, cool nights, and wet foliage encourage development. To control, clean up dead leaves and infected plants, avoid overhead watering late in the day, or spray with traditional fungicides. Heavier fertilization and more frequent mowing will help control rust in lawns.

Ruta (roo'duh) *n.* A genus of 40 species of aromatic perennials or subshrubs (Rutaceae). *R. graveolens* (rue), is the only one commonly grown. (See **rue.**)

rutabaga (roo'tuh bay'guh) *n.* A root vegetable, larger than the common turnip, and with yellow flesh. It is a member of the *Rapifera* group of *Brassica Rapa.* The leaves are smooth and dusty looking, and the roots are almost round. The rutabaga is more nutritious than the common turnip and has a much stronger flavor.

Rutaceae (roo tay'see ee) *n.* The rue family, consisting of about 150 genera and 1,600 species of trees or shrubs, evergreen or deciduous. The best known plants in the family are the species of *Citrus,* although there are other ornamental and useful genera.

ryegrass *n.* (See **Lolium.**)

rynia (righ'nee uh) *n.* A slow-acting botanical insecticide derived from the stems of tropical rynia. Relatively long-lasting (up to 2 weeks) and toxic in concentrated forms. Often combined with other botanicals.

sabadilla (sa ba dee'yuh) *n.* A broad-spectrum, short residual (2 days in sunlight) botanical insecticide derived from a South American lily. It can be very toxic to humans in purified form.

Sabal (sah'bahl) *n.* A genus of more than a dozen species of slow-growing subtropical palms (Palmae) native to the southwestern United States, the Caribbean, Mexico, and Central America. They grow from 6 to 90 feet. Some common species include *S. bermudana* (Bermuda palm), to 40 feet; *S. Blackburniana* (Hispaniolan palmetto); *S. Palmetto* (cabbage palm), to 90 feet; and *S. uresana* (Sonoran palm), to 30 feet. Commonly known as palmetto.

Sabal Palmetto
(Cabbage palm)

Sabbatia (sub bah'tee uh) *n.* A genus of 17 species of annual or hardy perennial plants (Gentianaceae) native to North America. They grow to 3 feet, with opposite leaves at the base and rose or white flowers in rounded clusters. Commonly known as American centaury, sea pink, marsh pink, rose pink, and bitter bloom.

Sabbatia
(American Centaury)
1 upper plant and flowers *2* root and lower stem

Sabiaceae (sa bee ay'see ee) *n. pl.* A family of 4 genera of vines, shrubs, and trees. They have simple or divided leaves, small flowers, and berrylike fruit. *Meliosma* is the only genus used as an ornamental.

sabicu (sahb eh koo') *n.* A common name for *Lysiloma latisiliqua,* a tropical tree growing to 50 feet.

sabulous (sahb'uh luhs) *a.* In botany, sandy; gritty. Also sabulose, sabuline.

saccate (sak'at) *a.* In botany, furnished with or having the form of a bag, pouch, or sac, as a saccate petal. Also saccated.

sacciform (sak'si form) *a.* Resembling a pouch.

Saccolabium (sk oh la'bi uhm) *n.* A genus of 6 species of epiphytic tropical flowering orchids (Orchidaceae), some species native to the East Indies. They have leathery leaves and small flowers on loose spikes or in clusters.

Sadleria (sad leh'i uh) *n.* A genus of 6 species of tropical tree ferns (Polypodiaceae) native to Hawaii. They grow to 5 feet or more.

safety glasses *n.* (See **goggles**.)

safflower (sa'flaw uhr) *n.* A plant, *Carthamus tinctorius;* also, a dyestuff consisting of its dried florets. The safflower is a thistlelike herb, 1 or 2 feet high, somewhat branching, with orange-red heads. It is sometimes planted in herb and flower gardens in the United States. Safflower is occasionally used as a substitute for saffron for its color, although it does not add a saffron flavor. As a dye, it imparts bright tints of red, but these are not permanent. It is sometimes used to adulterate saffron. Also called African saffron, false saffron, and dyer's saffron.

safflower

saffron (saf'ruhn) *n.* 1. The dried stigmas of the flowers of the autumn crocus, *Crocus sativus,* which is used as a seasoning, especially for rice dishes. The product of more than 4,000 flowers is required to make 1 ounce. It has a sweetish, aromatic odor, a faintly pungent taste, and a deep orange color. 2. The plant that produces saffron, a low bulbous herb, *Crocus sativus,* the autumn crocus. The saffron resembles the ordinary spring crocus, with handsome purple flowers.

saffron, bastard (saf'ruhn) *n.* Same as safflower.

saffron-crocus (saf'ruhn kroh'kuhs) *n.* (See **Saffron**.)

saffron, meadow (saf'ruhn) *n.* A common name for *Colchium autumnale,* a bulblike plant. It has narrow, pointed leaves that appear in spring and purple, pink, or white flowers that bloom in late summer after the leaves have died back. The corms are extremely poisonous, though they are a source of the drugs colchium and colchicine. Also known as autumn crocus, fall crocus, mysteria, and wonder bulb.

sage *n.* A plant of the genus *Salvia,* especially *S. officinalis,* the common garden sage. This is a shrubby perennial, sometimes treated as an annual, with rough, light green leaves and blue flowers, variegated with white and purple, arranged in groups along a tall stem. The main use of sage is as a condiment in flavoring poultry dressings, sausages, and cheeses. Sage is a favorite in herb gardens, where it will thrive as far north as central New England.

sage
1 slower stalk *2* stem with leaves

sage, black *n.* 1. A common name for *Trichostema lanatum,* a hardy shrub native to California. It grows 3 to 5 feet high, with long, narrow leaves that are fragrant when bruised, and striking blue flowers in clusters at the ends of stems in late spring and summer. Also known as woolly blue curls. 2. A common name for *Salvia mellifera,* a hardy shrub native to California. It grows to 7 feet, with oblong leaves, green and crinkled above, white and downy beneath, and very small lavender-blue flowers, the source of sage honey. 3. A common name for *Artemesia tridentata,* a hardy shrub native to dry areas west of the Rocky Mountains, from British Columbia to Baja California. It grows to 12 feet tall, with highly aromatic wedge-shaped silvery-gray leaves. Also known as common sage, basin sage, and big sagebrush.

sagebrush *n.* A collective name of various species of *Artemisia,* which cover immense areas on the dry, often alkaline, plains and mountains of the western United States. They are dry, shrubby, and bushy plants with a hoary, sagelike aspect, but without botanical affinity with the sage. The most characteristic species is *A. tridentata,* which grows from 1 to 6, and even 12 feet high, and is prodigiously abundant. A smaller species is *A. arbuscula,* that grows to only 1 foot tall.

sagebrush

sage, Jerusalem *n.* 1. A common name for *Phlomis fruticosa,* a hardy shrubby perennial. It grows to 4 feet, with gray-green leaves, and produces many dense whorls of rich yellow flowers. 2. A common name for *Pulmonaria officinalis,* a hardy perennial flowering plant. It grows to 1 foot, with oval or heart-shaped leaves and rose-violet or blue flowers. Also known as Jerusalem cowslip and blue lungwort.

Sageretia (sahj uh re′tee uh) *n.* A genus of more than 30 species of hardy shrubs (Rhamnaceae). They have opposite leaves and clusters or spikes of small white flowers.

sage, scarlet *n.* 1. A common name for *Salvia splendens,* a subtropical perennial flowering subshrub, often grown as an annual. It grows to 8 feet, with pointed oval leaves and brilliant scarlet flowers. It blooms from early summer to frost. 2. A common name for *Salvia coccinea,* a sub-tropical perennial, usually grown as an annual. It grows to 2 feet, with scalloped-edged leaves and deep scarlet flowers with purple overtones. Also known as Texas sage.

sage tree *n*. A common name for *Vitex agnus-castus,* a subtropical shrub or small tree. It grows to 20 feet, with narrow leaves, dark green above and gray on the underside. The lilac to lavender flowers appear in thick, long spikes in summer and fall. Also known as chaste tree, hemp tree, Indian-spice tree, and wild pepper.

sage, white *n*. 1. A common name for *Artemesia ludoviciana,* a hardy perennial flower native to the Midwest south to Mexico. It grows to 3 feet, with narrow-pointed leaves, gray-green on the underside, and clusters of small white flowers. Also known as western mugwort, cudweed, winter fat, and chamiso. 2. A common name for *Salvia apiana,* a tender perennial small shrub. It grows to 8 feet, with narrow, oblong leaves, mostly at the base of branches, and clusters of small white or pale lavender flowers. Also known as greasewood.

sage, wood *n*. 1. A common name for *Teucrium corodonia,* a tender small shrub. It grows to 1½ feet, with heart-shaped leaves cut off at the base and pale yellow flowers. Also known as wood germander. 2. A common name for *Teucrium canadense,* a hardy flowering perennial. It grows to 3 feet, with narrow, oval leaves, with a grayish fuzz beneath, and pinkish-purple flowers. Also known as American germander.

Sagina (sah jee′nah) *n*. A genus of 25 species of hardy annual or perennial plants (Caryophyllaceae). Forming mats of mosslike mounds, they grow no more than a few inches high, with slender, grasslike leaves and single, scattered small white flowers. Good as a ground cover. Commonly known as pearlwort or Irish moss. A greenish-yellow form, 'Aurea', is known as Scotch moss.

Sagittaria (sahj ih tah′ree uh) *n*. A genus of 20 species of subtropical aquatic perennial plants (Lophotocarpus). The underwater leaves are long and narrow; the leaves above water are shaped like an arrowhead, hence the common name arrowhead. It has white flowers in whorls on leafless stalks. A few species *(S. subulata, S. graminea)* are used as aquarium plants; *S. latifolia,* a native of North America, has 1½-inch-wide flowers. Commonly known as arrowhead, swamp potato, and wapato.

Sagittaria
(arrowhead)

sagittate (sahj′ih tayt) *a*. Shaped like an arrowhead; specifically, in botany, of a leaf: triangular, with the basal lobes pointing downward.

sagittate leaf

sago palm (say′goh) *n*. 1. A common name for *Cycas revoluta,* a somewhat hardy palm tree. It grows slowly to 10 feet, with featherlike leaves growing in rosettes from the top of the trunk. A good container plant or bonsai specimen. Also known as Japanese fern palm. 2. A common name for *Cycas circinalis,* a subtropical palm tree. It grows to 20 feet, with leaves to 8 feet long. Also known as fern palm and queen sago. 3. A common name for *Caryota urens,* a fast-growing tropical palm tree to 40 feet. Also known as wine palm, jaggery palm, and toddy palm.

saguaro (sah gwahr′oh) *n*. A common name for *Carnegiea gigantea,* a subtropical giant cactus. It grows slowly to 50 feet and has night-blooming flowers in May, followed by edible fruit. Suitable as a dramatic container plant. Also known as sahuaro and giant cactus.

sainfoin (sahn′foin) *n*. A common name for *Onobrychis viciifolia,* a hardy perennial ground cover. It grows to 2 feet with pink flowers in clusters. Also known as holy clover and saintfoin.

sainfoin
1 flower stalk 2 leaves

Saint-Bernard's-lily *n.* 1. A common name for *Anthericum Liliaigo,* a subtropical flower. It grows to 3 feet, with long narrow leaves and loose spikes of white flowers. 2. A common name for the genus *Chlorophytum,* a genus of tender perennial plants. They grow to less than 2 feet, with narrow pointed leaves and white flowers. Often grown indoors or in greenhouses. The most widely grown species is *C. comosum,* also called spider plant.

Saint-Bruno's-lily *n.* A common name for *Paradisea Liliastrum,* a hardy flower. It grows to 2 feet, with long, narrow leaves and white flowers in loose clusters. Also known as paradise lily.

Saint-Catherine's-lace *n.* A common name for *Erioganum giganteum,* a hardy shrub native to southern California. It grows to 8 feet, with gray-green leaves and thick clusters of white, woolly flowers.

saintfoin (saynt'foin) *n.* (See **sainfoin**.)

Saint-James's-lily *n.* A common name for *Sprekelia formosissima,* a subtropical flowering bulb. It grows to 1 foot, with long, narrow leaves and bright crimson flowers. Also known as Jacobean lily, aztec lily, and orchid amaryllis.

Saint-John's-bread *n.* A common name for *Ceratonia siliqua,* a hardy (to 18° F) evergreen tree. It grows to 50 feet, with divided, dark green leaves and small red springtime flowers, followed by flat, dark brown fruit pods, which are ground and used as a substitute for chocolate. Also known as carob.

Saint-John's-wort *n.* A common name for the genus *Hypericum,* a somewhat-hardy group of pe-

rennials and shrubs. They grow from 1 to 4 feet tall, with generally green oval leaves and bright yellow flowers. Used as informal hedges and ground covers.

Saintpaulia (saynt pohl'ee uh) *n.* A genus of 21 species of subtropical flowering perennial plants (Gesneriaceae), the best known of which is *S. ionantha,* commonly known as African violet. It has gray to gray-green heart-shaped fleshy leaves that grow in rosettes and are covered with soft, fuzzy hairs. Many cultivars provide a rich palette of choices of flower color and foliage size and color. Extremely popular, relatively trouble-free houseplants in North America.

salad burnet (ber neht') *n.* The perennial salad herb, *Poterium Sanguisorba.* Its leaves are used fresh for their mild cucumber flavor, which is lost in drying. The plant grows to about 12 inches, with pairs of small oval, notched leaves growing from delicate stems. The blossom is a green-to-purple head, ripening to seeds, which self-sow. Popular in herb gardens for its feathery foliage and compact shape.

salad rocket *n.* The arugula, *Eruca sativa.*

salal (sah lahl') *n.* A common name for *Gaultheria shallon,* a hardy small shrub native to southern California. It grows from 2 to 10 feet tall, depending on the amount of sun and water it receives, with oval to nearly round bright green leaves, tiny white flowers in summer, and small, edible (but unremarkable) black fruit. Cut branches used by florists, who call it lemonleaf.

Salicaceae (sahl ee kah'see ee) *n. pl.* A family of 3 genera and 500 species of shrubs and trees. They have simple deciduous leaves and flowers borne in catkins. The ornamental genera are *Populus* and *Salix.*

Salicornia (sahl ee kohr'ne uh) *n.* A genus of 10 species of hardy plants (Chenopodiaceae). *S. europaea* grows to 2 feet, with scalelike leaves that turn a briliant red in fall. Commonly known as glasswort and samphire.

saligot (sahl'ee goht) *n.* A common name for *Trapa natans,* a hardy aquatic plant naturalized in many rivers in the eastern United States. The edible fruit is frequently used in Oriental cuisine. Also known as water chestnut.

saline-alkali soil *n.* Soil having a combination of a harmful quantity of salts and a high degree of alkalinity.

saline soil *n.* A soil containing enough soluble salts to impare its productivity.

Salix (say'lihks) *n.* A genus of about 300 species of very hardy, fast-growing shrubs and trees (Salicaceae) native to all northern and cold regions, rare in the tropics, and very few in the Southern Hemisphere. They grow from 3 to 75 feet, depending on the species, with long, narrow leaves and erect catkins. Most species grow along streams, and many are widely planted to consolidate banks, and thus have become extensively naturalized. Commonly known as willow and osier.

sallow thorn *n.* A common name for *Hippophae rhamnoides,* a very hardy tree. It grows to 30 feet, with willowlike leaves and bright orange-yellow edible fruit, which remains on the tree throughout winter.

salmonberry (sahm'uhn ber'ee *n.* A common name for *Rubus chamaemorus, R. parviflorus,* and *R. spectabilis,* hardy perennial brambles of easy culture. *R. chamaemorus* makes a good rock-garden plant, growing to 10 inches high, and it is very hardy.

Salpiglossis (sahl pee glos'ihs) *n.* A genus of about 5 species of flowering annuals or somewhat-hardy perennials (Solanaceae), usually treated as annuals. The most commonly grown species is *S. sinuata,* which grows to 2½ feet, with 4-inch-long narrow leaves and petunialike flowers ranging from dark red, through yellow, to pink, with a variety of color combinations. There are many named cultivars. Commonly known as painted tongue.

salsify *n.* An old-fashioned garden vegetable, *Tragopogon porrifolius.* It was formerly extensively cultivated for its long root. Its flavor has given rise to the name of oyster plant or vegetable oyster. Its seeds are sown in spring and the plant is left in the ground until the following spring, when the roots are dug. Black salsify, *Scorzonera Hispanica,* is a related plant, with a root like that of salsify but black on the outside. It is similarly used, and its flavor is preferred by some. Black salsify, although a perennial, is treated as an annual in vegetable gardens. Its leaves, which grow to more than 1 foot tall, may be used in salads.

salsify, flowering stalk

salsuginous (sahl suh'gih nuhs) *a.* In botany, growing naturally in soils with a high salt content; halophytic.

saltation *n.* The movement of soil and mineral particles by intermittent leaps from the ground when the particles are being moved by wind or water.

saltbush *n.* A common name for *Atriplex,* a genus of hardy plants and shrubs, many species native to the western United States. They grow from 3 to 6 feet, with silver or gray leaves. Used as fire-retardant plantings on hillsides. Also known as orache.

salt tree *n.* A common name for *Halimodendron halodendron,* a hardy shrub. It grows to 6 feet, with gray leaves on spiny branches and has lavender, pealike flowers that bloom in early June. Well adapted to alkaline soils or near the seashore.

salverform (sahl'vehr form) *a.* In botany, noting a corolla with the outer edge spreading out flat, as in the primrose and phlox; hypocrateriform. Also salver-shaped.

salverform corolas of phlox flowers

Salvia (sahl'vee uh) *n*. A large genus including more than 750 species of annuals, perennials, or shrubs (Labiatae), of various degrees of hardiness, many species native to all parts of the United States. They have a generous palette of flower colors in summer that only excludes yellow. The foliage is equally varied and often provides great horticultural interest. Generally of easy culture and able to flourish in dry, rocky locations. Commonly known as sage or ramona.

Salvinia (sahl vihn'ee uh) *n*. A genus of 10 species of tropical aquatic ferns (Salviniaceae) that grow on the surface of lakes or ponds. *S. rotundifolia* is commonly known as floating moss.

Salviniaceae (sahl vihn ee uh'see ee) *n. pl*. A family of 2 genera and about 18 species of aquatic ferns. Both the genera *Azolla* and *Salvinia* are grown in aquariums and pools.

Samanea (sahm ahn ee'uh) *n*. A genus of 20 species of tropical shrubs and trees (Leguminosae). The most commonly grown species is *S. Saman*, a fast-growing tree, to 80 feet tall and 100 feet wide, with divided leaves and clusters of yellow flowers with long, pink stamens. Commonly known as rain tree, saman, monnkeypod, and zamang.

samara (sah mahr'uh) *n*. In botany, a dry, usually 1-seeded fruit provided with a wing, as in the ash, elm, or birch. Also called key and key fruit.

samariform (sahm'uh ree form) *a*. In botany, having the form of a samara.

Sambucus (sahm boo'khus) *n*. A genus of 20 species of hardy deciduous shrubs and trees (Caprifoliaceae), many native to North America. They grow to 50 feet, with divided leaves, clusters of white flowers, and blue-black to scarlet fruit, edible in some species. Commonly known as elder and elderberry. *S. caerulea* (blue elder), native to the northwestern United States, grows to 50 feet and bears edible fruit. *S. canadensis* (American elderberry), native to the eastern United States, is very hardy; grows to 8 feet, and bears prolific summer fruit. There are many cultivars. *S. pubens* (American red elderberry), native to eastern United States, is a shrub that grows 10 to 15 feet and bears scarlet fruit in late spring. *S. racemosa* (European red elderberry) is a vigorous, bushy shrub to 10 feet, with small yellowish flowers in clusters in May, followed by red fruit.

Sambucus canadensis
(American elderberry)
a flower *b* fruit

Samolus (sahm'oh luhs) *n*. A genus of 10 species of hardy aquatic or moisture-loving plants (Primulaceae). They grow to 2 feet, with simple leaves and small white flowers. Used as plants in aquariums. Commonly known as water pimpernel or brookweed.

samphire
(*Crithmum maritimum*)

474

samphire (sahm′fihr) *n.* 1. A common name for *Crithmum maritimum,* a hardy perennial. It grows to 2 feet, with long, narrow, fleshy leaves and small white flowers. Used as a salad plant. 2. A common name for *Salicornia europaea,* an annual often found growing in salty marshes, with foliage that turns bright red in autumn. Also known as chicken-claws or pigeonfoot.

Sanchezia (sahn chee′zee uh) *n.* A genus of 60 species of tropical plants and vines (Acanthaceae). They grow to 6 feet, with 12-inch- long oval leaves and yellow flowers in spikes.

sandalwood, bastard *n.* A common name for *Myoporum sandwicense,* a subtropical tree. It grows to 60 feet, with oval leaves and small white or pink flowers. Also known as naio.

sandlewood

sandalwood, red *n.* 1. A common name for *Pterocarpus santalinus,* a tropical tree with showy orange-yellow flowers. Also known as red sanderswood. 2. A common name for *Adenanthera pavonina,* a tropical tree. It grows to 50 feet, with large leaves and loose spikes of small white and yellow flowers, followed by dramatic-looking coiled seedpods. Also known as coralwood, redwood, peacock flower-fence, Barbados-pride, or coral pea.

sandalwood, white *n.* A common name for *Santalum album,* a tropical small tree. It grows to 30 feet, with oval leaves and yellowish flowers. The fragrant wood is used to build chests. Also known as sandalwood.

sandarac-tree (sahn′dah rak) *n.* A common name for *Tetraclinis articulata,* an evergreen, cone-bearing tree. It grows to 20 feet, with whorls of scalelike leaves. Also known as arar tree.

sandarac-tree, with cone

sand blackberry *n.* A common name for *Rubus cuneifolius,* a hardy bramble native to the eastern seaboard of United States. Often used as a ground cover in poor soil.

sandbox tree *n.* A common name for *Hura crepitans,* a tropical tree. It grows to 100 feet, with broad oval leaves and red flowers, folowed by ribbed fruit. The fruit explodes with a sharp noise to spread the seeds when ripe. Also known as monkey-pistol, javillo, or monkey's dinner-bell.

sandbox tree fruit

sand cherry *n.* A common name for 1 of a number of different species of *Prunus.* Most are hardy trees. *P. Besseyi* does particularly well in its native habitat of the midwestern United States. Good for pies, jams, and jellies. *P. pumila* (also called dwarf cherry) is grown as a hardy ornamental for its weeping habit and white flowers. *P. depressa* is a similar low-growing species.

sand jack *n.* A common name for *Quercus incana,* a deciduous oak shrub or small tree (to 25 feet) native to the southwestern United States. Also known as bluejack oak, turkey oak, or high-ground willow oak.

sandpaper vine *n.* A common name for *Petrea* (Verbenaceae), a genus of about 30 species of subtropical deciduous woody trees, shrubs, and vines native to the Americas. They grow to 35 feet, with small oblong leaves and blue-to-purple and white flowers in loose clusters. Also known as purple wreath, queen's wreath, or blue bird vine.

sand spurry *n.* A common name for *Spergularia* (Caryophyllaceae), a genus of annual or perennial low-growing plants, with thin leaves and clusters of small, pink flowers. As the common name implies, it grows well by the seashore.

sand verbena (ver bee'nuh) *n.* A common name for *Abronia* (Nyctaginaceae), a genus of low-growing annual or perennial plants (usually grown as annuals) native to the western United States. *A. cycloptera* has bright pink flowers; *A. latifolia,* lemon-yellow flowers; *A. maritima,* dark red flowers; and *A. umbellata,* pink flowers.

sandweed *n.* A common name for *Hypericum fasciculatum,* an evergreen shrub native to the southeastern United States. It grows to 2 feet, with long, narrow leaves and brilliant orange-yellow flowers.

sandwort *n.* A common name for about 150 species of low-growing annual or perennial plants of the genus *Arenaria* (Caryophyllaceae), some species native to North America. they have small white flowers that bloom in late spring and summer. Used as a ground cover.

sandy clay loam *n.* A texture class of soil that contains 20% to 35% clay, less than 28% silt, and 45% or more of sand.

sandy clay soil *n.* A texture class of soil that contains 35% or more of clay and 45% or more of sand.

sandy soil *n.* Soil material with more than 70% sand and less than 15% clay.

Sanguinaria (sang gwih nah ree uh) *n.* A genus of 1 species, *S. canadensis* (Papaveraceae), of hardy perennial plants native to eastern North America. It grows to 6 inches, with a rounded, irregularly lobed gray leaf and early spring white flower. The cultivar 'Multiplex' is a double-flowered form. Commonly known as bloodroot or red puccoon.

Sanguisorba (sang gwih zor'buh) *n.* A genus of 5 species of hardy perennial plants (Rosaceae). They grow to 6 feet with divided leaves and spikes of white, or deep-red to purple flowers that bloom in fall. Commonly known as burnet.

sanicle (sayn'ih kuhl) *n.* A common name for a plant of the genus *Sanicula,* hardy perennials native

to the western United States. Also known as snakeroot.

sanicle

sanicle, American (sayn'ih kuhl) *n.* A common name for *Heuchera americana,* a hardy perennial native to the midwestern United States. It grows to 3 feet, with lobed basal leaves and greenish-white flowers. Also known as rock geranium.

sanicle, Indian or white (sahn'ih kuhl) *n.* A common name for *Eupatorium rugosum,* a hardy perennial native to eastern North America. It grows to 5 feet, with long thin, oval leaves and clusters of white flowers. Also known as white sanicle and white snakeroot.

Sanicula (say nihk'oo luh) *n.* A genus of 37 species of hardy perennials (Umbelliferae). They grow to 2½ feet, with divided leaves and clusters of greenish-white, yellow, or purple flowers. Commonly known as snakeroot or sanicle.

sanitation *n.* The process of cleaning up the garden-removing dead debris, refuse, and diseased or infested plant parts-to eliminate hiding places and breeding and overwintering sites.

Sansevieria (sans'sehv ih eh'rhee uh) *n.* A genus of 60 species of tender perennial plants (Agavaceae). They grow to 6 feet, with fleshy, narrow leaves and pink-to-white flowers in loose clusters. Used as a houseplant in North America. The most common species is *S. trifasciata,* commonly known as snake plant or mother-in-law's tongue.

Santalum (san'tuh luhm) *n.* A genus of 9 species of tropical shrubs and trees (Santalaceae). (See **sandalwood, white**.)

Santolina (san toh lee'nah) *n.* A genus of 8 species of somewhat hardy shrubs and trees (Compositae). They grow to 2⅕ feet with grayish aromatic leaves and yellow flowers. In the far north, plants may die back in winter, but will resprout in spring. Used as ground covers, and edging plants. *S. Chamaecyparissus* (lavender cotton) which is widely available, can be sheared as small hedge.

Sanvitalia (san vih teh'lee uh) *n.* A genus of 7 species of annuals and tender perennials (Compositae). The most commonly grown species is *S. procumbens,* which grows to less than 6 inches high but with twice the spread. It has short oval leaves and profuse zinnialike yellow and orange flowers. Commonly known as creeping zinnia.

Sapindaceae (sahp ihn day'see ee) *n. pl.* A family of 150 genera and about 2,000 species of evergreen and deciduous shrubs and trees; the soapberry. They have mostly divided leaves and clusters or spikes of flowers. The ornamental genera are *Cardiospernum, Dodnaea, Euphoria, Harpullia, Koelreuteria, Litchi, Melicoccus, Sapindus,* and *Ungnadia.*

Sapindus
(soapberry)

Sapindus (sa pihn'duhs) *n.* A genus of 12 species of tropical shrubs and trees (Sapindaceae) that grow to 50 feet. The most widely grown species in North

America is *S. Saponaria,* a small evergreen tree 1-foot long leaves divided into leaflets, white flowers, and round, orange-brown, glossy fruits which can be used as soap. Commonly known as soapberry or chinaberry.

Sapium (sah'pee uhm) *n.* A genus of more than 100 species of somewhat hardy trees (Euphorbiacceae). They grow to 40 feet, with round leaves that taper to a point. The most widely grown species, *S. sebiferum,* makes a good street tree, poplarlike in appearance, with fine fall color. Commonly known as Chinese tallow tree.

sapling *n.* A young tree: especially applied to an immature forest tree when its trunk is less than 4 inches in diameter.

sapodilla (sahp oh dihl'uh) *n.* A common name for *Manilkara Zapota,* a tropical tree. It grows to more than 100 feet, with oval leaves nearly 6 inches long, small, whitish flowers, and 4-inch-long brown fruit. Also known as mispero, chicozapote, or naseberry.

sapodilla
a fruit *b* fruit showing interior

Saponaria (sahp oh nah'ree uh) *n.* A genus of 30 species of hardy annual and perennial plants (Caryophyllaceae). They grow to 3 feet or less, with simple leaves and pink or white flowers. Used as a rock garden plant, of easy culture. Commonly known as soapwort. *S. calabrica* is a low-growing annual with rose-colored flowers. *S. Ocymoides* is a low-growing perennial with small leaves and bright pink flowers. *S. officinalis* is taller (2 to 3 feet), with pale pink flowers.

Sapotaceae (sahp oh tayh'see ee) *n. pl.* A family of 40 genera and about 800 species of tropical and subtropical shrubs and trees; the sapodilla family.

They have oval leaves, flowers, and berrylike fruit. The ornamental genera are *Bumelia, Chrysophyllum, Manilkara, Mimusops,* and *Pouteria.*

sapote (sahp oh′tay) *n.* A common name for *Pouteria Sapota* a tropical tree that grows to 90 feet. It has oval leaves, nearly two feet long, that taper toward the stem, white-to-yellow flowers in clusters, and oval, reddish-brown edible fruit. Also known as mammee sapote, sapota, mamey colorado, or marmelade plum.

sapote, white (sahp oh′tay) *n.* A common name for *Casimiroa edulis,* a subtropical tree. It grows to 50 feet, with glossy green leaves divided into leaflets, light green, fragrant flowers, and sweet, 3 to 4-inch-round fruit. Also known as Mexican apple or zapote blanco.

saprophyte (sahp′roh fight) *n.* In botany, a plant that grows on dead or decaying organic matter, as in the *Monotropa.*

saprophytic (sahp roh fight′ihk) *a.* Getting nourishment from the products of decaying organic matter.

saprophytism (sahp′roh figh tihsuhm) *n.* The state of being saprophytic.

sapucia nut (sahp oh kee′uh) *n.* A common name for *Lecythis Zabucayo,* a tropical tree. It grows to 70 feet, with leathery, simple leaves, white flowers, and nearly globular fruit, 6 inches long. Also known as paradise nut or monkey-nut.

sarcocarp (sahr′koh kahrp) *n.* In botany, the fleshy part of certain fruits, between the epicarp and the endocarp; mesocarp; that part of fleshy fruits usually eaten, as in the peach, plum, etc.

Sarcococca (sahr′koh koh kuh) *n.* A genus of 14 species of somewhat hardy, slow-growing evergreen shrubs (Orchidaceae). They grow to 6 feet, with glossy, dark green leaves, tiny, fragrant, white flowers, and small red or black fruit. *S. Hookerana* grows to less than 1½ feet high and spreads by runners. Used as low hedges in shady areas. Commonly known as sweet box.

Sarcostemma (sahr koh stehm′uh) *n.* A genus of 10 species of subtropical and tropical succulent twining vines (Asclepiadaceae). They have tiny scalelike leaves and flat-topped clusters of greenish or yellow flowers.

Saritaea (sahr′ih tee uh) *n.* A genus of 2 species of tender vines (Bignoniaceae). They climb to 10 feet, with leathery oval leaves and spectacular trumpet-shaped rose-pink to pale purple flowers.

sarment (sahr′mehnt) *n.* In botany, a runner; a slender running stem, as that of the strawberry. Also sarmentum (*pl.* sarmenta).

sarmentose (sahr mehn′tohs) *a.* In botany, having long sarments or runners; having the form or character of a runner. Also sarmentous; sarmentaceous.

sarmentose stem of strawberry plant

Sarracenia (sahr uh seh′nee uh) *n.* A genus of 8 species of hardy plants (Sarraceniaceae) native to moist or swampy places in the southeastern United States. They grow to 4 feet, with leaves similar to hollow tubes or pitchers. The leaves trap and digest small insects. Can be a somewhat fussy houseplant in cold climates. Commonly known as pitcher plant.

Sarraceniaceae (sahr uh seh nee uh′seh ih) *n. pl.* A family of 3 genera and 15 species of flowering perennials. They have erect, hooded leaves that trap insects; solitary red, to pink, to yellow flowers; and fruit. The ornamental genera are *Darlingtonia* and *Sarracenia.*

sarsaparilla, bristly (sahr′sa pah rihl uh) *n.* A common name for *Aralia hispida,* a very hardy perennial. It grows to 3 feet, with bristly leaves and small greenish flowers.

sarsaparilla, wild (sahr′sa pah rihl uh) *n.* 1. A common name for *Aralia nudicaulis,* a hardy perennial. It grows to more than 1 foot and has compound leaves with oval leaflets and greenish-yellow flowers produced in umbels growing from the base of the plant. Also known as shotbush. 2. A common name for *Smilax glauca,* a hardy vine native to southeastern and midwestern North America. It has oval leaves are 2 to 3 inches long and, whitish flowers. 3. A common name for *Schisandra coccinea,* a tender vine native to southeastern North America. It has oval, fleshy leaves and small crimson flowers.

sartage (sahr'tahj) *n.* The clearing of woodland for agricultural purposes, as by setting fire to the trees.

Sasa (sah'sah) *n.* A genus of more than 150 species of hardy woody grasses (Gramineae). They grow to 8 feet (though there are many shorter species), with grasslike leaf blades clustered at the ends of stems and inconspicuous flowers. Used as informal hedges and edging plants; the rhizomes must be contained to prevent invasive action. Commonly known as bamboo.

sasanqua (sah sahng'kwuh) *n.* A common name for *Camellia sasanqua,* a somewhat hardy shrub with glossy, dark green foliage. A wide variety of cultivars provide a smorgasbord of flower colors and forms. Can be espaliered, made into a hedge plant, or ued as a free-standing tree. Accepts hard pruning most successfully just after blooming.

Sassafras (sas'ah fras) *n.* A genus of 3 species of hardy deciduous trees (Lauraceae). They grow to more than 60 feet, with 3-lobed leaves that sometimes produce good fall color. The leaves and twigs are aromatic when crushed. *S. albidum,* native to eastern United States and Texas is most widely available.

Sassafras
a, b, and *c* various shapes of the leaf

satinflower *n.* 1. A common name for a hardy biennial or perennial plant of the genus *Lunaria.* It grows to 4 feet, with simple leaves and white or purple flowers. The dried flower stalks with their round, translucent seedpods, are often used in arrangements for a dramatic effect. Also known as money plant. 2. A common name for *Clarkia amoena,* an annual flowering plant native to northwestern California. It grows to 3 feet, with narrow, pointed leaves and brilliant pink-to-lavender flowers. Also known as farewell-to-spring, godetia, or herald-of-summer.

satinleaf *n.* A common name for *Chrysophyllum oliviforme,* a tropical evergreen tree. It grows to 30 feet and has oval, 6-inch-long leaves, with a brown or reddish fuzz on the underside, and small white flowers in clusters, followed by small purple fruit. Also known as damson plum.

satinwood *n.* 1. A common name for *Chloroxylon Swietenia,* a tropical deciduous tree. It grows to 50 feet with divided leaves and small clusters of white flowers. Also known as East Indian satinwood. 2. A common name for *Zanthoxylum flavum,* a hardy tree. It grows to 30 feet, with divided leaves and small clusters of whitish flowers. 3. A common name for *Murraya paniculata,* a subtropical shrub or small tree. It grows to 12 feet, with glossy green leaves, rounded clusters of fragrant white flowers, and small, red, berrylike fruit. Also known as orange jasmine, orange jessamine, cosmetic-bark tree, or Chinese box.

satsuma orange (saht'su mah) *n.* A common name for a horticulural class of *Citrus reticulata* oranges from Japan. It is a somewhat hardy small tree, with pointed oval leaves, typical citrus blossoms, and tangerinelike fruit. In a warm climate, an excellent ornamental tree with the bonus of a crop.

Satureja (saht ohh ree'ih uh) *n.* A genus of 30 species of annual and hardy perennial plants (Labiatae). They grow to 2 feet, with square stems and opposite leaves. Many are grown as culinary aromatic mints. *S. Douglasii* (yerba buena), native to western North America has long trailing stems that root as it grows. *S. hortensis* (summer savory) is a summer annual. The leaves may be used fresh or dried as mild seasoning. *S. montana* (winter savory) is a low, spreading shrub. Its leaves have greater bite than those of *S. hortensis.*

Sauromatum (sah ruhm′at uhm) *n.* A genus of 4 species of hardy perennial plants (Araceae). The most widely known species is *S. guttatum.* It has a greenish-yellow bract, with purple marking, that surrounds a dull purple central spike and has deeply lobed leaves, which appear later. Commonly known as voodoo lily, red calla, or monarch-of-the-East.

Saururaceae (sah roh′ray see ee) *n. pl.* A family of 4 genera of plants, some species native to North America; the lizard's-tail family. They have smooth-edged leaves and loose spikes of small whitish flowers. The ornamental genera are *Anemopsis, Houttuynia,* and *Saururus.*

Saururus (saw ror′ruhs) *n.* A genus of 2 species of hardy perennial plants (Saururaceae) found in swampy locations. They grow to 5 feet, with deeply lobed leaves and 12-inch racemes of white, fragrant flowers. Commonly known as lizard's-tail.

Saururus
(lizard's tail)

sausage tree *n.* A common name for *Kigelia pinnata,* a subtropical or tropical tree. It is a large tree, with whitish bark and spreading branches that grow to 50 feet, large, divided alternate leaves, loose, drooping clusters of showy orange-to-red flowers, and bizarre-looking seedpods that resemble huge salamis. The fruit is often 2 feet or more in length, hanging from a long stalk.

Saussurea (sahw suh′reh uh) *n.* A genus of 130 species of very hardy, low-growing, flowering plants (Compositae) frequently found at high altitudes. They have a variety of leaf shapes and purple- to-bluish flowers.

savin (sahv′ihn) *n.* A common name for *Juniperus Sabina,* a hardy shrub native. It grows to 10 feet, and many cultivars offer a variety of foliage texture and color. Also spelled savine.

savory *n.* A plant of the genus *Satureja,* chiefly *S. hortensis* (annual summer savory), and *S. montana* (perennial winter savory), both commonly grown in herb gardens. They are low, aromatic herbs, cultivated for their leaves, which are used to flavor soups, stews, and bean dishes. Winter savory grows in a compact, somewhat woody, low shrub and has a stronger, more peppery flavor. Summer savory tends to be very spindly and sparse and needs to be supported to keep it from falling over.

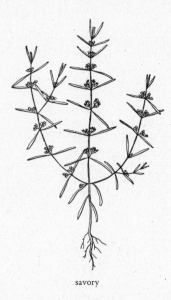

savory

savoy *n.* A variety of the common cabbage with a compact head and wrinkled leaves. It is favored by many gardeners for its fine flavor and resistance to splitting.

sawbrier (saw′brigh er) *n.* A common name for *Smilax glauca,* a hardy, thorny vine native to southeastern and midwestern North America. It has oval leaves to 2 to 3 inches long and whitish flowers. Also known as wild sarsaparilla.

saw cabbage palm *n.* A common name for *Acoelorrhaphe Wrightii,* a tropical fan palm native to the Caribbean and Central America. It grows slowly to 25 feet, with fronds 2 to 3 feet across with a silvery underside. Likes lots of water. Also known as Everglades palm or silver saw palm.

saw fern *n.* A common name for *Blechnum serrulatum,* a tropical fern native to the Americas. In a warm, moist environment, it grows over a wide area via creeping rhizomes with 2-foot leaves. Also known as swamp fern.

sawfly *n.* A wasplike insect whose wormlike larvae feed on the fruit and foliage of many trees and shrubs. The fruit is tunneled, the foliage skeletonized. Some plants can be completely defoliated. Control with insecticidal soap, horticultural oil, or traditional insecticides, or by tilling soil to kill overwintering larvae.

saw palmetto *n.* A common name for *Serenoa repens,* a tropical low- growing palm native to southeastern North America. It creeps over wide areas. Also known as scrub palmetto.

sawwort *n.* A common name for *Serratula tinctoria,* a hardy perennial flowering plant. It grows to 3 feet, with sharply serrated leaves and red-purple flowers. Also known as centaury.

saxicolous (sak sihk'uh luhs) *a.* Living or growing on or among rocks. Also saxicole; saxicoline.

Saxifraga (sak sihf ruh'guh) *n.* A genus of about 300 species of varying degrees of hardiness, usually low-growing, flowering perennials (Saxifragaceae); many species are hardy and are found in the Arctic. Growing from a base rosette of leaves, the flower stalks hold many small white, to pink, to purple, to yellow flowers. Common rock garden plants. Many cultivars of the most widely grown species are offered through specialty nurseries or gardening enthusiasts.

Saxifragaceae (sak suh fruh gay'see ee) *n. pl.* A family of 80 genera and about 1,200 species of flowering plants and shrubs. They have mostly alternate leaves and widely variable flowers and fruit. The ornamental genera are *Anopterus, Astilbe, Bauera, Bergenia, Bolandra, Boykinia, Carpenteria, Chrysosplenium, Decumaria, Deutzia, Escallonia, Fendlera, Francoa, Heuchera, Hydrangea, Itea, Lithophragma, Mitella, Parnassia, Philadelphus, Ribes, Rodgersia, Saxifraga, Schizophragma, Suksdorfia, Tiarella,* and *Tolmiea.*

saxifrage (sak'suh frihj) *n.* A common name for a plant of the genus *Saxifraga.*

saxifrage, golden (sak'suh frihj) *n.* A common name for a plant of the genus *Chrysosplenium,* hardy water-loving perennials. *C. americanum,* native to mid-North America, is low-growing, with small leaves and greenish-white flowers. Also known as water mat or water carpet.

saxifrage, meadow (sak'suh frihj) *n.* A common name for *Saxifraga granulata,* a hardy flowering perennial with 1-inch white flowers; 'Flore Pleno' has double flowers. Also known as fair-maids-of-France.

saxifrage, swamp (sak'suh frihj) *n.* A common name for *Saxifraga pensylvanica,* a hardy perennial native to eastern North America. It has 1-foot long leaves and tiny greenish flowers. A good bog plant. Also known as wild beet.

saxifragous (sak sihf'ruh guhs) *a.* Growing in rock crevices and bringing about the splitting of rock.

scab *n.* A fungal disease common in areas with summer rainfall. It is most troublesome on apples and crabapples, causing disfiguring lesions on the fruit, but it infects other plants as well. Control by planting resistant varieties, cleaning up debris in winter, or applying well-timed fungicidal sprays.

scaberulous (skuh ber'uh luhs) *a.* In botany, minutely scabrous, or rough-textured.

Scabiosa (skay bee oh'suh) *n.* A genus of more than 80 species of annual and hardy perennial plants (Dipsacaceae). They grow to 2⅓ feet, often with finely divided leaves, and have white, blue, rose, or yellow flowers that bloom above the foliage. A good cut flower. *S. atropupurea,* an annual, blooms from midsummer. *S. caucasuca* is a perennial that produces blue-to-lavender or white flowers starting in June. *S. ochroleuca* is a biennial with pale yellow flowers. Commonly known as pincushion flower or scabious.

scabious (skay'bee uhs) *n.* A common name for a plant of the genus *Scabiosa;* pincushion flower.

scabious, sweet (skay'bee uhs) *n.* A common name for *Scabiosa atropurpurea,* an annual flowering plant. It grows to 2 feet tall, with highly divided leaves and purple, rose, lilac, or white flowers. A good cut flower. Also known as mourning bride.

scabrid (skah′brehd) *a*. In botany, slightly rough to the touch, as a scabrid leaf.

scabrous (skah′bruhs) *a*. Rough, with rough little dots or scales.

scabrousness (skah′bruhs nehs) *n*. In botany, the state or property of being scabrous or rough.

Scaevola (see′vuh luh) *n*. A genus of more than 80 species of tropical plants and shrubs (Goodeni-aceae). The most frequently cultivated is *S. frutescens,* a spreading shrub that grows to 10 feet and has white flowers with purple streaks. Used as hedges and erosion control. Commonly known as beach naupaka.

scale *n*. 1. In botany, a small, rudimentary, often vestigial modified leaf, constituting the protective covering of the leaf buds of deciduous trees, the involucre of the Compositae, the bracts of the catkin, the imbricated and thickened leaves which constitute the bulb, and also applied in the Coniferae to the leaves or bracts of the cone. 2. A large group of many-colored insects, so called from their appearance; they are covered with a shieldlike scale under which they hide and feed. They stick fast to plants, often resembling small bumps on leaves or stems. Their armorlike cover makes them difficult to control with insecticides. They infest many plants and are often accompanied by ants and sooty mold. Infested plants are weakened, grow poorly; leaves are distorted or drop; branches or entire plants can die. To control, encourage or release beneficial insects (see **scale parasite**), handpick, exclude ants, and spray with insecticidal soaps, horticultural oils, or traditional insecticides. Sprays are most effective when insects are in the crawler stage.

scale parasite *n*. Any of several species of *Aphytis* wasps used as biological control of some species of scale. They can be purchased through the mail.

scallion *n*. Any of several onion varieties with long, narrow bulbs no wider than the leafstalks, grown for their tender, mild-flavored green tops. Usually called bunching onions in seed catalogs and sold as green onions or scallions in grocery stores.

scallopini (skahl uh pee′nee) *n*. Another name for the pattypan squash, referring to its scalloped outer edge.

scaly *a*. In botany, composed of scales lying over 1 another, as a scaly bulb; having scales scattered over it, as a scaly stem.

scammony (skah′muh nee) *n*. A common name for *Convolvulus Scammonia,* a perennial vine. It clambers to 12 feet with heart-shaped leaves and pink-to-white flowers.

scammony, showing root

scandent (skahn′duhnt) *a*. In botany, climbing.

scape *n*. In botany, a leafless peduncle or stem arising from the ground and bearing flowers, as in the narcissus, primrose, tulip, etc.

scapes (labeled S)

scar *n*. In botany, a mark on a stem or branch seen after the fall of a leaf, or on a seed after its separation from its stalk. (See **hilum.**)

scarab beetles (skar′uhb) *n. pl*. A large group of insects that includes the destructive plant pests rose chafer, Japanese beetle, and June beetle. (See individual pests for information.)

scarecrow *n*. An object, usually suggesting a human or an animal figure, designed to frighten crows or other birds away from gardens.

scarecrow snake *n.* A replica of a live snake, often inflatable, used to frighten birds and rabbits away from the garden.

scarious *a.* In botany, thin, dry, and membranous, as the whorl or set of bracts around the flowers or heads of many Compositae. Also scariose.

scarlet bugler *n.* 1. A common name for *Penstemon centranthifolius,* a tender perennial flowering plant native to California. It grows to 4 feet, with spatula-shaped lower leaves and narrow-pointed upper gray-green leaves and brilliant scarlet trumpet-shaped flowers. 2. A common name for *Cleistocactus Baumannii* a tender cactus. It grows to 6 feet, with a ribbed trunk and 2 to 3 inch S-shaped scarlet flowers.

scarlet bush *n.* A common name for *Hamelia patens,* a tender subtropical shrub. It grows to 25 feet, with soft gray oval leaves and small orange or scarlet flowers.

scarlet runner bean *n.* A common name *Phaseolus coccineus,* a tropical perennial usually grown as an annual. It grows 12 to 15 feet, with wide, oval leaves, bright scarlet 1-inch flowers, and black 1-inch seeds with red mottling. Also known as Dutch case-knife bean.

scarlet sage *n.* 1. A common name for *Salvia coccinea,* a somewhat hardy perennial, often grown as an annual. It grows to 2 feet, with small oval leaves and deep scarlet flowers. Also known as Texas sage. 2. A common name for *S. splendens,* a perennial, most often grown as an annual. It grows to 3 feet, with dark green leaves and the requisite scarlet flowers. There are many cultivars, including some with white flowers, as well as dwarf varieties.

scarred *a.* Marked by scars; exhibiting scars; specifically, in botany, marked by the scars left by leaves, fruits, etc., that have fallen off.

Schefflera (shehf'luh ruh) *n.* 1. A genus of 150 species of tropical shrubs and small trees (Araliaceae). They grow to 25 feet, with compound, rich green leaves and flat-topped clusters of white or greenish flowers. Used as foliage houseplants in cooler climates. Commonly known as umbrella tree, rubber tree, or starleaf. 2. A former name for *Brassaia actinophylla,* a tender shrub or small tree. It grows to 40 feet, with dark green compound leaves and small red flowers on separate small branches. Used as foliage houseplants; of easy culture. Also known as Australian umbrella tree, Queensland umbrella tree, Queen's umbrella tree, Australian ivy palm, octopus tree, or starleaf.

Schinus (skigh'nuhs) *n.* A genus of 28 species of tender evergreen trees (Anacardiaceae). The most widely planted species are *S. Molle* and *S. terebinthifolius. S. Molle* grows from 20 to 50 feet high, depending on its training. It has finely divided light green leaves on drooping branches, providing a graceful, lacy effect, and drooping, yellowish flowers in summer, followed by dark pink berries in fall and winter. Commonly known as pepper tree, California pepper tree, Peruvian pepper tree, Peruvian mastic tree, Australian pepper, molle, or pirul. *S. terebinthifolius* grows to 20 feet, with dark green, less-delicate leaves and showy, bright red berries in winter. Also known as Brazilian pepper tree or Christmas berry tree.

Schisandra (skeh zahn'druh) *n.* A genus of 25 species of sometimes hardy vines (Schisandraceae). They grow from 20 to 30 feet with oval leaves, white, pink, or crimson flowers, and red fruits which are decorative in winter. *S. coccinea* is native to southeastern North America. *S. chinensis* is hardy in the north. Need plants of both sexes for fruit. Commonly known as magnolia vine.

Schivereckia (skeh yuh rehk'ee uh) *n.* A genus of 5 species of hardy perennial plants (Cruciferae). The most widely grown species is *S. Doerfleri,* a low-growing plant forming a rosette of oblong leaves, with loose spikes of white flowers on 6-inch stalks.

Schizaea (skeh zee'uh) *n.* A genus of 30 species of ferns (Schizaeaceae). The most widely grown species is *S. pusilla* native to the northeastern seaboard of North America. It grows to 5 inches with grasslike, curly, sterile leaves around the base of the plant and fertile leaves held above on bare stems. Commonly known as curly grass.

Schizaeaceae (skihz ee ay'see ee) *n. pl.* A family of 4 genera and about 150 species of ferns, commonly known as the curly-grass family. They have simple or divided leaves. The ornamental genera are *Anemia, Lygodium,* and *Schizaea.*

Schizanthus (skeh zahn'thuhs) *n.* A genus of 10 species of annual or biennial flowering plants (Solanaceae). They grow to 4 feet with finely cut leaves and a profusion of clusters of purplish to yellowish orchidlike flowers. There are many cultivars with variations of sizes and colors of flowers. Commonly known as butterfly flower or poor-man's orchid.

schizocarp (skihz'oh kahrp) *n.* In botany, a dry compound fruit which at maturity, splits into 2 or more 1-seeded indehiscent carpels, as in most Umbelliferae.

schizocarpic (skihz'oh kahrp ik) *a.* In botany, resembling or belonging to a schizocarp. Also schizocarpous.

Schizoneura (skihz oh ner'uh) *n.* A notable genus of plant lice of the subfamily *Pemphiginae*, having the antennae 6-jointed, the third discoidal vein of the forewings with 1 fork, and the hind wings with 2 oblique veins. The genus is cosmopolitan and contains many species, nearly all of which excrete an abundance of flocculent or powdery white wax. Many live upon the roots of trees, and others upon the limbs and leaves. The best-known species is *S. lanigera,* known in the United States as the woolly root louse of the apple, and in England, New Zealand, and Australia as the American blight.

Schizopetalon (skihz oh pehd'uhl ahn) *n.* A genus of 5 species of annuals (Cruciferae). The most widely grown species is *S. Walkeri,* which grows to 2 feet, with gray hairy leaves and intensely fragrant white flowers.

Schizophragma (skihz oh frahg'muh) *n.* A genus of 4 species of hardy vines (Saxifragaceae). They grow to more than 30 feet, with broad, oval leaves and white flowers, 4 inches across. Commonly known as Japanese hydrangea vine.

Schizostylis (skihz oh'stigh luhs) *n.* A genus of 2 species of tender flowering plants (Iridaceae). The most widely grown species is *S. coccinea.* It grows to 2 feet, with narrow, stiff, evergreen leaves and showy, crimson fall flowers on 2 foot stems. Commonly known as crimson flag or Kaffir lily.

Schleichera (shligh'ker uh) *n.* A genus of one species, *S. oleosa* (Sapindaceae) a tropical tree. It grows to 60 feet, with divided leaves that are red when young, turning green with age, and yellowish-greenish flowers on 6-inch spikes. Commonly known as gum-lac, lac tree, or Ceylon oak.

Schlumbergera (shluhm ber'ger uh) *n.* A genus of 3 species of tender cacti (Cactaceae). *S. Bridgesii* and *S. truncata* are widely grown as houseplants; good in hanging baskets. *S. Bridgesii,* Christmas cactus, has flattened, bright-green stems that produce many 3-inch-long purple-red flowers at about Christmas time. The crab cactus, *S. truncata,* is so named because of the distinctive crab-claw-like joints at the ends of the branches. Many cultivars are available, with a broad range of colors.

Schomburgkia (shahm buhr'kee uh) *n.* A genus of about 15 species of tropical South American orchids (Orchidaceae). They grow to 2⅓ feet, with leathery, oblong leaves and racemes of flowers on long, slender stems. Commonly known as cowhorn orchid.

Schrankia (shrahn'kee uh) *n.* A genus of 20 to 30 species of hardy perennial low-growing plants (Leguminosae) native to North America. They have prickly stems with highly divided leaves and pink or purple flowers on short spikes. The many small leaflets that react to touch give it its common name of sensitive brier.

Schwalbea (shwahl'bee uh) *n.* A genus of 1 species, *S. americana* (Scrophulariaceae), a hardy perennial native to eastern North America. It grows to 2 feet, with oval, simple leaves and purplish-yellow flowers in a somewhat 1-sided wandlike spike at the ends of the stems. Commonly known as chaffseed.

Sciadopitys (sigh uh doh'pih tihs) *n.* A genus of 1 species, *S. verticillata* (Taxodiaceae), a hardy, slow-growing tree native to Japan. It grows to a 100 feet, with whorls of dark green fleshy needles. On mature trees, 3- to 5-inch cones may appear. A good specimen tree. Commonly known as umbrella pine and Japanese umbrella pine.

Scilla (skihl'uh) *n.* A genus of 80 to 90 species of hardy flowering bulbs (Liliaceae). They have straplike leaves and clusters of bell-shaped or starlike flowers in whites and blues and purples. Many species and cultivars provide a variety of blooming times and colors, and duration. They are good in beds with other plants, and their early bloom gets your gardening year off to a good start. They die back in summer. Commonly known as squill.

Scindapsus (sihn dap'sehs) *n.* A genus of 20 species of tropical vines (Araceae). The most widely available member of this genus is *S. pictus* 'Argyraeus', which climbs to 40 feet. It has 4-inch-long heart-shaped leaves, with silver spots on the tops of the leaves and insignificant flowers.

scion (sigh'uhn) *n.* A detached living shoot of a plant, especially 1 cut for the purpose of being grafted onto stock or another plant. Also spelled cion.

Scirpus (skuhr'puhs) *n.* A genus of about 200 species of hardy grasslike aquatic annual and perennial plants (Cyperaceae), more than a dozen species native to North America. They grow to 8 feet, with an insignificant flower near the top of the stalk. Commonly known as bulrush.

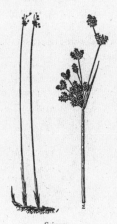

Scirpus
(bullrush)
1 whole plant *2* flowers

Scleranthus (skleh rahn'thuhs) *n.* A genus of 10 species of annual and perennial low-growing plants (Caryophyllaceae). They have long, narrow leaves and rounded clusters of small greenish flowers. Some species useful in rock gardens. Commonly known as knawe.

sclerenchyma (skleh rehng'kuh muh) *n.* In botany, in higher plants, the protective or supportive tissue made up of cells with lignified and thickened walls.

Scolymus (skahl'uh muhs) *n.* A genus of 3 species of somewhat hardy Mediterranean plants (Com-

positae). The most widely grown species is *S. hispanicus*, a thistlelike biennial. It grows to avigorously branched 4 feet, with spiny leaves and yellow flowers. Occasionally grown for its edible taproot. Commonly known as Spanish oyster plant and golden thistle.

scorch *n.* An injury to leaves caused by lack of water or excessive transpiration.

scorpioid (skor'pee oid) *a.* In botany, having parts arranged in a circinate form, as a scorpioid inflorescence in some of the Boraginaceae.

scorpoid flower

scorpioid cyme (skor'pee oid sighm) *n.* A coiled inflorescence in which the flowers arise 2-ranked on alternate sides of the axis, as in *Myosotis scorpioides*.

scorpion grass *n.* A common name for an annual or hardy perennial of the genus *Myosotis*, the most widely grown species are *M. scorpiodes*, a perennial, and *M. sylvatica*, an annual. Both grow to less than 2 feet with oblong leaves and blue, pink, or white flowers. Many cultivars of *M. sylvatica* are available. Also known as forget-me-not.

scorpion orchid *n.* A common name for an orchid of the genus *Arachnis*. It grows to 6 feet, with flowers on often tall, long, spectacular flower spikes.

scorpion senna *n.* A common name for *Coronilla Emerus*, a hardy shrub. It grows to 9 feet, with divided leaves and yellow flowers marked with red.

Scorzonera (skor zuh nihr'uh) *n.* A genus of 150 species of hardy perennial plants (Compositae). The most widely grown species is *S. hispanica*, a perennial grown as an annual or a biennial. It grows to 3 feet with long narrow leaves and yellow flowers. Commonly known as black salsify, Spanish salsify, viper's grass, or black oyster plant.

Scotch broom *n.* A common name for *Cytisus scoparius,* a hardy shrub. It grows to 10 feet, with small oval leaves and bright yellow flowers in loose bunches at the ends of branches. A weedy pest in parts of western North America.

Scotch elm *n.* A common name for *Ulmus glabra,* a hardy deciduous tree. It grows to 120 feet, with large saw-toothed leaves. Many cultivars provide a variety of tree shapes. Also known as wych elm or witch elm.

Scotch fir *n.* A common name for *Pinus sylvestris,* a very hardy tree. It grows to 100 feet or more, with bluish green needles covered with a pale, waxy powder and gray to reddish-brown cones, 2½ inches long. there are numerous cultivars, including 'Argentea' (with silvery needles), 'Compressa' (dwarf, conical), 'Nana' (a low, dense shrub), 'Pendula' (with drooping branches). Also known as Scots pine or Scotch pine.

Scotch heath *n.* A common name for *Erica cinerea,* a hardy shrub. It grows to 2 feet, with dark green leaves and purple flowers, fading to blue. Used as ground cover or in rock gardens. Also known as twisted heath or bell heather.

Scotch heather *n.* A common name for *Calluna vulgaris,* a hardy small shrub. The multitude of cultivars available provide combinations of size (from a few inches high to 3 feet), foliage color (various shades of green to yellows or grays), flower color (white, pink, lavender, or purple), and time of blooming (mid-to-late summer, fall). The smallest varieties are used in rock gardens; the larger varieties make good informal hedges.

Scotch moss *n.* 1. A common name for *Arenaria verna* 'Aurea' and *Sagina subulata* 'Aurea', hardy perennial ground covers. They grow to less than an inch high and produce tiny white flowers. 2. A common name for *Selaginella Kraussiana* 'Brownii', a tender, subtropical mosslike plant that grows to less than an inch high. Used as a ground cover. Appreciates warmth and lots of moisture.

scouring rush *n.* A common name for the genus *Equisetum.* The most widely found species is *E. hye-*

male, a hardy rushlike perennial. It grows to 4 feet in wet or boggy places. Its name derives from its use as a scouring agent for wood or metal. Also known as horsetail and shave grass.

screens *n. pl.* Plants grown to form a visual barrier, as in a hedge.

screw bean *n.* A common name for *Prosopis pubescens,* a tender large shrub or small tree. It grows to 24 feet, with narrow, gray green leaves and small spikes of yellowish flowers followed by seedpods, tightly coiled into a cylindrical shape. A close relative to the mesquite (P. glandulosa). Also known as tornillo.

screw pine *n.* A common name for plants of the genus *Pandanus,* tropical shrubs or trees. Their size ranges from 2 inches for P. *pygmaeus,* frequently used as a potted greenhouse plant, to 60 feet for P. *utilis,* the common screw pine. P. *Veitchii* is the most common container-grown species, with light green branches 2 to 3 feet long. The common name derives from the spiral arrangement of the needles on the branches.

screw-tree *n.* A common name for *Helicteres Isora,* a large tropical shrub. It grows to 12 feet, with oval, saw-toothed leaves and small clusters of blue flowers that later turn bright red.

Scrophularia
(figwort)
a leaf *b* flower

Scrophularia (skrahf yuh lah′ree uh) *n.* A genus of about 200 species of hardy biennial and perennial plants or small shrubs (Scrophulariaceae). They grow from 10 to 15 feet, with simple or compound scented leaves and small greenish, yellow, purple, or red flowers in clusters. *S. californica* is native to western North America and *S. marilandica* is native to eastern North America. Commonly known as figwort.

Scrophulariaceae (skrahf yuh lahr ee ay'see ee) *n. pl.* A family of 210 genera and nearly 3,000 species of annuals, perennials, and shrubs; the figwort family. The ornamental genera are *Alonsoa, Anarrhinum, Angelonia, Antirrhinum, Asarina, Bacopa, Besseya, Calceolaria, Castilleja, Celsia, Chaenorrhinum, Chelone, Chionophila, Collinsia, Cymbalaria, Diascia, Digitalis, Erinus, Galvesia, Hebe, Isoplexis, Leucophyllum, Lineria, Mazus, Mimulus, Nemesia, Orthocarpus, Parahebe, Pedicularis, Penstemon, Phygelius, Russelia, Scrophularia, Sutera, Syntheris, Torenia, Verbascum, Veronica,* and *Zaluzianskya.*

scrub *n.* 1. A bush; shrub; a tree or shrub seemingly or really stunted. 2. Collectively, bushes; brushwood; underwood; stunted forest. *a.* Of inferior breed or stunted growth.

scrub oak *n.* 1. A common name for *Quercus ilicigolia,* a hardy, deciduous shrub native to northeastern North America. It grows to 10 feet or more, with 2-lobed leaves with a whitish fuzz on the undersides. Also known as bear oak. 2. A common name for *Q. undulata* (Rocky Mountain scrub oak), a hardy, deciduous tree native to southwestern North America. It grows to 30 feet, with 3-inch oval, coarsely toothed leaves.

scrub palmetto *n.* 1. A common name for *Sabal Etonia,* a tropical palm native to Florida. It grows to less than 6 feet, with fronds 3 feet across. 2. A common name for *Sabal minor,* a somewhat hardy palm native to southeastern North America. It grows to 4 feet on a mostly underground trunk. Also known as dwarf palmetto or bush palmetto. 3. A common name for *Serenoa repens,* a tropical palm native to southeastern North America as far north as North Carolina. It creeps over wide areas. Also known as saw palmetto.

scrub pine *n.* 1. A common name for *Pinus Banksiana,* a very hardy tree. It can grow to 75 feet, but usually much less, with pairs of needles bright or dark green 1⅕ inches long. Tolerates poor soil that

other trees reject. Also known as jack pine or gray pine. 2. A common name for *P. virginiana,* a hardy tree native to southeastern North America. It grows between 30 and 50 feet, with pairs of 3-inch-long needles. Tolerates poor soil. Also known as Jersey pine, spruce pine, or poverty pine.

scuppernong (skuhp'er nahng) *n.* A cultivated variety of the muscadine, bullace, or southern foxgrape, *Vitis rotundifolia,* of the southern United States and Mexico. Its large purple berries are well flavored and peculiar in that all on a bunch do not ripen at once. The ripe berries fall from the vine and are gathered from the ground. They can be grown as far north as Delaware.

scurfy pea *n.* A common name for a member of the genus *Psoralea,* perennials and shrubs with varying degrees of frost hardiness. They grow mostly from 3 to 4 feet, though some shrubby species can grow to 12 feet. *P. bituminosa* a tender perennial, has light purple flowers in dense heads in spring and early summer. *P. esculenta,* a hardy perennial native to central North America has yellowish to bluish flowers on 4-inch stems. *P. Onobrychis,* native to mid-western United States, has pale purple or blue flowers on dense spikes during summer.

scuffle hoe *n.* A slicing weeder that cuts weeds just below the soil surface.

scurvy grass *n.* 1. A common name for *Barbarea verna,* a biennial weedy plant. It grows to 2 feet, with irregularly divided leaves and small yellow flowers in clusters in early spring. Often gathered as an edible green. Also known as early winter cress, Belle Isle cress, American cress, land cress, or upland cress. 2. A common name for *Cochlearia officinalis,* an annual formerly grown as a salad green. It grows to 1 foot, with heart-shaped leaves and small white flowers. Also known as spoon-wort. 3. A common name for *Crambe maritima,* a somewhat hardy coastal perennial. It grows to 3 feet, with large, 2-foot-long gray-blue leaves and clusters of white flowers. Also known as sea kale. 4. A common name for *Oxalis enneapphylla,* a hardy perennial ground cover. It grows to 6 inches, with more than a dozen leaflets in 2 whorls, and white flowers with lavender veins.

scutate (skyoo'tayt) *a.* In botany, shaped like a small shield; peltate; as a scutate leaf. Also scutated; scutiform.

Scutellaria (skyoo duhl ah′ree uh) *n*. A genus of approximately 300 species of mostly hardy perennials (Labiatae). There are both spreading and erect forms, with usually toothed leaves and rather large blue, violet, scarlet, or yellow flowers along the stem or in a terminal spike. Commonly known as skullcap.

scutiform (skyoo duh form) *a*. In botany, shield-shaped, scutate; peltate.

scythe *n*. An implement for cutting tall grass by hand, composed of a long, sharp, curving blade attached to a bent handle.

sea ash *n*. A common name for *Zanthoxylum clava-Herculis,* a somewhat hardy shrub or tree native to southeastern North America. It grows from 30 to 50 feet, with divided leaves, small thorns, and yellow flowers in clusters at the ends of the branches. Also known as southern prickly ash, Hercules′-club, or pepperwood.

sea beet *n*. A common name for *Beta vulgaris,* an annual or hardy biennial. This is the species from which the modern vegetables beets, chard, and sugar beets are derived. In the second year of growth, it produces a 4-foot stem with elongated oval leaves.

sea bindweed *n*. A common name for *Calystegia Soldanella,* a widely distributed hardy vine found near seashores. It twines over considerable sandy distances with kidney-shaped leaves and pale pink trumpet-shaped flowers.

sea buckthorn *n*. A common name for the genus *Hippophae.* The most widely planted species, *H. rhamnoides,* is a very hardy, spiny shrub or tree able to flourish in seashore growing conditions. It grows to 30 feet, with willowlike leaves and decorative bright orange fruit. Both sexes must be present to produce fruit. Also known as swallow thorn.

sea cushion *n*. A common name for *Armeria maritima,* a hardy perennial flowering plant native to the seashores of many continents, including the west coast of North America. It grows to less than 2 inches high in neat, dense little tufts of grasslike leaves and has pink or white tight clusters of flowers. Also known as thrift or sea pink.

sea daffodil *n*. 1. A common name for the genus *Hymenocallis,* a subtropical flowering bulb. It grows to no more than 3 feet, usually under 2 feet, with straplike leaves and white or yellow flowers similar to those of daffodils, with the central cup divided into segments. Also known as spider lily, crown beauty, or basket flower. 2. A common name for *Pancratium maritimum,* a subtropical flowering bulb with straplike leaves grow to 2½ feet long and very fragrant, white, summer-blooming flowers.

sea eringo (ih rihng′goh) *n*. A plant, *Eryngium maritimum.* Also known as sea holly. (See **Eryngium.**)

sea fig *n*. A common name used for *Carpobrotus chilenses,* a tender perennial succulent ground cover. It grows to 2 feet or more and easily roots. It has fleshy, 3-sided, dark green leaves and bright pinkish-purple flowers. Good for covering banks or a workhorse at the beach to stabilize dunes. Also known as ice plant.

Seaforthia (see fohr′thee uh) *n*. A former name for *Archontophoenix Cunninghamiana,* a tropical palm. It grows more than 50 feet, with 8- to 10-foot feathery fronds, gray-green on the underside. Also known as king palm.

sea grape *n*. A common name for *Coccoloba Uvifera,* a tropical tree. It grows to 20 feet or more, with round, thick leaves, 8-inches across, that have red veins. It has thick, 10-inch spikes of white flowers, followed by grapelike clusters of purple fruit. Also known as kino or platterleaf.

sea kale *n*. A common name for *Crambe maritima,* a somewhat hardy coastal perennial. It grows to 3 feet, with large, 2-foot-long gray-blue leaves and clusters of white flowers. Also known as scurvy grass.

sea lavender *n*. A common name for serveral plants of the genus *Limonium,* especially *latifolium,* also called marsh rosemary. The common wild species is a salt-marsh plant with a small rosette of leaves and a wiry, multi-branched stem, bearing at the top numerous small lavender-colored flowers. Several species are cultivated, the finest a perennial known as German statice, with somewhat larger, but still quite small, white blossoms. The flowers of the genus are of a dry texture, retain their color and shape long after being cut, and are popular for use in dried arrangements and wreaths.

sea lungwort *n.* A common name for *Mertensia maritima,* a tender perennial. It grows to 2 feet, with gray-green leaves and pink flowers.

sea onion *n.* 1. A common name for *Urginea maritima,* a somewhat hardy flowering bulb. It grows to 4 or 5 feet, with 1½ foot long gray-green leaves and dense spikes of whitish flowers. Also known as squill or red squill. 2. A common name for *Scilla verna,* a hardy flowering bulb. It grows to 6 inches, with narrow, straplike leaves and violet-blue flowers in dense clusters. Also known as spring squill.

sea orach (ahr′uhch) *n.* A common name for *Atriplex Halimus,* a somewhat hardy shrub. It grows to 6 feet, with oval, 2½-inch long leaves. A good coastal shrub.

sea pink *n.* A common name for a plant of the genus *Armeria,* hardy, evergreen, low-growing perennial plants. They grow in round clumps of stiff, thin, green leaves and have white, pink, rose, or red flowers in dense clusters on short stems. Also known as thrift.

sea poppy *n.* A common name for the genus *Glaucium,* a group of annual, biennial, and perennial flowering plants, usually grown as annuals. They grow to a maximum of 3 feet, with a basal rosette of divided leaves and large red or yellow flowers, singly on stems. Also known as horned poppy.

seaside pea *n.* A common name for *Lathyrus japonicus,* a hardy perennial vine often used as a ground cover. The stems grow to 2 feet long, with oval leaves and purple clusters of flowers. Also known as beach pea or heath pea.

seashore garden *n.* A garden plot modified to enable growth of certain plants adapted to sand, wind, and salt spray.

seashore mallow *n.* A common name for the genus *Kosteletzkya,* a group of somewhat hardy perennials and small shrubs. They grow as high as 10 feet, arrowhead-shaped leaves and white to yellowish, pink, or purplish flowers.

seashore paspalum (pas′puh luhm) *n.* (See **Paspalum.**)

season extender *n.* Any of various shelters, such as row covers, coldframes, or greenhouses, used to extend the growing season.

sea starwort *n.* A common name for *Aster Tripolinum,* an annual or short-lived perennial. It grows to 3 feet, with oval basal leaves that taper where they attach and blue-purple flowers.

sea-urchin cactus *n.* A common name for the genus *Echinopsis,* a tender, low-growing, round cactus native to South America. They produce brilliantly colored trumpet-shaped flowers in pink, red, yellow, or white. Easily grown in containers.

sea-urchin tree *n.* A common name for *Hakea laurina,* a somewhat hardy shrub or tree. It grows to 30 feet, with narrow, 6-inch-long pointed leaves and crimson flowers in round clusters.

sebaceous (seh bay′shuhs) *a.* In botany, having the appearance of fat, as the sebaceous secretions of some plants.

sebesten (seh best′uhn) *n.* A common name for *Cordia Sebestena,* a tropical shrub or evergreen tree. It grows to as much as 30 feet, with stiff, rough leaves, bright orange or scarlet flowers most of the year, and small white fruit. Also known as Geiger tree.

sebiferous (sehb ihf′uh ruhs) *a.* In botany, sebaceous; greasy.

Sechium (seek′ee uhm) *n.* A genus of 1 species of a tropical vine *S. edule* (Cucurbitaceae). It grows to 30 feet or more, given a structure on which to climb. It has squashlike triangular-shaped leaves, small white flowers, and pear-shaped, light green, vertically grooved edible fruit, 8 inches long. Grown as a vegetable in the tropics. Commonly known as chayote.

seckel (sehk′ihl) *n.* A small flavorful pear, ripening about the end of October, but keeping for a short time only. They are frequently preserved by pickling.

Securidaca (sehk uh rihd′ahk uh) *n.* A genus of about 70 species of tropical vines and small trees (Polygalaceae). They have alternate, smooth-edged leaves and red, purple, or yellow flowers. Many South American species climb trees to a great height.

sedge *n.* A common name for the genus *Carex,* hardy, grasslike perennial plants. They grow mostly to under 2 feet (an exception being *S. pen-*

dula, or sedge grass, that grows up to 5 feet with long, narrow leaves and inconspicuous flowers. Used as edging plants around water gardens or for green filler in borders; the smaller plants are excellent for rock gardens. Cultivars are available with varying shades of green and white. (See **Carex.**)

sedges

sedge, Fraser's *n.* A common name for *Cymophyllus Fraseri,* a hardy sedgelike perennial native to the United States from Pennsylvania south to South Carolina. It grows up to 1⅕ feet with flat, 2⅕-inch-wide leathery leaves and white brushlike flowers.

sedge peat *n.* The peat that results from decaying masses of several types of mosses.

sedimentary rock *n.* A rock composed of particles deposited from suspension in water, like sandstone, shale, limestone and conglomerates.

Sedum (see′duhm) *n.* A genus of close to 600 species of perennial succulents (Crassulaceae). Some are hardy north; most are low-growing, with a variety of textures and leaf colors, as well as attractive blossoms. Their generally compact habits make them well suited to rock gardens and container culture. Most sedums root readily from a broken stem. Most do well in poor soil, in hot, sunny exposures, requiring little water. Commonly known as stonecrop or orpine.

seed *n.* The fertilized and matured ovule of a flowering plant, containing an embryonic plant and, which, on being placed under favorable circumstances, develops into an individual similar to the one that produced it.

seedbox *n.* 1. A common name for *Ludwigia alternifolia,* a hardy perennial flowering plant native to eastern North America. It grows to 3 feet, with narrow, pointed leaves and yellow summertime flowers on single stalks from the base of the leaves. Also known as rattlebox. 2. In botany, a capsule.

seed-corn *n.* Corn or grain saved for seed; ears or kernels of maize set apart as seed for a new crop.

seeder *n.* Any of several devices used to distribute and plant seeds.

seed flat *n.* A boxlike structure for holding containers of seedlings. Also called flat.

seed leaf *n.* In botany, a cotyledon, which is the primary leaf or leaves in an embryo..

seedling guard *n.* A row cover to protect seeds or newly sprouted plants indoors or out.

seedling tray *n.* A tray, generally plastic, having individual compartments for planting and growing seeds. Also called seed starting tray.

seed sower *n.* Device for spreading and controlling the rate of distribution of seeds.

seed sowing *v.* The act of planting seeds, especially of planting with consideration for seed type and germination conditions.

seed starter kit *n.* A collection of materials such as pots, flats, soil, and seeds used for starting plants.

seed starting tray *n.* A container holding multiple individual cells; used for starting seeds or cuttings. Also called seedling tray.

seed tray heater *n.* (See **heat mat**.)

seed vessel *n.* In botany, the pericarp, or wall of the ripened ovary, which contains the seeds.

seepage (se′-pij) *n.* The escape of water through soil.

Selaginella (seh lahj uh nehl′uh) *n.* A genus of about 700 species of tropical and subtropical mosslike plants (Selaginellaceae). They usually are heavily branched and grow less than 12 inches high, with very small leaves. Good for hanging baskets in warm spots or ground covers. Commonly known as little club moss or spike moss.

Selaginella
(little club moss)

Selaginellaceae (seh lahj uh nuh lay'see ee) *n. pl.* A family of 1 genus, *Selaginella* and about 700 species of mosslike plants. They have very small, scalelike leaves and insignificant flowers.

Selago (sehl lay'goh) *n.* A genus of approximately 140 species of subtropical and tropical shrubs (Scrophulariaceae). They grow to 2 feet, with simple, heathlike leaves and tiny purple, blue, pink, or white flowers in spikes or clusters.

selective pesticide *n.* A pesticide that is effective only against a specific pest or a closely related group of pests.

Sevin (seh'vihn) *n.* (See **carbaryl**.)

Selenicereus (seh lee'nuh sih ruhs) *n.* A genus of about 20 species of tropical night-blooming cacti (Cactaceae) native to tropical America. They climb by aerial roots, and the ribbed stems produce large white flowers. Often grown as houseplant in colder climates. Commonly known as night-blooming cereus, moon cereus, or moon cactus.

self *n., pl.* **selfs** In horticulture, 1. An individual plant produced by self-fertilization, as opposed to cross-bred. 2. A self-colored flower; of a single color.

self-colored *a.* In horticulture, uniform in color, as self-colored flowers.

self-fertile *a.* In botany, fertile by means of its own pollen.

self-fertility *n.* In botany, ability to fertilize itself, possessed by many hermaphrodite flowers.

self-fertilization *n.* In botany, the fertilization of a flower by pollen from the same flower. Compare cross-fertilization.

self-heal *n.* A common name for *Prunella*, a genus of hardy perennials. Members of the mint family, they grow to less than 2 feet, with simple leaves and flowers in terminal spikes. Used in rock gardens and shady borders; can be weedy. *P. grandiflora* is the best of available species.

self-heal

self-sterile *a.* In botany, a term describing the inability of a plant to fertilize itself, as a self-sterile flower; opposed to self-fertile.

self-watering planter *n.* A plant pot with internal water reservoir from which plants can absorb moisture as required.

self-watering plant pot *n.* A container with a water storage area, from which a plant can absorb moisture as required.

self-watering tray *n.* A device for maintaining moisture in plant pots. The tray is lined with capillary matting, which absorbs water and makes it available to potted plants.

semaphore-plant (sehm'uh foh uhr) *n.* A common name for *Desmodium motorium*, a tropical perennial usually grown as an annual. It grows to 4 feet, with clusters of purple or violet flowers that appear in summer and very small leaflets that jerk in response to sunshine or warmth, hence the common name. Also known as telegraph plant.

Semecarpus (sehm uh kahrp′uhs) *n.* A genus of about 40 species of tropical trees (Anacardiaceae). The most widely available species is *S. Anacardium,* which grows to 15 feet, with large (to 1 foot or longer) oval leaves and clusters of greenish-white flowers. Commonly known as marking-nut tree or varnish tree.

semi- *prefix* 1. Half of. 2. Partly; to some extent; incompletely; having some of the characteristics of.

semi adherent *a.* In botany, having the lower half adherent, as a seed, stamen, etc.

semiamplexicaul (sehm′ee ahm plehks′uh kawl) *a.* In botany, half-amplexicaul; embracing half of the stem, as many leaves.

semiaquatic *a.* In botany, living in or adjacent to water, as semiaquatic plants that grow between tides, or in pools that periodically become dry.

Semiarundinaria (sehm′ee uh ruhn duh nah′ree uh) *n.* A genus of 3 species of somewhat hardy bamboos (Gramineae). The most widely available species is *S. fastuosa,* which grows to 25 feet, with leaf blades 1 inch wide and over 7 inches long, dark, shiny green above, dull below. It spreads slowly, so it can be kept under control with little effort. A good hedge plant. Commonly known as Narihira bamboo.

semi double *a.* In botany, having the outermost stamens converted into petals, while the inner ones remain perfect, as a semidouble flower.

seminiferous (sehm uh nihf′uh ruhs) *a.* Seed-bearing; producing seed.

sempervirent (sehm puh vigh′ruhnt) *a.* Always green or fresh; evergreen.

Sempervivum (sehm puh vigh′vuhm) *n.* A genus of approximately 40 species of hardy, low-growing, perennial succulents (Crassulaceae). They have leaves in rosettes and red, purple, white, or yellow flower clusters on spikes rising above the rosettes. They spread by offsets, miniature rosettes that reproduce around the older plant. The size of the mature rosettes can vary from the tiny ¾-inch-diameter *S. arachnoideum* to the 6-inch-diameter *S. tectorum* 'Robustum'. *S. tectorum* is widely available,

and many cultivars with varying size of rosettes and leaf color are offered. Commonly known as houseleek or live-forever.

Senecio (seh neesh′ee oh) *n.* A genus of perhaps as many as 3,000 species of annual and perennial plants (Compositae), estimated by some to be the largest genus of flowering plants. Representatives of this genus are found in widely distributed areas of the world in a wide-ranging variety of habitats. Commonly known as groundsel. Some widely available species include the following: *S. articulatus* (candle plant) is a tender succulent plant often grown as a houseplant. It has tall stalks with clusters of white flowers. *S. aureus* native to eastern North American swamps, produces deep yellow daisylike flowers in late spring. *S. Cineraria* (dusty miller) is an old favorite perennial, growing to 2⅓ feet with deeply cut woolly-white leaves and clusters of yellow flowers held above the foliage. *S. confusus* (Mexican flame vine or orangeglow vine) has light green leaves that may climb as high as 10 feet in warm areas, followed by clusters of daisylike orange-red flowers with gold centers. *S. Douglasii* (bush senecio) is a small (to 5 feet) shrub native to southwestern North America, with finely cut gray-green leaves and clusters of showy yellow, daisylike flowers. *S. xhybridus* (cineraria) is a staple of florist's wares and a stalwart in gardens in cool, dim spots where other plants balk. A perennial that is often grown as an annual, it can grow compactly or as high as 3 feet, producing bright clusters of daisylike springtime flowers in white, to pink, to blue, to purple, to red. *S. macroglossus* (Natal ivy, wax vine) has succulent stems and thick, waxy, ivylike leaves, producing tiny yellow daisylike flowers in summer. Suitable only as a houseplant in all but the warmest climates. *S. mikanoides* (German ivy) is an old-fashioned climbing or trailing houseplant with ivylike leaves and yellow buttonlike flowers. *S. Rowleyanus* (string-of-beads) is ideally suited to hanging baskets, producing long (to 6 feet) stems of ½-inch spherical gray-green leaves and small white flowers in summer.

senecioid (seh neesh′ee oid) *a.* Of, relating to, or resembling *Senecio.*

senna *n.* A common name for plants of the genus *Cassia,* subtropical or tropical annuals, perennials, shrubs, or trees. They have large compound leaves and golden-yellow flowers. Also known as shower tree.

senna

senna, apple-blossom *n.* A common name for *Cassia javanica,* a tropical tree. It grows to 20 feet, with feathery leaves and clusters of large apple-blossom-like flowers. Also known as apple-blossom cassia.

senna, bladder *n.* A common name for *Colutea arborescens,* a somewhat hardy, often weedy, shrub. It grows to 15 feet, with deciduous, compound leaves and small clusters of yellow-reddish flowers.

senna, candlestick *n.* A common name for *Cassia alata,* a tropical shrub. It grows to 8 feet, with large, finely divided leaves and spikes of golden-yellow flowers that bloom in winter. Also known as Christmas candle.

senna, flowery *n.* A common name for *Cassia corymbosa,* a tender flowering shrub. It grows to 10 feet, with dark green feathery leaves and profuse yellow flowers in rounded clusters.

senna, prairie *n.* A common name for *Cassia fasciculata,* an annual flowering plant. It grows to more than 2 feet, with feathery leaves that fold when touched and deep yellow flowers that come from the base of the leaf. Often grows as a vine if support is given. Also known as partridge pea, sensitive pea, or golden cassia.

senna, wild *n.* A common name for *Cassia hebecarpa* and *C. marilandica,* extremely similar hardy perennials native to eastern North America. They grow to 4 feet and then die back to the ground each fall. They have smooth, divided leaves and yellow pealike flowers in loose spikes.

sensitive fern *n.* A common name for *Onoclea sensibilis,* a somewhat hardy fern native to eastern North America. It grows to 2⅕ feet, with 4-foot-long sterile fronds and smaller fertile fronds. The common name is derived from the tendency of the segments of the fronds, after being detached and while wilting, to fold together.

sensitive pea *n.* 1. A common name for *Cassia fasciculata,* an annual flowering plant. It grows to more than 2 feet, with feathery leaves that fold when touched and deep-yellow flowers flowers that come from the base of the leaf. Often grows as a vine is support is given. Also known as partridge pea, golden cassia, and prairie senna. 2. A common name for *Cassia nictitans,* an annual flowering plant that grows to 18 inches, with feathery leaves and tiny yellow flowers. The leaflets fold together when touched. Also known as wild sensitive plant.

sensitive plant *n.* A common name for *Mimosa pudica,* a tender houseplant. It grows to 3 feet, with feathery leaves that fold up along the central rib when touched and small mauve flowers. Usually grown as a curiosity. Also known as touch-me-not, action plant, humble plant, shame plant, or live-and-die.

sepal (see'puhl) *n.* In botany, 1 of the individual modified leaves, usually green, that make up the calyx, or outer circle of floral envelopes.

sepals of various flowers (marked S)

sepaled (see'puhld) *a.* In botany, having sepals. Also spelled sepalled.

sepalody (sehp'uh loh dee) *n.* In botany, the metamorphosis of petals or other organs into sepals.

-sepalous (sehp'uhl uhs) *a. comb. form* Having sepals.

separate *n.* One of the individual size groups of mineral soil particles; sand, silt, or clay.

sept- or septi- *comb. form* Seven, as in septifolius, seven-leaved.

septate (sehp'tayt) *a.* In botany, divided by or having a septum or partition. Also septated.

septile (sep'tighl) *a.* In botany, of, belonging to, or relating to septa.

septum *n., pl.* **septa** or **septums**. In botany, a partition or dividing wall, as the septum in a compound ovary or fruit. Also dissepiment.

septa of cut poppy fruit

Sequoia (seh kwoy'uh) *n.* A genus of 1 species of hardy evergreen trees, *S. sempervirens* (Taxodiaceae) native to western North America. They grow to more than 300 feet, with reddish bark, leaves of 2 ranks of needles along a central rib, and soft cones less than an inch in length. Its large size and invasive roots make it suitable only in large gardens. Commonly known as redwood or coast redwood.

Sequoiadendron (seh kwoy'uh dehn druhn) *n.* A genus of 1 species of very hardy trees *S. giganteum* (Taxodiaceae) native to the western slopes of the Sierra Nevada mountain range of California. They grow to more than 250 feet, with thick, gray-green, overlapping, scalelike leaves and 3½-inch cones which mature on the tree over a 2-year period. Not a tree for anything less than a large garden. Com-

monly known as giant sequoia, big tree, or giant redwood.

Serenoa (seh ree'nuh wuh) *n.* A genus of 1 species of somewhat hardy (to North Carolina) low-growing palms *S. repens* (Palmae). It creeps over wide areas. Also known as saw palmetto and scrub palmetto.

sericeous (seh rihsh'uhs) *a.* In botany, silky.

serissa (seh rihs'uh) *n.* A genus of 3 species, the most widely grown of which is *S. foetida,* (Rubiaceae) a tender shrub. It grows to 2 feet, with small oval aromatic leaves and ½-inch trumpet-shaped flowers. A good container plant.

Serjania (suhr jayn'yuh) *n.* A genus of approximately 200 species of subtropical and tropical woody vines (Sapindaceae). They have divided leaves and loose spikes of small yellow flowers.

serotinal (sehr peh ter'ee) *a.* In botany, appearing or occurring in the latter part of the summer. Also serotinous.

serpentary (suhr pehn ter'ee) *n.* A common name for *Aristolochia Serpentaria,* a hardy vine native to the southeastern United States. It grows to more than 3 feet, with the signature heart-shaped leaves and greenish, J-shaped flowers. Also known as Virginia snakeroot.

serpent cucumber *n.* A common name for *Trichosanthes Anguina,* an annual vine. It grows to 15 feet, with large triangular-oval leaves and white flowers. The fruit is similar to a long (to 6 feet), coiled, thick, string bean. Requires a long, hot growing season and sturdy support. Also known as serpent gourd, snake gourd, club gourd, or viper's gourd.

serpent grass *n.* A common name for *Polygonum viviparum,* a hardy perennial plant. It grows to 1 foot, with both long and narrow and wide leaves, followed by loose spikes of small, light pink, or white flowers. Also known as Alpine bistort.

serpentine rock *n.* A rock consisting of acid magnesium silicate.

serpent's-tongue *n.* A common name for ferns of the genus *Ophioglossum,* a sometimes hardy, sometimes tropical low-growing fern. They have just a few fronds (sometimes only 1) and spikes that hold spore clusters. Also known as adder's-tongue fern or adder's tongue.

serpolet (suhr′puh leht) *n.* A common name for *Thymus Serpyllum,* a hardy perennial ground cover. It creeps at a relatively sedate pace, with tiny aromatic leaves and rosy-purple flowers that bloom all summer. Also known as lemon thyme, wild thyme, or mother-of-thyme.

serrate (seh′rayt) *a.* In botany, saw-toothed, with teeth along the margin pointing toward the apex, as a serrate leaf. Also serrated.

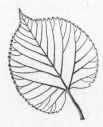

serrate leaf

serration (seh ray′shuhn) *n.* The state of being serrate. Also serrature.

Serratula (seh rach′uh luh) *n.* A genus of about 70 species of hardy perennial plants (Compositae). They grow as high as 5 feet, but usually less, with variably shaped leaves and tubular flowers in various shades of purple.

serrulate (sehr′yuh leht) *a.* Finely serrate; denticulate. Also serrulated.

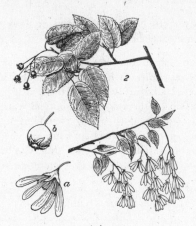

serviceberry
branch with flowers *2* branch with fruit *b* fruit *a* flowers

serviceberry *n.* A common name for hardy shrubs and small trees of the genus *Amelanchier* (Ro-

saceae), many are native to North America. Useful in the garden, particularly in the early spring when the small white flowers appear, sometimes all too fleetingly. Small red fruits, which birds love, appear in summer. Good foliage color in fall. Also known as shadblow, shadbush, or sugarplum tree.

service tree *n.* A common name for *Sorbus domestica,* a hardy deciduous tree. It grows to 60 feet, with divided pairs of leaflets, clusters of small white flowers in late spring, and green or brown fruit.

service tree, wild *n.* A common name for *Sorbus torminalis,* a tender deciduous tree. It grows from 30 to 45 feet with sharply lobed leaves and large clusters of white flowers.

sesame *n.* An annual herb, *Sesamum Indicum,* grown in tropical and subtropical areas. Its value lies chiefly in its seeds, from which is pressed sesame oil, widely used in cooking. The seeds are also used as food, especially in breads and crackers. The plant, which grows to 3 feet tall, thrives in sterile soil and is grown in the southern United States, where it has naturalized. Also called benne.

sesame

Sesbania (sehs bay′nee uh) *n.* A genus of close to 50 species of tender plants and shrubs (Leguminosae). They grow swiftly to as high as 20 feet, with fernlike leaves and drooping clusters of yellow to red sweet-pea-like flowers. Commonly known as scarlet wisteria tree.

seseli (sehs′uh lee) *n.* A genus of about 80 species of annual, biennial, or perennial plants (Umbelliferae). They grow to more than 3 feet, with rosettes of leaves and flat-topped clusters of white flowers.

sessile (sehs′uhl) *a.* In botany, attached directly without a stalk.

sessile attachments
1 sessile flower 2 sessile leaves

setaceous (seh tay'shuhs) *a.* In botany, having or consisting of bristles, or resembling a bristle; setiform.

setiform (seed'uh form) *a.* Bristle-like.

setose (see'tohs) *a.* In botany, bristly.

setterwort (sehd'uhr wert) *n.* A common name for *Helleborus foetidus,* a somewhat hardy perennial. It grows to 18 inches, with leathery, dark green divided leaves and light green flowers with purple margins appearing from February to April. Good for shady spots.

setula (sehch'uh luh) *n., pl.* **setulae**. A short seta, bristle, or hair. Also setule.

setulose (sehch'uh lohs) *a.* Finely setose; covered with small bristles or hairs.

severinia (sehv er rihn'ee uh) *n.* A genus of 5 or 6 species of tender shrubs and small trees (*Rutaceae*). The most widely grown species is *S. buxifolia,* which grows to 6 feet, with small, round, dark green leaves similar to box leaves, clusters of small white flowers and small black berries that appear in fall. Sharp thorns make this a good candidate for a barrier hedge. Commonly known as Chinese box orange.

sewage sludge *n.* An organic fertilizer that consists of dried processed sewage.

sexfoil *n.* In botany, a leaf with 6 leaflets; a flower with 6 perianth segments

shaddock *n.* A common name for *Citrus maxima,* a very tender tropical tree. It grows from 15 to 30 feet, with deep green, glossy 6- to 10-inch leaves, white, fragrant flowers, and huge (15- to 20-pound) yellow-orange fruit—more decorative than tasty. Also known as pomelo, pumelo, pommelo, or pompelmous.

shade cloth *n.* 1. A fabric stretched over young plants to protect them from excessive heat and moisture loss. 2. Any of various fabrics used in summer to lower soil temperatures, hasten germination of cool-season fall crops, prevent bolting, and protect against drying.

shade netting *n.* Mesh material that is stretched over a frame to shield plants from too much sun or heat.

shade, plants for *n.* Plants that will tolerate varying degrees of lack of light: light shade caused by tree branches, dense shade caused by a thick stand of trees, and intermittent shade caused by a building or tree near a spot in the garden.

shade tree *n.* A tree planted or valued for its shade, as distinguished from 1 planted or valued for its fruit, foliage, beauty, etc.

shagbark hickory *n.* A common name for *Carya ovata,* a hardy deciduous tree native to central and eastern North America. It grows to 120 feet with large compound leaves and separate male or female flowers on different trees. Flaking bark is the reason for its common name. Nuts are the best for this genus besides *C. illinoensis* (the pecan); many named varieties from which to choose. Also known as shellbark hickory.

shaggy *a.* In botany, pubescent or downy with long and soft hairs.

shallon (shahl'uhn) *n.* A common name for *Gaultheria shallon,* a hardy small shrub native to southern California. It grows from 2 to 10 feet tall, depending on the amount of sun and water it receives, with oval to nearly round bright green leaves, tiny white flowers in summer, and small, edible (but unremarkable) black fruit. Cut branches are used by florists, who call it lemonleaf.

shallot (shuh laht') *n.* A variety of the onion, *Allium cepa.* The bulb forms bulblets or cloves like the garlic and rocambole. The shallot is considered milder than the onion and is used in the same ways in cooking. The shallot, which rarely flowers or sets seed, is propagated from the cloves of the bulb. In the garden, it looks like a small onion plant.

shallow soil *n*. Soil that has little room for water storage and that can be easily moved by the weather.

shamrock *n*. A plant with 3-part leaves. The identity of the original shamrock. which St. Patrick used to illustrate the doctrine of the Trinity, is uncertain. These clovers are deep rooting and tough ground covers for full sun locations. The European wood sorrel, *Oxalis Acetosella,* is also called the Irish shamrock. Around St. Patrick's Day, florists often sell plants of *Medicago lupulina,* an annual also called hop clover, as shamrocks. When any of these plants are introduced to the garden care should be taken to prevent their becoming invasive pests.

shamrock pea *n*. A common name for *Parochetus communis,* a tender trailing perennial vine. It has compound leaves with 3 leaflets and cobalt-blue and pink flowers. Used in rock gardens and hanging baskets. Also known as blue oxalis.

sharpening stone *n*. A stone for sharpening tools by friction. (See also **tool sharpener.**)

shears *n*. Long-bladed scissors for cutting flower stems or grass borders.

sheath of grass leaf

sheath *n*. A tubular covering surrounding an organ or part of a plant, such as the basal part of a grass leaf surrounding the stem.

sheathed *a*. Enclosed in or having a sheath.

sheepberry *n*. 1. A common name for *Viburnum Lentago,* a deciduous hardy shrub or small tree na-tive to eastern North America. It grows to 30 feet, with oval, finely toothed leaves, white flowers in rounded clusters, and fruit that changes from green to red, to blue. A good screen or background plant. Also known as nannyberry, black haw, cowberry, nanny plum, sweetberry, tea plant, or sweet viburnum. 2. A common name for *Viburnum prunifolium,* a hardy deciduous shrub native to eastern North America. It grows to 15 feet, with oval, finely toothed leaves that turn a shiny red in autumn, clusters of white flowers, and blue-black fruit. Also known as black haw, sweet haw, nannyberry, or stagberry.

sheep bur *n*. A common name for members of the genus *Acaena,* a group of tender, low-growing trailing perennial ground covers. They have divided, gray-green leaves which make a handsome mat of foliage, insignificant flowers, and small burs, which are the marginally bothersome fruit.

sheep laurel *n*. A common name for *Kalmia angustifolia,* a hardy shrub native to eastern North America. It grows to 3 feet, with narrow, pointed leaves and clusters of purple-to-crimson flowers. Also known as dwarf laurel, pig laurel, lambkill, and wicky.

sheep manure *n*. A mixture of sheep excrement and straw used as humus to improve the texture of the soil.

sheep's-bit *n*. A common name for *Jasione perennis,* a somewhat hardy perennial. It grows to 18 inches, with oval, pointed leaves and ball-like clusters of blue flowers. Also known as shepherd's scabiosa.

sheep sorrel (saw'ruhl) *n*. A common name for *Rumex Acetosella,* a hardy perennial weed. It grows to 1 foot on spreading rootstocks, with 1-inch-long arrow-shaped leaves and small, red flowers. Can be invasive if given the slightest chance. Also known as red sorrel or common sorrel.

sheep's-parsley *n*. A common name for *Anthriscus sylvestris,* a hardy perennial or biennial green naturalized in North America. It grows to 3 feet with finely cut leaves divided into 3 parts. Closely related to chervil.

sheep's-tongue *n*. A common name for *Stomatium agninum,* a tender, low-growing succulent. It has dull gray-green leaves and light yellow flowers on short stalks. Also known as lamb's-tongue.

shellbark hickory *n.* A common name for 2 hickories, *Carya laciniosa* or *C. ovata,* native to southeastern and mid-North America. They grow slowly to 120 feet, with fernlike foliage. Both are handsome landscape trees with edible nuts.

shellflower *n.* 1. A common name for *Alpinia Zerumbet,* a tropical perennial. It grows to 12 feet, with large (2-foot long), shiny green leaves and fragrant purple flowers, with red and brown markings in drooping clusters that appear in late summer. Also known as shell ginger or pink porcelain lily. 2. A common name for *Molucella laevis,* an annual that grows to 2 feet, with 2-inch, almost round leaves and apple-green shell-like or bell-like flowers beginning almost from the base up the stem. The flower spikes are attractive dried, also. Also known as bells-of-Ireland or Molucca balm. 3. A common name for *Pistia stratiotes,* a tender subtropical and tropical aquatic perennial. It grows 6-inch rosettes, from which hang long, feathery roots and has fluted gray-green leaves that grow as long as 5 inches. Also known as water lettuce. 4. A common name for *Tigridia Pavonia,* a tender subtropical perennial bulb. It grows to 2 feet, with narrow, ribbed, swordlike leaves and showy, iris-like flowers in a wide selection of vivid colors. The flowers are short lived but profuse. Dig bulbs except in mild-winter areas. Also known as tiger flower.

shelterbelt *n.* A row or stand of trees, shrubs, or other thick growth planted as a barrier between a garden site and the prevailing wind or direction of storms.

she-oak *n.* A common name for tender shrubs and trees of the genus *Casuarina.* They grow from 6 to 70 feet, with inconspicuous leaves—that look like pine needles, but are actually small branchlets. The flowers are barely noticable, but produce small cones. Often used as a street tree or an attractive specimen plant. Also known as beefwood or Australian pine.

shepherd's clock *n.* A common name for *Anagallis arvensis,* an annual low growing weed, widely distributed. It has ¾-inch oval leaves and scarlet flowers. A form with blue flowers is also available.

Easily controlled. Common names allude to the closing of its flowers early in the afternoon or at the approach of bad weather. Also known as poor man's weatherglass, common pimpernel, or scarlet pimpernel.

Shepherdia (sheh puhr'dee uh) *n.* A genus of 3 species of very hardy deciduous shrubs and small trees (Elaeagnaceae) native to North America. They grow from 8 to 18 feet, with silvery leaves, small yellow flowers, and clusters of small red fruit. Tough plants for dry, rocky soils.

shepherd's club *n.* A common name for *Verbascum Thapsus,* a hardy biennial. It grows to 6 feet from a basal rosette, with gray-green, velvety leaves and yellow flowers blooming on a central stalk. Also known as common mullein, flannel plant, or velvet plant.

Shibataea (shihb uh'tay uh) *n.* A genus of 2 species of bamboo, the most widely distributed of which is *S. Kumasaca* (Gramineae), a hardy shrub. It grows slowly to 6 feet, with sharply pointed, unbamboolike oval leaves on unusual zigzag stems.

shield fern *n.* 1. A common name for *Dryopteris* and *Polystichum,* 2 genera of widely distributed ferns, many native to North America. Of easy culture in woodland gardens.

shingle oak *n.* A common name for *Quercus imbricaria,* a hardy, deciduous tree native to the southeastern United States. A handsome tree, it grows to 60 feet, with rectangular leaves that turn russet in the fall. Excellent as a windbreak; can be sheared when young. Also known as laurel oak.

shingle tree *n.* A common name for *Acrocarpus fraxinifolius,* a subtropical tree. It grows to great heights in its native habitat of Southeast Asia, but only 40 to 50 feet in the warmer areas of North America. It has divided leaves that are red when immature and dense clusters of scarlet flowers that appear before the leaves on the bare branches. Also known as pink cedar or red cedar.

shinleaf *n.* A common name for hardy perennials of the genus *Pyrola,* many of which are native to North America. They grow under 12 inches high, with rounded leaves at the base of the plant and white, greenish, pink, or purple flowers distributed on flowering stalks in late summer. Also known as wintergreen.

shittimwood (shihd'ehm wood) *n.* 1. A common name for *Bumelia lanuginosa,* a somewhat hardy deciduous tree native to southeastern North America. It grows to 45 feet, with rectangular leaves 2 to 3 inches long, small white flowers, and tiny black fruit. Also known as false buckthorn, gum elastic, or black haw. 2. A common name for *Halesia carolina,* a hardy deciduous tree native to eastern North America. It grows to 40 feet, with oval leaves and small, white, bell-shaped flowers in clusters in early spring. Also known as wild olive or oppossumwood.

shoeblack plant *n.* A common name for *Hibiscus Rosa-sinensis,* a subtropical flowering shrub. It grows to 15 feet with glossy green leaves and spectacular white, red, yellow, or apricot flowers. The flowers contain an astringent juice causing them to turn black or deep purple when bruised; used in Java for blacking shoes, whence the name. Also known as rose-of-China, China rose, or blacking plant.

shoes and stockings *n.* A common name for *Lotus corniculatus,* a hardy perennial ground cover. It grows to 2 feet, with leaves divided into 3 segments and clusters of red-tinged yellow flowers. Also known as bird's-foot trefoil.

shoestring fern *v.* A common name for *Vittaria lineata,* a grasslike tropical fern native to the southeastern United States and points south. It grows attached to trees, with fronds up to 3 feet or more and only a ¼-inch wide. Also known as beard fern, Florida ribbon fern, or old-man's-beard.

shooting star *n.* A common name for a hardy, small perennial of the genus *Dodecatheon,* native to, and widely distributed in North America. They grow on a basal rosette of leaves with leafless flowering stalks rising well above the leaves and small cyclamenlike magenta-to-lavender to white flowers. Also known as American cowslip.

shoreweed *n.* A common name for *Littorella uniflora,* a hardy aquatic grass. It grows to 4 inches or longer, with partially rounded or flat leaves. Used in aquariums. Also known as shore grass.

short-day plant *n.* A plant that tolerates short daylight hours; a plant which does not require long periods of sunlight. Chrysanthemums are examples of short-day plants.

Shortia (shord'ee uh) *n.* A genus of about 8 species of hardy perennial plants (Diapensiaceae). Low-growing, stemless plants with round or heart-shaped leaves and nodding bells of white, pink, or blue flowers on separate stalks. *S. galacifolia* is native to the mountains from Virginia to Georgia. Commonly known as oconee-bells or fringe bells.

Shortia galacifolia
(oconee bells)

shot hole *n.* A leaf-spot fungus infecting some fruit trees. The centers of the leaf spots fall out, creating small holes, which make the tree look as though it were hit by a shotgun blast. Good winter cleanup and well-timed fungicidal sprays are the most effective controls.

shovel *n.* Any of various implements consisting of a broad scoop or concave blade attached to a handle used for taking up and removing loose soil, compost, sand, etc.

shower tree, golden *n.* A common name for *Cassia fistula,* a tropical flowering tree. It grows to 30 feet, with feathery leaves and long clusters of pale yellow flowers. Also known as Indian laburnum, purging fistula, pudding-pipe tree, or goldenrain tree.

shredder *n.* A motorized device consisting of a container and blades or other cutting surface, used for cutting yard and garden waste, such as leaves and twigs, into small pieces. Also called shredder and composter.

shredder and chipper *n.* A motorized device composed of a container and blades, used for shredding leaves and twigs and chipping branches.

499

shredder and composter *n*. (See **shredder.**)

shrimp plant *n*. A common name for *Justica Brandegeana,* a subtropical flowering shrub. It grows to 3 feet, with soft, oval leaves and drooping spikes of bronze flowers that may resemble shrimp. Also known as Mexican shrimp plant, shrimp bush, or false hop.

shrub *n*. A woody plant, generally smaller than a tree, which produces several stems, rather than a single trunk from the base.

shrub althaea (ahl thee'uh) *n*. A common name for *Hibiscus syriacus,* a hardy flowering shrub. It grows to 10 feet, with small, triangular, deeply lobed leaves and small white, red, purple, or blue-lavender flowers with a red eye. Also known as rose-of-Sharon or althea.

shrubbery *n*. 1. Shrubs collectively. 2. A planting of shrubs, as in a garden.

shrubby *a*. 1. Shrublike, scrubby. 2. Abounding in shrubs.

shrub yellow root *n*. A common name for *Xanthorhiza simplicissima,* a hardy deciduous, shrub. It grows to 2 feet, with divided leaves that turn yellow to reddish-orange in fall and modest purple flowers in early spring. Used as a ground cover in damp shady spots. The roots are indeed yellow, as is the bark.

shuck *n*. An outer covering, such as the husk of corn or the shell of a walnut. *v*. To remove the husk, pod, or shell from.

Siamese shutoff *n*. (See **Y connection.**)

Sibbaldia (seh bahld'ee uh) *n*. A genus of about 8 species of very hardy perennial plants (Rosaceae). They grow to less than 12 inches with small, wedge-shaped leaflets and rounded clusters of tiny yellow flowers. Good rock-garden plants.

Siberian crab *n*. A common name for *Malus baccata,* a hardy flowering tree. It grows to more than 15 feet, with oval leaves, shiny above, pure white, fragrant 1½-inch flowers, and red and yellow fruit.

Siberian lily *n*. A common name for *Ixiolirion tataricum,* a tender flowering bulb. It grows to 16 inches, with narrow, straplike leaves arising from the base and flat-topped clusters of light blue to dark blue flowers.

Siberian pea tree *n*. A common name for *Caragana arborescens,* a very hardy shrub or small tree. It grows swiftly to 20 feet, with 3-inch pairs of leaflets and bright yellow, sweet-pea-like flowers in spring. Tough in hot or cold climates; good hedges or windbreak. Also known as Siberian pea shrub.

Siberian spruce *n*. A common name for *Picea obovata,* a very hardy tree. It grows to more than 100 feet, with dull green or bluish-green needles and 2½-inch cones.

Siberian squill *n*. A common name used for *Scilla sibirica,* a very hardy flowering bulb. It grows to 6 inches, with straplike leaves and spikes of deep blue flowers. Cultivars of white, purplish-pink, and violet-blue flowers are available. Dependable early spring color; colonies naturalize easily.

Siberian wallflower *n*. A common name for *Erysimum hieraciifolium,* a hardy biennial or perennial flowering plant, often grown as an annual. It grows to 3½ feet high with narrow gray or green leaves and deep orange springtime flowers.

Sicana (seh kay'nuh) *n*. A genus of 1 species *S. odorifera* (Cucurbitaceae) of tropical vines. It grows to more than 40 feet, with large (up to 1 foot) round leaves, yellowish flowers, and 2-foot-long, orange-crimson, cylindrical fruit, which is fragrant and edible. Grown as an annual in far southern climates. Commonly known as curuba, curua, coroa, or cassabanana.

sickle *n*. An implement consisting of a curved metal blade with a handle. Heavier sickles are used for cutting brush, lighter-weight ones for cutting long grass.

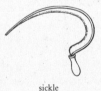

sickle

sicklepod *n*. A common name for *Cassia Tora,* an annual flowering plant. It grows to 3 feet, with pairs of oval leaflets and yellow flowers, followed by long, narrow seedpods.

Sicyos (ihs'ee uhs) *n.* A genus of more than 30 species of vines, the most widely available of which, *S. angulatus* (Cucurbitaceae), is native to eastern North America. It grows to more than 20 feet, with rounded, heart-shaped, deeply lobed leaves and small white or greenish flowers, followed by small burs. A fast-growing screen plant. Commonly known as bur cucumber or star cucumber.

Sida (sigh'duh) *n.* A genus of about 150 species of tender plants and shrubs (Malvaceae). The most widely available plant is *S. hermaphrodita,* native to the eastern United States. It grows from 2 to 3 feet, with large maplelike leaves and loose clusters of white flowers. Commonly known as Virginia mallow.

Sidalcea (sigh dahlsh'ee uh) *n.* A genus of 22 species of annual or hardy perennial plants (Malvaceae) native to western North America. They grow from 3 to 6 feet, with almost circular, softly toothed leaves and white, pink, or purple flowers on spikes at the end of the stalk. Commonly known as checker mallow.

side dressing *n.* An application of manure or fertilizer, around plants as they are growing.

Sideritis (sihd uh righd'ehs) *n.* A genus of about 100 species of annuals and hardy perennials and shrubs (Labiatae). They grow to 3 feet, often with woolly leaves and spikes of yellow flowers.

side saddle flower *n.* A common name for *Sarracenia purpurea,* a hardy perennial native to moist or swampy places in the southeastern United States. They grow to 1 foot, with leaves similar to hollow tubes splotched with red-purple. The leaves trap and digest small insects. Greenish-purple flowers are on separate stalks. Also known as common pitcher plant, sweet pitcher plant, southern pitcher plant, huntsman's cup, or Indian cup.

Sierra laurel *n.* A common name for *Leucothoe Davisiae,* a somewhat hardy shrub native to the northwestern United States. It grows to 5 feet, with 3-inch, glossy leaves and clusters of white, summertime flowers.

sigillate (sihj'uh layt) *a.* In botany, having markings that resemble seals, for example, on roots or stems.

Silene (sigh lee'nee) *n.* A genus of about 500 species of annual and hardy biennial and perennial plants (Caryophyllaceae) many native to North America. They range in size from less than 6 inches to 2 to 3 feet, with opposite leaves and white, pink, or red flowers. Easy to grow. Commonly known as campion or catchfly.

silica (sihl'ehk uh) *n.* An important soil constituent composed of silicon and oxygen.

silica gel (sihl'ehk uh) *n.* A fluffy powder used as a barrier to household pests, such as ants. It can also be used outdoors.

silicle (sihl'eh kuhl) *n.* In botany, a short silique, usually about twice as long as wide.

silique (seh'leek) *n.* In botany, the long, podlike fruit that is characteristic of plants of the family Cruciferae.

siliques of various plants

silk-cotton tree *n.* 1. A common name for *Ceiba pentandra,* a tropical deciduous tree. It can grow to 150 feet, with a 9-foot- diameter trunk from which extend thin buttresses. It has feathery leaves and yellowish, rose or white flowers that appear before the leaves. Kapok, once extensively used as an insulating or cushioning material, surrounds the seeds in their pod. Also known as kapok tree. 2. A common name for *Bombax Ceiba,* a tropical tree. It grows to 75 feet or more, with divided leaves and red flowers. 3. A common name for *Cochlospermum religiosum,* a tropical tree. It grows to 18 feet, with deeply lobed leaves, shiny green on top, and bright yellow flowers.

silk grass *n.* A common name for *Pityopsis graminifolia* and *P. nervosa,* somewhat hardy perennials native to North America. They grow to 2 or 3 feet, with narrow, soft, silvery leaves and yellow, daisylike flowers.

silk plant, Chinese *n*. A common name for *Boehmeria nivea*, a tender perennial. It grows from 3 to 5 feet, with hairy stems and large, oval leaves with a gray coating on the underside. Also known as China grass.

silk-tassel bush *n*. A common name for hardy evergreen shrubs or small trees of the genus *Garrya*, native to western North America. They grow to 15 feet, with oval leaves with a gray undercoating and greenish-yellow flowers in elegant catkins.

silk tree *n*. A common name for *Albizia Julibrissin*, a marginally hardy flowering deciduous tree. It grows quickly to 40 feet, with feathery, acacialike leaves and clusters of pale rose flowers, like pincushions above the foliage. An excellent and elegant shade tree. Also known as mimosa.

silk vine *n*. A common name for somewhat hardy deciduous vines of the genus *Periploca*. They grow to 40 feet, with dark green glossy leaves and clusters of greenish-yellow flowers.

silkweed *n*. A common name for mostly hardy perennials of the genus *Asclepias*, native to North America. They grow from 2 to 6 feet, with alternate or whorled leaves and often showy clusters of green or purplish or orange flowers. The seeds are borne by silky white hairs. Also known as milkweed or butterfly flower.

Silphium (sihl'fee uhm) *n*. A genus of about 20 species of hardy perennial plants (Compositae) native to central and southern North America. They grow to 6 feet or more, with rough, often large leaves and large, yellow, daisylike flowers. Commonly known as rosinweed.

silt loam *n*. 1. Soil material haviing 50% or more silt and 12% to 27% clay. 2. Soil material having 50 to 80% silt and less than 12% of clay.

silty clay *n*. A texture class of soil that has 40% or more clay and 40% or more silt.

silty clay loam *n*. A texture class of soil that has 27% to 40% of clay and less than 20% of sand.

silver-back fern *n*. A common name for *Pityrogramma triangularis* var.*viscosa*, a small hardy fern native to western North America. It grows to 12 inches, with triangular fronds with a silvery sheen on the undersides.

silver bell *n*. A common name for plants of the genus *Halesia*, a flowering tree native to eastern North America. *H. carolina* and *H. monticola* are hardy north. They grow to 30 feet or more, with finely toothed, oval leaves and clusters of charming white bell-shaped flowers in late spring. Also known as snowdrop tree.

silverberry *n*. A common name for various species of the genus *Elaeagnus* (*E. angustifolia, E. commutata,* or *E. pungens*), hardy, often spiny shrubs. They grow between 12 and 20 feet, and have alternate leaves, covered with small silvery or brown dots, small, fragrant flowers and small berries, often silvery. Tough, undemanding plants useful as barrier plantings.

silver buffalo berry *n*. A common name for *Shepherdia argentea,* a very hardy shrub or small tree native to North America. It grows to 18 feet with silvery leaves, small yellowish flowers, and edible fruit. A stalwart hedge plant.

silverbush *n*. 1. A common name for *Convolvulus Cneorum,* a tender shrub. It grows to 4 feet, with smooth gray leaves and white or pinkish summertime flowers. 2. A common name for *Sophora tomentosa,* a tender shrub or small tree. It grows to less than 20 feet, with leaves divided into many furry leaflets and pale yellow flowers in flowing clusters.

silver-crown *n*. A common name for *Cotyledon undulata,* a tender succulent. It grows to 4 feet, with broad, thick leaves, heavily dusted with white powder, and drooping clusters of orange flowers. Also known as silver-ruffles.

silver-dollar gum *n*. A common name for *Eucalyptus polyanthemos,* a marginally hardy tree. It grows to 60 feet, with new, gray-green leaves that are almost round and that become narrow and long as they mature, and small, creamy-white flowers.

silver-dollar tree *n*. A common name for *Eucalyptus cinerea,* a somewhat hardy tree. It grows to 50 feet, in an irregular shape, with new, gray-green leaves that are almost round and that become narrow and long as they mature, and small, whitish unimpressive flowers. Pruning encourages new foliage. Also known as spiral eucalyptus.

silver fern *n*. 1. A common name for plants of the genus *Pityrogramma*, tender, low-growing ferns. with the undersides of fronds covered with a silvery coating. 2. A common name for *Pteris quadriaurita* 'Argyraea', a tropical fern. It grows from 2 to 4 feet, with coarsely divided fronds splotched with white. Also known as silver-lace fern or striped brake.

silver king/silver queen *n*. Varieties of *Artemisia*, grown for their tall spikes of pale green foliage and beadlike flower heads, which dry well for winter arrangements. Both varieties are highly prized by wreath makers because they can be shaped into circles while fresh and then will dry into a firm base suitable for decoration with other herbs.

silver lace vine *n*. A common name for *Polygonum Aubertii*, a hardy, fast-growing, perennial vine. It grows 20 to 30 feet in a growing season, with glossy, heart-shaped leaves and sprays of creamy-white flowers in summer. Likes full sun; good for covering just about anything. Also known as China fleece vine.

silver-leaved mountain gum *n*. A common name for *Eucalyptus pulverulenta*, a tender tree. It grows to 30 feet, with silvery-gray new, almost circular leaves that appear to be pierced by the stem. The mature leaves are long and pointed. Also known as money tree.

silver linden *n*. A common name for *Tilia tomentosa*, a hardy tree. It grows to 90 feet, with roundish-oval 4-inch leaves with a saw-tooth edge and a white fuzz on the underside, which gives it a silvery appearance.

silverling *n*. 1. A common name for *Baccharis halimifolia*, a hardy deciduous shrub native to the Atlantic and Gulf coasts. It grows to 12 feet, with small, gray-green leaves and clusters of small, whitish flowers. Good seashore planting. Also known as groundsel tree, groundselbush, sea myrtle, or consumption weed. 2. A common name for *Paronychia argyrocoma*, a hardy low-growing perennial native to eastern North America. It grows to 12 inches, with small, narrow, pointed leaves and fuzzy silver flowers. Also known as silver whitlowwort.

silver mound *n*. A compact perennial plant, *Artemisia schmidtiana*, grown for its feathery gray-green foliage. It may be planted singly or in a row to define the borders of an ornamental or herb bed.

silverrod *n*. A common name for *Solidago bicolor*, a hardy perennial native to the northeastern quarter of North America. It grows to 4 feet, with oval leaves at the base and summertime clusters of white flowers at the top of the stalk. Also known as white goldenrod.

silver thistle *n*. A common name for *Onopordum Acanthium*, a hardy biennial thistle. It grows to 9 feet, with white downy stems and leaves and reddish-purple flowers. Also known as cotton thistle, Scotch thistle, oat thistle, silvery thistle or Argentine thistle.

silver torch *n*. A common name for *Cleistocactus Struasii*, a subtropical columnar cactus. It grows to 6 feet, with white bristlelike spines and red with green flowers.

silver tree *n*. A common name for *Leucodendron argentum*, a subtropical tree grown for its foliage. It grows to 30 feet, with silvery, soft, narrow leaves that completely cover the plant.

silver-vein creeper *n*. A common name for *Parthenocissus henryana*, a hardy deciduous vine. It grows to 20 feet, with leaves that start out purplish and mature to a bronzy green with silver veins; good red autumn foliage also. It has undistinguished flowers, followed by blue berries in the fall.

silver vine *n*. A common name for *Actinidia polygama*, a hardy flowering vine. It grows to 15 feet, with oval leaves rounded at the base, some white or yellowish on the upper half, and single or samll clusters of white flowers.

silverweed *n*. A common name for *Potentilla Anserina*, a very hardy, low-growing perennial ground cover. It has divided leaves, with a silvery underside, that grow in a rosette and 1-inch, roselike yellow flowers that appear 1 to a stem. Also known as goose grass or goose tansy.

Simmondsia (sihm uhnd'zee uh) *n*. A genus of 1 species, *S. chinensis* (Buxaceae), of tender (less so when mature) evergreen shrubs native to southwestern North America. It grows to 7 feet, with leathery, dull green leaves, small flowers, and nutlike fruit. The oil from the nut is used as a substitute for whale oil and for skin emollients. A good hedge plant in desert areas. Commonly known as goat nut or jojoba.

single grain soil *n.* A structureless soil in which each particle exists separately, as in a dune.

sinistrorse (sihn eh straw'uhrs) *a.* Of a plant, twining upward around an axis in a counter-clockwise direction, as applied to such phenomena as the arrangement of leaves around a stem, or branches around the trunk of a tree.

Sinningia (seh nihn'jee uh) *n.* A genus of more than 75 species of tropical flowering perennial plants (Gesneriaceae). The most widely available species is *S. speciosa* (gloxinia), mostly grown as a houseplant. It is low-growing, with dark green, toothed, velvet-textured leaves and white, red, pink, violet, purple, or blue flowers. Many cultivars are offered in a variety of color combinations. Of undemanding culture. Commonly known as violet slipper.

sinuate (sihn'yuhweht) *a.* Having a strongly wavy margin, as the leaves of *Pittosporum eugenioides*. Also sinuated.

sinuate leaf

sinuate-dentate (sihn'yuh weht) *a.* In botany, having a toothed margin that is also strongly wavy; used especially to describe leaves.

sinus *n.* In botany, an indentation or hollow in a margin, for example, between 2 divisions of a leaf.

Sisyrinchium (sihs uh ring'kee uhm) *n.* A genus of about 75 species of perennial plants (Iridaceae), not all of them consistently hardy; widely distributed, many native to North America. They usually grow under 2 feet, with small, irislike leaves and blue, yellow, or white flowers. *S. angustifolium* is native to eastern North America; *S. californicum* and *S. Douglasii* are native to the western United States. Commonly known as blue-eyed grass.

Sium (sigh'uhm) *n.* A genus of maybe 10 species of hardy perennial plants (Umbelliferae). They grow to 3 or 4 feet, with divided leaves and small white flowers. A native species, *S. suave,* grows in boggy meadows.

Skimmia (skihm'ee uh) *n.* A genus of about 10 species of somewhat hardy shrubs (Rutaceae). They grow to 6 feet with handsome, oval, 4- to 5-inch leaves, clusters of white flowers, and bright hollylike berries (male and female plants are sometimes required to produce berries).

skirret

skirret (skihr'iht) *n.* A species of water parsnip, *Sium Sisarum,* cultivated as a vegetable for its sweet-flavored root. The plant is 1 to 2 feet tall, with sparse leaves, a hardy perennial, but grown as an annual. The root is composed of small, fleshy, potatolike tubers, each the size of the little finger, and is eaten boiled served with butter or parboiled and then fried. Skirret, once a staple of home vegetable gardens, has now nearly fallen into disuse. It is planted from seed or from small side shoots from the roots.

skullcap

skullcap *n.* A common name for mostly hardy perennials of the genus *Scutellaria*. There are both spreading and erect forms with usually toothed leaves and rather large blue, violet, scarlet, or yellow flowers along the stem or in a terminal spike.

skunkbush *n.* A common name for *Rhus trilobata,* a hardy deciduous shrub. It grows to 6 feet, with oval, 1-inch leaflets and greenish flowers in clustered spikes. The crushed leaves have an unpleasant odor.

skunk cabbage *n.* 1. A common name used for *Lysichiton americanum,* a hardy perennial native to northwest North America. It is stemless, with large (to 5 feet long) bright green leaves, a bright yellow flower covering, and greenish flowers. The leaves give off unpleasant odor when crushed. Also known as western skunk cabbage. 2. A common name for *Veratrum californicum,* a hardy perennial native to western North America. It grows to 6 feet, with large oval leaves becomming narrower toward the top of the plant, and long clusters of off-white flowers. Also known as corn lily.

sky flower *n.* 1. A common name for *Duranta repens,* a subtropical evergreen shrub or small tree. It is fast-growing, to 18 feet, sometimes with thorns, with oval, 4-inch leaves, hanging clusters of small tubular blue-violet flowers, and fruit. Also known as golden dewdrop, pigeonberry, or Brazilian sky flower. 2. A common name for *Thunbergia grandiflora,* a tender, twining, evergreen vine. It grows vigorously to 20 feet or more, with rough, oval, toothed leaves and long drooping clusters of blue flowers in spring. Also known as blue trumpet vine, clock vine, or sky vine.

skyrocket *n.* A common name for *Ipomopsis aggregata,* a hardy biennial native to the mountains of western North America. It grows to 2 feet, with finely divided 2-inch leaves and red, golden-yellow, pink, or white tubular flowers arranged at the end of the stems. Also known as scarlet gilia.

slaked lime *n.* A lime that is used to raise the pH of soil but is more caustic than dolomitic soil.

slat house *n.* An open sided structure used to provide shade to young tender or plants. The roof is constructed of narrow pieces of wood (slats), between which are spaces of approximately the same width.

sleekwort, mauve *n.* A common name for *Liparis liliifolia,* a hardy perennial native to eastern North America; a member of the Orchid family It grows to 9 inches, with 2 leaves at the base and small, purple flowers on a stalk. Good for a shady wild garden. Also known as large twayblade or purple scutcheon.

slip *n.* 1. In plant propagation, a cutting from a mother plant. 2. The down-slope movement of a mass of soil under wet or saturated conditions.

slipper flower *n.* 1. A common name for a member of the genus *Calceolaria,* somewhat tender annuals and perennials. Annuals are low-growing; the perennials grow to 2 feet or more, with dark green crinkled leaves and unusual, brightly colored pouchlike flowers, often with red or orange-brown spots. Also known as slipperwort, pocketbook flower, or pouch flower. 2. A common name for *Pedilanthus tithymaloides.* (See **slipper plant.**)

slipper plant *n.* A common name for *Pedilanthus tithymaloides,* a tropical succulent shrub. The stems, growing to 6 feet in a zigzag pattern, have fleshy leaves streaked with white and various shades of green and occasionally pink. Clusters of slipper-shaped red and yellow flowers appear in summer. The milky sap can cause skin irritantations. Also known as slipper flower, Japanese poinsettia, redbird flower, ribbon cactus, or devil's backbone.

slippery elm *n.* A common name for *Ulmus rubra,* a hardy deciduous tree native to eastern North America. It grows to 60 feet, with a broad, open crown and large, wide leaves that are rough on top, smooth on the underside. Also known as red elm.

sloe (sloh) *n.* A common name for a number of different species of *Prunus: P. alleghaniensis, P. americana,* and *P. spinosa.* The first 2 species are native to southeastern North America. *P. alleghaniensis* grows to 15 feet with oval, serrated leaves, small white flowers turning pink, and ½-inch fruit. *P. americana* grows to 25 feet, with shaggy bark, often thorny branches, oval, serrated leaves, 1-inch white flowers, and ¾-inch yellow-to-red fruit. *P. spinosa* grows thickly to 12 feet, with oval, serrated leaves, profuse white flowers, and ½-inch shiny black fruit; it can grow on very poor soil.

sloe
1 branch with flowers 2 leaves and fruit

slope *n.* The incline of the surface of a soil expressed in the percentage of slope, which equals the number of feet of fall per 100 feet of horizontal distance.

slug *n.* A snail without a shell; a slimy, night-feeding creature that chews on a variety of plants. It thrives in moist conditions. There are many methods of control, including trapping (under boards or other shelters) or handpicking at night, using physical barriers (copper stripping or salt-impregnated), eliminating hiding places, and setting out poisonous baits.

slug barrier *n.* A copper strip, typically about 3 inches wide, which deters slugs by giving them a mild shock. The strips may be stapled to raised beds, containers, or trees or may be looped around seedlings.

slug pub *n.* A trap, baited with beer, used to attract and drown slugs. Also called slug saloon.

slug trap *n.* A container and bait to lure, capture, and promote the demise of snails and slugs.

smartweed *n.* A common name for a member of the genus *Polygonum,* annuals and mostly hardy perennials. They grow in a range of forms from vining (*P. Aubertii* or silver-lace vine) to large clumps (*P. cuspidatum* or Japanese knotweed) to ground covers (*P. capitatum*) with small pink or white flowers. *P. coccineum,* or water smartweed, is a water plant native to North America, with small rose-colored flowers. Also known as knotweed or fleeceflower.

Smilacina (smih luh sih'neh) *n.* A genus of about 25 species of hardy perennial plants (Liliaceae), many native to North America. They grow to 3 feet, in shady spots, with rich green leaves to 6 inches long on either side of the stem and plumes of white, pink, or purplish flowers at the end of the stems, followed by small, perfectly round, red berries. Commonly known as false Solomon's-seal, Solomon's-feather, or Solomon's plumes.

Smilax (smigh'laks) *n.* A genus of about 200 species of hardy vines (Liliaceae), many native to North America. They grow by pairs of grasping tendrils with oval 4- to 6-inch leaves and greenish, whitish, or yellowish flowers in small clusters at the base of the leaf stems. What florists call smilax is actually *Asparagus asparagoides.* Suitable only for woodland gardens; if allowed to grow unchecked, can produce an impenetrable thicket. Commonly known as greenbrier or catbrier.

Smithiantha (smihth ee ahn'thuh) *n.* A genus of 4 species of tropical flowering perennials (Gesneriaceae). They grow to 2½ feet, with heart-shaped, velvety, purplish leaves and red bell-shaped flowers. Commonly known as temple-bells.

smoke plant *n.* (See **smoke tree**.)

smoke tree *n.* 1. A common name for shrubs or small trees of the genus *Cotinus.* The most widely available species is *C. Coggygria,* which grows to 15 feet, with 3-inch oval leaves and large clusters of small greenish flowers, which fade to a billowy purple fuzz. *C. obovatus,* native to central North America, grows to 30 feet, and although lacking dramatic plumes of 'smoke,' does have exceptional yellow to orange and red autumn color. Also known as smoke bush. 2. A common name for *Dalea spinosa,* a small desert tree native to southwestern North America. It grows to 12 feet (taller with regular irrigation), with small, narrow leaves which fall early, and fragrant violet-purple flowers in late spring. The densely branched silhouette resembles clouds of smoke.

smokeweed *n.* A common name for *Eupatorium maculatum,* a hardy perennial native to eastern North America. It grows to 6 feet, with coarse, narrow leaves clustered around the stem and clusters of purplish tubular flowers at the ends of stems. Also known as Joe-Pye weed.

Smyrnium (smuhr'nee uhm) *n*. A genus of about 7 species of hardy biennial plants (Umbelliferae). The most widely distributed species is *S. Olusatrum*. It grows to 4 feet, with 18-inch leaves and greenish-yellow flowers in flat-topped clusters. Commonly known as alexanders or horse parsley.

snail *n*. A type of shelled gastropod, closely related to slugs. It is a troublesome garden pest that feeds on many plants, mostly at night. (For control methods, see **slug**. Also see **decollate snail** for an alternative biological control.)

snail barrier *n*. A copper strip, typically about 3 inches wide, which deters snails by giving them a mild shock. the strips may be stapled to raised beds, containers, or trees or may be looped around seedlings.

snailflower *n*. A common name for *Vigna Caracalla*, a tropical perennial vine. It twines to 20 feet, with 5-inch oval leaves and fragrant, cream-colored flowers with purple accents. The common name derives from the bottom petal that is twisted like a snail's shell. Also known as corkscrew flower, snail bean, snail vine, or caracol.

snail-seed *n*. A common name for *Cocculus carolinus*, a somewhat hardy perennial vine native to southeastern North America. It grows to 12 feet, with 4-inch oval leaves, inconspicuous flowers, and showy red clusters of fruit in early summer. Also known as Carolina moonseed, red moonseed, or coral beads.

snake *n*. One of various limbless reptilians. Most garden varieties are useful in controlling rodents and insects.

snakehead *n*. A common name for *Chelone glabra*, a hardy perennial native to northeastern North America. It grows to 6 feet, with attractive 6-inch leaves and white or soft pink flowers in spikes at the ends of the stems. Also known as turtlehead or balmony. Used in wet streamside or boggy locations.

snake mouth *n*. A common name for *Pogonia ophioglossoides*, a hardy member of the orchid family native to shady, swampy spots in North America. It grows to 2½ feet, with a single pointed oval leaf at the base and a fragrant white to pink flower, with a fringed lower lip. Also known as adder's-tongue-leaved pogonia, adder's-mouth, ettercap, or rose crest-lip.

snakeroot *n*. 1. A common name for *Asarum canadense*, a hardy perennial deciduous ground cover. It creates a carpet of heart-shaped leaves, 6-inches wide and 4 to 6 inches high and has small and inconspicuous flowers, hidden in the leaves. Needs shade. Also known as wild ginger. 2. A common name for a plant of the genus *Sanicula*, a group of hardy perennials. They grow to 2½ feet, with divided leaves and clusters of white, greenish, yellow, or purple flowers. Also known as sanicle.

snakeroot, black *n*. A common name for *Cimicifuga racemosa*, a hardy perennial native to northeastern North America. It grows to 8 feet, with large divided leaves and tall spikes of white flowers during summer. Also known as black cohosh.

snakeroot, button *n*. 1. A common name for *Eryngium yuccifolium*, a hardy perennial native to eastern North America. It grows to more than 3 feet, with long, bristly, straplike leaves and small, whitish flowers. Also known as rattlesnake-master. 2. A common name for members of the genus *Liatris*, hardy perennials native to central and eastern North America. It grows from 2 to 6 feet, with thin, grasslike leaves and brilliantly colored plumes of rose, purple, or white flowers. Tough, easy-to-grow plants. Also known as blazing star or gay feather.

snakeroot, Sampson's *n*. A common name for 2 species of *Gentiana*, both hardy perennials native to southeastern North America. *G. Catesbaei* grows to 2 feet, with blue flowers in small clusters at the ends of the stems. *G. villosa* grows to 18 inches, with greenish-white flowers with violet tinges.

snakeroot, Seneca (sehn ih'kha) *n*. A common name for *Polygala Senega*, a very hardy perennial native to northeastern North America. It has several 18-inch stems, which grow from a thick root, with narrow 2-inch-long leaves and dense clusters of whitish or greenish flowers.

snakeroot, Virginia *n*. A common name for *Aristolochia Serpentaria*, a hardy perennial. It grows to 3 feet, with heart-shaped leaves and greenish J-shaped flowers.

snakeroot, white *n*. A common name for *Eupatorium rugosum*, a hardy perennial native to eastern

North America. It grows to 5 feet, with long, thin, oval leaves and clusters of white flowers. Also known as Indian sanicle or white sanicle.

snake's-head *n.* A common name for *Fritillaria Meleagris,* a hardy flowering bulb. It grows to 15 inches, with thin, grasslike leaves and stalks of reddish-brown, drooping, bell-like flowers veined with purple. An enchanting springtime flower. Also known as checkered lily or guinea-hen tulip.

snake's-head iris *n.* A common name for *Hermodactylus tuberosus,* a hardy perennial iris. It grows to 18 inches, with gray-green irislike leaves and reddish-purple velvety outer petals and light green inner petals.

snakeweed *n.* 1. A common name for plants of the genus *Gutierrezia. G. Sarothrae,* native to western North America, is a hardy perennial that grows to 2 feet, with small, thin, sticky leaves and flat-topped clusters of yellow flowers. Also known as matchweed, matchbrush, resinweed, broomweed, or turpentine weed. 2. A common name for *Polygonum Bistorta,* a hardy perennial. It grows to 2 feet with 10-inch-long oblong leaves and 2-inch spikes of densely clustered white or pink flowers. Also known as bistort.

snap adapter *n.* Plastic device that makes a clicking sound as it connects parts of a watering system, such as a nozzle to a hose. Also called quick-connect hose system or snap-together watering system.

snapdragon *n.* A common name for a plant of the genus *Antirrhinum.* The most widely available species is *A. majus,* a tender perennial, generally treated as an annual. A multitude of cultivars have been developed, in sizes ranging from less than 8 inches to 3 feet and in flower forms ranging from the usual 'dragon' shape to double flowers or bell-like blossoms.

snapdragon, dwarf *n.* A common name for *Chaenorrhinum minus,* an annual widely naturalized in central and northeastern North America. It grows less than 12 inches tall, with 1-inch-long leaves and stalks of loose, leafy clusters of white-to-lilac flowers.

snapjack *n.* A common name for *Stellaria Holostea,* a somewhat hardy weedy perennial. It grows to 2 feet with 2-inch pointed leaves and loose clusters of white flowers. This common name derives from the extreme brittleness of its stems; also known as greater stitchwort.

snap-together watering system *n.* An irrigation system having parts connected by snap adapters. (See **snap adapter.**)

snapweed *n.* A common name for plants of the genus *Impatiens,* a widely distributed group of annuals and perennials. This common name derives from the action of the ripe seedpod, which can explode with a report, scattering the seed. Also known as balsam, jewelweed, or touch-me-not.

sneezeweed *n.* 1. A common name for *Achillea Ptarmica,* a very hardy perennial. It grows to 2 feet, with short, narrow leaves and clusters of white flowers. 2. A common name for a plant of the genus *Helenium,* especially the common *H. autumnale.* It grows to 6 feet, with smooth, 6-inch-long oval leaves and 2-inch daisylike flowers in shades of yellow. There are numerous cultivars with various plant and flower sizes. Also known as sneezewort.

snow-apple *n.* An old variety of apple that has very white flesh.

snowball *n.* A common name for *Viburnum Opulus* 'Roseum', a hardy deciduous flowering shrub. It grows to 12 feet, with 4-inch maplelike leaves that turn a dull red in the fall and rounded 2- to 4-inch clusters of late-spring-blooming white flowers, which resemble snowballs.

snowball, Chinese *n.* A common name for *Viburnum macrocephalum macrocephalum,* a hardy flowering shrub. It grows to 12 feet, with oval, dull green leaves and spectacular rounded 6- to 8-inch clusters of white springtime flowers.

snowball, Mexican *n.* A common name for *Echeveria elegans,* a tender perennial succulent. It grows in tight rosettes of greenish-gray spoon-shaped leaves 1-inch wide, and pink flowers with yellow lining, borne on 7-inch pink stems. A good edging plant in warm climates or in windowsill pots in cool-winter climates.

snowberry *n.* A common name for plants of the genus *Symphoricarpus,* hardy low-growing shrubs native to North America. They have small oval leaves and white or pink clusters of flowers, followed by white or colored berrylike fruit, which hang on the plant after the leaves have fallen.

snowberry, creeping *n.* A common name for *Gaultheria hispidula,* a hardy slow growing ground cover native to North America. It has ¾-inch oval leaves and tiny white flowers, followed by small pure white fruit. Good for bog or wild gardens. Also known as moxie plum or maidenhair berry.

snowbush *n.* A common name for 2 species of *Ceanothus,* both native to western North America. *C. cordulatus* is a tender, spiny shrub that grows to 4 feet, with tiny oval leaves and white flowers. *C. velutinus* is a hardy shrub that grows to 25 feet, with 2½-inch- long leaves, glossy above and downy below, and white flowers.

snowdrop *n.* A common name for a hardy springtime bulb of the species *Galanthus.* It grows under 6 inches tall, with usually 2 or 3 narrow leaves and single, bell-like white flowers, tinged with green.

snowdrop tree *n.* A common name for a member of *Halesia,* a genus of deciduous trees or shrubs native to eastern North America and eastern China. They have alternate, toothed leaves and nodding, white bell-shaped flowers, appearing in spring before the leaves, and usually borne on slender branches, forming arches or rows of bells along the underside. *H. diptera* and *H. carolina* are both native to the South and Midwest; *H. diptera* is hardy to Zone 8, *H. carolina* hardy to Zone 5. Also known as silver-bell tree.

snowflake *n.* 1. A common name for a hardy flowering bulb of the genus *Leucojum.* It grows to less than 12 inches, with rich green, straplike leaves and nodding, bell-like white flowers, several to a stalk. Most species bloom in early springtime, but *L. autumnale* blooms in the fall. Easy to grow.

snowflower *n.* A common name for *Spathiphyllum floribundum,* a tropical flower similar to anthuriums or calla lilies. It grows less than 12 inches, with large, lush, velvety leaves and white flowers.

snow-in-summer *n.* A common name for *Cerastium tomentosum,* a hardy perennial ground cover. It grows to 10 inches, with tufts of woolly silver-gray leaves and masses of small, showy white flowers. Not long lived; bounces back after severe frost. Also known as snow-in-harvest.

snow-on-the-mountain *n.* A common name for *Euphorbia marginata,* an annual succulent native to central North America. It grows to 2 feet, with oval, light green leaves, the upper ones of which have a margin of white, and yellow and white flowers. the plant exudes a milky sap which can cause skin irritations to some people. Also known as ghostweed.

snow wreath *n.* A common name for *Neviusia alabamensis,* a somewhat hardy deciduous shrub native to Alabama. It grows to 6 feet, with 3-inch-long, sharply pointed leaves and feathery white flowers with no petals.

soaker *n.* Device attached to the end of a hose to break the flow of water, releasing it slowly and evenly into the ground.

soaker hose *n.* A porous garden hose used above or below ground to release tiny amounts of water slowly and evenly into the soil.

soap bark tree *n.* A common name for *Quillaja Saponaria,* a somewhat hardy tree. It grows to 60 feet, with 2-inch-long shiny leaves and clusters of white flowers in springtime.

soapberry *n.* 1. A common name for subtropical and tropical shrubs and trees of the genus *Sapindus.* The most widely grown species in North America is *S. Saponaria,* a small evergreen tree with has 1-foot-long leaves divided into leaflets, white flowers, and round, orange-brown, glossy fruits, which can be used as soap. Also commonly known as chinaberry. 2. A common name for *Shepherdia canadensis,* a very hardy shrub native to North America. It grows to 8 feet, with leaves, smooth and green on top and silvery with brown scales on the underside and small yellow flowers, followed by attractive clusters of red berries. Also known as buffalo berry.

soapberry family *n.* A family of 150 genera and 2,000 species of evergreen and deciduous shrubs and trees, Sapindaceae. They have mostly divided leaves and clusters or spikes of flowers. The ornamental genera are *Cardiospernum, Dodnaea, Euphoria, Harpullia, Koelreuteria, Litchi, Melicoccus, Sapindus,* and *Ungnadia.*

soap plant *n.* A common name for *Chlorogalum pomeridianum,* a hardy perennial native to Oregon and California. It has straplike, wavy-margined leaves that grow to 2½ feet long and a delicately structured flower stalk that supports dainty white flowers. When wet and rubbed, the root produces a lather that was reputedly used by native Americans. Also known as wild potato.

soap tree *n.* A common name for *Yucca elata,* a somewhat hardy desert tree native to southwestern North America. It grows slowly to 20 feet, with long, narrow, pale green, pointed leaves and tall spikes of cream-colored flowers. Also known as soapweed or palmella.

soapwort *n.* A common name for low-growing annuals or hardy perennials of the genus *Saponaria,* They grow in clumps, with mostly oval leaves and small white, pink, or red flowers.

soapwort

soapwort gentian (jehn′chuhn) *n.* A common name for *Gentiana Saponaria,* a hardy perennial native to southeastern North America. It grows to 30 inches, with narrow, pointed leaves and clusters of deep blue tubular flowers.

sobole (sah′buh lee) *n,, pl.* **soboles**. In botany, a shoot, stolon, or sucker. Also sobol.

soboliferous (sah buh lihf′uh ruhs) *a.* In botany, producing suckers or lateral shoots from the ground; usually applied to shrubs or small trees.

society, horticultural *n.* A horticultural organization whose members are interested in and exchange information about plants in general (the American Horticultural Society, for example) or about particular plants (Dahlias-All-Round or the American Rhododendron Society, for example).

sod *n.* 1. The upper stratum of grassland, containing the roots of grass and any other herbs that may be growing in it; the sward or turf. 2. A piece of this grassy layer pared or pulled off; a turf; a divot or fail.

sod corer *n.* An implement used to treat compacted lawns by removing small (typically ½ inch) plugs of soil.

sodium nitrate *n.* An inorganic fertilizer that adds nitrogen to the soil.

Sodom apple *n.* A common name for *Solonum sodomeum,* a hardy, spiny shrub. It grows to 6 feet, with divided leaves, clusters of violet flowers, and glossy, plumlike fruit. Also known as yellow popolo or Dead Sea apple.

sod webworm *n.* The night-feeding larva of a tan moth. It chews grass blades off at the surface, causing gradually expanding dead spots in lawns. The moths fly in a herky-jerky pattern above the lawn when disturbed during the day. Look for the wormlike larvae at night with a flashlight, or, if you suspect infestation, flood a 1- foot-square area of turf with soapy water (1 tablespoon liquid detergent in a gallon of water). The worms will come to the surface in 10 to 15 minutes. Control with *Bacillus thruringiensis,* parasitic nematodes, resistant grass varieties, or traditional insecticides.

softwood *n.* Wood consisting of still soft, immature tissue.

soil *n.* 1. The upper layer of earth that can be plowed, dug, or tilled; 2. The earth's loose surface material in which plants grow. 3. Land.

soil amendment *n.* 1. A soil additive. 2. What is needed for optimum plant productivity.

soil analysis *n.* A chemical examintion of a soil sample to find out its components in order to recommend amendments to improve the soil.

soil block maker *n.* Device for compressing blocks of soil into cubes used for starting seedlings.

soil characteristic *n.* A feature of a soil that can be seen and/or measured in a soil sample.

soil classification *n.* The systematic arrangement of soils into groups or categories according to the proportion of sand, silt, or clay that is in the soil.

soil climate *n.* The moisture and temperature conditions existing in the soil.

soil conservation *n.* The positive concept of improvement of soils for use as well as their protection and preservation.

soil mixture *n.* A term used to describe various different mixes of soil and amendments to grow different types of plants.

soil particles *n.* Grains that make up soil.

soil pasteurization *n.* A sterilization process of soil that destroys objectionable organisms without chemically altering the soil.

soil population *n.* The group of organisms that normmally live in the soil.

soil potentional *n.* The study of what plants the soil will support.

soil quality *n.* An attribute of a soil that is inferred from soil characteristics and soil behavior under defined conditions.

soil sample *n.* A multiple sample of soil taken from a depth of 5 to 1 inches, labeled, and sent to a local state experiment station to be analyzed for content.

soil sampler *n.* A tube with a cutting edge used in removing a soil core for testing.

soil sieve *n.* Any of variously sized mesh screens used to sift compost, potting soil, or sphagnum or to remove chaff and debris from seeds and grains. Also called riddle or soil sifter.

soil sterilization *n.* The act of destroying all living organisms in the soil.

soil survey *n.* A general term for the systematic examination of soils, their description, classification, and mapping of kinds of soil.

soil test kit *n.* An assortment of chemicals and calibrated tubes with instructions for evaluating nutrients—typically, nitrogen, phosphorous, and potassium—and determining the acidity or alkalinity (pH) of soil. Also known as pH test kit.

soil test tape *n.* Tape, similar to litmus paper, for evaluating the acidity or alkalinity (pH) of soil.

Solanaceae (soh luh nay'see ee) *n. pl.* A family of about 90 genera and 2,000 species of flowering plants, vines, shrubs, and trees; the nightshade family. They have simple or divided leaves, star- or saucer-shaped flowers, and berries or capsules. The family includes many significant food crops, such as eggplant, pepper, tomato, and potato. The ornamental genera are *Browallia, Brunfelsia, Capsicum, Cestrum, Datura, Fabiana, Lycium, Nicandra, Nicotiana, Nierembergia, Petunia, Physalis, Salpiglossis, schizanthus, Solandra, Solanum, Streptosolen,* and *Vestia.*

Solandra (soh lahnd'druh) *n.* A genus of about 10 species of tropical vines (Solanaceae). They grow to more than 30 feet with glossy, leathery leaves and large, showy, trumpet-shaped white-to-yellow flowers . Commonly known as chalice vine.

Solanum (suh lay'nuhm) *n.* A genus of about 1,700 species of shrubs and vines (Solanaceae) of varying degrees of hardiness. They grow to varying sizes with clusters of yellow, white, or violet flowers followed by berrylike fruit. Some species, such as *S. carolinense* and *S. Dulcamara* have become much despised pests in North America. Some widely cultivated species include the following: *S. aculeatissimum* (love apple or soda-apple nightshade), a tender perennial, grows quickly to more than 6 feet, with thorny stems and leaves and clusters of white star-shaped flowers, followed by burnt-orange to brownish-red plumlike fruit. *S. jasminoides* (potato vine), a tender climbs rapidly to more than 15 feet and produces clusters of pure-white star-shaped flowers from springtime onward. *S. Pseudocapsicum* (Jerusalem cherry), a small evergreen shrub, is a popular subject for container gardening. It grows 3 to 4 feet tall (smaller cultivars are available) with shiny green leaves and white flowers. The real attraction is the scarlet ½-inch fruit, which remains on the plant throughout fall (the fruit may be poisonous). *S. Rantonnetii* (blue potato bush) can grow to 6 feet and produces clusters of dark blue or violet flowers, followed by red, heart-shaped fruit.

solar-heated plant tepee *n.* A cone-shaped structure formed of pliable, water-filled plastic baffles. Water in the baffles stores daytime heat for release at night, thus extending the gardening season in cold climates.

solarization (soh'ler uh zay'shuhn) *n*. A process of sterilizing soil and killing soil pests by covering the moist planting area with clear plastic and letting it "bake" for up to 6 months. This process is most effective in hot summer areas.

solar vent *n*. An opening to regulate the temperature inside a sun-heated greenhouse or cold frame. Some solar vents are opened automatically by a temperature-sensitive control device.

Soldanella (sahl duh nehl'uh) *n*. A genus of about 7 species of small, hardy perennial plants (Primulaceae). They grow under 6 inches, with rounded, leathery leaves and nodding blue, violet, or white flowers. Often used in rock gardens. Commonly known as alpenclock.

Soleirolia (sohl uh rohl'ee uh) *n*. A genus of 1 species *S. Soleirolii* (Urticaceae), a tender, fast-growing perennial ground cover. It forms a mat of nearly round ¼-inch leaves, with hardly noticeable flowers. It roots easily and can be invasive. Commonly known as baby's tears, Pollyanna vine, angel's tears, Irish moss, Japanese moss, Corsican-curse, peace-in-the-home, or mind-your-own-business.

Solidago
(goldenrod)

Solidago (sahl uh day'goh) *n*. A genus of about 130 species of hardy flowering perennials (Compositae), most species native to east of the Rocky Mountains. They grow from 1 to 3 feet (though sometimes taller), with little branching, simple leaves, and summer- and fall-blooming, mostly yellow or gold flowers, grouped at the end of the stems. Commonly known as goldenrod.

Solidaster (sahl uh dahs'ter) *n*. A hybrid between the genera of *Solidago* and *Aster*. x*S. luteus* grows to 30 inches, with narrow, pointed leaves and daisy-like bright yellow flowers.

Sollya (sahl'ee uh) *n*. A genus of 3 species of tender perennial vines (Pittosporaceae). The most widely grown is *S. heterophylla,* which twines or sprawls to more than 6 feet, with glossy, green, narrow leaves and summertime clusters of brilliant blue, bell-shaped flowers. A good ground cover on banks. Commonly known as bluebell creeper or Australian bluebells.

Solomon's-seal *n*. A common name for hardy perennials of the genus *Polygonatum,* many species native to eastern North America. They grow to under 6 feet, with bright green leaves along a central stem and greenish-white, bell-shaped flowers that hang below the arching stem in spring. Suited for wild gardens.

Solomon's-seal
1 flowering stalk *2* root and low stem

Solomon's-seal, false *n*. A common name for hardy perennials of the genus *Smilacina,* many native to North America. They grow to 3 feet, with rich green leaves to 6 inches long on either side of the stem, plumes of white, pink, or purplish flowers at the end of the stems, followed by small, perfectly round, red berries. Used in shady spots. Also commonly known as Solomon's-feather or Solomon's-plumes.

solum (soh'luhm) *n*. The upper part of a soil profile, above the parent material in which the processes of soil formation are active. Roots, plants, and animal-life characteristics of the soil are largely confined to the solum.

somatotropic (soh'muhd uh trahp ihk) *a*. In botany, promoting growth.

Sonoma oak *n*. A common name for *Quercus Kelloggii,* a hardy deciduous tree native to Oregon and California. It grows to more than 40 feet, with small-lobed leaves that provide a measure of bright yellow to the western autumnal landscape. Also known as California black oak or Kellogg oak.

soola clover (soo'luh) *n*. A common name for *Hedysarum coronaria,* a hardy perennial. It grows to 4 feet, with compound leaves and fragrant dense clusters of deep red flowers. Also known as French honeysuckle or sulla sweetvetch.

Sophora (suh foh'ruh) *n*. A genus of about 50 species of shrubs and small trees (Leguminosae) of varying degrees of hardiness. *S. japonica* (Japanese pagoda tree or Chinese scholar tree), a hardy deciduous tree grows to about 40 feet, with long clusters of yellowish-white flowers that appear in late summer. *S. secundiflora* (mescal bean or Texas mountain laurel), an evergreen shrub or small tree, has large, violet-blue, fragrant flowers in short clusters that bloom in early spring, and woody seedpods that are poisonous. Needs winter protection in cold climates.

Sorbaria (saw bah'ree uh) *n*. A small genus of mostly hardy deciduous flowering shrubs (Rosaceae). The most widely available species is *S. sorbifolia,* a very hardy shrub that grows to more than 6 feet, with sets of bright green saw-toothed leaves and hefty spires of tiny white flowers in summer. Prune hard in early spring. Commonly known as false spirea.

Sorbaronia (sawr'bah roh nee uh) *n*. A hybrid of *Aronia arbutifolia* and *Sorbus Aucuparia,* a very hardy deciduous shrub or small tree (Rosaceae). It grows to 20 feet, and has divided leaves, with furry undersides, and pinkish-white flowers, followed by small, dark purple fruit.

Sorbus (sawr'buhs) *n*. A genus of about 85 species of very hardy, deciduous, fast-growing shrubs and trees (Rosaceae) of varying sizes. They usually have divided leaves, clusters of white flowers and red,

orange, or yellow fruit. Commonly known as mountain ash. Some widely available species include the following: *S. alnifolia* (Korean mountain ash) grows to 60 feet, with undivided leaves, gray bark, large flowers, and decorative scarlet-to-orange fruits; fine fall color, also. *S. americana* (American mountain ash or dogberry), native to eastern North America, can be grown as a large shrub or small tree; produces thick clusters of bright red berries. *S. aucuparia* (rowan, European mountain ash, or quickbeam) may swiftly grow to 30 feet or taller with clusters of orange-red berries that persist through winter. *S. hybrida* grows to 35 feet, with leaflets at the base of the leaves, but lobes at the tip and gray on undersides. *S. tianshanica* is a relatively slow-growing shrub or small tree, topping out at 16 feet, with clusters of large flowers that turn to bright red fruit. It is suitable for small gardens.

sorose (soh'rohs) *a*. In botany, bearing sori. (See **sorus.**)

sorrel (sawr'uhl) *n*. A common name for mostly hardy, weedy perennials of the genus *Rumex.* They grow mostly to under 3 feet, with large basal leaves and greenish or reddish flowers. *R. Acetosa* (garden sorrel) is sometimes grown as a salad green. Also known as dock.

sorrel, Indian (sawr'uhl) *n*. A common name for *Hibiscus Sabdariffa,* an annual flowering plant. It grows to more than 6 feet, with 3- to 5-lobed leaves and yellow flowers, surrounded at the base by a fleshy red collar, which is used as a flavoring. Needs long hot summers. Also known as roselle or Jamaica sorrel.

sorrel, mountain (sawr'uhl) *n*. A common name for *Oxyria digyna,* a very hardy perennial. It grows to 2 feet, with rounded leaves on long stems and profuse small, greenish flowers.

sorrel tree (sawr'uhl) *n*. A common name for *Oxydendrum arboreum,* a somewhat hardy deciduous tree native to southeastern North America. It grows to 70 feet, with narrow, pointed leaves and drooping clusters of creamy, bell-shaped flowers in late summer. The leaves turn scarlet in autumn. Also known as sourwood or titi.

sorrel vine (sawr'uhl) *n*. A common name for *Cissus trifoliata,* a somewhat hardy deciduous vine.

It grows swiftly to 15 feet by strong tendrils, with fleshy, ivy-shaped leaves and inconspicuous flowers. Drought-resistant. Also known as possum grape.

sorrel, wood (sawr'uhl) *n.* A common name for some annual, but mostly hardy, small bulbous plants of the genus *Oxalis.* They grow mostly under 6 inches, with cloverlike leaves and white, pink, yellow, or red flowers. Used as good houseplants in the north and as garden accents in warmer climates. Also known as lady's-sorrel.

sorus (soh'ruhs) *n., pl.* **sori.** A fruit dot, or cluster of reproductive bodies occurring on lower plants such as ferns, lichens, and fungi; a familiar example is found in the clusters of sporangia on the undersides of the fronds of ferns.

sori of various ferns

sotol (soh'tohl) *n.* A common name used for *Dasylirion,* a genus of tender shrubs or small treelike plants native to southwestern North American deserts. They grow mostly under 3 feet tall, with spiky, narrow leaves and very small, whitish flowers on a tall (10- to-15 foot) spike. Also known as bear grass.

sourberry *n.* A common name for *Rhus integrifolia,* a tender coastal shrub native to southwestern North America. It grows to 10 feet and almost as wide, with oval, dark green leaves and dense clusters of white-to-pink flowers in early spring, followed by sour-tasting berries. Can be used as a hedge or a ground cover. Also known as lemonade berry.

sour gum *n.* A common name for *Nyssa sylvatica,* a hardy tree native to southeastern North America. It grows to 90 feet, with 5-inch- long, oval, glossy, dark green leaves that turn a brilliant orange to scarlet in fall, even in mild climates, and inconspicuous flowers and fruit. Also known as tupelo or pepperidge.

southern buckthorn *n.* A common name for *Bumelia lycioides,* a somewhat hardy deciduous, or partially evergreen, tree native to southeastern North America. It grows to 30 feet, with narrow, oval leaves, thorns, and clusters of white flowers. Also known as ironwood or mock orange.

southern fox grape *n.* A common name for *Vitis rotundifolia,* a somewhat hardy, strongly climbing vine native to southern North America. It has rounded, glossy leaves and small clusters of dull purple 1-inch-long grapes. Spectacular yellow fall color. Also known as muscadine grape, scuppernong, bullace.

southernwood *n.* A shrubby-stemmed species of wormwood, *Artemisia Abrotanum.* It is cultivated in gardens for its pleasant but strong- scented, finely cut, feathery leaves. Also called old-man, probably for the gnarled appearance of its twigs in winter, lad's- love, and boy's-love.

southern yellow pine *n.* A common name for *Pinus palustris,* a tender tree native to southeastern North America. It grows to 100 feet with groups of 3 18-inch-long needles (only 9 inches long on mature trees) and cylindrical 10-inch cones that can remain on the trees for years before dropping. Also known as longleaf pine or Georgia pine.

sowbread *n.* An inelegant common name for the elegant plants of the genus *Cyclamen,* low-growing perennials of varying hardiness. They have attractive, rounded, leaves marked with silver and dark green, and very handsome, nodding, pink, white, red, or magenta reflexed flowers. Grown widely in beds, borders, and as outdoor container plants. The florist's cyclamen (*C. persicum*) is also a popular houseplant. Also known as Persian violet or Alpine violet.

sow bug *n.* A small crustacean very similar to a pill bug, except it does not roll into ball when disturbed. (For controls, see **pill bug**.)

sowing seed *v.* (See **seed sowing.**)

soy *n.* The soybean or soy-pea, *Glycine Max.* It is an annual plant of the same family as beans and peas, with stout, nearly erect or somewhat climbing stems covered with rusty hairs, 3-part leaves, and 2 or 3 pods 1½ or 2 inches long. The seeds are made into soy sauce and variously used in cooking; an oil is also pressed from them. It is a major commercial crop in the United States.

spade *n.* A long-handled tool with a D-shaped handle and a flat metal blade; used for digging, cutting, and turning soil. The blade is designed to be pressed into the ground with 1 foot. Compare with shovel. *v.* To dig or cut with a spade; dig up (the ground) by means of a spade.

spadiceous (spay dihsh'uhs) *a.* In botany, bearing flowers on a fleshy or succulent spike enclosed in a leaflike spathe, as do palms.

spadiciform (spay dis'uh form) *a.* Resembling a spadix.

spadicose (spay'duh kohs) *a.* In botany, having flowers on or comprising a spadix.

spading fork *n.* A 4-tined fork, lighter than a manure fork or pitchfork, used to cultivate loose soil. (See also **manure fork** and **pitchfork**.)

spadix (spay'diks) *n., pl.* **spadices**. In botany, a fleshy spike, usually surrounded by a leaflike spathe, on which the flowers of certain plants (such as palms) are borne.

Spanish bayonet *n.* A common name for 2 species of *Yucca, Y. aloifolia* and *Y. baccata.* Both have rosettes of stiff, sharp leaves, between 2 and 3 feet long, and white flowers in large clusters. *Y. aloifolia* is tender and grows to 10 feet or more. *Y. baccata* is hardy and closer to the ground, at a maximum of 3 feet.

Spanish bluebell *n.* A common name for *Endymion hispanicus,* a hardy perennial bulb. It grows to 20 inches, with narrow, straplike leaves and blue to rose-purple nodding flowers. Also known as Spanish Jacinth or bell-flowered squill.

Spanish broom *n.* 1. A common name for *Genista hispanica,* a hardy shrub. It grows to 2 feet, with spiny stems and bright yellow pealike flowers. 2. A common name for *Spartium junceum,* a somewhat hardy evergreen shrub. It grows to 10 feet, nearly leafless, and produces clusters of bright yellow fragrant flowers at the ends of the branches. Also known as weaver's broom.

Spanish buckeye *n.* A common name for *Ungnadia speciosa,* a tender deciduous tree native to southwestern North America. It grows to 30 feet, with divided, fernlike leaves and clusters of rose-colored fragrant flowers. Also known as Texan buckeye or false buckeye.

Spanish chestnut *n.* A common name for *Castanea sativa,* a hardy tree. It grows to more than 100 feet, with an equivalent spread, with 8-inch round, coarsely toothed leaves and creamy-white flowers in catkins. It produces large chestnuts. Not for the small garden. Also known as European chestnut or Eurasian chestnut.

Spanish jasmine (jahz'mehn) *n.* A common name for *Jasminum grandiflorum,* a somewhat hardy flowering vine. It grows quickly to 15 feet, with glossy, dark green leaves and loose clusters of fragrant white flowers. Also known as Catalonian jasmine or royal jasmine.

Spanish moss *n.* A common name for *Tillandsia usneoides,* a tender epiphyte of southern North America and South America. Part of the archetypal vision of the Old South, it grows to 20 feet long, festooning trees with its soft gray-green foliage. Also known as graybeard.

Spanish oyster plant *n.* A common name for *Scolymus hispanicus,* a thistlelike biennial. It grows to a vigorously branched 4 feet, with spiny leaves and yellow flowers. Occasionally grown for its edible taproot. Also known as golden thistle.

Spanish woodbine *n.* A common name for *Merremia tuberosa,* a tropical perennial vine. It has deeply cut, 6-inch-long leaves and yellow, morning-glorylike flowers. The fruit resembles a carved rose. Also known as wood rose or yellow morning glory.

Sparaxis (spuh rahks'ehs) *n.* A genus of about 6 species of tender flowering corms (Iridaceae). They grow to 2 feet or less, with soft, sword-shaped leaves and small trumpet-shaped flowers, 3 or 4 to a spike, in combinations of yellow, red, pink, purple, or white. Commonly known as wandflower.

Sparmannia (spahr mahn'ee uh) *n.* A genus of 3 species of subtropical evergreen shrubs (Tiliaceae). They grow quickly to 20 feet, with large, velvety, light green 9-inch-long leaves and a few clusters of pure-white 1-inch flowers. Try as a houseplant in cooler climates. Commonly known as African linden or indoor linden.

sparrowgrass *n.* A common name for *Asparagus officinalis,* a hardy perennial vegetable. It grows to 5 or 6 feet if allowed to grow, but young shoots of at least 1-year-old plants are usually harvested for eating.

Spartina (spahr teen'uh) *n.* A genus of about 15 species of perennial grasses (Gramineae) native mostly to mild-winter, marshy, coastal areas. *S. pectinata* (prairie cordgrass) is grown as an ornamental for its arching foliage, which turns yellow in fall, and for its attractive plumes.

Spartium (spahr'shee uhm) *n.* A genus of 1 species of a somewhat hardy evergreen shrub, *S. junceum* (Leguminosae). It grows to 10 feet, nearly leafless, and produces clusters of bright yellow, fragrant, pealike flowers at the ends of the branches. Commonly known as weaver's broom or Spanish broom.

spathaceous (spay thay'shuhs) *a.* In botany, having or resembling a spathe. Also spathal.

spathe (spayth) *n.* In botany, a bract or leaf enclosing a flower cluster or spadix.

spathed (spathd) *a.* In botany, having a spathe.

Spathiphyllum (spay thuh figh'luhm) *n.* A genus of about 35 species of tropical flowering and foliage plants (Araceae). They grow mostly under 3 feet, with large, dark green, oval leaves tapering to a point, each leaf growing on its own stalk, and flowers, on their own stalks, that resemble a fully opened calla lily. Many cultivars exist with variable size or variegated leaf color. Commonly known as spathe flower.

spatterdock *n.* A common name for hardy perennial aquatic plants of the genus *Nuphar.* Floating on the surface of muddy-bottomed waterways, the leaves can be more than a foot in diameter, with yellow or purplish flowers held above the surface of the water. At least 2 species, *N. advena* and *N. saggittifolium* are native to North America. Also known as cow lily, yellow pond lily, or water collard.

spatulate *a.* Spatula-shaped; oblong or rounded with a long narrow base, as a spatulate leaf or petal. Also spatuliform.

spatulate leaves

spearflower *n.* A common name for a tropical evergreen shrub of the genus *Ardisia.* Its leaves are often leathery, and it has clusters of white or pink flowers, followed by scarlet or black fruit.

spearmint *n.* An aromatic, *Mentha viridis,* the most common garden mint. Known chiefly in gardens or as an escape from them. Its intensely flavored leaves are used as tea and in salads; an oil used in candy making is prepared from them. Although its 1- to 2- foot-high plants are attractive in herb gardens, the plant's voracious spreading roots will invade neighboring plants. Spearmint can either be planted away from garden beds and lawns or its roots can be contained in a large drum or tub full of soil, submerged in the ground. Spearmint thrives in moist areas, 1 of the few cooking herbs whose roots can survive constant moisture.

spearmint

species *n.* The basic unit used in classifying and describing living organisms. It ranks below the genus and above the individual or specimen, and denotes a group of individuals having common attributes, reproducing according to their kind, and designated by the conventional latinized 2-word name indicating first the genus and then the species; for example, *Ilex Aquifolium* (English holly) and *Citrus sinensis* (sweet orange).

speedwell *n.* A common name for hardy perennials of the genus *Veronica,* Most species grow between 2 and 4 feet high, but many are less than 12 inches—good candidates for ground covers-and they bloom in summer. Many of the 'old favorites' species have flowers of a distinctive rich violet-blue, but the development of new cultivars has added white and pink to the palette. Also known as brooklime.

speedwell

Sphaeralcea (sfer rahp'tehr ehs) *n.* A genus of about 50 species of somewhat hardy, mostly perennial plants and shrubs (Malvaceae), many native to arid regions of western North America. They mostly grow less than 3 feet, with yellow, orange, lavender, or whitish cuplike flowers. Commonly known as globe mallow or false mallow.

Sphaeropteris (sfeh rahp'tehr ehs) *n.* A genus of about 120 species of tree ferns (Cyatheaceae). The most widely available is *S. Cooperi,* the Australian tree fern. It grows to 20 feet with finely cut fronds that can reach up to 12 feet long. Extremely tender; it survives temperatures to 2° F with some damage, but will does stand colder temperatures.

sphagnum peat (sfahg'nuhm) *n.* The decaying sphagnum moss.

spica (spigh'kuh) *n.* In botany, a spike.

spicate (spigh'kayt) *a.* In botany, arranged in or having the form of a spike. Also spicated; spicigerous.

spice *n.* One of the aromatic vegetable condiments used for the seasoning of food, such as pepper, allspice, nutmeg, ginger, cinnamon, and cloves; collectively, such substances as a class, as the trade in spices or spice.

spiceberry *n.* 1. A common name for *Ardesia crenata,* a tender small evergreen shrub. It grows slowly to 6 feet with shiny, 8-inch-long leaves, with wavy margins, and white or pink flowers in loose clusters. The long-lasting, brilliant coral-red, oval berries are a cheerful addition in fall and winter. Often grown as a container plant. Also known as coralberry. 2. A common name for *Gaultheria procumbens,* a hardy ground cover native to eastern North America. It grows to 3 feet, with 2-inch-long, oval, glossy leaves, white bell-shaped flowers (often hidden by the leaves), and scarlet berries. The leaves and berries have the flavor of wintergreen. Also known as wintergreen, checkerberry, teaberry, mountain tea, or ivory-leaves.

spicebush *n.* A common name for *Lindera Benzoin,* a hardy deciduous shrub native to woodlands of eastern North America. It grows to 15 feet, with 5-inch-long oblong aromatic leaves and small, fragrant yellow flowers in spring, followed by scarlet berries on female plants in fall. Golden yellow fall foliage. Also known as Benjamin bush.

spice tree *n.* A common name for *Umbellularia californica,* a hardy evergreen tree native to Oregon and California. It grows to 80 feet, with shiny oval leaves, which yield a pungent odor of bay leaves (*Laurus nobilis*), unremarkable flowers, and fruit. Also known as Calfiornia bay, myrtle, or pepperwood.

spicewood *n.* Same as spicebush.

spiciform (spigh'suh form) *a.* Shaped like a spike.

spicose (spigh'kohs) *a.* Having spikes. Also spicous.

spicosity (spigh kaws'ih ee) *n.* In botany, the state or condition of having spikes.

spicula (spighk'yuh luh) *n., pl.* **spiculae.** In botany, a small or secondary spike. Also spicula, spikelet.

spiculate (spighk'yuh layt) *a.* Covered with or divided into small spikes.

spider catcher *n.* A device for trapping and transporting live spiders.

spiderflower *n.* A common name for *Cleome Hasslerana,* a shrubby annual. It grows to 5 feet, with divided leaves and large loose spikes of pink, pur-

517

ple, or white flowers. A tough plant. There are many cultivars of various shades of flower color. 2. A common name for tender shrubs and trees of the genus *Grevillea*. They have finely cut leaves and clusters of red, orange, pink, or white flowers. Most are drought-tolerant; not fussy about soil.

spider mite *n*. A very small (extremely hard to see with the naked eye) spiderlike insect relative that sucks juices from the leaves of many plants, especially those of fruits and vegetables. It thrives in hot, dry weather and on dusty, drought-stressed plants. It causes stippled foliage, with a shiny yellow or silver coloration, and often covers the leaves with fine webbing. Infested plants are weakened and often die. Control with beneficial insects, insecticidal soaps, horticultural oils, sulfur sprays, or traditional insecticides.

spider plant *n*. 1. A common name for a subtropical flowering bulb of the genus *Anthericum*. It grows to 3 feet, or less with long, narrow leaves and loose spikes of white flowers. 2. A common name for *Chlorophytum comosum,* a tender perennial, often grown as a houseplant in the north. It grows to less than 12 inches, with clumps of gracefully arching narrow, pointed leaves and white flowers on long spikes above the foliage. Miniature plants (called offsets) form at the ends of the stems. 3. A common name for *Cleome Hasslerana,* a shrubby annual. (See **spiderflower.**)

spiderwort

spiderwort *n*. A common name for tender perennial plants of the genus *Tradescantia*. Mostly sprawl-ing or trailing, they are almost indestructible. Flower colors include pink, blue, purple, or white. Often used as house plants.

spiderwort family *n*. A family of herbaceous perennials, native mostly to warm climates; the Commelinaceae. They are of importance as ornamental plants, either for their flowers or foliage. The principal genera are *Tradescantia, Commelina,* and *Cyanotis.* Used as small-scale ground covers in warm winter gardens or as hanging- basket indoor/outdoor plants anywhere.

Spigelia (spigh jeel'yuh) *n*. A genus of about 30 species of tender perennials (Loganiaceae). The most widely grown species is *S. marilandica,* native to southeastern North America. It grows to 2 feet, with 4-inch oval leaves and rounded clusters of 2-inch tubular flowers that are red on the outside and yellow on the inside. Commonly known as Indian pink, pinkroot, or worm grass.

spike *n*. In botany, an elongated, stemlike prominence upon which multiple flowers are borne in certain plants, such as the snapdragon and *Acanthus mollis.*

spike of flowers

spike heath *n*. A common name for *Bruckenthalia spiculifolia,* a somewhat hardy evergreen, heathlike shrub. It grows to 10 inches with needlelike leaves and summer-blooming spikes of small pink flowers.

spikelet *n*. In botany, a secondary spike, especially applied to grasses, whose flowers are grouped on several small spikes attached to a central axis.

spikenard *n*. A common name for *Aralia racemosa,* a hardy shrubby perennial native to eastern and central North America. It grows to 6 feet, with a few compound leaves with toothed leaflets, and many dense clusters of small white flowers. Also known as America spikenard, petty morel, or life-of-man.

spikenard, false *n.* A common name for *Smilacina racemosa,* a hardy perennial native to woodlands of North America. It grows to 3 feet on an arching stem, with 6-inch-long oval leaves, with fuzzy undersides, and a plume of white flowers, followed by small red berries. Also known as Solomon's-zigzag or treacleberry.

spikenard tree *n.* A common name for *Aralia spinosa,* a somewhat hardy shrub or small tree native to southeastern North America. It grows to 30 feet, with nasty thorns, large 3-part compound leaves and many large clusters of white-to-greenish flowers. Also known as devil's-walking-stick, Hercules'-club, angelica tree, or prickly ash.

spike rush *n.* A common name for rushes of the genus *Eleocharis,* found in wet, boggy places. They are characterized by mostly cylindrical, bamboolike stems, closely sheathed at the base, and bisexual flowers appearing between closely overlapping scales.

spiking fork *n.* An implement similar to a pitchfork but having 4 shorter, straighter tines; used to aerate turf.

spinach *n.* 1. A garden vegetable, *Spinacia oleracea,* producing thick succulent leaves, served raw in salads or boiled or steamed. There are several cultivated varieties, 1 of which, with wrinkled leaves like savoy cabbage, is the savoy or lettuce-leaved spinach. Spinach is rich in vitamin A, potassium, and calcium. 2. One of the several other plants with leaves that produce a dish like spinach, such as New Zealand spinach.

spinach beet *n.* A type of beet grown for its greens, rather than its root, such as chard.

Spinacia (spigh nay'see uh) *n.* A genus of apetalous plants, (Chenopodiaceae). It is characterized by bractless and commonly dioecious flowers, the pistillate with a 2- to 4-toothed roundish perianth, its tube hardened and closed in fruit, covering the utricle and its single erect turgid seed. There are 4 species, all Oriental (see **spinach**). They are erect annuals, with alternate, stalked leaves, which are entire or sinuately toothed. The flowers are borne in glomerules, the fertile usually axillary, the staminate forming interrupted spikes.

spinach, Indian *n.* A common name for *Basella alba,* a tropical vine. It grows swiftly to 30 feet long, with broad, oval green or purplish leaves and spikes of white flowers. Also known as Malabar spinach.

spinach, mountain *n.* A common name for *Atriplex hortensis,* an annual traditionally grown for greens, but grown now also as an ornamental. It grows to 8 inches, with triangular leaves that range in color from dark green to yellow to dark red. Cultivars are offered that provide consistent red leaf color. Also known as orache or garden orache.

spinach, New Zealand *n.* A low-growing, slightly trailing plant, *Tetragonia tetragoniodes,* with triangular, fleshy, deep green leaves. It performs far better in hot weather and can be harvested over a long season without going to seed. In mild climates, it can be grown as a perennial. The leaves are used like spinach, which they resemble in flavor and nutrients.

spinach, wild *n.* A common name for *Chenopodium Bonus-Henricus,* a somewhat hardy perennial. It grows to 30 inches with 3-inch-long arrow-shaped leaves and clusters of small greenish flowers. Also known as good-King-Henry, Mercury, allgood, fat-hen, or goosefoot.

spindle *v.* 1. To shoot or grow in a long, slender stalk or body; to form a stem. 2. To grow a long stalk or stem rather than forming flowers or fruit.

spindle tree *n.* A common name for species of the genus *Euonymus,* usually hardy deciduous and evergreen shrubs. They are grown for their foliage texture and form, sometimes for their decorative fruit.

spine *n.* In botany, a stiff, sharp-pointed outgrowth of a stem (as in the hawthorn), leaf (as in many species of holly), or other organ of a plant.

spined soldier bug *n.* A beneficial insect, which is primarily used to control the Mexican bean beetle, although it feeds on a variety of other plant pests. Sold through the mail.

spinescent (spigh nehs'uhnt) *a.* In botany, terminating in a spine or sharp point; tending to be spiny or thorny.

spiniform (spigh'nuh form) *a.* Having the form of a spine or thorn.

spinose (spigh'nohs) *a.* Full of spines; armed with spines or thorns. Also spinous.

spinule (spigh'nyool) *n.* A small spine.

spinulescent (spigh'nyuh lehs uhnt) *a.* In botany, producing small spines; having the form of a small spine.

spinulose (spigh'nyuh lohs) *a.* In botany, having small spines. Also spinulous.

Spiraea (spigh ree'uh) *n.* A genus of almost 100 species of mostly hardy deciduous shrubs (Rosaceae), some species native to North America. They grow to varying heights, with alternate leaves and mostly white flowers, sometimes pink and red. Commonly known as spirea or bridal wreath. Some widely available species include *S. alba* (meadowsweet) and *S. prunifolia* (bridal-wreath)

Spiranthes (spigh rahn'theez) *n.* A genus of about 200 species of often hardy orchids (Orchidaceae), many native to North America. They grow to 30 inches, with either oval or grasslike leaves and small white or greenish white, sometimes fragrant, flowers, often distributed on the bloom stem in a corkscrew pattern. Commonly known as ladies' tresses or pearl-twist.

spittlebug *n.* A small insect that envelops itself in a frothy secretion. It rarely harms plants but can be controlled with insecticidal soaps.

spleenwort, various species

spleenwort *n.* A common name for hardy and tropical ferns of the genus *Asplenium*. The size of their fronds ranges from 4 feet to 3 inches. Two widely grown tropical species grown as houseplants are *A. bulbiferum*, (mother fern), which has lacy fronds that produce tiny offsets of miniature plants that can be planted; and *A. nidus*, (bird's-nest fern), native to southern Florida, whose undivided fronds grow upright from a clump. Other hardy natives, such as *A. platyneuron* or *A. Trichomanes,* are available only from specialty nurseries.

sponge tree *n.* A common name for *Acacia Farnesiana,* an evergreen tropical shrub or small tree. It grows to 10 feet, with thorny branches, very small, divided leaves and balls of bright yellow, fragrant flowers that bloom in early spring. Also known as sweet acacia, popinac, opopanax, huisache, cassie, or West Indian blackthorn.

spoonflower *n.* 1. A common name for *Dasylirion Wheeleri,* a barely hardy perennial succulent native to southwest North America. It produces a fountain of blue-gray 3-foot-long tapering, fleshy leaves, with small thorns on the margins, and, occasionally, a tall (to 15 feet) flower stalk, with many tiny, greenish-white flowers. The base of each leaf widens where it joins the trunk; when dried, these long-handled 'spoons' are often used in flower arrangements. 2. A common name for *Xanthosoma Lindenii,* a tropical perennial foliage plant. It grows to 3 feet, with arrow-shaped leaves, up to 3 feet long and half as wide, with striking white veins. The flowers are a white spathe, similar to a calla. A dramatic houseplant. Also known as Indian kale.

spoonwood *n.* A common name for *Kalmia latifolia,* a very hardy evergreen shrub or small tree native to eastern North America. It grows to 10 feet or more, with oval, leathery leaves and clusters of pale pink flowers in May and June. Many cultivars are offered, with red and white and differing shades of pink flowers or dwarf habits. Also known as mountain laurel, calico bush, or ivybush.

spoonwort *n.* A common name for *Cochlearia officinalis,* an annual or biennial grass. It grows to about 12 inches, with heart-shaped, basal leaves and small white flowers. Grown as a strong-flavored salad green. Also known as scurvy grass.

sporal (spoh'ruhl) *a.* Relating to or resembling a spore.

sporange (spuh rahnj') *n.* In botany, the case or sac in plants in which the spores, which are equivalent to the seeds of flowering plants, are produced or carried. Also called sporangium.

spore *n*. In botany, the reproductive cell of lower or nonflowering plants such as ferns. A spore usually consists of a mass of protoplasm with a nucleus. It has no embryo as a seed has, but is capable of developing into a gametophyte and producing a new individual.

spore case *n*. In botany, the sporangium, or immediate covering of the spores.

sporiferous (spuh′rihf uh ruhs) *a*. In botany, bearing or producing spores.

sporophyll (spoh′ruh fihl) *n*. In botany, the leaf or leaflike organ that bears the spores. Also sporophyl.

sporophyte (spoh′ruh fight) *n*. In botany, the stage of the life cycle of ferns and seed plants in which the nonsexual organs of reproduction are borne, as distinguished from *gametophyte*.

sporophytic (spoh′ruh fight ihk) *a*. In botany, belonging to, resembling, or characteristic of a sporophyte.

sport *n*. A branch, inflorescence, flower, or shoot exhibiting unusual spontaneous deviation from type; mutation.

spotted evergreen *n*. A common name for *Aglaonema costatum*, a tropical, but tough and slow-growing, plant. It grows to less than 5 feet, with dark glossy-green leaves with gray veins, and short, pale green, calla-lilylike flowers. Easy-to-grow houseplants, especially for dark corners.

sprayer *n*. Any of various perforated nozzles used to break a stream of water or other liquid into finer particles and blow it through the air.

spray gun *n*. A device with a perforated nozzle controlled by a trigger grip, used to break a stream of water or other liquid into finer particles and blow it through the air.

spray head *n*. A type of nozzle.

spraying *n*. The act of applying various insecticides, pesticides, or herbicides to plants, utilizing equipment designed to deliver a thin coating to each plant for the purpose of controlling plant pests or diseases.

spray wand *n*. A unit consisting of a perforated spout and a rigid tube, typically 2 to 3 feet long, which attaches to a garden hose and is used to mist or water hard-to-reach plants. (See also **watering wand**.)

spreader *n*. 1. A small-wheeled vehicle used to deliver a measured quantity of seed, fertilizer, lime, or other bulk material over a garden spot, usually before planting. Spreaders are of 2 basic types, *hopper* or *drop*. 2. A material added to pesticide sprays to improve their contact with plant tissue.

spreader sticker *n*. A gluey substance applied to prevent another substance, such as odor repellent, from washing off.

Sprekelia (spree keel′ee uh) *n*. A genus of 1 species *S. formosissima* (Amaryllidaceae) of subtropical bulbs. It grows to 1 foot, with long, narrow leaves and bright crimson flowers. Also known as Jacobean lily, St.-James's-lily, Aztec lily, or orchid amaryllis.

spring *v*. To emerge from the soil from a local spot.

spring beauty *n*. A common name for plants of the genus *Claytonia*, particularly for the species *C. virginica*, a somewhat hardy perennial native to eastern North America. It grows to 12 inches, with grasslike leaves and white flowers tinged with pink along the upper half of the stalk.

spring garden *n*. A garden featuring plants such as crocuses, daffodils, and tulips, which bloom in the spring.

springtail (sprihng′tail) *n*. A small hopping insect that sometimes feeds on the tender foliage of young seedlings, particularly vegetables. Rarely a serious problem requiring control measures.

sprinkler *n*. A perforated device, often a cylinder or ring, attached to a hose or watering can to spray water on lawns or gardens.

sprinkler gauge *n*. (See **rain gauge**.)

sprinkling *n*. The act of scattering drops or particles, as water; a small, scattered quantity.

spritzer *n*. A tubular device to dust or spray powder or liquid onto plants.

sprout *v*. 1. To shoot forth or begin to grow, as a bud from a seed or stock. 2. To put forth shoots; bear buds. *n*. 1. A shoot of a plant, as from a germinating seed, a rootstock, tuber, runner, etc., or from the root (a sucker), stump, or trunk of a tree.

sprouts of Brussels sprouts

sprouted *a*. Having sprouts; budded: as sprouted potatoes.

sprouter *n*. A container used to hold water and seeds during germination. (Germinated seeds, called sprouts, are eaten in salads.)

spruce *n*. A common name for hardy, needled, evergreen trees of the genus *Picea*. Some may grow to as high as 150 feet. Many dwarf cultivars perform well in smaller home gardens but care must be taken when planting taller-growing species or varieties. Grows best in cooler climates. Used as a specimen tree or windbreak; smaller species and varieties make good container plants for living Christmas trees.

spruce, black *n*. A common name for *Picea mariana*, a very hardy tree native to northern North America. It grows to less than 60 feet, with blue-green needles and 1½-inch cones. Also known as double spruce or bog spruce.

spruce, blue *n*. A common name for *Picea pungens* 'Glauca', a very hardy tree native to the Rocky Mountain states. It grows to 100 feet or more, with bluish needles and 4-inch cones.

spruce, hemlock *n*. A common name for somewhat hardy trees of the genus *Tsuga*, native to

North America and East Asia. They can grow to 150 feet, with flattened, needlelike leaves and small, brown cones.

spruce, Himalayan *n*. A common name for *Picea Smithiana*, a tender tree. It grows to 150 feet, with glossy, gray, slightly drooping branchlets.

spruce, red *n*. A common name for *Picea rubens*, a hardy tree native to northeast North America. It grows to 90 feet with the grayish brown branches with 2-inch cones. Thrives on the cooler air of the mountains. Also known as balsam.

spruce, tideland *n*. A common name for *Picea sitchensis*, a very hardy tree native to northwest North America. It grows to 120 feet with the grayish brown branches, flattened needles silver above andglossy green below, and 4-inch cones. Does best in cool, humid climates. Also known as Sitka spruce.

spruce, white *n*. A common name for *Picea glauca*, a very hardy tree native to northern North America. It grows to less than 100 feet, with drooping small branches, bluish-green needles, and 2-inch cones. Also known as cat spruce.

spur *n*. In botany: 1. A slender hollow projection from some part of a flower, as from the calyx of columbine and larkspur and the corolla of violets. 2. A short branch bearing fruit buds. 3. A branch kept short by regular pruning.

spurs of various flowers (marked S)

spur flower *n*. A common name for a tender perennial of the genus *Plectranthus*. It grows to less than 3 feet, with thick, oval leaves, often with scalloped edges and prominent veins, and loose spikes of small white, bluish, or purplish flowers. Usually grown as a houseplant. Also known as Swedish begonia, Swedish ivy, or prostrate coleus.

spurge *n.* 1. A common name for plants of the genus *Euphorbia,* mostly perennials and shrubs of varying degrees of hardiness. Sizes range from under 12 inches to almost 30 feet. Most have a milky sap that can cause skin irritations to some people. 2. A common name for a hardy perennial of the genus *Pachysandra.* It grows to less than a foot high with dark green oval leaves and small, fluffy spikes of white flowers in summer. Most often used as a ground cover in shady corners of a garden.

spurge
(*Euphorbia*)

spurge, Allegheny mountain *n.* A common name for *Pachysandra procumbens,* à hardy perennial ground cover native to southeastern North America. It grows to less than 12 inches, with almost round leaves and small whitish-to-purplish flower spikes that appear in the spring before the leaves.

spurge, caper *n.* A common name for *Euphorbia Lathyris,* an annual or biennial. It grows to 3 feet, with narrow, gray-green leaves at right angles to each other around the stem and homely, yellow summertime flowers. Its milky sap can be caustic to skin. A reputed deterrent for moles and gophers. Also known as myrtle spurge or mole plant.

spurge, cypress *n.* A common name for *Euphorbia Cyparissias,* a hardy perennial. It grows to less than

12 inches, with small narrow leaves (suggesting cypress) and clusters of yellow flowers that become reddish-purplish with age. Often used as a ground cover; a very aggresive spreader that can become invasive.

spurge flax *n.* A common name for *Daphne Gnidium,* a somewhat hardy flowering shrub. It grows to 4 feet, with 1½-inch-long oval, pointed leaves and clusters of small creamy-white flowers.

spurge, flowering *n.* A common name for *Euphorbia corollata,* a hardy perennial native to eastern North America. It grows to 3 feet, with narrow, oval leaves and clusters of long-lasting white flowers. Also known as tramp's spurge or wild hippo.

spurge, Indian tree *n.* A common name for *Euphorbia Tirucalli,* a tender shrub or small tree. It can grow to 30 feet, in a tangle of light green branches, with minute leaves and insignificant flowers. Also known as milkbush, rubber euphorbia, finger tree, or pencil tree.

spurge, ipecac (ihp'eh kahk) *n.* A common name for *Euphorbia ipecacuanhae,* a somewhat hardy perennial native to southeastern North America. It grows to 12 inches, with multibranching stems and narrow, oval, green-to-purple leaves. Also known as wild ipecac or Carolina ipecac.

spurge laurel *n.* A common name for *Daphne Laureola,* a somewhat hardy flowering shrub. It grows to 3 feet or more, with handsome 6-inch-long, oval leaves, tapering toward the stem, and clusters of yellowish-green fragrant flowers in early spring.

spurge, leafy *n.* A common name for *Euphorbia Esula,* a hardy perennial. It grows to 3 feet, with narrow, pale green leaves and flat-topped clusters of tiny yellow flowers. Weedy. Also known as wolf's-milk.

spurge olive *n.* A common name for *Daphne Mezereum,* a hardy, deciduous, flowering shrub. It grows to 5 feet, with 3½-inch-long oval leaves and clusters of reddish-purple flowers that appear before the leaves in early spring, followed by scarlet or yellow berries. Also known as February daphne or mezereon.

spurge, seaside *n.* A common name for *Euphorbia polygonifolia,* an annual ground cover native to sandy shores of eastern North America. It grows to less than a foot, often creeping, with small green leaves and inconspicuous flowers.

spurge, slipper *n.* A common name for a tropical succulent of the genus *Pedilanthus,* native to the Americas. The most widely grown species is *P. tithymaloides.* It grows to 6 feet, with 4-inch fleshy leaves and clusters of red-to-purple flowers. Also known as Japanese poinsetta, redbird flower, redbird cactus, or devil's backbone.

spur-pruning *n.* A mode of pruning trees, by which 1 or 2 eyes of the previous year's wood are left and the rest cut off, so as to leave spurs or short rods.

spurred *a.* In botany, producing or provided with spurlike shoots or spines.

spurred corolla *n.* (See **corolla.**)

spurred gentian *n.* A common name for an annual, biennial, or hardy perennial of the genus *Halenia.* The most widely grown species is *H. corniculata.* An annual or biennial, it grows to 2 feet, with 4-inch-long, narrow, oval leaves and small, bell-like yellow flowers.

squama (skway′muh) *n., pl.* **squamae.** In botany, a scale or scalelike structure.

squamaceous (skwuh may′shuhs) *a.* In botany, scaly. Also squamate.

squamella (skwuh mehl′uh) *n., pl.* **squamellae.** In botany, a small scale.

squamiform (skway′muh form) *a.* Having the shape, character, or appearance of a scale.

squamous (skway′muhs) *a.* In botany, scaly or scalelike. Also squamose.

squamous bulb (skway′muhs) *n.* In botany, a bulb in which the outer scales are distinct, fleshy, and overlapping; a scaly bulb. (See **bulb.**)

squamule (skwam′yool) *n.* In botany, a small scale. Also squamula.

squamuliform (skwam′yuh luh form) *a.* Having the form or character of a squamule (small scale).

squarrose (skwah′rohs) *a.* In botany, rough with spreading processes, as the whorls of small leaves of various Compositae. Also squarrous.

squarrulose (skwah′ryuh lohs) *a.* In botany, somewhat squarrose.

squash *n.* The fruit of an annual plant, 1 of several species of the genus *Cucurbita.* Most of the very numerous varieties of the cultivated squash belong to 3 species: *C. maxima,* which contains the hubbard, turban, and buttercup squashes; *C. Pepo,* including the pumpkin, acorn, zucchini, and yellow summer squashes; and *C. moschata,* the butternut types. The last has a club-shaped, pear-shaped, or long cylindrical fruit with a smooth, cream-colored skin. Squashes are, for practical purposes, divided into summer and winter types. Among the latter are acorn, butternut, turban, buttercup, and hubbard, with firm flesh and good keeping qualities. The summer squash has a shorter vine, hence sometimes called bush squash. Its fruit is smaller and is either long and thin, as in crooknecks and zucchinis, or round and flattened with a scalloped border, as in scallop squashes. These are colored yellow, white, green, or green and white and have a higher water content and less keeping quality. Squashes are grown in both temperate and tropical climates and are popular vegetables for home gardeners. The summer squash is eaten before maturity, usually prepared by boiling. The winter squash is boiled or roasted and often made into pies, where it resembles pumpkin.

squash borer *n.* A destructive, white, wormlike larva of a clear-winged moth; most common in eastern United States. It bores into the stems of cucurbits (mainly squash), leaving sawdustlike excrement near holes, causing leaves to wilt and stems to die. Once the borer is inside stem, it is hard to control. Protective row covers, handpicking moths and larvae, early or late planting, or regular sprays of traditional insecticides are the most effective controls. Releasing parasitic nematodes may also help.

squash bug *n.* A troublesome pest of cucurbits. It sucks the plant juices from the stems and leaves, causing wilting or discoloration. Can be controlled with floating row covers, handpicking, sanitation, traps, planting resistant varieties, soap sprays, botanicals, or traditional insecticides.

squawberry (skwah) *n.* A common name for *Mitchella repens,* a hardy perennial ground cover native to eastern North America. It grows easily, rooting 1-foot-long stems, with small, dark green, oval leaves, with whitish veins, and tubular pinkish-white flowers, followed by small, brilliant, red berries often used for Christmastime decorations. Also known as partridgeberry, two-eyed berry, running box, twinberry, or squaw vine.

squaw huckleberry (skwah) *n.* 1. A common name for *Vaccinium caesium,* a hardy deciduous shrub native to southeastern North America. It grows to 3 feet, with oval, 2-inch-long leaves, with a white powder on the underside, and small clusters of white flowers, followed by small, dark blue fruit. Also known as deerberry. 2. A common name for *Vaccinium stamineum,* a somewhat hardy deciduous shrub native to southeastern North America. It grows to 10 feet, with 4-inch-long, oval leaves and clusters of showy white, bell-shaped flowers, followed by small blue or purple fruit. Also known as deerberry.

squawroot (skwah) *n.* 1. A common name for *Perideridia Gairdneri,* a hardy perennial native to the mountains of western North America. It grows to 4 feet, with divided leaves and small white flowers. Also known as edible-rooted caraway or Indian caraway. 2. A common name for *Trillium erectum,* a hardy perennial flowering plant native to northeastern North America. It grows to 2 feet, with broad, 7-inch-long leaves and brownish-purple, ill-scented flowers. Uncommonly, some plants have white or yellow flowers. Also known as purple trillium, stinking Benjamin, or brown Beth.

squaw-weed (skwah) *n.* A common name for *Senecio aureus,* a hardy perennial flowering plant native to swamps of eastern North America. It grows to 2½ feet, with rounded basal leaves, divided leaves on the stem, and yellow daisylike flowers in late spring. Also known as golden groundsel or golden ragwort.

squill (skwihl) *n.* 1. A common name for hardy, low-growing, flowering bulbs of the genus *Scilla.* They have dark green straplike leaves and clusters of bell-shaped or starlike flowers in whites and blues and purples. Many species and cultivars provide a variety of blooming times and colors and duration. They die back in summer. 2. A common name for *Urginea maritima,* a tender perennial bulb. It grows to 4 feet, with fleshy, straplike leaves, which die back in summer, and dense clusters of whitish flowers which bloom in fall on their own

stalk. Often grown as a houseplant. Also known as sea onion or red squill.

squirrel corn *n.* A common name for *Dicentra canadensis,* a hardy perennial native to northeastern North America. It grows to 1 foot, with lacy basal leaves and clusters of greenish-white, fragrant, heart-shaped flowers in spring.

squirrel cup *n.* A common name for *Hepatica americana,* a hardy perennial native to woodlands of eastern North America. It grows to 6 inches, with rounded, heart-shaped leaves and pale lilac to pinkish-white flowers that appear very early in spring. Also known as liverleaf.

squirrel's-foot fern *n.* A common name for *Davallia trichomanoides,* a tender, low-growing fern. It has finely cut fronds that grow from a brown furry rhizome (the squirrel's foot), which grows along the soil surface and when potted, frequently over the side of the container. Often grown as a houseplant. Also known as ball fern.

Stachys (stay'kehs) *n.* A genus of about 300 species of mostly hardy perennial plants (Labiatae). They grow to 3 feet, with opposite leaves and spikes of small flowers. Commonly known as betony, hedge nettle, or woundwort. Some commonly grown species include the following: *S. byzantina* (woolly betony or lamb's ears) is a popular edging plant with very soft, white, fuzzy leaves. Pink or purple flower spikes are not unlovely, but take second place to the foliage. *S. grandiflora* forms rosettes of oval leaves and shaggy stems, topped by clusters of violet flowers. *S. officinalis* (betony) flourishes in hot, dry soils. It forms a rosette of 5-inch-long leaves, sometimes smooth and sometimes hairy. The main stalk grows to 3 feet, topped by a dense cluster of small, red-purple flowers.

Stachytarpheta (stak eh tahr fee'duh) *n.* A genus of about 65 species of subtropical and tropical perennial plants and small shrubs (Verbenaceae). They grow to 6 feet, with toothed, wrinkled leaves and blue or purple flower spikes.

Stachyurus (stak eh yoo'ruhs) *n.* A genus of 5 or 6 species of somewhat hardy shrubs and small trees (Stachyuraceae). The most widely grown species is *S. praecox,* a shrub which grows to 12 feet, with 5½-inch-long oval leaves and loose spikes of yellow, bell-like flowers that appear in early spring before the leaves.

staff vine *n*. A common name for *Celastrus scandens,* a very hardy deciduous vine native to North America. It grows to 20 feet, with light green oval leaves and clusters of red fruit. The flowers are inconspicuous, but male flowers are necessary to produce the highly decorative fruit. Good yellow fall foliage. Also known as American bittersweet, climbing bittersweet, or waxwork.

stagbush *n*. A common name for *Viburnum prunifolium,* a hardy deciduous shrub or small tree native to eastern North America. It grows to 15 feet, with finely toothed, oval, 3-inch-long leaves and clusters of white flowers, followed by edible blue-black fruit. Also known as black haw, sheepberry, or nannyberry.

staggerbush *n*. A common name used for *Lyonia mariana,* a somewhat hardy deciduous shrub native to swampy spots of southeastern North America. It grows to 6 feet, with 2½-inch-long leaves and flat-topped clusters of white or pink flowers.

stagger grass *n*. A common name for *Zephyranthes Atamasco,* a somewhat hardy flowering bulb native to southeastern North America. It grows to 1 foot, with long, narrow leaves and single stalks of white, trumpet-shaped flowers. Also known as Atamasci lily.

staggerwort *n*. A common name for *Senecio aureus,* a hardy perennial flowering plant native to swamps of eastern North America. It grows to 2½ feet, with rounded basal leaves, divided leaves on the stem, and yellow daisylike flowers in late spring. Also known as golden groundsel, golden ragwort, or squaw weed.

stag-headed *a*. Having the upper branches dead, as a stag-headed elm.

stag horn fern *n*. A common name for plants of the genus *Platycerium,* mostly tropical ferns, though *P. bifurcatum* tolerates cool temperatures (to 45° F.). Attached to trees or a slab of bark, the fronds at the base are flat and light green, aging to brown; bright green forked fronds grow up and outward from the base.

staghorn moss *n*. A common name for *Lycopodium clavatum,* a hardy, mosslike perennial native to North America. It grows on creeping stems as long as 9 feet, with many bristle-tipped leaves on ascending branches. Often used as Christmas greens. Also known as ground pine or running pine.

staghorn sumac (soo′mak) *n*. A common name for *Rhus typhina,* a very hardy shrub or small tree native to eastern North America. It grows to mostly 15 feet, but up to 30 feet, with the velvety twigs (similar to early-spring staghorns) and finely divided, dark green leaves with gray undersides. Clusters of small, greenish flowers bloom in early summer, followed by fuzzy red fruit. Robust autumn-foliage color. Also known as velvet sumac or Virginia sumac.

stake *n*. A piece of wood, metal, or plastic having one pointed end which is driven into the ground to support or mark. *v*. To support with stakes or poles, as to stake vines.

stalk *n*. 1. The stem or main axis of a plant, usually supporting the leaves, flowers, and fruit, as a stalk of wheat or hemp. 2. The pedicel of a flower or the peduncle of a flower cluster, the petiole of a leaf, the stipe of an ovary, or any similar supporting organ; in mosses, a seta.

stalklet *n*. A diminutive or secondary stalk.

stamens of various flowers

stamen (stay′mehn) *n., pl.* **stamens** or **stamina**. In botany, the male reproductive, pollen-bearing organ of flowering plants, consisting of the filament and the anther.

staminate (stay′muh neht) *a*. In botany: 1. Furnished with or producing stamens. 2. Male, producing stamens but no pistils.

staminodium (stam uh noh′dee uhm) *n., pl.* **staminodia**. A sterile or abortive stamen, or an organ resembling an abortive stamen. Also staminode.

staminody (stam uh noh′dee uhm) *n.* In botany, the metamorphosis of various floral organs, such as sepals, petals, bracts, and pistils, into stamens. Compare sepalody, petalody, pistilody.

standard *n.* In horticulture: 1. A tree or shrub that stands alone, without being attached to any wall or support, as distinguished from an espalier or a cordon. 2. A shrub, such as a rose, grafted on an upright stem or trained to a single stem in tree form.

standing cypress *n.* A common name for *Ipomopsis rubra,* a biennial or tender perennial native to southeastern North America. It grows to 6 feet, in a thin silhouette, with smooth, finely cut leaves and tubular, scarlet, summertime flowers, yellow with red dots on the inside.

Stanhopea (stan hoh′pee uh) *n.* A genus of about 200 species of tropical American orchids (Orchidaceae). They produce a single large leaf and a stalk of yellow, fragrant, fantastically shaped flowers in summer or fall. The flower stalks have the unusual tendency to grow downward, so they are best planted in open-sided hanging baskets.

Stanleya (stan′lee uh) *n.* A genus of about 6 species of hardy perennials native to western North America (Cruciferae). They grow to 5 feet, with leaves covered with a pale waxy powder and with spikes of white-to-yellow flowers, followed by seeds trailing a silky substance, hence the common name prince's-plume.

Stapelia
(carrion flower)

Stapelia (stuh pee′lee uh) *n.* A genus of about 90 species of tropical and subtropical perennial succulent plants (Asclepiadaceae). They grow to less than

12 inches, with thick, fleshy stems and large, star-shaped flowers with an elaborately colored center. The flowers have an unpleasant odor. Commonly known as carrion flower or starfish flower.

Staphylea (staf uh lee′uh) *n.* A genus of 11 species of mostly hardy shrubs and small trees (Staphyleaceae). They grow to 25 feet (usually less), with compound leaves and clusters of white, bell-like flowers, followed by puffy seed capsules. *S. trifolia* is mostly hardy, native to eastern North America. Commonly known as bladdernut.

Staphyleaceae (staf uh lee ay′see ee) *n. pl.* A family of 5 genera and about 60 species of shrubs and trees; the bladdernut family. They have divided leaves, clusters of flowers at the ends of the stems and swollen seed capsules. The most widely planted genus is *Staphylea.*

staple gun *n.* A device by which staples are used to fasten polyethylene sheets to frames. Also called stapling tacker.

star anise (an′ihs) *n.* 1. The aromatic fruit of *Illicium verum,* a Chinese shrub or small tree. The fruit is a star-shaped pod of 8 points, each of which contains a single brown shiny seed.

star-clusters, Egyptian *n.* A common name for *Pentas lanceolata,* a tender perennial often grown as an annual. It grows to 3 to 4 feet, with hairy leaves like elongated ovals and clusters of small, star-shaped flowers in white, pink, lilac, or magenta.

starflower *n.* 1. A common name for *Smilacina stellata,* a hardy perennial native to North America and Europe. It grows to 2 feet, with slender, oval leaves and whitish flowers in stubby clusters, followed by small, spherical berries, turning dark red as they mature. Also known as star-flowered lily-of-the-valley. 2. A common name for *Stapelia variegata,* a subtropical perennial. It grows to 6 inches, with succulent, leafless stems and large star-shaped, multihued flowers. Also known as toad cactus or starfish plant. 3. A common name for hardy perennials of the genus *Trientalis,* native mostly to northern North America. They grow to less than 12 inches, with narrow, pointed leaves and dainty white or pink flowers. Also known as chickweed wintergreen.

starglory *n.* A common name for *Ipomoea Quamoclit,* an annual vine native to tropical America. It grows to 20 feet, with leaves divided into thread-like leaflets and scarlet morning-glory-like flowers. Also known as cypress vine or cardinal climber.

star grass *n.* 1. A common name for hardy perennials of the genus *Aletris,* native to eastern North America and east Asia. They grow to 3 feet, with grasslike leaves and white or yellow, starlike flowers. Also known as colicroot. 2. A common name for *Chloris truncata,* a subtropical or tropical perennial grass. It grows to 1 foot, with grasslike leaves and flowers resembling a starburst. Also known as creeping windmill grass. 3. A common name for plants of the genus *Hypoxis. H. hirsuta* is native to eastern North America and is hardy, with hairy, grasslike leaves and yellow, starlike flowers.

star harrow *n.* A long-handled cultivating instrument with star- shaped disks; used for pulverizing soil.

star jasmine (jaz′mehn) *n.* A common name for a tender flowering vine. It grows to more than 30 feet, with 3-inch-long, dark green, glossy leaves and profuse small clusters of fragrant white flowers. Also known as Confederate jasmine.

star-of-Bethlehem *n.* 1. A common name for *Campanula isophylla,* a tender perennial or ground cover. The stems grow to 2 feet long, with heart-shaped, light green leaves and pale blue, star-shaped flowers in late summer and fall. Good for hanging baskets; white and lavender-blue cultivars are sold. Also known as Italian bellflower or falling stars. 2. A common name for 1 of 3 species of the genus *Ornithogalum,* tender Mediterranean bulbs with thin, straplike leaves, and winter or spring blooming flowers. *O. arabicum* grows to 2 feet, with rounded clusters of 1-inch, white, fragrant flowers. *O. pyrenaicum* grows to 3 feet, with greenish- white flowers in dense spikes. *O. umbellatum* grows to 1 foot, with rounded clusters of pure-white flowers; a weedy pest in the eastern United States.

star-of-the-earth *n.* A common name for *Plantago lanceolata,* a hardy perennial weed. It consists of 9-inch-long basal, heavily ribbed leaves and dense flower spikes more than 2 feet tall. Common in lawns. Also known as narrow-leaved plantain, ribgrass, ripplegrass, or buckhorn.

star pepper *n.* A common name for *Evodia Danielii,* a somewhat hardy small tree. It grows to 25 feet, with leaves divided into many 4-inch leaflets and clusters of small white flowers, followed by reddish fruit capsules. Also known as Korean Evodia or bitter pepper.

star pine *n.* A common name for *Pinus Pinaster,* a marginally hardy, rapidly growing tree. It grows to 100 feet or more in a pyramidal shape, with glossy-green 5- to 7-inch-long needles and 5- to 10-inch-long oval cones. A good pine for the seashore. Also known as cluster pine.

stars-of-Persia *n.* A common name for *Allium Christophii,* a hardy flowering bulb. It grows to less than 18 inches, with straplike leaves with a white coating on the underside and 6- to 12-inch globes of lilac, starlike flowers.

star tulip *n.* A common name for mostly hardy flowering bulbs of the genus *Clochortus,* native to western North America. They grow to less than 3 feet, with long, narrow basal leaves and lovely cup-shaped white, yellow, orange, brown, or lavender flowers. They require perfect drainage, and are somewhat difficult to grow. Also known as mariposa lily, sego lily, globe tulip, or butterfly tulip.

starwort *n.* 1. A common name for hardy perennials of the genus *Aster.* They grow in a variety of sizes, with usually yellow disk- shaped flowers, surrounded by purple, blue, violet, pink, or white ray flowers. Also known as Michaelmas daisy or frost flower. 2. A common name for annual and perennial weeds of the genus *Stellaria. S. media,* the most ubiquitous, is a low-growing invasive weed. *S. pubera* (star chickweed or great chickweed) is a showy perennial native to southeastern North America. (See cut under **Stellaria.**)

starwort, mealy *n.* A common name for *Aletris farinosa,* a hardy perennial native to eastern North America. It grows to 3 feet, with yellowish-green, grasslike leaves and white, tubular, late-spring flowers. Also known as unicorn root, crow corn, or agueroot.

starwort, yellow *n.* A common name for *Inula Helenium,* a hardy, robust perennial widely naturalized in the Northern Hemisphere. It grows to 6 feet, with irregularly toothed leaves, smooth on top and hairy beneath, and large, yellow, daisylike flowers. Also known as elecampane.

state flowers *n. pl.* Plants chosen by states as symbols.

state trees *n. pl.* Trees chosen by states as symbols.

Statice (stad'uh see) *n.* A former genus, most species of which are now classified either as *Armeria* (thrift or sea pink) or *Limonium* (sea lavender).

Stauntonia (stawn toh'nee uh) *n.* A genus of about 6 species of evergreen, woody vines (Lardizabalaceae). The most widely available species, *S. hexaphylla,* is a tender vine, growing to 40 feet, with divided leaves and small clusters of fragrant, violet-tinted white flowers.

staverwort *n.* A common name for *Senecio Jacobaea,* a hardy biennial. It grows to 4 feet, with divided leaves in a rosette and flat clusters of yellow daisylike flowers. Also known as ragwort or tansy ragwort.

steepgrass *n.* A common name for *Pinguicula vulgaris,* a hardy perennial carniverous plant, some species native to North America. It grows to 6 inches, with small oval leaves that are covered with a sticky substance that traps small insects. It has small violet flowers. Also known as steepweed and steepwort.

steeplebush *n.* A common name for *Spiraea tomentosa,* a hardy flowering shrub native to northeastern North America. It grows to 4 feet, with 3-inch-long, oval, yellow-downy leaves and crowded spikes of purple-rose flowers in summer. Also known as hardhack; also, *Spiraea salicifolia.* (See **Spiraea.**)

Stelis (stel'lis) *n.* A genus of about 300 species of tropical American orchids (Orchidaceae). The species most frequently found is *S. aprica,* which grows to less than 10 inches, with fleshy, 4-inch-long leaves and small, dark purple flowers.

Stellaria (stuh lah'ree uh) *n.* A genus of about 120 species of annual and hardy perennial plants (Caryophyllaceae). They grow to 2 feet, with oval leaves and white flowers. *S. media,* the most ubiquitous, is a low-growing invasive weed. *S. pubera* (star chickweed or great chickweed) is a perennial native to southeastern North America with large showy flowers. Commonly known as chickweed, starwort, or stitchwort.

Stellaria pubera
(star chickweed)

stellate (steh'layt) *a.* Star-shaped. Also stellated.

stellate leaves (steh'layt) *n. pl.* Leaves, more than two in number, surrounding the stem in a whorl, or radiating like the spokes of a wheel or the points of a star.

stem *n.* 1. The main (usually aerial) axis of a tree, shrub, or plant; trunk, stalk. 2. The plant part that supports the leaves, flowers, or fruits of a plant, as the peduncle of a fructification, or the pedicel of a flower; the petiole or leaf-stem.

stem-leaf *n.* A leaf growing from a stem; a cauline leaf.

stemless *a.* Having no stem; acaulescent.

Stenanthium (steh nan'thee uhm) *n.* A genus of about 4 species of grasslike hardy perennial plants (Liliaceae), some species native to North America. They grow to 5 feet, with 12-inch-long, narrow leaves and long spikes of greenish, whitish, or purplish flowers.

Stenochlaena (steh nahk lay'nuh) *n.* A genus of 5 species of climbing tropical ferns (Polypodiaceae). They have large (4- to 6-foot-long), leathery, divided leaves.

stenopetalous (steh nuh pehd'uh luhs) *a.* In botany, having narrow petals.

stenophyllous (steh nuh figh'luhs) *a.* In botany, having narrow leaves.

Stephanandra (stehf uh nan'druh) *n.* A genus of 4 species of somewhat hardy deciduous shrubs (Rosaceae). They grow to 8 feet, often with finely cut leaves and terminal clusters of small white or greenish flowers.

Stephanotis (stehf uh noh'dehs) *n.* A genus of about 15 species of tropical vines (Asclepiadaceae). The most widely grown species is *S. floribunda,* which twines to 15 feet, with leathery, glossy, oval leaves and very fragrant, white, waxy flowers. Commonly known as Madagascar jasmine, floradora, or waxflower.

sterile *a.* 1. Unfruitful; unproductive. 2. Not fertile; barren. 3. In botany, of a flower, staminate or male; of a fern frond, without sori.

sterility *n.* The state or character of being sterile.

sterilization *n.* The act or operation of making sterile; specifically, the process of freeing from living germs.

sterilize *v.* 1.To disinfect pruning tools to avoid transmitting disease. Usually done by dipping in a 5% solution of household bleach. 2. To kill all living organisms in soil to control pests; done with soil solarization or chemical treatment.

Sternbergia (stuhrn buhr'gee uh) *n.* A genus of 5 species of fairly hardy bulbs (Amaryllidaceae). They grow to less than 12 inches and have straplike leaves and yellow, crocuslike flowers.

sternotribe (stuhr'noh trighb) *a.* In botany, touching the sternum, as certain flowers, especially adapted for cross-fertilization by external aid, have stamens and styles so arranged as to touch the sternum of a visiting insect.

Stevia (stee'vee uh) *n.* A genus of perhaps 150 species of subtropical and tropical plants and shrubs (Compositae). *S. serrata* is a native of southwestern North America that grows to more than 3 feet, with many small, toothed leaves and rounded, dense clusters of white flowers.

Stewartia (styoo ahr'shee uh) *n.* A genus of 6 species of somewhat hardy deciduous shrubs and small trees (Theaceae). They grow to 40 feet, with simple, toothed leaves and produce camellialike white flowers in summertime. Good fall color. Two shrub species, *S. Malacodendron* and *S. ovata,* are native to southeastern North America.

stickseed *n.* 1. A common name for a plant of the genus *Hackelia. H. Jessicae,* a hardy native of north-

western North America, grows to 3 feet, with 6-inch-long basal leaves and clusters of pale blue flowers with yellow crests. The seed clusters, not surprisingly, have clinging barbs. Also known as beggar's-lice. 2. A common name for a plant of the genus *Lappula,* widely distributed hardy weeds. They usually grow more than 12 inches, with narrow leaves, clusters of blue or white flowers, and barbed clusters of seeds.

stick-tight *n.* A common name for annuals or hardy perennials of the genus *Bidens.* They grow to 5 or 6 feet, with toothed or divided leaves and yellow or white daisylike flowers. The seeds are a tremendous nuisance to remove from clothes or animal fur. Also known as beggar-ticks, burmarigold, water marigold, pitchforks, Spanish needles, or tickseed.

sticky card *n.* An adhesive-coated card, typically yellow, used to attract and trap insects in a greenhouse.

sticky ribbon *n.* An adhesive band, typically yellow, used to attract and trap insects in a greenhouse.

sticky trap *n.* Some type of sticky material (often sold as Tanglefoot) applied to trunks of trees to prevent the movement of pests such as ants. Often applied to yellow cards or tape. The yellow color attracts pests, such as whitefly, which land on the material and get stuck.

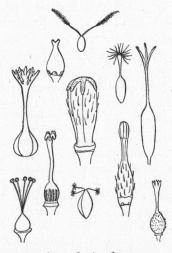

stigmas of various flowers

stigma *n.* In botany, the part of the pistil of a flower, usually on the tip of the style or ovary, which receives the pollen and on which it germinates.

stigmatic *a.* Having the character of, or pertaining to, a stigma.

stigmatiferous (stihg muh tihf'uh ruhs) *a.* Having a stigma.

Stillingia (stih lihn'jee uh) *n.* A genus of about 30 species of plants, shrubs, and trees (Euphorbiaceae). *S. Lyallii,* a small shrub native to southeastern North America, grows to 2 feet, with 4-inch-long, toothed green (or sometimes red) leaves and 5-inch-long spikes of yellow flowers. Commonly known as queen's-delight or queen's-root.

sting *n.* In botany, a sharp-pointed, hollow, glandular hair that secretes an irritating or poisonous fluid, as in the nettle.

stinging *a.* In botany, noting a plant furnished with stinging hairs. (See **sting.**)

stinging hair *n.* A sting.

stinging nettle *n.* 1. A common name for *Cnidoscolus texanus,* a perennial native to southern North America. It grows to 2 feet, covered with stiff, yellowish hairs, and has deeply cut leaves and rounded clusters of small white flowers. 2. A common name for *Urtica dioica,* a hardy perennial. It grows from 2 to 6 feet, with 6-inch-long, oval, toothed leaves and loose clusters of tiny white flowers.

stinkbugs *n. pl.* A large family of shield-shaped insects, including harlequin bugs, that give off a smelly secretion when disturbed. The adults and nymphs feed on a variety of plants, particularly fruit and vegetables, scarring the fruit and foliage. Control with row covers, handpicking, trapping, insecticidal soaps, sanitation, or traditional insecticides.

stinking cedar *n.* A common name for *Torreya taxifolia,* a tender tree native to Florida. It grows to 40 feet, with narrow, glossy, dark green yewlike leaves and cherrylike purple fruit with an unpleasant odor when bruised. Also known as stinking yew.

stinking chamomile (kam'uh mighl) *n.* A common name for *Anthenis Cotula,* an ill-smelling annual. It grows to 2 feet, with 2-inch-long fernlike leaves and small daisylike flowers, with a yellow center and white outer petals. Also known as mayweed, common dog fennel, or stinking mayweed.

stinking nightshade *n.* A common name for *Hyoscyamus niger,* an annual or biennial. The lower leaves are irregularly cut, and a leafy cluster of greenish-yellow, purple-veined flowers tops the spike. All parts of the plant are poisonous. Also known as henbane.

stipe *n.* In botany, a stalk or support, as the stalk-like prolongation of the receptacle of a flower, the petiole of a fern leaf, or the stem that supports the pileus of a mushroom.

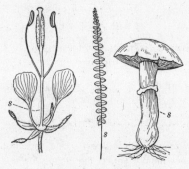

stipes of various plants

stipel (stigh'puhl) *n.* In botany, a secondary stipule situated at the base of the leaflets of a compound leaf.

stipellate (stigh'puhl leht) *a.* In botany, bearing or having stipels.

stipiform (stigh'puh form) *a.* In botany, having the form or appearance of a stipe; stalklike. Also stipitiform.

stipitate (stihp'uh tayt) *a.* In botany, having or supported by a stipe.

stipular (stihp'yuh luhr) *a.* In botany, of, having, or resembling stipules, as stipular glands.

stipulary buds (stihp'yuh lah ree) *n. pl.* Accessory buds in the axils of stipules, as in the apple and pear.

stipulate (stihp'yuh layt) *a.* In botany, having stipules, as a stipulate stalk or leaf.

stipule (stihp'yool) *n.* In botany, one of a pair of often leaflike lateral appendages found at the base of the petiole of many leaves.

stipules of various plants (labeled S)

stipuliform (stihp'yuh luh form) *a.* In botany, having the form of a stipule.

stirps (stuhrps) *n.* In botany, a race or permanent variety of plants.

stirrup hoe *n.* (See **oscillating hoe.**)

stitchwort *n.* A common name for annual and hardy perennial plants of the genus *Stellaria.* They grow to 2 feet, with oval leaves and white flowers. *S. media,* the most ubiquitous, is a low-growing invasive weed. *S. pubera* (star chickweed or great chickweed), native to southeastern North America is a perennial with large showy flowers. Commonly known as chickweed or starwort.

stock *n.* In botany: 1. The stalk, stem, or trunk of a tree or other plant, as distinguished from roots and branches. 2. A stem or root in which a bud or scion is inserted in grafting; also, a stem, tree, or plant that furnishes slips or cuttings.

Stokesia (stoh kee'zee uh) *n.* A genus of 1 species *S. laevis* (Compositae) of hardy perennial plants native to southeastern North America. They grow to 2 feet, with smooth, dark green leaves and aster-like lavender-blue flowers in late summer. Cultivars of white, blue, and lilac are available. Commonly known as Stokes' aster.

stolon (stoh'luhn) *n.* In botany, a prostrate branch from the base of a plant that runs along the ground or just below the surface and takes root, developing a new plant from its tips or nodes, as in the strawberry. Also called a runner.

stolons

stoma (stoh'muh) *n., pl.* **stomata**. In botany, any of the minute openings in the epidermis of a leaf, stem, or other plant organ through which gases are exchanged. Also stomate.

stone *n.* 1. The hard central portion of a drupe, as of a peach. 2. A small, hard, stonelike seed, as of a date.

stone brake *n.* A common name for *Cryptogramma crispa,* a hardy perennial fern. It grows to under 6 inches, with glossy, dark green fronds. The variety *C. c. acrostichoides* is native to the western half of North America. Also known as rock brake.

stonecress *n.* A common name for low-growing annual and perennial plants of the genus *Aethionema.* Small, stemless leaves clothe the stems that produce white, yellow, lilac, or pink flowers along the tips, mostly in spring.

stonecrop *n.* A common name for plants of the genus *Sedum,* perennial succulents. Some are hardy north; most are low-growing, with a variety of textures and leaf colors, as well as attractive blossoms. Their generally compact habits make them well suited to rock gardens and container culture. Also known as orpine. (See also **Sedum.**)

stonecrop, mossy *n.* A common name for *Sedum acre,* a hardy perennial succulent. It forms mats, with tiny, pointed, light green leaves and bright yellow flowers. Of extremely easy culture. Also known as golden-carpet or gold moss.

stone fruit *n.* In botany, a fruit with a hard endocarp enveloped in a pulp, as the peach, cherry, and plum; a drupe or drupelet.

stone mint *n.* A common name for *Cunila organoides,* a hardy perennial herb native to eastern North America. It grows less than 18 inches on multibranched stems, with pointed, oval leaves and rounded clusters of pinkish-purple flowers. Used as a culinary herb. Also known as American dittany, common dittany, or sweet horsemint.

stone oak *n.* A common name for *Quercus alba,* a hardy deciduous tree native to eastern America. It grows to 100 feet, with 3-inch-long oval, spiny-toothed leaves. Also known as white oak.

stone parsley *n.* A common name for annual, biennial, or perennial plants of the genus *Seseli.* They grow to more than 3 feet, with rosettes of leaves and flat-topped clusters of white flowers.

stone pine *n.* 1. A common name for *Pinus monophylla,* a somewhat hardy small tree native to southwestern North America. It grows to 25 feet, with dark green needles and nearly round cones. Also known as single-leaf pinyon pine or nut pine. 2. A common name for *Pinus pinea,* a marginally hardy tree. It grows to 80 feet, with a distinctive flat-topped silhouette and has 6-inche-long bright green needles and 5½-inch-long oval cones. Dramatic as a specimen tree. Also known as Italian stone pine or umbrella pine.

stoneroot *n.* A common name for *Collinsonia canadensis,* a hardy perennial native to eastern North America. It grows to 4 feet, with coarsely toothed oval leaves and clusters of yellow flowers. Both the flowers and the leaves (when crushed) are lemon-scented. Also known as citronella or richweed.

stoneseed *n.* A common name for hardy perennials of the genus *Lithospermum,* found throughout the world, many species native to North America. Characterized by a soft coat of hairs on the stems, They grow to 2 feet or less, with simple leaves, clusters of white, orange, or yellow flowers, and tough-shelled, almost porcelainlike, seeds. Also known as stoneweed, gromwell or puccoon.

stonewort *n.* A common name for a plant of the genus *Nitella,* widely distributed aquatic plants often grown in acquariums.

stool *n.* 1. The root or stump of a tree, or of a bush, cane, grass, etc., which annually produces shoots; also, the cluster of shoots thus produced. 2. The mother plant from which young plants are propagated by the process of layering. *v.* To produce shoots from the root; to form a stool.

storage capacity *n.* The amount of water that can be stored in the soil for future use.

storax (stoh′raks) *n.* A common name for marginally hardy shrubs or small trees of the genus *Styrax,* many species native to North America. The trees grow to 30 feet, the shrubs between 10 and 20 feet. They have roundish-oval leaves and drooping clusters of showy white flowers, often fragrant. Also known as snowbell.

storax flowering branch and leaf

storksbill *n.* 1. A common name for a plant of the genus *Erodium,* somewhat tender perennial members of the Geranium family. They are mostly low-growing, with deeply lobed leaves and rounded clusters of violet, white, yellow, purple, or pink flowers. Tough, moderately slow-growing plants for rock gardens. Also known as heron's-bill. 2. A common name for a plant of the genus *Pelargonium,* mostly tender flowering perennials. Most grow under 3 feet with rounded, deeply cut, or scalloped, sometimes fragrant, leaves and vibrantly colored flowers. Best bloom is produced by young plants. Also known as geranium. The name storksbill is derived from the distinctive shape of the seed capsule produced by

storksbill

stove plant *n*. A plant from a warm climate that must be cultivated in a greenhouse to allow it to survive.

strain *n*. A group of plants within a variety having some distinguishing quality, such as flower color, drought resistance, or high yield.

strainer-vine *n*. A common name for annual and tender perennial tropical vines of the genus *Luffa*. The most widely available is *L. aegyptiaca*, an annual that grows to 15 feet, with lobed leaves, yellow or white flowers, and cylindrical fruit, the fibrous core of which, when dried, is used as a bathing sponge. Also known as luffa, dishcloth gourd, rag gourd, or vegetable-sponge.

stramonium (struh moh′nee uhm) *n*. A common name for *Datura Stramonium*, an annual poisonous weed. It grows to 5 feet, with 8-inch-long oval, ill-smelling leaves and 4-inch white or violet trumpet-shaped flowers. All parts of the plant are poisonous. Also known as common thorn apple, Jimsonweed, or Jamestown weed.

Stranvaesia (stran vee′see uh) *n*. A genus of 4 or 5 species of tender evergreen shrubs and trees (Rosaceae). The most widely planted species is *S. Davidiana*, a shrub that grows to 20 feet, or more with 5-inch-long smooth leaves, colored purple and bronze and clusters of small white flowers in early summer, followed by red berries. Grows wide as well as tall.

strap fern *n*. A common name for *Polypodium phyllitidis*, a tropical fern that grows on trees. It has, not surprisingly, straplike leathery leaves, 3 feet long and 4 inches wide. Also known as ribbon fern.

stratification *n*. The germination or preservation of seeds by placing them between alternating layers of damp sand, earth, or other medium.

stratified *a*. Arranged in strata or layers. The term is confined to geological materials.

Stratiotes (strat ee oh′teez) *n*. A genus of 1 species *S. aloides* (Hydrocharitaceae) of hardy perennial water plants. It grows with partially submerged, stiff, sword-shaped, 1-foot-long leaves, in a spiral rosette, and 2-inch, white flowers. Commonly known as water soldier or water aloe.

strawberry *n*. The fruit of any of the species of the genus *Fragaria* or the plant itself. The plants are stemless, propagating by slender runners with 3-part leaves, bearing small white flowers, followed by the "berry," which consists of an enlarged fleshy cone, colored scarlet or other shade of red, with numerous tiny seeds on its surface. It is grown in great quantities in North America for its delicious, slightly acid fruit, which is used fresh for dessert and also frozen or made into jam, or a syrup for flavoring drinks, ice cream, etc.

strawberry, Alpine *n*. A European form of *Fragaria vesca*, sometimes distinguished as *F. collina*.

strawberry, barren *n*. A common name for *Waldsteinia fragarioides*, a hardy perennial strawberrylike ground cover native to northeastern North America. It grows to 3 inches, with glossy-green leaflets, toothed on the outer edges, and small yellow flowers in clusters, held above the leaves.

strawberry, bog *n*. A common name for *Potentilla palustris*, a hardy perennial native to northern North America. It creeps below 2 inches, with coarsely serrated compound leaves and loose clusters of red-to-purple flowers. Also known as marsh cinquefoil or marsh five-finger.

strawberry bush *n*. A common name for *Euonymus Americana*, a somewhat hardy shrub native to eastern North America. It grows to 7 feet, with 3-inch-long, oval leaves, turning red in the autumn, and clusters of small greenish flowers, followed by pink, warty seed capsules with scarlet seeds. Also known as bursting-heart.

strawberry cactus *n.* 1. A common name for *Echinocereus enneacanthus,* a tender cactus native to southwestern North America. It grows to 12 inches, with sharp spines and 3-inch purple or lavender flowers in spring, followed by red fruit. 2. A common name for *Ferocactus setispinus,* a tender cactus native to southwestern North America. It grows to 12 inches, with sharp spines and 3-inch trumpet-shaped yellow flowers with a red center followed by ½-inch round, red fruit. 3. A common name for a plant of the genus *Mammillaria,* tender flowering cacti. They grow less than 6 inches high in a squat cylinder or ball shape, with small red, white, yellow, or pink flowers arranged around the top of the plant. Good pot plants. Also known as pincushion.

strawberry clover *n.* A common name for *Trifolium fragiferum,* a hardy perennial ground cover. It creeps on rooting stems 12 inches long, with the usual 3 leaflets and pink-to-white flowers in long-stemmed globes. Also known as strawberry-headed clover.

strawberry-corn *n.* A small variety of popcorn with short ears and a bright red color.

strawberry fern *n.* A common name used for *Hemionitis palmata,* a tropical fern. It has 6-inch fronds with 5 triangular divisions.

strawberry geranium *n.* 1. A common name for *Pelargonium scabrum,* a tender perennial flower. Shrubby, it grows to 6 feet, with 1-inch-long 3-lobed leaves, smooth above and rough below, and rounded clusters of rose-to-white flowers, spotted and veined with red. Also known as apricot geranium. 2. A common name for *Saxifraga stolonifera,* a somewhat hardy—especially with protection—perennial. It mounds to 18 inches, with 4-inch-long, nearly round, white-veined leaves, reddish underneath, and loose clusters of white flowers. Easily grown as a houseplant or in mild climates as a ground cover. Also known as beefsteak geranium, strawberry begonia, creeping-sailor, or mother-of-thousands.

strawberry jar *n.* An urn, often of terra-cotta, having openings or molded pockets around the sides. Strawberries or other trailing plants are planted in the top and sides.

strawberry shrub *n.* A common name for *Calycanthus floridus,* a very hardy deciduous shrub. It grows to 10 feet, with 5-inch-long, glossy, dark green leaves and 2-inch, reddish-brown flowers in late spring. Also known as Carolina allspice or pineapple shrub.

strawberry tree *n.* A common name for *Arbutus Unedo,* a marginally hardy tree. It grows to 30 feet, with leathery, toothed, 6-inch-long leaves and clusters of small white, urn-shaped flowers, followed by red and yellow strawberrylike fruit that looks more attractive than it tastes. Undemanding once established. Also known as cane apples.

strawberry tomato *n.* A relative of *Physalis Alkekengi.* The berry, enclosed within an inflated husk, resembles a cherry or a very small tomato in appearance. Also called husk-tomato and ground-cherry.

strawberry, wild *n.* Any native strawberry, usually much smaller than cultivated varieties.

strawflower *n.* A plant with a flowerlike head that dries well, holding its shape and color. Although the term applies loosely to a number of everlasting flowers, it is most often used to describe members of the genus *Helichrysum.*

Strelitzia (streh liht′see uh) *n.* A genus of 4 species of subtropical perennial plants (Strelitziaceae). The most widely available species is *S. reginae,* whose leaves and flower stalks rise 3 feet from a clump. The leaves are oblong, leathery gray-green and the spectacular orange-and-blue flowers are instantly recognizable, providing an exotic, tropical feel. Good container plants, especially in colder areas where winter protection is necessary. Commonly known as bird-of-paradise, queen's bird-of-paradise, crane flower, or crane lily.

Streptocarpus (strehp toh kahr′puhs) *n.* A genus of 132 species of annual and tender perennial plants (Gesneriaceae). Some very interesting and lovely species plants may be available from specialty nurseries, but the most widely available are large- or small-flowered hybrids. They grow from a basal rosette, with 6- to 12-inch-long leaves, with wavy margins, and trumpet-shaped flowers with a long tube and a wide mouth. Good indoor container plants in cooler climates. Commonly known as Cape primrose.

streptomycin (strehp′toh migh′sihn) *n.* A bactericide used to control several plant diseases, including fire blight.

Streptopus (strehp′toh puhs) *n.* A genus of 7 species of hardy perennial plants (Liliaceae). They grow to less than 3 feet, with numerous oval leaves and purple, rose, pink, or white nodding flowers on twisted stalks. Commonly known as twisted-stalk.

Streptosolon (strehp toh soh′luhn) *n.* A genus of 1 species *S. Jamesonii* (Solanaceae), a tender shrub. It grows to 6 feet, with small, stubby, oval leaves and spikes of orange-red trumpet-shaped flowers. Commonly known as firebush, orange browallia, marmalade bush, or yellow heliotrope.

stress *n.* A term used for the total energy with which water is held in the soil. Expressed in any convenient pressure unit.

striate (strigh′ayt) *a.* Striped or streaked; marked with fine lines or channels.

striga (strigh′guh) *n., pl.* **strigae**. In botany, a sharp-pointed appressed bristle or hairlike scale.

strigose (strigh′gohs) *a.* In botany, rough with strigae; provided with sharp-pointed and appressed straight and stiff hairs or bristles, as a strigose leaf or stem. Also strigous.

strike *v.* In botany, to take root, as of a slip of a plant.

string bean *n.* A bean with green pods used for food, prepared before cooking by stripping off the tough thread along the back of the pods. Varieties of the common kidney bean, or French bean, are included, as well as a number of beans pickled at an immature stage, even those that do not have a "string" on the pod. The term snapbean or green bean is now more commonly used.

string trimmer *n.* A machine consisting of nylon line mounted on a wand, powered by a gas or electric motor, used to clip grass and weeds inaccessible to a lawn mower. The circular motion of the nylon line acts as a blade.

stringybark *n.* A group of trees of the genus *Eucalyptus* characterized by long, fibrous strands of bark. Included in this group are the following: *E. Blaxlandii* (Blaxland′s stringybark), *E. aggloerata* (blue-leaved stringybark), *E. alpina* (Grampian stringybark), *E. capitellata* (brown stringybark), *E. cinerea* (mealy stringybark), *E. globoidea* (white stringybark), *E. macrohyncha* (red stringybark), *E. muellerana* (yellow stringybark), and *E. obliqua* (messmate stringybark).

striolate (strigh′uh layt) *a.* In botany, minutely striate, or striped.

strobilaceous (strahb uh lay′shuhs) *a.* 1. Resembling or relating to a strobile. 2. Bearing strobiles. Also strobiline.

Strobilanthes (strahb uh lan′thuhs) *n.* A genus of between 200 and 300 species of tropical perennial plants and shrubs (Acanthaceae). Plants in the genus are variable, so it is difficult to define a type. The cultivated species are low shrubs, *S. Dyeranus* has 8-inch-long oval leaves, iridescent above and purple below, and spikes of violet flowers; *S. isophyllus* has 4-inch-long willowlike leaves and clusters of pinkish or blue and white flowers. Commonly known as Mexican petunia.

strobile (strahb′ehl) *n.* In botany, 1. A conelike structure of sporophylls, as in the horsetails and club mosses. 2. A gymnosperm cone or a hop inflorescence. Also strobilus.

strobiloid (strahb′uh loid) *a.* Resembling or relating to a strobile.

Stromanthe (stroh′mahnth) *n.* A genus of about 10 species of tropical flowering perennials (Marantaceae). They grow to 6 feet or less, with large, rectangular, heavily marked leaves and red or red-and-white flowers.

Strophanthus (struh fan′thuhs) *n.* A genus of about 40 species of tropical perennial vines (Apocynaceae). They climb to more than 25 feet or less, with oblong or oval leaves and rounded clusters of trumpet- or bell-shaped flowers in striking combinations of green, purple, white, yellow, and orange.

struma (stroo′muh) *n., pl.* **strumae**. In botany, a cushionlike swelling of or on an organ, especially at 1 side of the base of the capsule in many mosses.

strumose (stroo′mohs) *a.* In botany, bearing a struma or strumae. Also strumous.

Strychnos (strihk′nuhs) *n.* A genus of about 150 species of subtropical and tropical vines, shrubs, and trees (Loganiaceae). They grow as high as 40 feet, with oval or round leaves and rounded clusters of white or yellowish flowers. The seeds of *S. Nux-vomica* yield the drug strychnine.

stump tree *n.* A common name for *Gymnocladus dioica,* a hardy deciduous tree native to eastern North America. It grows to 100 feet, with divided leaves, clusters of greenish-white flowers, and beanlike fruit. Also known as Kentucky coffee tree, nicker tree, or chicot.

stunt *v.* To retard or stop plant growth or development, usually accidentally through exposure to harsh weather or lack of water or nutrients.

stupose (styoo′pohs) *a.* In botany, bearing tufts or matted filaments, like tow.

Sturt's desert pea *n.* A common name for *Clianthus formosus,* a tender clambering shrub. It grows to 4 feet, with dusty-gray leaflets and red sweet-pea-like flowers in loose, hanging clusters. Also known as desert pea or glory pea.

stylate (stigh′layt) *a.* In botany, having a persistent style.

style *n.* In botany, a narrow, usually elongated part of the pistil connecting the ovary with a stigma.

Stylidium
(trigger plant)

Stylidium (stigh lihd′ee uhm) *n.* A genus of about 90 species of mostly tender perennial plants (Stylidiaceae). The most widely available species, *S. graminifolium,* grows to 3 feet, with grasslike leaves and a spike of pink flowers. Commonly known as trigger plant.

styliferous (stigh lihf′uh ruhs) *a.* In botany, style-bearing; bearing one or more styles.

Stylomecon (stigh′loh meh kahn) *n.* A genus of 1 species *S. heterophylla* (Papaveraceae), of annual flowering plants native to western North America. They grow to 2 feet, with smooth, divided green leaves and brick-red flowers with a purple center. Commonly known as flaming poppy or wind poppy.

Stylophorum (stigh loh faw ruhm) *n.* A genus of less than 6 species of hardy perennial plants (Papaveraceae) native to eastern North America. The most widely available species is *S. diphyllum,*. which grows under 2 feet, with mostly basal, divided, light green leaves and clusters of deep-yellow, 2-inch flowers. Commonly known as celandine poppy or wood poppy.

stylopodium (stigh loh poh dee uhm) *n., pl.* **stylopodia.** In botany, 1 of the double fleshy disks from which the styles in the Umbelliferae arise.

stypticweed (stihp′tik) *n.* A common name for a hardy perennial native to eastern and southern North America. It grows to 3 feet, with feathery, divided leaves and showy clusters of yellow flowers. Also known as coffee senna, or stinking weed.

Styracaceae (stigh ruh say′see ee) *n. pl.* A family of 6 genera of shrubs and trees. They have alternate, simple leaves and mostly white flowers. The ornamental genera are *Halesia, Pterostyrax, Rehderodendron, Sinojackia,* and *Styrax.*

Styrax (stigh′raks) *n.* A genus of about 100 species of mostly tender shrubs and trees (Styraceae). The trees grow to 30 feet, the shrubs between 10 and 20 feet. Roundish-oval leaves are characteristic along with drooping clusters of showy white flowers, often fragrant. There are species native to both the east coast (*S. americanus* and *S. grandiflorus*) and the west coast (*S. officinalis officinalis*) of North America. Commonly known as snowbell or storax.

sub- *prefix* Below, under, or almost.

subaxillary *a.* In botany, situated under an axil, as a subaxillary bud.

subclass *n.* In plant and animal classification, a taxonomic category of related orders within a class.

subfamily *n.* A taxonomic group of related genera within a family.

subgenus *n., pl.* **subgenera**. A category in taxonomy of related species within a genus.

subherbaceous *a.* Herbaceous, but becoming more woody later in the growing season.

subirrigation *n.* The natural or deliberate irrigation through the control of the water table that will raise water into the root zone.

submerged *a.* 1. Under water. 2. Adapted to grow, or growing under water. Also called submersed.

subpetiolar (suhb pehd′ee oh luhr) *a.* In botany, situated under or within the base of the petiole, as the leaf buds of the plane tree.

subshrub *n.* A perennial plant having a woody base, but with herbaceous shoots that die back annually.

subsoil *v.* To till the soil below the normal plow depth.

subspecies *n., pl.* **subspecies**. A taxonomic subdivision of a species, often with a disinct geographic distribution.

subspecific *a.* Of the nature of a subspecies; not quite specific.

substrate *n.* The medium on which an organism lives, as soil or rock.

substratum *n.* A term for any layer lying beneath the subsoil or solum.

subsurface irrigation *n.* A watering system installed beneath the surface of the ground, as an in-ground sprinkler system.

subtend *v.* To occur below or close to, as a bract subtending a flower.

Subularia (soob yuh lah′ree uh) *n.* A genus of 2 species of hardy, widely distributed aquatic plants (Cruciferae). They grow to 4 inches high, with a rosette of many small, awl-shaped leaves and a stalk of undistinguished tiny white flowers. Commonly known as awlwort.

subulate *a.* Awl-shaped; slender, more or less cylindrical, and tapering to a point.

subulate leaves of juniper

subvarietal *a.* Varying slightly; having the character of a subvariety.

subvariety *n.* A subordinate variety; the further and minor modification of a variety, as a strain or line.

succession cropping *n.* Especially in a small vegetable garden, the practice of growing new plants in the space vacated by harvested ones.

succession of crops *n.* In agriculture, the rotation of crops. (See **rotation of crops.**)

succory (suhk′uh ree) *n.* A common name for *Chichorium intybus,* a hardy perennial naturalized as a roadside weed. It grows to 5½ feet, with crudely toothed basal leaves and blue ray flowers. Blanched, the leaves can be used in salads; the ground root is sometimes used as a substitute for coffee. Also known as swine's- succory, bluesailors, witloof, wild succory, or barbe-de-capuchin.

succory, blue (suhk′uh ree) *n.* A common name for *Catananchecaerula,* a mostly hardy perennial. It grows to 2 feet, with pointed, 1-foot-long woolly leaves clustered near the base, and blue ray flowers.

succubous (suhk′yuh buhs) *a.* In botany, overlapping, with the anterior margin of 1 leaf passing beneath the posterior margin of that succeeding it: opposed to incubous; said of leaves.

succulent *a.* Juicy, thick, and fleshy, as the leaves of the Cactaceae. *n.* A succulent plant, as a cactus or sedum.

sucker *n.* In botany, a rapidly growing shoot rising from an underground root or stem, often to the detriment of the plant.

suffrutescent (suh froo tehs'uhnt) *a.* In botany, somewhat or slightly woody at the base; sub-shrubby.

suffruticose (suh froo'duh kohs) *a.* In botany, having stems that are woody at the base and herbaceous above. Also suffruticous.

sugar beet *n.* A variety of beet grown for its high sugar content, a source of commercial sugar.

sugarberry *n.* A common name for plants of the genus *Celtis,* but most specifically *C. occidentalis,* a hardy tree native to eastern North America. The leaves are alternate and elmlike, the flowers small, with dark-purple or red fruit. Also known as nettle tree.

sugar bush *n.* 1. A common name for *Protea mellifera,* a subtropical shrub. It grows to 8 feet, with 4-inch-long smooth, narrow leaves and large, 5-inch-long white flowers. Also known as honey flower. 2. A common name for *Rhus ovata,* a tender shrub native to southwestern North America. It grows to 10 feet, with 3-inch-long, glossy, oval leaves and dense clusters of white or pinkish flowers in spring. Also known as sugar sumac. 3. A grove or orchard of sugar maples, or a woods in which sugar maples are predominant. Also called sugar orchard.

sugar gum *n.* A common name for *Eucalyptus cladocalyx,* a tender tree. It grows to 100 feet, with 5-inch-long, narrow, oval, reddish leaves and inconspicuous white flowers.

sugar orchard *n.* A collection or small plantation of sugar maples. Also called sugar bush.

sugar pea *n.* A variety of pea whose pod is tender enough to be eaten with the seeds.

sugar pine *n.* A common name for *Pinus Lambertiana,* a moderately hardy tree native to western North America. It grows to 200 feet or more, with clusters of dark bluish-green needles and large cylindrical cones. One of the tallest pines known.

sugar tree *n.* 1. Any tree from which sugar syrup or sugary sap can be obtained; particularly, the sugar maple. (See **maple.**) 2. An Australian shrub or small tree, *Myoporum platycarpum.*

sugi (soo'gee) *n.* A common name for *Crytomeria japonica,* a moderately hardy tree. It grows to 150

feet or more, with ½-inch curved blue-green needles, on gently pendulous branches, and round, 1-inch, reddish-brown cones. Also known as Japanese cedar.

sulcate (suhl'kayt) *a.* Having long, narrow lengthwise channels or grooves, as plant stems. Also sulcated.

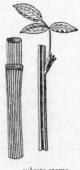

sulcate stems

sulfur *n.* A yellow mineral used as a dust or wettable powder for control of various diseases and insects, including powdery mildew, rust, and mites.

sulfur flower *n.* A common name for *Eriogonum umbellatum,* a hardy perennial native to the east side of the Rocky Mountains. It grows in spreading mats about 1 foot high, with 1-inch-long oval leaves, with woolly undersides, and stalks of tiny yellow flowers in flat-topped clusters.

sumac (soo'mak) *n.* A common name for shrubs, trees, and vines of the genus *Rhus.* Most deciduous species are hardy; the evergreen species are more problematic. They have alternate, compound leaves, frequently prized for their autumn color. Two widely distributed species—*R. radicans* (poison ivy) on the East Coast and *R. diversiloba* (poison oak) on the west coast—cause a severe rash in many people. Also spelled sumach.

sumac, Chinese (soo'mak) *n.* A common name for *Ailanthus altissima,* a moderately hardy tree. It grows rapidly to 60 feet, with compound, divided leaves and clusters of small, greenish flowers (those of male trees have an unpleasant odor). Also known as tree-of-heaven, copal tree, or varnish tree.

sumac, dwarf (soo'mak) *n.* A common name for a hardy shrub or tree native to the eastern United

States. It grows to 20 feet, with fernlike dark green leaves that turn a tapestry of colors in fall and dense clusters of greenish flowers that bloom in summer, followed by red berries. Also known as shining sumac, mountain sumac, or wing-rib sumac.

sumac, laurel (soo'mak, law'ruhl) *n.* A common name for *Rhus laurina,* a tender shrub native to southern California and Mexico. It grows from 10 to 20 feet, with light green, slightly aromatic leaves and dense clusters of small, greenish-white flowers, followed by small white berries. Also spelled as laural sumac.

sumac, poison (soo'mak) *n.* A common name for *Rhus vernix,* a hardy shrub native to eastern North America. It grows to 20 feet, with divided leaves, turning orange to scarlet in fall, and clusters of greenish-white flowers. Contact with skin may result in severe inflammation. Also known as swamp dogwood, swamp sumac, poison elder, or poison dogwood.

sumac, scarlet (soo'mak) *n.* A common name for *Rhus glabra,* a hardy shrub native to midwestern and western North America. It grows to 20 feet, often covered with a thin, waxy powder, with divided leaves with 5-inch leaflets and dense stalks of green flowers, followed by red berries. Extremely tough; takes drought and heat; good fall color. Also known as smooth sumac or vinegar tree.

scarlet sumac

sumac, Sicilian (soo'mak) *n.* A common name for *Rhus coriaria,* a moderately hardy shrub. It grows to 20 feet, with divided leaves with 2-inch leaflets, loose clusters of greenish flowers, and

brownish-purple, hairy berries. Also known as tanner's sumac or elm-leaved sumac.

sumac, smooth (soo'mak) *n.* A common name for *Rhus glabra,* a hardy shrub native to midwestern and western North America. Also known as scarlet sumac or vinegar tree. (See **sumac, scarlet.**)

summer cypress (sigh'prehs) *n.* A common name for *Kochia scoparia,* an annual foliage plant. It grows to 5 feet, with very narrow, light green leaves and inconspicuous flowers. Good for a quick hedge. Also known as belvedere.

summer hyacinth (high'uh sihnth) *n.* A common name for *Galtonia candicans,* a tender flowering bulb. It grows to 4 feet, with straplike leaves and spikes of drooping, trumpet-shaped 1½-inch pure-white, fragrant flowers.

summer oil *n.* (See **horticultural oil.**)

summer sweet *n.* A common name for *Clethra alnifolia,* a hardy shrub native to eastern North America. It grows to 10 feet, with 4-inch-long, oval, toothed leaves and spikes of fragrant white flowers in late summer and fall. Also known as sweet pepperbush.

sundew *n.* A common name for a plant of the genus *Drosera,* hardy small perennials of bogs and swamps. They grow under 12 inches, with basal leaves covered with fine hairs that trap and digest insects. Also known as daily-dew.

sundrops *n.* A common name for hardy perennials of the genus *Oenothera,* particularly *O. fruticosa, O. perennis,* and *O. pilosella,* native to eastern and central North America. They grow to around 2 feet, with oval lower leaves and pointed stem leaves and clear yellow flowers, which bloom during the day, as opposed to other members of the genus, the evening primroses.

sunflower *n.* 1. A common name for annual and moderately hardy perennials of the genus *Helianthus,* many native to North America. They grow as large as 10 feet, with coarsely toothed leaves and large, bright-yellow flowers, often harvested for their seeds. 2. A common name for moderately hardy perennials of the genus *Balsamorhiza,* native to western North America. They grow slowly to 3 feet, with basal leaves and typical sunflower blossoms. Also known as balsamroot.

sunflower

sunn (suhn) *n.* A common name for *Crotalaria juncea,* a tender shrub. It grows to 8 feet, with divided leaves on slender, wandlike, rigid branches and clusters of yellow flowers. Also known as sunn hemp.

sunn

sun plant *n.* A common name for *Portulaca grandiflora,* an annual flowering plant. It grows less than 6 inches, high with fleshy, pointed, 1-inch-long leaves and brilliantly colored open flowers, available in double flowers in a wide range of colors. Also known as rose moss or eleven-o'clock.

sunrose *n.* A common name for mostly tender perennials of the genus *Helianthemum. H. nummularium* is hardy in the north. It grows to 18 inches, with 2-inch-long, oval leaves, with gray undersides, and rounded clusters of pale yellow, white, or pink flowers. Also known as rock rose.

sun tree *n.* A common name for *Chamaecyparis obtusa,* a hardy tree. It grows slowly to 120 feet,

with dark green scalelike leaves and round ½-inch cones. Many cultivars offer elegant smaller-growing garden trees. Also known as Hinoki cypress or Japanese false cypress.

superior oil *n.* (See **horticultural oil**.)

superphosphate *n.* A fertilizer that supplies phosphorus and can force some plants to grow faster.

supplejack *n.* A common name for *Berchemia scadens,* a moderately hardy deciduous vine native to southeastern North America. It grows to 12 feet, with oval leaves with parallel veins and clusters of greenish-white flowers.

supplemental irrigation *n.* A general term used for irrigation during dry periods of time.

support rings *n. pl.* Two or more wire loops supported by stakes, used to prop and contain a cluster of weak-stemmed flowers such as delphiniums or peonies.

suprafoliaceous (soo pruh foh lee ay′shuhs) *a.* In botany, inserted on the stem above a leaf, as a peduncle or flower.

suprafoliar (soo pruh foh′lee uhr) *a.* In botany, growing above a leaf.

surculose (suhr′kyuh luhs) *a.* In botany, producing suckers. Also surculous.

surculus (suhr′kyuh luhs) *n., pl.* **surculi**. In botany, a sucker.

surface freeze *n.* A ground condition in which the moisture found on the surface freezes in cold temperatures, thus causing frost heaves.

surface soil *n.* 1. Soil that is ordinarily moved in tillage, 5- to 8-inches thick. 2. Soil found on top of the earth.

Surinam cherry (soo′ruh nam) *n.* A common name for *Eugenia uniflora,* a tropical shrub. It grows to 8 feet (but can reach 25 feet), with 2-inch-long coppery-green leaves and small, white, fragrant flowers, followed by small edible fruits that ripen from green to deep red. Also known as Brazil cherry, Barbados cherry, Cayenne cherry, or pitanga.

Sutera (soo teh′ruh) *n.* A genus of about 140 species of annual and subtropical perennial plants and shrubs (Scrophulariaceae). They grow compactly under 4 feet, with lobed or divided leaves and profuse spikes of white, pink, yellow, blue, or purple flowers.

Sutherlandia (suhth uhr luhnd'ee uh) *n.* A genus of 1 species *S. frutescens* (Leguminosae), a subtropical shrub. It grows to 3 feet, with finely divided leaves and short clusters of showy scarlet flowers.

suture *n.* In botany, the seam or line of junction between 2 edges, as where carpels of a pericarp join, marking the line of dehiscence, or opening.

Swainsona (swayn'soh'nuh) *n.* A genus of about 60 species of subtropical perennial plants (Leguminosae). The most widely available species, *S. galegifolia,* grows to 4 feet, with divided leaves with ½-inch leaflets and deep red flowers. Commonly known as swan flower, winter sweet pea, or darling pea.

swallowwort *n.* A common name for *Cynanchum Vincetoxicum,* a hardy vine. It clambers to 15 feet, with 5-inch narrow leaves and clusters of greenish-white flowers.

swallowwort, black *n.* A common name for *Cynanchum nigrum,* a hardy vine. It climbs to 15 feet, with 5-inch-longoval leaves and clusters of small purple-black flowers.

swamp beggar-ticks *n.* A common name for *Bidens connata,* an annual low-growing weed native to eastern North America. It has simple, toothed leaves, yellow flowers, and highly barbed seeds.

swamp cabbage *n.* A common name for *Symplocarpus foetidus,* a hardy low-growing perennial native to northeastern North America. It has heart-shaped leaves, 18 inches long and 12 inches wide, that give off a foul odor when bruised. The flower, a purple-brown and greenish-yellow callalike blossom, appears before the leaves. Also known as skunk cabbage or polecat weed.

swamp cottonwood *n.* A common name for *Populus heterophylla,* a somewhat hardy tree native to southeastern North America. It grows to 90 feet or less, with 7-inch-long, broad, pale green leaves and flowers in drooping, greenish catkins. Also known as black cottonwood or downy poplar.

swamp cypress (sigh'prehs) *n.* A common name for *Taxodium distichum,* a hardy deciduous tree native to eastern North America. It grows to as much as 150 feet, in wet places, with small, needlelike or spreading leaves. Only for large gardens.

swamp elm *n.* A common name for *Ulmus americana,* a hardy tree native to North America east of the Rocky Mountains. It grows to 120 feet, with 6-inch-long simple, toothed leaves and inconspicuous flowers. Highly suceptible to Dutch elm disease. Also known as American elm, white elm, or water elm.

swamp fly honeysuckle *n.* A common name for *Lonicera oblongifolia,* a hardy shrub native to northeastern North America. It grows to 5 feet, with 3-inch-long stubby leaves, gray beneath, and pairs of yellowish-white ½-inch flowers.

swamp globeflower *n.* A common name for *Trollius laxus,* a moderately hardy perennial native to eastern North America. It grows to 2 feet, with deeply lobed leaves and greenish-yellow flowers at the ends of the stems. Also known as spreading globeflower.

swamp gum *n.* A common name for *Eucalyptus ovata,* a tender tree. It grows to 90 feet, with peeling bark, long, narrow leaves, and small white flowers, followed by a hemispheric nut.

swamp hellebore (hehl'uh boh uhr) *n.* A common name for *Veratrum viride,* a hardy perennial native to North America. It grows to 7 feet, with broad, 12-inch-long leaves and long, drooping clusters of yellow-green flowers. Also known as white hellebore, itchweed, or Indian poke.

swamp hickory *n.* A common name for *Carya cordiformis,* a fairly hardy tree native to eastern North America. It grows to 90 feet, with divided leaves and 6-inch leaflets, and a smooth, round nut. Also known as bitternut or pignut.

swamp honeysuckle *n.* A common name for *Rhododendron viscosum,* a hardy, flowering deciduous shrub native to northeastern North America. It grows to 8 feet, with 2½-inch-long narrow, oval leaves and clusters of white or pink, fragrant, trumpet-shaped flowers. Also known as white swamp azalea or clammy azalea.

swamp laurel (law'ruhl) *n.* A common name for *Kalmia polifolia,* a hardy shrub native to North America east of the Rocky Mountains. It grows in a straggling manner to 2 feet, with 1½-inch-long, narrow leaves, white on the undersides, and rounded clusters of rose-purple flowers at the ends of the stems in late spring and summer. Also known as bog kalmia, bog laurel, or pale laurel.

swamp locust *n.* A common name for *Gleditsia aquatica,* a tender deciduous tree native to southeastern North America. It grows to 60 feet, with divided leaves and small greenish flowers in 4-inch spikes. Also known as water locust.

swamp loosestrife *n.* A common name used for *Decodon verticillatus,* a hardy perennial aquatic plant native to eastern North America. It grows to 8 feet or more, with 5-inch-long pointed leaves, deep pink flowers, and fruit. Arching branches that root may form a thicket. Also known as water willow or water oleander.

swamp magnolia (mag noh'lyuh) *n.* A common name for *Magnolia virginiana,* a somewhat hardy tree native to eastern North America. It grows to 60 feet, with 5-inch-long rounded-oval leaves and 3-inch white, fragrant flowers. Also known as sweet bay and swamp sassafras.

swamp mahogany (muh hahg'uh nee) *n.* A common name for *Eucalyptus robusta,* a somewhat hardy tree. It grows to 90 feet, with long, pointed, light gray-blue leaves and pink-tinted cream-colored flowers.

swamp maple *n.* A common name for *Acer rubrum,* a very hardy tree native to eastern North America. It grows rapidly to 120 feet, with 5-lobed leaves and clusters of red flowers that appear before the leaves. Also known as red maple, scarlet maple, or soft maple.

swamp moss *n.* A common name for moss of the genus *Sphagnum.*

swamp oak *n.* (See **swamp white oak.**)

swamp pine *n.* A common name used for *Pinus Elliottii,* a tender tree native to southeastern North America. It grows to 100 feet, with deep green, 5-inch-long needles and 6-inch oval cones. Also known as slash pine.

swamp pink *n.* 1. A common name for *Arethusa bulbosa,* a hardy orchid native to northeastern North America. It grows to 12 inches, with a single grass-like leaf and rose-purple flowers, with white, yellow, and purple markings. Also known as wild pink, dragon's-mouth, or bog rose. 2. A common name for *Calopogon,* a genus of hardy orchids native to northeastern North America. *C. tuberosus* grows to 18 inches, with grasslike leaves and clusters of pink to rose-purple flowers. Also known as grass pink. 3. A common name for *Helonias bullata,* a hardy perennial native to the central eastern seaboard. It grows to 3 feet, with long, straplike leaves and dense spikes of fragrant pink or purplish flowers.

swamp post oak *n.* A common name for *Quercus lyrata,* a hardy deciduous tree native to southeastern North America. It grows to 100 feet, with 8-inch-long, oval, deeply lobed leaves. The seed is almost totally enclosed by the cap. Also known as overcup oak.

swamp rose *n.* A common name for *Rosa palustris,* a very hardy shrub native to northeastern North America. It grows to 7 feet, with sharply toothed leaflets, gray underneath, and 2-inch pink flowers.

swamp rose mallow *n.* A common name for *Hibiscus Moscheutos,* a hardy shrub native to eastern North America. It grows to 8 feet, with oval, toothed leaves, gray underneath, and large white, pink, or rose flowers. Also known as common rose mallow, mallow rose, or wild cotton.

swamp sassafras (sas'uh fras) *n.* A common name for *Magnolia virginiana,* a marginally hardy tree native to southeastern North America. It grows to 60 feet, with 5-inch-long leaves, gray on the underside, and 3-inch white, fragrant flowers. Also known as sweet bay and swamp magnolia.

swamp saxifrage (saks'uh frihj) *n.* A common name for *Saxifraga pensylvanica,* a hardy perennial native to eastern North America. It has 1-foot-long leaves and tiny greenish flowers. A good bog plant. Also known as wild beet.

swamp Spanish oak *n.* A common name for *Quercus palustris,* a hardy deciduous tree native to mid-North America. It grows to 80 feet, with bright green, heavily lobed leaves, which turn a brilliant red in autumn. Excellent pyramidal form with low or drooping branches close to the ground. Also known as pin oak.

swamp tea tree *n*. A common name for *Melaleuca quinquenervia,* a tender tree. It grows to 25 feet, with peeling bark, narrow, oval, pale green leaves, and spikes of white flowers. Also known as paperbark tree, punk tree, or tea tree.

swamp white oak *n*. A common name for *Quercus bicolor,* a moderately hardy deciduous tree native to eastern North America. It grows to 70 feet, with 6-inch-long oval, lobed leaves, dark green above, gray underneath. The acorn cap covers ⅓ of the seed.

swamp willow *n*. A common name for *Salix discolor,* a hardy shrub or small tree native to eastern North America. It grows to 20 feet, with 4-inch-long leaves, gray beneath, and fuzzy gray catkins that appear before the leaves. Also known as large pussy willow.

swampwood *n*. A common name for *Dirca palustris,* a hardy shrub native to eastern North America. It grows to 6 feet, with 3-inch- long, oval leaves and clusters of yellow flowers that appear before the leaves. It has tough inner bark. Also known as leatherwood, wicopy, moosewood, or ropebark.

swanflower *n*. A common name for *Swainsona galegifolia,* a subtropical perennial. It grows to 4 feet, with divided leaves with ½-inch leaflets and deep red, white, or rose-violet sweet-pea-like flowers. Also known as winter sweet pea, or darling pea.

swan-neck rake *n*. An implement having curved and pointed tines attached to a transverse bar. The bar is attached to the handle by a metal piece in the shape of a swan's neck. Used for smoothing and evening newly cultivated soil.

Swan River everlasting *n*. A plant, *Helipterum Manglesii,* whose bright pink daisy-shaped flowers retain their color and form when dried.

Swedish ivy *n*. A common name for tender perennials of the genus *Plectranthus.* It grows to 12 inches, with round, scalloped-edged leaves and short spires of tiny white flowers. Often grown as a houseplant. Also known as Swedish begonia, prostrate coleus, or spur flower.

Swedish juniper (joo′nuh puhr) *n*. A common name for *Juniperus communis* ‘Suecica’, a hardy shrub. It grows to 15 feet, with sharp-pointed, narrow, glossy-green leaves (bronzy in winter). It has a dense columnar shape, with drooping branchlets.

sweet almond *n*. A common name for *Prunus dulcis dulcis,* a tender tree. It grows to 30 feet, with 5-inch-long, pointed, slightly toothed leaves and white to pinkish flowers. This is the commercially grown almond.

sweet alyssum (uh lihs′uhm) *n*. A common name for *Lobularia maritima,* a slightly hardy perennial, though mostly grown as an annual. It grows less than 12 inches, with small, thin, pointed leaves and many small globular clusters of flowers.

sweet annie *n*. A common name for *Artemisia annua,* a tall annual herb with fine, feathery, light green leaves. In a garden, the plants may reach 7 feet and are intensely fragrant, with tiny yellow flowers at the ends of their branches. It reseeds itself if allowed to mature in the garden. If cut young and hung to dry in a dark place, it may retain its green color; otherwise it turns a rich brown. It retains its intense sweet fragrance when dried, and although it is quite fragile, it is prized for use in herbal wreaths.

sweet balm *n*. A common name for *Melissa officinalis,* a hardy perennial. It grows to 2 feet, with light green lemon-scented leaves and small white flowers. Also known as common balm, bee balm, or lemon balm.

sweet basil (bays′uhl) *n*. A common name for *Ocimum Basilicum,* an annual herb. It grows to 2 feet, with 5-inch-long oval leaves and a spike of white or purplish flowers. Also known as common basil.

sweet bay *n*. 1. The victor's laurel, *Laurus nobilis,* which is also the common bay tree, in cooler regions grown as a shrub. Its evergreen leaves have a pleasant scent and an aromatic taste and are used for flavoring. (See **bay.**)

sweetbells *n*. A common name for *Leucothoe racemosa,* a moderately hardy shrub native to moist spots in southeastern North America. It grows to 12 feet, with 3-inch-long, finely toothed leaves and white-to-pinkish blueberrylike flowers.

sweet birch *n*. A common name for *Betula lenta,* a hardy tree native to eastern North America. It grows to 75 feet, with 5-inch-long oval leaves, soft on the undersides. The twigs and young branches are aromatic and yield oil of wintergreen. Also known as cherry birch, black birch, mahogany birch, or mountain mahogany.

sweetbrier

sweetbrier *n*. A common name used for *Rosa Eglanteria*, a moderately hardy flowering shrub. It grows from 3 to 6 feet, with 2 to 3 pairs of leaflets and 1-inch, bright pink flowers, followed by scarlet hips. Also known as eglantine.

sweet buckeye *n*. A common name for *Aesculus octandra*, a hardy tree native to the central and south-eastern United States. It grows to 90 feet, with leaves divided into 8-inch leaflets and erect clusters of yellow flowers at the ends of the branches. Also known as yellow buckeye.

sweet calabash (kal'uh bash) *n*. A common name for *Passiflora maliformis*, a tropical vine. It climbs by tendrils, with 4-inch- long oval leaves and 3-inch greenish flowers, mottled with reddish-purple, followed by round, 1½-inch yellowish fruit. Also known as sweetcup or conch apple.

sweet cicely (sihs'uh lee) *n*. A common name for *Myrrhis odorata*, a hardy perennial herb. The plant grows to 3 feet tall, with elegant, fernlike leaves and large flat heads of tiny white flowers, turning to long, shiny brown seeds with a spicy licorice flavor. The leaves have a sweet flavor and are used as a garnish; the roots may be dug and cooked like parsnips. Difficult to germinate from seed, sweet cicely is best planted in fall from freshly collected seeds. It can be grown throughout the United States and into southern Canada, although it is not as well known an herb. In places, it has naturalized from old gardens. Also known as myrrh and sweet chervil.

sweet corn *n*. A common name to distinguish corn grown for table use from those grown for drying and grinding or popping and those used for animal feed.

sweet fern *n*. 1. A fragrant shrub, *Myrica (Comptonia) asplenifolia*. Its fernlike leaves contain 9 or 10% of tannin. (See **Comptonia**.) 2. The European sweet cicely, *Myrrhis odorata* which has leaves dissected like those of a fern.

sweet fern

sweet flag *n*. A common name for *Acorus Calamus*, a hardy perennial bog plant. It grows to 6 feet, with irislike leaves and small greenish flowers. Also known as myrtle flag, calamus, sweet calamus, sweet cane. sweet rush, or flagroot.

sweet flag

sweet gale *n*. A common name for *Myrica Gale*, a hardy deciduous shrub native to northern North

545

America. It grows to 5 feet, with 2½-inch-long leaves and small green catkins. Also known as bog myrtle or meadow fern.

sweet goldenrod *n.* A common name for *Solidago odora,* a hardy perennial native to eastern North America. It grows to 5 feet, with thin, pointed leaves and large clusters of yellow flowers.

sweet gum *n.* A common name for *Liquidambar Styraciflua,* a hardy tree native to southeastern North America and Central America. It grows to 120 feet, with 7-inch-long, multilobed, toothed leaves that turn brilliant colors in autumn. Also known as red gum or bilsted.

sweetleaf *n.* A common name for tender shrubs and trees of the genus *Symplocos. S. paniculata* is most widely available and is somewhat hardy. It grows to 40 feet with 4-inch-long, oval, deciduous leaves and spikes of fragrant white flowers. Also known as Asiatic sweetleaf.

sweet pepperbush *n.* A common name for *Clethra alnifolia,* a hardy shrub native to eastern North America. It grows to 10 feet, with 4-inch-long, oval, toothed leaves and spikes of fragrant white flowers in late summer and fall. Also known as summer sweet.

sweet potato *n.* The plant *Ipomoea batatas,* a vine closely related to the morning glory. It is grown for its tubers, potatolike roots that have been eaten as a vegetable since ancient times. Two types are grown, 1 with dryer, yellow flesh and 1 with softer, orange flesh. In the southern United States, those with orange flesh are often called yams, although the true yam is a larger root vegetable of a different genus. The sweet potato needs 4 to 5 frost-free months to develop its roots to vegetable size, but it can be grown as far north as central New England in some years, depending on the weather. Plants are best started from vine cuttings, which are commercially available. The sweet potato is exceedingly rich in vitamin A.

sweet sedge *n.* A common name used for *Acorus Calamus,* a hardy perennial bog plant. It grows to 6 feet, with irislike leaves and small greenish flowers. Also known as sweet flag, myrtle flag, calamus, or flagroot.

sweet sultan *n.* A common name for *Centaurea moschata,* an annual flowering plant. It grows to 3 feet, with fernlike leaves and fragrant purple, pink, white, or yellow 2-inch flowers.

sweet viburnum (vigh buhr′nuhm) *n.* A common name for *Viburnum odoratissimum,* a tender evergreen shrub or small tree. It grows to 20 feet, with 6-inch-long, oval, leathery leaves and spikes of fragrant white flowers.

Sweet William *n.* A common name for *Dianthus barbatus,* a biennial, often grown as an annual. It grows to under 2 feet, with short, thin leaves and dense, flat-topped clusters of red, rose, pink, white, or purple flowers.

Sweet William, wild *n.* A common name for *Phlox divaricata,* a hardy spreading perennial native to North America. It grows to 18 inches, with 2-inch-long oval leaves and loose clusters of pale violet-blue to lavender flowers. Also known as blue phlox.

sweetwood *n.* A common name for *Glycyrrhiza glabra,* a tender perennial. It grows to 3 feet, with divided, sticky leaves and spikes of small bluish or violet flowers. Also known as licorice, which is made from its roots.

sweet woodruff *n.* A common name for *Galium odoratum,* a hardy low- growing perennial herb. It grows to 6 inches, with sweet-smelling thin oval leaves and loosely branched clusters of small white flowers in late spring. It thrives in shady woodland locations and moist areas. The foliage has a mild, sweet scent, which, when dried, resembles that of new-mown hay. Although it does not add a strong scent of its own, woodruff is used in potpourri as a fixative to intensify and hold the scents of other flowers and leaves. It can be used as a ground cover in shaded yards. Woodruff is combined with white wine to make May wine.

Swertia (swuhrsh′ee uh) *n.* A genus of about 50 species of annual and hardy perennial plants (Gentianaceae). They grow to 6 feet, with smooth-edged, mostly oval leaves and dense clusters of usually blue flowers.

Swietenia (swee tee′nee uh) *n.* A genus of about 5 species of tropical evergreen trees (Meliaceae). They grow to 150, feet with large, shiny, divided leaves. Commonly known as mahogany.

Swiss chard (chahrd) *n.* A leafy variety of the beet, *Beta vulgaris,* grown for its shiny dark green leaves and smooth white or red stalks. The stalks are usually cooked separately from the leaves, which are cooked and served like spinach. Among the easiest and most reliable garden vegetables to grow, chard produces a steady crop throughout the summer. If left in the garden through winter, chard produces one of the earliest spring vegetables. It is grown as far north as Zone 2; it withstands frost and thrives in nearly any soil. A variety with red-veined leaves, called rhubarb chard, is attractive enough to be grown in a flowering border as a background plant. Also known as spinach beet or leaf beet.

swivel hook *n.* A device from which hanging plants are suspended. The swivel facilitates even lighting of plants.

sword fern *n.* A common name for low-growing ferns of the genus *Nephrolepis,* widely distributed. They grow in clumps, with sword-shaped, evenly divided fronds. The widely grown houseplant, the Boston fern, is a variety of *N. exalta.*

sycamore (sihk'uh moh uhr) *n.* 1. A common name for *Acer pseudoplatanus,* a hardy deciduous tree. It grows to 100 feet, with 6-inch-long, 5-lobed, coarsely toothed leaves, dark green above, and yellowish-green flowers in hanging clusters. Also known as sycamore maple or mock plane. 2. A common name for mostly hardy, deciduous trees of the genus *Plantanus.* They grow to 150 feet, with 5-lobed leaves. Also known as buttonwood or plane tree.

sycamore fig
1 leaves *2* fruit

sycamore fig (sihk'uh moh uhr) *n.* A common name for *Ficus Sycomorus,* a tender tree. It grows to 60 feet, with nearly round leaves and 1-inch fruit. Also known as Egyptian sycamore or mulberry fig.

syconium (sigh koh'nee uhm) *n.* A multiple fleshy fruit composed of a hollow receptacle containing numerous reduced flowers, as in the fig.

symmetrical *a.* 1. In botany, having the same number of parts in each whorl, said of a flower. 2. Divided into 2 similar parts.

sympetalous (sihm pehd'uh luhs) *a.* The same as gamopetalous, having the petals joined at the base.

Symphoricarpos (sihmp fuhr uh kahr'pahs) *n.* A genus of 16 species of mostly hardy deciduous shrubs (Caprifoliaceae), most native to North America. They grow to 10 feet or less, with oval leaves and clusters or spikes of white or pink flowers, followed by white, purplish-red, coral-red, or rosy-pink berries. Commonly known as snowberry.

Symphyandra (sihmp fee an'druh) *n.* A genus of 8 species of somehat hardy biennial or perennial plants (Campanulaceae). They grow to 2 feet or less, with bell-shaped blue or white flowers. Commonly known as ring bellflower.

Symplocarpus (sihm ploh kahr'puhs) *n.* A genus of 1 species, *S. foetidus* (Araceae), a hardy perennial plant native to northeast North America. Its purple-brown, calla-like blossom, mottled with greenish-yellow, appears in early spring before the leaves. The leaves are 18 inches long and 12 inches wide, on short stalks, and give off a disagreeable odor when bruised. Commonly known as skunk cabbage or polecat weed.

Symplocos (sihm'pluh kahs) *n.* A genus of about 300 species of tender shrubs and trees (Symplocaceae). *S. paniculata* is the most widely available species and is somewhat hardy. It grows to 40 feet, with 4-inch-long, oval, deciduous leaves and spikes of fragrant white flowers.

sympodial (sihm poh'dee uhl) *a.* In botany, having the character of or resulting in a sympodium, as a sympodial stem or a sympodial growth.

sympodium (sihm poh'dee uhm) *n., pl.* **sympodia.** In botany, an apparent axis or stem that imitates a simple stem, but is made up of the bases of a number of secondary axes that arise successively as branches 1 from another, as the grapevine. Compare monopodium.

synacmic (sihn ak'mihk) *a.* In botany, of or pertaining to synacmy.

synacmy (sihn ak'mee) *n.* In botany, synanthesis; simultaneous maturity of the anthers and stigmas of a flower: opposed to heteracmy.

synantherous (sihn an'thuh ruhs) *a.* In botany, having the stamens coalescent by their anthers, as in the Compositae. Also symphyantherous.

synanthesis (sihn an thee'sihs) *n.* In botany, simultaneous anthesis; the synchronous maturity of the anthers and stigmas of a flower; synacmy.

synanthous (seh nan'thuhs) *a.* In botany, having flowers and leaves that appear at the same time; also, exhibiting synanthy.

synanthy (sih nan thee) *n.* In botany, the more or less complete union of several flowers that are usually distinct.

syncarp (sihn'kahrp) *n.* In botany: 1. An aggregate fruit, as the blackberry. 2. A multiple fruit, as the fig.

Syncarpia (sihn kahr'pee uh) *n.* A genus of 4 or 5 species of tender evergreen trees (Myrtaceae). They grow to 30 feet, with almost rectangular leaves and dense, rounded clusters of white flowers.

syncarpous (sihn·kahr'puhs) *a.* In botany: 1. Having the character of a syncarp. 2. Having carpels united.

syngenesious (sihn jeh nee'zhee uhs) *a.* In botany, having anthers united in a ring, as the stamens of Compositae.

Syngonium (sihn goh'nee uhm) *n.* A genus of about 20 species of tropical vines (Araceae). They clamber over trees with divided philodendronlike leaves and callalike greenish flowers.

synthetic pesticide *n.* A pesticide that is an artificially produced combination of various materials; not natural. Examples are carbaryl, diazinon, chlorpyrifos, and malathion.

Synthyris (sihn thigh'ruhs) *n.* A genus of 14 or 15 species of hardy perennials (Scrophulariaceae) native to western North America. Most grow under 12 inches, with basal, coarsely cut or toothed leaves and clusters of blue to violet-blue or white flowers on individual stalks.

syringa (seh rihn'guh) *n.* 1. A common name for hardy shrubs of the genus *Philadelphus,* many native to North America. The common species are vigorous, graceful shrubs of a bushy habit, with abundant, large, white, mostly clustered, flowers. Commonly known as mock orange. 2. A genus of about 30 species of hardy flowering shrubs or small trees (Oleaceae). They grow to 20 feet, with simple oval leaves and showy, fragrant clusters of small white, lilac, pink, red, or purple flowers. Commonly known as lilac.

systemic pesticide *n.* A pesticide that is absorbed by plant tissue and translocated throughout the plant. Consequently, if only a portion of the plant, such as the roots, receives a pesticide application, all of the plant would be toxic to a pest, including the leaves. Acephate and triforine are examples of systemic pesticides.

Tabebuia (tab ee boo'yuh) *n.* A genus of about 100 species of tender tropical large shrubs and trees (Bignoniaceae) native to the Americas. They grow from 12 to 100 feet, depending on the species, with opposite, usually fan-shaped, leaves and showy spikes or clusters of trumpet-shaped yellow, white, pink, purple, or red flowers. Used as patio trees, specimen flowering trees, or street trees. Commonly known as trumpet tree.

Tabernaemontana (tuh buhr nee mahn tay'nuh) *n.* A genus of 140 species of sometimes spiny tropical shrubs and small trees (Apocynaceae). They grow from 8 to 35 feet, with opposite, entire, leathery leaves and clusters of pinwheel-shaped yellow or white flowers, some fragrant at night. Used in frost-free gardens. Commonly known as red bay.

tacamahac (tak'uh muh hak) *n.* A common name for *Populus balsamifera,* a very hardy deciduous tree native to northern North America. It grows from 75 to 100 feet, with narrowly oval leaves and catkins. Also known as tacmahack, balsam poplar, and hackmatack.

Taccaceae (ta kay'see ee) *n. pl.* A family of 1 genus and 10 species of tropical perennials. The ornamental genus is Tacca.

Tagetes (taj′uh teez) *n*. A genus of 30 species of long-blooming strongly scented tender annuals and perennials (Compositae), native from Arizona to Argentina. They grow from 6 inches to 4 feet, depending on species, with opposite leaves and many-petaled yellow, orange, red-brown, or parti-colored flowers. One of the most widely grown bedding flowers in America, the short French marigolds, *T. patula,* are used massed in beds, for edging borders, and in pots. The tall African marigold, *T.erecta,* is used in annual borders or to fill in perennial borders for summer to fall color. Commonly known as marigold.

tahoka daisy (tuh hoh′kuh) *n*. A common name for *Machaeranthera tanacetifolia,* an annual perennial native to North America from Alberta to north-central Mexico. It is a densely leafy, bushy plant that grows to 2 feet, with fernlike leaves and large violet-blue or white daisylike flowers.

Talinum (tuh lee′nuhm) *n*. A genus of 50 species of annuals and perennials (Portulacaceae), mostly native to North America. They grow from a few inches to 2 feet, with more or less succulent narrow, basal, alternate leaves and showy clusters of short-lived pink, red, rose, yellow, or white flowers. Used in borders, rock gardens, or as pot plants. Commonly known as fameflower.

talipot (tal′uh paht) *n*. A common name for *Corypha umbraculifera,* a tropical palm. It grows to 80 feet, with a stout trunk 3 feet in diameter and huge fan-shaped leaves 16 feet across. The flower clusters are 20 feet long, the largest in the plant kingdom. Used as a specimen tree in tropical gardens. Also known as taliput and talipot palm.

tall fescue (tahl fehs′kyoo) *n*. (See **Festuca.**)

tallow shrub (ta′loh) *n*. A common name for *Myrica,* a genus of shrubs and small trees with waxy berries. (See **Myrica.**)

tallow tree (ta′loh) *n*. A common name for *Sapium sebiferum* and *Aleurites moluccana. S. sebiferum* is a dense, round-headed deciduous tree which has poplarlike leaves that color brilliant, translucent red or yellow in autumn. Also known as Chinese tallow tree. *Aleurites moluccana* is a large tropical tree grown ornamentally as a shade tree that appears white from a distance. Also called candlenut tree, candleberry tree, varnish tree, Indian walnut, country walnut, otaheite walnut, and tallow tree. (See **candlenut tree.**)

tamanu (tuh mah′noo) *n*. A common name for *Calophyllum inophyllum,* a tender tree. It grows to 60 feet, with evergreen, broadly oval leaves and spikes of very fragrant white flowers. Grown for its handsome leaves and fragrant flowers in frost-free gardens; especially useful in coastal gardens since it tolerates salt spray. Also known as Alexandrian laurel, Indian laurel, laurelwood.

tamarack (tam′uh rak) *n*. A common name for *Larix laricina,* a very hardy deciduous coniferous tree native to North America. It bright green scale-like spirally arranged needles and small, scaly, shiny cones. Also known as American larch, black larch, and hackmatack. Also a common name for *Pinus contorta latifolia,* a tall symmetrical, picturesque short-needled pine Also known as tamarack pine and lodgepole pine. (See **pine, lodgepole**.)

Tamaricaceae (tam uh reh kay′see ee) *n. pl.* A family of 4 genera and 100 species of shrubs and trees. The ornamental genera are *Myricaria* (false tamarisk), and *Tamarix* (tamarisk and salt cedar). Commonly known as the tamarisk family.

tamarind
a flowering branch *b* pod with seeds

tamarind (tam′uh rehnd) *n*. A common name for *Tamarindus indica,* a large subtropical tree. It grows to 80 feet, with delicate, finely cut leaves divided into many small leaflets, spikes of yellow flowers, and a long, hard cinnamon-brown pod used for flavoring. Used as a graceful shade tree in tropical gardens. Also known as tamarindo.

tamarind, black (tam'uh rehnd) *n.* A common name for *Pithecellobium arboreum,* a subtropical and tropical tree. It grows to 60 feet, with 16-inch-long leaves divided into tiny leaflets, small heads or spikes of white bottlebrushlike flowers, and a twisted pod red inside with black seeds.

tamarind, velvet (tam'uh rehnd) *n.* A common name for *Dialium guineense,* a subtropical and tropical tree. It grows to 60 feet, and has branches covered with a rusty-colored down. It has leaves divided into long oval or narrow leaflets and clusters of small white flowers, the buds of which are also covered with rust-colored down. The velvety oval fruit has red-orange edible pulp. Also known as Sierra Leone tamarind.

tamarind, wild (tam'uh rehnd) *n.* A common name for *Lysiloma bahamensis,* a subtropical tree native to southern Florida, the Caribbean and Central America. It grows to 50 feet, with large, feathery leaves divided into tiny leaflets, spikes of small white flowers, and hard flat brown pods 6 inches long.

Tamarindus (tam uh rihn'duhs) *n.* A genus of 1 species, *T. indica,* a subtropical and tropical tree (Leguminosae). Commonly known as tamarind. (See **tamarind.**)

tamarisk

tamarisk (tam'uh rehsk) *n.* A common name for *Tamarix,* a genus of deciduous shrubs or small trees. It grows from 9 to 30 feet and has green, jointed branchlets, small, scalelike leaves that secrete salt and showy spikes of tiny white, pink or rose flowers. Useful in coastal gardens, especially as windbreaks. Tolerates saline soils, wind, and salt spray. A superb desert tree. *T. africana* and *T. parviflora* flower in the spring, *T. chinensis* flowers in summer, and *T. aphylla* appears evergreen. Also known as salt cedar.

tamarisk, German (tam'uh rehsk) *n.* A common name for *Myricaria germanica,* a hardy deciduous shrub. It grows to 6 feet, and has scalelike leaves and dense spikes of small white or pink flowers. Also known as false tamarisk.

tamarisk family (tam'uh rehsk) *n.* A common name for *Tamaricaceae.* (See **Tamaricaceae.**)

Tamarix (tam'uh rihks) *n.* A genus of 54 species of deep-rooted shrubs and trees (Tamaricaceae) of varying degrees of hardiness. It grows from 9 to 30 feet and has green, jointed branchlets, small, scalelike leaves that secrete salt and showy spikes of tiny white, pink, or rose flowers. Many are native to dry desert regions, and they are choice trees for desert gardens. Commonly known as salt cedar and tamarisk. (See **tamarisk.**)

Tanacetum (tan uh seed'uhm) *n.* A genus of 50 species of mostly aromatic annuals and perennials (Compositae), some species native to western North America and others naturalized in North America. They grow from 1- to 3-feet tall and have alternate, aromatic leaves and clusters of either daisylike or buttonlike yellow flowers. Traditional in cottage and herb gardens. Good, long-keeping cut flowers. Commonly known as tansy.

Tanakaea (tan uh kay'uh) *n.* A genus of 1 species, *T. radicans,* an evergreen perennial that spreads by runners (Saxifragaceae). It grows to 1 foot, with fleshy, oval, hairy, long-stemmed basal leaves and dense clusters of small greenish-white flowers.

tanbark oak *n.* A common name for *Lithocarpus densiflorus,* a handsome tender tree native to the western United States. Also known as tanoak. (See **Lithocarpus.**)

tanekaha (tahn uh kah'hah) *n.* A common name for *Phyllocladus trichomanoides,* a tender evergreen coniferous tree. It grows to 70 feet, with reddish-brown, leathery leaflike branchlets and scalelike leaves and clusters of cones. Useful in mild-winter, cool-summer climates. Also known as celery pine. (See **Phyllocladus**.)

tangelo (tan jehl′oh) *n.* A hybrid citrus fruit, the product of crossing the tangerine with the grapefruit. It is grown in California and Florida; its culture is the same as that of oranges.

tangerine *n.* A relative of the orange, *Citrus reticulata,* a small spiny tree with orangelike fruits, smaller and more easily peeled than the orange. The tree is cultivated commercially and as a good yard ornament wherever citrus trees are grown, especially in Florida and California. Also called mandarin orange.

tangleberry *n.* A common name for *Gaylussacia frondosa,* a hardy deciduous shrub native to the eastern United States from New Hampshire to Florida; dwarf huckleberry. It grows to 6 feet, with alternate, simple, oval leaves, loose spikes of white bell-shaped flowers, and small, dark blue-gray berries. Used in woodland gardens. Also known as bluetangle and dangleberry.

tankage *n.* An organic fertilizer that leaves an alkaline reaction.

tansy

tansy (tan′zee) *n.* 1. A perennial herb, *Tanacetum vulgare,* a stout, erect plant 2 or 3 feet high, with deeply cut, toothed leaves, and yellow buttonlike flower heads in a flat cluster at the end of the stem. Having escaped from gardens, it is now a roadside weed in North America, thriving especially in

coastal areas. The acrid, strong-scented leaves and tops are used in herb blends to repel moths, ants, and other pests. The flower heads dry well, retaining their color and shape, and are prized for use in winter arrangements and herbal wreaths. The *Crispum* variety grows taller and has more luxurious foliage.

tanyah (tahn′yuh) *n.* A common name for *Colocasia esculenta* and *Xanthosoma,* both large tropical perennials with ornamental foliage and edible roots. (See **Colocasia** and **Xanthosoma**.)

tape grass *n.* A common name for *Vallisneria,* a genus of submersed, grasslike water plants with ribbonlike leaves, some species native to North America. Also known as eel grass. (See **Vallisneria**.)

taproot *n.* In botany, the main root of a plant, which grows downward to a considerable depth, giving off lateral roots in succession.

Taraxacum (tar′uhks uh kuhm) *n.* A genus of between 50 and 60 species of self-sowing taprooted biennials and perennials with milky sap (Compositae); dandelion. They grow from 8 to 18 inches, and have basal rosettes of leaves, cheerful yellow many-petaled flowers, and feathery silvery seedhead. *T. officinalis* is the common dandelion, America's most notorious lawn weed, but a nutritious pot-herb in the herb or vegetable garden. Commonly known as dandelion and blowballs.

Taraxacum officinalis
(dandelion)

tarnished plant bug *n.* A sucking, shield-shaped insect that damages the buds and fruit of a variety

551

of fruits and vegetables. Control with row covers, good sanitation, insecticidal soaps, sabadilla, or traditional insecticides.

taro (ta′roh) *n.* A food plant, *Colocasia esculenta,* grown for its starchy roots. It is a stemless plant, with the general habit of the caladiums of house and garden culture. The leaves are heart-shaped and about 1 foot long. Its chief value lies in its stemlike tuberous root, which is eaten boiled or baked or made into a bread or pudding. The leaves and leafstalks are also edible, with the character of spinach or asparagus. About 15 months are required to mature the root, so it is suitable only in far southern gardens.

tarp *n.* Waterproof sheet, typically of polyethylene, used to hold and move bulky yard material such as leaves.

tarragon (tar′uh gahn) *n.* A perennial culinary herb, *Artemisia Dracunculus.* Its leaves, unlike those of most artemisias, are lance-shaped and undivided, and they have an aromatic scent and taste, faintly like licorice. The plants are hardy into southern and central New England. For culinary use, only the smaller aromatic variety, known as French tarragon, should be used; it does not set viable seed and must be planted from root divisions. Tarragon seeds offered for sale will produce the coarse, flavorless Russian tarragon, an invasive weed.

tarweed *n.* A common name for *Grindelia,* a genus of perennials with alternate leaves, and heads of asterlike yellow flowers, often sweet-smelling and sticky. (See **Grindelia.**) Also a common name for *Madia,* a genus of heavy-scented sticky, hairy flowers native to western North America that grow from a few inches to 4 feet with sticky, richly aromatic leaves and small yellow daisylike flowers. (See **Madia.**) Also a common name for *Chamaebatia* (mountain misery), a genus of sticky, hairy shrubs native to California and northern Baja California. Also a common name for *Phacelia tanecetifolia,* (fiddleneck) an erect, bristly annual native to California and Arizona that has clusters of blue or lavender flowers that attract bees. (See **Phacelia.**)

Tasmanian laurel (law′ruhl) *n.* A common name for *Anopterus glandulosus,* a tender shrub or small tree. It grows to 30 feet, with glossy, thick, narrow, oval, simple alternate leaves and spikes of white flowers.

Tasmanian myrtle (muhr′duhl) *n.* A common name for *Nothofagus cunninghamii,* a tender broadleaf evergreen tree. It grows to 200 feet in the wild, with small, alternate leaves and nuts enclosed in a scaly cup.

tassel flower *n.* A common name for *Amaranthus* (see **Amaranthus**), *Petalostemon Brickellia grandiflora* (see **Brickella**), and *Emilia javanica* (See **Emilia**). *B. grandiflora* is a hardy perennial flower native to North America that grows up to 3 feet tall, and has toothed leaves and clusters of nodding white, yellow, or pink flowers. It thrives in shady, moist situations. *E. javanica* is an annual that grows to 2 feet, with oval leaves and brushlike red or yellow flowers; also known as Flora's-paintbrush.

Taxaceae (tak say′see ee) *n. pl.* A family of 5 genera of evergreen coniferous shrubs and trees; the yew family. The ornamental genera are *Taxus* (yew) and *Torreya.*

Taxodiaceae (taks oh dee ay′see ee) *n.* A family of 10 genera of evergreen or deciduous coniferous trees. The ornamental genera include *Cryptomeria, Cunninghamii* (China fir), *Glyptostrobus* (Chinese swamp cypress or Chinese water pine), *Metasequoia* (dawn redwood), *Sciadopitys* (Japanese umbrella pine), *Sequoia* (coast redwood), *Sequoiadendron* (giant sequoia and giant redwood), and *Taxodium* (cypress).

Taxodium
(cypress)

Taxodium (taks oh′dee uhm) *n.* A genus of 2 species of hardy to marginally hardy coniferous trees (Taxodiaceae). They grow to 150 feet, with graceful sprays of short, flat needlelike leaves and fragrant round, thick-scaled cones. Some species, such as bald cypress, are deciduous. Used as towering sentinal trees. Commonly known as cypress.

Taxus (taks′uhs) *n.* A genus of 8 species of hardy to very hardy slow-growing, long-lived densely-leaved evergreen coniferous shrubs and trees (Taxaceae), some species native to North America. They grow from 6 to 60 feet, depending on species, with spirally arranged, short, dark green needlelike leaves and fleshy scarlet berries only on female trees. Both fruit and foliage are poisonous. Commonly known as yew. (See **yew**.)

tea *n.* The tea plant, *Camellia sinensis,* a shrub from 3 to 6 feet high, grown in Asia and Africa. It is the source of the beverage tea. In the United States, it can be grown successfully in the South and in California, but it has thus far not been produced with economic success.

tea

teaberry *n.* The American wintergreen, *Gaultheria procumbens,* sometimes used to flavor tea and as a substitute for tea. Also called mountain tea, checkerberry and wintergreen.

tea family *n.* A common name for *Theaceae*. It includes tea and camillia. (See **Theaceae**.)

teak branch with flowers

teak *n.* A common name for *Tectona grandis,* a tall subtropical tree. It grows to 150 feet with large, drooping, oval, opposite, entire leaves and clusters of white or blue funnel-shaped flowers.

tea plant *n.* A common name for *Camellia sinensis* and *Viburnum Lentago*. *C. sinensis* is a densely leaved tender broadleaf evergreen shrub or tree that grows from 3 to 50 feet with glossy dark green oval leaves and nodding, white or pink cup-shaped flowers. A refined ornamental shrub and the source of both green and black tea that is made from the young leaves. Also known as tea tree. *V. lentago* is a very hardy deciduous massive shrub or small tree native to North America from Hudson Bay to Georgia and Mississippi. Also known as sweet viburnum, sheepberry, black haw, cowberry, nanny plum, sweetberry, wild raisin, and nannyberry. (See **nannyberry**.)

tea rose *n.* A common name for *Rosa odorata,* a parent of modern hybrid tea roses. Hybrid tea roses are tender shrub roses that bloom sporadically throughout the year during warm spells. Hybrid teas are the most poplar roses in America, and there are hundreds of named cultivars. They are valued for their reliable, recurrent bloom, refined, high-centered buds, range of colors (including white, yellow, red, lavender, blends and bi-colors) and some have a rich or spicy fragrance. They are excellent cut flowers. Unfortunately, they are vulnerable to almost innumerable pests and diseases.

teasel (teez′uhl) *n.* A plant of the genus *Dipsacus* (Dipsacaceae), chiefly *D. fullonum,* the fuller's teasel. It has naturalized in America, escaping from cultivation. The teasel is a coarse, stout hairy biennial. It grows to 6 feet, with large oval leaves, prickly beneath, and tall stalks with pale lilac flowers. The useful part is the oblong-conical fruiting head, thickly set with slender- pointed barbs, formerly widely used to raise a nap on woolen cloth. The dried flowerheads are used in everlasting arrangements. Often seen as a roadside weed; grown in historical herb or dyers' gardens. Also known as teazel.

teasel family (tee′zuhl) *n.* A common name for *Dipsacaceae*. Also known as teaselwort. (See **Dipsacaceae**.)

tea tree *n.* A common name for *Leptospermum* (see **Leptospermum**), *Melaleuca* (see **Melaleuca**) and *Camellia sinensis* (see **tea plant**).

tea tree, Ceylon *n.* A common name for *Cassine glauca,* a subtropical and tropical tree. It grows to 45 feet, with oval leaves and clusters of small yellow-green flowers.

tea tree, swamp *n.* A common name for *Melaleuca quinquenervia* and *M. Leucodendron,* both tender trees. (*M. quinquenervia* is often sold as *M. leucodendra. M. Leucodendron* is not grown in North America.) *M. quinquenervia* is a small tender tree or shrub with thick, spongy, peeling bark, long, narrow, leathery leaves and pale yellow, pink, or purple flowers that resemble bottlebrush. Used as a street tree or in pleasant groves. Also known as cajeput, paperbark tree, punk tree, and tea tree.

Tecoma (teh koh′muh) *n.* A genus of 16 species of tender evergreen shrubs and trees (Bignoniaceae) native from Florida to Mexico and Argentina. *T. stans* is a large shrub or small tree that grows to 20 feet with leaves divided into an odd number of oval, pointed leaflets and clusters of large bright yellow bell-shaped flowers. Used as a showy flowering long-blooming tree or large shrub. *Tecoma* is commonly known as trumpet bush and yellowbells. *T. stans* is commonly known as yellowbells, yellow trumpet flower, yellow elder, and yellow bignonia. (See **yellowbells** and **yellow elder**.)

Tecomaria (teh koh mah′ree uh) *n.* A genus of 3 species of tender and subtropical erect or trailing shrubs (Bignoniaceae). *T. capensis,* the Cape honeysuckle, grows to 6 feet unsupported, to 25 feet given support. It has leaves divided into glistening dark green leaflets and tight clusters of bright orange-red tubular flowers. Used as an espalier, an informal barrier hedge, or sprawling bank cover on hot, steep slopes. A tough, accommodating plant, it accepts full sun, light shade, wind, salt air, and drought once established.

Tectona (tehk toh′nuh) *n.* A genus of 4 species of tall deciduous tender trees (Verbenaceae). They grow to 150 feet, with opposite, entire leaves and clusters of white or blue funnel-shaped flowers. *T. grandis* is known as teak.

teil (tee′uhl) *n.* A common name for *Tilia* × *europea,* a tall, handsome, slow-growing very hardy deciduous tree. It grows to 120 feet, with broad, oval, pointed, toothed, dull dark green leaves that color soft yellow in autumn and clusters of fragrant white flowers that attract bees. Used as street trees and park trees in cold climates; they thrive in moist soils. Some feel that this hybrid's vices outweigh its virtues: it suckers enthusiastically and develops great whiskery knobs on the trunk. Also known as linden.

telegraph plant *n.* A common name for *Desmodium motorium,* a small tropical perennial with leaflets that jerk and twitch under the influence of warmth and sunshine. It has clusters of sweet pea-like flowers and a flat pod. Grown as a novelty in greenhouses.

Telephium (tehl uh′fee uhm) *n.* A genus of 6 species of woody perennial subshrubs (Caryophyllaceae). *T. imperati* is a dwarf shrub that grows to 16 inches with tiny, fleshy, alternate, gray-green leaves and clusters of white 5-petaled flowers. Used in rock gardens.

Tellima (tehl′uh muh) *n.* A genus of 1 species, *T. grandiflora,* a tender hairy, perennial (Saxafragaceae) native to western North America. It forms lush clumps of roundish leaves rising from the base of the plant and slender stalks of tiny fringed urn-shaped green flowers that turn red. Evergreen where winters are mild, deciduous elsewhere. Used in shady, moist situations and in woodland gardens. Choice combined with ferns, columbine, and bleeding heart. Commonly known as fringecups.

Templetonia (tehm puhl toh′nee uh) *n.* A genus of 7 species of tender shrubs (Leguminosae). *T. retusa,* coralbush, grows to 10 feet, with rigid, leathery leaves or no leaves at all, and sparse red or occasionally, yellow butterfly-shaped flowers.

tendril *n.* In botany, a spirally coiling, threadlike organ that attaches itself to another body for the purpose of support, as in the peavine, grapevine, or Virginia creeper. Morphologically, a tendril may be a modified stem, branch, stipule, or leaf.

tendriled *a.* Also known as tendrilled.

tension *n.* A term related to soil moisture and the equivalent negative pressure of suction of water in the soil.

tent caterpillar *n.* A moth larva that forms huge silken webs in the branches of trees and shrubs. It feeds on the foliage of many trees and shrubs, including fruit trees, often defoliating the plant. Control by handpicking and destroying webs with strong spray from a hose, *Bacillus thuringiensis,* releasing trichogramma wasps, or traditional insecticides.

tepal (tee′puhl) *n.* In botany, when the calyx and corolla are not clearly differentiated, as in tulips and begonias, the proper name for one of the petallike parts is tepal.

tepee (tee′pee) *n.* A cone shaped structure consisting of 3 or more stakes lashed together near the apex used to grow vine crops such as peas, beans, and cucumbers.

Tephrosia (teh froh′zhee uh) *n.* A genus of 300 to 400 species of mostly subtropical and tropical perennials and shrubs (Leguminosae), some species native to the United States. *T. virginiana* is a hardy perennial, native from Maine to Mexico, grows to 2 feet, with silky white new growth, alternate leaves divided into oval leaflets, silky beneath, and dense spikes of yellow and pink-purple flowers. Commonly known as hoary pea.

Tephrosia virginiana
(hoary pea)

terete (tuh reet′) *a.* Circular in cross section; cylindrical but usually tapering at both ends, as a terete seedpod.

terminal *a.* In botany, growing at the tip of a branch or stem.

Terminalia (tuhr muh nay′lee uh) *n.* A genus of 200 species of tall tropical trees (Combretaceae), some species deciduous in the dry or cool season.

They grow from 80 to 100 feet, with simple leaves crowded towards the ends of the branches and spikes of blue, yellow, red, green, white, or gray bell-shaped flowers. Used in tropical gardens and along frost-free seashores.

ternate (tuhr′nayt) *a.* In botany, arranged in 3s; used especially of a compound leaf with 3 leaflets, or of leaves whorled in 3s. If the 3 divisions of a ternate leaf are subdivided into 3 leaflets each, the leaf is biternate, and a still further subdivision produces a triternate leaf.

ternate leaves

ternatisect (tuhr nat′uh sehkt) *a.* In botany, cut into 3 lobes or partial divisions.

Ternstroemia (tuhrn stree′mee uh) *n.* A genus of 85 species of tropical broadleaf evergreen shrubs and trees (Theaceae). *T. gymnanthera* is a slow-growing tender evergreen shrub that takes a long time to reach 6 feet and as wide. It has red-stalked glossy, leathery, oval leaves that are bronzy-red when new, deep green at maturity, and bronzy-green or purplish red depending on season and situation. It has creamy-yellow fragrant flowers. Used as an informal hedge, near swimming pools, as a speciman shrub, and as a tub plant.

terrace *n.* 1. A ridge constructed across sloping soil on the contour or at a slight angle to the contour that intercepts and retards surplus runoff for infiltration into the soil. All excess water may be forced to flow slowly into prepared outlets. 2. A raised level faced with masonry or turf; an elevated flat space: as, a garden terrace; also, a natural formation of the ground resembling such a terrace.

terracotta *n.* A brownish-orange earthenware used to make pots.

terracotta hose pot *n.* A clay container in which a garden hose may be stored and hidden.

terrarium *n., pl.* **terrariums,** or **terraria.** An enclosed environment for land animals; a place where such animals are kept alive for study or observation.

tessellated (tehs'uh layt ehd) *a.* In botany, checkered. Also tesselate.

testa (tehst'uh) *n.; pl.,* **testae.** In botany, the hard outer coating of a seed; episperm.

tetra- *comb. form* Signifying 4; having 4, as in tetrachord, tetragon, tetramerous, tetrapetalous, tetraspermous.

tetradynamous (teh truh digh'nuh muhs) *a.* Having 6 stamens, 4 of which are long, as in the *Cruciferae.*

Tetragonia (teh truh goh'nee uh) *n.* A genus of 50 species of tender perennials and small shrubs (Tetragoniaceae). They grow from 2 to 10 feet, depending on the species, with alternate, entire, sometimes fleshy leaves, and tiny yellow flowers. *Tetragonia tetragonioides,* New Zealand spinach, has edible fleshy leaves used as a summer substitute for spinach. It has naturalized widely and tolerates heat, seashore conditions, or cool, humid conditions. It is perennial in mild-winter climates, grown as an annual elsewhere.

tetragynous (teh truh jigh'nuhs) *a.* Having 4 pistils or carpels.

tetramerous (teh tram'uh ruhs) *a.* In botany, having the parts in sets or multiples of 4s; frequently written 4-merous.

tetrandrous (teh tran'druhs) *a.* In botany, having 4 stamens.

Tetrapanax (teh truh'pah naks) *n.* A genus of 1 species, *T. papyriferus,* a fast-growing tropical evergreen shrub (Araliaceae). It grows to 10 to 15 feet, with big, bold, deeply lobed leaves, fuzzy white beneath, and big, branched clusters of creamy-white December-blooming flowers. The white fuzz can irritate eyes and skin. Used in mild-winter climates in moist soils. Makes a bold silhouette against walls, striking on patios or near pools. Commonly known as rice paper plant.

tetterwort *n.* A common name for *Chelidonium majus,* the common celandine, which stands 4 feet tall, has deeply divided leaves, and clusters of yellow flowers. (See **Chelidonium.**) Also a common name for *Sanguinaria canadensis,* a hardy perennial

native to eastern North America that grows to 6 inches, with a single, rounded, irregularly lobed, gray leaf 11 inches across, and and large white flowers in early spring. Commonly known as bloodroot or red puccoon because it has red sap. (See **Sanguinaria.**)

Teucrium (tyoo'kree uhm) *n.* A genus of 300 species of perennials and shrubs (Labiatae), some species native to the United States. They grow from 8 inches to 8 feet, depending on species, with opposite leaves and showy blue, red, lilac, pink, white, yellow, or cream bell-shaped or tubular flowers in whorls on the flower stalk. Used as edging, for dwarf hedges, massed, or in rock gardens. They are traditional in herb gardens and cottage gardens. Some species attract bees. They thrive in sun, heat, and poor rocky soils; drought tolerant once established. Commonly known as germander.

Teucrium
(germander)

Texas plume *n.* A common name for *Ipomopsis rubra,* a biennial or short-lived tender perennial. It is a striking tall, slender plant that grows to 6 feet, with finely divided, threadlike leaves and clusters of tubular flowers that are scarlet on the outside and yellow on the inside. Most effective massed at the back of the border. Drought tolerant once established. Also known as standing cypress.

Texas root rot *n.* A soil-borne disease common in high heat and alkaline soils of the Southwest. It kills plant roots, causing wilting and, possibly, death. Control by adding soil sulfur to decrease pH and adding abundant organic matter to the soil when planting.

textural class *n.* The type or classification of soil material determined by the proportion of sand, silt, and clay in its makeup.

thalamus (thal'uh muhs) *n.* In botany, a receptacle; the end of the flower stalk where the flowers are carried, which is often slightly enlarged.

thale cress *n.* A common name for *Arabidopsis thaliana*, a annual that grows to 18 inches, with leaves in basal rosettes and spikes of tiny white flowers. It has naturalized in the United States. Also known as mouse-ear cress.

Thalia (thay'lee uhh) *n.* A genus of 7 species of tender and tropical water plants (Marantaceae). They have long-stemmed, basal leaves and spikes of purple flowers. Used in wet soils or in shallow water.

Thalictrum (thuh lihk'truhm) *n.* A genus of 100 species of hardy, graceful, airy perennials (Ranunculaceae), some species native to North America. They grow from 5 inches to 8 feet, depending on the species, with basal, 3-part leaves resembling columbine or maidenhair, and delicate clusters or spikes of small white, yellow, purple, rose, or mauve flowers. Useful in moist soils, excellent along streams or pools. Grown in woodland gardens. Commonly known as meadow rue.

thalliform (thal'uh form) *a.* In botany, having the form of a thallus.

thalloid (tha'loid) *a.* In botany, of, resembling, or consisting of a thallus. Also thallose.

thallus (tha'luhs) *n.* In botany, the body of mosses, lichens, algae, and fungi, plants without leaves, roots, or stems.

thatch palm *n.* A common name for tropical and subtropical palms of the genera *Sabal* and *Thrinax*. *Thrinax* is not widely grown as an ornamental in the United States. Some species of *Sabal* (palmetto) are native to the southeastern and southwestern United States. *S. palmetto*, the cabbage palm, is slow-growing to 20 feet, with large, fan-shaped leaves and huge clusters of flowers that appear at maturity. Also known as thatch tree.

Theaceae (thee ay'see ee) *n. pl.* A family of 25 genera of mostly subtropical and tropical shrubs and trees. The ornamental genera include *Camellia*, *Cleyera, Eurya, Franklinia* (Franklin tree), *Gordonia, Stewartia,* and *Ternstroemia.* Commonly known as the tea family.

theca (thee'kuh) *n.* In botany, a case or sac; in a general sense, the same as capsule.

Thelesperma (thuh luh spuhr'muh) *n.* A genus of 12 species of annuals, biennials, and perennials (Compositae), many native to western North America. *T. burridgeanum* is a Texan annual that grows to 18 inches with finely divided leaves 4-inches long, and orange-yellow or red daisylike flowers.

Thelocactus (thuh loh kahk'tuhs) *n.* A genus of 20 species of small, rounded, spiny cacti (Cactaceae) native to the southwestern United States. *T. bicolor,* glory-of-Texas, is a stubby, chubby cactus 8 inches high and 3 inches thick. It has a profusion of curved spines 1¼ inches long and large purple bell-shaped flowers that close at night. Grown in pots by collectors.

Thelypteris (thuh lihp ter'uhs) *n.* A genus of 500 species of ferns (Polypodiaceae), mostly tropical, but some native to North America. They grow from 9 inches to 6 feet, depending on the species, with fronds divided into leaflets, narrow at the base, and sometimes hairy. (See **fern, New York**.)

Theobroma (thee uh broh'muh) *n.* A genus of 20 species of tropical trees (Byttneriaceae) native to lowland tropical America; chocolate. *T. cacao* is a broadleaf evergreen tree that grows to 25 feet or more, with large, leathery, oval leaves, small, yellow 5-petaled flowers borne on the trunk and branches, and a large, woody capsule 12 inches long, that contains seeds that are made into chocolate. Commonly known as cacao.

Theophrastaceae (thee uh fras tay'see ee) *n.* A family of 4 genera and 60 species of tropical broadleaf evergreen shrubs and trees native to tropical America and the Hawaiian Islands. The ornamental genus is *Jacquinia.* Commonly known as the theophrasta family. (See **Jacquinia**.)

thermometer *n.* An instrument used to measure temperature. (See also **maximum-minimum thermometer**.)

Thermopsis (thuhr mahp'sehs) *n.* A genus of 20 species of bushy perennials (Leguminosae), some species native to North America. They grow from 1 to 5 feet, with fan-shaped leaves divided into 3 oval leaflets and spikes of yellow pealike flowers. *T. caroliniana* is useful in the hot, muggy summers of the southeast, and hardy elsewhere. Commonly known as false lupine.

thermotropic (thuhr moh trahp′ihk) *a*. In botany, plant movement that is determined by temperature.

Thespesia (the spee′zhee uh) *n*. A genus of 15 species of tropical shrubs and trees (Malvaceae). They grow from 8 to 60 feet, depending on the species, with simple or lobed leaves and large, cup-shaped, red or red-purple flowers with a dark purple center.

Thespesia

Thevetia (theh vee′shee uh) *n*. A genus of 8 species of tender to tropical shrubs and trees (Apocynaceae), native to the Americas. *T. thevetioides*, giant thevetia, grows to 15 feet, with long, narrow dark green leaves and clusters of large, brilliant yellow pinwheel-shaped flowers 4 inches across. *T. peruviana* is also known as yellow oleander (see **yellow oleander**). All parts of both plants are poisonous. They tolerate heat and full sun, but not wind, drought, or frost. Used for background planting, as a screen or hedge.

thimbleberry *n*. A raspberry.

thimbleflower *n*. A common name for *Prunella vulgaris* (see **Prunella** and **hookweed**) and *Digitalis purpurea* (see **Digitalis** and **foxglove**). Blue thimbleflower is a common name for *Gilia capitata,* an annual native to western North America that grows from 8 to 30 inches, with finely cut leaves and pincushionlike blue flowers with blue pollen. (See **Gilia**). Used in borders or in wild gardens.

thimbleweed *n*. A common name for *Anemone cylindrica* (long-headed anemone) and *A. riparia,* both hardy perennial wildflowers native to North America. They grow from 1 to 3 feet, with lobed basal leaves and tall stalks with several white flowers. Used in wild gardens, woodland gardens, or in moist situations.

thinning shears *n*. Small shears with narrow, pointed blades for cutting flowers, dead-heading, and trimming.

Thiodan (thigh′oh dan) *n*. (See **endosulfan**.)

thistle *n*. A common name for prickly spiny plants of several genera most frequently *Cirsium, Onopordum,* and *Carduus*. Thistles often have bold, striking foliage and showy flowers, however their prickliness and propensity to self-sow have caused most of them to be considered weeds rather than ornamentals. (See **Cirsium,** and **Onopordum**.)

thistle, blessed *n*. A common name for *Cnicus benedictus,* a branching, thistlelike annual. Also known as cursed thistle. (See **Cnicus**.)

thistle, bull *n*. A common name for *Cirsium vulgare,* a tall biennial that grows to 5 feet, with prickly leaves and stems and large rose-purple flowers. Most commonly seen as a roadside weed; it has naturalized in North America. Also known as common thistle and spear thistle.

thistle, Canada *n*. A common name for *Cirsium arvense,* a prickly perennial that grows to 3 feet, with pink-purple flowers. It is a noxious weed that has naturalized in North America.

Canada thistle

thistle, Carline *n*. A common name for *Carlina acanthifolia,* a stemless perennial with prickly, divided leaves in a basal rosette and yellow or white flowers. Also known as acanthus-leaved thistle.

thistle, cotton *n.* A common name for *Onopordum Acanthium*, a hardy self-sowing perennial that grows to 9 feet, with spiny, lobed leaves and red-purple or white flowers. It has naturalized in parts of North America. Also known as Scotch thistle, silver thistle, oat thistle, and Argentine thistle.

thistle, fishbone *n.* A common name for *Cirsium diacantha*, a biennial that grows to 3 feet, with long, narrow, toothed leaves with 2 stiff, yellow spines on each tooth and purple flowers.

thistle, fuller's *n.* A common name for *Dipsaca sativus*, a prickly biennial. Also known as fuller's teasel. (See **teasel**.)

thistle, globe *n.* A common name for *Echinops*, a genus of biennials and hardy perennials that have divided leaves with prickly edges and rounded this-tlelike blue or white flowers. *E. exaltata* is a drought-tolerant, rugged-looking perennial that grows to 5 feet, with prickly, pointy gray-green leaves and steel-blue round flowerheads. Effective in clumps, beds and borders.

thistle, golden *n.* A common name for *Scolymus hispanicus*, a tall, prickly biennial that grows to 4 feet, with prickly stems and leaves and yellow this-tlelike flowers. Occasionally grown for its edible taproot. Also known as Spanish oyster plant.

thistle, holy *n.* A common name for *Silybum marianum*, a self-sowing spiny annual or biennial that has naturalized in the United States. It grows to 4 feet, with spiny-tipped leaves 2½ feet long and as much as 12 inches wide and purple flowers. Also known as blessed thistle, milk thistle, Our Lady's thistle, and St. Mary's thistle.

thistle, horse *n.* A common name for *Lactuca Serriola*, a biennial or winter annual, generally considered a weed. It grows to 5 feet, with oval, spiny leaves and clusters of yellow flowers. Also known as prickly lettuce.

thistle, melancholy *n.* A common name for *Cirsium heterophyllum*, a hardy perennial that grows to 4 feet, with narrow, oval leaves, felty beneath, edged by soft prickles and red-purple or white flowers 2 inches across.

thistle, milk *n.* A common name for *Silybum marianum*, a self-sowing spiny annual or biennial that has naturalized in the United States. Also known as blessed thistle, St. Mary's thistle, and holy thistle. (See **thistle, holy**.)

thistle, mountain *n.* A common name for *Acanthus montanus*, a tropical perennial that grows to 6 feet, with glossy, dark green, deeply cut, prickly tipped leaves and tall spikes of rose or red flowers. Grown for its large attractive leaves in frost-free climates. Also known as bear's-breech and mountain acanthus.

thistle, mountain sow *n.* A common name for *Lactuca alpina*, a very hardy stout, erect perennial that grows to 6 feet, with bristly lower stems, shiny, divided leaves and clusters of pale blue flowers.

thistle, oat *n.* A common name for *Onopordum acanthium*, a hardy self-sowing perennial that grows to 9 feet, with spiny, lobed leaves and red-purple or white flowers. (See **thistle, cotton**.)

thistle, Our Lady's *n.* A common name for *Silybum marianum*, a self-sowing spiny annual or biennial that has naturalized in the United States. Also known as blessed thistle, milk thistle, St. Mary's thistle, and holy thistle. (See **thistle, holy**.)

thistle, plume *n.* A common name for *Cirsium*, a genus of tall, spiny perennials. Most are noxious weeds; a few are grown ornamentally for their bold effect and large purple flowers. Also known as thistle.

thistle, plumeless *n.* A common name for *Carduus*, a genus of plants not grown in the United States.

thistle, saffron (saf'ruhn) *n.* A common name for *Carthamus tinctorius*, an annual that grows to 3 feet, with spiny-toothed leaves and rounded orange-yellow flowers that bloom in autumn. Used as cut flowers or dried for everlasting arrangements. Flowers can be used to give a saffronlike color and flavor to food. Also known as safflower, false saffron, and bastard saffron.

thistle, spear *n.* A common name for *Cirsium vulgare*, a tall biennial to 5 feet, with prickly leaves and stems and large rose-purple flowers. Most commonly seen as a roadside weed. Also known as bull thistle. (See **thistle, bull**.)

thistle, Scotch *n*. A common name for *Onopordum Acanthium*, a hardy self-sowing perennial that grows to 9 feet, with spiny, lobed leaves and red-purple or white flowers. Also known as cotton thistle. (See **thistle, cotton**.)

thistle, silver *n*. A common name for *Onopordum Acanthium*, a hardy self-sowing perennial that grows to 9 feet, with spiny, lobed leaves and red-purple or white flowers. Also known as cotton thistle. (See **thistle, cotton**.)

thistle, small globe *n*. A common name for *Echinops ritro*, a hardy perennial. It grows to 2 feet, with long, narrow, spiny-toothed leaves and round bright blue flowers. Grown in large clumps or in borders.

thistle, stemless *n*. A common name for *Carlina acaulis*, a low-growing hardy perennial. It has spiny-tipped leaves in a basal rosette and large white or red flowers 2 to 5 inches across.

thistle, thornless *n*. A common name for *Centaurea americana*, a tall annual that grows to 6 feet, with large, entire leaves 4 inches across, and rose-colored flowers. It is native to the central and southwestern United States south to Mexico. It is a good cut flower and dries well for everlasting arrangements. Also known as basket flower.

thistle, white *n*. A common name for a *Atroplex lentiformis*, a densely branched tender shrub native to alkaline deserts of the western United States. Also known as lens-scale and quail bush. (See **quail bush**.)

thorn *n*. 1. A sharp, rigid, woody, spine, usually on a plant branch or stem. 2. A common name for *Crataegus*, a genus of hardy, enthusiastically thorny, shrubs and small trees (Rosaceae), many native to North America. Also known as hawthorn, thornapple, and red haw.

thornbush *n*. A common name for any spiny shrub, such as *Crataegus*.

thorn, cockspur *n*. A common name for *Crataegus crus-galli*, a hardy, thorny, widespreading shrub or small tree, native to eastern North America, that grows to 30 feet, with 3-inch-long thorns, shiny, leathery toothed rounded oval leaves that turn red or yellow in autumn. It has clusters of white flowers that attract bees and red berries that attract birds. Also known as cockspur.

thorn, evergreen *n*. A common name for *Crataegus laevigata*, a thorny shrub or small tree, much used in hedges. (See **hawthorn** and **Crataegus**.)

thorn, Glastonbury *n*. A common name for *Crataegus monogyna* 'Biflora', a hardy deciduous tree that grows to 30 feet, with oval lobed leaves, gray felty beneath, masses of white flowers that bloom in mild climates during mid-winter and spring, and small bright red berries. Used as dense, narrow screen.

thorn, lily *n*. A common name for *Catesbaea spinosa*, a spiny subtropical shrub native to Cuba. It grows to 15 feet, with 1-inch-long spines, small, oval, pointed leaves and creamy white funnel-shaped flowers 6 inches long. Grown in frost-free gardens as a flowering shrub.

thorn, pear *n*. A common name for *Crataegus calpodendron*, a hardy, deciduous thorny shrub or small tree native to eastern North America. Also known as blackthorn.

thorn, sallow *n*. A common name for *Hippophae rhamnoides*, a very hardy deciduous thorny shrub or small tree. It grows to 30 feet, with alternate, willowlike leaves, inconspicuous yellow flowers, and bright yellow-orange edible berries that persist all winter. Male trees must be present for female trees to set fruit.

thorn sleeves *n*. Protective sleeves extending from wrist to elbow or above to prevent scratched arms or snagged clothing when pruning roses or picking berries.

thorn, Washington *n*. A common name for *Crataegus phaenopyrum*, a light, airy, hardy thorny deciduous small tree. It grows to 25 feet, with glossy small maplelike leaves that turn a beautiful orange and red in fall. It has broad clusters of small white flowers in late spring or early summer, and shiny red fruit that hangs on through winter. This is the most graceful and delicate of the hawthorns, widely used as a street or lawn tree.

washington thorn
a leaf *b* berries

thorn, white *n.* A common name for *Crataegus laevigata,* a thorny shrub or small tree, much used in hedges (see **hawthorn** and **Crataegus**). Also a common name for *Crataegus biltmoriana,* a very hardy stout, often thorny, shrub or tree native to the eastern United States that grows to 25 feet, with oval, lobed leaves, clusters of white flowers, and red berries. Also a common name for *Ceanothus incanus,* a tender spiny evergreen shrub native to California that grows to 12 feet, with oval, pointed leaves and clusters of white flowers.

thoroughwax *n.* A common name for *Bupleurum,* a genus of perennials and shrubs. The species grow from 16 inches to 6 feet, with simple, entire leaves and clusters of yellow or purple flowers. Used most often in dry soils in warm climates.

thoroughwort *n.* A common name for *Eupatorium,* also known as boneset. (See **boneset**.)

threadflower *n.* A common name for *Nematanthus,* a genus of South American epiphytic shrubs. (See **Nematanthus**.)

threadleaved *a.* Having long slender, threadlike leaves; filiform.

threadleaved sundew *n.* A common name for *Drosera filiformis,* a tender carnivorous perennial native to the southeastern United States. It grows to 9 inches, with threadlike leaves covered with purple hairs and clusters of 4 to 16 purple 5-petaled flowers. The hairs on the leaves trap and digest small insects unfortunate enough to land on them.

Occasionally grown in bog gardens or as a novelty houseplant. Also known as dewthread.

three-leaved *a.* In botany, having 3 leaves or leaflets, as many species of *Trifolium*; trifoliate or trifoliolate.

three-leaved ivy *n.* A common name for *Rhus toxicodendron,* also known as poison ivy and poison oak. (See **Rhus** and **poison oak**.)

three-men-in-a-boat *n.* A common name for *Rhoeo spathaceae,* a low-growing subtropical succulent perennial. Also known as purple-leaved spiderwort, oyster plant, Moses-on-a-raft, Moses-in-a-boat, Moses-in-the-cradle, Moses-in-the-bulrushes, man-in-a-boat, two-men-in-a-boat, three-men-in-a-boat, and boat lily. (See **lily, boat**.)

three prong weeder *n.* A hoe-shaped implement having 3 claw-shaped tines used to grab and pull weeds.

thrift *n.* A common name for *Armeria,* a genus of about 35 subspecies of low-growing, tufted, widely adapted, evergreen perennials. (See **Armeria**.)

thrift, common *n.* A common name for a *Armeria maritima,* a hardy low-growing, tufted, widely adapted, evergreen perennial with stiff, narrow leaves and long-blooming white-to-rose-pink flowers. (See **Armeria**.)

thrift, lavender *n.* A common name for *Limonium,* a genus of fairly hardy, mostly perennial, low-growing flowers. Also known as sea lavender, marsh rosemary, and statice. (See **Limonium**.)

thrift, prickly *n.* A common name for *Acantholimon,* a genus of hardy, tufted evergreen perennials with leaves in basal rosettes, and white, pink, or purple flowers either single or in clusters. (See **Acantholimon**.)

thrip (thrihp) *n.* A tiny (hard to see with the naked eye), fast-moving insect that scraps fruit, leaf, and flower tissue and feeds on the resulting plant juices. It causes misshapened new growth and flower buds and scarred fruit. Particularly troublesome on roses and gladiolus. It is a favorite food of many predaceous insects but can also be controlled with insecticidal soaps, botanicals, and traditional insecticides.

throat *n*. In botany, the mouth or orifice of a co-rolla or calyx, being the place at which the tube joins or expands into the limb.

throat of the corollas of various flowers

throatwort *n*. A common name for *Trachelium,* a genus of tender perennials, sometimes grown as annuals (Campanulaceae). *T. caeruleum* grows from 2 to 4 feet, with narrow, sharply toothed, alternate, simple, dark green leaves and tall stalks topped with broad, dome-shaped clusters of blue-violet flowers. A tough, undemanding plant used in beds and borders, and a good cut flower. Also a common name for *Campanula trachelium,* a perennial that has naturalized in North America. It grows to 3 feet, with broad, oval, pointed basal leaves and leafy clusters of blue-purple flowers. Also known as nettle-leaved bellflower.

thrumwort *n*. A common name for *Amaranthus caudatus,* a large, vigorous, much-branched tropical annual that grows to 3 to 8 feet, with large leaves to 10 inches long and red flowers in drooping, tassel-like clusters. Also known as love-lies-bleeding and tassel flower. (See **Amaranthus** and **love-lies-bleeding**.)

thrumwort, great *n*. A common name for *Alisma plantago-aquatica,* a hardy bog plant native to North America that grows to 3 feet, with long-stemmed oval leaves and whorled clusters of white flowers with purple-tipped petals. Grown as a bog plant for its attractive foliage and many flowers. Also known as water plantain and mad-dog weed.

Thuja (thyoo´juh) *n*. A genus of 5 species of neat, symmetrical, hardy, evergreen coniferous shrubs and trees (Cupressaceae), some species native to North America. They grow from 35 to 200 feet, depending on the species, with flat, graceful sprays of needlelike leaves and small cones. There are a myriad of hybrids, many dwarf cultivars, and these range in color from deep green to golden yellow. Used as screens, hedges, specimen plants, and dwarf varieties are excellent in pots. Commonly

known as arborvitae. Sometimes spelled thuya. (See **arborvitae**.)

Thuja
(arborvitae)

Thujopsis (thyuh jahp´sehs) *n*. A genus of 1 species, *T. dolabrata,* (Cupressaceae), a slow-growing hardy pyramidal evergreen coniferous tree that tends to be shrubby in cultivation. It grows to 50 feet, often less, with staghornlike sprays of scalelike leaves and round, flat-topped cones with wedge-shaped scales. Grown as a specimen or as a container plant. Thrives in cool, humid summers. Commonly known as false arborvitae and Hiba arborvitae.

Thunbergia (thuhn buhr´jee uh) *n*. A genus of more than 100 species of tropical flowering perennial vines (Acanthaceae). They grow to 20 feet or more, with opposite leaves and showy blue, yellow, orange, or white flowers. Used in hanging-baskets, as indoor/outdoor plants, and as houseplants. Some are grown as annuals.

thunderflower *n*. A common name for *Silene alba,* an annual, biennial, or short-lived perennial that grows to 3 feet, with oval, hairy leaves and faintly fragrant white 5-petaled flowers that open in the evening. Used in borders, and on rock walls. Also known as white campion, white cockle, evening lychnis, and evening campion.

thunder plant *n*. A common name for *Sempervi-vum tectorum,* a perennial succulent with a rosette of very thick, fleshy leaves and slender stalks of small pink flowers. Also known as houseleek, common houseleek, hen and chickens, roof houseleek, and old-man-and-woman. (See **houseleek**.)

thyme (tighm) *n*. A plant of the genus *Thymus.* The common garden thyme is *T. vulgaris,* a bushy shrub from 6 to 10 inches high, with many stems and very small oval leaves. It is pungent and aromatic and is largely cultivated as a seasoning for soups, sauces, etc. The wild or creeping thyme, or mother-of-thyme, is *T. Serpyllum,* a less erect plant forming broad, dense tufts, similar to *T. vulgaris,* but less flavorful and rarely cultivated for culinary use. The lemon or lemon-scented thyme, *T. × citriodorus,* is a hybrid of *T. vulgaris,* used especially in its variegated varieties as border or rock-garden plants. A number of thyme varieties available at herb nurseries are mislabeled as other species, when they are simply varieties of 1 of these.

Wild thyme

Thymelaeaceae (thighm uh lay′see ee) *n. pl.* A family of 40 genera and 50 species of shrubs and trees. The best known genus *Daphne.* Commonly known as the mezereum family.

Thymus (thigh′muhs) *n*. A genus of 300 to 400 species of mostly tender low-growing aromatic perennial herbs (Labiatae). They have tiny, simple, entire, oval leaves and short spikes with white, rose pink, or palest lavender flowers in whorled clusters. Grown primarily as culinary herbs, their aromatic leaves used for flavoring. Essential in the herb garden, grown as small-scale ground covers, traditional in cottage gardens, and grown as kitchen windowsill plants. Commonly known as thyme.

thyrse (thuhrs) *n*. In botany, a flower cluster with a central spike that has side branches also clustered with flowers, such as horse chestnut and lilac. Also thyrsus.

thyrsiform (thuhrs′uh form) *a*. In botany, thyrse-shaped.

thyrsoid (thuhr′soid) *a*. In botany, resembling a thyrse.

Thysanocarpus (thigh suh noh kahr′puhs) *n*. A genus of 5 species of annual wildflowers (Cruciferae) native to Western North America. *T. curvipes* grows to 20 inches, with oval, entire leaves in basal rosettes, slender spikes of tiny white or purple flowers, and round, flattened, winged pods, the edges of which are fringed. Also called lacepod and fringepod.

ti (tee) *n*. A common name for *Cordyline terminalis,* a tropical treelike plant with a slender stem topped by a head of long, narrow, drooping leaves, and large clusters of small flowers. Used most often as a houseplant or in frost-free gardens. Also known as tree-of-kings, good-luck plant, ti palm, ti tree, and Hawaiian good-luck plant.

Tiarella (tee uh rehl′uh) *n*. A genus of 6 species of variably hardy spring-blooming perennials (Saxifragaceae) native to North America. They grow from 12 to 18 inches, with basal leaves either lobed or divided into 3 leaflets that color brilliantly in autumn and spikes of small white or red 5-petaled flowers. Used as in wild gardens or rock gardens. Commonly known as false mitrewort.

Tibouchina (tihb uh kigh′nuh) *n*. A genus of 350 species of open-branched tender shrubs and subshrubs (Melastomataceae) native to South America. *T. urvilleana* grows from 5 to 15 feet, with fuzzy, oval pointed strongly ribbed leaves often with red margins and large, showy deep-purple flowers with red stamens. Used as specimens, foundation plants, in shrub borders, and as a tubbed indoor/outdoor plants. *T. urvilleana* is commonly known as princess flower, lasiandra, glorybush, pleroma, and purple glory tree. *Tibouchina* is commonly known as glorybush.

tick bean *n*. A common name for *Vicia faba,* a tall annual bean. Also known as faba bean, horse bean, broad bean, Windsor bean, English bean, and European bean. (See **Vicia** and **horsebean**.)

tickseed *n.* A common name for *Coreopsis,* a genus of mostly herbaceous perennials, many quite hardy, the ornamental species of which are native to the Americas. *C. tinctoria* is an annual species that grows to 4 feet, with showy bronze, yellow, orange, maroon, or red daisylike flowers banded with contrasting colors and with purple-brown centers. *C. tinctoria* is also known as coreopsis and annual calliopsis.

tidy-tips *n.* A common name for *Layia platyglossa,* a low-growing annual that grows from 5 to 16 inches, with entire, toothed, or lobed leaves, and yellow daisylike flowers with white-tipped petals. Used in flower gardens as a bedding plant, or in containers.

tigella (teh jehl′uh) *n.* In botany, a short stem. Also tigelle.

tigellate (teh′jehl ayt) *a.* In botany, having a short stalk, such as that of a bean.

tigerflower *n.* A common name for the genus *Tigridia* (see **Tigridia**) and specifically, *T. pavonia. T. pavonia* is a tender bulb that grows to 2½ feet, with narrow, ribbed swordlike leaves and showy, triangular orange, red, pink, yellow, or white flowers with a spotted center cup. Used in clumps, in borders, or in pots. Also known as Mexican shell flower

Tigridia (tigh grihd′ee uh) *n.* A genus of 27 species of tender perennial bulbs (Iridaceae). *T. pavonia,* tiger flower, is the only species in cultivation. Commonly known as tiger flower, shell flower, and one-day lily. (See **tigerflower**.)

Tilia
a flower *b* fruit

Tilia (tihl′ee uh) *n.* A genus of 30 species of hardy deciduous trees (Tiliaceae), some species native to North America. They grow from 35 to 100 feet, depending on the species, with pairs of alternate, heart-shaped leaves and drooping clusters of fragrant, white flowers that attract bees. The species are hopelessly susceptible to aphids, whose honeydew blackens the leaves and drips stickily onto everything below. The search continues for a resistant hybrid. Also known as lime tree and linden.

Tiliaceae (tihl ee ay′see ee) *n. pl.* A family of 50 genera of perennials (rarely) and flowering shrubs and trees. The ornamental genera include *Belotia, Grewia, Sparmannia,* and *Tilia.*

tiliaceous (tihl ee ay′shuhs) *a.* Belonging to the family *Tiliaceae.*

tillage *n.* The operation, practice, or art of tilling land, or preparing it for seed, and keeping the ground free from weeds that might impede the growth of crops; cultivation; culture; husbandry. Tillage includes manuring, plowing, harrowing, and rolling land, or whatever is done to bring it to a proper state to receive the seed, and the operations of plowing, harrowing, and hoeing the ground to destroy weeds and loosen the soil after it is planted.

Tillandsia (teh lahnd′zee uh) *n.* A genus of 374 species of subtropical and tropical epiphytic plants (Bromeliaceae) native to the Americas. They grow from 4 inches to 5 feet, depending on the species, with leaves in crowded basal rosettes and spikes, heads, or clusters of blue, green, purple, red, orange, or white flowers. Used most often as houseplants or greenhouse specimens, outdoors in subtropical gardens, or in pots or on bark slabs as indoor/outdoor plants.

tiller *n.* A hand or machine powered implement having a tined wheel or wheels used for plowing, cultivating, and mixing soil.

tilth *n.* The physical condition of a soil in respect to its fitness to support the growth of a specific type of plant.

tinker's root *n.* A common name for *Triosteum perfoliatum,* a hardy North American perennial wildflower that grows to 4 feet, with large oval leaves, purple tubular flowers, and yellow-orange fruit. Also known as wild coffee and tinker's weed.

Tipuana (tihp oo an'uh) *n*. A genus of 1 species, *T. tipu*, a fast-growing tender deciduous or semi-evergreen tree (Leguminosae). They grow from 35 to 50 feet, with leaves divided into many small light green leaflets, clusters of apricot to yellow sweet-pea shaped flowers and small pods. Used as a shade tree, lawn tree, park tree, and street tree. Flowers thrive best when they are away from coastal areas. Commonly known as tipu tree, rosewood, and pride-of-Bolivia.

Tipularia (tihp yuh lah'ree uh) *n*. A genus of 6 species of hardy terrestrial orchids (Orchidaceae), some species native to North America. *T. discolor,* native to the eastern United States, grows to 2 feet, with slender-stemmed heart-shaped dull green leaves with purple blotches and spikes of nodding green, yellow, rust-bronze, purple flowers. Used in shady, woodland gardens. *T. discolor* is commonly known as cranefly orchid, crippled-cranefly, mottled cranefly, and elfin-spur.

Tipularia discolor
(cranefly orchid)
1 flower stalk 2 root and leaf

tissue culture *n*. A means of asexual propagation used by commercial growers to produce clones of a particular plant in large quantities. It produces marketable plants much faster than growing them from seed. Meristem cells are grown in nutrient solutions in laboratory flasks until they have recognizable leaves and roots. They are then transplanted into a suitable potting medium. The process is much used in commercial orchid growing, and is sometimes called meristem culture.

Tithonia (teh thoh'nee uh) *n*. A genus of 10 species of tropical and subtropical annuals, perennials, and shrubs (Compositae) native to Mexico and Central America. *T. rotundifolia* is a husky, gaudy robust annual that grows to 6 feet, with velvety green oval leaves and large spectacular 3- to 4-inch flowers with orange petals and yellow centers. Used in the back of the border. Tolerates drought and heat; a good choice for desert gardens. Commonly known as Mexican sunflower.

toad *n*. A small, tailless amphibian desirable in gardens for controlling insects.

toadflax *n*. A common name for *Linaria*, a genus of tender annuals and perennials. Also known as spurred snapdragon. (See **Linaria**.)

common toadflax

toadflax, ivy-leaved *n*. A common name *Cymbalaria muralis,* a creeping perennial ground cover that has small, rounded, scalloped leaves and tiny snapdragonlike blue flowers. Used as a small-scale ground covers on stone walls or in hanging-baskets. Also known as Kenilworth ivy, coliseum ivy, and pennywort. See **Cymbalaria.**

toadstool *n*. 1. A common name for any fungus having a fruiting body with an umbrella-shaped cap. 2. An inedible mushroom, especially a poisonous one.

tobacco *n*. A common name for the genus *Nicotiana,* specifically *N. rustica* (wild tobacco) and *N. tabaccum* (cultivated tobacco). *Nicotiana* is a genus of annual or tender perennials, rarely shrubs, with some species native to the warm regions of the Americas. *N. rustica,* wild tobacco, is used to proe the natural insecticide nicotine. *N. tabaccum,* tivated tobacco, is grown to make cigarettes and gars.

tobira (tuh bigh'ruh) *n.* A common name for *Pittosporum tobira,* an evergreen shrub with dense, leathery, dark green leaves and clusters of small creamy-white fragrant flowers, with a fragrance like orange blossoms. Also known as mock orange and Japanese pittosporum. (See **Japanese pittosporum.**)

Toddalia (toh dah'lee uh) *n.* A genus of 1 species, *T. asiatica,* a tropical broadleaf evergreen trailing shrub (Rutaceae). It has prickly stems, with 3-part leaves, clusters of white 5-petaled flowers and fleshy, orange, fruit.

toddy palm *n.* A common name for any of several palms used to make wine, including *Caryota urens,* also known as kittul. (See **kittul.**)

Tofieldia (tuh feel'dee uh) *n.* A genus of 14 species of rhizomatous perennials (Liliaceae), some species native to the Americas. They grow from 6 to 20 inches, with basal grasslike leaves and white, yellow, or brown flowers. Used in bog gardens with moist, acid soils. Commonly known as false asphodel.

Tolmiea (tohl mee'uh) *n.* A genus of 1 species, *T. Menziesii,* a tender perennial (Saxifragaceae) native to western North America. They grow in attractive leafy clumps with soft furry, heart-shaped, shallowly lobed basal leaves. New plantlets appear on the leaves where the leaf stalk and leaf meet. Used in woodland gardens, as a small-scale ground cover in shady locations, and most often as a houseplant. Commonly known as piggyback plant, thousand-mothers, and youth-on-age.

Tolpis (tohl'puhs) *n.* A genus of 20 species of flowers (Compositae). They grow to 2½ feet, with mostly basal, toothed leaves and sulfur-yellow flowers that are reddish-brown inside.

tomato *n.* The fruit of a garden vegetable, *Lycopersicon Lycopersicum,* widely cultivated for its juicy red fruit in temperate as well as tropical climates. The stem, which is ordinarily weak and reclining, much branched and becoming 4 feet long and is often staked to keep it upright. The fruit is a berry, 2-celled in the Italian (plum) varieties and many-celled in the slicing varieties. A single pear-shaped form exists. In 1 very distinct variety, *cerasiforme,* the cherry tomato, the cherry-sized fruit is borne in long clusters. The color is commonly some tint of red, sometimes yellow. The tomato is of a soft, pulpy texture and has a slightly acid flavor. It is nutritious and rich in vitamin C.

tomato cage *n.* A device, usually of galvanized wire, used to contain and hold tomato vines upright. Also called tomato support.

tomato early blight *n.* A fungal disease common to tomatoes and potatoes that causes irregular circular spots or lesions on leaves, stems, and fruit. The spots often have a bull's-eye pattern of concentric rings. Common when dew is heavy or with overhead watering. To control, avoid overhead watering, keep plants growing vigorously, rotate crops, or spray with liquid copper.

tomato hornworm *n.* A large (up to 5 inches long), bright green moth larva with a hornlike hook at 1 end. It feeds on the leaves and fruit of tomatoes and other vegetables, including eggplant, potatoes, and peppers and can quickly defoliate portions of the plant and heavily scar the fruit. To control, handpick the worms (look for black droppings and eaten leaves), plant under row covers, release trichogramma wasps, or spray with *Bacillus thuringiensis* or traditional insecticides.

tomentose (tuh mehn'tohs) *a.* In botany, covered with densely matted woolly hairs. Also known as tomentous.

tomato support *n.* (See **tomato cage.**)

tomentum (tuh mehn'tuhm) *n.* In botany, a covering composed of short, densely matted, woolly hairs.

tongue fern *n.* A common name for *Pyrrosia lingua,* a tropical fern. It has dense clusters of broad, undivided, lance-shaped fronds that grow to 15 inches long. The fronds are felty brown on the underside. Used in pots and hanging-baskets or as a small-scale ground cover. Also known as Japanese felt fern.

tongue grass *n.* A common name for *Lepidium,* a genus of annuals, perennials, and subshrubs. (See **Lepidium.**)

tongueleaf *n.* A common name for *Glottiphyllum,* a genus of free-flowering dwarf, perennial succulents. (See **Glottiphyllum.**)

tool rack *n.* Any of several devices used to organize and hold garden tools.

tools *n.* Any of numerous implements such as shovels, rakes, and sprayers, either hand or machine powered, that are useful for working in a garden; garden tools.

tool sharpener *n.* A beveled grinding wheel that attaches to an electric drill. Variously shaped tool sharpeners are used to sharpen hoes, spades, edgers, weeders, etc. (See **sharpening stone.**)

toon *n.* A common name for *Cedrela Toona,* a subtropical tree that grows to 70 feet, with leaves divided into narrow, oval pointed leaflets and clusters of fragrant white flowers. Used in frost-free gardens.

toon branch with flowers

toothache tree *n.* A common name for *Zanthoxylum americana,* a very hardy, spiny, deciduous, aromatic shrub or tree, native to North America from Quebec to Florida. It grows to 25 feet, with large leaves divided into oval leaflets and clusters of green-yellow flowers that appear before the leaves. Also known as northern prickly ash.

toothwort *n.* A common name for *Dentaria,* a genus of perennial wildflowers with scaly creeping or tuberous roots, deeply cut leaves, and large, white or light purple flowers. Many species are native to North America. Used in rock gardens, wild gardens, or woodland gardens. Also known as pepperroot.

top dressing *n.* The application of fertilizer, compost, manure, or other soil amendment to the soil's surface.

topiary *a.* In gardening, clipped or cut into ornamental shapes; also, of or pertaining to such trimming. Topiary work is the clipping and trimming of trees and shrubs into regular or fantastic shapes.

topography *n.* The shape of the ground's surface like hills, valleys, plains, and slopes.

top soil *n.* A term for a presumed fertile soil. 2. The surface plow layer of soil; 3. Upper soil to 3 feet deep; 4. The A-horizon or surface soil; 5. The surface or upper part of the soil.

torchwort *n.* A common name for *Verbascum Thapsis,* a biennial roadside weed. (See **Verbascum.**)

Torenia (tuh ree′nee uh) *n.* A genus of 40 species of low-growing annuals and perennials (Scrophulariaceae). *T. fournieri,* blue wings or wishbone flower, grows to 12 inches, with toothed leaves and light blue flowers with dark blue markings and a bright yellow throat. Used in beds, pots and windowboxes or as edging for a border. Commonly known as wishbone flower.

tormentil (tawr′muhn tihl) *n.* A common name for *Potentilla,* a genus of mostly hardy low-growing annuals, perennials, and a few shrubs. They have fan-shaped or fernlike leaves and yellow, white, or red 5-petaled flowers. Used in borders, in rock gardens, and as small-scale ground covers. Also known as cinquefoil and five-finger.

tormentil

tornillo (tawr nee′yoh) *n.* A common name for *Prosopis pubescens,* a tender shrub or small tree native to the southwestern United States and north-western Mexico. It grows from 6 to 32 feet, with leaves divided into tiny oval downy leaflets, spikes of yellow flowers that attract bees, and a tightly twisted pod. A tough, adaptable plant, useful in desert gardens. Also known as screwbean.

torose (toh′rohs) *a.* Knobbed.

Torreya (tawr′ee uh) *n.* A genus of 6 species of slow-growing, open, marginally hardy shrubs and trees (Taxodiaceae), some species native to the United States. They grow from 15 to 75 feet, depending on the species, with short, needlelike leaves and fleshy purple fruit.

Torreya
1 branch with fruit *2* branch with male flowers

tortoise plant *n.* A common name for *Dioscorea elephantipes,* a tender twining vine with pointed leaves growing from a tuber, a member of the yam family. Also known as elephant's-foot and Hottentot bread.

totara (toh′duh rah) *n.* A common name for *Podocarpus totara,* a slow-growing, virtually pest-free, tender coniferous tree that resembles yew. It grows to 25 or 30 feet in cultivation, and has silvery-gray bark, stiff, leathery, gray-green pointed leaves, and small, red yewlike fruit. Used in mild-climate gardens and will live for years in containers. Also known as totara pine and mahogany pine.

touch-me-not *n.* A common name for *Impatiens,* a genus of annuals and tender perennials, some species native to North America. They have succulent stems, simple leaves, and often showy flowers, some species having 5-petaled blooms, others hav-

ing clusters of almost orchidlike curiously shaped blossoms. The pods have 5 segments, which coil elastically and eject the seeds by popping open violently. Also known as snapweed, balsam, and jewelweed. (See **Impatiens**.) Also a common name for *Ecballium Elaterium,* the squirting cucumber, which takes its common name from the fact that the ripe fruit separates suddenly from its stalk, forcibly squirting its seeds and juice through the hole left by the stalk. (See **Ecballium**.)

tower cress *n.* A common name for *Arabis turrita,* a low-growing perennial. It grows to 2½ feet, with oval, toothed leaves in basal rosettes that are blue-violet beneath, and dense spikes of yellow flowers. Used in borders, rock gardens, and pattern plantings.

tower mustard *n.* A common name for *Arabis glabra,* a hardy perennial. It grows to 4 feet, with oval, toothed, basal leaves and spikes of yellow flowers. It has naturalized in North America.

Townsendia (town zehn′dee uh) *n.* A genus of 20 species of variably hardy low-growing annuals, biennials, or perennials (Compositae) native to western North America. They grow from a few inches to 1 foot, with alternate leaves and daisylike white, pink, or purple flowers with yellow centers. Used in wild gardens or rock gardens. *T. exscapa,* native from Manitoba to New Mexico, is commonly known as Easter daisy.

toyon (toi′ahn) *n.* A common name for *Heteromeles arbutifolia,* a shrub or small tree, with simple, dark, shining, evergreen, sharply toothed leaves, and flat clusters of small white flowers, native to California and Baja California. (See **Heteromeles**.) Also known as California holly.

trace elements *n.* A chemical element found in plant tissue in very small amounts.

Trachelium (truh kee′lee uhm) *n.* A genus of 7 to 10 species of tender perennials, sometimes grown as annuals (Campanulaceae). They grow from 6 inches to 4 feet, depending on the species, with alternate, simple leaves and clusters of small purple, blue, or white flowers. A tough, undemanding plant used in beds and borders, and a good cut flower. Commonly known as throatwort.

Trachelospermum (trak uh loh spuhr′muhm) *n.* A genus of more than 10 species of tender, broadleaf, evergreen, twining woody vines or sprawling shrubs (Apocynaceae). *T. jasminoides* grows to 30 feet or more, with attractive, glossy, entire, opposite leaves and richly fragrant white pinwheel-shaped flowers that attract bees. Used as climbing vines on eaves, walls and fences, and as ground covers. *T. jasminoides* is commonly known as star jasmine and Confederate jasmine.

trachycarpous (trak ee kahr′puhs) *a.* In botany, having rough fruit.

Trachycarpus (trak ee kahr′puhs) *n.* A genus of 6 species of tender, slender palms (Palmae). They grow to 40 feet, with fiber-covered trunks, and fanlike leaves. Used in mild-climate gardens. Commonly known as fan-palm.

Trachymene (trak ee mee′nee) *n.* A genus of 12 species of annuals (Umbelliferae). They grow from 6 inches to 2 feet, with 3-part leaves and clusters of blue or white flowers, sometimes lacy in appearance. Used in annuals beds.

trachyspermous (trak ee spuhr′muhs) *a.* In botany, rough-seeded.

tractor *n.* (See **lawn tractor**.)

Tradescantia (trad eh skan′chee uh) *n.* A genus of 20 or more species of variably hardy erect or trailing perennials (Commelinaceae), some species native to the United States. They have succulent stems, often oval, pointed leaves and small blue, rose, purple, or white flowers. Used as small-scale ground covers, in hanging-baskets, and in pots. May be invasive in moist soils. Commonly known as spiderwort.

Tragopogon (trag uh poh′gahn) *n.* A genus of 50 species of hardy tap-rooted biennials and perennials with long, feathery bristles attached to the seeds (Compositae). They grow to 4 feet, with narrow, grasslike leaves and yellow or purple asymmetrical flowers. Several species have naturalized in North America and are generally regarded as weeds, including *T. porrifolius* (salsify). Commonly known as goatsbeard.

trailing arbutus (ahr byoo′duhs) *n.* A common name for *Epigaea repens,* a broadleaf evergreen prostrate or creeping shrub, with hairy stems, bright green oval, pointed leaves and waxy, fragrant rose-colored or white spring-blooming flowers. A choice woodland ground cover, particularly under pines, but difficult to grow without ideal conditions such as rich, moist, fast-draining, acid soils in shady locations. Also known as mayflower. (See **Epigaea**.)

training *n.* In gardening, the art or operation of forming young trees to a wall or espalier, or causing them to grow in a desired shape.

transpiration *n.* In botany, the loss of watery vapor from the surface of plant leaves.

transpire *v.* In botany, to exhale watery vapor.

transplanting *n.* 1. The act or process of removing and resetting, as a plant; transplantation. 2. That which is transplanted.

trap *n.* Any material or object used to capture plant pests. The pests either die in the trap or can easily be gathered and disposed of. Traps include boards, where snails can gather during the day; sticky materials, in which pests get stuck (see **sticky trap**); and rolled-up paper, where earwigs congregate during the day.

Trapa (tray′puh) *n.* A genus of 3 or 4 species of annual water plants (Trapaceae). They have rosettes of floating leaves with puffy, inflated stems and white or light purple flowers. Grown in ponds, but can become weedy. Commonly known as water nut and water chestnut. (See **ling**.)

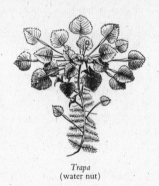

Trapa
(water nut)

Trautvetteria (traht yeh ter′ee uh) *n.* A genus of a few species of hardy perennials (Ranunculaceae), some species native to North America. They grow to 3 feet, with broad, divided, palm-shaped leaves and clusters of small white flowers. Used in wild gardens. Commonly known as false bugbane.

traveler's-joy *n.* A common name for *Clematis,* especially *C. vitalba. Clematis* species are mostly deciduous climbers with dark green leaves, often divided into leaflets, and the curling, clinging leaf stalks and showy large, flowers. The feathery, silky seed-heads are also ornamental. Some species are native to North America.

traveler's palm *n.* A common name for *Ravenala madagascariensis,* a subtropical treelike plant that grows in clumps to 30 feet or more. It has a fanlike trunk formed from the stems of bananalike leaves about 10 feet long and white flowers in canoelike bracts that hold rain water. Used in frost-free gardens for dramatic effect. Also known as traveler's tree.

treasure flower *n.* A common name for *Gazania rigens,* a low-growing tender creeping perennial. It grows from a rhizome with stems to 16 inches long, with narrow shiny green leaves, downy beneath, and masses of showy yellow or orange daisylike flowers with dark centers. The flowers close at night and do not open in cloudy weather. Used as small-scale ground cover, in rock gardens, on steep banks, trailing over a wall, and in hanging-baskets.

tree *n.* 1. A perennial plant that grows from the ground with a single permanent, usually tall, woody, self-supporting trunk or stem, and an elevated crown of branches and foliage (or, in the palms, only foliage). 2. An herb or shrub growing naturally in or trained into the form of a tree.

tree aloe (a'loh) *n.* A common name for *Aloe dichotoma,* a tender treelike succulent. Also known as quiver tree. (See **quiver tree**.)

tree, big *n.* A common name for *Sequoiadendron giganteum,* an evergreen tree native to the central Sierra Nevada Mountains of California. It grows up to 250 feet or more, has a trunk 30 feet in diameter, and lives for thousands of years. Because of these characteristics, it is among the world's oldest living things. Its bark is cinnamon colored while its leaves are scalelike, dense, and overlapping. Also known as Siena redwood, mammoth tree, giant sequoia, and giant redwood.

treebine *n.* A common name for *Cissus,* a tender broadleaf evergreen vine. Also known as grape ivy. (See **Cissus**.)

tree, blueberry *n.* A common name for *Elaeocarpus,* a genus of tropical and subtropical trees and shrubs with simple leaves, spikes of small white flowers, and blue-purple round, fleshy fruit. Used in frost-free gardens.

tree cactus *n.* A common name for any treelike cactus, but often used specifically for *Carnegiea gigantea,* a tall, tender columnar, ribbed, branched cactus. Also known as saguaro and Arizona giant. (See **Carnegiea**.)

tree celandine (sehl'uhn dighn) *n.* A common name for *Macleaya cordata,* a large stately hardy perennial. Also known as plume poppy. (See **Macleaya**.)

tree clover *n.* A common name for *Melilotus alba,* a tall aromatic biennial that has naturalized in North America. It grows to 10 feet, with cloverlike leaves and slender spikes of small, fragrant, white flowers that attract bees. Grown as a bee plant, then plowed under as green manure. Also known as white sweet clover, white melilot, and Bukhara clover.

tree fuchsia (fyoo'shuh) *n.* A common name for *Fuchsia excorticata,* a tender shrub or small tree. It has loose, papery bark, alternate, oval, pointed leaves and small, narrow, purplish-red flowers.

tree guard *n.* A foam-backed band of adhesive material typically about 3½ inches wide that is wrapped around a tree trunk to form a barrier preventing crawling insects, caterpillars, snails, and slugs from crossing. Can also be applied to wood frames of raised beds to keep out slugs, snails, and caterpillars. (See also **caterpillar tape**.)

tree heath *n.* A common name for the genus *Dracaena* and *Erica arborea. Dracaena* is a genus of tropical shrubs or trees with large, entire, often somewhat fleshy leaves that grow in tufts at the ends of the branches. (See **Dracaena**.) *Erica arborea* is a slow-growing tender evergreen shrub that grows to 20 feet, with tiny bright green needlelike leaves and large clusters of tiny fragrant white flowers. The burls are used to make briar pipes.

treehopper *n.* An unusual-shaped insect that wounds the bark of trees and shrubs when laying eggs, sometimes spreading secondary diseases. The nymphs suck the juices of some vegetables, including corn and tomatoes. Control measures are seldom required unless populations are very high. If necessary, control with horticultural oil sprays in fall.

tree lupine (loo′pehn) *n.* A common name for *Lupinus arboreus,* a tender bushy shrub native to California coastal areas. It grows from 5 to 8 feet, and has fan-shaped leaves with 5 to 12 leaflets and loose spikes of sulfur yellow flowers (occasionally lilac-blue or white). Useful in beach cottage gardens.

tree of heaven *n.* A common name for *Ailanthus altissima,* a hardy, deciduous tree. Also known as varnish tree, copal, and tree of the gods. (See **Ailanthus**.)

tree of sadness *n.* A common name for *Nyctanthes arbor-tristis,* a shrub or small tree with heart-shaped leaves and orange tubular fragrant flowers that open at night. Grown in mild climates for its heavily perfumed flowers. Also known as night jasmine.

tree orchid *n.* A common name for *Epidendrum,* a genus of mostly epiphytic orchids, native to tropical and subtropical America. They vary greatly in habit, but the stems are often pseudo-bulbs, with straplike, leathery leaves, and spikes or clusters of attractive, intriguing multi-colored flowers. Commonly known as buttonhole orchid.

tree paint *n.* A black asphalt emulsion used to seal and protect tree wounds, especially after pruning. Also called wound dressing, tree wound dressing, and pruning seal.

tree peony (pee′uh nee) *n.* A common name for *Paeonia suffruticosa,* a hardy deciduous shrubby perennial. It grows to 7 feet, with leaves divided into deeply cut leaflets and rose pink to white flowers. The orange and salmon-flowered hybrids are the result of crosses betweeen *P. suffruticosa* and *P. lutea,* a yellow-flowered peony. A choice perennial in the back of the hardy border. Tree peonies will bloom well with less winter chill than herbaceous peonies, making them a better choice for mild winter climates.

tree poppy *n.* A common name for *Dendromecon rigida* and *Romneya coulteri* both drought-tolerant, sun-loving natives of California. *D. rigida* is a perennial evergreen shrub, also known as bush poppy. (See **Dendromecon**.) *R. Coulteri* is a tall,

tough, fairly hardy perennial that grows to 8 feet or more, and has beautiful, deeply cut gray-green leaves and huge, showy fragrant poppylike flowers. The flowers grow 9 inches across with crepe paperlike white petals and bright yellow centers. Tolerates, indeed thrives, in poor, dry soil, full sun, and heat or cold. Spreads by underground rhizomes (enlarged roots), and can be invasive. Spectacular in the back of borders, *R. Coulteri* is especially useful on dry, steep banks and other difficult sites. *R. Coulteri* is also known as Matilija poppy, California tree poppy, and fried eggplant, the latter because the flowers look like eggs sunny-side-up.

tree primrose *n.* A common name for *Oenothera biennis,* a hardy perennial native to eastern North America. It grows from 1 to 6 feet, with long, narrow, flat leaves in a basal rosette and clusters of yellow 2-inch 4-petaled flowers that fade to the color of old gold. May be weedy. Traditional in the cottage garden. Also known as evening primrose and German rampion.

tree-protector *n.* Any device placed about a tree-trunk to prevent insects from crawling up the bark. It may be a circular trough kept filled with water or other fluid, or a band of paper or fabric coated with tar, etc.

tree ring *n.* A circle of cells just under the bark. The width of the ring indicates the amount of lateral growth the tree has undergone in any given year.

tree, Santa Maria *n.* A common name for *Calophyllum brasiliense,* a broadleaf evergreen subtropical tree. It grows to 65 feet or more, with leathery oval leaves and spikes of small, white fragrant flowers. Grown in mild-winter and frost-free gardens. Also known as Santa Maria.

tree soaker *n.* A short length of porous hose looped around the drip line of a tree or shrub to release tiny amounts of water slowly and evenly into the soil. May be used above or below ground.

tree surgery *n.* Any of various pruning, bracing, and rot removal procedures designed to improve the health of a tree.

tree tomato *n.* A common name for *Cyphomandra betacea,* a bushy subtropical treelike shrub that may reach 10 feet, usually less, with large oval, pointed leaves, small pink flowers, and red egg-shaped edible fruit. Grown mostly as a novelty indoor/outdoor plant and for its fruit that resembles tomatoes somewhat in appearance and flavor. Also known as tomato tree.

tree, trembling *n.* A common name for *Populus tremula* (European aspen or trembling poplar) and *P. tremuloides* (American aspen or quaking aspen). They are hardy deciduous trees with flat-stemmed leaves that twist and flutter in every breeze.

tree wound dressing *n.* A substance for sealing tree wounds and grafts. (See **tree paint**.)

trefoil (tree'foil) *n.* A common name for *Trifolium,* also known as clover, a low-growing plant with leaves divided into 3 oval leaflets. (See **clover** and **Trifolium**.)

trefoil, bird's-foot (tree'foil) *n.* A common name for *Lotus,* a genus of trailing, prostrate plants and subshrubs that grow from 2 to 4 feet, depending on the species, with leaves divided into leaflets, pealike red or yellow flowers, and narrow pods. (See **Lotus**.)

trefoil, marsh (tree'foil) *n.* A common name for *Menyanthes trifoliata,* a bog plant used in bog gardens. Also called water trefoil, bogbean and buckbean. (See **Menyanthes**.)

trefoil, shrubby (tree'foil) *n.* A common name for *Ptelea trifoliata,* a very hardy deciduous shrub or small tree with aromatic 3-part leaves, clusters of small greenish-white flowers, and papery, winged fruit. Also called wafer ash and hop tree.

trellis *n.* A latticework frame or structure used to support vines, roses, or other climbing plants. (See **vegetable trellis**.)

Trema (tree'muh) *n.* A genus of 20 species of tropical shrubs and trees (*Ulmaceae*). *T. guineensis* grows to 15 feet, and has oval, pointed leaves and clusters of small flowers.

trench *v.* To furrow deeply, especially with the spade; dig deeply and turn over thoroughly by means of a succession of contiguous trenches.

Trevesia (treh veh see'uh) *n.* A genus of 4 species of tropical evergreen shrubs and small trees (Araliaceae). *T. palmata* 'Micholitzii' grows from 10 to 20 feet, with large beautifully cut lobed leaves resembling a lacy snowflake. Used as a houseplant. *T. palmata* 'Micholitzii' is commonly known as snowflake tree.

triandrous (trigh an'druhs) *a.* Having 3 stamens.

Tribulus (trihb'yuh luhs) *n.* A genus of 12 species of subtropical and tropical annuals and perennials (Zygophyllaceae). *T. terrestris* grows to 3 feet, with opposite leaves divided into small, oval leaflets, tiny yellow flowers, and sharply spined fruit. It is a troublesome weed in California and the southeastern United States. Commonly known as puncture vine and burnut. The genus is commonly known as caltrop.

tri- *comb. form* Meaning 3, as tricapsular, 3-capsuled.

triadimefon (trigh ad'ih muh fahn) *n.* A synthetic, systemic fungicide used against a variety of diseases of lawns, rust, and powdery mildew. Common trade name: Bayleton.

tricarpellary (trigh kahr'puh leh ree) *a.* In botany, having 3—usually fused—carpels. Also tricarpellate.

Trichilia (trigh kihl'ee uh) *n.* A genus of 240 species of tropical shrubs and small trees (*Meliaceae*), some species native to the Americas. They grow from 15 to 30 feet, depending on the species, most with leaves divided into 3 leaflets, clusters of small white or yellow flowers, sometimes fragrant, and a seedpod that opens to expose orange or red seeds.

Trichocereus (trihk uh sih'ree uhs) *n.* A genus of 25 species of spiny ribbed cylindrical cacti (Cactaceae). The stems can be erect or prostrate, simple or branched, and they grow from 5 to 25 feet, depending on the species. They have large, fragrant, white, funnel-shaped flowers that bloom at night. Used in frost-free gardens. Unusually tough, these cacti tolerate both heat to 120° F. and cold to 25° F.

Trichodiadema (trihk oh dee'uh deh muh) *n.* A genus of 36 species of low-growing, tender, tufted, short-stemmed, or shrubby succulents (Aizoaceae). They have small, fleshy, cylindrical leaves and small magenta, white, or yellow daisylike flowers. Used as a small-scale groundcover in frost-free gardens; shrubby tuberous-rooted species make intriguing bonsai subjects.

Trichogramma wasp (trihk oh gram′uh) *n.* A beneficial insect whose larvae develop within the eggs of moths and caterpillars, killing the future pest. Can be used to control number of pests, including coddling moths, corn earworms, and tomato hornworms. Sold through the mail.

Trichosanthes (trihk uh san′theez) *n.* A genus of 40 or more species of tropical annuals and perennials (Cucurbitaceae). *T. anguina* is an annual climbing or sprawling vine with large, broad leaves, white, fringed female flowers and spikes of male flowers, and long, slim, coiled, fleshy edible fruit 1 to 6 feet long. Grown mostly as a novelty, *T. anguina* is commonly known as serpent cucumber, serpent gourd, snake gourd, club gourd, and viper's gourd.

Trichostema (trihk oh stee′muh) *n.* A genus of 16 species of annuals or shrubs (Labiatae) native to North America. *T. dichotomum,* an annual native to the eastern United States, grows from 4 to 30 inches, with oval leaves and spikes of blue, pink, or white flowers in whorls. Grown in wild gardens or rock gardens. *T. dichotomum* is commonly known as bastard pennyroyal. *T. lanatum* is a much-branched, neat, tender evergreen shrub, native to California, that grows from 3 to 5 feet, with narrow, dark green strongly aromatic leaves, woolly beneath, and spikes of blue flowers in whorls. Drought-tolerant, it is a choice plant for dry, sunny hillsides. *T. lanatum* is commonly known as woolly blue-curls.

tricostate (trigh kaws′tayt) *a.* In botany, 3-ribbed.

tricotyledonous (trigh kahd uh lee′duh nuhs) *a.* In botany, having 3 seed leaves.

Tricyrtis (trigh sehr′tuhs) *n.* A genus of between 10 and 15 species of marginally hardy perennials (Liliaceae). They grow from 2 to 3 feet, with alternate leaves and small, curiously shaped white or yellow flowers mottled with purple. Used in rock gardens, in moist, shady locations, or in pots. Commonly known as toad lily. (See **lily, toad**.)

Trientalis (trigh ehn tal′ehs) *n.* A genus of 4 species of very hardy perennials (Primulaceae), some species native to arctic and subarctic North America. They grow to a few inches high, with whorls of long, narrow leaves clustered at the tops of stems and small, star-shaped white or pink flowers. Used in gardens of the Far North and in alpine collections. Commonly known as starflower or chickweed wintergreen.

trifoliate (trigh foh′lee ayt) *a.* In botany, having 3 leaves, as in *Trillium.* Also trifoliated.

trifoliate orange (trigh for′lee ayt) *n.* A common name for *Poncirus trifoliata,* a deciduous citrus tree with stiff, angled, thorny branches and large, powerfully fragrant white flowers that appear before the leaves. Also known as hardy orange. (See **hardy orange**.)

Trifolium (trigh foh′lee uhm) *n.* A genus of 300 species of mostly low-growing annuals and short-lived perennials (Leguminosae); clover. They may grow up to 3 feet, with leaves divided into 3 oval leaflets and fragrant clusters of tiny white, yellow, red, pink, rose, or purple flowers that attract bees. Grown mostly as a cover crop or green manure to enrich soil with its nitrogen-fixing roots; some species are grown ornamentally, such as *T. fragiferum* (strawberry clover) and *T. repens* (white clover or Dutch white clover). Commonly known as clover and trefoil.

triforine (trigh′for een) *n.* A synthetic, systemic fungicide widely used to control diseases of roses and other plants. Very caustic. Common trade name: Funginex.

trifurcate (trigh′fuhr kayt) *a.* In botany, divided into 3 branches or forks.

trigamous (trigh′guh muhs) *a.* In botany, having 3 sorts of flowers in the same head—male, female, and hermaphrodite.

trigger grip *n.* A gunlike lever that actuates and locks a mechanism, as a nozzle, in one position.

trigger nozzle *n.* (See **pistol grip nozzle**.)

trigger plant *n.* A common name for *Stylidium,* a genus of tender perennials. *S. graminifolium* grows to 3 feet, with basal grasslike leaves 1 foot long, and long spikes of small, pink 5-petaled flowers that have a curved part that springs up when touched.

Triglochin (trigh gloh′kehn) *n.* A genus of 15 species of water plants (Juncaginaceae). They grow in bogs and marshes with basal, fleshy, semicylindrical leaves and spikes of flowers. Used in aquariums and bog gardens. Commonly known as arrow grass.

Trigonella (trihg uh nehl′uh) *n.* A genus of 70 species of annuals (Leguminosae). *T. Foenum-graecum* grows to 2 feet, with leaves divided into 3 oval leaflets and pairs of white flowers. It also has long pods with aromatic seeds that are the fenugreek used to flavor food, especially curries. Traditional in herb or cottage gardens. (See **fenugreek**.)

Trigonella foenum-graecum
(fenugreek)
a fruit

trijugate (trigh′juh gayt) *a.* In botany, having 3 pairs of leaflets.

Trillium (trihl′ee uhm) *n.* A genus of 30 species of hardy to very hardy perennials (Liliaceae), some species native to North America. They grow from 10 inches to 2½ feet, with 3 leaves in a whorl at the top of the stem and single, 3-petaled white, yellow, green, pink, or purple flowers in the middle of the whorl. Used in wild or woodland gardens; a choice plant for cool, moist, shady locations. Commonly known as wake-robin and birthroot.

trilobate leaf

trilobate (trigh′luh bayt) *a.* Three-lobed, as a leaf. Also trilobated, trilobed.

trimerous (trihm′uh ruhs) *a.* In botany, having the parts in 3s, and frequently written 3-merous.

trimorphism (trigh mawr′fizm) *n.* In botany, the occurrence of 3 distinct forms of flowers, leaves, or other parts upon the same plant, or upon plants of the same species.

trimorphous (trigh mawr′fuhs) *a.* Of, pertaining to, or characterized by trimorphism; having 3 distinct forms.

trioecious (trigh ee′shuhs) *a.* In botany, having male, female, and hermaphrodite flowers, each on different plants. Also triecious.

Triosteum (trigh ahs′tee uhm) *n.* A genus of 5 or 6 species of hardy perennials (Caprifoliaceae), some species native to North America. They grow to 4 feet, with opposite, simple, entire leaves and clusters of yellow or purple tubular flowers. Not widely grown as it is inclined to be weedy. Commonly known as horse gentian and feverwort.

tripetaloid (trigh pehd′uh loid) *a.* In botany, appearing as if furnished with 3 petals, as a tripetaloid perianth.

tripetalous (trigh pehd′uh luhs) *a.* In botany, 3-petaled.

Triphasia (trigh fay′zee uh) n. A genus of 3 species of spiny evergreen tropical shrubs and small trees (Rutaceae). *T. trifolia* grows to 15 feet, with leaves divided into 3 oval, pointed leaflets, fragrant, white flowers and small, dull red fruit with sticky pulp. Used as specimen shrubs and hedges in mild-winter climates. *T. trifolia* is commonly known as limeberry.

tripinnate (trigh pih′nayt) *a.* In botany, threefold pinnate, as when the leaflets of a bipinnate (doubly divided) leaf are themselves pinnate. Also tripinnated.

tripinnatisect (trigh peh nad′uh sehkt) *a.* In botany, parted nearly to the base or midrib in a tripinnate (triply divided) manner, as a leaf.

Tripleurospermum (trihp luhr oh spuhr′muhm) *n.* A genus of 25 species of annuals and fairly hardy perennials (Compositae). They grow from being mat-forming to 2 feet, depending on the species, with alternate, finely divided leaves and white or yellow daisylike or buttonlike flowers.

triploid (trip'loid) *a.* In botany, having 3 complete sets of chromosomes.

tripod sprinkler *n.* A sprinkler supported by a 3-legged structure, typically about 4-feet tall, for watering plants from above.

Tripogandra (trih poh gahn'druh) *n.* A genus of 20 or more species of tender and tropical creeping or draping perennials (Commelinaceae). *T. multiflora* grows to 3 feet with semi-succulent stems, dainty, oval, pointed dark green leaves, purple beneath, and many delicate clusters of tiny white flowers. Used mostly as houseplants and hanging-basket plants. *T. multiflora* is commonly known as bridal veil, fernleaf wandering Jew, and fernleaf inch plant.

Tripterygium (trihp tuhr'ee juhm) *n.* A genus of 2 species of deciduous shrubs, one tender (*T. wilfordii*) and one hardy (*T. regelii*) (Celastraceae). *T. Wilfordii* is a shrubby climbing vine that grows from 30 to 40 feet, with oval leaves and large clusters of white 5-petaled flowers. *T. Regelii* is a shrub that grows from 6 to 30 feet, with broad oval toothed leaves and large clusters of white flowers, the clusters 10 inches across.

tristachyous (trigh stay'kee uhs) *a.* In botany, 3-spiked.

Tristania (trehs stay'nee uh) *n.* A genus of 20 species of tender evergreen shrubs and trees (Myrtaceae). They grow from 6 to 60 feet, depending on the species, with interesting peeling bark, brightly colored in some species, alternate, simple leaves and clusters of small yellow or white 5-petaled flowers with many stamens. Hardy to 26° F., they are used as background plantings, screens, or in large tubs.

tristichous (tris'teh kuhs) *a.* In botany, arranged in 3 vertical rows or ranks.

tristylous (trigh stigh'luhs) *a.* In botany, 3-styled.

Triteleia (trigh duh ligh'uh) *n.* A genus of 14 species of mostly tender perennial bulbs (Amaryllidaceae) native to the western United States. They grow from 1 to 3 feet, with 1 or 2 narrow, pointed basal leaves and slim spikes of white, yellow, purple, or light blue trumpet-shaped flowers. These are choice specimens in wild gardens or in rock gardens.

triternate (trigh tuhr'nayt) *a.* In botany, a leaf divided into 3 parts, each of which is divided into 3 parts and then again divided into 3 leaflets; each complete leaf having 27 leaflets.

Trithrinax (trigh thrigh'naks) *n.* A genus of 5 species of small to medium-sized tender and tropical spiny-leaved palms (Palmae). *T. acanthocoma* grows to 15 feet, with a densely spiny trunk covered with stout 3-to 6-inch spines, and rounded fan-shaped leaves.

Tritonia (trigh toh'nee uh) *n.* A genus of 50 species of tender bulbs (corms) (Iridaceae). They grow to 2 feet, with narrow sword-shaped leaves and spikes clustered with brilliant red, orange, pink, yelow or apricot broadly funnel-shaped flowers. Used in beds, borders, rock gardens, and pots. Excellent cut flowers.

Trochodendron (trahk oh dehn'druhm) *n.* A genus of 1 species, *T. aralioides,* a tender broadleaf evergreen tree (Trochodendraceae). It grows to 60 feet, with pointed, simple, alternate leaves clustered at the ends of branches and spikes of small bright green flowers with many stamens. Commonly known as wheel tree.

Trollius (trah'lee uhs) *n.* A genus of 20 species of hardy perennials (Ranunculaceae), some species native to North America. They grow from 3 inches to 3 feet, depending on the species, with shiny, finely cut dark green leaves and bright yellow or orange globular flowers. Useful in moist, shady locations, particularly near pools or streams. Commonly known as trollflower and globeflower.

Tropaeolum (troh pee'uh lehn) *n.* A genus of 50 species of low-growing or scrambling self-sowing annuals and tender perennials (Tropaeolaceae). They grow from 6 inches to 15 feet, with long-stemmed round gray-green leaves and showy bright yellow, orange, or red flowers. Mostly grown as annuals, they flourish in coastal conditions, but will tolerate some drought. The erect species are grown as edging or in beds, and the sprawling types as ground covers, on steep banks, or over walls. The leaves of *T. majus* (nasturtium or Indian cress) are used in salads and the buds pickled as capers. The genus is commonly known as nasturtium, trophy cress, and trophywort. (See **Indian cress**.)

tropical almond *n.* A common name for *Terminalia catappa,* a tropical deciduous tree that grows to 80 feet, with long, stiff leaves crowded at the ends of the branches that turn red before falling in the dry season and spikes of small, white bell-shaped flowers. Used in tropical gardens, thriving especially at the seashore. Also known as Indian almond, kamani, and myrobalan.

trowel *n.* A scoop-shaped, short-handled instrument used for digging up or setting in small plants.

Truckee pine (truh'kee) *n.* A common name for *Pinus Jeffreyi,* a drought-tolerant hardy evergreen coniferous tree that grows to 120 feet, with bark that smells like vanilla, long, blue-green needles in bundles of 3, and smooth reddish-brown oval cones 6 to 8 inches long. Best used in mountain gardens, it is also an excellent bonsai subject. Also known as Jeffery pine.

truffle (truh'fuhl) *n.* A common name for the underground fungus of the genus *Tuber,* an edible wild mushroom that is prized above all others. The most valued are *T. melanosporum* (black truffle), *T. aestivum,* and *T. magnatum* (white truffle), all of which grow in France and Italy where they are sniffed out by pigs and dogs and dug up by truffle collectors. Truffles look a lot like small potatoes or rocks, but reveal pale canals, veins, and/or cavities when sliced. Their distinctive fragrance and flavor, makes one of the most cherished essences of French cuisine. Truffles rarely grow in great quantities and efforts to cultivate them have not been very successful. They tend, therefore, to be expensive.

trug *n.* A shallow basket, traditionally made from strips of wood but now also of polyethylene, used to carry flowers and produce.

trumpet creeper *n.* A common name for *Campsis,* specifically, *Campsis radicans,* a fast-growing self-clinging hardy deciduous woody vine, native to the eastern United States. It climbs by aerial rootlets to 40 feet or more, with leaves divided into toothed leaflets and clusters of large orange and scarlet flowers 3 inches long and 2 inches wide. Used as a quick summer screen. Also known as cross vine, common trumpet creeper, trumpet vine, cowitch, and trumpet honeysuckle.

trumpet flower *n.* A common name for any plant having trumpet shaped flowers such as trumpet creeper *Campsis radicans,* vanilla trumpet vine, *Distictis laxiflora,* and angel's trumpet, *Brugmansia.*

trumpet leaf *n.* A common name for *Sarracenia flava,* a carnivorous pitcher plant native to wetlands, bogs, and marshes of the southern Atlantic States. It has erect, trumpet-shaped red-veined leaves 2 to 4 feet long and large yellow flowers on tall stalks. Not easy to grow: they will not tolerate hard water (water containing dissolved mineral salts), dry air, dry soil, or strong fertilizers. Also known as yellow pitcher plant, trumpets, or umbrella-trumpets.

trumpet tree *n.* A common name for *Cecropia peltata,* a subtropical flowering tree. It grows to 60 feet, with hollow stems usually inhabited by vicious biting ants, dark green leaves palmately divided into 7 to 9 large oval leaflets, silvery white beneath, that flash like mirrors in the breeze, and spikes of yellow flowers. Used in frost-free gardens. Also known as trumpetwood.

trumpet vine *n.* A common name for any vine with trumpet-shaped flowers, such as *Campsis radicans* (cross vine), *Distictis buccinatoria* (blood-red trumpet vine), and *Clytostoma callistegioides* (violet trumpet vine).

trumpet vine, blood-red *n.* A common name for *Distictis buccinatoria,* a robust tender climbing woody vine that climbs by tendrils to 20 or 30 feet, with glossy, oval leaves and clusters of red trumpet-shaped flowers with yellow throats. The flowers bloom sporadically whenever the weather is warm, and fade to bluish red. It is hardy to 24° F. Used to cover arbors, porches, high fences, or walls, or as a sprawling ground cover on steep slopes. Also known as blood-trumpet.

truncate leaf

truncate *a.* In botany, appearing to have the end cut off square or straight, such as the leaf of the tulip tree, *Liriodendron tulipifera.*

truss *n.* In horticulture, a compact terminal flower cluster or fruit cluster, such as lilac or tomato.

tryma (trigh′muh) *n., pl.* **trymas.** In botany, a nutlike drupe (small fruit with a single seed) with the outer part of the seed covering fleshy, leathery, or fibrous, and with a stony endocarp (inner shell), as in the walnut and hickory nut.

Tsuga
(hemlock)

Tsuga (tsoo′guh) *n.* A genus of 10 species of hardy and very hardy, mostly gigantic, evergreen coniferous trees (Pinaceae), some species native to North America. They grow from 50 to 200 feet, depending on the species, with delicate, flat sprays of small needlelike leaves and small cones that hang down from the branches. Smaller species are good lawn trees, background trees, or can be sheared into a dense, outstandingly beautiful hedge. Taller species are best on very large properties where they are picturesque specimen trees. Hemlocks thrive in cool, moist climates, and tend to be smaller in hot, dry climates. Commonly known as hemlock or hemlock-spruce.

tub *n.* A wooden container, generally redwood or cedar, composed of staves held together around a round, flat bottom by metal hoops. Used in patio gardens or other landscapes where surface soil is inadequate or plants need to be rotated or moved.

tube *n.* In botany, any hollow elongated body or part of an organ, applied especially to a gamopetalous corolla or gamosepalous calyx, and also to a united circle of stamens.

tubeflower *n.* A common name for *Clerodendrum,* specifically *C. indicum. C. indicum* is a tender subtropical woody perennial or shrub that grows to 8 feet, with shiny, long, narrow, pointed, entire leaves and clusters of white tubular 4-inch-long flowers. It has naturalized in the southern United States. *C. indicum* is also known as turk's turban. *Clerodendrum* is also known as glory-bower, Kashmir-bouquet, and cashmere bouquet.

tuber *n.* 1. In botany, a short, thickened, usually subterranean stem or rhizome bearing buds or "eyes," each of which is capable of developing into a new plant, as in the potato or Jerusalem artichoke.

tubers on roots of plant

tubercle (tyoo′buhr kuhl) *n.* In botany; 1. Any knoblike outgrowth or projection. 2. A very small tuber. 3. A tuberous root bearing adventitious buds, and functioning like a tuber. Also tubercule.

tuberose (tyoo′brohz) *n.* A common name for *Polianthes tuberosa,* a tender bulblike perennial native to Mexico. It grows from a rhizome to 3½ feet, with basal, grasslike leaves and tall spikes of waxy white sweetly fragrant tubular flowers. Grown in frost-free gardens, or lifted in cold climates; also grown as an indoor/outdoor plant, and can be forced for early bloom. It is an excellent cut flower. No longer known in the wild.

tuberous (tyoo′buhr uhs) *a.* In botany, of the nature of or resembling a tuber; bearing tubers. Also tuberose.

tuberous begonia (tyoo′buhr uhs beh goh′nyuh) *n.* A common name for *Begonia × tuberhybrida,* a spectacular tender stemless perennial that grows from a tuber to 2½ feet, with semi-succulent, fleshy leaves and magnificently showy red, scarlet, carmine, yellow, orange, apricot, peach, white, or pink flowers. There are, in addition, fibrous begonias, low-growing semi-succulent perennials usually grown as annuals in beds or as edging, and Rex begonias grown for their large, strikingly patterned leaves, as houseplants or indoor/outdoor plants. Tuberous begonias can be either erect or draping. The draping varieties are dramatic in hanging-baskets with their brilliantly colored, saucer-sized flowers; the erect varieties are equally spectacular in pots and planters.

tubuliflorous (tyoo byuh lihf′uh ruhs) *a.* In botany, having the flowers of a head all with tubular corollas, as in the Campanulaceae and the Compositae.

tuckahoe (tehk′uh hoh) *n.* A common name for *Peltandra virginica* (Virginia wake-robin) and *Orontium aquaticum* (golden-club), both bog plants native to the United States. (See **Virginia wake-robin** and **Orontium**.)

tucum (too′koom) *n.* A common name for *Astrocharyum aculeatum*, a tall, spiny, slender-trunked subtropical palm that grows to 75 feet or more, with much-divided leaves 10 feet long and round, yellow-orange fruit.

tufted hair grass *n.* (See **Deschampsia**.)

Tulbaghia (tuhl bag′ee uh) *n.* A genus of 24 species of tender perennial bulbs (Amaryllidaceae). They grow into broad clumps 1½ to 2½ feet tall, with narrow, basal leaves that smell like onion or garlic when bruised, and slender stalks topped by clusters of lilac, lavender-pink, or violet star-shaped flowers. Grown in mild-climate gardens in sunny beds and borders or in cold climates in pots as indoor/outdoor plants.

tulip *n.* A common name for the genus *Tulipa,* a hardy perennial bulb. It grows from 4 to 24 inches, depending on the species, with broad, pointed basal leaves and deep cup-shaped flowers, sometimes striped or streaked, in virtually every color but blue. Tall formal tulips are best massed in beds or borders, the smaller species tulips are excellent in rock gardens. Tulips do best in cold winter climates.

Tulipa *n.* A genus of between 50 and 150 species of hardy perennial bulbs (*Liliaceae*) most native to central Asia. They grow from 4 to 24 inches, depending on the species, with broad, pointed basal leaves and chalicelike flowers in every color of the rainbow except blue. Used in beds, borders, rock gardens, and pots. Commonly known as tulip.

tulip, African *n.* A common name for *Haemanthus,* a genus of tender subtropical perennial bulbs. Also known as African blood lily and blood lily. (See **Haemanthus** and **lily, African blood**.)

tulip, bizarre *n.* A common name for breeder or cottage tulips. Both have flowers that are yellow with strange bronze, brown, maroon, or purple markings. The patterns of color are the result of a mosaic virus disease that cane be transmitted to other tulips and lilies. Do not plant them near prized solid color tulips and lilies if you wish them to retain their solid colors. (See **tulip, breeder** and **tulip, cottage**.)

tulip, breeder *n.* A common name for the tulips that Dutch growers once used to breed variegated tulips before it was understood that the variegations they prized were not a genetic variation, but the effect of a mosaic virus disease. They are hardy perennial bulbs that grow to 3 feet, with broad, pointed, basal leaves and large oval to globular flowers in unusual shades of bronze, mahogany, purple, and orange often with a flush of a contrasting shade. Used in beds and borders, and as cut flowers.

tulip, butterfly *n.* A common name for *Calochortus,* a genus of variably hardy perennial bulbs native to western North America from the Dakotas and British Columbia to Mexico. Also known as mariposa, sego lily, star tulip, globe tulip, wild tulip, and mariposa lily. (See **Calochortus** and **lily, mariposa**.)

tulip, cottage *n.* A common name for a hardy perennial bulb that grows to 2½ feet, with broad, pointed basal leaves and long oval, egg-shaped, or vase-shaped flowers, often with pointed petals. The flowers come in nearly every color but blue. Used in beds, borders, and pots. They are also superb cut flowers.

tulip, Darwin *n.* A common name for a hardy perennial bulb that grows to 2½ feet, with broad, pointed, basal leaves and tall stalks of large oval or egg-shaped flowers in clear, beautiful colors of white, cream, yellow, pink, red, mauve, lilac, purple, maroon, and nearly black. Used massed in beds, gardens, and parks around the world.

tulip, lily-flowered *n.* A common name for graceful, slender-stemmed hardy perennial bulbs that grow to 2 feet with narrow, basal leaves and long narrow flowers with pointed petals in the full range of tulip colors, which includes nearly every color but blue. Used in beds and borders, and makes a fine cut flower.

tulipomania (tyoo lehp uh may'nee uh) *n.* A craze for the cultivation or acquisition of tulips; specifically, that which arose in the Netherlands about the year 1634. Tulip marts were established in various towns, where roots were sold and resold as stocks on the exchange. A single root of *Semper augustus* was sold for 13,000 florins. After several years the government found it necessary to interfere.

tulip, parrot *n.* A common name for a hardy perennial tulip that grows from a bulb. It has broad, pointed leaves that grow from the base, and large long, deeply fringed and ruffled flowers, streaked and splashed with various colors. The patterns of color are the result of a mosaic virus disease that can be transmitted to other tulips and lilies. Do not plant them near prized solid color tulips and lilies if you wish them to retain their solid colors. They are best used in pots and planters.

tulip poplar (pahp'luhr) *n.* A common name for *Liriodenron tulipfera*, a hardy deciduous tree native to the eastern United States. Also known as tulip tree and whitewood. (See **Liriodendron**.)

tulip poppy *n.* A common name for *Papaver glaucum*, an annual that grows to 4 feet, with leaves divided into leaflets and large red flowers 4 inches across with a black eye at the base.

tulip, Rembrandt *n.* A common name for a hardy perennial tulip that grows from a bulb to 2½ feet. These are Darwin tulips that have been infected with the mosaic virus that causes colors to break, streak, and feather. These are the curiously streaked and striped tulips often depicted by the Dutch painters, such as Rembrandt. They are dramatic cut flowers.

tulip tree *n.* A common name for the genus *Liriodendron*, specifically *Liriodendron tulipifera*. (See **Liriodendron**.)

tulip tree, Chinese *n.* A common name for *Liriodendron chinense*, a hardy deciduous tree that grows to 50 feet, with leaves with pointed lobes and small olive-green flowers with a splash of yellow at the base. Useful in moist soils.

tulip, Turkish *n.* A common name for *Tulipa acuminata*, a small hardy perennial bulb that grows to 18 inches, with narrow, wavy-edged basal leaves and flowers with long, twisted, spidery petals in shades of red and yellow. Grown in beds, as edging, in rock gardens, and in pots.

tulip, wild *n.* A common name for *Tulipa sylvestris*, a hardy perennial bulb that grows to 1 foot, with 2 or 3 basal leaves and fragrant yellow flowers. These bloom well even in mild-winter climates, and may naturalize to form large colonies.

tumbler *n.* A vented barrel having an axle mounted on a frame used to mix compost components.

tumbleweed *n.* A common name for *Amaranthus albus*, a much-branched annual weed, native to the United States, that grows to 3 feet, with white stems, oval leaves and small clusters of green flowers. Most often seen tumbling along roadsides blown by the wind.

tump *v.* In horticulture, to form a mass of earth or a hillock round (a plant): as, to tump teasel.

tunic flower *n.* A common name for *Petrorhagia saxifraga*, a marginally hardy perennial with a woody base that has narrow leaves and clusters of tiny white or pink flowers with 4 bracts. Used in mild-winter climates. Also known as coat flower.

tupelo (tyoo'puh loh) *n.* A common name for *Nyssa*, a genus of hardy deciduous trees, some species native to the eastern North America. (See **Nyssa**.)

turban buttercup *n.* A common name for *Ranunculus asiaticus*, a hardy perennial that grows from a tuber to 18 inches, with fresh, rather fernlike bright green leaves and semi-double to fully double 3 to 5 inch-wide ball-shaped flowers in many shades of red, orange, pink, yellow, cream or white. Each flower stalks carries 1 to 4 flowers. Used in borders with Iceland poppies, snapdragons and nemesia.

Excellent cut flower. Also known as Persian ranunculus and Persian buttercup.

turbinate (tuhr'buh nayt) *a.* In botany, shaped like a top or a cone, narrow at the base and broad at the top.

turf *n.* 1. The surface or sward of grassy land, consisting of earth or mold filled with the roots of grass and other small plants, so as to adhere and form a kind of mat; earth covered with grass. 2. A piece of such earth or mold dug or torn from the ground; a sod. 3. In Ireland, same as peat.

turf edger *n.* (See **edging tool**.)

turfing daisy *n.* A common name for *Tripleurospermum tchihatchewii*, a mat-forming perennial with delicate leaves divided into leaflets and daisylike white flowers with yellow centers.

turgid (tuhr'jehd) *a.* Swollen; bloated; tumid; distended beyond its natural or usual state by some internal agent or expansive force: often applied to an enlarged part of the body.

turkey beard *n.* A common name for *Xerophyllum asphodeloides*, a hardy perennial native to the eastern United States. It grows to 5 feet, with grasslike basal leaves and spikes of tiny white flowers. Also known as mountain asphodel.

turkey berry tree *n.* A common name for *Mitchella repens*, a hardy low-growing, trailing, evergreen perennial native to eastern North America from Nova Scotia to Mexico. It grows to 12 inches long with glossy, dark green opposite leaves, little white funnel-shaped flowers in pairs, and scarlet or white edible berries. Also known as partridge berry. (See **Mitchella**.) Also a common name for *Symphoricarpos orbiculatus*, a very hardy shrub native to the eastern and central United States. It has elliptic leaves, small white, bell-shaped flowers, and coral red berries. Also known as coralberry and Indian currant.

turkey pea *n.* A common name for *Dicentra canadensis*, a very hardy perennial native to eastern North America. It grows to 12 inches, with finely-cut basal leaves and fragrant, heart-shaped greenish-white flowers tinged with purple. Also known as squirrel corn.

Turnera (tuhrn'uh ruh) *n.* A genus of 60 species of tropical perennials and low shrubs (Turneraceae), some species native to tropical America. *T. ulmifolia* grows to 2 feet, with narrow, oval, pointed leaves and yellow flowers 2 inches across that open only in the morning. Grown in frost-free climates. Commonly known as yellow alder.

Turneraceae (tuhrn uh ray'see ee) *n. pl.* A family of 8 genera of mostly tropical perennials, shrubs, and trees. The ornamental genus is *Turnera*.

turnip *n.* The thick, fleshy root of the plant *Brassica Rapa*, group *Rapifera*, a common garden and field crop. The rutabaga, or Swedish turnip, has smooth leaves and a round large root with yellow flesh and a strong flavor. The turnip proper has a smaller root with white flesh and a milder flavor. The turnip was cultivated by the Greeks and Romans and is now widely grown in temperate climates for use in soups and stews or as a boiled vegetable, mashed or whole, and for feeding cattle and sheep. The young shoots of the second year, known as turnip tops, are used for early greens and are more nutritious than the root, rich in vitamin A and calcium.

turnip, Indian *n.* A common name for *Arisaema triphyllum*, a North American perennial that has a root resembling a small turnip. Also called dragonroot and jack-in-the-pulpit.

turpentine tree *n.* A common name for *Syncarpia glomulifera*, a tender broadleaf evergreen tree that grows to 30 feet, with oval, opposite leaves and clusters of white 5-petaled flowers. Grown in mild climates as a shade tree.

turtlehead *n.* A common name for *Chelone*, a small genus of 5 or 6 species of perennials native to North America. (See **Chelone**.) Also a common name for *C. glabra* that grows to 6 feet, with narrow, 6-inch leaves, and spikes of inflated, arched, and nearly closed pink or white flowers; also known as snakehead.

Tussilago (tuuhs uh lay'goh) *n.* A genus of 1 species, *T. farfara*, a hardy low-growing perennial (Compositae) widely naturalized in North America. It grows to 6 inches, with long-stemmed basal leaves and pale yellow daisylike flowers. Rarely grown ornamentally as it is capable of becoming a pernicious weed. Commonly known as coltsfoot.

tussock (tuhs'ehk) *n.* A clump, tuft, or small hillock of growing grass.

tussock moth (tuhs'uhk) *n.* A destructive insect whose brightly colored larvae feed on the foliage of many trees (sometimes roses), working from the top of the plant to the bottom, skeletonizing the leaves and sometimes damaging the fruit. Spray with *Bacillus thuringiensis* to control young caterpillars or release trichogramma wasps; use traditional insecticides to control adults.

tutsan (tuht'suhn) *n.* A common name for *Hypericum Androseaemum*, a marginally hardy tidy-looking shrub that grows to 3 feet, with oval, pointed leaves, clusters of small golden yellow flowers with a sunburst of stamens in the center, and red berry-like fruits that turn purple or black. Useful as a tall groundcover at the edge of woods, shaded slopes, or in wild gardens.

twayblade *n.* A common name for *Liparis*, a genus of orchids, some native to North America. (See **Liparis**.) Also a common name for *Listera*, a genus of hardy to very hardy wild orchids, some species native to North America. (See **Listera**.)

twayblade
(*Liparis*)

twinberry *n.* A common name for *Mitchella repens*, a hardy low-growing, trailing, evergreen perennial, native to eastern North America. Also known as partridgeberry and turkey berry.

twine *n.* A string made of sisal, nylon, jute, or polypropylene used to tie stems to stakes or to mark garden   rows.

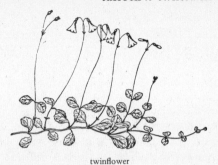

twinflower

twinflower *n.* A common name for *Linnaea borealis*, a very hardy trailing evergreen subshrub native to the Arctic and subarctic. It has small, wrinkled leaves, fragrant rose or white flowers, and yellow fruit. Used in wild gardens in very cold climates. *L. b. longiflora*, native from British Columbia to California, has somewhat larger leaves and longer flowers, and can be grown in mild-climate gardens.

twining *a.* Twisting, winding, or coiling.

twining stems

twinleaf *n.* A common name for *Jeffersonia diphylla*, a very hardy perennial native to eastern North America, from Ontario to Alabama. It grows from a rhizome to 18 inches, and has basal leaf blades divided into 2 kidney-shaped parts, white flowers 1 inch across on slender, leafless stalks, and a seed capsule that opens near the top as if by a lid. (See **Jeffersonia**.)

twin shutoff *n.* (See **Y connection**.)

twinspur *n.* A common name for *Diascia Barberae*, an erect annual that grows to 1 foot, with oval, toothed leaves and spikes of small rosy-pink flowers, with a yellow spot in the throat. Used in flower beds and pots.

twisted flower *n.* A common name for *Strophanthus*, a genus of tropical shrubs with opposite or whorled leaves and showy clusters of white or yellow funnel-shaped or belllike flowers, sometimes fragrant. Grown in frost-free gardens or in greenhouses.

twisted pine *n.* A common name for *Pinus contorta,* a hardy, picturesque, fairly fast-growing short-needled coniferous evergreen tree native to the Pacific Coast from Alaska to California. It grows to 35 feet or less, with dense, short, dark green needlelike leaves and and small yellow-brown cones. Useful in small gardens and in containers. Also known as beach pine and shore pine.

twisted-stalk *n.* A common name for *Streptopus,* a genus of hardy leafy rhizomatous perennials, some species native to North America. They grow from 18 inches to 3 feet, depending on the species, with narrow, oval, pointed leaves and white, pink, rose, or purple flowers on twisted stalks. *S. roseus,* rose mandarin, is a very hardy perennial native from Newfoundland south to Pennsylvania and Michigan. It grows to 2½ feet, with narrow, oval pointed leaves, rose to purple flowers, and red berries. Easily grown in wild gardens.

two-way hose shutoff *n.* (See **Y connection**.)

tying *v.* To support, as in tomato vines, by lashing with twine, fabric, or paper-covered wire to a stake.

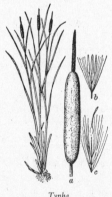

Typha
(cattail)

Typha (tigh'fuh) *n.* A genus of 15 species of hardy perennials (Typhaceae) that grow in wetlands, marshes, streams, and at the edges of lakes, some native to North America. They grow from 6 to 10 feet, depending on the species, with tall, flat, narrow, pointed leaves and tall, slender leafless stalks topped by soft, furry, dark brown flowers that look exactly like a cat's tail. Used in bog gardens, but can become weedy. They are best planted in pots and then buried in underwater. Commonly known as cattail, cattail flag, reedmace, and bulrush.

Typha (tigh'fuh) *n.* A genus of about 13 species of grasslike perennial plants (Typhaceae) native to marshes and wetlands. *T. latifolia* is sometimes grown as an ornamental for its erect, tight seed head referred to as a cattail. Very vigorous, often invasive. Commonly called cattail, cat's-tail, or bulrush.

Typhaceae (tigh fay'see ee) *n. pl.* A family of 1 genus, *Typha,* and 10 to 15 species of water-loving perennials. Commonly known as the cattail family.

ugli fruit (oo'glee) *n.* A Jamaican citrus fruit, probably a hybrid between the grapefruit and the tangerine.

Ugni (oog'nee) *n.* A genus of 5 to 15 species of tender shrubs (Myrtaceae), native to Central and South America. *U. molinae* is a tidy, restrained shrub to 6 feet, with small, oval, pointed bronze-tinted leaves, rose-tinted white bell-shaped flowers that attract bees, and tiny, dark red, edible fruit. Useful in moist soils near paths or patios and in containers.

Ulex (yoo'lehks) *n.* A genus of 25 species of hardy much-branched spiny shrubs (Leguminosae). They grow to 6 feet with small, spine-tipped, often scale-like leaves and fragrant yellow sweet-pea-shaped flowers. Grown as cover on poor, sandy soil. Commonly known as furze and gorse. (See **furze** and **gorse**.)

Ulex
(furze)

Ulmaceae (uhl may'see ee) *n. pl.* A family of 15 genera and 150 species of usually deciduous trees and shrubs; the elm family. The ornamental genera include *Celtis* (hackberry), *Ulmus* (elm), and *Zelkova*.

ulmaceous (uhl may'shuhs) *a.* In botany, of or pertaining to the Ulmaceae.

ulmo (ool'moh) *n.* A common name for *Eucryphia cordifolia,* a large tender broadleaf evergreen shrub or tree, native to Chile. It grows to 120 feet, much less in cultivation, with simple, heart-shaped leaves and showy, pretty white 4-petaled flowers up to 2 inches across in summer and autumn. They are quite rare. Also known as muermo.

Ulmus (ohl'muhs) *n.* A genus of 18 species of hardy to very hardy deciduous trees (Ulmaceae). They grow from 50 to 120 feet, depending on the species, with feather-veined oval, pointed, toothed leaves, inconspicuous flowers, and pale gold winged fruit. *U. americana* (American elm) was once widely used for lawn trees, shade trees, and street trees; now largely decimated throughout the United States by Dutch elm disease carried by the elm beetle. Planting of *U. americana* is no longer recommended, but other species are valuable ornamentals. Commonly known as elm. (See **elm**.)

umbel (uhm'buhl) *n.* A flower cluster, usually rounded, with all stems springing from the same point, as in Queen Anne's lace. Also umbella.

umbellate (uhm'buh layt) *a.* In botany, bearing umbels; arranged in umbels; umbellike, as umbel-late plants, flowers, or clusters. Also umbellar, umbellated.

umbellifer (uhm behl'uh fuh) *n.* In botany, a plant of the family Umbelliferae.

Umbelliferae (uhm buh lif'uh ree) *n. pl.* A family of 250 genera and 2,800 species of plant; the carrot or parsley family. Many of the species are widely grown for food or flavoring including carrots, parsley, parsnips, coriander, dill, caraway, anise, and fennel. The cultivated genera include *Anethum* (dill), *Carum* (caraway), *Coriandrum* (coriander), *Daucus* (carrot), *Foeniculum* (fennel), *Petroselinum* (parsley), *Pastinaca* (parsnip), and *Pimpinella* (anise). Apiaceae is a synonym.

umbelliferous (uhm buh lif'uh ruhs) *a.* In botany, bearing umbels; of or pertaining to the Umbelliferae.

umbelliform (uhm buh'lee form) *a.* Resembling an umbel.

Umbellularia (uhm buh loo lair'ee uh) *n.* A genus of 1 species, *U. californica* (Lauraceae), a large broadleaf evergreen tree native to California and Oregon. It grows to 80 feet, with long, narrow, pointed richly aromatic leaves, small yellowish flowers and olivelike fruit. Commonly known as bay tree, California laurel, California olive, and pepperwood.

umbellulate (uhm buh'loo layt) *a.* In botany, provided with or arranged in umbellules or umbellets.

umbellule (uhm'buh lool) *n.* A secondary umbel of a compound umbel. Also umbellet.

umbrella fern *n.* A common name for thicket-forming, sun-loving tropical ferns of the genus *Gleichenia*. (See **Gleichenia**.)

umbrella leaf *n.* A common name for *Diphylleia cymosa,* a hardy perennial native to wet places of the mountains of the southeastern United States, from Virginia to Georgia to Tennessee. It grows to 3 feet, with huge, lobed leaves and clusters of white flowers. Used in wild gardens or shaded rock gardens.

umbrella palm *n.* 1. A common name for *Hedyscepe canterburyana,* a subtropical and tropical palm that grows to 30 feet with arching, featherlike leaves clustered at the top of the slender trunk. Used as a houseplant, an indoor/outdoor plant, in containers, or in frost-free climates. 2. A common name for *Cyperus alternifolius,* a tender perennial that grows in or out of water to 4 feet, with narrow, firm leaves that spread out like the ribs of an umbrella at the top of slender stems. Used near streams or in containers. Can self-sow to the point of becoming a weed. Also known as umbrella plant and umbrella sedge.

umbrella pine *n.* A common name for 3 different plants: *Sciadopitys verticillata* (see **Japanese parasol fir**), *Pinus pinea* (nut pine), and *P. densiflora* 'Umbraculifera' (see **Japanese umbrella pine**). *P. pinea* is a slow-growing evergreen conifer that grows to 80 feet, flat-topped at maturity with long, stiff bright green needles and oval cones, 5 inches long, that produce edible seeds.

umbrella tree *n.* A common name for several different trees, including the genus *Schefflera* (see **Schefflera**) and *Magnolia tripetala. M. tripetala* is a North American tree native from Pennsylvania to Alabama and Mississippi. It grows to 40 feet, with huge 2-foot-long oval leaves, crowded at the ends of the branches. The immense white flowers are 10 inches across, but somewhat diminished in their appeal by their awful smell.

umbrella tree, ear-leaved *n.* A common name for *Magnolia Fraseri,* a deciduous North American tree native to the mountains of Virginia, south to Georgia and Alabama. It grows to 50 feet, with ear-shaped leaves, 18 inches long, and huge sweet-scented white or pale yellow flowers, 10 inches across.

umbrella tree, Queensland *n.* A common name for *Schefflera (Brassaia) actinophyla,* a handsome subtropical shrub or small tree. It grows to 20 feet or more, with long-stalked glossy-green leaves, divided into large leaflets resembling the ribs of an umbrella. Used most often as a houseplant or greenhouse specimen; in frost-free climates to create a tropical effect. Also known as Australian umbrella tree, Queensland umbrella tree, queen's umbrella tree, Australian ivy palm, octopus tree, and star-leaf.

underbrush *n.* Shrubs and small trees growing under large trees in a wood or forest; brush; undergrowth.

underbush *n.* Same as underbrush.

underground sprinkler system *n.* A subsurface irrigation system composed of piping and controls.

undergrowth *n.* That which grows under; especially, shrubs or small trees growing beneath or among large ones.

undershrub *n.* A plant of shrubby habit, but scarcely attaining the dimensions of a shrub; a very small shrub.

undulate *a.* In botany, having a wavy surface or edge. Also undulated.

Ungnadia (uhn nayd′ee uh) *n.* A genus of 1 species, *U. speciosa* (Sapindaceae), a tender deciduous shrubby tree native to Texas, New Mexico, and northern Mexico. It grows to 30 feet, with leaves divided into narrow leaflets and clusters of fragrant rose-colored 4-petaled flowers, 1 inch across. Commonly known as Texan buckeye, Mexican buckeye, Spanish buckeye, and false buckeye.

unhumidified *a.* A term used to describe organic matter prior to its decomposition into humus.

uni- *prefix.* One; single.

unicorn plant *n.* A common name for *Proboscidia,* an American genus with large purple flowers and fruit that can be pickled like cucumbers.

unicorn root *n.* A common name for 3 different plants *Aletris farinosa* (see **Aletris**), *Chamaelirium luteum* (see **Chamaelirium**), and *Helonias bullata* (see **Helonias**). Also known unicorn's horn.

uniflorous *a.* In botany, having only 1 flower. Also unifloral.

unifoliate *a.* 1. In botany, having 1 leaf. Also unifoliar.

unifoliolate *a.* Having a leaf that is compound in structure, but has only 1 leaflet, such as the orange tree.

uniparous *a.* In botany, having 1 branch.

unisexual *a.* In botany, said of a flower containing the organs of 1 sex: stamens or pistil, but not both; diclinous.

upas (yoo′puhs) *n.* A common name for *Antiaris toxicaria,* which is poisonous, and for species of

Strychnos, some of which are highly poisonous. Also known as upas tree. (See **Antiaris** and **Strychnos**.)

upland *n.* High ground.

urceolate (uhr see′uh leht) *a.* Urn-shaped; swelling out below and contracted at the mouth, as a calyx or corolla.

Urceolina (uhr see uh ligh′nuh) *n.* A genus of a few species of perennial bulbs (Amaryllidaceae) native to the Andes. *U. peruviana* grows to 18 inches, with long, narrow leaves and tall stalks topped by clusters of drooping scarlet flowers that appear before the leaves. Also known as urnflower.

urceolus (uhr see′uhl uhs) *n.,pl.* **urceoli**. In botany, any urn-shaped organ or part of a plant.

Urginea (uhr jihn′ee uh) *n.* A genus of between 30 and 40 species of moderately hardy perennial bulbs (Liliaceae). *U. maritima* grows to 4 or 5 feet, with long, fleshy, straplike leaves and densely flowered spikes of small white flowers that appear in autumn after summer dormancy.

urn *n.* A container, usually a vase with a pedestal, used for growing flowers.

Ursinia (uhr sin′ee uh) *n.* A genus of 40 species of annuals, perennials, and shrubs (Compositae). They grow from 14 inches to 3 feet, depending on the species, with alternate leaves, usually divided, and yellow or orange daisylike flowers on long stems. Used in beds and borders.

Urtica (uhrd′eh kuh) *n.* A genus of 50 species of annuals and perennials (Urticaceae). Commonly known as nettle, they are considered weeds. Some species cause a stinging rash.

Urticaceae (uhrd uh kay′see uh) *n. pl.* A family of more than 40 genera and 500 species of annuals, perennials, vines, shrubs, and trees, some with stinging hairs.

urticaceous (uhrd uh kay′shuhs) *a.* In botany, of or pertaining to the Urticaceae.

USDA An abbreviation commonly used for the United States Department of Agriculture.

utility cart *n.* (See **cart**.)

utility knife *n.* Any of various cutting tools having replaceable blades; used to cut twine, black plastic, etc.

utricle (yoo′treh kuhl) *n.* In botany, a small, bladderlike, usually dry, 1-seeded fruit with a thin, loose, tissuelike covering that does not open when ripe, such as that of an amaranth.

utricular (yoo trihk′yuh luh) *a.* Of, pertaining to, containing, or resembling a utricle.

Utricularia (yoo trik yuh lah′ree uh) *n.* A genus of about 200 species of water plants (Lintibulariaceae). They have submersed stems, simple leaves dissected into many hairlike segments, with many small bladders, and yellow flowers. Used in aquariums. Commonly known as bladderwort. (See **bladderwort**.)

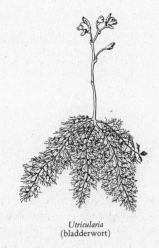

Utricularia
(bladderwort)

utriculiferous (yoo trihk′yuh lihf′uh ruhs) *a.* In botany, bearing or producing utricles.

utriculiform (yoo trihk′yuh luh form) *a.* In botany, having the form of a utricle.

utriculoid (yoo trik′yuh loid) *a.* Having the form of a bladder. Also utriculose.

uva (yoo′vuh) *n., pl.* **uvas** or **uvae**. In botany, a succulent fruit having a central placenta, as a grape.

Uvaria (yoo vair′ee uh) *n.* A genus of about 100 species of vines (Anonaceae). They have alternate, entire leaves, clusters of dark red flowers, and many-seeded fruit, often edible.

Uvularia (yoov yuh lair′ee uh) *n.* A genus of 5 species of hardy perennials (Liliaceae) native to eastern North America, from Quebec and Minnesota to Florida and Louisiana. They grow from rhizomes to 2½ feet, with long, narrow leaves and drooping yellow bell-shaped flowers that bloom in spring. Used in wild gardens and in shady places. Commonly known as bellwort, merrybells, haybells, and cowbells.

Uvularia
(bellwort)

Vaccaria (va kah′ree uh) *n.* A genus of 4 species of annuals (Caryophyllaceae). *V. pyramidata* grows to 2 feet, with narrow, oval leaves and pink to dark purple 5-petaled flowers. Naturalized as a weed in grain fields in North America. Commonly known as cockle, cow herb and dairy pink.

Vaccinium (vak sihn′ee uhm) *n.* A genus of 150 species of hardy deciduous or evergreen shrubs (Ericaceae), many species native to North America. They grow from 1 to 15 feet, depending on the species, with oval, pointed, simple, alternate leaves, white, green, red, or purple urn-shaped bell-like flowers and white, black, red, purple, or dark blue fruit that attracts birds. The genus includes blueberries, huckleberries, lingonberries, and cranberries. Used in woodland gardens, as fruiting hedges, as specimen shrubs, and for their fruit. Commonly known as blueberry, huckleberry, bilberry, and cranberry.

vagina *n.*, *pl.* **vaginae** or **vaginas**. In botany, a sheath; specifically that formed by the basal part of certain leaves where they embrace the stem.

vaginate *a.* Forming or formed into a sheath. Also vaginated.

valerian, garden (vuh lih′ree uhn) *n.* (See **Valeriana**.)

valerian, Greek (vuh lih′ree uhn) *n.* A common name for *Polemonium caeruleum,* a very hardy perennial flower. It grows to 3 feet, with lush rosettes of finely divided, fern-like leaves and clusters of blue bell-shaped or funnel-shaped flowers in summer. Used in moist, shady beds and borders. Combines well with hellebores, bellflowers, bleeding heart, hostas, lilies, and ferns. Also known as Jacob's ladder.

valerian, long-spurred (vuh lih′ree uhn) *n.* A common name for *Centranthus macrosiphon,* an annual flower. It grows to 2 feet, with oval, pointed leaves and clusters of deep rose flowers. Used in beds.

Valerian
1 entire plant
2 flower and upper stem

valerian, red (vuh lih′ree uhn) *n.* A common name for *Centranthus ruber,* a tender perennial. Also known as Jupiter's-beard. (See **Centranthus**.)

Valeriana (vuh lih ree an′uh) *n.* A genus of about 200 species of hardy perennials, subshrubs, or shrubs (Valerianaceae), some species native to North America. They grow from 6 inches to 5 feet, depending on the species, often with leaves in a basal rosette, and clusters of small white, pink, rose, or yellow flowers, sometimes fragrant. Used in beds and borders, traditional in cottage gardens. Also known as garden heliotrope, and valerian.

Valerianaceae (vuh lih ree uh nay'see ee) *n. pl.* A family of 10 genera and about 400 species of perennial flowers and shrubs; the valerian family. The ornamental genera include *Centranthus* (centranth), *Valeriana* (valerian), and *Valerianella* (corn salad or lamb's-lettuce).

valerianaceous (vuh lih ree uh nay'shuhs) *a.* Of, or characteristic of, the family Valerianaceae.

Valerianella (vuh lih ree uh nehl'uh) *n.* A genus of 50 to 60 species of annuals and biennials (Valerianaceae), some species native to North America, and other species naturalized in North America. They have simple, opposite, succulent leaves and headlike clusters of white, red, or blue tubelike flowers. Grown mostly for salad greens, useful in the vegetable plot or for edible landscaping. Also known as corn salad and lamb's-lettuce.

Vallaris (val'uh ruhs) *n.* A genus of 6 species of woody, twining, tropical vines (Apocynaceae). *V. solanacea* is a tall climbing vine with narrow, oval leaves, clusters of small, fragrant white trumpet-shaped flowers, and large, woody seed pods. Used to cover porches and arbors.

Vallesia (val'uh see uh) *n.* A genus of 8 species of tropical shrubs and small trees (Apocynaceae). *V. flexuosa* grows to 30 feet, with long, oval leaves and clusters of small, white, star-shaped flowers.

Vallisneria (val uh snih'ree uh) *n.* A genus of 8 to 10 species of submersed, grasslike water plants (Hydrocharitaceae), some species native to North America. They have ribbonlike leaves, male and female flowers, and curved fruit on a coiled stalk. Occasionally grown in aquariums or garden pools. Commonly known as eel grass and tape grass.

Vallota (vuh loh'duh) *n.* A genus of 1 species, *V. speciosa* (Amaryllidaceae), a tender perennial bulb. It grows to 2 feet, with straplike leaves, up to 2 feet long, and clusters of bright scarlet, funnel-shaped flowers. Grown in frost-free gardens or in small pots; blooms best when roots are crowded. Commonly known as Scarborough lily.

Valparaiso oak (val puh righ'zoh) *n.* A common name for *Quercus chrysolepis,* a handsome, round-headed tender evergreen tree native to the slopes and canyons of California and southern Oregon. Also known as canyon oak and canyon live oak. (See **oak, canyon**.)

valvate (val'vayt) *a.* In botany: 1. Opening as if by doors or valves, as in certain capsules or anthers. 2. Meeting at the edges without overlapping, as in certain sepals or leaves.

valve *n.* In botany, in flowering plants, 1 of the segments into which a capsule or legume splits at maturity, or which opens like a lid, as in the barberry.

Vancouveria (van koo vih'ree uh) *n.* A genus of 3 species of tender perennials (Berberidaceae) native to western North America, from British Columbia to California. They grow to 18 inches, with leaves divided into heart-shaped leaflets, rather resembling maidenhair fern, and clusters of attractive, small yellow or white flowers, with petals curved sharply backward. Used as a small-scale ground cover in dappled shade. The cut foliage is attractive in bouquets.

Vanda (van'duh) *n.* A genus of 60 species of tropical epiphytic orchids (Orchidaceae). They grow from 1 to 7 feet, depending on the species, with leathery or fleshy, strap-shaped leaves and large, showy multicolored flowers. These are the orchids traditionally used to make Hawaiian leis. Grown in greenhouses or in humid areas of Hawaii.

Vandopsis (van dahp'suhs) *n.* A genus of 20 species of tropical orchids (Orchidaceae). They grow from 1 to 6 feet, depending on the species, with broad, strap-shaped fleshy leaves and spikes of large, thick-petaled multicolored flowers. Grown by collectors in greenhouses.

Vangueria (van gwih'ree uh) *n.* A genus of 27 species of tropical shrubs and trees (Rubiaceae). *V. edulis,* tamarind-of-the-Indies, grows to 15 feet, with opposite leaves, clusters of very small, green, bell-shaped or tubular flowers, and edible, fleshy, apple-shaped fruit.

Vanheerdia (van heerd'ee uh) *n.* A genus of 4 species of dwarf, clump-forming succulents (Aizoaceae). They grow to a few inches high, with opposite, paired, symmetrical leaves and clusters of small, many-petaled yellow or orange flowers. Grown mainly by collectors.

Vanilla *n.* A genus of 90 species of robust, tropical epiphytic, branching, vinelike orchids (Orchidaceae) native to tropical America. *V. planifolia* has nar-

oval, leathery or fleshy leaves 8 inches long, low and orange flowers and an 8-inch-long aromatic pod, which produces the flavoring vanilla. The flowers are naturally pollinated by hummingbirds. When planted outside the American tropics, they must be hand-pollinated to bear fruit. Also known as vanilla plant.

Vanilla

vanilla trumpet vine *n.* A common name for *Distictis laxiflora,* a tender vine native to Mexico. It has deep green leaves divided into oval leaflets, and clusters of large, vanilla-scented trumpet-shaped violet flowers that fade first to lilac, then to white.

variegated *a.* Varied in color; irregularly marked with different colors.

variegation *n.* In botany: 1. The conjunction of 2 or more colors in the petals, leaves, or other parts of plants. 2. Being variegated; the act of variegating.

variety *n.* A subdivision of a species officially ranking between subspecies and forma. It is indicated in botanical nomenclature by its position following the species name, for example, Japanese flowering cherry, *Prunus serrulata serrulata,* or bitter almond, *Prunus dulcis amara.* A cultivar is a horticultural variety that is produced by selective breeding, rather than by natural selection, and persists only in cultivation (not found in the wild). Cultivars are indicated in botanical nomenclature by single quotes; for example, sunset lily, *Lilium pardalinum* 'Giganteum'. Hybrids are created by

crosses between 2 different species or 2 different forms of the same species. Hybrids may occur through natural selection or selective breeding (hybridization). Hybrids are indicated in botanical nomenclature by a multiplication sign between the two parents, such as *Abelia chinensis* × *A. uniflora* or *Abelia* × *grandiflora.* (These last 2 examples are 2 ways of describing the same plant.)

varnish tree *n.* A common name for *Ailanthus altissima* (tree of heaven or copal tree; see **Ailanthus**), *Koelreuteria paniculata* (see **Koelreuteria**), *Rhus verniciflua* (lacquer tree or Japanese lacquer tree), and *Semecarpus anacardium* (marking-nut tree). Neither *Rhus verniciflua* nor *Semecarpus anacardium* are grown ornamentally. The sap of *R. verniciflua* is used to make the shiny finish on Japanese lacquer boxes, and *S. anacardium* is used to produce an ink or dye.

vascular *a.* In botany, referring to a plant's circulatory system, which consists of, or relates to, the specialized conducting tissues of plants—xylem and phloem—which circulate sap.

vascular plants *n. pl.* Plants in which the structure is made up in part of vascular tissue or vessels. They include the flowering plants (angiosperms), cone-bearing plants (gymnosperms, such as conifers, ginkgos, and cycads), and ferns and fern allies (spore-producing). Nonvascular plants include fungi, algae, lichens, mosses, and liverworts.

vase *n.* Any of variously shaped containers for holding cut flowers.

Vauquelinia (vow'kuh leh nee uh) *n.* A genus of evergreen shrubs and small trees (Rosaceae), some species native to North America. *V. californica* is an open-growing evergreen shrub to 20 feet, with dark gray to red-brown bark, narrow, pointed, leathery, bright green leaves, woolly beneath, clusters of tiny, white, 5-petaled flowers, and persistent woody seed capsules. Useful in desert gardens; thrives despite drought, heat, and extremes of temperature. *V. californica* is commonly known as Arizona rosewood.

vegetable *n.* Typically, an herbaceous cultivated plant used for food, such as turnips, potatoes, spinach, peas, and beans.

vegetable fern *n.* A common name for *Diplazium esculentum,* a tender fern with an erect, trunklike rhizome. It has triangular, doubly divided fronds, 4 to 6 feet long. Grown in greenhouses with high humidity.

vegetable marrow *n*. A British name for zucchini and other green summer squashes.

vegetable oyster *n*. Salsify.

vegetable trellis *n*. A frame structure covered by nylon netting, used to support peas, pole beans, cucumbers, or squash.

vegetative *a*. Having the power to produce or support growth in plants, as the vegetative properties of soil.

vegetative propagation *n*. Propagation by asexual means, such as stem cuttings, leaf cuttings, layering, root division, or bulblets. African violets are propagated by leaf cuttings; roses and fruit trees are propagated by stem cuttings (also called slips); iris and daylilies are propagated by root division; strawberries and ivies can be propagated by layering; lilies can be propagated by bulblets.

vein *n*. In botany, a fibrovascular bundle at or near the surface of a leaf. Also nerve; rib.

Veitchia (vay chee′uh) *n*. A genus of 18 species of attractive tropical palms (Palmae). They grow from 15 to 100 feet, depending on the species, with divided leaves, male and female flowers, and orange to crimson fruit. *V. merrillii*, the Christmas palm or Manila palm, grows to 15 feet, with 6-foot-long leaves, with up to 63 leaflets on each side, and clusters of tiny crimson fruit. Grown in mild-winter climates or as a greenhouse specimen.

Veltheimia (vehl thay′mee uh) *n*. A genus of 5 species of tender perennial bulbs (Liliaceae). They grow to 15 inches, with narrow, basal leaves and spikes of nodding, tubular pale pink or purple flowers. Grown outdoors in mild-winter climates, in greenhouses elsewhere.

velutinous (veh loo′tuh nuhs) *a*. In botany, velvety; having dense, silky hairs.

velvet flower *n*. A common name for *Amaranthus caudatus,* a large, vigorous, much-branched annual flower. Also known as love-lies-bleeding. (See **love-lies-bleeding.**)

velvet groundsel *n*. A common name for *Senecio Petasitis,* a large tender perennial. It grows to 8 feet

and has wide, with lobed, fanlike, velvety leaves 8 inches across, and large clusters of daisylike bright yellow flowers, held well above the foliage. Useful for creating a tropical effect; grows well in big pots or tubs. Also known as California geranium.

velvetleaf *n*. A common name for *Abutilon Theophrasti* and *Kalanchoe beharensis. A. Theophrasti* is a large annual that grows from 2 to 6 feet, with rounded, heart-shaped, velvety leaves, up to 1 foot across, and yellow 5-petaled flowers. It has naturalized as a weed in the United States. Also known as butter print, pie marker, Indian mallow, and China jute. *K. beharensis* is a succulent that grows to 12 feet, with large, thick, triangular, velvety leaves, wavy and crimped at the edges. Grown outdoors in mild climates, as a houseplant anywhere. *K. beharensis* is also known as felt plant and velvet elephant-ear.

velvet plant *n*. A common name for *Gynura aurantiaca,* a trailing tropical perennial. The plushy purple stems grow to 9 feet long, with soft, velvety, purple oval leaves, to 8 inches, and orange-yellow flowers that fade to purple. Unfortunately, the flowers smell awful and should be pinched out as buds. Grown most often as a houseplant or sometimes as an indoor/outdoor hanging basket plant. Also known as purple velvet plant and royal velvet plant.

venation *n*. In botany, the arrangement of veins in the blade of a leaf.

Venidium (veh nihd′ee uhm) *n*. A genus of 20 or 30 species of annuals or tender perennials (Compositae). They grow to 3 feet, with alternate, usually woolly leaves and daisylike golden-yellow or orange flowers with dark centers. Usually grown as annuals in summer borders. Commonly known as Namaqualand daisy.

venous (vee′nuhs) *a*. In botany, having numerous veins; veiny, as a venous leaf. Also venose.

ventilator *n*. A device to draw in fresh air and expel stagnant air from a greenhouse or cold frame.

ventilator regulator *n*. A temperature-activated controller for opening or closing vents in a greenhouse or cold frame.

ventral (vehn truhl) *a*. In botany, belonging to the front or inner surface of anything; the opposite of dorsal.

ventricose (vehn'treh kohs) *a.* In botany, swollen or inflated on one side; distended.

Venus's-flytrap *n.* A common name for *Dionaea muscipula,* a tender carnivorous bog plant native to the southeastern United States, from North Carolina to South Carolina. It grows to a few inches tall, with long, hinged leaves, which snap shut when the sensitive hairs are triggered by insects, and clusters of small, white 5-petaled flowers. Grown as a novelty houseplant.

Venus's looking-glass *n.* A common name for *Legousia speculum-Veneris,* a small annual flower. It grows to 18 inches, with shiny leaves, shaped like a hand mirror, and clusters of 3 small blue or white 5-petaled flowers. Used in borders as edging, in beds, and in rock gardens.

Venus's-shoe *n.* A common name for *Cypripedium Calceolus pubescens,* a very hardy robust North American wild orchid, native from Newfoundland to the Yukon Territory, south to Georgia, Louisiana, Arizona, and Oregon. It grows to 2 feet, with oval, pointed leaves, 8 inches long, and large green-yellow or purple-brown slipper-shaped flowers. Also known as large yellow lady's-slipper, large yellow moccasin flower, Venus's-slipper, golden-slipper, whippoorwill-shoe, American valerian, umbil root, nerveroot, yellow Indian-shoe, and Noah's-ark.

Veratrum
(false hellebore)

Veratrum (veh ray'truhm) *n.* A genus of 45 species of hardy perennials that grow from rhizomes (Liliaceae), some species native to North America. They grow from 2 to 7 feet, depending on the species, with alternate, pleated leaves and clusters of white, green, brown, maroon, or purple flowers. The species are poisonous, and the poisons are used to make an organic pesticide. Commonly known as false hellebore. (See **hellebore, false**.)

Verbascum (vuhr bas'kuhm) *n.* A genus of about 250 species of hardy biennials (Scrophulariaceae); mullein. They grow from 3 to 7 feet, depending on the species, with alternate, simple, often furry, leaves and tall spikes of typically yellow 5-petaled flowers. Most often seen as a roadside weed, mulleins are sometimes grown in the back of a border for their bold effect, silvery leaves, or tall spikes of flowers.

Verbena (vuhr bee'nuh) *n.* A genus of about 200 species of mostly tender or short-lived perennials (Verbenaceae), some species native to North and South America. They grow from 6 inches to 4 feet, depending on the species, with usually opposite, toothed or cut leaves and clusters of white, pink, purple, blue, or multicolored flowers. Grown as annuals in cold climates, as drought-tolerant perennials in mild climates. Thrive in heat, useful in desert gardens. *V.officinalis* is traditional in cottage gardens. Commonly known as vervain.

Verbenaceae (vuhr buh nay'see ee) *n. pl.* A family of 75 to 98 genera and 2,600 to 3,000 species of annuals, perennials, subshrubs, and trees. The ornamental genera include *Aloysia, Callicarpa* (beautyberry), *Caryopteris* (bluebeard), *Clerodendrum* (glory-bower or Kashmir-bouquet), *Lantana* (shrub verbena), *Nyctanthus, Oxera* (royal climber), *Petrea* (bluebird vine or queen's wreath), *Verbena* (vervain), and *Vitex.*

verbenaceous (vuhr buh nay'shuhs) *a.* Pertaining to or having the characters of the Verbenaceae.

verbena, lemon (ver been'uh) *n.* (See **lemon verbena**.)

Verbesina (vuhr buh sigh'nuh) *n.* A genus of about 200 species of annuals, perennials, shrubs, and trees (Compositae) native to the Americas. They grow from 3 to 9 feet, depending on the species, with toothed leaves and usually yellow, daisylike flowers. Commonly known as crown-beard.

vernation (vuhr nay′shuhn) *n.* In botany, the disposition of leaves within a bud. Compare aestivation.

Vernonia (vuhr noh′nee uh) *n.* A genus of between 500 and 1,000 species of perennials, vines, subshrubs, shrubs, and trees (Compositae), many species native to the Americas. They grow from 6 inches to 10 feet, depending on the species, with typically alternate leaves and heads of tubular purple flowers that bloom in late summer or fall. Commonly known as ironweed. (See **ironweed**.)

Veronica (veh rahn′eh kuh) *n.* A genus of about 250 species of annuals and perennials (Scrophulariaceae). They grow from a few inches to 2 feet, with opposite, simple leaves and spikes or clusters of small white, rose, pink, deep blue, or purple flowers. Used in beds, sunny borders, and rock gardens; traditional in herb gardens. Commonly known as speedwell and brooklime.

Veronica
(speedwell)

Veronicastrum (veh rahn uh kas′truhm) *n.* A genus of 2 species of very hardy perennials (Scrophulariaceae) resembling *Veronica*; *V. virginicum* is native to eastern North America. *V. virginicum* grows to 7 feet, with toothed, narrow leaves and 9-inch spikes of tiny pale blue or white flowers.

Sometimes grown in herb gardens and cottage gardens. Commonly known as Culver's physic.

verrucose (vehr′yuh kohs) *a.* Warty.

verrucous (veh roo′kuhs) *a.* Of, relating to, or resembling a wart.

verruculose (veh roo′kyuh lohs) *a.* Minutely verrucose.

versatile *a.* In botany, swinging or turning freely on a support, especially as an anther fixed at the middle on the apex of the filament, and swinging freely.

Verschaffeltia (vehr shaf fehl′tee uh) *n.* A genus of 1 species, *V. splendida* (Palmae), a tall, slender tropical palm. It has a slim trunk, covered with black spines, that grows to 75 feet or more, with divided leaves 9 feet long. Used in frost-free gardens.

verticil (vuhr′duh sihl) *n.* In botany, a whorl, as leaves or flowers that are disposed in a circle or ring around an axis.

verticillaster (vuhr duh seh las′tuhr) *n.* In botany, a form of inflorescence in which the flowers are arranged in a seeming whorl, consisting of a pair of opposite axillary, usually sessile, cymes or clusters, as in many of the mints (Labiatae).

verticillastrate (vuhr duh seh las′trayt) *a.* In botany, bearing or arranged in verticillasters.

verticillate (vuhr duh seh′layt) *a.* Whorled; arranged in a verticil, as leaves or flowers; having organs so disposed. Also verticillated.

Verticordia (vuhr duh kawr′dee uh) *n.* A genus of 50 species of tender evergreen heatherlike shrubs (Myrtaceae). They grow to 3 feet, with small, narrow, entire, opposite leaves and showy white, pink, or yellow 5-petaled flowers. Commonly known as feather flower.

vervain family (vuhr′vayn) *n.* A common name for Verbenaceae. Also called the verbena family. (See **Verbenaceae**.)

vervain mallow (vuhr′vayn) *n.* A common name for *Malva Alcea*, a fast-growing, short-lived hardy perennial that has naturalized in the eastern United States. It grows to 4 feet, with small, dense, rounded leaves and pink hollyhocklike flowers. Used in perennial borders.

very coarse sand *n.* Soil particles measuring 1.0 to 2.0 millimeters.

very fine sand *n.* Soil particles measuring 0.05 to 0.10 milimeter.

vespertine (vehs'puhr tighn) *a.* In botany, opening in the evening, such as a flower.

Vestia (vehs'tee uh) *n.* A genus of 1 species, *V. lycioides* (Solanaceae), a tender evergreen shrub. It grows to 12 feet, with shiny, small, oval, entire leaves and clusters of open, drooping yellow-green flowers. It is reported to smell bad.

vetch *n.* A common name for *Vicia,* a genus of mostly trailing annuals, biennials, and perennials, many of them roadside weeds, some native to North America. They grow from 1 to 6 feet, with leaves divided into leaflets and terminating in a tendril. They have spikes of purple, rose, reddish-purple, white, or blue pealike flowers and long, thin pods resembling pea pods. Grown mostly as forage crops; often seen as roadside weeds. Also known as tare.

vetch

vetch, hairy *n.* A common name for *Vicia villosa,* naturalized as a weed in the United States. Also known as winter vetch and large Russian vetch.

vetch, horseshoe *n.* A common name for *Hippocrepis comosa,* a tender perennial ground cover. It forms a mat 3 inches high and spreads to 3 feet wide. It has leaves divided into many small leaflets and loose clusters of yellow sweet pealike flowers.

Used as a small-scale ground cover or in rock gardens. Fairly drought-tolerant and useful for controlling erosion.

vetch, milk *n.* A common name for *Astragulus,* a genus of mostly hardy perennials. (See **Astragalus**.)

vetch, tare (tah'uhr) *n.* A common name for *Vicia sativa,* an annual or biennial weed naturalized in North America. Also known as spring vetch.

vetch, tufted *n.* A common name for *Vicia Cracca,* a hardy perennial wildflower native to North America. It has stems to 6 feet long, with leaves divided into 4 or 6 pairs of small narrow leaflets and many-flowered spikes of purple to white sweet-pea-like flowers, all on 1 side of the spike. Also known as bird vetch, cow vetch, and Canada pea.

Viburnum
(arrowwood)
a flower *b* fruit

Viburnum (vigh buhr'nuhm) *n.* A genus of 225 species of hardy to very hardy shrubs and small trees (Caprifoliaceae), some species native to North America. They grow from 5 to 40 feet, depending on the species, though most are 10 to 12 feet tall. They have opposite, simple leaves that color spectacularly in autumn in many species. They also have large, showy clusters of white or pink flowers, sometimes fragrant, and fleshy red, yellow, purple, or black fruit that attracts birds. They are extremely adaptable plants, growing in sun or shade, in acid or alkaline soils, and willing to thrive in a wide range of climates. Many are choice garden plants. Individual species and cultivars are grown for their showy flowers, flower fragrance, fall color, attractive winter fruit, attraction to birds, or some combination of these qualities. Used as foundation plants, specimen shrubs and small trees, or as a screen. Commonly known as arrowwood.

Vicia (vih′shee uh) *n.* A genus of about 150 species of mostly hardy climbing or spreading annuals, biennials, and perennials (Leguminosae). They grow from 1 to 6 feet, depending on the species, with alternate leaves divided into an even number of paired leaflets, with a tendril at the end of the leaf, and white, purple, or magenta sweet pealike flowers. Some, such as *V. Fava,* are grown for food, many are grown as cover crops or as forage, and a few are grown ornamentally. Commonly known as vetch or tare.

Victoria *n.* A genus of 2 species of tropical water lilies (Nymphaeaceae) native to South America. They have huge, circular, floating, platter-shaped leaves 3 to 6 feet across, heavily ridged beneath, and floating, fragrant flowers that open white in the afternoon and fade to pink by the next day. Used in very large garden pools in tropical climates or grown as annuals. Commonly known as giant water lily and water-platter. (See **lily, giant water** and **lily, Santa Cruz water**.)

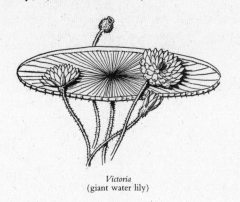

Victoria
(giant water lily)

Victorian box *n.* A common name for *Pittosporum undulatum,* a tender shrub or tree. It grows quickly to 15 feet, then slowly to 30 or 40 feet, with glossy, wavy-edged oval, pointed leaves, clusters of fragrant creamy-white flowers in early spring, and yellow-to-orange fruit that split to reveal sticky, bright orange seeds. Used as a lawn or street tree, screen, or container plant. Also known as mock orange.

Victory plant *n.* A common name for *Cheiridopsis candidissima,* a tender, dwarf, mat-forming succulent. It has thick, fleshy leaves, tipped with red, and white or light pink flowers 2 inches across. Grown mainly by collectors. Also known as goat's-horns.

Vigna (vigh′nuh) *n.* A genus of more than 200 species of mostly twining or sprawling annuals and perennials (Leguminosae). They grow from 2½ to 20 feet, depending on the species, with leaves divided into 3 leaflets, white, yellow, or purple sweet-pea-shaped flowers, and long pods. Azuki bean, mung bean, black-eyed pea, and yard-long (asparagus) bean are all in this genus. Most species are grown as food, forage, or cover crops. *V. car-acalla,* the snail vine, is grown ornamentally. It climbs to 20 feet, with 3-part leaves and fragrant cream-colored flowers marked with purple. The flowers, coiled at the edges, look like a snail's shell.

Villadia (vihl′uh dee uh) *n.* A genus of 30 species of tender succulent perennials (Crassulaceae), native to the Americas from Texas to Peru. They grow from 6 to 20 inches, with small, thick, fleshy, cylindrical, alternate leaves and spikes or clusters of small white, pink, red, orange, yellow, green, or purple flowers.

Villebrunea (vihl uh broo′nee uh) *n.* A genus of 8 species of shrubs or trees (Urticaceae). *V. pedunculata* is a small, slender-branched tree, with simple, narrow, oval, alternate leaves and male and female flowers.

villous (vihl′uhs) *a.* In botany, having long, soft, not interwoven hairs. Also villose.

villus (vihl′uhs) *n.* In botany, 1 of the long, straight, and soft hairs that sometimes cover the fruit, flowers, and other parts of plants.

Viminaria (vihm uh nah′ree uh) *n.* A genus of 1 species, *V. denudata* (Leguminosae), a tender shrub with long, arching branches. It grows to 20 feet, with alternate, threadlike leaves and long spikes of small orange-yellow sweet pealike flowers.

Vinca (vihng′kuh) *n.* A genus of 12 species of tender trailing evergreen perennials (Apocynaceae). The stems grow to several feet, mounding to 24 inches, with glossy, oval, pointed leaves and small clusters of lavender-blue flowers up to 2 inches across. Used as tough, tolerant, large-scale ground covers, or trailing from window boxes. Extremely persistent; can be invasive. Commonly known as periwinkle and myrtle. *V. rosea* is now classified as *Catharanthus rosea*; also called Madagascar periwinkle, rose periwinkle, and old maid. (See **Catharanthus**.)

vine *n.* A vine is a climbing plant with woody or herbaceous stems that climbs, twines, adheres, or scrambles over other taller objects—shrubs, trees, walls, fences, arbors, porches, gazebos, etc.—in order to reach sunlight. Vines climb by twining stems (honeysuckle and wisteria), twining leaf stalks (clematis), by tendrils (grapes, peas, and beans), by aerial roots (ivy and trumpet creeper), by adhesive disks (Boston ivy and Virginia creeper), and by hooks (climbing roses and cat's-claw). Vines that climb under their own power are described as self-clinging. Some plants used as vines merely sprawl and must be supported by being secured to an upright support such as a trellis or wall, for example, bougainvillea and star (Confederate) jasmine. Often used as a common name for *Vitis* (grapevine).

vine cactus *n.* A common name for *Fouquieria splendens*, a curious tender spiny shrub native to American deserts. Also known as coach-whip, Jacob's staff, and ocotillo. (See **ocotillo**.)

vine-culture *n.* Same as viticulture.

vinegar tree *n.* A common name for *Rhus glabra,* a hardy deciduous large shrub or small tree native to North America, from British Columbia to eastern Oregon. It grows to 20 feet, often less, with deep green leaves divided into many narrow, toothed leaflets that turn brilliant scarlet in autumn, inconspicuous flowers, and conical clusters of scarlet fruit that hangs on through winter. Tolerates heat, cold, drought, and all but the most alkaline soils. Grown for its fall color, winter fruit, and interesting silhouette. Excellent among coniferous evergreens or in containers. Also known as smooth sumac.

vine, India-rubber *n.* A common name for *Cryptostegia grandiflora*, a vigorous tropical woody vine. It has shiny, oval, simple, opposite leaves and clusters of lilac-purple trumpet-shaped flowers, 2 to 3 inches long. Used as a vine in frost-free climates. The sap has been used as a source of rubber. Also known as purple allamanda and rubber vine.

vine, red-bead *n.* A common name for *Abrus precatorius,* tropical twining evergreen woody vine. It grows to 10 feet, with alternate leaves divided into many small leaflets, spikes of small sweet pea-shaped rose, purple, or white flowers, and pods containing glossy, scarlet, poisonous seeds. Also known as rosary pea, love pea, Indian licorice, wild licorice, licorice vine, weather plant, weather vine, prayer-beads, coral-bead plant, and crab's-eye.

vine support *n.* (See **leaded wall nail**.)

vine, wonga-wonga (whan′guh wahn′guh) *n.* A common name for *Pandorea pandorana,* a large, tender twining evergreen vine. It has glossy leaves divided into oval, pointed leaflets and clusters of trumpet-shaped cream-colored flowers with a purple throat. Useful on arbors and lanais.

Viola (vigh oh′luh) *n.* A genus of about 500 species of low-growing perennials (Violaceae). They grow from a few inches to 16 inches, depending on the species, with variously shaped leaves and flowers. The family includes the pansy, viola, and violet. Pansies are much loved for the "faces" in their multicolored flowers, sweet violets for their fragrance. The genus has been much hybridized, giving rise to huge, long-stemmed solid-color pansies such as 'Royal Robe', in pale pastels such as 'Antique Shades', etc. Many species are grown as annuals. The genus is commonly known as violet.

Viola tricolor
(viola)

Violaceae (vigh oh lay′see ee) *n. pl.* A family of 18 genera and about 800 species of perennials, shrubs, and, rarely, vines or trees. The ornamental genera include *Hymenanthera, Melicytus,* and *Viola* (violet). Commonly known as the violet family.

violaceous (vigh uh lay'shuhs) *a*. Of, resembling, or pertaining to the family Violaceae.

violet *n*. A common name for the genus *Viola*. (See **Viola**.) Specifically used for *V. odorata,* also known as sweet violet. (See **violet, sweet**.)

violet, African *n*. A common name for *Saintpaulia,* a genus of semisucculent, low-growing, fuzzy-leaved tropical plants. A wildly popular houseplant, it grows to 8 inches, often smaller, with thick, fuzzy, rounded, heart-shaped leaves and clusters of purple, violet, white, pink, or bicolored flowers. There are nearly incalculable numbers of hybrids and named cultivars with single or double flowers, ruffled or variegated leaves, standard size or miniature, or any imaginable combination thereof. Probably America's most familiar windowsill plant.

violet, American dog *n*. A common name for *Viola conspersa,* a very hardy perennial wildflower native to eastern North America, from Quebec to Minnesota to Georgia. It grows to 8 inches, with rounded, heart-shaped leaves and many pale violet to white flowers.

violet, arrow-leaved *n*. A common name for *Viola sagittata,* a stemless, low-growing, very hardy perennial wildflower native to the eastern United States, from Maine to Minnesota to east Texas. It grows to 4 inches, with narrow, arrow-shaped leaves and violet-purple flowers, 1-inch across.

violet, Australian *n*. A common name for *Viola hederacea,* a tender tufted perennial that spreads by stolons. It grows to 4 inches, with small, kidney-shaped leaves and tiny white or blue flowers. Used as a small-scale ground cover in mild climates. Also known as ivy-leaved violet and trailing violet.

violet, bird's-foot *n*. A common name for *Viola pedata,* a stemless hardy perennial wildflower native to the eastern United States. It grows to 6 inches, with leaves divided like a bird's foot, with 3 or 5 toes, and variously colored, sometimes multicolored flowers. Also known as pansy violet and crowfoot violet.

violet, California golden *n*. A common name for *Viola pedunculata,* a tender perennial wildflower native to California. It grows from a stout rhizome to 2 feet tall, with round to oval leaves and orange-yellow flowers with purple veins on the inside.

violet, Canada *n*. A common name for *Viola canadensis,* a hardy perennial wildflower native to North America, from New Brunswick to Alabama and west to Washington and Arizona. It grows from a thick rhizome to 1 foot tall with heart-shaped, toothed leaves and with white flowers, yellow at the base and often tinged violet outside. Also known as tall white violet.

violet, Confederate *n*. A common name for a form of *Viola sororia* that has blue-gray flowers. *V. sororia,* the woolly blue violet, is a self-sowing stemless hardy perennial wildflower, the most widespread species of *Viola* native to the eastern United States. It grows from a thick fleshy rhizome, with large, heart-shaped leaves and small, open-faced blue, white, red, purple, or gray-blue flowers. Used as a ground cover under rhododendrons or in woodland gardens.

violet, dogtooth *n*. A common name for *Erythronium* (Liliaceae), a genus of low-growing, spring-blooming perennials with 2 smooth leaves, which are often mottled, and a stalk with 1 or more large yellow, pink, purple, rose, or white nodding, lily-like flowers. Also known as adder's-tongue, trout lily, and fawn lily. (See **Erythronium**; **lily, trout** and **lily, fawn**.)

violet, English *n*. A common name for *Viola odorata,* a tufted, stemless, hardy perennial that spreads by runners. It grows to a few inches tall, with dark green heart-shaped leaves and delicately fragrant, deep purple, blue-rose, or white flowers. Used as an edging in beds and borders, in woodland gardens, in window boxes, and in pots. Also known as sweet violet, garden violet, and florist's violet.

violet family *n*. A common name for Violaceae. (See **Violaceae**.)

violet, horned *n*. A common name for *Viola cornuta,* a tufted hardy perennial. It grows 6 to 8 inches, with smooth, oval leaves and purple, pansylike flowers, 1 inch across. Cultivars come in many different colors, such as purple, blue, yellow, apricot, ruby red, and white. Used in beds, borders, and pots. Also known as tufted pansy or viola.

595

violet, lance-leaved *n.* A common name for *Viola lanceolata,* a very hardy perennial wildflower native to North America, from Nova Scotia to Florida and Texas. It grows from a rhizome to 9 inches, with narrow leaves and white flowers. Also known as Eastern water violet.

violet, long-spurred *n.* A common name for *Viola rostrata,* a very hardy perennial wildflower native to North America, from Quebec to Michigan and Georgia. It has leafy stems to 15 inches, with shiny, spiny heart-shaped leaves and lilac flowers with dark spots.

violet, marsh *n.* A common name for *Viola palustris,* a stemless hardy perennial wildflower native to wet places in North America. It grows from a rhizome, with shiny heart-shaped or kidney-shaped leaves and small, pale lilac flowers with darker veins. Also known as alpine marsh violet.

violet, pale *n.* A common name for *Viola striata,* a hardy perennial wildflower native to the eastern United States. It has leafy stems to 2 feet, with oval, toothed leaves and small, cream-colored flowers with purple veins. Also known as striped violet, cream violet, and pansy violet.

violet, Parma *n.* A common name for *Viola alba,* a marginally hardy tufted perennial. It forms leafy clumps to 6 inches high, with dark green heart-shaped leaves and sweetly fragrant, small, double, blue-purple flowers. Used as a small-scale ground cover in woodland gardens.

violet, Philippine *n.* A common name for *Barleria cristata,* a tender flowering shrub. It grows to 4 feet, with oval, pointed leaves and loose clusters of showy blue or white flared tubular flowers, prickly at the base. Used as an indoor/outdoor plant, in containers, or in sunny borders in mild-winter climates.

violet, primrose-leaved *n.* A common name for *Viola primulafolia,* a very hardy perennial wildflower native to eastern North America, from New Brunswick to Minnesota, south to Florida and Texas. It grows to 10 inches, with oval leaves and white flowers with purple veins.

violet, round-leaved yellow *n.* A common name for *Viola rotundifolia,* a very hardy stemless perennial wildflower native to eastern America, from Maine to Georgia. It grows from a rhizome to 4 inches, with thick, oval leaves and bright yellow flowers with brown lines.

violet, sweet white *n.* A common name for *Viola blanda,* a stemless very hardy perennial wildflower native to eastern North America, from Quebec to Georgia and Louisiana. It has oval, hairy leaves and white flowers with petals turned backward.

violet trumpet vine *n.* A common name for *Clytostoma callistegioides,* a vigorous tender evergreen vine that climbs by tendrils. It has leaves divided into 2 shiny, oval leaflets and sprays of violet, lavender, or purple trumpet-shaped flowers 3 inches long. Often sold under the former name *Bignonia violacea.* Used on fences, walls, arbors, porches, or almost anything strong enough to bear its weight.

viper's bugloss (byoo′glohs) *n.* A common name for *Echium,* a genus of tall, hairy, somewhat shrubby plants with simple, alternate leaves and clusters of blue, purple, red, pink, or white flowers. *E. vulgare,* the common viper's bugloss, or blueweed, has showy blue flowers and is naturalized in the United States. (See **Echium.**)

Virgilia (vuhr jihl′ee uh) *n.* A genus of 2 species of tender broadleaf evergreen trees (Leguminosae). They grow to 30 feet, with alternate leaves divided into leathery, oval leaflets and showy spikes of fragrant sweet pealike deep pink or mauve flowers. Used as a flowering tree in frost-free gardens.

Virginia bluebells *n.* A common name for *Mertensia virginica,* a hardy perennial native to the eastern United States. It grows to 2 feet, with shiny, oval leaves and clusters of nodding pink or lavender buds that open into blue bell-shaped flowers. Used in shady borders, in woodland gardens, or mixed with shade-loving woodland ferns. Also known as bluebells, cowslip, Virginia cowslip, and Roanoke-bells.

Virginia creeper *n.* A common name for *Parthenocissus quinquefolia,* a vigorous, self-clinging, hardy woody vine. It has handsome, glossy, dark green 5-part leaves that turn flaming scarlet in autumn, inconspicuous flowers, and clusters of small black fruit that attract birds. Used to cover walls or fences or as a ground cover. Excellent for masking undistinguished architecture. Grown for its leafy summer green and spectacular fall color. Also known as woodbine, American ivy, and five-leaved ivy.

Virginia mallow *n.* A common name for *Sida hermaphrodita,* a rare perennial wildflower native to streambanks of the eastern United States. It grows to 10 feet, with large, lobed leaves, 10 inches long, and loose clusters of small white hibiscuslike flowers.

Virginia poke *n.* A common name for *Phytolacca americana,* a hardy perennial wildflower native to the United States. It grows to 12 feet, with narrow, oval leaves, 14 inches long, and spikes or clusters of small white or purple flowers. All parts of the plant are poisonous particularly the root. Also known as poke, scoke, pocan, garget, and pigeonberry.

Virginia stock *n.* A common name for *Malcolmia maritima,* an annual. It grows to 15 inches, with oval leaves and masses of white, yellow or pink (many shades through magenta) 4-petaled flowers. Used in sunny flower beds or as a bulb cover.

Virginia sumac (soo'mak) *n.* A common name for *Rhus typhina,* a hardy deciduous shrub or small tree native to eastern North America. It grows from 15 to 30 feet, and is wider than tall, with velvety branches covered with short brown hairs. It has deep green leaves divided into many toothed leaflets that turn rich red in fall, and clusters of fuzzy, crimson fruit that hangs on all winter. Used as a specimen tree, especially mixed with coniferous evergreens; also a good container tree. Tolerates heat, cold, and a wide range of soils. Also known as staghorn sumac and velvet sumac.

Virginia wake-robin *n.* A common name for *Peltandra virginica,* a hardy perennial wildflower native to streamsides and pond banks of eastern North America. It grows from a stout rhizome to 3 feet, with glossy, arrow-shaped leaves, green flowers, and green berries. Useful in moist soils for its attractive foliage. Also known as arrow arum and tuckahoe.

willow, Virginia *n.* A common name for *Itea virginica,* a hardy deciduous shrub native to the eastern United States. It grows to 10 feet, with alternate, simple leaves that color brilliant red in autumn and spikes of white fragrant flowers. Also known as sweet spire and tassel-white.

virgin's bower *n.* 1. A common name for *Clematis,* a genus of spectacular hardy flowering vines. (See **Clematis**.) 2. A common name for *C. virginiana,* a very hardy flowering vine native to eastern North America, from Nova Scotia to Manitoba and south to Georgia and Louisiana. It climbs to 10 or 20 feet, with leaves divided into 3 oval, pointed leaflets, masses of cream-white flowers in clusters, and silky, feathery seeds. *C. virginiana* is also known as woodbine, leatherflower and devil's darning needle.

virgin's bower

virgin soil *n.* A soil that has not been significantly disturbed from its natural environment.

viscid (vihs'ehd) *a.* Sticky; having a sticky layer.

Viscum (vihs'kuhm) *n.* A common name for a genus of parasitic plants, commonly known as mistletoe. *V. album* is the mistletoe of Europe.

vista *n.* A view or prospect, especially through an avenue, as between rows of trees; hence, the trees or other things that form the avenue.

Vitaceae (vigh tay'see ee) *n. pl.* A family of 12 genera of woody vines that climb by tendrils; the grape or vine family. The cultivated genera are *Ampelopsis, Cissus* (grape ivy or treebine), *Parthenocissus* (woodbine), *Rhoicissus* (African grape), and *Vitis* (grape).

Vitex (vigh'tehks) *n.* A genus of 270 species of shrubs and trees (Verbenaceae), some species native to South America. They grow from 10 to 100 feet, depending on the species, with opposite, fan-shaped leaves divided into 3 to 7 leaflets and spikes or clusters of pink, white, yellow, blue, or purple trumpet-shaped flowers, sometimes showy. Used in shrub borders for summer color or as a small shade tree. *V. Agnus-castus* is commonly known as chaste tree.

Vitex Agnus-castus
(chaste tree)

Viticipremna (vih duh sih prehm′nuh) *n.* A genus of 2 species of tropical shrubs and trees (Verbenaceae). *V. novae-pommeraniae* is a large shrub or tree, with leaves divided into 3 to 5 oval, pointed leaflets and long spikes of yellow-green flowers.

viticulture *n.* The cultivation of vines, especially the grapevine.

Vitis (vigh′dehs) *n.* A genus of long-lived tendril-climbing, mostly hardy deciduous woody vines (Vitaceae), many species native to North America; the grape. They have shredding bark on the trunk, lobed leaves that color red, orange, or yellow in autumn, inconspicuous flowers, and clusters of round, crisp grapes. *V. vinifera* is the European grape, long grown for both wine and table grapes. *V. Labrusca* is the slipskin grape, native to the eastern United States. Both species have been extensively hybridized. Grown primarily for their fruit, grapes are handsome ornamentals with shaggy, twisted trunks of great character, beautiful summer foliage, handsome, heavy clusters of grapes, rich fall color, and interesting winter silhouette. Wonderful grown over arbors for summer shade, along leaves, or on fences and walls. Commonly known as grape.

Vitis Labrusca
(grape)
a flower *b* vine with tendrils *c* leaf

Vittadinia (vihd uh dihn′ee uh) *n.* A genus of 8 species of tender perennials or subshrubs (Compositae). *V. australis* is a bushy shrublet to 1 foot, with oval, alternate leaves and small, daisylike white flowers with yellow centers.

Vittaria (veh tah′ree uh) *n.* A genus of about 50 species of tender subtropical and tropical epiphytic ferns (Polypodiaceae), some species native to the Americas. *V. lineata,* native to the southeastern United States, has densely clustered, narrow, simple, grasslike fronds. Grown in hanging-baskets in greenhouses or as an indoor/outdoor plant. Commonly known as grass fern. *V. lineata* is commonly known as shoestring fern, beard fern, Florida ribbon fern, and old-man's-beard.

Voandzeia (voh and zee′yuh) n. A genus of 1 species, *V. subterranea* (Leguminosae), an annual cultivated for its edible groundnuts which grow underground like peanuts. Commonly known as bambara groundnut.

Vriesea (vree′zhee uh) n. A genus of 240 species of large, showy, epiphytic bromeliads (Bromeliaceae) native to tropical America. They grow to 3 feet, with stiff, spiny-edged, beautifully patterned leaves and striking, long-lasting spikes of colorful bracts and flowers. Most often grown as tough, handsome houseplants. Can be grown outdoors in pots in frost-free climates or as indoor/outdoor plants.

Wachendorfia (wok uhn dorf′ee uh) *n.* A genus of several species of perennial herbs (Haemodoraceae). *W. thyrsiflora* is an evergeen plant with 3-foot-long pleated leaves arising from a corm. A tall, narrow flower cluster rises to 6 feet, with many yellow flowers opening from reddish buds. It can take little frost and needs moisture throughout the year.

wafer ash *n.* A common name for *Ptelea,* a genus of large deciduous shrubs or small trees (Rutaceae). *P. trifoliata,* which grows to 25 feet, is native to much of the eastern United States. *P. crenulata* is native to California. Leaves are divided, usually into 3 leaflets, with a strong aroma. Inconspicuous flowers are followed by flat, roundish seeds. Also called water ash, stinking ash, hop tree, or shrubby trefoil.

wahoo (wah′hoo) *n.* A common name for *Euonymus atropurpurea,* a shrub or small tree (Celastraceae) native to the eastern and central United States and Canada. It is also known as burning bush, a name it shares with *E. occidentalis,* western burning bush, and *E. alata* 'Compacta'. The common names spring from the brilliant red autumn color of the foliage.

wake-robin *n.* A common name for several plants, especially the species of *Trillium.* The trilliums are perennials with stems rising from an underground rhizome. Stems are topped by a whorl of 3 leaves, this in turn topped by a flower with 3 petals. They eventually form handsome clumps and are used in woodland gardens.

wake-robin, nodding *n.* A common name for *Trillium cernuum,* a plant with drooping blossoms. (See **Trillium.**)

wake-robin, purple *n.* A common name for *Trillium recurvatum.* (See **Trillium.**)

wake-robin, Virginian *n.* A common name for *Peltandra undulata,* a perennial plant (Araceae). Also known as arrow arum or tuckahoe. (See **Trillium.**)

wake-robin
a flower *b* fruit

wake-robin, white *n.* A common name for *Trillium grandiflorum.* (See **Trillium.**)

Waldsteinia (wawld stighn′ee uh) *n.* A genus of 6 species of strawberrylike perennials (Rosaceae). Leaves are divided into 3 leaflets. Flowers are small, yellow, 5-petaled, and followed by inconspicuous fruits. *W. fragarioides,* native to the eastern United States, is called barren strawberry. *W. ternatea* is an evergreen with shining foliage. It is often used as a ground cover.

walking fern *n.* A common name for ferns that root from the tip of the fronds, producing new plants. *Adiantum caudatum,* also known as trailing maidenhair fern, is one. Another is *Asplenium rhizophyllum (Camptosorus rhizophyllus),* a small fern with undivided leaves.

walking fern
(Camptosorus rhizophyllus)
a entire plants *b* single frond

walking leaf *n.* (See **walking fern.**)

wall basket *n.* (See **English wall basket.**)

wall bracket *n.* A metal device attached to a wall or other structure used to support a hanging planter.

wall fern *n*. A common name for *Polypodium vulgare,* a small evergreen fern that grows on walls or rocks. It is also called European polypody and adder's fern.

wallflower *n*. A common name for several biennials and perennials of the genus *Erysimum* (Cruciferae). The best known is common wallflower, *E. cheiri,* a biennial, or sometimes perennial, with fragrant single or double flowers that appear in a wide range of colors, including yellow, orange, red, brown, mauve, and mixtures of the above. It thrives best in cool-summer climates.

wallflower

wallflower, beach *n*. A common name for *Erysimum suffrutescens,* a yellow-flowered perennial native to California. (See **Erysimum**.)

wallflower, coast *n*. A common name for *Erysimum capitatum,* a white- or cream-flowered biennial native to the western United States. (See **Erysimum**.)

wallflower, Siberian *n*. A common name for *Erysimum xallionii,* a biennial, or perennial, with bright orange flowers. (See **Erysimum**.)

wall pot *n*. A half-round pot mounted on a wall used for growing decorative plants. Also known as wall planter

wall rockcress *n*. A common name for *Arabis caucasica* (*A. albida*), a low, spreading perennial (Cruciferae) with whitish, furry leaves and white flowers. There are variegated, double-flowered, and pink-flowered varieties. Widely used as a rock garden plant.

wall rue *n*. A common name for *Asplenium ruta-muraria,* a small fern that grows on rocks and cliffs.

wallwort *n*. A common name for *Sambucus ebulus,* an herbaceous perennial with many stems, divided leaves, and broad clusters of white flowers followed by deep blue-black fruits. Also known as dwarf elder and danewort.

walnut *n*. 1. The fruit of a number of species of *Juglans,* (Juglandaceae). Also the wood and the tree itself. 2. The fruit of *Juglans regia,* the English or Persian walnut. 3. A name applied to similar or related trees, fruits, or woods.

walnut
showing nutmeat, nut in husk, and nut

walnut, Arizona *n*. A common name for *Juglans major,* a 60-foot tree native to the southwestern United States. (See **Juglans**.)

walnut, black *n*. A common name for *Juglans nigra,* a tree of the eastern United States that grows up yo 150 feet and has valuable wood and thick-shelled edible nuts. (See **Juglans**.)

walnut, English *n*. A common name for *Juglans regia,* the common walnut of commerce. Also known as the European Walnut. (See **Juglans**.)

walnut family *n*. The common name for *Juglandaceae,* numbering 6 genera and about 60 species of hardy deciduous trees with divided leaves and hard, nutlike fruits. Walnuts, hickories, and pecans are prominent members. Also known as the hickory family.

walnut husk fly *n*. A type of fruit fly whose larvae infest developing walnuts, causing the husks to turn a streaked or blotchy black, but which do not harm the nut meat. Critical spray timing and tree size make it hard to control for most home gardeners.

Consult your local cooperative extension office for assistance.

walnut, little *n.* A common name for *Juglans microcarpa (J. rupestris)*, a small tree or large shrub native to the American Southwest. (See **Juglans.**)

walnut, white *n.* A common name for *Juglans cinerea*, better known as butternut. (See **butternut** and **Juglans.**)

wampee (wahm'pee) *n.* A common name for *Clausena lansium*, a small evergreen tree (Rutaceae) that has leaves divided into 5 to 9 leaflets, and clustered white or greenish flowers that are followed by clusters of fuzzy fruits about the size and flavor of grapes. It is cultivated for its fruits. Also known as wampi.

wandering Jew *n.* The common name for a number of related trailing herbaceous perennials (Commelinaceae). Among them are *Tradescantia albiflora, T. fluminensis, Zebrina pendula, Callisia elegans* (striped inch plant), and *Tripogandra multiflora* (fernleaf inch plant). All are trailing houseplants.

wandflower *n.* A common name for *Galax urceolata (G . aphylla)* a hardy evergreen perennial (Diapensiaceae) that is native to the southern Appalachian Mountains. It is noted more for its shining green foliage (bronze in winter) than for its narrow spikelike clusters of small white flowers. It is also known as wand plant, beetleweed, galaxy, and coltsfoot.

Washingtonia (wawsh ihng toh'nee uh) *n.* A genus of 2 species of palms (Palmae) native to the southwestern United States. Both are widely used for landscaping in California, Arizona, and parts of Nevada. *W. filifera*, California or desert fan palm, is a heavy-trunked tree that grows to 60 feet. In nature, its trunk is partially covered by a heavy skirt of drooping dead leaves. Broad, fan-shaped leaves form an open crown. It tolerates heat and wind, but needs some water at the root. *W. robusta (W. sonorae)*, is a taller tree that grows up to 100 feet and has a more slender trunk (sometimes curved in older plants), and a shaggier skirt of dead fronds. Both are sometimes called Washington palm.

watch owl *n.* An artificial owl mounted on a post or tree limb to frighten rabbits, squirrels, mice, and birds from the garden.

water arum (ahr'uhm) *n.* A common name for *Calla palustris*, a hardy perennial bog plant (Araceae). It has 6-inch arrow-shaped leaves that top 10-inch stalks and flower spikes that are surrounded by a 2-inch spathe that is green on the outside and white on the inside. It somewhat resembles the florist's calla (Zantedeschia). Also called wild calla and water dragon.

water ash *n.* A common name for *Fraxinus caroliniana (F. platycarpa)*, a small deciduous tree (Oleaceae). It grows in swamps in the southeastern United States. Also known as Carolina ash or pop ash.

water-avens (ayv'ehnz) *n.* A common name for *Geum rivale*, a perennial (Rosaceae) that grows up to 2 feet. It has divided leaves and dull orange-pink flowers that are about 1½ inches wide. Also called purple avens, Indian chocolate, and chocolate root.

water beech *n.* A common name for *Carpinus caroliniana*, a hardy deciduous tree (Betulaceae) native to the southeastern United States. It grows to 40 feet, with smooth gray bark, 4-inch oval leaves, and hard, heavy wood. Also known as American hornbeam and blue beech.

water caltrop (kal'truhp) *n.* A common name for *Trapa natans*, an aquatic annual (Trapaceae). It has floating leaves, 1½-inch white flowers, and large, hard seeds with edible flesh and 4 horns. The plant can become a weed. Also called Jesuit nut, trapa nut, ling, water chestnut, water nut, and saligot.

water chestnut, Chinese *n.* A common name for *Eleocharis dulcis*, an aquatic, rushlike plant (Cyperaceae). It has stems 1 to 3 feet tall, and brown-skinned, white-fleshed edible tubers or corms that are crisp and delicious.

watercress *n.* A creeping herb of springs and streams, *Nasturtium officinale*, from antiquity used as a spring salad and now very widely cultivated. It grows in running water in temperate climates, including all zones in the United States. The deep green leaves add a slightly peppery, crisp flavor to salads. Its flavor becomes very sharp as it matures and the tiny white flowers form. It is rich in vitamins A and C and in calcium.

water crowfoot *n.* A common name for *Ranunculus aquatilis*, an aquatic perennial (Ranunculaceae).

It has white flowers that are less than ½ inch wide, underwater leaves that are finely cut, and floating leaves that are roundish and lobed.

water distributor *n*. A water faucet attachment which converts a single tap into multiple taps (4 of more), each with its own shut-off valve. A water distributor enables several water or drip irrigation systems to operate simultaneously.

water dock, giant *n*. A common name for *Rumex hydrolapathum,* a large perennial (Polugonaceae) that grows up to 6 feet tall, and has 2-foot-long leaves. It is sometimes planted near streams or ponds. Also called water dock.

water-farming *n*. The cultivation of plants in water, instead of soil. Also known as hydroponic gardening.

water fern *n*. 1. A common name for members of *Azolla,* a genus of tiny floating ferns. *A. caroliniana* is familiar as a floating carpet of tiny green or red plants seen on still water. It is sometimes called mosquito plant. 2. A common name for members of *Ceratopteris,* a genus in the water-fern family (Parkeriaceae). *C. thalictroides* and *C. pteridoides* are occasionally planted in ponds or aquariums. *C. pteridoides* is also known as floating fern.

water gardening *n*. A form of ornamental horticulture in which plants, especially water lilies, are cultivated in pools, ponds or, tubs.

water hawthorn *n*. A common name for *Aponogeton distachyus,* an aquatic plant (Aponogetonaceae). It has floating narrow oval leaves and ½-inch fragrant white flowers in 2-forked clusters standing above the water. It is also known as Cape pondweed and Cape asparagus.

water hemlock *n*. A common name for *Cicuta maculata,* a perennial weed (Umbelliferae) that grows up to 6 feet or more. It has spotted stems, finely divided leaves, and white flowers in small flat-topped clusters. It is a deadly poison. Also called spotted water hemlock, or spotted hemlock.

water-holding capacity *n*. The ability of the soil to absorb and hold water, expressed in inches of water per verticle foot of soil.

water hyacinth (high'uh sihnth) *n*. A common name for several species of *Eichhornia* (Pontederi-

aceae). They have rosettes of roundish, fleshy leaves and attractive blue-purple flowers in spikes. *E. azurea,* sometimes called peacock hyacinth, has leafstalks that are not inflated. *E. crassipes,* the common water hyacinth, has leaves with bulbous, inflated leafstalks. Although much used in water gardens, *E. crassipes* rapidly becomes a weed in warm, still waters.

watering *v*. Irrigating; to apply water carried either in a container or through pipes or hoses to a lawn or garden.

watering can *n*. A container for water having a spout with attached or detachable perforated nozzle, called a rose, used to sprinkle plants.

watering tray *n*. A rimmed, flat bottomed container to hold moisture for propagating chamber, propagator, or plant pots.

watering wand *n*. A garden hose attachment for watering seedlings, potted plants, or hard-to-reach garden plants. A watering wand consists of a rose and tube (the wand) with a shut-off device.

waterleaf *n*. Any plant in the genus *Hydrophyllum* (Hydrophyllaceae). Of the 8 species, 2 are occasionally planted in wild gardens. *H. capitatum,* a perennial that grows to 18 inches, with grayish lobed leaves and blue to white flowers in clusters, is sometimes called cat's breeches. *H. virginianum,* called Virginia waterleaf, Shawnee-salad, or Indian salad, grows to 3 feet, and has deeply divided leaves and white or purple flowers.

waterleaf family *n*. The common name for *Hydrophyllaceae,* a family of 25 genera and perhaps 300 species of annuals, perennials, or shrubs, usually hairy or bristly, with flowers displayed singly or in clusters. Best known ornamental genera are *Nemophila* and *Phacelia.*

water lemon *n*. A common name for *Passiflora laurifolia* (Passifloraceae), a tropical evergreen vine related to the passionflower. It has showy purple-red flowers and an edible, 3-inch orange or yellow fruit.

water lemon, wild *n*. A common name for *Passiflora foetida,* a tropical vine with white, pink, or purple flowers and small edible yellow or red fruit.

water lettuce *n*. A common name for *Pistia stratiotes,* a floating perennial (Araceae). It forms

6-inch-wide rosettes of leaves that resemble open heads of lettuce. It is sometimes used in pools. Also known as shellflower.

water lily *n.* (See lily, water.)

water lily family *n.* A common name for *Nymphaeaceae*, a family of aquatic plants including *Nymphaea*, the genera *Nuphar, Euryale*, and *Nelumbo*, along with less well known genera.

water lobelia (loh bee'lyuh) *n.* A common name for *Lobelia dortmanna,* an aquatic, nearly leafless plant with small blue flowers borne above the water.

water locust *n.* A common name for *Gleditsia aquatica* (Leguminosae), a deciduous tree that grows up to 60 feet. It has large spines, divided leaves, inconspicuous flowers, and thin, beanlike pods. It is also known as swamp locust.

water logged *a.* A condition of soil in which the soil is completely saturated with water. Water-logged soil has little or no oxygen. The roots of many plants will rot in water-logged soil. (See **water mold**.)

water lotus *n.* A common name for *Nelumbo,* 2 species of large aquatic plants (Nymphaeaceae) more commonly known as lotus. Sacred bean is another common name.

watermelon *n.* A common name for *Citrullus lanatus,* and its fruit. The plant is a slender trailing vine, requiring a warm soil. The fruit is large, sometimes spherical, usually oval, 1½ or 2 feet long, smooth and green, or sometimes variegated on the outside, containing a rose-colored or sometimes yellowish sweet pulp and a refreshing, sweet watery juice. Miniature varieties, developed for northern climates, require a shorter growing season to mature. The thick, white rind of watermelon is preserved as a pickle.

watermelon begonia (beh goh'nyuh) *n.* A common name for *Peperomia argyreia* (Piperaceae), a houseplant with dark green, gray striped leaves.

water meter *n.* A device to stop the flow of water after a set volume, typically about 1,000 gallons, has passed through a hose. They are often used to conserve water and prevent water-logged soil.

water mint *n.* The strong scented mint *Mentha aquatica,* an aromatic herb of wet places, growing occasionally in the eastern United States. Its aroma resembles that of spearmint.

water miser *n.* A nozzle that conserves water by automatically stopping the flow of water through a hose.

water mold *n.* A fungus that thrives in overly wet soil, causing plant roots to turn dark and mushy. Plants lose vigor, turn yellow, wilt, and often die. To control, improve drainage, plant at the right depth, and water properly. Soil solarization and other forms of soil sterilization kill fungi, but cultural techniques are the best controls.

water nut *n.* A common name for plants of the genus *Trapa,* as well as the seeds of such plants. (See **water caltrop**.)

water oak *n.* An American oak that grows best in wet soil, especially the possum oak. (See **oak, water** and **Quercus**.)

water parsnip *n.* A common name for 2 species of *Sium,* aromatic perennials (Umbelliferae). *S. latifolium* and *S. suave* have edible roots, divided leaves, and clustered small flowers.

water pennywort *n.* A common name for 50 to 60 species of *Hydrocotyle,* low, creeping plants with round leaves and inconspicuous white or greenish flowers. They inhabit wet ground and are sometimes used as ground cover in such places. *H. sibthorpioides,* lawn water pennywort, sometimes invades lawns.

water plantain (plant'uhn) *n.* A common name for any member of the genus *Alisma* (Alismataceae). *A. plantago-aquatica (A. plantago)* is sometimes grown in bogs or at the edge of ponds. The 6-inch leaves resemble those of plantain (*Plantago*) but are less ridged. The half-inch white flowers form in whorls in narrow spikelike clusters.

water plantain family (plant'uhn) *n.* A common name for Alismataceae, which includes, in addition to the previous, several other genera of marsh or water plants, of which *Sagittaria* (the arrowheads or swamp potatoes) is best known.

water platter *n.* A common name for *Victoria regia* and *V. cruziana,* water lilies with huge leaves that are turned up at the edges. (See **lily, Victoria water.**)

water poppy *n.* A common name for *Hydrocleys nymphoides,* a tropical aquatic perennial (Butomaceae). It has roots that grow in mud, 2- to 3-inch oval leaves that float on the water, and showy clustered yellow flowers that are 2 inches across. It is grown in pools or aquariums.

water purslane (puhrs'lehn) *n.* A common name for *Ludwigia palustris* (Onagraceae), an aquatic plant. It has narrow 1- to 4-inch leaves and small yellow flowers. It is sometimes planted in pools or at the waterside.

water ratio *n.* The fraction of the total bulk volume of soil that is filled with water.

water requirement *n.* A term used for units of water required by plants during growing season. Knowledge of how much water a plant needs helps prevent both over and underwatering.

watershed *n.* In the United States, the term refers to the total area above a given point on a stream that contributes water to the stream's flow. Watershed land is often forested or covered with native brush.

water soluble fertilizer *n.* An organic or chemical fertilizer which can be dissolved in water, such as manure. Water soluble fertilizer may be applied through a watering system or sprinkled in with a watering can.

water star grass *n.* A common name for *Heteranthera dubia* (Pontederiaceae), an aquatic perennial. Its underwater stems bear very narrow 6-inch leaves and small starry yellow flowers.

water table *n.* The upper limit of the part of the soil or underlying rock material that is wholly saturated with water. A high water table might limit the plants that can be grown successfully.

water timer *n.* Any of various devices to stop and/or start the flow of water through a hose for either a predetermined period of time or a set amount of water.

water timer, electronic *n.* A clock attached to a hose or faucet which may be set to start and stop the flow of water in multiple segments of minutes or hours throughout a period of time, typically one week.

water timer, wind up *n.* A clock attached to a hose or faucet to stop the flow of water automatically after a set period of time.

water violet *n.* A common name for *Hottonia palustris* (Primulaceae), an aquatic perennial with 4-inch, deeply cut leaves. The 1-inch lilac, yellow-throated flowers are on a narrow, spikelike cluster that may grow over 1 foot tall.

water willow *n.* 1. A common name for *Baccharis glutinosa* a 10-foot evergreen shrub (Compositae) that grows near water in Southwestern America and Mexico. It has 4-inch glossy, sticky leaves and whitish flowers of little beauty. It is sometimes planted for erosion control. Also called sticky baccharis, seep willow, water-motie, and water-wally. 2. *Decodon verticillatus,* an 8-foot perennial (Lythraceae) native to wet places in the eastern United States. It has opposite or whorled 5-inch leaves and clusters of small purple flowers. Also called swamp loosestrife and water oleander.

water yam *n.* A common name for *Dioscorea alata,* a twining tropical vine (Dioscoreaceae). Its huge roots are grown for food. Also called white yam.

Watsonia (waht soh'nee uh) *n.* A genus of 70 or so species of plants (Iridaceae) with swordlike leaves and trumpet-shaped flowers on tall, branched stems. *W. beatricis* is an evergreen with 3-inch flowers on 3½ foot stalks. *W. pyramidata* and its hybrids are deciduous, with 4- to 6-foot stems bearing pink, red, rose, or lavender flowers. The variety *ardernei (W. ardernei)* is pure white.

wattle *n.* A common name for many species of *Acacia* (Leguminosae). All have tiny yellow, cream, or white flowers in tight clusters that are often combined into larger clusters. Their leaves are either finely divided or lacking, their place being taken by leaflike stalks.

wattle, bower *n.* A common name for *Acacia subporosa* (A. cognata), a graceful 20- to 30-foot tall tree with weeping branches. Also called river wattle.

wattle, broom *n.* A common name for *Acacia calamifolia,* a tall shrub also known as wallowa.

wattle, coastal *n.* A common name for *Acacia cyclopis,* a 10- to 15-foot tall shrub with dark green foliage and black seeds surrounded by a red ring.

wattle, Cootamundra (kood uh muhn'druh) *n.* A common name for *Acacia baileyana,* a tree that is widely grown in California. It has gray-green finely cut leaves and abundant winter golden yellow flowers. Also known as golden mimosa and Bailey acacia.

wattle, graceful *n.* A common name for *Acacia decora,* a 6- to 8-foot shrub with abundant yellow flowers.

wattle, orange *n.* A common name for *Acacia cyanophylla,* an 18-foot shrub. Also known as golden willow, Port Jackson wattle, and blue-leaf wattle.

wattle, silver *n.* A common name for *Acacia dealbata,* a tree that grows up to 60 feet tall, with silvery gray leaves and abundant, fragrant yellow flowers. Also known as mimosa.

wattle, water *n.* A common name for *Acacia retinodes,* a hardy 20-foot tall shrub with nearly continuous bloom. Sometimes sold as *A. floribunda.*

wax bean *n.* A common name for a yellow variety of the edible snap bean widely gronw in vegetable gardens.

waxberry *n.* 1. A common name for *Gaultheria hispida,* a tender shrub (Ericaceae). It has 2-inch leaves and clustered white flowers followed by white berries. 2. A common name for the bayberry, *Myrica cerifera.* (See **wax myrtle.**)

waxflower *n.* 1. A common name for *Chamelaucium,* a tender evergreen shrub (Myrtaceae). It has needlelike foliage and white, pink, or purple inch-wide flowers. *C. uncinatum,* Geraldton waxflower, is a splendid cut flower. 2. Plants in the genus *Chimaphila,* subshrubs (Pyrolaceae). 3. A common name for *Stephanotis floribunda* (Asclepiadaceae), a tropical twining evergreen vine with dark green leaves and clusters of fragrant waxy white flowers 1 to 2 inches wide. It is also called Madagascar jasmine.

wax gourd (goo'uhrd) *n.* A common name for *Benincasa hispida* (B. cerifera), a tropical annual vine (Cucurbitaceae). It has vines that climb by tendrils or sprawl, and yellow flowers that are followed by heavy waxy white fruit that may grow up to 16 inches long and has a hairy covering. It is much used in Oriental cooking. It is also called white gourd, Chinese watermelon, hairy melon, Chinese preserving melon, winter melon, and white pumpkin.

wax myrtle (muhr'duhl) *n.* A common name for *Myrica cerifera* a large evergreen shrub or small tree native to the southeastern United States. It produces grayish white fruit coated with a wax used in candlemaking. Also called waxberry and candleberry.

wax myrtle, California (muhr'duhl) *n.* A common name for *Myrica californica,* an evergreen tree that grows to 35 feet or more with purple fruit.

wax plant *n.* A common name for *Hoya carnosa,* an evergreen tropical vine (Asclepiadaceae). It has thick, dark green leaves and rounded clusters of waxy white and red flowers. Also known as honey plant from its copious nectar. Sometimes called porcelain flower.

wax plant, miniature *n.* A common name for *Hoya bella,* a small shrub grown in hanging baskets. Its leaves are an inch long or a little more, and its white and red flowers are miniatures of *H. carnosa.*

wax tree *n.* A common name for *Rhus succedanea,* a 30-foot tall deciduous tree (Anacardiaceae). Its leaves are divided into as many as 15 4-inch leaflets. It flowers are greenish, and followed by clusters of white fruits that yield a commercial wax. The stems also yield varnish. In the fall, the tree displays brilliant color.

wax vine *n.* 1. Plants in the genus *Hoya.* (See **wax plant.**) 2. A common name for *Senecio macroglossus,* an evergreen vine (Compositae). It has glossy leaves with 3 to 5 lobes, that resemble ivy leaves in form and flowers (not often seen on small plants) that are like yellow daisies. There is a white and green form, 'Variegata'.

wayfaring tree *n.* A common name for *Viburnum lantana,* a 15-foot hardy deciduous shrub (Caprifoliaceae). It has 4 inch clusters of white flowers that are followed by red fruit which turns black with age. It is also called twistwood.

wayfaring tree, American *n.* A common name for *Viburnum alnifolium,* a 10-foot shrub with 5-inch flower clusters and red fruit that turns black. It is also called Devil's-shoestrings, dogberry, dog-hobble, moosewood, moose bush, mooseberry, tanglefoot, tangle-legs, trip-toe, white mountain dogwood, and witch-hobble.

weather *n.* The combination of wind, temperature, cloudiness, moisture, and pressure which affect and, together with soil type, determine the growing conditions of plants.

weathering *v.* The physical and chemical disintegration and decomposition of rocks and mineral.

weather plant *n.* A common name for *Abrus precatorius*, the rosary vine. It is so-called because of its (largely mythical) ability to predict weather by its leaf behavior. (See **Abrus**.)

Wedelia (weh dee'lee uh) *n.* A genus of 70 tropical or subtropical annuals, perennials, or shrubs (Compositae). *W. trilobata*, is a trailing plant with fleshy evergreen leaves and inch-wide yellow flowers that resemble miniature zinnias. It is used as a ground cover in tropical regions or wherever frosts are rare and light.

weeder *n.* Any of variously shaped tools used to remove unwanted plants from the soil.

weed mat *n.* A multi-layered fabric placed around plants to control growth of weeds and conserve soil moisture.

weed puller *n.* A implement consisting of a pinching mechanism mounted on a tube, typically 2 to 3 inches long, used for gripping and pulling weeds from cultivated land or in a rockery.

weed trimmer *n.* (See **string trimmer**.)

weeping bottlebrush *n.* A common name for *Callistemon viminalis*, a large shrub or small evergreen tree. It grows up to 30 feet, with drooping branches thickly set with 6-inch narrow leaves and bright red flowers that gather in a bottlebrush formation at the ends of branchlets.

weeping cherry *n.* A common name for *Prunus serrulata* 'Pendula', a weeping form of the Japanese flowering cherry or Oriental cherry.

weeping cherry, double *n.* A common name for *P. subhirtella* 'Yae-shidare-higan'. (See **Prunus**.)

weeping cherry, single *n.* A common name for *Prunus subhirtella* 'Pendula'. (See **Prunus**.)

weeping Chinese banyan (ban'yuhn) *n.* A common name for *Ficus benjamina*, an evergreen tropical tree. It is sometimes grown as a house plant.

weeping fig *n.* A common name for *Ficus benjamina*. (See **Ficus**.)

weeping laurel (law'ruhl) *n.* A common name for *Ficus benjamina*. (See **Ficus**.)

weeping myall (migh'awl) *n.* A common name for *Acacia pendula*, an evergreen tree that grows up to 25 feet. It has pendulus weeping branches and puffs of yellow flowers.

weeping spruce *n.* A common name for *Picea brewerana*, a tree (Pinaceae) that grows up to 100 feet, with drooping branchlets and short, dark green needles.

weeping tea tree *n.* A common name for *Melaleuca quinquenervia*, (often sold as *M. leucadendron*) an evergreen tree (Myrtaceae) that grows to 40 feet tall. It has thick, spongy, peeling white bark and narrow leaves on drooping branches, and white flowers in clusters. It is also called river tea tree, cajeput tree, and in Florida, where it is considered a pest, punk tree.

weevils (wee'vuhlz) *n. pl.* A large group of beetle larvae that feed on the leaves and roots of many plants. They include plum curculio, strawberry root weevil, and black vine weevil. Difficult to control. Proper identification is very important. Sanitation, rotenone, parasitic nematodes, and traditional insecticides are common controls.

Weigela (wigh jee'lee uh) *n.* A genus of 10 to 12 hardy deciduous shrubs (Caprifoliaceae). All have clusters of pink, red, white (rarely yellow) 5-lobed flowers. Most are garden hybrids with descriptive cultivar names like Bristol Ruby, Bristol Snowflake, and Newport Red. *W. florida* 'Variegata' has variegated leaves along with its pink flowers. *W. middendorffiana* has yellow flowers with orange markings.

Wellington boots *n.* Mid-calf waterproof rubber boots used while gardening. Also called Wellies.

Welsh onion *n.* A common name for *Allium fistulosum*, a bunching onion with clustered bulbs barely thicker than the stems. Widely grown under many names: ciboule, Spanish onion, two-bladed onion, and Japanese bunching onion.

western dog violet *n*. A common name for *Viola adunca*, a 4-inch-tall violet with roundish leaves and purple flowers. Also called hook-spur violet.

western holly fern *n*. A common name for *Polystichum scopulinum*, a fern (Polypodiaceae). Also called Eaton's fern.

western hound's tongue *n*. A common name for *Cynoglossum grande*, a perennial (Boraginaceae) with broad, hairy basal leaves and a tall, loose cluster of blue flowers that resemble the flowers of the forget-me-not.

western laurel (law'ruhl) *n*. A common name for *Kalmia microphylla*, a small evergreen shrub (Ericaceae). It has 1½-inch leaves and rounded clusters of ½-inch purplish pink flowers. Also called alpine laurel.

western red cedar *n*. A common name for *Thuja plicata*, a coniferous tree (Cupressaceae) that grows up to 200 feet. Also called giant arborvitae and giant cedar.

western round-leaved violet *n*. A common name for *Viola orbiculata*, a 3-inch round-leaved violet with yellow flowers.

western sand cherry *n*. A common name for *Prunus besseyi*, a very hardy shrub (Rosaceae), with edible purple-black cherries that are larger than ½ inch in diameter.

western sweet white violet *n*. A common name for *Viola macloskeyi*, a violet that grows up to 6 inches, with roundish leaves and white flowers.

western sword fern *n*. A comon name for *Polystichum munitum*, a large evergreen fern (Polypodiaceae) that grows up to 6 feet. Also known as giant holly fern.

Westringia (wehst rihng'ee uh) *n*. A genus of evergreen shrubs (Labiatae). *W. rosmariniformis* grows up to 6 feet, and has light green to gray green leaves that are lighter on their undersides, and white flowers. It somewhat resembles a paler, less dense rosemary. Effective in wind and drought. It tolerates sea wind.

wet soil plants *n*. Plants, such as willow, cranberry, and Japanese iris, which can withstand a great deal of moisture in the soil.

wetting agent *n*. 1. Material that reduces amount of water needed by increasing water penetration into the soil. 2. A material added to pesticide sprays so that they spread easily over the plant surface.

wheelbarrow *n*. A tringular metal or wooden box with one wheel in front, 2 legs in back on which it rests, and 2 handles by which a person lifts the legs from the ground and pushes the load in the box. Used to move soil, sand, gravel and other garden materials from place to place.

wheeled cultivator *n*. (See **high wheel cultivator**.)

wheel hoe *n*. A long handled implement consisting of blades mounted behind a wheel, typically 12 inches in diameter, used in cultivating the soil in preparation for planting.

whetstone *n*. (See **sharpening stone**.)

whin (hwihn) *n*. Another name for *Ulex europaeus*. (See **Ulex**.)

whinberry (hwihn beh'ree) *n*. A common name for *Vaccinium myrtillus*, a deciduous shrub (Ericaceae) that grows up to 2 feet, with small white to pink flowers and edible blue-black fruit. Also called whortleberry and bilberry.

whippoorwill-flower (hwih puhr wihl') *n*. A common name for *Trillium cuneatum*, a woodland perennial that grows up to 10 inches tall. It has deep maroon or brown flowers that are at least 4½ inches long.

whippoorwill's shoe (hwih puhr wihl') *n*. A common name for *Cypripedium calceolus pubescens*, a hardy woodland perennial (Orchidaceae). It resembles the yellow lady's slipper, but is larger.

whirligig *n*. A whimsical piece of statuary having wind-activated parts, such as waving arms, which may frighten unwanted birds from the garden.

whirling sprinkler *n*. A 2 to 4 armed sprinkler head resembling the upturned tentacles of an octupus which revolves and sprays water through the nozzles at the end of each arm. Also called a revolving or rotating sprinkler.

whiskey barrel planter *n.* A container made of wood or plastic, shaped like half a whiskey barrel. It is used for growing flowers, shrubs or small trees.

whispering bells *n.* A common name for *Emmenanthe penduliflora,* an annual (Hydrophyllaceae) native to the southwestern United States. It can grow up to 1½ feet. It has deeply cut leaves and drooping yellow to light pink flowers. Also known as yellowbells or golden bells.

whistlewood *n.* A common name for *Acer pensylvanicum,* a small maple tree (Aceraceae) that grows from 20 to 35 feet. It is distinguished by bark that is strongly striped with white, and by brilliant yellow fall color. Also called striped maple, Pennsylvania maple, and moosewood.

white cedar *n.* A common name for *Chamaecyparis thyoides,* a hardy, coniferous tree (Cupressaceae) that grows up to 90 feet. It has flattened branchlets and scalelike leaves. It grows in acidic, moist soils. A few horticultural varieties are sometimes cultivated.

white clover *n.* A common name for *Trifolium repens,* a dwarf, creeping perennial (Leguminosae). Its leaves are divided into 3 (rarely 4) leaflets, and its small white flowers are in dense, round heads. It is an important lawn and pasture plant, and a source of honey. Also called white Dutch clover.

whitecup *n.* A common name for *Nierembergia repens,* a low-growing creeping perennial (Solanaceae). It has bright green inch-long leaves and white cup-shaped flowers that are 2 inches across. Used as a ground cover in mild-winter regions.

whitefly *n.* A tiny, white, plant-sucking insect that infests many plants, congregating on the undersides of leaves. Whiteflies are particularly troublesome in warm weather and in greenhouses. They cause plants to lose vigor and leaves to turn yellow. They also produce abundant honeydew, resulting in sooty mold and ants. Control with beneficial insects, including Encarsia wasps. Horticultural oils, insecticidal soaps, yellow sticky traps, row covers, botanical sprays, and traditional insecticides are other control measures.

whitefly parasite *n.* (See **Encarsia wasp.**)

white forsythia (fuhr sihth'ee uh) *n.* A common name for *Abeliophyllum distichum,* a hardy deciduous shrub (Oleaceae) that grows to 3 feet, with fragrant white flowers that grow in short clusters in early spring.

white gossamer *n.* A common name for *Tradescantia sillamontana,* a perennial houseplant (Commelinaceae). It resembles a compact wandering Jew plant, but the leaves are covered with a furry white cobwebbing. Also called white velvet.

white jewel *n.* A common name for *Titanopsis schwantesii,* a clump-forming succulent pot plant (Aizoaceae). It has thick, fleshy, gray-white dotted brown leaves and pale yellow flowers.

white mugwort *n.* A common name for *Artemisia lactiflora,* a hardy perennial (Compositae) that grows from 2 to 4 feet tall. It has large, loose clusters of small white flowers. Used in flower borders.

white-plush plant *n.* A common name for *Echeveria leucotricha,* a rosette-forming fleshy plant (Crassulaceae). The 8-inch rosettes of thick leaves are densely covered with white hairs. Also called chenille plant.

white popinac (pahp'uh nak) *n.* A common name for *Leucaena glauca* (Leguminosae), a fast-growing tropical shrub or tree that grows up to 30 feet, with finely divided leaves, fluffy flowers in inch-wide heads, and 6-inch beanlike seed pods.

white sapota (suh poh'dee) *n.* A common name for *Casimiroa edulis,* an evergreen tree (Rutaceae) that grows up to 50 feet. It has leaves that are divided into 5 5-inch leaflets, greenish flowers, and yellow-green 3- to 4-inch fruits with a sweet, white, custardlike pulp.

white trailing ice plant *n.* A common name for *Delosperma 'Alba',* a trailing succulent perennial (Aizoaceae). It has many-petaled white flowers. Used as ground cover in dry, mild-winter areas.

whiteweed *n.* Any of several weeds that have a white or whitish flower, especially the common daisy.

whitewood *n.* 1. A name given to a number of trees that produce a white timber, such as *Liriodendron tulipifera,* a large tree (Magnoliaceae) that is commonly known as the tulip tree or yellow poplar. 2. Trees in the genus *Tilia* (Tiliaceae), especially *T. americana,* the American linden or basswood.

whitlavia (hwiht la'vee uh) *n.* A common name for *Phacelia minor,* an annual flowering plant (Hydrophyllaceae) native to California. It has coarsely toothed leaves and bell-shaped violet flowers.

whitlowwort (hwiht'loh wort) *n.* A common name for several species of the genus *Paronychia* (Caryophyllaceae). They are low annuals or perennials with tufted growth and inconspicuous flowers sheltered by conspiculous silvery bracts. *P. argentea* and *P. argyrocoma* (silverling or silver whitlowwort) are sometimes grown in rock gardens.

whorl (hwurl) *n.* In botany, a circle of radiating leaves, flowers, or other organs around a common center, on the same plane. Also whirl.

whorled (hwurld) *a.* In botany, furnished with or arranged in whorls.

wide row planting *n.* The practice of sowing seeds, usually of the same plant, in multiple rows. For instance, 2 or 3 lines of beans can be planted together, often on a raised row, with deep, wide parallel channels for irrigation.

Wigandia (wihg and'ee uh) *n.* A genus of large shrubs or small trees (Hydrophyllaceae) native to tropical America. They have large leaves covered with stinging hairs and big bell-shaped blue flowers. *W. caracasana* grows to 10 feet, and has leaves 1½ feet long. *W. urens* can reach 20 feet or more, and has foot-long leaves. Naturalized in waste places in Southern California.

wig tree *n.* A common name for *Cotinus coggygria.* Also called smoke bush, smoke plant, and Venetian sumac. (See **smoke tree.**)

wild almond *n.* A common name for *Prunus fasciculata.* (See **Prunus.**)

wild cherry *n.* A common name for *Prunus pensylvanica* (wild red cherry, pin cherry), and *P. serotina* (wild black cherry).

wild crab apple *n.* A common name for *Malus angustifolia, M. coronaria,* and *M. ioensis.* (See **Malus.**)

wild garlic *n.* A common name for *Allium canadense,* a garlic relative (Liliaceae). Also known as wild onion and meadow leek.

wild ginger *n.* A common name for *Asarum caudatum.* (See **Asarum.**)

wild hyacinth (high'uh sihnth) *n.* 1. A common name for *Camassia scilloides,* a bulb native to the eastern United States. It has white or blue flowers on 2½-foot narrow, spikelike clusters. Also called meadow hyacinth, eastern Camassia, and indigo squill.

wild lilac *n.* A common name for *Ceanothus.* (See **Ceanothus.**)

wild pink *n.* 1. A common name for *Silene caroliniana,* a perennial (Caryophyllaceae) that grows to 8 inches. It has white to pink flowers more than 1 inch wide. 2. A common name for *Arethusa bulbosa,* a small perennial (Orchidaceae). It has a single grasslike leaf and a 2-inch pink-purple flower with white and yellow markings.

wild potato *n.* A common name for *Ipomoea pandurata.* Also known as wild sweet potato, wild potato vine.

wild sweet William *n.* A common name for *Phlox divaricata,* a perennial phlox (Polemoniaceae) that grows to 18 inches. It has broad clusters of 1½-inch pale blue or white flowers.

wild-thyme azalea (uh zay'lyuh) *n.* A common name for *Rhododendron serpyllifolium,* a low evergreen shrub (Ericaceae). It has small (⅔ inch) leaves and rose-pink flowers that are ¾ inch across.

willow *n.* A common name for any plant in *Salix,* a genus (Salicaceae) that includes about 300 species of deciduous trees and shrubs with narrow leaves and tiny flowers borne in dense clusters (catkins). Many are planted for ornament, while others have value as erosion control, windbreaks, or as wood for fuel, light construction, basketry, or the manufacture of small items. 2. Any of a number of plants with a real or fancied resemblance to willows.

willow, Arctic *n.* A common name for *Salix arctica,* a creeping shrub sometimes planted in rock gardens.

willow, basket *n.* A common name for *Salix purpurea,* a 9-foot shrub with slender purplish branches turning gray. It is sometimes used as a hedge, especially the dwarf variety 'Nana', because it tolerates cold, wet soil. Also called purple osier and Alaska blue willow.

willow, black _n_. A common name for _Salix nigra_, a 35-foot tree native to the United States.

black willow

willow, black pussy _n_. A common name for _Salix gracilistyla melanostachys_, a shrubby pussy willow with black catkins and red anthers.

willow, coral bark _n_. A common name for _Salix alba_ Britzensis, a tree with coral red bark that is cut back annually for its production of new shoots.

willow, creeping _n_. A common name for _Salix repens_, a creeping shrub sometimes seen in rock gardens.

willow, cricket-bat _n_. A common name for _Salix alba_ 'Caerulea', a 75-foot tree with blue-green foliage.

willow, desert _n_. A common name for _Chilopsis linearis_, a large shrub or small tree (Bignoniaceae) that is native to the Southwestern desert regions of the United States. It is willowlike in appearance, but has clusters of trumpet-shaped flowers in white, pink, or purple.

willow, dragon's-claw _n_. A common name for _Salix matsudana_ 'Tortuosa', a variety of Hankow or Pekin willow with contorted branches. Also called twisted Hankow willow.

willow family _n_. A common name for the family Salicaceae, with 2 genera of woody plants _Salix_ (the willows), and _Populus_ (poplars and aspens)

willow, fan giant weeping _n_. A common name for _Salix blanda_ 'Fan', a weeping tree resistant to heat and wind.

willow, florists' _n_. A common name for _Salix caprea_, a shrub that produces the familiar pussy willows sold at the florists' shops. Also called French pussy willow, goat willow, pink pussy willow, pussy willow, and sallow.

willow, globe _n_. A common name for _Salix matsudana_ 'Umbraculifera', an umbrella-shaped willow useful in difficult conditions.

willow, globe Navajo _n_. A common name for _Salix matsudana_ 'Navajo', a 70-foot willow that tolerates heat and drought.

willow, Hankow _n_. A common name for _Salix matsudana_, an erect willow that grows from 40 to 50 feet. It has bright green leaves, and needs less moisture than other willows. It also tolerates heat.

willow herb _n_. A common name for any species of the genus _Epilobium_ (Onagraceae). _Epilobium angustifolium_, the great willow herb, is a 3- to 5-foot perennial with rosy purple flowers that grow in a long spikelike cluster. It often springs up on land after wild fires, and for this reason is commonly called fireweed.

willow herb

willow, large pussy _n_. A common name for _Salix discolor_, similar to other pussy willows, but its catkins are ½ inch longer.

willow-leaved jessamine (jeh′suh mehn) *n.* A common name for *Cestrum parqui,* an evergreen subtropical or tropical shrub (Solanaceae) that grows from 10 to 12 feet tall. It has long, narrow leaves, and clustered greenish-white flowers that are intensely fragrant at night. Also called night-blooming jessamine, a name properly belonging to *C. nocturnum.*

willow myrtle (muhr′duhl) *n.* A name given to evergreen trees and shrubs in the genus *Agonis* (Myrtaceae). Best known is *A. flexuosa,* a tree that grows to 35 feet, with weeping branches, small white flowers, and a strong peppermint fragrance. Also known as peppermint tree or Australian willow myrtle. *A. juniperina,* the juniper myrtle, is similar in size but more open in growth habit, with smaller leaves.

willow, Niobe *n.* A common name for *Salix alba* 'Tristis', a large weeping willow with golden yellow first-year branchlets. Also known as *S. babylonica* aurea 'Niobe'.

willow oak *n.* A common name for *Quercus phellos,* a 60-foot deciduous tree (Fagaceae). Its name comes from its narrow, smooth-edged leaves. It is a favored street tree in many regions. (See **oak, willow**.)

willow, Pekin *n.* (See **willow, Hankow**.)

willow, ringleaf *n.* A common name for *Salix babylonica* 'Crispa' or 'Annularis', a weeping tree with leaves twisted into a near-circle. Also called corkscrew willow.

willow, rose gold pussy *n.* A common name for *Salix gracilistyla,* a shrub that grows to 10 feet, with gray catkins showing pink and gold anthers.

willow, weeping *n.* A common name for *Salix babylonica,* a strongly weeping tree that grows up to 50 feet, the classic willow of Chinese gardens.

willow, Wisconsin weeping *n.* A common name for *Salix blanda,* less strongly weeping than other pendulous forms.

willow, yellow *n.* A common name for *Salix alba vitellina,* with bright yellow young branches.

wind *n.* Air in motion, a factor gardeners must consider in choosing varieties of plants for some sites.

wind-break *n.* Something to break the force of the wind, as a hedge, a board fence, or a row of evergreen trees; any shelter from the wind. (See **shelterbelt**.)

windflower *n.* A common name applied loosely to all species of *Anemone,* a genus of perennials (Ranunculaceae). It particularly refers to *A. nemorosa,* also known as the European wood anemone, and to *A. fulgens,* the scarlet windflower.

windmill jasmine (jaz′mehn) *n.* A common name for *Jasminum nitidum,* a tender evergreen shrubby vine (Oleaceae) with fragrant white flowers. It is also called angel-wing jasmine, star jasmine, and Confederate jasmine, the last two names more properly belonging to *Trachelospermum jasminoides.*

window plant *n.* 1. One of many common names for *Monstera deliciosa* (*Philodendron pertusum*), a large vine (Araceae), so called because the leaves have large holes in addition to its deep lobes. It is a familiar house plant, or garden plant in warm climates. It is also called split-leaf philodendron, ceriman, Swiss cheese plant, breadfruit vine, hurricane plant, Mexican breadfruit, fruit-salad plant, and cut-leaf philodendron. 2. Any of a number of succulent plants that have transparent upper leaf surfaces to shelter the chlorophyll-bearing surface from heat, sun, or wind. Genera include *Fenestraria* (Aizoaceae), and *Haworthia* (Liliaceae).

windmill palm *n.* A common name for *Trachycarpus fortunei,* sometimes sold as *Chamaerops excelsa,* a hardy fan palm that grows up to 30 feet. Its trunk is covered with dense blackish fiber.

window box *n.* A container for growing decorative plants outside a window.

window hayrack *n.* (See **English planter**.)

windowsill tray *n.* A long, narrow, shallow container for holding potted plants on a windowsill.

wineberry *n.* 1. A common name for *Rubus phoenicolasius,* a raspberrylike shrub (Rosaceae). It has long canes and small, bright red raspberrylike fruit. 2. A Japanese variety of raspberry.

wing *n.* In botany, a dry membranous expansion or thin extension of any kind, such as that on certain seed capsules or stems, such as the winged seed of *Acer*; also, one of the two side petals of certain flowers.

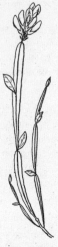

wings on stems

winged pea *n.* 1. A common name for *Lotus tetragonolobus,* an annual (Leguminosae) with trailing stems, red flowers, and 3-inch-long, 4 angled pods that are edible when young. 2. A common name for *Lotus berthelotii,* a tender ornamental trailing plant with silvery leaves and orange-scarlet, 1-inch flowers. 3. A common name for *Psophocarpus tetragonolobus,* a twining tender perennial with reddish flowers and 4-winged pods that grow to 9 inches long, and are edible when young. It is also called winged bean, asparagus pea, princess pea, Goa bean, Manila bean, and four-angled bean.

winter aconite (ak'uh night) *n.* A common name for *Eranthis,* 7 species of small tuberous perennials (Ranunculaceae), with finely divided basal leaves and yellow or white flowers with many petallike sepals. *E. hyemalis* grows from 2 to 6 inches tall. It has inch-wide yellow flowers, that are among the first flowers to appear in late winter or early spring.

winterberry *n.* Any of several species of holly in the genus *Ilex.* They are shrubs that are notable for a show of red or black berries in winter.

winterberry, common *n.* A common name for *Ilex verticillata* and *Ilex glabra.* *I. verticillata* is a deciduous shrub that grows up to 15 feet, and has smooth leaves and red ¼-inch fruits. Also known as black alder. *I. glabra* is an evergreen shrub that grows up to 10 feet and has black fruit that is larger than ¼ inch in diameter. Also known as gallberry, bitter gallberrry, inkberry, and Appalachian tea. (See **Ilex**.)

winterberry, Japanese *n.* A common name for *Ilex serrata,* a 4- to 10-foot tall deciduous shrub that has red fruits. (See **Ilex**.)

winterberry, mountain *n.* A common name for *Ilex ambigua montana,* a deciduous shrub that has up to 7-inch-long leaves and red fruits. Also known as large-leaved holly and mountain holly. (See **Ilex**.)

winter cherry *n.* 1. A common name for *Cardiospermum halicababum,* (Sapindaceae). It has inflated, inch-wide fruit. Better known as balloon vine or heart pea. 2. A common name for *Physalis alkekengi (P. franchetii),* a perennial (Solanaceae). It has an inflated orange-red 2-inch calyx. It is better known as Chinese lantern, Japanese lantern, and alkekengi.

wintercreeper *n.* A common name for *Euonymus fortunei radicans,* a hardy trailing or climbing evergreen shrub or vine (Celastraceae). It is used as a ground cover or wall cover, climbing by rootlets.

winter cress *n.* A common name for *Barbarea vulgaris,* a biennial (Cruciferae) that grows to 3 feet, and has yellow flowers. It is sometimes grown as a salad green, although it is more commonly a weed. Also called rocket (but not the salad rocket *Eruca vesicaria*).

wintergreen
(*Gaultheria procumbens*)

wintergreen *n.* Any of several small woodland plants with evergreen foliage. The best known is *Gaultheria procumbens,* a low-growing plant (Ericaceae) that has erect stems that grow from underground creeping rhizomes. It has aromatic leaves that taste like wintergreen, tiny flowers, and mildly aromatic red berries. It is also known as checkerberry.

wintergreen, alpine *n.* A common name for *Gaultheria humifusa,* a wintergreen native of the western United States. It has edible red berries.

wintergreen, arctic *n.* A common name for *Pyrola grandiflora,* an evergreen shrublet (Pyrolaceae), that grows to 8 inches. It has roundish leaves and creamy, pink-tinged flowers that are arranged spirally. Also called arctic pyrola.

wintergreen, chickweed *n.* A common name for *Trientalis,* a small perennial herb (Primulaceae) with white or pink flowers. Also commonly known as starflower.

wintergreen, flowering *n.* A common name for *Polygala paucifolia,* a small evergreen shrublet (Polygalaceae) native to the mountain woodlands of the northern United States. It grows up to 6 inches tall and bears oddly shaped purplish pink flowers. Also called fringed polygala and bird-on-the-wing.

wintergreen, pink *n.* A common name for *Pyrola asarifolia,* a foot-tall plant that has spirally arranged pink to red flowers. Also called pink pyrola.

wintergreen, spotted *n.* A common name for *Chimaphila maculata,* a 10-inch shrublet. It has leaves marked with white along the veins and fragrant white flowers.

winter hazel *n.* A common name for several species of *Corylopsis* (Hamamelidaceae). All are deciduous shrubs with fragrant yellow flowers that dangle in clusters from bare branches in late winter or early spring. *C. paucifolia,* buttercup winter hazel, grows up to 6 feet, and has flowers in clusters of 2 or 3. *C. spicata,* spike winter hazel, is a coarse shrub with large leaves and spikes of 6 to 12 flowers.

winter purslane (puhrs′lehn) *n.* A common name for *Montia perfoliata* (Portulacaceae), an annual with fleshy, long-stalked, narrow, inconspicuous leaves. The flowers resemble a large round leaf with tiny white flowers in the center. Its foliage is edible. Also known as miner's lettuce or Cuban spinach.

winter-sweet *n.* A common name for *Chimonanthus praecox (C. fragrans),* a 10-foot deciduous shrub (Calycanthaceae) with intensely fragrant inchwide, many-petaled flowers of pale yellow with brown markings. It blooms in midwinter in mild regions, and early spring elsewhere.

wireworms *n. pl.* The hard-shelled, jointed larvae of click beetles. They feed on roots of many plants, particularly root crops, and are hard to control. Soil sterilization, tilling, parasitic nematodes, trapping, and traditional insecticides are control measures.

Wisteria (wehs′tih ree uh) *n.* A genus of 9 or 10 species of deciduous woody vines (Leguminosae) some species native to eastern North America. They have compound pinnate leaves and ornamental blue, white, purple or rose petalike flowers in drooping racemes that are followed by long flattened pods.

wisteria, Chinese (wehs′tih ree uh) *n.* A common name for *Wisteria sinensis,* a vine that grows up to 50 feet. It has abundant 1-foot- long clusters of violet-blue pea-shaped flowers that appear in spring before the foliage arrives. Two varieties are cultivated: the white variety, 'Alba', and a double-flowering blue variety.

wisteria, evergreen (wehs′tih ree uh) *n.* A common name for *Millettia reticulata,* a woody vine (Leguminosae) that grows to 15 feet or more, with evergreen leaves that are divided into many leaflets, and dark rose-purple flowers in dense clusters that have an odd, attractive fragrance.

wisteria, Japanese (wehs′tih ree uh) *n.* A common name for *Wisteria floribunda.* It has 1½-foot clusters of violet or violet-blue flowers that begin to appear at the top of the cluster, gradually opening toward the end of the cluster, making the Japanese wisteria a longer-blooming plant than the Chinese wisteria, whose buds open nearly all at once. There are also other varieties of Japanese wisteria that differ from the original species by having a 3-foot long cluster and white or pinkish flowers.

wisteria, silky (wehs′tih ree uh) *n.* A common name for *Wisteria venusta.* It has short, fat clusters of comparatively large, fragrant, pealike flowers that open all at once. The common variety is white; there is also a blue variety, *W. venusta* 'Violacea'.

witch alder *n.* A common name for *Fothergilla gardenii,* a 3-foot tall deciduous shrub (Hamamelidaceae), with white flowers that appear in brushlike spikes at the ends of the branches. It displays outstandingly brilliant fall foliage color.

witch hazel *n.* A common name for several species of the genus *Hamamelis,* hardy deciduous large shrubs or small trees. They have fragrant flowers with 4 narrow, often twisted, strap-shaped petals. They bloom in fall, winter, or early spring. All have outstanding fall foliage color.

witch hazel
(*Hamamelis virginiana*)

witch hazel, Chinese *n.* A common name for *Hamamelis mollis,* a shrub or tree that grows to 30 feet, with golden yellow flowers and yellow fall foliage color. It blooms in winter.

witch hazel, common *n.* A common name for *Hamamelis virginiana.* It grows up to 15 feet, with yellow flowers blooming in late autumn and bright yellow fall foliage.

witch hazel family *n.* A common name for the family Hamamelidaceae, 23 genera of woody plants, including many ornamentals such as *Hamamelis, Fothergilla,* and *Loropetalum.*

witch hazel, Japanese *n.* A common name for *Hamemelis japonica.* It grows up to 30 feet, with yellow flowers that appear in winter or early spring.

witch hazel, vernal *n.* A common name for *Hamemelis vernalis.* It grows up to 6 feet, with dull,

fragrant yellow flowers that bloom in winter or early spring.

withe rod (wihth) *n.* One of the common names for *Viburnum cassinoides,* a deciduous shrub (Caprifoliaceae) that grows up to 12 feet. It has white flowers in 5-inch clusters followed by black, edible fruits. Also called Appalachian tea, swamp haw, teaberry, and wild raisin.

witloof chicory (chihk'uh ree) *n.* A variety of chicory having large roots and forming a close, elongated head of white leaves. These heads are cooked as a vegetable or eaten raw in salads. (See **Belgian endive.**)

woad (wohd) *n.* A common name for *Isatis tinctoria,* an herb formerly cultivated for the blue dye extracted from its fermented leaves. It is now grown in herb gardens, chiefly for its historical interest.

woad

woadwaxen (wohd'waks'uhn) *n.* The dyer's-broom, *Genista tinctoria.*

wolfberry *n.* A common name for *Symphoricarpos occidentalis,* a deciduous shrub (Caprifoliaceae) that grows up to 5 feet and has small pinkish flowers followed by white berries.

wolfsbane *n.* A common name for plants in the genus *Aconitum,* especially *A. lycoctonum.* Garden wolfs' bane is *Aconitum napellus.* All are are poisonous.

wood ashes *n.* A fertilizer containing potash.

wood betony (beht'uh nee) *n.* A common name for a species of *Pedicularis,* a genus of about 350 annuals, biennials, or perennials (Scrophulariaceae). Although some are attractive, many are semiparasitic and hard to grow. They are also called lousewort.

woodbine *n.* A common name for several species of honeysuckle (Lonicera). The name is originally applied to *Lonicera periclymenum,* a vine with yellowish-white flowers, but has also been used for *Clematis virginiana* (also called leather flower, virgin's bower, and devil's darning needle) and Virginia creeper, *Parthenocissus quinquefolia.*

woodbine, Dutch *n.* A common name for *Lonicera periclymenum belgica,* a form of woodbine with purple flowers that become yellowish.

woodbine, Italian *n.* A common name for *L. caprifolium,* a honeysuckle with white or purplish flowers.

woodbine, Spanish *n.* A common name for *Merremia tuberosa,* a perennial morning glory vine (Convolvulaceae). It has yellow flowers and a woody seed capsule shaped like a flower. It is better known as wood rose, Hawaiian wood rose, yellow morning glory, or Ceylon morning glory.

wood fern *n.* A common name for ferns of the genus *Dryopteris.* There are 150 species, many native to the United States. They are called *Aspidium* by some authorities, and are also known as shield ferns.

wood germander (juhr man'duhr) *n.* A common name for *Teucrium scorodonia,* a dwarf shrubby perennial (Labiatae). It has dark green, somewhat rough leaves and pale yellow flowers. A variety 'Crispum', with ruffled leaf edges is sometimes grown in gardens.

wood hyacinth (high'uh sihnth) *n.* A common name for *Endymion non-scriptus (Scilla non-scripta),* a bulbous plant (Liliaceae) with spikes of violet blue flowers. There are pink and white varieties. It is also known as English bluebell or harebell.

wood rose *n.* 1. A common name for *Rosa gymnocarpa,* a wild rose of the western United States. It has inch-wide single pink flowers that grow on an 8-foot tall shrub. 2. A common name for *Merremia tuberosa,* a perennial vine (Convolvulaceae). Its woody seed capsule resembles that of roses.

woodruff *n.* A shade-loving herb, *Gallium odoratum,* also called sweet woodruff. (See also **sweet woodruff**.) The name is also applied to species of the genus *Asperula,* particularly *A. tinctoria* (dyer's woodruff), whose roots sometimes served as a red dye.

Woodsia (wood'zee uh) *n.* A genus of 40 species of small ferns (Polypodiaceae). Best known is *W. ilvensis,* the rusty or fragrant woodsia, a finely cut fern to 8 or 10 inches tall.

wood sorrel (saw'ruhl) *n.* Loosely applied, any member of the genus *Oxalis.* Strictly applied, it pertains to *O. acetosella,* and *O. violacea. O. acetusella* is a woodland perennial with 3-parted leaves and small white flowers with purple streaks. *O. violacea,* the violet wood sorrel, is similar, but with pink or purplish (rarely white) flowers.

wood spurge *n.* A common name for *Euphorbia amygdaloides,* a hardy perennial (Euphorbiaceae) that grows to 1 foot tall. It has crowded narrow leaves along the stems and broad clusters of greenish yellow flowers. There is a variety 'Purpurea' ('Rubra') that has dark reddish purple foliage.

wood violet *n.* A common name for *Viola riviniana,* an 8-inch tall violet plant with 1-inch blue violets. It is also called dog violet.

Woodwardia virginiana
(Virginia chain fern)
a entire plant *b* single pinnule of a frond

Woodwardia (woo dwar'dee uh) *n.* A genus of 12 species of large ferns, the chain ferns (Polypodiaceae). *W. fimbriata,* the giant chain fern of the Pacific coast, can reach 9 feet tall. *W. virginiana,* the Virginia chain fern, grows to 2 feet tall. *W. radicans,* the European chain fern, has arching fronds that grow up to 7 feet; it sometimes forms new plants at the tips of the fronds. Oriental chain fern, *W. orientalis,* is similar in size, but produces many plantlets along its fronds.

woolly bear *n.* A common name for *Begonia leptotricha,* a houseplant with woolly 1- to 3-inch leaves and white flowers. It is also called Manda's woolly bear and woolly bear caterpillar.

worm grass *n.* A common name for *Spigelia marilandica,* a perennial (Loganiaceae). It is better known as pinkroot or Indian pink.

wormseed *n.* 1. A common name for *Artemisia maritima,* a strongly scented 2-foot tall woolly subshrub (Compositae). 2. A common name for *Chenopodium ambrosioides,* a strong-scented 3½-foot annual or perennial (Chenopodiaceae). Its leaves are used in Mexican cookery under the name epazote. Other names are Mexican tea, Spanish tea, and American wormseed.

wormwood *n.* A name applied to *Artemisia* (Compositae), several species of aromatic perennials or subshrubs. Common wormwood is *A. absinthium,* also known as absinthe, a 4-foot perennial with finely cut, silvery, silky foliage and inconspicuous whitish flowers. *A. frigida,* a 1 to 1½-foot perennial with finely cut white leaves is called fringed wormwood. *A. pontica,* which grows up to 4 feet, is known as Roman wormwood. *A. stellerana* is beach wormwood, a woolly perennial that grows up to 2½ feet. It is also known as old woman and dusty miller.

wort *n.* A plant; an herb; a vegetable. The word -wort is very frequently a part of old common names of plants, as in bonewort, bloodwort, liverwort, lungwort, etc, often indicating its use as medicine.

wound dressing *n.* (See **tree paint.**)

woundwort *n.* 1. A name applied to species of *Stachys,* perennials or subshrubs (Labiatae). *S. germanica* is called downy woundwort. They are also known as betony and hedge nettle. 2. A common name for *Anthyllis vulneraria,* an annual or perennial plant (Leguminosae) with divided leaves and yellow to red flowers. It is also known as kidney vetch and lady's-fingers.

Wulfenia (wool feh'nee uh) *n.* A genus of several species of hardy perennials (Scrophulariaceae). All are smooth, tufted plants with thick rootstocks and blue flowers that grow in spikelike clusters. *W. carinthiaca,* which grows to 2 feet, is the best known. Sometimes planted in rock gardens or flower borders.

Wyethia (wigh ee'thee uh) *n.* A genus of coarse perennials (Compositae) native to the mountains of the western United States. They have heavy rootstocks, large, glossy basal leaves, and big, 3 to 5 inch-wide golden daisylike flowers that appear on 3 foot tall stalks. They are showy, but seldom grown in gardens, because the flower reaches its full size slowly. Three species sometimes grown are *W. amplexicaulis, W. angustifolia,* and *W. helenioides.*

xanth-/xantho- *comb. form.* Yellow.

Xantheranthemum (zan ther an'thuh muhm) *n.* A genus of 1 species, *X. igneum* (Acanthaceae), trailing houseplants. They have opposite, yellow-veined, dark green leaves, purple beneath, and spikes of yellow tubular flowers. Grown for their foliage as houseplants.

Xanthisma (zan thihz'muh) *n.* A genus of 1 species, *X. texana* (Compositae), an annual native to Texas. It grow to 3 feet, with narrow, divided leaves and yellow daisylike flowers with yellow centers that close at night. Used in wild gardens or native-plant collections. Commonly known as sleepy daisy.

Xanthoceras (zan thahs'er uhs) *n.* A genus of 2 species of hardy deciduous shrubs and trees (Sapindaceae). They grow to 15 feet, with narrow, pointed, divided alternate leaves and spikes of 5-petaled white flowers with a red or yellow blotch.

Xanthorhiza (zan thuh rih'zuh) *n.* A genus of 1 species, *X. simplicissima* (Ranunculaceae), a hardy deciduous shrublet native to the eastern United States from New York to West Virginia south to Florida and Alabama. It grows to 2 feet, with leaves divided into leaflets and drooping spikes of tiny brownish-purple flowers. Useful in damp, shady locations. Commonly known as shrub yellow root.

Xanthorrhoea (zan thuh ree'uh) *n.* A genus of 12 species of slow-growing subtropical woody perennials (Liliaceae). They grow to 15 feet, with a thick, woody, black stem topped by a tuft of stiff, linear leaves, and tall spikes dense with white flowers. Grown in dry situations in sandy soil; good with yucca and century plant (*Agave*). Commonly known as grass tree.

Xanthosoma (zan thuh soh'muh) *n.* A genus of 40 species of tender tuberous perennials (Araceae) native to tropical America. They grow from tuberous rootstocks to 6 feet, with large arrow-shaped or triangular leaves and green or yellow callalike flowers that are more curious than attractive. Grown for their foliage to create tropical effects in mild-winter climates, as indoor/outdoor plants, as houseplants, or in greenhouses. Commonly known as yautia, malanga, tannia, tannier, tanyah, and ocumo.

Xeranthemum (zih ran'thuh muhm) *n.* A genus of annual herbs, characterized by long-stalked, solitary flower heads of a daisy shape, rose-colored or silvery white. *X. annuum,* the most frequently cultivated species, is known as annual everlasting or immortelle, both names commonly given to a number of different flowers that dry well for use in winter bouquets.

xeriscape (zer ih'skayp) *n.* A landscape designed with drought-tolerant plants.

xerophilous (zer ahf'ih luhs) *a.* In botany, loving dryness; denoting plants that are characteristic of, tolerant of, or thriving in the presence of dry climates. Also xerophile, xerophilic, xerophil.

Xerophyllum (zer ah figh'luhm) *n.* A genus of 2 species of American perennial wildflowers (Liliaceae): *X. asphodeloides* (turkey beard and mountain asphodel) is native to the eastern United States, and *X. tenax* (bear grass or fire lily) is native to the western United States. They grow from 5 to 6 feet, with basal grasslike leaves and tall spikes of small white flowers. Used in wild gardens or native-plant collections.

xerophyte (zer'oh fight) *n.* A plant adapted structurally to living and growing with limited water by means that limit transpiration or provide water storage, for example, cactus and succulents.

xyl-/xylo- *comb. form.* Woody.

Xylobium (zigh loh'bee uhm) *n.* A genus of 30 species of tropical epiphytic (living on a host without deriving nourSihment from it) orchids (Orchidaceae) native to Central and South America and the West Indies. They grow from pseudobulbs to 1 inch, with long, narrow leathery leaves and erect or arching spikes of variously patterned multicolored flowers. Grown by collectors in warm greenhouses.

Xylococcus (zigh loh kohk'uhs) *n.* A genus of 1 species, *X. bicolor* (Ericaceae), a hardy evergreen much-branched shrub native to California and Baja California. It grows to 6 feet, with shiny, dark green leaves, downy-gray beneath, and clusters of white or pink heatherlike flowers.

Xylosma (zigh lahs'muh) *n.* A genus of about 100 species of large tender semievergreen shrubs or small trees (Flacourtiaceae). *X. congestum* grows from 8 to 10 feet, with bronzy new growth that matures into shiny, yellow-green, long, oval, pointed leaves and inconspicuous flowers. Used as a shrub, hedge, screen, espalier, and in containers.

Xyridaceae (zigh rih day'see ee) *n. pl.* A family of 2 genera of rushlike perennial bog plants. The cultivated genus is *Xyris*.

Xyris (zigh'rihs) *n.* A genus of 240 species of perennials (Xyridaceae), some species native to eastern North America from Newfoundland to Ontario, south to Florida and Texas. They grow to 2½ feet, with rushlike leaves and yellow flowers. Used in wild gardens in moist or wet soils. Commonly known as yellow-eyed grass.

yam *n*. 1. A tuberous (potatolike) root of a plant of the genus *Dioscorea*, particularly 1 of numerous species cultivated for their edible roots; also, such a plant itself. The plant is commonly a slender, twining, high-climbing vine, in some species prickly; the root is fleshy, often very large, sometimes a shapeless mass, sometimes long and cylindrical, varying in color from white through purple to nearly black. The yam is propagated by cuttings from the root or also, in some species, by axillary bulblets. The root, which contains a large amount of starch, is nutritious. It is cooked by baking or boiling and is sometimes converted into a meal used for making cakes and puddings. *D. sativa* is hardy in the southern United States, but the true yam is rarely cultivated, except for its fast-growing vines, which are useful as screening plants. 2. The orange-fleshed varieties of sweet potato, grown in the southern United States.

yam vine

yam bean *n*. A common name for *Pachyrrhizus erosus* and *P. tuberosus,* subtropical and tropical perennial vines. *P. erosus* has naturalized in Southern Florida. They grow from tuberous roots to 20 feet or more, with leaves divided into leaflets, clusters of butterfly-shaped purple or white flowers, and long pods. The seeds are poisonous. Grown for their edible tubers.

yam family *n*. A common name for Dioscoreaceae. (See **Dioscoreaceae.**)

yam, wild *n*. Any native species of yam; specifically, the wild yam- root, *Dioscorea villosa,* a delicate and pretty twining vine of North America, growing from Virginia north to Canada.

yang-tao (yahng tah′oh) *n*. A common name for *Actinidia deliciosa* (kiwifruit or Chinese gooseberry) and *A. arguta* (hardy kiwi or tera vine). *A. arguta* is much like *A. deliciosa* (see **Actinidia**) but is much hardier and has smaller leaves, flowers, and fuzzless fruit. Grown ornamentally and for their fruit (the vines will not fruit without both male and female plants).

yard-long bean *n*. (See **asparagus bean.**)

yarrow (yar′oh) *n*. The perennial herb *Achillea Millefolium* and other plants of the same genus. The tiny flowers form a flat head, white in the common variety, which has naturalized throughout much of North America. Pink and magenta varieties are grown in perennial borders and herb gardens. The yellow *A. filipendulina* is taller, often reaching 3 feet, and has fernlike leaves, larger than the fine, feathery foliage of other varieties. Its yellow flower heads dry well for use in winter arrangments and wreaths.

yarrow

yate tree *n*. A common name for *Eucalyptus cornuta,* a large-headed, spreading, tender broadleaf evergreen tree. It grows from 30 to 60 feet, with peeling bark, a dense crown of lance-shaped shiny leaves (the juvenile leaves are round), clusters of fuzzy, greenish-yellow flowers, and clusters of seed capsules with short horns. Used as a shade tree; extremely adaptable to a variety of soils and degrees of moisture.

yaupon (yaw′pahn) *n.* A common name for 2 species of *Ilex*, (holly), *I. Cassine* and *I. vomitoria,* hardy North American evergreen shrubs or trees native from southeastern Virginia, south to Florida and west to Texas. They have attractive red berries in winter. Also spelled yapon, yapa, or youpon. (See **Ilex**.)

Y connection *n.* A device in the shape of an inverted "Y" having dual shutoff levers; used to run 2 hoses from 1 faucet. Also called two-way hose shutoff, twin shutoff, or Siamese shutoff.

yedda hawthorn (yehd′duh) *n.* A common name for *Rhaphiolepis umbellata,* a thick, full, bushy, tender broadleaf evergreen shrub. It grows from 4 to 6 feet, sometimes more, with roundish, leathery, dark green leaves and clusters of small white fragrant flowers. Used as a specimen shrub, background shrub, foundation plant, or hedge.

yellow archangel *n.* A common name for *Lamiastrum galeobdolon,* a tender evergreen ground cover. (See **Lamiastrum**.)

yellow bells *n.* 1. A common name for *Emmenanthe penduliflora,* an annual flower native to western North America. (See **Emmenanthe**.) 2. Also a common name for the genus *Tecoma* and *T. stans* (yellow elder), showy yellow-flowering vines native from Florida to Mexico and Argentina. (See **Tecoma**.)

yellow elder *n.* A common name for *Tecoma stans,* a fast-growing, bushy, tender American flowering vine, native from Florida to Mexico and Argentina. It grows to 20 feet, with leaves divided in long, pointed leaflets and spectacular clusters of bright yellow trumpet-shaped flowers. Used as a showy landscape specimen. Also known as yellow bignonia, yellow trumpet flower, and yellow bells.

yellow flax, Indian *n.* A common name for *Reinwardtia indica,* a tender, spreading long-blooming, bushy, shrublike perennial. It grows to 4 feet, with

small, simple leaves and masses of large brilliant-yellow flowers in late fall and winter. Used in perennial borders or with shrubs.

yellow oleander (oh′lee an der) *n.* A common name for *Thevetia peruviana,* a tender evergreen shrub. It grows to 8 feet, with long, narrow leaves, with edges rolled under, and clusters of fragrant yellow-to-apricot flowers. Used as a hedge, screen, or background planting in mild-winter climates. Tolerates high heat and full sun, but no wind. It is poisonous. Also known as be-still tree and lucky nut.

yellow rocket *n.* A common name for *Barbarea vulgaris,* a biennial naturalized in North America. Generally considered a weed. Also known as winter cress and rocket.

yellowroot *n.* 1. A common name for the genus *Xanthorhiza.* (See **Xanthorhiza**.) 2. A common name for *Hydrastis Canadensis,* a North American plant. Also called orangeroot, yellow puccoon, Indian paint, turmeric root, and goldenseal. (See **Hydrastis**.)

yellow sticky trap *n.* (See **sticky trap**.)

yellowwood *n.* A common name for 2 trees, *Cladrastis lutea,* (See **Cladrastis**) and *Rhodosphaera rhodanthema. R. rhodanthema* is a tender Australian tree. It grows to 40 feet, with leaves divided into leathery leaflets and dense clusters of tiny red flowers.

yellowwood
a pod

yerba buena (yer′bah bway′nah) *n.* A common name for *Satureja Douglasii,* a tender, creeping, subtropical perennial native from British Columbia to Southern California. It has stems to 18 inches, with aromatic light green rounded leaves, with scalloped edges and spikes of whorled white to pale lavender flowers. Used in herb gardens or to tumble over stone walls.

yerba mansa (yer'buh mahn'suh) *n.* A common name for *Anemopsis californica,* a perennial with thick, aromatic rootstocks, native from California and Nevada to Texas and Baja California. It grows to 2 feet, with large oval, mostly basal leaves and spikes of white flowers. Grows well in wet, alkaline soils.

yerba mate (yer'buh mah'tay) *n.* A common name for *Ilex paraguariensis,* a small tender evergreen holly tree, native to South America. It grows to 20 feet, with leathery, flat dark green oval leaves, greenish-white flowers, and red berries. The source of the famous mate tea of the Argentinean gauchos. Also known as Paraguay tea and mate.

yerba santa (yer'buh sahn'tuh) *n.* A common name for *Eriodictyon,* a genus of evergreen shrubs native to the American West and adjacent Mexico. (See **Eriodictyon**.)

yew *n.* A common name for slow-growing and long-lived trees of the genus *Taxus,* hardy or very hardy evergreen conifers. They grow to 50 feet, with spirally arranged short, needlelike, dark green leaves and fleshy scarlet berries (only on female trees). Both fruit and foliage are poisonous. Used as hedges, screens, or specimen trees.

yew, American *n.* A common name for *Taxus canadensis,* a very hardy North American shrub native from Newfoundland to Virginia and Iowa. It grows to 6 feet, with creeping branches, pointed dark yellow-green leaves, and round fruit. Also known as ground hemlock. (See **ground hemlock.**)

yew, Chinese *n.* A common name for *Taxus chinensis,* a hardy evergreen conifer. It grows to 50 feet, with curved, pointed, glossy-green leaves and small, fleshy fruit.

yew, Chinese plum *n.* A common name for *Cephalotaxus Fortunii (Fortuneii),* a hardy slow-growing evergreen shrub or small tree. It grows to 10 feet, with soft, needlelike leaves, to 3 inches long, and fruit resembling small green or brown plums. Useful in moist, shady places.

yew, English *n.* A common name for *Taxus baccata,* a slow-growing hardy evergreen tree. It grows

to 40 feet or more, with glossy, short, needlelike dark green leaves and small, round, fleshy fruit. There are many cultivars, some hardier than the species. Used for hedges, screens, or as specimen trees.

English yew

yew family *n.* A common name for Taxaceae. (See **Taxaceae**.)

yew, Florida *n.* A common name for *Taxus floridana,* a tender spreading shrub or tree native to Florida. It grows to 25 feet, with small, curved, needlelike leaves.

yew, golden *n.* A common name for a cultivar of English yew, *Taxus baccata* 'Aurea', a hardy evergreen coniferous tree. It grows to 60 feet, with golden yellow new growth from spring to autumn, turning green in fall and winter.

yew, Harrington plum *n.* A common name for *Cephalotaxus Harringtonia,* a hardy evergreen shrub or tree. It grows to 30 feet, with dark green needlelike leaves, 2 inches long, and plumlike fruit on the stalks. Used as hedges and screens in shady places.

yew, Irish *n.* A common name for a cultivar of English yew, *Taxus baccata* 'Stricta', a hardy slim, columnar tree. It grows to 20 feet or more, with dark green leaves. Striking against a light wall or as a background plant.

yew, Japanese plum *n.* A common name for *Cephalotaxus Harringtonia drupacea,* a hardy evergreen tree similar to *Cephalotaxus Harringtonia* (Harrington plum yew). (See **yew, Harrington plum**.) *C. H. drupacea* has showier fruit than the species. Also known as plum-fruited yew.

yew, Prince Albert *n.* A common name for *Saxigothea conspicua,* a tender evergreen coniferous tree or shrub. It grows to 40 feet, with peeling bark and short, dark green needlelike leaves. Grown in Florida and other warm regions.

yew, Western *n.* A common name for *Taxus brevifolia,* a hardy tree native from Alaska south to California, east to Montana. Most plants sold under this name are cultivars of *T. baccata. T. brevifolia* is rare in the wild and difficult to grow in cultivation. Also known as Oregon yew.

ylang-ylang (ee lahng' ee lahng') *n.* A common name for *Cananga odorata,* a flowering tropical tree. It grows to 80 feet, with large oval leaves, 8 inches long, and clusters of drooping greenish-yellow very fragrant flowers. The flowers are the source of ylang-ylang oil, prized for perfume. Grown in warm climates for its showy flowers and sweet fragrance. Also spelled ilang-ilang.

York-and-Lancaster rose *n.* A common name for *Rosa damascena* 'Versicolor', a hardy antique rose; a cultivar of the damask rose. It grows to 8 feet, with leaves divided into 5 oval, pointed leaflets and all white, all pink, or white-and-pink fragrant semi- double flowers, all colors appearing on the same plant. Named for the roses symbolic of the York and Lancaster families in the War of the Roses.

youngberry *n.* A common name for *Rubus ursinus* 'Young', a hardy shrub. It is a blackberry, similar to boysenberry, with white flowers and sweet, large blackberries. There is a thornless variety. Grown for its summer fruit.

youth-and-old-age *n.* A common name for 2 plants, *Aichryson domesticum* and *Zinnia elegans* (common zinnia). (See **Zinnia.**) *A. domesticum* is a succulent that grows to 12 inches, with small, thick, fleshy leaves and small golden flowers.

youth-on-age *n.* A common name for *Tolmiea menziesii,* a North American perennial native to the west coast from Alaska to northern California. It forms a leafy clump to 24 inches, with soft, maplelike leaves on which new plants sprout and inconspicuous reddish-brown flowers. Used as a houseplant, in shaded window boxes, hanging baskets, containers, and as a small-scale ground cover in shady, moist places. Also known as piggyback plant and thousand-mothers.

Yucca (yuhk'uh) *n.* A genus of about 40 species of evergreen perennials, shrubs, and trees (Agavaceae) native to North America. They grow from 28 inches to 40 feet, depending on the species, with stiff, swordlike or stillettolike leaves and large clusters of showy white or cream-colored flowers. The hardy species are grown as specimens in cold-winter climates, others in hot, dry regions, and in containers. Young yuccas can be grown as indoor plants.

Yucca

yulan (yoo'lahn) *n.* A common name for *Magnolia denudata* (*M. conspicua, M.heptapeta*), a spreading deciduous tree. It grows to 35 feet or more, with broad, blunt leaves, 7 inches long, large, fragrant white tulip-shaped flowers, 6 inches across, that appear before the leaves, and fruit. Used as a specimen where its irregular winter silhouette and fragrant flowers can be enjoyed, and in woodland gardens.

Z

Zaluzianskya (zahl oo zee an'skee yuh) *n.* A genus of 40 species of annual or tender perennials (Scrophulariaceae). They grow to 18 inches, with simple, entire leaves and spikes of white and purple tubular flowers that exude their fragrance toward evening. Grown for their fragrance.

Zamia (zuh'mee uh) *n.* A genus of 40 species of short, slow-growing, wide-spreading palmlike tropical plants (Zamiaceae), technically primitive conifers. They grow 3 to 4 feet wide, with stiff, frondlike leaves, closely resembling a coarse, leathery fern. Used as handsome houseplants, in greenhouses, excellent in containers as indoor/outdoor plants, or outdoors in frost-free climates.

zamia

Zannichellia (zan ih kehl′ee uh) *n.* A genus of 1 species, *Z. palustris*, (Zannichelliaceae), a slender, branched water plant. It has threadlike leaves and a horned nutlet. Grows in fresh or brackish water; a common ditch weed. Commonly known as horned pondweed.

Zantedeschia (zanh tuh dehs′kee uh) *n.* A genus of 6 species of tender perennials (Araceae). *Z. aethiopica* grows 3 to 4 feet, with wide, glossy, arrow-shaped leaves on long, thick stems and tall, dramatic, milky-white flaring flowers with a yellow central spike; the calla lily. Used in moist borders and containers; the smaller species are used as houseplants. Commonly known as calla or calla lily.

Zanthoxylum (zan thahk′suh luhm) *n.* A genus of about 200 species of prickly shrubs and trees with aromatic bark (Rutaceae), some species native to North America. They grow from 20 to 60 feet, depending on the species, with alternate leaves, usually divided into leaflets, and clusters of small greenish flowers. Commonly known as prickly ash.

Zauschneria (zahsh nih′ree uh) *n.* A genus of 4 species of self-sowing, spreading, semievergreen woody perennials or subshrubs (Onagraceae) native to California. They grow to 2 feet, with small, narrow, gray leaves and many slim scarlet-red trumpet-shaped flowers that attract hummingbirds. Some varieties have white or pink flowers. Used in wild gardens, native plant gardens, on banks or

slopes, or as a small-scale ground cover. Inclined to scruffiness in maturity. Commonly known as California fuchsia and hummingbird flower.

Zea (zee′uh) *n.* A genus of 1 to 4 species of mostly annual grasses (Gramineae). *Z. mays,* sweet corn, is most familar as a widely grown vegetable. Some variegated varieties are also used as ornamentals. (See **corn**.)

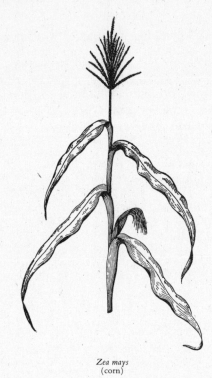

Zea mays
(corn)

zebra plant *n.* A common name for *Calathea zebrina,* a perennial native to tropical America. It grows to 3 feet, with large, yellow-veined, velvety-green oval leaves, purple beneath. Grown for its dramatically colored foliage. Used as a houseplant, greenhouse specimen, or indoor/outdoor plant.

Zebrina (zuh bree′nuh) *n.* A genus of 2 species of subtropical trailing semisucculent plants (Commelinaceae) native to Mexico and Guatemala. They have leaves striped in several colors, including red, purple, pink, white, or cream, depending on the variety. Used in hanging baskets or as a ground cover in frost-free climates, but most often grown as a houseplant for its foliage.

Zelkova (zehl koh′vuh) *n.* A genus of 5 species of large hardy deciduous trees (Ulmaceae). They grow to 60 feet or more, with smooth gray bark and alternate, wavy-toothed leaves with conspicuous veins that turn yellow or red in fall. Used as a shade tree or street tree; a good substitute for elms where Dutch elm disease is decimating elms.

Zenobia (zehn oh′bee uh) *n.* A genus of 1 species, *Z. pulverulenta* (Ericaceae), a slow-growing deciduous flowering shrub native to the southeastern United States. It grows to 6 feet, with pale green oval, pointed leaves, the new growth covered with a white powder that turns the leaves pearly gray, and clusters of bell-shaped white flowers. Used in shady, moist woodland gardens.

Zephyranthes (zehf ih ran′theez) *n.* A genus of 40 species of tender perennial bulbs (Amaryllidaceae). They grow from 1 to 2 feet, with slim, narrow, leaves growing from the base, and funnel-shaped white, yellow, deep orange, or rose-pink flowers on hollow stems. Used in rock gardens, in the foreground of perennial borders, or in pots. Commonly known as fairy lily, rain lily, zephyr flower, or zephyr lily. (See **fairy lily** and **lily, zephyr**.)

Zigadenus (zihg uh deen′uhs) *n.* A genus of 15 species of mostly North American perennial wildflowers (Liliaceae), some very hardy. They grow from bulbs or rhizomes to 3 feet, with straplike leaves and tall spikes or clusters of yellow, green, white, or purple flowers. Used in wild gardens or native-plant collections. Commonly known as death camas and zygadene. (See **death camas**.)

zinc *n.* A trace element usually present in most soils.

Zingiber (zihn′jih ber) *n.* A genus of 85 species of tropical or subtropical perennials (Zingiberaceae). They grow from aromatic rhizomes from 20 inches to 6 feet, depending on the species, with narrow, glossy bright green leaves and spikes of yellow-green flowers. The rhizome of *Z. officinale* is the source of culinary ginger. Ginger root purchased from a grocery store and planted will grow as a windowsill plant. Used in moist, shady situations in frost-free climates. Commonly known as ginger.

Zingiberaceae (zihn′jih buh ray′see uh) *n. pl.* A family of 40 genera of rhizomatous tropical flowers. The cultivated genera include *Hedychium, Kaempferia,* and *Zingiber.*

zingiberaceous (zihn′jih buh ray′shuhs) *a.* Of or pertaining to ginger, or the Zingiberaceae.

Zinnia (zihn′ee uh) *n.* A genus of 17 species of annuals, perennials, and subshrubs (Compositae) native to the Americas, mostly Mexico. They grow from 6 inches to 3 feet, depending on the species, with opposite, entire leaves and showy, colorful, single or double flowers in a wide range of colors, in fact, every color but blue. Used in beds, borders, and pots. Commonly known as zinnia and youth-and-old-age. (See **youth-and-old-age**.)

Zizia (zihz′ee uh) *n.* A genus of 4 species of hardy North American perennials (Umbelliferae) native from New Brunswick to Florida and west to Texas. They grow to 2½ feet with 3-part leaves and rounded clusters of small yellow flowers.

Ziziphus (zihz′ih fuhs) *n.* A genus of 40 species of deciduous or evergreen shrubs and trees (Rhamnaceae), some species native to the American West. They grow from 12 to 40 feet, depending on the species, with alternate, simple leaves, clusters of small green, yellow, or white flowers and fleshy fruit, sometimes edible. *Z. Jujuba* produces the datelike jujube fruit, which has a sweet applelike flavor, but the fruit ripens only in hot summer climates. Sometimes spelled Zizyphus.

zonal (zohn′uhl) *a.* 1. Relating to the form of a zone. 2. Relating to a major soil group marked by the well-developed characteristics that are determined by the action of climate and/or organism.

zone *n.* An area that differs significantly from adjoining areas.

zones of hardiness *n.* A map denoting areas of like temperatures and growing conditions with which the cultural requirements (hardiness) of various plants may be correlated. By comparing the hardiness rating listed in catalog, stock, or seed packet with the zone number of his or her locale, a gardener can determine the likelihood of a particular variety's ability to survive.

Zoysia (zoi′see uh) *n.* A genus of about 5 species of low-growing perennial grasses (Gramineae). Several are grown as lawn grasses or ground covers. The most common is *Z. tenuifolia* (Korean grass).

zucchini (zoo kee'nee) *n.* A green-skinned summer squash, *Cucurbita pepo* of the variety *Melopepo,* a fast-growing garden vegetable. It is a bush squash, with large cut leaves and bright orange blossoms, which form the squashes at their base. The still-open blossoms with or without the newly formed miniature squash are also steamed or batter-fried as a vegetable. This squash is among the eas-iest to grow and the most popular of garden vegetables. Also known as cocozelle, courgette, and vegetable marrow.

Zygopetalum (zigh goh peht'uh luhm) *n.* A genus of 20 species of epiphytic orchids (Orchidaceae) native to Central and South America. They grow from pseudobulbs to 30 inches, with long, narrow, leaves that grow from the base, and spikes of showy multicolored flowers, variously spotted or striped. Grown by collectors in warm greenhouses.

Common Name Index

The Common Name Index includes every common name referred to within the text of *The Dictionary of Horticulture*. If a common or genus name appears as a main entry in the dictionary, it is bolded in the index for the user's convenience.

Users should further note that genus names have been bolded in the index only if their main entries contain specific references to particular common names. Users can refer to genus entries throughout the dictionary to obtain general information about, and characteristics of, the plants within them.

A

Aaron's-beard: *Hypericum calycinum* (See rose-of-Sharon.)

abaca: *Musa textilis*

abele: *Populus alba*

absinthe: *Artemisia absinthium* (See **wormwood.**)

Abyssinian sword lily: *Acidanthera, Gladiolus callianthus*

acajou: *Meliaceae*

aceituno: *Simarouba glauca* (See **mountain damson.**)

achillea: *Achillea*

aconite: *Aconitum*

acorn squash: *Cucurbita Pepo* (See **squash.**)

action plant: *Mimosa pudica* (See **sensitive-plant.**)

Adam-and-Eve: *Aplectrum hyemale, Arum maculatum* (See **lords-and-ladies.**)

Adam's flannel: *Verbascum olympicum* (See **mullein.**)

Adam's-needle: *Yucca filamentosa, Y. Smalliana*

adder's fern: *Polypodium vulgare* (See **polypody.**)

adder's mouth: *Malaxis, Pogonia ophioglossoides* (See **snake mouth.**)

adder's spear: *Ophioglossum vulgatum* (See **adder's-tongue.**)

adder's-tongue: *Erythronium, Ophioglossum,* (See **serpent's tongue.**), *O. vulgatum* (See **violet, dog-tooth.**)

adder's-tongue fern: *Ophioglossum* (See **serpent's tongue.**)

adder's-tongue-leaved pogonia: *Pogonia ophioglossoides* (See **snake mouth.**)

adder's violet: *Goodyera*

adder's-wort: *Polygonum*

allgood: *Chenopodium Bonus-Henricus*
(See **spinach, wild**.)

almond, desert: *Prunus fasciculata* (See
peach, wild.)

almond, earth: *Cyperus esculentus* (See
rush nut.)

almond tree: *Prunus*

almond, wild: *Prunus fasciculata* (See
peach, wild.)

alpenclock: *Soldanella*

alpencross: *Hutchinsia alpina*

alpine azalea: *Loiseleuria procumbens*

Alpine bistort: *Polygonum viviparum*
(See **serpent grass**.)

alpine forget-me-not: *Eritrichium*

alpine laurel: *Kalmia microphylla* (See
western laurel.)

alpine rose: *Rosa pendulina* (See
mountain rose.)

Alpine violet: *Cyclamen* (See **sowbread**.)

althaea: *Hibiscus syriacus* (See
rose-of-Sharon and **shrub
althea**.)

aluminum plant: *Pilea* Cadierei

alumroot: *Geranium maculatum,
Heuchera*

amaranth: *Gomphrena globosa*

amaryllis: *Hippeastrum* (See **lily,
barbados**.)

amatungulu: *Carissa grandiflora, C.
macrocarpa* (See **natal plum**.)

Amazon lily: *Eucharis*

Amazon water-platter: *Victoria
amazonica* (See **lily, Amazon
water**.)

amber bell: *Erythronium americanum*
(See **lily, trout**.)

amboyna: *Pterocarpus indicus* (See
kiabooca.)

America spikenard: *Aralia racemosa*
(See **spikenard**.)

American aloe: *Agave*

American arborvitae: *Thuja occidentalis*
(See **arborvitae**.)

American aspen: *Populus tremula* (See
tree, trembling.)

American beech: *Fagus grandiflora* (See
beech.)

American bittersweet: *Celastrus scadens*
(See **staff vine**.)

American centaury: *Sabbatia*

American chestnut: *Castanea dentata*
(See **chestnut**.)

American cowslip: *Dodacatheon* (See
cowslip and **shooting star**.)

American cress: *Barbarea verna* (See
scurvy grass.)

American dittany: *Cunila organoides*
(See **stone mint**.)

American dogwood: *Cornus sericea* (See **osier, red**.)

American elderberry: **Sambucus** *canadensis*

American elm: *Ulmus americana* (See **elm** and **swamp elm**.)

American false hellebore: *Veratrum viride* (See **itchweed**.)

American fly honeysuckle: **Lonicera** *canadensis*

American germander: *Teucrium canadense* (See **sage, wood**.)

American ginseng: *Panax quinquefolius* (See **ginseng**.)

American hop hornbeam: *Ostrya virginiana* (See **leverwood**.)

American hornbeam: *Carpinus caroliniana* (See **water beech**.)

American ipecac: **Gillenia**

American larch: *Larix larcina* (See **hackmatack**.)

American laurel: **Kalmia** (See **laurel**.)

American linden: *Tilia Americana* (See **linden**.)

American lotus: **Nelumbo** *lutea*

American mangrove: *Rhizophora Mangle* (See **mangrove**.)

American mountain ash: **Sorbus** *americana*

American pellitory: *Parietaria Pennsylvanica* (See **pellitory**.)

American pennyroyal: **Hedeoma**

American plane: *Platanus occidentalis* (See **plane tree**.)

American red elderberry: **Sambucus** *pubens*

American spikenard: *Aralia racemosa* (See **Indian root** and **spikenard**.)

American valerian: *Cypripedium Calceolus pubescens* (See **Venus's-shoe**.)

American wall fern: **Polypodium** *virginianum*

American wayfaring tree: *Viburnum alnifolium* (See **hobblebush** and **moosewood**.)

American white hellebore: **Helleborus** *viride* (See **hellebore**.), *Veratrum viride* (See **Indian poke**.)

American wormseed: *Chenopodium ambrosioides* (See **Mexican tea**.)

amethyst flower: **Browallia**

ammobium: **Ammobium** *alatum*

anacua: *Ehretia Anacua* (See **knackaway**.)

anagua: *Ehretia elliptica*

anaphalis: **Anaphalis** *margaritacea*

anaqua: *Ehretia Anacua* (See **knackaway**.)

angelica tree: *Aralia spinosa* (See
Hercules'-club and **spikenard tree**.)
angelin: *Andira*
angelique: *Angelica, A. archangelica*
angel's-fishing-rods: ***Dierama***
angel's-tears: *Datura sanguinea,*
Narcissus triandrus, **Soleirolia**
Soleirolii
angel's trumpet: *Brugmansia, B.*
arborea, B. sanguinea, B. suaveolens,
Datura inoxia
anglepod: ***Gonolobus***, *G. gonocarpos*
Angola pea: ***Cajanus*** *cajan*
animated oat: *Avens sterilis*
anise: ***Myrrhis*** *odorata, Pimpinella An-*
isum
Anise hyssop: *Hyssopus Foeniculus* (See
Hyssop.)
anise tree: *Illicium*
annatto: *Bixa Orellana* (See **Arnotto**.)
annual beard grass: ***Polypogon*** *monspe-*
liensis
annual calliopsis: *Coreopsis tinctoria* (See
tickseed.)
annual everlasting: ***Xeranthemum*** *ann-*
uum
annual phlox: ***Phlox*** *drummondii*
antelope brush: *Purshia tridentata*
antelope bush: ***Purshia***
Apache plume: ***Fallugia*** *paradoxa*

apostle plant: *Neomarica gracilis, N.*
Northiana
Appalachian tea: *Ilex glabra* (See **win-**
terberry, common.), *Viburnumcass-*
inoides (See **withe rod**.)
apple blossom cassia: *Cassia javanica*
apple haw: *Crataegus* (See **Mayhaw**.)
apple mint: *Mentha suaveolens*
apple-of-peru: ***Nicandra*** *Physaloides*
apple tree: ***Malus***
apricot: *Prunus armeniaca*
apricot geranium: *Pelargonium scabrum*
(See **strawberry geranium**.)
aquatic banana plant: *Nymphoides aquat-*
ica (See **lily, fairy water**.)
aralia ivy: ***Fatshedera***
arar tree: *Tetraclinis articulata* (See
sandarac-tree.)
arbutus: *Arbutus*
areca palm: ***Chrysalidocarpus***
Argentine thistle: *Onopordum Acanthium*
(See **silver thistle**.)
Arizona giant: *Carnegiea gigantea* (See
tree cactus.)
Arizona plane: *Platanus wrightii* (See
plane tree.)
arnotta: *Bixa Orellana* (See **Arnotto**.)
Arnotto: *Bixa Orellana*
aroeira: *Schinus terebinthifolius*
arrow arum: ***Peltandra,*** *P. virginica,*

P. undulata (See **wake-robin, Virginian**.)

arrow bamboo: *Pseudosasa*

arrow grass: *Triglochin*

arrowhead: *Sagittaria latifolia*

arrowleaf: *Sagittaria montevidensis*

arrowroot plant: *Maranta arundinacea* (See **arrowroot**.)

arrowwood: *Viburnum* (See **mealy tree**.)

artichoke: *Cynara scolymus*

artic pyrola: *Pyrola grandiflora* (See **wintergreen, arctic**.)

artillery plant: *Pilea microphylla*

artist's acanthus: *Acanthus mollis*

arugula: *Eruca vesicaria* (See **rocket**.)

asarabacca: *Asarum canadense* (See **heart snakeroot**.), *A. europaeum* (See **hazelwort**.)

ashweed: *Aegopodium Podagraria* (See **herb Gerard**.)

Asiatic poppy: *Meconopsis betonicifolia*

Asiatic sweetleaf: *Symplochos paniculata*

asparagus: *Asparagus officinalis*

aspen: *Populus tremuloides*

asphodel: *Asphodeline lutea* (See **king's spear**.)

asp-of-Jerusalem: *Isatis tinctoria*

assai palm: *Euterpe edulis, E. oleracea*

Atamasci lily: *Zephranthes Atamasco* (See **stagger grass**.)

Australian banyan: *Ficus macrophylla* (See **Moreton Bay fig**.)

Australian bluebell creeper: *Sollya heterophylla* (See **bluebell, Australian**.)

Australian bluebells: *Sollya heterophylla*

Australian brake: *Pteris tremula*

Australian finger lime: *Microcitrus australasica* (See **orange, native**.)

Australian flame tree: *Chorizema cordatum* (See **oak, flowering**.)

Australian fuchsia: *Correa*

Australian ivy palm: *Brassaia actinophylla* (See **Schefflera**.)

Australian pepper: *Schinus Molle*

Australian pine: *Casuarina* (See **sheoak**.)

Australian tea tree: *Leptospermum laevagatum*

Australian tree fern: *Sphaeropteris Cooperi* (See **Cyathea**.)

Australian umbrella tree: *Brassaia actinophylla* (See **Schefflera**.)

Australian willow myrtle: *Agonis, A. flexuosa* (See **willow myrtle**.)

autumn crocus: *Colchicum autumnale* (See **saffron, meadow**.)

avens: *Geum, G. urbanum* (See **herb Bennet**.)

avocado: *Persea americana* (See **pear, alligator**.)

awl tree: ***Morinda*** *citrifolia* (See **mulberry, Indian**.)

awlwort: ***Subularia***

Aztec lily: ***Sprekelia*** *formosissima* (See **Saint-James's-lily**.)

B

baboon flower: *Babiana*

baboonroot: *Babiana*

baby orchid: *Odontoglossum grande*

baby pepper: *Rivina* humilis

baby pine of China: *Crassula tetragona* (See **pine tree, miniature**.)

baby's breath: *Gypsophila* elegans, **G.** paniculata

baby's tears: *Soleirolia* Soleirolii

baby sun rose: *Aptenia* cordifolia

bachelor's button: *Centaurea* Cyanus (See **bluebottle** and **knapweed**.)

bacon-and-eggs: *Pultenaea*

bald cypress: *Taxodium distichum* (See **cypress**.)

Balfour aralia: *Polyscias* balfouriana

ball cactus: *Notocactus*

ball fern: *Davallia trichomanoides* (See **squirrel's-foot fern**.)

balloon flower: *Platycodon,* P. grandiflorus

balloon vine: *Cardiospermum halicacabum*

ballroot: *Quercus ilex rotundifolia* (See **oak, ballota**.)

balm: *Melissa*

balm of Gilead: *Populus balsamifera,* P. candicans (See **necklace poplar** and **poplar, balsam**.)

balmony: *Chelone glabra* (See **snakehead**.)

balsa: *Ochroma* pyramidale

balsam: *Impatiens* (See **snapweed** and **touch-me-not**.) *Picea rubens* (See **spruce, red**.)

balsam apple: *Clusia rosea* (See **monkey apple**.), *Momordica Balsamina*

balsam pear: *Momordica Charantia* (See **bitter melon**.)

balsam poplar: *Populus balsamifera* (See **necklace poplar** and **tacamahac**.)

balsamroot: *Balsamorhiza* (See **sunflower**.)

balsam tree: *Abies balsamea, A. concolor, A. Fraseri, Populus balsamifera, P. trichocarpa*

bambara groundnut: *Voandzeia subterranea*

bamboo: *Polygonum cuspidatum* (See **Japanese knotweed** and **Mexican bamboo**.), *Sasa*

bamboo-brier: *Smilax rotundifolia*

banana: *Musa*

banana passion fruit: *Passiflora mollissima* (See **passionflower**.)

banana plant: *Nymphoides aquatica* (See **lily, fairy water**.)

banana shrub: *Michelia figo*

baneberry: *Actaea*

banner plant: *Anthurium*

banyan: *Ficus benghalensis*

barbados cherry: *Bunchosia, Eugenia uniflora* (See **Surinam cherry**.), *Malpighia glabra*

Barbados gooseberry: *Pereskia aculeata* (See **gooseberry**.)

barbados lily: *Hippeastrum puniceum*

Barbados-pride: *Adenanthera, A. pavonina* (See **sandalwood, red**.), *Caesalpinia pulcherrima* (See **flower-fence**.)

barbe-de-capuchin: *Chichorium intybus* (See **succory**.)

barberry: *Berberis vulgaris* (See **jaundice-berry**.)

barometer bush: *Leucophyllum frutescens*

barrel cactus: *Echinocactus garusonii, E. multiplex* (See **lily, pink Easter**.) *Ferocactus, F. ancanthoides, F. wislizenii*

barren oak: *Quercus marilandica* (See **oak, jack**.)

basil: *Ocimum, Ocimum basilicum*

basin sage: *Artemesia tridentata* (See **sage, black**.)

basket fern: *Nephrolepis pectinata*

basket flower: *Centaurea americana* (See **thistle, thornless**.), *Hymenocallis* (See **sea daffodil**.)

basket-of-gold: *Aurinia saxatilis* (See **golden tuft** and **madwort, rock**.)

basket willow: *Salix viminalis* (See **osier**.)

basswood: *Tilia Americana* (See **linden**.)

bastard pennyroyal: *Trichostema di-chotomum*

bastard saffron: *Carthamus tinctorius* (See **thistle, saffron.**)

bay: *Laurus* nobilis

bayberry: *Myrica* californica, *M. Faya*, *M. pensylvanica, Pimenta racemosa* (See **myrtle, candleberry.**)

bay laurel: *Laurus nobilis* (See **laurel.**), *Umbellularia californica* (See **pepper-wood.**)

bay-rum tree: *Pimenta* racemosa

bay tree: *Laurus nobilis*, *Pimenta race-mosa, Umbellularia californica* (See **mountain laurel, myrtle, Oregon** and **myrtle.**)

beach heather: *Hudsonia, H. tomentosa* (See **poverty plant.**)

beach naupaka: *Scaevola frutescens*

beach pea: *Lathyrus japonicus* (See **sea-side pea.**)

beach pine: *Pinus contorta* (See **pine, twisted.**)

beach wormwood: *Artemisia stellerana* (See **wormwood.**)

bead plant: *Nertera granadensis*

bead tree: *Melia Azedarach* (See **lilac, Indian.**)

bead vine: *Crassula rupestris* (See **neck-lace vine.**)

beam tree: *Sorbus Aria*

bean, Azuki: *Vigna*

bean, four-angled: *Psophocarpus tet-ragonolobus* (See **pea, winged.**)

bean, Goa: *Psophocarpus tetragonolobus* (See **pea, winged.**)

bean, Manila: *Psophocarpus tetragonolo-bus* (See **pea, winged.**)

bean, mung: *Vigna*

bean tree: *Castanospermum australe, La-burnum* (See **Moreton Bay chest-nut.**)

bean, winged: *Psophocarpus tetragonolo-bus* (See **pea, winged.**)

bean, yard-long: *Vigna*

bearberry: *Arctostaphylos* Manzanita, *A. Uva-ursi* (See **foxberry** and **kinni-kinnik.**)

beard fern: *Vittaria lineata* (See **shoe-string fern.**)

bear grass: *Dasylirion*, **Nolina, Xero-phyllum** *tenax* (See **sotol.**)

bear oak: *Quercus ilicifolia* (See **oak, barren** and **scrub oak.**)

bear's-breach: *Acanthus, A. montanus, A. spinosus* (See **thistle, mountain.**)

beaumont root: *Gillenia trifoliata, Veronicastrum virginicum*

beautyberry: *Callicarpa americana* (See **mulberry, French.**)

beautybush: *Kolkwitzia* amabilis

beauty-of-the-night: *Maribilis Jalapa* (See **marvel-of-Peru** and **four-o'clock**.)

beaver poison: *Cicuta maculata* (See **mushquash root**.)

beaverwood: *Celtis occidentalis* (See **hackberry**.)

bedstraw: *Galium* (See **loveman**.)

bee balm: *Melissa officinalis* (See **sweet balm**.) *Monarda,* *Monarda didyma* (See **mountain mint**.)

bee orchid: *Cleome* (See **beeflower**.)

bee orchis: *Cleome lutea, C. serrulata* (See **gnatflower**.)

bee tree: *Tilia Americana* (See **linden**.)

beech: *Fagus*

beechdrops: *Epifagus Virginiana*

beech fern: *Phegopteris* connectilis, *Thelypteris phegopteris*

beeflower: *Cleome lutea, C. serrulata*

beefsteak geranium: *Saxifraga stolonifera* (See **strawberry geranium**.)

beefsteak plant: *Acalypha Wilkesiana* (See **copperleaf**.), *Perilla*

beefwood: *Casuarina* (See **he-oak, pine, Australian** and **she-oak**.)

beetleweed: *Galax* (See **wandflower**.)

beggar's-lice: *Bidens, Hackelia Jessicae* (See **stickseed**.)

beggar's-ticks: *Bidens* (See **beggar's-lice** and **stick-tight**.)

belladonna: *Atropa belladonna* (See **nightshade**.)

belladonna lily: *Amaryllis* hallii

Belle Isle cress: *Barbarea verna* (See **scurvy grass**.)

bell heather: *Erica cinerea* (See **Scotch heath**.)

bellflower: *Campanula*

bell-flowered squill: *Endymion hispanicus* (See **Spanish bluebell**.)

bellote: *Quercus ilex rotudnifolia* (See **oak, ballota**.)

bells-of-Ireland: *Molucella laevis* (See **Molucca balm** and **shellflower**.)

bellwort: *Uvularia* (See **merrybells**.)

Belmore sentry palm: *Howea*

belvedere: *Kochia* scoparia (See **Mexican fireweed** and **summer cypress**.)

bene: *Sesamum Indicum* (See **benne**.)

Benjamin bush: *Lindera* Benzoin (See **spicebush**.)

benne: *Sesamum Indicum* (See **sesame**.)

benni: *Sesamum Indicum* (See **benne**.)

bergamot: *Monarda didyma* (See **bee balm**.)

Bermuda palm: *Sabal* bermudana

be-still tree: *Thevetia peruviana* (See **yellow oleander**.)

betel palm: *Areca catechu*

betony: *Stachys,* *S. grandiflora*, *S. officinalis*

bhang: *Cannabis sativa* (See **hashish** and **marijauna**.)

bible leaf: *Chrysanthemum Balsamita* (See **costmary**.)

big cone spruce: *Pseudotsuga macrocarpa*

big sagebrush: *Artemesia tridentata* (See **sage, black**.)

bigtooth maple: *Acer saccharum grandidentatum* (See **maple, sugar**.)

big tree: *Sequoiadendron giganteum* (See **redwood, giant**.)

bilberry: *Vaccinium* (See **blueberry**.), *V. myrtillus* (See **whinberry**.)

bilimbi: *Averrhoa Bilimbi*

bilsted: *Liquidambar Styraciflua* (See **sweet gum**.)

bindweed: *Calystegia sepium* (See **hedge bindweed** and **morning glory, wild**.), *Convolvulus* (See **hellebore**.), *C. arvensis* (See **morning glory, wild**.)

birch, black: *Betula nigra* (See **birch, river**.)

birch, red: *Betula nigra* (See **birch, river**.)

birch, river: *Betula nigra*

bird cherry: *Celtis australis* (See **hackberry**.), *Prunus Padus* (See **hagberry**.), *P. pensylvanica* (See **pin cherry**.)

bird-foot violet: *Viola pedata* (See **horse violet**.)

bird of paradise: **Heliconia**, **Strelitzia** *reginae* (See **lily, crane**.)

bird-on-the-wing: *Polygala pauciflora* (See **wintergreen, flowering**.)

bird-plant: *Heterotoma lobelioides*

birdseed grass: **Phalaris** *canariensis*

bird's-eye: *Adonis annua, Primula farinosa, Veronica Chamaedrys*

bird's-foot trefoil: *Lotus corniculatus* (See **shoes and stockings**.)

bird's-nest: *Asplenium nidus, Daucus Carota, Neottia Nidusavis*

bird's-nest fern: *Asplenium nidus* (See **spleenwort**.)

birthroot: *Trillium* (See **Indian balm**.)

birthwort: *Aristolochia A. californica* (See **pipe vine**.)

bishop's cap: *Astrophytum myriostigma*, *Mitella*

bishop's-weed: *Aegopodium Podagraria* (See **goatweed, goutweed** and **herb Gerard**.)

bistort: *Polygonum Bistorta* (See **snakeweed**.)

bitterbloom: *Sabbatia*, *S. angularis*

bitter cassava: *Manihot esculent*

bitter cress: *Cardamine pratensis* (See **lady's-smock** and **meadow cress**.)

bitter gallberry: *Ilex glabra* (See **winterberry, common**.)

bitter gourd: *Momordica charantia* (See **bitter melon**.)

bitter-herb: *Chelone glabra*, *Erythroea centaurium*

bitter melon: *Momordica charantia*

bitternut: *Carya cordiformis* (See **pignut** and **swamp hickory**.)

bitter pepper: *Evodia Danielii* (See **star pepper**.)

bittersweet: *Celastrus* (See **fevertwig**.), *Celastrus scandens*, *Solanum Dulcamara* (See **nightshade**.)

bitterwood: *Quassia amara*, *Simarouba glauca* (See **mountain damson**.)

black acacia: *Acacia melanoxylon* (See **lightwood**.)

black alder: *Alnus glutinosa* (See **alder**.), *Ilex verticillata* (See **winterberry, common**.)

black bamboo: *Phyllostachys nigra*

black bean: *Castanospermum australe* (See **Moreton Bay chestnut**.)

black birch: *Betula lenta* (See **mahogany birch, mountain mahogany** and **sweet birch**.)

black calla: *Arum palaestinum* (See **lily, Solomon's**.)

black cherry: *Prunus serotina* **(See rum cherry**.)

black cohosh: *Cimicifuga racemosa* (See **rattlesnake root** and **snakeroot, black**.)

black cottonwood: *Populus heterophylla* (See **swamp cottonwood**.)

black crowberry: *Empetrum nigrum* (See **crowberry**.)

black cumin: *Nigella sativa*

blackening plant: *Hibiscus rosa-sinensis*

black-eyed Susan: *Rudbeckia hirta* (See **oxeye**.)

black-eyed susan vine: *Thunbergia alata* (See **clock vine**.)

black gum: *Nyssa sylvatica* (See **pepperidge**.)

black haw: *Bumelia*, *Viburnum Lentago* (See **nannyberry**.), *V. prunifolium* (See **sheepberry, stagbush**, and **tea plant**.)

black hellebore: *Helleborus niger* (See **hellebore**.)

black henbane: *Hyoscyamus niger* (See **henbane**.)

blacking plant: *Hibiscus Rosa-sinensis* (See **shoeblock plant**.)

blackjack: *Quercus marilandica* (See **oak, barren**.)

blackjack oak: *Quercus marilandica* (See **oak, barren**.)

black knapweed: *Centaurea nigra* (See **horse knob**.)

black larch: *Larix larcina* (See **hack-matack** and **larch, American**.)

black laurel: *Gordonia Lasianthus* (See **loblolly bay**.)

black locust: *Robinia Pseudoacacia* (See **locust**.)

black mountain ash: *Eucalyptus Sieberi* (See **mountain ash**.)

black mustard: *Brassica nigra* (See **mustard**.)

black nightshade: *Solanum nigrum* (See **nightshade** and **poisonberry**.)

black oak: *Quercus velutina* (See **quercitron**.)

black olive tree: ***Bucida***

black oyster plant: ***Scorzonera*** *hispanica*

black persimmon: *Diospyros texana* (See **Mexican persimmon** and **persimmon**.)

black salsify: ***Scorzonera*** *hispanica* (See **salsify**.)

black snakeroot: ***Cimicifuga*** *racemosa* (See **rattlesnake root**.)

black swallowwort: **Cynanchum**

blackthorn: *Crataegus calpodendron* (See **thorn, pear**.), *C. tomentosa* (See **pear haw**.), *Prunus spinosa*

black titi: *Cyrilla racemiflora* (See **leatherwood**.)

black truffle: *Tuber melanosporum* (See **truffle**.)

blackwood: *Acacia melanoxylon* (See **lightwood**.)

bladder campion: *Silene vulgaris* (See **rattlebox** and **rattleweed**.)

bladder fern: *Cystopteris*

bladdernut: ***Staphylea***, *S. trifolia*

bladderpod: *Alyssoides*

bladder senna: ***Colutea***

bladder snout: *Utricularia vulgaris*

bladderwort: ***Utricularia***

blanketflower: ***Gaillardia***

blanket leaf: *Verbascum olympicum* (See **mullein**.)

blanket plant: *Verbascum olympicum* (See **mullein**.)

Blaxland's stringybark: *Eucalyptus Blaxlandii* (See **stringybark**.)

blazing star: ***Chamaelirium*** *luteum*, ***Liatris***, *L. spicata* (See **gayfeather**

and **snakeroot, button**.), *Mentzelia laevicaulis*

bleeding heart: ***Clerodendrum****, Dicentra* (See **love-lies-bleeding**.)

blessed thistle: *Cnicus benedictus, Silybum Marianum* (See **milk thistle**.)

blister cress: *Cheiranthus, Erysimum*

blood berry: ***Rivina*** *humilis* (See **rougeberry**.)

bloodflower: *Asclepias curassavica*

bloodleaf: *Iresine*

blood lily: ***Haemanthus*** (See **tulip, African**.)

blood-red trumpet vine: *Distictis buccinatoria* (See **trumpet vine**.)

bloodroot: ***Sanguinaria*** *canadensis* (See **puccoon** and **tetterwort**.)

blood trumpet: *Distictis buccinatoria* (See **trumpet vine, blood-red**.)

bloodwort: ***Haemodoraceae***

bloody bark: *Lonchocarpus* (See **lance-pod**.)

blooming-sally: *Epilobium angustifolium*

blowballs: ***Taraxacum*** (See **lion's-tooth**.), *T. officinalis*

blubell creeper: *Sollya heterophylla* (See **bluebell, Australian**.)

blue agapanthus: *Agapanthus africanus* (See **lily, African**.)

blue barberry: *Mahonia Aquifolium* (See **Oregon grape**.)

blue bead lily: *Clintonia borealis* (See **lily, corn**.)

bluebeard: *Caryopteris*

blue beech: *Carpinus caroliniana* (See **water beech**.)

bluebell: *Endymion non-scriptus*

bluebell, Australian: *Sollya heterophylla*

bluebell, California: *Phacelia campanularia*

bluebell, Clanwilliam: *Ixia incarnata*

bluebell creeper: ***Sollya*** *heterophylla*

bluebell, English: *Endymion non-scriptus*

bluebells: *Mertensia virginica* (See **Virginia bluebells**.)

bluebell, Spanish: *Endymion hispanicus*

blueberry: ***Vaccinium***

blue bird vine: ***Petrea***

blueblossom: *Ceanothus thyrsiflorus*

bluebonnet: *Lupinus subcarnosus*

bluebottle: *Centaurea Cyanus*

bluebush: *Eucalyptus macrocarpa*

blue cohosh: ***Caulophyllum*** *thalictroides* (See **cohosh** and **papoose root**.)

blue creeper: *Bredemeyera volubilis*
blue-curls: *Phacelia congesta, Trichostema*
blue daisy: *Felicia ameloides* (See **marguerite, blue**.)
blue-dicks: *Dichelostemma pulchellum*
blue elder: *Sambucus caerulea*
blue-eyed grass: *Sisyrinchium, S. californicum, S. bellum*
blue-eyed Mary: *Omphalodes verna, Tradescantia virginiana*
blue false indigo: *Baptisia australis* (See **indigo**.)
blue fescue: *Festuca ovina glauca*
blue flag: *Iris versicolor*
blue ginger: *Dichorisandra thyrsiflora*
bluegrass: *Poa*
blue gum: *Eucalyptus Globulus* (See **gum**.)
blue-gum tree: *Eucalyptus globulus*
blueheart: *Buchnera*
blue hibiscus: *Alogyne* (See **Malvaceae**.)
blue huckleberry: *Gaylussacia frondosa* (See **huckleberry**.)
bluejack: *Quercus cinerea, Q. incana* (See **oak, bluejack**.)
bluejack oak: *Quercus incana* (See **sand jack**.)

blue-leaved stringybark: *Eucalyptus aggloerata* (See **stringybark**.)
blue lotus: *Nymphaea caerulea* (See **lily, Egyptian water**.)
blue lungwort: *Pulmonaria officinalis* (See **sage, Jerusalem**.)
blue mahoe: *Hibiscus elatus* (See **mahoe**.)
blue marguerite: *Felicia*
blue oxalis: *Parochetus communis* (See **shamrock pea**.)
blue palm: *Brahea armata, Sabal minor*
blue palmetto: *Rhapodophyllum hystrix*
blue passionflower: *Passiflora caerulea* (See **passionflower**.)
blue phlox: *Phlox divaricata* (See **Sweet William, wild**.)
blue pine: *Pinus wallichiana* (See **pine, Bhutan**.)
blue poppy: *Meconopsis betonicifolia*
blue potato bush: *Solanum Rantonnetii* (See **Solanum**.)
blue-sailors: *Chichorium intybus* (See **succory**.)
bluestar: *Amsonia*
bluet: *Centaurea cyanus*
bluetangle: *Gaylussacia frondosa* (See **huckleberry**.)

blue thimbleflower: *Gilia capitata* (See **thimbleflower**.)

blue trumpet vine: *Thunbergia grandiflora* (See **sky flower**.)

bluets: ***Hedyotis*** *caerulea* (See **Quakerladies**.)

blueweed: ***Echium*** *vulgare* (See **viper's bugloss**.)

blue wild ryegrass: ***Elymus***

blue wings: ***Torenia*** *fournieri*

blushwort: *Aeschynanthus*

boat lily: *Rhoeo spathacea* (See **oyster plant**.)

bog asphodel: ***Narthecium***

bogbean: ***Menyanthes*** *trifoliata* (See **trefoil, marsh**.)

bogberry: *Vaccinium Oxycoccus*

bog kalmia: *Kalmia polifolia* (See **swamp laurel**.)

bog laurel: *Kalmia polifolia* (See **swamp laurel**.)

bog myrtle: *Myrica Gale* (See **sweet gale**.)

bog rhubarb: ***Petasites*** *hybridus*

bog rose: ***Arethusa*** *bulbosa* (See **swamp pink**.)

bog rosemary: ***Andromeda*** (See **moorwort**.)

bog rush: *Juncus*

bog spruce: *Picea mariana*

bog stars: ***Parnassia***

bog twayblade: *Liparis Loeselii* (See **orchid, fen**.)

Bok choy: *Brassica Rapa*

Bokhara fleece-vine: ***Polygonum*** *baldschuanicum*

bolbonac: *Lunaria annua* (See **pennyflower**.)

boneset: *Eupatorium* (See **hemp agrimony** and **thoroughwort**.)

bonnet bellflower: ***Codonopsis***

Boston fern: *Nephrolepis exaltata* (See **sword fern**.)

Boston ivy: *Parthenocissus quinquefolia, P. tricuspidata*

botanical-wonder: ***Fatshedera***

bo tree: ***Ficus*** *religiosa*

bottlebrush: ***Melaleuca***, ***Metrosideros***

bottle-brush: ***Callistemon***

bottlebrush grass: ***Hystrix*** *patula*

bottle gentian: *Gentiana Andrewsii*

bottle palm: ***Beaucarnea***

Bowles' golden grass: ***Milium*** *effusum*

bowman's root: ***Gillenia***, G. *trifoliata* (See **Indian root**.), *Veronicastrum virginicum*

bowwood: ***Maclura*** *pomifera*

box elder: *Acer Negundo* (See **elder** and **maple, ash-leaved**.)

box holly: *Ruscus aculeatus* (See **Jew's myrtle**.)

box huckleberry: *Gaylussacia brachycera*

box sand myrtle: **Leiophyllum** *buxifolium* (See **myrtle, sand**.)

box thorn: *Lycium* (See **matrimony vine**.), *L. europaeum*

boy's-love: *Artemisia Abrotanum* (See **southernwood**.)

bracken: *Pteridium aquilinum*

brake: *Pteridium aquilinum*

brakes: *Pteris*

Brazil cherry: *Eugenia uniflora* (See **Surinam cherry**.)

Brazilian flame bush: *Calliandra*

Brazilian pepper: *Schinus terebinthifolius* (See **aroeira** and **pepper tree**.)

Brazilian pepper tree: *Schinus* *terebinthifolius*

Brazilian plume flower: *Jacobinia carnea, Justicia carnea* (See **plume flower**.)

Brazilian sky flower: *Duranta repens* (See **sky flower**.)

breadfruit tree: *Artocarpus altilis* (See **breadfruit**.)

breadfruit vine: *Monstera deliciosa* (See **Mexican bamboo** and **window plant**.)

bread palm: *Cycas*

breadroot: *Psoralea esculenta* (See **pomme blanche**.)

breath-of-heaven: *Diosma*

bridal bouquet: **Porana** *paniculata*

bridal veil: **Tripogandra** *multiflora*

bridal veil broom: **Retama** *monosperma*

bridal wreath: *Francoa ramosa,* **Spirea**, *S. prunifolia*

brier, Austrian: *Rosa foetida*

brisbane box: *Tristania conferta*

bristly locust: *Robinia hispida* (See **moss locust** and **rose acacia**.)

brittlebush, white: *Encelia farinosa*

brittle fern: *Cystopteris fragilis*

broad bean: *Vicia Faba* (See **horse-bean** and **tick bean**.)

broad beech fern: **Phegopteris** *hexagonoptera*

brooklime: *Veronica* (See **speedwell**.)

brookweed: *Samolus*

broom: *Genista*

broomcorn: *Sorghum bicolor* (See **hirse**.)

broom crowberry: *Corema*

broom hickory: *Carya glabra* (See **hognut** and **pignut**.)

broom, Spanish: *Spartium junceum*

broomweed: *Gutierrezia*, *G. Sarothrae* (See **snakeweed**.)

brown Beth: *Trillium erectum* (See **squawroot**.)

brown-eyed-Susan: *Gaillardia aristata, Rudbeckia hirta*

brown stringybark: *Eucalyptus capitellata* (See **stringybark**.)

Brussels sprout: *Brassica oleracea*

buchu: *Diosma*

buckbean: *Menyanthes trifoliata* (See **marsh trefoil**.)

buckeye: *Aesculus* (See **horse chestnut**.), *A. Hippocastanum*

buckeye, false: *Ungnadia speciosa*

buckeye, Mexican: *Ungnadia speciosa*

buckeye, Spanish: *Ungnadia speciosa*

buckeye, Texan: *Ungnadia speciosa*

buckhorn: *Plantago lanceolata* (See **star-of-the-earth**.)

buckhorn plantain: *Plantago lanceolata*

buckler fern: *Nephrolepsis exaltata*

buckthorn: *Rhamnus cathartica* (See **hart's-thorn**.)

buckwheat tree: *Cliftonia monophylla*

Buddhist pine: *Podocarpus macrophyllus*

buffalo berry: *Shepherdia canadensis* (See **soapberry**.)

bugbanes: *Cimicifuga* (See **rattleweed**.)

bugleweed: *Ajuga, A. reptans, Lycopus americanus, L. europaeus*

bugloss: *Anchusa officinalis*

Bukhara clover: *Melilotus alba* (See **tree clover**.)

bullace: *Vitis rotundifolia* (See **southern fox grape**.)

bullbrier: *Smilax rotundifolia* (See **bamboo-brier** and **horse brier**.)

bullock's-heart: *Annona reticulata*

bull thistle: *Cirsium vulgare* (See **thistle, spear**.)

bulrush: *Scirpus, Typha, T. latifolia*

bunchberry: *Cornus canadensis*

bunchflower: *Melanthium virginicum*

bunny ears: *Opuntia microdasys* (See **rabbit-ears**.)

bur cucumber: *Sicyos angulatus* (See **Sicyos**.)

burdock: *Arctium, A. Lappa* (See **hurr-bur**.)

burhead: *Echinodorus*

bur-marigold: *Bidens* (See **stick-tight**.)

Burmese plumbago: *Ceratostigma*

Burmese rosewood: *Pterocarpus indicus*

burnet: *Poterium, Sanguisorba*

burnet saxifrage: *Pimpinella saxifraga*

burning bush: *Dictamnus albus* (See **Fraxinella**.), *Euonymus atropurpurea* (See **Indian arrow**.), *Kochia trichophylla*

bur reed: *Sparganium*

bur sage: *Ambrosia* (See **ragweed**.)

bursting heart: *Euonymus Americana* (See **strawberry bush**.)

bush anemone: ***Carpenteria*** *californica*

bush clover: ***Lespedeza***

bush, cranberry: *Viburnum Opulus Roseum* (See **marsh elder**.)

bush honeysuckle: ***Diervilla, D. Lonicera***

bush moonflower: *Ipomoea leptophylla* (See **manroot**.)

bush morning glory: *Ipomoea leptophylla* (See **manroot**.)

bush palmetto: *Sabal minor* (See **scrub palmetto**.)

bush poppy: *Dendromecon, D. rigida* (See **tree poppy**.)

bush senecio: ***Senecio*** *Douglasii*

bush violet: ***Browallia***

bustic: *Dipholis salicifolia*

busy Lizzy: ***Impatiens***

butcher's broom: ***Ruscus*** *aculeatus* (See **Jew's myrtle**.)

butter-and-eggs: *Linaria vulgaris*

butterbur: ***Petasites*** *hybridus*

buttercup: ***Ranunculus***, *R. acris, R. bulbosus* (See **goldcup**.), *R. repens* (See **kingcup**.)

buttercup, creeping: ***Ranunculus*** *repens*

buttercup squash: *Cucurbita maxima* (See **squash**.)

buttercup winter hazel: *Corylopsis pauciflora* (See **winter hazel**.)

butterfly bush: ***Buddleia***

butterfly flower: *Asclepias* (See **silkweed**.), ***Schizanthus***

butterfly ginger: *Hedychium coronarium* (See **lily, butterfly**.)

butterfly iris: *Dietes* (See **lily, Natal**.), ***Moraea***

butterfly lily: ***Calochortus***

butterfly orchid: *Epidendrum tampense*

butterfly pea: *Clitoria* (See **pigeonwings**.)

butterfly tree: *Bauhinia purpurea* (See **orchid tree**.)

butterfly tulip: *Calochortus* (See **lily, mariposa** and **star tulip**.)

butterfly weed: ***Asclepias*** (See **milkweed**.), *A. tuberosa* (See **pleurisy root**.)

butternut: *Juglans cinerea* (See **lemon walnut**.)

butternut squash: *Cucurbita moschata* (See **squash**.)

butter-plant: *Abutilon Theophrasti* (See **velvetleaf**.)

butterwort: ***Penguicula***

buttonbush: ***Cephalanthus*** *occidentalis* (See **pond dogwood**.)

button fern: ***Pellaea*** *rotundifolia*

buttonhole orchid: ***Epidendrum*** (See **tree orchid**.)

button snakeroot: *Eryngium yuccaefolium,* ***Liatris*** (See **rattlesnake master**.), *L. spicata* (See **gayfeather**.)

buttons-on-a-string: *Crassula rupestris*

buttonwood: *Plantanus* (See **sycamore**.), *P. occidentalis* (See **plane tree**.)

C

cabbage palm: *Euterpe edulis, E. oleracea, Sabal palmetto* (See **thatch palm**.)

cabbage rose: *Rosa centifolia* (See **moss rose** and **Provence rose**.)

cabbage tree: *Cordyline australis* (See **lily, palm**.)

cacao: *Theobroma cacao*

cactus, crown: *Rebutia*

cactus, Easter: *Rhipsalidopsis gaertneri*

cactus, mistletoe: *Rhipsalis*

cajan: *Cajanus, C. cajan* (See **pea, Angola**.)

cajeput: *Melaleuca Leucadendron, M. quinquenervia* (See **tea tree, swamp**.), *Umbellaria californica*

cajeput tree: *Melaleuca quinquenervia* (See **weeping tea tree**.)

calabar: *Muntingia Calabura*

calabash: *Crescentia Cujete, Lagenaria vulgaris*

calabash tree: *Crescentia Cujete*

calamint: *Calaminthia* (See **mountain mint**.)

calamondin: *Citrofortunella mitis*

calamus: *Acorus Calamus* (See **myrtle, flag** and **sweet flag**.)

calico bush: *Kalmia latifolia* (See **mountain laurel** and **spoonwood**.)

calico flower: *Aristolochia elegans, Kalmia latifolia*

California bay: *Umbellularia californica* (See **mountain laurel, myrtle, Oregon, pepperwood**, and **spice tree**.)

California bayberry: *Myrica Californica* (See **bayberry** and **myrtle, California wax**.)

California black oak: *Quercus Kelloggii* (See **Sonoma oak**.)

California bluebell: *Phacelia* campanularia, and *P. minor*
California coffee tree: *Rhamnus californica* (See **coffee tree**.)
California fern: *Conium maculatum*
California fuchsia: *Zauschneria*
California holly: *Heteromeles arbutifolia* (See **Christmas berry**.)
California laurel: *Umbellularia californica* (See **mountain laurel, myrtle, Oregon**, and **pepperwood**.)
California lilac: *Ceanothus thyrsiflorus*
California live oak: *Quercus agrifolia* (See **live-oak**.)
California nutmeg: *Torryea californica*
California olive: *Umbellularia californica* (See **mountain laurel** and **myrtle, Oregon**.)
California pepper tree: *Schinus Molle* (See **pepper tree**.)
California pitcher plant: *Darlingtonia californica* (See **pitcher plant**.)
California plane tree: *Platanus racemosa* (See **plane tree**.)
California poppy: *Eschscholzia californica*
California rape: *Brassica Kabe* (See **mustard, wild**.)
California tree poppy: *Romneya coulteri* (See **tree poppy**.)

California wax myrtle: *Myrica californica* (See **bayberry**.)
calla: *Zantedeschia aethiopica*
calla lily: *Zantedeschia aethiopica*
caltrop: *Tribulus*
calypso: *Calypso*
camas: *Camassia Leichtlinii, C. Quamash*
camomile: *Anthemis*
campion: *Lychnis*
Canada moonseed: *Acer circinatum* (See **vine maple**.)
Canada plum: *Prunus Americana* (See **plum, wild**.) (See **mountain holly**.)
Canadian holly: *Nemopanthus mucronatus* (See **mountain holly**.)
canaigre: *Rumex hymenosepalus*
canary: *Phalaris canariensis*
canary bird bush: *Crotalaria agatiflora*
Canary Island date palm: *Phoenix canariensis*
candleberry: *Myrica cerifera* (See **myrtle, candleberry**, and **myrtle, wax**.), *M. pensylvanica* (See **bayberry**.)
candleberry myrtle: *Myrica cerifera* (See **myrtle, wax**.)
candleberry tree: *Aleurites moluccana* (See **tallow tree**.)

candlenut tree: *Aleurites moluccana* (See **tallow tree**.)

candle plant: *Plectranthus articulatus, P. Oertendahlii,* **Senecio** *articulatus*

candle tree: **Parmentiera** *cereifera*

candlewick mullen feltwort: *Verbascum olympicum* (See **mullein**.)

candlewood: *Fouquiera*

candytuft: *Iberis*

cane apples: *Arbutus Unedo* (See **strawberry tree**.)

cannonball tree: **Couropita** *guianensis*

canterbury bell: *Campanula Medium*

canyon live oak: *Quercus chrysolepis* (See **live-oak**.)

Cape belladonna: *Amaryllis belladonna* (See **lily, Belladonna**.)

cape chestnut: *Calodendron capense* (See **chestnut**.)

Cape cowslip: *Lachenalia*

Cape fuchsia: **Phygelius** *aequalis, P. capensis*

Cape gooseberry: **Physalis** *peruviana* (See **gooseberry**.)

Cape honeysuckle: **Tecomaria** *capensis*

Cape jasmine: **Gardenia** *jasminoides*

Cape marigold: **Dimorphotheca**

Cape myrtle: **Myrsine** *africana*

Cape plumbago: **Plumbago** *auriculata, P. Capensis* (See **leadwort, Cape**.)

Cape pondweed: **Aponogeton** *distachyus*

Cape primrose: **Streptocarpus**

caper spurge: *Euphorbia Lathyris* (See **mole plant**.)

cape weed: **Arctotheca** *calendula*

caprifig: *Ficus arica sylvestris*

caracol: *Vigna Caracalla* (See **snailflower**.)

carambola: **Averrhoa** *Carambola*

caraway: *Carum Carvi*

cardamom: *Eletaria cardomomum*

cardinal climber: *Ipomea Quamoclit* (See **starglory**.), **Lobelia** *Cardinalis* (See **pink, Indian**.)

cardinal's guard: **Pachystachys** *coccinea*

cardoon: *Cyanara cardunculus*

caricature plant: *Graptophyllum pictum*

carnation: *Dianthus caryophyllus* (See **gillyflower**.)

carnauba palm: **Copernicia** *prunifera*

carob: *Ceratonia siliqua* (See **locust** and **Saint-John's-bread**.)

carob tree: **Ceratonia** *siliqua* (See **honey bread**.)

Carolina allspice: *Calycanthus floridus* (See **strawberry shrub**.)

Carolina ash: *Fraxinus caroliniana* (See **water ash**.)

Carolina hemlock: *Tsuga Caroliniana*
(See **hemlock spruce**.)

Carolina ipecac: *Euphorbia ipecacuanhae*
(See **spurge, ipecac**.)

Carolina jessamine: *Gelsemium sempervirens* (See **jasmine, Carolina**.)

Carolina moonseed: ***Cocculus*** *carolinus*
(See **snail-seed**.)

Carolina rhododendron: ***Rhododendron***
carolinianum

carosella: *Foeniculum vulgare*

carpet bugle: ***Ajuga***

carpet grass: ***Axonopus***

carpet pink: *Silene acaulis* (See **moss
campion**.)

carrion flower: *Smilax herbacea,*
Stapelia

carrot: *Daucus, D. carota*

cart-track plant: ***Plantago*** *major*

cashew: *Anacardium occidentale*

cashew nut: *Anaardium occidentale*

cashew tree: *Anacardium* (See
acajou.)

cashmere bouquet: *Clerodendrum*
(See **tubeflower**.)

cassabanana: *Sicana odorifera* (See
Sicana.)

cassandra: ***Chamaedaphne*** *calyculata*
(See **leatherleaf**.)

cassava: ***Manihot***, *M. esculent*

cassie: *Acacia Farnesiana* (See **sponge
tree**.)

cassina: *Ilex Cassine* (See **dahoon**.)

cassine: *Ilex Cassine* (See **dahoon**.)

cast-iron plant: ***Aspidistra***, *A. eliator*

castor bean: *Ricinus communis*

castor oil plant: ***Ricinus***, *R. communis*
(See **castor oil**.)

castor oil tree: ***Ricinus***

Catalonian jasmine: *Jasminum grandiflorum* (See **Spanish jasmine**.)

catawba: *Catalpa* (See **Indian bean**.)

Catawba rhododendron: ***Rhododendron***
catawbiense

catawba rose: *Rhododendron catawbiense*
(See **mountain rose**.)

catberry: ***Nemopanthus*** *mucronatus* (See
mountain holly.)

catbrier: ***Smilax***

catchfly: ***Lychnis***, *L. Viscaria, Silene*

catch-me-if-you-can: *Acalypha Wilkesiana* (See **copperleaf**.)

catclaw: *Acacia*

Catesby lily: *Lilium Catesbaei* (See
southern red lily.)

catgut: *Tephrosia* (See **pea, hoary**.)

catjang: *Cajanus cajan* (See **pea, Angola**.)

catmint: ***Nepeta***

catnip: ***Nepeta*** *Cataria*

cat's-claw: **Macfadyena**

cat's-claw creeper: **Macfadyena**

cat's-claw trumpet: **Macfadyena**

cat's-foot: *Antennaria plantaginifolia* (See **mouse-ear**.)

cat spruce: *Picea glauca*

cat's tail: *Typha, T. latifolia*

cattail: **Typha**, *T. latifolia*

cattail flag: **Typha** (See **flag**.)

cauliflower: *Brassica oleracea*

Cayenne cherry: *Eugenia uniflora* (See **Surinam cherry**.)

ceci: *Cicer arietinum* (See **chick-pea**.)

cedar: *Cedrus*

cedar, canoe: *Thuja plicata* (See **cedar, red**.)

cedar, giant: *Thuja plicata* (See **cedar, red**.)

cedar, incense: *Calocedrus decurrens* (See **cedar, red**.)

cedar-of-Goa: *Cupressus lusitanica* **(See Mexican cypress**.)

cedar-of-Lebanon: *Cedrus libani*

cedar, red: *Juniperus virginiana*

cedar, salt: **Tamarix** (See **tamarisk**.)

cedar, western red: *Thuja plicata* (See **cedar, red**.)

cedar, white: *Chamaecyparis thyoides*

celadine poppy: **Stylophorum** *diphyllum*

celery: **Apium** *dulce, A. graveolens*

celery pines: **Phyllocladus** *trichomanoides*

celestial lily: **Nemastylis**

ceniza: **Leucophyllum** *frutescens*

centaury: **Centaurium**, *Serratula tinctoria* (See **sawwort**.)

Centifolia rose: *Rosa centifolia* (See **Provence rose**.)

centipede plant: **Homalocladium**, *H. platycladium* (See **ribbon bush**.)

century plant: **Agave**, *A. Americana*

cepe: **Boletus** *edulis*

ceriman: *Monstera deliciosa* (See **window plant**.)

Ceylon merrimia: **Merremia** *tuberosa*

Ceylon morning glory: *Merremia tuberosa* (See **woodbine, Spanish**.)

Ceylon oak: **Schleichera** *oleosa*

chaffseed: **Shwalbea** *americana*

chain fern: *Woodwardia*

chain-of-love vine: **Antigonon** *leptopus* (See **mountain rose**.)

chain orchid: **Dendrochilum**

chalice vine: *Solandra, S. guttata, S. maxima*

chamiso: *Artemesia ludovicinia* (See **sage, white**.)

chamomile: *Anthemis tinctoria* (See **marguerite, golden**.), **Chamaemelum**, **Matricaria** *recutita*

champignon: **Agaricus** *campestris*

chanterelle: *Cantharellus cibarius*

chaparral mallow: *Malacothamnus*

chard: *Beta Vulgaris Cicla*

chardoon: *Cyanara cardunculus* (See **cardoon**.)

charlock: *Brassica Kabe* (See **mustard, wild**.)

chaste tree: *Vitex agnus-castus* (See **hemp tree**, **pepper, wild**, and **sage tree**.)

chaulmoogra: *Hydnocarpus Kurzii* (See **chaulmoogra**.)

chayote: *Sechium edule*

checkerberry: *Gaultheria procumbens* (See **spiceberry** and **teaberry**.)

checkerbloom: *Sidalcea malvaflora*

checkered lily: *Fritillaria Meleagris* (See **guinea-hen** and **snake's-head**.)

checker mallow: *Sidalcea* (See **Sidalcea**.)

cheeses: *Malva sylvestris* (See **mallow, high**.)

chenar tree: *Platanus orientalis* (See **chinar tree**.)

chenille plant: *Acalypha hispida*, *Echeveria leucotrichia*, *E. pulvinata*

cherimoya: *Annona cherimola* (See **cherimoyar**.)

cherry: *Prunus avium*, *P. cerasus*

cherry birch: *Betula lenta* (See **mahogany birch**, **mountain mahogany**, and **sweet birch**.)

cherry laurel: *Prunus caroliniana* (See **orange, wild**.), *P. Laurocerasus* (See **laurel, cherry**.)

cherry tomato: *Lycopersicon cerasiforme* (See **tomato**.)

cherry, wild: *Prunus pensylvanica*

chestnut: *Castanea sativa*

chestnut oak: *Quercus Muehlenbergii*, *Q. prinus* (See **oak, basket**.)

chiccory: *Cichorium Intybus* (See **chicory**.)

Chickasaw plum: *Spondias Mombin* (See **hog plum**.)

chicken-claws: *Salicornia europaea* (See **samphire**.)

chickory: *Cichorium Intybus* (See **chicory**.)

chick-pea: *Cicer*, *C. arietinum*

chickweed: *Cerastium*, **Stellaria** (See **starwort** and **stitchwort**.)

chickweed wintergreen: *Trientalis* (See **starflower**.)

chicory: *Cichorium Intybus*

chicot: *Gymnocladus dioica* (See **stump tree**.)

chicozapote: *Manilkara Zapota* (See **sapodilla**.)

Chilean bellflower: *Lapageria* rosea (See **Chile-bells**.)

Chilean fire tree: *Embothrium* coccineum

Chilean jasmine: *Mandevilla laxa*

Chilean pine: *Araucaria* araucana (See **monkey puzzle tree**.)

Chile-bells: *Lapageria* rosea

chimney bellflower: *Campanula pyramidalis*

china fir: *Cunninghamia lanceolate*

Chinaberry: *Melia Azedarach* (See **lilac, Indian**.), *Sapindus* Saponaria (See **soapberry**.)

Chinaberry tree: *Melia Azedarach* (See **paradise tree**.)

China fleecevine: *Polygonum Aubertii* (See **fleecevine, silver** and **silver lace vine**.)

China grass: *Boehmeria nivea* (See **ramie** and **silk plant, Chinese**.)

China jute: *Abutilon Theophrasti* (See **velvetleaf**.)

China rose: *Hibiscus* Rosa-sinensis (See **shoeblock plant**.), *Rosa chinensis* (See **noisette**.)

chinar tree: *Platanus orientalis*

China silk plant: *Boehmeria nivea* (See **ramie**.)

China tree: *Melia* Azedarach (See **lilac, Indian**.)

chin cactus: *Gymnocalycium*

chincherinchee: *Ornithogalum thyrsoides*

Chinese photinia: *Photinia serrulata*

Chinese bellflower: *Abutilon* (See **flowering maple**.)

Chinese bottle tree: *Firmiana simplex* (See **parasol tree**.)

Chinese box: *Murraya* paniculata (See **satinwood**.)

Chinese box orange: *Severinia* buxifolia

Chinese date: *Ziziphus Jujuba* (See **Jew's thorn**.)

Chinese evergreen: *Aglaonema modestum*

Chinese flame tree: *Koelrueteria* bipinnata

Chinese gooseberry: *Actinidia* chinensis (See **kiwi**.), *A. deliciosa* (See **yang-tao**.)

Chinese ground orchid: *Bletilla striata*

Chinese hat plant: *Holmskioldia*, *H. sanguinea*

Chinese-houses: *Collinsia*, *Collinsia heterophylla*

Chinese lantern: *Abutilon* (See **flowering maple**.), *A. hybridum*, **Physalis** (See **winter cherry**.), *P. alkekenii*, *P. franchetii*

Chinese mustard: *Brassica Rapa*

Chinese mustard cabbage: *Brassica Rapa* (See **Bok choy**.)

Chinese pagoda tree: *Sophora japonica* (See **pagoda tree**.)

Chinese parasol tree: *Firmiana, F. simplex* (See **parasol tree**.)

Chinese peony: *Paeonia lactiflora* (See **peony**.)

Chinese pine: *Crassula tetragona* (See **pine tree, miniature**.)

Chinese plumbago: **Ceratostigma**

Chinese preserving melon: *Benincasa hispida* (See **wax gourd**.)

Chinese sacred lily: *Narcissus Tazetta*

Chinese scholar tree: *Sophora japonica* (See **Japanese pagoda tree** and **pagoda tree**.)

Chinese tallow tree: *Sapium sebiferum* (See **tallow tree**.)

Chinese water chestnut: *Eleocharis dulcis* (See **ling**.)

Chinese watermelon: *Benincasa hispida* (See **wax gourd**.)

chinquapin: *Castanea pumila*, **Castanopsis**, *C. chrysophylla*

chive: *Allium Schoenoprasum*

chocolate: **Theobroma**

chocolate-root: *Geum rivale* (See **water avens**.)

chocolate tree: *Theobroma Cacao*

chokeberry: **Aronia**

choke cherry: *Prunus virginiana*

Christmas bells: *Sandersonia aurantiaca* (See **lily, Chinese lantern**.)

Christmas berry: *Heteromeles arbutifolia*

Christmas berry tree: **Schinus** *terebinthifolius*

Christmas cactus: **Schlumbergera** *Bridgesii*

Christmas candle: *Cassia alata* (See **senna, candlestick**.)

Christmas fern: **Polystichum** *acrostichoides*

Christmas flower: *Helleborus niger* (See **Christmas rose**.)

Christmas rose: **Helleborus** *niger* (See **hellebore**.)

Christ's-thorn: **Paliurus** *Spina-Christi* (See **Jew's thorn**.)

chufa: *Cyperus esculentus* (See **rush nut**.)

ciboule: *Allium fistulosum* (See **Welsh onion**.)

cici: *Cicer arietinum* (See **chick-pea**.)

cider gum: *Eucalyptus Gunnii* (See **gum**.)

cigar flower: *Cuphea ignea* (See **cigar plant**.)

cigar plant: *Cuphea ignea*

cigar tree: *Catalpa* (See **Indian bean**.)

cineraria: *Senecio hybridus*

cinnamon jasmine: *Hedychium coronarium* (See **lily, butterfly**.)

cinnamon vine: *Dioscorea batatas*

cinquefoil: *Potentilla* (See **five-finger**, **five-leaf**, and **tormentil**.)

circle onion: *Allium cepa* (See **Egyptian onion**.)

citronella: *Collinsonia canadensis* (See **stoneroot**.)

clammy azalea: *Rhododendron viscosum* (See **swamp honeysuckle**.)

clammy chickweed: *Cerastium* (See **mouse-ear**.)

clammy locust: *Robinia viscosa*

classic myrtle: *Myrtus communis*

clearweed: *Pilea* (See **richweed**.)

cleavers: *Galium* (See **goosetongue**, **gripgrass**, and **loveman**.), *G. aparine*

cliff brake: *Pellea*

cliff date palm: *Phoenix rupicola*

cliff-green: *Paxistima canbyi* (See **mountain lover**.)

climbing bittersweet: *Celastrus scandens* (See **bittersweet**, **climbing staff tree**, and **staff vine**.)

climbing fern: *Lygodium*, *L. japonicum* (See **Hartford fern**.)

climbing fumitory: *Adlumia*, *A. fungosa* (See **fumitory** and **mountain fringe**.)

climbing hempweed: *Mikania*

climbing hydrangea: *Hydrangea anomala petolaria* (See **hydrangea**.)

climbing lily: *Gloriosa rothschildiana*

climbing onion: *Bowiea*

climbing staff tree: *Celastrus scandens*

cloak fern: *Notholaena*

clock vine: *Thunbergia alata*, *T. grandiflora* (See **sky flower**.)

cloudberry: *Rubus Chamoemorus*

cloud grass: *Agrotis nebulosa*

clove: *Syzygium aromaticum*

clove gillyflower: *Dianthus caryophyllus* (See **gillyflower**.)

clove pink: *Dianthus caryophyllus* (See **gillyflower**.)

clover: *Trifolium* (See **trefoil**.)

clover, strawberry: *Trifolium fragiferum*

clover, white: *Trifolium repens*

clover, white Dutch: *Trifolium repens* (See **white clover**.)

club gourd: *Trichosanthes anguina* (See **serpent cucumber**.)

club moss: *Lycopodium* (See **ground pine** and **moss**.)

cluster pine: *Pinus Pinaster* (See **pinaster** and **star pine**.)

coachwhip: *Fouquieria* splendens (See **ocotillo** and **vine cactus**.)

coachwood: *Ceratopetalum apetalum* (See **leatherwood**.)

coast live oak: *Quercus agrifolia* (See **live-oak**.)

coast redwood: *Sequoia* sempervirens

coat flower: *Petrorhagia saxifraga* (See **tunic flower**.)

cob cactus: *Lobivia*

cobnut: *Corylus avellana grandis*

cobra lily: *Darlingtonia californica* (See **pitcher plant**.)

coca: *Erythroxylum* Coca

cocaine plant: *Erythroxylum* Coca

cockle: *Vaccaria*

cocklebur: *Agrimonia*, *Xanthium*

cocksfoot orchard grass: *Dactylis* glomerata

cockspur: *Crataegus crusgalli* (See **thorn, cockspur**.), *Pisonia* aculeata

coco: *Cocos*

coco-de-mer: *Lodoicea* maldivica

coconut palm: *Cocos* nucifera (See **coco** and **coconut**.)

coco plum: *Chrysobalanus icaco* (See **icaco**.)

cocozelle: *Cucurbita pepo* (See **zucchini**.)

codlins-and-cream: *Epilobium hirsutum*

coffee: *Coffea, Rubia* (See **madderwort**.)

coffee fern: *Pellaea* andromedifolia

coffee tree: *Coffea arabica*, *Polyscias* guilfoylei

cohosh: *Actaea pachypoda*

cola nut: *Cola acuminata* (See **kola nut**.)

colicroot: *Aletris* (See **star grass**.)

coliseum ivy: *Cymbalaria* muralis (See **toadflax, ivy-leaved**.)

colonial bent grass: *Agrotis* tenuis

coltsfoot: *Galax* (See **wandflower**.), G. urceolata, *Tussilago* Farfara (See **foalfoot** and **horsefoot**.)

columbine: *Aquilegia*

columbo: *Frasera*

common aubrietia: *Aubrietia* deltoidea

common avens: *Geum urbanum* (See **avens**.)

common balm: *Melissa officinalis* (See **sweet balm**.)

common basil: *Ocimum Basilicum* (See **sweet basil**.)

common calla: *Zantedeschia aethiopica* (See **lily, arum**.)

common carrot: *Daucus Carota* (See **carrot**.)

common catbrier: *Smilax rotundifolia* (See **horse brier**.)

common club moss: *Lycopodium clavatum* (See **ground pine**.)

common dittany: *Cunila organoides* (See **stone mint**.)

common dog fennel: *Anthenis Cotula* (See **stinking chamomile**.)

common edible plum: *Prunus domestica* (See **plum**.)

common fennel: ***Foeniculum*** *vulgare*

common fig: ***Ficus*** *Carica*

common geranium: *Pelargonium hortorum* (See **Geranium**.)

common guava: ***Psidium*** *guajava*

common hoarhound: ***Marrubium*** *vulgare*

common houseleek: *Sempervivum tectorum* (See **thunder plant**.)

common lousewort: ***Pedicularis*** *canadensis*

common meadow beauty: *Rhexia virginica* (See **deer grass**.)

common mullein: *Verbascum Thapsus* (See **sheperd's club**.)

common myrtle: ***Myrtus*** *communis*

common nightshade: *Solanum nigrum* (See **poisonberry**.)

common pasqueflower: ***Anemone*** *pulsatilla*

common pea: ***Pisum*** *sativum*

common peony: *Paeonia lactiflora* (See **peony**.)

common periwinkle: *Vinca minor* (See **myrtle** and **myrtle, running**.)

common persimmon: ***Diospyros***

common pimpernel: *Anagallis arvensis* (See **sheperd's clock**.)

common pitcher plant: *Sarracenia purpurea* (See **side saddle flower**.)

common plantain: ***Plantago*** *major*

common princess palm: ***Dictyosperma*** *album*

common red poppy: *Papaver rhoeas* (See **poppy**.)

common rose mallow: *Hibiscus moscheutos* (See **rose mallow** and **swamp rose mallow**.)

common sage: *Artemesia tridentata* (See **sage, black**.)

common snowdrop: *Galanthus nivalis* (See **fair-maids-of-February**.)

common sorrel: *Rumex Acetosella* (See **sheep sorrel**.)

common trumpet creeper: ***Campsis***, *C. radicans* (See **trumpet creeper**.)

common viper's bugloss: ***Echium***, *E. vulgare* (See **viper's bugloss**.)

common wallflower: *Erysimum cheiry* (See **wallflower**.)

common weed: ***Plantago*** *lanceolata*

common white jasmine: ***Jasminium*** *officinale*

common wormwood: *Artemisia absinthium* (See **wormwood**.)

compass plant: *Silphium laciniatum* (See **rosin plant**.)

conch apple: *Passiflora maliformis* (See **sweet calabash**.)

coneflower: *Echinacea purpurea*, ***Ratibida*** *columnifera*, *R. pinnata*, *R. pulcherrima*, ***Rudbeckia***, *R. fulgida*

coneflower, prairie: ***Ratibida*** *columnifera*, *R. pinnata*, *R. pulcherrima*

cone-plant: ***Conophytum***

Confederate jasmine: ***Trachelospermum*** *jasminoides*

Confederate vine: ***Antigonon***, *A. leptopus* (See **mountain rose**.)

Congo pea: ***Cajanus***, *C. cajan* (See **pea, Angola**.)

consumption weed: *Baccharis halimifolia* (See **myrtle, sea** and **silverling**.)

convulsion root: ***Monotropa*** *uniflora* (See **corpse plant**.)

copal: *Ailanthus altissima* (See **tree of heaven**.)

copal tree: *Ailanthus altissima* (See **sumac, Chinese** and **varnish tree**.)

copey: *Clusia rosea* (See **monkey apple**.)

copperleaf: ***Acalypha***, *A. Wilkesiana*, ***Alternanthea***

copper leaves: *Anacampseros telephiastrum* (See **love plant**.)

coquelicot: *Papaver*

coquito: *Jubaea chilensis*

coral-bead plant: *Abrus precatorius* (See **pea, rosary** and **vine, red-beard**.)

coral beads: *Cocculus carolinus* (See **snail-seed**.)

coral bean: ***Erythrina*** *corallodendron* (See **frijolillo**.), *E. herbacea*

coralbells: ***Heuchera***, *H. sanguinea*

coralberry: *Ardesia crenata* (See **spiceberry**.), *Symphoricarpus orbiculatus* (See **turkey berry tree**.)

coralbush: ***Templetonia*** *retusa*

coral drops: ***Bessera*** *elegans*

coral gem: *Lotus berthelotii*

coral gum: *Eucalyptus torquata* (See **gum**.)

coral honeysuckle: ***Lonicera*** *sempervirens*

corallita: ***Antigonon*** *leptopus* (See **mountain rose**.)

coral pea: ***Adenanthera***, *A. pavonina*

(See **sandalwood, red**.), *Hardenbergia violacea* (See **lilac, Australian**.)

coral plant: *Jatropha multifida*, ***Russelia***

coralroot: ***Corallorhiza***

coral tree: ***Erythrina***, *E. caffra* (See **kaffir boom**.)

coralvine: ***Antigonon*** *leptopus* (See **mountain rose**.)

coralwood: ***Adenanthera***, *A. pavonina* (See **sandalwood, red**.)

coralwort: *Dentaria*

coreopsis: *Coreopsis tinctoria* (See **tickseed**.)

coriander: *Coriandrum sativum*

cork elm: *Ulmus Thomasii* (See **elm**.)

cork oak: *Quercus Suber* (See **cork tree**.)

corkscrew flower: *Vigna Caracalla* (See **snailflower**.)

cork tree: ***Phellodendron***, *P. amurense*, *Quercus Suber*

corkwood: ***Leitneria*** *floridana*

corn: *Zea mays* (See **maize**.)

corn-adonis: ***Adonis***

cornbind: *Convolvulus*

cornbottle: *Centaurea Cyanus*

corn chrysanthemum: *Chrysanthemum segetum* (See **marigold, corn**.)

corn cockle: ***Agrostemma***

corn crowfoot: *Ranunculus arvensis* (See **hellebore**.)

cornel: *Cornus*

cornelian cherry: *Cornus mas*

corn flag: *Gladiolus*, *G. segetum* (See **flag**.)

cornflower: ***Centaurea*** *cyanis* (See **bluebottle**, **knapweed**, and **Quaker-ladies**.)

corn lily: *Veratrum californicum* (See **skunk cabbage**.)

corn marigold: *Chrysanthemum segetum* (See **golden flower**.)

corn poppy: *Papaver rhoeas* (See **poppy**.)

corn salad: *Fedia*, *Valerianella olitoria*

coroa: *Sicana odorifera* (See **Sicana**.)

corozo: *Phytelephas macrocarpa* (See **ivory nut**.)

corpse plant: ***Monotropa*** *uniflora* (See **Indian pipe** and **pinesap**.)

Corsican-curse: ***Soleirolia*** *Soleirolii*

Corsican sandwort: *Arenaria balearica* (See **pearlwort, Corsican**.)

cosmetic-bark tree: ***Murraya*** *paniculata* (See **satinwood**.)

costmary: ***Chrysanthemum*** *Balsamita*

cotton: *Gossypium* (See **Malvaceae**.)

cotton thistle: *Onopordum Acanthium* (See **silver thistle**.)

cottonweed: *Abutilon, A. margaritacea, A. Theophrasti, Otanthus maritimus,* **Populus**

cottonwood: *Populus, P. deltoides*

cottonwood, black: *Populus trichocarpa*

cottonwood, Fremont: *Populus Fremontii*

cottonwood, lanceleaf: *Populus acuminata*

cottonwood, narrowleaf: *Populus angustifolia*

Coulter pine: *Pinus coulteri* (See **pine, big-cone**.)

country walnut: *Aleurites moluccana* (See **tallow tree**.)

courgette: *Cucurbita pepo* (See **zucchini**.)

coventry bell: *Anemone pulsatilla, Campanula Medium*

cowbells: **Uvularia** (See **merrybells**.)

cowberry: *Viburnum Lentago* (See **nannyberry, sheepberry**, and **tea plant**.)

cowherb: **Vaccaria**, *V. pyramidata*

cow-horn orchid: **Schomburgkia**

cow itch: *Campsis radicans* (See **cross vine** and **trumpet creeper**.)

cow itch tree: **Lagunaria** *Patersonii*

cow lily: **Nuphar** (See **spatterdock**.)

cow oak: *Quercus Michauxii* (See **oak, basket**.)

cow parsnip: *Heracleum* (See **meadow parsnip**.)

cowpea: *Vigna unguiculata* (See **pea, black-eyed**.)

cowslip: **Caltha** *palustris* (See **lily, cow, marsh marigold**, and **May blob**.), *Mertensia virginica* (See **Virginia bluebells**.)

coyoli palm: **Acrocomia** *mexicana*

coyote bush: *Baccharis pilularis* (See **kidneywort**.)

crab apple: *Malus*

crabapple tree: **Malus**

crab cactus: **Schlumbergera** *truncata*

crab's eye: **Abrus** *precatorius* (See **pea, rosary** and **vine, redbeard**.)

crab tree: *Malus* (See **crab apple**.)

crakeberry: **Empetrum** *nigrum* (See **crowberry**.)

crampbark: *Viburnum trilobum* (See **cranberry bush**.)

cranberry: **Vaccinium**, *Viburnum opulus*

cranberry bush: *Viburnum Opulus* (See **cranberry tree**.), *V. trilobum*

cranberry, European: *Viburnum Opulus Roseum* (See **marsh elder**.)

cranberry tree: *Viburnum trilobum* (See **cranberry tree**.)

crane flower: *Strelitzia reginae* (See **lily, crane**.)

cranefly orchid: *Tipularia discolor*

crane lily: *Strelitzia reginae*

cranesbill: *Geranium*

crane's bill: *Erodium* (See **muskflower**.)

crape gardenia: *Tabernaemontana divaricata* (See **crape jasmine**.)

crape jasmine: *Tabernaemontana divaricata*

crape myrtle: *Lagerstroemia indica* (See **lilac, Indian**.)

crazyweed: *Oxytropis* (See **locoweed**.)

creambush: *Holodiscus discolor*

creamcups: *Platystemon, P. californicus*

creeping Charley: *Peperomia rotundifolia*

creeping Charlie: *Glechoma hederacea, Lysimachia Nummularia, Malva sylvestris, Pilea nummulariifolia, Plectranthus*

creeping forget-me-not: *Omphalodes verna* (See **forget-me-not**.)

creeping grass: *Agrotis stolonifera*

creeping Jennie: *Convolvulus arvensis, Echinocystus lobata, Lycopodium clavatum, L. complanatum, L. obscurum,*

Lysimachia Nummularia (See **creeping Charlie**.)

creeping Jenny: *Lysimachia nummularia* (See **moneywort** and **motherwort**.)

creeping mint: *Meehania cordata*

creeping phlox: *Phlox nivalis*

creeping-sailor: *Saxifraga stolonifera* (See **strawberry geranium**.)

creeping St.-John's-wort: *Hypericum calycinum* (See **rose-of-Sharon**.)

creeping windmill grass: *Chloris truncata* (See **star grass**.)

creeping zinnia: *Sanvitalia procumbens*

creosote bush: *Larrea*

crested dwarf iris: *Iris cristata*

Cretan bear's-tail: *Celsia*

Cretan brake: *Pteris cretica*

Cretan mullein: *Celsia*

Crete dittany: *Origanum dictamnus* (See **hart's-eye**.)

crimson flag: *Schizostylis coccinea*

crinum lily: *Crinum*

crippled-cranefly: *Tipularia discolor* (See **orchid, cranefly**.)

crocus, autumn: *Colchicum*

crocus, celandine: *Crocus Korolhowii*

crocus, Chilean: *Tecophilaea cyanocrocus*

crocus, Dutch: *Crocus vernus*

crocus, iris-flowered: *Crocus byzantinus*

crocus, saffron: *Crocus sativus*

crocus, Scotch: *Crocus biflorus*

crocus, tropical: *Kaempferii rotunda*

crocus, wild: *Anemone nuttalliana*

cross vine: *Ampelopsis arborea, Bignonia capreolata* (See **quartervine**.), *Campsis radicans* (See **trumpet creeper** and **trumpet vine**.)

crosswort: *Crucianella*

croton: *Codiaeum*

crowberry: *Arctostaphylos uva-ursa, Corema, Empetrum, Vaccinium macrocarpon, V. Myrtillus*

crow corn: *Aletris farinosa* (See **starwort, mealy**.)

crownbeard: *Verbesina*

crown beauty: *Hymenocallis* (See **sea daffodil**.)

crown daisy: *Crysanthemum coronarium*

crown fritillary: *Fritillaria imperialis*

crown imperial: *Fritillaria imperialis*

crown-of-thorns: *Euphorbia Milii*

crown-pink: *Lychnis Coronaria* (See **mullein pink**.)

crown plant: *Campsis*

crown vetch: *Coronilla varia*

cruel plant: *Cynanchum*

crystal tea: *Ledum palustre* (See **marsh tea**.)

cuckooflower: *Cardamine* pratensis (See **lady's-smock**, **Mayflower**, and **meadow cress**.), *Lychnis Flos-cuculi* (See **meadow campion**.), *Lychnis floscuculis* (See **ragged robin**.)

cuckoopint: *Arum maculatum* (See **lords-and-ladies**.)

cucumber: *Cucumis sativus*

cucumber root: *Medeola virginica*

cucumber tree: *Magnolia acuminata* (See **mountain magnolia**.)

cudweed: *Artemesia ludovicinia* (See **sage, white**.), *Gnaphalium*

culinary bay: *Laurus* nobilis

cultivated tobacco: *Nicotiana tabaccum* (See **tobacco**.)

Culver's physic: *Veronicastrum*

cumin: *Cuminum Cyminum*

cup-and-saucer: *Campanula medium*

cup-and-saucer plant: *Holmskioldia, H. sanguinea* (See **Chinese hat plant**.)

cup-and-saucer vine: *Cobaea* scandens (See **cup-and-saucer**.)

cupey: *Clusia rosea* (See **monkey apple**.)

cup fern: *Dennstaedtia*

cupflower: *Nierembergia*

Cupid's bower: ***Achimenes***

cupid's-dart: ***Catananche***, *C. caerulea*

cup-of-gold: *Solandra guttata*

cup plant: *Silphium perfoliatum*

curlew berry: *Empetrum nigrum* (See **crowberry**.)

curly grass: ***Schizaea*** *pusilla*

curly palm: ***Howea***

currant: ***Ribes***

currant, black: ***Ribes*** *nigrum*

currant, Catalina: ***Ribes*** *laurifolium, R. viburnifolium*

currant, Missouri: ***Ribes*** *aureum, R. odoratum*

currant, red: ***Ribes*** *silvestre, R. spicatum*

currant, winter: ***Ribes*** *sanguineum*

curry plant: *Helichrysum angustifolium*

curtain plant: *Kalanchoe pinnata* (See **love plant, Mexican**.)

curua: *Sicana odorifera* (See **Sicana**.)

curuba: *Sicana odorifera* (See **Sicana**.)

cushaw: *Cucurbita maxima, C. moschata*

cushion aloe: ***Haworthia***

cushion pink: *Silene acaulis* (See **moss campion**.)

custard apple: ***Annona*** *Cherimola*

cut-leaf philodendron: *Monstera deliciosa* (See **window plant**.)

cypress: ***Cupressus, Taxodium***

cypress, bald: *Taxodium distichum*

cypress, false: *Chamaecyparis*

cypress, mourning: *Chamaecyparis funebris, C. Lawsoniana*

cypress pine: ***Callitris***

cypress, standing: *Ipomopsis rubra* (See **Texas plume**.)

cypress vine: *Ipomoea Quamoclit* (See **starglory**.)

cyps: ***Paphiopedilum***

cythera: ***Calypso***

D

daffadilly: *Narcissus Pseudonarcissus* (See **daffodil**.)

daffadowndilly: *Narcissus Pseudonarcissus* (See **daffodil**.)

daffodil: *Narcissus*, *N. Pseudonarcissus*

daffodil, checkered: *Fritillaria Meleagris*

daffodil, hoop-petticoat: *Narcissus Bulbocodium*

daffodil, Peruvian: *Hymenocallis narcissiflora*

daffodil, rush: *Narcissus Jonquilla*

dahl: *Cajanus cajan* (See **pea, Angola**.)

dahoon: *Ilex Cassine*

daikon: *Raphanus sativus* (See **radish**.)

daily-dew: *Drosera* (See **sundew**.)

dairy pink: *Vaccaria*, *V. pyramidata* (See **cowherb**.)

daisy, blue: *Felicia ameloides*

daisybush: *Olearia*

daisy, Dahlberg: *Dyssodia tenuiloba* (See **marigold, fetid**.)

daisy, English: *Bellis perennis* (See **marguerite**.)

daisy, globe: *Globularia trichosantha*

daisy, Michaelmas: *Aster nova-angliae*, *A. nova-belgii*

daisy, Namaqualand: *Venidium*

daisy, oxeye: *Chrysanthemum Leucanthemum* (See **marguerite**.)

daisy, paper: *Rhodanthe*

daisy, Paris: *Chrysanthemum frutescens* (See **marguerite**.)

daisy, Shasta: *Chrysanthemum maximum*, *Leucanthemum maximum*

daisy, Swan River: *Brachycome iberidifolia*

daisy, tahoka: *Machaeranthera tanacetifolia*

daisy, Transvaal: *Gerbera jamesonii*

daisy tree: ***Montanoa*** *grandiflora, Olearia* (See **daisybush**.)

daisy, white: *Chrysanthemum Leucanthemum* (See **marguerite**.)

dame's rocket: ***Hesperis*** *matronalis*

dame's violet: ***Hesperis*** *matronalis*

dammar pine: *Agathis*

damson: *Prunus insititia*

damson plum: *Chrysophyllum oliviforme* (See **satinleaf**.)

dandelion: ***Taraxacum*** (See **lion's-tooth**.), *T. officinale*

daneflower: *Anemone Pulsatilla* (See **pasqueflower**.)

Dane's blood: *Anemone Pulsatilla, Sambucus Ebulus* (See **Danewort**.)

Daneweed: *Sambucus Ebulus* (See **Danewort**.)

Danewort: *Sambucus Ebulus*

dangleberry: *Gaylussacia frondosa* (See **tangleberry**.)

darling pea: ***Swainsona*** *galegifolia* (See **swampflower**.)

dasheen: *Colocasia esculenta*

date palm: ***Phoenix***, *P. dactylifera* (See **date**.)

date plum: *Diospyros, D. virginiana* (See **lotus tree**.)

dawn redwood: ***Metasequoia*** *glyptostroboides*

daylily: ***Hemerocallis*, Hosta**

deadly nightshade: *Atropa belladonna* (See **nightshade**.)

deadman's hand: *Dryopteris filix-mas, Laminaria digitata*

deadman's toe: *Laminaria digitata* (See **deadman's hand**.)

dead-men's-fingers: *Orchis latifolia, O. mascula, O. maculata, O. morio*

dead nettle: ***Lamium***

Dead Sea apple: *Solonum sodomeum* (See **Sodon apple**.)

death camas: ***Zigadenus***, *Z. venenosus* (See **camas**.)

death's-herb: *Atropa Belladonna*

deerberry: *Vaccinium* (See **squaw huckleberry**.)

deer-foot: *Achlys triphylla*

deer grass: ***Rhexia*** (See **meadow beauty**.), *R. virginica*

deer-tongue fern: ***Phyllitis*** *scolopendrium*

deodar: *Cedrus deodara*

deodar cedar: ***Cedrus*** *Deodara*

desert candle: ***Eremurus***

desert marigold: ***Baileya***

desert olive: ***Forestiera***

desert pea: *Clianthus formosus* (See **Sturt's desert pea**.)

desert plume: *Stanleya pinnata* (See
prince's-plume.)

desert willow: *Chilopsis linearis*

devil's backbone: **Pedilanthus** *tithyma-loides* (See **slipper plant** and **spurge, slipper**.)

devil's-claw, common: *Probiscidea jussieui*

devil's club: **Oplopanax** *horridus*

devil's-darning-needle: *Clematis virginiana* (See **virgin's-bower**.)

devil's ivy: **Epipremnum**

devil's paintbrush: *Hieracium*

devil's-plague: *Daucus carota carota* (See **Queen Anne's lace**.)

devil's shoestring: *Tephrosia virginiana, Viburnum alnifolium* (See **hobble-bush, moosewood**, and **wayfaring tree, American**.)

devil's-walking-stick: *Aralia spinosa* (See **Hercule's-club** and **spikenard tree**.), *Zanthoxylum clava-Herculis*

devilwood: **Osmanthus**, *O. americanus*

dewberry: *Rubus macropetalus*

dewdrop: **Dalibarda**

dew plant: *Aptenia, Carpobrotus, Cephalophyllum, Delosperma, Drosanthemum, Drosera rotundifolia, Lampranthus, Malephora, Mesembryanthemum, Oscularia* (See **ice plant**.)

dewthread: *Drosera filiformis* (See **threadleaved sundew**.)

dhak: *Butea monosperma*

dhal: *Cajanus cajan* (See **pea, Angola**.)

dhauri: *Woodfordia fruticosa*

diamond flower: **Ionopsidium**, *I. acaule*

dicondra: **Dicondra** *micanthra*

dill: *Anethum graveolens*

dilly: *Mimusops emarginata*

dishcloth gourd: *Luffa aegyptiaca* (See **strainer-vine**.)

ditch grass: *Ruppia* (See **pondweed, tassel**.)

dittany: **Dictamnus** *albus* (See **fraxinella**.)

dittany of Crete: *Origanum Dictamnus* (See **hop marjoram**.)

dock: **Rumex**, *R. Acetosa* (See **sorrel**.)

dodder: *Cucutus* (See **hellebore**.)

dogbane: **Apocynum**, *A. androsaemifolium*

dogberry: **Sorbus** *americana, Viburnum alnifolium* (See **hobblebush, moosewood** and **wayfaring tree, American**.)

dogberry tree: *Cornus sanguinea*

dog brier: *Rosa canina* (See **rose, brier**.)

dog fennel: *Anthemis tinctoria* (See **marguerite, golden.**)

dog-hobble: *Viburnum alnifolium* (See **hobblebush, moosewood,** and **wayfaring tree, American.**)

dog rose: *Rosa canina*

dog's bane: *Apocynum androsaemifolium* (See **dogbane.**)

dog tooth violet: *Erythronium*

dog tree: *Alnus, Cornus, Euonymus, Sambucus, Viburnum*

dog violet: *Viola riviniana* (See **wood violet.**)

dogwood: *Cornus florida, C. sanguinea* (See **dogberry tree.**)

doom palm: *Hyphaene thebaica*

double coconut: *Lodoicea maldivica*

double spruce: *Picea mariana* (See **spruce, black.**)

Douglas fir: *Pseudotsuga menziesii*

doum palm: *Hyphaene thebaica* (See **doom palm.**)

doveflower: *Peristeria elata* (See **holy ghost flower.**)

dove orchid: *Peristeria elata* (See **dove flower** and **holy ghost flower.**)

dove's-foot: *Geranium molle*

dove tree: *Davidia involucrata*

down tree: *Ochroma pyramidale*

downy poplar: *Populus heterophylla* (See **swamp cottonwood.**)

dragon flower: *Huernia*

dragonhead: *Dracocephalum* (See **lion's-heart.**)

dragon-mouth: *Horminum*

dragonroot: *Arisaema Dracontium, A. triphyllum* (See **Indian turnip, jack-in-the-pulpit,** and **turnip, Indian.**)

dragon's-mouth: *Arethusa bulbosa* (See **swamp pink.**)

drooping melaleuca: *Melaleuca armillaris* (See **myrtle, bracelet honey.**)

dropwort: *Filipendula vulgaris*

Drummond phlox: *Phlox drummondii*

drumstick tree: *Cassia fistula*

duckweed: *Lemna*

dudder grass: *Adiantum capillus-veneris* (See **fern, Venus's-hair.**)

dulcamara: *Solanum Dulcamara*

dumb cane: *Dieffenbachia*

durmast: *Quercus peterea*

dusk's-meat: *Lemna*

dusty miller: *Artemisia stellerana* (See **wormwood.**), *Centaurea cineraria* (See **knapweed.**), *Chrysanthemum ptarmiciflorum, Lychnis Coronaria* (See **mullein pink** and **rose campion.**), *Senecio Cineraria, S. vira-vira* (See **ragwort, sea.**)

Dutch case-knife bean: *Phaseolus coccineus* (See **scarlet runner bean**.)

Dutchman's-breeches: *Dicentra Cucullaria*

Dutchman's pipe: ***Aristolochia*** *californica, A. durior, A. macrophylla* (See **pipe vine**.)

Dutch-mice: *Lathyrus tuberosus* (See **pea, tuberous**.)

dwarf blueberry: *Vaccinium Pennsylvanicum* (See **blueberry**.)

dwarf cherry: *Prunis pumila* (See **sand cherry**.)

dwarf dandelion: ***Krigia***

dwarf elder: *Sambucus Ebulus* (See **elder**.)

dwarf fan palm: ***Chamaerops*** *humilis*

dwarf gingseng: *Panax trifolius* (See **ginseng**.)

dwarf iris: ***Iris*** *Douglasiana*

dwarf laurel: *Kalmia angustifolia* (See **sheep laurel**.)

dwarf palmetto: *Sabal minor* (See **scrub palmetto**.)

dwarf plumbago: ***Ceratostigma***

dwarf poinciana: *Caesalpinia pulcherrima* (See **flower-fence**.), *Poinciana pulcherrima* (See **pride of Barbados**.)

dwarf snapdragon: ***Chaenorrhinum***

dye root: ***Lachnanthes*** *caroliana* (See **redroot**.)

dyer's broom: *Genista tinctoria* (See **green broom**.)

dyer's greenweed: ***Genista*** *tinctoria*

dyer's madder: *Rubia tinctorum* (See **madder**.)

dyer's saffron: *Carthamus tinctorius* (See **safflower**.)

dyer's woad: ***Isatis*** *tinctoria*

E

eardrop: *Dicentra*

ear-leaved umbrella tree: *Magnolia fraserii* (See **mountain magnolia**.)

early winter cress: *Barbarea verna* (See **scurvy grass**.)

earth ball: *Tuber melanosporum*

earthnut: *Arachis*, A. *hypogaea*

earth-star: *Cryptanthus*

Easter daisy: *Townsendia exscapa*

Easter flower: *Anemone pulsatilla, Narcissus*

Easter-heralds-trumpet: *Beaumontia grandiflora*

Easter lily: *Lilium candidum, L. longiflorum eximium*

Easter lily cactus: *Echinopsis multiplex* (See **lily, pink Easter**.)

Easter-lily vine: *Beaumontia grandiflora* (See **Easter-heralds-trumpet**.)

eastern camassia: *Camassia scilloides* (See **hyacinth, wild**.)

East Indian holly fern: *Arachniodes aristata* (See **holly fern**.)

East Indian lotus: **Nelumbo** *nucifera*

East Indian satinwood: *Chloroxylon Swietenia* (See **satinwood**.)

ebony spleenwort: **Asplenium** *platyneuron*

edelweiss: *Leondontopodium alpinum* (See **lion's-foot**.)

edible fig: **Ficus** *carica* (See **fig tree**.)

edible-rooted caraway: *Perideridia Gairdneri* (See **squawroot**.)

eel grass: **Vallisneria** (See **tape grass**.)

eggplant: *Solanum Melongena*

eglantine: *Rosa Eglanteria* (See **sweetbrier**.)

egret flower: **Pecteilis** *radiata, P. susannae*

egret orchid: ***Pecteilis*** *radiata, P. susannae*

Egyptian bean: ***Dolichos*** *Lablab*

Egyptian lotus: *Nymphaea Lotus* (See **lily, Egyptian water**.)

Egyptian onion: *Allium cepa*

Egyptian privet: *Lawsonia inermis* (See **henna**.)

Egyptian star-cluster: ***Pentas*** *lanceolata*

Egyptian sycamore: *Ficus Sycomorus* (See **sycamore fig**.)

Egyptian water lotus: *Nymphaea Lotus* (See **lily, Egyptian water**.)

elder: *Sambucus*

elderberry: *Sambucus*

elecampane: ***Inula*** *Helenium* (See **horseheal** and **starwort, yellow**.)

elephant apple: ***Feronia*** *limonia*

elephant creeper: *Argyreia nervosa*

elephant ear: *Alocasia, Colocasia*

elephant-ear fern: *Elaphoglossum crinitum*

elephant garlic: *Alium sativum*

elephant-heads: ***Pedicularis*** *groenlandica*

elephant's ear: *Alocasia,* Begonia, Caladium, **Enterolobium**, *E. cyclocarpum*

elephant's foot: ***Dioscorea*** *elephantipes* (See **Hottentot bread** and **tortoise plant**.)

eleven-o'clock: *Portulaca grandiflora* (See **sun plant**.)

elf dock: *Inula Helenium*

elfin-spur: ***Tipularia*** *discolor* (See **orchid, cranefly**.)

elkhorn fern: ***Platycerium***

elk tree: *Oxydendrum arboreum*

elkwood: *Oxydendrum arboreum* (See **elk tree**.)

elm: ***Ulmus***

elm, American: ***Ulmus*** *americana*

elm-leaved sumac: *Rhus coriaria* (See **sumac, Sicilian**.)

emblic: ***Phyllanthus*** *emblica*

Emodi pine: *Pinus roxburghii* (See **pine chir**.)

empress tree: ***Paulownia***, *P. tomentosa*

enchanter's nightshade: *Circaea*

encino: *Quercus agrifolia*

endive: *Cichorium Endivia*

English bean: *Vicia faba* (See **tick bean**.)

English bluebell: *Endymion nonscriptus* (See **hyacinth, wood**.)

English elm: *Ulmus procera* (See **elm**.)

English fern: ***Polystichum*** *setiferum*

English hawthorn: *Crataegus laevigata*

English ivy: ***Hedera*** *Helix* (See **ivy**.)

English laurel: *Prunus Laurocerasus* (See **laurel, cherry**.)

English pea: **Pisum** *sativum*

English plantain: **Plantago** *lanceolata*

English violet: *Viola odorata* (See **sweet violet**.)

English walnut: *Juglans regia* (See **nut, Madeira**.)

epazote: *Artemisia maritima* (See **wormseed**.)

eryngo: **Eryngium**, *E. maritimum* (See **holly, sea**.)

ettercap: *Pogonia ophioglossoides*

eulalia grass: **Miscanthus** *sinensis*

Eurasian chestnut: *Castanea sativa* (See **Spanish chestnut**.)

European aspen: *Populus tremula* (See **tree, trembling**.)

European bean: *Vicia faba* (See **tick bean**.)

European beech: **Fagus** *sylvatica* (See **beech**.)

European chain fern: **Woodwardia** *radicans*

European chestnut: *Castanea sativa* (See **Spanish chestnut**.)

European filbert: *Corylus Avellana* (See **hazel, European**.)

European grape: *Vitis vinifera* (See **Hamburg**.)

European hackberry: *Celtis australis* (See **hackberry**.)

European hazelnut: *Corylus Avellana* (See **filbert**.)

European mountain ash: **Sorbus** *Aucuparia* (See **quickbeam** and **rowan**.)

European nettle tree: *Celtis australis* (See **honeyberry** and **lotus tree**.)

European parsley fern: **Cryptogramma** *crispa* (See **mountain parsley**.)

European polypody: *Polypodium vulgare* (See **polypody**.)

European red elderberry: **Sambucus** *racemosa*

European spindle tree: *Euonymus europaea* (See **louseberry**.)

European white birch: *Betula alba, B. pendula* (See **poplar birch**.)

European white water lily: *Nymphaea alba* (See **nenuphar**.)

European wood anemone: **Anemone** *nemorosa* (See **windflower**.)

European wood sorrel: *Oxalis Acetosella* (See **shamrock**.)

evening campion: *Silene alba* (See **campion** and **thunderflower**.)

evening lychnis: *Silene alba* (See **thunderflower**.)

evening primrose: **Oenothera**, *O. biennis* (See **tree primrose**.)

Everglades palm: **Acoelorrhaphe** *wrightii* (See **saw cabbage palm**.)

evergreen cherry: *Prunus ilicifolia* (See **mountain holly**.)

evergreen sumac: *Rhus vireus* (See **kinnikinnik**.)

everlasting: **Antennaria, Gnaphalium, Helichrysum**, *Helipterum*

everlasting pea: *Lathyrus sylvestris* (See **pea, perennial**.)

everlasting, pearly: **Anaphalis** *margaritacea*

everlasting, winged: *Ammobium alatum*

F

faba bean: *Vicia faba* (See **tick bean**.)

fair-maids-of-February: *Galanthus nivalis*

fair-maids-of-France: *Saxifraga granulata* (See **meadow saxifrage**.)

fairy bells: *Disporum*

fairy duster: *Calliandra*

fairy lantern: *Calochortus albus* (See **lily, globe**.)

fairy lily: *Zephyranthes*

fairy slipper: *Calypso*

fairy wand: *Chamaelirium* luteum, *Dierama*

fall crocus: *Colchicum autumnale* (See **crocus, autumn** and **saffron, meadow**.)

falling stars: *Campanula isophylla* (See **star-of-Bethlehem**.)

fall phlox: *Phlox* paniculata

false acacia: *Robinia Pseudoacacia* (See **locust**.)

false aloe: *Manfreda*

false aralia: *Dizygotheca*

false arborvitae: *Thujopsis* dolabrata

false asphodel: *Tofieldia*

false bird-of-paradise: *Heleconia* (See **lobster-claw**.)

false buckeye: *Ungnadia speciosa* (See **Mexican buckeye** and **Spanish buckeye**.)

false bugbane: *Trautvetteria*

false cypress: *Chamaecyparis*

false dragonhead: *Physostegia* (See **lion's-heart**.)

false elm: *Celtis occidentalis* (See **hackberry**.)

false flag: *Neomarica* (See **lily, toadcup**.)

false garlic: *Nothoscordum*

false goatsbeard: *Astilbe biternata* (See **goatsbeard.**)

false heather: *Fabiana imbricata*

false hellebore: *Veratrum viride* (See **Indian poke.**)

false hop: *Justica Brandegeana* (See **shrimp plant.**)

false indigo: *Amorpha fruticosa*, *Baptisia*, *B. australis* (See **indigo.**)

false lily-of-the-valley: *Maianthemum* (See **mayflower, Canada.**)

false loosestrife: *Ludwigia*

false lupine: *Thermopsis caroliniana*

false mallow: *Sphaeralcea* (See **mallow, globe.**)

false mesquite: *Calliandra*

false mitrewort: *Tiarella*

false saffron: *Carthamus tinctorius* (See **safflower** and **thistle, saffron.**)

false solomon's seal: *Smilacina*

false spirea: *Astilbe*, *Sorbaria*, *S. sorbifolia*

false tamarisk: *Myricaria*, *M. germanica* (See **tamarisk, German.**)

false violet: *Dalibarda repens*

false wintergreen: *Pyrola rotundifolia* (See **lily-of-the-valley, wild** and **lettuce, Indian.**)

fameflower: *Talinum*

fan iris: *Neomarica* (See **lily, toad-cup.**)

fan palm: *Chamaerops*, *C. humilis*, *Sabal*, *Trachycarpus*, *Washingtonia*

fanweed: *Thlaspi arvense* (See **mustard, mithridate** and **penny cress.**)

fanwort: *Cabomba*

farewell-to-spring: *Clarkia*, *C. amoena* (See **satinflower.**)

farkleberry: *Vaccinium arboreum*

fat-hen: *Chenopodium Bonus-Henricus* (See **spinach, wild.**)

fava bean: *Vicia Fava* (See **horsebean.**)

feather bells: *Stenanthium gramineum* (See **feather-fleece.**)

feather bush: *Lysiloma Thornberi*

feather-fleece: *Stenanthium gramineum*

feather flower: *Verticordia*

featherfoil: *Hottonia*

feather geranium: *Chenopodium Botrys* (See **oak, Jerusalem.**)

feathertop: *Pennisetum villosum*

February daphne: *Daphne mezereum* (See **mezereon** and **spurge, olive.**)

felon herb: *Hieracium Pilosella* (See **mouse-ear.**)

felonwort: *Solanum Dulcamara*

felt plant: *Kalanchoe beharensis* (See **velvetleaf.**)

feltwort: *Verbascum Thapsus*

675

fennel: *Faeniculum vulgare*

fennel-flower: *Nigella*, *N. damascena* (See **love-in-a-mist**.)

fenugreek: *Trigonella Foenum-graecum*

fern, basket: *Nephrolepis pectinata*

fern, beard: *Vittaria lineata*

fern, bear's-foot: *Davallia, Humata tyermannii, Polypodium* (See **rabbit's-foot fern**.)

fern, Boston: *Nephrolepsis exaltta*

fern, cinnamon: *Osmunda cinnamonea*

fern, climbing: *Lygodium*

fern, cloak: *Notholaena*

fern, common rasp: *Doodia media* (See **rasp fern**.)

fern, crested: *Dryopteris cristata*

fern, Eaton's: *Polystichum scopulinum* (See **fern, Western holly**.)

fern, felt: *Pyrrosia*

fern, Florida ribbon: *Vittaria lineata*

fern, flowering: *Osmunda, O. regalis* (See **king fern**.)

fern, giant holly: *Polystichum munitum* (See **fern, western sword**.)

fern, gold: *Notholaena, Pityrogramma*

fern, grape: *Botrychium virginianum* (See **fern, rattlesnake**.)

fern, grass: *Vittaria lineata*

fern, hacksaw: *Doodia aspera* (See **rasp fern**.)

fern, hare's-foot: *Davallia, Humata tyermannii, Polypodium* (See **rabbit's-foot fern**.)

fern, Hartford: *Lygodium palmatum* (See **climbing fern**.)

fern, hart's-tongue: *Phyllitis scolopendrium*

fern, hay-scented: *Dennstaedia punctilobula*

fern, holly: *Polystichum Lonchitis*

fern, interrupted: *Osmunda claytoniana*

fern, iron: *Rumohra adantiaformis* (See **marsh fern**.)

fern, Japanese felt: *Pyrrosia lingua* (See **tongue fern**.)

fern, lady: *Athyrium Filix-femina*

fernleaf inch plant: *Tripogandra multiflora*

fernleaf wandering Jew: *Tripogandra multiflora*

fern, leather: *Rumohra adiantiformis*

fern, leatherleaf: *Rumohra adiantiformis* (See **marsh fern**.)

fern, maidenhair: *Adiantum, A. capillus veneris* (See **fern, Venus-hair**.)

fern, New York: *Thelypteris noveboracensis*

fern-of-the-desert: *Lysiloma Thornberi*

fern, ostrich: *Matteuccia*

fern palm: *Cycas circinalis* (See **sago palm**.)

fern, parsley: *Tanacetum vulgare*

fern pine: ***Podocarpus*** *gracilior*

fern prickly rasp: *Doodia aspera* (See **rasp fern**.)

fern, rabbit's-foot: *Davallia Fijeensis*

fern, rattlesnake: ***Botrychium*** *virginianum*

fern, resurrection: *Polypodium polypodioides*

fern rhapis: *Rhapsis excelsa* (See **palm, hemp**.)

fern, royal: *Osmunda regalis* (See **king fern**.)

fern, sensitive: *Onoclea sensibilis*

fern, shield: *Aspidium* (See **fern, wood**.)

fern, shoestring: ***Vittaria*** *lineata*

fern, small rasp: *Doodia caudata* (See **rasp fern**.)

fern, squirrel's-foot: *Davallia trichomanoides*

fern, staghorn: *Platycerium bifurcatum*

fern, sword: *Nephrolepsis, Polystichum munitum*

fern, ten-day: *Rumohra adantiaformis* (See **marsh fern**.)

fern, tongue: *Pyrrosia lingua*

fern, umbrella: *Gleichenia*

fern, vegetable: *Diplazium esculentum*

fern, Venus's-hair: *Adiantum capillus-veneris*

fern, walking: *Camptosorus*

fern, wall: *Polypodium vulgare*

fern, water: *Azolla, Ceratopteris*

fern, western holly: *Polystichum scopulinum*

fern, western sword: *Polystichum munitum*

fern, wood: *Aspidium, Dryopteris*

feterita: *Sorghum bicolor*

fetterbush: *Andromeda floribunda*, ***Leucothoe*, Pieris** *floribunda*

fever bark: *Pinckneya pubens* (See **fever tree**.)

feverfew: ***Chrysanthemum*** *parthenium* (See **motherwort** and **pellitory**.)

feveroot: ***Triosteum***, *T. perfoliatum*

fever tree: *Pinckneya pubens*

fevertwig: *Celastrus scandens*

feverweed: *Eryngium*

feverwort: *Eupatorium perfoliatum, Triosteum perfoliatum*

fiddle-leaf fig: ***Ficus*** *lyrata*

fiddleneck: *Phacelia tanecetifolia* (See **tarweed**.)

field maple: *Acer campestre* (See **mazer tree**.)

field penny cress: *Thlaspi arvense* (See

flamboyant: ***Delonix***, *D. regia* (See
peacock flower.)

flameflower: *Pyrostegia venusta* (See
golden shower.)

flame-of-the-forest: ***Butea*** *monosperma* (See **palas tree**.), ***Spathodea***
campanulata

flame-of-the-woods: *Ixora coccinea*

flame pea: ***Chorizema***

flame tree: *Brachychiton acerifolius* (See
lacebark.), *B. australis*

flame vine: *Pyrostegia venusta* (See
flameflower and **golden shower**.)

flamingo flower: *Anthurium Scherzeranum*

flamingo plant: *Anthurium andraeanum*
(See **lily, flamingo**.), *Hypoestes phyllostachya*, *Jacobinia carnea* (See **plume
flower**.)

flaming poppy: ***Stylomecon*** *heterophylla*

flaming trumpet: *Pyrostegia venusta* (See
flameflower and **golden shower**.)

Flanders poppy: *Papaver rhoeas* (See
poppy.)

flannelbush: ***Fremontodendron***

flannelflower: *Actinotus helianthi*,
Verbascum olympicum (See **mullein**.)

flannel plant: *Verbascum Thapsus*
(See **hare's-beard** and **sheperd's
club**.)

flat pea: *Lathyrus sylvestris* (See **pea,
perennial**.)

flax: ***Linum***

flaxweed: *Linaria vulgaris*

fleabane: ***Erigeron***

fleaseed: *Plantago Psyllium* (See
fleawort.)

fleawort: *Plantago Psyllium*

fleeceflower: *Polygonum*

fleecevine, silver: *Polygonum Aubertii*

fleur-de-lis: *Iris germanica* (See **flag**.)

flintwood: *Eucalyptus pilularis*

floating bur reed: *Sparganium angustifolium* (See **bur reed**.)

floating fern: ***Ceratopteris***, *C. pteridoides* (See **fern, water**.)

floating heart: ***Nymphoides***

floating moss: *Salvinia rotundifolia*

flooded gum: *Eucalyptus rudis* (See
gum.)

floppers: *Kalanchoe pinnata* (See **love
plant, Mexican**.)

floradora: ***Stephanotis*** *floribunda*

Flora's paintbrush: ***Emilia*** *javanica*

Florence fennel: *Foeniculum vulgare*

Florida holly: *Schinus terebinthifolius*
(See **pepper tree**.)

Florida mahogany: ***Persea*** *borbonia*

Florida maple: *Acer barbatum* (See **maple, Southern sugar**.)

Florida ribbon fern: *Vittaria lineata* (See **shoestring fern.**)

florist's calla: *Zantedeschia aethiopica* (See **lily, arum.**)

florist's chrysanthemum: *Dendrathema morifolium* (See **Chrysanthemum.**)

florist's violet: *Viola odorata* (See **sweet violet.**)

flossflower: *Ageratum*

floss-silk tree: *Chorisia*, *C. speciosa*

flower fence: *Caesalpinia pulcherrima*, *Poinciana pulcherrima* (See **pride of Barbados.**)

flowering almond: *Prunus glandulosa* (See **almond tree.**)

flowering crab: *Malus* (See **crab apple.**)

flowering dogwood: *Cornus florida* (See **dogwood.**)

flowering fern: *Osmunda*

flowering Judas: *Cercis* (See **redbud.**)

flowering maple: *Abutilon*

flowering quince: *Chaenomeles*, *C. speciosa* (See **Japanese quince.**)

flowering rush: *Butomus umbellatus*

flowering stones: *Dinteranthus*, *Lithops*

flowering willow: *Chilopsis linearis* (See **desert willow.**)

flower-of-an-hour: *Hibiscus Trionum* (See **mallow, Venice.**)

fluellen: *Veronica Chamaedrys*, *V. officinalis*

fly honeysuckle: *Lonicera canadensis*, *L. Xylosteum*

fly orchid: *Ophrys insectifera*

fly poison: *Amianthium*, *A. muscitoxicum*

foalfoot: *Tussilago Farfara*

foamflower: *Tiarella cordifolia*

foenugreek: *Trigonella Foenum-graecum* (See **fenugreek.**)

fool's-stones: *Orchis*

forage bamboo: *Phyllostachys aureosulcata*

forget-me-not: *Myosotis* (See **mouse-ear.**), *M. scorpioides*, *M. sylvatica* (See **scorpion grass.**)

forget-me-not, Chinese: *Cynoglossum amabile*

forget-me-not, true: *Myosotis*

Formosa rice plant: *Fatsia japonica*

Forster sentry palm: *Howea*

fortnight lily: *Dietes*

fountain bush: *Russelia*

fountain dracena: *Cordyline australis* (See **lily, palm.**)

fountain grass: *Pennisetum ruppellii*, *P. setaceum*

fountain plant: *Russelia*

four-o'clock: *Mirabilis Jalapa* (See **marvel-of-Peru**.)

foxbane: *Aconitum Lycoctonum, A. Napellus* (See **monkshood**.)

foxberry: *Arctostaphylos Uva-ursi*

foxglove: *Digitalis* (See **lion's-mouth**.), *D. purpurea* (See **fingerflower** and **ladyfinger**.)

fox grape: *Vitis Labrusca*

foxtail: *Alopecurus*

foxtail lily: *Eremurus* (See **desert candle**.)

Franceschi palm: *Brahea*

frangipani: *Plumeria, P. rubra* (See **jasmine, red** and **nosegay**.)

frangipani tree: *Plumeria* (See **frangipani**.)

frankincense pine: *Pinus Taeda* (See **loblolly pine**.)

Franklin tree: *Franklinia*

fraxinella: *Dictamnus albus* (See **gas plant**.)

freckleface: *Hypoestes phyllostachya* (See **flamingo plant**.)

Fremontia: *Fremontodendron*

French bean: *Phaseolus vulgaris* (See **bean** and **kidney bean**.)

French honeysuckle: *Centranthus ruber, Hedysarum coronarium* (See **soola clover**.)

French hydrangea: *Hydrangea macrophylla* (See **hydrangea**.)

French lavender: *Lavandula Spica* (See **lavender**.)

French mulberry: *Callicarpa americana*

French rose: *Rosa gallica* (See **gallica rose**.)

French turpentine pine: *Pinus pinaster* (See **pinaster**.)

French weed: *Thlaspi arvense* (See **mustard, mithridate** and **penny cress**.)

friar's-cap: *Aconitum Napellus* (See **monkshood**.)

fried egg plant: *Romneya coulteri* (See **tree poppy**.)

friendship plant: *Pilea involucrata*

frijolillo: *Erythrina corallodendron*

frijolita: *Sophora secundiflora* (See **mescal bean**.)

fringe bells: *Shortia galacifolia* (See **shortia**.)

fringe cups: *Tellima grandiflora*

fringed gentian: *Gentianopsis*

fringed orchid: *Habenaria* **(See meadow pink**.)

fringed orchid, large purple: *Habenaria psycodes*

fringed polygala: *Polygala pauciflora* (See **wintergreen, flowering**.)

G

galaxy: *Galax* (See **wandflower**.), *G. urceolata*

gallberry: *Ilex glabra* (See **winterberry, common**.)

gallica rose: *Rosa gallica*

ganjah: *Cannabis sativa* (See **hashish**.)

garbanzo: *Cicer, C. arietinum* (See **chick-pea**.)

garden balm: *Melissa officinalis*

garden balsam: *Impatiens Balsimina* (See **lady's slipper**.)

garden calla: *Zantedeschia aethiopica* (See **lily, arum**.)

garden cress: *Lepidium sativum* (See **pepper, poor man's**.)

gardener's-garters: *Phalaris picta*

garden-gate: *Geranium robertianum* (See **herb Robert**.), *Viola, V. arvensis, V. ocellata*

garden lovage: *Levisticum officinale* (See **lovage**.)

garden orache: *Atriplex hortensis* (See **mountain spinach**.)

garden patience: *Rumex patientia*

garden pea: *Pisum sativum*

garden rocambole: *Allium cepa* (See **rocambole**.)

garden saxifrage: *Chrysosplenium*

garden sorrel: *Rumex Acetosa* (See **sorrel**.)

garden violet: *Viola odorata* (See **sweet violet**.)

garget: *Phytolacca americana* (See **poke, Virginian**.)

garland flower: *Daphne Cheorum, Erida persoluta, Hedychium coronarium* (See **lily, butterfly**.)

garlic: *Allium, A. sativum*

garlic chive: *Allium tuberosum*

garlic mustard: ***Alliaria***

garlic, serpent: *Allium Scorodoprasum* (See **rocambole**.)

garlic shrub: *Adenocalymna alliacea*

garlic vine: ***Cydista*** *aequinoctialis*

garlic, wild: *Allium canadense*

gas plant: ***Dictamnus*** *albus*

gayfeather: *Liatris* (See **snakeroot, button**.), *L. spicata*

geebung: ***Persoonia***

geiger tree: *Cordia Sebestena* (See **sebesten**.)

genip: ***Melicoccus*** *bijugatus* (See **mamoncillo**.)

genipe: ***Melicoccus*** *bijugatus* (See **mamoncillo**.)

gentian: *Gentiana*

gentianella: *Gentiana acaulis*

gentian, spurred: *Halenia*

Georgia bark: *Pinckneya pubens* (See **fever tree**.)

Georgia pine: *Pinus palustris* (See **southern yellow pine**.)

geranium: *Pelargonium* (See **stork's-bill**.)

geranium, California: *Senecio Petasitis* (See **velvet groundsel**.)

geranium, ivy: *Pelargonium peltatum*

geranium leaf aralia: ***Polyscias*** *guilfoylei*

Gerardia: ***Agalinis***

German ivy: ***Senecio*** *mikanioides*

German myrtle: *Myrtus communis*

German rampion: *Oenthera biennis* (See **tree primrose**.)

German statice: ***Limonium*** (See **sea lavender**.)

germander: ***Teucrium***, *T. Canadense*

ghost gum: *Eucalyptus papuana, E. pauciflora* (See **gum**.)

ghost plant: *Graptopetalum paraguayense*

ghostweed: *Euphorbia marginata* (See **snow-on-the-mountain**.)

giant allium: *Allium giganteum*

giant arborvitae: *Thuja plicata* (See **cedar, red**.)

giant cactus: *Carnegiea gigantea* (See **saguaro**.)

giant chain fern: ***Woodwardia*** *fimbriata*

giant chestnut: ***Castanopsis***

giant chincherinchee: *Ornithogalum Saundersiae* (See **chincherinchee**.)

giant daisy: *Chrysanthemum serotinum, Wytheia*

giant dracena: *Cordyline australis* (See **lily, palm**.)

giant fennel: ***Ferula*** *communis*

giant gum: *Eucalyptus regnans* (See **mountain ash**.)

giant redwood: ***Sequoiadendron*** *giganteum*

giant reed: ***Arundo*** *donax*

giant sequoia: ***Sequoiadendron*** *giganteum* (See **redwood, giant**.)

giant sunflower: *Helianthus giganteus*

giant thevetia: ***Thevetia*** *thevetiodes*

giant water dock: *Rumex hydrolapathum* (See **horse sorrel**.)

gilliflower: *Dianthus caryophyllus* (See **gillyflower**.)

gill-over-the-ground: *Glechoma hederacea*

gillyflower: *Dianthus caryophyllus, Matthiola incana*

gimlet gum: *Eucalyptus salubris* (See **gum**.)

ginger: ***Zingiber*** *officinale*

gingerbread palm: ***Hyphaene*** *thebaica*

gingerbread tree: *Hyphaene thebaica* (See **doom palm**.)

ginger, wild: *Asarum caudatum*

gingko: *Ginkgo biloba* (See **maidenhair tree**.)

ginseng: ***Panax***, *P. pseudoginseng, P. quinquefolius*

gipsywort: *Lycopus europaeus*

glade mallow: ***Napaea*** *dioica*

gladiole, water: *Butomus umbellantus* (See **rush, flowering**.)

glasswort: *Salicornia europaea* (See **pickleweed, pigeonfoot** and **Salicornia**.)

Glastonbury thorn: *Crataegus monogyna*

globe amaranth: ***Gomphrena***, *G. globosa*

globeflower: ***Trollius***, *T. Europaeus*

globe mallow: ***Sphaeralcea***

globe thistle: *Echinops*

globe tulip: ***Calochortus*** (See **lily, mariposa**.), *Clochortus* (See **star tulip**.)

glory-bower: ***Clerodendron*** (See **tubeflower**.)

glorybush: ***Tibouchina***, *T. urvilleana*

glory-bush, Brazilian: *Tibouchina Urvilleana*

glory flower: ***Eccremocarpus***

glory-flower, Chilean: *Mocarpus*

glory-of-Texas: ***Thelocactus*** *bicolor*

glory-of-the-snow: *Chionodoxa*

glory-of-the-sun: *Leucocoryne ixioides*

glory pea: ***Clianthus***, *C. formosus* (See **parrot's beak** and **Sturt's desert pea**.), *C. puniceus* (See **parrot's beak**.)

glory tree: ***Clerodendrum***

glory vine, crimson: *Vitis Coignetiae*

gloxinia: *Sinningia* (See **Gloxinia**.)

gloxinia, common: *Sinningia*

gnatflower: *Cleome lutea, C. serrulata*

goat nut: *Simmondsia* chinensis

goatsbeard: *Aruncus, Tragopogon*

goatsfoot: *Oxalis caprina*

goat's-horns: *Cheiridopsis candidissima* (See **victory plant**.)

goat's rue: *Galega officinalis, Tephrosia* (See **pea, hoary**.), *Tephrosia virginiana* (See **devil's shoe-string**.)

goatweed: *Aegopodium Podagraria* (See **goutweed**.)

godetia: *Clarkia, C. amoena* (See **satinflower**.)

goldback fern: *Pityrogramma triangularis*

goldcup: *Caltha palustris, Ranunculus acris, R. bulbosus, Solandra guttata* (See **cup-of-gold**.)

golddust: *Aurinia saxatilis* (See **mad-wort, rock**.)

gold-dust plant: *Acuba japonica*

gold-dust tree: *Acuba serratifolia* (See **gold-dust plant**.)

golden aster: *Chrysopsis* (See **aster**.)

golden bamboo: *Phyllostachys aurea*

golden bells: *Emmenanthe penduliflora* (See **whispering bells**.)

golden brodiaea: *Triteleia ixioides* (See **pretty face**.)

golden buffalo: *Ribes aureum, R. odoratum*

golden candle: *Pachystachys lutea*

golden-carpet: *Sedum acre* (See **stone-crop, mossy**.)

golden cassia: *Cassia fasciculata* (See **partridge pea, senna, prairie** and **sensitive pea**.)

golden chain: *Laburnum, L. anagyroides*

golden chain tree: *Laburnum*

golden club: *Orontium* aquaticum (See **tuckahoe**.)

golden crownbeard: *Verbesina encelioides* (See **crownbeard**.)

golden cup: *Hunnemannia, H. fumariifolia* (See **Mexican tulip poppy**.)

golden dewdrop: *Duranta repens* (See **pigeonberry** and **sky flower**.)

golden eardrops: *Dicentra chrysantha* (See **eardrop**.)

golden feather palm: *Chrysalidocarpus lutescens*

golden-fleece: *Dyssodia tenuiloba* (See **marigold, fetid**.)

golden flower: *Aurinia saxatile, Chrysanthemum segetum*

golden garlic: *Allium moly*

golden glow: *Rudbeckia lacinata*

golden groundsel: *Senecio aureus* (See **liferoot, squaw-weed** and **stagger-wort**.)

golden larch: *Pseudolarix*, P. *kaempferi*

golden marguerite: *Anthemis tinctoria*

golden mimosa: *Acacia baileyana* (See **wattle, Cootamundra**.)

goldenpert: *Gratiola aurea*

golden polypody: *Polypodium aureum*

golden ragwort: *Senecio aureus* (See **liferoot, squaw-weed** and **stagger-wort**.)

goldenrain tree: *Cassia fistula* **(See shower tree, golden**.)

golden rain tree: *Koelreuteria*, K. *paniculata*

goldenrod: *Solidago*

goldenrod, hybrid: *Solidago*

golden saxifrage: *Chrysosplenium*

goldenseal: *Hydrastis*, H. *canadensis* (See **orangeroot** and **yellow-root**.)

golden shower: *Cassia fistula*, *Pyrostegia venusta* (See **flameflower**.)

golden-slipper: *Cypripedium*, *Calceolus pubescens* (See **Venus's-shoe**.)

golden star: *Chrysogonum virginianum*

golden stars: *Bloomeria*, B. *crocea*

golden thistle: *Scolymus hispanicus* (See **Spanish oyster plant**.)

golden tuft: *Aurinia saxatile* (See **madwort, rock**.), *Helichrysum orientale*

golden tuft alyssum: *Aurinia saxatilis* (See **madwort, rock**.)

golden wood millet: *Milium effusum*

golden yarrow: *Achillea millefolium*

goldfern: *Pityrogramma chrysophylla* (See **gold fern**.)

gold fields: *Lasthenia chrysotoma*

goldflower: *Helichrysum orientale*, *Hymenoxys Cooperi*

goldilocks: *Aster linosyris*, *Chrysocoma*

goldthread: *Coptis*

goldylocks: *Aster linosyris* (See **goldilocks**.), *Chrysocoma* (See **goldilocks**.)

gold moss: *Sedum acre* (See **stonecrop, mossy**.)

gold of pleasure: *Camelina sativa*

gomuti: *Arenga pinnata*

gomuto: *Arenga pinnata* (See **gomuti**.)

goober: *Arachis*

good-king-harry: *Chenopodium Bonus-Henricus* (See **good-king-henry**.)

good-king-henry: *Chenopodium*, C. *Bonus-Henricus* (See **goosefoot** and **spinach, wild**.)

good-luck leaf: *Kalanchoe pinnata* (See **love plant, Mexican**.)

good-luck plant: *Cordyline terminalis* (See **ti**.)

gooseberry: ***Ribes***

gooseberry, common: ***Ribes*** *grossularia, R. uva-crispa*

gooseberry, fuschia-flowered: ***Ribes*** *speciosum*

gooseberry tree: ***Phyllanthus*** *acidus*

goosefoot: ***Chenopodium***, *C. Bonus-Henricus* (See **spinach, wild**.)

goosegrass: *Galium* (See **loveman**.)

goose grass: *Bromus mollis, Potentilla Anserina* (See **silverweed**.)

goose tansy: *Potentilla Anserina* (See **goose grass** and **silverweed**.)

goosetongue: *Achillea Ptarmica, Galium*

gopher plant: *Euphorbia Lathyris* (See **mole plant**.)

gopherwood: *Cladrastus lutea*

gorgon: *Euryale ferox* (See **furze** and **lily, prickly water**.)

gorse: *Genista anglica* (See **furze**.), *Ulex, U. Europaeus*

goutweed: ***Aegopodium*** *Podagraria* (See **goatweed** and **herb Gerard**.)

governor's plum: *Flacourtia indica*

grace garlic: ***Nothoscordum***

Grampian stringybark: *Eucalyptus alpina* (See **stringybark**.)

granadilla: *Passiflora quadrangularis* (See **passionflower**.)

grape: ***Vitis***

grape, European: ***Vitis*** *vinifera*

grape fern: *Botrychium*

grapefruit: *Citrus maxima*

grape hyacinth: ***Muscari*** (See **muskflower**.), *M. botryoides*

grape ivy: ***Cissus*** (See **treebine**.), *C. rhombifolia*

grape, slipskin: ***Vitis*** *Labrusca*

grassnut: *Triteleia laxa* (See **lily, triplet**.)

grass nut: ***Arachis***

grass-of-Parnassus: ***Parnassia***

grass palm: *Cordyline australis* (See **lily, palm**.)

grass pink: ***Calopogon***, *C. tuberosus* (See **swamp pink**.)

grass tree: ***Xanthorrhoea***

grassy-bells: *Edraianthus*

grassy-leaved sweet flag: ***Acorus*** *gramineus*

gravel plant: *Epigaea repens*

gravelroot: *Collinsonia canadensis, Eupatorium purpureum*

graybeard: *Tillandsia usneoides* (See **hanging moss, long moss** and **Spanish moss**.)

gray pine: *Pinus Banksiana* (See **scrub pine**.)

greasewood: *Salvia apiana* (See **sage, white**.)

great angelica: *Archangelica atropupurea* (See **masterwort**.)

great chickweed: *Stellaria pubera* (See **starwort**.)

greater burnet saxifrage: *Pimpinella major*

greater stitchwort: *Stellaria Holostea* (See **snapjack**.)

great laurel: *Rhododendron maximum* (See **laurel**.)

Grecian laurel: *Laurus nobilis*

Greek myrtle: *Myrtus communis* (See **myrtle**.)

Greek valerian: *Polemonium caeruleum*

green amaranth: *Amaranthus retroflexus* (See **pigweed**.)

green bean: *Phaseolus vulgaris*

greenbrier: *Smilax*, *S. rotundifolia* (See **bamboo-brier** and **horse brier**.)

green broom: *Genista tinctoria*

green dragon: *Dracunculus*

green-dragon: *Arisaema Draconitum*

green gentian: *Frasera*

greening-weed: *Genista tinctoria* (See **green broom**.)

green pea: *Pisum sativum*

green-stem Joe-Pye-weed: *Eupatorium purpureum* (See **Joe-Pye weed**.)

green-weed: *Genista tinctoria* (See **green broom**.)

grim-the-collier: *Hieracium aurantiacum*

gripgrass: *Galium*

gromwell: *Lithospermum* (See **stoneseed**.)

ground ash: *Aegopodium Podagraria* (See **herb Gerard**.)

ground cedar: *Juniperus communis*

ground cherry: *Physalis Alkekengi* (See **strawberry tomato**.), *P. peruviana*

ground elder: *Aegopodium Podagraria* (See **herb Gerard**.)

ground hemlock: *Taxus canadensis*

ground ivy: *Glechoma*, *G. hederacea* (See **gill-over-the-ground**.)

groundnut: *Apios tuberosa*, *Arachis*, *A. hypogaea* (See **earthnut**.)

ground pine: *Lycopodium*, *Lycopodium clavatum* (See **staghorn moss**.), *L. obscurum*

ground pink: *Phlox subulata*

ground plum: *Astragalus crassicarpus*

groundsel: *Senecio*

groundsel bush: *Baccharis halimifolia* (See **myrtle, sea, groundsel tree** and **silverling**.)

groundsel, golden: *Senecio aureus* (See **ragwort, golden**.)

groundsel tree: *Baccharis halimifolia* (See **myrtle, sea** and **silverling**.)

grugru: *Acrocomia* (See **macaw palm**.)

grugru palm: *Acrocomia*

Guadalupe palm: *Brahea*, *B. edulis*

guanabana: *Annona muricata*

guango: *Samanea Saman*

guarabu: *Astronium*

guava: *Psidium*, *P. Guayava*

guelder rose: *Viburnum opulus*, *V. Opulus Roseum* (See **marsh elder**.)

guinea-hen: *Fritillaria Meleagris*

guinea-hen flower: *Fritillaria Meleagris* (See **guinea-hen**.)

guinea-hen tulip: *Fritillaria Meleagris* (See **daffodil, checkered, lily, checkered** and **snake's-head**.)

gum: *Eucalyptus, Liquidambar, Nyssa*

gumbo: *Abelmoshus esculentus* (See **okra**.)

gumbo-limbo: *Bursera Simaruba*

gum elastic: *Bumelia*

gum-lac: *Schleichera oleosa*

gum plant: *Grindelia* (See **rosin plant**.)

gumweed: *Grindelia* (See **gum plant** and **rosin plant**.)

gumwood: *Commidendron rugosum*

gypsyweed: *Veronica officionalis*

gypsywort: *Lycopus americanus*, *L. europaeus*

H

habbel: *Juniperus drupacea* (See **plum juniper**.)

hackberry: *Celtis* (See **one-berry**.), *C. occidentalis*

hackia: *Tabebuia*

hackmatack: *Larix laricina* (See **tamarack**.), *Populus balsamifera* (See **necklace poplar** and **tacamahac**.)

haekaro: *Pittosporum umbellatum*

hagberry: *Celtis australis* (See **hackberry**.), *Prunus Padus*

hag-taper: *Verbascum olympicum* (See **mullein**.)

hair grass: *Koelaria*

hair palm: *Chamaerops humilis*

hair-trigger flower: *Stylidium*

hairy melon: *Benincasa hispida* (See **wax gourd**.)

Hamburg: *Vitis vinifera*

hammock fern: *Blechnum occidentale*

handkerchief tree: *Davidia involucrata* (See **dove tree**.)

hanging moss: *Ramalina, Tillandsia usneoides, Usnea*

harbinger-of-spring: *Erigenia bulbosa*

hard fern: *Blechnum*

hard heads: *Centaurea nigra* (See **horse knob**.)

hardhack: *Spirea tomentosa* (See **steeplebush**.)

Harding grass: *Phalaris tuberosa*

hardock: *Arctium*

hardy ageratum: *Eupatorium coelestinum* (See **mistflower**.)

hardy kiwi: *Actinidia arguta* (See **yang-tao**.)

hardy orange: *Poncirus, P. trifoliata* (See **orange, wild** and **trifoliate orange**.)

harebell: *Campanula rotundifolia, Endy-*

mion nonscriptus (See **hyacinth, wood**.)

harefoot: *Trifolium arvense*

hare's-bane: *Aconitum lycoctonum*

hare's-beard: *Verbascum olympicum* (See **mullein**.), *V. Thapsus*

hare's-ear: *Bupleurum rotundifolium*

hare's-foot: *Polypodium aureum*

hare's-tail grass: *Lagurus ovatus*

haricot: *Phaseolus vulgaris* (See **bean** and **kidney bean**.)

haricot bean: *Phaseolus vulgaris*

harlock: *Actium Lappa*

harpula: *Harpullia cupanioides*

Hartford fern: *Lygodium, L. palmatum* (See **climbing fern**.)

hart's-eye: *Origanum dictamnus*

hart's-thorn: *Rhamnus cathartica*

hart's-tongue: *Phyllitis Scolopendrium, Polybotria cervina*

hart's-tongue fern: *Asplenium scolopendrium* (See **Phyllitis**.), *Phyllitis scolopendrium*

hasheesh: *Cannabis sativa* (See **hashish**.)

hashish: *Cannabis sativa*

Hawaiian good-luck plant: *Cordyline terminalis* (See **ti**.)

Hawaiian wood rose: *Merremia tuberosa* (See **morning glory, Ceylon** and **woodbine, Spanish**.)

hawk's-beard: *Crepis*

hawkweed: *Hieracium, H. aurantiacum* (See **king devil**.), *Hieracium venosum* (See **rattlesnake weed**.)

hawthorn: *Crataegus* (See **Maybloom, Maybush** and **thorn**.), *C. laevigata*

haybells: *Uvularia* (See **merrybells**.)

hay-scented fern: *Dennstaedtia punctilobula*

hazel: *Corylus* (See **filbert**.)

hazel alder: *Alnus rugosa* (See **alder**.)

hazel, European: *Corylus Avellana*

hazelnut: *Corylus*

hazelwort: *Asarum europaeum*

head betony: *Pedicularis canadensis*

heal-all: *Collinsonia canadensis, Habenaria orbiculata, Prunella vulgaris, Sedum Rosea*

healing herb: *Symphytum officinale*

heart liverleaf: *Hepatica*

heartpea: *Cardiospermum Halicacabum*

heartsease: *Viola, V. tricolor* (See **love-in-idleness**.)

heartseed: *Cardiospermum*

heart snakeroot: *Asarum canadense*

heath: *Erica*

heath pea: *Lathyrus japonicus* (See **seaside pea**.)

heather: *Calluna vulgaris* (See **ling**.)

heather bell: *Erica cinerea*
heathwort: *Calluna, Erica*
heavenly bamboo: *Nandina domestica*
heavy pine: *Pinus ponderosa*
hedge apple: *Maclura pomifera*
hedge bindweed: *Calystegia sepium*
(See **morning glory, wild**.)
hedge fern: *Polystichum aculeatum, P.
setiferum*
hedgehog cactus: *Echinocereus*
hedge maple: *Acer campestre* (See **mazer tree**.)
hedge nettle: *Stachys*
hedge pink: *Saponaria officinalis*
hedge plant: *Ligustrum*
he-huckleberry: *Cyrilla racemiflora,
Lyonia ligustrina* (See **maleberry**.)
heliotrope: *Heliotropium, Valeriana
officinalis*
heliotrope, garden: *Valeriana* (See
valerian.)
hellebore, false: *Helleborus, Veratrum*
helleborine: *Cephalanthera, Epipactis*
hellweed: *Cucutus*
helmetflower: *Aconitum Napellus*
(See **monkshood**.), *Coryanthes,
Scutellaria*
helmet orchid: *Galeandra lacustris*
hemlock: *Conium maculatum* (See
poison hemlock.), *Tsuga*

hemlock, spotted: *Cicuta maculata* (See
hemlock, water.)
hemlock, spotted water: *Cicuta maculata*
(See **hemlock, water**.)
hemlock spruce: *Tsuga*
hemlock, water: *Cicuta maculata*
hemp: *Cannabis, C. sativa* (See **marijuana**.)
hemp agrimony: *Eupatorium*
hemp dogbane: *Apocynum cannabinum*
(See **Indian hemp**.)
hemp nettle: *Galeopsis*
hemp tree: *Vitex Agnus-castus* (See
chaste tree, pepper, wild and **sage
tree**.)
hempweed: *Eupatorium cannabinum*
hempweed, climbing: *Mikania scandens*
hen and chickens: *Sempervivum tectorum*
(See **houseleek** and **thunder plant**.)
henbane: *Hyoscyamus* (See **nightshade**.), *H. niger* (See **stinking
nightshade**.)
henna: *Lawsonia inermis* (See **mignonette, Jamaica**.)
he-oak: *Casuarina*
herald-of-summer: *Clarkia amoena* (See
satinflower.)
herald's-trumpet: *Beaumontia grandiflora*
(See **Easter-heralds-trumpet**.)

herb Barbara: *Barbarea vulgaris*

herb Bennet: *Geum urbanum*

herb carpenter: *Prunella vulgaris*

herb Christopher: *Filipendula ulmaria, Osmunda regalis, Stachys officinalis*

herb Gerard: ***Aegopodium*** *Podagraria*

herb-grace: *Ruta graveolens* **(See herb-of-grace.)**

herb lily: *Alstroemeria haemantha*

herb Louisa: *Aloysia triphylla*

herb Margaret: *Bellis perennis*

herb-of-grace: *Ruta* (See **rue**.), *R. graveolens*

herb-of-repentance: *Ruta graveolens* (See **herb-of-grace**.)

herb patience: ***Rumex*** *patientia*

herb-repentance: *Ruta graveolens* (See herb-of-grace.)

herb Robert: *Geranium Robertianum* (See **garden-gate** and **kiss-me**.)

herb, southernwood: ***Artemisia*** *Abrotanum*

herb, trinity: *Hepatica, Viola tricolor*

herb twopence: *Lysimachia Nummularia* (See **moneywort**.)

Hercule's-club: *Aralia spinosa* (See **spikenard tree**.), *Zanthoxylum clava-Hercules* (See **orange, wild, pepperwood** and **sea ash**.)

heronbill: ***Erodium*** (See **heron's-bill**.)

heron's bill: ***Erodium*** (See **stork's-bill**.)

hesper palm: ***Brahea***

Hiba arborvitae: ***Thujopsis*** *dolabrata*

Hiba cedar: *Thujopsis dolabrata* (See **false arborvitae**.)

hibiscus, Chinese: ***Hibiscus*** *rosa-sinensis*

hibiscus, Hawaiian: ***Hibiscus*** *rosa-sinensis*

hickory: ***Carya***

hickory acacia: *Acacia leprosa*

hickory elm: *Ulmus Thomasii*

hickory pine: *Carya ovata* (See **shagbark hickory**.), *Pinus aristata*

hickory, shagbark: *Carya ovata*

hidden lily: ***Curcuma***

highbush cranberry: *Viburnum Opulus* (See **cranberry tree**.), *Viburnum trilobum* (See **cranberry bush**.)

high-ground willow oak: *Quercus incana* (See **oak, bluejack** and **sand jack**.)

high mallow: *Malva sylvestris*

hill goosebery: *Rhodomyrtus tomentosa* (See **myrtle, downy**.)

hill guava: *Rhodomyrtus tomentosa* (See **myrtle, downy**.)

hillock tree: *Melaleuca hypericifolia*

hills-of-snow: *Hydrangea arborescens*

hillwort: *Mentha pulegium*

Himalayan honeysuckle: ***Leycesteria*** *formosa*

Himalayan white pine: *Pinus wallichiana* (See **pine, Bhutan**.)

hinoki cypress: *Chamaecyparis obtusa* (See **Japanese cypress** and **sun tree**.)

hirse: *Sorghum bicolor*

Hispaniolan palmetto: ***Sabal Blackburniana***

hive vine: *Mitchella*

hoary alyssum: ***Berteroa*** *incana*

hoary pea: ***Tephrosia*** *virginiana* (See **Alyssum**.)

hobblebush: *Viburnum alnifolium* (See **moosewood**.)

hog-bean: *Hyoscyamus niger* (See **henbane**.)

hog cranberry: *Arctostaphylos Uva-ursi* (See **kinnikinnik**.)

hognut: *Carya glabra*

hog peanut: ***Amphicarpaea***

hog plum: *Prunus angustifolia*

hog's-bean: *Hyoscyamus niger* (See **henbane** and **hog bean**.)

holly: *Ilex*

holly barberry: *Mahonia Aquifolium* (See **Oregon grape**.)

holly, box: *Ruscus aculeatus*

holly, California: ***Heteromeles***, *H. arbutifolia* (See **toyon**.)

holly, English: *Ilex Aquifolium*

holly fern: ***Cyrtomium***, *C. falcatum, Polystichum Lonchitis*

holly grape: ***Mahonia***

hollyhock: ***Alcea*** (See **Malvaceae**.)

hollyhock-rose: *Selaginella lepidophylla*

holly, laurel: *Prunus ilicifolia*

hollyleaf cherry: *Prunus ilicifolia* (See **mountain holly**.)

hollyleaf sweetspire: ***Itea*** *ilicifolia*

holly-leaved cherry: *Prunus ilicifolia* (See **mountain holly**.)

holly mahonia: *Mahonia Aquifolium* (See **Oregon grape**.)

holly, rose: *Turnera ulmifolia*

holly, sea: *Eryngium maritimum*

holm: *Quercus Ilex*

holy clover: *Onobrychis viciifolia* (See **sainfoin**.)

Holy-Ghost: *Angelica sylvestris*

Holy Ghost flower: ***Peristeria*** *elata*

holy herb: *Verbena officinalis*

holy thistle: *Silybum Marianum* (See **milk thistle**.)

honesty: ***Lunaria***, *L. annua* (See **pennyflower**.), *L. rediviva*

honey bell: ***Hermannia*** *verticillata*

honeyberry: *Celtis australis* (See **lotus tree**.), *Melicoccus bijugatus* (See **mamoncillo**.)

honeybloom: *Apcynum androsaemifolium*

honey bread: *Ceratonia siliqua*

honeybush: *Melianthus*

honeybush, large: *Melianthus major*

honeydew: *Cucumis melo*

honeyflower: *Lambertia formosa, Melianthus major, Protea mellifera* (See **sugar bush**.)

honey locust: *Gleditsia, G. triacanthos*

honey mesquite: *Prosopis juliflora*

honey myrtle: *Melaleuca*

honeysuckle: *Aquilegia, Lonicera, L. Periclymenum, Rhododendron nudiflorum* (See **pinxter flower**.), *R. periclymenoides* (See **pinxter flower**.), *R. prinophyllum*

honey vine: *Cynanchum*

honeywort: *Cerinthe*

Hong Kong orchid tree: *Bauhinia blakeana*

hookweed: *Prunella vulgaris*

hook-spur violet: *Viola adunca* (See **western dog violet**.)

hoop ash: *Celtis occidentalis* (See **hackberry**.), *Fraxinus sambucifolia*

hoop-petticoat daffodil: *Narcissus Bulbocodium*

hoop pine: *Araucaria cinninghamii* (See **Moreton Bay pine**.)

hop: *Humulus Lupulus*

hopbush: *Dodonaea*

hop clover: *Medicago lupulina* (See **shamrock**.)

hop hornbeam: *Ostrya*

hop marjoram: *Origanum Dictamnus*

hop tree: *Ptelea trifoliata* (See **trefoil, shrubby**.), *Ptelea* (See **wafer ash**.), *Pteles trifoliata*

hop trefoil: *Trifolium procumbens*

horehound: *Marrubium vulgare*

hornbeam: *Carpinus*

horned pondweed: *Zannichellia*

horned poppy: *Argemone, Glaucium,* (See **sea poppy**.)

horned rampion: *Phyteuma*

horn-of-plenty: *Fedia cornucopiae*

hornwort: *Ceratophyllum*

horse balm: *Centaurea* (See **knapweed**.), *Collinsonia, Collinsonia canadensis* (See **balm** and **gravelroot**.)

horse bean: *Vicia faba* (See **tick bean**.)

horse brier: *Smilax rotundifolia*

horse chestnut: *Aesculus, A. Hippocastanum* (See **chestnut**.)

horse daisy: *Chrysanthemum Leucanthemum*

horse elder: *Inula Helenium*

horsefly weed: *Baptisia tinctoria*

horsefoot: *Tussilago Farfara*

horse gentian: *Triosteum*

horse gowan: *Chrysanthemum Leucanthemum, Crepis, Hypochoeris, Matricaria recutita, Taraxacum officinale*

horsehair vine: *Muehlenbeckia complexa* (See **necklace vine**.)

horseheal: *Inula Helenium* (See **horse elder**.)

horseheel: *Inula Helenium* (See **horseheal**.)

horsehoof: *Tussilago Farfara* (See **horsefoot**.)

horse knob: *Centaurea nigra* (See **horse knob**.)

horsemint: *Monarda*, *M. punctata*

horse nettle: *Solanum carolinense*

horse parsley: *Smyrnium Olusatrum*

horseradish: *Armoracia rusticana*

horseradish tree: *Moringa pterygosperma*

horseshoe vetch: *Hippocrepis*

horse sorrel: *Rumex hydrolapathum*

horse sugar: *Symplocos*

horsetail: *Equisetum, E. hyemale* (See **scouring rush**.)

horsetail tree: *Casuarina equisetifolia*

horse violet: *Viola pedata*

horseweed: *Collinnsinia Canadensis* (See **horse balm**.)

hot apple: *Aptenia cordifolia*

Hottentot bread: *Dioscorea elephantipes* (See **tortoise plant**.)

Hottentot fig: *Carpobrotus edulis*

hound's-tongue: *Cynoglossum*

house iris: *Neomarica* (See **lily, toadcup**.)

houseleek: *Sempervivum tectorum* (See **thunder plant**.)

houseleek, common: *Sempervivum tectorum* (See **houseleek**.)

hubbard squash: *Cucurbita maxima* (See **squash**.)

huckleberry: *Cyrilla racemiflora* (See **leatherwood**.), *Gaylussacia, G. frondosa, Vaccinium*

huisache: *Acacia Farnesiana* (See **sponge tree**.)

hulver: *Ilex Aquifolium*

humble plant: *Mimosa pudica* (See **sensitive-plant**.)

hummingbird flower: *Zauschneria*

huntsman's-cup: *Sarracenia* (See **Indian cup**.), *Sarracenia purpurea* (See **side saddle flower**.)

huntsman's-horn: *Sarracenia flava*

hurr-bur: *Acrtium Lappa*

hurricane plant: *Monstera deliciosa* (See **Mexican bamboo** and **window plant**.)

husk-tomato: *Physalis Alkekengi* (See **strawberry tomato**.)

hyacinth: *Hyacinthus* (See **jacinth**.)

hyacinth bean: ***Dolichos*** *Lablab*

hyacinth, fringe: *Muscari comosum* (See **hyacinth, tassel**.)

hyacinth, grape: *Muscari*

hyacinth, meadow: *Camassia scilloides* (See **hyacinth, wild**.)

hyacinth, musk: *Muscari racemosum*

hyacinth, nutmeg: *Muscari racemosum*

hyacinth-of-Peru: *Scilla peruuviana* (See **hyacinth, Peruvian** and **lily, Cuban**.)

hyacinth, Peruvian: *Scilla peruuviana*

hyacinth, scilla, large: *Scilla hyacinthoides*

hyacinth, star: *Scilla amoena*

hyacinth, starry: *Scilla autumnalis*

hyacinth, tassel: *Muscari comosum*

hyacinth, water: *Eichhornia* (See **hemlock, water**.)

hyacinth, wild: *Camassia scilloides*

hyacinth, wood: *Endymion, E. nonscriptus*

hydrangea vine, Japanese: *Schizophragma hydrangeoides*

hyssop: ***Hyssopus***, *H. officinalis*

I

icaco: *Chrysobalanus Icaco*

Iceland poppy: *Papaver nudicaule* (See **poppy**.)

ice plant: *Aptenia,* ***Carpobrotus****, C. edulis* (See **Hottentot fig**.) *C. chilensis* (See **pig's-face** and **sea fig**.), ***Cephalophyllum****, Delosperma, Drosanthemum,* ***Lampranthus****, Malephora,* ***Mesembryanthemum****, Oscularia*

icicle plant: ***Mesembryanthemum***

icicle radish: *Raphanus sativus* (See **radish**.)

ilang-ilang: ***Cananga*** *odorata* (See **ylang-ylang**.)

immortelle: ***Helichrysum,*** ***Helipterum,*** ***Xeranthemum*** *annuum*

immortelle, mountain: *Erythrina Poeppigiana*

incense cedar: *Calocedrus* (See **Libocedrus**.), *C. decurrens, Libocedrus*

India date palm: ***Phoenix*** *sylvestris*

Indian almond: *Terminalia catappa* (See **tropical almond**.)

Indian apple: *Podophyllum peltatum*

Indian arrow: *Euonymus atropurpurea*

Indian balm: *Trillium, T. recurvatum*

Indian bean: *Catalpa*

Indian beech: ***Pongamia***

Indian caraway: *Perideridia Gairdneri* (See **squawroot**.)

Indian cherry: *Amelanchier, Rhamnus caroliniana*

Indian chocolate: ***Geum*** *rivale* (See **water avens**.)

Indian corn: *Zea mays*

Indian cress: ***Tropaeolum*** *majus*

Indian cucumber: *Medeola virginica*

Indian cucumber root: *Medeola virginica* (See **cucumber root** and **Indian cucumber**.)

Indian cup: *Sarracenia, S. purpurea* (See **side saddle flower**.)

Indian currant: *Symphoricarpus orbiculatus* (See **turkey berry tree**.)

Indian elm: *Ulmus rubra*

Indian fig: *Opuntia Ficus-indica*

Indian hemp: *Apocynum cannabinum* (See **hashish**.)

Indian kale: *Xanthosoma Lindenii* (See **spoonflower**.)

Indian laburnum: *Cassia fistula* (See **shower tree, golden**.)

Indian lettuce: *Pyrola rotundifolia* (See **lily-of-the-valley, wild**.)

Indian licorice: *Abrus precatorius* (See **pea, rosary** and **vine, red-beard**.)

Indian madder: *Rubia* cordifolia

Indian mallow: *Abutilon Theophrasti* (See **velvetleaf**.)

Indian mulberry: *Morinda* citrifolia

Indian paint: *Hydrastis Canadensis* (See **yellowroot**.)

Indian-paintbrush: *Castilleja californica, C. coccinea*

Indian physic: *Gillenia , G. trifoliata* (See **Indian root**.)

Indian pink: *Spigelia marilandica* (See **spiderwort**.)

Indian pipe: *Monotropa uniflora* (See **fitroot** and **pinesap**.)

Indian plum: *Oemleria cerasiformis* (See **osoberry**.)

Indian poke: *Helleborus viride* (See **hellebore**.), *Veratrum viride* (See **swamp hellebore**.)

Indian rhododendron: *Melastoma malabathricum*

Indian root: *Aralia racemosa, Gillenia trifoliata*

Indian sanicle: *Eupatorium rugosum* (See **snakeroot, white**.)

Indian's-dream: *Pellaea atropurea*

Indian shoe: *Cypripedium* (See **moccasin flower**.)

Indian shot: *Canna*

Indian sorrel: *Hibiscus sabdariffa* (See **roselle**.)

Indian spice: *Vitex agnus-castus* (See **chaste tree** and **pepper, wild**.)

Indian-spice tree: *Vitex Agnus-castus* (See **hemp tree** and **sage tree**.)

Indian tobacco: *Lobelia inflata*

Indian turnip: *Arisaema triphyllum* (See **jack-in-the-pulpit**.), *Psoralea esculenta* (See **pomme blanche**.)

Indian walnut: *Aleurites moluccana* (See **tallow tree**.)

Indian warrior: *Pedicularis densiflora*

India-rubber plant: *Ficus elastica* (See **rubber plant**.)

India rubber vine: *Cryptostegia grandiflora* (See **rubber vine**.)

India wheat: *Fagopyrum tataricum*

indigo: *Indigofera*

indigo broom: *Baptisia australis*

indigo squill: **Camassia** *scilloides* (See **hyacinth, wild**.)

indigo, wild: *Baptisia australis*

indoor linden: **Sparmannia**

inkberry: *Ilex glabra* (See **winterberry, common**.)

inkberry-weed: *Phytolacca* (See **pokeweed**.)

ink plant: *Cloriaria myrtifolia*

innocence: **Hedyotis** *caerulea*

interior live oak: *Quercus Wislizeni* (See **live-oak**.)

interrupted fern: *Osmunda Claytoniana*

Irish furze: *Ulex europaeus strictus*

Irish heath: **Daboecia** *cantabrica*

Irish moss: *Arenaria verna* (See **pearlwort**.), *Sagina* (See **moss**.), *S. subulata* (See **pearlwort**.), *Soleirolia Soleirolii*

Irish shamrock: *Oxalis Acetosella* (See **shamrock**.)

ironbark tree: *Eucalyptus*

iron fern: *Rumohra adantiaformis* (See **leather fern**.)

ironheads: *Centuarea nigra*

iron oak: *Quercus stellata*

irontree: **Metrosideros**

ironweed: **Vernonia**

ironwood: *Bumelia lycioides* (See **southern buckthorn**.), *Cyrilla racemiflora* (See **leatherwood**.)

ironwort: *Sideritis*

islay: *Prunus ilicifolia* (See **mountain holly**.)

Italian bellflower: *Campanula isophylla* (See **star-of-Bethlehem**.)

Italian buckthorn: **Rhamnus** *alaternus*

Italian lovage: *Levisticum officinale* (See **lovage**.)

Italian stone pine: *Pinus pinea* (See **parasol fir** and **stone pine**.)

ita palm: **Mauritia** *flexuosa*

itchweed: **Helleborus** *viride* (See **hellebore**.), *Veratrum viride* (See **Indian poke** and **hellebore**.)

Ithuriel's spear: *Triteleia laxa*

ivory-leaves: *Gaultheria procumbens* (See **spiceberry**.)

ivory nut: *Phytelephas macrocarpa*

ivory tree: *Wrightia tinctoria*

ivy: *Hedera, Kalmia latifolia* (See **mountain laurel**.)

J

jaboticaba: *Myrciaria cauliflora*

jacinth: *Hyacinthus*

jackfruit: *Artocarpus heterophyllus*

jack-in-the-bush: *Umbilicus rupestris*

jack-in-the-pulpit: *Arisaema triphyllum* (See **Indian turnip**.)

jack oak: *Quercus marilandica* (See **oak, barren**.)

jack pine: *Pinus Banksiana* (See **scrub pine**.)

jack tree: *Artocarpus heterophyllus* (See **jackfruit**.)

jackwood: *Cordia dentata* (See **loblolly tree**.)

Jacobean lily: *Sprekelia formosissima* (See **Saint-James's-lily**.)

Jacob's-coat: *Acalypha Wilkesiana* (See **copperleaf**.)

Jacob's ladder: *Pedilanthus tithymaloides*, **Polemonium**, *P. caeruleum*, (See **valerian, Greek**.)

Jacob's-rod: **Asphodeline**

Jacob's staff: *Fouquieria splendens* (See **ocotillo** and **vine cactus**.)

jade plant: *Crassula arborescens, C. argentea*

jaggery palm: *Caryota, C. urens* (See **sago palm**.)

Jamaica: *Hibiscus sabdariffa* (See **roselle**.)

Jamaica nutmeg: *Monodora myristica*

Jamaica sorrel: *Hibiscus Sabdariffa* (See **sorrel, Indian** and **roselle**.)

jambolan: *Arisaema triphyllum* (See **jack-in-the-pulpit**.)

jambolana: *Syzygium cumini*

jambu: *Syzygium cumini*

Jamestown weed: *Datura Stramonium*

jamrosade: *Syzygium Jambos*

Japan clover: *Lespedeza striata*
Japanese angelica tree: *Aralia elata*
Japanese apricot: *Prunus Mume*
Japanese arborvitae: *Thuja Standishii*
Japanese artichoke: *Stachys affinis*
Japanese ash: *Fraxinus manchurica*
Japanese ashberry: *Mahonia japonica*
Japanese aspen: *Populus Sieboldii*
Japanese azalea: *Rhododendron*
Japanese banana: *Musa Basjoo*
Japanese barberry: *Berberis Thunbergii*
Japanese bead tree: **Melia** *Azedarach* (See **lilac, Indian**.)
Japanese beautyberry: *Callicarpa japonica*
Japanese beech: *Fagus crenata*
Japanese bittersweet: *Celastrus orbiculatus*
Japanese black pine: *Pinus Thunbergiana*
Japanese carnelian cherry: *Cornus officinalis* (See **Japanese cornel dogwood**.)
Japanese cedar: *Crytomeria japonica* (See **sugi**.)
Japanese cherry: *Prunus serrulata*
Japanese chestnut: *Castanea crenata*
Japanese climbing fern: *Lygodium japonicum*

Japanese cornel: *Cornus officinalis* (See **Japanese cornel dogwood**.)
Japanese cornel dogwood: *Cornus officinalis*
Japanese cypress: *Chamaecyparis obtusa*
Japanese false cypress: *Chamaecyparis obtusa* (See **sun tree**.)
Japanese fatsia: **Fatsia** *japonica*
Japanese felt fern: **Pyrrosia** *lingua*
Japanese fern palm: *Cycas revoluta* (See **sago palm**.)
Japanese flowering cherry: *Prunus serrulata* (See **Japanese cherry**.)
Japanese flowering plum: *Prunus Mume* (See **Japanese apricot**.)
Japanese flowering quince: *Chaenomeles speciosa* (See **quince**.)
Japanese hawthorn: *Rhaphiolepis umbellata*
Japanese hazel: *Corylus Sieboldiana*
Japanese hemlock: *Tsuga diversifolia, T. Sieboldii*
Japanese holly: *Ilex crenata*
Japanese honeysuckle: *Lonicera japonica*
Japanese hop: *Humulus japonicus*
Japanese hydrangea vine: **Schizophragma**
Japanese iris: *Iris ensata*
Japanese ivy: *Parthenocissus tricuspidata*

Japanese knotweed: *Polygonum cuspidatum* (See **Mexican bamboo** and **smartweed**.)

Japanese lacquer tree: *Rhus verniciflua* (See **varnish tree**.)

Japanese lantern: **Physalis** (See **winter cherry**.), *P. alkekengi*, *P. franchetii*

Japanese lantern plant: *Hibiscus schizopetalus*, *Physalis alkekengi*

Japanese laurel: *Acuba japonica*, *Crassula argentea*

Japanese lilac: *Syringa reticulata* (See **Japanese tree lilac**.) *S. villosa*

Japanese linden: *Tilia japonica*

Japanese live oak: *Quercus myrsinifolia* (See **live-oak**.)

Japanese maple: **Acer** *palmatum*

Japanese mint: *Mentha arvensis piperescens*

Japanese moss: **Soleirolia** *Soleirolii*

Japanese oak: *Lithocarpus glaber*

Japanese pagoda tree: **Sophora** *japonica* (See **pagoda tree**.)

Japanese pansy: **Achimenes**

Japanese parasol fir: *Sciadopitys verticillata*

Japanese pear: *Pyrus pyrifolia*

Japanese pepper: *Zanthoxylum piperitum* (See **pepper, Chinese**.)

Japanese persimmon: *Diospyros Kaki* (See **persimmon**.)

Japanese photinia: **Photinia** *glabra*

Japanese pink: *Dianthus chinensis*

Japanese pittosporum: *Pittosporum Tobira* (See **tobira**.)

Japanese plum: *Eriobotrya japonica*, *Prunus Japonica* (See **plum**.), *P. salicina*

Japanese poinsettia: *Pedilanthus tithymaloides* (See **slipper plant** and **spurge, slipper**.)

Japanese privet: *Ligustrum japonicum*, *L. lucidum*

Japanese quince: *Chaenomeles speciosa*

Japanese raisin tree: **Hovenia** *dulcis* (See **raisin tree**.)

Japanese red pine: *Pinus densiflora*

Japanese rose: **Kerria**, *K. japonica*

Japanese rubber plant: *Crassula argentea*

Japanese silver grass: **Miscanthus** *sinensis*

Japanese snowbell: *Styrax japonicus*, *Viburnum plicatim*

Japanese snowflower: *Deutzia gracilis*

Japanese spruce: *Abies Mariesii*, *Picea jezoensis*

Japanese spurge: **Pachysandra** *terminalis*

Japanese star anise: *Allicium anisatum*

Japanese storax: *Styrax japonicus* (See **Japanese snowbell**.)

Japanese tree lilac: *Syringa reticulata*

Japanese umbrella pine: *Pinus densiflora*, **Sciadopitys** *verticillata* (See **Japanese parasol fir** and **parasol fir**.)

Japanese walnut: *Juglans ailantifolia*

Japanese white pine: *Pinus parviflora*

Japanese wisteria: *Wisteria floribunda*

Japanese witch hazel: *Hamemelis japonica*

Japanese yew: **Podocarpus** *macrophyllus*, *Taxus cuspidata*

Japan globeflower: **Kerria**, *K. japonica* (See **Japanese rose**.)

Japan pepper: *Zanthoxylum piperitum* (See **pepper, Chinese**.)

japonica: *Camellia japonica*, *Chaenomeles speciosa* (See **Japanese quince**.), *Lagerstroemia indica*

jarool: *Lagerstroemia speciosa* (See **myrtle, queen's crape**.)

jasmine: *Jasminum*

jasmine, bastard: *Cestrum*

jasmine, Cape: *Gardenia jasminoides*

jasmine, Carolina: *Gelsemium sempervirens*

jasmine, Chilean: *Mandevilla laxa*

jasmine, night: *Nyctanthes arbor-tristis*

jasmine, red: *Plumeria rubra*

jaundice-berry: *Berberis vulgaris*

jaundice tree: *Berberis vulgaris* (See **jaundice-berry**.)

Java glory bean: **Clerodendrum**

javillo: *Hura crepitans* (See **sandbox tree**.)

jellico: *Angelica sylvestris*

jelly palm: **Butia**

jequirity: **Abrus**

Jersey pine: *Pinus virginiana* (See **scrub pine**.)

Jersey tea: *Ceanothus americanus*

Jerusalem artichoke: *Helianthes tuberosus*

Jerusalem cherry: *Solanum Pseudocapsium* (See **Solanum**.)

Jerusalem cowslip: *Pulmonaria officinalis* (See **sage, Jerusalem**.)

Jerusalem pine: *Pinus halepensis* (See **pine, Aleppo**.)

Jerusalem sage: **Phlomis** *fruticosa*, **Pulmonaria**

Jerusalem thorn: **Paliurus** *Spina-Christi* (See **Jew's thorn**.), **Parkinsonia** *aculeata*

jessamine, willow-leaved: *Cestrum pargui*

Jesuit nut: *Trapa natans* (See **water caltrop**.)

jetbead: *Rhodotypos scandens*

jewelweed: *Impatiens* (See **snapweed** and **touch-me-not**.), *I. capensis*, *I. pallida* (See **quick-in-the hand**.)

Jew's mallow: *Corchorus olitorius*

Jew's myrtle: *Ruscus aculeatus*

Jew's thorn: *Paliurus Spina-Christi*, *Ziziphus Jujuba*

jicama: *Pachyrhizus erosus*, *P. tuberosus*

jimpson: *Datura Stramonium* (See **jimsonweed**.)

jimpson-weed: *Datura Stramonium* (See **jimsonweed**.)

jimson: *Datura Stramonium* (See **jimsonweed**.)

jimsonweed: *Datura Stramonium* (See **Jamestown weed**.)

Job's tear's: *Coix Lacryma*

Joe-Pye weed: *Eupatorium purpureum* (See **gravelroot, motherwort** and **smoke weed**.) *Eupatorium maculatum*

joewood: *Jacquinia Barbasco*

John Crow beans: *Abrus*

John-go-to-bed-at-noon: *Tragopogon pratensis*

Johnny-jump-up: *Viola tricolor* (See **herb trinity, love-in-idleness** and **pansy**.)

joint fir: *Ephedra*

jointweed: *Polygonella*

jojoba: *Simmondsia chinensis*

jonquil: *Narcissus Jonquilla*

Joseph-and-Mary: *Pulmonaria officinalis*

Joseph's coat: *Alternanthera* (See **copperleaf**.), *Amaranthus tricolor*

Joshua tree: *Yucca brevifolia*

joss flower: *Narcissus Tazetta orientalis*

Jove's-fruit: *Lindera melissifolia*

Judas tree: *Cercis* (See **redbud**.), *C. Siliquastrum* (See **love tree**.)

jujube: *Ziziphus Jujuba* (See **Jew's thorn**.)

jumble-beads: *Abrus*

jumping bean: *Sapium, Sebastiana*

jumping seed: *Sapium* (See **jumping bean**.), *Sebastiana* (See **jumping bean**.)

juneberry: *Amelanchier* (See **Indian cherry**.)

jungle-flame: *Ixora coccinea* (See **flame-of-the-woods**.)

jungle geranium: *Ixora coccinea* (See **flame-of-the-woods**.)

juniper: *Juniperus*

jupiter's-beard: *Anthyllis*, **Centranthus** *ruber* (See **lilac, German** and **valerian, red**.), *Sempervivum tectorum*

jute: *Corchorus*

K

kaffir boom: *Erythrina caffra*
kaffir lily: *Clivia*, ***Schizostylis*** *coccinea*
kaffir plum: *Harpephyllum caffrum*
kahika: ***Podocarpus*** *dacrydioides* (See **kahikatea**.)
Kahikatea: *Podocarpus dacrydioides*
Kai apple: *Dovyalis caffra* (See **Kei apple**.)
kaki: *Diospyros Kaki*
kale: *Brassica oleracea*
kale, Indian: *Colocasia esculenta, Xanthosoma sagittifolium*
kale, wild: *Brassica Kaber*
kamani: *Terminalia catappa* (See **tropical almond**.)
kangaroo acacia: *Acacia armata* (See **kangaroo thorn**.)
kangaroo apple: *Solanum aviculare*
kangaroo grape: *Cissus antarctica*
kangaroo thorn: *Acacia armata*

Kangaroo treebine: ***Cissus*** *anarctica*
kangaroo vine: *Cissus antarctica* (See **kangaroo grape**.)
kaoliang: *Sorghum bicolor*
kapok: *Ceiba pentandra*
kapok tree: *Ceiba pentandra* (See **silk cotton tree**.)
karo: *Pittosporum crassifolium*
Karoo rose: ***Lapidaria*** *margaretae*
karum tree: ***Pongamia***
Kashmir bouquet: ***Clerodendrum*** (See **tubeflower**.)
katsura tree: ***Cercidiphyllum***, *C. Japonicum*
kauri pine: *Agathis*
kava: *Piper methystichum*
kawakawa: ***Macropiper*** *excelsum*
Kei apple: ***Dovyalis***, *D. caffra*
Kellogg oak: *Quercus Kelloggii* (See **Sonoma oak**.)

kenaf: *Hibiscus cannabinus*

Kenilworth ivy: *Cymbalaria* muralis (See **toadflax, ivy-leaved**.), *Linaria cymbalaria* (See **pennywort**.)

Kentia palm: *Howea*

Kentucky bluegrass: *Poa* pratensis

Kentucky coffee tree: *Gymnocladus dioica* (See **coffee tree, nicker tree** and **stump tree**.)

keyaki: *Zelkova serrata*

khair: *Acacia Catechu*

khat: *Catha edulis*

ki: *Cordyline terminalis*

kiabooca: *Pterocarpus indicus*

kidney bean: *Phaseolus vulgaris* (See **bean**.)

kidney vetch: *Anthyllis*, *A. Vulneraria* (See **lady's-finger** and **woundwort**.)

kidneywort: *Baccharis pilularis, Umbilicus rupestris*

kikar: *Acacia nilotica*

kimono plant: *Achimenes*

king bolete: *Boletus edulis* (See **mushroom**.)

kingcup: *Caltha palustris* (See **goldcup** and **lily, cow**.) *Ranunculus acris, R. bulbosus, R. repens*

king devil: *Hieracium aurantiacum*

king fern: *Osmunda regalis*

kingfisher daisy: *Felicia Bergeriana*

king nut: *Carya laciniosa*

king palm: *Archontophoenix, A. Cunninghamiana* (See **seaforthia**.)

king protea: *Protea* cynaroides

king's crown: *Jacobinia carnea, Justicia carnea* (See **plume flower**.)

king's spear: *Asphodeline lutea Eremurus* (See **desert candle**.)

kinnikinic: *Rhus vireus* (See **kinnikinnik**.)

kinnikinnik: *Arctostaphylos* Uva-ursi, *Cornus sericea, Rhus vireus*

kino: *Coccoloba Uvifera* (See **sea grape**.)

kiss-behind-the-garden-gate: *Viola* (See **garden gate**.)

kisses: *Viola tricolor* (See **kiss-me**.)

kiss-me: *Geranium robertianum, Saxifraga umbrosa, Viola tricolor*

kiss-me-over-the-garden-gate: *Polygonum* orientale (See **prince's-feather**.)

kittul: *Caryota urens* (See **toddy palm**.)

kiwi: *Actinidia chinensis*

kiwifruit: *Actinidia* deliciosa (See **kiwi** and **yang-tao**.)

knackaway: *Ehretia Anacua*

knapweed: *Centaurea, C. nigra* (See **horse knob** and **ironheads**.)

knawel: *Scleranthus*

knight's-spur: *Delphinium*
knobweed: *Centaurea* (See **knapweed**.)
knockaway: *Ehretia Anacua* (See
 knackaway.)
knotweed: ***Polygonum***, *P. capitatum*
 (See **smartweed**.)
koa: *Acacia koa*
kohlrabi: *Brassica oleraceae*

kola nut: *Cola acuminata*
Korean Evodia: *Evodia Danielii* (See
 star pepper.)
Korean mountain ash: ***Sorbus*** *alnifolia*
kudzu: *Pueraria lobata*
kudzu vine: *Pueraria lobata* (See
 kudzu.)
kumquat: ***Fortunella***

L

Labrador tea: ***Ledum*** *groenlandicum*

lacebark: *Brachychiton acerifolius, B. discolor,* **Hoheria** *populnea*

lace fern: *Cheilanthes gracillima*

lace flower, blue: *Trachymene coerulea*

laceleaf: *Aponogeton madagascariensis* (See **latticeleaf**.)

lacepod: ***Thysanocarpus*** (See **fringe-pod**.)

lacquer tree: *Rhus verniciflua* (See **varnish tree**.)

lac tree: *Schleichera oleosa*

ladies'-smock: ***Cardamine*** *pratensis* (See **lady's-smock** and **meadow cress**.)

ladies'-tobacco: ***Antennaria***

ladies'-tresses: ***Spiranthes*** (See **lady's-tresses**.)

lad's-love: *Artemisia Abrotanum* (See **southernwood**.)

ladybells: *Adenophora*

lady fern: ***Athyrium*** *Filix-femina*

ladyfinger: *Digitalis purpurea*

lady-of-the-night: *Brunfelsia americana*

lady's bedstraw: *Galium verum*

lady's bower: *Clematis Vitalba*

lady's-delight: *Viola tricolor*

lady's eardrops: *Fuschia* (See **eardrop**.)

lady's-earrings: ***Impatiens***

lady's-finger: *Abelmoschus esculentus,* ***Anthyllis***, *A. Vulneraria* (See **kidney vetch** and **woundwort**.)

lady's-glove: *Digitalis purpurea*

lady's leek: *Allium cernuum* (See **onion, wild**.)

lady-slipper: *Cypripedium* (See **lady's slipper**.)

lady's mantle: ***Alchemilla*** *vulgaris*

lady smock: *Cardamine pratensis* (See **lady's-smock** and **meadow cress**.)

lady's slipper: *Cypripedium* (See **Indian shoe**.), *Impatiens balsamina*, ***Phragmipedium***

lady's slippers: ***Paphiopedilum***

lady's sorrel: ***Oxalis*** *corniculata* (See **sorrel, wood**.)

lady's traces: *Spiranthes* (See **lady's-tresses**.)

lady's-tresses: *Spiranthes*

lambkill: *Kalmia angustifolia* (See **sheep laurel**.)

lamb's ears: ***Stachys*** *byzantina, S. officinalis*

lamb's lettuce: ***Valerianella***

lamb's-quarters: *Chenopodium album* (See **goosefoot**.)

lamb's-tongue: *Stomatium agninum* (See **sheep's-tongue**.)

lancepod: ***Lonchocarpus***

land cress: *Barbarea verna* (See **scurvy grass**.)

larch: *Larix*

larch, American: *Larix laricina* (See **tamarack**.)

larch, black: *Larix laricina* (See **tamarack**.)

larch, Chinese: *Larix Potaninii*

larch, Dahurian: *Larix Gmelinii*

larch, Dunkeld: *Larix Eurolepsis*

larch, European: *Larix decidua*

larch, golden: *Pseudolarix Kaempferi*

larch, Japanese: *Larix Kaempferei*

larch, Western: *Larix occidentalis*

large autumn scilla: *Scilla autumnalis* (See **hyacinth, starry**.)

large-fruited red-flowering gum: *Eucalyptus leucoxylon* (See **gum**.)

large-fruited rose apple: *Syzygium malaccensis* (See **malay apple**.)

large pussy willow: *Salix discolor* (See **swamp willow**.)

large twayblade: *Liparis liliifolia* (See **sleekwort, mauve**.)

large yellow lady's-slipper: *Cypripedium Calceolus pubescens* (See **Venus's-shoe**.)

large yellow moccasin flower: *Cypripedium Calceolus pubescens* (See **Venus's-shoe**.)

larkspur: *Consolida ambigua* (See **rocket larkspur**.), *Delphinium* (See **knight's-spur**.)

lasiandra: ***Tibouchina*** *urvilleana*

latan palm: ***Latania***

latticeleaf: ***Aponogeton*** *madagascariensis*, ***Goodyera***

lattice plant: ***Aponogeton*** *madagascariensis* (See **latticeleaf**.)

laural sumac: *Rhus laurina* **(See Sumac, laurel**.)

laurel: *Kalmia, Laurus nobilis, Prunus Laurocerasus, Rhododendron maximum*

laurel, Alexandrian: *Calophyllum inophyllum* (See **tamanu**.)

laurel cherry: *Prunus Laurocerasus*

laurel, great: *Rhododendron maximum*

laurel, Indian: *Calophyllum inophyllum* (See **tamanu**.)

laurel oak: *Quercus* (See **acajou**.), *Q. imbricaria* (See **shingle oak**.)

laurel, purple: *Rhododendron catawbiense*

laurel tree: *Persea borbonia*

laurelwood: *Calophyllum inophyllum* (See **tamanu**.)

laurustine: *Viburnum Tinus* (See **laurustinus**.)

laurustinus: *Viburnum Tinus*

lavender: *Lavandula, L. vera*

lavender cotton: *Santolina chamaecyparissus*

lavender mist: *Thalictrum*

lavender, sea: *Limonium* (See **thrift, lavender**.)

lavender starflower: *Grewia occidentalis*

lavender thrift: *Limonium latifolium*

lawn water pennywort: *Hydrocotyle sibthorpiodes* (See **water pennywort**.)

Lawson's cypress: *Chamaecyparis lawsoniana* (See **cypress** and **Port Orford cedar**.)

lawyer's-tongue: *Gasteria*

lazy daisy: *Aphanostephus*

lead plant: *Amorpha canescens*

lead tree: *Leucaena glauca*

leadwort: *Plumbago*

leadwort, Cape: *Plumbago auriculata, P. Capensis*

leadwort, Ceylon: *Plumbago zeylanica*

leaf beet: *Beta vulgaris* (See **Swiss chard**.)

leather fern: *Acrosticum aureum, Rumohra adantiaformis*

leatherflower: *Clematis, C. versicolor, C. Viorna* (See **love-in-a-mist**.), *C. virginiana* (See **old-man's-beard** and **virgin's-bower**.)

leatherleaf: *Chamaedaphne calyculata, Polypodium Scouleri*

leatherleaf fern: *Rumohra adantiaformis* (See **leather fern**.)

leatherwood: *Ceratopetalum apetalum, Cyrilla racemiflora* (See **myrtle**.), *Dirca, D. palustris* (See **swampwood**.), *Eucryphia lucida*

leathery polypody: ***Polypodium*** *sconleri*

leek: ***Allium***, *A. Ampeloprasum*

lemon: *Citrus Limon*

lemonade berry: *Rhus integriflia* (See **sourberry**.)

lemon balm: *Melissa officinalis* (See **garden balm** and **sweet balm**.)

lemon-flowered gum: *Eucalyptus woodwardii* (See **gum**.)

lemongrass: *Cymbopogon citratus*

lemonleaf: *Gaultheria shallon* (See **salal** and **shallon**.)

lemon-scented gum: *Eucalyptus citriodora* (See **gum**.)

lemon thyme: *Thymus Serpyllum* (See **serpolet**.)

lemon verbena: ***Aloysia*** *triphylla*

lemon vine: ***Pereskia*** *aculeata*

lemon walnut: *Juglans cinerea*

lens-scale: *Atriplex lentiformis* (See **quail bush** and **thistle, white**.)

Lenten rose: ***Helleborus*** *orientale* (See **hellebore**.)

lentil: ***Lens*** *culinarus*

lentiscus: *Pistacia Lentiscus*

lentisk: *Pistacia Lentiscus* (See **lentiscus**.)

leopard flower: *Belamcanda chinensis* (See **lily, blackberry** and **Pardanthus**.), ***Pardanthus***

leopard lily: ***Lachenalia***, *Lilium Catesbaei* (See **southern red lily**.)

leopard palm: ***Amorphophallus***

leopard plant: *Ligularia tussilaginea*

leopard's bane: *Doronicum, D. cordatum, D. Pardalianches*

lesser celandine: *Ranunculus Ficaria* (See **celadine** and **pilewort**.)

lettuce: ***Lactuca***, *L. sativa*

lettuce, Indian: *Frasera carolinensis, Montia, Pyrola rotundifolia*

lettuce, lamb's: *Valerianella*

levant madder: ***Rubia*** *peregrina*

leverwood: *Ostrya virginiana*

licorice: *Glycyrrhiza glabra* (See **sweetwood**.)

licorice fern: ***Polypodium*** *californicum, P. glycyrrhiza*

licorice vine: ***Abrus*** *precatorius* (See **pea, rosary** and **vine, red-beard**.)

life-of-man: *Aralia racemosa* (See **spikenard**.)

life plant: *Biophytum sensitivum, Kalanchoe pinnata* (See **love plant, Mexican**.)

liferoot: *Senecio aureus*

lightwood: *Acacia melanoxylon*

lignum vitae: *Acacia*

lignum vitae: *Eucalyptus*, ***Guaiacum***, *Metrosideros, Vitex*

lilac: *Ceanothus thyrsiflorus, Melia Azederach,* **Syringa**

lilac, **Australian**: *Hardenbergia violacea*

lilac, **German**: *Centranthus ruber*

lilac, **Hungarian**: *Syringa Josikaea*

lilac, **Indian**: *Lagerstroemia indica, Melia Azedarach*

lilac, Persian: **Melia** *Azedarach*

lilac, **wild**: *Ceanothus*

lilli-pilli tree: **Acmena** *smithii*

lillypilly: **Acmena** *Smithii*

lillypilly tree: **Acmena** *Smithii* (See **lillypilly**.)

lily: **Lilium**

lily, **adobe**: *Fritillaria pluriflora*

lily, **African**: *Agapanthus africanus*

lily, **African blood**: *Haemanthus*

lily, **African corn**: *Ixia* (See **lily, corn**.)

lily, **alligator**: *Hymenocallis Palmeri*

lily, **alp**: *Lloydia*

lily, **alpine**: **Lilium** *parvum*

lily, **Amazon**: *Eucharis grandiflora*

lily, **Amazon water**: *Victoria amazonica*

lily, **American Turk's-cap**: **Lilium** *superbum*

lily, **arum**: *Zantedeschia aethiopica* (See **lily, calla** and **lily, trumpet**.)

lily, **Atamasco**: *Zephyranthes Atamasco*

lily, **Australian water**: *Nymphaea gigantea*

lily, **avalanche**: *Erythronium grandiflorum*

lily, **Aztec**: *Sprekelia formosissima*

lily, **Backhouse hybrid**: **Lilium** ×*Backhousei*

lily, **Barbados**: **Hippeastrum**

lily, **bell**: **Lilium** *Grayi*

lily, **Belladonna**: *Amaryllis belladonna*

lily, Bermuda: **Lilium** *longiflora eximium* (See **lily, Bermuda Easter**.)

lily, **Bermuda Easter**: **Lilium** *longiflora eximium*

lily, **blackberry**: *Belamcanda chinensis* (See **lily, leopard**.)

lily, **blood**: *Haemanthus* (See **lily, African blood**.)

lily, **blue bead**: *Clintonia borealis*

lily, **blue funnel**: *Androstephium coeruleum*

lily, **boat**: *Rhoeo spathaceae* (See **three-men-in-a-boat**.)

lily, **bugle**: *Watsonia*

lily, **butterfly**: *Hedychium coronarium*

lily, **calla**: *Zantedeschia aethiopica* (See **lily, arum**.)

lily, **Canada**: **Lilium** *canadense*

lily, **candlestick**: **Lilium** *pensylvanicum*

lily, Cape blue water: *Nymphaea capensis*

lily, Cape Cod pink water: *Nymphaea odorata rosea*

lily, Carolina: *Lilium* *Michauxii*

lily, Caucasian: *Lilium* *Monadelphum*

lily, celestial: *Nemastylis*

lily, chamise: *Lilium* *rubescens*

lily, chaparral: *Lilium* *rubescens* (See **lily, chamise.**)

lily, checker: *Fritillaria lanceolata*

lily, checkered: *Fritillaria Meleagris*

lily, Chinese lantern: *Sandersonia aurantiaca*

lily, Chinese white: *Lilium leucanthum*

lily, climbing: *Gloriosa, G. rothschildiana* (See **lily, gloriosa.**)

lily, coast: *Lilium* *maritimum*

lily, cobra: *Arisaema speciosum, Darlingtonia*

lily, Columbia: *Lilium* *columbianum*

lily, corn: *Clintonia borealis* (See **lily, blue bead.**), *Ixia, Veratrum californicum*

lily, cow: *Caltha palustris, Nuphar*

lily, crane: *Strelitzia reginae*

lily, crinum: *Crinum*

lily, Cuban: *Scilla peruuviana* (See **hyacinth, Peruvian.**)

lily, desert: *Hesperocallis undulata*

lily, dwarf ginger: *Kaempferia Roscoana*

lily, Easter: *Lilium* *longiflorum eximium* (See **lily, Bermuda Easter.**)

lily, Egyptian water: *Nymphaea caerulea, N. Lotus*

lily, Eucharist: *Eucharis grandiflora* (See **lily, Amazon.**)

lily, Eureka: *Lilium* *occidentale*

lily, European white water: *Nymphaea alba*

lily, fairy: *Zephyranthes, Z. candida* (See **lily, rain.**), *Z. citrina* (See **lily, rain.**), *Z. grandiflora* (See **lily, rain.**)

lily, fairy water: *Nymphoides aquatica*

lily, fawn: *Erythronium* (See **violet, dog-tooth.**), *E. californicum*

lily, fire: *Cyrtanthus, Zephyrathes tubiflora, Zerophyllum tenax*

lily, flamingo: *Anthurium andraeanum*

lily, flax: *Dianella, Phormium*

lily, fortnight: *Dietes* (See **lily, Natal.**)

lily, fragrant plantain: *Hosta plantanginea*

lily, fragrant water: *Nymphaea odorata*

lily, garland: *Hedychium*

lily, giant: *Cardiocrinum gigantum, Doryanthes excelsa*

lily, giant water: *Victoria*

lily, ginger: *Hedychium* (See **lily, gar-**

lily, milk-and-wine: *Crinum latifolium zeylanicum*

lily, minor Turk's-cap: *Lilium pomponium* (See **lily, lesser Turk's-cap**.)

lily, mountain: *Leucocrinum montanum*, *Lilium auratum*

lily, narrow-leaved plantain: *Hosta lancifolia*

lily, Natal: *Dietes*

lily-of-China: *Rohdea japonica*

lily-of-the-Altai: *Ixiolirion*

lily-of-the-Amazon: *Eucharis grandiflora* (See **lily, Amazon**.)

lily-of-the-field: *Anemone, Sternbergia lutea*

lily-of-the-Nile: *Agapanthus africanus* (See **lily, African**.)

lily-of-the palace: *Hippeastrum aulicum*

lily-of-the-valley: *Clethra arborea, Convallaria majalis* (See **May blossom**.)

lily-of-the-valley bush: *Pieris japonica*

lily-of-the-valley, false: *Maianthemum*

lily-of-the-valley shrub: *Pieris japonica* (See **lily-of-the-valley bush**.)

lily, of-the-valley, star-flowered: *Smilacina stellata*

lily-of-the-valley tree: *Crinodendron patagua*

lily-of-the-valley, wild: *Mianthemum canadensem, Pyrola elliptica, P. rotundifolia*

lily, one-day: *Tigridia pavonia*

lily, orange: *Lilium bulbiferum*

lily, orange-bell: *Lilium Grayi* (See **lily, bell**.)

lily, orange-cup: *Lilium philadelphicum*

lily, Oregon: *Lilium columbianum* (See **lily, Columbia**.)

lily, palm: *Cordyline australis, Yucca gloriosa*

lily, Palmer spear: *Doryanthes Palmerii*

lily, panther: *Lilium pardalinum* (See **lily, leopard**.)

lily, paradise: *Paradisea Liliastrum*

lily, peacock: *Kaempferia Roscoana* (See **lily, dwarf ginger**.)

lily, perfumed fairy: *Chlidanthus fragrans*

lily, pig: *Zantedeschia aethiopica* (See **lily, arum**.)

lily, pine: *Lilium Catesbaei*

lily, pinewoods: *Eustylis purpurea*

lily, pink Easter: *Echinopsis multiplex*

lily, pink porcelain: *Alpinia Zerumbet*

lily, plantain: *Hosta*

lily, pond: *Nymphaea odorata* (See **lily, fragrant water**.)

lily, pot-of-gold: *Lilium iridollae*

lily, prickly water: *Euryale ferox*

lily, pygmy water: *Nymphaea tetragona*

lily, queen: *Curcuma petiolata*

lily, rain: *Zephyranthes* (See **lily, fairy**.), *Z. candida, Z. citrina, Z. grandiflora*

lily, red ginger: *Hedychium coccineum*

lily, red spider: *Lycoris radiata*

lily, redwood: *Lilium rubescens* (See **lily, chamise**.)

lily, regal: *Lilium regale*

lily, Resurrection: *Kaempferia rotunda, Lycoris squamigera* (See **lily, magic**.)

lily, roan: *Lilium Grayi* (See **lily, bell**.)

lily, rock: *Dendrobium speciosum*

lily, royal: *Lilium regale* (See **lily, regal**.), *L. superbum*

lily-royal: *Lilium superbum* **(See lily, American Turk's-cap** and **swamp lily**.)

lily, royal water: *Nymphaea amazonica, Victoria amazonica* (See **lily, Amazon water**.)

lily, sand: *Leucocrinum*

lily, Santa Cruz: *Victoria*

lily, Santa Cruz water: *Victoria Cruziana*

lily, Scarborough: *Vallota* speciosa

lily, scarlet ginger: *Hedychium coccineum* (See **lily, red ginger**.)

lily, scarlet Turk's-cap: *Lilium chalcedonicum* (See **lily, Nankeen**.)

lily, seersucker plantain: *Hosta seiboldii*

lily, sego: *Calochortus* (See **lily, mariposa** and **tulip, butterfly**.) *C. nuttallii*

lily, Shasta: *Lilium Washingtonianum*

lily, showy: *Lilium speciosum* (See **lily, showy Japanese**.)

lily, showy Japanese: *Lilium speciosum*

lily, Siberian: *Ixiolirion tatarica*

lily, Sierra: *Lilium parvum* (See **lily, alpine**.)

lily, small tiger: *Lilium parvum* (See **lily, alpine**.)

lily, snake: *Dichelostemma volubile*

lily, Solomon's: *Arum palaestinum*

lily, southern red: *Lilium Catesbaci*

lily, spear: *Doryanthes*

lily, speckled wood: *Clintonia umbellulata*

lily, spider: *Crinum, Hymenocallis, Lycoris radiata* (See **lily, red spider**.)

lily, star: *Calochortus* **(See tulip, butterfly**.) *Leucocrinum, Lilium concolor, Zigadenus Fremontii*

lily, St.-Bernard's-: *Anthericum Liliago, Chlorophytum*

lily, St.-Bruno's-: *Paradisea Liliastrum* (See **lily, paradise**.)

lily, St. James's: *Sprekelia formosissima* (See **lily, Aztec**.)

lily, St.-Joseph's-: *Hippeastrum reginae, H. vittatum*

lily, sunset: *Lilium Humboldtii, L. pardalinum*

lily, swamp: *Lilium superbum* (See **lily, American Turk's-cap**.), *Saururus cernuus* (See **lizard's-tail**.)

lily, thimble: *Lilium Bolanderi*

lily, tiger: *Lilium Catesbaei, L. lancifolium,*

lily, toad: *Tricyrtis*

lily, toad-cup: *Neomarica*

lily, torch: *Kniphofia*

lily, triplet: *Triteleia laxa*

lily, trout: ***Erythronium**,* (See **violet, dog-tooth**.), *E. americanum*

lily, trumpet: *Lilium longiflorum, Zantedeschia aethiopica* (See **lily, arum**.)

lily, tuberous water: *Nymphaea tuberosa* (See **lily, magnolia water**.)

lily, turban: *Lilium Martagon* (See **lily, Martagon**.), *L. pomponium* (See **lily, lesser Turk's-cap**.)

lilyturf: ***Liriope, Ophiopogon***

lilyturf, big blue: *Liriope muscari*

lilyturf, creeping: *Liriope spicata*

lilyturf, dwarf: *Ophiopogon japonicus*

lilyturf, white: *Ophiopogon Jaburan*

lily, turk's cap: *Lilium Matagon* (See **lily, Martagon**.), *L. Michauxii* (See lily, Carolina.), *L. pomponium* (See lily, lesser Turk's-cup), *L. superbum* (See **lily, American turk's-cap**.)

lily, Victoria water: *Victoria regia*

lily, voodoo: *Sauromatum venosum*

lily, Washington: *Lilium Washingtonianum*

lily, water: *Nymphaea*

lily, Western: *Lilium occidentale* (See **lily, Eureka**.)

lily, wheeled: *Lilium medeoloides*

lily, white trumpet: *Lilium longiflorum* (See **lily, trumpet**.)

lily, white water: *Nymphaea odorata* (See **lily, fragrant water**.)

lily, wild orange-red: *Lilium philadelphicum* (See **lily, orange-cup**.)

lily, wild yellow: *Lilium canadense* (See **lily, Canada**.)

lily, wood: *Lilium philadelphicum* (See **lily, orange-cup**.)

lily, yellow: *Lilium canadense* (See **lily, Canada**.)

lily, yellow-bell: *Lilium canadense* (See **lily, Canada**.)

lily, yellow pond: *Nuphar* (See **lily, cow**.)

lily, yellow Turk's-cap: *Lilium pyrenaicum*

lily, yellow water: *Nuphar luteum*

lily, zephyr: *Zephyranthes* (See **lily, fairy**.), *Z. candida, Z. citrina, Z. grandiflora* (See **lily, rain**.)

lima bean: ***Phaseolus*** *lunatus* (See **bean**.)

lime: *Tilia*

limeberry: ***Triphasia*** *trifolia*

lime tree: ***Tilia***

lime, wild: *Zanthoxylum Fagara*

linden: ***Tilia***

ling: *Calluna vulgaris, Eleocharis dulcis, Trapa bicornis, T. natans* (See **nut, Jesuits** and **water caltrop**.)

lingberry: *Vaccinium Vitis-Idaea minus* (See **mountain cranberry**.)

lintisco: *Rhus vireus* (See **kinnikinnik**.)

lion's-ear: *Leonotis, L. Cardiaca, L. Leonurus*, (See **lion's-tail**.)

lion's-foot: *Leontopodium alpinum, Prenanthes*

lion's-heart: *Dracocephalum, Physostegia*

lion's-mouth: *Antirrhinum, Digitalis, Linaria*

lion's-tail: *Leonotis* (See **lion's-ear**.) *L. Cardiaca, L. Leonurus*

lion's-tooth: *Taraxacum*

lip fern: *Cheilanthes*

Lisianthus: ***Eustoma***

litchi: ***Litchi***

litchi nut: ***Litchi***

little bluestem: ***Andropogon*** *scoparius*

little club moss: *Selaginella* (See **moss**.)

little-pickles: ***Othonna*** *capensis*

live-and-die: *Mimosa pudica* (See **sensitive-plant**.)

live-forever: ***Sempervivum*** *tectorum*

live-oak: *Quercus agrifolia, Q. chrysolepis, Q. myrsinifolia, Q. virginiana Q. Wislizeni*

liverleaf: *Hepatica, H. americana* (See **squirrel cup**.)

liverwort: *Hepatica* (See **liverleaf**.)

liverwort, noble: *Hepatica nobilis*

living-rock: ***Ariocarpus***

Livingstone daisy: ***Dorotheanus***

lizard's-tail: ***Saururus***, *S. cernuus*

lizardtail: *Saururus cernuus* (See **lizard's-tail**.)

loblolly bay: ***Gordonia***, *G. Lasianthus*

loblolly pine: *Pinus Taeda*

loblolly tree: *Cordia dentata*

lobster-claw: *Heliconia*

lobster-claws: *Cheiridopsis Pillansii, Vriesea carinata*

locoweed: *Chrysothamnus, Cicuta, Eu-*

patorium rugosum, Haplopappus, **Oxytropis**

locust: *Ceratonia siliqua, Robinia, R. Pseudoacacia*

locust, black: **Robinia** *pseudacacia*

locust, bristly: **Robinia** *hispida*

locust, clammy: **Robinia** *viscosa*

locust, honey: *Gleditsia, G. triacanthos*

locust, moss: **Robinia** *hispida*

locust, swamp: *Gleditsia aquatica* (See **locust, water**.)

locust tree: *Robinia*

locust, water: *Gleditsia aquatica*

locust, yellow: **Robinia** *pseudacacia*

Loesel's twayblade: *Liparis Loeselii* (See **orchid, fen**.)

loganberry: *Rubus ursinus*

lollipop flower: **Pachystachys** *lutea*

Lombardy poplar: *Populus nigra*

London pride: *Dianthus barbatus, Lychnis chalcedonica, Saxifraga umbrosa*

long beach fern: *Phegopteris connectilis, Thelypteris phegopteris (Polyodium phegopteris)* (See **mountain fern**.)

longan: *Euphoria Longan*

long-headed anemone: *Anemone cylindrica* (See **thimbleweed**.)

long-headed poppy: *Papaver dubium* (See **poppy**.)

longleaf mahonia: *Mahonia nervosa* (See **Oregon grape**.)

longleaf pine: *Pinus palustris* (See **southern yellow pine**.)

long moss: *Tillandsia usneoides*

long purples: *Lythrum Salicaria*

looking-glass plant: *Coprosma repens*

loosestrife: **Lysimachia**, *L. vulgaris,* **Lythrum**

loosestrife, purple: *Lythrum Salicaria*

loquat: **Eriobotrya**, *E. japonica* (See **Japanese plum**.)

lords-and-ladies: *Arum maculatum*

Lord's-candlestick: *Yucca gloriosa* (See **lily, palm**.)

lote tree: *Celtis australis* (See **honeyberry** and **lotus tree**.)

lotus: *Nelumbo* (See **water lotus**.), *N. nucifera, Nymphaea, N. Lotus* (See **lily, Egyptian water**.)

lotus, blue: *Nymphaea caerulea, N. stellata*

lotus, Egyptian: *Nymphaea caerulea, N. Lotus*

lotus tree: *Celtis australis, Diospyros Lotus, D. virginiana*

louseberry: *Euonymus europaea*

lousewort: *Pedicularis* (See **wood betony**.), *P. canadensis* (See **head betony**.)

lovage: *Levisticum officinale*

love apple: *Solanum aculeatissimum*

love grass: *Eragrostis*

love-in-a-mist: *Cerastium tomentosum, Clematis Viorna, Nigella damascena, Passiflora foetida*

love-in-idleness: *Viola tricolor*

love-lies-bleeding: *Adonis annua, Amaranthus caudatus* (See **thrumwort** and **velvet flower**.), *Dicentra*

loveman: *Galium*

love pea: *Abrus precatorius* (See **pea, rosary**.)

love plant: *Anacampseros telephiastrum*

love plant, Mexican: *Kalanchoe pinnata*

love tree: *Cercis Siliquastrum*

love vine: *Antigonon leptopus* (See **mountain rose**.)

low-bush blueberry: *Vaccinium vacillans* (See **blueberry**.)

lucky nut: *Thevetia peruviana* (See **yellow oleander**.)

luffa: *Luffa aegyptiaca* (See **strainer-vine**.)

lungan: *Euphoria Longan* (See **longan**.)

lungwort: *Hellebore, Hieracium, Mertensia, Pulmonaria, P. officinalis* (See **Joseph and Mary**.), *Verbascum*

lupine: *Lupinus*

lustwort: *Drosera rotundifolia*

M

macaw tree: *Acrocomia* **(See macaw palm.)**

Mackaya: *bella*

Madagascar jasmine: *Stephanotis floribunda* (See **waxflower**.)

Madagascar lace plant: *Aponogeton madagascariensis*

Madagascar palm: *Pachypodium lamerei*

Madagascar periwinkle: *Catharanthus, C. rosea* (See **old maid**.), *C. roseus* (See **periwinkle**.)

Madagascar plum: *Flacourtia indica* (See **governor's plum**.)

Madagascar rubber vine: *Cryptostegia madagascariensis* (See **rubber vine**.)

madar: *Calotropis* (See **mudar**.)

madder: *Rubia, R. tinctoria*

Madeira vine: *Anredera, A. cordifolia* (See **mignonette vine**.)

madrona: *Arbutus menziesii* (See **madrone**.)

madrone: *Arbutus menziesii* (See **arbutus**.)

madrono: *Arbutus menziesii* (See **madrone**.)

madwort: *Alyssum, Aurinia saxatilis*

madwort, rock: *Aurinia saxatilis*

mad-dog weed: *Alisma plantago-aquatica* (See **thrumwort, great**.)

magic flower: *Achimenes,* Cantua buxifolia

magic-flower-of-the-Incas: *Cantua buxifolia* (See **magic flower**.)

magic tree: *Cantua buxifolia* (See **magic flower**.)

magnolia vine: *Schisandra chinensis*

maguey: *Agave*

maho: *Hibiscus elatus* (See **mahoe**.)

mahoe: *Hibiscus tiliaceus* (See **mountain mahoe.**)

mahogany: *Swietenia*

mahogany birch: *Betula lenta* (See **mountain mahogany** and **sweet birch.**)

mahogany pine: ***Podocarpus*** *totara*

mahogony, swamp: *Eucalyptus robusta*

mahogany, West Indies: *Swietenia Mahogoni*

maidenhair: *Andiantum*

Maidenhair berry: *Gaultheria hispidula* (See **snowberry, creeping.**)

maidenhair ferns: ***Adiantum*** *Capillus-Veneris*

maidenhair tree: ***Ginkgo****, G. biloba*

maidenhair vine: ***Muehlenbeckia*** *complexa* (See **necklace vine.**)

maiden pink: *Dianthus deltoides*

maiden's wreath: ***Francoa***

Malabar plum: *Syzygium malaccensis* (See **Malay apple.**)

Malabar spinach: *Basella alba* (See **spinach, Indian.**)

malanga: *Colocasia esculenta*, ***Xanthosoma****, X. sagittifolium* (See **kale, Indian.**)

malay apple: *Syzygium jambos, S. malaccensis*

malcolm stock: ***Malcolmia*** *maritima*

maleberry: *Lyonia ligustrina*

male blueberry: *Lyonia ligustrina* (See **maleberry.**)

male fern: *Dryopteris Filix-mas*

mallow: ***Malva*** (See **muskflower.**)

mallow, curled: *Malva verticillata*

mallow, glade: *Napaea dioica*

mallow, globe: *Sphaeralcea*

mallow, high: *Malva sylvestris*

mallow, marsh: *Althaea officinalis, Hibiscus Moscheutos* (See **mallow, rose.**)

mallow, musk: ***Malva****, M. moschata*

mallow, prairie: *Sphaeralcea coccinea*

mallow, red false: *Sphaeralcea coccinea* (See **mallow, prairie.**)

mallow, rose: *Hibiscus, H. Moscheutos* (See **swamp rose mallow.**)

mallow, sleepy: *Malvaviscus*

mallow, swamp rose: *Hibiscus Moscheutos*

mallow, tree: *Lavatera arborea*

mallow, Venice: *Hibiscus Trionum*

mallow, Virginia: *Sida hermaphodita*

mallow, wax: *Malvaviscus*

mallow, white: *Althaea officinalis* (See **mallow, marsh.**)

Maltese cross: *Lychnis chalcedonica* (See **London pride.**)

mamey: ***Mammea*** *Americana*

mamey colorado: *Pouteria sapota* (See **marmalade plum, mammee sapota** and **sapote**.)

mamey sapota: *Pouteria sapota* (See **mammee sapota** and **marmalade plum**.)

mammee: ***Mammea*** *Americana*

mammee apple: ***Mammea*** *Americana*

mammee sapota: *Pouteria sapota* (See **marmalade plum**.)

mammee sapote: *Pouteria Sapota* (See **sapote**.)

mammoth tree: *Sequoiadendron giganteum* (See **tree, big**.)

mamoncillo: *Melicoccus bijugatus*

mandarin orange: *Citrus reticulata*

Mandarin's hat: ***Holmskioldia*** *sanguinea* (See **Chinese hat plant**.)

Manda's woolly bear: *Begonia leptotricha* (See **woolly bear**.)

mandrake: ***Mandragora*** *officinarum, Podophyllum peltatum* (See **Mayapple** and **raccoon-berry**.)

mangel-wurzel: *Beta vulgaris*

mango: ***Mangifera***

mangosteen: ***Garcinia*** *Mangostana*

mangostine: *Garcinia Mangostana* (See **mangosteen**.)

mangrove: *Rhizophora Mangle*

mangrove, American: ***Rhizophora*** *mangle*

mangrove, button: *Conocarpus*

manioc: *Manihot* (See **cassava**.), *M. esculent*

maniocca: *Manihot* (See **cassava**.)

manna gum: *Eucalyptus viminalis* (See **gum**.)

manroot: *Ipomoea leptophylla*

manyberry: *Celtis occidentalis* (See **hackberry**.)

manzanita: *Arctostaphylos*

man-in-a-boat: *Rhoeo spathaceae* (See **lily, boat** and **three-men-in-a-boat**.)

man-of-the-earth: *Ipomoea leptophylla* (See **manroot**.)

maple: *Acer*

maple, Amur: *Acer Ginnala*

maple, ash-leaved: *Acer Negundo*

maple, big-leaf: *Acer macrophyllum*

maple, coliseum red: *Acer cappadocicum*

maple, David's: *Acer Davidii*

maple, evergreen: *Acer oblongum*

maple, field: *Acer campestre* (See **maple, hedge**.)

maple, flowering: *Abutilon*

maple, Formosan: *Abutilon morrisonense*

maple, full-moon: *Acer japonicum*

maple, hard: *Acer saccharum* (See **maple, rock** and **maple, sugar**.)

maple, hedge: *Acer campestre*

maple, Japanese: *Acer japonicum, A. palmatum*

maple, mountain: *Acer spicatum*

maple, Mt. Morris: *Abutilon morrisonense* (See **maple, Formosan**.)

maple, Norway: *Acer platanoides*

maple, paperbark: *Acer griseum*

maple, Pennsylvania: *Acer pensylvanicum* (See **whistlewood**.)

maple, red: *Acer rubrum*

maple, river: *Acer saccharinum* (See **maple, silver**.)

maple, rock: *Acer saccharum* (See **maple, sugar**.)

maple, Rocky Mountain: *Acer glabrum*

maple, scarlet: *Acer rubrum* (See **maple, red**.)

maple, silver: *Acer saccharinum*

maple, soft: *Acer rubrum* (See **maple, red** and **maple, silver**.)

maple, Southern sugar: *Acer barbatum*

maple, striped: *Acer pensylvanicum* (See **whistlewood**.)

maple, sugar: *Acer saccharum* (See **maple, rock**.)

maple, swamp: *Acer rubrum* (See **maple, red**.)

maple, sycamore: *Acer pseudoplatanus*

maple trident: *Acer Buergeranum*

maple, vine: *Acer circinatum* (See also **maple**.)

maple, white: *Acer saccharinum* (See **maple, silver**.)

maqui: *Aristotelia chilensis*

marbleleaf: **Peristrophe** *hyssopifolia*

mare's tail: **Hippurus**, *H. vulgaris*

margosa: **Melia** *Azedarach* (See **lilac, Indian**.)

marguerite: *Argyranthemum frutescens* (See **Paris daisy**.), *Chrysanthemum frutescens*

marguerite, blue: *Felicia amelloides*

marguerite, golden: *Anthemis tinctoria*

marigold: *Calendula officinalis,* **Tagetes**

marigold, African: **Tagetes** *erecta* (See **marigold**.)

marigold, American: **Tagetes** *erecta* (See **marigold**.)

marigold, aztec: **Tagetes** *erecta* (See **marigold**.)

marigold, corn: *Chrysanthemum segetum* (See **oxeye, yellow**.)

marigold, fetid: *Dyssodia*

marigold, fig: **Mesembryanthemum**

marigold, French: ***Tagetes*** *patula* (See **marigold**.)

marigold, pot: *Calendula officinalis* (See **marigold** and **marigold, fig.**)

marigold, signet: *Tagetes tenufolia*

marigold, sweet-scented: *Tagetes lucida*

marijuana: ***Cannabis*** *sativa* (See **hashish**.)

marine ivy: *Cissus incisus*

marine vine: *Cissus incisus* (See **marine ivy**.)

mariposa: *Calochortus* (See **lily, mariposa** and **tulip, butterfly**.)

mariposa lily: ***Calochortus***, *C. leichtlinii*, *Clochortus* (See **star tulip**.)

maritime pine: *Pinus pinaster* (See **pinaster**.)

marjoram: ***Origanum***

marjoram, common: *Origanum vulgare* (See **marjoram**.)

marjoram, Sweet: *Origanum Majorana* (See **marjoram**.)

marjoram, wild: *Origanum vulgare* (See **marjoram**.)

marking-nut tree: ***Semecarpus***, *S. Anacardium* (See **varnish tree**.)

marlberry: *Ardisia escallonoides*

marmalade bush: ***Streptosolon*** *Jamesonii*

marmalade fruit: *Pouteria sapota* (See

mammee sapota and **marmalade plum**.)

marmalade plum: *Pouteria sapota* (See **mammee sapota**.)

marmalade tree: *Pouteria sapota* (See **mammee sapota** and **marmalade plum**.)

marri: *Eucalyptus calophylla* (See **red gum**.)

marsh bellflower: *Campanula aparinoides*

marsh cinquefoil: *Pontentilla palustris* (See **strawberry, bog**.)

marsh collard: ***Nuphar*** (See **lily, cow**.)

marsh elder: *Viburnum Opulus*

marsh fern: *Rumohra adantiaformis*

marsh five-finger: *Pontentilla palustris* (See **strawberry, bog**.)

marsh-mallow: ***Althaea*** *officinalis*, *Hibiscus moscheutos palustris*

marsh marigold: ***Caltha*** *palustris* (See **goldcup, lily cow, kingcup, May blob, Mayflower** and **meadow bright**.)

marsh pennywort: *Hydrocotyle* (See **pennywort**.), *H. vulgaris*

marsh pink: ***Sabbatia***

marsh rosemary: *Limonium* (See **thrift, lavender**.), *L. latifolium* (See **sea lavender**.)

marsh tea: *Ledum palustre*

marsh trefoil: *Menyanthes trifoliata*

Martha Washington geranium: *Pelargonium domesticum* (See **Geranium**.)

marvel-of-Peru: *Mirabilis jalapa* (See **four-o'clock**.)

mask flower: *Alonsoa*

masterwort: *Archangelica atropurpurea*, **Astrantia**, *Heracleum Sphondylium*

mastic tree: *Pistacia Lentiscus* (See **lentiscus**.)

matchbrush: *Gutierrezia*, *G. Sarothrae* (See **snakeweed**.)

matchweed: *Gutierrezia*, *G. Sarothrae* (See **snakeweed**.)

mate: *Ilex paraquariensis* (See **yerba mate**.)

Matilija poppy: *Romneya coulteri* (See **tree poppy**.)

matrimony vine: *Lycium*

matrimony vine, common: *Lycium halimifolium*

mattress vine: *Muehlenbeckia complexa* (See **necklace vine**.)

Mayapple: *Podophyllum peltatum* (See **raccoon-berry**.)

May blob: *Caltha palustris* (See **lily, cow**.)

Maybloom: *Crataegus*

May blossom: *Convallaria majalis*

maybush: *Crataegus* (See **Maybloom**.)

May cherry: *Amelanchier*

Mayduke: *Amelanchier* (See **May cherry**.)

mayflower: *Cardamine pratensis* (See **lady's-smock** and **meadow cress**.), *Epigaea repens* (See **gravel plant** and **trailing arbutus**.)

Mayflower, Canada: *Maianthemum canadense*

Mayhaw: *Crataegus*

may lily: *Convallaria majalis* (See **May blossom**.)

maypop: *Passiflora incarnata*

mayten: *Maytenus Boaria*

Maythorn: *Crataegus* (See **Maybloom**.)

mayweed: *Anthenis Cotula* (See **stinking chamomile**.)

mazer tree: *Acer campestre*

meadow beauty: *Rhexia*, *R. virginica*,

meadow bright: *Caltha palustris* (See **lily, cow**.)

meadow campion: *Lychnis Flos-cuculi*

meadow cress: *Cardamine pratensis* (See **lady's-smock**.)

meadow fern: *Dryopteris, Myrica Gale* (See **myrtle, bog** and **sweet gale**.), *Polypodium vulgare*

meadow foam: *Limnanthes*

meadow foxtail: **Alopecurus**

meadow hyacinth: **Camassia** *scilloides*

meadow leek: *Allium canadense* (See **onion, wild**.)

meadow parsnip: *Heracleum*

meadow pea: *Lathyrus pratensis*

meadow pine: *Pinus caribaea, P. Taeda*

meadow pink: *Dianthus deltoides, Hibenaria, Lynchnis Flos-cuculi*

meadow queen: *Filipendula, Spirea*

meadow rue: **Thalictrum** (See **lavender mist**.)

meadow saffron: *Colchicum autumnale* (See **crocus, autumn**.)

meadow sage: *Salvia pratensis*

meadow saxifrage: *Saxifraga granulata*

meadowsweet: *Astilbe,* **Filipendula,** *Spirea, S. alba*

mealberry: *Arctostaphylos Uva-ursi* (See **kinnikinnik**.)

mealy stringybark: *Eucalyptus cinerea* (See **stringybark**.)

mealy tree: *Viburnum*

Mediterranean hackberry: *Celtis australis* (See **honeyberry** and **lotus tree**.)

medlar: **Mespilus** *germanica, Vangueria infausta*

Medusa's head: *Euphorbia Caput-Medusae*

melancholy thistle: *Cirsium heterophyllum*

melilot: **Melilotus**

melon: *Cucumis Melo*

melon cactus: *Melocactus communis*

Mercury: *Chenopodium Bonus-Henricus* (See **spinach, wild**.)

Merlin's-grass: *Isoetes lacustris*

mermaid weed: **Proserpinaca**

merrybells: **Uvularia**

mescal bean: **Sophora** *secundiflora*

mesquite: **Prosopis**

mesquite, screw-pod: *Prosopis pubescens*

messmate stringybark: *Eucalyptus obliqua* (See **stringybark**.)

Mexican apple: *Casimiroa edulis* (See **sapote, white**.)

Mexican bamboo: **Polygonum** *cuspidatum* (See **Japanese knotweed**.)

Mexican blue palm: **Brahea** *armata*

Mexican breadfruit: *Monstera deliciosa* (See **window plant**.)

Mexican buckeye: *Ungnadia speciosa*

Mexican creeper: **Antigonon** *leptopus* (See **mountain rose**.)

Mexican cypress: *Cupressus lusitanica*

Mexican feather palm: **Astrocaryum**

Mexican fire bush: **Kochia** *trichophylla*

Mexican fire plant: *Euphorbia hetero-phylla* (See **poinsettia, annual**.)

Mexican fireweed: *Kochia scoparia*

Mexican flame vine: *Senecio confusus*

Mexican ivy: *Cobaea scandens*

Mexican orange: *Choisya ternata*

Mexican palo verde: *Parkinsonia aculeata*

Mexican persimmon: *Diospyros texana*

Mexican petunia: *Strobilanthes isophyllus* (See **Strobilanthes**.)

Mexican pinon pine: *Pinus cembroides*

Mexican poppy: *Argemone mexicana* (See **poppy, prickly**.)

Mexican privet: *Forestiera*

Mexican rose: *Portulaca grandiflora*

Mexican scammony: *Ipomoea orizabensis*

Mexican shellflower: *Tigridia Pavonia* (See **lily, one-day** and **tigerflower**.)

Mexican shrimp plant: *Justica Brandegeana* (See **shrimp plant**.)

Mexican star: *Milla biflora*

Mexican star-of-Bethlehem: *Milla*

Mexican stone pine: *Pinus cembroides* (See **Mexican pinon pine**.)

Mexican sunflower: *Tithonia, T. rotundifolia*

Mexican tea: *Chenopodium ambrosioides*

Mexican tulip poppy: *Hunnemannia, H. fumariifolia*

Mexican white pine: *Pinus ayacahuite*

mezereon: *Daphne mezereum* (See **spurge, olive**.)

Michaelmas daisy: *Aster* (See **starwort**.) *A. novi-begii, A. novae-angliae*

Michigan rose: *Rosa setigera* (See **prairie rose**.)

Mickey Mouse plant: *Ochna serrulata*

mignonette: *Reseda, R. odorata*

mignonette, common: *Reseda odorata*

mignonette, Jamaica: *Lawsonia inermis*

mignonette tree: *Lawsonia inermis* (See **henna** and **mignonette, Jamaica**.)

mignonette vine: *Anredera, A. cordifolia*

milfoil: *Achillea Millefolium, Myriophyllum* (See **parrot's-feather**.)

milkbush: *Euphorbia tirucalli* (See pencil tree and **spurge, Indian tree**.)

milkmaids: *Dentaria californica* (See **pepper-root**.)

milk thistle: *Silybum Marianum*

milk tree: *Mimusops*

milk vetch: *Astragalus*

milkweed: *Asclepias* (See **silkweed**.), *A. tuberosa*

milkwort: *Campanula, Polygala*

mimicry plants: *Pleiospilos*

mimosa: *Acacia dealbata* (See **wattle, silver**.), *Albizia Julibrissin* (See **silk tree**.), *Leguminosae*

Mindanao gum: *Eucalyptus deglupta* (See **gum**.)

mind-your-own-business: *Soleirolia Soleirolii*

miner's lettuce: *Montia* (See **lettuce, Indian**.)

Ming aralia: *Polyscias fruticosa*

miniature palm: *Phoenix roebelenii*

mint: *Mentha*

mintbush: *Prostanthera*

mint, corn: *Mentha arvensis* (See **mint**.)

mint, Corsican: *Mentha requienii* (See **mint**.)

mint geranium: *Chrysanthemum Balsamita* (See **costmary**.)

mint, pennyroyal: *Mentha Pulegium* (See **mint**.)

mintshrub: *Elsholtzia Stauntonii*

miracle leaf: *Kalanchoe pinnata* (See **love plant, Mexican**.)

miriti palm: *Mauritia flexuosa*

mirror plant: *Coprosma repens* (See **looking-glass plant**.)

mispero: *Manilkara Zapota* (See **sapodilla**.)

mistflower: *Eupatorium coelestinum*

mistletoe: *Phoradendron serotinum, Viscum album*

miterwort: *Mitella* (See **bishop's-cap**.)

miterwort, false: *Tiarella*

mithridate mustard: *Thlaspi arvense* (See **penny cress**.)

moccasin flower: *Cypripedium* (See **Indian shoe** and **lady's slipper**.)

mock apple: *Echinocystis lobata*

mock azalea: *Menziesia*

mock cucumber: *Echinocystis lobata* (See **mock apple**.)

mock orange: *Bumelia, B. lycioides* (See southern buckthorn.), *Maclura pomifera, Philadelphus* (See **syringa**.), *Pittosporum tobira* (See **tobira**.), *P. undulatum, Prunus caroliniana, P. laurocerasus, Styrax americanus*

mock orchid: *Philadelphus*

mock pennyroyal: *Hedeoma pulegioides* (See **pennyroyal, American**.)

mock plane: *Acer pseudo-platanus* (See **maple, sycamore**.)

mock strawberry: *Duchesnea*

mockernut: *Carya tomentosa*

mockernut hickory: *Carya tomentosa* (See **mockernut**.)

mole plant: *Euphorbia Lathyris* (See **spurge, caper**.)

molle: **Schinus** *Molle*

Molucca balm: *Moluccella laevis* (See **shellflower**.)

monarch-of-the-East: **Sauromatum** *guttatum, S. venosum* (See **voodoo lily**.)

monarda: *Monarda didyma* (See **bee balm**.)

monastery bells: **Cobaea** *scandens*

mondo grass: **Ophiopogon** (See **lily-turf**.)

moneyflower: *Lunaria annua*

moneyplant: **Lunaria** (See **satinflower**.), *L. annua* (See **pennyflower**.)

money tree: **Crassula** *argentea, Eucalyptus pulverulenta* (See **silver-leaved mountain gum**.)

moneywort: *Lysimachia nummularia* (See **motherwort**.)

monkey apple: *Clusia rosea*

monkey flower: **Mimulus** (See **muskflower**.)

monkey nut: **Arachis**, *Lecythis Zabucayo* (See **sapucia nut**.)

monkey plant: **Ruellia** *makoyana*

monkey pod: *Samanea saman* (See **rain tree**.)

monkey pot: **Lecythis**

monkey pot tree: **Lecythis**

monkey-pistol: **Hura**, *H. crepitans* (See **sandbox tree**.)

monkey puzzle: *Araucaria araucana* (See **pine, Chilean**.)

monkey-puzzle tree: **Araucaria** *araucana*

monkey's dinner-bell: **Hura**, *H. crepitans* (See **sandbox tree**.)

monkshood: **Aconitum**, *A. Napellus* (See **helmetflower**.)

monkshood-vine: **Ampelosis** *aconitifolia*

monk's pepper tree: *Vitex Agnus-castus* (See **hemp tree** and **pepper, wild**.)

monk's rhubarb: *Rumex alpinus* (See **mountain rhubarb**.)

monox: *Empetrum nigrum* (See **crowberry**.)

montbretia: **Crocosmia**

Monterey cypress: *Cupressus macrocarpa*

Monterey pine: *Pinus radiata*

moon cactus: **Selenicereus**

moon cereus: **Selenicereus**

moon daisy: *Chrysanthemum Leucanthemum*

moon fern: *Botrychium Lunaria* (See **moonwort**.)

moonflower: *Anemone nemorosa, Chrysanthemum Leucanthemum* (See **moon**

daisy and **moonflower**.), *Ipomoea alba*

moonpenny: *Chrysanthemum Leucanthemum* (See **moon daisy** and **moonflower**.)

moonseed: *Menispermum*

moonseed, Canadian: *Menispermum canadense*

moonseed, Carolina: *Cocculus carolinus*

moonwort: *Botrychium Lunaria, B. virginianum* (See **fern, rattlesnake**.), *Lunaria, L. annua* (See **pennyflower**.)

moorwort: *Andromeda*

mooseberry: *Viburnum alnifolium* (See **hobblebush, moosewood** and **wayfaring tree, American**.)

moose bush: *Viburnum alnifolium* (See **hobblebush, moosewood** and **wayfaring tree, American**.)

moose elm: *Ulmus rubra*

moosewood: *Acer pensylvanicum* (See **maple, striped** and **whistlewood**.), *Dirca palustris* (See **swampwood**.), *Viburnum alnifolium* (See **hobblebush** and **wayfaring tree, American**.)

morel: *Morchella, M. esculenta* (See **mushroom**.)

Moreton Bay chestnut: *Castanospermum australe*

Moreton Bay fig: *Ficus macrophylla*

Moreton Bay pine: *Araucaria cunninghamii*

morning campion: *Lychnis dioica* (See **campion**.)

morning flag: **Orthrosanthus** (See **morning flower**.), *O. chimboracensis*

morning flower: **Orthrosanthus**, *O. chimboracensis*

morning glory: *Argyreia, Calystegia, Convolvulus, Ipomoea, I. tricolor, I. nil, Merremia*

morning glory, beach: *Ipomoea Pescapra*

morning glory, Brazilian: *Ipomoea setosa*

morning glory, bush: *Convolvulus cneorum*

morning glory, Ceylon: *Merremia tuberosa*

morning glory, common: *Ipomoea purpurea*

morning glory, dwarf: *Convolvulus tricolor*

morning glory, ground: *Convolvulus mauritanicus*

morning glory, Imperial Japanese: *Ipomoea Nil*

morning glory, red: *Ipomoea coccinea*

morning glory, silver: *Argyrea splendens*

morning glory, wild: *Calystegia sepium, Convolvulus arvensis* (See **morning glory, wild**.)

morning glory, woolly: *Argyrea nervosa*

morning glory, yellow: *Merremia tuberosa* (See **morning glory, Ceylon**.)

moschatel: *Adoxa Moschatellina*

Moses-in-a-boat: *Rhoeo spathaceae* (See **lily, boat** and **three-men-in-a-boat**.)

Moses-in-the-bulrushes: *Rhoeo spathaceae* (See **lily, boat** and **three-men-in-a-boat**.)

Moses-in-the-cradle: *Rhoeo spathaceae* (See **lily, boat** and **three-men-in-a-boat**.)

Moses-on-a-raft: *Rhoeo spathaceae* (See **lily, boat** and **three-men-in-a-boat**.)

moso bamboo: *Phyllostachys pubescens*

mosquito plant: *Azolla, A. caroliniana* (See **water fern**.), *Cynanchum*

moss, Allegheny: *Robinia kelseyi*

moss campion: *Silene acaulis* (See **campion**.)

moss, flowering: *Pyxidanthera barbulata, Sedum pulchellum*

moss locust: *Robinia hispida* (See **locust, bristly** and **rose acacia**.)

moss phlox: *Phlox subulata* (See **ground pink** and **moss pink**.)

moss pink: *Phlox subulata* (See **ground pink**.)

moss rose: *Rosa centifolia* (See **Provence rose**.)

mossy-cup oak: *Quercus macrocarpa* (See **oak, bur**.)

mossy locust: *Robinia hispida* (See **moss locust**.)

mother fern: *Asplenium bulbiferum* (See **fern, mother, parsley fern** and **spleenwort**.)

mother-in-law: *Kalanchoe pinnata* (See **love plant, Mexican**.)

mother-in-law's-tongue: *Gasteria, Sansevieria trifasciata*

mother-of-pearl plant: *Graptopetalum paraguayense* (See **ghost plant**.)

mother-of-thousands: *Saxifraga stolonifera* (See **strawberry geranium**.)

mother's-tears: *Achimenes*

motherwort: *Artemisia, Chrysanthemum parthenium, Eupatorium purpureum, Leonurus, L. Cardiaca* (See **lion's-ear**

and **lion's-tail**.), *Lysimachia nummularia*

mother-of-thyme: *Thymus Serpyllum* (See **serpolet**.)

moth mullein: *Verbascum Blattaria*

moth orchid: *Phalaenopsis*

moth plant: *Phalaenopsis*

mottled-cranefly: *Tipularia discolor* (See **orchid, cranefly**.)

mountain acanthus: *Acanthus montanus* (See **thistle, mountain**.)

mountain ash: *Eucalyptus regnans, Eucalyptus Sieberi, Fraxinus texensis, Sorbus*

mountain asphodel: *Xerophyllum aspodeloides* (See **turkey beard**.)

mountain avens: *Dryas octopetala* (See **avens**.)

mountain balm: *Eriodictyon californicum*

mountain cranberry: *Vaccinium Vitis-idaea minus* (See **lingberry**.)

mountain daisy: *Arenaria groenlandica*

mountain damson: *Simarouba glauca*

mountain devil: *Lambertia formosa* (See **honeyflower**.)

mountain dogwood: *Cornus Nuttallii* (See **dogwood**.)

mountain ebony: *Bauhinia variegata* (See **orchid tree**.)

mountain fern: *Thelypteris Oreopteris, T. phegopteris*

mountain flax: *Phormium colensoi*

mountain fleece: *Polygonum amplexicaule*

mountain fringe: *Adlumia fungosa*

mountain garland: *Clarkia*

mountain grape: *Mahonia Aquifolium* (See **Oregon grape**.)

mountain heath: *Phyllodoche caerulea*

mountain heather: *Phyllodoce breweri, P. caerulea* (See **mountain heath**.)

mountain hemlock: *Tsuga Mertensiana* (See **hemlock spruce**.)

mountain holly: *Ilex ambigua, Nemopanthus mucronatus, Prunus ilicifolia*

mountain laurel: *Kalmia latifolia* (See **spoonwood**.), *Umbellularia californica* (See **myrtle, Oregon**.)

mountain lily: *Leucocrinum montanum* (See **star lily**.)

mountain lover: *Paxistima Canbyi, P. Myrsinites*

mountain magnolia: *Magnolia acuminata, M. fraserii*

mountain mahagony: *Betula lenta* (See **mahogany birch** and **sweet birch**.), *Cercocarpus, Taxus brevifolia*

mountain mahoe: *Hibiscus tiliaceus*

mountain maple: *Acer circinatum,*

A. spicatum, A. glabrum douglasii, Alnus rhombifolia

mountain mint: ***Pycnanthemum***

mountain papaya: *Carica pubescens* (See **papaya**.)

mountain parsley: *Cryptogramma crispa*

mountain parsley fern: ***Cryptogramma crispa*** (See **mountain parsley**.)

mountain phlox: ***Phlox*** *subulata* (See **ground pink** and **moss pink**.)

mountain pieris: *Andromeda floribunda* (See **Pieris**.), ***Pieris*** *floribunda* (See **fetterbush**.)

mountain pride: *Penstemon Newberryi*

mountain rhubarb: *Rumex alpinus*

mountain ribbonwood: ***Hoheria*** *glabrata*

mountain rose: ***Antigonon*** *leptopus, Rosa pendulina, Rhododendron catawbiense*

mountain rosebay: ***Rhododendron*** *catawbiense* (See **mountain rose**.)

mountain sandwort: *Arenaria groenlandica*

mountain sorrel: ***Oxyria***

mountain spinach: *Atriplex hortensis* (See **orache**.)

mountain spray: ***Holodiscus*** *dumosus*

mountain tea: *Gaultheria procumbens* (See **spiceberry** and **teaberry**.)

mountain tobacco: ***Arnica*** *montana*

mountain winterberry: *Ilex ambigua* (See **mountain holly**.)

mountain wood fern: *Thelypteris Oeopteris* (See **mountain fern**.)

mourning bride: *Scabiosa atropurpurea* (See **scabious, sweet**.)

mourning cypress: *Chamaecyparis Lawsoniana* (See **Lawson's cypress**.)

mouse-ear: ***Hieracium*** *pilosellais*

mouse-ear: *Antennaria plantaginifolia, Arabidopsis Thaliana, Cerastium,* **Hieracium** *Pilosella, Myosotis*

mouse-ear chickweed: *Cerastium* (See **mouse-ear**.)

mouse-ear cress: *Arabidopsis Thaliana* (See **mouse-ear** and **thale cress**.)

mouse-ear everlasting: *Antennaria plantaginifolia* (See **mouse-ear**.)

mouse-ear hawkweed: *Hieracium Polosella* (See **mouse-ear**.)

mouse-ear plantain: *Antennaria plantaginifolia* (See **mouse-ear**.)

mouse plant: *Arisarem proboscideum*

moxie plum: *Gaultheria hispidula* (See **snowberry, creeping**.)

mudar: *Calotropis*

mud plantain: *Alisma, Heteranthera*

muermo: *Eucryphia cordifolia* (See **ulmo**.)

mugwort: *Artemisia* (See **motherwort**.), *A. vulgaris*

mulberry: *Morus*

mulberry fig: *Ficus Sycomorus* (See **sycamore fig**.)

mulberry, French: *Callicarpa americana*

mulberry, Indian: *Morinda citrifolia*

mullein: *Verbascum, V. Thapsus* (See **feltwort** and **hare's-beard**.)

mullein pink: *Lychnis Coronaria* (See **rose campion**.)

Murray red gum: *Eucalyptus calophylla* (See **red gum**.), *E. camaldulensis* (See **gum**.)

muscadine grape: *Vitis rotundifolia* (See **southern fox grape**.)

mushquash root: *Cicuta maculata*

musk clover: *Erodium moschatum* (See **muskflower**.)

musk hyacinth: *Muscari racemosum* (See **muskflower**.)

musk mallow: *Abelmoschus moschatus, Malva moschata*

muskmellon: *Cucumis Melo*

musk plant: *Mimulus moschatus* (See **muskflower**.)

musk rose: *Rosa moschata* (See **noisette**.)

muskroot: *Adoxa Moschatellina*

mustard: *Brassica*

mustard, mithridate: *Thlaspi arvense*

mustard, tower: *Arabis glabra*

mustard, wild: *Brassica Kabe*

mustard, wormseed: *Erysimum cheiranthoides*

myrobalan: *Phyllanthus emblica, Terminalia catappa* (See **tropical almond**.)

myrrh: *Myrrhis odorata* (See **sweet cicely**.)

myrtle: *Cyrilla racemiflora* (See **leatherwood**.), *Umbellularia californica* (See **mountain laurel, pepperwood** and **spice tree**.), *Vinca, V. minor* (See **myrtle, running**.)

myrtle, Australian willow: *Agonis flexuosa*

myrtle, blue: *Ceanothus thyrsiflorus, Vinca minor*

myrtle, bog: *Myrica Gale*

myrtle, bracelet honey: *Melaleuca armillaris*

myrtle, California wax: *Myrica californica*

myrtle, candleberry: *Myrica*

myrtle, cape: *Myrsine africana*

myrtle, classic: *Myrtus communis*

myrtle, crape: *Lagerstroemia indica*

myrtle, downy: *Rhodomyrtus tomentosa*

myrtle, Dutch: *Myrica gale*

myrtle, dwarf: *Myrtus communis*

myrtle, flag: *Acorus calamus* (See **sweet flag**.)

myrtle, Greek: *Myrtus communis*

myrtle, gum: *Angophora*

myrtle, honey: *Melaleuca*

myrtle, Jew's: *Ruscus aculeatus*

myrtle, Oregon: *Umbellularia californica*

myrtle, polish: *Myrtus communis*

myrtle, queen's crape: *Lagerstroemia speciosa*

myrtle, running: *Vinca minor*

myrtle, sand: *Leiophyllum*

myrtle, sand-verbena: *Backhousia*

myrtle, scent: *Darwinia*

myrtle, sea: *Baccharis halimifolia*

myrtle spurge: *Euphorbia Lathyris* (See **mole plant** and **spurge, caper**.)

myrtle Swedish: *Myrtus communis*

myrtle, Tasmanian: *Nothofagus Cunninghamii*

myrtle, wax: *Myrica cerifera*

myrtle, Western tea: *Melaleuca nesophylla*

myrtle, willow: *Agonis*

mysteria: *Colchicum autumnale* (See **crocus, autumn** and **saffron, meadow**.)

N

naiad: *Naias*

nailwort: *Paronychia*

naio: *Myoporum sandwicense* (See **sandalwood, bastard**.)

naked lady: *Amaryllis belladonna, Colchicum autumnale*

naked-lady lily: *Amaryllis belladonna* **(See lily, Belladonna.)**

nakedwood: *Canella, Colubrina*

Namaqualand daisy: *Venidium*

nandin: *Nandina domestica*

nannyberry: *Viburnum prunifolium* (See **sheepberry** and **stagbush**.), *V. Lentago* (See **Sheepberry** and **tea plant**.)

nanny plum: *Viburnum Lentago* (See **nannyberry, sheepberry**, and **tea plant**)

Napa cabbage: *Brassica rapa*

nap-at-noon: *Ornithogalum umbellatum, Tragopogon pratensis*

Narihira bamboo: *Semiarundinaria fastuosa*

narrow beech fern: *Phegopteris connectilis*, Thelypteris phegopteris

narrow-leafed perennial pea: *Lathyrus sylvestris* (See **pea, perennial**.)

narrow-leaved fritillaria: *Fritillaria lanceolata* (See **lily, checker**.)

narrow-leaved plantain: **Plantago** lanceolata (See **star-of-the-earth**.)

naseberry: Manilkara zapota (See **sapodilla**.)

nasturtium: **Tropaeolum** majus, *T. tuberosum*

Natal ivy: *Senecio macroglossus*

Natal lily: *Moraea*

Natal plum: *Carissa grandiflora, C. macrocarpa*

native fuchsia: *Correa*

navelseed: Omphalodes (See **navelwort**.)

navelwort: *Cotyledon umbilicus,* **Hydrocotyle**, *H. vulgaris (see* **marsh pennywort**.*),* **Omphalodes**, *Umbilicus
rupestris* (See **kidneywort** and **pennywort**.)

Nebraska fern: **Conium** *maculatum*

necklace poplar: *Populus balsamifera,
P. deltoides*

necklace tree: **Ormosia**

necklace vine: *Crassula rupestris,*
Muehlenbeckia *complexa*

needle furze: *Genista anglica* (See
furze.)

neem tree: *Azadirachta indica* (See
neem.)

nenuphar: *Nuphar luteum, Nymphaea
alba*

nerveroot: *Cypripedium, Calceolus pubescens* (See **Venus's-shoe**.)

nettle: *Urtica*

nettle, false: *Boehmeria*

nettle, flame: *Coleus*

nettle-leaved bellflower: *Campanula
trachelium* (See **throatwort**.)

nettle tree: *Celtis occidentalis, C. australis*
(See **hackberry** and **sugarberry**.)

New Jersey tea: *Ceanothus americanus*
(See **redroot**.)

New York fern: *Thelypteris nevadensis*
(See **Parathelypteris**.), *T. noveboracensis*

New Zealand brass buttons: **Cotula**
squalida

New Zealand Christmas tree: *Metrosideros excelsis, M. robustus*

New Zealand Flax: **Phormium** *tenax*

New Zealand hempel: **Phormium**
tenax

New Zealand laurel: **Corynocarpus**,
C. laevigata

New Zealand pepper tree: **Macropiper**
excelsum

New Zealand spinach: *Tetragonia tet-
ragonioudes*

nibung: *Oncosperma tigillarium*

nibung palm: *Oncosperma tigillarium*

nicker tree: *Caesalpinia, Gymnocladus
dioica* (See **stump tree**.)

niger seed: *Guizotia abyssinica* (See
ramtil.)

night blooming cereus: *Hylocereus
undatus, Nyctocereus serpentinus, Selenocereus, S. grandiflorus*

night-blooming jasmine: *Cestrum nocturnum* (See **jasmine**.)

night jasmine: *Cestrum nocturnum,*
Nyctanthes *arbor-tristis* (See **tree of
sadness**.)

night jessamine: *Cestrum nocturnum*
nightshade: *Solanum, Trillium*
ninebark: *Physocarpus*, P. opulifolius
Nippon-bells: *Shortia uniflora*
nitta tree: *Parkia, P. biglobosa, P. filicoidea*
Noah's-ark: *Cypripedium Calceolus pubescens* (See **Venus's-shoe**.)
noble fir: *Abies procera* (See **fir**.)
nodding onion: *Allium cernuum* (See **onion, wild**.)
noisette: *Rosa chinensis, R. moschata*
noonflower: *Ornithogalum umbellatum, Tragopogon pratensis* (See **nap-at-noon**.)
Nootka cypress: *Chamaecyparis Nootkatenis* (See **cypress**.)
nopal: *Nopalea, Opuntia*
Norfolk Island pine: *Araucaria heterophylla*, (See **pine, Australian** and **pine, house**.)
northern beech fern: *Phegopteris connectilis*
northern prickly ash: *Zanthoxylum americana* (See **toothache tree**.)
northern red oak: *Quercus rubra*

Norway pine: *Pinus resinosa*
Norway spruce: *Picea abies*
nosegay: *Plumeria* , P. rubra
nun's orchid: *Phaius grandifolius*, P. tankervilliae, *Phajus grandifolius*, P. tankervilliae
nut grass: *Cyperus esculentus* (See **rush nut**.)
nut, Jesuits': *Trapa natans*
nut, Madeira: *Juglans regia*
nutmeg: *Myristica fragrans*
nutmeg, California: *Torreya Californica*
nutmeg flower: *Nigella sativa*
nutmeg hyacinth: *Muscari racemosum* (See **muskflower**.)
nutmeg tree: *Myristica fragrans* (See **nutmeg**.)
nut orchid: *Achimenes*
nut pine: *Pinus cembra, P. cembroides, P. edulis P. monophylla*, (See **stone pine**.), *P. Pinea*
nut sedge: *Cyperus esculentus* (See **rush nut**.)
nut, Spanish: *Gynadriris Sisyrinchium*
nut tree, Australian: *Macadamia*

O

oak: *Quercus*

oak, Australian turkey: *Quercus cerris austriaca*

oak, ballota: *Quercus ilex rotundifolia*

oak, barren: *Quercus ilicifolia, Q. marilandica*

oak, basket: *Quercus Michauxii, Q. prinus* (See **oak, chestnut** and **oak, swamp chestnut**.)

oak, bear: *Quercus ilicifolia*

oak, black: *Quercus velutina* (See **oak, yellow-barked**.)

oak, blue: *Quercus Douglasii*

oak, bluejack: *Quercus incana*

oak, bur: *Quercus macrocarpa*

oak, California black: *Quercus Kelloggii*

oak, California field: *Quercus agrifolia* (See **oak, California live**.)

oak, California live: *Quercus agrifolia*

oak, California scrub: *Quercus dumosa*

oak, California white: *Quercus lobata* (See **oak, valley**.)

oak, canyon: *Quercus chrysolepis* (See **oak, Valparaiso**.)

oak, canyon live: *Quercus chrysolepis* (See **oak, canyon** and **oak, Valparaiso**.)

oak, Catesby: *Quercus laevis*

oak chestnut: *Castanopsis, Quercus Muehlenbergii* (See **oak, yellow**.), *Q. prinus*

oak, chinquapin: *Quercus prinoides*

oak, cork: *Quercus Suber*

oak, cow: *Quercus Michauxii*

oak, Daimyo: *Quercus dentata*

oak, Darlington: *Quercus laurifolia*

oak, deer: *Quercus Sadlerana*

oak, durmast: *Quercus petraea*

oak, dwarf chestnut: *Quercus prinoides*

obedience plant: ***Physostegia*** (See
lion's-heart.), *P. virginiana*

obedient plant: *Physostegia*

Oconee-bells: *Shortia galacifolia* (See
shortia.)

ocotillo: ***Fouquieria*** *splendens* (See
vine cactus.)

octopus tree: *Brassaia actinophylla*
(See **Schefflera**.), *Schefflera actinophylla* (See **umbrella tree, Queensland**.)

ocumo: ***Xanthosoma****, sagittifolium* (See
kale, Indian.)

oilcloth flower: *Anthurium andraeanum*
(See **lily, flamingo**.)

okra: ***Abelmoschus*** *esculentus* (See
lady's-finger.)

old-field pine: *Pinus Taeda* **(See
loblolly pine**.)

old maid: *Catharanthus rosea* (See
Vinca.), *Zinnia elegans*

old-man: *Artemisia Abrotanum* (See
southernwood.)

old-man-and-woman: *Sempervivum tectorum* (See **houseleek** and **thunder
plant**.)

old-man cactus: ***Cephalocereus*** *senilis*

old-man-of-the-Andes: *Borzicactus
Trollii*

old-man's-beard: ***Chionanthus*** *virginicus* (See **clematis**.), *Clematis virginiana, C. vitalba,* ***Vittaria*** *lineata* (See
shoestring fern.)

old plainsman: ***Hymenopappus*** *scabiosaeus*

old woman: *Artemisia stellerana* (See
wormwood.)

oleander: ***Nerium****, N. oleander* (See
rosebay.)

oleander, common: *Nerium
oleander*

oleaster: *Elaeagnus*

olive: *Olea Europaea*

olive plum: *Cassine*

olive, Russian: *Elaeagnus*

olive scutcheon: *Liparis Loeselii* (See
orchid, fen.)

olive wood: *Cassine*

one-berry: *Celtis, Mitchella repens*

one-flowered pyrola: ***Moneses***
uniflora

one-flowered shinleaf: ***Moneses***
uniflora

onion: ***Allium****, A. Cepa*

onion, Japanese bunching: *Allium fistulosum* (See **Welsh onion**.)

onion, sea: *Ornithogalum caudatum,
Scilla verna, Urginea maritima*

onion, Spanish: *Allium fistulosum* (See
Welsh onion.)

onion, two-bladed: *Allium fistulosum*
(See **Welsh onion**.)

onion, wild: *Allium canadense, A. cernuum*

opium poppy: *Papaver somniferum* (See **poppy**.)

opopanax: *Acacia Farnesiana* (See **sponge tree**.)

opposumwood: *Halesia carolina* (See **shittimwoood**.)

orache: *Atriplix* (See **saltbush**.), *A. hortensis* (See **spinach, mountian**.)

orange: *Citrus sinensis*

orange, bigarade: *Citrus sinensis* (See **orange**.)

orange, bitter: *Citrus sinensis* (See **orange**.)

orange browallia: **Streptosolon** *Jamesonii*

orange flower: *Choisya ternata, Trillium erectum*

orange flower, Mexican: *Choisya ternata*

orangeglowe vine: *Senecioconfusus*

orange grass: *Hypericum gentianoides* (See **pineweed**.)

orange jasmine: **Murraya** *paniculata* (See **satinwood**.)

orange jessamine: *Murraya paniculata* (See **satinwood**.)

orange lily: *Lilium bulbiferum*

orange, mandarin: *Citrus reticulata* (See **tangerine**.)

orange, Mexican: *Choisya ternata* (See **orange flower**.)

orange, mock: *Pittosporum undulatum* (See **Victorian box**.)

orange, native: *Microcitrus australasica*

orange, Osage: *Maclura pomifera*

orangeroot: *Hydrastis*, *H. canadensis* (See **goldenseal** and **yellowroot**.)

orange, Seville: *Citrus sinensis* (See **orange**.)

orange, sweet: *Citrus sinensis* (See **orange**.)

orange, wild: *Poncirius trifoliata, Prunus caroliniana, Zanthoxylum clava-Herculis*

orchid amaryllis: **Sprekelia** *formosissima* (See **lily, Aztec** and **Saint-James's-lily**.)

orchid, buttonhole: *Epidendrum*

orchid cactus: *Epiphyllum*

orchid, cranefly: *Tipularia discolor*

orchid, dancing-lady: *Oncidium*

orchid, fen: *Liparis Loeselii*

orchid, fringed: **Habenaria** (See **rein orchis**.)

orchid foxtail: *Rhynchostylis*

orchid, gold-lace: **Haemaria**

orchid, green fringed: *Habenaria lacera* (See **orchid, ragged**.)

orchid, ladyslipper: *Cypripedium, Paphiopedilum*

orchid, moth: *Phalaenopsis*

orchid pansy: ***Achimenes***, *Miltonia*

orchid, ragged: *Habenaria lacera*

orchid, ragged fringed: *Habenaria lacera* (See **orchid, ragged**.)

orchid, rein: ***Habenaria***

orchid tree: *Bauhinia purpurea, B. variegata*

orchid, vanda: *Vanda*

oregano: ***Origanum*** *vulgare*

Oregon boxwood: *Paxistima Myrsinites* (See **mountain lover**.)

Oregon crab apple: *Malus fusca* (See **powitch**.)

Oregon grape: *Mahonia* (See **hollygrape**.), *M. Aquifolium, M. nervosa*

Oregon myrtle: *Umbellularia californica* (See **mountain laurel** and **pepperwood**.)

organ-pipe cactus: ***Lemaireocereus*** *marginatus*

Oriental arborvitae: ***Platycladus***

Oriental chain fern: ***Woodwardia*** *orientalis*

Oriental pear: *Pyrus pyrifolia*

Oriental poppy: *Papaver orientale* (See **poppy**.)

orpine: *Sedum* (See **stonecrop**.)

orpine, evergreen: *Sedum Anacampseros*

Osage orange: ***Maclura*** *pomifera*

osier: ***Salix***, *S. viminalis*

osier, red: *Cornus sericea*

osmund: ***Osmunda***

osoberry: *Oemleria cerasiformis*

ostrich fern: *Matteuccia*

oswego tea: ***Monarda,*** *M. didyma* (See **bee balm**.)

otaheite gooseberry: ***Phyllanthus*** *acidus*

otaheite walnut: *Aleurites moluccana* (See **tallow tree**.)

our lady's bedstraw: *Galium verum* (See **lady's bedstraw**.)

overcup oak: *Quercus lyrata* (See **swamp post oak**.)

owl's clover: ***Orthocarpus***

oxeye: *Chysanthemum Leucanthemum,* ***Heliopsis*** *helianthoides*

oxeye, creeping: *Wedelia trilobata*

oxeye daisy: *Chrysanthemum Leucanthemum* (See **horse daisy, moon daisy, moonflower**, and **oxeye**.)

oxeye, yellow: *Chrysamthemum segetum, Rudbeckia hirta*

oxlip: *Primula elatior*
oxtongue: *Anchusa, A. Gasteria, A. officinalis, A. Picris,* **Gasteria**
oyster plant: *Mertensia maritima, Rhoeo* *spathaceae* (See **lily, boat** and **three-men-in-a-boat**.), *Tragopogon porrifolius* (See **salsify**.)

P

Pacific wax myrtle: Myrica californica (See **myrtle, California wax**.)

padauk: **Pterocarpus**, *P. indicus* (See **kiabooca**.)

pagoda flower: **Clerodendrum**

pagoda tree: **Plumeria**

paintbrush: **Castilleja**

painted cup: *Castilleja*

painted daisy: *Pyrethrum coccineum, Tanacetum coccineum* (See **pyrethrum**.)

painted lady: *Echeveria derenbergii, Lathyrus odoratus*

painted tongue: **Salpiglossis** *sinuata*

paint rock: **Lachnanthes** *caroliana*

paint root: *Lachnanthes caroliana* (See **redroot**.)

palas tree: *Butea monosperma*

pale laurel: *Kalmia polifolia* (See **swamp laurel**.)

pale snapweed: *Impatiens pallida* (See **quick-in-the-hand**.)

pale touch-me-not: *Impatiens pallida* (See **quick-in-the-hand**.)

palm, Australian ivy: *Schefflera actinophyla* (See **umbrella tree**.)

palma christi: **Ricinus**, *R. communis* (See **castor bean**.)

palm, bamboo: *Rhapis excelsa* (See **palm, hemp**.)

Palm-Beach-bells: **Kalanchoe**

palm, California: **Washingtonia** *filifera*

palm, Caribee royal: **Roystonea** *oleracea*

palm, Chilean wine: **Jubaea**

palm, Christmas: **Veitchia** *merrillii*

palm, coquito: **Jubaea**

palm, Cuban royal: **Roystonea** *regia*

palm, desert fan: **Washingtonia** *filifera*

palm, dwarf: *Chamaerops humilis* (See **palm, hemp**.)

palmella: *Yucca elata* (See **soap tree**.)

palmetto: Chamaerops humilis (See **palm, hemp**.), *Sabal*

palm, fan: *Chamaerops humilis* (See **palm, hemp**.)

palm, fishtail: *Caryota urens* (See **jaggery palm**.)

palm grass: *Curculigo* capitulata

palm, hemp: *Chamaerops humilis, Rhapsis excelsa*

palm, honey: *Jubaea*

palm, ita: *Mauritia flexuosa*

palm, ivory: *Phytelephas macrocarpa*

palm, lady: *Rhapis* excelsa

palm lily: *Cordyline*

palm, little cokernut: *Jubaea*

palm, Manila: *Veitchia* merrillii

palm, miniature fan: *Rhapsis excelsa* (See **palm, hemp**.)

palm, needle: *Rhapidophyllum hystrix*

palm, peach: *Bactris gasipaes, Gulielma gasipaes*

palm, pindo: *Butea capitata*

palm, rattan: *Rhapis humilis*

palm, royal: *Roystonea, R. elata*

palm, slender-lady: *Rhapis excelsa* (See **palm, hemp**.), *R. humilis* (See **rattan**.)

palm, syrup: *Jubaea*

palm, talipot: *Corypha umbraculifera* (See **talipot**.)

palm, umbrella: *Cyperus alternifolius* (See **umbrella plant**.)

palm, Washington: *Washingtonia*

palm, windmill: *Trachycarpus fortunei*

palmyra palm: *Borassus flabellifer* (See **palmyrae**.)

palmyra tree: *Borassus flabellifer* (See **palmyrae**.)

pampas grass: *Cortaderia, C. jubata, C. selloana*

panamiga: *Pilea involucrata*

panamigo: *Pilea involucrata* (See **panamiga**.)

panda plant: *Kalanchoe tomentosa*

pansy: *Viola* (See **heartsease**.), *V. ocellata* (See **garden-gate**.), *V. tricolor* (See **herb trinity, kiss-me**, and **lady's-delight**.)

pansy orchid: *Miltonia*

pansy, tufted: *Viola cornuta* (See **violet, horned**.)

pansy, wild: *Viola pedunculata*

papaw: *Asimina triloba* (See **paw paw**.)

papaya: *Carica papaya* (See **melon tree**.)

paperbark: *Melaleuca quinquenervia*

paperbark tree: *Melaleuca quinquenervia* (See **swamp tea tree**.)

paper birch: *Betula papyrifera*
paper mulberry: ***Broussonetia*** *papy-rifera*
paper reed: *Cyperus papyrus*
paper-shrub: *Daphne bholua*
paper tree: *Broussonetia papyrifera* (See **paper mulberry**.)
paphs: ***Paphiopedilum***
papoose root: ***Caulophyllum*** *thalic-troides*
papyrus: ***Cyperus*** *papyrus*
papyrus, dwarf: *Cyperus haspan, C. iso-cladus*
papyrus, miniature: *Cyperus haspan, C. isocladus*
paradise lily: *Paradisea Liliastrum* (See **Saint-Bruno's-lily**.)
paradise nut: *Lecythis Zabucayo* (See **sapucia nut**.)
paradise plant: *Jacobinia carnea, Justicia carnea* (See **plume flower**.)
paradise tree: ***Melia*** *Azedarach* (See **li-lac, Indian**.), *Simarouba glauca* (See **mountain damson**.)
Paraguay tea: *Ilex paraquariensis* (See **yerba mate**.)
parasol fir: *Pinus densiflora, P. pinea, Sciadopitys verticillata*
parasol tree: *Firmiana simplex*
Paris daisy: *Argyranthemum frutescens*

parlor maple: *Abutilon* (See **flowering maple**.)
parlor palm: ***Chamaedorea*** *elegans*
parrot's-beak: ***Clianthus*** *puniceus* (See **pea, glory**.), *Lotus berthelotii* (See **coral gem**.)
parrot's-bill: *Clianthus puniceus* (See **pea, glory**.)
parrot's-feather: *Myriophyllum aquati-cum, M. proserpinacoides*
parrot's-flower: *Heliconia psittacorum*
parsley: ***Petroselinum*** *crispum*
parsley fern: *Asplenium bulbiferum, Cryptogramma acrostichoides, C. crispa, Tanacetum vulgare*
parsley haw: *Crataegus apiifolia, C. marshallii*
parsley piert: *Alchemilla microcarpa*
parsnip: *Pastinaca sativum*
partridgeberry: ***Mitchella***, *M. repens* (See **hive vine**, **one-berry**, **squaw-berry**, **turkey berry tree**, and **twin-berry**.)
partridge pea: *Cassia fasciculata* (See **senna, prairie** and **sensitive pea**.), *Chamaecrista fasciculata*
pasqueflower: *Anemone pulsatilla* (See **daneflower** and **Easter flower**.), ***Pulsatilla***
passionflower: ***Passiflora***

patience: *Rumex patientia*

patience dock: ***Rumex*** *patientia* (See
patience.)

patience plant: *Impatiens wallerana*,
Rumex patientia (See **patience**.)

patient Lucy: *Impatiens wallerana* (See
patience plant.)

paw paw: ***Asimina*** *triloba*

pea: *Pisum sativum*

pea, Angola: *Cajanus cajan*

pea, asparagus: *Psophocarpus tetragonolobus* (See **pea, winged**.)

pea, beach: *Lathyrus japonicus*

pea, black-eyed: ***Vigna***, *V. unguiculata*

pea, butterfly: *Centrosema virginianum*,
Clitoria

pea, Canada: *Vicia Cracca* (See **vetch,
tufted**.)

peace-in-the-home: ***Soleirolia*** *Soleirolii*

peach: *Prunus Persica*

peach, desert: *Prunus andersonii*

peach oak: *Quercus phellos*

peach protea: ***Protea*** *grandiceps*

peach, wild: *Prunus fasciculata*

peacock flower: ***Delonix***, *D. regia*

peacock flower-fence: ***Adenanthera***
pavonina (See **sandalwood,
red**.)

peacock iris: *Moraea pavonia*, *M.
neopavonia*

pea, Congo: *Cajanus cajan* (See **pea,
Angola**.)

pea, earthnut: *Lathyrus tuberosus* (See
pea, tuberous.)

pea, glory: *Clianthus*

pea, hoary: *Tephrosia*

pea, Lord Anson's blue: *Lathyrus
nerosus*

pea, love: *Abrus precatorius* (See **vine,
red-beard**.)

pea, no-eye: *Cajanus cajan* (See **pea,
Angola**.)

peanut: ***Arachis***, *A. hypogaea*

peanut cactus: *Chamaecereus*

pea, partridge: *Cassia fasciculata*

pea, perennial: *Lathyrus latifolius*, *L.
sylvestris*

pea, pigeon: *Cajanus cajan* (See **pea,
Angola**.)

pea, princess: *Psophocarpus tetragonolobus*
(See **pea, winged**.)

pear: *Pyrus communis*

pear, alligator: *Persea americana*

pear fruit: ***Margyricarpus*** *setosus* (See
pearl-berry.)

pear, garlic: *Crateva religiosa*

pear haw: *Crataegus tomentosa*, *C.
calpodendron*

pearl-berry: ***Margyricarpus*** *setosus*

pearlbush: *Exochorda*

pearl millet: ***Pennisetum*** *americanum*

pearl plant: *Haworthia margaritifera*

pearl-twist: *Spiranthes*

pearlwort: ***Sagina***, *S. subulata*

pearlwort, Corsican: *Arenaria balearica*

pearly everlasting: *Anaphalis margaritacea* (See **povertyweed**.)

pea, rosary: *Abrus precatorius* (See **vine, red-beard**.)

pea shrub: *Caragana frutex* (See **pea tree**.)

pea, sweet: *Lathyrus odoratus*

pea, Tangier: *Lathyrus tingitanus*

pea tree: *Caragana*

pea, tuberous: *Lathyrus tuberosus*

pea, winged: *Lotus berthelotii, L. tetragonolobus, Psophocarpus tetragonolobus*

pebble plant: ***Mesembryanthemum***

pecan: *Carya illioensis, C. pecan*

peepal: *Ficus religiosa* (See **pipal tree**.)

peepul: *Ficus religiosa* (See **pipal tree**.)

pelican flower: *Aristolochia grandiflora*

pellitory: *Parietaria officinalis*

pencil bush: *Euphorbia tirucalli* (See **pencil tree**.)

pencil tree: *Euphorbia Tirucalli* (See **spurge, Indian tree**.)

Pennsylvania maple: *Acer pensylvanicum* (See **maple, striped**.)

penny cress: ***Thlaspi***, *T. arvense* (See **mustard, mithridate**.)

pennyflower: *Lunaria annua*

penny grass: *Rhinanthus crista-galli, Thlaspi arvense* (See **penny cress**.)

pennyroyal, American: *Hedeoma pulegioides*

pennyroyal, bastard: *Trichostema dichotomum*

pennywort: *Cotyledon umbilicus,* ***Cybmalaria*** *muralis,* (See **toadflax, ivy-leaved**.), *Umbilicus rupestris* (See **kidneywort** and **navalwort**.)

peony: *Paeonia*

pepper-and-salt: *Erigenia bulbosa* (See **harbinger-of-spring**.)

pepper-bush, sweet: *Clethra alnifolia*

pepper, Celebes: *Piper ornatum*

pepper, Chinese: *Zanthoxylum piperitum*

pepper cress: *Lepidium* (See **peppergrass**.)

peppergrass: *Lepidium, L. sativum* (See **pepper, poor man's**.), ***Pilularia***

peppermint: *Mentha piperita*

peppermint tree: ***Agonis***, *A. flexuosa* (See **myrtle, Australian willow** and **willow myrtle**.)

pepper, poor man's: *Lepidium sativum*

pepperidge: *Nyssa sylvatica* (See **sour gum**.)

pepperroot: *Dentaria*, (See **tooth-wort**.)

pepper tree: *Schinus*, *S. Molle*

pepper vine: *Ampelopsis* arborea, *Piper nigrum*

pepper, wild: *Vitex agnus-castus*

pepperwood: *Umbellularia* californica (See **mountain laurel**, **myrtle, Oregon** and **spice tree**.), *Zanthoxylum clava-Hercules* (See **sea ash**.)

pepperwort: *Lepidium*, *L. sativum* (See **pepper, poor man's**.), **Marsilea peregrina**: *Jatropha integerrima*

perennial hibiscus: *Hibiscus Moscheutos*

perennial phlox: *Phlox* paniculata

perennial ryegrass: *Lolium* perenne

perfumed fairy lily: *Chlidanthus* fragrans

periwinkle, Madagascar: *Catharanthus rosea* (See *Vinca*.)

periwinkle: *Catharanthus roseus*, *Vinca*, *V. major*

periwinkle, rose: *Catharanthus rosea* (See *Vinca*.)

Persian buttercup: *Ranunculus asiaticus* (See **turban buttercup**.)

Persian lilac: *Melia Azedarach* (See **lilac, Indian**.)

Persian ranunculus: *Ranunculus asiaticus* (See **turban buttercup**.)

Persian violet: *Cyclamen* (See **sow-bread**.)

persimmon: *Diospyros*

Peruvian jacinth: *Scilla peruviana* (See **hyacinth, Peruvian** and **lily, Cuban**.)

Peruvian lily: *Alstroemeria*

Peruvian mastic tree: *Schinus Molle*

Peruvian pepper tree: *Schinus Molle*

petticoat daffodil: *Narcissus Bulbocodium* (See **daffodil, hoop-petticoat**.)

petty morel: *Aralia racemosa* (See **spikenard**.)

pheasant's-eye: *Adonis*, *A. annua* (See **bird's-eye**.), *Narcissus poeticus*

philodendron, bird's-nest: *Philodendron bipinnatifidum*, *P. cannifolium*, *P. selloum*, *P.wendlandii*

philodendron, dubia: *Philodendron radiatum*

philodendron, heart-leaf: *Philodendron scandens*

philodendron, red-leaf: *Philodendron erubescens*

philodendron, spade-leaf: *Philodendron domesticum*

philodendron, split-leaf: *Monstera deliciosa*, *Philodendron pertusum*

phoenix tree: *Firmiana simplex* (See **parasol tree**.)

piccabean bangalow palm: ***Archontophoenix***

piccabean palm: ***Archontophoenix***

pickaback plant: *Tolmiea menziesii*

pickerel weed: ***Pontederia***, *P. cordata*

pickleweed: *Salicornia, S. europaea* (See **pigeonfoot**.)

pie-marker: *Abutilon Theophrasti* (See **velvetleaf**.)

pieplant: ***Rheum*** *Rhabarbarum*

pigeonberry: *Duranta repens* (See **sky flower**.), ***Phytolacca***, *P. americana* (See **pokeweed** and **poke, Virginian**.)

pigeonfoot: *Salicornia europaea* (See **pickleweed**, **pigeonfoot**, and **samphire**.)

pigeon pea: ***Cajanus***

pigeon plum: *Coccoloba diversifolia*

pigeon-wings: *Clitoria*

pigface: *Carpobrotus aequilaterus* (See **pig's-face**.)

piggyback plant: ***Tolmiea*** *menziesii* (See **pickaback plant** and **youth-on-age**.)

pig laurel: *Kalmia angustifolia* (See **lambkill** and **sheep laurel**.)

pignut: *Carya cordiformis* (See **swamp hickory**.), *C. glabra* (See **hognut**.)

pignut hickory: *Carya glabra* (See **pignut**.)

pig's-face: *Carpobrotus aequilaterus, C. chilensis*

pigweed: *Amaranthus retroflexus*, ***Chenopodium*** (See **goosefoot**.), *Chenopodium album* (See **lamb's-quarters**.)

pilewort: *Ranunculus Ficaria* (See **lesser celandine**.)

pillwort: ***Pilularia***, *P. globulifera*

pimpernel: ***Anagallis***

pinaster: *Pinus pinaster*

pin cherry: *Prunus pensylvanica*

pin clover: *Erodium cicutarium* (See **pin grass**.)

pincushion: *Leucospermum*, ***Mammillaria*** (See **strawberry cactus**.), *Scabiosa atropurpurea* (See **mourning bride**.)

pincushion cactus: *Mammillaria*

pincushion flower: *Leucospermum*, *Scabiosa* (See **pincushion cactus**.), *S. ochroleuca*

pincushion tree: ***Hakea***

pindar: ***Arachis***

pine: *Pinus* (See **fir tree**.)

pine, Afghan: *Pinus eldarica*

pine, African fern: *Podocarpus gracilior*
pine, air: *Aechmea*
pine, Aleppo: *Pinus halepensis*
pineapple: *Ananas, A. comosus*
pineapple flower: *Eucomis*
pineapple guava: *Feijoa sellowiana*
pineapple lily: *Eucomis* (See **pineapple flower**.)
pineapple shrub: *Calycanthus floridus* (See **strawberry shrub**.)
pine, Australian: *Araucaria heterophylla, Casuarina* (See **he-oak**.)
pine, Austrian: *Pinus nigra*
pine-barren-beauty: *Pyxidanthera barbulata* (See **moss, flowering**.)
pine, beach: *Pinus contorta*
pine, Bhutan: *Pinus wallichiana*
pine, big-cone: *Pinus coulteri*
pine, bishop: *Pinus muricata*
pine, black cypress: *Pinus muricata*
pine, Bosnian: *Pinus leucodermis*
pine, bristlecone: *Pinus aristata*
pine, Buddhist: *Podocarpus macrophyllus*
pine, Canary Island: *Pinus canariensis*
pine, cedar: *Pinus glabra*
pine, celery: *Phyllocladus trichomanoides* (See **tanekaha**.)
pine, Chilean: *Araucaria araucana*
pine, Chilghoza: *Pinus gerardiana*

pine, Chinese: *Crassula tetragona, Pinus tabuliformis*
pine, Chinese water: *Glyptostrobus lineatus*
pine, Chinese white: *Pinus armandii*
pine, chir: *Pinus roxburghii*
pine, cluster: *Pinus pinaster*
pine, common screw: *Pandanus utilis*
pine, cow's-tail: *Cephalotaxus harringtoniana*
pine, cypress: *Callitris*
pine, dammar: *Agathis*
pine, digger: *Pinus sabiniana*
pine, dwarf Siberian: *Pinus pumila*
pine, dwarf stone: *Pinus pumila* (See **pine, dwarf Siberian**.)
pine, dwarf white: *Pinus strobus*
pine, eastern white: *Pinus strobus*
pine, Formosa: *Pinus taiwanensis*
pine, foxtail: *Pinus balfouriana*
pine, frankincense: *Pinus taeda*
pine, French turpentine: *Pinus pinaster* (See **pine, cluster**.)
pine, Georgia: *Pinus palustris*
pine, Gerard's: *Pinus gerardiana* (See **pine, Chilghoza**.)
pine, giant: *Pinus lambertiana*
pine, gray: *Pinus banksiana*
pine, hickory: *Pinus aristata* (See **pine, bristlecone**.)

pine, hoop: *Araucaria Cunninghamii*

pine, house: *Araucaria heterophylla*

pine, imou: *Dacrydium cupressinum*

pine, Indian longleaf: *Pinus roxburghii* (See **pine, chir**.)

pine, Italian stone: *Pinus pinea*

pine, jack: *Pinus banksiana* (See **pine, gray**.)

pine, Japanese umbrella: *Pinus densiflora* (See **pine, umbrella**.)

pine, Jeffery: *Pinus Jeffreyi* (See **pine, truckee**.)

pine, Jelecote: *Pinus patula*

pine, Jersey: *Pinus virginiana*

pine, jointed: *Polypodium subauriculatum*

pine, knobcone: *Pinus attenuata*

pine, Korean: *Pinus koraiensis*

pine, lacebark: *Pinus bungeana*

pine lily: *Lilium Catesbaei* (See **southern red lily**.)

pine, limber: *Pinus flexilis*

pine, loblolly: *Pinus taeda* (See **pine, frankicense**.)

pine, lodgepole: *Pinus contorta latifolia* (See **tamarack**.)

pine, longleaf: *Pinus oocarpa, P. palustris*

pine, long-tag: *Pinus echinata*

pine, Macedonian: *Pinus peuce*

pine, mahogany: *Podocarpus totara* (See **totara**.)

pine, maritime: *Pinus pinaster* (See **pine, cluster**.)

pine, Mexican stone: *Pinus cembroides*

pine, Mexican yellow: *Pinus patula* (See **pine, Jelecote**.)

pine, mountain: *Pinus mugo*

pine, mugho: *Pinus mugo* (See **pine, mountain**.)

pine, Nepal nut: *Pinus gerardiana* (See **pine, Chilghoza**.)

pine, New Caledonian: *Araucaria columnaris*

pine, Norway: *Pinus resinosa*

pine, nut: *Pinus monophylla, P. edulis, P. pinea* (See **umbrella pine**.)

pine, old-field: *Pinus taeda* (See **pine, frankicense**.)

pine, pinon: *Pinus quadrifolia*

pine, pitch: *Pinus rigida*

pine, poverty: *Pinus virginiana*

pine, prickly: *Pinus pungens*

pine, princess: *Crassula pseudolycopodioides, Lycopodium obscurum*

pine, red: *Pinus resinosa* (See **pine, Norway**.)

pine, Riga: *Pinus sylvestris rigensis* (See **fir, riga**.)

pine, Rocky Mountain yellow: *Pinus ponderosa scopulorum*

pine, rough-barked Mexican: *Pinus montezumae*

pine, running: *Lycopodium clavatum*

pine, sand: *Pinus clausa*

pinesap: *Monotropa uniflora* (See **Indian pipe**.)

pine, Scotch: *Pinus sylvestris*

pine, Scots: *Pinus sylvestris* (See **pine, Scotch**.)

pine, screw: *Pandus veitchii, P. utilis* (See **pandanus** and **pine, common screw**.)

pine, scrub: *Pinus banksiana* (See **pine, gray**.)

pine, shortleaf: *Pinus echinata* (See **pine, long-tag**.)

pine, slash: *Pinus elliottii*

pine, Soledad: *Pinus torreyana*

pine, spruce: *Pinus glabra* (See **pine, cedar**.)

pine, stone: *Pinus monophylla* (See **pine, nut**.), *P. pinea* (See **pine, Italian stone**.)

pine, sugar: *Pinus lambertiana* (See **pine, giant**.)

pine, Swiss mountain: *Pinus mugo* (See **pine, mountain**.)

pine, Swiss stone: *Pinus cembra*

pine, table-mountain: *Pinus pungens* (See **hickory pine**.)

pine, tamarack: *Pinus contorta latifolia* (See **tamarack**.)

pine, tanyosho: *Pinus densiflora*

pine, thatch screw: *Pandanus tectorius*

pine, totara: *Podocarpus totara* (See **pine, mahogany** and **totara**.)

pine tree, miniature: *Crassula tetragona*

pine, truckee: *Pinus Jeffreyi*

pine, twisted: *Pinus contorta*

pine, twisted-leaf: *Pinus teocote*

pine, two-leaved nut: *Pinus edulis* (See **pine, nut**.)

pine, umbrella: *Pinus densiflora, P. pinea* (See **pine, Italian stone**.), *Sciadopitys verticillata*

pine, Veitch screw: *Pandanus veitchii*

pineweed: *Hypericum gentianoides* (See **orange grass**.)

pine, western white: *Pinus monticola*

pine, western yellow: *Pinus ponderosa*

pine, white: *Pinus strobus* **(See pine, eastern white**.)

pine, white bark: *Pinus albicaulis*

pin grass: *Erodium cicutarium* **(See pin clover**.)

pink: *Dianthus*

pink, California Indian: *Silene californica*

pink cedar: *Acrocarpus fraxinifolius* (See **shingle tree**.)

pink, Cheddar: *Dianthus gratianopolis*

pink, clove: *Dianthus caryophyllyus*

pink, cluster-head: *Dianthus carthusianorum*

pink, cottage: *Dianthus plumarius*

pink, cushion: *Silene acaulis*

pink, Deptford: *Dianthus armeria*

pink, fire: *Silene virginica*

pink fritillary: *Fritillaria pluriflora* (See **lily, adobe**.)

pink, grass: *Calopogon pulchellus* (See **cottage pink**.)

pink, Indian: *Spigelia marilandica* (See **worm grass**.)

pink melaleuca: *Melaleuca nesophylla* (See **myrtle, Western tea**.)

pink mountain heather: *Phyllodoce empetriformis*

pink needle: *Erodium cicutarium* (See **pin grass**.)

pink pokers: *Phylliostachys Suworwii* (See **Russian statice**.)

pink polka-dot plant: *Hypoestes phyllostachya* (See **flamingo plant**.)

pink porcelain lily: *Alpinia Zerumbet* (See **shellflower**.)

pinkroot: *Spigelia marilandica* (See **pink, Indian**, **spiderwort**, and **worm grass**.)

pink slipper orchid: *Calypso*

pinkster flower: *Rhododendron nudiflorum, R. periclymenoides* (See **pinxter flower**.)

pink trumpet vine: *Podranea ricasoliana*

pink vine: *Antigonon leptopus* (See **mountain rose**.)

pink, wild: *Arethusa bulbosa, Silene caroliniana*

pin oak: *Quercus palustris* (See **swamp Spanish oak**.)

pinwheel: *Aeonium haworthii*

pinxterbloom: *Rhododendron nudiflorum, R. periclymenoides* (See **pinxter flower**.)

pinyon: *Pinus quadrifolia* (See **pine, pinon**.)

pipal tree: *Ficus religiosa*

pipe vine: *Aristolochia californica, A. durior, A. macrophylla*

pipewort: *Eriocaulon*

pipsissewa: *Chimaphila umbellata*

pipul: *Ficus religiosa* (See **pipal tree**.)

pirul: *Schinus Molle*

pistache, Chinese: *Pistacia chinensis*

pitahaya: *Echinocereus*

pitanga: *Eugenia uniflora*

pitaya: *Echinocereus* (See **pitahaya**.)

pitcher plant: *Nepenthes*, *Sarracenia* (See **huntsman's-cup** and **Indian cup**.)

pitchforks: *Bidens* (See **stick-tight**.)

plane tree: *Plantanus* (See **sycamore**.)

plantain: *Musa*, *M. paradisiaca*, *Plantago*, *P. lanceolata* (See **ribgrass, ribwort**.)

plantain, rattlesnake: *Goodyera*

platter dock: *Nymphaea alba* (See **lily, European white water**.)

platterleaf: *Coccoloba Uvifera*

Platyphyllum: *Lilium auratum*

pleroma: *Tibouchina urvilleana*

pleurisy root: *Asclepias tuberosa*

plum, beach: *Prunus maritima*

plum, Chickasaw: *Prunus angustifolia*

plume flower: *Jacobinia carnea*, *Justicia carnea*

plume poppy: *Macleaya cordata* (See **tree celadine**.)

plumeria: *Plumeria*, *P. rubra* (See **nosegay**.)

plum fir: *Podocarpus andinus*

plum-fruited yew: *Cephalotaxus Harringtonia* (See **yew, Japanese plum**.)

plum juniper: *Juniperus drupacea*

plum, wild: *Prunus Americana*, *P. spinosa*

plum yew: *Cephalotaxus*

pocan: *Phytolacca americana* (See **poke, Virginian**.)

pocketbook flower: *Calceolaria* (See **slipper flower**.)

poet's jasmine: *Jasminium officinale*

poha: *Physalis peruviana*

Poinciana, dwarf: *Caesalpinia pulcherrima*

Poinciana, royal: *Delonix regia*

poinsettia: *Euphorbia pulcherrima*

poinsettia, annual: *Euphorbia cyathophora*, *E. heterophylla*

poisonberry: *Solanum nigrum*

poison bulb: *Crinum asiaticum*

poison dogwood: *Rhus vernix* (See **sumac, poison**.)

poison elder: *Rhus vernix* (See **sumac, poison**.)

poison flag: *Iris versicolor* (See **flag, blue**.)

poison hemlock: *Cicuta* maculata, **Conium** maculatum

poison ivy: *Rhus* radicans (See **sumac**.), *R. Toxicodendron* (See **oak, poison**.)

poison oak: *Rhus diversiloba* (See **sumac**.), *R. diversilobum*

poisonous nightshade: *Solanum Dulcamara* (See **nightshade**.)

poke: ***Phytolacca*** (See **pokeweed**.),
P. americana (See **pigeonberry**,
poke, Virginian, and **red-ink
plant**.)

poker plant: *Kniphofia, Tritoma*

poke, Virginian: *Phytolacca americana*

pokeweed: ***Phytolacca***, *P. americana*
(See **red-ink plant**.)

polecat weed: *Lysichiton americanum,
L. camtschatcense,* ***Symplocarpus*** *foetidus*
(See **swamp cabbage**.)

Pollyanna vine: ***Soleirolia*** *Soleirolii*

polypody: *Polypodium, P. vulgare*

pomegranate: ***Punica*** *granatum*

pomelo: *Citrus grandis, C. maxima* (See
grapefruit, **pummelo**, and **shaddock**.)

pomerac jambos: *Syzygium malaccensis*
(See **malay apple**.)

pomme blanche: ***Psoralea*** *esculenta*

pomme-de-prairie: ***Psoralea*** *esculenta*

pommelo: *Citrus maxima* (See **shaddock**.)

pompelmous: *Citrus maxima* (See
shaddock.)

pond apple: *Annona glabra*

pond dogwood: *Cephalanthus occidentalis*

pond-lily cactus: ***Epiphyllum***

pond nuts: ***Nelumbo*** *Lutea*

pond spice: ***Litsea***, *L. aestivalis*

pondweed: ***Potamogeton***

pondweed, Cape: *Aponogeton distachyus*

pondweed, choke: *Elodea canadensis*

pondweed, horned: *Zannichellia
palustris*

pondweed, tassel: *Ruppia*

poonga-oil tree: ***Pongamia***

poor-man's orchid: ***Schizanthus***

poor man's weatherglass: *Anagallis
arvensis* (See **pimpernel** and **sheperd's clock**.)

Poor Robin's plaintain: *Erigeron pulchellus* (See **robin's plantain**.)

pop ash: *Fraxinus caroliniana* (See **water
ash**.)

popinac: *Acacia Farnesiana* (See **sponge
tree**.)

poplar: ***Populus***

poplar, balsam: *Populus balsamifera*

poplar birch: *Betula alba, B. pendula*

poplar, Carolina: *Populus deltoides*

poplar, downy: *Populus heterophylla*

poplar, silver: *Populus alba*

poplar, trembling: *Populus tremula* (See
tree, trembling.)

poplar, weeping: *Populus grandidentata*

poppy: *Papaver*

poppy anemone: *Anemone coronaria*

poppy, celandine: *Stylophorum diphyllum*

poppy mallow: *Callirhoe*

poppy, matilija: *Romneya*

poppy, prickly: *Argemone mexicana*

porcelain ampelopsis: *Ampelopsis brevipunduculata*

porcelain flower: *Hoya, H. carnosa* (See **wax plant**.)

porcini: *Boletus edulis*

Portia tree: *Thespesia populnea*

Port Orford cedar: *Chamaecyparis lawsoniana* (See **cedar** and **Lawson's cypress**.)

Portuguese cedar: *Cupressus lusitanica* (See **Mexican cypress**.)

portulaca: *Portulaca grandiflora* (See **rose moss**.)

possum grape: *Cissus incisus* (See **marine ivy**.), *C. trifoliata* (See **sorrel vine**.)

post oak: *Quercus stellata* (See **iron oak**.)

pot: *Cannabis sativa* (See **hashish** and **marijauna**.)

potato tree: *Solanum macranthum*

potato vine: *Solanum jasminoides* (See **Solanum**.)

potato, wild: *Ipomoea pandurata*

potato, wild sweet: *Ipomoea pandurata* (See **potato, wild**.)

pothos: *Epipremnum, E. aureum, Rhaphidophora aurea, Scindapsus aurens*

pouch flower: *Calceolaria* (See **slipper flower**.)

pound spice: *Litsea geniculata*

poverty pine: *Pinus virginiana* (See **scrub pine**.)

poverty plant: *Hudsonia tomentosa*

povertyweed: *Anaphalis margaritacea, Iva hayesiana*

powderpuff: *Calliandra*

powitch: *Malus fusca*

prairie apple: *Psoralea esculenta*

prairie burdock: *Silphium terebinthinaceum* (See **prairie dock**.)

prairie cordgrass: *Spartina pectinata*

prairie dock: *Silphium terebinthinaceum*

prairie gentian: *Eustoma grandiflorum*

prairie iris: *Nemastylis acuta* (See **lily, celestial**.)

prairie potato: *Psoralea esculenta* (See **pomme blanche**.)

prairie rose: *Rosa setigera*

prairie senna: *Cassia fasciculata* (See **sensitive pea**.)

prairie turnip: *Psoralea esculenta*

prayer-beads: *Abrus precatorius* (See **pea, rosary** and **vine, red-beard**.)

prayer plant: *Maranta leuconeura kerchovianat* (See **rabbit tracks**.)

pregnant onion: *Ornithogalum caudatum* (See **onion, sea**.)

pretty face: *Triteleia ixioides*

prickly ash: *Aralia spinosa* (See **spikenard tree**.), *Zanthoxylum, Z. americanum*

prickly cucumber: *Echinocystis, E. lobata* (See **mock apple**.)

prickly lettuce: *Lactuca Serriola* (See **thistle, horse**.)

prickly pear: *Opuntia* (See **nopal**.)

prickly pole: *Bacris guineensis*

prickly poppy: *Argemone A. mexicana* (See **Mexican poppy**.)

prickly shield fern: *Polystichum aculeatum*

prickly thrift: *Acantholimon*

prickly water lily: *Euryale*

pride of Barbados: *Caesalpinia pulcherrima* (See **flower-fence**.), *Poinciana pulcherrima*

pride-of-Bolivia: *Tipuana tipu*

pride of California: *Lathyrus splendens*

pride of China: *Melia Azedarach* (See **lilac, Indian**.)

pride-of-India: *Lagerstroemia speciosa* (See **myrtle, queen's crape,**

queen's-flower.), *Melia Azedarach* (See **lilac, Indian**.)

prim: *Ligustrum vulgare* (See **privet**.)

primrose: *Primula, P. vulgaris*

primrose, bird's-eye: *Primula farinosa, P. laurentiana, P. mistassinica*

primrose, Chinese: *Primula sinensis*

primrose, drumstick: *Primula cashmeriana, P. denticulata*

primrose, fairy: *Primula malacoides*

primrose, Himalayan: *Primula sikkimensis*

primrose, Japanese: *Primula Japonica*

primrose tree: *Lagunaria Patersonii*

Prince-of-Wales'-feather: *Amaranthus erythrostachys, A. hypochondriacus* (See **prince's-feather**.)

Prince-of-Wales fern: *Leptopteris superba*

Prince-of-Wales plume: *Leptopteris superba*

prince's-feather: *Amaranthus erythrostachys, A. hypochondriacus, Polygonum orientale*

prince's pine: *Chimaphila umbellata* (See **pipsissewa**.)

prince's-plume: *Stanleya* (See **standing cypress**.), *S. pinnata*

princess feather: *Polygonum orientale* (See **prince's-feather**.)

princess flower: *Tibouchina* urvilleana
princess palm: *Dictyosperma*
princess tree: *Paulownia*
prism cactus: *Leuchtenbergia* principis
privet: *Ligustrum*
privet, Texas: *Ligustrum japonicum*
proboscis flower: *Proboscidea*
propeller flower: *Eustylis purpurea* (See **lily, pinewoods**.)
prophet flower: *Arnebia echioides, A. griffithii*, **Echioides** longifliorum
prostrate coleus: *Plectranthus* (See **spur flower** and **Swedish ivy**.)
Provence rose: *Rosa centifolia*
Provins rose: *Rosa centifolia* (See **Provence rose**.)
puccoon: *Lithospermum* (See **stoneseed**.), *Sanguinaria canadensis*
pudding grass: *Hedeoma pulegioides* (See **pennyroyal, American**.)
pudding-pipe tree: *Cassia fistula* (See **shower tree, golden**.)
pumelo: *Citrus grandis, C. maxima* (See **pummelo** and **shaddock**.)
pummelo: *Citrus grandis, C. maxima*
pumpkin: *Cucurbita Pepo* (See **squash**.)
punk tree: *Melaleuca quinquenervia* (See **paperback, swamp tea tree, tea tree, swamp**, and **weeping tea tree**.)

purging cassia: *Cassia fistula*
purging fistula: *Cassia fistula* (See **shower tree, golden**.)
purple allamanda: *Cryptostegia grandiflora* (See **rubber vine** and **vine, India-rubber**.)
purple avens: *Geum rivale* (See **water avens**.)
purple cliff brake: *Pellaea atropurea* (See **Indian's-dream**.)
purple false eranthemum: *Pseuderanthemum*
purple fountain grass: *Pennisetum setaceum*
purple foxglove: *Digitalis purpurea* (See **lady's-glove**.)
purple fringe tree: *Cotinus Coggygria* (See **fringe tree**.)
purple glory tree: *Tibouchina* urvilleana
purple horned poppy: *Rosemeria*
purple laurel: *Rhododendron catawbiense* (See **mountain rose**.)
purple-leaved spiderwort: *Rhoeo spathaceae* (See **lily, boat** and **three-men-in-a-boat**.)
purple moon grass: *Molinia* caerulea
purple osier: *Salix purpurea* (See **willow, basket**.)
purple pleatleaf: *Eustylis purpurea* (See **lily, pinewoods**.)

 **Q**

quailbush: *Atroplex lentiformis* (See **thistle, white**.)

Quaker-ladies: *Centaurea cyanis, Hedyotis caerulea*

quaking aspen: *Populus tremula* (See **tree, trembling**.)

quaking grass: ***Briza***

quartervine: *Bignonia capreolata*

quebracho: *Pithecellobium arboreum*

Queen Anne's lace: ***Daucus***, *D. carota carota*

queen lily: *Curcuma petiolata* (See **lily, hidden**.)

Queen of Sheba vine: ***Podranea*** *brycei*

queen of the meadow: *Eupatorium purpureum, Filipendula ulmaria, Spirea*

queen of the night: **Hylocereus** un-datus, *Selenicereus grandiflorus*

queen-of-the-prairie: ***Filipendula*** *rubra*

queen palm: ***Arecastrum*** *romanzoffianum*

queen sago: *Cycas circinalis* (See **sago palm**.)

queen's bird-of-paradise: *Strelitzia reginae* (See **lily, crane**.)

queen's-delight: ***Stillingia***, *S. sylvatica*

queen's-flower: *Lagerstroemia speciosa*

queen's jewels: ***Antigonon*** *leptopus* (See **mountain rose**.)

queen's-lace: *Daucus carota carota* (See **Queen Anne's lace**.)

Queensland lacebark: *Brachychiton discolor* (See **lacebark**.)

Queensland nut tree: *Macadamia* (See **nut tree, Australian**.)

Queensland pittosporum: *Pittosporum rhombifolium*

Queensland umbrella tree: *Brassaia actinophylla* (See **Schefflera**.)

queen's-root: ***Stillingia***, *S. sylvatica* (See **queen's-delight**.)

Queen's umbrella tree: *Brassaia actinophylla* (See **Schefflera**.)

queen's wreath: ***Antigonon*** *leptopus* (See **mountain rose**.), **Petrea, P.** volubilis

quercitron: *Quercus velutina* (See **oak, black**.)

quickbeam: ***Sorbus*** *aucuparia* (See **rowan**.)

quick-in-the-hand: *Impatiens pallida*

quillaja: *Quillaja Saponaria*

quillwort: *Isoetes, I. lacustris* (See **Merlin's-grass**.)

quince: *Chaenomeles speciosa, Cydonia oblonga*

quinine: *Rubia* (See **madderwort**.)

quinoa: *Chenopodium Quinoa* (See **goosefoot**.)

quiver tree: *Aloe dichotoma* (See **tree aloe**.)

R

rabbitberry: *Shepherdia argentea*

rabbitbrush: *Chrysothamnus* (See **lo-coweed**.)

rabbit-ears: *Opuntia microdasys*

rabbit's-foot: ***Polypodium*** *aureum*

rabbit's-foot fern: *Davallia, Humata tyermannii, Polypodium*

rabbit's pea: *Tephrosia* (See **pea, hoary**.)

rabbit tracks: *Maranta leuconeura kerchovianat*

raccoon-berry: *Podophyllum peltatum* (See **Mayapple**.)

radish: *Raphanus sativus*

radish, common: ***Raphanus*** *sativus*

radish, rat-tail: ***Raphanus*** *caudatus*

raffia: *Raphia farinifera*

ragged robin: *Lychnis Flos-cuculi* (See **meadow campion** and **meadow pink**.), *L. floscuculis*

rag gourd: *Luffa aegyptiaca* (See **strainer-vine**.)

ragweed: *Ambrosia, A. artemisiifolia, A. trifida*

ragweed, common: *Ambrosia artemisiifolia* (See **ragweed**.)

ragwort: *Senecio, S. Jacobaea* (See **staverwort**.)

ragwort, common weedy: *Senecio jacobaea* (See **ragwort**.)

ragwort, golden: *Senecio aureus*

ragwort, purple: *Senecio elegans*

ragwort, sea: *Senecio cineraria, S. viravira*

railroad vine: *Ipomoea Pes-capra* (See **morning glory, beach**.)

rain lily: ***Zephyranthes***

rain tree: ***Samanea*** *saman*

raisin tree: *Hovenia dulcis*

ramie: *Boehmeria nivea*

ramona: *Salvia*

rampion: *Campanula rapunculus*

rampion, German: *Oenothera biennis*

rampion, horned: *Phyteuma*

ram's-head: *Cypripedium arietinum*

ram's-head orchid: *Cypripedium arietinum* (See **ram's-head**.)

ramtil: *Guizotia abyssinica*

ramtilla: *Guizotia abyssinica* (See **ramtil**.)

Rangoon creeper: *Quisqualis indica*

rape: *Brassica napus*

Rapunzel: *Campanula rapunculus* (See **rampion**.)

raspberry: *Rubus, R. calycinoides, R. Idaeus*

raspberry, black: *Rubus odoratus* (See **raspberry**.)

raspberry, flowering: *Rubus odoratus*

raspberry, Rocky mountain: *Rubus deliciosus*

raspberry, Rocky mountain flowering: *Rubus deliciosus* (See **raspberry, Rocky mountain**.)

raspberry, wild red: *Rubus Idaeus* (See **raspberry**.)

rasp fern: *Doodia, D. aspera, D. caudata, D. media*

rat-poisin plant: *Hamelia patens*

rattail cactus: *Aporocactus flagelliformis*

rattan: *Calamus, Daemonorops*

rattan, ground: *Rhapis excelsa*

rattle: *Rhinanthus*

rattlebox: *Crotalaria, Halesia carolina, Ludwigia alternifolia* (See **sedge**.), *Rhinanthus, Rhinanthus crista-galli* (See **pennygrass**.), *Silene vulgaris*

rattlebush: *Baptisia tinctoria, Crotalaria*

rattlesnake grass: *Briza*

rattlesnake master: *Eryngium yuccaefolium, Liatris, Manfreda virginica*

rattlesnake plantain: *Goodyera*

rattlesnake root: *Chamaelirium luteum, Cimicifuga racemosa, Polygala, Prenanthes* (See **lion's-foot**.)

rattlesnake weed: *Eryngium yuccaefolium, Goodyera, Hieracium venosum, Liatris*

rattle-top: *Cimicifuga*

rattleweed: *Astragalus, Baptisia tinctoria* (See **horsefly weed**.), *Crotalaria, Oxytropis*

rayless goldenrod: *Haplopappus* (See **locoweed**.)

red alder: *Alnus oregona* (See **alder**.)

red alpine campion: *Lychnis alpina* (See **campion**.)

red angel's trumpet: *Brugmansia*

red bay: *Persea borbonia, Tabernaemontana*

red-bead vine: *Abrus precatorius* (See **pea, rosary**.)

red-berried elder: *Sambucus racemosa* (See **elder**.)

redberry: ***Rhamnus*** *crocea*

redberry, hollyleaf: ***Rhamnus*** *ilicifolia*

redbird cactus: *Pedilanthus tithymaloides* (See **spurge, slipper**.)

redbird flower: *Pedilanthus tithymaloides* (See **slipper plant** and **spurge, slipper**.)

redbud: *Cercis*

red calla: ***Sauromatum*** *guttatum* (See **monarch-of-the-East**.)

red campion: *Lychnis dioica* (See **campion**.)

red-cap gum: *Eucalyptus erythrocorys* (See **gum**.)

red cedar: *Acrocarpus fraxinifolius* (See **shingle tree**.)

red currant: *Ribes rubrum* (See **currant**.)

red cypress pine: *Callitris endlicheri* (See **pine, black cypress**.)

red elm: *Ulmus rubra* (See **elm** and **slippery elm**.)

red fescue: ***Festuca*** *rubra*

red gram: *Cajanus cajan* (See **pea, Angola**.)

red gum: *Eucalyptus calophylla* (See **gum**.), *E. camaldulensis, Liquidambar Styraciflua* (See **sweet gum**.)

red haw: ***Crataegus*** (See **thorn**.)

red heather: ***Phyllodoce*** *breweri*

red hot poker: *Kniphofia, Tritoma* (See **poker plant**.)

red-ink plant: *Phytolacca americana*

red jasmine: *Plumeria rubra* (See **frangipani**.)

red kowhai: *Clianthus puniceus* (See **parrot's beak**.)

red maple: *Acer rubrum* (See **swamp maple**.)

red moonseed: *Cocculus carolinus* (See **snail-seed**.)

red osier dogwood: ***Cornus*** *sericea* (See **kinnikinnik**.)

red oxalis: ***Oxalis*** *corniculata*

red pine: *Dacrydium cupressinum* (See **pine, imou.**), *Pinus resinosa* (See **Norway pine**.), ***Podocarpus*** *dacrydioides* (See **kahikatea**.)

red plum: *Prunus Americana* (See **plum, wild**.)

red puccoon: ***Sanguinaria*** *canadensis* (See **puccoon** and **tetterwort**.)

red ribbons: *Clarkia concinna*

red robin: *Geranium Robertianum* (See **herb Robert**.)

redroot: *Amaranthus retroflexus* (See

pigweed.), *Ceanothus americanus,*
Lachnanthes *caroliana*

redroot pigweed: *Amaranthus retroflexus*
(See **pigweed**.)

red rose of Lancaster: *Rosa gallica* (See
rose, French.)

red sandalwood: **Pterocarpus** *santalinus*

red sanderswood: *Pterocarpus santalinus*
(See **sandalwood, red**.)

redshanks: *Adenostoma sparsifolium*

red sorrel: *Hibiscus sabdariffa* (See
roselle.), *Rumex Acetosella* (See **sheep
sorrel**.)

red-spotted gum: *Eucalyptus mannifera*
(See **gum**.)

red squill: *Urginea maritima* (See **sea
onion**.)

red-stemmed filaree: *Erodium cicutarium*
(See **pin grass** and **pin clover**.)

red stringybark: *Eucalyptus macrohyncha*
(See **stringybark**.)

red titi: *Cyrilla racemiflora* (See **leatherwood**.)

redtwig dogwood: *Cornus sericea* (See
osier, red.)

red valerian: **Centranthus** *ruber* (See
lilac, German.)

redwood: *Adenanthera pavonina* (See
sandalwood, red.), **Sequoia** *sempervirens*

redwood, dawn: *Metasequoia
glyptostroboides*

redwood, giant: *Sequoiadendron
giganteum* (See **tree, big**.)

redwood, Siena: *Sequoiadendron
giganteum* (See **tree, big**.)

reed canary grass: **Phalaris**
arundinacea

reed grass: *Phalaris arundinacea*
(See **Calamagrotis**.)

reedmace: **Typha**

rein orchid: *Habenaria* (See **meadow
pink**.)

rein orchis: *Habenaria*

resinweed: **Gutierrezia** *Sarothrae* (See
snakeweed.)

rest-harrow: **Ononis**, *O. arvensis, O.
spinosa*

Resurrection lily: *Kaempferii rotunda*
(See **crocus, tropical**.)

resurrection plant: **Anastatica** *hierochuntina, Selaginella lepidophylla* (See
hollyhock rose.)

rhodora: **Rhododendron** *canadense*

rhubarb: **Rheum** *palmatum, R. rhabarbarum*

rhubarb dock: *Rumex patientia* (See
patience.)

rhubarb, monk's: **Rumex** *patientia*

rhubarb, wild: **Rumex** *hymenosepalus*

ribbon bush: *Homalocladium* platycladium

ribbon cactus: *Pedilanthus tithymaloides* (See **slipper plant**.)

ribbon fern: *Polypodium phyllitidis* (See **strap fern**.)

ribbon grass: *Phalaris* picta

ribgrass, ribwort: *Plantag, P. lanceolata* (See **star-of-the-earth**.)

riceflower: *Pimelea, P. coarctata, P. prostrata*

rice paper plant: *Tetrapanax papyriferus*

rice paper tree: *Tetrapanax papyriferus* (See **rice paper plant**.)

richweed: *Collinsonia Canadensis* (See **horse balm**, **gravelroot** and **stoneroot**.)

rimu: *Dacrydium cupressinum* (See **pine, imou**.)

ring bellflower: *Symphyandra*

ripple-grass: *Plantago lanceolata* (See **star-of-the-earth**.)

river red gum: *Eucalyptus camaldulensis* (See **gum**.)

river tea tree: *Melaleuca quinquenervia* (See **weeping tea tree**.)

Roanoke-bells: *Mertensia virginica* (See **Virginia bluebells**.)

Robin-run-away: *Dalibarda* repens

robin's plantain: *Erigeron pulchellus*

roble: *Quercus lobata*

rocambole: *Allium sativum*

rock brake: *Cryptogramma, C. acrostichoides, C. crispa* (See **brake** and **stone brake** and **parsley fern**.)

rock chestnut oak: *Quercus prinus* (See **oak, basket**.)

rock cotoneaster: *Cotoneaster horizontalis*

rockcress: *Arabis*

rockcress, California: *Arabis blepharophylla*

rockcress, mountain: *Arabis alpina*

rockcress, purple: *Arabis blepharophylla*

rockcress, wall: *Arabis causcasia*

rock elm: *Ulmus thomasii* (See **elm**.)

rocket: *Barbarea vulgaris* (See **yellow rocket**.), *Diplotaxis, Eruca vesicaria* (See **arugula**.)

rocket, dame's: *Hesperis matronalis* (See **violet, dame's**.)

rocket, dyer's: *Reseda luteola*

rocket larkspur: *Consolida ambigua*

rocket, sweet: *Hesperis matronalis* (See **violet, dame's**.)

rocket, white: *Hesperis matronalis* (See **rocket, dame's**.)

rock geranium: *Heuchera americana* (See
sanicle, American.)

rock jasmine: ***Androsace***

rock nettle: ***Eucnide***

rock palm: ***Brahea***

rock polypody: ***Polypodium*** *virginianum*

rock purslane: ***Calandrinia***

rockrose: *Clistus*

rock rose: ***Helianthemum*** *canadase, H.
nummularium* (See **sunrose**.)

rock spiraea: ***Holodiscus*** *dumosus,
Petrophytum*

rock spray: *Cotoneaster horizontalis* (See
rock cotoneaster.)

Roebelin palm: ***Phoenix*** *roebelenii*

Roman candle: *Yucca gloriosa* (See **lily,
palm**.)

Roman coriander: ***Nigella*** *sativa*

Roman wormwood: *Artemisia pontica*
(See **wormwood**.)

roof houseleek: *Sempervivum tectorum*
(See **houseleek** and **thunder
plant**.)

ropebark: *Dirca palustris* (See **moosewood** and **swampwood**.)

roquette: *Eruca vesicaria* (See **arugula**
and **rocket**.)

rosa de montana: ***Antigonon*** *leptopus*
(See **mountain rose**.)

rosary plant: *Crassula rupestris* (See
necklace vine.)

rosary vine: ***Ceropegia***, ***Crassula
rupestris*** (See **necklace vine**.)

rose: ***Rosa***

rose acacia: ***Robinia*** *hispida* (See **moss
locust**.)

rose, Alpine: *Rosa pendulina*

rose, apothecary: *Rosa gallica* (See
rose, French.)

rose apple: *Syzygium Jambos, S. malaccensis* (See **jamrosade**.) (See **malay
apple**.)

rose, Austrian brier: *Rosa foetida*

rose, Austrian copper: *Rosa foetida*

rose, baby: *Rosa multiflora*

rose balm: *Impatiens Balsimina* (See
garden balsam.)

rose balsam: *Impatiens balsamina* (See
lady's slipper.)

rose, Banksia: *Rosa Banksiae*

rose, Banksian: *Rosa Banksiae* (See
rose, Banksia.)

rosebay: *Nerium oleander* (See **oleander**.), ***Rhododendron*** *maximum*

rosebay, Lapland: *Rhododendron lapponicum*

rose, Bengal: *Rosa roulettii* (See **rose,
China**.)

rose, brier: *Rosa canina*

rose, burnet: *Rosa pimpinellifolia*
rose, cabbage: *Rosa centifolia*
rose, California: *Rosa californica*
rose campion: *Lychnis coronaria* (See **campion** and **mullein pink**.)
rose, Cherokee: *Rosa roxburghii*
Rose, chestnut: *Rosa roxburghii*
rose, China: *Rosa chinensis*
rose, Christmas: *Helleborus niger*
rose, cinnamon: *Rosa cinnamomea*
rose, climbing: *Rosa setigera*
rose, cluster: *Rosa pisocarpa*
rose crest-lip: *Pogonia ophioglossoides*
rose, damask: *Rosa damascena*
rose, dog: *Rosa canina* (See **rose, brier**.)
rose, eglantine: *Rosa eglanteria*
rose, evergreen: *Rosa sempervirens*
rose, fairy: *Rosa chinensis minima*
rose, Father Hugo's: *Rosa hugonis*
rose, French: *Rosa gallica*
rose geranium: *Pelargonium graveolens*
rose, ground: *Rosa spithamea*
rose, guelder: *Viburnum opulus*
rose, Himalayan musk: *Rosa brunonii*
rose, hundred-leaved: *Rosa centifolia* (See **rose, cabbage**.)
rose, hybrid musk: *Rosa moschata*
rose, Japanese: *Rosa rugosa*

rose, Lady Banks': *Rosa Banksiae* (See **rose, Banksia**.)
rose, Lancaster: *Rosa damascena* (See **rose, damask**.)
rose leek: *Allium canadense* (See **onion, wild**.)
roselle: *Hibiscus Sabdariffa* (See **sorrel, Indian**.)
rose, Macartney: *Rosa bracteata*
rose mallow: *Hibiscus*
rose mallow, great: *Hibiscus grandiflorus*
rose mallow, halberd-leaved: *Hibiscus militaris* (See **rose mallow, soldier**.)
rose mallow, soldier: *Hibiscus militaris*
rose mandarin: *Streptopus roseus* (See **pine, twisted**.)
rosemary: *Rosmarinus officinalis*
rosemary, bog: *Andromeda polifolia*
rosemary, wild: *Ledum palustre*
rose, memorial: *Rosa wichuraiana*
rose moss: ***Portulaca*** *grandiflora* (See **Mexican rose** and **sun plant**.), *Rosa centifolia*
rose, musk: *Rosa moschata*
rose, Nootka: *Rosa nutkana*
rose-of-China: ***Hibiscus*** *Rosa-sinensis* (See **shoeblock plant**.)
rose-of-heaven: *Lychnis coeli-rosa*
rose-of-Jericho: ***Anastatica*** *hierochuntina*

rose-of-Sharon: **Hibiscus** *syriacus*
rose-of-Venezuela: *Brownea grandiceps*
rose, pasture: *Rosa carolina*
rose periwinkle: *Catharanthus rosea* (See **old maid**.)
rose, Persian yellow: *Rosa foetida*
rose pink: **Sabbatia**
rose pogonia: **Pogonia** *ophioglossoides*
rose, polyantha: *Rosa rehderana*
rose, prairie: *Rosa setigera* (See **rose, climbing**.)
rose, Provence: *Rosa centifolia* (See **rose, cabbage**.)
rose, Provins: *Rosa centifolia* (See **rose, cabbage**.)
rose, pygmy: *Rosa chinensis minima* (See **rose, fairy**.)
roseroot: **Rhodanthe**
rose-scented geranium: *Pelargonium capitatum*
rose, Scotch: *Rosa pimpinellifolia* (See **rose, burnet**.)
rose, swamp: *Rosa palustris*
rose, tea: *Rosa odorata*
rose, wood: *Rosa gymnocarpa*
rosewood, Arizona: **Vauquelinia** *californica*
rosewood: **Pterocarpus, Tipuana** *tipu*
rose, York: *Rosa damascena* (See **rose, damask**.)

rosin plant: *Grindelia, Siliphium*
rosinweed: *Grindelia* (See **compass plant**, **gum plant** and **rosin plant**.), **Silphium** *laciniatum* (See **compass plant**.)
rougeberry: **Rivina** *humilis*
rouge plant: **Rivina** *humilis* (See **rougeberry**.)
round-leaf wintergreen: *Pyrola rotundifolia* (See **lettuce, Indian** and **lily-of-the-valley, wild**.)
round-leafed snow gum: *Eucalyptus perriniana* (See **gum**.)
round-leafed sundew: *Drosera rotundifolia* (See **lustwort**.)
rowan: **Sorbus** *aucuparia*
rowan tree: *Sorbus aucuparia* (See **quickbeam** and **rowan**.)
royal climber: **Oxera** *pulchella*
royal jasmine: *Jasminum grandiflorum*
royal poinciana: **Delonix**, *D. regia* (See **peacock flower**.)
royal velvet plant: *Gynura aurantiaca* (See **velvet plant**.)
rubber euphorbia: *Euphorbia Tirucalli* (See **spurge, Indian tree**.)
rubber plant: **Ficus** *elastica*
rubber tree: **Schefflera**
rubber vine: **Cryptostegia**
rubygrass: **Rhynchelytrum** *repens*

rucola: *Eruca vesicaria* (See **arugula** and **rocket**.)

rue: *Ruta*

rue anemone: *Anemonella A. thalictroides*

rue, goat's: *Galega officinalis*

rue, wall: *Asplenium rutamuraria*

rum cherry: *Prunus serotina*

run away-robin: *Glechoma hederacea* (See **gill-over-the-ground**.)

runner bean: *Phaseolus vulgaris*

running box: *Mitchella repens* (See **hive vine**, **partridgeberry** and **squawberry**.)

running pine: *Lycopodium clavatum* (See **ground pine** and **staghorn moss**.)

running pop: *Passiflora foetida* (See **love-in-a-mist**.)

rupturewort: *Herniaria, H. glabra*

rush: *Juncus*

rush, flowering: *Butomus umbellantus*

rush nut: *Cyperus esculentus*

rush, soft: *Juncus effusus*

rush, spiral: *Juncus effusus*

rush, zebra: *Juncus effusus*

russet-witch: *Liparis Loeselii* (See **orchid, fen**.)

Russian olive: *Elaeagnus angustifolia*

Russian statice: *Phylliostachys Suworwii*

Rutland beauty: *Calystegia sepium* (See **hedge bindweed** and **morning glory, wild**.)

S

sabicu: *Lysiloma latisiliqua*

sacaline: ***Polygonum*** *sachalinense*

sacred bamboo: ***Nandina*** *domestica* (See **nandin**.)

sacred bean: ***Nelumbo*** (See **water lotus**.), *N. nucifera*

sacred-flower-of-Peru: ***Cantua*** *buxifolia* (See **magic flower**.)

sacred-flower-of-the-Incas: ***Cantua*** *buxifolia* (See **magic flower**.)

sacred-lily-of-China: *Rohdea japonica* (See **lily-of-China**.)

sacred lotus: ***Nelumbo*** *nucifera*

safflower: *Carthamus tinctorius* (See **thistle, saffron**.)

saffron: *Crocus sativus*

saffron, bastard: *Carthamus tinctorius*

saffron, false: *Carthamus tinctorius*

saffron, meadow: *Colchium autumnale*

sage: ***Salvia****, S. officianalis*

sage, black: *Artemesia tridentata, Salvia mellifera, Trichostema lanatum*

sagebrush: *Artemesia* (See **motherwort**.), *A. arbuscula, A. tridentata*

sage, Jerusalem: *Phlomis fruticosa, Pulmonaria officinalis*

sage, scarlet: *Salvia coccinea, Salvia splendens*

sage tree: *Vitex Agnus-castus* (See **chaste tree, hemp tree** and **pepper, wild**.)

sage, white: *Artemesia ludoviciana, Salvia apiana*

sage, wood: *Teucrium canadense, T. corodonia*

sago palm: *Arenga pinnata* (See **gomuti**.), ***Caryota****, C. urens,* ***Cycas****, C. circinalis, C. revoluta*

saguaro: *Carnegiea gigantea* (See **tree cactus**.)

sahuaro: *Carnegiea gigantea* (See **saguaro**.)

sainfoin: *Onobrychis viciifolia*

Saint-Bernard's-lily: *Anthericum Liliaigo, A. Liliastrum, Chlorophytum, C. comosum*

Saint-Bruno's-lily: *Paradisea Liliastrum*

Saint-Catherine's-lace: *Erioganum giganteum*

saintfoin: *Onobrychis viciifolia* (See **sainfoin**.)

Saint-James's-lily: *Sprekelia formosissima*

Saint-John's-bread: *Ceratonia siliqua* (See **honey bread**.)

Saint-John's-wort: *Hypericum*

salad burnet: *Poterium Sanguisorba*

salad rocket: *Eruca sativa*

salal: *Gaultheria Shallon*

saligot: *Trapa natans* (See **nut, Jesuit's** and **water caltrop**.)

sallow: *Salix caprea* (See **willow, florist's**.)

sallow thorn: *Hippophae rhamnoides*

salmonberry: *Rubus chamaemorus* (See **cloudberry**.), *R. parviflorus, R. spectabilis*

salmon gum: *Eucalyptus salmonophloia* (See **gum**.)

salsify: *Tragopogon porrifolius* (See **oyster plant**.)

saltbush: *Atriplix*

salt tree: *Halimodendron, H. halodendron*

saman: *Samanea Saman* (See **rain tree**.)

samfire: *Crithmum maritimum*

samphire: *Crithmum maritimum, Salicornia europaea* (See **pickleweed, pigeonfoot** and **Salicornia**.)

sandalwood: *Santalum album* (See **sandalwood, white**.)

sandalwood, bastard: *Myoporum sandwicense*

sandalwood, red: *Adenanthera pavonina, Pterocarpus santalinus*

sandarac-tree: *Tetraclinis articulata*

sandberry: *Arctostaphylos Uva-ursi* (See **kinnikinnik**.)

sand blackberry: *Rubus cuneifolius*

sandbox tree: *Hura crepitans*

sand cherry: *Prunus, P. Besseyi, P. depressa, P. pumila*

sandjack: *Quercus incana* (See **oak, bluejack**.)

sandlewood, white: *Santalum album*

sand lily: *Leucocrinum montanum* (See **star lily**.)

sand myrtle: *Leiophyllum buxifolium*

sandpaper vine: *Petrea*, *P. volubilis*

sand phlox: *Phlox* bifida

sand rose: *Anacampseros telephiastrum* (See **love plant**.)

sand spurry: *Spergularia*

sand verbena: *Abronia*, *A. cycloptera*, *A. latifolia*, *A. maritima*, *A. umbellata*

sandweed: *Hypericum fasciculatum*

sandwort: *Arenaria*

sanicle: *Sanicula* (See **snakeroot**.)

sanicle, American: *Heuchera americana*

sanicle, Indian or white: *Eupatorium rugosum*

Santa Cruz water platter: *Victoria Cruziana* (See **lily, Santa Cruz water**.)

Santa Maria: *Calophyllum brasiliense* (See **tree, Santa Maria**.)

sapodilla: *Manilkara* Zapota (See **naseberry**.)

sapota: *Pouteria sapota* (See **mammee sapota**, **marmalade plum** and **sapote**.)

sapote: *Pouteria sapota* (See **mammee sapota** and **marmalade plum**.)

sapote, white: *Casimiroa edulis*

sapucia nut: *Lecythis Zabucayo*

sarsaparilla, bristly: *Aralia hispida*

sarsaparilla, wild: *Aralia nudicaulis*, *Schisandra coccinea*, *Smilax glauca*

sasanqua: *Camellia sasanqua*

satinflower: *Clarkia amoena*, **Lunaria**, *L. annua* (See **pennyflower**.)

satinleaf: **Chrysophyllum** oliviform

satinwood: *Chloroxylon Swietenia*, **Murraya** paniculata, *Zanthoxylumm flavum*

satsuma orange: *Citrus reticulata*

sausage tree: **Kigelia** pinnata

savin: *Juniperus Sabina*

savine: *Juniperus Sabina* (See **savin**.)

savory: **Micromeria**, *Satureja*

sawbrier: *Smilax glauca*

saw cabbage palm: **Acoelorrhaphe** wrightii

saw fern: *Blechnum serrulatum*

saw palmetto: **Serenoa** repens (See **scrub palmetto**.)

sawwort: *Serratula tinctoria*

saxifrage: *Saxifraga*

saxifrage, golden: *Chrysosplenium*, *C. americanum*

saxifrage, meadow: *Saxifraga granulata*

saxifrage, swamp: *Saxifraga pensylvanica*

scabious: **Scabiosa** ocheroleuca

scabious, sweet: *Scabiosa atropurpurea*

scabwort: **Inula** Helenium

scammony: *Convolvulus Scammonia*

Scarbrough lily: *Vallota speciosa*
scarlet bugler: *Cleistocactus Baumannii*, *Pentsemon centranthifolius*
scarlet bush: *Hamelia* patens (See **rat poison plant**.)
scarlet-flowering gum: *Eucalyptus ficifolia* (See **gum**.)
scarlet gilia: *Ipomopsis* aggregata (See **skyrocket**.)
scarlet gum: *Eucalyptus phoenicia* (See **gum**.)
scarlet maple: *Acer* rubrum (See **swamp maple**.)
scarlet pimpernel: *Anagallis* arvensis (See **pimpernel** and **sheperd's clock**.)
scarlet runner bean: *Phaseolus* coccineus
scarlet sage: *Salvia coccinea, S. splendens*
scarlet sumac: *Rhus glabra* (See **sumac, smooth**.)
scarlet windflower: *Anemone fulgens* (See **windflower**.)
scarlet wisteria tree: *Sesbania*
Schefflera: *Brassaia actinophylla*
scoke: *Phytolacca* americana (See **poke, Virginian**.)
scorpion grass: *Myosotis* (See **mouse-ear**.), *M. scorpiodes, M. sylvatica*

scorpion orchid: *Arachnis*
scorpion senna: *Coronilla Emerus*
Scotch attorney: *Clusia rosea* (See **monkey apple**.)
Scotch broom: *Cytisus*, *C. scoparius*
Scotch elm: *Ulmus glabra* (See **elm**.)
Scotch fir: *Pinus sylvestris*
Scotch heath: *Erica cinerea*
Scotch heather: *Calluna vulgaris*
Scotch moss: *Arenaria verna* (See **pearlwort**.), *Sagina subulata* (See **pearlwort**.), *Selaginella Kraussiana*
Scotch pine: *Pinus sylvestris* (See **Scotch fir**.)
Scotch thistle: *Onopordum Acanthium* (See **silver thistle**.)
Scots fir: *Pinus sylvestris* (See **pine, Scotch**.)
Scots pine: *Pinus sylvestris* (See **Scotch fir**.)
scouring rush: *Equisetum*, *E. hyemale*
screw bean: *Prosopis pubescens* (See **mesquite, screw-pod** and **tornillo**.)
screw pine: *Pandanus P. pygmaeus, P. utilis* (See **pine, common screw**.), *P. Veitchii*
screw-tree: *Helicteres Isora*
scrub oak: *Quercus ilicifolia* (See **oak, barren**.), *Q. undulata*
scrub palmetto: *Sabal Etonia, S. mi-*

semaphore-plant: *Desmodium motorium*

Senegal date palm: *Phoenix reclinata*

senega root: *Polygala* (See **rattlesnake root**.)

senna: *Cassia*

senna, apple blossom: *Cassia javanica*

senna, bladder: *Colutea arborescens*

senna, candlestick: *Cassia alata*

senna, flowery: *Cassia corymbosa*

senna, prairie: *Cassia fasciculata* (See **partridge pea**.)

senna, wild: *Cassia hebecarpa, C. marilandica*

sensitive brier: **Schrankia**

sensitive fern: **Onoclea** *sensiblilis*

sensitive pea: *Cassia fasciculata* (See **senna, prairie**.), *C. nictitans*

sensitive plant: *Mimosa pudica* (See **humble plant**.)

sequoia, giant: *Sequoiadendron giganteum* (See **tree, big**.)

serpentary: *Aristolochia Serpentaria*

serpent cucumber: *Trichosanthes Anguina*

serpent gourd: *Trichosanthes Anguina* (See **serpent cucumber**.)

serpent grass: *Polygonum viviparum*

serpent's tongue: *Ophioglossum*

serpolet: *Thymus Serpyllum*

serviceberry: *Amelanchier* (See **Indian cherry** and **May cherry**.)

service tree: *Sorbus domestica*

service tree, wild: *Sorbus torminalis*

sesame: *Sesamum Indicum* (See **benne**.)

setterwort: *Helleborus foetidus*

seven-bark: *Hydrangea arborescens* (See **hills-of-snow**.)

Seychelles nut: **Lodoicea** *maldivica*

shadblow: *Amelanchier* (See **May cherry** and **serviceberry**.)

shadbush: *Amelanchier* (See **Indian cherry** and **serviceberry**.)

shaddock: *Citrus grandis* (See **pummelo**.), *C. maxima* (See **pummelo**.)

shagbark: **Carya**

shagbark hickory: **Carya** *ovata*

shallon: *Gaultheria shallon*

shallot: **Allium**, *A. cepa*

shame plant: *Mimosa pudica* (See **sensitive-plant**.)

shamrock: *Medicago lupulina, Oxalis Acetosella, Trifolium procumbens, T. repens*

shamrock pea: *Parochetus communis*

Shasta daisy: **Leucanthemum** *maximum*

shave grass: **Equisetum**, *E. hyemale* (See **scouring rush**.)

shaving-brush tree: **Pachira** *aquatica*

sheepberry: *Viburnum Lentago, V.*

prunifolium (See **nannyberry, stag-bush** and **tea plant**.)

sheep burr: *Acaena*

sheep laurel: *Kalmia angustifolia* (See **lambkill**.)

sheep's-bit: *Jasione perennis*

sheep sorrel: *Rumex Acetosella*

sheep's-parsley: *Anthriscus sylvestris*

sheep's-tongue: *Stomatium agninum*

shellbark: *Carya laciniosa* (See **king nut**.)

shellbark hickory: *Carya laciniosa* (See **king nut**.), *C. ovata* (See **shagbark hickory**.)

shellflower: *Alpinia* Zerumbet (See **lily, pink porcelain**.), *Moluccella laevis* (see **Molucca balm**.), *Pistia stratiotes* (See **water lettuce**.), *Tigridia Pavonia* (See **lily, one-day**.)

shell ginger: *Alpinia* Zerumbet (See **lily, pink porcelain** and **shellflower**.)

she-oak: *Casuarina* (See **he-oak** and **pine, Australian**.)

shepherd's clock: *Anagallis arvensis* (See **pimpernel**.)

shepherd's club: *Verbascum Thapsus*

shepherd's purse: *Capsella*

shepherd's scabiosa: *Jasione perennis* (See **sheep's-bit**.)

shield fern: *Dryopteris*, *Polystichum*

shingle oak: *Quercus imbricaria*

shingle plant: *Marcgravia* rectiflora

shingle tree: *Acrocarpus fraxinifolius*

shinleaf: *Pyrola*, *P. elliptica* (See **lily-of-the-valley, wild**.)

shittimwood: *Bumelia lanuginosa*, *Halesia carolina*

shoeblack plant: *Hibiscus Rosa-sinensis*

shoes and stockings: *Lotus corniculatus*

shoestring fern: *Vittaria lineata*

shoo-fly plant: *Nicandra*

shooting star: *Dodacatheon*

shore grass: *Littorella uniflora* (See **shoreweed**.)

shore pine: *Pinus contorta* (See **pine, twisted**.)

shoreweed: *Littorella uniflora*

shotbush: *Aralia nudicaulis* (See **sarsaparilla, wild**.)

shower-tree: *Cassia* (See **senna**.)

shower tree, golden: *Cassia fistula*

shrimp bush: *Justica Brandegeana* (See **shrimp plant**.)

shrimp plant: *Justica Brandegeana*

shrub althaea: *Hibiscus syriacus* (See **rose-of-Sharon**.)

shrubby althaea: *Althaea*

shrubby trefoil: *Ptelea* (See **wafer ash**.)

shrub verbena: *Lantana*

shrub yellow root: *Xanthorhiza, X. simplicissima*

Siberian bugloss: ***Brunnera***

Siberian crab: *Malus baccata*

Siberian lily: *Ixiolirion tataricum*

Siberian pea shrub: *Caragana arborescens* (See **Siberian pea tree**.)

Siberian pea tree: *Caragana arborescens* (See **pea tree**.)

Siberian spruce: *Picea obovata*

Siberian squill: *Scilla sibirica*

Siberian wallflower: *Erysimum hieraciifolium*

sicklepod: *Cassia Tora*

sidesaddle flower: *Sarracenia* (See **huntsman's-cup** and **Indian cup**), *S. purpurea*

Sierra laurel: *Leucothoe Davisiae*

Sierra Leone tamarind: *Dialium guineense* (See **tamarind, velvet**.)

Sierra water fern: *Thelypteris nevadensis* (See **Parathelypteris**.)

silk-cotton tree: *Bombax Ceiba*, ***Ceiba** pentandra* (See **kapok**.), ***Cochlospermum** religiosum*

silk grass: *Pityopsis graminifolia, P. nervosa*

silk plant, Chinese: *Boehmeria nivea*

silk-tassel bush: ***Garrya***

silk tree: ***Albizia** Julibrissin*

silk vine: ***Periploca**, P. graeca*

silkweed: *Asclepias*

silky oak: ***Grevillea** robusta*

silver-back fern: *Pityrogramma triangularis*

silver bell: ***Halesia**, H. carolina, H. monticola*

silver-bell tree: ***Halesia*** (See **snowdrop tree**.), *H. carolina, Rhinanthus* (See **rattlebox**.)

silverberry: ***Elaeagnus**, E. angustifolia, E. commutata* (See **oleaster**.), *E. pungens*

silver buffalo berry: *Shepherdia argentea*

silverbush: *Convolvulus Cneorum*, (See **morning glory, bush**.) *Sophora tomentosa*

silver-crown: *Cotyledon undulata*

silver dollar: *Lunaria annua* (See **pennyflower**.)

silver-dollar gum: *Eucalyptus polyanthemos* (See **gum**.)

silver-dollar tree: *Eucalyptus cinerea*

silver fern: ***Pityrogramma**, Pteris quadriaurita*

silver fir: ***Abies** alba* (See **fir**.)

silver king: *Artemisia*

silver lace: ***Chrysanthemum** ptarmiciflorum*

silver-lace fern: *Pteris quadriaurita* (See **silver fern**.)

silver lace vine: *Polygonum* Aubertii (See **fleecevine, silver** and **smartweed**.)

silver-leaved mountain gum: *Eucalyptus pulverulenta*

silver-leaved poplar: *Populus alba* (See **abele**.)

silver linden: *Tilia toomentosa*

silverling: *Baccharis halimifolia* (See **myrtle, sea**.), *Paroniychia argyrocoma*

silverling whitlowwort: *Paronychia argentea* (See **whitlowwort**.), *P. argyrocoma* (See **whitlowwort**.)

silver mound: *Artemisia schmidtiana*

silver-mountain gum: *Eucalyptus pulverulenta* (See **gum**.)

silver queen: *Artemisia*

silverrod: *Solidago bicolor*

silver-ruffles: *Cotyledon undulata* (See **silver-crown**.)

silver saw palm: *Acoelorrhaphe Wrightii* (See **saw cabbage palm**.)

silver thistle: *Onopordum Acanthium*

silver torch: *Cleistocactus Struasii*

silver tree: *Leucodendron* argenteum

silver-vein creeper: *Parthenocissus henryana*

silver vine: *Actinidia polygama*

silverweed: *Potentilla Anserina* (See **goose grass**.)

silver whitlowwort: *Paroniychia argyrocoma* (See **silverling**.)

Singapore plumeria: *Plumeria* obtusa

single-leaf pinyon pine: *Pinus monophylla* (See **stone pine**.)

Sitka spruce: *Picea sitchensis* (See **spruce, tideland**.)

skirret: *Sium Sisarum*

skullcap: *Scutellaria* (See **helmetflower**.)

skunkbush: *Rhus* trilobata

skunk cabbage: *Lysichiton*, L. americanum, *Symplocarpus* foetidus (See **swamp cabbage**.), *Veratrum californicum* (See **lily, corn**.)

sky flower: *Duranta repens* (See **pigeonberry**.), *Thunbergia grandiflora*

skyrocket: *Ipomopsis* aggregata

sky vine: *Thunbergia grandiflora*

slash pine: *Pinus Elliottii* (See **swamp pine**.)

sleekwort, mauve: *Liparis liliifolia*

sleepy catchfly: *Silene antirrhina* (See **catchfly**.)

sleepy daisy: *Xanthisma*

slipper flower: *Calceolaria*, Pedilanthus tithymaloides

slipperwort: *Calceolaria* (See **silpper flower**.)

slippery elm: *Ulmus rubra* (See **elm** and **moose elm**.)

sloe: *Prunus alleghaniensis, Prunus americana, Prunus spinosa*

small celandine: *Ranunculus Ficaria* (See **celadine, lesser celandine** and **pilewort**.)

small-fruited hickory: *Carya glabra* (See **pignut**.)

small-leaved elm: *Ulmus alata* (See **elm**.)

smartweed: *Polygonum* (See **fleeceflower**.)

smoke bush: *Cotinus* (See **smoke tree**.), *C. coggygria* (See **wig tree**.)

smoke plant: *Cotinus coggygria* (See **wig tree**.)

smoke tree: *Cotinus, C. coggygria* (See **fringe tree**.), *C. obovatus, Dalea spinosa*

smokeweed: *Eupatorium maculatum* (See **Joe-Pye weed**.)

smooth hydrangea: *Hydrangea arborescens* (See **hills-of-snow**.)

smooth sumac: *Rhus glabra* (See **sumac, scarlet**.)

snail bean: *Vigna Caracalla* (See **snailflower**.)

snailflower: *Vigna Caracalla*

snail-seed: *Cocculus carolinus*

snail vine: *Vigna Caracalla* (See **Phaseolus** and **snailflower**.)

snake gourd: *Trichosanthes Anguina* (See **serpent cucumber**.)

snakehead: *Chelone glabra* (See **turtlehead**.)

snake lily: *Dichelostemma volubile*

snake mouth: *Pogonia ophioglossoides*

snake palm: *Amorphophallus rivieri*

snake plant: *Sansevieria trifasciata*

snakeroot: *Asarum canadense* (See **heart snakeroot**.), *Sanicula* (See **sanicle**.)

snakeroot, black: *Cimicifuga racemosa*

snakeroot, button: *Eryngium yuccifolium, Liatris*

snakeroot, Sampson's: *Gentiana, G. Catesbaei, G. villosa*

snakeroot, Seneca: *Polygala Senega*

snakeroot, Virginia: *Aristolochia Serpentaria*

snakeroot, white: *Eupatorium rugosum*

snake's-head: *Fritillaria Meleagris* (See **daffodil, checkered** and **guinea-hen**.)

snake's-head iris: *Hermodactylus tuberosus*

snake's-head tulip: *Fritillaria Meleagris* (See **lily, checkered**.)

snakeweed: ***Gutierrezia***, *G. Sarothrae*, *Polygonum Bistorta*

snap bean: ***Phaseolus*** *vulgaris*

snapdragon: ***Antirrhinum*** (See **lion's-mouth**.), *A. majus*

snapdragon, dwarf: *Chaenorrhinum minus*

snapjack: *Stellaria Holostea*

snapweed: ***Impatiens*** (See **touch-me-not**.)

sneezeweed: *Achillea Ptarmica*, ***Helenium***, *H. autumnale*

sneezewort: *Achillea ptarmica* (See **goosetongue**.), *Helenium autumnale* (See **sneezeweed**.)

snottygobble: ***Persoonia***

snowball: *Viburnum Opulus*

snowball bush: *Viburnum Opulus* (See **guelder rose** and **marsh elder**.)

snowball cactus: ***Pediocactus*** *simpsonii*

snowball, Chinese: *Viburnum macrocephalum*

snowball, Mexican: *Echeveria elegans*

snow bark tree: *Quillaja Saponaria*

snowbell: ***Styrax*** (See **storax**.)

snowberry: ***Chiococca, Symphoricarpos***

snowberry, creeping: *Gaultheria hispidula*

snowbush: *Ceanothus, C. cordulatus, C. velutinus*

snow gum: *Eucalyptus niphophila* (See **gum**.)

snowdrop: ***Galanthus***

snowdrop tree: ***Halesia*** (See **silver bell**.) *H. diptera, H. carolina*

snowflake: ***Leucojum***, *L. autumnale*

snowflake tree: ***Trevesia*** *palmata*

snowflower: *Spathiphyllum floribundum*

snow-in-harvest: ***Cerastium*** *tomentosum* (See **snow-in-summer**.)

snow-in-summer: ***Cerastium*** *tomentosum* (See **love-in-a-mist**.), *Clematis Viorna* (See **love-in-a-mist**.)

snow-on-the-mountain: *Euphorbia marginata*

snow poppy: ***Eomecon*** *chionantha*

snow wreath: ***Neviusia*** *alabamensis*

soapbark tree: *Quillaja Saponaria* (See **quillaja**.)

soapberry: ***Sapindus***, *S. Saponaria, Shepherdia canadensis*

soap plant: *Chlorogalum pomeridianum*

soap tree: *Yucca elata*

soapweed: *Yucca elata* (See **soap tree**.)

soapwort: ***Saponaria***, *S. calabrica, S.*

Ocymoides, S. officinalis (See **fuller's herb** and **hedge pink**.)

soapwort gentian: *Gentiana Saponaria*

soda-apple nightshade: ***Solanum*** *aculeatissimum*

Sodom apple: *Solonum sodomeum*

soft chess: *Bromus mollis* (See **goose grass**.)

soft maple: *Acer saccharinum* (See **maple, silver, maple, red** and **swamp maple**.), *A. rubrum*

soft-tip yucca: *Yucca gloriosa* (See **lily, palm**.)

solitaire palm: ***Ptychosperma*** *elegans*

Solomon's-feather: ***Smilacina (See* Solomon's-seal, false**.)

Solomon's-plumes: ***Smilacina*** (See **Solomon's-seal, false**.)

Solomon's-seal: *Polygonatum*

Solomon's-seal, false: *Smilacina*

Solomon's-zigzag: *Smilacina racemosa* (See **spikenard, false**.)

Sonoma oak: *Quercus Kelloggii*

Sonoran palm: ***Sabal*** *uresana*

soola clover: *Hedysarum coronaria*

sorrel: ***Rumex***

sorrel, common: ***Rumex*** *acetosella*

sorrel, dock: ***Rumex***

sorrel, French: ***Rumex*** *acetosa, R. scutatus*

sorrel, garden: ***Rumex*** *acetosa, R. scutatus*

sorrel, Indian: *Hibiscus Sabdariffa*

sorrel, mountain: *Oxyria digyna*

sorrel, sheep: ***Rumex*** *acetosella*

sorrel tree: ***Oxydendrum*** *arboreum* (See **elk tree**.)

sorrel vine: *Cissus trifoliata*

sorrel, wood: *Oxalis*

sotol: *Dasylirion*

sourberry: *Rhus integrifolia*

sour gum: ***Nyssa*** *sylvatica* (See **gum** and **pepperidge**.)

soursop: ***Annona*** *muricata*

sourwood: ***Oxydendrum*** *arboreum* (See **elk tree** and **sorrel tree**.)

South American Apricot: ***Mammea*** *Americana*

southern beech fern: ***Phegopteris*** *hexagonoptera*

southern blue flag: ***Iris*** *virginica*

southern buckthorn: *Bumelia lycioides*

southern fox grape: *Vitis rotundifolia*

southern live oak: *Quercus virginiana* (See **live-oak**.)

southern maidenhair: *Adiantum capillus-veneris* (See **fern, Venus's- hair**.)

southern pitcher plant: *Sarracenia purpurea* (See **side saddle flower**.)

southern prickly ash: *Zanthoxylum clava-Herculis* (See **pepperwood** and **sea ash**.)

southern red lily: *Lilium Catesbaei*

southernwood: *Artemisia Abrotanum*

southern yellow pine: *Pinus palustris*

southern yew: ***Podocarpus*** *macrophyllus*

Southwestern tepary bean: ***Phaseolus*** *acutifolius*

sowbread: *Cyclamen, C. persicum*

soy: *Glycine Max*

Spanish bayonet: *Yucca aloifolia, Y. baccata*

Spanish bluebell: *Endymion hispanicus*

Spanish broom: *Genista hispanica,* ***Spartium*** *junceum*

Spanish buckeye: *Ungnadia speciosa* (See **Mexican buckeye**.)

Spanish buttons: *Centaurea nigra* (See **horse knob**.)

Spanish chestnut: *Castanea sativa*

Spanish dagger: *Yucca gloriosa* (See **lily, palm**.)

Spanish flag: ***Mina*** *lobata*

Spanish Jacinth: *Endymion hispanicus* (See **Spanish bluebell**.)

Spanish jasmine: *Jasminum grandiflorum*

Spanish lime: ***Melicoccus*** *bijugatus* (See **mamoncillo**.)

Spanish moss: *Tillandsia usneoides* (See **hanging moss** and **long moss**.)

Spanish needles: *Bidens* (See **sticktight**.)

Spanish oyster plant: ***Scolymus*** *hispanicus* (See **thistle, golden**.)

Spanish salsify: ***Scorzonera*** *hispanica*

Spanish tea: *Chenopodium ambrosioides* (See **Mexican tea**.)

Spanish woodbine: ***Merremia*** *tuberosa* (See **morning glory, Ceylon**.)

sparrowgrass: *Asparagus officinalis*

spathe flower: ***Spathiphyllum***

spatterdock: ***Nuphar*** **(See lily, cow**.), *N. advena, N. saggittifolium*

spearflower: *Ardisia*

spear lily: *Doryanthes, D. Palmerii* (See **lily, Palmer spear**.)

spearmint: *Mentha viridis*

speedwell: *Veronica, V. Chamaedrys* (See **bird's-eye**.)

spiceberry: *Ardesia crenata*

spicebush: *Lindera Benzoin* (See **linden**.)

spice tree: *Umbellularia californica*

spicy jatropha: *Jatropha integerrima* (See **peregrina**.)

spider flower: ***Cleome*** *Hasslerana, C. spinosa, Grevillea*

spider lily: **Crinum**, *Hymenocallis* (See **sea daffodil**.), **Lycoris**

spider orchids: **Brassia**

spider plant: *Anthericum*, *A. Liliago* (See **lily, St.-Bernard's-**.), **Chlorophytum** (See **lily, St.-Bernard's-**.), *C. comosum, Cleome Hasslerana*

spiderwort: **Commelina**, **Tradescantia**

spiked loosestrife: *Lythrum Salicaria* (See **loosestrife, purple**.)

spiked rampion: **Phyteuma** *spicatum*

spike heath: **Bruckenthalia**, *B. spiculifolia*

spike moss: **Selaginella** (See **moss**.)

spikenard: *Aralia racemosa*

spikenard, false: *Smilacina racemosa*

spikenard tree: *Aralia spinosa*

spike rush: *Eleocharis*

spike winter hazel: *Corylopsis spicata* (See **winter hazel**.)

spinach: **Spinacia**, *S. oleracea*

spinach beet: *Beta vulgaris* (See **Swiss chard**.)

spinach dock: **Rumex** *patientia*

spinach, Indian: *Basella alba*

spinach, mountain: *Atriplex hortensis*

spinach, New Zealand: *Tetragonia tetragoniodes*

spinach, wild: *Chenopodium Bonus-Henricus*

spindle tree: **Eunymus**, *E. europaeus*

spiral eucalyptus: *Eucalyptus cinerea* (See **silver-dollar tree**.)

spiral flag: **Costus**

spleenwort: **Asplenium**, *A. platyneuron, A. Trichomanes*

split-leaf philodendron: *Monstera deliciosa* (See **Mexican bamboo** and **window plant**.)

splitrocks: **Pleiospilos**

sponge tree: *Acacia Farnesiana*

spoonflower: *Dasylirion Wheeleri, Xanthosoma Lindenii*

spoonwood: *Kalmia latifolia* (See **mountain laurel**.)

spoonwort: *Cochlearia officinalis* (See **scurvy grass**.)

spotted cat's-ear: **Hypochoeris** *radicata*

spotted cowbane: *Cicuta maculata* (See **mushquash root**.)

spotted evergreen: *Aglaonema costatum*

spotted gum: *Eucalyptus maculata* (See **gum**.)

spotted hemlock: **Conium** *maculatum* (See **poison hemlock**.)

spreading dogbane: *Apcynum androsaemifolium* (See **honeybloom**.)

spreading globeflower: *Trollius laxus* (See **swamp globeflower**.)

spring beauty: **Claytonia**, *C. virginica*

spring gold: *Lomatium utriculatum*

spring meadow saffron: ***Bulbocodium*** *vernum*

spring squill: *Scilla verna* (See **onion, sea** and **sea onion**.)

sprouting leaf: *Kalanchoe pinnata* (See **love plant, Mexican**.)

spruce: ***Picea (See* fir tree**.)

spruce, black: *Picea mariana*

spruce, blue: *Picea pungens*

spruce fir: *Picea Abies* (See **spruce, Norway**.)

spruce, hemlock: *Tsuga*

spruce, Himalayan: *Picea Smithiana*

spruce, Norway: *Picea Abies*

spruce pine: *Pinus virginiana* (See **pine, Jersey** and **scrub pine**.)

spruce, red: *Picea rubens*

spruce, tideland: *Picea sitchensis*

spruce, white: *Picea glauca*

spur flower: ***Plectranthus*** (See **Swedish ivy**.)

spurge: ***Euphorbia***, *Pachysandra*

spurge, Allegheny mountain: *Pachysandra procumbens*

spurge, caper: *Euphorbia Lathyris*

spurge, cypress: *Euphorbia Cyparissias*

spurge flax: *Daphne Gnidium*

spurge, flowering: *Euphorbia corollata*

spurge, Indian tree: *Euphorbia Tirucalli*

spurge, ipecac: *Euphorbia ipecacuanhae*

spurge laurel: *Daphne Laureola*

spurge, leafy: *Euphorbia Esula*

spurge, olive: *Daphne Mezereum*

spurge, seaside: *Euphorbia polygonifolia*

spurge, slipper: *Pedilanthus, P. tithymaloides*

spurred butterfly pea: *Centrosema virginianum* (See **pea, butterfly**.)

spurred gentian: ***Halenia***, *H. corniculata*

spurred snapdragon: ***Linaria (See* toadflax**.), *L. vulgaris* (See **flaxweed**.)

squarenut: *Carya tomentosa* (See **mockernut**.)

squash: *Cucurbita*

squawberry: *Mitchella repens* (See **partridgeberry**.)

squaw huckleberry: *Vaccinium caesium, V. stamineum*

squawroot: *Perideridia Gairdneri, Trillium erectum*

squaw vine: *Mitchella repens* (See **partridgeberry** and **squawberry**.)

squaw weed: *Senecio aureus* (See **staggerwort**.)

squill: *Scilla, Urginea maritima* (See **sea onion**.)

squirrel corn: *Dicentra canadensis* (See **turkey pea**.)

squirrel's cup: *Hepatica americana*

squirrel's-foot fern: *Davallia trichomanoides*

squirting cucumber: *Ecballium elaterium* (See **touch-me-not**.)

staff vine: *Celastrus scadens*

stagberry: *Viburnum prunifolium* (See **sheepberry**.)

stagbush: *Viburnium prunifolium*

staggerbush: *Lyonia mariana*

stagger grass: *Zephranthes Atamasco*

staggerwort: *Senecio aureus*

staghorn: *Platycerium*

stag horn fern: *Platycerium*

staghorn moss: *Lycopodium clavatum*

staghorn sumac: *Rhus typhina*

standing cypress: *Ipomopsis rubra* (See **cypress**.)

star anemone: *Anemone hortensis*

star anise: *Illicium verum* (See **anise**.)

star cactus: *Ariocarpus, Astrophytum ornatum, Haworthia*

star chickweed: *Stellaria pubera* (See **starwort**.)

star-cluster: *Pentas lanceolata*

star-cluster, Egyptian: *Pentas lanceolata*

star cucumber: *Sicyos angulatus* (See **Sicyos**.)

starfish flower: *Stapelia*

starfish plant: *Stapelia variegata*

starflower: *Smilacina stellata* (See **lily, of-the-valley, star-flowered**.), *Stapelia variegata, Trientalis* (See **wintergreen, chickweed**.)

star-flowered lily-of-the-valley: *Smilacina stellata* (See **starflower**.)

starglory: *Ipomoea Quamoclit*

star grass: *Aletris, Chloris truncata, Hypoxis, H. hirsuta*

star ipomoea: *Ipomoea coccinea* (See **morning glory, red**.)

star jasmine: *Trachelospermum jasminoides* (See **jasmine**.)

starleaf: *Brassaia actinophylla, Schefflera, S. (Brassaia) actinophyla* (See **umbrella tree, Queensland**.)

star lily: *Leucocrinum montanum, Lilium concolor, Zigedenus Fremontii*

star-of-Bethlehem: *Campanula isophylla, Ornithogalum, O. arabicum O. pyrenaicum, O. umbellatum* (See **nap-at-noon**.), *Tragopogan prantensis* (See **nap-at-noon**.)

star of the desert: ***Amberboa***

star-of-the earth: *Plantago lanceolata*

star pepper: *Evodia Danielii*

star pine: *Araucaria heterophylla* (See **pine, house**.), *Pinus Pinaster*

starry campion: *Silene stellata* (See **campion**.)

stars-of-Persia: *Allium Christophii*

star tulip: ***Calochortus*** (See **lily, mariposa**.)

starwort: *Aster,* ***Stellaria****, S. media, S. pubera*

starwort, mealy: *Aletris farinosa*

starwort, yellow: *Inula Helenium*

star zygadene: *Zigedenus Fremontii* (See **star lily**.)

statice: ***Limonium*** (See **thrift, lavender**.)

staverwort: *Senecio Jacobaea*

steepgrass: *Pinguicula vulgaris*

steeplebush: *Spiraea salicifolia, S. tomentosa*

steepweed: *Pinguicula vulgaris* (See **steepgrass**.)

steepwort: *Pinguicula vulgaris* (See **steepgrass**.)

steinpilz: ***Boletus*** *edulis*

step palm: ***Archontophoenix***

stickseed: *Hackelia, Lappula*

stick-tight: ***Bidens***

sticky baccharis: *Baccharis glutinosa* (See **water willow**.)

sticky-heads: ***Grindelia*** (See **gum plant**.)

stinging nettle: *Cnidoscolus texanus, Urtica dioica*

stinking ash: ***Ptelea*** (See **wafer ash**.), *P. trifoliata*

stinking Benjamin: *Trillium erectum* (See **squawroot**.)

stinking cedar: *Torreya taxifolia*

stinking chamomile: *Anthenis Cotula*

stinking mayweed: *Anthenis Cotula* (See **stinking chamomile**.)

stinking nightshade: *Hyoscyamus* (See **nightshade**.), *H. niger* (See **henbane**.)

stinking yew: *Torreya taxifolia* (See **stinking cedar**.)

stinkweed: *Thlaspi arvense* (See **mustard, mithridate** and **penny cress**.)

stitchwort: ***Stellaria***

St. Mary's thistle: *Silybum Marianum* (See **milk thistle**.)

stock: ***Matthiola*** *longipetala bicornis*

stock, Virginia: *Malcolmia maritima*

Stoke's aster: ***Stokesia*** *laevis*

stone brake: *Cryptogramma crispa*

stonecress: *Aethionema*

stonecrop: ***Sedum***

stonecrop, mossy: *Sedum acre*
stone mint: *Cunila organoides*
stone oak: *Quercus alba*
stone parsley: *Seseli*
stone pine: *Pinus monophylla, P. pinea*
stoneroot: *Collinsinia canadensis* (See **horse balm**.)
stoneseed: *Lithospermum*
stoneweed: *Lithospermum* (See **stoneseed**.)
stonewort: *Nitella*
storax: *Styrax*
stork's-bill: *Erodium* (See **heron's-bill**.), *E. cicutarium* (See **pin clover** and **pin grass**.), *Pelargonium*
strainer-vine: *Luffa, L. aegyptiaca*
stramonium: *Datura Stramonium*
strap fern: *Polypodium phyllitidis*
strawberry: *Fragaria*
strawberry, Alpine: *Fragaria collina, F. vesca*
strawberry, barren: *Walsteinia fragarioides*
strawberry begonia: *Saxifraga stolonifera* (See **strawberry geranium**.)
strawberry, bog: *Potentilla palustris*
strawberry bush: *Euonymus Americana*
strawberry cactus: *Echinocereus enneacanthus, Ferocactus setispinus, Mammillaria* (See **pincushion cactus**.)

strawberry clover: *Trifolium fragiferum*
strawberry fern: *Hemionitis palmata*
strawberry geranium: *Pelargonium scabrum, Saxifraga stolonifera* (See **Geranium**.)
strawberry guava: *Psidium litorale*
strawberry-headed clover: *Trifolium fragiferum* (See **strawberry clover**.)
strawberry shrub: *Calycanthus, C. floridus*
strawberry tomato: *Physalis Alkekengi*
strawberry tree: *Arbutus Unedo* (See **arbutus**.)
strawflower: *Helichrysum, H. bracteatum, Helipterum*
string-of-beads: *Senecio Rowleyanus*
string-of-hearts: *Ceropegia*
stringybark: *Eucalyptus*
striped brake: *Pteris quadriaurita* (See **silver fern**.)
stump tree: *Gymnocladus dioica*
Sturt's desert pea: *Clianthus formosus* (See **pea, glory** and **parrot's beak**.)
succory: *Chichorium intybus*
succory, blue: *Catananchecaerula*
sugar apple: *Annona squamosa*
sugarberry: *Celtis, Celtis occidentalis* (See **hackberry**.)
sugar bush: *Protea mellifera* (See **honeyflower**.), *Rhus ovata*

Surinam cherry: *Eugenia uniflora*

Surinam quassia: *Quassia amara*

swallow thorn: *Hippophae rhamnoides* (See **sea buckthorn**.)

swallowwort: *Cynanchum Vincetoxicum*

swallowwort, black: *Cynanchum nigrum*

swamp beggar-ticks: *Bidens connata*

swamp cabbage: *Symplocarpus foetidus*

swamp chestnut oak: *Quercus Michauxii* (See **oak, basket**.), *Q. prinus* (See **oak, basket**.)

swamp cottonwood: *Populus heterophylla*

swamp cypress: *Taxodium distichum*

swamp dogwood: *Rhus vernix* (See **sumac, poison**.)

swamp elm: *Ulmus americana*

swamp fern: *Blechnum serrulatum* (See **saw fern**.)

swamp fly honeysuckle: *Lonicera oblongifolia*

swamp globeflower: *Trollius laxus*

swamp gum: *Eucalyptus ovata*

swamp haw: *Viburnum cassinoides* (See **withe rod**.)

swamp hellebore: *Veratrum viride*

swamp hickory: *Carya cordiformis* (See **pignut**.)

swamp honeysuckle: *Rhododendron viscosum*

swamp laurel: *Kalmia polifolia*

swamp lily: *Lilium superbum*

swamp locust: *Gleditsia aquatica* (See **water locust**.)

swamp loosestrife: *Decodon* verticillatus (See **water willow**.)

swamp magnolia: *Magnolia virginiana* (See **swamp sassafras**.)

swamp mahogany: *Eucalyptus robusta*

swamp maple: *Acer rubrum*

swamp moss: *Sphagnum*

swamp paperbark: *Melaleuca ericifolia* (See **paperback**.), *M. rhaphiophylla* (See **paperback**.)

swamp pine: *Pinus Elliottii*

swamp pink: *Arethusa* bulbosa, Calopogon, C. tuberosus, *Helonias*, H. bullata

swamp post oak: *Quercus lyrata*

swamp potato: *Sagittaria* latifolia

swamp red bay: *Persea* borbonia

swamp rose: *Rosa palustris*

swamp rose mallow: *Hibiscus Moscheutos*

swamp sassafras: *Magnolia virginiana* (See **swamp magnolia**.)

swamp saxifrage: *Saxifraga pensylvanica*

swamp Spanish oak: *Quercus palustris*

swamp sumac: *Rhus vernix* (See **sumac, poison**.)

swamp tea tree: *Melaleuca quinquenervia* (See **paperback**.)

swamp white oak: *Quercus Michauxii* (See **oak, basket**.), *Quercus bicolor*

swamp willow: *Salix discolor*

swampwood: *Dirca palustris*

swanflower: *Swainsona galegifolia*

Swan River daisy: *Brachycome iberidifolia*

Swan River everlasting: *Helipterum Manglesii*

Swedish begonia: *Plectranthus* (See **spur flower** and **Swedish ivy**.)

Swedish ivy: *Plectranthus* (See **spur flower**.)

Swedish juniper: *Juniperus communis*

sweet acacia: *Acacia Farnesiana* (See **sponge tree**.)

sweet almond: *Prunus dulcis dulcis*

sweet alyssum: *Lobularia* maritima (See **Alyssum**.)

sweet annie: *Artemesia annua*

sweet balm: *Melissa officinalis*

sweet basil: *Ocimum Basilicum*

sweet bay: *Laurus* nobilis (See **bay**.), *Magnolia virginiana* (See **swamp magnolia** and **swamp sassafras**.), *Persea borbonia*

sweetbells: *Leucothoe racemosa*

sweetberry: *Viburnum Lentago* (See **nannyberry, sheeperry** and **tea plant**.)

sweet birch: *Betula lenta* (See **mahogany birch** and **mountain mahogany**.)

sweet box: *Sarcococca Hookerana*

sweetbrier: *Rosa Eglanteria* (See **rose, eglantine**.)

sweet buckeye: *Aesculus octandra*

sweet calabash: *Passiflora maliformis*

sweet calamus: *Acorus Calamus* (See **sweet flag**.)

sweet cane: *Acorus Calamus* (See **sweet flag**.)

sweet chervil: *Myrrhis* odorata (See **sweet cicely**.)

sweet cicely: *Myrrhis* odorata, *Osmorhiza*

sweet clover: *Melilotus*

sweetcup: *Passiflora maliformis* (See **sweet calabash**.)

sweet fern: *Comptonia* peregrina, *Myrica (Comptonia) asplenifolia*, *Myrrhis odorata*

sweet flag: *Acorus* Calammus (See **flag** and **myrtle, flag**.)

sweet gale: *Myrica Gale* (See **myrtle, bog**.)

sweet goldenrod: *Solidago odora*

sweet gum: *Liquidambar*, *L. Styraciflua* (See **gum**.)

sweet haw: *Viburnum prunifolium* (See **sheepberry**.)

sweet horsemint: *Cunila organoides* (See **stone mint**.)

sweet Joe-Pye weed: *Eupatorium purpureum* (See **Joe-Pye weed**.)

sweetleaf: *Symplocos* (See **horse sugar**.)

sweetleaf, Asiatic: *Symplocos paniculata*

sweet mace: *Tagetes lucida* (See **marigold, sweet scented**.)

sweet marjoram: *Origanum Majorana*

sweet pea: *Lathyrus odorata*

sweet pepperbush: *Clethra alnifolia* (See **sweet pepperbush**.)

sweet pitcher plant: *Sarracenia purpurea* (See **side saddle flower**.)

sweet potato: *Ipomoea batatas*

sweet-potato tree: *Manihot esculent*

sweet rocket: *Hesperis matronalis*

sweet rush: *Acorus Calamus* (See **sweet flag**.)

sweet scabious: *Scabiosa atropurpurea* (See **mourning bride**.)

sweet sedge: *Acorus Calamus*

sweetsop: *Annona squamosa*

sweetspire: *Itea virginica* (See **willow, Virginia**.)

sweet sultan: *Centaurea moschata* (See **knapweed**.)

sweet vernal grass: *Anthoxanthum*

sweet viburnum: *Viburnum Lentago* (See **nannyberry, sheepberry** and **tea plant**.), *V. odoratissimum*

sweet violet: *Viola odorata*

Sweet William: *Dianthus barbatus* (See **London pride**.)

Sweet William, wild: *Phlox divaricata*

sweetwood: *Glycyrrhiza glabra*

sweet woodruff: *Galium odorata*

swine's-succory: *Chichorium intybus* (See **succory**.)

Swiss chard: *Beta Vulgaris* (See **chard**.)

Swiss cheese plant: *Monstera deliciosa* (See **Mexican bamboo** and **window plant**.)

switch grass: *Panicum virgatum*

sword fern: *Nephrolepis*

sword lily: *Gladiolus*

sycamore: *Acer pseudoplatanus* (See **maple, sycamore**.), *Plantanus*, *P. occidentalis* (See **plane tree**.)

sycamore fig: *Ficus Sycomorus*
Sydney blue gum: *Eucalyptus saligna*
  (See **gum**.)
Syrian bead tree: ***Melia*** *Azedarach* (See
  lilac, Indian.)

Syrian juniper: *Juniperus drupacea* (See
  plum juniper.)
syringa: *Philadelphus*
Szechwan pepper: *Zanthoxylum piperi-*
  tum (See **pepper, Chinese**.)

T

table mountain pine: *Pinus pungens* (See **pine, prickly**.)

tacamahac: *Populus balsamifera* (See **necklace poplar**.)

tacamahack: *Populus balsamifera* (See **poplar, balsam** and **tacamahac**.)

tackahoe: *Pelatandra virginica* (See **wake-robin, Virginian**.)

tagua nut: *Phytelephas macrocarpa* (See **palm, ivory**.)

talipot: *Corypha umbraculifera*

talipot palm: *Corypha umbraculifera*

taliput: *Corypha umbraculifera* (See **talipot**.)

tall fescue: *Festuca*, *F. elatior*

tallow shrub: *Myrica*

tallow tree: *Aleurites moluccana*, *Sapium sebifeum*

tamanu: *Calophyllum inophyllum*

tamarack: *Larix laricina*, *L. occidentalis*, *Pinus contorta* (See **hackmatack** and **larch, Western**.)

tamarind: *Tamarindus indica*

tamarind, black: *Pithecellobium arboreum*

tamarindo: *Tamarindus indica* (See **tamarind**.)

tamarind-of-the-Indies: *Vangueria edulis*

tamarind, velvet: *Dialium guineense*

tamarind, wild: *Lysiloma bahamensis*

tamarisk: *Tamarix*

tamarisk, German: *Myricaria germanica*

tanbark oak: *Lithocarpus densiflorus*

tanekaha: *Phyllocladus*, *P. trichomanoides*

tangerine: *Citrus reticulata*

tangleberry: *Gaylussacia frondosa*

tanglefoot: *Viburnum alnifolium* (See

hobblebush, moosewood and **wayfaring tree, American**.)

tangle-legs: *Viburnum alnifolium* (See **hobblebush, moosewood,** and **wayfaring tree, American**.)

tanner's dock: *Rumex hymenosepalus*

tanner's sumac: *Rhus coriaria* (See **sumac, Sicilian**.)

tannia: *Xanthosoma, X. sagittifolium* (See **kale, Indian**.)

tannier: *Xanthosoma*

tanoak: *Lithocarpus densiflorus* (See **tanbark oak**.)

tansy: *Tanacetum, T. vulgare*

tansy ragwort: *Senecio Jacobaea* (See **staverwort**.)

tanyah: *Colocasia esculenta, Xanthosoma*

tape grass: *Vallisneria*

tapeworm plant: *Homalocladium*

tapioca: *Manihot esculent*

tare: *Vicia* (See **vetch**.)

taro: *Colocasia,* (See **elephant ear**.), *C. esculenta*

tarragon: *Artemisia Dracunculus*

tarragon, French: *Artemisia Dracunculus* (See **tarragon**.)

Tartar lily: *Ixiolirion tatarica* (See **lily, Siberian**.)

tarweed: *Chamaebatia, Grindelia,* (See **gum plant** and **rosin plant**.) *Madia, Phacelia tanecetifolia*

Tasmanian laurel: *Anopterus glandulosus*

Tasmanian myrtle: *Nothofagus cunninghamii*

Tasmanian tree fern: *Dicksonia antarctica*

tassel flower: *Amaranthus, A. caudatus,* (See **thrumwort**.), *Brickellia grandiflora, Emilia javanica, Petalostemon*

tassel-white: *Itea virginica* (See **willow, Virginia**.)

Tatarian honeysuckle: *Lonicera Tatarica*

tea: *Camellia sinensis*

teaberry: *Gaultheria procumbens* (See **spiceberry**.), *Viburnum cassinoides* (See **withe rod**.)

teak: *Tectona grandis*

tea, Mexican: *Chenopodium ambrosioides* (See **wormseed**.)

tea plant: *Camellia sinensis, Viburnum Lentago* (See **nannyberry** and **sheepberry**.)

tea rose: *Rosa odorata*

teasel: *Dipsacus, D. fullonum, D. sativus* (See **fuller's teasel**.)

tea, Spanish: *Chenopodium ambrosioides* (See **wormseed**.)

tea tree: *Camellia sinensis* (See **tea**

plant.) *Leptospermum*, *L. scoparium*, *Melaleuca*, *M. quinquenervia* (See **tea tree, swamp**.)

tea tree, Ceylon: *Cassine glauca*

tea tree, swamp: *Melaleuca Leucodendron*, *M. quinquenervia*

teazel: *Dipsacus* (See **teasel**.)

teddy bear: *Cyanotis* kewensis

telegraph plant: *Desmodium motorium* (See **semaphore-plant**.)

temple-bells: *Smithiantha*

temple plant: *Crateva religiosa* (See **pear, garlic**.)

temple tree: *Plumeria*

ten-day fern: *Rumohra adantiaformis* (See **leather fern**.)

tera vine: *Actinidia* arguta (See **yang-tao**.)

tetterwort: *Chelidonium majus*, *Sanguinaria canadensis*

Texan buckeye: *Ungnadia speciosa* (See **Mexican buckeye** and **Spanish buckeye**.)

Texas ash: *Fraxinus texensis* (See **mountain ash**.)

Texas bluebell: *Eustoma*

Texas bluebonnet: *Lupinus subcarnosus* (See **bluebonnet**.)

Texas ebony: *Pithecellobium* flexicaule

Texas mountain laurel: *Sophora* secundiflora (See **mescal bean**.)

Texas plume: *Ipomopsis rubra*

Texas ranger: *Leucophyllum* frutescens

Texas sage: *Salvia coccinea* (See **sage, scarlet**.)

thale cress: *Arabidopsis thaliana*

thatch palm: *Howea*, Sabal, Thrinax

thatch tree: *Sabal palmetto* (See **thatch palm**.)

thick-leaved phlox: *Phlox* carolina

thimbleberry: *Rubus occidentalis* (See **raspberry**.)

thimbleflower: *Digitalis purpurea*, *Prunella vulgaris*

thimbleweed: *Anemone cylindrica*, *A. riparia*

thistle: *Carduus*, *Cirsium* (See **thistle, plume**.), *Onopordum*

thistle, acanthus-leaved: *Carlina acanthifolia* (See **thistle, Carline**.)

thistle, Argentine: *Onopordum Acanthium* (See **thistle, cotton**.)

thistle, blessed: *Cnicus benedictus*, *Silybum marianum* (See **thistle, holy** and **thistle, milk**.)

thistle, bull: *Cirsium vulgare*

thistle, Canada: *Cirsium arvense*

thistle, Carline: *Carlina acanthifolia*

thistle, common: *Cirsium vulgare* (See **thistle, bull**.)

thistle, cotton: *Onopordum Acanthium*

thistle, cursed: *Cnicus benedictus* (See **thistle, blessed**.)

thistle, fishbone: *Cirsium diacantha*

thistle, fuller's: *Dipsaca sativus*

thistle, globe: *Echinops*

thistle, golden: *Scolymus hispanicus*

thistle, holy: *Silybum marianum* (See **thistle, milk**.)

thistle, horse: *Lactuca Serriola*

thistle, melancholy: *Cirsium heterophyllum*

thistle, milk: *Silybum marianum* (See **thistle, holy**.)

thistle, mountain: *Acanthus montanus*

thistle, mountain sow: *Lactuca alpina*

thistle, oat: *Onopordum Acanthium* (See **thistle, cotton**.)

thistle, Our Lady's: *Silybum marianum* (See **thistle, holy**.)

thistle, plume: *Cirsium*

thistle, plumeless: *Carduus*

thistle, saffron: *Carthamus tinctorius*

thistle, Scotch: *Onopordum Acanthium* (See **thistle, cotton**.)

thistle, silver: *Onopordum Acanthium* (See **thistle, cotton**.)

thistle, small globe: *Echinops ritro*

thistle, spear: *Cirsium vulgare* (See **thistle, bull**.)

thistle, stemless: *Carlina acualis*

thistle, St. Mary's: *Silybum marianum* (See **thistle, holy** and **thistle, milk**.)

thistle, thornless: *Centaurea americana*

thistle, white: *Atroplex lentiformis*

thorn: *Crataegus*

thorn apple: *Crataegus* (See **thorn**.), *Datura*, *D. Stramonium* (See **jimsonweed**.)

thornbush: *Crataegus*

thorn, cockspur: *Crataegus crus-galli*

thorn, evergreen: *Crataegus laevigata*

thorn, Glastonbury: *Crataegus monogyna*

thorn, lily: *Catesbaea spinosa*

thorn, pear: *Crataegus calpodendron*

thorn, sallow: *Hippophae rhamnoides*

thorn, Washington: *Crataegus phaenopyrum*

thorn, white: *Ceanothus incanthus*, *Crataegus biltmoriana*, *C. laevigata*

thoroughwax: *Bupleurum*

thoroughwort: *Eupatorium* (See **hemp agrimony**.)

thousand-mothers: *Tolmiea menziesii* (See **pickaback plant** and **youth-on-age**.)

threadflower: *Nematanthus*

threadleaved sundew: *Drosera fili-formis*

three-leafed nightshade: *Trillium* (See **nightshade**.)

three-leaved ivy: *Rhus toxicodendron*

three-men-in-a-boat: *Rhoeo spathaceae* (See **lily, boat**.)

thrift: *Armeria* (See **sea pink**.), *A. maritima* (See **sea cushion**.)

thrift, common: *Armeria maritima*

thrift, lavender: *Limonium*

thrift, prickly: *Acantholimon*

throatwort: *Trachelium*

thrumwort: *Amaranthus caudatus*

thrumwort, great: *Alisma plantago-aquatica*

thunderflower: *Silene alba*

thunder plant: *Sempervivum tectorum*

thyme: *Thymus, T. vulgaris* (See **lemon thyme**.)

thyme, creeping: *Thymus Serpyllum* (See **thyme**.)

thyme, mother-of-: *Thymus Serpyllum* (See **thyme**.)

thyme, wild: *Thymus Serpyllum* (See **thyme**.)

ti: *Cordyline terminalis* (See **ki**.)

tick bean: *Vicia faba*

tickseed: *Bidens* (See **stick-tight**.), *Coreopsis*

tidy-tips: *Layia, L. platyglossa*

tigerflower: *Tigridia, T. Pavonia* (See **lily, one-day** and **shellflower**.)

tiger's-jaw: *Faucaria*

timber bamboo: *Phyllostachys bambusoides*

tinker's root: *Triosteum perfoliatum*

tinker's weed: *Triosteum perfoliatum* (See **feveroot** and **tinker's root**.)

ti palm: *Cordyline terminalis* (See **ti**.)

tipu tree: *Tipuana tipu*

tisswood: *Persea borbonia*

titi: *Cyrilla racemiflora* (See **leatherwood**.), *Oxydendrum arboreum* (See **sorrel tree**.)

ti tree: *Cordyline terminalis* (See **ti**.)

toad cactus: *Stapelia variegata* (See **starflower**.)

toad-cup lily: *Neomarica*

toadflax: *Linaria* (See **lion's-mouth**.), *L. vulgaris* (See **flaxweed**.)

toadflax, ivy-leaved: *Cymbalaria muralis*

toad lily: *Tricyrtis*

tobacco: *Nicotiana, N. rustica, N. tabacum*

tobacco sumac: *Rhus vireus* (See **kinnikinnik**.)

Tobago cane: *Bactris guineensis* (See **prickly pole**.)

tree celadine: *Macleaya cordata*

tree clover: *Melilotus alba*

tree cranberry: *Viburnum trilobum* (See **cranberry bush.**)

tree fern: *Alsophila, Blechnum, Cibotium, Cyathea, Dicksonia* (See **fern, tree.**)

tree fuchsia: *Fuchsia excorticata*

tree heath: *Dracaena, Erica arborea*

tree lupine: *Lupinus arboreus*

tree mallow: *Lavatera* (See **lavender.**)

tree of heaven: *Ailanthus altissima* (See **sumac, Chinese** and **varnish tree.**)

tree-of-kings: *Cordyline terminalis* (See **ti.**)

tree-of-life: *Mauritia flexuosa*

tree of sadness: *Nyctanthes arbor-tristis*

tree of the gods: *Ailanthus altissima* (See **tree of heaven.**)

tree orchid: *Epidendrum*

tree peony: *Paeonia suffruticosa*

tree poppy: *Dendromecon rigida, Romneya coulteri*

tree primrose: *Oenthera biennis*

tree, Santa Maria: *Calophyllum brasiliense*

tree tomato: *Cyphomandra betacea*

tree trembling: *Populus tremula, P. tremuloides*

trefoil: *Trifolium*

trefoil, bird's foot: *Lotus*

trefoil, marsh: *Menyanthes trifoliata*

trefoil, shrubby: *Ptelea trifoliata*

trifoliate orange: *Poncirus trifoliata* (See **hardy orange.**)

trigger plant: *Stylidium graminifolium*

Trinidad flame bush: *Calliandra*

trip-toe: *Viburnum alnifolium* (See **hobblebush, moosewood,** and **wayfaring tree, American.**)

tritoma: *Kniphofia, Tritoma* (See **poker plant.**)

Tritonia: *Crocosmia*

trollflower: *Trollius*

trophy cress: *Tropaeolum*

trophywort: *Tropaeolum*

tropical almond: *Terminalia catappa*

tropical crocus: *Kaempferia rotunda* (See **lily, Resurrection.**)

true fir: *Abies* (See **fir.**)

true myrtle: *Myrtus communis*

true Oriental plane: *Platanus orientalis* (See **plane tree.**)

truffle: *Tuber*

trumpet bush: *Tecoma*

trumpet creeper: *Campsis, C. radicans* (See **creeper** and **cross vine.**)

trumpet flower: *Bignonia capreolata* (See **quartervine.**), *Campsis radicans*

trumpet honeysuckle: *Campsis radicans* (See **cross vine** and **trumpet creeper**.), *Lonicera sempervirens*

trumpet leaf: *Sarracenia flava* (See **huntsman's-horn**.)

trumpets: *Sarracenia flava* (See **huntsman's-horn** and **trumpet leaf**.)

trumpet tree: *Cecropia peltata*, *Tabeuia*

trumpet vine: *Campsis*, *C. radicans* (See **trumpet creeper**.), *Clytostoma callistegioides*, *Distictis buccinatoria*

trumpet vine, blood-red: *Distictis buccinatoria*

trumpetwood: *Cecropia peltata* (See **trumpet tree**.)

tubeflower: *Clerodendrum*, *C. indicum*

tuberose: *Polianthes tuberosa*

tuberous vetch: *Lathyrus tuberosus* (See **pea, tuberous**.)

tuckahoe: *Orontium aquaticum*, *Peltandra undulata* (See **wake-robin, Virginian**.), *P. virginica*

tucum: *Astrocharyum aculeatum*

tulip: *Tulipa*

tulip, African: *Haemanthus*

tulip, butterfly: *Calochortus*

tulip, globe: *Calochortus* (See **tulip, butterfly**.)

tulip poplar: **Liriodendron**, *L. tulipfera*

tulip poppy: *Papaver glaucum*

tulip tree: *Liriodenron tulipfera* (See **tulip poplar**.)

tulip tree, Chinese: *Liriodendron chinense*

tulip, Turkish: *Tulipa acuminata*

tulip, wild: *Calochortus* (See **tulip, butterfly**.), *Tulipa sylvestris*

tumbleweed: *Amaranthus albus*

tunic flower: *Petrorhagia saxifraga*

tupelo: **Nyssa**, *N. sylvatica* (See **pepperidge** and **sour gum**.)

turban buttercup: *Ranunculus asiaticus*

turban squash: *Cucurbita maxima* (See **squash**.)

turfing daisy: *Tripleurospermum tchihatchewii*

turkey beard: **Xerophyllum** *aspodeloides*

turkey berry: *Mitchella repens* (See **twinberry**.)

turkey berry tree: *Mitchella repens*, *Symphoricarpus orbiculatus*

turkey oak: *Quercus incana* (See **oak, bluejack** and **sand jack**.)

turkey pea: *Dicentra canadensis*

Turkish filbert *Corylus Colurna* (See **filbert**.)

Turk's-cap: *Lilium Martagon* (See **lily,**

Martagon.), *L. superbum* (See **lily, American Turk's-cap**.)

Turk's-cap lily: *Lilium superbum* (See **swamp lily**.)

turk's turban: ***Clerodendrum**, C. indicum* (See **tubeflower**.)

turmeric root: *Hydrastis Canadensis* (See **yellowroot**.)

turnip: *Brassica Rapa*

turnip, Indian: *Arisaema triphyllum*

turpentine tree: *Syncarpia glomulifera*

turpentine weed: ***Gutierrezia**, G. Sarothrae* (See **snakeweed**.)

turtlehead: *Chelone, C. glabra* (See **snakehead**.)

tutsan: *Hypericum Androseaemum*

twayblade: *Liparis* (See **lion's-tooth**.), *Listera*

twelve-apostles: ***Neomarica*** (See **lily, toad-cup**.)

twinberry: *Mitchella repens* (See **hive vine, partridgeberry**, and **squawberry**.)

twinflower: *Linnaea borealis* (See **lingberry**.)

twining brodiaea: *Dichelostemma volubile* (See **snake lily**.)

twinleaf: ***Jeffersonia*** *diphylla*

twinspur: ***Diascia**, D. Barberae*

twist arum: ***Helicodiceros*** *muscivorus*

twisted flower: *Strophanthus*

twisted heath: *Erica cinerea* (See **Scotch heath**.)

twisted stalk: ***Streptopus***

twistwood: *Viburnum lantana* (See **wayfaring tree**.)

two-eyed berry: *Mitchella repens* (See **hive vine, partridgeberry**, and **squawberry**.)

two-men-in-a-boat: *Rhoeo spathaceae* (See **lily, boat** and **three-men- in-a-boat**.)

U

ulmo: *Eucryphia cordifolia*

umbil root: *Cypripedium Calceolus pubescens* (See **Venus's-shoe**.)

umbrella leaf: *Diphylleia cymosa*

umbrella palm: ***Cyperus, Hedyscepe***

umbrella pine: *Pinus densiflora* (See **parasol fir**.), *P. pinea* (See **stone pine**.), *Sciadopitys verticillata* (See **parasol fir**.)

umbrella plant: *Cyperus alternifolius* (See **umbrella palm**.), *Eriogonum*

umbrella sedge: *Cyperus alternifolius* (See **umbrella palm**.)

umbrella tree: *Magnolia tripetala, Schefflera*

umbrella tree, Australian: *Schefflera (Brassaia) actinophyla* (See **umbrella tree, Queensland**.)

umbrella tree, ear-leaved: *Magnolia Fraseri*

umbrella tree, queen's: *Schefflera (Brassaia) actinophyla* (See **umbrella tree, Queensland**.)

umbrella tree, Queensland: *Schefflera (Brassaia) actinophyla*

umbrella-trumpets: *Sarracenia flava* (See **huntsman's-horn** and **trumpet leaf**.)

umbrellawort: *Mirabilis*

umkokolo: ***Dovyalis***

unicorn plant: ***Proboscidea***

unicorn root: *Aletris farinosa* (See **starwort, mealy**.), *Chamaelirium luteum, Helonias bullata*

unicorn's horn: *Aletris farinosa* (See **unicorn root**.), *Chamaelirium luteum* (See **unicorn root**.), *Helonias bullata* (See **unicorn root**.)

upas: *Antiaris toxicaria, Strychnos*
upas tree: ***Antiaris*** *toxicaria*
 (See **upas**.), *Strychnos* (See
 upas.)

upland cress: *Barbarea verna* (See
 scurvy grass.)
upland tupelo: ***Nyssa*** *sylvatica*
urnflower: *Urceolina*

V

valerian: *Valeriana*

valerian, Greek: *Polemonium caeruleum*

valerian, long-spurred: *Centranthus macrosiphon*

valerian, red: *Centranthus ruber*

valley oak: *Quercus lobata* (See **oak, California white**.)

vanilla plant: *Vanilla planifolia*

vanilla trumpet vine: *Distictis laxiflora* (See **trumpet flower**.)

varnish tree: *Ailanthus altissima* (See **sumac, Chinese** and **tree of heaven**.), *Aleurites moluccana* (See **tallow tree**.), *Koelreuteria* paniculata, *Rhus* verniciflua, *Semecarpus, S. Anacardium*

vase plants: *Aechmea*

vase vine: *Clematis Viorna* (See **love-in-a-mist**.)

vegetable marrow: *Cucurbita pepo* (See **zucchini**.)

vegetable oyster: *Tragopogon porrifolius* (See **salsify**.)

vegetable-sponge: *Luffa aegyptiaca* (See **strainer-vine**.)

velvet elephant-ear: *Kalanchoe beharensis* (See **velvetleaf**.)

velvet flower: *Amaranthus caudatus*

velvet grass: *Holcus*

velvet groundsel: *Senecio Petasitis*

velvetleaf: *Abutilon Theophrasti, Kalanchoe beharensis*

velvet plant: *Gynura, Gynura aurantiaca, Verbascum Thapsus* (See **hare's-beard** and **sheperd's club**.)

velvet sumac: *Rhus typhina* (See **staghorn sumac**.)

Venetian sumac: *Cotinus coggygria* (See **wig tree**.)

Venus's-flytrap: *Dionaea muscipula*

venus's-hair: *Adiantum capillus-veneris* (See **fern, Venus's-hair**.)

Venus's-looking-glass: *Legousia speculum-Veneris*

Venus's-shoe: *Cypripedium Calceolus pubescens*

Venus's-slipper: *Cypripedium Calceolus pubescens* (See **Venus's-shoe**.)

vervain: *Verbena, V. officinalis*

vervain mallow: *Malva Alcea*

vetch: *Vicia*

vetch, bird: *Vicia Cracca* (See **vetch, tufted**.)

vetch, cow: *Vicia Cracca* (See **vetch, tufted**.)

vetch, hairy: *Vicia villosa*

vetch, horseshoe: *Hippocrepis comosa*

vetch, large Russian: *Vicia villosa* (See **vetch, hairy**.)

vetch, milk: *Astragulus*

vetch, spring: *Vicia sativa* (See **vetch, tare**.)

vetch, tare: *Vicia sativa*

vetch, tufted: *Vicia Cracca*

vetch, winter: *Vicia villosa* (See **vetch, hairy**.)

Victorian box: *Pittosporum undulatum*

victory plant: *Cheiridopsis candidissima*

vine: *Vitis*

vine cactus: *Fouguieria splendens* (See **ocotillo**.)

vinegar tree: *Rhus glabra* (See **sumac, scarlet** and **sumac, smooth**.)

vine, grape: *Vitis*

vine, India-rubber: *Cryptostegia grandiflora*

vine lilac: *Hardenbergia violacea* (See **lilac, Australian**.)

vine maple: *Acer circinatum*

vine, red-beard: *Abrus precatorius*

vine, rubber: *Cryptostegia grandiflora* (See **vine, India-rubber**.)

vine, vanilla trumpet: *Distictis laxiflora*

vine, weather: *Abrus precatorius* (See **vine, red-beard**.)

vine, wonga-wonga: *Pandorea pandorana*

viola: *Viola cornuta* (See **violet, horned**.)

violet: *Viola, V. odorata*

violet, African: *Saintpaulia*

violet, alpine marsh: *Viola palustris* (See **violet, marsh**.)

violet, American dog: *Viola conspersa*

violet, arrow-leaved: *Viola sagittata*

violet, Australian: *Viola hederacea*

violet, bird-foot: *Viola pedata* (See **violet, pansy**.)

Virginia bluebells: *Mertensia* virginica (See **cowslip**.)

Virginia chain fern: *Woodwardia* virginiana

Virginia cowslip: *Mertensia virginica* (See **cowslip** and **Virginia bluebells**.)

Virginia creeper: *Parthenocissus quinquefolia* (See **creeper**.)

Virginia mallow: *Sida hermaphrodita* (See **Sida**.)

Virginian stock: *Malcolmia* maritima

Virginian sumac: *Rhus typhina* (See **staghorn sumac**.)

Virginia snakeroot: *Aristolochia Serpentaria* (See **serpentary**.)

Virginia wake-robin: *Peltandra virginica* (See **tuckahoe**.)

Virginia willow: *Itea virginica*

virgin's bower: *Clematis*, *C. virginiana* (See **old-man's-beard**.)

voodoo lily: *Sauromatum* guttatum (See **monarch-of-the-East**.), *S. venosum*

W

wafer ash: *Ptelea, P. trifoliata* (See **tre-foil, shrubby**.)

wahoo: *Euonymus atropurpurea* (See **Indian arrow**.)

wahoo elm: *Ulmus alata* (See **elm**.)

wake-robin: *Trillium*

wake-robin, nodding: *Trillium cernuum*

wake-robin, purple: *Trillium recurvatum*

wake-robin, Virginian: *Peltandra undulata, P. virginica*

wake-robin, white: *Trillium grandiflorum*

walking fern: *Camptosorus rhizophyllous* (See **fern, walking**.)

walking iris: *Neomarica* (See **lily, toad-cup**.)

walking onion: *Allium cepa* (See **Egyptian onion**.)

wall fern: *Polypodium vulgare* (See **polypody**.)

wallflower: *Cheiranthus Cheiri, Erysimum*

wallflower, beach: *Erysimum suffrutescens*

wallflower, coast: *Erysimum capitatum*

wallowa: *Acacia calamifolia* (See **wattle, broom**.)

wall-pellitory: *Parietaria officinalis* (See **pellitory**.)

wall rockcress: *Arabis caucasia*

wall rue: *Asplenium rutamuraria*

walnut, Arizona: *Juglans major*

walnut, black: *Juglans nigra*

walnut, English: *Juglans regia*

walnut, little: *Juglans microcarpa*

walnut, white: *Juglans cinerea*

wampee: *Clausena lansium*

wampi: *Clausena*

wandering Jew: *Callisia elegans*, **Commelina**, *Iradescantia Albiflora*, *Tradescantia fluminensis*, *Tripogandra multiflora*, *Zebrina pendula*

wandflower: *Dierama*, *Galax*, *G. urceolata*, **Sparaxis**

wand plant: *Galax* (See **wandflower**.)

wapato: *Sagittaria latifolia*

wart plant: *Haworthia*

water aloe: *Stratiotes aloides*

water arum: *Calla palustris*

water ash: *Fraxinus*, **Ptelea** (See **wafer ash**.), *P. trifoliata* (See **hop tree**.)

water-avens: *Geum rivale* (See **avens**.)

water beech: *Carpinus caroliniana*

water caltrop: *Trapa natans* (See **nut, Jesuits**.)

water carpet: *Chrysosplenium americanum* (See **saxifrage, golden**.)

water chestnut: **Pachira** *aquatica*, **Trapa**, *T. bicornis* (See **ling**.), *T. natans* (See **saligot** and **water caltrop**.)

water chestnut, Chinese: *Eleocharis dulcis*

water chinquapin: **Nelumbo** *lutea*

water clover: *Marsilea*

water collard: **Nuphar** (See **lily, cow** and **spatterdock**.)

watercress: **Naturtium** *officinale*

water crowfoot: *Ranunculus aquatilis*

water dock: *Rumex hydrolapathum* (See **water dock, giant**.)

water dock, giant: *Rumex hydrolapathum*

water dragon: *Calla palustris* (See **water arum**.), *Saururus cernuus* (See **lizard's-tail**.)

water elm: *Ulmus americana* (See **elm** and **swamp elm**.)

water fern: *Ceratopteris*

water flag: *Iris Pseudacorus* (See **flag, yellow**.)

water gladiolus: *Butomus umbellatus*

water hawthorn: *Aponogeton distachyus* (See **pondweed, Cape**.)

water hemlock: *Cicuta* (See **locoweed**.), *C. maculata* (See **poison hemlock**.)

water horehound: *Lycopus americanus*, *L. europaeus*

water hyssop: *Bacopa*

water lemon: *Passiflora laurifolia*

water lemon, wild: *Passiflora foetida*

water lettuce: *Pistia stratiotes* (See **shellflower**.)

water lobelia: *Lobelia dortmanna*

water locust: *Gleditsia aquatica* (See **swamp locust**.)

water lotus: **Nelumbo**, *N. nucifera*

water maize: *Victoria amazonica* (See **lily, Amazon water**.)

water marigold: *Bidens* (See **stick-tight**.)

water mat: *Chrysosplenium americanum* (See **saxifrage, golden**.)

watermelon: *Citrullus lanatus*

watermelon begonia: *Pellionia daveauana*, *Peperomia argyreia*

watermelon pilea: *Pilea cadierei*

water milfoil: *Myriophyllum* (See **parrot's-feather**.)

water mint: *Mentha aquatica*

water-motie: *Baccharis glutinosa* (See **water willow**.)

water nut: *Trapa*

water nymph: *Naias*

water oleander: *Decodon verticillatus* (See **swamp loosestrife** and **water willow**.)

water parsnip: *Sium*

water pennywort: *Hydrocotyle* (See **navelwort** and **pennywort**.), *H. vulgaris* (See **marsh pennywort**.)

water pimpernel: *Samolus*

water plaintain: *Alisma*, *A. plantago-aquatica* (See **thrumwort, great**.)

water platter: *Victoria* (See **lily, giant water**.), *V. cruziana*, *V. regia*

water poppy: *Hydrocleys* nymphoides

water purslane: *Ludwigia palustris*, *Peplis* diandra

water smartweed: *Polygonum coccineum* (See **smartweed**.)

water soldier: *Stratiotes* aloides

water star grass: *Heteranthera dubia*

water trefoil: *Menyanthes trifoliata* (See **trefoil, marsh**.)

water-trumpet: *Cryptocoryne*

water violet: *Hottonia* (See **featherfoil**.), *H. palustris*

water-wally: *Baccharis glutinosa* (See **water willow**.)

waterweed: *Anacharis*

water willow: *Baccharis glutinosa*, *Decodon* verticillatus, (See **swamp loosestrife**.)

waterwort: *Elatine*

water yam: *Dioscorea alata*

wattle: *Acacia*, *A. cornigera*

wattle, blue-leaf: *Acacia cyanophylla* (See **wattle, orange**.)

wattle, bower: *Acacia*

wattle, broom: *Acacia calamifolia*

wattle, coastal: *Acacia cyclopis*

wattle, Cootamundra: *Acacia baileyana*

wattle, graceful: *Acacia decora*

wattle, orange: *Acacia cyanophylla*

wattle, Port Jackson: *Acacia cyanophylla* (See **wattle, orange**.)

wattle, river: *Acacia* (See **wattle, bower**.)

wattle, silver: *Acacia dealbata*

wattle, water: *Acacia retinodes*

wax bean: *Phaseolus vulgaris*

waxberry: *Gaultheria hispida, Myrica cerifera* (See **myrtle, wax**.)

waxflower: *Chamelaucium, Hoya, Stephanotis floribunda*

wax gourd: *Benincasa hispida*

wax myrtle: *Myrica cerifera*

wax myrtle, California: *Myrica californica*

wax palm: *Ceroxylon alpinum*

wax plant: *Hoya, H. carnosa*

wax plant, miniature: *Hoya bella*

wax tree: *Rhus succedanea*

wax vine: *Hoya, Senecio macroglossus*

waxwork: *Celastrus scadens* (See **staff vine**.)

wayfaring tree: *Viburnum lantana*

wayfaring tree, American: *Viburnum alnifolium*

weather plant: *Abrus precatorius* (See **pea, rosary** and **vine, red-beard**.)

weaver's broom: *Spartium junceum* (See **Spanish broom**.)

Weddell palm: *Microcoelum weddellianum*

wedelia: *Wedelia trilobata* (See **oxeye, creeping**.)

weeping bottlebrush: *Callistemon viminalis*

weeping cherry: *Prunus serrulata*

weeping cherry, double: *Prunus subhirtella*

weeping cherry, single: *Prunus subhirtella*

weeping Chinese banyan: *Ficus benjamina*

weeping fig: *Ficus benjamina*

weeping laurel: *Ficus benjamina*

weeping myall: *Acacia pendula*

weeping spruce: *Picea brewerana*

weeping tea tree: *Melaleuca quinquenervia*

Welsh onion: *Allium fistulosum*

Welsh poppy: *Meconopsis cambrica*

Western balsam poplar: *Populus trichocarpa* (See **cottonwood, black**.)

Western catalpa: *Catalpa* (See **Indian bean**.)

Western cottonwood: *Populus fremontii* (See **cottonwood, Fremont**.)

western dog violet: *Viola adunca*

western hound's tongue: *Cynoglossum grande*

western laurel: *Kalmia microphylla*

western mugwort: *Artemesia ludoviciana* (See **sage, white**.)

western redbud: *Celtis occidentalis* (See **nettle tree**.)

western sand cherry: *Prunus besseyi*

western sword fern: ***Polystichum*** *munitum*

western yew: *Taxus brevifolia* (See **mountain mahogany**.)

West Indian birch: *Bursera Simaruba* (See **gumbo-limbo**.)

West Indian blackthorn: *Acacia Farnesiana* (See **sponge tree**.)

wheatgrass: ***Agropyron***

wheel tree: ***Trochodendron*** *aralioides*

whin: *Ulex Europaeus* (See **gorse**.)

whinberry: *Vaccinium myrtillus*

whippoorwill-flower: *Trillium cuneatum*

whippoorwill's-shoe: *Cypripedium Calceolus pubescens* (See **Venus's-shoe**.)

whispering bells: ***Emmenanthe*** *penduliflora*

whistlewood: *Acer pensylvanicum* (See **maple, striped**.)

white alder: *Alnus rhombifolia*

white campion: *Silene alba* (See **thunderflower**.)

white cedar: *Chamaecyparis thyoides* (See **cedar**.)

white clover: *Trifolium repens*

white cockle: *Silene alba* (See **thunderflower**.)

whitecup: *Nierembergia repens*

white elm: *Ulmus americana* (See **swamp elm**.)

white-flowered plumbago: *Plumbago zeylanica* (See **leadwort, Ceylon**.)

white forsythia: ***Abeliophyllum***, *A. distichum*

white ginger: *Hedychium coronarium* (See **lily, butterfly**.)

white goldenrod: *Solidago bicolor* (See **silverrod**.)

white goosefoot: *Chenopodium album* (See **lamb's-quarters**.)

white gossamer: *Tradescantia sillamontana*

white gourd: *Benincasa hispida* (See **wax gourd**.)

white-heart hickory: *Carya tomentosa* (See **mockernut**.)

white heather: ***Cassiope*** *Mertensiana*

white hellebore: *Veratrum viride* (See **swamp hellebore**.)

white hoarhound: ***Marrubium*** *vulgare*

white jewel: *Titanopsis schwantesii*

white lotus: *Nymphaea Lotus* (See **lily, Egyptian water**.)

white-man's-foot: ***Plantago*** *major*

white melilot: *Melilotus alba* (See **tree clover**.)

White Mountain dogwood: *Viburnum alnifolium* (See **hobblebush, moosewood** and **wayfaring tree, American**.)

white mugwort: *Artemisia lactiflora*

white mustard: *Brassica alba* (See **mustard**.)

white oak: *Quercus alba* (See **stone oak**.)

white pine: ***Podocarpus*** *dacrydioides* (See **kahikatea**.)

white-plush plant: *Echeveria leucotricha*

white popinac: *Leucaena glauca* (See **lead tree**.)

white poplar: *Populus alba* (See **poplar, silver**.)

white pumpkin: *Benincasa hispida* (See **wax gourd**.)

white sandalwood: ***Santalum*** *album*

white sanicle: *Eupatorium rugosum* (See **sanicle, Indian** and **sanicle, white**.)

white sapota: *Casimiroa edulis*

white sapote: ***Casimiroa***

white snakeroot: *Eupatorium rugosum* (See **locoweed, sanicle, Indian** and **sanicle, white**.)

white-stemmed filaree: *Erodium moschatum* (See **muskflower**.)

white stringybark: *Eucalyptus globoidea* (See **stringybark**.)

white swamp azalea: *Rhododendron viscosum* (See **swamp honeysuckle**.)

white sweet clover: *Melilotus alba* (See **tree clover**.)

white thistle: *Atriplex lentiformis* (See **quail bush**.)

whitethorn: *Crataegus* (See **maybush**.)

white titi: *Cyrilla racemiflora* (See **leatherwood**.)

white trailing ice plant: *Delosperma*

white truffle: *Tuber aestivum* (See **truffle**.), *T. magnatum* (See **truffle**.)

white velvet: *Tradescantia sillamontana* (See **white gossamer**.)

white walnut: *Juglans cinerea* (See **lemon walnut**.)

whiteweed: *Chrysanthemum Leucanthemum* (See **marguerite**.)

whitewood: ***Liriodendron***, *L. tulipfera* (See **tulip poplar**.), *Tilia*

white yam: *Dioscorea alata* (See **water yam**.)

whitlavia: *Phacelia minor*

whitlowwort: *Paronychia*

whitten tree: *Viburnum Opulus Roseum* (See **marsh elder**.)

whortleberry: *Vaccinium myrtillus* (See **whinberry**.)

wicky: *Kalmia angustifolia* (See **lambkill** and **sheep laurel**.)

wicopy: *Dirca palustris* (See **moosewood** and **swampwood**.)

widow's-tears: ***Achimenes***

wig tree: ***Cotinus*** *coggygria*

wild angelica: *Angelica sylvestris* (See **Holy-Ghost**.)

wild balsam apple: ***Echinocystis***, *E. lobata* (See **mock apple**.)

wild bean: ***Apios*** *tuberosa*

wild beet: *Amaranthus retroflexus* (See **pigweed**.), *Saxifraga pensylvanica* (See **saxifrage, swamp**.)

wild bergamot: ***Monarda***

wild black cherry: *Prunus serotina* (See **rum cherry**.)

wild black currant: *Ribes americanum* (See **currant**.)

wild buckwheat: ***Eriogonum***

wild calla: *Calla palustris* (See **water arum**.)

wild carrot: ***Daucus***, *D. carota carota* (See **Queen Anne's lace**.)

wild cherry: *Prunus ilicifolia* (See **mountain holly**.)

wild cinnamon: *Canella Winterana* (See **nakedwood**.)

wild coffee: *Colubrina arborescens* (See **nakedwood**.), ***Polyscias*** *guilfoylei*, ***Psychotria***, *Triosteum perfoliatum* (See **feveroot** and **tinker's root**.)

wild cotton: *Hibiscus Moscheutos* (See **mallow, rose** and **swamp rose mallow**.)

wild date palm: ***Phoenix*** *sylvestris*

wild fennel: ***Nigella***

wild garlic: *Allium canadense* (See **onion, wild**.)

wild ginger: ***Asarum*** *canadense* (See **heart snakeroot** and **snakeroot**.), *A. caudatum* (See **ginger, wild** and **hazelwort**.), *A. europaeum*

wild hippo: *Euphorbia corollata* (See **spurge, flowering**.)

wild hydrangea: *Hydrangea arborescens* (See **hills-of-snow** and **hydrangea**.)

wild indigo: ***Amorpha*** *fruticosa*, *Baptisia tinctoria* (See **horsefly weed** and **rattlebush**.)

wild ipecac: *Euphorbia ipecacuanhae* (See **spurge, ipecac**.)

wild jalap: *Podophyllum peltatum* (See **Mayapple** and **raccoon- berry**.)

wild Johnny-jump-up: *Viola pedunculata* (See **pansy**.)

wild lemon: *Podophyllum peltatum* (See **Mayapple** and **raccoon- berry**.)

wild lettuce: *Pyrola rotundifolia* (See **lettuce, Indian** and **lily- of-the-valley, wild**.)

wild licorice: *Abrus precatorius* (See **pea, rosary** and **vine, red- beard**.)

wild lilac: *Ceanothus thyrsiflorus*

wild lily-of-the-valley: *Pyrola rotundifolia* (See **lettuce, Indian**.)

wild madder: *Rubia peregrina*

wild mandrake: *Podophyllum peltatum*

wild mock cucumber: *Echinocystis lobata* (See **mock apple**.)

wild morning glory: *Calystegia sepium* (See **hedge bindweed**.)

wild musk: *Erodium cicutarium* (See **pin clover** and **pin grass**.)

wild olive: *Elaeagnus angustifolia, Halesia carolina* (See **shittimwood**.)

wild pansy: *Viola tricolor* (See **love-in-idleness**.)

wild pepper: *Vitex Agnus-castus* (See **chaste tree, hemp tree** and **sage tree**.)

wild pineapple: *Bromelia Pinguin* (See **pineapple**.)

wild pink: *Arethusa bulbosa* (See **swamp pink**.)

wild potato: *Chlorogalum pomeridianum*

wild potato vine: *Ipomoea pandurata* (See **manroot** and **potato, wild**.)

wild raisin: *Viburnum Lentago* (See **nannyberry** and **tea plant**.), *V. cassinoides* (See **withe rod**.)

wild red cherry: *Prunus pensylvanica* (See **pin cherry**.)

wild rosemary: *Ledum palustre* (See **marsh tea**.)

wild sarsaparilla: *Smilax glauca* (See **sawbrier**.)

wild sensitive plant: *Cassia nictitans* (See **sensitive pea**.)

wild succory: *Chichorium intybus* (See **succory**.)

wild Sweet William phlox: *Phlox divaricata*

wild thyme: *Thymus Serpyllum* (See **mother of thyme** and **serpolet**.)

wild-thyme azalea: *Rhododendron serpyllifolium*

wild tobacco: *Nicotiana rustica* (See **tobacco**.)

wild water lemon: *Passiflora foetida* (See **love-in-a-mist**.)

wild yellow plum: *Prunus Americana* (See **plum, wild**.)

willow: *Salix*

willow, Alaska blue: *Salix purpurea* (See **willow, basket**.)

willow, Arctic: *Salix arctica*
willow, basket: *Salix purpurea*
willow, black: *Salix nigra*
willow, black pussy: *Salix gracilistyla melanostachys*
willow, coral bark: *Salix alba*
willow, cricket-bat: *Salix alba*
willow, desert: *Chilopsis linearis*
willow, dragon's-claw: *Salix matsudana*
willow, fan giant weeping: *Salix blanda*
willow, florist's: *Salix caprea*
willow, French pussy: *Salix caprea* (See **willow, florist's**.)
willow, globe: *Salix matsudana*
willow, globe Navajo: *Salix matsudana*
willow, goat: *Salix caprea* (See **willow, florist's**.)
willow, golden: *Acacia cyanophylla* (See **wattle, orange**.)
willow, Hankow: *Salix matsudana*
willow herb: *Epilobium*
willow, large pussy: *Salix discolor*
willow-leaved jessamine: *Cestrum parqui*
willow myrtle: *Agonis, A. flexuosa* (See **myrtle, Australian willow**.)
willow, Niobe: *Salix alba*

willow oak: *Quercus phellos* (See **peach oak**.)
willow, pink pussy: *Salix caprea* (See **willow, florist's**.)
willow, pussy: *Salix caprea* (See **willow, florist's**.)
willow, ringleaf: *Salix babylonica*
willow, rose gold pussy: *Salix gracilistyla*
willow, twisted Hankow: *Salix matsudana* (See **willow, dragon's-claw**.)
willow, Virginia: *Itea virginica*
willow, weeping: *Salix babylonica, S. repens*
willow, Wisconsin weeping: Salix blanda
willow, yellow: *Salix alba vitellina*
windflower: *Anemone, A. fulgens, A. nemorosa*
windmill jasmine: *Jasminum nitidum*
windmill palm: *Chamaerops* humilis
window leaf: *Monstera*
window plant: *Monstera deliciosa* (See **Mexican bamboo**.)
wind poppy: *Stylomecon* heterophylla
wind rose: *Rosemeria*
Windsor bean: *Vicia faba* (See **tick bean**.)
wineberry: *Rubus phoenicolasius*

wine palm: *Caryota urens* (See **sago palm**.)

winged elm: *Ulmus alata* (See **elm**.)

wingnut: *Pterocarya*

winter aconite: *Eranthis*

winterberry: *Ilex*

winterberry, common: *Ilex glabra, I. verticillata*

winterberry, Japanese: *Ilex serrata*

winterberry, mountain: *Ilex ambigua montana*

winter cherry: *Cardiospermum* (See **heartseed**.), *C. halicababum, Physalis*

wintercreeper: *Euonymus fortunei radicans*

winter cress: *Barbarea, B. vulgaris* (See **rocket** and **yellow rocket**.)

winter fat: *Artemesia ludovicinia* (See **sage, white**.)

winter fern: *Conium maculatum*

wintergreen: *Gaultheria procumbens* (See **spiceberry** and **teaberry**.), *Pyrola* (See **shinleaf**.)

wintergreen, American: *Gaultheria procumbens* (See **mountain tea**.)

wintergreen, arctic: *Pyrola grandiflora*

wintergreen, chickweed: *Trientalis*

wintergreen, flowering: *Polygala pauciflora*

wintergreen, pink: *Pyrola asarifolia*

wintergreen, spotted: *Chimaphila maculata*

winter hazel: *Corylopsis*

winter heliotrope: *Petasites fragrans*

winter melon: *Benincasa hispida* **(See wax gourd**.)

winter purslane: *Montia perfoliata*

winter savory: *Satureja montana* (See **savory**.)

winter's bark: *Drimys Winteri*

winter-sweet: *Chimonanthus, C. praecox*

winter sweet pea: *Swainsona galegifolia* (See **swanflower**.)

wire plant: *Muehlenceckia*

wire vine: *Muehlenbeckia*

wishbone flower: *Torenia fournieri*

wisteria, Chinese: *Wisteria sinensis*

wisteria, evergreen: *Millettia reticulata*

wisteria, Japanese: *Wisteria floribunda*

wisteria, silky: *Wisteria venusta*

witch alder: *Fothergilla, F. gardenii*

witch elm: *Ulmus glabra* (See **Scotch elm**.)

witch hazel: *Hamamelis*

witch hazel, Chinese: *Hamamelis mollis*

witch hazel, common: *Hamamelis virginiana*

witch hazel, Japanese: *Hamamelis japonica*

witch hazel, vernal: *Hamamelis vernalis*

witch hobble: *Viburnum alnifolium* (See **hobblebush, moosewood** and **wayfaring tree, American**.)

withe rod: *Viburnum cassinoides*

witloof: *Chichorium intybus* (See **succory**.)

woadwaxen: **Genista** *tinctoria*

wolfberry: *Symphoricarpos occidentalis*

wolfsbane: *Aconitum, A. lycoctonum, A. Napellus* (See **friar's-cap, helmetflower** and **monkshood**.)

wolf's-milk: *Euphorbia Esula* (See **spurge, leafy**.)

wonder bulb: *Colchicum autumnale* (See **crocus, autumn** and **saffron, meadow**.)

wonkapin: **Nelumbo** *Lutea*

wood betony: *Pedicularis, P. canadensis* (See **head betony**.)

woodbine: *Clematis virginiana* (See **virgin's-bower**.), **Lonicera** *Periclymenum* (See **honeysuckle**.), *Parthenocissus quinquefolia* (See **Virginia creeper**.)

woodbine, Dutch: *Lonicera periclymenum belgica*

woodbine, Italian: *Lonicera caprifolium*

woodbine, Spanish: *Merremia tuberosa*

wood fern: **Dryopteris**

wood germander: *Teurium corodonia* (See **sage, wood**.), *T. scorodonia*

wood hyacinth: **Endymion**, *E. nonscriptus* (See **harebell**.)

wood mint: **Blephilia** *hirsuta*

wood poppy: **Stylophorum** *diphyllum*

wood rose: **Merremia** *tuberosa* (See **morning glory, Ceylon, Spanish woodbine** and **woodbine, Spanish**.), *Rosa gymnocarpa*

wood rush: **Luzula**

wood sorrel: **Oxalis** *corniculata*

wood spurge: *Euphorbia amygdaloides*

wood violet: *Viola riviniana*

woodwaxen: *Genista tinctoria*

woolly bear: *Begonia leptotricha*

woolly bear caterpillar: *Begonia leptotricha* (See **woolly bear**.)

woolly betony: **Stachys** *byzantina*

woolly blue curls: **Trichostema** *lanatum* (See **sage, black**.)

woolly sunflower: **Eriophyllum**

worm grass: *Spigelia marilandica* (See **pink, Indian** and **spiderwort**)

wormseed: *Artemisia maritima, Chenopodium ambrosioides* (See **Mexican tea**.)

XYZ

yam: *Dioscorea*, *D. batatas*

yam bean: *Pachyrhizus* erosus, *P. tuberosus*

yam, wild: *Dioscorea Villosa*

yang-tao: *Actinidia* arguta, *A. deliciosa*

yanquapin: *Nelumbo Lutea*

yantia: *Xanthosoma sagittifolium* (See **kale, Indian**.)

yapa: *Ilex* (See **yaupon**.)

yapon: *Ilex* (See **yaupon**.)

yarrow: *Achillea*, *A. Millefolium* (See **milfoil**.)

yate tree: *Eucalyptus cornuta*

yaupon: *Ilex*, *I. Cassine* (See **dahoon**.), *I. vomitoria*

yautia: *Xanthosoma*

yedda hawthorn: *Rhaphiolepis umbellata*

Yeddo spruce: *Picea jezoensis* (See **Japanese snowbell**.)

yellow adder's tongue: *Erythronium americanum* (See **adder's-tongue** and **lily, trout**.)

yellow ageratum: *Lonas annua*

yellow alder: *Turnera ulmifolia* (See **holly rose**.)

yellow archangel: *Lamiastrum* galeobdolon

yellow avens: *Geum urbanum* (See **avens**.)

yellow-barked oak: *Quercus velutina* (See **oak, black** and **quercitron**.)

yellow bells: *Emmenanthe* penduliflora (See **whispering bells**.), *Tecoma*, *T. stans*

yellow bignonia: *Tecoma stans* (See **yellow elder**.)

yellow buckeye: *Aesculus octandra* (See **sweet buckeye**.)

828

yellow chamomile: *Anthemis tinctoria* (See **golden marguerite**.)

yellow clover: *Trifolium procumbens* (See **hop trefoil**.)

yellow elder: *Tecoma stans*

yellow-eyed grass: *Xyris*

yellow flag: *Iris Pseudacorus* (See **flag, water**.)

yellow flame: *Peltophorum pterocarpum*

yellow flax, Indian: *Reinwardtia indica*

yellow guava: *Psidium litorale*

yellow heliotrope: *Streptosolon Jamesonii*

yellow horn-poppy: *Glaucium flavum*

yellow Indian-shoe: *Cypripedium Calceolus pubescens* (See **Venus's-shoe**.)

yellow jasmine: *Gelsemium sempervirens* (See **jasmine, Carolina**.)

yellow jessamine: *Gelsemium sempervirens*

yellow locust: *Robinia Pseudoacacia* (See **locust**.)

yellow morning glory: *Merremia tuberosa* (See **Spanish woodbine** and **woodbine, Spanish**.)

yellow nelumbo: *Nelumbo Lutea*

yellow nut grass: *Cyperus esculentus* (See **nut rush**.)

yellow nut sedge: *Cyperus esculentus* (See **nut rush**.)

yellow oleander: *Thevetia peruviana*

yellow parilla: *Menispermum canadense* (See **moonseed, Canadian**.)

yellow pitcher plant: *Sarracenia flava* (See **huntsman's-horn** and **trumpet leaf**.)

yellow poinciana: *Peltophorum pterocarpum*

yellow pond lily: *Nuphar* (See **spatter-dock**.)

yellow popolo: *Solonum sodomeum* (See **Sodom apple**.)

yellow puccoon: *Hydrastis, H. canadensis* (See **goldenseal** and **yellow-root**.)

yellow rattle: *Rhinanthus, R. crista-galli* (See **pennygrass**.)

yellow rocket: *Barbarea vulgaris*

yellowroot: *Hydrastis, H. Canadensis, Xanthorhiza*

yellow stars: *Bloomeria crocea*

yellow stringybark: *Eucalyptus muellerana* (See **stringybark**.)

yellow summer squash: *Cucurbita Pepo* (See **squash**.)

yellow trumpet flower: *Tecoma stans* (See **yellow elder**.)

yellow trumpet vine: *Macfadyena*

yellow twayblade: *Liparis Loeselii* (See **orchid, fen**.)

yellow water iris: *Iris Pseudacorus* (See **flag, yellow**.)

yellow water lily: *Nuphar luteum* (See **nenuphar**.)

yellowwood: *Cladrastis lutea, Rhodosphaera rhodanthema*

yerba buena: *Satureja Douglasii*

yerba linda: *Peperomia rotundifolia*

yerba mansa: *Anemopsis californica*

yerba mate: *Ilex paraquariensis*

yerba santa: *Eriodictyon*

yesterday-today-and-tomorrow: *Brunfelsia australis, B. floribunda*

yew: *Taxus*

yew, American: *Taxus canadensis*

yew, Chinese: *Taxus chinensis*

yew, Chinese plum: *Cephalotaxus Fortunii*

yew, English: *Taxus baccata*

yew, Florida: *Taxus floridana*

yew, golden: *Taxus baccata*

yew, Harrington plum: *Cephalotaxus Harringtonia*

yew, Irish: *Taxus baccata*

yew, Japanese plum: *Cephalotaxus Harringtonia drupacea*

yew, Oregon: *Taxus brevifolia* (See **yew, Western**.)

yew, Prince Albert: *Saxigothea conspicua*

yew, Western: *Taxus brevifolia*

ylang-ylang: *Cananga odorata*

York-and-Lancaster rose: *Rosa damascena*

youngberry: *Rubus ursinus*

youpon: *Ilex* (See **yaupon**.)

youth-and-old-age: *Aichryson domesticum, Zinnia elegans*

youth-in-old-age: *Zinnia elegans* (See **old maid**.)

youth-on-age: *Tolmiea Menziesii* (See **pickaback plant**.)

yucca: *Manihot esculent*

yulan: *Magnolia denudata*

zamang: *Samanea Saman*

zapote blanco: *Casimiroa edulis* (See **sapote, white**.)

zebra plant: *Aphelandra squarrosa, Calathea zebrina, Cryptanthus zonatus*

zedoary: *Curcuma Zedoaria*

zephyr flower: *zephyranthes*

zinnia: *Zinnia elegans* (See **old maid**.)

zucchini: *Cucurbita Pepo* (See **squash**.)

Zulu potato: *Bowiea*

zygadene: *Zigadenus*

USDA
Plant
Hardiness
Zone
Map

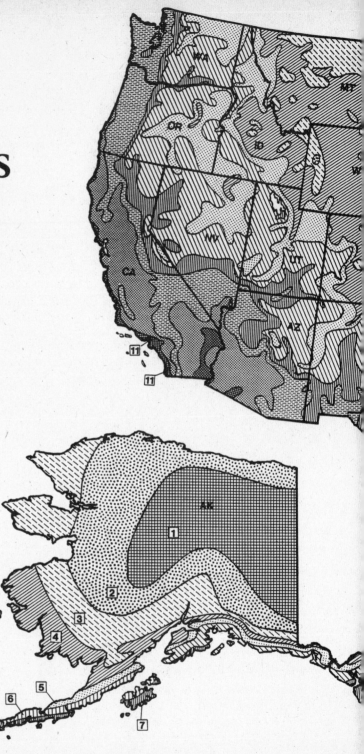

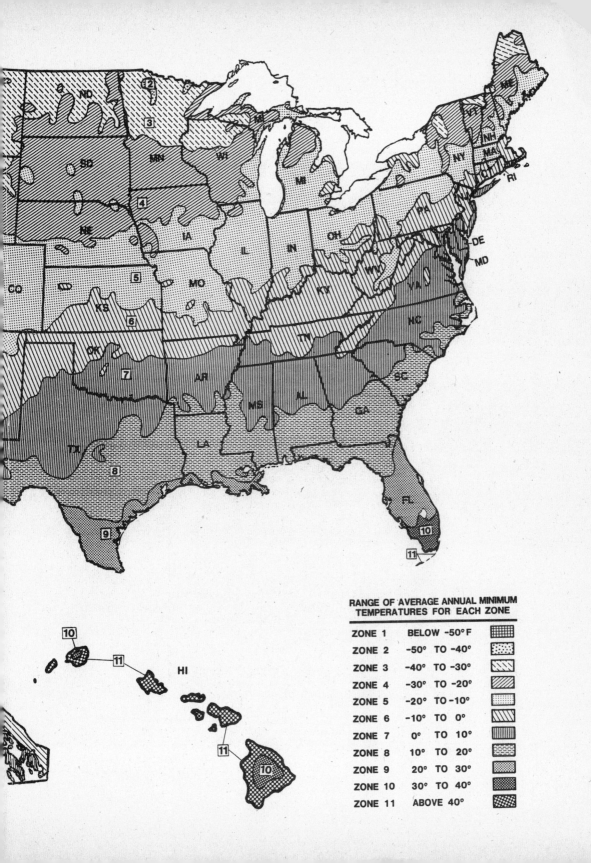

**RANGE OF AVERAGE ANNUAL MINIMUM
TEMPERATURES FOR EACH ZONE**

ZONE 1	BELOW -50°F	
ZONE 2	-50° TO -40°	
ZONE 3	-40° TO -30°	
ZONE 4	-30° TO -20°	
ZONE 5	-20° TO -10°	
ZONE 6	-10° TO 0°	
ZONE 7	0° TO 10°	
ZONE 8	10° TO 20°	
ZONE 9	20° TO 30°	
ZONE 10	30° TO 40°	
ZONE 11	ABOVE 40°	

FOR THE BEST IN PAPERBACKS, LOOK FOR THE

In every corner of the world, on every subject under the sun, Penguin represents quality and variety—the very best in publishing today.

For complete information about books available from Penguin—including Puffins, Penguin Classics, and Arkana—and how to order them, write to us at the appropriate address below. Please note that for copyright reasons the selection of books varies from country to country.

In the United Kingdom: Please write to *Dept. JC, Penguin Books Ltd, FREEPOST, West Drayton, Middlesex UB7 0BR*.

If you have any difficulty in obtaining a title, please send your order with the correct money, plus ten percent for postage and packaging, to *P.O. Box No. 11, West Drayton, Middlesex UB7 0BR*

In the United States: Please write to *Consumer Sales, Penguin USA, P.O. Box 999, Dept. 17109, Bergenfield, New Jersey 07621-0120*. VISA and MasterCard holders call 1-800-253-6476 to order all Penguin titles

In Canada: Please write to *Penguin Books Canada Ltd, 10 Alcorn Avenue, Suite 300, Toronto, Ontario M4V 3B2*

In Australia: Please write to *Penguin Books Australia Ltd, P.O. Box 257, Ringwood, Victoria 3134*

In New Zealand: Please write to *Penguin Books (NZ) Ltd, Private Bag 102902, North Shore Mail Centre, Auckland 10*

In India: Please write to *Penguin Books India Pvt Ltd, 706 Eros Apartments, 56 Nehru Place, New Delhi 110 019*

In the Netherlands: Please write to *Penguin Books Netherlands bv, Postbus 3507, NL-1001 AH Amsterdam*

In Germany: Please write to *Penguin Books Deutschland GmbH, Metzlerstrasse 26, 60594 Frankfurt am Main*

In Spain: Please write to *Penguin Books S. A., Bravo Murillo 19, 1° B, 28015 Madrid*

In Italy: Please write to *Penguin Italia s.r.l., Via Felice Casati 20, I-20124 Milano*

In France: Please write to *Penguin France S. A., 17 rue Lejeune, F-31000 Toulouse*

In Japan: Please write to *Penguin Books Japan, Ishikiribashi Building, 2-5-4, Suido, Bunkyo-ku, Tokyo 112*

In Greece: Please write to *Penguin Hellas Ltd, Dimocritou 3, GR-106 71 Athens*

In South Africa: Please write to *Longman Penguin Southern Africa (Pty) Ltd, Private Bag X08, Bertsham 2013*